50

THE WORLD GUIDE TO
AUTOMOBILE
MANUFACTURERS

THE WORLD GUIDE TO
AUTOMOBILE
MANUFACTURERS

NICK BALDWIN
G. N. GEORGANO
MICHAEL SEDGWICK
BRIAN LABAN

Facts On File Publications
New York, New York ● Oxford, England

First published in Great Britain in 1987
by Macdonald & Co (Publishers) Ltd
London & Sydney

A member of BPCC plc

This edition published in 1987 by Facts
On File by arrangement with Macdonald
& Co (Publishers) Ltd

Library of Congress cataloging-in-publication data

The World guide to automobile manufacturers.

   Includes index.
   1. Automobile industry and trade — Dictionaries.
I. Baldwin, Nick.
HD9710.A2W6686   1987   338.7'6292222'0321   87-81834
ISBN 0-8160-1844-8

Project editors: Mary Davies, Richard Williams

Copy-editor: Sam Elder

Designed by Design 23

Picture research by Mirco Decet

Chronology by David Burgess-Wise

Filmset by SX Composing Ltd, Rayleigh, Essex

Printed and bound in Yugoslavia by Mladinska Knjiga

Title-page photograph: BMW 327 coupé of 1937

CONTENTS

INTRODUCTION

Over the past 20 years numerous dictionaries and encyclopedias have been published, covering the cars of various countries, or, in some cases, of the whole world. They have usually neglected any analysis of the manufacturing background – who produced and designed the cars, and why they turned out as they did – and in this volume we have tried to redress the balance.

The motor car did not grow up in isolation from the general engineering life of the country, and few companies have been devoted solely to the manufacture of passenger cars. While not ignoring the cars themselves, the entries in this Guide examine the industries from which the companies sprang, and the rise and fall of the makers' fortunes brought about by good or bad management, or changing economic conditions. Particular reference is usually made to the origins and extent of the companies' backing, their corporate status, changes of company name, structure or ownership, mergers, takeovers, and bankruptcies. Often, the number of employees, capital value and extent of the production facilities are described as part of the overall picture. Most entries contain specific details of the number of vehicles produced by individual companies, either in total or as annual figures, or occasionally as output of specific models.

Many car manufacturers grew from the coachbuilding or cycle industries, but they have also followed less likely apprenticeships, such as the making of telephones (Ader), plumbers' supplies (Buick), whalebone corsets (Peugeot), birdcages (Pierce Arrow), and sheep-shearing equipment (Wolseley). Sometimes car making has been supported by other kinds of business, such as the aero-engines of Rolls-Royce and Alvis, or the commercial vehicles and military contracts of Berliet.

The importance of dominant personalities is not forgotten, nor the sources of finance. While it would be impossible, as well as tedious, to give annual balance sheets for every make, significant changes in profit and loss, as well as production figures, are frequently mentioned. Participation in sport often brings glory but little profit, and this is noted as well. Finally, many companies have continued to be active in other fields after car manufacture ceased, and this is traced, wherever possible, up to the present.

Choice of Makes

More than 4000 makes of car have come and gone during the past 100 years, but many of these survived for only a year or two, with production not even reaching double figures. They could not be said to have company histories, and are therefore not included in our Guide. Instead we have carefully selected 1000 makes, on the basis of their importance to the growth of the motor industry, both in design and numbers manufactured. Every make of car with a life of ten years or more is listed, and many with less, where their design or other contributions to motoring history have been exceptional. These include DeLorean, whose financial and political involvement have exceeded the car's technical interest, and Trumbull, which was the most successful of the American cyclecars, despite a lifespan of only three years.

Two phenomena of recent years have been the proliferation of kit car and replicar makes. Most of these will not be found in the Guide, simply because they have not been in business long enough to establish their credentials. However, there are exceptions, such as the British kit-car makers, Dutton and NG, and the doyenne of American replicars, the Excalibur.

Chronology and Index

An important feature of the book is the Chronology, which contains details of technical advances, the growth of the industry and of the number of vehicles in use around the world, the social, political and economic events which have influenced the shape of cars and the industry, and all general milestones in the history of motoring.

Names of companies, marques, component suppliers, and significant individuals which appear elsewhere than under their own headings are listed in the Index. A number of well-known marque names, which do not have individual company histories, can be traced either through the Index or by cross-references in the main text. One example is Mercury, which is included in the Lincoln entry as it has always been part of Ford's Lincoln-Mercury Division.

Michael Sedgwick

The original team of contributors to the Guide included the late Michael Sedgwick, and in his inimitable way he quickly became the team's coordinator and mentor. The difficult task of selecting the top 1000 makes was largely Michael's work, and he was keenly anticipating contributing some 175 entries. Sadly, he died in October 1983, having written only one entry. However, his drive and inspiration behind the planning of the book must not go unrecognized. It is a fitting conclusion to a lifetime of recording motoring history.

G. N. Georgano
Guernsey, March 1987

ABADAL
SPAIN 1912-1923; 1930

Don Francisco Serramelera y Abadal, a Spanish racing motorist, was Hispano-Suiza's agent in Madrid from 1904, virtually from the marque's Spanish origins. From 1908 he also represented the company in Barcelona and in 1912 F. S. Abadal y Cia of Barcelona began to market cars under its own name.

The first Abadals were a 3.6-litre four-cylinder 18/24hp and a 4.5-litre 45hp six. The sporty, long-stroke four in particular was mechanically very similar to the contemporary Hispano Alfonso, but had a distinctive vee radiator. Although the cars were designed by Francisco Abadal and assembled in Barcelona, the company bought its four-cylinder engines and chassis from the Belgian company Automobiles Impéria in Liège, maker of Im-péria cars. Impéria sold some of the Abadal designed cars in Belgium, with Belgian-built bodywork, under its own name and a few were sold in France by M. Magne, a dealer in Paris.

Abadal showed two cars with boat-style bodywork at the 1913 Paris Salon, one by Labourdette and one by Alin and Liautard, creating great interest, but up to the outbreak of World War I, when production in Belgium stopped, the company had built fewer than 90 cars.

During the war Abadal built a few light cars in Spain but concentrated on building coachwork for other makes, including Mercédès, Peugeot and, of course, Hispano-Suiza. The company did not resume Abadal production *per se* after World War I, but from 1916 it had been agent for the six-cylinder Buick and from 1919 to 1923 it modified these cars in small numbers as the sporty Abadal-Buick.

Impéria did resume production of the four-cylinder Abadals, sold under that name, and production continued when Impéria was taken over in 1920 by Mathieu Van Roggen. Impéria also built three or four 5.6-litre straight-eight prototypes of what would have been the Impéria-Abadal, but this excellent design went no further. In total, Impéria built about 170 post-war Abadals before abandoning the small-volume high-price concept in 1923 in favour of smaller cars under its own name.

Francisco Abadal built one more car under his own name. This was an American-style saloon with a 3.5-litre six-cylinder Continental engine and four-speed gearbox, but it never went into production and the marque name disappeared. BL

ABARTH
ITALY 1949-1971

Carlo Abarth was born of Italian parents in Yugoslavia on 15 November 1908 but grew up in Austria. He trained as a mechanic and enjoyed a brief motorcycle racing career that was prematurely ended by an accident. At the conclusion of World War II Abarth moved to Merano in Italy, whence his family originated and, through a family friendship established in Austria with Ferry (son of Ferdinand) Porsche, became Italian representative of the Porsche design bureau in association with Rudolf Hruska.

Another family friend, the legendary racing driver Tazio Nuvolari, put Abarth and Hruska in touch with Turin industrialist Piero Dusio, among whose various business interests was the racing-car manufacturer Cisitalia. Dusio, anxious for Cisitalia to break into Grand Prix racing, met the bond which released Porsche from internment by the French – and Porsche provided Cisitalia's Grand Prix design.

As Dusio pursued his ultimately abortive course of building the advanced, flat-twelve, rear-engined racer, Abarth, as Cisitalia's chief mechanic, prepared and raced the less exotic but more successful series production D46 racers, designed by Fiat's gifted chief designer, Dante Giacosa. In 1949, funds exhausted, Dusio moved Cisitalia to Argentina in the hope of new funding and Abarth & Cie was effectively born of the Cisitalia collapse.

Carlo Abarth went into partnership with Armando Scagliarini to continue Cisitalia racing operations, including those of Armando's

Abadal four-seat tourer of 1914

Fiat-Abarth 1000 racer of 1966

Fiat-Abarth 500 coupé of 1961

successful son, Guido. The company opened a factory in Turin on 15 April 1949; it had 32 employees and planned to develop Abarth competition cars and tuning equipment for other marques. For the company's symbol Carlo adopted his birth sign, the Scorpion.

The first Abarths soon appeared alongside the Cisitalia Squadra Abarth cars, whose racing successes continued with 18 wins in Abarth's first year of patronage. Ironically, it was a racing failure which prompted Abarth to expand the component side of his company. At the 1949 Madrid Grand Prix the prototype 204 was a surprising flop, and although its poor showing was later attributed to deterioration in transit of the alcohol fuel, Abarth lost valuable orders. Silencers, valve springs, manifolds and even column gearchange conversions then became Abarth's stock in trade.

The 204 was a success elsewhere, however, and in 1950 Nuvolari scored the last win of a magnificent career with an Abarth-prepared 204 Spyder in the Monte Pellegrino hillclimb. Also in 1950, Abarth introduced the 114mph (183kph) 204 Berlinetta, with Abarth-modified 1090cc Fiat power and Porsche-inspired torsion bar suspension.

Abarth continued to expand through prototype and 'special edition' production, invariably based on Fiat Millecento mechanicals and with exceptional aerodynamic styling. He now also added record breaking to his interests and expanded his racing activities, for publicity as much as for development.

The company formed more formal links with Fiat with the 1956 introduction of a road-

going 750cc version of the diminutive 600, followed by the 850TC for which Fiat supplied shells and part-finished cars. In return, Abarth gave Fiat excellent publicity by dominating the smaller classes of the European Touring Car Championships and capturing some 113 world records with Fiat-powered Abarths, clothed by the likes of Pininfarina and Bertone.

Abarths gradually became more Abarth and less Fiat as Abarth developed his own engines in the early 1960s, starting with a 1300 and moving through 1600cc to a full 2-litre. In spite of this and brief flirtations with Alfa Romeo in 1958, Porsche in 1960 and Simca between 1961 and 1966, the Fiat link remained strong.

Helped by particularly apposite championship rules, Abarth piled up a huge list of competition successes, with over 7200 class and outright wins by 1972, according to Fiat. These netted three successive European Touring Car Challenge 1-litre class wins, seven 1000- and 1300-class World Manufacturers' Championships, a European Alpine Championship and two successive European Hillclimb Championships.

Although sporting success made the Abarth name, racing ambition also brought major financial problems. In 1967 Abarth invested heavily in developing a 6-litre V12 engine to chase victory in the World Manufacturers' Championship, only to see his project killed by the late imposition of a 3-litre capacity limit. A 3-litre Grand Prix engine was never completed.

In 1970 Abarth signed agreements to pro-

duce tuned versions of the Autobianchi A112, but by 1971 Abarth's financial problems were such that, on 1 August, Fiat took over the tuning part of the company with Carlo himself retained as a technical consultant and the Abarth name still used for special production cars, the national Formula Italia single-seater racers and Fiat's successful rally cars. Fiat relinquished the former competition side of Abarth, including the services of chassis engineer Arrigo Tomaini and engine man Jacaponi, to Osella Servizio Corse, which continued to use Abarth engines with mixed success in various formulae up to 1974.

Abarth Fiats won the World Rally Championship in 1977, 1978 and 1980 and Abarth also developed the Lancia which won the title in 1983. Since 1979 the company has built a number of tuned and supercharged engines for Fiat and Lancia and in 1985 one of the hottest of the hot hatchbacks was the Fiat Strada Abarth 130TC.

Just as Abarth had started out with Cisitalias, Osella had been founded in 1965 to prepare and race customer Abarths, its young founder, Vincenzo Osella, acquiring his love for racing during 1963 – while building a house for Carlo Abarth. BL

ABBOTT/ABBOTT-DETROIT
USA 1909-1918

The Abbott Motor Co was organized in Detroit in 1909 with a capital of $300,000, making conventional cars with four-cylinder Continental engines. Prices were in the range $1500 to $2350 and the cars were badged as Abbott-Detroits.

Production in the first year was about 100 cars. By 1911 there were two models, the four-cylinder 30 and the six-cylinder 44; the cars' slogan 'Built for Permanence' was not very appropriate for the company, which was reorganized in 1914 and again in 1915 when it was acquired by the Consolidated Car Co. In 1916 it dropped the four-cylinder car and added an eight, powered by a Herschell-Spillman V8. Production was 15 to 20 a day, and it was to improve on this figure that the company moved to a larger plant at Cleveland, at the same time increasing capitalization to $1,250,000 and changing the name to the Abbott Corporation.

The move took place in April 1917, a few days before America entered World War I. This proved fatal for the new company, which struggled on through 1917 making Continental-engined sixes – very few of the 8-80 were made, and none at Cleveland – before going bankrupt in January 1918. The name and goodwill were purchased by the Standard Motor Parts Co and the plant by the National Electric Lamp Works, both of Cleveland. It is believed that employees of the latter company assembled one or two Abbotts from parts left behind by the Abbott Corporation. GNG

ABC
GB 1920-1927

ABC 1203cc two-seater of c.1921

The ABC had its origins in a small factory at Redbridge, near Southampton, making motor boat and aero engines. In 1910 Granville Bradshaw became chief designer changing the name to the All British Engine Co. To be nearer to the aircraft makers it moved to Brooklands in 1911, later adding flat-twin engines for motorcycles and cyclecars to its products. Complete motorcycles were then made by ABC Road Motors Ltd of Walton-on-Thames, Surrey, and this company also made aero engines, from 1917 under the name Walton Motors Ltd. The engines included the ABC Dragonfly, Wasp and Gnat. War contracts led to a considerable expansion of the factory, which covered 22 acres (9 hectares) by the end of hostilities.

In 1919 ABC began to make the single-cylinder Skootamota, one of the first motor scooters, and Bradshaw also designed a flat-twin motorcycle which was made under the name ABC by the Sopwith Aviation and Engineering Co at nearby Kingston-on-Thames. This arrangement continued until 1921.

In 1920 a new company, ABC Motors (1920) Ltd, was formed with a capital of £500,000 to manufacture aero engines, motorcycles and a new light car, all to be powered by Bradshaw's engines. Castings, stampings and drop forgings for the car were to be supplied by Harper Bean Ltd up to a total of 5000 sets a year, hence the presence on the ABC board of J. Harper Bean, managing director of the well-known Midlands firm.

The car had a 1203cc overhead-valve air-cooled engine, and shaft drive. It performed well, being capable of 65mph (104kph) in Super Sports form, but was noisy, hard to start and very prone to breaking push rods. Hoped-for sales of 5000 a year never materialized and not more than 1500 were sold in seven years.

In 1923 the company went into liquidation and a new concern, ABC Motors Ltd, was formed under the leadership of the former company secretary, T. A. Dennis. The car was made more reliable but the damage to its reputation stuck, and sales dwindled until 1927 when they ceased. Skootamota production had ended in 1922, but the flat-twin motorcycles were made until 1924.

ABC Motors Ltd continued in business under T. A. Dennis, making Scorpion flat-twin aero engines (modified versions of the car engine) and from 1932 a flat-twin auxiliary engine designed by Lord Ridley, who had joined ABC in 1929. This was widely used during World War II for driving dynamos and compressors. In 1929 ABC built one complete aircraft, the Robin monoplane, and from 1938 was active in making variable pitch propellers. It became part of Vickers Ltd in 1951 and remained so until it was closed down in 1971. GNG

AC
GB 1908-1985

The history of AC dates back to 1904, when Autocars and Accessories Ltd was founded at West Norwood in south London to manufacture a three-wheeled trade carrier suitable for businesses which wanted to replace their pony and trap but could not afford a full-size four-wheeled van. The partners were engineer John Weller, who had designed an advanced 20hp car in 1903, and John Portwine, owner of a chain of butcher shops who provided the initial capital of £200.

Weller also designed a motorcycle and the Hitchon-Weller car which was made by the Hitchon Gear and Automobile Co of Accrington, Lancashire, and was sold under the name Globe. Probably because of his association with this company, production of the Autocarrier tri-van did not begin until 1907, but it finally caught on at a price of only £80 and well-known customers included the Great Western Railway, Maples, Selfridges and Associated Newspapers. Export orders took the Autocarrier as far afield as Argentina and China.

In 1908 a passenger version of the Autocarrier was launched under the name AC Sociable and remained in production until 1914. The original company was renamed Auto Carriers Ltd in 1907 and Auto Carriers (1911) Ltd four years later, when capital was increased to £25,000. In the same year new premises were acquired at Thames Ditton, Surrey, in which town the company and its successors have been located ever since. An attractive four-wheeled light car with three-speed gearbox in unit with the rear axle and a French-built 10hp four-cylinder Fivet engine (made in the former Tony Huber works at Billancourt) were launched in 1913, but fewer than 100 were made before production was stopped by the outbreak of World War I.

The factory was enlarged during the war, when it made large quantities of shells and fuses, and a post-war model was announced in October 1918, two weeks before the Armistice. This was similar to the pre-war car, but with a larger Fivet engine soon replaced by a 1496cc Anzani engine, for which AC placed an order for 2000 units with British Anzani. In return for what was a very important order for a struggling firm, Portwine and Weller became directors of British Anzani. In 1919 Weller's 1½-litre six-cylinder engine was announced, and this unit, increased to 1991cc in 1922, became the staple AC power unit until 1963, by which time power had risen from 35 to 103bhp.

In February 1921 S. F. Edge of Napier fame joined the board of AC, together with Thomas Gillett, who was to drive ACs in a number of record-breaking races, and Lieutenant-Colonel John S. Napier. In 1921 AC had 900 employees and a capital of £330,000. In September 1922 Weller and Portwine both resigned, leaving Edge in total command of AC's policies. Their places on the Anzani board were taken by Edge and Gillett, but shortly afterwards Edge began to manufacture engines of Anzani design in the Cubitt factory which he also owned, and the AC order of 2000 engines was never fulfilled. This caused a great deal of recrimination and was one of the reasons why British Anzani went into liquidation in 1925.

AC Autocarrier three-wheeler of 1903

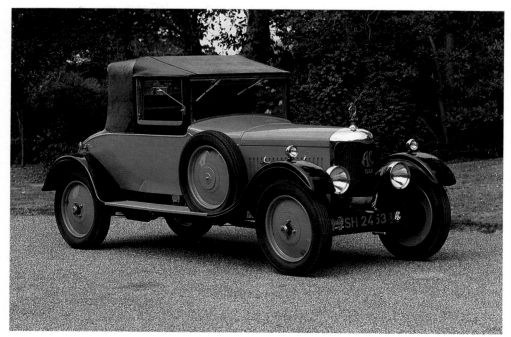

AC 2-litre Six of 1925

By this time AC was itself in trouble. It was saved only by the intervention of Edge, who put in a lot of his own money and in 1925 bought up the 80,000 shares in the company that were owned by Vauxhall Motors. His investment in AC totalled £135,000. The cars had sold well in the early 1920s, but with very little modernization – front-wheel brakes were an extra until 1927, and they had only three speeds up to 1933 – they fell behind their competitors. The four-cylinder model in particular became hard to sell and was dropped after 1927. A six-cylinder model driven by the Hon Victor Bruce gave Britain its first Monte Carlo Rally victory in 1926.

The company name had changed from Auto Carriers (1911) Ltd to AC Cars Ltd in 1922, and a further reorganization in 1927 led to the formation of AC (Acedes) Ltd. During 1929 this company went into liquidation and car manufacture ceased. Edge and Gillett left, both having lost their sizeable investments. Only the service department continued, one of its jobs being the production of two six-cylinder engines to drive the dynamos on the airship *R100*.

In the spring of 1930 the Thames Ditton factory was bought by the Hurlock brothers, William and Charles, who operated a successful business in Brixton, London, selling and servicing cars and commercial vehicles. They had no intention of becoming manufacturers, planning to use the AC factory as a depot. However, when the AC service manager assembled a car for William Hurlock's personal use, Hurlock was sufficiently pleased to recommend the make to his friends, with the result that a trickle of cars, each built to special order, left the factory between 1930 and 1933.

Production then began to build up, aided by the use of a Standard 16 chassis as supplied to SS Cars Ltd. Weller's classic single-overhead cam 2-litre six was retained, now made in unit with a four-speed gearbox supplied by ENV. This was supplemented by a Wilson preselector box from 1934 and a synchromesh box from 1935, although the two-seater sports models could be had with all three types of gearbox up to 1939.

Most components on 1930s ACs were bought from outside suppliers, but coachwork was made by AC, as it had been in the 1920s. A variety of attractive bodies was made, two- and four-door saloons, coupés, sports tourers and short wheelbased two-seater sports cars. It is remarkable that such a variety was available with such small production, much lower than under the Edge regime. Indeed, only 631 cars were made from 1933 to 1939. AC had about 100 workers in 1938.

The Hurlock brothers were keen rally drivers and gained much useful publicity with victories in the RAC Rally and other events. The 1933 RAC was won by Kitty Brunell and her all-girl team in AC sports tourers, and in 1935 T. V. Selby only just missed winning the Monte Carlo Rally.

Car production ceased soon after the outbreak of war in September 1939, and a wide variety of war work occupied both the Thames Ditton and Taggs Island factories for the next six years. The Taggs Island premises were bought in 1940, by which time AC had already contracted to make parts for Fairey Aviation and this work became increasingly important during the 1940s and 1950s. Other war work included fire-pump trailers, bodies and cabs for Ford and Bedford fire-engines, six-pounder guns, glider undercarriages and flame-throwers.

Fulfilment of war contracts prevented an immediate return to car manufacture and it was not until October 1947 that the first post-war cars left the factory. These used pre-war engines and chassis with attractive streamlined saloon bodies. The saloons and a few drop-head coupés were made at Thames Ditton, joined for 1950 by the Buckland sports tourer made by Buckland Body Works of Buntingford, Hertfordshire, an important location in the future history of AC.

In October 1951 AC became a public company, increasing its capital by £50,000 in one shilling shares. The continuing substantial contracts with Fairey Aviation were mentioned by the financial press as the main reason for confidence in the company, which had averaged more than £52,000 profit annually for the preceding 10 years.

Sales of the handsome but increasingly old-fashioned 2-litre saloon were sluggish by 1951 and AC was diversifying into different fields. These included three-wheeled invalid carriages, for which AC received a major contract from the Ministry of Pensions, four electric trains for use on Southend pier (in service up to 1979), and the 'Bag Boy' golfclub carrier. All these came from Taggs Island, the parts for the invalid carriages being machined at Thames Ditton. A development of the invalid carriage was the Petite, a two-seater three-wheeler, of which about 2000 were made from 1953 to 1958.

The significance of Buntingford emerged in 1953 when visiting AC managers were attracted by an advanced sports car, built by John Tojeiro, that had a tubular ladder chassis, transverse leaf independent suspension and a simple Ferrari-like aluminium body. Powered by a 2-litre Bristol engine and driven by Cliff Davis, it was highly successful in competitions.

AC duly acquired the right to make the car at Thames Ditton, powered by its own 2-litre engine. It was known as the Ace, and it was joined in 1954 by the Aceca coupé and in 1959 by the Greyhound four-seater sports saloon. The Bristol engine was an alternative from 1956 and after Bristol ceased making its own engines in 1959 the 2.6-litre Ford Zephyr engine was adopted.

The Ace had many competition successes, winning the 2-litre class at Le Mans in 1957 and Sports Car Club of America Championships from 1957 to 1961. This attracted the attention of American racing-driver Carroll Shelby, who persuaded Ford to supply V8 engines for mounting in AC chassis. The result was the Cobra, of which 1070 were made from 1962 to 1969.

Ace production ceased in 1963, the company concentrating on supplying chassis to Shelby until 1966 when it launched the AC 428, a luxury GT coupé or open two-seater using a lengthened Cobra chassis, 7-litre Ford V8 engines and bodies from Frua in Italy. They were never bestsellers, only 80 being made in seven years, and the energy crisis of 1973 killed them off completely. The invalid three-wheeler was discontinued in 1976 but commercial trailers and vehicle bodybuilding kept the company going.

Derek Hurlock, son of William, was too

much of an enthusiast to abandon car production, however. As with Tojeiro 20 years earlier, he found his answer in a one-off prototype, this time the mid-engined coupé built by Peter Bohanna and Robin Stables. First shown in 1972 with a British Leyland Maxi engine and gearbox, the AC ME3000 version eventually appeared with Ford 3-litre V6 power and AC's own five-speed gearbox. Development problems and difficulties in obtaining Type Approval delayed production until January 1979 and the small dealer network gradually crumbled, so that sales were now handled direct from the factory. Only eight development cars were made between 1973 and 1980, and 68 production cars from 1980 to 1984.

Non-car activities pushed profits up from £123,000 in 1974 to £218,000 in 1977, the year in which AC bought the specialist commercial-vehicle manufacturer Unipower, but in 1979 and 1980 losses of over £200,000 were recorded. The factory which the company had occupied since 1911 was sold for £1.2 million and smaller premises elsewhere in Thames Ditton were acquired. Unipower was also sold.

In April 1984 came the news that a Scottish businessman had bought the car interests of AC and formed a new company, AC (Scotland) Ltd. A factory was acquired at Cardonald Industrial Estate, Glasgow, with a capacity of 400 cars a year. AC Cars plc has a small shareholding in the new company and will continue to sell the Scottish-built cars, and to service older ACs.

Thirty Ford-engined cars were made in Scotland between September 1984 and June 1985, when it was announced that they were to be replaced by a re-styled car called the Ecosse, powered by an Alfa Romeo 2½-litre V6 engine. Later in 1985 the company went out of business. GNG

ACADIAN
see McLaughlin

ACE
see Ryknield

ADAMS/ADAMS-HEWITT, HEWITT
GB, USA 1905-1914

Edward Ringwood Hewitt was a talented American inventor from a wealthy background who was educated at Princeton and in Germany. From 1891 he designed propellers for Vickers in England and worked with Maxim on his steam aeroplane of 1894. His grandfather, Peter Cooper, had made America's pioneer steam loco 'Tom Thumb' and had founded a glue factory where Hewitt became chief chemist.

After visiting France in 1899 to examine its motor industry, Hewitt began experimenting with a motor vehicle and in 1903 was ready for production. With financial backing from a member of the Rockefeller family and $40,000 from his mother he founded the Hewitt Motor Co. In 1905 he acquired US Long Distance/Standard Motor Construction Co of New Jersey.

Meanwhile in England, A. H. Adams had obtained the American Cutler-Hammer electrical equipment agency and set up Igranic Works of Bedford in 1899. When Adams met Hewitt the two men agreed on a joint programme of car production, the idea being that engines and foot-change planetary gearboxes would be made by Adams, and axles

and other parts would be made in New York. About 50 sets of parts were supplied from England before US assembly was discontinued.

The Adams-Hewitt car was launched in England in 1905 with a single-cylinder horizontal engine, and 'pedals to push, that's all'. Twins and fours followed, plus a remarkable V8, based on an Antoinette aero engine and designed by chief engineer Reg Smith in late 1906. Possibly 11 V8 cars were built. Two V8 engines were also mounted on a common crankcase to make a V16 racing-boat engine for a New Zealand customer in 1908.

Marcus Inman-Hunter, who had been apprenticed at the Great Northern Railway with W. O. Bentley, became designer and chief engineer in 1907 and an enormous assortment of models followed. They carried the name Adams and had A-shaped radiators.

Adams-Hewitt of 1906

Hewitt in the United States produced a similar V8 but from 1908 was best known for commercial vehicles. Hewitt merged with the makers of the Everitt car in 1911 and the following year joined a consortium that included Mack. E. R. Hewitt became a director of Mack and remained technical adviser to the company until after World War II.

At Bedford, sliding-mesh gearboxes were introduced, a car was supplied to the Emperor of Abyssinia as early as 1907, and compressed-air starters that also worked a jacking system and tyre inflator came in 1911. Coventry-Simplex and Aster engines were used on some models. Financial difficulties were looming, however, and in 1911 Inman-Hunter left to design the Cheswold car while J. M. Strachan, later well-known for bus bodies, joined the Aberdonia company. E. Talbot, the chief draughtsman, perfected his steel Zephyr piston while at Adams.

A. H. Adams was lost in the *Titanic* disaster in 1912 and a receiver was appointed to his firm, which continued to make cars until 1914. Total production including vans has been estimated at 3000. Igranic Works resumed activity in the electrical component industry and as Brookhirst-Igranic, part of the Metal Industries group, remains in Bedford where the Adams car test-track still exists and a 1907 car is preserved. NB

AC ME3000 3-litre coupé of 1977

ADAMS-FARWELL
USA 1905-1913

The Adams Co of Dubuque, Iowa, was founded in 1883 and manufactured park benches, milling and foundry equipment. In about 1887 Fay Oliver Farwell became superintendent and a decade later began to tinker with an air-cooled rotary engine as a power unit for horseless carriages. Between 1898 and 1905 he built five such vehicles, all powered by three-cylinder engines.

In February 1905 his Model 5 was shown at the Chicago Automobile Show and small-scale production began, although the cautious Adams brothers, Eugene and Herbert, did not commit the whole of their works to the new-fangled invention. For 1906 a five-cylinder model was announced, using the same principle of a horizontal rotary engine whose cylinders and crank case revolved around a fixed shaft. Transmission was by a four-speed gearbox – three speeds from 1908 – and a short chain to the rear axle. The engine was mounted in the rear of the frame, and the cars could be driven either from the front seat or the rear; moving the pedals and steering tiller took less than a minute.

As the years passed, prices rose from $2000 to $3500 and the cars became more conventional looking, with a frontal bonnet, even though the engine remained at the rear. The dual steering position was abandoned. Sales dwindled and in 1913 the Adams brothers gave up manufacture after about 52 cars had been made. Their company survives to the present day.

Farwell left in 1921 and showed his devotion to the rotary idea by trying to sell a merry-go-round to fairground operators. When this venture failed he set up a gear-cutting business in Toledo, Ohio, where he worked until his death in 1942. GNG

ADER
FRANCE 1900-1907

Born at Muret near Toulouse in 1841, Clément Ader achieved more fame with aeroplanes than with cars, not that the latter were lacking in interest. He was also a successful bicycle manufacturer from 1869. He made a considerable fortune from his Société Générale des Téléphones Ader, which installed many of the most important telephone lines in France and elsewhere in Europe.

The money derived from this business enabled him to build three steam-powered aeroplanes between 1890 and 1897, for which he received a subsidy from the French War Office. He had little success with these, although they were the first attempts in France to fly with a heavier-than-air machine.

In 1900 he created a separate branch of the telephone company to make cars, giving it

Adler Trumpf Junior sports of c.1936

the clumsy title of Société Industrielle des Téléphones-Voitures Automobiles, Système Ader. His first car had a 6hp V-twin engine of 904cc, chain drive and a tubular frame. With a four-seater tonneau body, it sold for 6000 francs. In 1901 he replaced the tubular chassis with a channel steel one and built his first shaft-driven car, although he also continued with chain-drive models.

His first four-cylinder engine of 1902 was, in effect, two of the 904cc two-cylinder units linked together, and when he built a team of V8 racing cars for the 1903 Paris-Madrid race, these used two of the V4s. These engines were never used in production cars but were important as being the first roadgoing V8 engines ever made. A shaft-drive motorcycle powered by a 479cc V-twin engine was offered under the name Moto-Cardan in 1903.

In 1904 Ader separated car production completely from telephones, forming the Société des Automobiles Ader, although the factory remained at Levallois Perret. For 1904 he made a 10hp vertical twin and two models of 14/20hp four-cylinder cars, one with in-line cylinders, the other a V4, hedging his bets as to the popularity of the two systems. He continued to do this until 1907 when he went over entirely to in-line engines with two four-cylinder cars, a 16/20 of 2923cc and a 28/32 of 5398cc. He continued to make V engines for use in motor boats, while his engines were also supplied to other firms including Royal Enfield in England.

In 1904 he obtained some English capital, forming the Société Anonyme des Automobiles Ader Ltd; Ader cars were sold in England under the name Pegasus. Sales dwindled from 1905 and in 1907 Ader abandoned car production. He died in 1925 at the age of 84. GNG

ADLER
GERMANY 1900-1939

The Adler was one of Germany's most respected cars for much of its life. It had its origins in the bicycle business founded in Frankfurt-am-Main by Heinrich Kleyer in 1880. At first he imported American

machines which he sold under the name Herold. By 1885 he had acquired a six-storey building, at that time the tallest business premises in Frankfurt, in which he manufactured cycles, with the top floor reserved for riding lessons for new owners.

In 1895 he changed the name of his cycle to Adler (Eagle) and during the 1890s he began to make wire wheels which he supplied to Benz, then the world's largest car manufacturer. He also founded the German branch of Dunlop and entered the typewriter manufacturing field, which was to outlast his motor cars by many years.

He acquired a licence to make De Dion-Bouton tricycles in 1898, but did not do much with it, proceeding to a light car powered by a De Dion-Bouton engine. This voiturette was designed by Franz Starkloph and went into production in 1900.

Three years later Starkloph left Adler for the Polyphon company, which made the Curved Dash Olds under licence, and in his place came Edmund Rumpler, later to achieve fame with his rear-engined 'teardrop' cars. His contributions to Adler were not so spectacular, but he kept the company at the forefront of contemporary design, with four-cylinder engines in-unit with gearboxes, light-alloy crankcases and, from 1905, pressure lubrication.

In 1904 Adler expanded its premises but still could not keep up with demand, so it imported French-built Clément-Bayards in the same way that Opel had been doing with Darracqs. In 1906 the company name was changed from Heinrich Kleyer AG to Adlerwerke. The range of models grew in the years up to World War I, and in 1911 ran from a 1-litre V-twin to a 9.1-litre four, commercial vehicles up to a 3-ton chassis, motorcycles and also the bicycles on which the company's prosperity was founded.

In 1912 and 1913 the company built additional factory space and purchased the works in Frankfurt of the electrical equipment manufacturer AEG. It had also set up an Austrian subsidiary and was exporting to many European countries as well as to Russia and Asia. In Britain Adler was represented by coachbuilders Morgan and Co of Leighton Buzzard, which often mounted its own

13

Adler Trumpf Junior cabriolet of c.1936

3-litre six-cylinder Diplomat.

Shortly after the Trumpf was introduced in 1932, Heinrich Kleyer died at the age of 79. He was succeeded by his son Erwin, whose interest in streamlining led to some very advanced competition versions of the Trumpf, and a new series of 2½-litre six-cylinder cars with aerodynamic bodies was introduced in 1938.

Like most Adlers of the 1930s, these cars had bodies by Ambi-Budd. Only 5295 were made before World War II once again turned Adler's attention to military products, in particular staff cars and ambulances based on the Diplomat, and half-tracked vehicles of Demag design powered by four-cylinder Maybach engines. Adler 2½-litre engines were used in the Trippel amphibious cars.

The factory was largely destroyed during the war, and although prototypes of a post-war Trumpf Junior were built, the company decided not to resume car production. Instead, when its new factory was completed, it concentrated on typewriters and, from 1949 to 1957, a range of motorcycles from 98 to 250cc. Adler's considerable dealer network was taken up by Volkswagen. Typewriter production continues to the present day, latterly as part of the Grundig group for which Adler also makes calculators. In 1969 Grundig was bought by the American Litton Industries Inc, which sold it to Volkswagenwerk AG in 1979. GNG

bodies and sold the cars under the name Morgan-Adler. German-sold Adlers generally used bodies by Schebera of Berlin.

During World War I Adler built trucks, transmissions for tanks, and aero engines under licence from Benz. Heinrich Kleyer made an interest-free war loan of 4 million marks to the government, but the loan was never fully repaid so that in 1920 the company passed into the control of the Deutsche Bank. The post-war car range was smaller than previously, a 5-ton truck chassis was introduced but motorcycles were not revived although bicycles continued to be made until 1939.

Assembly-line production began in 1925 with the 1½-litre four-cylinder Favorit whose 25bhp engine had detachable head and aluminium pistons, while the chassis had four-wheel brakes. More than 30,000 Favorits were made until 1934.

Adler's first straight-eight appeared in 1928, powered by a 3.9-litre side-valve unit and carrying handsome coachwork by Neuss, Gläser and others. It was also used as the basis for unusual functional coachwork designed by Walter Gropius, founder of the Bauhaus movement. A total of 1720 Eights was made between 1928 and 1934.

By 1928 Adler had a workforce of 6000 and was turning out 60 cars a day. Despite financial problems the following year, they were the third best-selling German car in 1930 behind Opel and BMW. The directors decided to move towards a more popular market, and after considering a rear-engined minicar designed by Josef Ganz, they opted for front-wheel drive and appointed as designer Hans Gustav Röhr, who had left the company bearing his name in 1930.

The result was the most famous Adler yet made, the 1½-litre Trumpf which appeared at the 1932 Geneva Motor Show. With all-round independent suspension and all-steel body made by Ambi-Budd of Berlin, the Trumpf soon became a bestseller. In 1933 2000 were being made every month, and total sales to 1939 of the Trumpf and its smaller brother, the 1-litre Trumpf Junior, were 128,443. The design was made under licence in Belgium by Impéria and in France by Rosengart. The Standard Eight was dropped in 1933, and the biggest Adler in production thereafter was the

Aero Type 50 sports of c.1938

AERO/ENKA
CZECHOSLOVAKIA 1929-1947

One of the more successful two-stroke cars from central Europe, the Aero design began life in 1924 as the Disk, designed by Bretislav Novotny. It had a 499cc single-cylinder engine, started by pulling a rope, and a punt-type frame. With backing from a friend named Koland, Novotny managed to start small-scale production of the car in Prague under the name Enka (the phonetic sound of NK, Novotny and Koland).

In 1929 production was taken up by the Aero company of Prague which made light aircraft, Weymann coachwork and sidecars

Aero Type 30 of 1933

for motorcycles. A 662cc two-cylinder model followed in 1931, enlarged to 998cc in 1932. From 1934 onwards front-wheel drive was adopted in a new series of Aeros, designed by Basek. They were low and handsome cars, whose length of bonnet belied their small engine capacity, which was still only 998cc.

In 1937 this Type 30 was joined by the similar looking Type 50 which had four cylinders of the same dimensions as the 30's (85×88mm) giving 1997cc. The wheelbase was only 3½in (90mm) longer than that of the Type 30, and with a roadster body, the Type 50 was good for 75mph (120kph).

During the 1930s Aero ranked fourth among Czech car producers, with annual output not much above 1000; in 1937 the company sold 1277, including a few light vans on the Type 30 chassis. Exports were confined to neighbouring countries such as Hungary, Poland and Romania. After the war the Type 30 was revived for a short time, and was offered on the Swiss market in 1947.

The factory was testing prototypes of new designs, the 750cc two-cylinder Ponny and 1½-litre four-cylinder Record, when car production ceased. A Skoda-designed 1½ ton van was made from 1946 to 1951, after which production of the design was transferred to Praga. Aero also built bodies for the Aero Minor of 1946-51, though this was not an Aero design, being developed from the pre-war Jawa Minor.

Together with other Czech aircraft firms, Aero was nationalized after the war. It became part of Letecke zavody and has made a variety of machines, including the Ae 45 twin-engined five-seater (1947 to 1958) and more recently MIG, Dolphin and Albatros fighters, the last-named being still in production in the 1980s. GNG

AGA
GERMANY 1919-1928

The German manufacturer AGA began life in Sweden as Svenska AB Gasaccumulator, making welding equipment. A German subsidiary, Autogen Gasaccumulator AG, was founded in Berlin-Lichtenberg in 1915, making machine gun parts during World War I. When the war ended, the relatively prosperous parent company looked for ways to expand into central Europe. In 1919 the company began to build cars, not initially of its own designs, but under licence from the Belgian manufacturer FN. From May 1920 the company was known as Aktiengesellschaft für Automobilbau, or AGA.

The first car, based on the pre-war FN 6PS, was introduced in October 1919 as the four-cylinder 1418cc 6/16PS Type A. From 1921 the unsuccessful Type A was replaced by the 1420cc 6/20PS and AGA offere a limousine, a two-seater and even a delivery truck. In 1920 Thulinverken, a Swedish aeronautical company based in Landskrona, began to manufacture cars under licence as Thulins, but only about 300 were built before the firm in this form went bankrupt in 1924.

From an early stage, AGA pursued a competition programme, although the production cars were said to have tricky handling and terrible brakes and were widely used as taxis. In 1921 works driver Philipp won the 6hp class in the inaugural meeting at Berlin's spectacular Avus track, at almost 70mph (112kph). In 1924 three 1495cc 6/30PS cars were sent to the Targa Florio where they took second and third places in their class.

From 1922, after the parent company had run into financial problems, AGA became part of the Stinnes corporation, which also included Dinos, Rabag-Bugatti and Vorster & Stolle. After Hugo Stinnes' death, towards the end of 1924, AGA had cash problems, aggravated by the fact that in straitened post-war Germany almost 90 per cent of car sales were under hire purchase agreements, but cautious banks had little inclination to provide credit for the smaller manufacturers.

In November 1925, in spite of earlier showing what was claimed to be the 10,000th AGA at the Berlin exhibition, the original company went bankrupt. AGA Kraftwerken Verwertungs GmbH continued limited production and the Dinos factory was taken over in 1926, ostensibly to increase production. A new company, AGA Fahrzeugwerke GmbH, was founded and produced up-dated versions of the 6/20PS. There were also plans to manufacture an 850cc competitor for the Dixi, under licence from the British Singer company, but these came to nothing.

In 1928 the company was still exhibiting cars at the shows, including a proposed six-cylinder 10/45PS cabriolet, but production stopped at the end of the year and in 1929 the new company was also declared bankrupt. The company continued, however, to make car parts in the early 1930s and carries on today with its initial activity of producing welding equipment. BL

AIREDALE
GB 1912-1924

In 1911 fellmonger George Barker provided a corner of his premises, 'The Skinyard', for his son Norman and a friend, Guy Nanson, to set up Nanson, Barker and Co and build the Tiny cyclecar. Between 1912 and the war three were made, one JAP-engined van for a local stationer and two Chater Lea-powered cars. Nanson left the company in 1913 and Noel Barber became a partner before going off for the duration of the war, through which the company made trench pumps and shell noses. With modest wartime profits, Nanson, Barker and Co resumed car manufacture in 1919, and with further financial help from Bradford mill owner Sam Ambler the company was reorganized in 1922 as Airedale Cars Ltd, named after the Aire valley where they were built and with the eponymous terrier as a mascot.

Norman Barker designed his first car around a Rubery-Owen chassis, a three-speed gearbox and one of four American Stirling engines which the firm had acquired during the war. The prototype was assembled in 'The Skinyard's' old scullery, whose wall had then to be knocked down to let the car out.

Production cars, first with Dorman and later Meadows engines, were assembled on the first floor of an old cornmill. The chassis were then lowered to the ground on a block and tackle, to be bodied by Jimmy Rock of Bingley or, later, by a firm in Bradford on a frame built by a local joiner.

In its brief heyday, the firm employed eight fitters and an apprentice, had a small forge and made its own gearboxes and back axles—although most castings were bought in. Airedale's car for the 1922 Olympia Show, hand polished by a local fireplace maker, was finished at 8pm on the eve of the show and was pushed to the local station to catch a train to London.

After almost 100 cars had been made, mostly two-seaters with dickeys, but also some four-seaters, the Amblers withdrew their support. No cars were built after 1924, although Noel Barber bought all the remaining spares to maintain a supply for Airedale owners. BL

AJS
GB 1930-1933

Around the turn of the century the four Stevens brothers began making small engines for motorcycles in Wolverhampton, one of their main customers being the Wearwell Motor Carriage Co, maker of the Wolf. In 1909 they began making their own motorcycles under the name AJS (Albert John Stevens), when a new private company, A. J. Stevens and Co Ltd, was formed. Five years later it became a public company, A. J. Stevens (1914) Ltd, with a capital of £250,000 and by the early 1920s was among the leading

AJS Nine fabric saloon of 1931

British motorcycle makers, with a workforce of 600.

In 1924 the brothers added radio sets to their products and in 1929 brought out a range of buses powered by six-cylinder Coventry-Climax engines. These were made for two years only. They were joined in 1930 by a 9hp light car powered by a 1018cc Coventry-Climax engine and available as an open two-seater for £210, fabric saloon (£230) or coach-built saloon (£240). It was rumoured to be based on the Clyno Nine, but although AJS had acquired some patents from their fellow Wolverhampton firm when it went into liquidation, there were very few close similarities between the two cars.

The AJS Nine was a quality light car, and considering its high price and the effects of the Depression on the market, did well to sell 3000 units in 18 months. However, in October 1931 AJS went into liquidation, due to losses on the motorcycle and bus side of the business, and all production at Wolverhampton ceased. Rights to the motorcycles were bought by the Collier brothers, makers of the Matchless, and production of the AJS was resumed at Plumstead in south-east London, where they were made until 1969.

The buses were dropped but manufacture of the car was taken over by Willys-Overland-Crossley Ltd of Stockport, which made a further 300, all coach-built saloons. At £229 they were competing closely with Crossley's own Ten at £265, and the AJS was reduced to £189 in March 1932. They tried to launch a larger, 1½-litre, car at £375 but it got no further than the 1932 Olympia Show. Willys-Overland-Crossley went into liquidation a year later.

In 1934 the Stevens brothers founded a new company, Stevens Brothers (Wolverhampton) Ltd, which made motorcycles and three-wheeler light vans until 1937. The original works were still in use in 1985 in the light engineering field and were still being run by a member of the Stevens family. GNG

ALBANY
GB 1903-1905

The short-lived Albany Manufacturing Co Ltd of Willesden, north-west London, was nothing if not versatile: in its three brief seasons it made both petrol- and steam-powered cars and established a reputation as supplier of its own silencers and 'Venetian' radiators, which *The Autocar* in 1904 remarked 'have a neat appearance and are widely used'.

The company was constituted in 1903 and the steam car was offered for that year only. Designed by Frederick Lamplough, who had built a steam car as early as 1896, it appeared at the Crystal Palace Show in February as the Lamplough-Albany. The 24hp four-cylinder car had a semi-flash boiler, fuelled by either petrol or kerosene and running at a pressure of 300-400psi. Outwardly it looked much like any contemporary petrol car and was available with wheel or tiller steering.

In December of the same year A. Christophe showed a 10hp two-seater petrol-engined Albany at the Paris Show, priced at 5000 francs or about £200. The company also offered a 16hp twin and the light petrol car was dubbed the Silent Safety; it had an Albany-designed silencing system in which the exhaust gases passed first through a turbine which drove the cooling fan and then to a silencer. The clutch control was connected to the carburettor in such a way that the engine slowed automatically as the clutch was withdrawn.

The Motor described the 10hp single-cylinder car as being 'of an extremely simple construction and of very strong build ... its appearance vies with that of the most expensive cars and it ought to be just the thing for automobilists who look to economy in the first cost and upkeep of their vehicles'. Not enough automobilists did look to Albany, however, and in mid-1905 the company

ceased car manufacture and reverted to making radiators and selling the rather more long-lived Talbot cars. BL

ALBANY
GB 1971-1980

The prototype of the Albany replica Edwardian roadster, with side-valve Ford Popular engine and much Morris Minor running gear, was conceived by Brian Shepherd in 1971 and built in a modern factory in Christchurch, Hampshire, which normally made materials for the construction industry. In December 1971 it was offered as a production model, with cast alloy artillery style wheels, a brass radiator shell and replica lamp units carrying modern lights, by the newly formed Albany Motor Carriage Co.

The first cars were delivered early in 1972, now with Morris Minor engines governed to limit top speed to about 40mph (64kph), at a basic price of £1987. The sixth Albany, delivered in September, used a Triumph 1300 engine, which was subsequently offered as standard as sales rose to about two cars a month. The American specification Triumph Spitfire engine was adopted in 1974, when about a dozen cars were sold in the United States before the dealer there went out of business.

The Albany sold steadily, if only in small numbers. A four-seater prototype of 1976 went into production alongside the two-seater late in 1977, but production stopped in 1980 as the novelty wore off. BL

ALBERT
see Gwynne

ALBION
GB 1900-1913

Norman Osborne Fullerton and T. Blackwood Murray worked together at the Mo-Car Syndicate, which produced the Arrol-Johnston, as works and commercial managers respectively. Blackwood Murray had formerly been with electrical engineers Mavor and Coulson, where he worked on an electrical ignition system for Coventry Daimler and invented the low tension magneto. The two men left in 1899 to develop their own car prototypes and on 30 December 1899 they formed the Albion Motor Car Co, working from upstairs rooms in Finnieston Street, Glasgow. There were seven employees.

Early in 1900 the first opposed-twin 8hp engines, with low tension magneto and Blackwood Murray's patent governor, were ready for installation in Arrol-Johnston-like dogcarts. A total of 159 dogcarts, with wheel steering from 1902, were produced until 1903. Some had van bodies and several were exported.

THE 12 h.p. "LAMPLOUGH-ALBANY" STEAM TONNEAU CAR.

Lamplough-Albany steam tonneau of 1902

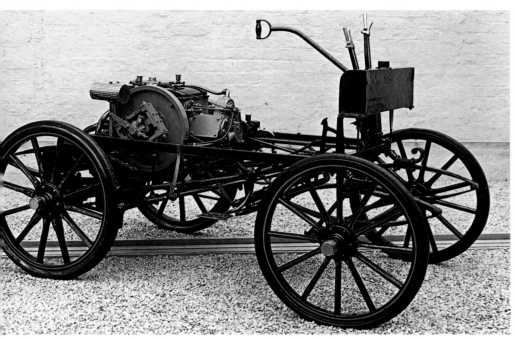

Albion dogcart chassis of c.1900

Albion 24/30hp A6 of 1906

several models carried on into the 1980s. The Albion plant by that time was concentrating on components, notably axles, for other Leyland vehicle factories. NB

ALBRUNA
see Brown

ALCO
USA 1905-1913

The American Locomotive Co was created in 1901 by the merger of eight railway locomotive builders, the oldest dating from 1835, whose combined output by 1906 totalled 40,000 steam locos. In June 1905 the company's president, Albert S. Pitkin, announced that it had negotiated with Berliet in France to build cars under licence in a rolling stock factory at Providence, Rhode Island. Berliet was paid 500,000 francs, and 200 cars were

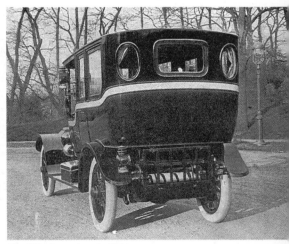

Alco 60hp limousine of c.1911

In July 1903 Albion moved into a factory at Scotstoun and the Finnieston Street premises were acquired by Walter Bergius, who made a few Kelvin cars there from 1904 before deciding in 1906 that a better future lay in marine engines. In 1904 came a 1-ton Albion truck and dogcart production ceased.

Two-cylinder vertical-engined chassis had appeared in 1903 and were joined in 1906 by a four-cylinder 24hp model, still with chain drive. In 1906 221 chassis were made and the workforce had risen to 283; by 1910 there were 450 employees. Albions were very popular as ¾ to 2-ton vans in London, where sales were in the hands of the Lacre Motor Car Co until Albion opened its own factory-staffed branch in 1909, Lacre having earned disfavour for selling Albion 'as sure as sunrise' vehicles as Lacres.

In 1912 only about 150 of the 554 Albions built that year were cars; a four-cylinder 15hp chassis was the first with shaft drive. The workforce had reached about 1000 when the four joint managing directors, each an expert

in different areas, decided at the end of 1913 to concentrate on commercial vehicles alone. Although a few chassis were sold for estate duties as shooting brakes, the overall decision was vindicated during World War I, when some 6000 Albions were supplied to the fighting services. T. Blackwood Murray remained closely involved at Scotstoun until his death in 1929, and by the end of that year his company had produced a total of 20,942 vehicles.

Albion outlasted all other pioneer Scottish car-makers. It built on its reputation of simple, frugal, well-made, long-lasting vehicles and became a major producer of lorries and buses. It produced its own diesel engines from 1933 and in 1935 acquired the Glasgow factory of Halley Motors Ltd.

In 1951 Albion was acquired by Leyland Motors Ltd for nearly £3 million but retained its separate identity until the 1960s, by which time its factories employed 3500 people. In 1972 the Albion name on commercial vehicles was replaced by that of Leyland, but

planned in the first year using a mixture of French and American parts.

No expense was spared to achieve perfection, and vanadium steel – described as 'the mystic, anti-fatigue metal' – was widely used for the first time on an American car. Each car took 19 months to complete; the casing for the live rear axle, first introduced on smaller models in 1907, was forged in one piece by the largest drop-hammer in the world and accounted for about a third of this period.

The earliest cars were 24 and 40hp fours with chain drive, two-speed differentials (until 1907), and camshaft drive by Renolds chain. The word automobile was dropped from the car division's name of American Locomotive Automobile Co in 1909 and the cars, which had been called American Locomotive Berliet, American Berliet or simply Berliet, became Alcos after the Berliet licence was discontinued in September 1908. B. D. Gray was now chief engineer. Taxis became an important product in 1909 and Berliet-based cabover trucks, which had been in experimental service since 1907, were also adopted. Within a couple of years commercials accounted for 85 per cent of output and Alco was the largest American taxi builder.

Little effort was made to capitalize on the remarkable success of an Alco car in winning the Vanderbilt Cup in both 1909 and 1910, although in 1912 the company announced that as it was 'unable to build a better car' it would 'make a more beautiful one'. Harry S. Houpt, previously champion salesman for the E. R. Thomas Motor Car Co and maker of the 1909-10 Houpt car, ran the racing team and then became general sales manager, boosting agencies from 4 to 89 and sales by 365 per cent. He left in 1912 to represent Lozier. Another Alco employee was Walter P. Chrysler.

Having made about 1000 trucks and 4000 passenger vehicles Alco announced in September 1913 that it was discharging its 1200 motor factory employees and would concentrate exclusively on the railroad industry. Even if the cars were no longer viable the company's showing in the commercial field had been spectacular and earnings from road and rail interests in 1913 were $35 million. The road vehicle side had consistently lost money but stockholders had wanted it to be sold as a going concern, and forced management changes. The new team concentrated on railway equipment.

Alco stuck to steam for too long and introduced diesels too late to compete successfully with General Motors. Its diesel loco and generator business was bought by the Worthington Corporation in 1964, Alco becoming a holding corporation under the name Citadel Industries, which is owned by General Tire and Rubber Co. The renamed Studebaker-Worthington company sold its Alco engine line to White in 1969. NB

ALCYON
FRANCE 1906-1928

Alcyon racer of 1908

Edmond Gentil made Alcyon motorcycles at Neuilly, Seine, from 1902, many of the early machines using Zédel and Buchet engines. In 1906, when capital stood at 500,000 francs, light cars were added and a year later there were models of up to 2.7 litres capacity. Zurcher engines were used in several models

and also in the single-cylinder 1912 Isle of Man Tourist Trophy motorcycle entries. A move was made to Courbevoie in 1912 and the firm's car side became Société des Automobiles Alcyon in 1914.

Its post-war efforts were limited to cyclecars and a short-lived 2-litre model, various sporting versions of which were sold with Alcyon GL badges by agent Giroux of Lyons. From 1925 the cyclecars were largely identical to Sima-Violets. Some were marketed under the name of the recently acquired Armor motorcycle firm.

After 1928 only motorcycles were made and Alcyon acquired many of its former rivals, also creating new brands. Names that became involved included Olympique (a neighbour in Courbevoie), Thomann, La Française and Labor. Labor lasted until 1960 and Alcyon itself stopped trading a few years later, having concentrated most of its efforts on mopeds. NB

ALDA
FRANCE 1912-1922

The prime mover behind the French Alda was Fernand Charron, former bicycle racer turned auto racer and one of the recurring names in French automobile history. Charron, born in Angers in 1866, was one of France's earliest motor dealers, having set up shop in Paris in 1897 with fellow racers Léonce Girardot and Emile Voigt as Panhard agents under the name L'Agence Générale des Automobiles. Charron, Girardot and Voigt progressed from being salesmen to being manufacturers, showing their first, Panhard-like, CGV car in 1901 and establishing a company to build them at Puteaux, Seine, in February 1902.

Towards the end of 1906, CGV was bought out by British financier David Dalziel after negotiations with another British group had fallen through. He reconstituted CGV as a British company, Charron Ltd, although the majority of shares in the hugely overcapitalized company were held in France. Fernand Charron managed Charron Ltd's Puteaux works and from 1907 the company's cars were known as Charrons.

With the 1908 recession profits fell from over £73,000 in 1907 to less than £6500, and although the company would continue until 1930, Charron left. He took over the management of the neighbouring Clément-Bayard company – only partly on the strength of having recently married the daughter of founder and former Panhard director Adolphe Clément.

Two years later Charron went back to his original dealership in Paris's Avenue de la Grande Armée, but in 1912, after brief involvements with Hurtu, Reyrol, SCAR and Théophile Schneider, he acquired the patents to the Henriod rotary valve as used, abortively, in the contemporaneous Darracqs. He also acquired works in Courbevoie

Alda 3-litre Coupe de l'Auto model of 1913

which had formerly belonged to the English car and aero-engine company E. N. V. Motors Ltd, and in 1912 began marketing four-cylinder 15 and 25hp rotary- and poppet-valve-engined cars known as Aldas. Alda was an acronym derived from 'Ah, la Délicieuse Automobile' and was chosen in favour of the originally intended F. Charron to avoid confusion with the still extant Charron.

The rotary-valve engines and 25hp car were dropped for 1913 and 1914 but the big, expensive Aldas did not sell in large enough numbers to establish the company – in spite of an ambitious racing programme, started in 1913 when Tabateau finished sixth in the Coupe de l'Auto and even extending to Grand Prix racing in the 1914 French Grand Prix.

When World War I intervened the Alda works were requisitioned and the company worked for national defence, mostly as an importer of American-built Federal trucks. It returned to car manufacture in 1920 with a 20hp 3.5-litre car built in the Farman brothers' factory at Billancourt, albeit only until 1922 when the company ceased trading. BL

ALES
see Otomo

ALFA ROMEO
ITALY 1910 to date

Italy's oldest sporting make grew from the failure of Darracq to sell cars in Italy. Societa Italiana Automobili Darracq (SIAD), a branch of the French company, was founded in Naples on 26 February 1906, moving to a site at Portello near Milan and its more ready supply of labour before the end of the year. Portello, still an Alfa factory in the 1980s, was intended to employ some 200 workers and assemble 600 cars and cabs a year from parts imported from Darracq's Suresnes factory.

Alexandre Darracq was in business more for love of money than for love of motors and soon became embarrassingly aware that his fragile, underpowered, underbraked cars were patently unsuited to the Italian market. Darracq built just 300 cars in 1908, at a loss of

156,000 lire, doubling that loss in 1909 when only 61 cars were built, and almost going bankrupt.

Darracq was no doubt relieved to liquidate SIAD in 1909 and sell Portello at the turn of the year to a group of local businessmen who were keen to build a more appropriate, all-Italian car. They were headed by former SIAD managing director, Cav. Ugo Stella. With a 500,000-lire loan from the Banca Agricola di Milano, Anonima Lombardo Fabbrica Automobili – or ALFA – was formed on 24 June 1910. It had a nominal capital of 1.2 million lire.

ALFA's first cars were probably Darracq based, but the company quickly produced its own very different cars. Sturdy, powerful and well-braked, the 24hp 4.1-litre and 12hp 2.4-litre were designed by former Marchant, Bianchi and Fiat designer Giuseppe Merosi. The ALFA badge combined the St George's Cross of the coat of arms of Milan with the more bizarre device of the Visconti family, a biblical serpent devouring a boy. The *quadrifoglio* or four-leaved clover appeared initially on the chassis and engine number plates.

The cars were popular and within a few years ALFA was employing some 300 people to make up to 3500 cars a year. ALFA's sporting aspirations surfaced in 1911, the same year as those of Bugatti, when two 24hp cars were entered in the Targa Florio, works test-driver Franchini leading briefly but both cars retiring. The first modest racing success was in 1914, when Campari and Franchini finished third and fourth in the Coppa Florio with 40/60hp models, introduced in 1913. ALFA had even built a Merosi-designed four-cylinder twin-cam Grand Prix car in 1914, but war intervened before it could be raced.

World War I also saw the beginning of the Romeo connection. Nicola Romeo had been born at San Antimo, Naples, on 28 April 1876 and graduated in civil engineering from Naples Polytechnic in 1900 before moving to Liège to gain a degree in electrical engineering. In 1902 he started business in Milan, prospering to the extent that in 1911 he founded Accomandita Ingegner Nicola Romeo & Co, making mining machinery.

During the war Romeo's company made portable compressors known as 'The Little Italian' and expanded rapidly from 100 employees in June 1915 to 2500 in 1916. The expansion included taking over ALFA's Portello works in December 1915 by arrangement with ALFA's major shareholder, Banca di Sconto, to build tractors, ploughs and Isotta aero engines.

In February 1918 Romeo formally absorbed ALFA into Societa Anonima Italiana Ing Nicola Romeo, with himself as managing director and ambitions to continue building, and racing, cars. When the war ended in November 1918, Merosi went back to designing cars under a new badge which now read Alfa-Romeo.

Alfa Romeo (without the hyphen) made its racing début in the 1919 Targa Florio, with

Alfa Romeo 8C-2300 Mille Miglia of 1931

three re-badged pre-war 40/60s, all of which retired. The 24hp car re-emerged as the 20/30 and the 12hp as the 15/20 but the first car actually designed as an Alfa Romeo was the luxurious six-cylinder G1.

Racing remained a passion for Alfa Romeo and from the early 1920s the team was run by the driver Enzo Ferrari, who on 1 December 1929 founded Scuderia Ferrari in Modena to oversee all Alfa's racing activity and maintain customers' competition cars. He went on to achieve fame for his own racing activities.

Under Ferrari and with engineer Luigi Bazzi and designer Vittorio Jano, both brought from Fiat, Alfa's competition successes would soon mount. The marque's first outright win was for Giuseppe Campari in the 1920 Circuit of Mugello, repeated in 1921, and victory in the 1923 Targa Florio for Ugo Sivocci, the last in a racing version of Merosi's 3-litre six-cylinder RL, introduced in 1921. Sivocci was killed at Monza in 1923 while practising for the European Grand Prix in the Merosi-designed six-cylinder twin-overhead cam 2-litre P1, a car which subsequently never raced.

In 1924 Alfa set up a British concessionaire, Alfa Romeo British Sales Ltd, and also produced the magnificent, Jano-designed P2 Grand Prix car, a supercharged 2-litre straight-eight which won on its début, driven by Ascari in the Circuit of Cremona, won again on its first Grand Prix appearance, with Campari at Lyons, and never looked back. The only low spot in the remarkable career of the P2 was Antonio Ascari's death in one of the cars at Montlhéry in 1925. The team completed the season to claim the first ever world championship and the Alfa badge grew a laurel wreath border in celebration. Nicola Romeo became president of the company in 1925, a position he held until his retirement in 1930.

Merosi left in 1926 and Jano began to complement his racing work with some outstanding road cars, starting in 1927 with a six-cylinder single-overhead cam 1500 tourer, a 1750 derivative and then 1500 and 1750 twin cams, supercharged or otherwise. In 1931 Jano produced the 2.3-litre supercharged straight-eight 8C-2300, and when Earl Howe and Sir Tim Birkin won the first of the 8C's four consecutive Le Mans that year they re-

Alfa Romeo 6C-2500 Freccia d'Oro of 1947

ceived a telegram from Mussolini congratulating them on their victory 'for Italy'.

Also in 1931 Jano produced a Grand Prix development of the 8C, another début winner, in the European Grand Prix at Monza; it was known ever after as the Alfa Romeo Monza. That was followed by the twin-engined Tipo A and the classic Tipo B Monoposto, or P3, of 1932, with 2.6-litre twin supercharged, twin-overhead cam straight-eight engine. Yet again an Alfa won its Grand Prix début, this time the 1932 Italian. The P3 won that year's championship and went on to win over 40 major races, including Nuvolari's epic 1935 Nürburgring victory against the increasingly dominant German teams.

The P3's career, however, was dogged by Alfa's mounting financial problems. In 1931 the majority shareholding passed from the Banco di Sconto, which had its own problems, to Consorzio per le Sovvenzioni Industriali, a government organization making grants to industry. The shares then passed to the Istituto di Liquidazione and in 1933 the company was taken over by the newly founded and government-sponsored Istituto Reconstruzione Industriale, which revamped the company as Societa Anonima Alfa Romeo. The company then branched into commercial vehicle manufacture; there was already an aviation section, in Naples, whose Fiat-engined RO5 two-seater monoplane had won a government competition in 1929 for the best light aeroplane.

The on-off racing programme included V12 and V16 Grand Prix cars and in 1935 the thoroughly dangerous *bi-motore*, with P3 engines front and back, but with Germany in Grand Prix racing in earnest there were few wins. In sports car racing, however, Alfa dominated, winning every Mille Miglia from

1928 to 1938 with the exception of 1931. Before Jano left for Lancia (and ultimately Ferrari) in 1938, he designed the 1934 2.3-litre twin-cam six, the 6C-2300, which, developed by Bruno Treviso into the 2500, saw production until after World War II.

Alfa suffered badly during the war, which Nicola Romeo did not live to see, having died on 15 August 1938. The Portello factory, engaged entirely on war work and employing some 8500 people, was bombed first on St Valentine's Day 1943, again in August and yet again in October 1944, by which time it was two-thirds destroyed. The company's post-war recovery, however, was remarkable, both on road and track.

Production continued of marine and aero engines, some of the latter under licence for the British Bristol Aeroplane Co, which was itself moving into car production. Even before Alfa's roadgoing manufacture was due to resume in 1947 with the Freccia d'Oro, an updated version of the pre-war six, the company resumed racing.

Its latest and ultimately most remarkably successful racer was the Tipo 158 Alfetta, based on a pre-war voiturette designed by Gioacchino Colombo, around half the old V16 engine. The 1½-litre supercharged straight-eight and its derivative the 159 totally dominated immediate post-war Grand Prix racing with over 25 wins and the first two official World Drivers' Championships, for Giuseppe Farina and Juan Mañuel Fangio in 1950 and 1951. After that the company rested on its laurels for almost three decades, confining its racing activities to only partially successful sports car racing and the many touring car classes, these with enormous success.

By 1950 Alfa was changing direction as it introduced what was obviously a mass-market car, the four-cylinder 1900, with unitary construction and designed by Alessio. Super and Sprint versions followed and the engine found its way into the company's remarkable record and publicity seeker the *Disco Volante*, or Flying Saucer. The mass-market trend was continued in 1954 with the introduction of the 1300cc twin-cam four-cylinder Giulietta which, in increasingly potent two- and four-door versions, styled by Pininfarina, Bertone and Zagato, lasted until the more powerful and larger Giulia appeared in 1962. There were also a 2000, six-cylinder

2600, and numerous bodywork styles to choose from, and in the late 1950s Alfa was even making the humble Renault Dauphine under licence at Portello.

Because Alfa needed to increase its volume and expansion at Portello was curbed by the proximity of housing, a new plant was started at Arese, near Milan, in 1963. The plant would occupy half a square mile (1.3sq km) and aim at an ultimate capacity of 150,000 cars a year; it would also house an Alfa museum.

The first car to be assembled at Arese was the Giulia Sprint GT, introduced at the factory in September 1963 but built from parts made in Portello. In 1969 production at Arese topped 100,000 for the first time – a marked difference from Alfa's pre-war production peak of 1110 cars in 1925. In 1966-67 the company had perceived a need to double production over the next 15 years and to do so it took another major new direction, with the Alfasud.

Helped by government willingness to back firms providing labour in the south, Alfa had already established a factory at Pomigliano d'Arco, near Naples, initially making aero engine and commercial vehicle parts. The expansion of the car factory to a fully automated plant occupying some 100 acres (40 hectares) of the 590-acre (238-hectare) site and aiming at 1000 cars a day was entrusted to Viennese engineer Rudolf Hruska, who was also given the task of originating a smaller, cheaper Alfa, the front-wheel-drive Alfasud. The Alfasud was in production by 1972 when Pomigliano had 16,000 employees and its own test-track, complementing the 3½-mile (5.6-km) Balocco test-track that had become fully operational in 1964.

The Alfasud proved popular enough, growing to 1.5 litres and with various styling op-

tions. It dovetailed into the range alongside a new Alfetta, introduced in 1972, the 1976 Giulietta, the rapid GTV6 of 1979 and the Alfa 6, due to be replaced in 1986 by the Pininfarina styled 164. A new small car, the 33, appeared in 1983 and the end of the line for the Alfasud came late that year when it was announced that production had ceased except for Ti models, which would be available only until 1984.

The Pomigliano plant changed over to production of the successful 33 and the new Arna, built in association with Nissan. Early in 1984 a four-wheel-drive 33 Estate and saloons were introduced.

In commercial terms the Alfasud operation had been a nightmare. The southern plant had dreadful labour problems, suffering up to one fifth absenteeism and no less than 78 major strikes and 882 minor ones in 1977 alone. Production losses then amounted to as many as 100 cars a day, the company's £70 million losses equating to almost £50 per car. Between 1973 and 1978 Alfasud was responsible for some 80 per cent of the company's overall losses, borne with increasing reluctance by the government as a penalty for their own policies. Alfa still showed losses from 1977 to 1984 averaging about £50 million a year, and as the government started to withhold further support it began to look to possible industry links, perhaps with Chrysler or Nissan, ostensibly only for technical collaboration. From 1981 to 1984 the workforce at Arese fell from 16,000 to around 7000, although efficiency improved dramatically as the company aimed for a much reduced break-even capacity of about 200,000 cars a year. In 1985, Alfa production totalled about 157,600 cars.

At the end of 1980 Alfa announced that it was co-operating with Nissan in a new small

Alfasud 1.5TiX of 1982

Alfa Romeo Arna 1.5Ti of 1984

Alfa Romeo Giulia Sprint GT of 1963

Alfa Romeo 90 saloon of 1985

Alfa Romeo 2.5-litre GTV6 of 1983

Alfa Romeo 33 four-wheel-drive estate of 1984

car. It was to be built in a new factory with some 2500 workers and Japanese machinery, with Alfasud running gear and 80 per cent total Alfa content but having a Japanese-built shell. The car, identical to the Nissan Cherry Europe, appeared at the 1984 Geneva Show as the Arna Ti, with an uprated Alfasud flat-four engine and a question mark over whether it would be marketed outside Italy under the Alfa or Nissan flags. The Arna, due to be rebodied in 1986, never looked a commercial success and by late 1985 Alfa's future depended mainly on new models, notably the up-market 90 saloon, which replaced the Alfetta, and the sporty four-cylinder or V6 75, which was named for the company's 75th anniversary. BL

ALLARD
GB, CANADA 1937-1959; 1981 to date

Born in June 1910, Sydney Allard went into business in 1930 under the name of Adlards Motors Ltd, a small service garage in Putney, south London. The name came from Roberts Adlard, a building firm which Sydney's father had acquired, and the similarity between that and the Allard family name was pure coincidence. The share capital was £2000 and the original partners were Sydney Allard, his mother Celia and Alfred Briscoe, who had been foreman at the garage where Sydney had served his apprenticeship.

In 1934 a Ford dealership was acquired, and Reginald Canham joined the firm, working mainly on the sales side. He was to stay with them until long after car manufacture ceased. Sydney Allard spent a lot of time engaging in trials, at first with a Ford V8 which had been built for the 1934 Tourist Trophy, and then with another Ford V8 which he modified and fitted with a Bugatti tail. He

had innumerable successes with this car, and in 1937 another was built for an outside customer, David Gilson.

The sale of this car marked the début of Allard the car manufacturer, although production was very limited and the bulk of the firm's income still came from Ford sales. In 1938 new premises were acquired for the manufacture and sale of the competition cars and share capital was increased to £20,000.

Between 1937 and September 1939, 12 Allards were built, including three with Lincoln-Zephyr V12 engines. They ranged from fierce trials specials to quite civilized four-seater sports tourers. The chassis was now a distinctive Allard product with Leslie Ballamy split-axle independent front suspension, while coachwork was by Coachcraft, Ranalah and Whittingham & Mitchel.

Before the end of 1939 Allards had turned over entirely to war work, initially converting laundry vans to run on town gas, but later they concentrated on the servicing and repair of army vehicles, specializing (at Allard's request) in Fords. New premises were acquired at Fulham.

World War II did not put an end to Sydney Allard's ambitions, and his first step towards realizing these was to form a new company devoted to car manufacture. Named the Allard Motor Co Ltd, it was formed on 14 February 1945 with initial capital of £100; but it did not replace Adlards Motors Ltd, which remained in business up to 1976.

The post-war range of cars, now no longer called Allards Specials, was announced in January 1946, and new premises were acquired in Clapham, about 3 miles (5km) from Putney; the works totalled 30,000sq ft (2800sq m). The new cars used mainly Ford components, including the 3.6-litre V8 engine, three-speed gearbox, torque tube rear axle, modified front axle and springs, wheels and hubcaps (the latter on the first few cars only). The striking bodies were by Whittingham & Mitchel or Paramount Sheet Metal.

The first production cars were ready by July 1946, and seven cars left the factory during the year. The following year 173 units were delivered, nearly all with the 3.6-litre V8 engine, K two-seaters, L four-seaters and M drop-head coupés, although a few short-chassis J1 two-seaters with Mercury 3.9-litre engines were supplied.

October 1948 saw Allard's first appearance at a British Motor Show when the P-type saloon was added to the range. It was now established as one of the leading makers of British sports cars, and although its output was still relatively small – 432 cars were delivered in 1948 – the striking appearance of its cars and sporting successes kept the company in the public eye. It had obtained Ford's permission to list all the UK Ford dealerships as Official Allard Agents, while overseas it was represented in Switzerland, Sweden, Finland, the USA and several other countries.

Unfortunately for Allard the 1948 London Show also saw the arrival of the brand-new Jaguar XK120, equally striking in appearance, with a sophisticated twin-overhead cam engine, and very close in price. Subsequent sales never equalled the 1948 figure, reaching only 265 in 1949, 305 in 1950 and 337 in 1951. Thereafter they dropped badly, 132 and 123 in 1952 and 1953 respectively, and only 44 from 1954 onwards. During this

Allard 4.4-litre V12 special of 1937

period the proportion of cars exported rose dramatically, from 7 per cent in 1949 to 99 per cent (119 out of 123) in 1953.

Ironically, while sales were dropping, the Allard name was earning increasing fame in competitions. Cadillac- and Chrysler-engined J2s scored many race victories in the United States between 1950 and 1952, and in 1952 Sydney Allard won the Monte Carlo Rally in a P-type saloon, the first and only time that this event has been won by a man driving his own make of car. All competition cars were sold to the USA as rolling chassis, to be fitted there with a wide variety of locally-made V8 engines such as Cadillac, Chrysler, Dodge and Ardun-tuned Mercury. In Britain, Allards continued to be powered by the old 3.6-litre side-valve V8, but in 1950 Ford had abandoned this unit in favour of smaller short-stroke overhead-valve four- and six-cylinder engines.

Sydney Allard decided to follow suit, and in 1952 announced an open two-seater powered by a choice of the Ford engines and christened the Palm Beach. It was aimed at the US market, and there were plans for it to be given a fibreglass body made by Graham-Paige. These never materialized, and only 74 Palm Beaches were made.

In 1954 Sydney Allard ventured into a completely new field, that of the motorcycle-engined three-wheeler. The product was named the Clipper and a separate company was formed under the name Allard Clipper Co. The chassis were to be made at Allard's Fulham premises, with fibreglass bodies coming from Haddenham, Buckinghamshire. Various power units including British Anzani and JAP were tried but the project was abandoned before the bugs could be ironed out. Estimates of Clipper production vary from 12 to 20, with not more than one or two actually being sold to customers. The designer Gottlieb was later responsible for two other three-wheelers, the Powerdrive and the Coronet.

Production of the larger cars dwindled from 1954 onwards, totalling a mere six in 1955, and seven more from 1956 to 1959. The final three cars had 3.4-litre Jaguar engines, ironic in view of the fact that it was the success of the Jaguar, as much as anything, which took away Allard's market. With hindsight it is clear that the Allard was a car ideally suited to the immediate post-war period; it had a striking appearance that appealed to a car-starved public and was able to make use of available, though even then dated, components, but it really had no hope of competing in the 1950s with firms such as Jaguar and Aston Martin, which had much greater resources for development.

In 1959 the company secured a contract from the London Ambulance Service for the conversion of BMC and Bedford chassis to De Dion axles, these having been used on the Allard J2. This proved very profitable, and further orders from provincial cities and from Singapore kept the factories active for several years. Other work included the fitting of sunshine roofs and the tuning of Ford Anglias, sold as Allardettes; Allard also became world distributors and later manufacturers of the Shorrock supercharger. In 1962 Sydney Allard built a powerful Chrysler-engined dragster, and later made for sale a few smaller models known as Dragons, with supercharged four-cylinder Ford engines.

Sydney Allard died in April 1966, but the businesses were carried on by Reg Canham, who looked after the flourishing Ford dealership of Adlards, and Sydney's son Alan, who concentrated on superchargers, tuning and sunroofs. Canham died in 1973 and Adlards closed down in 1976. Alan Allard operated a factory at Daventry until 1975 when he moved to Ross-on-Wye, where he founded Allard Turbochargers. Production of a replica Allard J2, powered by a Chrysler V8 engine, began in Mississauga, Ontario in 1981, but only a handful have been made to date. GNG

ALLDAYS/ENFIELD
GB 1898-1918

The Alldays and Onions Pneumatic Engineering Co Ltd of Birmingham had the longest ancestry of any British motor manufacturer, tracing its history back to two Birmingham engineering firms, Onions established in 1650 and Alldays in 1720. By the 1880s it had extensive premises covering more than 8 acres (3 hectares) and was a specialist supplier to blacksmiths, foundries, engineering and railway companies. The Pneumatic Engineering Co Ltd was established in December 1889 to acquire Alldays and Onions Ltd, for £95,000, and shortly afterwards began the manufacture of bicycles.

The company's first motor vehicle was the Alldays Traveller of 1898, a wheel-steered quadricycle powered by a 4hp De Dion-Bouton engine. Cars proper followed in 1903, as did motorcycles which were made under the name Alldays-Matchless until 1915. They had no connection with the well-known London-built Matchless motorcycle, but were named after the Matchless works where they were made.

The most successful car was the two-cylinder 10/12 made from 1905 to 1913, but Alldays also made four- and six-cylinder cars up to a 30/35hp Six built from 1911 to 1914. In 1906 the company entered the commercial vehicle market with a van on the 10/12 chassis, later making lorries up to 5 tons capacity, and a tri-van on the lines of the Autocarrier. It also made a number of railway inspection trolleys, continued general engineering work and built the chassis for Railless trolleybuses between 1911 and 1914.

In 1908 Alldays acquired the Enfield Autocar Co of Redditch and thereafter the ranges of the companies were rationalized, although both companies and cars retained their individual names until 1918. The Alldays Midget and Enfield Nimble Nine light cars of 1913-15 were virtually identical.

In 1918 the motor interests of the two companies were merged in a new firm, Enfield-Alldays Motors Ltd. Alldays and Onions continued with general engineering and motorcycles which were marketed under the name Allon from 1915 to 1924. The chairman was Hyam Marks who was also a director of Austin. In 1925 the company was re-formed as New Alldays and Onions Ltd, but ceased trading two years later. GNG

ALPINE
FRANCE 1955 to date

Between 1952 and 1954, when viable French competition cars were something of a rarity, Jean Redélé, a young engineer whose father owned a Renault dealership in Dieppe, used a modified 750cc Renault 4CV in virtually any

Allard J2 roadster of 1950

type of competition he could find. What Redélé loved most was rallying in the Alps or racing in the Mille Miglia. He won a Coupe des Alpes in 1954 and the 750cc class of the Italian race three times, from 1952 to 1954. When he decided that his cars should go into modest production, the marque became Alpine and the first model became the Mille Miles.

Redélé was born in 1922 in Dieppe. He gained a degree in engineering before joining his father's firm to help rebuild the company after World War II, not by selling new cars, because there were none, but by repairing old ones and agricultural machinery.

In 1955 Société Automobiles Alpine was formed as a limited liability company and the first 'production' car, officially the A106, appeared. Uprated 4CV running gear was used, including the platform chassis onto which was bonded a stubby, glassfibre body,

Renault-Alpine GTA V6 of 1986

Alpine A110 1600S of 1969

styled by Michelotti and made initially by Chappe Frères in Paris. The car was available with either a Renault three-speed gearbox or the five-speed developed by Redélé (and Claude engineering) for his original cars. A106s soon went into competition and in 1956 Maurice Michy won his class in, appropriately, the Mille Miglia.

At this stage production was very limited and a steel-bodied car, the A107, did not go beyond the prototype stage. Further versions of the A106 appeared with the 850cc (later 904 and 948) Dauphine engine from 1956, and the model survived until 1960. Alongside it, the A108 appeared in 1957 as a mechanically similar cabriolet, joined in 1959 by a 'Sport' version, built around Alpine's own first chassis, a tubular backbone.

By 1959 Alpine was becoming fairly well established, with a production of around 100 a year, including cars for export, at $3300. Further body styles were added in 1961, a 2+2 coupé and the Berlinette Tour de France.

In 1963 the classic Alpine shape was introduced on the A110, with R8 mechanicals including engine options of up to 1108cc and 87bhp. The car remained in production for 15 years, growing by stages to 1800cc and building an outstanding competition record, helped in rallying by its rear-engine, rear-drive layout. A110s finished 1-2-3 in the 1969 Coupe des Alpes and in 1971, by which time Alpine was officially responsible for Re-

nault's competition programme, Ove Andersson led an Alpine 1-2-3 in the Monte. In 1973 the car, in 170bhp, 1800 form, won the World Rally Championship. The government petrol company, Elf, was another Alpine backer.

Alongside rallying and production, Alpine began a racing programme in 1963 with the Len Terry-designed A210 sports racer, coded by year as M63, then M64, M65 etc. These were regularly successful at Le Mans in the Index of Performance but Alpine was less successful with the V8-engined A220 of 1967 and, briefly, in single-seater racing, first tackled in 1964 with a Ron Tauranac-designed car for Formula 2 and Formula 3. A later return to single-seaters was rather more productive. Finance for the racing programme came largely from Renault but when, in 1967, the government decided to fund a 'national' Grand Prix project, they gave their £400,000 backing not to Renault but to Matra and Redélé shelved his Formula 1 plans.

In April 1969 when the company had just moved into a new, larger factory with 200 staff, production was at 500 to 600 cars a year, growing steadily from the 350 of 1964. The cars were officially sold through all Renault dealerships and even carried a standard Renault guarantee. Renault's just reward for their backing came in 1978 when Jaussaud and Pironi won Le Mans with the Renault Alpine A442. Four years earlier Renault had officially taken over Alpine.

Plans for the A110's successor were already in hand before the Renault takeover and in July 1971 the Institut de Développement Industriel made a grant which resulted in the 2+2 A310. The car was introduced at the 1971 Geneva Show with a 140bhp R16TX engine but this was later upgraded to the twin-cam 2664cc V6 of the Renault 30. The next generation Alpine, with turbocharged or normally aspirated V6 engines, suffered several delays in its launch but was eventually announced in 1985. It was slightly larger than its predecessor although broadly similar. It is marketed as part of the Renault range, under the name Renault Alpine V6.

A310s were formerly also built and marketed by Renault assembly plants in Spain, Mexico, Brazil and Bulgaria to bring peak production up to around 2000 cars a year. Jean Redélé continued to be very much a part of Alpine in a management capacity for Renault Sport at its headquarters in Paris, while the Alpine name has latterly been associated with the successful Renault rally car and the sporting, roadgoing R5, which was in many ways a 1980s version of Redélé's original theme. BL

ALTA
GB 1930-1947

When Geoffrey Taylor decided to build his own sports car he decided to build *entirely* his own sports car, not a special for someone else's engine; and if he had no machine tools to build his own engine then he would make it by hand. Taylor had been born in 1904 and in the early 1920s made car and motorcycle components such as pistons and valve gear on a small scale, much of his output being for the local firm, ABC, of Hersham, Surrey. In 1927 he decided to build his own 'ideal' sports car and he set up shop in the stables adjoining his father's house at Kingston Hill.

His first car, built between 1928 and 1930,

23

was to all intents and purposes hand-made. Taylor designed the light alloy, 1074cc twin-overhead camshaft four-cylinder engine, made wooden patterns and sent them to a local foundry for casting. His toolroom comprised a lathe, a drill and a grinder, water-driven from the domestic supply in typically anachronistic style. The house's central heating boiler served for small heat treatment jobs and the crank and rods were roughed out of solid stock with a handsaw before being beautifully hand finished.

The first car, PK4053, was finished in 1930 and Taylor used it to win a bronze medal in the London to Land's End Trial. PK4053 still exists, in Cleveland, Ohio. Taylor called the car Alta, a contraction of Alberta, Canada, a place name he had read in a novel and liked the sound of.

Having decided to produce a small number of Altas, he formed the Alta Car and Engineering Co, and having failed to find a factory he bought land on the Kingston bypass at Tolworth. With the aid of a couple of labourers he spent three months building a 115×25ft (35×7.6m) workshop where replicas of PK4053 were built on roughly the same one-off basis but around Rubery Owen frames. The new bypass was regularly used as an impromptu test-track.

Virtually all subsequent Altas were competition cars, from trials cars to full Grand Prix cars. Their first success was in 1932 when a supercharged Alta-engined Frazer-Nash took the Shelsley Walsh 1100 record.

Manufacture of alloy heads for Austin Sevens supplemented Alta's meagre income, for the philanthropic Taylor had little time for financial considerations and often sold his cars at, or even below, cost. In the 1930s an 1100 Alta cost around £350 and even the single-seater racers of 1937 could be had for as little as £850.

Regular, if relatively minor, competition successes made Alta's name and by 1935 the company was outgrowing its original buildings and moving into single-seater racing, eventually to challenge ERA supremacy until interrupted by World War II. During the war Alta made prototype aircraft components, jigs, tools and airframe parts.

Almost as soon as the war ended, Taylor showed drawings for a new Grand Prix car but material shortages delayed the appearance of the rubber sprung car until 1948, by which time it was outclassed. Alta's one brief flirtation with pure road cars occurred shortly after the war with a proposed 2-litre saloon, which apparently progressed no further than the prototype stage. Including the original trials type cars, probably no more than 15 road usable Altas were made.

Alta engines continued their competition success, principally with Connaught and HWM, the latter founded in 1950 by long-time Alta exponents John Heath and George Abecassis and in many ways a logical continuation of Alta. Geoffrey Taylor, however, died in 1966 after a long illness. BL

ALVIS
GB 1920-1967

A former naval architect and aero engine designer at Siddeley-Deasy, T. G. John formed his own engineering company in Coventry in 1919 with paid-up capital of £4250. T. G. John Ltd made a small number of stationary engines, carburettor bodies for Zenith, and the Stafford Mobile Pup, a 140cc scooter of which about 100 were built. Late in 1919 John was approached by engineer G. P. H. de Freville – who had imported the DFP before Bentley did – with a design for a 1½-litre four-cylinder engine with aluminium pistons, and this became the Alvis 10/30 when put into production by John in 1920. The car was assembled in a new factory in Holyhead Road, Coventry, which was to remain the home of the Alvis Car and Engineering Co until it was destroyed in the Blitz of 1940.

From the start the Alvis had a good reputation as a light car of above average quality, although quite expensive at £750 to £870. In 1920 120 cars were made, rising to 344 in 1921 and 733 in 1922. In the latter year Alvis took over the manufacture of the Buckingham cyclecar from another Coventry firm. Designed by L. F. Buckingham, inventor of the incendiary bullet, this was one of the better cyclecars, but their day was coming to an end, hastened by the arrival in July 1922 of the Austin Seven, and not more than 30 Buckinghams were made by Alvis.

In 1923 came the launch of the 12/50, probably the most famous Alvis model ever made. It had a 1496cc (sports models) or 1598cc (touring models) overhead-valve four-cylinder engine designed by Captain G. T. Smith-Clarke (formerly of Daimler), and it put the company firmly in the public eye by winning the 1923 Brooklands 200-Mile Race, which was the leading event for light cars.

As a result of this win, sales jumped from 710 to 933 between 1923 and 1924, but this apparent success merely underlined T. G. John's chronic lack of capital. A petition by the coachbuilder Cross & Ellis brought the company into the hands of receivers, but the 12/50's reputation led creditors to agree to

payment in cash and the issue of debentures. The company prospered during the later 1920s, production exceeding 1000 for the first time in 1927. For 1928 a small six-cylinder engine was introduced, the model acquiring the name Silver Eagle in 1929.

A more dramatic departure was a series of front-wheel-drive cars with four- and eight-cylinder engines. This principle had been first tried on the Alvis racing cars in 1925, and the roadgoing cars were marketed from 1928 to 1930; they were not such a disaster for the company as has sometimes been claimed, but the Depression had a bad effect on the sales of all Alvises and it was decided to kill off the front-wheel-drive after 140 had been made.

An interesting addition to the company's income at this time came from royalties on the patents owned by G. T. Smith-Clarke. Thus they received two shillings and sixpence from Vauxhall for each rubber engine mounting used, and five shillings each from Daimler for oiling patents on sleeve-valve engines.

During the 1930s the workforce remained fairly static at around 500, turning out a maximum of 20 chassis a week. Coachwork still came from outside suppliers, Vanden Plas and Charlesworth being the leading coachbuilders on the Speed 20 chassis and its successors, the Speed 25, 3½-litre and 4.3. The smaller four-cylinder cars such as the Firefly, Firebird and 12/70 were bodied by Cross & Ellis, Holbrook and Mulliner.

The introduction in 1931 of the Speed 20

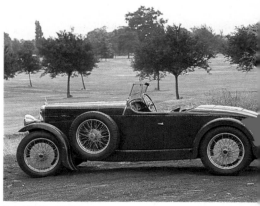

Alvis 12/60 of 1932

Alvis TF21 of 1966

marked a new departure for Alvis; its engine was an enlarged version of the Silver Eagle's but the chassis was longer and lower, and gave the car an appearance rivalling that of the SS1. For 1934 two important innovations appeared on the Speed 20: these were an all-synchromesh gearbox, the first on a British car, and independent front suspension. The Speed 20 was succeeded by larger and more luxurious models in the same image which took Alvis into the world of the elegant luxury car, used by film stars and able to hold its own in the company of Bentley and Lagonda. T. G. John made a £35,000 bid to buy Lagonda when it went into receivership, but his bid was too low and the company went to Alan Good.

In 1936 the company changed its name to Alvis Ltd with an increase of issued capital to £700,000. The car market was declining and so Alvis turned to other fields, notably aero engines, for which a new factory was built, and armoured cars built to the design of the Hungarian, Nicholas Straussler. For them a new company, Alvis-Straussler Mechanisation Ltd, was formed and three bays in the aero engine factory were allocated.

The first aero engine, a fourteen-cylinder radial, based on Gnome et Rhône designs and named the Pelides, was completed in March 1937. The company later made its own-design nine-cylinder Leonides radial engine as well as doing important subcontracting work for Rolls-Royce. This diversification was a blessing for the company, which recorded losses from 1936 to 1938 but was back in profit by mid-1939.

Smith-Clarke now felt that the range of cars was too great and recommended a move away from the luxury end of the market. Thus, although production of the Speed 25 and 4.3-litre continued to 1940, it is unlikely that they would have survived for many more seasons. It is somewhat surprising that a total of 108 new cars were delivered in 1940, consisting of 77 12/70s, 18 Speed 25s, nine 4.3s, three Silver Crests and one Crested Eagle.

After the November air-raids during which the car factory was destroyed by bombing, work was dispersed through 21 factories which were responsible for the manufacture and overhaul of Rolls-Royce aero engines, the manufacture of undercarriages and a wide variety of other military equipment. Alvis did not build any of its own design of aero engine as these were more suited to civil aircraft, nor did it receive any contracts for armoured vehicles, though these were to come soon after the end of the war.

Early in 1946 a merger with Lagonda was once more in the air when Alan Good offered a new design and spares and goodwill to the value of £75,000. However, Alvis's post-war plans were already laid and the offer was declined.

Only one car model, the TA14, was put into production in 1946. This was based on the 12/70 and was available with Mulliner saloon or Tickford drophead coupé bodies. A total of

3311 were made, plus 100 of the controversially-styled TB14 roadster, and in 1950 it was replaced by the 3-litre six-cylinder 21 Series. These were made until October 1954 when Mulliner was taken over by Standard and no longer supplied bodywork to Alvis.

While the search for alternative body suppliers took place there was virtually an interregnum in car production, yet a record net profit of over £150,000 was made in 1954-55. This shows how small a part motor cars played in Alvis's affairs by this time, the bulk of production being devoted to the nine-cylinder Leonides and fourteen-cylinder Leonides Major aero engines, and to the new range of six-wheeled high mobility vehicles.

The Leonides had proved particularly successful in helicopters and for several years virtually every helicopter in the UK was Alvis powered. Fixed-wing aircraft which used these engines included the Percival Provost and Pembroke, Scottish Aviation Prestwick Pioneer and Twin Pioneer and Canadian De Havilland Husky. A Leonides also powered the original Saunders Roe Hovercraft.

The military vehicles were made in four basic models, the Saladin armoured car, Saracen armoured troop-carrier, Salamander fire tender and Stalwart amphibious load-carrier. Powered by Rolls-Royce B80 eight-cylinder engines, they had Wilson five-speed preselector gearboxes and six-wheel drive. A total of 4262 were made between 1952 and 1971 and they were exported to 23 countries. The 1963 marketing agreement between Alvis and Berliet led to plans to build the Stalwart in France under the name Auroch, but these were aborted by the Alvis takeover by British Leyland in 1967.

Car manufacture was resumed in 1958 when Alvis concluded a successful agreement with the London coachbuilder Park Ward, which built a two-door saloon and convertible designed by Graber of Switzer-

land on the 3-litre chassis. This elegant car was made with only a few modifications until September 1967, when all car production ceased. During the 1960s car production occupied the works for just two weeks in each year, being either fitted in all at once or spaced out in intervals between military production.

In 1965 Alvis was acquired by Rover and a prototype mid-engined sports car, powered by a 3½-litre Rover V8 engine, was built by Alvis. However, it did not fit into the British Leyland marketing philosophy and was never commercialized.

Production of both aero engines and the Saracen/Stalwart family ceased in 1971, but in the meantime Alvis had received a contract to build the Scorpion and Scimitar light tanks, in which it has been engaged ever since. In 1981 British Leyland disposed of the company to United Scientific Holdings for £27 million. Pretax profits the previous year had been £7 million, vastly greater than they had ever been with Alvis as a motor car manufacturer. GNG

AMÉDÉE BOLLÉE
FRANCE 1873-1922

Amédée Bollée, born in 1842 the son of a Le Mans bell-founder, built his first vehicle, the famous 12-seater *L'Obéissante*, in 1873. There followed several other large steam carriages and buses, including the *Marie-Anne* of 1879. This was a four-wheeler with additional two-wheel tender which had chain drive to both hindmost axles and the first-known Cardan shaft between them. There was also a 4×4 and, in 1876, a four-wheel-steered bus with independent suspension. In 1878 came a lighter steam carriage, *La Mancelle* – which, like *L'Obéissante*, still exists. It

Bollée 20hp Tour de France of 1899

had independent front suspension and a vertical steam engine at the front, under a bonnet, but with the boiler at the rear.

An early customer, Léon Le Cordier, acquired exclusive rights to vehicles for public service while Bollée looked after private sales and production. A manufacturing licence was sold to an Austrian consortium, which soon sold it to German interests who created Dampfwagen Centralgesellschaft in 1880.

A workshop specifically for vehicles was built away from the bell foundry and in 1880 it employed 17 men. A press campaign against Bollée's traitorous behaviour in helping the German enemy during the Franco-Prussian war damaged the company's prospects in France and the German company got into financial difficulty.

A son, also called Amédée, had been born in 1867 and at the age of 18 was running the steam department. In 1887 he made a prototype petrol engine, initially intended for airships, and after several experiments began building internal combustion engined cars in 1896 with his brother Camille. Another brother, Léon, also made rival vehicles from 1895 in a factory provided by Amédée Sr.

In March 1897 Baron de Turkheim paid 500,000 francs for a licence for De Dietrich to make Amédée Bollée cars, and engines for several of these were made at Le Mans. A licence was also acquired by Leesdorfer in Austria. Up to 100 Amédée Bollées were sold annually in the late 1890s although then, as later, Amédée Bollée was more concerned with experiments than series production. He built boat-shaped racing cars in 1898, probably the first with streamlining and one of which was driven by Ferdinand Charron, and the following year made a pioneering monobloc four-cylinder engine, using the resources of his father's foundry.

For about two years from 1900 few, if any, cars were made, although engine production continued. Thereafter car production was small and probably seldom exceeded 20 expensive and high quality cars a year. A fuel injection system was invented in 1903 and, in the quest for silence, hydraulic tappets were adopted after about 1910.

Amédée Bollée Jr made shells in World War I and in 1914 perfected a vehicle-mounted machine able to detect the whereabouts of guns from their sound waves. His father died in 1917 and, although a few more cars were made between 1919 and 1922 from pre-war components, the firm's speciality became piston rings; it was making 20,000 of these a day in 1937.

Amédée Bollée Jr died in 1926 and his son Pierre has continued the firm, known as Les Segments Amédée Bollée. Another branch of the Bollée family still makes bells at Orléans. NB

AMERICAN

see American Underslung

26

American Bantam Austin Seven of 1930

AMERICAN AUSTIN/BANTAM
USA 1929-1941

The American Austin Car Co was founded in July 1929 in the former Standard Steel Car plant at Butler, Pennsylvania, to build modified British Austin Sevens under licence. Engineering was directed by A. J. Brandt, a former Oakland vice-president, and Alexis de Sakhnoffski did the styling. Even before production started, in May 1930, orders were impressive, peaking at nearly 185,000 that August. Alas, the little Austin, although frequently photographed with movie stars, did not sell and the first season's 8558 units represented the best-ever performance.

Early in 1932 the factory closed, but was reopened by the efforts of Georgia car dealer Roy S. Evans, who remaindered-off unsold stock through his own chain at $295 each, good enough to finance further production until the parts inventory ran out. When this happened, in 1934, bankruptcy supervened after some 19,500 cars and light commercials had been made.

With local financial support Evans bought the firm and reconstituted it as American Bantam in 1936. Work on refrigerator stampings and marinized Austin/Bantam engines kept the factory going until the 1938 cars were ready, tooled on a shoestring $216,000, including $300 to de Sakhnoffski for a restyle. Australian (and even British) licence production was rumoured, but by 1940 only 6700 Bantams had been sold at a loss of $50 per car. Even the improved 1940 three-bearing engine did not help.

The cars had been tested by the army in 1933, and in 1940 Bantam bid on a new light 4×4 military vehicle, the future Jeep. Karl H. Probst had a prototype on the road in 49 days and this Continental-powered machine won the contest, even if rivals Ford and Willys made most of the production versions. Bantam built 2675 in 1940-41, turning thereafter to two-wheeled trailers, which they had tried to civilian account in 1938. Production of these continued until the firm was taken over by American Rolling Mills in 1956. Evans had sold out in 1946, after seeing his firm become profitable. MCS

AMERICAN MOTORS
USA 1954 to date

American Motors Corporation was formed on 1 May 1954 through a merger of Hudson and Nash. It was masterminded by George Mason of Nash, which was very much the senior partner with larger premises and a better selling line of cars (135,000 to 76,000 from Hudson in 1953). Unfortunately, Mason saw little of his new venture as he died suddenly in October 1954, to be succeeded as chairman, president and general manager by George Romney.

Hudson's Detroit plant was sold and all production concentrated at the Nash factory at Kenosha, Wisconsin. Individual lines of Nash and Hudson models were continued for three years, albeit with an increasing amount of badge engineering, but for 1958 all AMC cars were badged as Ramblers with the exception of the Austin A40 powered sub-compact Metropolitan. The big 5.8-litre V8 powered car was the Rambler Ambassador, but the bulk of sales went to the smaller Rambler American, which was a revival of the original Nash Rambler of 1950-54. This car sold over 42,000 units in its first year, 1958, and put American Motors into profit for the first time for two years. In 1958 the industry was in recession and AMC was the only group that increased its sales and market share. In 1959 sales doubled to 401,446, giving AMC fourth place in the production league, largely because Romney had anticipated the public demand for a compact car before any of the Big

Three were ready. In 1961 a Canadian plant was opened at Brampton, Ontario.

In 1960 and 1961 AMC was up to third place, but after that competition from cars such as the Pontiac Tempest, Oldsmobile F85 and Plymouth Valiant pushed it further down the league. Romney left in 1962 to run successfully for Governor of Michigan and was succeeded by Roy Abernethy, who stayed with AMC only five years before giving way to William V. Luneburg.

In 1966 American Motors launched an unsuccessful fast-back coupé called the Marlin, to compete with Ford's Mustang and Plymouth's Barracuda; two years later came a much more successful replacement, the Javelin. This and its short wheelbased two-seater version, the AMX, gave American Motors good entries in the Pony Car and Muscle Car stakes, backed up by the Ambassador and Rebel in the less sporting market.

The Kelvinator Division of AMC was sold off in 1968 and the Rambler name was dropped from 1970 except for export models of the compact Hornet, successor to the old Rambler American. A new model for the 1970s was the sub-compact Gremlin, on an 8ft (2.4m) wheelbase and with a choice of 3.2- or 3.8-litre six-cylinder engines.

In February 1970 American Motors bought the Kaiser Jeep Corporation, which had used Rambler V8 engines since 1965 in its most powerful Jeeps. This brought heavy trucks into American Motors' orbit, as Kaiser Jeep manufactured 6×6 2½-ton military trucks which had been made by Reo and Studebaker since 1950. In March 1971 a new wholly-owned subsidiary, AM General, was formed, and this has been responsible for the manufacture of the M-Series military trucks and also postal delivery vehicles and buses. The latter were made at Mishawaka, Indiana, until 1978 and thereafter at Marshall, Texas. Other diversification was signalled by the acquisition in 1974 of Wheel Horse Products of South Bend, Indiana, a company that manufactured garden tractors.

Full-size cars disappeared from the American Motors line up in 1974 with the end of the Ambassador, and the Javelin was also drop-ped. In their place came the controversially-styled Pacer two-door sedan, originally planned to use a General Motors-built Wankel engine driving the front wheels. GM's cancellation of this engine forced American Motors to power the Pacer with its own six-cylinder engine. The Pacer was made until 1980 when it was replaced by the Spirit, a more conventional sub-compact powered by a choice of Audi four-cylinder 2-litre engine or GM 2½-litre four.

True to George Mason's philosophy of the 'different car', American Motors came out in 1981 with the four-wheel-drive Eagle range, a sedan and a station wagon, powered by a 4.2-litre six. These were America's first regular cars, as opposed to Jeep-type vehicles, with four-wheel drive.

In 1978 Renault began to buy into American Motors, eventually acquiring a 46.9 per cent interest and in 1982 an Americanized Renault 9 went into production at Kenosha under the name American Motors Alliance. AM's current president, José Dedeurwaerder, comes from Renault. During the first quarter of 1983 the Alliance accounted for 91 per cent of AMC's car sales. It was joined later by the Encore, an Americanized Renault 11.

A further international link was announced in the summer of 1983 when AMC signed a contract with the Chinese government to form a new company, the Beijing Jeep Corporation, in which AMC has a 31.6 per cent interest. This will give technical assistance to improve the ageing BJ212 design.

American Motors badly needed additional sources of revenue, for despite the success of the Alliance, the company lost $66 million in the first quarter of 1983 compared with $51 million for the same period in 1982. The last year the car division showed a profit was 1979. The AM General Division was bought by LTV of Texas in 1983 for $170 million.

Production in 1985 was 111,138 Alliances and Encores, 11,311 Eagles and 225,824 Jeeps. The Eagles were dropped from the 1986 range.

In 1987 a merger between AMC and Chrysler was announced whereby Chrysler was to pay $600 million for AMC stock. GNG

AMERICAN SIMPLEX/
AMPLEX
USA 1905-1917

The American Simplex was made by the Simplex Motor Car Co of Mishawaka, Indiana. The company was organized in 1904 and started operating in October of that year, but the first car did not make its appearance until July 1905, the year in which Indiana introduced licensing of automobiles.

The first American Simplex cars used four-cylinder 40hp two-stroke engines and these were soon uprated to 6.8 litres and 50hp, as in the 'Valveless' 1908 Model D touring roadster, capable of a lively 70mph (112kph). By 1910 the range included three open and two closed cars, at prices up to $5400. Also in 1910 the company became the Amplex Motor Car Co; the name was changed again, in 1914, to the Amplex Manufacturing Co but the company stayed in Mishawaka. The marque, too, became known as Amplex, ostensibly to avoid confusion with the rather more successful and prestigious Simplex from New Brunswick, better known for its New York-built Crane-Simplex cars.

Only the name really changed, however, as Amplex continued to produce its overpriced 40 and 50hp two-stroke cars. Amplex entered two 60hp four-cylinder two-stroke cars, with oversquare engine dimensions, in the very first Indianapolis 500-mile race in May 1911. One car ran well but the other was involved in the 500's first fatal accident. A rear tyre and rim came off the Amplex driven by Arthur Greiner; the car crashed heavily and Greiner's riding mechanic, Arthur Dickson, was killed.

Amplex's commercial fortunes were no better; a 1913 four-stroke design was a failure and in 1916 the company was taken over again. The new owner was King C. Gillette, of razor fame, who organized the Gillette Motors Co. Gillette was no more successful than Simplex or Amplex, in spite of trying a sleeve-valve two-stroke rotary engine, and a receiver was appointed in September 1917, after which no more cars were made. BL

AMC Gremlin X of 1978

American Motors Jeep Comanche of 1986

AMERICAN UNDERSLUNG/
AMERICAN
USA 1906-1914

The Indianapolis-based American Motor Car Co was founded by V. A. Longaker and D. S. Menasco, who had made a fortune in the lumber business. They engaged Harry C. Stutz as chief engineer and for 1906 brought out a well-made, conventional touring car with a 35-40hp four-cylinder engine. This was to have been made by Continental, but the company was too busy.

However, Stutz was told that if his company could find a firm to assemble the engines, Continental would supply most of the principal components. The contract went to a small company owned by the Teetor brothers and set them on the path to becoming important engine manufacturers under the name Teetor-Hartley. Frames for the first Americans came from A. O. Smith and axles from Garford.

Shortly after the first production cars were made, early in 1906 Stutz left American to join the Marion Motor Car Co, also of Indianapolis. His place was taken by Fred I. Tone who came from Marion. Tone designed the underslung model after seeing a conventional frame being carried into the factory upside down, and this first American Underslung was put into production in 1907. It had a two-seater roadster body and a larger engine, of 40-50hp, which, with the gearbox, was mounted on a sub-frame. This and the 35-40hp tourer were the only models for 1907, when about 100 cars were made.

Larger engines of 50 and 70hp were used in some models from 1908, all these engines being built by Teetor to Tone's design. Body styles included two- and four-seaters on the underslung chassis, known as the Speedster and Traveler respectively, and a range of open and closed bodies on the conventional chassis. Prices ran as high as $5000. In 1908 John North Willys founded the American Motor Sales Co to market American cars and his own Overlands.

Fred Tone left in 1911 after a disagreement, and the company was reorganized under J. I. Handley who became president of American and also of Marion. The company now had three factories, one for production of the Traveler, another for production of the Tourist and Scout, and a third for bodies. The Scout was a smaller and cheaper model with 22.4hp engines made by American, and selling for $1250. The conventional chassis were dropped for 1912, which was American's best year, with about 1000 cars made, compared with an average of 150 to 200 for previous years. The cars were now officially called American Underslungs.

In September 1912 the company began to publish a house journal, *Underslung News*, and approached 1913 with great optimism and its biggest line yet. This ran from the

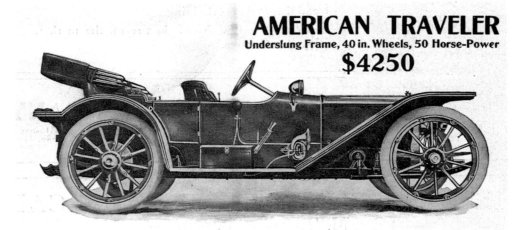

AMERICAN TRAVELER
Underslung Frame, 40 in. Wheels, 50 Horse-Power
$4250

American Underslung Traveler of 1911

Scout, now priced at $2000, to the Traveler limousine at $6000. However, the new range, which included electric starters, had involved heavy capital expenditure and when the hoped-for spring boom in sales failed to materialize American was quickly in trouble.

In a desperate attempt to stimulate sales it announced its 1914 models in April 1913. These included its first six-cylinder car, powered by a Teetor-designed and built 60hp engine. Production was almost at a standstill by August and the company was in the hands of a receiver by November 1913, along with Marion.

Few, if any, cars were made in 1914, and in April the premises and unsold cars were put up for sale. There were some bargains to be had, including four-cylinder engines for $100, Scout roadsters for $600 and full-size roadsters for $900. The factories were sold for $70,000 to the Indianapolis Cordage and Implement Co. GNG

AMILCAR
FRANCE 1921-1939

The birth of Amilcar was partly a result of the birth of Citroën. In 1918 Jules Salomon, designer of the world's first real mass-market small car, Le Zèbre, was employed by André Citroën to design the car which would bring him into the motor industry in the 1920s – the 5CV. Salomon's design for Citroën so undercut Le Zèbre's four-cylinder trendsetter that in 1919, the year of the Citroën's introduction, Le Zèbre's makers, Borie and Co, were in trouble.

A 36-year-old Le Zèbre technician and former Berliet test driver, André Morel, had racing ambitions which he thought could be pursued through a design for a small sporting car by Edmond Moyet, a colleague of Salomon at Citroën. Morel was friendly with a Le Zèbre shareholder, Emil Akar, the son of a wealthy Paris clothier and then manager of a chain of grocery stores, and in Akar he saw a source of finance. Morel introduced Moyet to Akar and another Le Zèbre shareholder,

Joseph Lamy. Akar agreed to provide 100,000 francs to build two examples of Moyet's car, which were labelled Borie cyclecars.

These were demonstrated to enthusiastic Le Zèbre dealers who in 1919, through an agent in Lyons, invested 1 million francs in the new project. Lamy and Akar invested a further 2 million and in 1921 founded the Société Nouvelle pour l'Automobile Amilcar, at St Denis, a popular district for smaller manufacturers. The name Amilcar was coined by Maurice Puech, one of those to see the first cars, from the names of Lamy and Akar – who became, respectively, sales director and managing director.

Amilcar's intention was to build a real car but small enough to invoke the French tax advantages for light weight. Moyet's first design, the 903cc four-cylinder CC, with solid rear axle, was launched in 1921. By mid-July production of the very basic, lightweight cars was five a day.

On 27 November the Amilcar first appeared in competition, when Morel began to fulfil his sporting ambitions by setting a flying kilometre class record at over 56mph (90kph). In 1922 the factory entered three cars (there was also a private entry) in the inaugural Bol d'Or 24-hour race and Morel beat Robert Benoist's Salmson to victory at an average of over 37mph (60kph).

By 1924, and the CGS, Amilcars were becoming more 'conventional', with pressure lubrication, front-wheel brakes and larger engines, partly compensated for by lighter bodies, but showing that Amilcar was already eschewing the cyclecar rules. Amilcar had had a specialized competition department since 1923, with a million-franc budget, and certainly success sold cars, more than 15,000 of the side-valve four-cylinders to date.

In 1925, when Amilcar built 3700 cars, the company moved into larger premises in St Denis and invested heavily in new machinery and impressive testing and research facilities. The Margyl bodywork company, owned by Amilcar technical director Marcel Sée, also became part of Amilcar and in 1926 1200 employees built some 4800 cars.

Against this background Moyet could afford to engage two assistants, one from Sunbeam and one from Fiat's racing department, to produce, predictably, a six-cylinder engine for the 1925 competition car, the CO. The superb engine developed 75bhp in Roots supercharged form and the car was an immediate success, finishing first and second in the 1926 Grand Prix de Provence, with Morel winning. In 1927 a single-seater CO, the MCO Record, became the first 1100cc car to exceed 125mph (200kph) and subsequently took many other records. Some 50 examples of a productionized CO, the C6, were sold to private entrants.

Amilcar CGS of c.1926

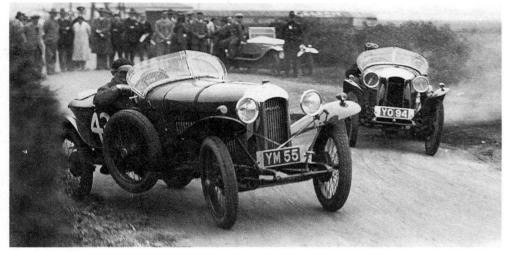
Amilcar C6 of 1926

The CGS and the low chassis CGS 'Surbaissé' models continued to sell well and were built under licence in several countries, as the Amilcar Italiana in Italy, the Grofri in Austria and the Pluto in Germany. Amilcars were exported to Australia and to the United States, where they were distributed by Maybach Motors of New York.

Amilcar could not, however, escape the Depression and from early 1927 the works racing programme was radically cut back, with only sporadic official competition involvement, principally in record breaking, from that season on. The growing financial problems led to the departure of both Lamy and Akar, who could no longer afford to back the company, and in July 1927 Amilcar was reorganized with new management and 10 million francs nominal capital as Société Anonyme Français de l'Automobile.

The company, fatefully, now decided to concentrate on touring cars such as the Types L and M and the rather fragile C8. In October 1928 it seemed that Amilcar might be absorbed by the Durant Motor Corporation, an idea thwarted by William Durant himself being caught in the Wall Street crash. In 1929 Morel, finding himself starved of racing, left the company.

A return to small cars with the 621cc Type C of 1933 could not reverse Amilcar's decline and in 1935 the company moved to much smaller premises in Boulogne, to be reorganized once again as the Société Financiers pour l'Automobile, with Marcel Sée in charge. For a couple of seasons the company built the N7 Pégase, which used a Delahaye 12CV engine, before being taken over by Hotchkiss in 1937.

Under Hotchkiss and with J. A. Grégoire as designer, Amilcar in 1938 launched the technically interesting, aluminium chassised, front-wheel-drive 'Compound', but only some 700 cars were built before World War II intervened. By the time peace returned the Amilcar name had been laid to rest. BL

AMPHICAR
GERMANY 1961-1968

The Amphicar was the only true amphibian ever to go on general sale and was the brainchild of the amphibian's most stalwart exponent, Hans Trippel. Trippel began designing amphibians in 1932, starting production under his own name in 1934 with the four-wheel- and propeller-drive SG6. His early cars were ostensibly for estate and forestry use but, with World War II approaching, his designs had an obvious military appeal. Trippel became a member of Hitler's advisory staff and took over the Bugatti factory at Molsheim to produce military amphibians.

After the war Trippel produced one, unsuc-cessful, conventional car, but by 1957 that project had been abandoned and at the 1959 Geneva Show he exhibited a new amphibian known as the Eurocar – so-named probably because parts were bought in from all over Europe.

In 1961 Deutsche Industrie-Werke was formed in Lübeck-Schlutup to produce the Eurocar in quantity as the Amphicar. Although the show car had had an Austin A35 engine, production cars used the 1147cc Triumph Herald unit, rear-mounted and driving through the rear wheels, with power take off from the gearbox to twin propellers, selected by a simple lever.

The car had already made its American début at the 1960 New York Motor Show and an American financed branch, the Amphicar Corporation, planned to sell the cars in the USA. The German company was renamed Amphicar Vertriebs GmbH and production transferred to Wuppertal-Elberfield, Berlin, where production remained until the end, in 1968, the company name having changed again in 1963 to Deutsche Waggons und Maschinenfabriken. In fact, the majority of a probable total production of 800 cars went to the USA, some 600 being exported there and the rest being spread around Europe.

By most accounts the Amphicar was dreadful on the road because of its narrow tyres, high centre of gravity and tail-heavy weight distribution – but it was truly amphibian. On the road it could achieve 68mph (109kph) and in water it would do 6½ knots, steered by the front wheels as rather rudimentary rudders. Braking in the water was achieved by selecting reverse and revving hard!

Amphicar publicity stunts were plentiful. On 16 September 1965 two British Army officers, a sergeant, and Amphicar owner Timothy Dill-Russell, a professional escapologist, crossed the English Channel in two Amphicars from Dover to Calais. Although one car eventually had to tow the other, the crossing was completed in 7 hours and 20 minutes and cost only £4 in fuel for the two cars and four passengers. The cars then toured Europe, visiting the Frankfurt Show and the works in Berlin. Another publicity stunt had a less happy ending when an Amphicar was run down by a ship in the Straits of Gibraltar.

None of the many backers of the Amphicar companies ever saw a profit from the venture and Amphicar found it increasingly difficult to meet road and marine regulations, while owners who used their cars in salt water not surprisingly found that they were encountering horrific corrosion problems. The novelty wore off and in 1968 the company ceased trading. BL

AMPLEX
see American Simplex

ANADOL
TURKEY 1966 to date

The Anadol was the first car designed to be manufactured in Turkey, and car, factory and organization were set up as a package deal by the British Reliant company. Reliant's role as purveyors of ready made motor industries began with Autocars in Israel, which placed a trial order for 100 three-wheelers in 1959 and subsequently negotiated a deal for Reliant to design a four-wheel car (the company's first) to be built near Haifa. Production of the Ford Anglia-powered car began in 1959.

In the autumn of 1963 the Turkish Koç Holdings group approached Reliant to undertake a similar operation and in the same year it inspected the Haifa plant. On 13 January 1964 in Athens, Koç and Reliant began negotiations which resulted in the adoption of a basic design and commercial terms by August. As a client of the Koç subsidiary Otosan, Reliant would design a car to meet local requirements, plan a factory, provide detailed assembly manuals, train key personnel, supply moulds and jigs, provide advice on developing local content and back up the whole operation with paperwork in the local language.

Koç invested £600,000 in the project and Reliant £100,000, although under Turkish law Reliant was not allowed a stake in Otosan. The project did, however, represent an income of about £250 per car to the British company, local content initially being responsible for 50 per cent of the product by value and Reliant supplying much of the rest.

In December 1965 the prototype four-door saloon, styled by Ogle, was *driven* to Istanbul to be presented for government approval, which it formally received in February 1966. Reliant's project FW5 was renamed Anadol after a national competition to name the car.

On 1 March 1966 the production design was finalized and Reliant personnel travelled to Turkey to supervise developments. In May a 60,000sq ft (5600sq m) factory was started alongside the Otosan truck works and near the Ankara road on the outskirts of Istanbul. The Otosan Otomobil Sanayii AS factory was opened on 16 December by Koç president Vehbi Koç, who declared, 'We are at the

Anadol 1.3 saloon of c.1970

threshold of the automotive industry'; at this time, Turkey's 33 million people had only 60,000 cars. The new factory employed 280 staff at around £9 for a 48-hour week.

The final pre-production car had been assembled in England in July 1966 and the first Otosan-built Anadol was completed on 7 December. Within a week three cars were ready for proving runs and by the time the factory opened 31 cars had been built and 15 delivered to showrooms in five cities. Some 250 firm orders, accompanied by deposits, were taken on the day the car was announced and, not being subject to the 136 per cent prevailing import duty, the car was competitively priced and well received.

The initial production target was 2500 cars a year, with 5000 a year being achieved by November 1970 – close to the factory's 6000 annual capacity; total production by the end of that year was 10,000. The Ford 1300 engine had been adopted as standard in 1969 and a 1600 option was added in 1974 along with a coupé model, the cars continuing with only minor changes and the addition of a station wagon. They were built, however, in much smaller numbers, the output for 1982 being quoted as just 407 cars from over 1800 workers. In 1986 the Anadol 16 was replaced by the Otosan Ford Taunus 1.6, which used the body of the obsolete Taunus Cortina with a 1.6 litre Ford engine. BL

ANDERSON
USA 1916-1925

The most successful car to be built in the southern United States, the Anderson appealed to local patriotism with its slogan 'A Little Bit Higher in Price BUT Made in Dixie!' The company had its origins in the Hollier and Anderson Buggy Co of Rock Hill, South Carolina, founded in 1889. John Gay Anderson became sole proprietor in 1905, by which

time the factory was turning out one buggy every 25 minutes. In 1910 he launched his first car, a conventional 35hp four-cylinder tourer, the Rock Hill 35, but buyers were so few that he never put it into production.

After 1912 the buggy business began to decline and Anderson turned to making truck bodies for Model T Fords. In 1915 he made his second entry into the automobile business with the Anderson Model 6-40-6, an assembled car powered by a Continental six-cylinder engine, which was brought out as a 1916 model. A separate company, the Anderson Motor Co, was formed to handle this side of the business, capitalized at $1.5 million.

Bodywork was, naturally, made in-house from oak and ash grown in Anderson's own woods. Two body styles were offered initially, a tourer and roadster, priced at $1250, but sedans were added later.

Anderson's contribution to the war effort was the making of aircraft-carrying trailers and 100 light trucks. Sales were encouraging in the early post-war years, with 1180 recorded for 1920, but thereafter they dropped to 481 in 1921 and 630 in 1922. Specification changed little, although for 1923 a smaller Continental engine was used, the 3.2-litre Model 6Y compared with the 3.7-litre Model 7R of previous years. Aluminium bodies were now offered, prices running from $1195 for the tourer to $1595 for the sedan. The larger car was still listed at $1945 for the tourer.

Anderson's best year was 1923, when 1875 cars were made, but the Continental 6Y engines gave a lot of trouble due to cylinder block warpage which seriously damaged the Anderson's reputation. In 1924 sales dropped to 616, while a mere 136 cars were delivered in 1925, the last year of production.

In September 1926 the assets were sold for $63,000 to trustees of the stockholders. The factory remained empty until 1928 when it was reopened for textile manufacture. The premises are still active today as the Rock Hill Printing and Finishing Co. GNG

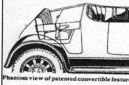

Anderson 6 convertible of 1920

ANDRÉ
see Marlborough

ANGUS-SANDERSON
GB 1918-1927

The Angus family had been coachbuilders from about 1750 and Sanderson had been apprenticed to their firm before starting a factory in St Thomas Street, Newcastle-upon-Tyne, where the Hugh Mason-designed NUT motorcycle, named after the city, was built at the rate of six to eight a week from 1912. An offshoot of the original carriage and body

Angus-Sanderson 14.2hp of 1925

firm had built a few Aster-engined Sandersons in Carlisle in 1905-6.

Sanderson built up successful car sales agencies with the Angus family and, as Sir William Angus, Sanderson and Co Ltd, produced a small batch of assembled cars in the NUT factory in 1918-19. The cars had radiators styled by Cecil Kimber (later of MG fame), Wrigley gearboxes and axles (from the Birmingham firm that would be acquired by William Morris in 1923-24 and become the home of his Morris-Commercial) and 14.3hp four-cylinder 2.3-litre Tylor engines.

During 1919 car production was moved to a factory at Birtley, 6 miles (9km) from Newcastle, where 6000 Belgians had made armaments in World War I. The Angus-Sanderson was intended for mass production and nearly all the metal parts were bought in, although elaborate machinery was installed to prepare the timber for framing the attractive, spray-painted bodies. It looked set to become the highest-production British car, but there were interminable teething troubles and production hold-ups caused by unskilled labour and out-of-balance component stocks.

Sir William Angus, Sanderson and Co was in serious financial difficulties in less than two years and Tylors, the engine-makers, were behind a rescue attempt that created Angus-Sanderson (1921) Ltd, at Hendon, Middlesex. Cars were built for a time there in the old Grahame-White factory. An additional 8hp model was planned for 1923 but the project never got off the ground. Sales of the 14.3hp continued until 1927, many going overseas. Total output was in the region of 3000 cars. NB

ANSALDO
ITALY 1919-1936

Founded in 1852, Ansaldo was one of Italy's largest engineering combines with interests in ordnance, aero engines, railway locomotives and shipbuilding. Its headquarters were in Genoa, with aero engine works in Turin, foundries at Aosta and naval yards at Sestri

31

Ponente and Voltri. At the end of World War I the workforce totalled 80,000. Up to that time the only road vehicles made were armoured cars on the Lancia 1Z chassis.

In 1919 Guido Soria, the chief engineer, suggested that the spare capacity in the aero engine plant could be put to good use making motor cars, and produced an up-to-date four-cylinder single-overhead cam engine of 1847cc capacity, installed in an American type chassis with three-speed gearbox and central change. The bodies were rather utilitarian but this Tipo 4 sold quite well, with 287 finding buyers in 1920 and 443 in 1921. The 2-litre 4CS followed in 1922, and a 2-litre six, the GAN, in 1923.

In 1922 Ansaldo was threatened by the failure of the Banco di Sconto, which brought down SPA, but it was rescued by Varese financial interests, and in 1927 Ansaldo Auto-

Ansaldo 4A of 1919

Ansaldo 4C Torpedo of 1923

mobili was formed under the control of the aircraft company Macchi. This was because the Ansaldo group, described at that time as the biggest engineering concern in Europe, was divided up at the order of Mussolini's government. The aeronautical section devolved to Fiat.

Car production continued at between 1000 and 2000 a year in the mid-1920s; the 1847cc and 2-litre fours lasted up to 1930 under various designations, there was a cheaper 1½-litre four from 1926 to 1929, the Tipo 10, and six-cylinder cars were also made. In 1924 the 4C at 28,000 lire was a competitor for Fiat's 501 at 32,000 lire, although Fiat was making five times as many cars.

Soria left Ansaldo in 1927 but all subsequent cars were to his design, as it took two years to get them into production. These were the 2.8-litre six-cylinder Tipo 18, and the 3½-litre straight-eight Tipo 22. They were made from 1929 to 1932, 400 being laid down. However, it took until 1936 before all were sold, by which time Ansaldo had been reorganized as CEVA (Costruzioni e Vendite Automobili Ansaldo). A small number of 2-

and 3-ton lorries were also made from 1930 to 1932, while Ansaldo sold a licence to the Czech Wikov company for production of its overhead cam engine.

CEVA sold out in 1937 to Viberti; its interests included bus bodies, and a few Viberti-bodied trolleybuses carried the Ansaldo name up to about 1950. There were also some Fiat-Ansaldo six-wheeled armoured cars made in the 1930s, but these had no connection with CEVA, being the products of another branch of Ansaldo at Genoa. GNG

ANSBACH
see Faun

APOLLO/PICCOLO
GERMANY 1904-1925

The Apollo name originated in 1910 with a reorganization of A. Ruppe & Sohn AG when its Piccolo cars changed name to Piccolo-

Apollo (or sometimes Apollo-Piccolo) and later to plain Apollo. Arthur Ruppe had started business in 1854 as an iron founder and went on to make agricultural machinery. In 1902 the company started producing motorcycles, known as Apoldanias, and in 1904 Ruppe built the first Piccolo car, with an air-cooled V-twin motor. The car was cheap – as little as 2000 marks in 1905 – and popular, and by 1906 Ruppe & Sohn employed more than 600 people.

In 1908 the firm was reorganized as a limited company in Apolda, but in the same year the son, Hugo, left to form his own company building similar, air-cooled cars under the name MAF with reasonable success. In 1910, when Piccolo brought out its smallest and cheapest model, the Mobbel, the firm was renamed as Apollo-Werke AG. The air-cooled cars continued as Piccolos until 1912 when they became Apollo-Piccolos; the larger, water-cooled cars became Piccolo-Apollos and then plain Apollos. The first car from Apollo-Werke was the model G7/20PS which was built from the end of 1910 to 1912, when it was replaced by the 6/18PS Model C, which, with an increase to 20bhp from 1914, lasted until 1920.

Apollo engaged the talented designer and racing enthusiast Karl Slevogt, formerly of Laurin-Klement and Puch, and Slevogt designed several sporty Apollos. The Type B 4/10PS was shown at the 1911 Berlin Motor Show and in 1912 a 20bhp version, the Type B Special, appeared. Slevogt's Type F 8/28PS was available in competition trim and was quite competitive with contemporary Bugattis, occasionally with Slevogt driving.

Before World War I, Apollo was forced by financial constraints to limit its competition activities, but after the war the company returned to building sports cars. The 4/20PS, introduced in 1920, was the first German production car with a front swing-axle and it continued until 1925.

In 1921 Apollo took over Hugo Ruppe's ailing MAF works and built a prototype V8 engine. The engine did not go into production, however, as Apollo was gradually declining. The company ceased trading in 1926. BL

APPERSON
USA 1901-1926

The Apperson brothers, Elmer and Edgar, were born in Indiana in 1861 and 1870 respectively. They were great-great-grandsons of the famous Kentucky pioneer Daniel Boone and came from farming stock. They founded the Riverside Machine Shop in Kokomo, Indiana, in 1888 and helped Elwood Haynes build his first car in 1894. From 1898 to 1901 they were in partnership with Haynes making the Haynes-Apperson car, and in October 1901 set up on their own as the Apperson Brothers Automobile Co.

The company took its first order at the New York Automobile Show in November 1901, although production did not begin until the following spring; initial production was two cars a week. The car had a 16hp horizontally-opposed two-cylinder engine and was expensive at $2500. A horizontally-opposed four followed in 1903; the company changed to vertical engines in 1904.

The name Jackrabbit was first used for a sporting model for 1906, but this soon became an unofficial name for all Appersons; indeed, its factory bore a large sign that read 'Jack Rabbit Motor Cars'. By 1907 there were four four-cylinder models, of 24/30hp, 40hp, 50hp and the 60hp Jackrabbit roadster, at prices up to $7500 for a 50hp limousine. In 1908 the company was incorporated with a paid-up capital of $400,000; the factory was expanded and production reached about 2500 cars a year. A number of lower priced models were introduced, the cheapest being a 26hp four for only $1350 in 1915.

A more significant offering for 1915 was a 5.4-litre V8 designed by Burrt J. Hubbard. With a four-seater 'chummy' body this sold for a remarkably low $2000. The V8, which continued to 1925, was advertised as 'The Eight with Eighty less parts', although it was never actually spelt out what these parts were. In 1917 some special models known as Silver-Appersons were made; the name did not come from their colour but from the New York dealer Conover T. Silver who also designed special bodies for Willys and was later responsible for the Kissel Gold Bug.

Elmer Apperson died in 1920, aged 58. He was replaced as president by Edgar, who sold out to a syndicate called the Pioneer Automobile Co in 1924, by which time production had dropped from more than 2000 in 1916 to fewer than 1000. A smaller car with a six-cylinder Falls engine had joined the V8 in 1923, but not many were sold. In 1924 it was rumoured that Apperson would join forces

Aquila Italiana sports two-seater of 1914

again with Haynes, but the latter went out of business before serious negotiations could start.

Apperson struggled on until December 1925, announcing 1926 models which featured six-cylinder Velie or straight-eight Lycoming engines and front-wheel brakes. All assets were sold by the receiver in July 1926. Edgar Apperson lived to see a Kokomo street renamed Apperson Way in 1955, and died four years later at the age of 89. GNG

AQUILA ITALIANA
ITALY 1906-1917

The Aquila Italiana, or Italian Eagle, was built between 1906 and 1917 by Fabbrica Italiana d'Automobili Aquila in Turin. The first Aquila appeared in 1906, when Societa Anonima Aquila Italiana was registered with capital of 1.2 million lire, Giuseppe Bozzi as president and Giulio Pallavicino as general manager. The first car was designed by technical director Ing Giulio Cesare Cappa, who later worked for both Fiat and Itala, and it possessed very advanced engineering.

Later cars had four- or six-cylinder engines, pioneering the use of monobloc casting, a ball-bearing crankshaft and – by the time the cars made a delayed production appearance in 1908 with the four-cylinder model K – the first known use of aluminium pistons in a car engine. The engine and gearbox were carried on a common mount and were thus effectively in unit. The delays were caused partly by the death of the company's main backer, in 1906, and partly by other production problems which included moving to a larger site sufficient for projected needs.

In 1912 Cappa produced a 4.2-litre 60hp six-cylinder car which, driven by Marsaglia, finished second in the 1913 Targa Florio and won several important hillclimbs. The smaller, four-cylinder 12/15, driven by Eugenio Beria d'Argentina and with streamlined aluminium bodywork, was very successful in hillclimbs and sprints.

Aquila sporting successes continued through Cav Vincenzo Florio, of Targa Florio connection, and Bugatti exponent Barto-

lomeo Costantini. In 1914 Aquila entered three typically advanced single-overhead cam six-cylinder cars for the French Grand Prix, although only one started, for Costantini – who retired after 10 laps. The cars were built virtually unchanged, alongside aero engines under Salmson and SPA licences, until 1917 when the company ceased trading, to be absorbed by the expanding SPA company. BL

Arab two-seater of c.1927

ARAB
GB 1926-1930

This 2-litre sports model emanated first from the KL steel foundry and then from part of the Phoenix factory in Letchworth in 1926 and was the work of Reid Railton, who later found fame with the Brooklands Riley Nine, the Railton land speed record machines and transmissions for ERA. Railton had been assistant to J. G. Parry Thomas, the chief experimental engineer at Leyland Motors in World War I.

Railton and Thomas shared rented accommodation and filled spare moments with sketches of their ideas for high-performance cars. The outcome was the Leyland 8 and a 2-litre engine sharing valve gear, hemispherical head and other features with the big Leyland. Fifty sets of 2-litre castings were ordered by Leyland and one was used for competition in an Enfield-Alldays chassis – apparently with Leyland approval as it was called the Spurrier-Railton, Henry Spurrier being the Leyland managing director. Other engines were used by Parry Thomas in the racing cars he worked on after leaving Leyland in 1923.

Railton departed soon afterwards and formed Arab Motors in March 1925 with the Henry Spurriers, senior and junior, as his fellow directors. He built a few cars related to the Spurrier-Railton 'prototype' and then appeared to lose interest in the project after Thomas was killed during a land speed record attempt in the chain-drive, aero-engined Babs in 1927.

Railton moved to join Thomas's backer, Kenneth Thomson, at Thomson and Taylor and it seems likely that one or two more Arabs were completed there in 1929-30. Only about 10 Arabs appear to have been built, two with low chassis and a top speed of 90mph (145kph). NB

ARGUS
GERMANY 1902-1906

Argus cars were made by Paul Jeannin who set up the Internationale Automobilzentrale KG Jeannin and Co in Berlin in 1901. He began by importing Panhards from France, and the first Argus cars of 1902 used Panhard engines and components, assembled in Berlin. In 1903 Jeannin changed the name of his company to Argus Motorenbaugesellschaft and began to make engines of his own design. These were of two, four or six cylinders and were intended for boat and stationary engine work as well as for cars.

Complete cars were made as well as engines, but they were rare and expensive. They were made in three models, a 12PS two-cylinder of 2380cc, a 20hp four-cylinder of 4960cc and a 40hp four-cylinder of 9260cc.

In 1906 Jeannin left the Argus company to set up, with his brother Emil, the Sun Motorengesellschaft Jeannin and Co KG, which made Sun cars for two years. Argus gave up cars at about the same time, and began making aero engines. By 1912 the Argus was the most widely used aero engine

in Germany. The company abandoned these after 1918 but re-entered the field in 1926, continuing until the end of World War II. It had one further involvement with cars, making straight-eight engines for Horch from 1926 to 1929. This was logical, as it had bought the Horch company in 1920. During the 1930s and World War II Argus made inverted V12 aero engines. GNG

ARGYLL
GB 1899-1928; 1976 to date

While he was works superintendent at the Eadie Manufacturing Co of Redditch, Alexander Govan undertook a study of continental cars with the intention of designing a vehicle incorporating their best features. He later transferred to the Scottish Cycle Co of Hozier Street, Bridgeton, Glasgow, and designed a shaft-drive, Renault-inspired light car in 1899.

Financial backing came from W. A. Smith of the National Telephone Co; he was also a director of the Bryant and May match firm, which would subsequently use Argyll vans. Smith and Govan formed Hozier Engineering Co Ltd in 1900 with a capital of £15,000, and the first cars were sold in April. MMC and Simms engines were used after the first 90 voiturettes appeared with 2¾hp De Dion engines. In 1902 production was running at six to eight cars a week. Clément, De Dion and Aster engines were soon also used, followed by an Argyll-built three-cylinder 12/14hp unit in late 1903.

Argyll opened an engine factory employing 300 in 1904, although designs were Aster-based until 1907. The firm was producing 15 vehicles a week, which made it one of the most prolific European producers. Govan, the managing director, was an adept publicist and his cars were seen in many reliability trials and record attempts. A London branch provided regular engineers' reports for its customers and cars were being sold over-

seas, notably in Australia, where the agent Tarrant made some crypto-Argylls under his own name.

An output of 1200 cars was forecast for 1905 and a dividend of 35 per cent to shareholders underlined the firm's confidence. Commercial vehicles, including taxis, became increasingly important and this department was under the control of John Brimlow, formerly of Stirling Motor Carriages Ltd.

In March 1905 a new company, Argyll Motors Ltd, was formed to increase capital and take over Hozier Engineering. Nearly half the proceeds of its £500,000 share issue were used to build an imposing factory at Alexandria, near Dumbarton, complete with three gold-leaf domes and marble floors. Potential output was 2500 vehicles a year, although 800 was more like the actual achievement. The model range included taxis and other commercial vehicles and 10 to 26hp cars. Each received 30 to 35 coats of paint and varnish and was subjected to a 100-mile (160-km) road test.

In 1907 Argyll Motors suffered a disastrous loss when Govan died from food poisoning. The company's over-capacity at a time of recession led to difficulties and 1500 men were laid off at Alexandria. In November 1907 assets were written down by 50 per cent and a new firm, Argylls Ltd, was formed. One of the chief creditors, Dunlop, succeeded in putting in Colonel J. S. Mathew as managing director in an attempt to retrieve the situation. At this time A. Davidson, formerly of MMC, was works manager and Henri Perrot from Brasier was chief engineer.

Perrot gave reluctant support to the single-sleeve-valve engine introduced by Peter Burt to Colonel Mathew in 1909, but once convinced of its advantages he did everything possible to make it practicable. It proved costly to produce, however, yet two versions were made, of 15/30 and 25/50hp. This occurred at a time when the production of 240 vehicles in 1909 and 452 in 1910, from a factory that had overheads of £12,000 a

Argus Beaufort 20hp of 1903 (right) with 20hp Humber

Argyll limousine of 1913

month, could not sustain expensive development.

When attempting to patent the Burt engine Argyll discovered that the Canadian J. H. K. McCollum had already protected many of its features. The company reached an understanding with Burt and McCollum and sold a licence for production of the engine to Piccard-Pictet, whereupon the latter's British agents were sued in 1911 by the holders of the Knight sleeve-valve patents. £50,000 was allegedly spent by Argyll in extricating itself from the morass, though its sleeve-valve cars were undoubtedly good when they reached the public in 1912 and they continued the Argyll features of excellent workmanship, refinement and good looks. The 12hp, launched in October 1911, had the added distinction of Rubery front-wheel brakes, the rights to which Henri Perrot acquired for £200 in 1914 and put to good use when four-wheel brakes became commonplace in the 1920s.

Sales grew slowly, but in 1913 a 2614cc sleeve-valve car drove around Brooklands for 14 hours at an average speed of 76.43mph (122.97kph). Despite the introduction of 120bhp Burt-McCollum aero engines in 1914, Argylls Ltd was tottering – and finally collapsed in June that year.

The Alexandria factory was sold to the Admiralty for £153,000 and thereafter made torpedoes. The former Hozier Engineering/ Argyll factory in Bridgeton then became a store place for the remnants of the firm. After World War I small scale production of cars, initially of the pre-war 15/30hp, was resumed there under the direction of John and Charles Brimlow.

Only about a dozen 15/30s were made before efforts were concentrated on a 1½-litre, 12hp car in 1921 with side-valve or sleeve-valve engines. Some Burt-McCollum units were used, made by Wallace, which soon

collapsed when its three-wheel-drive Glasgow tractors failed commercially. Engines and axles were also supplied by Greenwood and Batley of Leeds, the makers of motorized factory trucks. An 18/50 2.4-litre sleeve-valve six was also offered. In all, some 200 to 300 of the post-war Argylls are believed to have been made until about 1928, after which Bridgeton and a London depot continued in business for a number of years providing spares and servicing.

In 1983 a Scottish-built Argyll V6 or V8 sports car, successor to a new Argyll coupé built in limited numbers from 1976, was launched, to be built at a rate of one a month initially and hopefully thereafter at about 30 cars a year. The new company, Argyll Turbo Cars Ltd of Lochgilphead, had six employees under aviation engineer Bob Henderson, also maker of the Minnow-Fish carburettor who built the 1976 Argyll. When the car was unveiled by the Duke of Argyll, a 1907 Argyll was on hand to remind purchasers of the name's past history. NB

ARIEL
GB 1898-1916; 1922-1925

The name Ariel is one of the oldest in the vehicle industry and dates from 1847 when Whitehurst & Co of London began marketing, unsuccessfully, the Ariel wheel, intended for horsedrawn vehicles and fitted with what is widely considered to be the world's first pneumatic tyre, Thompson's Pneumatic Belt. By 1871 the name had been taken up by James Starley who, with William Hillman, of later car fame, was building lightweight 'ordinary' Ariel bicycles (as well as sewing machines) in Coventry.

Around 1874 Starley's company moved into the Ariel Works in Coventry but the name

disappeared briefly from the cycle industry before being re-registered on 1 November 1893 by safety bicycle manufacturers Guest & Barrow, a company that was promptly dissolved four months later.

The Ariel name was then taken up by Harvey DuCros's Dunlop group of companies, which registered the Ariel Cycle Co Ltd in London in November 1897. The Ariel and Dunlop badges were similar renderings of two entwined serpents forming a tyre on a wheel.

A conglomerate company, Cycle Components Manufacturing, run by Charles Sangster and S. F. Edge, made parts for Ariel, among others, and in or around 1897 Dunlop sold Ariel to the company. In 1898 the Ariel Motor Co Ltd was formed in Birmingham as a subsidiary of Cycle Components Manufacturing and on 18 November 1898 the first powered Ariel, a 1¾hp De Dion type three-wheeler, made under licence, was shown at the Crystal Palace Show.

Late in 1899 Charles Jarrott took an Ariel to the United States and demonstrated it on a track in what may have been America's first ever motorcycle race. As a result the Spalding Bidwell Cycle Depot set up a New York agency in 1900.

Ariel soon moved from tricycles to quadricycles, showing a 3hp model at the 1901 National Show, and at the same show unveiled a 9/10hp vertical-twin engined car with tonneau body. In August 1902 a 16hp four-cylinder Ariel, designed by Sangster, was entered for the Automobile Club's Reliability Trial but crashed while on test and could not start.

Alongside the cars Ariel was starting its better known and longer lived role as a motorcycle manufacturer. From 1904 the Ariel Cycle Co would seem to have controlled the motorcycle side of Cycle Components while the Ariel Motor Co confined its activities to cars.

In 1906, after flagging sales, the company was reorganized as Ariel Motors Ltd and concentrated on a new range of large, conventional cars marketed as Ariel-Simplexes. Financial problems remained, however, and the company was rescued by cash from Société Lorraine de Dietrich, which was looking for a plant in Britain and bought Ariel's Selly Oak factory from Components Ltd for £36,000. By April 1908 it was supposedly making three chassis a week, with plans to build Antoinette aircraft alongside the cars, but all mention of British Lorraine-Dietrichs ceased in 1910 and a receiver was appointed the following year.

Meanwhile, Ariel made arrangements for its cars to be built in Coventry by the Coventry Ordnance Co, a branch of Cammell Laird. Production continued with six models in 1913 and two four-cylinder models in 1914, one of which continued until 1916 when war production took over completely, Ariel making motorcycles, bombs and other armaments.

In 1915 the car and motorcycle companies were registered jointly for the first time as Ariel Works Ltd, but after the war no car production was attempted until 1922. As Ariel concentrated on motorcycles, a design by Jack Sangster (son of Charles) for an air-cooled, flat-twin 8hp car was taken up by Rover as the Rover 8, with Sangster as assistant works manager.

Jack soon rejoined Components Ltd as assistant managing director to his father, and worked on the design of the Ariel Nine, with which the company made its post-war re-appearance. The air-cooled, flat-twin engine of the Nine was made by A. Harper Sons & Bean Ltd, which had connections with Charles Sangster dating back to his cycle days.

Alas, the noisy, vibration-prone Nine and its four-cylinder successor of 1924, the Ten, were not a success and after they were dropped from production in 1925 Ariel concentrated on two wheels instead of four. From 1927 Edward Turner worked for Ariel until he moved to Triumph in 1936, when both motorcycle factories were under Jack Sangster's control. Both firms later joined the BSA-Daimler group and Ariel motorcycle production continued until 1970. BL

ARIÈS
FRANCE 1903-1938

Baron Charles Petiet founded the Société Anonyme Ariès at the age of 24 in 1903, having worked briefly for Panhard et Levassor. Ariès had a capital of 500,000 francs, increased to 1 million by 1905, and a small factory at Villeneuve-la-Garenne, not far from the Aster factory at St Denis which supplied many of its engines. It employed about 100 men and was best known for commercial vehicles, although cars of good quality were made in small numbers, some being sold in England by Sydney Begbie as Asters while others were sold by a firm in Beccles from 1904 to 1906 as Anglians.

Initially most had chain drive, although Cardan drive and separate drive shafts above a dead axle were soon adopted. Chain drive persisted on the largest commercials into the 1930s. Six-cylinder and V4 cars were available in 1908 and were joined by the world's smallest six in 1910.

The firm opened an additional factory at Courbevoie and up to World War I made consistent, albeit modest, profits averaging about 100,000 francs a year. Production in 1913 totalled 350 vehicles. Shortly before the war Aster-engined lorries were approved for government subsidy and the company produced 3000 of these plus searchlight vehicles for the armed services. Hispano-Suiza aero engines were also produced.

Cars were promoted with the slogan 'Made with the precision of an aero engine and the strength of a lorry'. They continued to play only a small part in the affairs of Ariès. In 1924 the export manager, Louis Carle, travelled to Britain offering the trade overhead camshaft 5/8, 8/10, 12/15 and 15/20 models, without much success. New models were designed for 1931 by H. Toutée, who had been responsible for mid-1920s Chenard-Walckers.

The company was in severe financial difficulties by 1932 and gave up heavy commercials soon afterwards, although a 10hp chassis, for car or van use and with the unusual feature of a two-speed back axle, remained in production until 1938. The Ariès founder, Baron Petiet, died in 1958. NB

ARMSTRONG-SIDDELEY
GB 1919-1960

Armstrong-Siddeley Motors Ltd was formed through a merger between John Siddeley's Siddeley-Deasy Motor Manufacturing Co and Armstrong-Whitworth, both of which companies had been well-known for cars before World War I. In fact Armstrong-Whitworth acquired Siddeley-Deasy for £419,750, forming the Armstrong-Whitworth Development Co Ltd, of which Armstrong-Siddeley Motors Ltd was a subsidiary. Siddeley-Deasy was also celebrated for its aircraft engines, particularly the Siddeley Puma made during the war, and this side of the business continued to be important to the Coventry company.

Its first car was a substantial vehicle with a 30hp six-cylinder overhead-valve engine of 4960cc capacity and 60bhp. A five-seater sold for £960 complete – Armstrong-Siddeley always made its own coachwork – and customers included two royal dukes, the Duke of York (later King George VI) and the Duke of Gloucester. It was joined by a smaller, 2.3-litre 18hp in 1922 and a 1.8-litre 14hp four-cylinder car in 1924. The latter had a flat radiator, instead of the massive vee of the larger Armstrongs. These sold well, total sales reaching 4000 a year by the mid-1920s.

At the other end of the scale was the Stoneleigh light car powered by a 9hp vee-twin engine, with an unusual feature on the early models of a central driving position, ahead of the two passengers. This lasted only from 1922 to 1924. In 1922 more than 3000 employees worked at Armstrong-Siddeley on cars and aero engines.

In 1926 Siddeley bought back his business from Armstrong-Whitworth for £1.5 million. This included the aircraft side of Armstrong-Whitworth, as the parent Sir W. G. Armstrong, Whitworth and Co Ltd concentrated on armaments, later merging with Vickers. Siddeley's new holding company, the Armstrong-Siddeley Development Co Ltd, therefore controlled Armstrong-Whitworth Aircraft Ltd, Armstrong-Siddeley Motors Ltd and later another well-known aircraft firm, A. V. Roe Ltd, as well as the bodybuilding firm Burlington Carriage Co.

Armstrong-Siddeley had a number of military contracts in the 1920s, including 350hp tank engines supplied to Vickers in 1926, and the licence production of the Italian Pavesi tractor that drove and steered on all four wheels. They also made, in 1929 and 1930, some experimental eight-wheeled derivatives of the Pavesi design, powered by A. S. Genet radial aero engines.

In 1929 Armstrong-Siddeley adopted the

Armstrong-Siddeley Sapphire of 1954

Armstrong-Siddeley Hurricane of 1947

Wilson epicyclic gearbox which had been developed by Colonel Walter G. Wilson as an aid to gear changing in tanks. Wilson had designed the Wilson-Pilcher car in 1901, which had later been taken over by Armstrong-Whitworth. Known as the Wilson Self Changing Gearbox, it was a pre-selector system and an important step towards the modern automatic transmission.

Siddeley acquired the rights from Wilson and set up a separate company called Self Changing Gears Ltd, which supplied gearboxes to a number of other car makers including Daimler, Riley, Talbot, AC, Lagonda and Invicta. This was a substantial business, nearly 13,000 gearboxes going to Riley alone. Continental and American rights to the Wilson gearbox were taken on by Anthony Lago.

Armstrong-Siddeley entered the 1930s with four basic models, the 1½-litre 12/6, 1.9-litre 15/6, 2.8-litre Twenty and the old 4.9-litre Thirty, of which only 70 were made to 1933. Total production was running at around 3000 a year and the make had a well-established position in the upper middle-class bracket. The cars seemed utterly unsporting, but some sports tourers based on the 12 and 20hp chassis did well in Alpine Trials and RAC Rallies.

In 1933 the company challenged the Rolls-Royce and Daimler market with the Siddeley Special, a luxury car with a 4.9-litre six-cylinder engine derived from the original Thirty, though now with most of the engine made of Hiduminium alloy. This was a Rolls-Royce product, and one of their few alloys which other firms have been permitted to use. Despite its elegant appearance and 95mph (152kph) top speed, the Siddeley Special never really caught on and only 235 were sold between 1933 and 1937.

Aero engines continued to play a vital part in the company's business, and Armstrong-Siddeley was the second most important maker of radial engines in Britain, after Bristol. In 1935 the company merged with Hawker Engineering to form the Hawker-Siddeley Aircraft Co, which after the war became the Hawker-Siddeley group and in 1959 merged with its main rival to become Bristol-Siddeley Motors. J. D. Siddeley was knighted in 1932 and five years later was created Baron Kenilworth for his contributions to the aero engine industry. Among the most important engines of the 1930s and 1940s were the Lynx and Cheetah seven-cylinder radials, and the Tiger fourteen-cylinder radial. More than 40,000 Cheetah engines were made.

Hawker-Siddeley flourished during World War II, controlling not only Armstrong-Whitworth and Hawker but also A. V. Roe and the Gloster Aircraft Co. Despite its busy aircraft engine programme, Armstrong-Siddeley found time to develop its post-war cars, which were announced in the second week of May 1945, just as the war in Europe ended.

They had 2-litre engines similar to those in the 1939 Sixteen (enlarged to 2.3 litres in 1949) with attractive modern styling by Cyril Siddeley, J. D.'s elder son. Initially two bodies were available, the Hurricane drophead coupé and the Lancaster saloon, but these were later joined by the Typhoon fixed-head coupé and Whitley four-light saloon. For the first time in 13 years an alternative to the Wilson box was offered in the shape of a Rootes-made four-speed synchromesh gearbox.

These cars sold well, a total of 12,570 being made between 1945 and 1953, when they were replaced by a larger car aimed at the Jaguar market. This was the 3.4-litre Sapphire saloon, which never achieved the success of its rival although 8187 of it and its 4-litre development, the Star Sapphire, were sold. In 1960 Bristol-Siddeley decided that production of Armstrong-Siddeley motor cars was no longer an economic proposition, and the last Star Sapphires were made in June of that year.

Bristol-Siddeley continued the production of Armstrong-Siddeley aero engines until 1983 while the Viper 8 was still being made intermittently in early 1984. GNG

ARMSTRONG-WHITWORTH/WILSON-PILCHER
GB 1904-1919

William Armstrong, later knighted and subsequently Lord Armstrong, began his career as a solicitor but became interested in hydraulics and started the Elswick works at Scotswood on the Tyne in 1847 to produce his patented hydraulic machinery. He made a 3lb (1.3kg) gun in 1855 followed by a rifled barrel three years later and this led to sizeable armaments contracts. Shipbuilding became another speciality and more than 1000 fighting vessels were launched between 1885 and 1907, the later ones having Sir W. G. Armstrong, Whitworth and Co steam turbines. The Whitworth referred to Sir Joseph Whitworth, pioneer of the standard screw thread in 1841, whose firm merged with Armstrong in 1897.

Gottlieb Daimler had worked for Whitworth for a time, and Armstrong-Whitworth was a breeding ground for other famous motor industry names. C. R. F. Englebach, prominent at Austin and a member of its board in the 1920s, began at Armstrong-Whitworth by helping to establish a motor department at Scotswood under chairman Sir Andrew Noble, who had succeeded Lord Armstrong on his death in 1900.

The Elswick works built engines, components and gun tractors, and in 1902 added the Roots and Venables heavy-oil-engined car to its range and produced it at an initial rate of one a week for two years. This was succeeded in 1904 by the Wilson-Pilcher, an advanced car that had been made in London since 1901 to the design of Percy Pilcher and W. G. Wilson of epicyclic gearbox fame who went on to design the Hallford lorry and was jointly credited with Britain's World War I tank.

The Armstrong-Whitworth motor department had dealings with the Motor Omnibus Construction Co, which made London buses, and an Armstrong-Whitworth 3-ton lorry took part in trials in 1907. Output in 1907 was some 300 cars and 200 commercials.

The Wilson-Pilcher had a horizontally-opposed engine, epicyclic gearbox and other such unusual technical features as overlapping piston ring ends. At Scotswood it was made under Wilson's supervision in four- and six-cylinder versions.

Meanwhile, Englebach as works manager reorganized the factory in 1906 to make a more conventional car, known as the Armstrong-Whitworth. The first was a 28/36 and the range soon included 30 and 40hp four-cylinder models and a 30/50 six from 1912. In 1913 production was at 10 to 12 chassis a week, factory area was up three-fold to 48,400sq ft (4500sq m) and the motor department had a staff of about 750.

Other Armstrong-Whitworth involvements included aircraft engines from 1912 and an 'aerial department' from June 1913 where airships and then planes were made in a disused skating rink at Gosforth. Cars were quickly forgotten in the rush to produce armaments during World War I, when Armstrong-Whitworth made about 1000 aircraft, hundreds of engines, 21 million cartridge cases, 14.5 million shells, 13,000 guns, 69 ships and 18 million fuses – among other things.

In 1919 a return to car production was considered and 150 cars were laid down at Elswick. In May of that year, however, Sir W. G. Armstrong, Whitworth bought the Siddeley-Deasy Motor Manufacturing Co of Coventry for £419,750 and transferred its aircraft and car interests to the newly created Armstrong-Whitworth Development Co, whose subsidiary became Armstrong-Siddeley Motors Ltd.

With the loss of armaments contracts Sir W. G. Armstrong, Whitworth subsequently ran into financial difficulties and sold the car and aircraft firm to John Siddeley in 1926. In 1927 Armstrong-Whitworth merged with Vickers, which was in similar difficulties and was disposing of its Wolseley subsidiary to raise cash.

The resulting Vickers-Armstrong Ltd of 1927 subsequently made a wide range of military and civilian vehicles including Carden-Loyds at Elswick. From 1931 the factory was also the home of Saurer commercial vehicles, built under licence as Armstrong-Saurers until 1937. NB

ARNOLD
GB 1896-1898

Arnold's agricultural engineering and milling machinery business was founded in 1844 in

East Peckham, then a village to the south of London. Walter Arnold visited Germany in 1895 and brought back a Benz. An exclusive licence to sell and build them in Britain was obtained and under the name Arnold Motor Carriage Co about a dozen cars were built between 1896 and 1898, being available in 1897 with 3, 5 or 8½hp engines.

The prototype, which still exists and differs from a Benz in having wet-liners, was fitted by its first owner with possibly the world's first electric self-starter, which could apparently also assist the car on hills. It was a dynamotor and was patented in 1896. An Arnold took part in the Emancipation Run to Brighton in 1896.

A subsidiary, Hewetsons, named after Arnold's sales manager, retained a Benz agency for some years. George Mercy and chief engineer W. A. Gladwin who worked on the cars were still with the firm in the 1930s, when it was run by the widow of one of the Arnold brothers. NB

ARNOLT
see Bristol

ARROL-ASTER
see Arrol-Johnston

ARROL-JOHNSTON/ARROL-
ASTER, ASTER, GALLOWAY
GB 1896-1929

George Johnston, who received his engineering training at the Hydepark Locomotive Co in Glasgow, built an experimental steam tram in 1894 and bought various continental cars before building his own prototype dogcart in 1895 which had a two-cylinder petrol engine, with four opposed pistons, mounted under the floor. Production of these 'high-wheelers' with six seats started at Camlachie in 1896-97 under the name Mo-Car or Arrol-Johnston.

The Mo-Car Syndicate, formed at the end of 1895, had financial backing from Sir William Arrol, a famous consulting engineer and architect of the Forth Bridge. Arrol was chairman, Johnston managing director, N. O. Fulton was works manager and T. Blackwood Murray was commercial manager. The last two soon left and formed the Albion Motor Car Co in 1899, the same year in which the Mo-Car Syndicate became a joint stock company with £50,000 capital. The Camlachie factory was destroyed by fire in 1901 and in 1902 production restarted in a thread factory at Paisley owned by the Coats family, who were shareholders.

J. S. Napier, later of Cubitt and no relation to the London car builders of the same name, became managing director of the newly situated and named Arrol-Johnston and Co, with

Arrol-Aster saloon of 1927

William Beardmore of the vast Beardmore engineering group the largest shareholder. Napier designed a conventional 18hp car and drove it to victory in the first Tourist Trophy Race in 1905, although updated versions of the dogcarts still continued in production.

The New Arrol-Johnston Car Co Ltd, with Beardmore as chairman, was formed in 1906 and George Johnston, who had become less involved, departed to plan the abortive All British Car Co. Capital was £500,000. In 1907 a Beardmore employee named Ernest Shackleton had a special air-cooled Arrol-Johnston with Simms engine made for him to take on his Antarctic expedition – and named a glacier after Sir William Beardmore in honour of his support. The car had great difficulties in the ice and is chiefly notable for being the first Arrol-Johnston with a coffin nose, a feature of the successful 15.9hp of 1909.

An estimated 700 cars had been made in 1907 and the 15.9hp, early examples of which had four-wheel brakes, notched up sales of about 300 a year. Commercial vehicles were an important sideline and included several early forward control designs on a range of vehicles from double-deck buses to dogcart-based vans.

T. C. Pullinger took over as general manager in April 1909, bringing with him unrivalled motor experience gained in France and also at Hallford, at Sunbeam and as manager of the Beeston Humber factory. Numerous other ex-Humber men joined him.

Production moved to a new factory at Dumfries in 1913 to be nearer the English market, while the Paisley factory made about 50 electric vehicles intended as a British version of the Detroit Electric. Paisley was subsequently bought by Beardmore in 1915 for aero engine production and Beardmore taxis after World War I. The Heathhall factory in Dumfries was a very modern ferro-concrete building with its own facilities for aluminium and iron casting, two steam engines generating power for the latest electric machine tools and compressed air throughout the building, which had lifts to bring light assemblies down through the floors.

The Beardmore-Halford-Pullinger (BHP) aero engine, based on an Austro-Daimler design, was worked on by an Arrol-Johnston subsidiary, Galloway Engineering at Tongland, Kirkcudbright. Shortages of labour and materials led to Siddeley-Deasy taking over the project, moving much of it to Coventry and evolving the famous Puma and other aero engines. After the war Galloway Motors was formed to make light, Fiat 501-inspired cars at Kirkcudbright from 1920.

Arrol-Johnston returned to peacetime production in 1919, when it employed 1400 at Heathhall and 1000 at Tongland, with an advanced Victory model. The Victory was designed by G. W. A. Brown, late of Clément-Talbot, who had designed Percy Lambert's 100mph (160kph) car of 1913. It had an overhead-cam 2.8-litre four-cylinder engine and centre gearchange. Chief draughtsman was L. J. Shorter, who had formerly held the same position with Sunbeam and been with Humber before that.

The Victory was not a success, however, and the 15.9 was soon revived with Victory-style radiator. Fifty cars a week were produced at the peak of 1920. Thereafter Arrol-Johnston's outdated and sober cars sold with increasing difficulty, although a detachable-head monobloc four and in-unit gearbox were adopted for a new 20 in 1922. To fill the surplus capacity at Heathhall the Galloway was moved there in 1922 and in 1924 the largest Galloway and smallest Arrol-Johnston shared the same 12hp engine.

It has been suggested that as early as 1913 Arrol-Johnston gained control of Aster Engineering Co Ltd of Wembley. Whether the link between the two companies dates from that year or later, the well-known proprietary engine maker had grown from a licensed offshoot of the famous French Ateliers de Construction Mécanique l'Aster of St Denis, Paris, which opened an English operation at Wembley in 1899 under the control of Sydney Begbie. Edwardian cars bearing the Aster name in Britain were Ariès imported by Begbie, but in 1922 came a new breed of refined and attractive London-built Asters. These initially had six-cylinder overhead-valve 2.6-litre engines and were followed in 1924 by the 2.9-litre 20/55, which was available as a 20/70 sports when the Duke of York, later George VI, bought one in 1925. From 1927 Aster used Burt-McCollum single sleeves.

In April of that year the Aster Engineering Co Ltd formally allied with Arrol-Johnston. The new company was called Arrol-Johnston and Aster Engineering Co Ltd. Galloway Motors was liquidated in 1928 and all car production subsequently took place at Heathhall.

The Arrol-Aster range was a rationalized assortment from the former separate offerings and included a remarkable straight-eight sleeve-valve 3.15-litre 23/70, some of which were supercharged. In 1928-29 the company found time to reconstruct Sir Malcolm Campbell's Bluebird, but from July 1929 it was insolvent, yet staggered on for about a year. The empire of Sir William Beardmore, now Lord Invernairn, was in almost equally serious difficulties, so he was unable to come to the rescue. NB

ASA
ITALY 1962-1967

The ASA was born from Enzo Ferrari's desire to make a small car with the performance, quality and good looks of his V12s. He built a prototype of the Ferrarina, as it was nicknamed, in 1958; this had an 850cc twin-overhead cam four-cylinder engine and Pininfarina coupé body. It was never Ferrari's intention to make it himself and eventually he found a constructor in Oronzio de Nora, of the de Nora petro-chemical group, whose son Niccolo was a great Ferrari enthusiast.

The de Noras provided the manufacturing facilities in Milan but the new company was organized by a group of racing drivers including Lorenzo Bandini and Giancarlo Baghetti, with technical expertise provided by Giotto Bizzarini, a Ferrari engineer who was also responsible for the Iso Grifo and Bizzarini cars. The company was called ASA (Autocostruzione Societa per Azione); it was incorporated in May 1962, but it was not until two years later that any cars were built. They were attractive little coupés, powered by a 96bhp

Aston Martin Le Mans of 1933

1000cc four-cylinder twin-overhead cam engine, with disc brakes all round and a body by Bertone. Most were GT coupés, but there were a handful of convertibles as well.

Unfortunately the ASA was too expensive to compete with cars like the hotter Alfa Romeo Giulias or Abarths, while in the United States, which was approaching the muscle car era, 96bhp was too puny to get excited about. By 1966 ASA was in financial trouble and the following year it closed.

At its best, production never exceeded one car a week, and the total made has been estimated at between 50 and 75. The best export market was the United States, which took 32. Two six-cylinder cars with roll-bar tops were made in 1967, one 1300cc and one 1800cc, but they never saw production. GNG

ASCOT
GB 1928-1930

The Ascot Motor and Manufacturing Co Ltd of Letchworth, Hertfordshire, was formed to exploit the patents of Eugene Fejes, a Hungarian who had devised a car with a chassis and engine made of pressed and welded sheet steel, eliminating the need for castings. It was said that several hundred Fejes vehicles were in use with the Hungarian postal service and that railcars had also been constructed under this system. The patents were to cover the Fejes system in the making of tractors, aeroplanes, airships and engines as well as motor cars.

A factory was acquired from the recently-defunct Phoenix Motor Co and a company floated with nominal capital of £400,000. Initial production of 1500 cars a year was planned, at which figure a unit cost of £105 was estimated. With annual production of 50,000 the unit cost would come down to £85. On the basis of this, a selling price of £130 was chosen for a 10hp four-cylinder tourer. However, the necessary finance was never raised and only a few prototypes were ever made at Letchworth.

The next venture of the Ascot company was a much more conventional car called the Gold Cup Six. This used a 2¼-litre six-cylinder engine, probably a Continental, Warner three-speed gearbox and Dewandre servo

brakes. It was available as a coupé, fabric saloon or two-seater sports, but very few were made and production ended in 1930. Another short-lived project was the advanced Ascot-Pullin motorcycle which itself did not last beyond 1930. GNG

ASTER
see Arrol-Johnston

ASTON MARTIN
GB 1922 to date

The origins of Aston Martin lay in a small car repair business set up in Kensington, London, by an engineer, Robert Bamford, and a wealthy car enthusiast, Lionel Martin. The company was registered in September 1913 with capital of £1000 and the following year Martin evolved a hybrid competition car consisting of a 1400cc four-cylinder Coventry-Simplex engine in the chassis of a 1908 Grand Prix des Voiturettes Isotta-Fraschini.

Martin named this car Aston Martin because he had been successful at the Aston Clinton, Buckinghamshire, hillclimb in his 10hp Singer. This first Aston Martin was never able to prove itself in competition because of the outbreak of World War I; the Kensington works was closed but Martin used the car throughout the war years.

In May 1920 Bamford resigned, his share being taken up by Martin's wife. New premises were acquired at 53 Abingdon Road, also in Kensington, and a development programme was started on the post-war cars. These used a 1½-litre four-cylinder engine in a Rubery Owen chassis. Several racing cars were built including two twin-overhead cam versions ordered by Count Louis Zborowski, but it was 1923 before any cars were sold to the public.

It has been estimated that Lionel Martin spent between £100,000 and £150,000 of his own money on the firm, despite a contribution of £10,000 from Zborowski for the Grand Prix cars. Between 1923 and 1925 about 50 cars were built by a staff not exceeding 20. Competition activities brought considerable honour but no profit, and in November 1924 the company went into receivership, despite the injection of fresh capital from the Hon John Benson and his mother, Lady Charnwood.

The receiver had discussions with a number of concerns, including Vauxhall, the Bristol Aeroplane Co and the French manufacturer Donnet et Zédel, but eventually Bamford and Martin was acquired by a Birmingham firm of consulting engineers, Renwick and Bertelli. A. C. Bertelli had designed the 10hp Enfield Allday and in partnership with William Renwick built one car before acquiring Aston Martin. The four-cylinder overhead-cam engine from this car was the basis for the

39

Aston Martin DB2 prototype of 1949

new Aston Martin which was announced in time for the 1927 Olympia Show.

A new factory was acquired at Feltham, Middlesex, in part of the wartime Whitehead Aircraft works, which had been used by Citroën for its first UK assembly plant, but the new company expended its small capital in getting the car into production and Benson and Renwick soon withdrew their support. Bertelli struggled on, gaining backing from various sources including P. C. Kidner of Vauxhall.

Only 19 cars were made of the first series, nine saloons, eight tourers and two works competition two-seaters, with bodies designed and built by Bertelli's brother Harry. The works cars won the Rudge Whitworth Cup in the 1928 Le Mans race and modified versions of these with three-seater bodies became the forerunners of the famous International model made from 1929 to 1932.

The racing programme was an important means of development but was very costly, and in 1931 the company was in trouble again. It was owned briefly by H. J. Aldington of Frazer Nash who sold it to London motor distributor Lance Prideaux-Brune. He invested considerable capital and was joined later by R. Gordon Sutherland, son of the wealthy ship-owner, Sir Arthur Sutherland. Bertelli remained with the company until 1937 when he retired to become a farmer and champion pig breeder; he died in 1979.

With Sutherland's money and Bertelli's design skill, Aston Martin flourished in the early 1930s, with several successes at Le Mans and in the Tourist Trophy. Cars such as the International, Le Mans, Mark II and Ulster won rallies and Concours d'Elegance and have become highly prized collectors' cars. Only one engine was offered, the 1½-litre, based on the original Renwick and Bertelli design of 1926. Saloon, tourer and sports bodies were made, mostly by Harry Bertelli, who had premises next door to the Feltham factory, but the cars could be supplied in chassis

Aston Martin V8 of 1986

form for other coachbuilders to work on. A total of 105 cars were made in 1933, double the best figure for the pre-Sutherland era.

In 1936 a new overhead-cam 2-litre engine replaced the faithful 1½. Designed by Bertelli and Claude Hill, it powered a new range of saloons and two-seaters which took Aston Martin up to World War II. About 140 of these 2-litre cars were made. The final pre-war design was the Atom, a streamlined saloon with independent front suspension, a Cotal gearbox and, in its final stages, a completely new pushrod engine which was used in the postwar DB1 Aston Martin.

Work was already advanced on this new engine, and a chassis to go with it, when tractor manufacturer David Brown acquired a controlling interest in Aston Martin in February 1947. The first David Brown Aston Martin, the 2-litre DB1, went into production in 1948, but only 15 were made as David Brown had acquired a larger engine with more development potential when he bought the Lagonda car company in 1947. This W. O. Bentley-designed 2½-litre, twin-overhead cam six went into the DB2, a fast-back coupé whose body was derived from a Le Mans Special on

the DB1 chassis. The DB2 went into production in May 1950 and began a long line of David Brown Aston Martins, the DB2/4, DB3 sports racers, and DB4. In 1959 Aston Martin became the only British manufacturer to win the sports car constructors' championship.

Originally Aston Martins and Lagondas were assembled at Feltham with engines, chassis and gearboxes coming from the David Brown factory at Farsley, near Leeds, and bodies from Tickford at Newport Pagnell. In 1955, however, all production was transferred to Newport Pagnell.

The introduction of the 3.7-litre DB4 in 1959 marked the end of the cars whose ancestry dated back to the Atom chassis and Bentley-designed engine; but it began a new line, the influence of which can still be seen in the Aston Martin of today. They were all two-door fast-back coupés or convertibles, but for customers who wanted four doors David Brown revived the Lagonda name with the Rapide, with 4-litre DB4 engine and Superleggera body. The 3.7-litre DB4 grew into the 4-litre DB5, DB6 and DBS, and in September 1969 came a brand new 5.3-litre V8 engine in the DBS body.

In February 1972 Sir David Brown decided that the losses sustained by Aston Martin Lagonda – it was £450,000 in debt – could no longer be carried by his company, so he sold out to Company Developments Ltd. In fact he merely divested himself of debts, for all he gained was £100 for the shares and a nominal £1 for the debts. Company Developments pruned the workforce and trimmed the range, dropping the six-cylinder cars entirely. In 1974 it revived the Lagonda name on what was a lengthened DBS V8 with four doors, but only seven of these were made. The company was in deep trouble, having spent £350,000 on making the V8 acceptable for the American market and this, coupled with escalating costs, brought Aston Martin to insolvency by December 1974.

Aston Martin Vantage Zagato of 1986

Aston Martin Lagonda of 1982

Six months later a new group came to the rescue, Canadian Rolls-Royce distributor George Minden and American 'company doctor' Peter Sprague, who formed a new company, Aston Martin Lagonda (1975) Ltd; additional capital came from Sheffield steel manufacturer Denis Flather and property developer Alan Curtis.

For five years sales were reasonably satisfactory, averaging six a week. There was the V8 saloon, the Vantage (a high performance version of the saloon) and the Volante (convertible), and in 1976 they were joined by yet another Lagonda revival, this time a striking four-door saloon with completely new body, styled by Bill Towns. This car's complex electronics gave teething troubles but by 1980 it was outselling the Aston Martins, despite a rise in price from £24,570, when it was announced, to £49,933.

In 1980 the company changed hands once again, being bought by Victor Gauntlett, chairman of Pace Petroleum, and Tim Healey, chairman of CH Industrials. Gauntlett not only encouraged the return of Aston Martin to racing with the Nimrod Group C car, but also diversified by establishing Aston Martin Tickford, a company which produces limited edition luxury versions of production cars and offers specialist advice to the industry on the building of prototypes. Operating from a new factory at Milton Keynes, its first products were the Hi-Fi Lancia and Frazer Tickford Metro, followed by the turbocharged Tickford Capri. In 1983 it set up a separate

division in Coventry to build the Jaguar XJ-S cabriolet.

In July 1983 the American distributor Automotive Investments of Connecticut purchased Pace Petroleum's 55 per cent holding although Victor Gauntlett continued to run Aston Martin and seven months later bought out CH Industrials' 45 per cent holding, to become sole owners. Current production at Newport Pagnell consists of the Aston Martin Vantage saloon and Volante convertible, and the Lagonda saloon, at prices ranging from £51,275 for the cheapest Aston Martin saloon to £74,994 for the Lagonda, although a specially equipped version of the latter is priced at £85,000. In the autumn of 1985 production was running at four cars a week. The 10,000th Aston Martin was completed in April 1984.

In April 1985 former journalist Michael Bowler became engineering director responsible for developing a new range of smaller Aston Martins to appear in about 1989. The last big V8 is the Zagato-bodied coupé of 1986. In September 1987 Ford acquired control of the company. GNG

ASTRA
see Westinghouse

ATLAS
see Knox

ATS/SERENISSIMA
ITALY 1962-1970

ATS was created to build a Grand Prix car for Scuderia Serenissima, relying heavily on various talented engineers who had recently departed from Ferrari and elsewhere, and doomed to a very short history. In 1961 Ferrari had won the World Championship with a car designed by Carlo Chiti, but following a row with Ing Ferrari, Chiti walked out of the team and into backing from Serenissima patron Count Volpi di Misurata to build *his* Grand Prix car.

Automobili Serenissima SpA, Bologna, was founded on 11 February 1962, backed by Volpi, knitting-machine manufacturer Giorgio Billi and Jaime Ortez-Patino, nephew of a Bolivian copper king. A factory was started at Pontecchio Marconi, near Bologna, where Chiti, five design staff and six others began construction of the new car with parts from all over Italy. They worked in a shed on the site pending completion of the factory.

Volpi withdrew from the project very early, and on 30 November 1962 Chiti's operation became Automobili Turismo Sport SpA, or ATS. On 15 December the ATS Tipo 100 Formula 1 car was unveiled at a Bologna hotel; at the unveiling, Billi announced plans for a production GT car and Chiti's ATS 2500GT was shown for the first time at the Geneva Show in March 1963. It was an interesting design, the first road car to use the racing-type, mid-engine layout, and powered by a 210bhp V8 engine. Bodywork was by the long established Turinese house of Allemano.

A slightly modified car later appeared at the Paris Salon in October when one M. Thépenier agreed to market ATS in France. In December 1963 a factory was under construction outside Modena with room for 400 workers. A foundry and machine shop were already making castings for Colotti gearboxes, but the factory would never go into production. Although a GTS version was shown in Turin in 1964, only 12 cars were built and probably no two were identical.

ATS Formula 1 car of 1962

The Formula 1 car was tested in March 1963, raced at the Belgian Grand Prix in June and was a resounding flop. The Formula 1 operation was separated from the road cars in June 1964 and entrusted to Alf Francis (who had connections with Colotti) as the ATS-Alf Francis Racing Team, with Chiti as engineering consultant. The car was always an also-ran and the final racing connection was when an ATS-derived engine powered a Cooper in the 1966 British Grand Prix.

After forays into GT racing, ATS ceased trading in 1964, Chiti moving on to Alfa Romeo's Autodelta racing operation. Count Volpi attempted a revival under the Serenissima name but failed, and Moreno Baldi tried again in 1970 but was soon left with a pile of spares and little else. BL

AUBURN
USA 1903-1936

The Eckhart Carriage Co was an old-established family firm in Auburn, Indiana, founded by Charles Eckhart and operated by him and his sons Frank and Morris. In 1900 the sons built a single-cylinder tiller-steered runabout, and to make these commercially they established the Auburn Automobile Co with initial capital of $2500. Production began modestly in 1903, with 50 cars sold in 1904, and a two-cylinder model added in 1905. These had 24hp horizontally-opposed engines, quite substantial five-passenger tonneau bodies and sold for $1250.

In 1910 came Auburn's first four-cylinder car, powered by a Rutenber engine, followed in 1912 by a six with electric lights. In 1911 Auburn became associated with the Zimmerman Manufacturing Co, which had made its name with high wheelers but since 1910 was making conventional cars. The 40hp Zimmerman four-cylinder car was made by Auburn. From 1914 to 1919 Auburn offered conventional four- and six-cylinder cars in the $895 to $2200 price range, powered by Continental, Rutenber or Teetor engines.

In 1916 John Zimmerman joined Auburn and established a new company within Auburn called the Union Automobile Co. For one year the four-cylinder Auburns were marketed as Unions, and carried the Union badge, but from 1917 they reverted to the Auburn name. Whether Union or Auburn, they were well made and reliable but pedestrian in appearance and offered nothing that could not be found in many other makes. Charles Eckhart died in 1915, and three years later his sons sold the business to a Chicago group headed by Ralph Austin Bard that included on its board William Wrigley Jr of chewing gum renown.

In 1919 came the Auburn Beauty Six with improved styling, followed in 1921 by the 6-51 sports model with cycle-type wings, step plates instead of running boards, and the unusual feature of a small luggage compartment behind the nearside front wheel. This sold for $895, but sales picked up very slowly and did not exceed 2500 a year in 1923 or 1924. Then the owners brought in as general manager 30-year-old Erret Lobban Cord, who had already made – and lost – several fortunes in the auto business. Cord found 700 unsold cars, and by some judicious and inex-

pensive repainting and nickel-plating he managed to move them within a very short time.

For 1925 Cord had the range completely re-styled by J. M. Crawford. The new Auburns had rounded tops to their radiators, two-tone colour schemes and used six-cylinder Continental or (from mid-1925) straight-eight Lycoming engines.

Two years later, Cord, now president of Auburn, bought Lycoming, together with Duesenberg of Indianapolis and the Limousine Body Co of Kalamazoo, Michigan, which had supplied Auburn with bodies for several years. Total assets of Lycoming, which included an important heating equipment company, were said to be $5 million, and of Duesenberg about $1 million. He also bought the Connersville, Indiana, body-making company and the Central Manufacturing Co, assuring himself ample facilities for the expanded production he looked forward to.

The new eight-cylinder Auburns were fast, good-looking and well-equipped, appearing much more expensive than they actually were. Sales increased dramatically, and by mid-1927 Auburn was making more than 100 cars a day and still had a waiting list for some models. The 8-88 speedster with pointed tail, two-seater body was particularly stylish. Sales benefited from the fact that Mercer had recently gone out of production while the Stutz speedster cost nearly three times the $1695 asked for the Auburn. In 1928 power was upped to 115bhp, hence the new speedster's name, 8-115. The last year for the Continental engine was 1927, all subsequent Auburns being powered by Lycoming, as

Auburn roadster of 1917

Auburn S1 of 1931

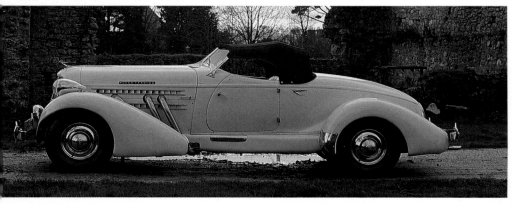

Auburn 851 Speedster of 1935

were the associated makes Duesenberg and (from 1929) Cord.

More than 22,000 Auburns were sold in 1929, a ninefold increase over 1924. The Depression did not immediately hit Auburn as drastically as many other makers and after a dip to 11,270 in 1930, sales climbed to a record 28,103 in 1931. For 1932 the Eights were joined by a 160bhp V12 of 6.4 litres, available in a variety of body styles, the cheapest of which, a two-passenger coupé, sold for only $975. This was the only twelve-cylinder car ever to sell for under $1000, way below rival V12s such as Cadillac ($3495), Lincoln ($4700) or Pierce-Arrow ($3450). Even the beautiful speedster body on the V12 chassis cost only $1600.

In 1932 the Depression began to bite; only 11,646 cars were sold and Auburn lost nearly $1 million. The next year was even worse, with sales of only 6000. The V12 was dropped after 1934 but there were two new, cheaper models, an 85bhp six and a 100bhp eight. Cord was devoting much of his attention elsewhere now, particularly to his aviation interests which included the Stinson and Vultee aircraft corporations. Day to day management of Auburn fell to Harold T. Ames, Duesenberg's president, who brought with him August Duesenberg as chief engineer and Gordon Buehrig as stylist. They were responsible for the 1935 models which included the Type 851 speedster.

This harked back to the great days of Auburn speedsters, and had a pointed tail,

two-seater body, and outside exhaust pipes. A Switzer-Cummins supercharger boosted power to 150bhp, and each speedster sold carried a plaque certifying that it had exceeded 100mph (160kph) in the hands of racing driver and record breaker Ab Jenkins. At $2245 the 851 speedster lost money on every car sold, but it drew people into the showrooms – and one of the other Auburns might well be sold as a result. About 500 speedsters were made in the years 1935 and 1936; total production in these years was 7011, with only a meagre 1848 sales recorded in 1936.

No Auburns were made in 1937 and in August of that year the last Cord car left the factory. The only vehicle-making part of the Cord empire that survived was the Pak-Age-Car Corporation division of Auburn Central Co of Connersville, Indiana, which made the Pak-Age-Car rear-engined delivery van from 1938 to 1941. Most of these were sold and serviced by Diamond T, the Chicago truck builders, and carried Diamond T badges.

From the 1960s the Auburn 851 speedster became a popular subject for replicas. The best known American versions were those made by Glenn Pray's Auburn-Cord-Duesenberg Co of Tulsa, Oklahoma, the California Custom Coach Corporation of Pasadena, and Elegant Motors Inc of Indianapolis. Some of these were dual-cowl phaetons of a type never made by Auburn. There was also a short-lived Australian version, which was made at Melbourne. GNG

AUDI
GERMANY 1910-1939; 1965 to date

The word audi is the Latinized version of the German horch (hark), and the Audi company was founded in 1910 as Audi Automobilwerke GmbH, in Zwickau, by August Horch. A pioneer of the motor industry in Germany, Horch had been an engineer with Benz from 1896 to 1899 before setting up on his own as A. Horch & Co in 1899 in an abandoned stable in Cologne-Ehrenfeld, where he produced his first car in 1900.

After a short period in another factory at Reichenbach, Saxony, he moved to Zwickau in 1903, having so far produced just three cars. Horch eventually became established through sporting success and engineering quality but August left the first company bearing his name in June 1909 after long-running arguments over policy.

On 16 July 1910 he founded August Horch Automobilwerke GmbH, also in Zwickau, with a capital of 200,000 marks. He was promptly sued in the court of Lipsia by A. Horch & Co Motorwagenwerke and hastily Latinized the new company's name to Audi.

The first Audi car, the Type B, 10/28PS, was delivered early in 1910 and the light, modern design soon became popular. Publicity-conscious Horch revived his sporting involvements, leading a team which included Audi engineers Graumuller and Lange as drivers. He contested the 1911 and 1912 Austrian Alpine Trials with a Type B and the 1913 and 1914 events with the even more sporting, 62mph (100kph), Type C, 14/35PS, introduced in 1912. He did so to such effect that the car became known as the Alpensieger (Alpine Victor).

Other pre-war Audis included the larger Type D, 18/45PS and the Type E, 22/50, each produced in fairly limited numbers. From 1913 the cars could be equipped with Bosch electric lighting and starter motors.

From 1914 and the start of World War I, Audi built 2-ton lorries based on strengthened 14/35 chassis and although there were no private cars there were military versions of the 14/35 Type C. The war affected Audi badly, with design standing still and August himself losing interest in the company, eventually to leave officially in 1920, retaining only a nominal seat on the board. Types C, D and E continued and the Type G, 8/28PS was added.

Six- and eight-cylinder cars were introduced from 1924 and the 1928 eight-cylinder Type R Imperator was the last true Audi before the cars became more and more 'assembled'. The Imperator was a very uninspiring car and up to 1932 sold only 150 units, helping Audi into a very parlous financial state.

In 1928 J. S. Rasmussen became Audi's major shareholder, in the year when his own DKW motorcycle company introduced its first car at the Leipzig Fair. Rasmussen had acquired the design rights and manufacturing machinery for the respected American Rickenbacker engine when that company went out of business in 1927 and he now began assembling Audis around German-built versions of the Rickenbacker engines. The six-cylinder Dresden sold only about 100 units between 1931 and 1932 and the eight-cylinder Zwickau some 400 from 1929 to 1932.

A smaller Audi, introduced in 1931 with Peugeot engine and DKW chassis, was the last Audi before the company was absorbed into the Auto Union in 1932, along with Horch, Wanderer and DKW, the four companies symbolized by the four rings of the

Audi Alpensieger 14/35PS of c.1912

every major honour to be won and prompted a four-wheel-drive 80 Quattro, various four-wheel-drive Volkswagens and the eventual promise of a four-wheel-drive option for every car in the Volkswagen-Audi range.

Audi had fulfilled that promise by 1985 with four-wheel drive available on all its seven model ranges but had been overtaken in rallying by the compact Peugeot 205 based rally car.

For the road cars, plans were afoot to replace the five-cylinder engine by a new range of V6s and V8s by 1988 and to build larger luxury saloons directly to challenge the prestige market. August Horch would have approved. BL

Audi 225 Front of 1937

Auto Union badge. Two Wanderer-engined, front-wheel-drive models became the company's biggest pre-war sellers, the UW selling some 2000 units from 1933 to 1934 and the UW 225 selling 2600 from 1935 to 1938.

After the war, in 1945, Auto Union was nationalized as part of the combine Industrie-Vereinigung Volkseigner Fahrzeugwerke, which built DKW-based IFA cars in the former Audi works at Zwickau. In 1949 Auto Union regained its independence, in Düsseldorf, and in 1956 Mercedes-Benz became the majority shareholder, but the Audi name would not be revived until after 1964, when Volkswagen took over the conglomerate as Auto Union GmbH, based at Ingolstadt. Audi reappeared with a 1.7-litre front-wheel-drive saloon introduced in 1965 and has continued ever since.

In 1969, Audi NSU Auto Union AG was formed by the merger of Auto Union and NSU Motorenwerke AG. NSU ceased production in 1977 but, under VW, Audi prospered, the two marques making the most of joint technical developments. Audi produced the series 60 and 90, introduced in 1969, the 80, from 1973, and the 1970 100. The millionth Audi was sold in May 1973, in which year the company, with 33,600 employees, built 409,743 cars (in 1985, 35,700 employees built 392,000 cars).

In the late 1970s and early 1980s Audi con-

Audi Quattro of 1984

tinued to develop technologically-advanced ideas such as a five-cylinder engine, introduced in the 100 series in 1977, turbocharging (as an option on the same engine from 1980 in the 200 series), aerodynamic styling, and, most impressively, four-wheel drive on the remarkable Quattro.

This four-seater coupé with turbocharged, injected, five-cylinder engine had permanent four-wheel drive and even in standard guise was capable of 137mph (220kph). When Audi went rallying with the Quattro it won

AUREA
ITALY 1920-1933

The Aurea light car was originally built by the Societa Italiana Ferrotaie of Turin. Designed by Effren Magrini, it was a conventional light car powered by a 15/18hp four-cylinder engine of 1460cc, which developed 22bhp in the normal version and 30-35bhp in the sports models. In 1922 the Societa Ferrotaie changed its name to Fabbrica Anonima Torinese Automobili (FATA) with a capital of 500,000 lire. In 1925 capital was increased to 2 million lire and the company moved to larger premises which had formerly been occupied by the Nazzaro company.

Design changed little, though front-wheel brakes were adopted in 1925 and a slightly larger, 1497cc, engine with overhead valves came in 1927. This and a companion model with the same capacity but side valves were made in dwindling numbers until 1933. The previous year FATA had been acquired by Giovanni Ceirano who ended car production in favour of the manufacture of spare parts. An important contract to supply components for Alfa Romeo continued until the factory was irreparably damaged during World War II. Ceirano closed the business in April 1945. GNG

AUSTIN/MINI, VANDEN PLAS
GB 1906 to date

Born in 1866, Herbert Austin was the son of a Buckinghamshire farmer who moved to Yorkshire to be farm bailiff for the Earl Fitzwilliam, who later backed the Sheffield-Simplex car. Herbert went to Rotherham Grammar School and then Bampton Commercial College and was to have been apprenticed to the Great Northern Railway. Instead he was invited to visit relatives in Australia and worked there for an engineering workshop in Melbourne, where an uncle was works manager.

Two years later he joined the Australian agents for Crossley gas engines and after various jobs moved to an engineering shop developing mechanical sheep shears invented by F. Y. Wolseley. The intricate mechanism required Birmingham metal-working skills and Wolseley established a company there which Herbert Austin managed from 1893.

He developed the first Wolseley cars in 1896 and remained with the company until disagreeing with the policy of its new owners, Vickers Ltd, in 1905. With Frank Kayser of Sheffield steel manufacturers Kayser, Ellison & Co, he formed the Austin Motor Co; much of its £50,000 share capital was held by Harvey DuCros, who owned the Dunlop patents and had extensive financial interests in the French motor industry. A derelict works was bought on a 2½-acre (1-hectare) site at Longbridge, on the western outskirts of Birmingham, for £7750. Production of two cars a week was planned.

Despite his earlier adherence to horizontal engines, the first Austin cars of 1906 had four-cylinder vertical engines. In the first full year 31 were made and 270 men were employed. About 200 cars a year were built in the next three years and then there was rapid growth to 1912, when 1100 sales were attained, the workforce reached 1800 and profits of £56,000 were earned.

The range in this period included everything from single-cylinder 7hp cars to various fours and sixes, the largest being three 100hp racers developed in 1908. The singles were Swifts in disguise, as the two firms were financially linked via the DuCros family; Austin also made Gladiators, another DuCros marque, for the British market.

In 1914 Austin became a public limited liability company with the issue of 400,000 £1 shares. As the Austin Motor Co (1914) Ltd it employed 2638, which was to rise to over 22,000 men and women in World War I. A £500,000 order was obtained from Russia for vehicles and equipment and dozens of Austin's 2 to 3-ton lorries with separate shaft drive to each rear wheel were supplied.

Total wartime production included 2000 aircraft, 8 million shells, 650 heavy guns, 2500 aero engines, 1600 2 to 3-ton lorries, some 3000 cars, ambulances and armoured cars, 1600 limber wagons and 4762 generating sets. Turnover in 1918 was £10 million compared with a maximum of £426,000 a year before the war.

Herbert Austin was knighted in 1917 and was a Unionist Member of Parliament for six years from 1924. In the later years of the war he had driven a Hudson Super Six and came to espouse the virtues of American cars. This was reflected in his post-war Twenty, a substantial 3.6-litre side-valve monobloc four with centre gearchange. To gain the advantages of mass-production all Austin's re-

Austin/Swift 7hp of 1910

sources went into this one model, plus commercial vehicles and tractors using the same engine.

One hundred and fifty a week were planned but the problems of transition to peacetime production as well as strikes and other labour difficulties caused only about 200 to be built in 1919, although 463 commercial vehicles were produced. The following year 4319 cars were made plus up to 66 tractors a week and a few commercials.

Sir Herbert Austin and the DuCros family still held a controlling interest in the company, despite a share capital increased to £1.65 million. A £5 million flotation in 1920 proved a disastrous failure, however, and in 1921 the firm went into receivership after two years of heavy losses.

It was restructured and handed back to Sir Herbert and DuCros in 1922 with a new board which included Hyam Marks of Alldays and C. R. F. Englebach from Coventry Ordnance and formerly of Armstrong-Whitworth. The tractor and lorry market was proving to be too competitive due to the growing presence of Ford, so Austin transferred tractor production to a factory at Liancourt north of Paris, where it continued for 20 years, and ended production of all but car-based vans.

Something was needed to keep fully occupied the 58-acre (20-hectare) floor space of what was called 'the largest motor factory in the Empire'. A one-model policy based on a car as large as the Twenty was plainly not the answer. The factory by now possessed the latest automated tooling and had facilities for spray-painting all cars.

The Twelve, a scaled-down Twenty, appeared at the 1921 Olympia Show. It provided almost half the company's 2500 sales in 1922 and reached a peak production of 14,000 in 1927. A few Twelves and Twenties also provided the chassis for Sizaire-Berwick, an Anglo-French car firm that Sir Herbert unwisely purchased in 1923. Even more significant than the Twelve was the Seven, which was intended to compete with the air-cooled

Austin's 1920s race team at Avus

OV 9806

OV 9818

Rover 8 and end motorcycle competition.

This diminutive, four-cylinder, water-cooled car appeared in July 1922 and was Austin's most popular model from 1924. It helped to give Austin 37 per cent of the British car market in 1929, the year in which the 100,000th Seven was made. In addition the Seven was built under licence in the United States by American Austin (later Bantam), by Rosengart in France, by Gotha Waggonfabrik of Eisenach in Germany as the Dixi, and it was the inspiration for Datsun in the early 1930s. The Seven's engine lived on at Reliant until 1962 after production ceased at Longbridge in 1938.

The workforce totalled 11,000 in 1928, by which time Englebach had streamlined production and improved quality, quantity and output with an incentive scheme introduced in the mid-1920s. One car was a week's work for 16 people in 1926 compared with 104 people in 1910 – and four in 1958.

A vast factory expansion programme was undertaken in the late 1920s and Herbert Pepper of Star and Guy joined the board. Austins, apart from the remarkable Seven, were often more expensive than their rivals, but they were better equipped and arguably better made; indeed, there was some justification for the slogan 'Invest in an Austin'.

New in 1926 was a six-cylinder 20 followed by a six-cylinder 16-18 and a whole spate of 10, 12 and 14hp four- or six-cylinder cars in the early 1930s. Styling in the 1930s was handled by Dicki Burzi, formerly with Lancia, and it was he who finally replaced the winged wheel trade mark with a flying A in 1946. A version of the Twelve was developed in late 1929 as the start of a successful 50-year line of London taxis.

The Depression held few terrors for Austin, which earned net profits of £350,000 to £660,000 each year in the 1930s. In contrast with the 1920 share issue, that of 1933 was oversubscribed eight times. In 1933, too, the Hayes infinitely variable transmission was offered on the 16 and 18 while synchromesh spread to the manual cars.

Herbert Austin became Lord Austin of Longbridge in 1936, a year in which his factories employed 25,000. Over at Morris, L. P. Lord resigned as managing director and in 1938 joined the Austin board, taking over as chairman on Lord Austin's death in 1941.

A medium-weight range of trucks was launched in 1938 after a lapse of over 15 years. The timing was opportune and 82,500 were produced during World War II in addition to 108,500 cars and utilities, 600,000 jerry cans, 2.5 million tin helmets, 3500 lifeboat engines, thousands of air frames and complete planes (Stirling, Battle, Hurricane and Lancaster), 110,000 Churchill tank suspension units, plus millions of other items including crankshafts for Bristol aero engines. The aircraft were made at Cofton Hackett, which later received a £20 million refit to produce Maxi and subsequent engines.

Various pre-war cars were revived in 1946

Austin 12hp special-bodied of c.1927

and there was a new 16, using a 12 chassis with the long lasting 2.2-litre engine developed in the war. This engine popped up again in the A70 replacement for the 16 and went into the Healey 100.

In 1947 the millionth Austin was made. The A40 appeared later that year with over a third of the first 30,000 going to the USA, followed by an A90 developed specially for that market. Materials were initially allocated to makers in relation to their export performance and one of Austin's greatest achievements in this respect was the Metropolitan, which was made for Nash Motors for 10 years from 1952 and sold a peak 22,000 in the USA in 1959. The car had bodywork by Fisher and Ludlow, which soon became part of Austin.

An earlier foray into bodywork takeovers had brought Vanden Plas into the Austin camp in 1946, Vanden Plas being responsible for the truck-engined A120 limousines that came to be known as Princesses. The firm had its origins in 1870, when Guillaume Van den Plas inherited a wheelwright's shop in Brussels and from 1884 made complete carriages in Antwerp. In 1913 a British licensee was incorporated with a capital of £2650, soon raised to £22,750; during World War I it was part of the Aircraft Manufacturing Co.

In 1923 Vanden Plas – as it was always spelled in England – came under new ownership and moved into the former works of Kingsbury engineering in north-west London, where aircraft and then Kingsbury light cars and scooters had been made from 1919 to 1923. High-quality coachwork and aircraft subcontracts kept the firm busy for 20 years and by mid-1948 five Austin limousines were being turned out each week.

From 1958 the complete chassis was assembled there and in 1960 Vanden Plas Princess became a marque in its own right, subsequently producing in 1964 the Rolls-Royce-engined Princess 4-litre R and luxury versions of several BMC and then BL models. In 1967 Vanden Plas had a workforce of 287. In October 1975 the Austin Princess front-wheel-drive range became known simply as Princess, and then the Austin Ambassador which ceased production in 1983. Among the luxury models it now produces are versions of the Metro and Maestro.

Austin Ten Lichfield of 1935

Post-war Austin production averaged about 50,000 cars a year, but this jumped to 117,000 in 1949 – when Morris production was 90,000 – and continued climbing. Commercials averaged about 15,000 a year. Net profits in 1951 were almost £3 million.

After George Harriman from Morris became deputy managing director in 1950, discussions took place between Austin and Morris in an effort to avoid nationalization. These talks culminated in the creation, in 1952, of the British Motor Corporation, which was the fourth largest motor firm in the world with 42,000 employees and roughly 35 per cent of the British market.

The transverse-front-engined, front-wheel-drive Mini, designed by Alec Issigonis, was the first of the technically advanced new breed of BMC cars in 1959 and received various group badges before becoming a marque in its own right in 1970. The four millionth Mini was delivered in November 1976, and 25 years after its inception it had changed little in outward appearance. The Mini and the 1100, introduced in Britain in 1963, were also made in Italy by Innocenti.

Few models were sold exclusively as Austins following the formation of BMC, although notable exceptions included the company's first unitary construction car, the A30 of 1952, its successor the A35, the Gipsy 4×4 of 1967, the Farina-styled A40 of 1959, the Maxi of 1969, the Allegro (which also had a Vanden Plas clone) of 1973, the Metro of 1980 (of which 500,000 were sold in its first three years) and the Ambassador of 1982-83. From 1971 the Austin emphasis was on the front-drive, independently-sprung cars, while Morris generally took care of the conventional, rear-drive market.

Austins were assembled in Australia from 1948 and in 1951 the A40 was that country's second most popular car. Austin's market share was 30.7 per cent in 1951 but this, including the rest of the Leyland group, had sunk to 6.2 per cent 20 years later and a loss of more than £1 million that led to the closure of the assembly plant in 1974. Some specifically Australian models were evolved, the final ones going under the name Leyland.

There was also the 1300-based Apache in South Africa and the 1100/1300-based Authi, with protruding boot, in Spain. The Mini-Moke carried on in Australia to the early 1980s, when its production moved to Portugal. A South African assembly plant made special Austins for local requirements for much of the 1970s, and in Chile the Mini and 1100 were built with fibreglass bodies to avoid humidity problems.

In Britain in 1955 Austin had 21,000 employees and a factory area of 155 acres (72 hectares). By 1964 BMC was making profits of £21 million and both profits and sales rose by almost 40 per cent between 1963 and 1966. Exports by BMC constituents in the 20 years since the war were 4,250,000 vehicles, worth £1800 million. Yet in 1968, despite being the sixth largest motor manufacturer in the world and the largest commercial vehicle-maker in Europe, the Austin-Morris division made only 720,000 cars in factories manned for an output of at least 850,000; profits were just £6 million on sales of £400 million. BMC had merged with Jaguar-Daimler to create British Motor Holdings in December 1966, and in 1968 Leyland – which already controlled Triumph, Rover and Alvis – took over BMH.

There had been political pressure for many years to create a single, sizeable British motor firm and Lord Stokes of Leyland was seen as the man to carry through the task. It was he who returned Austin and Morris to an internally competitive footing with distinct car ranges, and it was intended that each

should make 10,000 cars a week. In 1972 this was almost achieved at Longbridge with 9000 cars produced each week.

There were dogged battles to increase competitiveness throughout the 1970s, when the group was saved by government funding and the arrival of the dynamic Michael Edwardes as chief executive towards the end of the decade. Growing emphasis was placed on the Austin name, and in 1982 BL Cars Ltd became the Austin Rover Group Ltd, the only other car division being that of Jaguar.

Losses since then have been trimmed and the overall Leyland group traded profitably in 1983, making £2 million on a turnover of £1800 million; the workforce of 107,000 was nearly 20,000 down on 1981. Car sales in 1983 totalled 450,500 and Austin-Rover had 18 per cent of the British market.

Some 100,000 of the all-new Maestro hatchback had been made by January 1984 and a saloon sharing many mechanical elements, the Montego, appeared in April. Component orders for the car, worth £180 million up to the end of the year, were also placed for production in Britain.

In the latter half of 1984 the Jaguar/Daimler business was sold off and, without the profits contributed by this division, Austin Rover lapsed into losses again. Worldwide sales declined to 421,000 but market share in the UK was little changed. The range of models was supplemented during 1984 by the introduction of five-door Metros and the Montego Estate. In August the Mini celebrated its 25th birthday with some 4,960,000 having been produced to that date. The extensive programme of model renewal pursued in the 1980s gave the group a competitive range of products covering 95 per cent of the market for the first time for more than a decade.

The year 1985 began well with market share in the UK being marginally increased and the government approving Austin Rover's corporate plan involving investment of £18,000 million. Of long term significance was the announcement of still closer ties with Honda, involving plans to develop jointly a

new middle range car to replace the Maestro. Some £250 million was allocated to the development of a new Austin engine which was deemed to be vital to ensure the group's future as a manufacturer rather than a mere assembler. In September 1985 the 10 millionth car left the assembly line at Longbridge and the one millionth Metro was made in October 1986. However, corporate losses of £60 million in the first half of 1986 led to the departure of chairman Harold Musgrave and several of his staff. The new chairman was Graham Day. NB

AUSTIN
USA 1902-1918

James E. Austin and his son Walter S. Austin had a number of inventions to their credit, including a shingle cutting machine and a chainless bicycle, before they set up as car makers in their home town of Grand Rapids, Michigan. They formed the Austin Automobile Co in the summer of 1902, but their first car was not completed until December. It was fairly typical of American practice, with a 16hp two-cylinder engine under the seat, planetary transmission and chain drive. It was priced at $2000 and 11 cars were sold during 1903.

For 1904 a larger two-cylinder engine was featured, with shaft drive replacing chains, but the Austins really got into their stride in 1905, with front-mounted 35hp and 50hp, vertical, four-cylinder engines with triple automatic inlet valves. Larger models followed, a 60hp four-cylinder and 90hp six-cylinder, now with mechanically operated inlet valves.

The 90 was one of the largest cars in the United States, with a capacity of nearly 13 litres and capable of pulling away from 7 to 90mph (11 to 145kph) in top gear. List price was $7000, though at least one owner managed to get his for $5000 in cash, paid on the stand at the 1909 Chicago Auto Show.

Production was strictly limited and probably did not exceed 30 cars a year up to 1914. The workforce varied between 13 and 35. Engines were made by Austin to start with, but later they were Continental, Teetor-Hartley and Weidely power units, the last named in the 90.

In 1913 a two-speed axle was introduced, giving different ratios for town or country work; a similar design was adopted by Cadillac the following year which resulted in a lawsuit by Austin for infringement of patent. It was settled in the Austins' favour in 1916.

Some lower priced six-cylinder Austins were offered in 1915 and 1916, the Model 36-66 at $2800 and the Model 48-66 at $3600, but for 1917 all the sixes were dropped in favour of a V12. This used a 6.4-litre Weidely engine and was offered with a variety of open and closed bodywork, priced from $3400 to $5250. Very few were made, and the Austins ceased to build cars in 1918.

Austin A90 Atlantic of c.1947

Walter continued to promote his two-speed axle as an accessory for Fords and Chevrolets, and later went into real estate. Both Austins were very long lived, James dying in 1936 at the age of 95, and Walter in 1965 at the age of 99. GNG

AUSTIN-HEALEY
see Healey

AUSTRALIAN SIX
AUSTRALIA 1919-1924

Frederick Hugh Gordon, born in 1880, was a descendant of a Scottish family who had become large Australian landowners and sheep farmers. Educated to be a banker, he soon set his eyes on the motor trade and started selling imported Packards, Wolseleys and Fords from a building in Castlereagh Street, Sydney, owned by his mother.

In 1916 he began importing American Mitchells, assembling the cars in Australia, but there were enormous wartime transport problems so Gordon decided to build his own cars. On 12 June 1918 he formed F. H. Gordon & Co with four shareholders, £20,000 capital and a plant in Rushcutters Bay, New South Wales. He immediately advertised for dealers.

Production started in July 1919 and the first, Rutenber-engined cars were completed in September. The Hughes and Martin elements of Sydney shipbuilders Hughes, Martin & Washington backed Gordon to form Australian Motors Ltd. While still building cars at the old plant, the company acquired a 7-acre (3 hectare) site at Ashfield, where a new factory was started in November 1919, financed by debentures.

Martin went to the United States and bought 500 Rutenber engines and other running gear, although in 1921 his company claimed 75 per cent local content. The company had its own foundry and machine shops, with 200 employees, and was building a car a day.

The engines were delivered, and 500 more ordered and paid for, before quality problems showed up in many returned cars. Subsequently, engines were rebuilt before use, which was financially crippling. Gordon sought further investors, but none was forthcoming; nor would the government help, so Australian Motors had to increase prices from £535 to £600, when importers were cutting theirs. Six cars shipped to Singapore were returned damaged after three months without being collected, Martin died, and a car displayed at the 1922 Royal Easter Show was vandalized.

After two years without a profit, the company printed a booklet admitting its problems and outlining remedies, but it did not help. Production stopped towards the end of 1923,

when creditors resumed assembly from remaining parts. Late in 1924 Harkness & Hillier, who had bought 10 cars for their hire business, and Properts bodybuilders were engaged to make what they could from stock; they built six or seven cars, with Ansted engines, before the buildings and equipment were sold. A saddened Gordon reverted to selling imports and died on 12 February 1931, aged 51. BL

AUSTRO-DAIMLER/MAJA
AUSTRIA 1899-1934

Gottlieb Daimler vies with Karl Benz as the inventor of the motor car, having developed the high-speed petrol engine and built his first mobile test-bed in 1885. His first real car ran in Cannstatt in 1886 and by 1890 he had founded Daimler Motoren Gesellschaft. Daimler left his own company in 1893 but returned two years later to build Daimler cars in quantity until his death in 1900.

In 1899 Daimler made arrangements with the Austrian company Bierenz-Fischer & Co, founded in 1848 in Vienna Neustadt, to build about 100 cars a year as copies of the German Daimlers. An Austrian company, Österreichische Daimler Motoren Gesellschaft, was registered in 1899 but output was small and by no means profitable. In 1902 Daimler's son Paul was sent to oversee the operation, which became essentially independent of the German company, although it did not achieve financial independence until 1906.

Since 1902 German Daimlers had been built under the name Mercédès, in honour of the eldest daughter of Emile Jellinek, consul-general of the Austro-Hungarian Empire in Nice and a director of the Daimler company since 1900. In 1906 Jellinek founded Österreichische Automobil Gesellschaft with a capital of 900,000 krone and between 1907 and 1908 he engaged Österreichische Daimler Motoren Gesellschaft to build Maja cars (named after his younger daughter). When Österreichische Automobil Gesellschaft went bankrupt the Maja design was taken up by Österreichische Daimler Motoren Gesellschaft and produced until 1914 as the rather staid 28/36PS.

In 1905 Paul Daimler returned to Germany and Ferdinand Porsche took over in Vienna, concentrating his creative efforts first on aero engines, specifically for airships. In 1910, capitalizing on aero engine technology, Daimler introduced the five-valve four-cylinder 22/80PS Prince Henry, designed to win the trial of the same name and successful in doing so. The production Prince Henry, an open four-seater, was capable of 81mph (130kph) and about 200 were delivered to the United States. A smaller sporting car, the 16/25 Alpine, was derived from the 16/18 which won the 1911 Austrian Alpine Tour.

From 1910 the company had only loose connections with its German parent and these were severed completely in 1911, after which the cars were known officially as Austro-Daimlers. A new symbol was adopted, designed by bodywork-designer Ernst Neumann-Neander around the two-headed black eagle, copied with the emperor's permission from the heraldic device of the royal house.

In 1912 the company acquired the former Westinghouse plant in Hungary, when the French car-making branch of the American electrical giant went bankrupt. There some 500 cars were built under the brand name Marta until 1914. Austro-Daimler also sold Lohner-Porsche petrol and petrol-electric cars on behalf of Jellinek, and at the outbreak of war Austro-Daimler was Austria's largest car manufacturer. During the war Austro-Daimler built four-wheel-drive trucks and heavy road trains to haul howitzers. Some had detachable road wheels for which rail

Austro-Daimler ADM sports of 1926

Autocar buggy of 1901

wheels could be substituted, an early example of road-rail operation. Austro-Daimler also built a Porsche-designed petrol-electric road train. When the war ended, a few cars were assembled in Liège from pre-war parts by a M. Klinkhamers, and sold as Alfa-Legias. Austro-Daimler itself reverted to building the pre-war 16/18 and 20/30 models and also introduced the six-cylinder AD617.

In 1919 Porsche produced an exciting 1100cc twin-overhead cam voiturette racer, the Sascha. Before he left the company in 1923, bound for Mercédès, he also designed the 2½-litre ADM. This developed as the sporting ADMII of 1925 and the 3-litre ADMIII from 1926, which in sports form was the first production Austro-Daimler to exceed 100mph (160kph). Hans Stuck Sr won the European Hillclimb Championship in 1930 with a special ADMIII, as well as numerous other races and hillclimbs. Also in 1925, Austro-Daimler began an association with Austro-Fiat, another Viennese company.

Karl Rabe took over as designer and produced the ADR, whose tubular backbone chassis and swing-axle rear suspension brought legal action against Austro-Daimler from the Czechoslovakian Tatra company, which accused Austro-Daimler of copying Hans Ledwinka's classic Type 11 design. The ADR continued, however, with the imposing 3.6-litre ADR6 Bergmeister of 1929 and the company's one and only eight-cylinder car, the 1930 ADR8.

In 1928 Austro-Daimler merged with Puch-Werke AG, which had given up production of Puch cars in 1925, to form Austro-Daimler-Puchwerke AG and in 1929 began an association with Steyr-Werke AG which led to a full amalgamation in 1934 as Steyr-Daimler-Puch AG. Austro-Daimler production stopped in 1934, because the merger was largely prompted by the fact that both companies had the same bankers, who could see little point in backing two versions of what was essentially the same product. Austro-Daimler was the marque that disappeared. BL

AUSTRO-FIAT
AUSTRIA 1911-1936

The Österreichische Fiat Werke of Vienna was the first foreign branch of the famous Italian firm. Although the company was founded in 1907, early vehicles were imported from Italy and Austrian manufacture did not get going until 1911. The Fiat Models 1 and 2 were made, both with four-cylinder monobloc engines, of 1.8 and 2.6 litres respectively. Austro-Fiat also built vans and chain-drive trucks of up to 3 tons capacity, the latter not of purely Fiat design.

In 1921 Austro-Fiat brought out a new model which was no longer based on Fiat designs. This Typ C1 had a 2½-litre four-cylinder engine with four-speed gearbox, front-wheel brakes and a vee radiator which gave it a typically German look. It was made in small numbers until 1928 when it was replaced by the Typ 1001, a 1.3-litre light car with swing-axle rear suspension which it shared with the Steyr and Austro-Daimler. This is not surprising, as in 1925 Austro-Fiat had become associated with Austro-Daimler, and sales of Fiats in Austria were taken over by another company. The company name became Österreichische Automobilfabrik AG in 1921.

Car production by Austro-Fiat dwindled in the 1930s, as the Typ 1001 was paralleled by the smaller models of Steyr, which had joined forces with Austro-Daimler in 1934. The Typ 1001 was also made in landaulette-taxi form with a conventional rear axle, and as a 20cwt (1000kg) delivery van or truck.

Commercial vehicles had always been more significant for Austro-Fiat, and these continued in production under the name OAF. They became associated with the German firm MAN in 1938 and merged with fellow Austrian truck- and bus-maker Gräf & Stift in 1970. After 1975 they became indistinguishable from MANs, although still wearing OAF badges. GNG

AUTOAR
ARGENTINA 1950-1962

Piero Dusio was a wealthy Italian industrialist who made a considerable personal fortune from textile manufacture, banking, hotels and from Cisitalia, initially a sporting goods manufacturer. Dusio also used the Cisitalia name on highly successful 'production' racing cars, but when he attempted to break into Grand Prix racing with a Porsche-designed Cisitalia he lost huge sums of money.

When the company went bankrupt in mid-1949, Dusio sold most of the assets of Cisitalia to Automotores Argentinos in Buenos Aires, partly in the hope that with these connections the Argentine government would provide backing for his racing plans.

Autoar produced not sports cars but Jeep-engined utility vehicles, starting in 1950, and a similarly-powered saloon from 1951 – all with Cisitalia badges. On several occasions in 1952 and 1953 Autoar ran the one complete example of the Grand Prix car which Dusio had imported into Argentina, but with many mechanical problems and little success.

Dusio returned to Italy in 1952 where his son Carlo had reconstituted Cisitalia. Autoar production continued, on and off, alongside licensed assembly of the NSU Prinz, until 1962, when the company ceased trading. BL

AUTOBIANCHI
see Bianchi

AUTOCAR
USA 1898-1911

Louis S. Clarke formed the Pittsburgh Motor Vehicle Co on 23 September 1897, and its first products were tricycles with single-cylinder engines mounted vertically between the rear wheels. A four-wheel buggy was made in 1898 and on 28 August 1899 a new firm, the Autocar Co, was incorporated by the founder and his brother, John S. Clarke, and it took over the earlier firm. In 1900 27 cars were made and the factory was moved to the Philadelphia suburb of Ardmore. The next year Autocar produced the first two-cylinder, shaft-drive car in the United States; other firsts claimed by the firm in its early years were porcelain spark plugs, double reduction gearing and circulatory oil system.

Contrary to horse-drawn tradition, steering was in the position of current American cars, on the left, whereas Autocar's rivals favoured the other side. The Clarke brothers maintained that their design was best for safety, but their dealers were at the sharp end of so much sales resistance that Autocar was forced to adopt right-hand steering.

The Type X 12hp of 1906 looked rather like

a contemporary French car with coal scuttle bonnet and underslung radiator. Both 12hp two- and 24hp four-cylinder cars were made, the latter with conventional bonnet and radiator. The ignition control and throttle were mounted as part of the steering-wheel rim. The emergency brake also disengaged the clutch.

In 1907 a 2000lb (907kg) capacity, shaft-drive commercial vehicle chassis was developed, wtih double-reduction rear axle, three-speed 'progressive' transmission and horizontally-opposed two-cylinder engine mounted under the seat, which was above and slightly to the rear of the front axle. From 1908 this and updated versions became Autocar's main product until 1919, although a few cars were sold up to 1911. By 1920 some 25,000 Autocar commercials were in use and the total of two-cylinder models was more than 30,000 when production ended in 1926. In 1919, four-cylinder versions for higher payloads had been introduced.

Electric trucks were made for a time in the early 1920s and in 1926 conventional (normal control) trucks joined the traditional cabover (forward control) models. In the late 1920s some stylish vans, little bigger than the typical car-based models of its rivals, were produced with chrome radiator shells that were more rounded than the classic Autocar radiators of the 1930s.

Having built its own gasoline engines, including the Blue Streak six, Autocar adopted some proprietary diesels from 1935 and heavy vehicles were increasingly made. During World War II Autocar produced thousands of military half-tracks.

The company's best year was 1946, with sales exceeding 5000 vehicles, but the slump that followed left it vulnerable and it was acquired by White in 1953. Production moved to Exton, Pennsylvania, in 1954 and Autocar became the heavy-duty, custom-built vehicle division of White. In 1980 White was declared bankrupt and Volvo acquired the company and its Autocar subsidiary in May 1981, both ranges being continued. NB

AUTOCRAT
GB 1912-1926

The Autocrat Light Car Co of Gough Road, Balsall Heath, Birmingham, was founded in 1912 by W. Ivy Rogers, who had previously made bicycles for the trade. To begin with, a 7/9hp Peugeot air-cooled V-twin was mounted fore-and-aft but later in 1912 the Autocrat emerged with JAP water-cooled V-twin with crankshaft now parallel with the frame. Alternatively, a four-cylinder water-cooled engine was offered, all versions having chain drive.

No cars were made from 1915 to 1918, and in the latter year it was announced that future models would have Coventry-Simplex 11.9hp engines. However, the conventional assem-

Autocrat convertible of 1923

bled light cars that emerged from a new address at Edward Road, Balsall Heath, had various engines, including 11.9hp units from Dorman and 12hp Meadows in 1922.

A coupé, with detachable hard top, was offered from 1919 and an ultra-basic Service model with oil lamps joined the range in 1921. In late 1923 came a 10/12hp Meadows overhead valve-engined model and the address was now given as Spring Road, Hall Green.

Autocrat was rescued from financial difficulties in 1926 by the Calthorpe Motor Co, which itself promptly hit problems. Autocrat was discontinued and its factory was then to have been the home of the Derby motorcycle, but this project failed to materialize. Despite the company's optimism, production had always been modest. NB

AUTOGEAR
see Stanhope

AV
GB 1919-1924

Made by Ward and Avey Ltd of Teddington, Middlesex, the first AV car was the 1914 Carden Monocar re-named. Prices ran from £146 5s for a 5hp to £156 7s 6d for an 8hp. JAP engines were mostly used, but some cars had Blackburne or MAG power units. Bodies, supplied by the Thames Valley Pattern Works, were of plywood, mahogany or compressed paper.

In 1920 a tandem-seater Bicar version appeared, still with rear-mounted V-twin JAP engine, priced at £235. The following year a

side-by-side two-seater appeared under the name Runabout and the Bicar was dropped. The last year for the Monocar was 1922 and the Runabout became the only model for 1923 and 1924, after which the company announced, in the sad litany of so many moribund firms, that it was making cars to special order only.

At its peak the company employed 80 people. Several hundred Monocars were made, and about 50 two-seaters. The company name was changed to AV Motors in 1923 and to AV Motors Ltd in 1926. Although the latter included manufacturing in its list of activities, it seems that its business was restricted to repairs and general garage work. From 1924 to 1952 it held a Jowett agency, and when Jowetts closed down, the company began selling Rootes Group cars. GNG

AVANTI II
USA 1965 to date

Studebaker ended production of its striking Avanti coupé in 1963 but two South Bend Studebaker dealers, Nathan Altman and Leo Newman, were so enthusiastic for the model that they tried to interest other manufacturers in building it. When this brought no results they went into business themselves, buying the dies and parts, and the right to use the Avanti name, as well as part of the Studebaker factory. For an engine they used the 300bhp Chevrolet Corvette unit, while the bodies were made by Molded Fiberglass of Ashtabula, Ohio, which also made the Corvette body. Annual output first exceeded 100 in 1968 and peaked at 276 in 1983. Bought by property developer Steve Blake in 1982, the firm halted production in October 1985, but in April 1986 it started up again as the New Avanti Motor Corporation owned by Texas businessman Michael E. Kelly.

Very little change has taken place in the Avanti II since it was introduced, for its timeless appearance is one of its leading assets. The original 5.3-litre engine was replaced by a 5.7-litre unit from 1971. Borrani wire wheels were an option from 1972. The base price of the first Avanti II was $6500, and by 1985, when a 5-litre Chevrolet engine was used, this had risen to $37,995. A convertible was introduced at $39,900. GNG

Avanti II coupé of c.1965

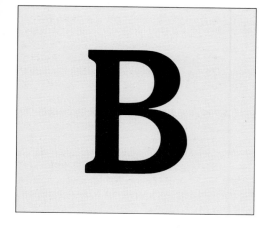

B

BAGULEY
see Ryknield

Baker Electric runabout of c.1902

BAKER ELECTRIC
USA 1899-1916

Walter C. Baker was president of the Cleveland-based American Ball Bearing Co when he organized the Baker Motor Vehicle Co in 1898. The president of the new company was his father-in-law, Rollin H. White of the White Sewing Machine Co, later to become famous as a car and truck manufacturer. Baker was vice-president and his brother-in-law, Frederick R. White, was treasurer. Their first car, a light two-seater electric buggy, was bought by the inventor Thomas A. Edison and by March 1900 sales justified a move to larger premises, still in Cleveland. Also in 1900 Baker Electrics featured shaft drive, the first application of this principle to an American-made car.

Production grew rapidly over the next few years, reaching 400 annually in 1905 and 800 a year later. In 1905-6 a new factory was built

at West 80th Street which is still occupied by the descendant of the Baker company, the street now being called Baker Avenue.

By 1906 a wide range of electric vehicles was being made, from a light two-seater called the Imperial, at $1200, to an Outside Brougham with seating at the rear for driver and footman, at $4000. Trucks were introduced in 1907 and were made in sizes ranging from 1000lb (453kg) to 5 tons until 1916, as well as electric cars with the larger bonnetted appearance of petrol cars.

The company was at its peak in the years 1910 to 1914, when it could justifiably advertise that it was the foremost maker of electric vehicles in the world. Customers included the King of Siam and Mrs William Howard Taft, wife of the President of the United States. By late 1912 more than 200 companies were operating fleets of Baker Electric trucks. Demand for electrics was dropping, however,

and in 1915 Baker merged with another Cleveland firm, Rauch and Lang, to concentrate production and seek other fields of manufacture. The Baker as a make survived for only one further season, and the 1916 models of cars and trucks were the last. In 1919 Walter Baker was on the board of Peerless. Later products of the new organization are described under Owen Magnetic and Rauch and Lang. GNG

BALLOT
FRANCE 1921-1933

E. Ballot had been an engineer in the merchant marine before founding Ballot et Cie in Paris in 1906 to make marine engines with the insignia of EB on either side of an anchor. Car and commercial vehicle engines were soon being made, important customers including Delage, Mass and La Licorne. An interesting departure from normal practice in 1910 was a four-cylinder engine with an oscillating slipper in the head, opening and closing the ports.

A limited liability company with capital of 500,000 francs was formed in 1910 and a year later Etablissements Ballot SA was floated with a capital of 1.8 million francs. E. Ballot was administration director with little financial involvement, the actual backers including Adolphe Clément, Fernand Charron and a future Minister of Public Works, Pierre Forgeot. Jean Lacoste and Marc Birkigt, of Hispano-Suiza fame, held executive positions. Soon afterwards a new factory was opened on the Boulevard Brune; it had the latest machinery and a workforce of 400.

Hispano-Suiza aero engines were produced during the war while the workforce increased to 1000 and capital to 12.6 million francs. There was also a diesel marine engine

Ballot 2-litre racer (Jules Goux) of 1922

section, which Fernand Vadier joined from Panhard at the end of hostilities; he then went on to help Ernest Henry design Ballot's racing cars from 1919.

After making only racers until 1921 the company produced a roadgoing, four-wheel-braked 2LS, of which between 50 and 100 were sold in the next two to three years. In 1923 came the first true touring Ballot, designed by Henry's successor, Vadier. Some 1500 of this 2LT four-cylinder 2-litre car and 500 of the more sporting 2LTS, which joined it in 1924, were made until 1928, when fours were discontinued. In 1926 Dewandre servo brakes were adopted and Fernand Vadier left the company to sell these to other French manufacturers.

A six-cylinder Ballot appeared in 1927 followed by a straight-eight at that year's Salon. The market was small for such machines in the Depression, Ballot himself was dismissed by Forgeot and the firm came under the control of Hispano-Suiza in 1930. It installed its own 4.6-litre six in a Ballot chassis to create the Hispano-Suiza Junior and then, in 1933, closed the Ballot factory. NB

BANTAM
see American Austin

BARDON
FRANCE 1899-1906

On the Rothschild estate at Puteaux in 1899 Louis Bardon built light cars which were powered by underfloor-mounted, opposed-piston engines with no less than four flywheels. In 1901 his firm, Société Anonyme des Automobiles et Traction (Système Bardon), merged with the makers of the Gaillardet proprietary engines, which also made a few cars. Financial backing came from Pierre de La Ville le Roulx, who soon became in-

volved with Westinghouse. In 1901 a twin-cylinder opposed-piston car appeared and in 1904 the range included a 3-ton forward control lorry.

In November 1906 Bardon joined forces with Georges Richard to create Unic, which moved into Bardon's Puteaux factory and had as chairman Pierre de La Ville le Roulx. Jules Salomon, who was later associated with Le Zèbre and Citroën, also worked for the Bardon company. NB

BARKAS
see Framo

BARRON-VIALLE
FRANCE 1923-1929

This was a short-lived, high-quality French car made by A. Barron and Antoine Vialle. Barron was a former Berliet engineer who began making lorries of his own design at Lyons in 1912, in partnership with coachbuilder Vialle, who had set up in business at Tulle in 1900, moving to Lyons in 1909. They made a number of Ballot-engined chain-drive lorries up to 1920 when they turned to railway carriage repairs as a more profitable business.

In 1923 the Gadoux brothers designed a 2-litre overhead-valve six-cylinder car which was made briefly by the Société des Automobiles Six of Strasbourg. The design was taken over by Barron-Vialle in 1924 and made in the Lyons factory, at first under the name Six and then as Barron-Vialle. During the summer of 1924 a 2.7-litre straight-eight was added to the range, followed by the Super Six Sport which used the straight-eight engine in the six chassis.

At about this time Barron resigned from the business, although his name was retained. He began to make the American-designed

Campbell gearbox, but did not succeed in selling any except to his own company.

In 1926 the Gadoux brothers left and the railway carriage business faded away, so that Vialle was forced to concentrate on cars. He attempted to manufacture Sintesi bicycles, which were not a success, and battery-electric buses for the city of Lyons, but the contract for these went to De Dion-Bouton.

The next three years were the most successful for the company, although production did not exceed 50 to 60 cars a year. It had agents in Switzerland, Belgium, Italy and Britain. The same basic designs of six- and eight-cylinder cars were made, development being in the hands of Emile Lachanary, who came from another Lyons car-maker, SLIM. Engines and chassis were made in-house but bodies were bought from outside suppliers.

The cars were last produced in 1929, then Vialle moved to Arandon, Isère, where he resumed the manufacture of commercial vehicles on a small scale. This lasted until 1937 when the factory became a camp for Spanish Civil War refugees. GNG

BAYARD-CLÉMENT
see Clément-Bayard

BAYLISS-THOMAS
GB 1919-1929

With a partner called Thomas, Bayliss formed a company in 1874 and made bicycles under the name Excelsior. This name was picked from a popular Victorian ballad based on a Longfellow poem which contained the lines: 'A youth who bore, 'mid snow and ice, a banner with the strange device, Excelsior.' The bicycles, and the motorcycles that joined them in 1896, had as their emblem a youth on a mountain-top carrying a banner bearing the word Excelsior.

In 1919 Bayliss, Thomas and Co experimented in Coventry with an air-cooled three-wheeled car with independent front suspension and in 1921 made an Excelsior four-wheeler. By then, however, the company had been acquired by ships' lamp-makers R. Walker and Sons Ltd of Tyseley, Birmingham, which also made motorcycles for Gamages and its own Monarch models. Under the name Excelsior Motor Co Ltd, registered in April 1920, Bayliss, Thomas was transferred to Tyseley, its Coventry factory becoming the home of Francis-Barnett motorcycles.

In October 1921 its first production car appeared, using the old but now hyphenated name Bayliss-Thomas, possibly to avoid confusion with the Belgian Excelsior. The car had a Coventry-Simplex 10.8hp engine and Wrigley gearbox. Some had Bowden sliding-door saloon bodywork made by Bowden Brakes, although from 1925 all bodies were from Mulliner.

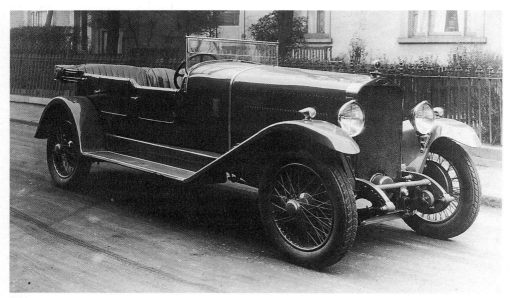

Barron-Vialle open tourer of c.1925

Eric Walker, the managing director, believed in buying most components from specialists, but non-ferrous castings, sheet metal and all plating as well as nuts and bolts were made in-house. The company also stove-enamelled all wings and offered stoved rubber in place of plating on basic models. Proprietary chassis were also protected with stoved rubber. Superior to the commercial model and the so-called 'British' model, which had a modicum of brightwork, was the 'East' version, which made much use of polished aluminium and plating.

From 1923 Meadows engines and gearboxes were used, although the range was always restricted to between 8 and 13hp. At least 500 Meadows-engined cars were made and in 1926 the erecting shop was stated to be capable of handling 40 cars a week. This figure was never achieved, however, production being fewer than 1000 a year. Bayliss-Thomas production ceased about 1929, although the car continued to be listed in buyers' guides until 1931.

The Excelsior motorcycle, early 1920s examples of which had detachable wheels made under licence from Lea-Francis, carried on until 1964. Its makers, Excelsior-Britax, became well-known for seat belts and other car accessories. Britax now belongs to BSG International Ltd, and the old factory is run by export merchants Walker-Tyseley International in association with Seafarer Marine. NB

BEAN
GB 1919-1929

A. Harper and Sons was registered in 1901 with £16,000 capital and made stampings, castings and forgings in the Black Country to the west of Birmingham. The Bean family had been metal workers since 1826. In 1879 George Bean married into the Harper family, joining the company in 1901 and six years later creating A. Harper, Sons and Bean Ltd. By the 1920s it was supplying nearly half of Britain's motor manufacturers with 500 tons of castings and similar supplies each week. By then, too, it had acquired the Perry Motor Co Ltd, which had introduced an 11.9hp car in the early years of World War I.

The Perry was redesigned for mass production by an American named Tom Conroy from Willys-Overland, and Harper Bean Ltd was formed in November 1919 to produce the car and to purchase outright, or buy holdings in, allied companies involved in component manufacture. It acquired the British Motor Trading Corporation to sell its vehicles, a majority share in Vulcan, a 50 per cent holding in Swift and a 44 per cent stake in ABC.

Only about 10 per cent of the £46 million required for this ambitious programme was forthcoming from the stock market so that Harper Bean Ltd was in trouble from the moment Bean car production started at Tipton in 1919.

The company planned to make 50,000 cars a year. A National Projectile factory in Dudley that had been built and equipped by Bean in World War I and with a workforce of 10,000 was acquired from the government as a bodyworks, and at Tipton there was a moving track in three assembly bays each of 450×90ft (137×27m). Boys on roller skates whirred about carrying messages, though they need hardly have rushed as output was just five cars a day in early 1920. Production of 505 was achieved in July 1920, the car being the cheapest 11.9 at the London Motor Show, but by the year's end Harper Bean Ltd had gone into liquidation.

One of the major shareholders, Colonel Sir Thomas A. Polson, now formed a new board and attempted to salvage the situation. Very little production took place in 1921 but in 1922 it frequently reached 80 to 100 a week from a single shift potential of 250, and by then Polson had managed to sell most of the holdings in the other companies. Even so, 90 per cent of the parts in a contemporary Bean were now produced in-house.

By 1924, when some 7000 of the smaller cars had been sold, a 14hp car was produced and its components were also used in a 1¼-ton commercial chassis which, by 1927, accounted for 60 per cent of production. Beans were inexpensive and sound cars and were better equipped than the average Morris or Clyno.

H. Kerr Thomas, who had started with Dennis and spent many years in the United States with Pierce-Arrow, arrived to strengthen the board. R. H. Rose found time between two stints at Sunbeam to be technical adviser. Chief draughtsman was Harold Radford, who, like many other employees, had worked at Austin.

In 1926 Bean Cars Ltd was formed and a year later the steel-producer Hadfields took over the company. The Twelve had by then been discontinued, after some 3000 sales, the Fourteen having reached nearly 4000. Only 500 of a Meadows-engined, six-cylinder Bean were sold, and redesigned Hadfield-Bean cars gave way totally to commercial vehicles in 1929. The last of the line was to be an optimistically named New Era one-tonner, but it never appeared before a receiver was appointed in June 1931.

It took the receiver almost three years to sort out the company's affairs, but some parts survived. Beans Industries Ltd was the name adopted by one section which, in 1937, made George Eyston's Thunderbolt land speed record contender. This section became a part of Standard-Triumph and ultimately passed into British Leyland. The current title is Beans Engineering, a subsidiary of Leyland's SU-Butec components business which remanufactures diesel engines for worldwide customers. NB

BEARDMORE
GB 1920-1928

William Beardmore became a partner in the Parkhead Forge, Glasgow, in 1861 and after his death in 1877 his son William took over and began to produce steel. From 1890 armour plate was a speciality and with the acquisition of a site at Dalmuir in 1900 Beardmore became a major builder of warships. William Beardmore was also chairman of J. I. Thornycroft from 1901 to 1907, and Thornycroft steam vehicles were built in Scotland by Duncan Stewart and Co, of which Beardmore was a director. In 1902 William Beardmore and Co Ltd was formed, with Vickers, Sons and Maxim Ltd subscribing 50 per cent of the equity. This Vickers held until its merger with Sir W. G. Armstrong-Whitworth and Co in 1927.

William Beardmore was the largest shareholder in Arrol-Johnston from 1902 and retained close ties with the car firm until its liquidation in 1929. His company was a major maker of car chassis frames for several firms

Bean 14hp of 1926

Beardmore 'Hyper' Taxi of 1929

including Arrol-Johnston, and these provided up to 20 per cent of Parkhead's revenue for many years.

In 1913 Beardmore Austro-Daimler Aero Engines Ltd was formed. During World War I Beardmore companies constructed airships, maritime vessels, 650 aeroplanes, armaments, tank tracks, and BHP (Beardmore, Halford, Pullinger) aero engines.

At the end of the war G. H. Allsworth and F. M. Luther, the Austro-Daimler importers who had interested Beardmore in aero engines, joined the recently knighted Beardmore and J. G. Girdwood on the board of the Beardmore Motor Co Ltd. The company's 11hp cars were to be made in a former fuse factory at Anniesland, Glasgow, 15hp cars in Arrol-Johnston's former Underwood works, Paisley, and 30hp cars at Coatbridge. In addition, Beardmore bought Alley and MacLellan, started a steam locomotive department and made Beardmore Precision motorcycles in Birmingham and Dunelt motorcycles in Sheffield.

In 1920 the company lost £115,000, and losses on a smaller scale persisted throughout the decade. Most of the firm's peripheral interests in transport were therefore closed down or disposed of after the arrival of Lewis Ord from Armstrong-Whitworth as joint managing director in 1928.

The cars had been promoted under the slogan 'A better car is outside the range of practical engineering' but few sold apart from the 15, most of which became taxis. By 1928 more than 6000 taxis had been supplied to London; but car production ended soon afterwards, taxi production then moving briefly to Anniesland. In 1932 half the taxi business was sold and production transferred to north London. Beardmore severed its connection with taxis in 1939 – but they were revived in

name at least from 1954 until 1967.

Vans had been made in the 1920s – 250 were produced in 1926, for example – and in 1930-32 some 200 Beardmore road tractor/trailer outfits were made in Clapham, London, under licence from Chenard-Walcker. A few were tried with Beardmore's diesel engines, made in Dalmuir, which were sold as proprietary units for commercial vehicles. The most famous Beardmore diesels were those in the ill-fated *R101* airship.

Sir William Beardmore became Lord Invernairn in 1921, but by the time of his death in 1936 he had relinquished control over his company. With the coming of rearmament in the late 1930s the company reverted to its special area of interest. Beardmore was bought by the Firth-Brown steel group in 1957, made the propeller shaft brackets for the *Queen Elizabeth 2* in 1966, and at the end of 1975 lost its separate identity. NB

BEAUMONT
see McLaughlin

BECKMANN
GERMANY 1900-1926

In 1882 Otto Beckmann helped found the Erste Schlesische Velociped Fabrik in Breslau, Germany. The company produced bicycles, but during the 1890s Beckmann became increasingly interested in cars and in 1900 the company produced a single-cylinder De Dion-powered voiturette. At the same time the company name was changed to Erste Schlesische Velociped und Automobil-Fabrik Otto Beckmann & Cie.

The voiturette continued in production until about 1905, and from 1901 to 1902 Beckmann introduced strong, Panhard-like two- and four-cylinder cars, generally using French Buchet or Aster proprietary engines. Like many early makers, Beckmann used competition for promotion and several Beckmanns, 6½hp, 700cc singles, competed successfully in the Schlesische Automobil-Club Breslau-Vienna event of 1902.

From 1904 Beckmann offered its own two-, four- and six-cylinder engines, ranging from 10 to 50hp. In 1905 a four-cylinder 16/20PS coupé cost 15,000 marks. The founder's son, Paul Beckmann, led the Beckmann entries in the 1906 and 1907 Herkomer Trials with a 40hp 8600cc four-cylinder car which as a direct consequence became known as the 'Herkomer type'.

Beckmann only ever sold cars in relatively small numbers, especially after World War I when limited production was resumed until 1926, when the former cycle works was taken over by Opel, then Germany's largest automobile manufacturer and the world's biggest cycle-maker. BL

BÉDÉLIA
FRANCE 1909-1925

In France, shortly after the turn of the century, petrol shortages promoted legislation which encouraged smaller and smaller cars. The credit for inventing the logical conclusion to the trend, the cyclecar, goes to Bédélia.

In 1909 an 18-year-old engineering student, Robert Bourbeau, assembled a tiny, low-slung four-wheeler, essentially an oblong box powered by a motorcycle engine. The driver sat behind the passenger, both on rudimentary canvas seats, and the entire front axle pivoted about a single vertical coil spring, steered by cord and bobbin. The tiny car had two-speed belt drive, weighed around 425lb (190kg) and became known as a cyclecar.

Bourbeau's friend Henri Devaux provided working capital for manufacturing cars to sell at about 1200 francs during 1910, and in November a company, Bourbeau et Devaux, was formed in Rue St Felicien-David, Paris, with a capital of 10,000 francs.

The cars had ash frames, panelled in steel and with a wooden floor. To change gear, the driver moved the rear axle forward by lever and the passenger moved the long side-belts. There was no reverse gear. Bédélia cars were both cheap and popular, especially in Britain, where they were imported by Palmer's Garage of Merton at prices from 56 guineas for a 3½hp single-cylinder to £108 for a 10hp V-twin.

In January 1913 an advertisement proclaimed Bédélia to be 'the largest producers of cyclecars in the world'. In spite of a flimsy appearance the cars had a reputation for reliability and speed. Bédélias performed well

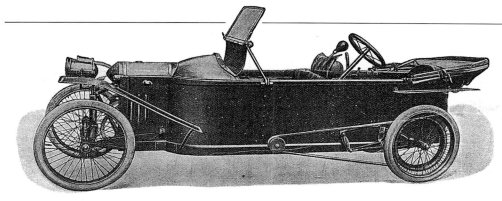

Bédélia two-seat Torpedo of c.1911

in their class at Le Mans, three times broke the cyclecar hour record in 1912, and established 2-hour and 100-mile records, usually with Bourbeau as driver. In 1913 Bédélia won the Grand Prix des Cyclecars at Amiens.

During World War I Bédélias were used as field ambulances, with a single casualty carried on a horizontal stretcher rigged above the petrol tank, which was itself above the engine! As the cyclecar boom faded after the war with the advent of the true light car, Bédélia fared better than most, adopting more conventional side-by-side seating and three-speed transmission. In 1920 Bourbeau and Devaux sold the company to a former distributor, M. Binet, who had the cars built for him by L. Mahieux et Cie of Levallois-Perret until 1925, when production stopped. BL

BEIJING/PEKING
CHINA 1958 to date

Said to have been founded in 1940, there is no trace of this company until 1949 when the Beijing Automobile Repair Works was set up. This became the Beijing Automobile Accessories Works in 1954, replaced in turn by Beijing Automobile Works in 1958 when two models of car were announced. The Jingganshan, named after the mountains where Mao Tse-tung set up a revolutionary base in 1927, was a four-door unitary construction saloon with rear-mounted 36bhp four-cylinder engine; there was also a large Beijing saloon powered by a V8 engine. Very few of these were made, but several hundred of the Jingganshans were built.

In 1960 a few examples of the Dongfanghong BJ760 (East is Red) were made. This was a four-door saloon powered by a 2½-litre Volga engine, and in 1963 came the BJ210E,

Beijing BJ212 4×4 pickup of c.1985

4×4 Jeep-type vehicle, also Volga-powered and forerunner of the larger BJ212.

In 1966 came the factory's best-known product, the BJ212 4×4 Jeep-type vehicle, based on the Russian UAZ family and powered by a four-cylinder overhead-valve engine similar to that used in the Volga car. This has been made with little change ever since, the 1984 model using a 2.4-litre 75bhp petrol engine, with the option of a 2½-litre Perkins diesel. In 1979 it was briefly offered on the British market with a 2.3-litre Vauxhall engine. The 2.4-litre engine is also used in a four-door saloon, the BJ750, and a forward control 2-ton truck, the BJ130.

The Beijing name is also found on buses and heavy dump trucks, while the BJ212 and BJ130 are made in a number of other factories in China. The workforce at the Beijing car factory is about 10,000; production was about 17,000 in 1984, most of these being BJ212s.

In 1983 an important agreement was signed between Beijing and American Motors Corporation by which the latter would give technical assistance with development of the BJ212, followed by Chinese production of a Jeep by 1988. The agreement gave AMC a 31.6 per cent stake in the newly formed Beijing Jeep Corporation. GNG

BELGICA
BELGIUM 1899-1909

The Société des Cycles Belgica was founded in 1885 in Molenbeek-St Jean, a suburb of Brussels. Among its bicycles was a folding model which was supplied in large numbers to the Belgian Army and brought great prosperity to the firm. The company's chairman, Louis Mettewie, turned to cars in 1899, showing electric cars alongside his cycles at the Brussels Exposition that year. His first petrol car appeared in 1901, a two-cylinder light car with bodywork by De Ruyter Demissine, and in 1902 the range was extended to include two single-cylinder models, three twins and a four, which were designed by Georges Desson.

In June 1902 the SA des Cycles et Automobiles Belgica became the SA Franco-Belges de Construction Automobiles, with offices in Paris and Brussels and a capital of 1.5 million French francs. Development of

the cars followed conventional lines, with shaft drive coming in 1905 and the first six-cylinder model in 1907.

The Brussels factory had become too small by 1906, and Belgica merged with the Usine de Saventhem, where cars were made under the name US Brevets Mathieu. Here, under a new company title, Usine de Saventhem SA, were made cars, trucks, buses, fire engines, marine engines and electrical generating equipment, while the smaller Brussels factory was retained for the manufacture of components. The president of this new company was the Baron van Zuylen de Nyefelt, a founder of the Automobile Club de France.

The company overreached itself with this large factory, however, and lack of capital forced it to close its doors in 1909. The Saventhem factory was bought by Excelsior. GNG

BELL/CWS BELL
GB 1905-1927

In 1905 the Calder Ironworks at Ravensthorpe, Yorkshire, run by Bell Brothers, introduced the first of a series of solid cars designed by Edwin Humphreys and these soon earned a sound reputation for tackling the steep hills of the area. The range was quite extensive but was produced in very limited quantities under the slogan 'Sound as a Bell'. The cars were seldom seen outside their native county.

Bell ceased vehicle production in 1914 but had new designs on the stocks when the Co-operative Wholesale Society (CWS) in Manchester acquired its business in 1919 and moved it to the former premises of Cotton Industry Motor Transport Ltd in Chorlton Road, Alexandra Park, Manchester. A. H. Freeman, in charge of the society's engineering department and formerly of Crossley, Argyll, Halley and Austin, looked after the new manufacturing interests. Soon a range of ¾-ton, 1- and 1½-ton lorries was introduced.

Bell had intended to make 16, 20 and 30hp cars after World War I but the 250 CWS workforce concentrated initially on the commercials in the hope of replacing the thousands of horse-drawn vehicles in the Co-op movement with motors. In 1920 a 16hp car was built and, as the 16/20, a few were sold for use by Co-operative societies. Lighter vehicles in the shape of motorcycles and cyclecars were made by the CWS at Tyseley, Birmingham, usually under the names Federal or Federation, the bikes surviving to 1937. The Co-op fell foul of the motor trade by offering these vehicles through their exclusive outlets and also by tackling general motor repairs, Chorlton Road offering Model T Ford repairs to outside customers.

In 1922 a competitive Dorman-powered 1½/2-ton commercial chassis became the staple product and a car based on many of its components was offered. The 16/20 became the 15.9 in 1923, when 80 men were employed in the motor car department. Hopes of increasing the workforce to 300 were never achieved and car production ended in 1927. CWS Bell commercials, particularly small charabancs, were made until 1930, but despite exhortations to carry Co-op goods on Co-op vehicles they could not compete with mass-produced and much cheaper rivals. NB

BELL/RIESS-ROYAL
USA, CANADA 1915-1922

The Bell Motor Car Co was formed in York, Pennsylvania, in 1915 and began building a small, four-cylinder tourer, the Model 16, which was advertised as 'The sensation of the year 1915' and which sold for $775. Between 1916 and 1918, Bell cars were also built under licence in Canada at Barrie, Ontario.

Early cars used Golden, Belknap and Schwartz, or Continental proprietary engines, but from 1919 Bells were powered by Herschell-Spillman engines. In 1922 the cars became known as Riess-Royals, after the company president, Charles E. Riess. Only a very few were built before the company ceased trading that year. BL

BELLANGER
FRANCE 1912-1928

Born in 1884, Robert Bellanger set up in business in 1906 under the name Hagnauer et Bellanger, acting as the Paris agent for Westinghouse and Delaunay-Belleville cars. In 1912 he acquired a factory at Neuilly-sur-Seine, and began to make a medium-sized car powered by a four-cylinder English Daimler sleeve-valve engine. They had imposing bull-nose radiators, overhead worm drive and Riley detachable wire wheels. Their slogan was 'Son capot est d'argent et son silence est d'or' ('Her bonnet is silver and her silence

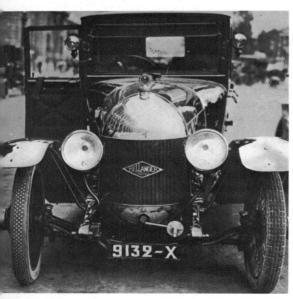

is golden'). The first models used Daimler engines of 2.6- and 3.3-litre capacity, but by 1914 these had been joined by a 2-litre (actually the BSA Stoneleigh engine) and a 6.3-litre.

Bellanger prospered during World War I, expanding into aircraft, farm equipment and armoured cars, and also acquiring a shipyard at St Malo, the SA des Chantiers Navals de l'Ouest, which made a wide variety of sea and river craft. After the war he continued with this business, and also the tool-making firm, Forges et Ateliers de Juvisy, while other Bellanger-owned companies made cycle components and marine and industrial semi-diesel engines.

The Société des Automobiles Bellanger abandoned sleeve valves and began to make a conventional car on American lines using a 3.2-litre four-cylinder Briscoe engine with unit three-speed gearbox and wooden wheels with detachable rims. About 2000 of these were made between 1919 and 1923, and a number were used as taxis in Paris. Bellanger also made a few larger cars designed by Valentin Laviolette who had been with Spyker. These had 4.3-litre, four-cylinder or 6.4-litre, V8 engines, with horizontal valves. Like the smaller car they used large bull-nose radiators.

Few of the Laviolette-designed cars were made, and all production seems to have stopped in 1923, although some lists carried the Bellanger through to 1925. In that year the Neuilly factory was sold to Peugeot, which in turn sold it to Rosengart in 1928. The Bellanger name returned briefly when De Dion-Bouton sought to encourage sales of its 1.3-litre Model JP by fitting a V radiator and selling the result as a Model B1 Bellanger. This venture lasted less than a year.

Robert Bellanger became a member of the Chamber of Deputies, later a senator. He spent his retirement restoring a ruined 11th-century Provençal fortress, using a tractor of his own construction made out of bits of various Bellanger cars. He died in 1966. GNG

BELSIZE/MARSHALL
GB 1897-1925

In 1903 the Belsize Motor Car and Engineering Co Ltd was formed in Manchester with a capital of £30,000. It had evolved from a merger of the Belsize Works of Walter Radermacher and engineers Marshall and Co. Marshall, run by James Hoyle Smith, had built Hurtus under licence since 1897. In 1905 Belsize-Ryknield buses were supplied to Leeds, an association probably limited to engines.

In 1906 the firm was re-formed with £100,000 capital and a major expansion programme started. G. T. Richards joined as designer from Rolls-Royce and by 1911 there were 1200 men, 7 acres (2.8 hectares) of factory and 200 cars and commercials in the course of manufacture at any one time. Out-

put was said to be 1200 a year.

The Belsize name had been used on cars since 1901, and on bicycles before that. Buchet engines were employed in early Manchester-designed cars but Belsize was soon making its own engines, including an overhead-valve six in 1906 and fours for taxis, vans and various car models. It built fire-engine chassis with engines of up to 14½-litre capacity in 1911 for the local fire engineers John Morris and Son Ltd, and earned healthy profits of £13,250 in 1909 and £40,000 in 1913. Experiments were made with sleeve valves and in 1912 an overhead-chain-driven-cam six with in-unit gearbox was offered as well as marine engines. By 1914 the workforce totalled 1500 and wartime output soon built up to 50 vehicles a week, plus shells and aero engines.

The company found post-war trading conditions difficult. It lost £171,000 in 1920-21 and a receiver was appointed in 1923. In an effort to appeal to the mass market a 1.1-litre V-twin oil-cooled Belsize-Bradshaw had been added in 1921, designed by Granville Bradshaw. It did not sell well, however, and neither did the company's lorries nor the 1.7-litre six and 2.5-litre eight-cylinder cars added in 1924.

Production that year was at a virtual standstill due to lack of money and the factory ground to a halt early in 1925. James Hoyle Smith was still managing director, but after he died later that year his company finally collapsed with liabilities of £500,000. NB

BENJAMIN/BÉNOVA
FRANCE 1921-1931

Designed and built by Maurice Jeanson of Asnières, the Benjamin was a typical French light car with sporting proclivities, in the style of Amilcar or Sénéchal, although it never became so well known. The first Benjamin had a 750cc four-cylinder engine, three-speed gearbox integral with the rear axle, and transverse front suspension. Overall weight was just under 770lb (350kg), which meant that it could be taxed as a cyclecar. One of these Benjamins won its class in the 1922 Bol d'Or race. There were soon several varieties, including a long wheelbase four-seater, a taxi-cab and delivery van, and an overhead-cam sports model capable of 60mph (96kph).

In 1924 Jeanson also offered a true cyclecar, with rear-mounted 525cc vertical-twin two-stroke engine in a punt-type frame, joined by a three-cylinder version the following year. The cyclecar era was practically over in France, and they did not sell well. Jeanson soon wisely replaced them with conventional cars powered by 985cc Ruby or 1095cc Chapuis-Dornier engines, with quarter-elliptic springing all round and worm drive. These were offered with open or closed bodies, and as light commercial vehicles.

In 1927 the company was reorganized and

Bellanger 'Bull-nose' of c.1914

the products renamed Bénova. For the following season one model was offered with a small straight-eight SCAP engine of 1492cc, but this lasted only two years, and the final Bénovas were four-cylinder cars with capacities from 945cc to 2.1 litres. In the mid-1920s Jeanson advertised that he also made bicycles and motorcycles, but these never became at all well known. GNG

BENTALL
GB 1905-1912

The Bentall family were Essex farmers. In 1797 William Bentall established a company to make a special plough that he had developed and in 1806 came the first steam thresher. Farm machinery was exported throughout the world in Victorian times, as was screw-cutting machinery. William's grandson, E. E. Bentall, developed stationary petrol engines in about 1900 for farm use and became an enthusiastic motorist, favouring

Georges Richard and Richard-Brasier cars. In 1904 two-cylinder versions of the stationary engines were installed in Dupressoir chassis.

Bentall had its own foundry, and following the success of the prototype cars in 1905, an automobile department was set up at Maldon with £60,000 worth of special tools and equipment. Bentall's chauffeur, Ernest Linnett, was chief engineer. Dupressoir chassis and other French components were used until Bentall components could be substituted. The bonnet and circular Molineaux radiator were reminiscent of Hotchkiss. Two- and four-cylinder 8-16hp engines were offered.

The cars were mostly sold locally, although Lacre represented Bentall in London and sold a number overseas. Both sleeve-valve and Bingham's silent piston-valve engines were tried in 1908-10, and an Aster engine was used in Miss Bentall's wedding car in 1910. Production was unprofitable and ended in 1912, by which time about 100 cars had been made. Bentall is still well known today as a make of agricultural machinery. NB

BENTLEY
GB 1919-1931

Born in 1888, Walter Owen Bentley was apprenticed to the Great Northern Railway works at Doncaster but soon turned to the motor trade, selling DFP cars in London's West End. He greatly improved the performance of these by using aluminium pistons, and during World War I he was engaged by the Technical Board of the Royal Naval Air Service to work on an improved version of the French Clerget rotary engine, using aluminium pistons. He did this first at Gwynnes Engineering works at Hammersmith and later at Humber in Coventry, both also car manufacturers, the modified Clerget engines being known as BR1 and BR2.

In 1919 Bentley returned to selling DFPs, but with the help of F. T. Burgess, an ex-Humber draughtsman, he planned to build a car bearing his own name. Bentley Motors Ltd was formed in August 1919, being a successor to a previous company of the same name, which was concerned with sales. Nominal share capital was £200,000 but cash in the bank was only £18,575; factory premises at Cricklewood, north-west London, were built by means of a mortgage, the first of many, and the company was desperately under-capitalized from the start.

Nevertheless, a prototype 3-litre four-cylinder single-overhead cam engine was running by October 1919 and a complete car two months later. Development work took 21 months, and the first sale was not made until September 1921. The price of a 3-litre chassis was £1050 and of an open four-seater tourer

Bentley 3-litre (Isle of Man TT) of 1922

'W.O.' in a Bentley 4½-litre of 1928

£1350, which put it among the most expensive cars on the British market. Launching a brand new car at the top end of the market has never been easy, but sales built up encouragingly, reaching 122 in 1922, 204 in 1923 and 402 in 1924.

By the middle of the decade Bentley cars had already gathered much of the mystique which they still have today, helped by their first Le Mans victory in 1924. Early customers were mostly enthusiastic young sportsmen, of whom Prince George, later the Duke of Kent, was one, but the marque soon attracted show-business figures such as Gertrude Lawrence and Beatrice Lillie.

Despite the surface success and newspaper adulation, Bentley Motors was still seriously under-capitalized, and in 1925 W.O. approached the millionaire sportsman Woolf Barnato for help. This was forthcoming, but only at the expense of Bentley's control of his company, for Barnato's help was not an injection of capital but a takeover, which involved the winding up of Bentley Motors Ltd and the formation of a new company of the same name with Barnato as chairman. His position in the new company can be assessed by his holding of 109,400 £1 preference shares and 114,000 one-shilling ordinary shares, compared with Bentley's 6000 and 3000 shares, although W.O.'s brother H. M. Bentley and one or two others held a number of shares as well.

The years 1926 to 1931 brought the greatest glory to Bentley's reputation with four successive Le Mans victories (1927-30) and the best year for production (408 in 1928). The 3-litre had been joined by a more 'touring' six-cylinder car, the 6½-litre, which soon had its sporting version in the Speed Six, and by a new four-cylinder sports car, the 4½-litre. The 3-litre was dropped in 1929, after 1622 had been made, and at the 1930 London Show there appeared the finest and most expensive Bentley yet. This was the 8-litre, with 220hp six-cylinder engine and a chassis price of £1850. Aimed straight at the Rolls-Royce Phantom II market, the 8-litre was a casualty of Bentley's collapse and only 100 were made.

In June 1931 the company's debts were such that it could no longer continue trading. Barnato was unable or unwilling to meet the debts, which amounted to £103,675, and a receiver was appointed. It was thought that Napier, with whom Bentley had discussions about a new car, would acquire the company, but in November a mystery 'organization' called the British Central Equitable Trust Ltd made a higher bid than Napier – £125,256 against £104,775 – and became the owner of Bentley Motors Ltd.

Several days passed before even W.O. himself learned that British Central represented Rolls-Royce, and that by the terms of his contract with Bentley Motors, he was to become a Rolls-Royce employee. He was never happy at Rolls-Royce, and when his contract came up for renewal in 1935 he left, to join Lagonda

where he remained for 11 years. A new company was formed, Bentley Motors (1931) Ltd, which was a wholly-owned subsidiary of Rolls-Royce.

The fruit of the Rolls-Royce/Bentley alliance was the 3½-litre for which the phrase 'The Silent Sports Car' was coined. It had a modified Rolls-Royce 20/25 engine in the chassis intended for a new small Rolls. Although old-school Bentley enthusiasts were disappointed, the new car sold well, as did its successor, the 4¼, which used the 25/30 Rolls-Royce engine and was made from 1936 to 1939.

From 1931 onwards Bentley has no company history separate from that of Rolls-Royce, under whose entry further details of Bentley will be found. W. O. Bentley died in 1971. GNG

BENZ
GERMANY 1885-1926

Although arguments have raged about the maker of the first motor car, there is really no dispute that the creator of the first successful car which led directly to production cars built for sale was Karl Benz. Born in 1844, Benz studied at the Karlsruhe Polytechnic and worked as a fitter in various engineering concerns before setting up his own workshop in Mannheim in 1872. By 1880 he had made a working two-stroke engine, and after many vicissitudes he set up, with friends, a new company called Benz und Cie: Rheinische Gasmotorenfabrik.

He made a single-cylinder four-stroke gas engine and in 1885 fitted one of these to a tubular-framed three-wheel carriage, which he designed specifically for his engine, as existing horsedrawn carriages were not suitable. (In this he was one step ahead of Gottlieb Daimler who did use a horse-carriage for his first car.) Final drive was by chain to the rear wheels. Advanced features which were not adopted by all car-makers for many years were electric ignition, a mechanically operated inlet valve and a differential.

The car was completed some time in 1885, but no exact records exist of the first time it ran. He took out a patent for the car on 30 January 1886; by the spring Benz had ventured onto the streets of Mannheim and the occasion was recorded in the local paper in May. During 1886 and 1887 Benz worked to improve his car, devoting to it practically all of the time he should have been giving to his business, to the despair of his partners.

His first sale of a car was probably to Emile Roger, a Parisian bicycle-maker who had obtained the licence to Benz stationary engines in France, and who ordered a car on a visit to Mannheim in 1887. Roger later added Benz cars to the engines he was offering, and in the 1890s sold several hundred.

The first long-distance journey in the car was made by Benz's wife Bertha, who drove

with her two sons from Mannheim to Pforzheim and back, a round trip of 102 miles (164km). This was in August 1888 and shortly afterwards Benz drove 200 miles (320km) to Munich to show his car at the International Exhibition.

The Benz three-wheeler had been offered for sale since 1887, but buyers were very few, if any, except for Roger. It was not until Benz obtained two new partners that he was able to find customers.

The new partners were Friedrich von Fischer, who looked after internal administration, and Julius Ganss, who became the salesman. Benz's former partners preferred to concentrate on stationary engines, now fuelled with petrol rather than town gas.

A number of three-wheelers, substantially similar to the 1885 car, though with wooden spokes in place of wire wheels, were sold in 1890 and 1891, and in 1892 Benz brought out his first four-wheeled car, the Viktoria. Sales gradually picked up, 69 cars for the years 1886-93 and 67 in 1894.

The car that really sparked off Benz's success was the Velo, a two-seater with wire wheels and a 1045cc engine which developed around 2bhp. Introduced in 1894, this was much lighter and cheaper than the Viktoria, costing 2000 marks (£500) compared with 4000 marks (£1000) for the Viktoria. Thanks to the Velo, sales reached 135 in 1895 and 181 in 1896, which was more than the combined efforts of all the other car-makers in Europe and the United States. In 1897 Emile Roger sold nearly 350 cars in France, which was Benz's best export market, followed by Great Britain where about 200 had been sold by early 1898.

Quite apart from their success under their own name, Benz cars were important in that they were the means by which many other manufacturers entered the motor industry. Hurtu in France, Arnold, Marshall and Star in England and Mueller in the USA all began with cars based on the Benz Velo design.

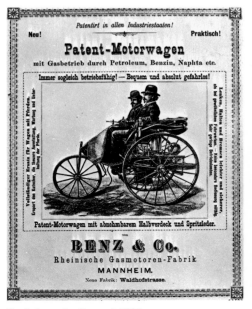

The first car advertisement, 1888

Benz 'Comfortable' of 1898

A two-cylinder Benz with horizontally-opposed cylinders appeared in 1896, and commercial vehicles the same year. However, the basic designs showed very little change up to 1900, by which time the tiller steering, belt transmission and 18mph (29kph) top speed of the Velo were distinctly outdated, a fact reflected in a drop in sales from 603 in 1900 to 385 the following year and only 226 in 1902.

Karl Benz, like Henry Ford with the Model T, was reluctant to modernize what he saw as a sound design, but his fellow directors eventually prevailed on him to change, and a new designer was brought in, a Frenchman named Marius Barbarou who had been works manager for Adolphe Clément. He designed a conventionally up-to-date car with front-mounted two- or four-cylinder engine and chain or shaft drive, known as the Parsifal.

In 1899 the original Benz und Cie: Rheinische Gasmotorenfabrik became a joint stock company, adding 'AG' to its name, with capital of 3 million marks; the work area increased from 4800 to 36,000sq yd (4000 to 30,100sq m). This had been planned by Friedrich von Fischer, shortly before he died, as an essential for expansion and also in order to give more power to those who opposed Karl Benz's conservatism. Dissension reached a peak in 1903 when Benz resigned from the firm altogether.

Julius Ganss struggled on with the Parsifal cars for a year, but although more modern, they did not perform well and sales were very disappointing. The year 1903-4 showed a loss of 500,000 marks, and shortly afterwards Ganss and Barbarou resigned, the latter returning to France where he went to work for Delaunay-Belleville.

Benz had designed a new four-cylinder engine before he left, so he was invited back, and this engine was put into production in place of the Parsifal designs. In 1906 he and

his two sons left for good, however, forming a new company, C. Benz Sohne, at Ladenburg am Neckar.

The new chief designer was Hans Nibel, who also drove Benz racing cars and remained with the company until the merger with Mercédès in 1926. Benz now settled down to a range of conventional high quality cars, ranging from a 2-litre 8/20PS to a 10-litre 39/100PS. They were favoured by many German and other aristocratic families, headed by Prince Henry of Prussia (although his brother the Kaiser preferred Mercédès, as did their uncle King Edward VII). The first six appeared in 1914.

Commercial vehicle production increased after the acquisition in 1907 of the Süddeutsche Automobil-Fabrik of Gaggenau. From 1911 its heavy trucks were sold under the Benz name, and the Gaggenau plant is still operated by Mercedes-Benz today.

In 1908 a young Frenchman, Prosper l'Orange, joined Benz to help with development of the diesel engine. This did not have immediate results, but Benz was a pioneer with this motive power, putting a diesel-powered truck and agricultural tractor on the market in 1923.

Between 1903 and 1914 the company was a keen participant in motor sport, fielding a team of three in the 1908 Grand Prix and successfully attacking the world land speed record with the 21-litre Blitzen (Lightning) Benz in which Bob Burman achieved a speed of 141.7mph (228kph) at Brooklyn, New York, in 1911. A few road cars powered by this enormous four-cylinder engine were made, selling in England for £1800 in 1912.

In 1912 Benz entered the aero engine field with a 100bhp four-cylinder unit with which it won the Kaiser's Prize that year. This was developed into the six-cylinder B23 engine, and in January 1914 Benz had developed a 250bhp V12. Aero engines formed a very important part of Benz's war work, and by 1918 it had produced a supercharged V12 developing 675bhp, as well as smaller engines of six and eight cylinders.

After World War I Benz built a reduced range of cars. Some were continuations of pre-war designs such as the 2-litre 8/20PS and 4.7-litre 18/45PS; others were new models, including the 1½-litre 6/18PS and 7-litre 27/70PS six-cylinder.

Throughout the years of car development, Benz had continued to build stationary engines, and in April 1922 this department changed its name to Motorenwerke vorm Benz Abtl Stationarer Motorenbau AG (Motor Works, formerly Benz Stationary Engines Department), commonly known as MWM. It concentrated on the development of industrial diesel engines developing up to 15bhp per cylinder at a maximum of 400rpm. High-speed diesels were also developed for trucks and tractors, and, as Mercédès was working on similar engines, the companies were well placed to lead the field when they merged in 1926.

The steady decline of Benz was caused by the fact that speculator Jacob Schapiro had managed to gain at first 40 per cent, later 60 per cent, of the Benz shares. In addition he stipulated that up to 30 per cent of Benz cars be fitted with bodies of his own coachbuilding firm Schebera and that he be appointed Benz representative for Berlin and the surrounding provinces.

The Benz financial director, Wilhelm Kissel, strongly disapproved of Schapiro's dealings. To finance his extensive bill dealings Schapiro did these transactions between his numerous firms. Kissel therefore joined forces with Dr Emil Georg von Stauss, general manager of the Deutsche Bank, and bought as many Schapiro bills as he could with money lent by the bank; and as these bills were not prolonged, Schapiro was forced to sell most of his Benz shares to Deutsche Bank. This bank, on the other hand, already owned a large number of Daimler shares, so Kissel successfully combined both companies in a merger of interests at first, and into a full merger on 1 July 1926.

Kissel became the first general manager of the new Daimler-Benz AG, a post he held until his death in 1942. Three brilliant engineers, Nibel of Benz, and Porsche and Nallinger of Daimler went on to the board of the new company. Only two Benz models, the 10/30PS and 16/50PS, appeared with Mercedes-Benz badges and these were gone by 1927. Karl Benz died in 1929 at the age of 85 while his widow, Bertha, survived until 1944, when she was 95. GNG

BERGMANN/BERGMANN-MÉTALLURGIQUE
GERMANY 1907-1922

Born in 1851, Sigmund Bergmann emigrated to the United States as a young man and went into partnership with Thomas A. Edison. In 1889 they formed General Electric and two years later Bergmann returned to Germany where he founded Sigmund Bergmann and Co in Berlin. In 1900 this became Bergmann Elektrizitätswerke AG and was a major manufacturer of electrical equipment of all kinds.

In 1907 the company began to make electric cars and trucks which were sold under the brand name Fulgura. Two years later it acquired a licence to build Belgian Métallurgique cars; these were made in various sizes from a 6/18PS of 1½ litres up to a 7.3-litre 29/70PS, equivalent to the 38/90CV by Belgian rating. During World War I the Bergmann factory made trucks, which continued until 1922.

Licence production of Métallurgiques was resumed in 1920 with one model, the 2.6-litre 10/30PS, which Belgians knew as the 14CV. Pre-war cars had Vanden Plas bodies, but the post-war bodies were German made. In 1922 Métallurgique introduced the new Bastien-designed 2-litre, but this was not taken up by

59

Bergmann Fulgura Luxus Elektromobil of c.1907

Bergmann, which ceased car production that year. From 1922 to 1939 Bergmann made electric vans and trucks which were widely used by the German Post Office.

In 1912 Siemens-Schuckert, another large electrical firm, began to buy into Bergmann, and by 1941 it owned 89 per cent of the shares. The factory was located in what became East Berlin in 1945, and was nationalized, but Bergmann became active again in West Berlin, and is today a holding company controlling five major firms. These make cables, telecommunication equipment, postal meter machines and a wide variety of electric motors and transformers. Bergmann shares are held today by two banks and Siemens-Schuckert. GNG

BERKELEY
GB 1956-1961

Berkeley Foursome of 1960

In 1956 at the request of Charles Panter of the Berkeley Coachwork Co, a well-established caravan manufacturer, Laurie Bond designed the first Berkeley car. Bond had been a manufacturer in his own right since 1949 when he designed a Villiers-powered three-wheeler with a unitary alloy body. In 1956 he also began work on the rear-engined glassfibre Unicar for S. E. Opperman of Elstree, a car which sold sporadically up to 1959.

As caravan manufacturers, Berkeley was skilled in the use of glassfibre and as he was increasingly using the material in his own cars as well as the Unicar, Bond developed an alloy-reinforced glassfibre tub bonded to a steel chassis for the newly-formed Berkeley Cars Ltd. The biggest difference from the Bond, however, was that the two-seater Berkeley had four wheels.

It predated the Mini, albeit crudely, in having a transverse engine (a 328cc Anzani or Excelsior) and front-wheel drive (by chain from a motorcycle-type gearbox). The car, 10ft 3in (3.1m) long, weighed around 700lb (317kg), but with only 15hp it was hardly quick, in spite of its sporty looks and all-independent suspension.

A 492cc three-cylinder Excelsior-engined model was introduced in the autumn of 1957 and a four-seater version, the Foursome, on a lengthened chassis, followed in 1958. More performance was available when the B95 and B105 versions replaced the originals in 1959, with 40bhp Royal Enfield Super Meteor and 50bhp Constellation engines respectively hiding under a redesigned nose. The type numbers ostensibly referred to top speeds but were probably rather optimistic, although Berkeleys did achieve class wins in the 1959 Mille Miglia and Monza 12-Hours, defeating several Abarths among others.

A few cars were exported to California, but with Berkeleys as expensive as Austin-Healey's newly introduced Sprite, sales were poor although the company reckoned 3000 Berkeleys were on the road by 1960. In an attempt to overcome the downmarket, motorcycle-engined image, Berkeley worked on a Ford 105E-engined car, the Bandit. This was designed by sports-racing expert John Tojeiro, who became part-time technical director at Berkeley while simultaneously working on the similarly ill-starred Britannia GT for Britannia Cars Ltd. Only one Bandit was built before 1961, when a proposed merger between Berkeley and Bond fell through. Tojeiro returned to Tojeiro Automotive Developments and Berkeley returned to building caravans. BL

BERLIET
FRANCE 1895-1939

Lyons has always been the second city of France as far as the motor industry is concerned, and its leading make for more than 70 years has been Berliet. Marius Berliet was born there in 1866 and was apprenticed to his father's profession of weaver. He was more interested in the mechanics of silk weaving than in the trade as a whole, and in 1893 he designed a machine for cutting ribbon. In 1894 he began work on his first car, which was not completed until the following year. It had a single-cylinder horizontal engine and tandem seating for two; this layout was chosen because the narrow doorway of his workshop obliged him to make a narrow car.

It was not a success, but news of it reached a local businessman who ordered another car and gave Berliet a deposit of 10,000 francs. This car was completed at the beginning of 1898, but although the customer found it satisfactory, he gave it back to Berliet so that he could make further tests with a view to starting manufacture.

Berliet bought a small workshop in 1899 and working with only three employees he managed to make, and sell, six cars during the year. They had conventional seating, rear-mounted two-cylinder engines and wheel steering. The workshop was so small that final assembly of the cars took place on the pavement outside. Only five cars were delivered in 1899, but in 1900 Berliet rented larger premises and production was able to expand. The 1901 models had front-mounted two- or four-cylinder engines under a De Dion bonnet, four-seater tonneau bodies and chain drive.

In 1902 Berliet purchased the premises of Audibert et Lavirotte, which had been making a small number of heavy cars in Lyons since 1894, and which had rejected Berliet when he proposed a partnership in 1897. Maurice Audibert went to another Lyons firm, Rochet-Schneider, but Emile Lavirotte became the manager of Berliet's Paris agency, and later set up a sales organization in Moscow.

He was now able to expand further, and by the beginning of 1905 he had 250 employees turning out 300 cars a year. The cars were now on Mercédès lines, with honeycomb radiators, four-cylinder engines, pressed steel chassis and chain drive. There were four models from 14 to 60hp and these continued for several years, with a six-cylinder 60hp arriving in 1907.

In 1905 Berliet signed an important agreement with the American Locomotive Co of Providence, Rhode Island, whereby certain Berliets would be made in the United States and sold under the name Alco. For this licence Berliet received $100,000, which enabled him to purchase a new factory. To celebrate the alliance the Berliet radiator badge adopted the front view of a typical American locomotive, complete with cow-catcher.

The new factory not only turned out more cars, but also the first commercial vehicles, which were to outlive the cars by more than 40 years. These were initially a forward control chassis for truck or bus bodies, and in 1908 a taxicab chassis. Another feature of the new factory was a maintenance and driving school for chauffeurs, which was open to anyone whether or not they or their employers owned a Berliet car. This was opened in 1906, four years before the much better known Rolls-Royce school.

Berliet was never very active in motor sport, although cars were entered in the 1906 and 1907 Targa Florios, Bablot, the company's Marseilles agent, finishing third in the 1906 event. Porporato won the 1908 Targa Bologna, while victory in the second Monte Carlo Rally went to the German sportsman Julius Beutler in a 16hp Berliet limousine.

Production in 1906 was 450 cars, but the following year it shot up to 1200, plus about 100 commercial chassis. By 1913 Berliet was making 3000 cars a year, which put it in fourth place among French firms, beaten only by Renault, Peugeot and Darracq.

Design did not change greatly during the pre-1914 era, although chain drive was gradually phased out and disappeared altogether after 1910. An 8hp two-cylinder car was launched in 1909, but otherwise Berliets were conventional fours (sixes to special order only), with monobloc engines standardized from 1913 onwards. The company's export market was one of the most successful of any European manufacturer: the cars were sold as far afield as Brazil, Java and the Philippines, as well as having a keen following in Russia and most European countries.

As soon as World War I broke out Marius Berliet stopped car production and threw his firm into the war effort. The chief contribution was the CBA 4-ton truck. By 1918 this was being made at the rate of 1000 a month. Total wartime production of this robust vehicle was 25,000, and it continued to be made in smaller numbers up to the late 1920s. Other Berliet contributions included 75mm shells

tives. Even this did not help, and in April 1921 his company passed into the hands of the banks which had bailed him out. It was to be eight years before he regained control.

The unfortunate VB was hastily replaced by the VL, which was an improved version with strengthened rear axle. For 1923 this became the VF, with shorter wheelbase and smaller-bore engine, which made it a 12CV instead of 15CV. There was also a short-lived 4-litre 22CV.

During the 1920s Marius Berliet became very interested in alternative sources of power, specifically producer gas and electricity. For the former he obtained a licence for the Imbert system from Lorraine-Dietrich, and after trying it out on a 12CV car he offered it as a production model of the CBA truck in 1927. The original Imbert gas producer used charcoal fuel, but Berliet modified this to operate

but shunting locomotives, railcars, boats and electric generating sets.

Commercial vehicles assumed increasing importance during the 1930s, helped by big military contracts. By 1939 there were 12 models of truck, from a car-based 15cwt (760kg) van to a 15-ton six-wheeler, all the larger models being available with a choice of petrol, diesel or gazobois engines, and a wide range of buses as well. In contrast the car models were only three and these shared the same engine.

Car production in the 1930s centred on two models, the 1.6-litre 9CV and the 2-litre 11CV. From 1933 these were known as the 944 (9CV, four cylinders, four speeds) and the 1144 (11CV, four cylinders, four speeds). There was also a three-speed SV model, the 943. For 1935 Berliet offered a 3.3-litre four-cylinder car running on gazobois, but very few were

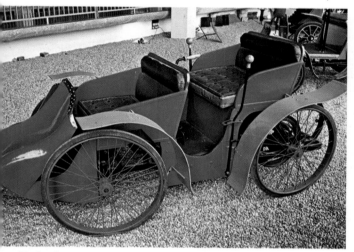

The first Berliet, 1895

Berliet 944 of 1933

and Renault tanks. To provide for all this production, Berliet built its largest factory yet, the 1000-acre (400-hectare) Vénissieux plant on the outskirts of Lyons.

For his post-war programme Berliet decided on precisely one model each of car and truck. The latter was to be the well-tried CBA, but for his car Berliet chose a new design on American lines with 3.3-litre four-cylinder engine, which owed much to a Dodge Four that he had acquired and dismantled. Unfortunately he used inferior steel for many of the components of this VB model, and it soon gained a bad reputation as claims under guarantee poured in.

Berliet hoped to make 100 VBs a day, but at best no more than 15 were made daily, and these did not find buyers easily. His aim for the CBA was 40 trucks a day, and although this figure was reached for a while it was to little avail as they did not sell, due to the enormous number of war surplus trucks available at low prices. During the winter of 1920 more than 600 unsold CBAs sat in the snow outside the Vénissieux works.

This double blow wiped out the prosperity Berliet had achieved during the war. Some 2500 employees were dismissed, and the factory took on work repairing railway locomo-

on wood, thus avoiding the need for reducing it to charcoal first. The 'Gazobois Berliet' was offered on most commercial vehicles up to World War II and on some passenger cars. Less successful was his venture into electric power: although a wide range of battery electrics from a town car to a 30-seater bus was proposed, the only ones made were a few ¾-ton delivery vans.

Two new cars were launched at the 1923 Paris Salon, a 1-litre 7CV and a 4-litre 18CV, both with overhead valves and the larger car having aluminium pistons. An 11CV 1.8-litre six-cylinder car was launched for the 1927 season, but it was the success of the little 7CV and the commercial vehicles that restored Berliet to prosperity and enabled Marius to regain complete control of his firm in 1927. He was now 62 years old, but was very much the autocrat as Ettore Bugatti was at Molsheim. His eldest son, Jean, was seen as the 'crown prince' but it was Marius who made the major decisions.

One of the most important of these was to equip his trucks with diesel engines, which became available from 1932. More than 22,000 diesel engines were made in the eight years before the outbreak of World War II, and these powered not only road vehicles,

sold. In 1936 the 9CV received the name Dauphine and two years later this was also used for the 11CV.

The 1939 range consisted of three models, an old-fashioned looking 'commerciale' with opening rear for commercial travellers, the so-called Super Dauphine, which was similar to the 1938 models, and the Dauphine 39 which used the body of the Peugeot 402B with Berliet's own radiator grille. All these models were powered by the 11CV engine. The Dauphine 39 only went into production in March, and fewer than 200 were made before the outbreak of war.

Like Louis Renault, Marius Berliet was imprisoned in 1944 for having been too successful in making trucks for the Nazis, but was soon released. He died in 1949, aged 83. Passenger cars were not revived in 1946, but Berliet went from strength to strength with its commercial vehicles, which were made in all sizes from four to 100 tons. It merged with Citroën in 1967 but the latter sold its holdings to Renault in 1974, and since 1977 Berliet has been a division of Renault Véhicules Industriels. The Berliet name was gradually phased out in favour of Renault, except in certain export markets where Berliet is better known. GNG

BERNA
see Saurer

BEVERLEY BARNES
GB 1924-1931

The owners of this very English-sounding make were Belgians, Messrs Dolphens and Flamand, and Count Lenaerts. In 1914 they took over the works at Barnes, south-west London, where the Eagle light car had been made, and began a general engineering business under the name Lenaerts and Dolphens. Aero engines were made during the war, by the end of which the workforce numbered about 1800, many of whom were Belgian. In the early 1920s the company did all the machining work for Bentley Motors, other customers at this time including Beardmore and Lagonda.

In September 1923 it built a prototype car, powered by its own make of 3994cc 90bhp straight-eight engine with gear driven overhead cam. It proved unacceptably rough in running, and not more than six were made. Subsequent models included a larger car, the 4826cc 30/90 and a 2½-litre, all straight-eights. Car production was only a sideline to the contract work for other companies, and largely a hobby for M. Dolphens.

Only 14 cars are known to have been built, but there may have been six or seven more. The last Beverley made – Barnes was dropped in 1929 – was a 2½-litre 22/90, shown at Olympia in 1929 and 1930 and sold in 1931.

The failure of Bentley in 1931 hit the company badly, and of a contract from Invicta for 500 chassis only 12 were made. A few 3-litre engines were made for Sir Dennistoun Burney's Burney Streamline car, and the Beverley works was sold in 1934 to Omes Ltd, metal founders. GNG

BIANCHI/AUTOBIANCHI
ITALY 1899 to date

Edoardo Bianchi was the greatest pioneer of the bicycle and motorcycle in Italy, and also an important producer of cars and commercial vehicles for more than 40 years. He was born in Milan in 1865, and set up a small machine shop for bicycle manufacture when he was 20 years old. He moved to bigger premises in 1888 when he made the first Italian bicycles with pneumatic tyres. His business expanded greatly during the 1890s, when cycling became as fashionable in Italy as elsewhere, and in 1897 he began experiments with motor tricycles.

His first car of 1899 had a single-cylinder De Dion engine and tubular frame, and was generally similar to the pioneer efforts of another great Italian car company, Isotta-Fraschini. Further prototypes with single- and two-cylinder engines followed, but no serious car production began before 1905.

Meanwhile, Bianchi had bought a big factory in the Via Nino Bixio of 538,000sq ft (50,000sq m) in area, and here he began serious manufacture of motorcycles in 1903. Giuseppe Merosi, later famous for the Alfa Romeo RL series, joined Bianchi in 1904 and stayed with them until 1909. It was he who was responsible for the first four-cylinder Bianchis, large chain-driven Mercédès-like cars with 4½-litre and 7.6-litre engines.

In April 1905 a new company, Fabbrica Automobili e Velocipedi Edoardo Bianchi and Co, was formed, which was quoted on the Italian stock exchange the following year. A separate company, Camions Bianchi of Brescia, was also set up in 1906 to make trucks, but there was little demand yet in Italy for goods vehicles and the company was wound up in 1909. More serious production of Bianchi trucks was taken up in 1912.

Entries in the 1907 Kaiserpreis and Coppa

Florio races led to more sporting Bianchis such as the enormous 11.4-litre Tipo E. Bianchi's drivers were Carlo Maserati, who was also chief tester and whose brothers later made competition cars (he himself died in 1911), and Gian Fernando Tommaselli, a racing cyclist who progressed through the Bianchi company to become managing director.

A new factory was opened in 1907 in the Viale Abruzzi; this became the main plant for cars, and the Via Nino Bixio factory was henceforth devoted to bicycles and motorcycles. By 1909 Bianchi had a flourishing export market, with sales offices in Paris, London, Zurich, Vienna, Berlin, New York and Buenos Aires. In 1910 the company sold 450 cars, making it the largest Italian manufacturer after Fiat (with 1698 sales). In 1913 it set up its own body shops, and thereafter most Bianchis had factory bodies.

In 1914 a new small car was introduced, the Tipo S with 1244cc monobloc four-cylinder engine. It was available in one body style only (tourer) and one colour (black), but the result of this austerity was that at 5000 lire it undercut the Fiat Tipo Zero by 3000 lire and most other rivals by even more.

There were several larger Bianchis as well, 2.1-litre and 4.4-litre cars, and the range was headed by the 9-litre 60/75hp with Mercédès-type V-radiator and chain drive. This was still available in 1916, when it must have been one of the last large chain-driven cars in the world. Since 1909 Antonio Santoni had been chief designer in succession to Merosi.

During World War I Bianchi concentrated on aero engines but also supplied motorcycles and 30cwt (1524kg) to 3½-ton trucks for the army. Truck production stopped in 1919, and for the next 14 years the only Bianchi commercial vehicles were light vans and taxicabs on the S4 and S5 car chassis.

The staple car models of the early 1920s were the 1.7-litre Tipo 12 and 16, and the 2-litre Tipo 18. They were solid family cars with no sporting pretensions, and the two

Bianchi advertisement, 1907 *Autobianchi Y10 of 1986*

Bianchi S5 Torpedos on parade in c.1927

twin-overhead cam racing cars driven by Costantini and Conelli in 1922 and 1923 events had little success and no influence on touring car design. In contrast, Bianchi motorcycles had a good competition record, one of their riders being the great Tazio Nuvolari.

In 1925 came Santoni's greatest success, the 1287cc four-cylinder Tipo S4, a much neater and more compact car than its predecessors, and an obvious rival to the recently introduced Fiat 509. However, the enormous resources of Fiat enabled it to price its car somewhat lower than the Bianchi, sales of which never reached its maker's expectations. Its successor, the S5, sold 6600 units from 1928 to 1934, about 10 per cent of Fiat's sales of comparable models.

In 1928 Bianchi moved up-market again with a 2.7-litre straight-eight, the S8. This was enlarged to 2.9 litres in 1930 and to 3 litres on the short chassis S8*bis* sports model of 1933, but never sold very well.

The S8 and the S5 were replaced in 1934 by Bianchi's last passenger car, the 1½-litre S9. This had rather Fiat-like styling but retained old-fashioned beam axles. Even though some long-wheelbase versions found favour as taxicabs, the S9 was clearly not a viable model and production ceased in 1939.

Cycles and motorcycles continued to prosper, however, with a new factory at Desio opened in 1939. In 1934 Bianchi had returned to truck-making, with the encouragement of the Fascist government which was greatly expanding military spending. The new trucks were 3-tonners powered by Mercedes-Benz-type diesel engines. These were made in large numbers for the war effort, as were generating sets, motorcycles and motorcycle-based three-wheelers.

Passenger cars were not revived after World War II, although a number of different prototypes with four- and six-cylinder engines were tested between 1939 and 1950. Diesel trucks, bicycles and motorcycles were made in some quantity, but by the mid-1950s two-wheeler sales were falling. Bianchi attempted to diversify into the manufacture of fibreglass boats, but this was a failure.

In 1955 Ferrucio Quintavalle, a Milanese industrialist, organized a new joint company involving Fiat, Bianchi and tyre-makers Pirelli. It was called Autobianchi SpA, and initially continued the manufacture of trucks, with motorcycles being made by a separate company, Edoardo Bianchi SpA. The Viale Abruzzi factory was closed and demolished, production being centred on Desio.

In 1957 came the first fruits of the new combine, a small car called the Bianchina. This was a two-seater coupé based on the Fiat 500 floorpan and was joined later by a saloon, estate car and van. Giuseppe Bianchi sold his holdings in Autobianchi SpA in 1958, and by 1963 the company was wholly owned by Fiat, which used the Desio factory for making overdrive gearboxes for Fiat cars as well as for Bianchina production. Trucks were dropped in 1966 and motorcycles in 1967; in April 1968 Autobianchi lost all independence, becoming Fiat SpA (Sezione Autobianchi).

As well as making certain Fiat models, such as the 500 estate car (Giardinera), Autobianchi acted as a testing house for new Fiat models; the transverse-engined front-wheel-drive Primula of 1964 paved the way for Fiat's 128 introduced in 1969, while the Autobianchi A112 front-wheel-drive two-door saloon of 1969 did the same for the Fiat 127 of 1971. Not that the Autobianchis did not have successful careers in their own right: the A112 in particular has been made in Abarth-tuned sports versions, and was still in production in 1986. Its best year was 1972 when 113,399 were sold, and total production to the end of 1984 was more than 1 million.

Sales are now handled by Lancia (owned by Fiat since 1969) and the A112 carries Lancia badges in some markets such as Switzerland. It is currently made in four versions, with engines of 903cc, 965cc and 1150cc, the latter being the Abarth-tuned model giving 70bhp and a top speed of 100mph (160kph). In 1985 Autobianchi began to manufacture the Lancia Y10 small car, which is badged as an Autobianchi in some markets. GNG

BIDDLE
USA 1915-1922

The Biddle Motor Car Co of Philadelphia bore the name of one of the city's leading families, and its founder R. Ralston Biddle was a member of that family. Launched in October 1915, the car was very much an assembled product, with Buda four-cylinder engine, Warner transmission and many other bought-in components.

From the start it had a distinguished appearance due to imaginative body styling and a Mercédès-type V-radiator made by English and Mersick. Prices started at a modest $1700 for a tourer, but rose to $2600 by 1918, when the Duesenberg four-cylinder 'walking beam' engine could be had at a cost of $1000 more than the Buda-powered chassis. Very few Biddles were made with this engine, owing to shortage of supply as well as the high price.

Biddle's best years were 1917-19, when sales may have reached 500 a year, but in the latter year it moved from Philadelphia to New York. This resulted in a shortage of capital, and in 1920 it sold out to a syndicate which included Stephen Bourne, formerly Secretary of the US Shipping Board, maker of the Bourne Magnetic truck, G. H. Stetson of hat fame, and H. C. Maibohm, president of the Maibohm Motors Co, which made conventional cars at Sandusky, Ohio. Maibohm failed to provide the $189,000 he had promised to keep Biddle going, and his partners filed for bankruptcy, leaving some 40 cars uncompleted.

A new group came to the rescue headed by F. L. Crane of Crane-Simplex and Ralph R. Owen of Owen Magnetic. They continued the Buda-powered Biddles, now with bodies by Rauch and Lang and priced from $3475 to $4350. Planned production by the new Biddle-Crane Motor Car Co was 200 cars a year, but it is unlikely that it made as many as that between 1920 and the closure of the firm in mid-1922. Like the Daniels, the Biddle carried no radiator badge, being identified only by the name on its hub caps. GNG

BIGNAN
FRANCE 1919-1931

Jacques Bignan and M. Picker set up an engine firm in 1911 which in 1919 offered its first complete car, the 17 Bignan. This was made for them in the Grégoire factory at Poissy and had a de la Fournaise chassis. Later versions of the model were sold in England as the Grégoire-Campbell. Other engines were developed for racing with help from Nemorin Causan, who had designed early Delage racing engines and then worked for Corre La Licorne. Many of the sporting Bignans had Rudge-Whitworth wheels and servo front-wheel brakes with only a transmission brake serving the rear wheels. Causan and Bignan converted pre-war designed side-valve engines to successful high performance engines and in 1921-22 developed their famous desmodromic-valve 2-litre car.

A factory with space to make complete cars was opened in Rue Normandie, Courbevoie, from which variations on the sporting chassis

Bignan 2-litre desmodromic-valve racer of 1922

emerged. They often had cheaper Ballot, SCAP and CIME proprietary engines in apparently sporting chassis, exploiting the competition image. Salmson cyclecars and EHP light cars were also sold under the Bignan name. The latter started with the D4 model of 1923, developed by Bignan for EHP's owner, CGA, which built bodies for Bignan.

In 1923 a sixteen-valve 2-litre, giving more power than the desmodromic engine, powered a class-winning Bignan at Le Mans. A year later, 124bhp was extracted from a 3-litre six, which entered production as a 2½-litre touring car.

The company's finances were just as complex as its model range and in 1926 the firm collapsed. It was kept in business until 1930 by a trust named after the flying stork radiator badge, Société La Cigogne. Jacques Bignan by then had left, and won the Monte Carlo Rally of 1928 at the wheel of a Fiat. Badge-engineered EHPs plus the 2½-litre tourer continued after his departure, and the final new models had SCAP 1.8- and 2.3-litre straight-eight engines. The last cars, in 1931, went under the name Bignan-MOP. NB

BIRCH/BUSH
USA 1916-1925

Birch Motor Cars Inc of Chicago and the neighbouring Bush Motor Co both sold only cars built to their specifications by other companies, and both sold cars exclusively by mail order. J. H. Bush originally had cars built to be presented to graduates of his Bush Auto Mechanics School in Chicago, but in 1916 he organized the Bush Motor Co to market Bush

cars commercially. Birch was set up in 1917 to the same ends.

The appropriately badged but otherwise identical Birch and Bush cars were built to tender by several companies, principally Crow-Elkhart of Elkhart, Indiana; Huffman, also of Elkhart; Sphinx and Pullman of York, Pennsylvania; and Piedmont and Norwalk, both from Virginia. These companies also often marketed the same designs under their own badges and built further copies for yet other companies. Norwalk and Piedmont, for example, probably both built Stork Kars, and Piedmont certainly built very similar cars for Alsace and Lone Star. The cars variously used Leroi, Lycoming, Beaver or Herschell-Spillman four- and six-cylinder engines.

All these clones make it extremely difficult to establish which companies sold how many of what, but Bush certainly sold hundreds of cars and quite possibly thousands. The cars were cheap but not very attractive; until 1921 they were only offered as open models but a sedan was then also offered. Birch ceased trading in 1923 but Bush continued until 1925. BL

BISCUTER
SPAIN 1951-1958

Gabriel Voisin made a few buckboards after World War I and following World War II he returned to the theme with a 125cc cyclecar, produced in collaboration with motorcycle maker Gnome et Rhône with bodies by the aircraft firm Potez. A few were made in 1946 in the Boulevard Exelmans in Paris, but although 1500 orders with deposits were

placed for the 'Mini Voisin' at the Cycle and Motocycle Salon, Voisin could find no firm willing to put them into production.

In 1950, however, a delegation from the Spanish Autonacional SA, with engineer Damien Casanova, visited Voisin and acquired a licence to produce what became known as the Biscuter. Production started in 1951 with locally-produced, but British-designed, Hispano-Villiers 197cc engines. Biscuters were made by Autonacional SA at San Adrian de Besos following prototypes from Biscuter Autonacional Voisin in Cataluna. They had front-wheel drive, four-wheel independent suspension and two- or three-seat passenger or van bodywork. A version of 1956-58 had glassfibre sports coupé bodywork. Biscuter production may have continued as late as 1962 and production estimates range as high as 20,000. NB

BIZZARINI
ITALY 1965-1969

Giotto Bizzarini graduated from the University of Pisa in 1953 with a degree in mechanical engineering and began work with Alfa Romeo before moving to Ferrari, where he worked on what would eventually become the 250GT Berlinetta. In November 1961, in company with several other disenchanted engineers including Carlo Chiti, Bizzarini left Ferrari. While Chiti and others set up ATS to build racing and sports cars, Bizzarini organized Prototipi Bizzarini Srl in Livorno to perform engineering and design consultancy work.

He worked initially for Lamborghini and for refrigerator manufacturer Renzo Rivolta, who had just launched Iso SpA in Bresso, Milan. Bizzarini designed the Iso Grifo A3C GT and also worked for Ferrari on the abortive ASA 100 'mini-Ferrari', essentially a scaled-down version of the 250GT Berlinetta, built for Ferrari by Oronzio de Nora in Milan between 1964 and 1967.

Giotto Bizzarini raced a lightweight Iso Grifo at Le Mans in 1964 and won the GT class, but while Rivolta concentrated his efforts on the four-seater A3L, Bizzarini negotiated a deal to manufacture a version of the two-seater A3C under his own name. From 1965 Bizzarini offered the 160mph (257kph) GT Strada 5300, powered, like the Iso by Chevrolet's 5.3-litre, 365bhp V8.

The original bodies, built by Piero Drogo, had serious quality problems and later bodies were built by BBM in Modena, which also worked on a scaled-down Bizzarini to be powered by a 1.9-litre, four-cylinder Opel engine. This car was presented at the Turin Show in 1966 and was eventually given a glassfibre body and redesigned suspension; known as the GT Europa, less than a dozen were ever built. Nor did Bizzarini sell many of the bigger model, which had formidable competition from the likes of the De Tomaso Mangusta, AC Cobra, the Corvette and its own sibling, the Grifo.

In 1969 Prototipi Bizzarini closed down, but shortly after, in 1970, Giotto Bizzarini was paid, apparently handsomely, by American Motors to produce three prototypes of the ultimately rejected, mid-engined AMX/3 sports car, and his name was later linked again with Iso. A non-functional Iso prototype, the Varedo, shown at the 1973 Turin Show, was said to be designed by Giotto Bizzarini, but Iso too was bankrupt in 1975 and the Varedo was never produced. BL

BLACK CROW
see Crow-Elkhart

BLAKELY
USA 1972 to date

D. Blakely founded the Blakely Auto Works at Davis Junction, Illinois, in 1972 to build an attractive glassfibre kit-car known as the Bantam. The tubular-spaceframed car had a four-cylinder Ford Pinto or V6 engine.

In 1973 Blakely introduced the uprated Bearcat and in 1976 unveiled the 100mph (160kph), 2.3-litre, Pinto-engined Bearcat S, a two-door two-seater with optional automatic transmission. Blakely production was claimed to be some 125 cars a year during the late 1970s, when the small factory employed about 36 people. By 1980 production had been increased to 200 cars a year, with a staff of 59, and in 1982 the plastic-bodied Bearcat S sold for $16,000. BL

BLERIOT-WHIPPET
GB 1920-1927

During World War I, George Herbert Jones and W. D. Marchant worked at the Zenith motorcycle factory in Hampton Court on the Zenith Gradua drive, an infinitely variable system using vee belts and movable pulleys. Jones and Marchant believed that the system could be adapted to a cyclecar and they built a 6hp JAP vee-twin engined prototype, which was completed at Marchant's house in Weybridge, Surrey. Although Zenith had helped in the building of the prototype it could not put the design into production so Jones and Marchant began looking for a potential manufacturer.

In 1917 the British government took over the Bleriot Flying School at Brooklands aerodrome, near Weybridge, and subsequently built a new factory at a cost of £75,000 in nearby Addlestone for the Air Navigation and Engineering Co Ltd, makers of Bleriot and Spad aircraft. As wartime production tailed off, the company began to look for something to produce alongside aircraft, and the French works manager, Norbert

Chereau, eventually accepted the Jones and Marchant car, which was to be called the Bleriot-Whippet.

The only significant change from the prototype was the adoption of an air-cooled, vee-twin Blackburne engine instead of the JAP, in deference to Air Navigation's wartime connections. After early problems, Jones and Marchant modified the Blackburne engines with roller bearing big ends to give reliable, 45mph (72kph) performance.

Delivery of the ash-framed cars started in April 1920, and in May 50 examples were pictured together outside the factory. A two-seater version sold for £250 as did a 'sports' version, which Marchant drove in competition; the de luxe cost £350.

In 1921 Jones left the company to work with Granville Bradshaw on advanced motorcycle engines. In 1923 a new model Bleriot-Whippet appeared, at £155, later cut to £125. In spite of such cuts and steady technical development through chain to shaft drive, sales were limited by the availability of ever cheaper 'real' cars and production ended in 1927. The factory also made Eric-Longden light cars until 1927 and ultralight aircraft, but it was eventually sold for just £16,000 and taken over by the French coachbuilder Weymann as a British depot. BL

BMF
see Oryx

BMW
Germany 1929 to date

The Bayerische Motoren Werke (Bavarian Motor Works) had a flourishing career as a maker of aircraft engines and motorcycles long before starting car manufacture. It sprang from the merger in 1913 of the aero engine makers, the Karl Rapp Motorenwerke München GmbH and the Gustav Otto Flugmotorenfabrik, which became the Bayerische Flugzeugwerke in 1916 and the Bayerische Motoren Werke the following year.

Among the leading architects of the new combine were Italian-born Austrian banker Camillo Castiglione, who was a major shareholder in Austro-Daimler, and a young Austrian flying officer, Franz-Joseph Popp, who arranged a major contract for BMW to build aero engines for Austro-Daimler. He later became managing director of BMW up to 1940 and father-in-law of the British racing driver Dick Seaman.

Large military contracts for aero engines quickly brought prosperity to the new firm, which was capitalized at 12 million marks in August 1918. By October 1918 it was making 150 engines a month, and its design was licence-built by Adler, NAG and MAN.

After the Armistice of November 1918 BMW was forbidden to make aero engines, but it branched out into other fields including railway braking systems and, from 1921, motorcycle engines and large truck engines. The former were of flat-twin design, made mainly for Victoria but also used by some small German and Austrian motorcycle-makers. The 8-litre 45/60PS truck engine was unusual in having a single-overhead cam; it was used by MAN and Zypen among others. In 1923 BMW produced its first complete motorcycle, the 500cc side-valve IZ 32; two of its features, a horizontally-opposed flat-twin engine and shaft drive, are still found on BMW motorcycles today.

The engines found their way into a few German light cars, including the three-wheeled Wesnigk, the two-wheeled Mauser Einspurwagen, the BZ and the Maja. In 1922 BMW experimented with a car using this flat-twin engine, but did not proceed with it, and when the company entered car manufacture

BMW Dixi roadster of c.1928

it was with the licence-built Austin Seven, which was made by the Dixi Werke at Eisenach. This had been made as the Dixi 3/15PS since December 1927; BMW officially acquired Dixi Werke for around 1 million marks on 1 October 1928, and from 1 January 1929 the cars were badged as BMW 3/15s.

The 3/15 continued to be made at Eisenach while BMW's Munich factories concentrated on motorcycles and aero engines, both of which enabled them to ride out the Depression more successfully than many firms. As well as its own aero engine designs it made the American Pratt and Whitney Hornet nine-cylinder radial, which powered Junkers and Messerschmitt planes. A total of 15,948 BMW 3/15s were made, to which should be added 9208 made under the Dixi regime for a grand total of 25,156 of the Austin Seven based cars.

Their successor was the 3/20PS, little larger in engine capacity or overall length, but all new, with a central backbone frame and swing axle rear suspension. It was no coincidence that there were similarities with the Mercedes-Benz 170, for the two firms shared several directors and many Mercedes-Benz dealers sold the small BMWs as well.

In 1933 came the Type 303, a small six-cylinder car of 1.2 litres which began the pattern of BMWs for the rest of the 1930s; the tubular frame was retained up to 1936 and engines grew in size to 2 litres on the most famous Types 326, 327 and 328 and to 3.5

326s, and 335s until May 1941, after which motorcycles were the only road vehicles it was permitted to build. As bombing threatened Munich, motorcycle production was transferred to Eisenach. Aero engines, including pioneer gas turbines, were made mainly at Allach and Berlin-Spandau.

By the end of the war the Munich car plant was in ruins, BMW generally was to be dismantled as part of war reparations, while Eisenach was now in the Russian zone of Germany. Eisenach returned to car production first, with pre-war BMW designs sold under the name EMW. Motorcycle production resumed at Munich in 1948, and by the end of 1950 more than 26,000 single-cylinder R24s had been made.

Car production took much longer to be re-established. After experimenting with a flat-twin coupé resembling a Fiat Topolino, the company reverted to a 2-litre six-cylinder engine of pre-war design, clothed in a rather bulbous four-door saloon body. Known as the Type 501 this went into production in December 1952; the first 2000 had bodies by Baur of Stuttgart as BMW's presses were not ready. The 501 was made in various forms until 1958, being joined in 1954 by the 502 which had a 2.6-litre V8 engine in the 501 body. There were also sports models 503 and 507, made in small numbers, and these and the 502 took the company into the 1960s.

A complete contrast was the BMW-Isetta,

an Italian-designed bubble car built under licence from Iso of Milan and powered by BMW's 245cc R25 motorcycle engine. A total of 161,728 were made between 1955 and 1962, and they led on to the 600, a four-seater bubble car, and its successor, the 700. This was a 'proper car' in appearance, although still using a rear-mounted flat-twin air-cooled engine. The bodies were styled by Giovanni Michelotti, hence their Triumph Herald-like lines.

Despite quite respectable sales of the Isetta, BMW was going downhill in the late 1950s due to a disastrous slump in motorcycle sales from a peak of 29,699 in 1954 to 5400 in 1957. Most of the Allach factory was sold to truckmaker MAN but the company might still have gone under had it not obtained 10 million marks of government investment in 1959. This was earmarked for development of the 700. A plan for joint ownership of BMW by Daimler-Benz and a consortium of banks was rejected by dealers and shareholders, and after many changes at boardroom level the company managed to survive independently, aided by a 20 million mark loan from MAN.

The 700 sold well, with 188,000 units delivered up to September 1965, but meanwhile a completely new middle-class range of cars had been launched, beginning with the 1500 of 1961. These sophisticated yet compact cars with 1499cc single-overhead cam engines and modern simple lines filled a vital gap between the mass production Opels and Fords and the larger Mercedes-Benz. Gradually the other models were phased out – the Isetta in 1962, and the V8 and the 700 in 1965.

By the end of 1963 BMW was making profits again, and in 1966 it achieved record sales of over 74,000 cars. The same year it acquired Hans Glas GmbH, maker of Goggomobil and Glas cars. Two Glas models were carried on by BMW with the latter's badges, the 1600GT which received a BMW 1600 engine, and the 3-litre V8 which was largely unchanged apart from badging. These were made until 1968, after which the Glas factory at Dingolfing was modernized and has become one of BMW's leading plants.

BMW 507 cabriolet of 1956

litres for the Type 335, the last pre-war design. In 1933 Fritz Fiedler joined BMW from Horch and soon made his mark with an ingenious cylinder head incorporating hemispherical combustion chambers with a single side-camshaft. This was used in the 328 two-seater sports car, 327/328 coupé and the post-war Bristol, Frazer-Nash and AC cars.

Bodies for the 3/20PS and the first 303s came from Daimler-Benz's Sindelfingen factory, but from 1933 onwards BMW relied mainly on Ambi-Budd of Berlin for its saloon bodies, and Autenrieth and Reutter for its cabriolets. From 1935 to 1939 several models of BMW were sold in Britain under the name Frazer-Nash-BMW.

Production of cars for civilian owners ceased in early September 1939, but BMW continued to make a small number of 321s,

BMW 327 coupé of 1937

BMW 735i of 1986

The Glas 1700 bodyshell found its way to South Africa where it was used for the first South African-built BMWs of 1968. These hybrid cars used BMW 1800 and 2000 engines and were made until 1975, when they were replaced by variations of standard German cars.

In 1968 BMW launched its first six-cylinder cars since the 501. These were the 2500 and 2800 series which took the company into the big Mercedes class. The following year saw a new production record of 144,788 cars established; in order to make room for car production, motorcycles were transferred to a plant in West Berlin.

The 1970s were years of almost uninterrupted growth and success for BMW; even the oil crisis of 1973-74 hit the firm less than others, and in 1975, when world car production was 16 per cent down on the previous year, German production was up by 5 per cent and BMW by 23 per cent. That year 221,298 cars were made and 25,566 motorcycles. From a specialist producer of luxury cars in the 1950s, BMW had become a quantity manufacturer whose sales among German cars were exceeded only by VW, Opel and Ford, and yet it retained a cachet which put it well ahead of these makes.

Its best seller was the 2002, with 339,084 made between 1968 and 1976, as well as 56,863 of its sporting derivatives such as the 2002tii and turbo. At the top of the range were the 3.0-series cars, big 3- and 3.3-litre saloons and coupés, which rivalled the best that Mercedes-Benz could offer.

Like its rivals from Stuttgart, BMW believes in gradual development and improvement rather than dramatic innovation, and the current range has grown from the models of the 1970s. It now consists of four ranges, the 3 Series of saloons and cabriolets with four-cylinder 1.7- or 2.5-litre engines, the 5 Series of four-door saloons with engines from a 1.7-litre four to a 3.4-litre six, the 6 Series of coupés with 2.8- or 3.4-litre six-cylinder engines, and the 7 Series of four-door saloons with six-cylinder engines of 3 and 3.4 litres, and a 5-litre V12. Diesel engines are available in the 3 and 5 Series, and there are also high-performance M models, the 2.3-litre M3

and the 3.4-litre M535. A four-wheel-drive version of the 3 Series was introduced in 1985, with the likelihood of a similar 7 Series car in 1986.

Car production is now concentrated in two plants, in Munich where the 3 Series is made, and Dingolfing which makes the 5, 6 and 7 Series. Motorcycles are still made in Berlin, although light alloy castings for these engines come from Munich. All coupé bodies since the 2000C/CS are made by Karmann of Osnabrück.

Capacity in 1985 was nearly 1000 vehicles a day from Munich and Dingolfing, and 165 a day from Berlin. Car production in 1985 was 445,233 plus 37,100 motorcycles, all made by a total workforce of around 46,800. A new factory is currently being built at Regensburg to provide additional capacity for future growth. GNG

BNC
FRANCE 1923-1931

The BNC sports car was made by Bollack, Netter et Cie of Levallois-Perret, Seine. The first cars were designed by Jacques Muller, an Alsatian who had worked for Anzani, Berliet and Hispano-Suiza, and who launched his own car in 1920. This was a cyclecar powered by a 995cc vee-twin Train engine, or an 892cc four-cylinder SCAP. After two years of small-scale production Muller sold out to the Bollack brothers and Netter in 1922, joining the new firm for a few years. He later worked on aircraft re-fuelling machinery and built a prototype microcar after World War II.

The first BNC had a Ruby engine of 750cc or 970cc and a three-speed gearbox in place of the Jacques Muller two-speed. Touring, sports and delivery van models were made. Export sales were particularly directed towards Belgium and Spain, although some cars were sold in England. They gradually increased in size, with closed bodies available in 1925.

A range of successful sports models followed, with 1100cc SCAP engines which could be had with a Cozette supercharger.

This was probably the first supercharged French car to be sold to the public. From 1927 their appearance was characterized by sloping radiators and frames which were underslung at the rear. Ruby engines of 1088cc or 1097cc were also available, and some touring BNCs were offered with 1½-litre Meadows 4ED engines. Only three of these were actually made.

In 1928 Lucien Bollack left the company to set up a business importing Lycoming engines. In connection with this he built a very attractive straight-eight car, Lycoming-powered, with other American components such as Warner gearbox and Gemmer steering. He planned to sell this under his own name, but the Depression struck before he could get into production and it is likely that only one car was made.

Bollack's place at BNC was taken by Charles de Ricou, who had had an adventurous career as an entrepreneur in Indo-China and elsewhere. He bought up the Lombard sports car company and also the rights to AER-Mercier pneumatic suspension. He acquired at great expense a factory at Rueil-Malmaison, which had been used by Hurtu for making components. Although the small BNC sports cars continued to be made, de Ricou followed Bollack's example in offering large touring cars powered by straight-eight Lycoming engines of 4 or 4.9 litres. They had frames bought from Delaunay-Belleville, which was also using American engines at this time, and the AER suspension was tested but not used commercially. Not more than six of these big BNC Aigles were made.

Meanwhile, de Ricou continued his empire building by buying up Rolland-Pilain of Tours. He launched another marque the AER, which appeared at the 1930 Paris Salon as a handsome low-slung coupé with Mercier suspension. The show car was powered by a six-cylinder Citroën engine, but de Ricou planned to use a six-cylinder Rolland-Pilain in the production AER. These never appeared, and in 1931 the whole business collapsed, bringing about the end of BNC, Lombard and Rolland-Pilain.

Spares for the BNC sports cars were bought by garage owner and well-known racing driver for the make, André Siréjols. He assembled a small number of sports cars, using SCAP or Ruby engines, until 1939. GNG

BOBBI-KAR
see Keller

BOLIDE
FRANCE 1899-1907

Bolide cars were designed by Léon Lefebvre who had designed an earlier car, the Léo, in 1896. This had a horizontal-twin Pygmée engine, and this layout was used on the first

Bolides. The earliest of these were privately built, but in 1900 he formed a company, Léon Lefebvre et Cie, with capital of £7000.

Three models of Bolide were made at this time, an 8hp twin, 16hp twin and 40hp four, the last with an enormous engine of square dimensions (155×155mm) giving a capacity of 11,692cc. This was employed mainly for racing, and was one of the Bolide designs made under licence in Belgium by Snoeck, a textile machinery company at Ensival-les-Verviers.

In 1902 Lefebvre abandoned his horizontal-engined cars and brought out a range of much smaller and more conventional machines with proprietary engines by De Dion-Bouton, Aster or Tony Huber. In 1905 he formed a new company, the Société des Automobiles Prima, which made Prima cars until 1909. Bolides continued to be made under new ownership, the company being called the Société L'Auto Reparation. They were conventional cars with four- or six-cylinder engines and shaft drive, and were made in very small numbers until 1907. GNG

BOND
GB 1948-1974

The Bond Minicar, designed by Laurie Bond and built by Sharps Commercials Ltd of Preston, Lancashire, was announced in May 1948 in the motoring and motorcycling press, each feeling an affinity with the tiny vehicle. At the time, Britain still had post-war fuel restrictions and the motorcycle-engined Bond car was intended primarily for local use, within a 20 to 30 mile (32 to 48km) radius, with a top speed of just 30mph (48kph), but with 100mpg (35km per litre) fuel economy.

The original car was a chassis-less, open, two-seater three-wheeler with a stressed skin aluminium body. Bond already had experience of stressed skin construction through his four-wheeled 500cc racing cars. The three-wheeler used a Villiers 125 single-cylinder two-stroke engine, driving the single front wheel through a three-speed gearbox and chain. With no rear suspension other than its tyres, the car weighed only 195lb (88kg) and

Bond Bug 700ES of 1970

was intended to sell at approximately £150 plus tax.

The car as announced had solid, high sides, but cutaway sides (still without doors) were planned. Production of 'several cars a week' was to begin in August 1948.

The Bond soon became quite popular. In 1952 electric starting was offered – there had originally been a kickstart under the bonnet – and in 1953 rear-wheel suspension and a front brake became available. By 1954 the Bond was well established and with increased production was making more use of glassfibre for body parts – now including separate front 'wings'. In 1954 four-seaters appeared and Lieutenant-Colonel Michael Crosby and Captain T. Mills took part 'unofficially' in the Monte Carlo Rally.

From 1959 a 246cc Villiers engine and four-speed gearbox were available and these soon became standard. From 1965, when the company changed its name to Bond Cars Ltd, the three-wheeler really grew up, with a rear-mounted four-cylinder 875cc Hillman Imp engine.

There was an even bigger change in 1963 when Bond introduced the four-wheeler Equipe. This glassfibre-bodied coupé was based on a Triumph Herald chassis (this being one of the few cars which still had a separate chassis) with a Triumph Spitfire engine. The project had Triumph's full co-operation and Bond Equipes were sold through Triumph dealerships.

In 1968 the six-cylinder Vitesse-based Equipe 2-litre GT was introduced, but in spite of appearances Bond had problems and late in 1969 was taken over by the most successful of the three-wheeler manufacturers, Reliant. At the time, Reliant could claim to be the biggest all-British manufacturer, with some 20,000 sales a year.

Bond's Preston factory was closed and both three- and four-wheeled ranges dropped, to be replaced by a single Reliant-developed model, the futuristic Bug. This sporty two-seater used the excellent 700cc (later 750cc) four-cylinder, all-alloy Reliant engine, but lasted only until 1974, when the Bug and the Bond name were finally dropped. BL

Borgward P100 of 1960

BORGWARD
GERMANY, MEXICO 1939-1961; 1961-1970

Carl F. Borgward was born in Hamburg but began work in Bremen as an apprentice locksmith. In the early 1920s he became involved in car component manufacture and began his empire building. In 1927 he took over the Gartner bodybuilding company and Goliath, of Bremen, which had controlled the Bremen commercial vehicle manufacturer Hansa-Lloyd since 1924. In 1929 the Borgward-Goliath combine also took over Hansa, the private car building associate of Hansa-Lloyd. Borgward transferred Hansa production from Varel to Bremen, and having stopped its minimal private car production, left Hansa-Lloyd to build commercials.

Goliath and Hansa continued to produce cars under their own names, Goliath from 1931 to 1934 and again after 1950, and Hansa up to 1938, after which the cars were marketed as Borgwards. The amalgam of companies became Carl F. Borgward Automobil und Motoren-Werke, Bremen, in 1939. Borgward would also revive the Lloyd name during the 1950s.

The first Borgward was a six-cylinder 2300 version of the Hansa 1700, made briefly before World War II forced the Bremen factories over to war work. Although the factories were virtually destroyed during the war, Borgward, aided by outside capital, was back in production by 1948.

In 1949 the company was restructured as Carl F. Borgward GmbH and Borgward introduced the Hansa 1500, the first post-war German car to reach production, at the Geneva Show. It was an attractive, modern car and was followed by 1800 and six-cylinder 2400 models.

Borgward looked to competition involvement for publicity and in 1950 used a streamlined, 66bhp version of the 1500 to take 12 international class records at Montlhéry, including 1000 miles (1609km) at an average of over 107mph (172kph). The modified engine went into production in 1951.

Borgward also pursued a dominant circuit

racing programme, with a competition department run by former Mercedes-Benz Grand Prix team member Hans Hugo Hartmann. Mainstays of the competition programme were various versions of the Isabella, a unitary construction development of the 1800, launched in 1954.

The Isabella became generally available in a 75bhp TS (Touring Sport) coupé version, and for racing a 115bhp fuel-injected engine was developed, enabling Borgwards to win the 1954 Eifelrennen and take a class win in the 1955 Mille Miglia. An even more advanced, twin-cam four-valve injected racing engine, introduced in 1956, with 150bhp, was less successful in the small, open RS but still scored some reasonable results.

In spite of the competition successes and generally high regard for the road cars, Borgward production was never quite enough to ward off serious financial problems. In 1958, after a Borgward helicopter designed by Kurt Focke had all but drained resources, Borgward stopped racing.

In 1960 Borgward put its name on the smaller Lloyd Arabella in a bid to generate volume sales, but still had to negotiate a loan from the government of 30 million marks, payable in three equal instalments. The third instalment was due in February 1961, but rumours that it would be withheld brought the creditors crowding in. On 4 February 1961 Carl Borgward retired, surrendering his factories, 19,000 unsold cars and liabilities equivalent to some £17 million to the government of Bremen in order, he said, 'to safeguard the jobs of 20,000 workers'.

The officials treated Borgward, Goliath and Lloyd as separate entities, confusing creditors even further, and set up an experimental shop under Herr Ueblacker to produce military vehicles and some rather strange design exercises which it was hoped might help the company. Carl Borgward retained an option to repurchase the company within six months if he could raise the necessary 50 million marks and might have succeeded through potential military contracts or foreign capital. Prospective purchasers included Chrysler, Ford and BMC, but there was obvious resistance to links with the strongly socialist government.

After Bremen had injected the equivalent of some £4.2 million, Lloyd and Hansa production stopped and Borgward was reorganized again as plain Borgward-Werke AG. In July, shortly after the 200,000th Isabella was produced, the company was declared bankrupt.

By the end of 1961 the factories had been sold, mostly to commercial vehicle manufacturer Hanomag. Amazingly, the majority of the remaining Isabellas were sold at a premium, enabling Borgward eventually to pay its creditors in full.

A Mexican company, Impulsora Automotriz SA, bought the Isabella tooling and plant for $40 million and assembled Isabellas until 1966, while Fabrica Nacional Automoviles SA in Monterey eventually resumed manufacture of Borgward's last car, the 2.3-litre six-cylinder limousine. A total of 2613 Mexican 'Grosse Borgwards' were built between 1968 and 1970 before that company also closed. Carl Borgward, who had been a major influence on the post-war German industry, died in July 1963 aged 73. BL

BOYER
FRANCE 1898-1906

Noé Boyer was a former commercial director of the Phébus branch of the Clément-Gladiator and Humber bicycle company, a combine formed in 1896 by Harvey DuCros from Adolphe Clément's Clément company, the Gladiator cycle company (originally founded by Darracq) and Thomas Humber's British cycle company. The Phébus name was used on Aster- and De Dion-powered motor tricycles and later on the Phébus-Aster voiturette, built by Noé Boyer et Cie of Suresnes from 1898.

At the same time the company also built Boyer cars. It is uncertain when the Boyer name was first applied to the vehicles, but the company entered a car in the Paris-Rambouillet-Paris race of 1899 and by 1901 Boyer was marketing a tubular-framed, chain-drive voiturette with De Dion, Aster, Buchet or Meteor engines. According to contemporary advertising, the Boyer had a 'frame made to carry any desired form of bodywork'. In 1901 a Boyer car was driven from Paris to Barcelona 'without breakdown' – a remarkable feat if accurately reported.

Boyer cars were sold in England as Yorks by the British agent, the Colonial Motor Car Co Ltd of London. In 1902 a 6hp model sold for £190 but British imports were stopped that year due to quality problems.

From 1903 Boyer offered larger touring cars, of up to 24hp. In 1905 a 16hp Boyer won a Gold Medal for ease of starting, allegedly won in a remarkable 0.8 seconds. Boyer cars were later made in the Prunel factory in Puteaux, Seine, along with numerous other marques such as Gnome, Gracile and JP, complicating exact dating of Boyer's demise. The last car actually listed was a six-cylinder model shown at the Paris Salon of 1906, when there were also three four-cylinder models on offer in what was apparently the marque's last season. BL

BRADLEY
USA 1972-1982

Bradley Automotive of Minneapolis, Minnesota, was founded in 1971 as a division of the Thor Corporation, with G. Bradley as president. By May 1972 Bradley was advertising the Volkswagen-based Bradley GT coupé, with gullwing doors and pop-up headlights.

Unlike many buggy-type kits, the Bradley mounted directly onto a standard Beetle floorpan, without any shortening or welding, allegedly to give 100mph (160kph) performance with the twin-carburettor 1600 engine. This lively performance, ease of assembly, optional air conditioning and a choice of no less than 50 colours, helped Bradley to the claim of being America's biggest kit-car producer. In 1976 Bradley built over 2600 cars and by 1978 had 110 employees.

By 1981 the range had been extended with the GTII and replicas which variously evoked the MG TD, the 1955 Thunderbird, and the Mercedes-Benz SS or 540K. The MG, SS and GT kits were available with petrol or battery-electric power and the GTII was supposedly capable of 140mph (225kph) with available high power options, or 80mph (128kph) cruising and 28mpg (10km per litre) economy from a standard VW engine. BL

BRAMHAM
see Stanhope

BRASIER/GEORGES RICHARD, MICHEL IRAT, RICHARD-BRASIER
FRANCE 1897-1930

The Paris-based Richard firm, founded in about 1850, made pressure and electrical meters and photographic and optical equipment. It entered the bicycle market early and adopted the four-leaf clover trade mark in 1892, using famous artists for imaginative poster advertisements that are still widely reproduced.

Cars were mentioned in the 1893 prospectus of the Société Anonyme Georges Richard, run by Georges and his brother Max and capitalized at 500,000 francs. The first vehicles appeared four years later. Engines were Benz-inspired but the cars, like De Dietrich and Orleans, were soon produced under Vivinus licence. Goods vehicles were introduced in 1897.

Capital went up to 1 million francs that year and leapt to 3 million francs in 1899 when a Franco-Swiss investment house, Indusmine, re-financed the business. The additional money was used to build a factory at Ivry-Port, not far from Panhard et Levassor. It employed 300 men, had the latest American machine tools and a floor area of some 53,800sq ft (5000sq m). Electric Duc cars were followed by motorcycles designed by skate-maker Choubersky in 1901. That year, car output totalled 423.

Henri Brasier joined the company from Mors in 1901 and designed a 14hp car in 1902, when Arbel steel frames were adopted. Output reached 624 in 1904 when Brasier assumed control and Richard established a company that became Unic in 1906. Because Georges Richard's name could no longer be used on Richard-Brasier cars, in 1905, after

Brasier tourer of 1919

some 2000 had been sold in total, the make became known as Trèfle à Quatre Feuilles (Four-leaved Clover, after the trade mark) and, later, Brasier. Henri Brasier was also involved with the Krieger electric car firm that had come under Indusmine's wing in 1900.

At the 1904 Salon, exhibitors had included Société des Anciens Etablissements Georges Richard, Ajax, selling Poney light cars (a name used for several early Georges Richards), and H. Petit et Cie with Georges Richard bicycles and Four-leaved Clover motorcycles. Richard-Brasiers won both the 1904 and 1905 Gordon Bennett Cup races as well as providing winning engines for many power boat races. These marked the high point of the company's competition career.

In 1905 several key personnel left to design cars for E. R. Thomas in the United States while Henri Perrot went to Argyll. In 1906 a components factory was started in Reims, Brasiers were being made under licence in Italy under the name Fides, and the French company became Automobiles Brasier after further financial adjustments.

Demand for the firm's expensive cars was diminishing rapidly, but in 1910 the entire range contained a wide assortment of 10 to 50hp cars with two-, four- and six-cylinder engines, as well as taxis and various sizes of commercial vehicle. Engines from the heaviest models were also used by Mass. Cheaper vehicles boosted output to 628 in the year to April 1910 and 795 in the next 12 months.

During World War I lorries and Hispano-Suiza aero engines were made and in 1916 Brasier acquired Seat to boost its output of aero engines. After 1918 expensive and rather outdated cars and commercials were produced. In 1926 a change of ownership altered the firm's name to Société Chaigneau-Brasier, the Chaigneau family having been bicycle-makers. A 9CV light car was introduced, one of which covered 11,200 miles (18,500km) in north Africa in eight days. This was followed in 1928 by a remarkable straight-eight 3-litre overhead-cam front-wheel-drive luxury car. Commercials were discontinued that year.

Georges Irat then reorganized the firm,

which was run by his son Michel. A few CB2 1086cc sports cars were made under the name Michel Irat until 1930, when the firm collapsed. Its factory was later bought by Delahaye. NB

BRAUN
see Faun

BRENNABOR
GERMANY 1908-1933

The Brennabor was the product of Gebr Reichstein (Reichstein Brothers), a company which dated back to 1871 when Carl Reichstein set up a small business in Brandenburg to make basketwork prams. In 1885 bicycles were added to its products and, in 1902, motorcycles. These were named Brennabor, an old name for Brandenburg.

Its first car was a Fafnir-engined chain-drive three-wheeler called the Brennaborette, made from 1908 to 1911. A four-wheeler with 6/8PS two-cylinder engine was announced later in 1908, and various four-cylinder models up to a 28bhp 2½-litre were made in the years to 1914. In 1913 2400 cars were built, making the company the second most important German car manufacturer after Opel.

In 1917 Carl Reichstein, who was by then 70 years old, handed over control to his sons Walter, Carl Jr, Ernst and Eduard. Motorcycles were not revived after World War I but the Typ P four-cylinder side-valve 2-litre tourer was put into production in 1919; it was joined in 1922 by the 1½-litre overhead-valve Typ S. They were conventional cars of no great performance, but they sold well, and by 1925 Brennabor had made more than 10,000 postwar cars. In 1922 Brennabor joined with Hansa-Lloyd and NAG to form a combined sales organization, the GDA (Gemeinschaft Deutscher Automobilfabriken), this arrangement lasting until 1928.

By 1925 the workforce totalled 6000. American-style mass production methods were brought in by Eduard Reichstein, who

had spent eight years with General Motors. The best selling model was the Typ R, a derivative of the 1½-litre S, of which 20,000 were made from 1925 to 1928. In 1927 and 1928 Brennabor was again second only to Opel among German car-makers, with daily production of 100 cars, in addition to bicycles and prams. Both 1- and 2-ton trucks were also made from 1924 to 1932.

Six-cylinder cars came with the 2½-litre Types AK and AL, and the 3-litre Types ASK and ASL, of which about 10,000 were made from 1927 to 1930. These were followed by the 2½-litre six-cylinder Juwel 6 and 3½-litre straight-eight Juwel 8. At 6480 marks for a saloon, the Juwel was the cheapest German-made eight-cylinder car, yet not more than 100 were sold.

The Depression hit Brennabor hard, and in 1931 two new models were launched which, it was hoped, would recoup sales. One was a 4/20PS light car with a 995cc four-cylinder engine and the appearance of a BMW 3/20PS, although without the latter's independent suspension and backbone frame. The cheapest model cost only 1985 marks and sold 2000 units from 1931 to 1933. The other new Brennabor was a low-slung two-door saloon with a reversed Juwel 6 engine and gearbox driving the front wheels. There was insufficient capital to get this off the ground, however, and it never passed the prototype stage.

Production was suspended for eight months in 1932 due to financial problems, but two six-cylinder models were brought out for 1933. These were the 2-litre Type E and 2½-litre Type F, the latter based on the Juwel 6. About 200 of these were made during 1933, but by the end of the year all car production had ceased. The factory continued to make bicycles and prams until 1940, when it turned to armament manufacture. The works were destroyed by bombing towards the end of World War II. GNG

BREWSTER
USA 1915-1925; 1934-1935

Founded in 1810, Brewster and Co was, in its own words, 'Carriage Builders to American Gentlemen'. It had the same old-established reputation that Barker enjoyed in Britain. It built its first car bodies in 1905 and by 1910 its six-storey factory in Long Island City had 8 acres (3 hectares) of floor space. In 1914 the company became US agent for Rolls-Royce and the following year it began to make cars of its own. These were relatively small luxury cars powered by 4½-litre Knight sleeve-valve engines, carrying mostly town car bodies. The whole car was made in the Brewster factory.

About 300 of these quality small cars were made in a 10-year period, but their price – $10,200 for a limousine in 1923 – made them increasingly hard to sell, and Brewster lost a lot of money on the venture. On 1 January 1926 Rolls-Royce of America acquired control of Brewster, and although William Brewster remained as president and became vice-president and a director of Rolls-Royce of America, policy was dictated by Rolls-Royce. The Brewster car had been discontinued in 1925, and the whole of the Long Island City plant was devoted to bodybuilding, mostly on American Rolls-Royce chassis.

Production of the American Rolls-Royce virtually ceased in 1931, and Brewster had to look for new business. In 1934 the new president, John S. Inskip, announced a line of cars using Brewster-built bodies and distinctive radiator grilles on lengthened Ford V8 chassis. The idea behind the car was that chassis components might be replaced several times but the quality Brewster body would last indefinitely. Convertible and town car bodies were offered, all at the same price of $3500. A few cars used other chassis such as Buick or Lincoln.

In 1935 Rolls-Royce of America, renamed the Springfield Manufacturing Corporation the previous year, filed for bankruptcy and all its assets were sold off. The Brewster family regained control of the factory but remained in business for only three more years and the last Brewster-Ford car was made in 1935. A total of 135 were produced. GNG

BRICKLIN
USA, CANADA 1974-1975

Philadelphia-born Malcolm Bricklin made his first million with his hardware supply company, Handyman America Inc of Orlando, Florida. He went on to import Lambretta and Rabbit motor scooters, the latter made by Fuji Heavy Industries of Tokyo, the manufacturer of Subaru cars. Bricklin began importing the diminutive, rear-engined Subaru 360 in the early 1960s, before it was branded 'the most unsafe car' by *Consumer Report*. As sales plummeted, Bricklin established small commercial race tracks for his unsold Subarus and determined to build what he called 'the world's first safety sports car'. The Bricklin SV1, a gullwing 5.7-litre Ford-powered glassfibre coupé – the prototype used an AMC 5.9 engine – had safety bumpers and a rigid passenger cell.

Bricklin set up the Bricklin Vehicle Corporation in St John, New Brunswick, in 1974. The New Brunswick government, keen to ease local unemployment, arranged finance and two factories for the company. Bodies were made in Minto and cars were assembled at St John, Bricklin also taking advantage of the duty-free movement of Ford engines from Detroit, as allowed under the Auto Pact.

The company ran into problems with bonding the bodies, and with body fit; wastage ran at up to 25 per cent and so many hours were spent adjusting doors that labour costs alone averaged some $6300 per car.

The first 800 cars probably cost at least $16,000 each to build but were sold to Bricklin's US arm in Scottsdale, Arizona, for $5400 each.

Malcolm Bricklin was better as a promoter than as a manager, relying largely on family for staffing and exercising little or no financial control. When he needed more money he simply asked the New Brunswick government for it. Premier Richard Hatfield backed Bricklin's well-intended but wildly optimistic predictions for around $23 million, but a further request for $10 million was too much and the government began receivership proceedings on 25 September 1975. Malcolm Bricklin was also personally bankrupt; total production had been just 2875 cars.

Bricklin later became involved with Pininfarina and its 1980s version of what was originally the Fiat 124 Sport. The remaining company assets were bought by Ohio businessman Sol Shenk, president of Consolidated International Inc, of Columbus, which still supplies virtually any Bricklin spare part. Malcolm Bricklin continued his motor industry connections through Bricklin Industries and in October 1984 announced a $100 million contract with Zavodi Crvena Zastava to begin importing the Yugo 55 into the USA from the spring of 1985. BL

BRIGGS DETROITER
see Detroiter

BRIGGS & STRATTON
USA 1919-1924

The Briggs & Stratton was a motorized, two-seater buckboard powered by a fifth wheel which incorporated a single-cylinder air-cooled lawnmower-type engine. The fifth wheel, which bolted to the back of the rudimentary vehicle, started life in October 1914 as the Smith Motor Wheel, built by the A. O. Smith Corporation of Milwaukee.

Thousands of these Motor Wheels were built, and were even made under licence in Britain as the Wall Auto Wheel. They were mainly used as bolt-on power packs for bicycles, but in 1916 the American Motor Vehicle Co of Lafayette, Indiana, designed a buggy for A. O. Smith which that company sold as the Smith Flyer for $135. The Flyer was also available as a delivery wagon and a railway inspection car with flanged wheels.

In May 1919 the A. O. Smith Corporation sold the rights to build the Smith Flyer to the Briggs & Stratton Co, also of Milwaukee. The Briggs & Stratton buckboard used an enlarged and improved version of the Motor Wheel, giving around 2hp; probably several hundred were built. Claims of 40mph (64kph) and 100mpg (35km per litre) were slightly fanciful; 25mph (40kph) and 50mpg (17.5km per litre) may be more realistic.

Briggs & Stratton manufactured the buckboard until early 1924, when it sold the manufacturing rights to the Automobile Electric Service Co of Newark, New Jersey, which continued to build both petrol and electric models as the Red Bug or Auto Red Bug. Briggs & Stratton continued to market the Motor Wheel on a scooter and on a remarkable device for towing ice skaters. The company went on to make outboard motors, pumps and generators, and in 1979 built an experimental six-wheeled petrol-electric car, the Hybrid, in which a 694cc engine drove a generator to charge the battery pack. BL

BRILLIÉ
FRANCE 1903-1908

Eugène Brillié was born in Paris in 1863 and became the engineering partner of Gustave Gobron in 1898. He left Gobron-Brillié in 1903

Briggs & Stratton of 1922

to start his own Société des Automobiles Brillié in Paris.

In 1900 he had helped to found the short-lived Société Nanceienne d'Automobiles at Nancy and was its consulting engineer. One of its Gobron-Brillié-engined lorries had been inspected by the Portuguese army and the Schneider armaments firm hired Brillié to design a similar vehicle for a Portuguese contract. Brillié-Schneider went on to gain a large Paris bus order in 1905, commercials being made in Le Havre as well as Paris and Le Creusot. Meanwhile, Brillié's own vehicle company was not faring well with its range of forward control taxis and luxury cars, and it collapsed in February 1908.

Eugène Brillié then joined Schneider full-time and designed the first French tank to be used in World War I. Schneider merged all its vehicle interests into SOMUA in 1914 which became a constituent of SAVIEM 40 years later, this in turn becoming Renault Véhicules Industriels. NB

BRISCOE/EARL
USA 1914-1921

Benjamin Briscoe had plenty of involvement with the motor business before he began to make cars under his own name. His Briscoe Manufacturing Co, founded in 1886, had made radiators and sheet metal parts for Oldsmobile, and he also lent money to David Dunbar Buick to enable the latter to build his first car. Later he was involved with Jonathan Maxwell in the Maxwell-Briscoe car and in the unsuccessful combine, the United States Motor Co.

In 1913 he and his brother Frank set up Briscoe Frères in Billancourt, France, to make a cyclecar called the Ajax, but few cars were made. The small factory was used for shell manufacture during World War I, and the Briscoes returned to the United States where they put a modified Ajax into production under the name Argo. This grew into a conventional car, but the Briscoes sold off the Jackson, Michigan, plant to Mansell Hackett, who changed the car's name to his own and moved operations to Grand Rapids.

At the same time that he was making the Argo cyclecar Benjamin Briscoe had introduced a car under his own name. This had a 2½-litre four-cylinder side-valve engine of Briscoe manufacture, and a light body made of composition papier-mâché-type material. Its most unusual feature was a single, cyclops, headlamp set in the radiator shell, but this was abandoned after a year because it was illegal in a number of states.

The 1916 Briscoe had two headlamps and a conventional steel body on a wooden frame; it was now made by the Briscoe Motor Corporation with financial backing from the Swift meat-packing family. Chassis came from the Lewis Spring and Axle Co of Jackson, which was purchased by Briscoe. Also

in 1916 a Ferro V8 engine was offered as an alternative to the Briscoe-built four, although it was very little larger and gave no extra power for its additional $200 cost.

Briscoe production for 1916 was 7100 cars, for 1917 8100 including a new air-cooled four. War service took Benjamin Briscoe to France, where he made contact with the Bellanger company and became a director in return for co-operation which was to lead to a number of four-cylinder Briscoe engines being supplied to the French company for use in its post-war cars.

In 1919 Briscoe Motor Corporation made 11,000 cars but sales slumped to 6000 in 1920, and in October 1921 the car's name was changed to Earl, after the new vice-president Clarence A. Earl, who had come from Willys Overland. Despite the additional capital which he secured, the new company did not prosper, closing for good in 1923. From 1916 to 1921 Briscoes were made in Canada by the Canadian Briscoe Motor Co Ltd in the Brockville, Ontario, factory where the Brockville-Atlas car had been made. About 1000 a year were produced. Benjamin Briscoe turned to other fields including oil and gold mining, and was a prosperous man when he died in 1945, aged 78. GNG

Bristol Beaufort of 1985

BRISTOL/ARNOLT
GB 1947 to date

As World War II drew to an end, thoughts at the Bristol Aeroplane Co Ltd at Filton, Bristol, turned to uses for soon-to-be-redundant factory space. Chief Engineer Sir Roy Fedden, with the enthusiastic co-operation of George (later Sir George) White, son of the company founder, had already designed an up-market, sporting car. White had formerly been a British and world record holding speedboat driver, until his career was ended by a serious accident in 1938, after which he turned his interest to cars.

The streamlined, rear-radial-engined coupé reached the prototype stage and was tested on the airfield, displaying such excessive oversteer that it was soon wrecked. Nevertheless, a car division was established in 1945, the production decision being made

in June and factory space allocated on the edge of the Filton aerodrome. Major G. H. Abell, previously joint managing director of the Connaught Motor & Carriage Co and managing director of Invicta Car Sales Co, became general manager of the Cars Division, having been with Bristol since 1933.

Throughout the war H. J. Aldington, who had controlled Frazer-Nash since 1929, was a director of the Bristol Aeroplane Co. Before the war, Frazer-Nash imported BMW cars and used BMW engines in its own cars. After the war, Aldington resumed his liaison with BMW on behalf of Bristol as well as Frazer-Nash.

Bristol subsequently acquired many BMW designs as war reparation and Aldington pursued the release from military detention of former BMW designer Dr Fritz Fiedler. Fiedler was brought to Filton to develop a much-improved Bristol version of the six-cylinder BMW 328 engine, which was bench-run in May 1946. This was put into a lengthened 326-type chassis with a 327-based body which was first tested in July 1946 and the car made its début at the 1947 Geneva Show as the Bristol 400. Price was a hefty £2375. Initially seven complete sets of parts had been made, two chassis-only cars were tested, and

the remaining parts made four complete prototypes and one set of spares.

Some 700 400s were built until 1950, including one with a station wagon body to avoid purchase tax and export duty. The 400 began Bristol's competition career with third place overall in the 1948 Monte Carlo Rally; it was the first British finisher.

Late in 1949 the 401, styled by Touring of Milan and with Superleggera construction, went into production alongside the 400. The 401's aerodynamics, and improved engine, brakes, wheels and axles, were tested on the huge 8250ft (2515m) Filton runway built for the Brabazon airliner. Later in 1949 the drophead 402 was launched but only 25 were made.

Bristol enthusiast and successful racer Anthony Crook put 104 miles (167km) into an hour at Montlhéry with a standard 401 and returned the car to the London Motor Show within 12 hours. Crook was to have a long association with Bristol.

It was a busy year in 1953: in June the 403 evolved, and the company moved into more ambitious racing projects with the ERA G-type based 450, a finned coupé which retired from Le Mans with a broken crank. Bristol gave up racing after the 1955 Le Mans disaster, but Bristol engines were widely used by British Grand Prix and sports car racing manufacturers for many years.

In October 1953 the short chassis 404 was introduced at the London Motor Show. Domestic sales of the expensive 404 were poor; only 40 were built until 1956.

At the London Show, Bristol sales manager James Watt met S. H. 'Wacky' Arnolt, a Chicago-based car importer and vice-president of Bertone; the Arnolt-Bristol was conceived, originally based on the 404 chassis. Arnolt built rather ugly Bertone-bodied GT, touring and highly successful competition models around the 1971cc Bristol six. 'Wacky' Arnolt died in 1960 and the last Bristol chassis was delivered to Chicago in 1961, the final year for the Bristol six-cylinder engine, but according to most sources the last of some 142 Arnolts was sold in 1968.

At home Bristol quickly reverted to the longer wheelbase with the 1954 405, the last of the first generation Bristols. A total of 294 saloons and 46 drophead coupés, by Abbotts of Farnham, were built until 1958. In 1956 the 406 had indicated a move towards luxury and made the first use of Watts linkage suspension on a production car.

In 1960 the Bristol Aeroplane Co amalgamated with Hawker Siddeley and the Cars Division was reorganized as a separate, private company, Bristol Cars Ltd, jointly owned by Sir George White and Anthony Crook. As the company sought more power to haul improved creature comforts without losing the sporting touch, a 3-litre Armstrong Siddeley six was rejected in spite of the Hawker Siddeley connection and a Bristol-designed V8 was deemed too expensive. Instead, a long association with American power units began with the 1961 407, powered by a unique version of the 313cu in Chrysler V8, with Torqueflite automatic transmission.

Bristol headquarters remained at Filton but the aircraft company reclaimed the body shop and 407 and subsequent bodies were built by Park Royal Vehicles Ltd of Acton. Bristol evolved the American-engined cars through sequential numbers to the 1969 411 and its replacement in 1978, the sleek 603 saloon. There was also a Zagato-designed car, the 412, with a more angular body and the option of a Targa-type convertible, and a rapid, if bulky 5.9-litre turbocharged 412 derivative, the 1980 Beaufighter, reviving a former Bristol aircraft model name.

Since 1983, all the Bristol range has had names formerly used on aircraft; the V8 603 saloon became the Britannia and its turbocharged derivative is known as the Brigand. The 1987 range also included an export only version of the Beaufighter, known as the Beaufort. BL

British Ensign EP6 of 1920

BRITISH ENSIGN/ENSIGN
GB 1913-1927

Formed in 1913, Ensign Motors Ltd of Brompton Road, London, began by making a thoroughly conventional 22hp four-cylinder car followed by 15 and 18hp versions. In late 1914 the company, now known as British Ensign Motors, introduced a 3-ton Tylor-powered lorry from a new factory in nearby Willesden Green and was producing it at the rate of five or six a week a year later.

After World War I it continued with the lorries, which were now 4-tonners, until 1923. Several were sold to India and others were used as breakdown tenders by the London General Omnibus Co. The pre-war cars were not revived, however, and in their place came a remarkable luxury chassis known as the Ensign EP6 with an overhead-camshaft six-cylinder 6.8-litre, 96bhp engine, apparently based on aero-engine experience, and with non-detachable wheels.

The vehicle cost rather more than the contemporary Rolls-Royce Silver Ghost and very few were made, possibly only four. It was designed by Edward Gillett, formerly of the Gillett Motor Co, who had made steam commercial vehicles in the early years of the century. He was assisted by a six-man team including an American, H. P. Crown, whose father, J. L. Crown, bought British rights to the Entz magnetic transmission and made the Crown Magnetic in Chelsea using the transmission. Of the dozen or so built, one was an Ensign EP6 with Crown radiator and appeared at the 1922 Olympia Show as a Crown Ensign.

A 12hp Meadows-engined family car was introduced in 1922. This was called an Ensign, like the commercials, whereas the EP6 from 1920 was known as a British Ensign. Only 37 12s were made. A £100, 8hp, four-cylinder car produced by the firm, but sold under designer Gillett's name, fared no better in 1926-27, when only 25 were sold. This failure effectively put an end to British Ensign Motors. Its Willesden factory subsequently became Studebaker's British home. NB

BRITISH SALMSON
GB 1934-1939

British Salmson 20/90 of 1936

British Salmson Aero Engines Ltd was established in 1930 to make air-cooled radial engines of French Salmson design. Some Salmson engines had been built in Britain during World War I by the Dudbridge Iron Works in Stroud, Gloucestershire, which later built the Hampton car. With premises at Raynes Park, south-west London, British Salmson hoped to cash in on the light aircraft boom, but although it sold some engines to British Klemm and at least one powered a Cierva Autogiro, it needed alternative work and in 1934 began to make the Salmson S4C 1½-litre twin-overhead cam car, with British bodywork supplied by Ranalagh or Newns. About 250 of these were made between 1934 and 1938, together with 75 of the slightly larger S4D with a 1.6-litre engine.

The cars were made in batches, few exceeding 30. Aero engine manufacture continued, workers being transferred from cars to aero work according to demand. By 1938 the company was making very few complete aero engines, but was busy making components for other companies.

For 1936 came an all-British model, the 20/90 with a 2½-litre twin-overhead cam six-cylinder engine developing 90bhp. This was made in saloon and two-seater sports models, but only 15 cars left the factory up to 1939. The fours were no longer made after 1938, and the company imported French-built four-cylinder Salmsons.

British Salmson remained active as general engineers, and from 1950 to 1952 it made the Cyclaid 31cc engine for motorizing bicycles. The factory was bought by Napier in about 1947 and later used for jam manufacture. British Salmson moved to Glasgow where it was engaged in the manufacture of printing presses. GNG

BRITON
GB 1909-1928

In 1909 the Star Cycle Co Ltd, a wholly-owned subsidiary of Star Engineering Ltd, was sold off to become a separate company with a capital of £10,000 under the name Briton Motor Co Ltd. It had been run by Edward Lisle Jr, who continued to be managing director. Although separate financially it remained in the family as the chairman was Edward Lisle Sr, who was also chairman and managing director of Star Engineering on whose board Edward Jr had a seat.

The first Britons were two- and four-cylinder light cars which had previously been called Starlings, but the twin was dropped in 1911, and in 1913 the company introduced a new 10hp four-cylinder model with a stroke of 120mm which gave it a capacity of 1750cc. The company continued to make motorcycles under the Star name with its own or JAP engines until 1914. In 1912 the company was reorganized as the Briton Motor Co (1912) Ltd, with issued capital of £30,882, and the following year it moved to new premises in Walsall Street, Wolverhampton.

The 10hp sold well in 1913 and 1914, while World War I contracts enabled good profits to be made until the end of 1918. During the war Briton was agent for the American Scripps-Booth car.

Briton entered the post-war period with great optimism, pricing its 10hp car at £300, at which figure it expected a vast market. Unfortunately, when it reached the showroom the car cost £495 and had little to distinguish it from countless other light cars; sales foundered and by 1922 Briton had gone into voluntary liquidation.

It was bought by C. A. Weight who continued manufacture of the 10hp and a 10/12hp, and in 1925 increased the factory area. In 1928 Weight became agent and spares manufacturer for the Caterpillar tractor and ended production of the Briton. About 1000 cars were made between 1920 and 1928. GNG

BROCKLEBANK
GB 1927-1929

The Brocklebank was conceived, it was said at the time, as 'Birmingham's reply to the US challenge'. It had a 2-litre six-cylinder engine

74

made by Brocklebank and Richards Ltd of Oozells Street. American Warner rear axles, centre-change gearboxes and Lockheed-Bendix hydraulic brakes were installed in the chassis in one of the aero sheds that had been erected between Adderley Park and Bordesley Green by Wolseley for the making of Hispano-Suiza aero engines in World War I.

Major Frank Brocklebank was much impressed by Hudson cars and in 1921 he planned a vehicle on similar lines. He was joined by Richards, who had spent some time at the Hudson works in the United States. Chief draughtsman was an Australian named Waterman, who did much to foster sales in his native country.

Although a few cars were made from 1925, production proper did not start until 1927, by which time the locally built and overweight Watson bodies looked old-fashioned, a situation not rectified until Gordon England and Weymann bodies were specified. Four to five cars a week were made, but production ended in 1929 after about 600 had been sold, when financial backing was withdrawn.

Sir Herbert Austin visited the works but refused to pay the £18,000 asking price. Spares went to Smiths Garage in Bournbrook which bought one Meadows engine and where a Mk II Brocklebank might have been planned in 1930. NB

BROOKE
GB 1901-1913

J. W. Brooke & Co Ltd ran a foundry, boiler-making and general engineering business in the Suffolk coastal town of Lowestoft. Marine petrol engines were developed and in 1901 a three-cylinder 10hp example was fitted transversely in a car. Production started in 1903 and accounted for three-quarters of Brooke's business by 1905.

Early cars had a bowl in the centre of the steering wheel for gloves, goggles and other small items. A four was offered in 1904 and a six followed in 1906. S. F. Edge contracted to take a year's output for his sales organization, but the Brooke car department had all but ceased trading by 1910. The occasional vehicle was produced up to 1913, however, including in 1910 a curious swan-shaped car that hissed. Brooke certainly built the engine for this and may even have been responsible for the entire car. NB

BROOKS
CANADA 1924-1926

Oland J. Brooks of Buffalo, New York, moved to Toronto in 1920 to form the Banking Service Corporation, a company dealing primarily in second mortgage finance. On 14 March 1923 Brooks incorporated Brooks Steam Motors Ltd in the old railway town of

Stratford, Ontario.

He bought a local factory for $50,000. Having paid $5000 himself and raised a mortgage from the town council for the rest he moved into the works even before financing was complete. He also set up an American branch in Buffalo, but production was always in Stratford, where labour was plentiful due to lay-offs by the railway companies and where there was abundant enthusiasm for a steam car, which was what Brooks would build. It would be the first steam car built in Canada since 1911 and second in popularity only to the Stanley.

A prototype tourer was demonstrated in September 1923 and production of the 'Gentle Giant of Motion' began in 1924. There was only one production model, a fabric-bodied four-door with two-cylinder engine in unit with the rear axle. The Brooks car was similar to the Stanley but stronger, and very expensive at $3885. It was also complicated to start, but the boiler, wrapped in 3 miles (5km) of piano wire, was virtually unburstable. The Brooks performed quite well but had difficulty maintaining constant high speeds without using excess fuel.

Soon after production started, Brooks claimed to have enough parts in stock to build 200 cars. Within a year the company reported that $2 million in stock had been sold and that at least one executive was earning over $25,000. By 1925 Brooks employed 125 workers, including 20 in service departments in Ottawa, Montreal, London (Ontario), Toronto and Winnipeg.

Brooks also set up taxi companies in Stratford and Toronto, using Brooks steamers exclusively, but he was heavily criticized by stockholders for selling these cabs at half price. He was also criticized for low sales and high management turnover. Late in 1926, after three years without dividends, the stockholders tried to take over the company, but although they obtained a court order denying him his vote at meetings, Oland Brooks retained control.

Prices were cut to $2885 to promote sales, but production stopped in July 1926 after 180 cars had been built. Work continued on two steam buses, one of which was eventually sold to an outside buyer after Brooks himself failed to acquire it and stayed in service until 1937. In 1929 Brooks went into receivership and in 1931 all the assets were auctioned at the factory, 40 cars being sold for between $150 and $400 each. BL

BROTHERHOOD
see Sheffield-Simplex

BROUGH SUPERIOR
GB 1935-1939

The extrovert George Brough, born in April

1890, was the son of William Edward Brough, a Nottingham cycle manufacturer and proprietor of W. E. Brough & Co, precision engineers. William Brough built his first De Dion-powered car in 1898, and another car in 1908, but from 1902 his main product was the Brough motorcycle.

During World War I George worked on aero engine development and determined to put his experience to designing a better motorcycle. He claimed his one third share of his father's company (another brother had the other share) and set up a small workshop from which, in late 1919, came the first Brough Superior motorcycle. In November 1922 *The Motor Cycle* described the Brough Superior as 'this Rolls-Royce of motorcycles'. It was built until 1940.

George Brough in the meantime decided to build a Superior car, and the prototype appeared in 1932. This had a Dorman engine, but when the production car was shown in May 1935 it used American Hudson components.

The Brough Superior was designed by a committee, including Brough, the Duke of Richmond and Gordon (whose estate included what would become Goodwood circuit) and racing driver Freddy Dixon, who designed the suspension. The alloy, four-seater, drophead body was made by Acherleys of Birmingham and workmanship and materials throughout were of the very best. No name or other badge appeared on the outside of the car.

Brough initially used a Hudson Terraplane chassis, lowered by 7in (178mm), with a 4.1-litre 125bhp straight-eight engine, but in June 1936 he was forced to switch to Hudson's six-cylinder engine as Railton had negotiated exclusive rights to the eight for its own Anglo-American hybrid. At £695 the Brough Superior was less than half the price of a Bentley or Rolls-Royce. A four-door saloon and a rapid two-seater, some examples of which were equipped with supercharging, were also available in 1936.

In May 1938 Brough announced the Brough Superior 12, with a 4398cc Lincoln Zephyr V12 engine – and now with Brough badges in evidence. Only three twelves were built before World War II and George Brough crashed one of them. The car should have sold for £1250, compared to around £1600 that a purchaser would have paid for a contemporary Rolls or Bentley.

During the war, Brough machined crankshafts for Rolls-Royce aero engines and George Brough personally used a converted Brough Superior known as 'Old Faithful' as a high-speed delivery truck, regularly delivering half a ton of crankshafts at up to 90mph (145kph). After the war, there were no more Brough Superiors, either two-wheeled or four, and total car production was some 148 cars. George Brough had 'Old Faithful' rebodied in its original form and used the car enthusiastically until his death in January 1970. BL

BROUHOT
FRANCE 1898-1911

Towards the end of the 19th century Charles Brouhot started an agricultural machinery business in Vierzon, a town on the River Cher south of Paris. He was soon making threshing machines and barn engines, and in 1898 set up a separate department named Automobiles G. Brouhot to make a 3hp voiturette with ratchet differential. Horizontal twins of 7hp and with constant mesh and gear drive followed in 1899. Vertical-engined 15 to 40hp chain-drive models then appeared in 1903-4, one of which killed its mechanic and members of the crowd in the 1903 Paris-Madrid race and put an end to Brouhot's racing ambitions after an expensive legal wrangle.

Simms-Bosch magnetos were used, along with shaft drive and monobloc engines on some models from 1907, when taxi cabs and forward-control lorries were also produced. Brouhots were available in Britain under the names Smart and Club.

In 1906 a Paris financial syndicate had converted the car section into Société Anonyme des Usines G. Brouhot with a capital of 3.5 million francs, but sales difficulties and poor management led to chaos in 1908 and the firm never recovered. A curious regression in 1908 produced an 8hp car with vertical single-cylinder engine and belt drive while a modern monobloc 12 in 1910 was popular as a taxi. There was also a 60hp aero engine in 1909, but in 1911 the car side collapsed.

The agricultural machinery business continued until shortly before World War I when the financial difficulties of an associate in Argentina caused Brouhot's company to go bankrupt. The Société Française de Vierzon Matériel Agricole et Industriel took over Brouhot and made steam traction engines from 1915, and SFV farm tractors right up to 1959. NB

BROWN/ALBRUNA
GB 1901-1912

Brown Brothers Ltd of Great Eastern Street, London, is a famous cycle and motor factor, selling a wide variety of components and accessories of all kinds. The company was founded in 1888 by Ernest and Albert Brown, another brother, Frederick, joining them a year later. It became a limited company in 1897 and two years later added motor tricycles and light steam cars to its range of products. The steamers were American in origin, being made by the G. E. Whitney Motor Wagon Co of Boston, and sold in England under the name Brown-Whitney. The tricycles (and quadricycles from 1900) had De Dion engines but were possibly of Brown manufacture.

Certainly from 1901 Brown was selling motorcycles and light cars which it advertised as being of its own manufacture, although some of the cars seem to have been made by Star of Wolverhampton. In 1902 Brown advertised a light tonneau at £275 'in which almost any type of engine could be fitted', with optional chain or shaft drive.

A 1905 18/20hp tourer had a Brotherhood-Crocker engine and there was also a 12/16hp car powered by a four-cylinder Forman engine. It is almost certain that Brown never made its own engines. A 40hp six was listed for 1907, together with 18/20, 20/22 and 24hp four-cylinder models, all these being shown at Olympia in November 1906 alongside a wide range of accessories. In 1908 the company announced a smaller car called the Albruna, with 1.4-litre four-cylinder monobloc engine.

This was made until 1912 when Brown ceased car manufacture; the last car sold under the Brown name was made in 1911. Motorcycles were continued until 1929, the post-war ones being sold under the name Vindec. This name was found on bicycles sold by Brown up to the 1960s. Brown is also famous for its extensive catalogues of equipment and accessories, which have been issued annually from about 1895 to the present day. GNG

BRUNAU
see Fischer

BRUSH
GB 1902-1904

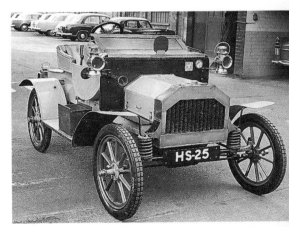

Brush two-seater of c.1900

The Brush car was a short-lived venture by a well-known electrical engineering company, which had been established in 1880 as the Anglo-American Brush Electric Light Corporation to exploit the patents of C. F. Brush of Cleveland, Ohio. In 1889 the name was changed to Brush Electrical Engineering Co Ltd. Its headquarters were at Loughborough, Leicestershire, where it had a 33-acre (13-hectare) factory.

In 1901 it took on the agency for the French

Sage car, and when it announced a car of its own manufacture in 1902 it bore some resemblance to the French product, with 10hp Abeille two-cylinder engine and a Sage gearbox. Larger cars with 12, 16 and 20hp engines followed in 1903. These, together with lorry and bus chassis, were made in Brush's London branch at Lambeth, but there was a parallel design called the Brushmobile, made at Loughborough. This was nothing more than a 6hp single-cylinder Vauxhall with a different bonnet to distinguish it from the Luton product, and in fact some Brushmobiles were made at Luton.

The last Brush cars were made in 1904 but commercial vehicles were continued until 1910. A subsidiary, Brush Coachwork Ltd of Loughborough, built a large number of bus and coach bodies until 1952, while the electrical engineering side continued to flourish. In 1946 it returned to road vehicles with a range of battery electric vans, which were made until 1968. GNG

BRUSH
USA 1907-1913

The Brush Runabout, as this unusual single-cylinder light car was often called, was designed by Alanson Partridge Brush and put into production by Frank Briscoe, who wanted to emulate the success of his brother Benjamin who was making the Maxwell-Briscoe car. Among the features of the Brush design were left-hand drive – most American cars before the Ford Model T had right-hand drive – counter-clockwise rotation of the engine, wooden axles and frame, and suspension by coil springs all round. The 1907 Brush had a curious friction clutch and no gearbox, but this was replaced by a two-speed planetary transmission the following year. The basic Runabout had solid tyres and cost $500, but pneumatics could be had for $50 extra, and from 1908 there was a 500lb (225kg) delivery van at $600.

At first the Brush Motor Car Co operated from Frank Briscoe's radiator factory in Detroit, but in 1909 he put up a new plant which he said would be the largest single factory in the automobile trade. About 2000 Runabouts and delivery vans were made in 1909, and 10,000 in 1910, the year in which Benjamin Briscoe formed the United States Motor Corporation. Capitalized at $16 million, this was an attempt to rival the recently-formed General Motors combine. It included Maxwell-Briscoe, Brush, Courier, Dayton and Alden-Sampson among its makes as well as about 130 smaller companies, mostly component suppliers.

In 1911 the Brush line was extended to include a closed coupé at $800 and the Titan taxicab, a four-seater landaulette which still used the 8hp single-cylinder engine. The Brush continued to be popular, but production was erratic as finance was juggled between the various companies in the US Motor Corporation.

For 1912 a new, cheaper model, the $350 Liberty-Brush, was announced, and this was the only car to be offered for 1913. US Motors collapsed that year, dragging Brush down with it, and the last cars were completed in the summer of 1913.

Alanson Partridge Brush had already left the company, in 1910 joining Oakland, for which he designed a two-cylinder engine, also with counter-clockwise rotation. He later set up a firm of consulting engineers with his brother William, and made many contributions to car design, including the double transverse rear suspension used on the Marmon 34 (1916-26), Monroe (1919), Saxon-Duplex and other cars, and the Z-section frame stiffened by the running boards, featured by Lexington, Marmon and others. He died in 1952 at the age of 74. GNG

BRÜTSCH
GERMANY 1951-1958

Although the company Egon Brütsch Fahrzeugbau of Stuttgart existed from 1951 to 1957 and built a range of mostly eccentric prototypes, production was never started under the Brütsch name, the only Brütsch cars going into production being built and marketed by others. Egon Brütsch raced bicycles from about 1929 to 1931 and from 1935 to 1950 he raced cars, including such substantial makes as Bugatti and Maserati, but his own designs were mostly for very small three-wheelers, with one-, two- or four-seater bodies.

His first design was the single-seater Eremit (or Hermit) of 1951 but although a prototype of this was built, no production cars appeared. The very similar 400 of 1952 met a similar fate.

In 1953 and 1954 Brütsch worked on the rather larger Brütsch 1200, based on the Ford Taunus 12M but with Brütsch-designed glass-fibre bodywork. Like the others, this car did not reach production and the prototype was the last car actually to use the Brütsch name.

Brütsch's next design, the three-wheeled 49cc single-seater Mopetta of 1956, was possibly the smallest car ever built. It was 5ft 7in (1.7m) long and weighed 134lb (61kg). With a 2hp motor it was claimed to do 28mph (45kph). The Mopetta actually did go into production in 1957, selling for 1050 marks as the Opelit Mopetta after Brütsch had founded Mopetta GmbH in Frankfurt in 1956. Georg von Opel acquired a licence to build the Mopetta but did not take up production. The Mopetta company also developed other Brütsch small car designs, mainly of three-wheelers but including the Pfeil (or Arrow, and actually designed in 1955) and the 1957 V2, all with glassfibre bodywork by Wendler of Reuttingen.

Brütsch was permanently in financial difficulties and it was only the sale of licences which kept the company going. Brütsch designs were built by the Swiss Belcar and French Avolette companies, but plans by Burgfalke to build cars in small numbers came to nothing.

Harald Friedmann, however, built another Brütsch design, the four-wheeled two-seater Spatz, under licence and in March 1956 formed Victoria Motorrad Werke in Nuremberg as part of the Bayerische Autowerke, with capital of 400,000 marks to build the Victoria Spatz. This was the most widely built Brütsch design, with 1487 made between 1956 and 1958, although only 63 examples were built in 1958 as demand collapsed and the company moved on to building motorcycles, as part of the Zweirad-Union. BL

BSA
GB 1907-1939

The Birmingham Small Arms Co was incorporated as a limited company in 1861, but its origins stretch back to a guild of gunsmiths formed during the reign of William III (1689-1702). Its business was the manufacture of rifles, shotguns and machine guns, but in 1880 it began to make bicycles, initially to other people's designs. Its own design of safety cycle appeared in 1885, and apart from a gap between 1888 and 1893, BSA bicycles were made continuously until about 1982, although under the ownership of Raleigh Industries from 1956.

BSA's first involvement with cars came in 1900 when it made components for Roots and Venables. The original factory was at Small Heath, Birmingham, but when car manufacture was planned BSA bought a former government arms factory at Sparkbrook. Manager of the new motor car department was Colonel E. E. Baguley, who had been with Ryknield in Burton-on-Trent. Working under him was Leslie Wilson, who later became secretary of the Midland Automobile Club and organizer of the Shelsley Walsh hillclimb from 1913 to 1958.

The first BSA car was a conventional four-cylinder machine with 18/23hp L-head engine and shaft drive. It went into small-scale production in 1907 but was not released to the press or exhibited at motor shows until the following year. About 150 18/23s were made, and it was joined in 1909 by a smaller 14/18hp, and by a larger 25/33hp which was a close copy of the 40hp Itala. Production of these, together with Drewry railcars, went ahead steadily into 1910, but in December of that year BSA took over Daimler, which was already making a wide range of cars.

The existing BSA range was dropped and Baguley returned to Burton-on-Trent, where he made cars under his own name. The only BSA listed for 1912 had a Daimler-built Knight sleeve-valve engine of 13.9hp and a pressed steel body made at Sparkbrook. An identical

BSA 10hp of 1934

BSA Scout of 1937

car with different radiator was made for Siddeley-Deasy and sold under the name Stoneleigh.

In 1910 BSA motorcycles began to be made in the Small Heath factory, and these soon earned a fine reputation, many seeing service during World War I. The Knight-engined car was not revived but in its place BSA offered a substantial-looking light car powered by an 1100cc vee-twin engine made by Hotchkiss of Coventry. About 2500 were made between 1922 and 1924, when it was replaced by a series of sleeve-valve cars which were, in fact, small Daimlers, distinguishable only by the radiators which were devoid of the Daimler 'flutes', and made at Coventry.

The Sparkbrook factory was turned over to machine tool manufacture, and no more cars came from it. The small role that cars played in the overall BSA picture can be gauged from the fact that in 1924 the area of Sparkbrook was 5 acres (2 hectares) and that of Small Heath more than 48 acres (19 hectares).

The crypto-Daimlers were dropped in 1926, and for three years there were no BSA cars. The company did, however, make a short-lived venture into the radio business in 1926, forming a separate company, BSA Radios Ltd.

In 1929 BSA Cycles Ltd launched an ingenious three-wheeler, designed by F. W. Hulse and powered by a 1021cc vee-twin engine based on the Hotchkiss. This drove the front wheels which were independently sprung by transverse springs. While it lacked the performance of the Morgan, it was a more comfortable three-wheeler and easier to drive, becoming even more civilized when it received a 1075cc four-cylinder engine in 1933. Both two- and four-cylinder three-wheelers were made until 1936, selling about 5200 and 1700 units respectively. There were also four-wheeler derivatives made in smaller numbers (about 100 twins and 300 fours).

In 1933 a new line of BSA cars appeared; this time they were variants on the Lanchester Ten with side-valve engines as opposed to Lanchester's overhead valve. However, the Lanchester's fluid flywheel transmission was retained, and at £230 for a six-light saloon they were the cheapest cars ever offered with this easy-change transmission. Standard saloon bodies were by Pressed Steel, but coachbuilt variants were also available: a

four-light saloon by Holbrook was called the Varsity when offered by BSA, but was also to be found in the Standard range as the Dorchester and in Vauxhall's as the Suffolk. BSA also offered a Light Six variant of the Lanchester with 1378cc overhead-valve engine. All these cars were built by Lanchester.

In 1935 they were joined by the Scout, a four-cylinder front-wheel-drive car made by BSA Cycles, and in the cause of rationalization the fluid flywheel cars were dropped at the end of 1936. The Scout was made up to the outbreak of World War II, an attractive little car with 1075cc engine (1203cc from 1936) which gave 32bhp and a top speed approaching 70mph (112kph) in its final form. It was available as a two- or four-seater sports, coupé or two-door saloon, and about 2700 were made.

Although BSA motorcycles survived into the 1970s, no cars were made after the war. A prototype three-wheeler, the Triumph Tigress-powered Ladybird, was tested in 1960 but never commercialized.

During the 1950s the motorcycle firms Ariel, New Hudson, Sunbeam and Triumph were absorbed into the BSA empire. Guns, small stationary power units and machine tools continued to be made by a variety of subsidiary companies. Motorcycle manufacture lasted until April 1973, and in July of that year the assets were acquired by Dennis Poore's Norton-Villiers-Triumph group. GNG

BUCCIALI
FRANCE 1922-1933

Bucciali two-stroke V4 of 1925

The brothers Angelo and Paul-Albert Bucciali built a couple of racing cars before setting up their own company, Bucciali Frères, in August 1922 with capital of 200,000 francs and a factory in the Paris suburb of Courbevoie. Their first cars used a 1496cc V4 two-stroke engine designed and built by Marcel Violet, but this unit did not prove very satisfactory and in 1925 they opted for a conventional 1.6-litre SCAP engine. About 105 cars were sold between 1925 and 1927.

In 1926 Paul-Albert Bucciali built the first of his front-wheel-drive cars, and this principle was to be his absorbing interest for the rest of his automotive career. SCAP four- and eight-cylinder engines were offered in the first of these TAV (Traction Avant) cars, but it is likely that only one four-cylinder car was built. A CIME six-cylinder engine powered the TAV 2 which also had Sensaud de Lavaud swash plate transmission. At most six of these were made, for Bucciali's ambitions to produce the ultimate luxury car led him to ever larger power units. These included a few 4-litre supercharged Mercedes-Benz engines, but mostly six- or straight-eight Continentals built in France by Hotchkiss.

Mystery surrounds the sixteen-cylinder *Double Huit* Bucciali, for the only survivor turned out to have a dummy engine stuffed with old newspapers. However, there may have been one or two others, which may have used Peerless sixteen-cylinder engines, as the Bucciali brothers were the Paris dealers for Peerless for a while, and the engines could have been supplied instead of cash when the Cleveland firm was paying off its creditors.

The last two Bucciali cars, known as TAV 12s, used V12 Voisin engines and were made in 1933. Total production of the front-drive Bucciali was about 38. In 1934 the brothers planned to make a four-wheel-drive sports coupé, but it was never built.

More successful was Paul-Albert's work on *gazogène* conversion, and had not the German invasion intervened, he might have seen to fruition a proposal to convert all French Army vehicles to *gazogène*. After the war he worked for Cotal, the gearbox manufacturer, for a number of years, and in 1957 he formed the Société de Mécanique et des Brevets Bucciali, which purchased Cotal. He died in 1981 at the age of 91. GNG

BUCHET
FRANCE 1911-1930

The Société Buchet was formed at Levallois-Perret in 1888 to make an electric arc lamp invented by E. V. Buchet. Production of petrol engines began in about 1899, when it was also making full overhead-valve conversions of De Dion's inlet-over-exhaust valve engines. In 1901 it built the engines for Santos Dumont's airship, and over the next few years supplied engines to at least 23 car-makers in France, Britain, Belgium and Austria. In 1902 the company made a monstrous racing tricycle powered by a 4245cc air-cooled vertical twin, but its engines were mostly smaller than this, and included some single-cylinder units for cyclecars. However, in 1906 it made a V8 aero engine.

The first complete Buchet car was a four-cylinder taxicab of 1910, followed by cars for private use in 1911. This was a conventional 12/16hp side-valve four of 2176cc capacity, joined by 1100cc and 1½-litre cars in 1913. The former was exported to England in chassis form, there to be fitted with bodies by the Hollingdrake company of Southport and sold under the name Ascot. This lasted from 1914 to 1915 only.

In 1919 Buchet was purchased by Gaston Sailly and the company name changed to Gaston Sailly Moteurs et Automobiles Buchet, with a new factory at Billancourt. During the 1920s a range of six conventional cars was made, ranging from an 1100cc four to a 1730cc six, made in 1928 and 1929 only. Overhead valves and front-wheel brakes came in 1924.

In the mid-1920s annual production ran at about 300 of the 1100cc cars and 100 to 150 of the 1½-litre. About 60 to 70 sixes were made all told. Production probably ended in 1930, although the make was carried on some lists as late as 1932. GNG

BUCKINGHAM/HAMARD
AUSTRALIA 1933-1934

Drastic, ostensibly protective, import tariffs in Australia in the early 1930s prompted several attempts to establish domestic car manufacture using Australian materials and labour as far as possible. Such a venture was undertaken by long-established motor engineers J. T. Buckingham and A. T. Ward of Victoria, who announced their intention to build an Australian car in 1931.

Production was to be based in Melbourne and the car, planned to sell for £400, was to be called the Hamard Six (from the last letters of the two names). It was to be an American-style car but built entirely in Australia. A new company, Buckingham & Ward Motors Pty (Australia) Ltd, was set up in Footscray, Victoria, with £10,000 from shareholders.

Initially, two cars were to be built under the scrutiny of time and motion experts to give production cost estimates for raising further capital. The first chassis were made by Mephan and Ferguson, castings were from the United Engineering and Malleable Co and gears were supplied by the Richardson Gear Co.

Buckingham & Ward took over the foundry and engineering works of Hamble & Sons Pty Ltd of Geelong, and at least one Buckingham Sixty was made – the Hamard name having been dropped. The first chassis was shown at the International Motor Show in Melbourne in June 1933 and subsequently underwent 30,000 miles (48,280km) of testing. In July it was evaluated by the Post Office authorities and a prospectus was issued soliciting capital to change from assembly to manufacture. The company sought nominal capital of £500,000 and proposed selling cars for between £225 and £295.

In October 1934 Buckingham & Ward announced that it would build the Buckingham with help in production of forgings and pressings from the government munitions works at Maribyrnong. The company started building four-cylinder cars and went on to sixes, but very few cars were built, the Australian public preferring to buy imports in spite of the levies, and the company closed in 1934. BL

BUGATTI
GERMANY, FRANCE 1909-1956

Ettore Bugatti was born in Milan in September 1881, and by the age of 18 he was competing successfully in races on a twin-engined tricycle. He designed and built a four-cylinder car in 1901 and subsequently worked as a designer for De Dietrich at Niederbronn, Alsace (1902-4), Emile Mathis at Graffenstaden, Alsace (1904-6), and Deutz at Cologne (1907-9). While working for Deutz he designed and built – it is said in the cellar of his house which was, in fact, inside the Deutz premises – a small car with four-cylinder eight-valve 1208cc engine and shaft drive. This was the prototype of the cars which Bugatti began to manufacture in 1910 after he had resigned from Deutz.

In December 1909 he rented a disused dye works at Molsheim, Alsace; machinery began to arrive in January 1910, and the first production car, with 1327cc engine, was delivered to a customer a few months later. Only five cars were made in 1910, but the following year 75 were delivered and the workforce had grown to 65 men.

Also in 1911 Bugatti built a smaller car with 855cc four-cylinder engine and a curious transmission with two concentric propeller shafts providing the two forward speeds. Apparently he had no intention of manufacturing this design; he offered it first to Wanderer in Germany and then to Peugeot, which took it up and manufactured it as the famous Bébé Peugeot. The company made 3095 examples from 1912 to 1914.

Meanwhile, Bugatti cars had begun to appear in racing, driven by his partner Ernst Friderich who won his class in the 1911 Grand Prix de France. In 1913 came a much larger car, with 5-litre engine and chain drive, the prototype of which Bugatti had completed in 1910. It is historically important as the engine had three valves per cylinder (two inlet, one exhaust), anticipating the three-valve Type 30 and Type 37 engines of the 1920s, but only seven of these large cars were made.

Production of the smaller cars, known as the Type 13, went ahead steadily in the years up to World War I, reaching 12 a month at the beginning of 1913, and 19 a month at the end of the year. About 345 had been built by the outbreak of World War I.

It seems that the Molsheim works was idle during the war as the machinery had been removed for the German war effort. (Alsace was a German province from 1871 to 1918, so all pre-1919 Bugattis were German cars.) Bodies were mostly by Gangloff of Colmar who did a lot of work on Bugattis right up to 1939, and also by some small firms like Durr of Colmar and Fossier of Strasbourg.

Ettore Bugatti and his family spent the war in Paris where he supervised the design of

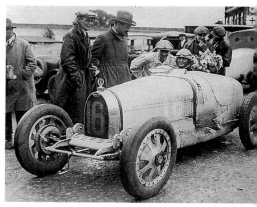

Bugatti Type 35 of c.1929

aero engines. The most famous of these was the sixteen-cylinder double bank 500hp engine which was made by Duesenberg Motors Corporation of Elizabeth, New Jersey. At the end of 1918 he returned to Molsheim, which was now once again in French territory, and restarted production of the Type 13 and its successor, the sixteen-valve model which came to be known as the Brescia after Friderich's victory in the 1921 Grand Prix des Voiturettes at Brescia.

About 2000 Brescias were made until 1926, and the model had the distinction of being the only Bugatti car design to be built under licence in foreign countries. Crossley in England, Rabag in Germany and Diatto in Italy all took out licences to manufacture the Brescia between 1919 and 1925, although not more than 25 cars were made by any of these firms. Rabag (Rheinische Automobilbau AG) was

Bugatti Type 41 Royale prototype of c.1926

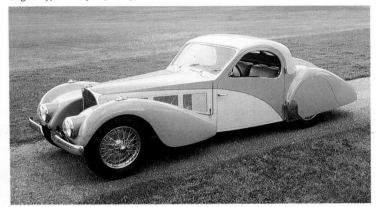

Bugatti Type 57SC Atlantic coupé of 1937

Bugatti Type 43 of 1927

Because of the railcars, the workforce rose to 1400 and this came at a very opportune time for Bugatti, as sales of its cars were badly hit by the Depression. The position was hardly helped by the fact that it was offering six different models, all of them expensive straight-eights. In addition Ettore Bugatti had made a number of unwise property speculations, and his personal and corporate prosperity of the 1920s was seriously eroded. In 1936 the Bugatti factory, in common with most others in France, suffered a serious strike. The autocratic Ettore was so offended that he retired from Molsheim to Paris (in 1939 he even considered transferring all production from Molsheim to Belgium), leaving

formed specifically to make Bugattis, and produced no other models, but for Crossley and Diatto the venture was a small sideline to their general production.

A 2-litre straight-eight Type 30 joined the Brescia in 1922, giving Bugatti an entry into the higher priced market and beginning a line of straight-eights which it was to make until the end of production. The Type 35 was the most successful racing car of the inter-war period and the only car capable of winning Grands Prix which could also be bought by the amateur. In 1926 the Type 35 won 12 major Grands Prix, and in 1927 Bugatti claimed to have won 2000 sporting events, although this figure presumably includes the successes of the Brescia.

Two four-cylinder models followed, the Type 37 1½-litre racing car for those who could not afford a Type 35, and the touring Type 40, nicknamed 'Ettore's Morris Cowley' because of its modest price and relatively low performance by Bugatti standards. About 830 Type 40s were made between 1926 and 1931, making it the third largest selling model after the Brescia and the Type 44 3-litre straight-eight.

Bugatti started building bodywork with the extraordinary 'tank' bodies on the 1923 Grand Prix cars. The beautiful Type 35 bodies were almost certainly made at Molsheim and by 1927 he had a fully fledged body shop, though Gangloff remained an important supplier of coachwork.

In complete contrast to the Type 40 was the Type 41, known as La Royale. Bugatti first

conceived the idea of building a supercar to outdo all possible rivals in 1913, but it was not until 1926 that his dream became a reality. The first car had a straight-eight engine of nearly 15 litres capacity developing a claimed 300hp at 1700rpm, but its successor used a slightly scaled-down unit of 12,763cc and 250hp. Although Bugatti claimed that King Alfonso XIII had ordered one, no Royales were sold to royalty, and of the six cars made, only three were ever sold, the others remaining with the Bugatti family.

It would be fair to describe the Royale episode – it took seven years to sell even the three cars – as Ettore's greatest folly, except that the left-over Royale engines formed the basis of a new business. A batch of 30 had been built, and even before the last car had been delivered it was obvious that an alternative use would have to be found for them. Ettore decided to enter the high speed railcar field, and with typical enthusiasm built extensions to the factory, transferred men from car production and devoted every effort to the new project.

The work began in 1930 and by the summer of 1933 the first Bugatti railcar went into service on the Paris-Deauville run. Two types were made, the 'light' using two engines, and the 'double' using four engines; bodies were by Gangloff. The batch of 24 car engines was soon used up, and between 1933 and 1939 a total of 186 engines and 79 railcars were built. They gave excellent service on a number of routes and the last was not withdrawn until 1958.

his 27-year-old son, Jean, in charge. In Paris he designed aircraft and boats.

It was Jean who was largely responsible for the last serious production Bugatti, the Type 57, with 3.3-litre twin-cam straight-eight engine. This was introduced in 1934 as competition for the other French *grands routiers* by Delage, Delahaye and Talbot. It was more refined than most previous Bugattis, offering comfort and modern lines as well as speed. The bodies were styled by Jean Bugatti, the closed models being made at Molsheim, and the open ones by Gangloff at Colmar. The 57 was also available as a chassis for outside coachbuilders to work on.

Supercharged models were available from 1937 to 1939 and a total of 683 Type 57s were made between 1934 and 1939. The Type 57's best year was 1936, despite the strike, when 149 cars were delivered, but by 1939 sales were down to 52. Bugatti was virtually a one-model company during this period, although a few of the large 5.3-litre straight-eight Type 46 were still being sold off up to 1936.

In August 1939 Jean was killed while testing a racing car near Molsheim, and less than a month later war broke out. Once again Molsheim had to contribute to the German war effort. This time the factory was divided into two parts, 'Trippel Werke' where amphibious cars were made, and 'Kriegsmarine' for the manufacture of torpedoes.

Ettore moved to Bordeaux where he continued all sorts of design projects including a small car powered by a 370cc twin-cam four-cylinder engine, of which only one was built.

After the war he and his younger son, Roland, worked on the Type 73, a 1½-litre overhead-cam touring and racing car. The Molsheim factory had not yet been returned to the family and development of the Type 73 went ahead in the La Licorne factory in Paris which Bugatti owned. Few complete cars were made and Ettore Bugatti's death in August 1947 put an end to the project.

In 1951 an up-dated Type 57 was put into production at Molsheim under the direction of Pierre Marco, but only about 20 were made. The company struggled several times to return to car manufacturing. In 1956 it produced a singularly unsuccessful Grand Prix car, and in 1963 Automobiles Bugatti was acquired by Hispano-Suiza, once a great car-maker itself, but by then involved with diesel and aircraft engines. It was later absorbed by SNECMA, the French nationalized aerospace industries combine, and the factory continues to make aircraft parts. GNG

BUICK/MARQUETTE
USA 1903 to date

David Dunbar Buick was born in Scotland in 1854 and at the age of two emigrated with his parents to the United States. After peddling newspapers in his schooldays in Detroit he joined the same engineering firm as Henry Ford and then got into the plumbing business where he developed a way of coating cast iron baths. In about 1900 he developed an engine that was sold to neighbouring Detroit firms by his Buick Auto-Vim and Power Co. He is believed to have developed an experimental car that was sold in 1901 to Walter L. Marr, the firm's chief engineer. Another early designer at Buick was Eugene Richard, formerly of Olds.

In 1902 the newly formed Buick Manufacturing Co took over the former Buick company but quickly ran into difficulties and was reorganized by the Briscoe brothers with $100,000 capital as the Buick Motor Co in May 1903. They soon lost interest and sold out to a wagon-builder in Flint.

The first production Buick, a horizontal twin with overhead valves and planetary transmission, appeared in 1903. A handful may have been made that year – estimates of 16 seem optimistic – and were reputedly followed in 1904 by 37 produced in a new 20,000sq ft (1858sq m) factory by a workforce of 50 men. Engines were also made for other car companies in the first few years.

William C. Durant of Durant-Dort wagons was impressed and raised investment in Buick to $1.5 million in 1904-5 and became chairman. Profits of $400,000 were earned on 1400 cars worth $2 million in 1906, but David Buick had soon had enough of the dynamic new regime. In 1910 he was advertising for investors to exploit the 'oil-bearing' land he had bought, but this, like all his subsequent endeavours, proved unsuccessful. For a time he ran Lorraine Motors of Grand Rapids, which made funeral and private cars, but he died in obscurity in 1929.

Fours had been added at Buick, followed by the famous 'square' 20hp of 1908, when 8487 cars were built. Durant created General Motors in September that year and promptly purchased Buick on 1 October.

Arthur and Louis Chevrolet worked for Durant and raced Buicks. The works manager, William H. Little, like Louis Chevrolet, wanted to make cars under his own name and both men were set up in business by Durant after he lost control of General Motors in 1910. C. W. Nash was briefly in charge at Buick before becoming president of General Motors and then acquiring Rambler. He was succeeded at Buick in 1912 by another budding motor magnate, Walter P. Chrysler.

Buick production in 1910 totalled 30,525 from 6500 men and rose to 44,000 cars a year by 1915. In 1913 the factory was described as the largest under one roof, the machine shop alone covering 6 acres (2.5 hectares), and Buicks were usually second or third in the American sales charts. Buick made virtually all its own parts and bought from component suppliers which were either General Motors-owned or in which it held stock options. Planetary transmission was discontinued in 1911, by which time Buicks were popular in both Britain and Canada, being assembled and bodied as British Bedfords then Bedford-Buicks in Britain, and by McLaughlin in Canada.

Buicks gradually grew in size and cost (and profitability) in order to escape Durant's fixation with a $1000 price ceiling. Apart from the fours to 1909, all had overhead valve engines. Sixes came in 1914. Two years later production reached almost 125,000 for third place behind Ford and Willys-Overland. Car output at a reduced rate continued during World War I – 115,000 in 1917 and 75,000 in 1918 – when 2500 Liberty aero engines were built in collaboration with Packard.

When General Motors was reeling in the post-war recession Buick helped to keep it

Buick Six tourer of 1924

Buick Roadmaster of 1936

Buick four-seater of 1906

Buick Electra Park Avenue of 1979

Buick Le Sabre of 1968

Buick Somerset Regal of 1985

afloat with its profitable 3.9-litre sixes and 2.8-litre fours. Average sales were around 100,000 cars, rising to 200,000 from 1923 when the millionth car left the line; the next million took just five years to achieve.

The Buick stand at the 1922 New York Show displayed one of the first 'bright' post-war cars, a red roadster, and front-wheel brakes were standardized in 1924. 'When better automobiles are built Buick will build them' became a famous slogan, and the new Packard-like radiator shape from 1925 strengthened middle-class respect for the marque. In 1926 sales reached 267,000, but an unfortunate styling aberration by General Motors led to the 'Pregnant Buick' of 1929, which proved to be a costly mistake.

In mid-1929 a name from General Motors' past was revived for a cheaper companion line to Buick. The Marquette had been the name adopted by General Motors in 1912 for the former Rainier and Welch cars, but had lasted only a year. It was little more enduring in the Depression, although 35,000 were sold before the 213cu in six was dropped in 1930. F. A. 'Dutch' Bower now became chief engineer and his straight-eight engines for 1931 remained a Buick hallmark until 1953.

Sales slumped to 41,500 in 1932, after which the sales operations of Buick, Oldsmobile and Pontiac were merged to cut overheads and streamline efficiency. Harlow 'Red' Curtice inaugurated a new regime that was to replace model numbers with dynamic names and make Buick the General Motors front-runner in terms of styling and performance. He spent $65 million improving production facilities up to World War II and added 2 million sq ft (185,000sq m) of production space soon after.

Charles A Chayne, the new chief engineer in 1936, was responsible for the adoption two years later of coil springs all round, the Dyna-flash engine and semi-automatics. Hydramatic was introduced in 1939 followed by the Fireball engine in 1941. A total of 316,250 cars were sold in 1941 and 16,600 the following year before the Buick factories reorganized to concentrate on military orders.

In 1948 the five millionth Buick was sold and a torque converter (Dynaflow Drive) was offered for the first time, soon accounting for three-quarters of all sales. The successful regime of Curtice ended that year and Ivan Wiles took over. The 'mouseholes' in the bonnet which would become as much a Buick trade mark as the straight-eight arrived soon afterwards, being the work of E. F. Nickles, chief designer for 12 years from 1947. When Chayne was promoted to GM Engineering's vice-presidency, Verne P. Matthews took his place in 1951 and was involved with the new overhead valve V8 in 1953.

Sales reached a record 553,000 in 1950 and then more than 780,000 in 1955 for third place behind Chevrolet and Ford. But a slide to 257,000 in 1958 required decisive action. Famous old names such as Roadmaster and Century were replaced by Electra, Invicta and Le Sabre with relatively restrained 'fin era' styling and massive V8s giving up to 300bhp. The names Riviera and Skylark from 1948 and 1953 lived on, the former on the industry's first mass-produced hardtop convertible. The 'Special' tag, first used before the war, was revived in 1961 for a new aluminium 3½-litre V8-engined car. In 1962 an iron V6 shared with Oldsmobile was adopted. Five years after the aluminium engine was dropped in 1963, when 750,000 had been made, Rover took up its production in Britain.

Car sales had recovered under Edward Rollert's direction from 1959, reaching 654,000 in 1965. They were helped from 1963 by the Riviera, widely held to be America's most attractive car which was to include versions giving up to 340bhp from 7 litres. The market was extremely volatile, however, in the 1970s. Sales of 826,000 in 1973 plummeted to 400,000 in 1974 before climbing again.

In the 1970s the typical Buick became smaller, and the convertibles that had been such a feature of the range were no longer produced after 1976. The Buick-Opel sales network marketed the Gemini, specially built by Isuzu, in 1976. In 1979 the Riviera became a relative of the Oldsmobile Toronado with front-wheel drive, and a year later there was the front-wheel-drive Skylark version of the Chevrolet Citation. The Skyhawk, a four-cylinder, 2-litre version of the General Motors 'World Car', appeared in 1982, by which time most larger Buicks were using a petrol or diesel V6, although 5-litre petrol and 5.7-litre diesels were also available.

Buick achieved record sales in 1984 with the Century being 10th in the US sales league. Four new models were introduced that year: the Electra, the Electra T Type, the Park Avenue and the sporty Somerset Regal, a four-seater two-door model of medium size. The 1986 range was similar, although the Buick Division no longer offered a diesel engine. Production in 1985 topped one million. NB

BURNEY
GB 1930-1933

Born in 1888, Sir Charles Dennistoun Burney achieved fame as the designer of the R100 airship which was built by the Airship Guarantee Co Ltd in 1929. His first car was, in fact, assembled at the airship station at Howden, Yorkshire. It had a streamlined aeroplane-type saloon body with all-independent suspension and a 12/75 Alvis engine mounted at the rear; the chassis was that of a front-wheel-drive Alvis turned back to front, with the steering locked, and the dead rear axle of the Alvis replaced by a conventional steering axle.

This prototype was completed in 1928, but 'production' Burney Streamlines were made from 1930 by Streamline Cars Ltd at Maidenhead, in the famous 'Jam Factory' where it shared premises with GWK and Impéria Motors Ltd. Burney did not envisage serious production here, for there was not the space, but 12 cars were assembled, nine using the 3-litre straight-eight Beverley engine, two the Armstrong-Siddeley 20hp six and one, which went to America as a demonstrator, a Lycoming straight-eight. They followed the same lines as the prototype, with very long, narrow bodies and stubby little bonnets with the option of a dummy radiator or a plain front.

At a price of £1500 they could not have expected to find many buyers, even though the Prince of Wales ran one briefly. In 1933 Burney sold his patents to Crossley, which made about 25 Crossley-Burneys powered by its own 2-litre engine. These were made at Stockport, and although Streamline Cars remained in business for several years longer, its work was purely experimental. GNG

BUSH
see Birch

BUTZ
see Gutbrod

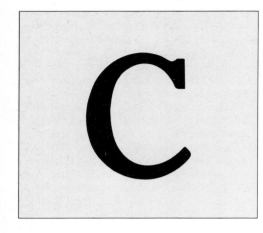

CADILLAC/LA SALLE
USA 1903 to date

Henry Martyn Leland, born in 1843, gained early experience in arms factories including Colt before joining the Brown and Sharpe tool and sewing machine firm. He set up an engineering company in Detroit in 1890 with his son Wilfred and partners Norton and Faulconer and in 1896 began to build engines. These were supplied to Olds, for which a single-cylinder motor was developed but not adopted. A customer was needed urgently.

At the Detroit Automobile Co, formed in 1899, the chief engineer was Henry Ford. Experimental vehicles were built until 1901, when a Ford two-cylinder design briefly entered production. After disagreements, Ford left the company and the remaining directors sold out to Leland in August 1902. A. P. Brush redesigned the Detroit to accept the single-cylinder Leland and Faulconer engine, and with its planetary gearbox it became an immediate success, 2500 selling by the end of 1903. In 1904 Leland and Faulconer joined forces with the Cadillac Automobile Co to create the Cadillac Motor Car Co. The name came from Antoine de la Mothe Cadillac, who had founded Ville D'etroit – which became Detroit – in 1701.

Early cars were extremely well made but very basic. Output for 1905 made Cadillac second only to Olds as the world's largest producer, and a year later the company claimed to have the biggest car factory in the world.

Fours had joined the singles in 1905 and the new four-cylinder 30 of 1909 replaced all previous models. In July that year William C. Durant acquired Cadillac for his General Motors Co, paying some $5.7 million. In 1910 closed Fleetwood bodies were used on nearly 10 per cent of the 8000 output. Towards the end of 1911 C. F. Kettering's Delco electric self starter became a standard fitment and in 1913 electric starting, lighting and ignition won Cadillac a Dewar Trophy from the Royal Automobile Club for engineering excellence.

In 1914 production totalled 14,000 and a 5.1-litre V8 was the first of this configuration to enter quantity production. The 5.6-litre fours were dropped and 13,000 V8s sold in 1915, followed by 18,000 in both 1916 and 1917, when Cadillac became the standard US Army officers' car.

Durant, like Ford a pacifist, had banned war material production in General Motors factories; but after Leland left Cadillac to develop the Liberty aero engine, Durant had a change of heart and 1157 V8 artillery tractor engines plus aero engines were made by Cadillac. Leland afterwards developed the Lincoln luxury car and sold the project to Ford.

At this stage Cadillac cars were technically advanced, well made and powerful. They were intended to simplify driving rather than appeal to the luxury market, where Packard held sway.

Having averaged annual sales of about 20,000 in the four years from 1917, Cadillac slumped to 5250 in 1921, so a decision was taken at General Motors to move the Cadillac, one of the few profitable areas of the group, up in price and specification. The inherently unbalanced V8 was given a completely redesigned crankshaft, which was developed at great expense in 1923 to enable it to equal Packard's straight-eight. Much of this was the work of William R. Strickland, who had worked on the Peerless V8 and became a vice-president of that firm.

Duco nitrocellulose paint was pioneered by Oakland and Cadillac in 1924, and in 1925 L. P. Fisher from Fisher Body became manager and bought the Fleetwood Custom Body Co. Cadillac had established a new factory at Clark Avenue, Detroit, in 1920 and $5 million was spent on modernization in 1925.

Ernest Seaholm had succeeded Benjamin Anibal as chief engineer in 1920 and was to hold the post until 1943. Frank Johnson was his engine designer until he left for Lincoln. With Harley J. Earl, a young stylist brought in by Fisher, Johnson developed in 1927 a cheaper V8 line which was named La Salle after the French explorer of Illinois. Production leapt from 20,419 in 1926 to 47,420 in 1927. The world's first synchromesh transmission, designed by Harley Thompson, was adopted in 1928 and safety glass also came as a standard fitment for the first time, followed by chrome plating.

Johnson's successor as engine designer was Owen Nacker whose 7.4-litre V16, modestly rated at 165hp and announced in December 1929, took the luxury market by storm. A V12 based on the V16 was introduced in September 1930. Although 41,000 Cadillacs and La Salles had been sold in the 1929 season, the Depression caused sales to fall to 30,000 in 1931 and plummet to an average of only 10,000 a year for the next four years. Yet innovation proceeded. Power brakes were introduced in 1931, ride regulator in 1932, 'no draft' ventilation in 1933, independent suspension and hidden spare wheel in 1934 when the La Salle was demoted to Olds's straight-eight engine, and 'turret top' all-steel bodies made their début on 1935 stock models.

In 1936 a new thin-walled iron V8 helped Cadillac sales overtake Packard. In that year almost half of all US sales of cars over $1500 were from Cadillac. Total sales of 26,000 rose to 46,153 in 1937, a figure not to be exceeded until 1941 when 66,130 cars were sold.

In 1938 running boards were finally deleted

Cadillac Model A of 1903

from the 60 Special, and three years later, having proved itself on cheaper General Motors cars, Hydramatic came to Cadillac. At the end of 1939 all but the V8s were discontinued, as was the La Salle the following year; it had had a V8 once more from 1937 and was selling well, but it was no longer a worthwhile marketing strategy as small Cadillacs could command higher prices.

Car production was suspended in February 1942 as Cadillac factories began the building of thousands of light tanks and gun carriages with V8 engines and Hydramatic. J. F. Gordon, who had been responsible for the final V16, took over as chief engineer in 1943 and then as general manager in 1946 on Nicholas

year for sales was 1969, when 266,798 cars were sold, helped by the success of the front-wheel-drive Eldorado of 1967 which notched up nearly 350,000 sales in a 10-year model run. It featured front disc brakes and self-levelling suspension with torsion bar independent front suspension. The V8s reached a peak of 8.2 litres in 1970 but the compact, unitary construction Seville of 1975 gave a pointer to the future of 'gas guzzlers' even in the top price range. Production in 1973 of 307,698 fell to 230,649 the following year and recovered only slowly.

The Eldorado ceased in 1976 and engine size diminished rapidly. There was even a diesel from Oldsmobile with British CAV in-

jection equipment available from 1978, a V6 for 1981 and a four-cylinder 1.8 (then 2-litre) front-wheel-drive car, the Cimarron, based on the General Motors J-car. A feature of the V8s, which had digital fuel injection, was their ability to run on four, six or eight cylinders. In 1984 two new models, the De Ville and the Fleetwood Sedan, were introduced, being Cadillac versions of the General Motors 'C cars'. Total car production for 1985 was 368,157. New for 1987 was the Allante, a $50,000 convertible whose bodies were built by Pininfarina in Italy and flown to Detroit for assembly with chassis and engine. Cadillac described this as the world's longest production line. NB

Cadillac 'Inside Drive' limousine of 1914

Cadillac La Salle coupé of 1935

Cadillac V8 convertible of 1954

Dreystadt's elevation to run Chevrolet.

A new overhead-valve oversquare V8, soon to feature in Allards, came into use in 1948, when fins made a tentative appearance. On 25 November 1949 the millionth Cadillac was produced and the following year annual car production exceeded 100,000 for the first time. Power steering was made standard on all models in 1954 and in 1957 the Eldorado Brougham was the first to have air suspension. The General Motors X-frame was used by Cadillac from that year until the perimeter frame was introduced 10 years later.

Throughout the 1960s Cadillac factories underwent continual expansion. The best

Cadillac Eldorado coupé of 1985

Calcott two-seater of 1916

CALCOTT
GB 1913-1926

Calcott Brothers and West was founded in Coventry in 1886 and in its early years made bicycles and roller skates. Enoch J. West departed for Progress Cycles, later making the Progress car and then the West from 1904 at his own components firm in Foleshill. His company made chassis for numerous small firms and built the Ranger cyclecar shortly before World War I.

Meanwhile, William and James Calcott together with James's father Jim formed a limited company in 1896 and did good business producing bicycles for the trade to sell under various names. Their company also made components and became exclusive subcontractor to Siddeley-Deasy. A factory in Far Gosford Street had replaced the original sheds and 120 to 150 were employed there in good years.

Motorcycles with White and Poppe or the company's own engines were made from 1910 to 1915, and in 1913 a 10.5hp car with a Calcott engine was produced. This had a radiator shape reminiscent of the Standard and was designed by Arthur Alderson, who had been with Singer and would later leave Calcott to design the first Cluley cars and the 1919 Lea-Francis.

A profit of £2243 was earned in the first year of car production and in 1914, when vans, cars, motorcycles and bicycles were offered, the figure rose to £10,032 and then £16,124 in 1915. Cars appear to have been made for the army until 1917, along with all sorts of other war material.

The war was followed by three very successful years when 10 and 12hp cars were produced. During this time high dividends were paid – 40 per cent in 1922 – but while the shareholders were being kept sweet, machinery was badly in need of replacement.

When L. J. Shorter arrived from Humber in 1924 to design the next generation of Calcott cars the machinery could not cope with the fine tolerances required. The 12/24 gained a notorious reputation for broken back axles, every one having to be replaced at considerable cost to Calcott. Although chassis frames were bought in from Mechans of Scotstoun most other parts were made by the Calcott company itself.

A 16hp model was produced in 1925 and a 24hp six was planned, but in 1926 the money ran out. When the shareholders were asked for £30,850 only £12,000 was forthcoming. Singer bought the factory in 1926, the spares going to R. H. Collier to help maintain the 2500 cars that had been made. All the company's liabilities were paid off in full. The factory was empty during the 1930s and was sold to a paint firm for £20,000 in 1939. It is still in use today. NB

CALTHORPE/HANDS, MOBILE
GB 1905-1926

One of the better quality British light cars, the Calthorpe was the product of a Birmingham company which grew out of the cycle industry. George W. Hands set up in business in the 1890s as Hands and Cake, the name being changed to the Bard Cycle Manufacturing Co Ltd in 1897. Four years later he founded the Minstrel Cycle Co and in 1904 began manufacture of a cheaper bicycle, the Rea (named after a local river), in the former Bard factory. The Minstrel and Rea Cycle Co was formed in October 1905, but meanwhile Hands had launched a light car, the 10hp four-cylinder Calthorpe, which made its public appearance at the Agricultural Hall Show in February 1905.

Few 10hp Calthorpes were made, but in July 1905 a slightly larger car with 12/14hp White and Poppe four-cylinder engine was introduced, and this remained in production for three years. The early Calthorpe cars were made in the same Barn Street, Birmingham, factory as the bicycles, but in 1906 the Calthorpe Motor Co became limited, with capital of £5000, and car production was moved to new premises at Cherrywood Road, Bordesley Green, Birmingham, where it remained for the rest of the company's life.

The Minstrel and Rea Cycle Co Ltd stayed at Barn Street; it introduced motorcycles in 1909 and later changed its name to the Calthorpe Motor Cycle Co Ltd. As such it outlived the cars by more than 13 years.

The 1907 range consisted of the 12/14 and a 28/40hp, also using a White and Poppe engine. In March of that year another Birmingham firm was bought, the Mobile Motor and Engineering Co Ltd, which had made light cars since 1903. Mobile's manager Louis Antweiler joined Calthorpe and was a director until the firm's closure. Owners of Mobiles were assured that Calthorpe would supply them with spare parts, but the single- and two-cylinder Mobiles were not continued. For 1908 Calthorpe's new model had a 16/20hp

Calthorpe 10.4hp of c.1922

Alpha engine. They were good looking cars with rounded bonnets and radiators, and a cab version was offered in 1909 on a new 12/14hp chassis.

Together with larger firms such as Vauxhall and Sunbeam, Calthorpe supported the Coupe de l'Auto races in France from 1909 to 1912 with modified versions of its production cars, though with no great success. By 1912 it was making its own 16/20hp four-cylinder engines, and a new company was formed, the Calthorpe Motor Co (1912) Ltd, with issued capital of £70,000. An important new model was the 9.5hp Calthorpe Minor, launched in November 1913. This was a beautifully-made light car which put the company on the map to a greater extent than the larger cars had done. Bodies were mostly made by Mulliners of Birmingham, and in 1917 Calthorpe bought up this firm, taking possession as soon as government contracts were completed in 1918. Calthorpe's wartime production was devoted to mines and grenades.

In 1919 a holding company, Calthorpe Investments Ltd, was formed to acquire the share capital of Calthorpe Motor Co (1912) Ltd and Mulliners Ltd. Post-war production was concentrated on one model, the 10.4hp, which could be fitted with sporting aluminium bodies by Calthorpe, or coachbuilt ones by Mulliners. The 10.4 became very popular, and at the peak of production in 1921 as many as 50 cars a week were being made by a workforce of 1200, but the success of Morris hit sales of Calthorpes as it did those of many other firms.

George Hands left the company in 1921 to make a light car of his own called the Hands. This was assembled in the Barn Street premises of the Calthorpe Motor Cycle Co, by now a separate concern, and used a 9.8hp Dorman engine and Wrigley gearbox. Hands also owned a garage and the Palace Hotel at Torquay, but was not successful as a car manufacturer on his own and he returned to Calthorpe in 1923.

The 10.4 was joined for that year by a new 12/20 designed by Hugh Rose, who was later responsible for the high-camshaft Riley Nine and Lea-Francis engines. Another new model was a 15hp six which Hands had originally planned to make under his own name, but hardly any of these were built. Production of the 12/20 never reached the heady figures of 1921, and the Bordesley Green factory closed suddenly towards the end of 1924. A number of 12/20s remained unsold, and these were used to pay off creditors.

Attempts were made to keep the firm going and although Hands announced the formation of a new company with nominal capital of £30,000 there is no record of this company trading. Calthorpe had a stand at the 1925 Olympia Motor Show on which three cars were shown, including one of the ephemeral sixes, but they were old stock and the public did not show sufficient interest to justify restarting production. In January 1926 the business was offered for sale as a going concern,

but there were no takers, and three months later the factory was put up for sale. The older part was sold for £9700 and the newer withdrawn at £14,000.

In June 1926 Calthorpe Motor Supplies Ltd was formed, but although it advertised 10/20 and 12/20 models as late as 1928, none were made. The unsold portion of the factory was eventually bought by Colmore for use as a Morris service centre.

The Calthorpe Motor Cycle Co continued in production until 1938, when it went into liquidation. It was bought by Bruce Douglas who intended to restart manufacture, but was prevented from doing so by the onset of war. Mulliners also survived the collapse of the Calthorpe Motor Co, becoming a supplier of coachwork to such companies as Standard and Lanchester. It was taken over by Standard-Triumph in 1957, and closed in 1960. Although the coachbuilding Mulliners were all related, there was no business connection between the Birmingham firm and Arthur Mulliner of Northampton or H. J. Mulliner of London. GNG

CAMERON
USA 1902-1921

Cameron air-cooled six of c.1909

Everett S. Cameron began his career in the bicycle trade and in 1901 developed a car which the ex-mayor of Pawtucket, Rhode Island, put into production in 1902 at his Brown Textile Machine Co, founded in 1829. About 1800 air-cooled shaft-driven light cars were made in the first five years. In 1905 the newly established Cameron Car Co moved to Brockton, Massachusetts, where larger cars with gearboxes in-unit with the back axle were made in the former Marsh Motor Co factory.

In 1908 there was another move, this time to the Beverly Manufacturing Co plant at Beverly, Massachusetts. Cameron as general manager set the target for 1 September 1909 to 1 July 1910 at 5000 air-cooled cars, split between Beverly and a factory at New London, Connecticut, which specialized in six-cylinder models. A batch of 100 cars was also built in 1909 by the Brown Cotton Gin Co, probably at Pawtucket. Use was also made of a plant at Attica, Ohio, and a factory at West Haven, Connecticut. Water-cooled cars under the name Yale Flyer joined the air-cooled Camerons in 1913, but in 1914 the company collapsed.

Three years later Cameron Motors Corporation was formed at Norwalk, Connecticut, and E. S. Cameron, after a stint working on

the Euclid cyclecar, now sought to revive his company's light air-cooled sixes. Smaller air-cooled fours were also to be used in Cameron tractors, made in Stamford, Connecticut, where the car firm moved, and by Coffyn-Taylor Motor Co of New York for its Cotay light car, in which Cameron had an interest but which was only produced in 1920 and 1921.

The final Cameron cars still had gearboxes on their back axles and were made until 1921 with six alternative cylinder sizes. There was also a 10hp four that is said to have been available in Britain. NB

CARDEN/SHERET
GB 1913-1925

John Valentine Carden was an incurable experimenter who dabbled with amphibious tanks and ultra-light aircraft as well as with cyclecars. His first cars were built in his private workshop at Farnham, Surrey. With low-slung, cigar-shaped single-seater bodies and 4hp rear-mounted JAP engines, they did well at Brooklands so Carden began to offer them for sale at £55 each.

Despite the absence of clutch, gearbox and differential – the driver pushed the car to start and them jumped in – the cars sold well enough to justify expansion. With backing from G. C. Holzapfel, Carden formed the Carden Engineering Co with new premises at Teddington, Middlesex, to which it moved in February 1914. Here it offered five models from a single-cylinder 3½hp at £59 10s, to a two-cylinder 4hp with two-speed gearbox, at £72 10s.

By 1916 Carden had sold his monocar design to Ward and Avey Ltd, which took over the Teddington premises. In *Light Cars and Cyclecars of 1916* it was still listed as the Carden, but in 1919 it reappeared as the AV.

In 1919 Carden opened new premises at Ascot, Berkshire, where he made a tandem two-seater, whose design he sold to Tamplin in November 1919. He then designed a side-by-side two seater with rear-mounted 707cc

Carden cyclecar of 1921

flat-twin engine driving the rear axle by reduction gearing. This sold for £100, rising to £134 in 1921.

In 1922 Carden Engineering was taken over by Arnott and Harrison of Willesden, London, and an improved design was made under the name New Carden. From 1924 to 1925 Arnott and Harrison made a more expensive version of this which was named the Sheret after its designer, A. H. Sheret. It had chain instead of spur gear drive, three speeds instead of two, and quarter-elliptic springs all round, instead of the New Carden's transverse semi-elliptic at the front.

Arnott and Harrison abandoned both models in 1925, but the company was still active as a toolmaker during World War II. Carden was later connected with the Carden-Loyd tracked vehicle, and died in an air crash in 1935. GNG

CARTERCAR
USA 1906-1915

Byron J. Carter was born in August 1863. When he was 21 he moved to Jackson, Michigan, first as a printer and later as proprietor of a bicycle shop. In August 1899, with his profits, he completed his first car. On 19 July 1902 Carter formed the Jackson Automobile Co with Charles Lewis, director of the Union Bank of Jackson, and George A. Matthews of the Fuller Buggy Co, who was also a director of Jackson City Bank. The company initially made both steam and petrol cars, called Jaxons, but although Carter patented his three-cylinder steam engine in 1903 no more Jaxon steamers were made after that year, and the petrol-engined cars continued as Jacksons.

Carter effectively left Jackson in September 1903 after building a buggy with a clever variable friction-drive, although he continued as manufacturing superintendent. He built 11 examples of his buggy and was granted a patent on his drive system in May 1904.

On 26 September 1905 Carter incorporated The Motorcar Co in Detroit with capital of $150,000 and leased the former Stearns factory to build Cartercar cars. He became second vice-president and in return for his patents received $75,000, mostly in stock. The first Cartercars were shown in 1906; 101 cars were built that year, 264 were built in 1907 and 325 in 1908.

According to folklore, Byron J. Carter died after being struck by a recoiling starting handle while helping a lady motorist, thereby prompting his friend Henry Leland of Cadillac, to redouble his efforts to perfect an automatic starter. Carter actually died of pneumonia, in April 1908.

In November 1908 The Motorcar Co combined with the Pontiac Spring and Wagon Co, which had made a car called the Pontiac from 1907, to form the Carter Car Co of Pontiac, Michigan. Capital was increased to $350,000.

About this time William C. Durant was in-

Case six of 1922

Case six of 1924

dustriously buying companies, especially companies with interesting patents, as part of a rapid expansion of his General Motors Co. Carter's friction drive prompted Durant to take control of the Carter Car Co on 26 October 1909 through the acquisition of 25,772 shares at $5.56 each, a total of around $143,000.

Cartercar production continued as normal for a while and the friction drive found a few commercial applications, but by 1914 General Motors was increasingly controlling Carter policy, specifically aiming at lower prices. By 1915 Carter Car Co was in trouble and ceased production, just another in the catalogue of disasters which, for a while, cost Durant control of General Motors for the second time.

The Carter Car Co's parts operation was sold for $44,000 and in February 1917 the company was officially wound up. The plant was used by General Motors to build a new car, the Oakland, which ultimately became the second, and more successful, Pontiac to emerge from the old works. BL

CASE
USA 1910-1927

Born in 1819, Jerome Increase Case founded the J. I. Case Threshing Machine Co in Rochester, Wisconsin, in 1842, moving shortly afterwards to Racine, Wisconsin, where the company is still located. By 1848 it was Racine's largest employer of labour, a posi-

tion it still holds. Case soon became the leading maker of threshing machines in the world, with exports to South America, Europe and Australia.

In 1869 the company made its first portable steam engine and in 1876 its first self-moving traction engine. About 36,000 traction engines were made between then and 1925. An experimental petrol-engined agricultural tractor had been built in 1892, but tractor production did not get going until 1911.

Case used its famous trade mark, 'Old Abe', for over 100 years, and its origin is worth recording. In the early spring of 1861, an eaglet chick too young to fly was captured by Chippewa Indians and exchanged for a bushel of corn from a settler, Dan McCann. He soon found that a growing eagle made a poor pet and sold the bird for $2.50 to Company C of the 8th Wisconsin Regiment. The men named him 'Old Abe' after President Abraham Lincoln. The bird became a famous mascot, giving a screaming battle cry whenever martial music was played at parades.

After the Civil War 'Old Abe' was given quarters in the State House at Madison, Wisconsin, and was visited by thousands every year. The eagle's last public appearance was at a great reunion of Civil War veterans in Milwaukee in 1880, where it shared the platform with General Ulysses S. Grant. During the winter a fire broke out in the State House, and although 'Old Abe' was rescued, the bird suffered badly from the smoke and died on 26 March 1881. Jerome Case had seen the famous eagle in 1861 and adopted it as his trade mark. In 1894 the trade mark reached its definitive form, with 'Old Abe' perched atop a globe of the world. This was used on all Case products until 1969.

In 1910 Case management decided to enter the car business, and purchased the factory of the recently defunct Pierce-Racine Motor Car Co. Its first 40hp four-cylinder tourer was, in fact, a Pierce-Racine renamed, and smaller fours of 25 and 30hp were added later. Engines were its own ex-Pierce-Racine design, but many components were bought in, such as Brown-Lipe transmissions, Rayfield carburettors and Weston-Mott rear axles. In 1916 production reached a peak, with 2000 cars sold; the make was widely distributed through the vast dealer network for Case tractors and threshers.

In 1918 the four was replaced by a six-cylinder model using a Continental engine. These were made in gradually increasing sizes until 1923; usually only one model a year was listed, but sometimes an overlap made two sizes available, as in 1923 when the Case could be had with the 55bhp 3.9-litre Continental 8R or the 70bhp 5.2-litre Continental 8T. They were in the medium price bracket, a seven-passenger touring car costing $1990 in 1923.

Production in 1920 was 1370 units and in 1923 1600, but thereafter numbers fell as the car was not sufficiently different from many other medium-priced machines on the market. Case did not want to expand its car plant at the expense of its traditional products, which would have been the only way to bring prices down, and in 1927 it withdrew from car manufacture altogether.

The company continued to expand in the agricultural field, buying rival tractor makers Emerson-Brantingham in 1928, and the Rock Island Plow Co in 1937. In 1967 it merged with Tenneco Inc, becoming a wholly-owned subsidiary of Tenneco three years later. Tenneco also bought the David Brown and International Harvester tractor ranges. GNG

CASTLE-THREE
GB 1919-1922

In their garage called the Castle Motor Co in the Midlands town of Kidderminster, the brothers Stanley and Loughton C. Goodwin had a well-equipped workshop that made shells, depth charge pistols, gun carriage hubs and Dragonfly aero engine components during World War I. Having seen the design faults in the light cars brought in for repair, Stanley Goodwin decided to make a high grade three-wheeler with water-cooled four-cylinder engine, epicyclic gearbox and shaft drive, to cater for discriminating motorists.

The first 11 Castle cars produced in late 1919 and early 1920 had Dorman engines although Belgian-made Peters units were later employed. No doubt on the strength of its Belgian content a Castle-Three was awarded a Gold Medal at the 1920 Antwerp International Exhibition.

At the 1919 London Motor Show 2300 orders were taken, but production was slow to pick up and only about 350 Castle-Threes were sold in the make's brief life. Many appear to have had sliding mesh rather than epicyclic transmissions.

In 1922 a four-wheeler was tried but not marketed, as the workshop was taken over by a local carpet magnate. As a consequence of this, spares and cars in various stages of manufacture were then sold to Elephant Motors in London. NB

CASTRO
see Hispano-Suiza (Spain)

CEIRANO/SCAT
ITALY 1901-1932

The Ceirano story is a complex one, as three Ceirano brothers were associated with at least seven makes of car. Their activities can best be summarized through the stories of the brothers themselves.

Ceirano publicity showing first car, 1899

Giovanni Battista Ceirano (1859-1912) was the eldest brother. He opened a bicycle shop in Turin in 1880, starting to make his own machines three years later. He gave these the name Welleyes, which was also used for the prototype car he built in 1899. This was a single-cylinder belt-driven two-seater designed by Aristide Faccioli. One of his financial backers was Cesare Gorio-Gatti who was also a partner in a group headed by Giovanni Agnelli. The group was looking for a suitable design of car to be made by its new company, Fabbrica Italiano Automobili Torino, and

within a few weeks of introducing Ceirano to the group, it acquired the Welleyes which became, with modifications, the first Fiat.

Ceirano was left with his factory and a reasonable amount of capital from the sale of his design. He continued to make bicycles and in 1901 began building small Renault-based cars with single-cylinder engines by Aster or De Dion. In 1903 Faccioli, who had gone to Fiat along with his design, returned to Ceirano for whom he designed a four-cylinder car.

Ceirano's younger brother, Matteo, had joined him in 1901, but in July 1903 he left to form his own company. Three months later the middle brother Giovanni joined Fratelli Ceirano, which in the following year changed its name to Societa Torino Automobili Rapid (STAR). Giovanni Battista retired with ill health in 1905, and STAR then passed out of Ceirano hands.

Meanwhile, after leaving STAR, Giovanni Ceirano (1865-1948) founded Giovanni Ceirano Junior which soon became Fabbrica Junior Torinese Automobili. In 1906 he left Junior to form the Societa Ceirano Automobili Torino (SCAT). Here he made a range of T-head four-cylinder cars of quite modest size by contemporary Italian standards; the largest was a 22/32hp of 3.8 litres, enlarged to 4.4 litres in 1910. These enabled the new company to ride out the depression of 1907-8 which killed off many of the smaller Italian companies.

By 1909 SCAT had made 500 cars and three years later annual production was up to 400. Ceirano hoped for 1000 a year by 1916, but instead his new factory in the Corso Francia turned to the manufacture of trucks and Hispano-Suiza aero engines for the war effort. SCAT achieved a number of sporting successes, in particular wins in the Targa Florios of 1911, 1912 and 1914.

In 1917 Ceirano sold out to a French financial group, and the production of cars, which must have been pretty limited anyway because of the war, came to an end. In 1919 the Banco di Sconto financed a return to SCAT car production, while Giovanni Ceirano, with his son Ernesto, formed yet another company, Ceirano Giovanni Fabbrica Automobili. It launched a 16/20hp 2.3-litre four-cylinder car based on the 1914 SCAT and made this and a 3-litre six until 1924, when the company bought back into SCAT.

It continued its previous designs for a while, but soon brought out a new, smaller car with 1460cc four-cylinder engine, four-speed gearbox and four-wheel brakes. Known as the Tipo 150, the tourer looked not unlike a small Lancia Lambda. Saloons and sporting models were made, the latter being the overhead-valve 150S. It sold well and was marketed in Britain as the Newton-Ceirano, being sold by Newton and Bennett of Manchester. The Tipo 150 was made under licence in Germany by Mollenkamp Werke of Cologne from October 1924 to 1926.

The Ceiranos also built trucks and buses from 1925, and these assumed greater importance than the cars in the late 1920s. The last car model, a version of the 150S with independent front suspension, was made in 1930 and 1931. From 1929 Ceirano had been in a consortium with Fiat for truck sales and in 1931 it sold out to SPA, a wholly-owned Fiat subsidiary. SPA continued to make Ceirano trucks until shortly before World War II.

Unlike his brothers, Matteo Ceirano (1870-1941) never made a car under his own name, but after he left Fratelli Ceirano in July 1903 he founded Matteo Ceirano & Co which became Itala the following year. He did not stay there long, joining Michele Ansaldi's FIAT-Ansaldi company in 1905 and moving on to form Societa Piemontese Automobili (SPA) in 1906. He stayed with this company until 1918. GNG

CEMSA-CAPRONI
ITALY 1946-1950

The large Caproni group was mainly concerned with aircraft, but it had controlled Isotta-Fraschini since 1933, and after World War II planned to make a small family car to complement the new rear-engined Isotta-Fraschini 8C. It was to be made by the Caproni Elettromeccanica Saronna (hence CEMSA) and was designed by Ing Franco Fessia, who also designed the pre-war Fiat Topolino.

The F11, as it was called, had a 1093cc flat-four engine mounted ahead of the driven front axle, coil independent suspension all round, and a four-door saloon body. It was a very promising design but was frustrated by political decisions.

The Caproni organization had been a major supplier to Mussolini's government, and the post-war Italian leaders, who included a

Cemsa F11s of c.1947

large number of socialists and communists, were not well-disposed towards Caproni. They blocked a merger between CEMSA and Isotta-Fraschini which would at least have put the group's two car divisions under one umbrella, if not literally under one roof. The Cemsa F11 was exhibited at a number of motor shows from 1947 to 1949, in two-door convertible as well as saloon form, but production never started.

The design was taken up by Minerva in 1953, but the Belgian firm was on its last legs and nothing came of this. However, in 1960 Fessia's design finally reached the production lines in the shape of the Lancia Flavia. It is a tribute to the advanced thinking behind it that the basic 14 year old design was quite acceptable in 1960, and remained in the Lancia range until 1975. GNG

CENTURY/EAGLE
GB 1903-1910

Ralph Jackson of Altrincham, Cheshire, began to manufacture Ralpho bicycles in that town in 1885 and formed the Ralpho Cycle Co. Next, Jackson built a three-wheeled two-seater, with 2¼hp engine, which he sold for £115 as the Century Tandem. In November 1899 he formed the Century Engineering & Motor Co Ltd, with Arthur Frith, to manufacture the Tandem.

The company remained in Altrincham but had a London office, and much of the £11,000 capital was spent on advertising. In May 1901 the company moved to Willesden, London, and in June, Sydney Begbie, the man who introduced Aster engines to England, joined the board.

By 1903 Century production had reached two tandems a week in three variants and Begbie, who owned most of the stock, now introduced the Century car. This used two-cylinder Aster engines, of 8 or 12hp, and much French running gear, but it had an En-

glish-built chassis. In 1904 Begbie changed the company name to Century Engineering Co Ltd and was building Tandems, Century cars and light vans.

In 1905 the company introduced the improved New Century Tandem and in 1906 the four-cylinder, 16hp Princess car. Production stopped in 1906 but the Century company continued trading as agent for other marques including Astahl and Clyde during 1907.

In the meantime, in June 1901, as Begbie took control of Century, Jackson had moved back to Altrincham and joined John Kenworthy and J. B. Bindloss to set up the Eagle Engineering & Motor Co Ltd with nominal capital of £6000, of which £4000 was taken up. This company, apparently oblivious to possible cries of plagiarism, marketed a very thinly-disguised Tandem as the Eagle Tandem. Also in 1901, Jackson patented a three-speed and reverse epicyclic gear for use in the larger Eagle cars which appeared in 1903.

In 1904 a fearsome 80mph (128kph) single-seater 16hp version of the Tandem, called the Eagle racer, was added to a range which included the Eagle Tonneau, Eagle light car, Eagle commercial vehicles and a £100, single-seater three-wheel Runabout.

Jackson's Eagles were good cars and competitively priced but the company still experienced financial problems and in February 1905, faced with mounting debts, Eagle went into voluntary liquidation, to be wound up by the receiver on 9 January 1907.

Undaunted as ever, Jackson found new associates and resumed limited manufacture, at Broadheath Generating Station and under his own name, of the New Eagle. These were sold through the St George's Motor Car Co of Leeds, which was formed with a capital of just £1500. The arrangement continued until 1910 when Jackson joined P. Edwards to open the Ralph Jackson and Edwards garage in Altrincham. In late 1913 Jackson made one further vehicle, a Jackson cyclecar, but World War I prevented production and after the war the garage concentrated on repair work. BL

CGV/CHARRON
FRANCE, GB 1901-1929

Charron, Girardot et Voigt (CGV) was formed by three successful racing drivers, Fernand Charron, Léonce Girardot and Emile Voigt. Charron, born at Angers in 1866, was a former bicycle racer, champion of France in 1891, and a director of the Rudge and Humber cycle firms. In 1900 he won the first Gordon Bennett Cup race for Panhard, in a team which included René de Knyff and Léonce Girardot.

Born in 1864, Girardot had been associated with Charron through the Paris Panhard agency, L'Agence Générale des Automobiles, since 1897, when the company was formed with a capital of 300,000 francs. The agency sold cars with a premium of 15 to 30 per cent for early delivery and thereby prospered to the extent that Charron and Girardot, joined by another Panhard racer, Voigt, born in 1872, were able to display their own CGV car in 1901.

The first CGV model resembled the larger Panhards, with four-cylinder 3.3-litre engine, four-speed gearbox and chain drive. In February 1902 Charron, Girardot et Voigt, with a capital of 2 million francs, was established in Rue d'Ampère, Puteaux, Seine. Production that year was 76 cars, sold at an average of 14,000 francs. One was sold to King Carlos of Portugal, who visited the CGV works after the Paris Salon. Charron and Girardot went to the United States in 1902 and arranged assembly under licence by Smith & Mabley (later the proprietor of Simplex) through the CGV Co of America, in Rome, New York.

In 1903 CGV built 196 cars, including a 7.2-litre racer with one of the first ever straight-eight engines. By 1905 the company employed some 400 workers and produced 265 cars, large four-cylinder models from 4.9 to 6.2 litres.

In November 1906 the London financier Davison Dalziel formed a British company, Automobiles Charron Ltd, with a capital of £380,000 (about 10 million francs) which bought out CGV. Dalziel's United Investment Corporation sold 300,000 preference shares for cash and received £44,000 plus half the 80,000 deferred shares. CGV received £64,000 cash, the remaining 80,000 £1 preference shares and the other half of the deferred shares, with a listed value of just over £132,000. This capitalization included almost a 50 per cent mark-up on assets for goodwill, and although the hugely overcapitalized company was now legally British, much of the stock was French-owned.

At CGV only one of the original trio, Charron, remained – as manager of the Puteaux works – and from 1907 the cars were known as Charrons. Girardot moved on to sponsor the GEM petrol-electric car, made by Société Générale d'Automobiles Electro-Mécanique, also in Puteaux, while Voigt joined the still independent CGV in New York.

With the 1908 recession, Charron profits plunged from 1907's £72,280 to £6445 and Fernand Charron left the company to join Clément, having recently married Adolphe Clément's daughter. He left after two years, however, and progressed via various other companies to form Alda in 1912. Charron was replaced at Charron by a Belgian, Georges Koenigswerther, and Réne Nagelmackers of the Belgian finance house Nagelmackers et Fils joined the Charron board.

With the addition of smaller cars in 1909 profits picked up to £51,686, representing approximately 700 cars sold, and for the next few years profits and output hovered around those levels. The smallest Charron, the 845cc Charronette, was introduced in 1912, in which year Dalziel restructured the company.

In October 1913 the company was refinanced with 210,000 £1 ordinary shares, allocated to existing shareholders. Capital was reduced by £172,000 and the goodwill account of some £102,000 written off. In an apparent reversal, 60,000 preference shares were sold in 1914 to raise fresh capital.

During World War I the Charron factory, with a reduced staff, made cars and military equipment, although being British-owned it escaped French requisition. After the war, Dalziel, expecting British import restrictions, bought control of the Sheffield engineering firm W. S. Laycock, which built cars for the British market in the 1920s.

Post-war Charrons fell behind the more progressive opposition. The last car, a 1.8-litre version of an earlier 2.8 six, was marketed until 1929 and the company ceased trading in 1930, the factory being bought by Unic in 1931. BL

CHADWICK
USA 1903-1915

The Chadwick was, for a while at least, a very good car indeed, mainly because its progenitor, Lee Sherman Chadwick, was not only an inventor but also a confirmed perfectionist. Born in 1875, Chadwick was trained as an engineer and in 1899 he invented an advanced laundry machine. He was then employed by the struggling Boston Ball Bearing Co as general superintendent, and moved the company into profit. While there he built two experimental cars to demonstrate the company's products.

When the company was sold, Chadwick went as a designer to the Searchmont Motor Co of Philadelphia, builders of low-powered buggies since 1900. There he designed a range of expensive 8 and 10hp front-engined twin-cylinder cars and again helped the company to expand, moving into a new plant in Chester, Pennsylvania, in 1902.

Chadwick then designed a four-cylinder car for Searchmont, supported by the company's backers, and 100 cars were ordered.

CGV racer of 1905

Charron saloon of 1922

Problems in Wall Street, however, caused Searchmont's backers to withdraw and the company went out of business in 1903, whereupon Chadwick bought the four-cylinder parts and set up on his own to produce the first Chadwick car in the same year. It was a 60mph (96kph) 24hp tourer, listed at $4000.

He moved his machinery into an old stable, which he named the Fairmount Engineering Works, repairing foreign cars as well as building Chadwicks. In 1905, after he had built some 15 cars, he moved into larger premises and built another 25 cars before introducing the 11.2-litre six-cylinder Great Chadwick Six in 1906.

On 7 March 1907 he incorporated the Chadwick Engineering Works in Pottstown, Pennsylvania, partly because of its proximity to the Light Foundry Co, a major supplier. In the spring of 1908 he opened a new factory with about 90 employees and planned to build four cars a week. The $5500 Chadwick was built to a standard, not a price, with hand-finished leather and hickory trim and alloy bodywork.

The Chadwick was a fast car: a stripped version had been timed at over 100mph (160kph), and by 1908 the company was entering competitions, starting with hillclimbs and progressing to racing. In October, Willie Haupt led the Vanderbilt Cup race on Long Island, against the world's best, until sidelined by magneto trouble. These Chadwick racers made the first recorded use of supercharging on a petrol engine but the system was never used on the road cars. Chadwick's first race win, at Fairmount Park, also marked a win for Firestone tyres on their first ever racing appearance. Chadwick engines were also used in racing speedboats.

By 1910 Chadwick was in financial trouble, and when the Light Foundry Co cut off supplies he was faced with the expensive prospect of setting up his own foundry. Moreover, he was in dispute with his backers over setting up a dealership network to increase low sales, and further improving the Perfected

Great Chadwick Six as it was now called.

In 1911 Chadwick, disillusioned, left his company and the motor industry to join the Perfection Stove Co. Chadwick production continued until 1915 and probably 264 cars were built in total before the company folded in 1916. BL

CHALMERS/CHALMERS-DE-TROIT
USA 1908-1923

Roy Chapin left his job at Olds in 1906 and with backing from E. R. Thomas of Buffalo set up the E. R. Thomas-Detroit Co of Detroit. They were joined in the venture by Howard Coffin, Fred Bezner and James Brady, all from Olds. Coffin's designs were used and E. R. Thomas contracted to take the first year's output of 500 cars. Two years later Chapin brought Hugh Chalmers, a former vice-president of National Cash Register, into the company, and after he had bought out Thomas's holding the firm was renamed Chalmers-Detroit.

Roscoe Jackson and George Dunham joined from Olds to develop a car costing less than $1000, and a subsidiary company called Hudson was formed to produce it in 1909. Hugh Chalmers lost interest in this project and sold his Hudson stock to Chapin, Coffin and Bezner for $80,000, but he bought their holdings in Chalmers for $788,000. Brady and Dunham remained with his enterprise, which had factories totalling 750,000sq ft (70,000sq m).

Progress was swift and in 1910 Chalmers sold 6350 cars to reach ninth place in the American sales league. Many of the firm's engines in the 1908-12 period came from Westinghouse. From 1910 it used the promotional gambit of giving cars to basketball champions, which earned Chalmers much publicity, as did a good many competition successes.

Output had reached almost 10,000 a year in

1915 and 21,000 in 1916. Sixes had been made from 1913 and were the only type offered from 1915. In 1913 Chalmers and 10 colleagues each put up $10,000 to make another cheap car, the Saxon, but Chalmers disposed of his financial interests two years later. Lady Duff-Gordon was hired to promote and colour-coordinate Chalmers cars in 1916, but more significant was the arrival of Walter E. Flanders as president of both Chalmers and Maxwell in 1917. Maxwell cars were then made in Chalmers' up-to-date plant but were marketed independently.

Despite Hugh Chalmers' brilliant salesmanship the company suffered from pressing financial problems and marked overcapacity. In 1920 Chase Securities, owed $26 million, brought in W. P. Chrysler who liquidated the Maxwell distribution network in 1921 and Chalmers in 1922. The entire operation was re-formed as the Maxwell Motor Corporation, which Chrysler headed from 1923. That year some 9000 Chalmers were made, having Maxwell bodywork and Lockheed hydraulic brakes. In 1924 the factory was reorganized to make Chrysler cars. NB

CHAMBERS/DOWNSHIRE
NORTHERN IRELAND 1904-1926

Jack Chambers, designer of the first Vauxhall car, worked closely with his brothers in Belfast in preparing their first Downshire car early in 1904. It was built in the workshop of the family's engineering business, founded in 1897. The car had a flat-twin 7hp engine and epicyclic gearbox in the back axle and was marketed in England by Alford and Alder of London from 1905, by which time it was known as a Chambers.

A flat-four engined car was developed in 1906 and in 1909 came a vertical-engined vehicle with Coventry-Simplex 12/14hp four, followed by a model with Chambers' own four-cylinder engine that lasted from 1910 to 1925. Commercial vehicles based on the car and larger chassis were also built, and several were supplied as ambulances during World War I.

The epicyclic gearbox was discontinued soon after the war and Meadows sliding mesh units substituted. It was not economic to design a new engine with the detachable head now demanded by customers and in 1925 Meadows four- and six-cylinder engines were adopted. Only two of the former cars and nine of the latter were sold, the last in 1927.

Total Chambers production was probably about 500 vehicles, but despite this small number the privately financed firm was by far the longest surviving Irish make. It had continued in business with a Karrier commercial vehicle agency and by reconditioning chassis after the war. Once car manufacture ended in 1926 a Renault agency was acquired, but in August 1929 the firm went into voluntary liquidation. NB

Chalmers Six of 1914

CHANDLER/CLEVELAND
USA 1913-1929

Born in 1874, Frederick C. Chandler worked for the H. A. Lozier Co from 1890 to 1913, by which time he had risen to vice-president. In January 1913 Chandler and four colleagues left Lozier and less than a month later set up the Chandler Motor Co in Cleveland to make a reasonably-priced six-cylinder car.

The first cars looked very like the Loziers, but were much cheaper at $1785 for a fully equipped six-cylinder five-passenger touring model complete with Westinghouse electric starter. The engines were designed and built by the company, the design being the work of one of the ex-Lozier men, John V. Whitbeck.

Magnificent Sixes as well as Eights

CHANDLER

Magnificent is the one word of words that fits this car—but there is nothing in English that expresses the supreme joy of driving it.
It gives you a new notion of smooth motion; quiet flight; boundless power. Everything about the car makes you feel that here, at last, is the last word in motoring.
All models embody the famous CHANDLER system of automatic chassis lubrication—merely press a plunger and the job is done!

The wide CHANDLER RANGE includes Sixes and Eights. We proudly ask you to see these cars. Take a drive—compare!

	COMPLETE CARS		CHASSIS.	
Prices :—	22 H.P. (Standard Six) 4-Door Saloon £380	22 H.P. Standard Six	.. .. £300	
	24 H.P. (Special Six) 4-Door Saloon £480	24 H.P. Special Six	.. .. £350	
	30 H.P. (Big Six) 4-Door Metropolitan Saloon.. £550	30 H.P. Big Six..	.. .. £450	
		33/80 H.P. 8-Cyl., 7 Passenger Saloon	.. .. £850	*All deliveries ex London.*

CHANDLER DISTRIBUTORS (Great Britain), LTD. 118, New Bond Street, LONDON, W.1.
Telephone : Mayfair 3305. Telegrams : "Chanlshub, Wesdo, London."

Chandler advertising, 1927

Success came quickly to the new company, with sales jumping from 550 in 1913 to 1950 in 1914, 7000 in 1915 and 15,000 in 1916. The last figure made Chandler the largest producer of cars in Cleveland, and 13th in the entire United States. Capitalization was now $7 million and shares were reported to have been 12 times over-subscribed.

Prices ran from $1295 for a tourer to $2595 for a limousine, all models using the same overhead-valve six-cylinder engine, and bodies by Fisher of Detroit. In 1917 the company made 15,000 cars as well as a large number of Holt 10-ton artillery tractors for the US Army.

Seeing the need for a cheaper car, Chandler organized a subsidiary company in 1919 called Cleveland Automobile Co and purchased a new 17-acre (7-hectare) site for the production of the Cleveland car. This was smaller all round than the Chandler but still had a six-cylinder engine, a monobloc that dispensed with the Chandler's pair-cast cylinders. Production began in the autumn of 1919

with prices starting at $1385 and $1795 for the cheapest Chandler.

Chandler's best year was 1920, with a total of nearly 40,000 cars of both makes delivered; Chandler was ahead of his time in using aeroplanes to deliver spare parts to dealers. The recession of the early 1920s hit Chandler hard, sales dropping to 20,500 in 1922 although rising slightly to 25,500 in 1923, in which year Cleveland outsold Chandler by 14,500 to 11,000 cars. Monobloc engines and coil ignition arrived on the Chandler in 1923, and in 1924 came the 'Traffic Transmission', a constant mesh system which eliminated clashing of gears. Company advertising urged: 'If you *really* want your wife to drive, telephone the Chandler dealer.'

From 1925 the phenomenal success story of 10 years earlier gradually soured, not because of any inherent fault in the company or its cars, but because the manufacturing capacity of giants such as General Motors and Ford enabled unit costs to be drastically reduced. Middle-sized firms like Chandler, Jordan and Paige were hit the hardest.

Chandler began by dropping the Cleveland line in 1926, in which year total production was 20,971, and in an attempt to keep up with prevailing fashion introduced a straight-eight for 1927, like all other Chandlers using the company's own engine. No profit was being made and in December 1928 the bulk of Chandler stock was acquired by the Hupp Motor Car Co of Detroit. Chandler production continued until May 1929 and prototypes for 1930 were built.

Frederick Chandler joined his son in Chandler Products Corporation, making cap screws, and remained with this company until his death in 1945. The company continues in business as a division of Monogram Industries, making specially engineered bolts and fasteners. GNG

CHARRON
see CGV

CHATER LEA
GB 1907-1922

Chater Lea was in business from the early 1890s manufacturing high-quality lugs and other fittings for bicycle and, later, motorcycle frames at its works in Golden Lane, London. In 1900 the firm was incorporated as the Chater Lea Manufacturing Co Ltd, with William Chater Lea as director.

Chater Lea had now developed from building components, which also included wheels and axles, to building complete motorcycle frames, tailor made for almost any make of engine. In 1903 Chater Lea produced its own motorcycle, complete except for tyres and saddle, whose choice was left to the rider.

In 1907 Chater Lea made a first, brief sortie into car building with the Carette. This was a light car with a 6hp twin-cylinder air-cooled engine mounted outside the offside of the body between the front and rear wheels and with three-speed transmission. It was shown alongside the motorcycles at the 1908 Stanley Show, priced at 95 guineas, but Chater Lea made no serious efforts at production of what was essentially just a prototype.

The next car did not appear until 1913, by which time the company had simplified its name to Chater Lea Ltd and moved into larger, nine-storey premises in Banner Street, London. This second car was a more conventional 8hp four-cylinder light car with front engine and shaft drive. Made almost entirely by Chater Lea, it sold in some numbers.

During World War I Chater Lea car and motorcycle production gave way to small shells, wire cutters, electrical terminals and other military equipment. After the war, motorcycle manufacture resumed in earnest in 1919 but only a few cars were built until 1922, after which Chater Lea committed itself entirely to motorcycles. These included some highly respected performance models and sidecar outfits widely used for commercial deliveries and by the Automobile Association, which would eventually be one of Chater Lea's last motorcycle customers in 1936.

William Chater Lea died in 1927 and his sons, John and Bernard, moved the works to Letchworth, Hertfordshire, in 1928, changing the company name back to Chater Lea Manufacturing and forming another company, Chater Lea Estates Ltd, to run the Banner Street property, which was subsequently damaged during World War II. Motorcycle production continued until 1936, although run down gradually from 1930, and the company, still family controlled, reverted to parts manufacture, which it continues to the present day. BL

CHECKER
USA 1959-1982

The Checker name will always be associated with taxicabs which had been in production for nearly 40 years before a private car version was marketed. The name was first seen in 1920 on the cab model of the four-cylinder Commonwealth car made at Joliet, Illinois. Bodies were supplied by the Markin Auto Body Corporation, also of Joliet, and the name came from the Checker Cab Co of Chicago, for which the cabs were built. Gradually cabs assumed the major part of Commonwealth's business, and in 1921 Morris Markin acquired control of the company, changing the name to Checker Cab Manufacturing Co in 1922, the year in which the Commonwealth car was discontinued.

In 1923 Markin moved his new company to Kalamazoo, Michigan, where it took over the plant where the defunct Handley-Knight car had been made and the Dart body plant which was also vacant. By 1925 cab production had reached 75 a week; Checkers were used in many American cities as well as being exported to England. Buda four-cylinder engines were used, joined in 1927 by a six, and in 1933 by a Lycoming straight-eight. In June 1933 E. L. Cord purchased sufficient stock from his friend Markin to gain control of Checker, which then took over production of the Saf-T-Cab made by Auburn, another Cord-owned company.

The Depression had hit Checker hard, and in 1934 only 1000 cabs were made compared with 4800 in 1928. Sales picked up gradually to some 2000 a year by 1939, but to keep the workforce employed Checker took on a number of contracts for outside firms, including building commercial bodies for Hudson in 1938-39, and truck cabs for Ford.

In 1936 Markin bought back his stock from Cord from his own personal resources. This was a heavy investment for him, but providential in view of the closure of all Cord car plants only a year later. The 1930s cabs used six-cylinder Continental engines.

During World War II Checker built large numbers of trailers and experimental four-wheel-drive and four-wheel-steering Jeeps. After testing cabs with rear engines and transverse-mounted front engines driving front wheels, the company settled for a conventional design with six-cylinder Continental engines in 1947, and this was gradually improved during the 1950s. These cabs were offered as 'pleasure cars' from 1948, but passenger cars were not officially marketed until the 1960 season.

From 1948 to 1953 Checker was active in the bus field, initially making chassis for Transit Buses Inc of Dearborn, Michigan, and from 1949 making complete buses of Transit design with six-cylinder Continental engines mounted transversely at the rear. About 500 were made.

A new model of cab, the A-8, appeared in 1958, with coil independent front suspension and power-assisted steering and brakes. This became the A-9 a year later, and a passenger car version was marketed for 1960 under the name Superba. The faithful side-valve Continental six remained the standard power unit for cabs and cars until 1965 when it was replaced by Chevrolet six or V8 engines. A long-wheelbase 12-passenger Aerobus was made from 1958 to 1974 and was very popular for airport limousine work.

During the 1960s production ranged from 5500 to more than 8000 units a year, but this dropped in the next decade to 4169 in 1974 and 3340 in 1980. Checker quality was working against it, as the small number of private buyers were not the sort of people who changed their cars often, and planned obsolescence was a phrase unknown at Kalamazoo. The taxi trade seemed to prefer mass-produced cabs from Dodge or Plymouth despite the Checker's longevity, with mileages of 300,000 or more not uncommon. On 9 July 1982 David Markin, son of founder Morris who had died in 1971, decided to call it a day and ended production of cars and cabs. GNG

CHENARD-WALCKER
FRANCE 1901-1946

Ernest Chenard set up as a bicycle-maker in Asnières in 1883, going into partnership in 1898 with Henri Walcker to make motor tricycles of De Dion type. In 1901 they built their first car, an 1160cc T-head twin with coil ignition. It had a double back axle in which the drive was taken by two cardan shafts independently of a dead axle beam. This system was used by Chenard-Walcker until the mid-1920s, although some of its cheaper models had conventional axles, and in 1904 there appeared a short-lived 10hp which had double chain drive.

The business expanded rapidly and by 1905 it was making 400 cars a year, as well as marine engines. In 1906 it moved to larger premises at Gennevilliers where it remained for the next 40 years. It also became a public company.

A light van was listed on the 16/20hp four-cylinder chassis, and taxicabs were made from 1908, but otherwise Chenard-Walcker concentrated on passenger cars in the medium size and price range, although there was a 942cc single-cylinder voiturette from 1909-10, and at the other end of the scale a large four of 5.9 or 6.3 litres, made from 1906 to 1911. Production reached 1200 cars in 1910, rising to 1500 in 1913 when a 4½-litre six joined the range. Henri Walcker died in 1910.

In 1919 the firm revived its pre-war 3-litre car, adding smaller cars over the next few years. It also entered the commercial vehicle market with a road tractor powered by a 3-litre car engine. Trailers were either made by Chenard-Walcker itself or the well-known trailer manufacturer Lagache et Glaszmann.

These tractors were marketed by a separate company. They grew in size and power, the largest being a 6×4 powered by two 7½-litre Panhard engines totalling 250bhp, made in 1931. Chenard-Walcker sold licences for manufacture of the tractors to Beardmore in Britain and to Minerva in Belgium.

Ernest Chenard died in 1922, being succeeded by his son Lucien. The company was now heavily supported by outside financial interests, the Donnay family and Lucien's brother-in-law Georges Stein. New designs appeared that year, notably a 3-litre single-overhead cam four with Hallot servo brakes which acted on the front wheels and on the transmission. This car was designed by Henri Toutée, who also produced a 2-litre model in 1923.

These sports Chenards were raced with some success, including winning the first Le

Chenard-Walcker 3-litre Le Mans of 1923

Mans 24-hour race in 1923, and were made until 1927. In 1924 there was a 4-litre straight-eight, but although this was raced and catalogued it seems that no cars reached private buyers. There were also some 1½-litre sports cars, with all-enveloping 'tank' bodies which did well in competitions. Touring Chenard-Walckers were more conventional machines, with 2- or 3-litre side-valve engines. The mid-1920s were the most successful years for Chenard-Walcker which was turning out about 100 cars a day, making it France's fourth largest car manufacturer.

During the 1920s Chenard-Walcker had several tie-ups with other firms, notably with Sénéchal; its small sports cars were made by a Chenard subsidiary, the Société Industrielle et Commerciale de Gennevilliers, from 1923 to 1927. Chenard-Walcker also made AEM front-wheel-drive electric vans and in 1927 entered into a consortium organized by Charles Weiffenbach of Delahaye. This also included Donnet and Unic but these firms soon dropped out.

The Delahaye connection brought about a close similarity between some models: Delahaye adopted the Chenard-Walcker ribbon radiator while Chenard's new six-cylinder inlet-over-exhaust engines owed much to Delahaye. The association also led to more commercial vehicles by Chenard, light vans on car chassis from 1927, and larger trucks and buses from 1932. In 1931 Chenard-Walcker was supplying engines to Ariès and in 1932 the agreement with Delahaye came to an end.

Apart from the sports models, Chenard-Walcker cars were very orthodox, not to say dull, but from 1933 they blossomed out with front-wheel drive, independent suspension and Cotal gearboxes. Jean Grégoire was responsible for the front-wheel-drive cars, of which there were two models, a 2.4-litre with independent front suspension and Chenard-Walcker gearbox (1933) and a 2-litre with Cotal gearbox (1935-36). Neither was a great success, although about 1000 of the first were sold and 300 of the second.

In 1934 Chenard-Walcker brought out a 3½-litre V8 of its own design, which must have been a considerable strain on its already troubled finances. A complicated range of four- and eight-cylinder cars was made from 1934 to 1936, with independent front suspension and Cotal gearboxes on some models. In 1936 they began to lose their individuality, as the saloon bodies were made by Chausson and identical to those supplied to Matford.

Chausson, a well-known maker of radiators and pressed-steel bodies, gained financial control of Chenard-Walcker in 1936. The following year the company lost its own engines, which were now provided by Citroën (1911cc four) and Matford (3622cc V8). The Aigle-8 could only be distinguished from the Matford by its radiator grille, although the convertibles had pillarless Vutotal windscreens made under Labourdette patents that were not shared by Matford. These models

were made until the outbreak of World War II in 1939, and some were assembled in 1946.

The Chenard-Walcker name survived for a few years after the war on a forward control 1/1¼-ton van; this had originally been made in 1941 with a 725cc flat-twin engine, but post-war models used a Peugeot four-cylinder engine, and from October 1950 these vans carried Peugeot badges. As such, the design lasted until 1965. GNG

CHEVROLET
USA 1911 to date

Louis Chevrolet was born in 1878 at La Chaux de Fonds, Switzerland, where his father was a watchmaker. When he was six years old Louis moved with his family to the Beaune region of France where, at an early age, he invented a pump for transferring wine from barrels. Later he worked for a bicycle repairer and followed that with a spell at Mors in Paris. With his brothers Gaston and Arthur he headed for the fresh opportunities of Canada and then went to New York, where he worked for the De Dion-Bouton importer and for William Walter, an émigré Swiss who made cars and, from 1911, his famous Walter 4×4 trucks.

Louis Chevrolet testing Classic Six of 1911

Louis moved on to the Pope empire and spent time with Pope-Toledo, Rambler and Waverley. He became a successful racing driver and built a Buick-based racer which brought him to the attention of William C. Durant. Arthur Chevrolet became Durant's chauffeur and both he and Louis raced in the Buick team.

Louis interested Durant in French-inspired four- and six-cylinder cars which he had designed in 1909-10 and after Durant lost control of General Motors the two men collaborated on a prototype car, the Chevrolet. The name appealed to Durant because of its foreign but easily Americanized sound and the fact that its designer was well-known to the public through racing.

A successful prototype 4.9-litre six was built in Grand River Avenue, Detroit, from March 1911 and on 3 November the Chevrolet Motor Car Co of Michigan was organized by Durant. In 1912, 2999 Chevrolets were made in a small plant in West Grand Boulevard, Detroit, while a new factory was built near Ford's Highland Park plant. Production costs at Durant's Little Motor Car Co in Flint were lower, however, so Chevrolet production was transferred there in 1913, and also to the former Maxwell-Briscoe plant at North Tarrytown, New York.

Louis Chevrolet left the company in December 1913 and went on to design Frontenac racing cars and the Cornelian cyclecar. He became president of the Frontenac Motor Co in partnership with V. R. Hefler, who was also president of Zenith carburettors, and J. Boyer of Springfield Metal Body.

In the early 1920s Chevrolet designed a Frontenac road car and Chevrolet Brothers Manufacturing Co made motor and aero components. All his efforts in the motor and aeroplane industry, including the Chevrolet Aircraft Corporation, met with disaster in the Depression. Louis worked briefly, and in a lowly position, for General Motors' Chevrolet division in the early 1930s but suffered from a

Chevrolet Royal Mail H2 of 1915

Chevrolet Sports Coupé AC of 1929

Chevrolet racer of 1921

brain disease for the last six years of his life and died in obscurity in 1941.

The cars bearing his name went from success to success, however. At first they were large and typically American cars with Mason motors, as found in the sister Little line, but in 1913 they started to head towards the mass-market, with the overheard-valve four-cylinder Baby Grand and Royal Mail models. Several others followed, including a Mason powered V8, but the car that established Chevrolet was the overhead-valve 490 (its price in dollars) of 1916. Chevrolet sales had doubled annually in the early years and reached 13,300 early in the war, 70,700 in 1916 and 150,000 in 1919.

Durant had meanwhile formed the Republic Motor Car Co with a capital of $65 million to run the operation and to attract further finance, and in October 1915 he incorporated the Chevrolet Motor Co in Delaware with a capital of $20 million. The Little, made by William Little, his former factory manager at Buick, was discontinued. In 1918 General Motors took over Chevrolet and two years later Durant was ousted.

Much of the early success of Chevrolet in the western states could be attributed to Norman De Vaux, who became California dealer in 1914 and built a Chevrolet assembly plant at Oakland in 1916 before selling out to General Motors for $4 million in 1921. In Canada, McLaughlin assembled Chevrolets from 1915. By 1920 Chevrolet had additional plants in the USA at St Louis, Fort Worth and Bay City. Light trucks had been added in 1918 but the post-war slump reduced total sales to 76,370 in 1921 causing a loss of $5 million.

A recommendation was made to General Motors to close Chevrolet on the grounds that it could not hope to compete against Ford in the low-price field. From February 1922, however, it was given another chance with William S. Knudsen, formerly production manager at Ford, in charge. That year saw sales of 243,500, which doubled in 1923. Thanks to the General Motors credit division, opened in 1919, many sales were made on 6 per cent credit, worth $6 million by 1926.

Chevrolet two-door of 1941

The GM 'copper-cooled' engine was shown by Chevrolet in January 1923, but last-minute problems caused cancellation and the recall of 759 cars. The K of 1924 was a hurried replacement for the 'copper-cooled' and the 490. Its Duco nitrocellulose finish was from du Pont, the owners of which were major General Motors shareholders. By now the old Samson tractor factory at Janesville, Wisconsin, was boosting capacity and overseas assembly was taking place in Antwerp, Copenhagen and London. The Superior Coach hard top version was an instant success.

Chevrolet production exceeded 750,000 in 1926 and topped 1 million in 1927, when it overtook Ford during that company's changeover from the Model T to the A. The five millionth Chevrolet was produced in 1928, and 1929 saw a peak of 1,328,605 that was unbeaten until 1941. Ford was again out-produced in 1931 and Chevrolet generally remained America's most popular car thereafter.

In December 1928 a 'Six for the price of a Four' marked the end of the four-cylinder Chevrolets and heralded the 'cast iron wonder' or 'stove bolt six' as it was colloquially known. This excellent engine went into the Chevrolet International 6 and various commercial vehicles and stayed in production until 1953. Having succeeded A. T. Sturt in 1921, O. E. Hunt was the chief engineer from the time of its conception until 1929.

William S. Knudsen became executive vice-president at General Motors in 1933, when his place at Chevrolet was taken by M. E. Coyle, a finance officer with the company since 1916. Harley J. Earl, who had come from Fisher Body and ran the corporate art and colour studios, devised the long, low, beaver-tail look with pointed grille on the 1933 Chevrolets – all now with synchromesh – and the turret top for 1935. In 1934 independent front suspension was introduced and almost half a million cars sold.

The 10 millionth Chevrolet came off the line in 1935 and marked the return to 1 million annual sales, which included some of the industry's first all-steel station wagons. In 1938 Chevrolet climbed to the top of the US truck sales and did likewise in Canada where, since 1930, its commercials had gone under the name Maple Leaf Chevrolets. US car sales that year were 490,000, considerably down on recent years but still ahead of Ford. During the year a new factory was built in Tonawanda, New York, and three years previously the opening of a Japanese plant led to the birth of the Toyota car.

Following a record-breaking 1.4 million sales in 1941 the Chevrolet plants switched to war production on 30 January 1942. Half a million military cars and trucks and armoured cars were built, along with 8 million shells, 60,000 Pratt and Whitney aero engines, 2 million lb (907,000kg) each of aluminium and grey iron and 5.7 million lb

(2.65 million kg) of magnesium components.

Nicholas Dreystadt, general manager of Cadillac, succeeded Coyle in 1946 and on his death two years later was succeeded by W. F. Armstrong, a General Motors vice-president, with T. H. Keating as general manager and John G. Wood as chief engineer. Keating took over at the top from 1949 to 1956. It was a time of expansion. In the late 1940s the Flint factories were expanded and vast new factories opened in Los Angeles and Cleveland. By 1952 2 million square feet (185,000sq m) of factory space had been added.

Powerglide had become available on Chevrolets in 1950, bringing fully automatic transmission to low-priced cars for the first time. In 1953 a glassfibre-bodied, Harley J. Earl 'dream car' became a production reality with help from Maurice Olley, a Briton who

Chevrolet Corvette of 1956

Chevrolet Sport cabriolet of 1936

had worked at Vauxhall and Cadillac and was now in charge of research and development.

The Corvette sports car was produced from mid-1953, initially more as an image-booster than as a serious sales project. A pilot batch of 300 was made at Flint before production was moved to St Louis when it became apparent that the Corvette was a success. In 1954 a total of 3640 were made but only 700 followed in 1955, after which a re-design brought V8 power and manual transmission instead of the straight-six and automatic. Annual Corvette production by 1965 was 23,562 and total sales of 500,000 were reached in 1977. A record 393,000 commercial vehicles had been made in 1955, when overhead-valve V8s came to many cars and trucks.

In October 1959 the unlucky Corvair went on sale. This technically interesting and unexpected compact model had a rear-mounted air-cooled flat-six, with fully independent suspension and Fisher monocoque construction. Some 250,000 were made in 1960 and 316,000 in its peak year of 1961. Author Ralph Nader decided that it was 'unsafe at any speed' in his book of the same name and Corvair sales were badly affected, just 2359 finding buyers in 1969.

Three years after the Corvair came the semi-compact Chevy II, which included an automatic option on a four-cylinder engine for the first time in America. It was followed by the Chevelle in 1964, the first Chevrolet with General Motors' perimeter frame, which

soon spread to other models. At the North Tarrytown plant the 50 millionth Chevrolet had been produced the year before and in 1966 a huge new plant was commissioned at Lordstown, Ohio. The Camaro sports coupé was added to the range in 1967 and five years later General Motors acquired a 34 per cent stake in Isuzu. Certain Japanese models were slotted into the Chevrolet lineup.

As a consequence of the 1973 oil crisis and subsequent recession Chevrolet car sales fell from 2.3 million in 1973 to 1.7 million in 1975. There was also a scaling down in the size of cars. In 1976 a compact 'world car' called the Chevette was launched by Chevrolet and in 1980 came the interesting front-wheel-drive transverse-engined Citation. Many of the large V8 cars were by then using an Oldsmobile diesel engine introduced in 1978.

Chevrolet, which had previously offered its own version of most GMC heavy trucks, focussed on light commercials and cars from 1981.

The year 1984 was an especially good one for General Motors, with Chevrolet spearheading the volume attack. Leading the charge was the 'world' model Cavalier, produced in the USA with a Chevrolet badge. In this form it enjoyed US bestseller status, followed by the Chevrolet Celebrity in third place and the Chevrolet Caprice/Impala in fifth. New models introduced during the year by Chevrolet were the Sprint, the Spectrum and the Astro Compact Van. The Sprint and Spectrum were imported from GM's Japanese affiliates Suzuki and Isuzu. New United Motor Manufacturing Inc, the joint venture with Japan's Toyota Motor Corporation, bore fruit in late 1984 when the Chevrolet Nova made its début at Fremont, California. This was available from 1985.

Chevrolet has 35 American factories and an estimated 25 million Chevrolets are in current use around the world, although the distinction of being the world's largest carmaker was lost to Toyota in 1980. NB

Chevrolet Caprice Classic of 1977

Chevrolet Citation X-11 of 1985

CHIC
AUSTRALIA 1925-1929

Although Australia in the 1920s was keen to establish a domestic motor industry, basic raw material shortages dictated that many 'Australian' cars were assembled rather than manufactured. One such was the Chic, built by Chic Cars Ltd, a company registered in January 1924 in Adelaide, South Australia.

The company's proprietor and managing director, Clarence W. Chick, spent eight months in Britain, France and the United States selecting possible component suppliers for the car, which was designed for Chic by F. W. Bond & Co of Brighouse, Yorkshire. Bond itself assembled American-style cars with Continental, Anzani or Meadows engines (among others), but the handsome little car which it designed for Chic was more British than American.

Although Bond designed the car, it did not supply the parts, nor did Chick's foreign travel bear much fruit. In October 1924 the company chairman, Sir Richard Butler, announced that because of supply problems from elsewhere, most parts would be made in Britain by the Monarch Motor Co Ltd of Castle Bromwich, Birmingham. Exceptions would be the Meadows engines and Australian-made tyres and bodywork.

The sporty and adaptable Meadows was used by the likes of Frazer-Nash, Lea-Francis and Bond itself, which even offered a potent, supercharged 1½-litre unit. Chic originally intended to use a 15/30hp Meadows, but after availability problems it adopted the 14/40 version. Later, an 18/48hp Meadows-engined six was also offered.

An assembly plant was opened at Millswood, South Australia, on 1 September 1924. By 1925 cars were being displayed, and well received, at Australian shows, badged with a winged circle around a map of Australia and the Chic name. A branch office was opened in Melbourne and, although almost no cars were built in the first six months, the company showed a half-year profit as expenses had been so low.

Chic advertising described the car as 'A Thoroughbred, For the Professional Man, The Owner Driver, The Outback, The Traveller, for the man who wants an *economical*, TROUBLE and FOOLPROOF CAR'. In spite of this suggested wide appeal, Chics sold in very limited numbers before the company ceased trading in 1929. Meadows engine supply figures suggest a total output of 25 Chic cars, several of which still exist. BL

CHILTERN
see Vulcan

CHIRIBIRI
ITALY 1913-1927

Antonio Chiribiri was a Venetian who had worked for the Florentia, Züst and Isotta-Fraschini companies before setting up his own aero engine works in Turin in 1910, building 40hp engines. Chiribiri was still also described as an aeroplane maker in August 1915.

In 1914 he was commissioned by Count Gustavo Brunetta d'Usseaux to build a light car named after the goddess Siva. About 100 of these were made before the Count lost interest, so Chiribiri began to make the car under his own name. It had an 8/10hp, monobloc four-cylinder engine, alloy pistons and worm drive. As Chiribiri was increasingly occupied with war work he sold the parts for this car to Alfredo Gallanzi, who tried to market it in 1918 under the name Ardita, but with little success.

In 1919 Chiribiri brought out a new 1.6-litre 12hp four-cylinder car, replaced in 1922 by a slightly smaller four of 1½-litre capacity. This was the basis of a very exciting twin-overhead cam competition car, the Monza Corsa, of which only three were made. Antonio Chiribiri's two sons drove them, and Tazio Nuvolari had one as his first racing car.

Chiribiri cars were sold on the British and French markets but production was never very large, as the firm was busy producing aero engines. In 1927 the company went into liquidation and the factory was taken over by Lancia. GNG

CHRISTIE
USA 1903-1908

Farmer's son John Walter Christie, born in New Jersey in May 1865 and of Scottish descent, was an innovator. Among his most radical innovations were his Christie cars, America's first serious front-wheel-drive cars, and legendary racers. From the age of 16, Christie worked in naval ordnance and marine engineering, and in 1897 in New York he set up as a marine design consultant. His most successful project was a much improved big-gun turret for the US battleship *Maine*, a design also adopted by the Royal Navy. Christie earned substantial royalties from his designs and married into a wealthy family, enabling him to set up the Walter Christie Machinery company in 1900.

In 1901 he expanded into the Christie Iron Works, building marine and stationary engines, and decided to build and race a car, essentially for publicity. He decided on front-wheel drive for simplicity, using the crankshaft as the front axle and driving the wheels by individual flywheels and clutches. He also felt it was more natural to pull a vehicle than to push it.

His first car, a four-cylinder 30hp racer, ran in 1903 and appeared in public at the Ormond Beach races in January 1904, finishing last. Another car was completed in October, using a 60hp engine with one exhaust and eight inlet valves per cylinder.

After this car appeared at Ormond Beach in 1905 several people expressed interest in a touring version of the Christie, and in February Walter formed the Christie Direct Action Motor Car Co in Hoboken, New Jersey, with capital of $330,000 – $299,000 of which was Christie's valuation of his drive patents. He personally contributed $1000 cash and sold the bulk of the stock to his wife.

He intended to build road cars, but only after further experience with his racers, which in September 1905 included a four-wheel-drive car, achieved by the simple expedient of adding a second engine for the rear wheels. In front-wheel drive only form this car was crashed by George Robertson in the Long Island elimination race for the 1905 Vanderbilt Cup, when he failed to make a bend and lost both front wheels. A liberal interpretation

Chiribiri Milan of 1925

John Christie and Christie 20-litre racer of 1907

of the rules allowed another Christie into the race but, driven by Walter himself, it was eliminated in an accident with Lancia's Fiat.

In 1906 he again moved to larger premises and began work on a four-cylinder 50hp seven-seater tourer. This was completed in the summer and sold for $7500.

In 1907 capital was increased to $1 million; Christie invested $20,450 of his own money and attracted some outside investors. He intended to build 30 100mph (160kph), 80hp runabouts to sell at $7000 each in 1907, increasing to 100 cars by 1908, but his ambitious plans were not supported by investors disillusioned by his racing failures. The biggest of the half dozen Christie racers, a monstrous 20-litre V4, failed on the fifth lap of the 1907 French Grand Prix, and the terminal understeer so spectacularly displayed on American dirt tracks was entertaining to watch but hardly calculated to encourage road car sales.

In September 1907 a court awarded one investor more than $19,000 reparations and during 1908 the company went into receivership. William Gould Brokaw took control, but in September 1908 Christie transferred what patents he still owned to a new company, Walter Christie Automobile Co, with wholly-owned nominal capital of $400,000. This company built one four-cylinder taxi in 1908, which sold for $2600, and one final racer, used by Barney Oldfield until 1915.

In 1910 Christie sold his remaining taxi patents for a nominal $1 and, blamed by his backers for his companies' failures, turned his back on cars. In 1912 he formed the Front Drive Motor Corporation, which built 600 highly-regarded fire engine tractor units. From 1915 he became obsessed with designing high-speed tanks, enthusiastically pursued by Britain, Germany and even Russia, but largely shunned by America. Saddened by years of rejection, Christie died in January 1944. BL

CHRYSLER/DE SOTO, IMPERIAL, PLYMOUTH
USA 1923 to date

Chrysler Six Imperial Sedan of 1925

Walter P. Chrysler rose from floor sweeper to millionaire in 20 years. After working for a railway company he became works manager of the American Locomotive Co before joining Buick in 1911. He eventually became its president and a vice-president of General Motors. In 1920 Chase Securities hired him for two years at $1 million a year to tackle the reorganization of the ailing Willys organization; he was also hired to restructure the Maxwell and Chalmers companies.

At Willys he brought in three Studebaker designers, Carl Breer, Fred Zeder and Owen Skelton, to produce a new six which later became the Flint car. The same team joined Chrysler at Maxwell/Chalmers, which he acquired in 1923, and designed a similar vehi-

cle, offering '$5000 performance for $1500'. Chase Securities lent Maxwell $50 million to make this car and in 1924 the former Chalmers plant in Detroit produced the six-cylinder Model B, which included Lockheed contracting, hydraulic, four-wheel brakes, a Chalmers feature. Some 32,000 were made that year and 162,000 in 1926.

Maxwell was discontinued in 1925 and in June the Chrysler Corporation was formed with the transfer of Maxwell's shares, valued at $400 million. As well as factories in Detroit and at nearby Highland Park, there were plants in New Castle and Evansville (Indiana), Dayton (Ohio), Helena (Arkansas) and Windsor (Ontario).

From the outset the Chrysler Six had pressure lubrication, shock absorbers and oil and air filters. Rubber engine mounts came in 1925, when almost 4000 dealers were handling the runaway success and pushing the new marque to seventh spot in sales.

In 1926 four models, the 58, 60, 70 and 80, marked the start of broader market coverage, the last-mentioned model being the first Imperial. It was designed by Chrysler himself and the original 'three musketeers', as he called his design team. It had stock bodies by General Motors' Fisher division and others by a variety of coachbuilders and stylists including Le Baron, a name that became synonymous with Chrysler. In late 1927 the 5080cc L-80 was the most powerful American car. K. T. Keller was hired from General Motors to run the manufacturing side and in 1935 became president. Styling was the work of Oliver A. Clark from Studebaker.

To tackle the cheaper end of the market two new brands were conceived in 1928, the six-cylinder De Soto and four-cylinder Plymouth. It was the takeover of Dodge, however, which pushed Chrysler up to third position in US sales and increased its factory space five times. With Dodge added, Chrysler now had its first trucks.

The company weathered the Depression

well enough. The only year that Chrysler lost money was in 1932, when it sold 25,300 Chryslers and Imperials, 30,200 Dodges, 121,500 Plymouths and 27,500 De Sotos; the figures for 1928 were 161,000 Chryslers, 67,300 Dodges, 52,500 Plymouths and 33,500 De Sotos.

Plymouth had notched up its millionth sale in 1934 under the control, since 1930, of Fred L. Rockelman, formerly of Ford. De Soto had climbed from 29th to 11th position and brought the world's cheapest eight-cylinder car to the masses in 1930. Dodge was the only other Chrysler division with this feature for a year. Imperial, however, soon came to favour straight-eights and the CD Chrysler used one for 1931. De Soto was being run by a former salesman Byron Foy, who became Chrysler's son-in-law and was president of the division between 1931 and 1941. It earned a reputation as the group's technical guinea pig.

Technical developments for 1932 included power brakes and a revolutionary engine mounting termed 'floating power', a licence for which was sold to Citroën. Automatic clutches and freewheels were also introduced, followed by synchromesh in 1933.

The notorious Airflow, which had been in development since 1928, appeared in 1934. It came with six cylinders as a De Soto and with eight as a Chrysler. Although its styling did not meet with public approval it was technically advanced, having unitary construction, automatic overdrive, seating low down within the wheelbase, faired-in headlamps and 40 per cent less wind resistance than ordinary cars. The eight-cylinder Chrysler version sold 11,000 in its first year and the six-cylinder De Soto 15,825; sales then declined until the models were discontinued in 1937.

The Chrysler division averaged about 10th in the American sales league, usually a little ahead of De Soto but way behind Plymouth, which consistently held third spot. In 1937, a good year for the industry, Plymouth sold

514,000, Chrysler with Imperial sold 108,000 and De Soto – which had new styling by Ray Dietrich, of Le Baron fame, for their S-3 – sold 86,500. These figures were broadly similar in 1940, a year after the introduction of fluid drive (torque converter), column change, and plastic on the dashboard.

Following Walter P. Chrysler's death in 1940, K. T. Keller became chief executive. It was a year that saw the use of vacuum operated dropheads and sealed beam lamps. In 1941 came the safety-lip wheel, which kept the tyre on when flat with the car in motion; it is still used by Chrysler today.

After civilian car production was ended in early 1942, Chrysler Corporation and its divisions made 28-ton tanks, military vehicles, anti-aircraft cannons, cartridge cases, shells and aircraft fuselages. In 1952 Chrysler took over the Detroit Tank Arsenal and has been a major producer ever since.

In 1946 car production was centred on Detroit, Evansville and Los Angeles; a plant at San Leandro, California, was added in 1950. De Sotos, which had settled into the price slot above Dodge, were made only in Detroit and Los Angeles, as were Imperials. Post-war cars featured Town and Country styling, with wooden exterior trim similar to that of station wagons. They were the trendsetters of the era, often used by film cads. Ignition key starting was a pioneering innovation in 1949. Four years later Chrysler acquired the bodywork plants and machinery of Briggs Manufacturing Co and in 1955 opened a new stamping plant in Twinsburg, Ohio.

Assembly quality has always been good and the interiors, particularly of Chryslers and Imperials, were excellent, but styling had stagnated. Accordingly, from 1950 the recently promoted Virgil Exner did his best to sharpen the image with a series of dream cars. These were turned into reality by Ghia and caught the public imagination – as well as ultimately leading to the Dual-Ghia.

By October 1952 $200 million had been spent on an all-new range, including a new 5.4-litre overhead-valve V8, announced in 1951. It was the most powerful of its day. The V8, also used by Allard and Cunningham, had been designed by chief engineer Rob Roger, Owen Skelton and James Zeder, who was for many years director of Chrysler research. In 300bhp form – initially it had developed 180bhp – it was installed in the 1955 C-300 Chrysler to make America's most powerful sedan.

In 1953 Power Flight automatic transmission had been introduced. The first of several experimental Chrysler gas turbine cars in 1954 helped boost Chrysler's prestige and market share, and Exner's 1955 Flite Sweep styling brought a hint of dream cars onto the parking lot. The side-valve six used by Plymouth finally gave way to the V8 that year.

In 1950 when L. L. Colbert became president, Chrysler (including Imperial) sold 167,300 cars, Plymouth sold 573,000 and De Soto sold 127,500. Ten years later the figures were 87,420, 610,000 and 19,400 (plus 16,830 Imperials, which had become a separate division in 1955). In 1958, for the first time since 1932, Chrysler lost money. Not surprisingly De Soto, which had slid badly since 1958 and had been put in the Plymouth division the following year, was finally dropped in 1960.

For 1960 Plymouth launched the compact Valiant range alongside the Chrysler Corporation's typical, large V8s. It did particularly well in export markets, especially Australia, where Chrysler had assembled cars since 1928 and had made its first indigenous model, the Royal, from 1956, using an old Plymouth body style. Plymouth was felt to be too colonial and old-fashioned a name, and most of those sold in Britain and elsewhere from the 1930s went under the Chrysler name. In 1961 Plymouth joined the Chrysler division.

The basic structure of the Valiant was also used for the successful V8 Barracuda fast-

Chrysler Airflow of 1934

Chrysler Town & Country of 1949

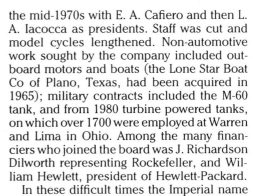

the mid-1970s with E. A. Cafiero and then L. A. Iacocca as presidents. Staff was cut and model cycles lengthened. Non-automotive work sought by the company included outboard motors and boats (the Lone Star Boat Co of Plano, Texas, had been acquired in 1965); military contracts included the M-60 tank, and from 1980 turbine powered tanks, on which over 1700 were employed at Warren and Lima in Ohio. Among the many financiers who joined the board was J. Richardson Dilworth representing Rockefeller, and William Hewlett, president of Hewlett-Packard.

In these difficult times the Imperial name was discontinued in 1975 after a losing battle

Chrysler New Yorker of 1979

Chrysler Fifth Avenue of 1985

back that first appeared in 1965, when styling was in the hands of Elwood P. Engel, formerly of Lincoln. Virgil Boyd became president of Chrysler in 1967 and clawed back Chrysler's corporate market share to 19 per cent in 1968. Total Chrysler Corporation car sales were 1.45 million in 1965, 1.27 million in 1970 but only 903,000 five years later, when the whole industry was struggling.

Attempts were made to increase overseas involvement and in 1964 the Rootes group in Britain was partially acquired, becoming Chrysler United Kingdom Ltd in 1970 and a wholly-owned subsidiary in 1973. Simca had joined the fold in 1963, Chrysler having taken a minority interest in the French firm in 1958. In 1967 Chrysler built up a majority stake in the Spanish Barreiros truck company.

Plymouth imported the Hillman Avenger as the Cricket from 1971 but most subsequent efforts centred on Japanese products. Chrysler acquired a 15 per cent stake in Mitsubishi Motors in 1970 and many of the group's small cars were based on these or Simcas throughout the decade. In 1978 alone, Mitsubishi made nearly 1 million vehicles, of which Chrysler sold a quarter.

After the 1973 oil crisis Chrysler offloaded some of its interests. In 1978 the French, British and Spanish factories were sold to Peugeot-Citroën for $230 million in return for 15 per cent equity in Peugeot-Citroën, which renamed the cars Talbot.

The Chrysler-owned former Rootes empire in Britain was saved from collapse in 1975 by a long-standing ckd deal with Iran and a massive injection of government money. Renault bought a half share in both the Spanish and British Dodge truck factories in 1981 and soon took them over completely.

Other manufacturing plants in Turkey

(sold in 1978), South America and South Africa were also affected. A two-thirds share in the Brazilian company was sold to Volkswagen in 1978 and Colombian and Venezuelan interests were sold to General Motors. The Canadian plant at Windsor was retained and in 1983 was given a £380 million boost, including 123 robots, primarily to make passenger utilities and Mini-Ram vans at the rate of 1600 a day.

In Europe the Chrysler name had been used on the Hillman-designed, Simca-built 180 announced in 1970 and transferred to Spain in 1978. Other 'Simcas' were sold (and in some cases also built) in Britain as Chryslers from the mid-1970s until the Peugeot-Citroën takeover. Between 1976 and 1979 in Britain, Hillman models became Chryslers and there was also a new model in the shape of a Chrysler Sunbeam hatchback from 1978. Various engines were available, including a sixteen-valve Lotus unit in 1979. In Australia, Mitsubishi took over the Adelaide plant in 1980, where some of its models had been assembled since 1974, and continued the Valiant.

In 1970 the Chrysler group worldwide had 228,332 employees. It made a loss that year of $7.85 million, having made only a small profit in the USA. It was then profitable until 1974, when the new loss amounted to $52.1 million. Peak worldwide Chrysler vehicle sales were recorded in 1973 at 3.45 million units. The comparable figure for 1984 was 2,034,348, of which 1,824,248 were produced in North America. Approximately 7 per cent of Chrysler's American sales in the mid-1980s came from Japan.

As the recession bit, Chrysler opened up lines of credit with 115 banks totalling $1000 million. John Ricciardo became chairman in

against Lincoln, which had been selling up to five times more cars each year. In 1977 6 per cent of Chrysler's US sales consisted of four-cylinder cars and the company predicted that this would reach 70 per cent by 1985. The Dodge Omni and Plymouth Horizon of 1978-80 used VW engines. The Imperial name was revived in 1981 and the new Chrysler Le Baron models of 1982 had Chrysler 2.2 or Mitsubishi 2.6-litre transverse fours and front wheel drive; 3.7 sixes and 5.2-litre V8s were still offered in the Cordoba and larger types. For 1985-86 Chrysler bought more than 500,000 2.6-litre four-cylinder engines from Mitsubishi and intends to use 2 million V6 3-litre units from Mitsubishi in five years commencing in 1986. A new model for 1986 was the Chrysler-Maserati, a convertible made in Italy with a 2.2 litre engine modified by the Italian firm to give greater power. The Plymouth range for 1986 included the long-lived Horizon, a new front-drive coupé called the Sundance which was also made as the Dodge Shadow, the Reliant and Caravelle sedans, equivalent to the Dodge Aries and 600, and one survivor of the large rear-driven sedans, the V8 Gran Fury.

Worldwide Chrysler sales in 1978 had fallen to 2.2 million units (1.25 million of them US cars) and employees to 158,000. Losses totalled $205 million. Since then there has been a gradual improvement as more cost-effective and fuel-efficient models have been developed. From the early 1980s most had front-wheel drive.

Chrysler returned to profitability in 1982, and in 1984 it employed a workforce of 100,435, including 80,233 in the USA when L. A. Iacocca was chairman. It still retained a 14 per cent interest in Peugeot SA plus 15 per cent in Mitsubishi Motors; its largest subsidiary outside the USA and Canada was Chrysler de Mexico SA. In North America Chrysler accounted for 10.4 per cent of the car and 12.6 per cent of the truck market in 1984. Having spent $650 million on the development programme of the Dodge Lancer and Chrysler Le Baron GTS for 1985, which included a new assembly plant at Sterling Heights, Chrysler announced that it intended to launch a new model every six months until 1989.

Many of the company's executive officers have come from senior positions elsewhere in the industry in the past five years. They include B. E. Bidwell (ex Ford and Hertz), R. E. Dauch and R. L. Stewart (formerly with Volkswagen of America) and T. G. Denomme, D. R. Platt and E. A. Reickert (all from Ford). A new appointment in 1985 was M. T. Stamper, also vice-chairman of Boeing.

In 1985 Chrysler celebrated 60 years of production, and two years later announced plans to take over American Motors in a deal worth more than $600 million. NB

CID
see Cottereau

CIEM
see Stella

CISITALIA
ITALY 1946-1965

Cisitalia was a rich man's dream which went wrong and ultimately cost its founder a substantial fortune, but which left behind some remarkable cars. It resulted from the financial success and personal determination of Piero Dusio, who had been an accomplished athlete and highly paid footballer whose career was cut short by injury.

The team's sponsor found Dusio a sales job in the Genoa branch of its textile business, where he proceeded to create hugely increased profits. He was recalled to Turin and put in charge of national sales, at an astronomical salary. Not only could he afford to race cars himself, but he founded Scuderia Torino to sponsor others. By 1939 he had created his own business empire, based on textiles, banking, hotels and manufacturing sporting goods, including bicycles. Dusio's sporting goods company was known as Consorzio Industriale Sportivo Italia, or Cisitalia.

During World War II Dusio planned to build and race cars when war ended and in 1944 he employed talented Fiat engineer Dante Giacosa to design a simple, Fiat-based racer which could be produced, profitably, in reasonable numbers. Rejecting first thoughts of a Fiat 500 chassis, Giacosa designed a tubular-framed racer, using, with Fiat's

approval, an 1100cc Fiat engine uprated from 32 to over 60bhp. The first prototype was completed in the summer of 1945 and, in August, Dusio employed former Fiat experimental engineer Dr Giovanni Savonuzzi as chief engineer to set up a production shop.

The first production prototype of the Cisitalia D46 was finished in the spring of 1946 and tested by Piero Taruffi, who became racing manager and chief tester. By August, Cisitalia SpA, the car company, had completed seven cars and in September D46s took the first three places in their race début.

Thus Cisitalia's reputation was made and many cars were ordered. Cisitalia also started a sports racing car project, based on the *monoposto*. After Dusio had rejected designs from several stylists, Savonuzzi designed a low, two-door coupé body. The second 1100 sports prototype was built by Vignale and two cars were also bodied by Farina, one of them being the first Cisitalia road car. Another chassis went to Pininfarina, which in September 1946 showed the definitive version of the coupé; this went on display in 1951 in the Museum of Modern Art in New York, as a work of artistic merit.

Farina also designed a convertible, but Cisitalia could not meet the substantial demand for both road cars and racers, a demand reinforced by successes including second, third and fourth places in the 1947 Mille Miglia. Production versions of the 'Mille Miglia' coupé and roadster were introduced later on.

Cisitalia sold 31 *monopostos* up to 1947 and created a further income from producing tools. But Dusio had set his sights on Grand Prix racing and now committed the company to a disastrous Formula 1 car project.

While Dusio was looking for a Grand Prix design, the Porsche design office was looking for work and Porsche's Turin representative, Carlo Abarth, introduced to Dusio by Nuvolari, put the two in touch. Dusio eventually paid 1 million francs to secure the release from French internment of Dr Ferdinand Porsche, who responded with Project T360 – a mid-engined twin-overhead cam, supercharged flat-12 1½-litre Grand Prix car, based on his pre-war Auto Unions and with two- or four-wheel drive. Porsche began work

on the car with brilliant racing engineers Ing Karl Rabe and Dr Eberan von Eberhorst, who worked in Turin, organizing the project.

Porsche's original cost estimate had been 20 million lire, but von Eberhorst spent almost 30 million simply in equipping Cisitalia to build the car. Savonuzzi ventured that the first car might cost 100 million lire and in October 1947, as Dusio insisted on continuing, Savonuzzi resigned. He was replaced as chief engineer by Abarth's associate Rudolf Hrushka. Dusio was committing all to the project, stopping lucrative tool sales to release workshop space and stopping D46 production as racing formulae changed in January 1948. Only the roadgoing coupés and convertibles were still built.

With Dusio all but bankrupt, a completed Grand Prix car was finally displayed at the Turin Show in February 1949, an ailing Nuvolari in the cockpit. Within months Cisitalia was indeed bankrupt, without the Grand Prix car ever having run and the second car being no more than a set of parts.

Dusio sold what was left to Automotores Argentinos, or Autoar, in Buenos Aires and moved there in the hope of raising backing from the Argentine government, but it did not happen. Autoar briefly built Cisitalia-badged, Jeep-based utilities and in 1952 and 1953 ran the one complete example of the Grand Prix car which Dusio had taken to Argentina. Alas, what might once have been the world's most advanced racer was hopelessly unreliable and quickly faded into obscurity.

In 1952 Dusio returned to Italy where his son, Carlo, was attempting to revive Cisitalia's road car operations. A 2.8-litre four-cylinder coupé was announced, but few of the 135mph (217kph) cars were built. In 1953 Cisitalia built some Ford-engined prototypes for Ford in America but Ford did not take up the option to manufacture.

Cisitalia built a rebodied Fiat 1900-based sports saloon, a 70bhp version of the 1100 coupé from 1954 (of which around 100 were made) and a Volvo-engined derivative of that car, known as the Radente. The final offering, built in small numbers from 1961 to 1965, was the Coupé Tourism Special, rebodied 750 and 850cc versions of the rear-engined Fiat 600. BL

Cisitalia 202 spider of 1949

Citroën B2 doctor's coupé of 1922

CITROËN
FRANCE 1919 to date

André Citroën's parents were rich Jewish diamond merchants of Dutch extraction who lived in Paris and who lost everything as a result of a complex swindle. In 1884, when André was six, his mother died and his father committed suicide. He lived for a time in Poland, where he acquired the French rights to manufacture an uncle's wooden cogwheels, which had the original feature of teeth in a vee-form for extra strength.

Soon after 1900 he established a gear cutting shop in Paris with Jacques Hinstin and by 1910 annual sales had reached 1 million francs. One of their most famous undertakings was the steering gear for the *Titanic*.

André Citroën was related by marriage to a director of Mors and retained close ties with that company until after World War I, introducing the firm to sleeve-valve engines. One brother, a diamond merchant, ran the Banque Automobiles, which provided money for car purchasers. Another represented Minerva in London.

By 1913 the gear firm with its chevron-tooth trade mark had made 500 engines for Sizaire-Naudin, had built a new factory on Quai Grenelle in 1911 and had become Société Anonyme des Engrenages Citroën with a capital of 3 million francs. Citroën had visited the United States in 1912 to study mass-production at Ford and this was put to valuable use in World War I for the output of shells from Mors and from his own plants, which included one on Quai Javel (now known as Quai André Citroën).

At the end of the war the armaments factory was converted for car production, Citroën having hired Jules Salomon, designer of the Zèbre while at Unic. A luxury car designed by M. Dufresne was commissioned at the same time but was soon sold as a complete project

to Voisin. Salomon came up with a design suitable for mass-production, the A-type Citroën, which had electric starting and lighting and was launched in 1919. Some 2000 were built that year and 8000 in 1920, more than any other European car of the time.

To keep pace with demand, Citroën acquired Adolphe Clément's factory at Levallois-Perret in 1922 along with part of the Mors plant. By 1924 150,000 of the inexpensive Citroëns were said to have found buyers. The following year they were joined by the first all-steel Budd-licensed saloons in Europe, which helped to revolutionize the industry. The bodies for these were produced at Citroën's new works at Saint-Ouen, where 250 US-built cold presses were installed.

By then the company's factories covered 200 acres (80 hectares), employed 35,000 workers and, in 1927, were turning out 400 cars a day, many being painted by the recently introduced nitrocellulose process in order to speed output. In 1928 Citroën captured 36 per cent of the French car market.

A British company had been formed in 1923 and a factory was opened at Slough

three years later, continuing in business until assembly was discontinued in 1965. Citroëns were soon being produced in Germany, Austria (by Gräf & Stift) and Italy as well as being unofficially copied by other firms, including Sima-Standard.

Various keenly priced models appeared, including the C-type 5CV from 1922. The company was also producing taxis and Kégresse-Hinstin half-track vehicles as well as 1-ton commercials from late 1926 with vacuum servo brakes.

In 1928 an influx of new American machine tools helped to produce the first six-cylinder Citroën car as well as a high speed 1.8-ton six-cylinder commercial chassis. Total sales were 100,000 in 1929, aided by clever advertising, special insurance schemes and standardized repair charges. An 8CV created a well-publicized endurance record of 186,000 miles (300,000km) in 134 days in 1932, the year Chrysler floating power engine mounts

Citroën 11AL of 1934

and part-synchromesh gears with freewheel were adopted on Citroëns.

A more modern factory was built on Quai Javel to produce the revolutionary front-wheel-drive and hydraulically braked cars, launched in 1934, with their electrically seamless-welded unitary construction and independent front suspension. The *traction avant* marked such an innovation that sales were initially slow, although of course it gradually confounded the sceptics and went on to great success, sixes being introduced in 1938. With identifiably similar styling the *traction avant* lasted until July 1957, by which time 708,339 of the four-cylinder types had been built.

The four-cylinder long-stroke engine soldiered on for another 10 years in the ID model. Engines and transmissions from the *traction* found their way into such French makes as Chenard-Walcker, Georges Irat, Rosengart – to where Jules Salomon had departed to make Austin Sevens in 1928 – and La Licorne. DAF used a 10CV engine in a 4×4 amphibious prototype and after the war DB favoured Citroën power.

101

Citroën DS of c.1968

ceeded for the first time in 1957 and the 400,000 mark was reached in 1963. These figures were largely a result of the popularity of the 2CV and its commercial derivatives.

In 1954 the H model Six tried the hydro-pneumatic self-levelling suspension that was to be a feature of the streamlined DS series introduced a year later. These had power-assisted brakes with discs at the front – the first in a mass-produced car – and power-assisted steering and gearchange, although in 1956 the less complex and less expensive ID was developed.

Citroën 2CV of 1986

Citroën CX estate of 1983

Citroën BX GTi of 1986

André Citroën died of cancer in 1935, having lost control of his company in December 1934 after creditors had petitioned for bankruptcy. A French government commission thereupon assumed control and persuaded the wealthy Michelin tyre family interests to acquire the company in 1935.

Conventional rear-drive cars, including diesels in 1937-38, continued to be produced and commercial vehicles were available for loads of up to 2½ tons with optional 3.05-litre diesels from 1937. These engines with enlarged bores lasted until 1971, when replaced by Berliet, by which time power output had grown from 55 to 108bhp.

In 1936 a market survey had concluded that demand existed for an extremely basic and cheap car, so Citroën responded by building

300 prototype two-cylinder air-cooled 2CV cars with hammock seats and front-wheel drive in 1938-39. Progress was halted by World War II, when Citroën factories came under Nazi control and produced more than 6000 2-tonners for Germany's army, but after 1945 work resumed.

Pierre Boulanger, the general manager, was closely involved with the development of the car that was said to seat 'four people under an umbrella'. It was he who unveiled it to an astonished public in 1948. After initial hesitation the French, and Francophiles everywhere, took it to their hearts; 5 million had been sold by 1976.

After the war sales picked up impressively, from 9439 in 1945 to 42,785 in 1948 and 101,161 in 1951. Sales of 200,000 were ex-

An association with Panhard was formed in April 1955 and led to a full integration of the two companies in July 1965. The former Mathis (Matford) factory was also purchased, and produced Citroën engines. From 1955 Panhard's surplus capacity was used to make 2CV vans, while the heavyweight Panhard commercials boosted Citroën's presence in the over 3-ton market, scoring sales of 5158 in 1958. The commercial vehicles division reaped benefits from the acquisition of Berliet in 1967.

The 2CV car became available with twin engines and 4×4 in 1958 and three years later a variation was introduced in the slightly less bizarre shape of the Ami-6, followed by the Dyane in 1968. A British Citroën Bijou was produced in 1960 with fibreglass body. In France that year work began on a vast new factory at Rennes-la-Janais, Brittany.

Maserati made a 2.7-litre four overhead-cam 170bhp V6 engine for the Citroën SM sports coupé of 1970. It was also used by Automobiles Ligier, a Vichy-based company that was acquired by Citroën in 1974 to assemble the SM. Another Italian connection at the time of the link-up with Maserati was a 15 per cent shareholding taken in Citroën by Fiat in an effort to improve management in the financially ailing French firm. Under this arrangement the Autobianchi range was sold in France by Citroën. In the early 1970s Renault was making twice as many cars a year as Citroën, and in 1973 Peugeot produced 656,000 against 607,000 by Citroën.

In 1975 the last of the D-series cars was produced, having sold 1.25 million. Thereafter the CX took its place, resembling an enlarged version of the GS that had been available since 1970. The GS had a flat-four engine, although a few used Wankel rotaries, a type also tried in 500 prototype M35 Ami-based coupés in 1969, following a joint development agreement with NSU in June 1964.

In 1974 the Fiat liaison came to an end, Michelin's shares in the loss-making Berliet were sold to state-supported Renault – and Citroën then became the property of Peugeot. This development was reflected in the production of various hybrid models such as the Visa, which had a Citroën air-cooled flat-twin engine in a Peugeot 104 structure, although Peugeot engines were later offered. In 1982 came the new BX16 with rearward-inclined four-cylinder transverse 1360 and 1580cc engines and widespread use of plastic in the body construction. 1986 saw a new small hatchback, the AK, powered by 954, 1124 or 1360cc 4-cylinder engines

Eight years earlier, in 1978, Peugeot-Citroën PSA had acquired Chrysler's European interests, which included Simca in France, and from 1979 the European Chrysler cars were known as Talbots. In 1981 Citroën and Peugeot, in conjunction with Fiat, developed a new van range at Sevel that is also marketed by Talbot and Alfa Romeo.

In 1980 Citroën production had dropped by 22 per cent from over 700,000 to 555,000, and sales continued to decline during the early 1980s, although 1985 production picked up to 553,100 from 511,000 the previous year. Exports remained steady at around 50 per cent of total production and Citroëns were produced in several countries under other names. In Yugoslavia they carried the Tomos name and in Romania versions of the Visa with 652cc two-cylinder or 1129cc flat-four engines were entitled Oltcit. NB

CLAN
GB 1970 to date

The Clan Crusader was the brainchild of Paul Haussauer, the son of a Swiss businessman. Haussauer, born in 1942, gained a degree in engineering science from Oxford while apprenticed to the General Electric Co. After a period with a plastics company he joined Lotus and eventually became an assistant projects engineer. In January 1970 he left, with various other Lotus personnel, to form the Clan Motor Co Ltd, largely financed by his father, René who had made the family fortune from Sadia water heaters and who now became chairman of Clan.

The company's first premises were a small shed in Norfolk, where a load-carrying glass-fibre monocoque body, requiring only two moulds, was devised and the body styled by another former Lotus man, John Frayling. The car met the EEC 30mph barrier impact test with impressive ease. Power would come from a rear-mounted Sunbeam Imp engine

and Chrysler guaranteed engine supplies for a number of years, even if Imp production should stop. The Crusader was planned as much as a second car as just another sports car.

The first example was built in September 1970 in a 3000sq ft (280sq m) interim workshop in the corner of a baked bean factory, but Haussauer always intended to build the Clan on a totally professional basis.

In March 1971 the company moved to a new, purpose-built, 23,000sq ft (2150sq m) government-owned factory in Washington New Town, County Durham, with local council aid via the Board of Trade and a proper production line was installed. The first production cars were completed in June 1971 and went on sale in September.

Sales started slowly but the car was well reviewed by virtually all testers for its construction quality and 100mph (160kph) performance. Early competition successes such as Andy Dawson's second place in the Manx Rally also brought welcome publicity. Haussauer's brother-in-law, Arthur Birchall, formerly Lotus's chief Indianapolis mechanic, ran a racing and development department for Clan.

Early production was held up by supply problems and power cuts but by October 1972, 32 staff were building five cars a week. Output to date was 130 cars against an expectation of 200, but Clan's 18 agents reported full order books.

More tooling was planned, to increase capacity to 20 cars a week. By now 70 per cent of Clan's output was finished cars and only 30 per cent were kits, the tax advantages of the latter having disappeared with the introduction of value added tax in April 1973, although Haussauer was never particularly keen on selling 'part-built' cars anyway.

In spite of the undoubted quality of the product and the businesslike operation, Clan went out of business through lack of finance. Brian Luff, another ex-Lotus man who was also part of the original Clan design team,

purchased the moulds and supplied Clan shells, as well as building his own, Mini-based kit car, the Status. When Luff transferred from Nazeing, Essex, to Jersey in 1977 the supply of Clan shells apparently dried up.

In February 1983 Peter McCandless bought the original moulds and moved Clan Cars to Newtownards, Northern Ireland, where he resumed production of a revised model. McCandless also planned to build an Alfa-Sud-powered mid-engined car under the Clan name by late 1985. In August 1984, however, Paul Haussauer also announced new plans for a Clan based on the original design which he intended to manufacture in Cyprus and reintroduce in Britain through his own venture, Phoenix Automotive. BL

CLÉMENT-BAYARD/BAYARD-CLÉMENT
FRANCE 1899-1922

Like that of many firms in the motor industry, the complex story of Clément and Clément-Bayard (or Bayard-Clément) cars had its origin in the 19th century cycle trade. Adolphe Clément was born in 1855, and after setting up a small bicycle shop in Paris in 1878 he soon became a leading manufacturer.

It was from the pneumatic tyre that he made his fortune, however, for he obtained French manufacturing rights to the Dunlop tyre in exchange for buying £2000 worth of Dunlop shares. These he later sold for £200,000, using the profit to set up a factory at Levallois-Perret for the manufacture of tyres.

In 1894 his bicycle firm became the Société Anonyme des Vélocipèdes Clément with capital of 4 million francs. Two years later the name Clément, and some of the factories, were bought by an English syndicate headed by Harvey DuCros of Dunlop and Ernest Terah Hooley, together with Alexander Darracq's Gladiator bicycle works and the French branch of Humber. Clément stayed

Clan Crusader of 1972

Two Cléments of the early 1900s

Clément-Bayard AL spider of c.1913

with this new combine, called Clément, Gladiator and Humber (France) Ltd, which added motorcycles and cars to its products in 1896. The cars were sold under the name Gladiator.

While remaining on the board of this company, Clément joined Panhard et Levassor in 1897, becoming its chairman in 1900, and established his own separate factory in 1897 at Levallois-Perret for the manufacture of bicycles, motorcycles and light cars.

Few of the latter were made until 1900 when Clément was building two distinct types of car, a light, rear-engined voiturette powered by a 2½hp De Dion-Bouton engine, and the Clément-Panhard. This was designed by Krebs of Panhard et Levassor and had a 3½hp single-cylinder engine, with the archaic features of hot tube ignition and centre pivot steering, in which the complete front axle turned with the wheels. It has been described as one of the worst cars ever made, but more than 100 were sold and it was even made under licence in Scotland by Stirling of Hamilton.

Clément also dabbled in electric cars at this time, importing Columbias from the United States, fitting them with French bodies and selling them under the name Electromotion. In 1900 Clément's Levallois works employed 400 men, while he had another factory at Mezières, near the Belgian border, which made components for bicycles and cars, and

104

Clément vans on duty in pre-World War I London

supplied Panhard and Levassor as well.

In 1903 Clément resigned from Panhard and Gladiator; as cars bearing the name Clément were still being made in the Gladiator factory, he decided to give his own products a new name. He chose Clément-Bayard, after the 16th century hero the Chevalier Bayard – 'le chevalier sans peur et sans reproche' – who had saved Mezières from the Duc de Nassau in 1521. He also changed his surname to Clément-Bayard. The cars were called Bayard, or Bayard-Clément.

These cars were sold in England by the British Automobile Commercial Syndicate, backed by the Earl of Shrewsbury and Talbot and managed by D. M. Weigel. In 1903 a factory was built at Ladbroke Grove, west London; the cars were at first identical to the French products and were called Clément-Talbot and later Talbot, although the company name remained Clément-Talbot Ltd up

to 1938. To confuse matters further, the Gladiator-built Cléments were imported into Britain by E. H. Lancaster who sold them as Cléments. Later cars sold under the Clément name were British made, by Swift of Coventry. From 1906 to 1910 certain Clément-Bayard models were made in Italy by Diatto of Turin, but annual production did not exceed 200.

By 1904 Adolphe Clément-Bayard had 1600 employees at Levallois turning out 1200 cars a year, making him a major European manufacturer. Most of the machinery at Levallois was American. Castings and other components came from Mezières which employed 400, and he had his own separate coachbuilding works.

Production of bicycles and motorcycles was carried on in separate factories at Levallois. The cars ranged from a 6hp single-cylinder to a 27hp four. Taxicabs became a speciality and in 1909 there were 456 Clément-Bayard cabs in Paris, where they were second in popularity only to Renault. Light vans had been made since 1903, but from 1906 the company made heavier trucks and buses which were continued until 1914.

Clément-Bayard played an active part in motor racing from 1903 to 1908, entering teams for Gordon Bennett trials and the Grand Prix, but the death of Adolphe's 22-year-old son Albert in practice for the 1907 Grand Prix led to an end of sporting involvement. Another field in which Clément-Bayard was active was that of aero engines and airships. In 1910 he began to manufacture the Demoiselle monoplane designed by Santos-Dumont, selling them for 7500 francs, less than his more expensive cars.

By 1914 production was running at 1500 cars a year, which meant that he was no longer a leading manufacturer although still in the top 24 European firms. Twelve models of car were being made, from a 7hp twin to a 30hp six. A 20hp four used the Knight sleeve-valve engine and all models featured dashboard radiators.

During World War I Clément-Bayard expanded its premises for the manufacture of munitions, but the post-war years saw a rapid contraction, largely due to the retirement in 1919 of the driving force, Adolphe Clément-Bayard. The Mezières factory was sold, and production of two models, an 8hp and a 17.9hp, was carried on at Levallois until 1922, when the factory was sold to Citroën. Clément-Bayard died in 1928 of a heart attack while at the wheel of his car. He was 73. GNG

CLÉMENT-TALBOT
see Talbot (GB)

CLÉNET/CORSAIR
USA 1976 to date

Clénet Coachworks Inc of Goleta, California, was established in 1976 by French-born Alain

J. M. Clénet, a graduate of the National Superior School of Design, Paris, to build nostalgically-styled sports cars which Clénet insisted were not replicas. Production was initially to be limited to 250 examples, numbered in silver, of each type.

The first Clénet resembled a Mercedes 540K roadster and was built on a new Lincoln Continental chassis and running gear, serviceable by Lincoln-Mercury dealers; the two-seater passenger compartment was based on an MG Midget centre section and the rest of the handbuilt, unitary construction body, with the exception of glassfibre wings, was of zinc-plated steel. Clénet offered every conceivable extra, although he insisted on personally approving all body colours.

Clénets were extremely expensive: the 1979, 5732cc 120mph (193kph) four-seater convertible Roadster sold for $65,000; the 1981 Mercury Marquis-based Series II cost $83,500; and the 1982 Series III Asha, with a 4950cc Lincoln-Mercury V8, cost $75,000 – for a two-door two-seater.

Clénet was able to sell about 125 cars a year in the early 1980s when the company had a workforce of 150, but the company had ceased trading in its own capacity by 1983 and versions of the cars were reincarnated by the Roaring Twenties Motor Car Co of El Cajon, California, as the Corsair.

In October 1984 Alain Clénet joined forces with Lands Design of Elkhart, Indiana, to build a luxury van, the Precedent, based on Chevrolet and Lincoln mechanical elements with Citroën doors and other parts in an otherwise purpose-built body. The car was expected to sell for about $40,000. In 1985 both the Corsair, at $49,500 with a choice of Ford or Chevrolet V8s, the Clénet Cabriolet Series II, at $98,000, and the Clénet Asha Series III, at $74,000 with Ford V8 power, were listed. The Clénet name had been revived in its own right by Alfred Di Mora, a former assembly line worker with the original Clénet Coachworks Inc, who had bought the assets of the firm and started production in a new factory near Santa Barbara, California, employing 43 workers and with plans to build six cars a month. BL

CLEVELAND
see Chandler

CLULEY
GB 1921-1928

Clarke, Cluley and Co was founded as a textile machine maker in Globe Works, Well Street, Coventry, in 1890 and quickly moved into the booming cycle trade. It made Globe motorcycles for 10 years from 1901 and a Riley-like three-wheel Cymocar in 1904.

A slump in textiles persuaded the brothers C. J. and N. F. Cluley to enter the car business

and A. Alderson, fresh from designing the 11.9 Lea-Francis, was hired to design a well-engineered 10hp model that appeared in 1921 and was produced largely in-house. It was joined by an 11.9hp version in 1922 and by a 16hp six in 1923.

A 14/30 was designed by E. Farbrother, formerly with Windsor; in 1927 this became the 14/50, with an overhead-valve 2120cc Meadows four-cylinder engine. Up to 1928, 49 of the 14/50 were built and in that year Clarke, Cluley became a limited company, abandoning cars in favour of textile machines once more. Car production may have been as high as 3000, but the company had been unable to reduce prices sufficiently to compete in the family car market.

The firm weathered the Depression with a workforce reduced to 17, and in 1934 began work as a subcontractor to Rolls-Royce on aero engines. Its factory was destroyed in the Blitz and the company subsequently moved to Kenilworth. The firm is once more under the private control of the Cluley family and nowadays makes helicopter components and its old speciality, textile equipment. NB

CLYDE
GB 1901-1932

George Henry Wait was a pioneer bicyclist who rode from Land's End to John O'Groats in 1888 on a Humber. In 1890 he went into partnership in a bicycle business in Leicester, and later in the decade floated the Clyde Cycle and Motor Car Co with capital of £25,000. An 1899 prospectus referred to a Clyde Pennington Victoria with 'mechanism not liable to get out of order' as well as a tricycle built by MMC, which also built Clyde's Bollée-type car.

The first Leicester-built Clyde motor vehicles were completed probably in 1901 and had Simms engines, although White and Poppe as well as Aster units were subsequently used. In 1905 the firm was wound up and extensive tooling, 60 motorcycle frames, 25 bicycles, 12 motorcycles and one two-cylinder car were disposed of.

In 1908 Wait and C. B. Warner were running a large garage with room for 60 cars in an

old tram depot in Belgrave Gate, Leicester. They were selling Talbots and Singers as well as Clydes, but made a loss of £2741 that year on a turnover of £10,000. In 1909 a Clyde with direct drive on all gears did well in the Scottish Trial and a London agent was appointed for the hitherto regional make in 1910. Bankruptcy loomed again, however, with money owed to Aster, Clément-Talbot, Bayliss-Thomas, Lea and Francis, New Imperial, JAP, Riley and White and Poppe.

The business was restructured as G. H. Wait and Co Ltd, which held an Austin agency. A small number of Clydes continued to be assembled, possibly until as late as 1932. Total output was reputed to be 4000 cycles, 470 motorcycles, 245 cars and 15 commercial vehicles. NB

CLYNO
GB 1922-1930

Cousins Frank and Alwyn Smith invented a variable transmission with inclined pulleys at their motorcycle accessory firm at Thrapston, Northamptonshire, and in 1909 incorporated it into a motorcycle that had a Stevens engine and Chater Lea forks. In honour of the transmission the motorcycle was called a Clyno and was so well received that in 1910 the Clyno Engineering Co moved to a larger factory in Pelham Street, Wolverhampton.

Sidecar outfits were a speciality and were adapted to carry machine guns and for other military purposes. Over 2000 were supplied in World War I, along with 1500 8hp combinations sold to Russia. The firm also made ABC Dragonfly aero engines and parts.

Clyno experimented with a light car before the war and was later introduced to C. M. van Eugen, who had worked for Simplex in his native Holland and then Daimler and ABC in England. In 1918 van Eugen designed a 10hp overhead-valve Clyno, but it failed to go into production because of mounting financial difficulties.

Van Eugen departed for Swift and then Lea-Francis and Riley. Other Clyno casualties were works manager Henry Meadows, who left to set up a successful proprietary engine and gearbox business in Wolverhampton, and chief engineer S. C. Poole, who went to Singer as chief designer and from there to Jowett.

A new firm, Clyno Engineering Co (1922) Ltd, with £100,000 share capital, was formed to mass-produce cars, although motorcycle production continued for another two years. William Smith was chairman and his son Frank was managing director; competition motorcyclist James Cocker ran the sales side and appointed an agent in every sizeable town.

The first 10.8hp cars were designed by George Stanley, detail work being done by A. G. Booth. Engines were by Coventry-Climax. Performance, quality and steering were all

Clyde tourer of 1906

excellent so that the car was soon a runaway success, becoming embroiled in a bitter price war with Morris.

Some 623 were built in the first year, 2126 in the 1924 season and almost 5000 in 1925. Cars were widely exported, largely because of the company's links with the Rootes distribution network. Engines for a larger 12hp model were now made by Clyno itself. In 1926 production averaged 225 cars a week and extra space was urgently needed.

A 4-acre (1.6-hectare) factory was commissioned at nearby Bushbury in 1927. During the transition, production dropped to under 10,000 for the year, compared with more than 12,000 previously, although a profit of £24,000 was earned on a turnover of £1¼ million.

A new mass-seller was needed to justify the capacity of Bushbury, and in the spring of 1928 the Clyno Nine fabric saloon entered production at the rate of 70 a week. That summer a more basic Nine appeared, known as the Century because of its price, which was not much over £100. This model was badly equipped, however, looked shoddy and failed to sell satisfactorily.

Major creditors such as Coventry-Climax, Lucas and Dunlop appointed a committee to supervise their interests. The 10.8 was discontinued as rising costs were making it uneconomic, and Rootes, which was now working with Hillman, stopped distributing Clyno. A receiver was appointed in February 1929 and in August the firm was wound up with debts of £175,000. Frank Smith became works manager of Star and A. G. Booth went to AJS, which had built some Clyno bodies, before going on to design the Singer Lē Mans. In all, some 40,000 Clyno cars and 15,000 Clyno motorcycles had been sold.

The machine tool firm Alfred Herbert Ltd bought Clyno primarily for the tooling, selling the goodwill, drawings and spares to R. H. Collier and Co Ltd of Birmingham. Among the items received by Colliers was a one-off straight-eight 18hp Clyno, but of more value were tons of spares that enabled the firm to build a few complete cars at its new Wolverhampton depot. It went on to deal in late model Clynos to maintain secondhand values and sustain a healthy demand for spares. NB

COLE
USA 1909-1925

Joseph J. Cole was a carriage salesman who began his career with the Parry Manufacturing Co of Indianapolis and afterwards worked with Moon Brothers Carriage Co of St Louis. Both of these companies were later to make cars. In 1904 he left Moon to acquire the Gates-Osborne Carriage Co of Indianapolis, the name of which he changed to the Cole Carriage Co in December 1905.

Business prospered, and in 1907 the com-

Clyno Royal Torpedo of 1926

pany made 3000 vehicles in 49 different models. In 1908 J. J. Cole built an experimental high-wheeler motor buggy that used many horse buggy components and was powered by a 14hp two-cylinder engine. The chief engineer was Charles S. Crawford, who had formerly been with the Lozier Automobile Co.

Between October 1908 and May 1909 Cole turned out 170 high-wheelers, selling at between $725 and $775. These were not entirely successful, however, so Crawford designed a conventional four-cylinder touring car. In July 1909 the Cole Motor Car Co was formed and carriage manufacture abandoned.

The first cars, made in 20 and 30hp models, were joined in 1913 by a six-cylinder 60hp with capacity of 7.3 litres. The paircast four-cylinder engines were made by Cole, a new four-storey factory with an assembly line being opened in March 1914. Car production rose rapidly, from 111 between September and December 1909 to 783 in 1910 and 3547 in 1913. Prices ranged from $1685 for the 40 to $2485 for the 60. Electric lights and starter were standard features in 1913, while left-hand steering and coil ignition were adopted in 1914.

In 1915 and 1916 the six-cylinder engines were made for Cole by Northway, and when Cole adopted a V8 power unit in 1915 this was also Northway-built. From 1917 the V8 was the only model – and it was a good performer, as the 5.3-litre engine developed 80bhp. It was particularly popular in hilly territory, such as the Rocky Mountains. In the early 1920s most of the taxis in Denver were Cole Aero Eights. Peak production year was 1919, when 6255 cars were sold. Body styling was quite unusual, with hexagonal windows in the rear quarters, while the names given to these bodies were also quite individual – 'tourosine', 'sportosine', and 'brouette'.

For 1924 balloon tyres were adopted, giving rise to the advertisement asking 'Have you gone ballooning in a Cole?'. By this time production was very much reduced, falling from 1522 in 1923 to only 632 in 1924, the year in which the last Coles were made. To sell off

stock the company continued to advertise until 1925.

J. J. Cole died in September 1925, but the company continued in business by sub-letting its sizeable premises and renting them out to small engineering concerns. In this way it kept going until 1967, when the assets were sold to the Service Supply Co Inc, a distributor of bolts, screws and nuts. GNG

COLIBRI
see Selve

COLUMBIA/LIBERTY
USA 1916-1924

The Columbia Motors Co was formed in 1916 in Detroit, Michigan, to assemble conventional, low-priced, six-cylinder cars. Two models were available, a roadster and a tourer, both powered by Continental proprietary engines.

In 1920 Columbia offered probably the first example of thermostatically-operated radiator blinds, which opened automatically as the radiator heated up. Columbias were highly regarded and sold well; in 1923, when a basic roadster cost $995, Columbia sold some 6000 cars. Late in the year, in an attempt to increase manufacturing capacity, it bought the Liberty Motor Co, also of Detroit.

Liberty had also been in business since 1916, initially using Continental engines but later building its own six and selling cars very similar to the Columbia. Columbia intended to sell both its own and Liberty models, but in spite of their apparent earlier promise, both marques ceased production in 1924. BL

COLUMBIA
see also Pope

COMET
CANADA 1907-1908

The main promoter and driving force behind Montreal's first successful car builder, the Comet Motor Co, was former bicycle racer Lou D. Robertson. Robertson was the manager of the Montreal branch of the Eastern Automobile Co, one of Canada's main motor dealerships, when in 1906 he began assembling the Comet company. Another director was Frank Anson, a founder member of the Automobile Club of Canada; Berne Nadall was production manager.

The Comet was supposedly so-named because of the expected return of Halley's Comet, due in 1910, but the cars appeared (and disappeared) before the real thing. A tourer and a landaulette were ready for the Montreal Show in April 1907 and both were bought on the spot at a hefty $5000 each.

The Comet's cloth-covered wooden bodies were made locally, but most of the running gear was European-made, mainly in France. Castings for the 24hp four-cylinder engine were made by Clément-Bayard. A Comet car, driven by Lou Robertson himself, was used to drive the Prince of Wales during a visit to Quebec.

In trying to add a 40hp four-cylinder and a more powerful six to the range, Comet over-extended itself. In 1908, in an attempt to generate more cash for expansion, Comet dropped the six and reduced the price of the 24hp 'Car of Canada' to $4000, at the same time extending the guarantee from 60 days to 12 months.

After a total production of between 50 and 200 cars, however, the company stopped production and began selling other makes, notably Packard, Peerless and Chalmers. Robertson went on to develop a system of dry-plate photography before opening a canned orange juice factory in California. BL

COMPOUND
USA 1904-1907

The Eisenuth Horseless Vehicle Co was originally incorporated in San Francisco by a Mr Eisenuth who demonstrated an experimental car in that city in 1896. Nominal capital was $1 million but this was increased to $10 million by the later purchase of the Keating Automobile & Wheel Co, and the company moved to New Jersey. The name Compound was chosen because the company's production cars used compound engines, notably the Graham-Fox.

Compound engines such as the Crossley and Sperry were quite popular in the early 1900s and Eisenuth exhibited a Graham-Fox car at the 1903 Madison Square Gardens Show, but when the cars went into production in 1904, following another company

move to Middletown, Connecticut, they were called Compounds.

The three-cylinder engine had two high compression, 4in (101mm) bore outer cylinders whose exhausts fed a central, 7in (177mm) bore, low compression cylinder which ultimately exhausted to the atmosphere. The four-stroke high compression cylinders fired alternately, making the low compression cylinder somewhere between a two- and a four-stroke, erring towards the former.

Early models were a two-seater 12/15hp Doctor Compound, a five-seater 24/28hp touring car, which sold for $2000, and a seven-seater 40hp six at $3750. All were produced in 1906. The six was made up of two three-cylinder engines on a common crankcase. In 1904 a Compound was sent to Britain to be demonstrated, but sales never really took off outside the United States.

These cars were advertised as 'The Quality cars, No Muffler, No Noise, Just Power' and magazines showed 'The Runabout that Climbs' (a 12/15hp) climbing a 40 per cent gradient, fully loaded. The car also won several economy tests and hillclimbs and was really becoming quite popular, but the recession of 1907 slowed sales to a trickle, the company could not afford any developments for 1908 and production stopped. BL

CONNAUGHT
GB 1949-1959

Although Connaught's main claim to fame was Tony Brooks's famous win in the 1955 Syracuse Grand Prix, the company did include a few road cars in its all too brief history. The marque was founded by Rodney Clarke, a qualified automobile engineer and racing enthusiast who was invalided out of the RAF in 1940. He set up Continental Cars Ltd in Send, Surrey, which sold Bugattis – Clarke raced a Type 59 – and in the early post-war years had a flourishing tuning and repair business. Clarke hoped to become an official Bugatti dealer, but was stopped by that company's rapid post-war decline so he

decided to build his own, specialized sports car.

He called the cars Connaughts, from Continental Autos, and the first was the 1949 racing sports car. It was based on modified Lea-Francis components, with a 1767cc Lea-Francis engine, developed by Continental Cars' works manager Mike Oliver, and John Wyer's Monaco Engineering company of Watford. The engine gave 107bhp compared to the standard 70 and the car had a rather ugly alloy body – removable in around four minutes – on a tubular steel frame.

It made its race début at Silverstone in June 1949 driven by Kenneth McAlpine, of the McAlpine construction family, a keen driver and friend of Clarke. In 1949 and 1950 the two of them regularly raced the first two examples of the Connaught in British events.

With McAlpine's backing, Connaught progressed to Formula 2 racing with the sports car based A-series, which appeared in 1950, and began limited production of a roadgoing version of the sports racer, the L3. This sold for £800 plus taxes and, up to 1953, 27 cars were built, including a few cycle-winged type L3/SRs, with bodies by Abbotts of Farnham.

In 1951 Clarke and McAlpine formed Connaught Engineering Ltd to build the Formula 2 car and subsequent racers. This operation initially used part of Continental Cars' premises before taking over completely in June 1951. The Formula 2 cars were quite successful, in spite of being underpowered, and by 1952 they were racing in Grands Prix run to Formula 2 regulations. Connaught now concentrated solely on racing, making its first continental appearance in Belgium in June 1952 and culminating in Brooks's Syracuse win.

Even with McAlpine's backing, however, racing was too expensive; in 1956 the company spent £20,000 and after the 1957 Monaco Grand Prix it withdrew. In September all the cars and equipment were auctioned, two cars going to Bernie Ecclestone, later of Brabham. The last Connaught racer, the C-Type, was completed by Paul Emery for the 1959 US Grand Prix and appeared as late as 1962, when it failed to qualify at Indianapolis. BL

Connaught Type B of 1954

CONTINENTAL
see De Vaux

CONY
JAPAN 1961-1966

The Cony was a product of the former aircraft company Aichi, which was reformed as Aichi Machine Industry Co Ltd after World War II. The first road vehicles were three-wheeled light vans and pick-ups, of a type very popular in Japan. These were joined by the four-wheeled 360 with 359cc two-cylinder engine. By 1960 Aichi was producing 400 three-wheelers and 1000 Model 360s a month, as well as 1000 stationary engines for farms.

In 1961 came a passenger car version of the Model 360, a four-seater, two-door saloon with rear-mounted engine developing 18bhp. An estate car version was added later, but car production was always quite limited compared with the commercial models. In 1966 Aichi was absorbed into the Nissan group, and production of Cony cars and commercials ended. GNG

COOPER/MINI COOPER
GB 1947-1971

In 1920 Charles Cooper, once apprenticed to Napier and having racing associations with Kaye Don and S. F. Edge, opened a garage in Surbiton, Surrey, which grew steadily until the outbreak of World War II. After the war, Charles's son John joined the firm and in July 1946, in just five weeks from drawing board to road, they built the prototype Cooper-JAP 500 racer.

The car won the 850 class at the Brighton Speed Trials and a replica was ordered by Eric Brandon. Twelve more orders followed and even before these were filled, 12 more.

In 1947, as racing car production took over the garage, the Cooper Car Co Ltd was formed. In 1947 Cooper built a roadgoing car, the Triumph-engined T4, developed from the Formula 3 chassis, and after two more experimental road cars in 1948 and 1949, built the MG-engined T14 sports racer in 1950.

This led to the 1952 T21, an MG TC/TD-powered road or racing car which was the quickest unblown car in its class. Other sports-car projects included a 1951 streamlined record breaker, the 2-litre Cooper-Bristol, various Cooper-Climax racers and the Cooper-Jaguar, first seen in 1955.

As well as producing more than 500 cars by January 1956 – including, amazingly, 360 500s – the self sufficient factory undertook outside work and built the prototype Vanwall chassis. Staff increased from three in 1947 to 24 by 1956.

In 1958 and 1959 Cooper considered several more road car projects, including the T47, an Anzani-engined, three-wheeler 'people's car', but it was never built. In 1959 the company built one 1250 Climax-engined version of the Renault Dauphine, but much more significant that year was the début of the car which would make Cooper famous, the Mini.

John Cooper was a friend of the Mini's designer, Alec Issigonis, through a long association with the British Motor Corporation as a consultant, and was fully aware of the car's potential. Almost casually, Cooper suggested to BMC chairman Sir George Harriman the idea of building, say, 1000 modified Minis – to which Harriman responded with surprising enthusiasm. The first Mini Cooper, the 55bhp 997, was announced in July 1961 and, after early production problems, was marketed from September. It was followed by the 1071cc Cooper S in March 1963 (to August 1964), the 998 in January 1964 and the 1275 and 970 S variants from March 1964.

By the time Cooper's agreement with BMC lapsed, in August 1971, 145,493 Cooper Minis had been built, the last in July 1971. Although BMC boss Donald Stokes would not renew Cooper's £2 per car royalty deal, preferring the free use of GT and Clubman designation, the Cooper name was carried for a further three years on Italian-built Innocenti Minis until the managing director of that subsidiary returned to a post at Jaguar.

Charles Cooper had died in 1965 and John joined forces with Marks and Spencer heir Jonathan Sieff's Chipstead Group, a major foreign car concessionaire. The company was renamed the Cooper Group and the road and racing sides were separated, with the Cooper Car Co remaining autonomous. Sieff effectively bought control of the racing side, which had won the world championship in 1959 and 1960. He paid £250,000 and guaranteed sponsorship of £100,000 a year, but the racing team was disbanded in 1969. BL

CORD
USA 1929-1937

Errett Lobban Cord was born in Warrensburg, Missouri, in 1894 and had, on his own admission, made and lost three fortunes before he reached 21. His ventures had included building racing bodies on Model T Fords and operating a trucking company. In 1924 he was vice-president and general manager of the Chicago distributor for Moon cars when he was invited to become general manager of the Auburn Automobile Co. In five years he turned this from a moribund to a highly successful company, buying up several other concerns on the way.

In 1929 he incorporated the Cord Corporation, a $125 million holding company which included Auburn and Duesenberg cars, various bodybuilding companies, Lycoming engines and Stinson aircraft. To this he added a radical new design of car bearing his own name.

The Cord L-29 had a 4.9-litre 115bhp straight-eight Lycoming engine, with front-wheel drive designed by Cornelius Van Ranst aided by racing-car designer Harry Miller. It had much lower lines than any contemporary American car and came in handsome open and closed body styles made by the Cord-owned Union City Body Co. Prices ran from $3095 to $3295, but there were few buyers in Depression-hit America for an unconventional car at that price. The L-29 was dropped in 1932 after some 5200 had been made.

The Cord Corporation made a very small profit in 1934 and a loss in 1935, but its

Cooper-Jaguar of 1955

Replica 'works' Mini Cooper

Cord L29 of 1929

Cord 812 phaeton of 1937

founder was still tempted by the dream of his own make of car. Some useful contracts for kitchen cabinets provided more than $500,000 for the new project, and the Cord Model 810 made it to the New York and Chicago Auto Shows in November 1935.

It was a very striking car, with 4.7-litre Lycoming V8 engine driving the front wheels and a Gordon Buehrig-designed streamlined body, with wrap-around grille and retractable headlamps. Despite many orders at the shows, the 810 did not go into production until February 1936, by which time many customers had become impatient and cancelled their orders. This fact, combined with problems with transmission and overheating, dented the new Cord's prospects, and only 1174 were sold in the United States in 1936.

For 1937 a longer wheelbase version with a chauffeur's division was offered, together with the option of a supercharger on all models, which were now called the 812. Only 1146 of these were sold before August 1937 when production ceased. Total US sales of the 810/812 were 2320, with about 650 going to overseas customers.

The Cord Corporation was in retreat now; no Auburns were made in 1937, and only a trickle of Duesenbergs. The Auburn plant had been reduced to a parts depot in May 1936

and all production of Auburns and Cords was at Connersville, Indiana. The body dies for the 812 were bought by Norman de Vaux and eventually appeared as the Graham Hollywood and Hupmobile Skylark. Connersville continued to make kitchen cabinets, electric fans and air conditioning units, and also a rear-engined delivery van called the Pak-Age-Car, which was built from 1938 to 1941 and marketed by Diamond T.

In February 1938 the Cord Corporation changed its name to the Aviation and Transportation Co. As AVCO it made Jeep bodies in World War II, and later bought Powel Crosleys' radio and refrigerator company. It added dishwashers to its products in the 1950s, selling out in 1959 to Design and Manufacturing Corporation, which is today the world's largest producer of dishwashers. Lycoming survives today as a division of AVCO, making aero engines, mainly for light aircraft.

Errett Lobban Cord sold all his holdings in 1937 and later built another empire on the West Coast based on real estate and uranium. He died in 1974 at the age of 79. GNG

CORNILLEAU ST BEUVE
see Straker-Squire

CORSAIR
see Clénet

COSWIGA
see Nacke

COTTEREAU/CID
FRANCE 1898-1914

Cottereau 5hp of 1903

Louis Cottereau, a racing cyclist, and Henry Cottereau made bicycles from 1891 and cars from 1898 in Dijon. Etablissement Cottereau et Cie chose to call its cars voiturines in place of the word voiturette coined by Bollée, and stuck to this name for many years. The first voiturines had air-cooled 5hp vee-twins.

A Benz-type car in 1901 was not so well received and larger vee-twins were added instead, as well as a vertical single-cylinder car called the Selecta, and a 10hp four. A licence to make Cottereaus was granted to the Brièrre company in Paris which in 1900 had made a single-cylinder car with Morisse engine and became Cottereau sales agent. In 1902 a water-cooled 5hp single called the Populaire was sold in England, where the name Citizen was also used. Both Cottereau and Brièrre raced their cars, the voiturines by now having partial water-cooling under a system perfected by T. C. Pullinger, later of Sunbeam.

In 1904 Cottereau adopted a camshaft adjustment that altered valve timing to increase engine braking. From 1903 to 1909 motorcycles were made and these had Cottereau, Minerva or Peugeot engines. Also produced were commercial vehicles based on the cars and even a 4-tonner in 1905. The cars also got larger, and in 1906, when Cottereau became a Société Anonyme with 1.5 million francs capital, the range included an 18.3-litre six.

Most components and bodywork were made by Cottereau, which at its peak employed 300 to 350 men, although Arbel chassis were used on a competitively priced three-cylinder model and later fours. A proliferation of Cottereau models, often with

Cottereau Populaire of 1904

choice of valve gear and final drive, did little to help profitability and a slump adversely affected the company.

An effort to break into the luxury car market was made in 1907 with a 26hp four, which had wooden wheels and an Arbel steel frame. To cater for the voiturine end of the market the company produced a 7hp water-cooled single with central chain drive and tubular frame; a similar 9hp followed in 1910. Experiments were made with four- and six-cylinder rotary-valve engines.

In 1910, too, Cottereau was taken over by Compagnie Industrielle Dijonaise, the initials of which were adopted for the cars of 1911. The use of single cylinders continued in an 8hp Buchet-engined Baby, which had friction transmission and shaft-drive, versions being sold in 1912 under the name Emeraude. Rotary-valve engines appeared in 14 and 16hp cars in 1912 and were joined by a luxury 22hp version in 1913. Technical as well as financial difficulties which the company was unable to solve caused CID to abandon car production the following year. Louis Cottereau died in 1917. NB

COTTIN-DESGOUTTES
FRANCE 1905-1933

Pierre Desgouttes worked for the pioneer Lyons car-maker Audibert et Lavirotte, which became part of the expanding Berliet organization in 1903. He transferred to Berliet and

there worked on the car that was to be adopted by Sunbeam.

In 1904 he left, however, and in the following year formed Société des Automobiles Pierre Desgouttes et Cie, with a small factory in Lyons. One of his main shareholders was Cyrille Cottin, who came from a rich textile family, and early in 1906 the firm became Automobiles Cottin et Desgouttes. The first car, a 24/40 four, was ready in October 1905 and had an Arbel steel frame.

This and subsequent models were well made and a little cheaper than rival Berliets. A 9.5-litre 30hp six was ready towards the end of 1906. Commercial vehicles were made from the outset, a speciality being shaft-drive Alpine buses and charabancs.

In 1908 the firm adopted its familiar star badge, carrying the wording Paris-Lyons in honour of a recently-opened Paris sales office. About 300 men were employed in 1910 and production had risen to 450 vehicles

Cottin-Desgouttes, French GP, 1911

110

Cottin-Desgouttes Sans Secousse of 1927

three years later. During World War I aero engines, six-cylinder command cars, 1½- to 4-ton lorries and engines of up to 150bhp for 'locotracteurs' were made.

A 4-litre 18CV car and various commercials were made after the war and were joined in 1922 by the first 'small' Cottin et Desgouttes, an M-type 12 with five-bearing crank and four-wheel brakes. Pierre Desgouttes resigned after designing this car, which soon came with various engine capacities, including a six in 1923. He was replaced by Paul Joseph from Berliet, although his name was retained on the cars and he himself lived on into the 1950s.

A sports version of the M, with three valves per cylinder, two carburettors and eight plugs, was developed and won the 1924 Grand Prix de Tourisme. About 20 Grand Prix models were sold and overall production was about 35 vehicles a month, of which perhaps a third were commercials. Several low chassis coaches were built and in 1925 these were offered in Britain by Cottin Commercial Cars of Hammersmith, London.

In 1927 Paul Joseph and Antoine Burlat produced their remarkable Sans Secousse (literally 'without jolts'), which had four-wheel independent suspension by transverse leaves, a low centre of gravity and inboard rear brakes. Initially a 12CV with angular Cottin bodywork, it soon came with various four- and six-cylinder engines including, in 1927, their first proprietary engined 10CV six. A Sans Secousse won the Comfort Concours in the 1927 Monte Carlo Rally although it did no better than 27th overall. The cars were advertised extensively and about 20 a month were sold.

A 14 six, new in 1929, won the gruelling Sahara Rally the following year, when Lockheed hydraulic brakes were adopted. Prices were almost double those of equivalent Citroëns and Renaults, and sales suffered accordingly. In 1931, with a SCAP 2.4-litre engined 14 straight-eight ready for production, Cyrille Cottin's company went into liquidation.

The Société Nouvelle des Automobiles Cottin-Desgouttes was then formed and cars built from a components stock worth 10 million francs were shown at the 1932 Salon. The last cars were assembled in 1933 and Cyrille Cottin died in 1942. NB

COURIER
see Stoddard-Dayton

COVENTRY-PREMIER
see Premier

COVENTRY-VICTOR
GB 1926-1938

Coventry-Victor three-wheeler of 1935

The forerunner of the Coventry-Victor Motor Co Ltd was formed in 1904 as Morton and Weaver Ltd and for many years specialized in horizontally-opposed two-cylinder engines for use in motorcycles, light cars and as mobile power plants of all kinds. The name was changed to Coventry-Victor in 1911. One of its more important customers before 1914 was the Coventry motorcycle maker, W. Montgomery and Co.

In 1919 the company launched a motorcycle of its own manufacture, powered by a 688cc flat-twin engine, and this unit was used in a prototype four-wheeled light car, designed by the company's managing director W. A. Weaver. Built in 1919 it never went into production, but Coventry-Victor engines were supplied to numerous cyclecar makers, including some as far afield as Belgium

(Jeecy-Vea) and Czechoslovakia (CAS). Its best customer in England was Grahame-White, which bought several hundred in the early 1920s.

In 1926 Coventry-Victor brought out a chain-driven three-wheeler using the 688cc engine, priced at £99 15s complete. A 749cc sports model at £110 followed in 1928, although the smaller engine was continued until 1933. In 1932 the three-wheelers were completely restyled by C. F. Beauvais, who had built a light car named the CFB in 1920-21 and who was also responsible for styling Avon Standards, Singers and Crossleys in the early 1930s. The new models, with Avon-built bodies and available in attractive dual-tone colour schemes, were made until 1938. They were powered by engines of 749, 850 or 998cc.

In 1932 Coventry-Victor formed a separate company, Victor Oil Engines (Coventry) Ltd, to make small flat-twin diesel engines which were sold under the name Victor Cub. These were popular as marine units, and at least one was installed in a Jowett van. Motorcycle production ended in 1930 and cars in 1938, but in 1949 the company experimented with a new car, code-named Venus, powered by a 747cc flat-four engine. However, the project was not judged a success and the car never

went into production.

Coventry-Victor made a large number of air-cooled petrol engines during World War II, and in the 1950s turned to single and horizontally-opposed twin diesel engines which were widely used in lifeboats and as auxiliary power units for yachts and fishing vessels. It also undertook a good deal of subcontract engineering work, including making the Martin V8 engine used in the prototype Deep Sanderson car which later became the Monica.

W. A. Weaver, one of the original partners, ran the company until his death in 1970 when it was reorganized by his son as A. N. Weaver (Coventry-Victor) Ltd. Under this name, and at new premises, the company is still in the business of making industrial and marine engines today. GNG

CRANE/CRANE-SIMPLEX
USA 1912-1924

Born in 1874, Henry Middlebrook Crane came from a wealthy family and was able to indulge his interest in speedboats and motor cars while working for the American Bell Telephone Co and then for Western Electric. With his brother, Clinton, he built several successful speedboats and in 1906 he founded the Crane and Whitman Co at Bayonne, New Jersey, to build motor cars.

The first Crane car, a large T-head four-cylinder, was completed in 1907 and two more cars were built in 1908, but production did not start until 1912, with the Model 3, a 9.2-litre 46hp six with four-speed gearbox and shaft drive. The chassis price was $9000, making it one of the most expensive American cars of its day. Crane favoured Brewster as a coachbuilder, and most Crane cars were probably bodied by that firm.

About 20 Crane Model 3s were made in 1912 and 1913, followed in 1914 by the Model 4 which differed in having the cylinders cast in two blocks of three instead of three pairs. This design attracted the attention of the Simplex Automobile Co of New Brunswick, New Jersey, which needed a more refined design than the large chain drive fours that it was making. It therefore purchased the Crane Motor Car Co, acquiring at the same time the services of Henry Crane.

For 1915 the company announced its new model, the Simplex, Crane Model 5 which was soon abbreviated to Crane-Simplex. Production was in the Simplex factory, and about 500 chassis were built until July 1917. Increased numbers enabled Simplex to get the price down to $5000 in 1915, although it rose again to $7000 two years later. Bodies were by a variety of the best American coachbuilders, including Brewster, Healey, Holbrook and Demarest.

America's entry into World War I put an end to the Crane-Simplex car, as the factory began production of the Hispano-Suiza V8 aero engine under the supervision of Henry Crane. Simplex became part of a newly-formed group, the Wright-Martin Aircraft Corporation, and no more cars were made at New Brunswick, although some Model 5s were still being sold off in 1920.

Rights to the Crane engine were acquired by Emlen S. Hare who was attempting to build an empire of high-quality cars including Locomobile and Mercer. This eventually collapsed in bankruptcy, and a new company, Crane-Simplex Co of New York, acquired the rights in 1923 and proposed to build 100 of the old-style chassis selling at $10,000. Few, if any, of these were actually built.

Meanwhile, Henry Crane built some experimental cars in his own workshop at Garwood, New Jersey, but he never returned to car manufacture. He had a distinguished career as an engineer with General Motors, being technical adviser to Alfred Sloan and instrumental in the launch of the Pontiac in 1926. Later he was an advocate of the large-bore short-stroke V8 engine that General Motors adopted in the 1950s. He died in 1956. GNG

CRAWFORD
USA 1904-1923

Robert S. Crawford was a wealthy bicycle manufacturer of Hagerstown, Maryland, whose company was acquired by the Pope organization in the early 1900s. The Pope Tribune car was made there. With the proceeds he set up a small car manufacturing company based on his private stables. Production of conventional two- and four-cylinder cars began in 1904, and over the next few years output and size of cars both increased.

In 1907 62 cars were made and the next year Crawford resigned, the majority of shares being acquired by a Danish-born local organ manufacturer, Mathias Peter Möller.

At first, practically all components were made in the factory, including tools such as socket wrenches. However, components from outside suppliers were increasingly used from 1910, including Continental six-cylinder engines. All bodies were made in-house.

Peak production year was 1910 with 275 cars built; output subsequently varied from 38 in 1917 – doubtless because of America's entry into World War I when the company made gun sights – to 142 in 1919. The labour force never exceeded 40 to 50 men.

The early 1920s saw a great mortality among undistinguished assembled cars such as the Crawford, and production dwindled to 55 in 1922 and then to precisely one in 1923. By this time Robert Crawford's brother George had left and the Crawford family was completely out of the business, but Möller had ambitious plans for car manufacture and these were realized in the Dagmar. GNG

CRESPELLE
FRANCE 1906-1923

The Crespelle was built by F. Crespelle of Paris from 1906 to 1923, but in spite of its relatively long existence the Crespelle achieved more sporting renown than sales success. The first cars used long-stroke single-cylinder Aster or De Dion engines and were successful in hillclimbs and minor races, most results coming from hillclimbs.

The Crespelle grew up until by 1913 it was using long-stroke four-cylinder engines of up to 3 litres, a Janvier unit, in a six model range. The post-war Crespelles mainly used four-cylinder Sergant engines in sizes ranging from 1.3 to 2.4 litres. BL

CROSLEY
USA 1939-1952

Born in 1886, Powel Crosley Jr became a pioneer of mass-produced radios and in 1922 was the largest radio manufacturer in the world. He also owned a radio station and the Cincinnati Redlegs baseball team, and manufactured refrigerators, making the first fridge to have shelves in the doors.

He had built a home-made electric car in 1900, and considered manufacture in 1907 with the low priced six-cylinder Marathon Six. Lack of capital put an end to this project, but the design was incorporated in the Lexington, made at Lexington, Kentucky, and Connerville, Indiana, from 1909 to 1928.

His first production car was launched in April 1939, a microcar by American standards, powered by a 15bhp 580cc flat-twin

Crane-Simplex six of c.1918

Crosley convertible coupé of 1941

Waukesha engine, a modified version of the unit used for powering orchard sprayers. Transmission was by three-speed non-synchromesh Warner gearbox. The two-seater convertible sold for $325, undercutting the cheapest American Bantam by $62. The cars were made at one of Crosley's factories in Richmond, Indiana.

Crosley sold 2017 cars to the end of 1939, but production problems brought the 1940 total down to 422. With a new chief engineer, Paul Klotsch, things improved in 1941, when 2289 cars were sold, the range now including a station wagon and delivery van.

Crosley prospered during the war, with a payroll of 10,000 people making anti-aircraft shell fuses, gun turrets, field radios and Waukesha-powered sledges. The company also made 36 examples of a mini Jeep intended for parachute dropping and, most important, a small four-cylinder engine with copper brazed cylinder block. This 722cc 26hp COBRA engine went into the post-war Crosley car, a four-seater sedan with all-steel body by Murray, which entered production in June 1946.

By this time Powel Crosley had shed his radio interests, marking this step by a change in company name from the Crosley Radio Corporation to Crosley Motors Inc. The post-war cars were made at Marion, Indiana.

Crosley hoped to sell 80,000 cars in 1946, but in fact only 5007 units left the factory. Business picked up later, though, with more than 16,000 sold in 1947 and 28,000 in 1948. This last figure included 23,000 station wagons, making Crosley the world's largest builder of station wagons.

The factory was extended by 40 per cent in 1948 but business dropped badly the following year, when only 8549 cars were sold. The COBRA engine proved to have serious faults

due to electrolysis acting on the copper, and was replaced by the CIBA (cast iron block assembly) for 1949. Another damaging factor was the availability of low-mileage full-size second-hand cars for no more than the $950 to $1000 price of a new Crosley. Despite the introduction of two novelties, the Hotshot sports car and Farm-O-Road utility vehicle, sales dropped to 7043 in 1950 and 4839 in 1951.

Powel Crosley was realist enough to see that sales were unlikely to pick up and ended production in July 1952, after 1522 vehicles had been made that year. The company was

bought by the General Taxi and Rubber Co of Akron, Ohio, which later merged with the Aerojet Engineering Corporation. The factory was used for the manufacture of parts for jet-assistance take-off rockets. Powel Crosley retained his interests in the Cincinnati Reds until his death in 1961. GNG

CROSSLEY
GB 1904-1937

William Crossley was honeymooning in Germany when he came to hear of the new 'atmospheric' engines. He summoned his engineering-trained brother Frank to meet inventor Nikolaus A. Otto and in 1869 they acquired patent rights to Otto and Langen's engines throughout the world, except for Germany. Only 87 were built in Germany that year but sales in both Britain and the continent expanded rapidly; when the type ended in 1876 Crossley had made almost as many as the 2649 of Deutz. Crossley then turned to the 'Otto cycle' four-stroke engines at his Otto Gas Engine works in Manchester and by 1900 had made 26,500 engines.

In London, car dealers Charles Jarrott and William Letts were keen to sell a large and luxurious British model alongside the imported Locomobile, De Dietrich and Oldsmobile cars they were selling. They persuaded J. S. Critchley from Daimler to design an 'English Mercédès' and he in turn took the plans to Crossley. The first car, with 4.6-litre engine, was ready in January 1904 and had a Belgian frame and other foreign components. Two years later came 'all British' types. In 1906 also the firm supplied petrol engines for Leyland buses and a car-making subsidiary of

Crossley 30/40hp (Charles Jarrott driving) of 1907

113

Crossley Brothers Ltd was formed.

At the end of 1910 the car business and Charles Jarrott and Letts Ltd were merged as Crossley Motors Ltd of Gorton, Manchester, with Kenneth Crossley as chairman. Thereafter the engine firm went its separate way, taking over first the Premier Gas Engine Co of Sandiacre in 1919 and then the Saunderson Tractor and Implement Co Ltd of Bedford in 1923. Its eventual output exceeded 100,000 oil and gas engines.

In 1909 the smaller 12/14 – soon called the 15 – and 20hp cars were designed by Walter Iden in conjunction with G. H. Woods, A. W. Reeve and the former Wolseley driver Cecil Bianchi, who was works manager and later chief engineer before joining Bean in 1929. Front-wheel brakes were tried in 1909 as well. Output in 1913 was about 650 cars.

The 20, later designated 20/25, was made from 1909 to 1925 and almost 10,000 were supplied as staff cars, ambulances, armoured cars and tenders during World War I. Complete drawings were sent to Russia for

times with five-cylinder radial engine. A. V. Roe and Co Ltd were sold to Armstrong-Siddeley in 1928.

William Letts, who had been on the board of Crossley Motors from the beginning, was, with former racing driver Charles Jarrott, the British Bugatti importer. It was not altogether surprising, therefore, when Crossley began to build the Type 22 in Gorton in 1922. A first batch of 500 was intended, but perhaps only two dozen were actually made.

Rather more productive was Letts's friendship with J. N. Willys, and Willys-Overland-Crossley Ltd was set up in December 1919 to make American-type cars. Despite ambitious plans for building 12,000 cars and light commercials a year, little more than assembly and the fitment of British trim and lighting took place. An all-British Overland with Morris-Oxford engine was developed and the Whippet Six was produced as the Palatine Six in 1931. Willys-based commercials did a better job of hiding their identity under the name Manchester from 1926. Short-

being hand-built at Gorton in May 1930. Two years later a Coventry-Climax powered Ten was made at the rate of 450 a year.

Crossley commercial vehicles were selling well and in 1928 the company tackled the bus and coach market. Ten years later almost 1000 buses had been sold to municipal operators alone. In 1930 Britain's first diesel double-decker was built by Crossley. This vehicle had a Gardner engine, although Crossley diesels were developed that year.

The Ten was restyled by C. F. Beauvais of New Avon bodyworks as the Regis 4 in 1935, although coachwork was made at Gorton, and was joined by a Coventry-Climax 1½-litre six-cylinder engined Regis 6. Production of the Ten and Regis 4 totalled 2000; the figure for the Regis 6 was about 500. In 1937 car production ceased.

AEC bought the company in 1948 to create Associated Commercial Vehicles Ltd, which Maudslay also joined. Crossley bus bodies and trolleybuses continued to be built until the factory was closed in 1958. NB

Crossley 10hp of 1933

manufacture at Lebedev before the Revolution. Crossley also made Beardmore and Bentley BR2 aero engines during the war and forged such strong links with the predecessor of the RAF that it remained its heavy vehicle supplier for 25 years.

In 1920, when car production was running at 20 chassis a week, Crossley acquired the A. V. Roe aircraft firm. The Avro light car introduced in 1919 with 1.3-litre four-cylinder engine was continued for a further year, some-

ly before the end of the marque and of Willys-Overland-Crossley in 1933, some versions had become all-British.

Meanwhile in 1925 Crossley had introduced a six-cylinder 18/50 and had received royal patronage in Britain, Siam, Japan and Spain. In 1925 the company made profits of £16,000 but a year later this was turned into a loss of £285,000.

In 1927 a 2-litre six was introduced, which accounted for most of the 35 to 50 cars a week

CROUCH
GB 1912-1927

John William Fisher Crouch was apprenticed at Maudslay and later worked for Daimler. After his father, also called John, sold his hat-making factory in Atherstone near Birmingham the two men formed Crouch Motors (1910) Ltd with the proceeds. They developed a three-wheel Crouch Carette with centrally mounted Coventry-Simplex 1-litre water-cooled vee-twin which was available from 1912 and was joined by a four-wheel version in 1913.

Having made war materials during World War I the company resumed car production in Coventry at the end of hostilities and soon some 400 men were making 20 to 30 cars a week. Bodies initially came from the Carbodies company but an old munitions factory was then taken over by Crouch for this work. The cars became more conventional, at least half having Anzani four-cylinder engines and the rest Coventry-Simplex and Coventry-Climax fours. All had Meadows gearboxes and Moss axles. They earned a sporting reputation, particularly in the hands of Stirling Moss's father Alfred, who handled London sales and in 1923 offered one year's free insurance and guarantee on the £225 four-cylinder tourer and promised 90mph (145kph) from the Anzani-engined sports model.

A serious blow was the despatch to Australia of 200 cars, none of which was paid for. John Crouch was forced to sell family property in Cardiff and Coventry to keep the firm going, but after about 3000 Crouch cars had been sold in all, the company collapsed in 1927. John Crouch Jr returned to Daimler as an engineer, having lost virtually everything. He died in about 1950. NB

Crouch Carette of 1912

Crouch (Alfred Moss driving) of c.1922

CROW-ELKHART/BLACK
CROW, MORRISS-LONDON
USA 1911-1925

This make had its origins in the Black Manufacturing Co of Fort Wayne, Indiana, which made high-wheel buggies from 1903 to 1910. In 1909 it took over the distribution of a new conventional four-cylinder car which it called the Black Crow, made by the Crow Motor Car Co of Elkhart, Indiana. Late in 1910 the Black Co was liquidated, and in the following year the name Crow-Elkhart was adopted.

A wide range of models with four different sizes of four-cylinder engine was offered for 1912, at prices from $875 to $2000. A Rutenber six-cylinder engine was added for 1913, and for 1914 there were two Lycoming-powered fours and the Rutenber six. These were conventional cars apart from the mounting of

the gearboxes on the rear axle.

In 1916 Crow-Elkhart made its most attractive-looking car, a three-seater cloverleaf roadster with four-cylinder Lycoming engine, vee-radiator and wire wheels, priced at a modest $795. This was made at least until 1918 and stood out in a range of otherwise very ordinary-looking cars. A four-cylinder Gray engine was used in 1919, but the following year the company reverted to Lycoming for the fours, with the six-cylinder unit still coming from Rutenber. From 1921 Herschell-Spillman engines were used, a four and a six to 1922, and fours only thereafter.

The Crow-Elkhart sold quite well in and around its home town but never became well-known nationally. Peak production was in 1916, when more than 1000 cars were sold; by 1920 sales were down to 600, dropping rapidly after that. There were two international ventures. About 120 four-cylinder models were assembled in Canada at Mount Brydges,

Ontario, in 1916 and 1917, and in 1919 an agreement was signed with London dealer F. E. Morriss whereby Morriss would import four-cylinder Crow-Elkhart chassis, fit them with English bodies and sell them under the name Morriss-London.

This was never very successful, and in 1922 69 chassis, which had stood in the open for nearly a year, were bought by Saunders Motors Ltd of Golders Green, London, for £75 each. They were refurbished, given tourer or landaulette bodies made by a small London firm, and sold under the name Saunders. This lasted until 1925 when Saunders went into liquidation, being re-formed as H. A. Saunders Ltd, Austin dealers.

The Crow-Elkhart company was re-formed in June 1923 as the Century Motor Co, but few cars were made and production ceased during 1924. Some Crow-Elkharts were made for Birch Motor Cars Inc, a mail-order firm which sold the cars under its own name. GNG

CROWDY
see Weigel

CROXTON/CROXTON-KEETON,
JEWEL(L), KEETON
USA 1905-1915

Herbert A. Croxton, born in 1872 and a prominent steel-maker, was head of the Forest City Motor Car Co of Cleveland (and later Masillon) Ohio, which built a high-wheeled buggy in 1905 with a two-stroke single-cylinder engine, two-speed chain drive and a $600 price tag. The car was sold as the Jewell and remained virtually unchanged for two years. In 1908 the Jewell was followed by the $3000 newly-spelled Jewel 40, which had a four-stroke Rutenber engine.

In 1909 the company became the Jewel Motor Car Co and in 1910 was reorganized again as the Croxton-Keeton Motor Co with working capital increased from $250,000 to $500,000. Keeton referred to Forrest M. Keeton of Detroit, born in 1874, and who from 1903 had worked as sales manager in the Pope-Toledo branch of the Pope Motor Car Co. In 1908 he had set up the Keeton Taxicab and Town Car Works, building taxis.

Herbert Croxton became president of Croxton-Keeton, which remained in Masillon. The former Jewel 40 was renamed the Croxton-Keeton 'German type' and was joined by a 30hp 'French type' with scuttle radiator.

In 1910 Croxton and Keeton separated to make cars under their own names. Keeton formed the Keeton Motor Co in Detroit in 1910 and built Keeton cars until 1913, beginning with a 3.7-litre four-cylinder landaulette and a 6-litre six selling for between $2500 and $2800. This Six-48 claimed to be the first car to offer wire wheels as standard. Keeton also built a prototype racer but gradually moved over to cyclecars, marketing the Car Nation alongside the Keeton in 1913 and continuing Car Nation production until 1915, having been taken over by the American Voiturette Co, also of Detroit.

Keeton cars were also built in Canada by Keeton Motors Ltd of Brantford, Ontario, a company formed by a local group. It built its first Keeton in 1913 and apparently outlived the American version by continuing into 1915.

Croxton set up the Croxton Motor Car Co in Cleveland, Ohio, in 1911 and continued to build the German 45 and the French 30. In March 1911 Croxton merged with the struggling Royal Tourist Motor Car Co of Cleveland to form the Consolidated Motor Car Co. In June 1912 this partnership was dissolved and Croxton reorganized again as the Croxton Motors Co and moved to Washington, Philadelphia, where he continued to build similar cars in small numbers alongside a new six, until late in 1913.

In February 1914 Croxton reorganized yet again, as the Universal Motor Car Co with $1 million capital, but a planned $475 cyclecar was never built. The plant was auctioned in 1915 for just $25,000. After the end of their companies and after World War I, Keeton returned to the auto trade as a salesman and not as a manufacturer, until his death in 1944. Herbert Croxton died in 1940. BL

CUBITT
GB 1920-1925

The Cubitt was one of several British attempts at mass production in the early post-war years, others including Angus-Sanderson and Ruston-Hornsby. The parent company, Holland, Hannen and Cubitt Ltd was well-known for its building and engineering work and could trace its origins to the building company founded by Thomas Cubitt in 1815, which was largely responsible for the development of the Belgravia district of London.

In 1919 it took over a munitions factory at Aylesbury, Buckinghamshire, owned by James Putnam, who received shares in the newly formed Cubitt's Engineering Co Ltd in

exchange for providing the 10-acre (4-hectare) factory. Authorized share capital was £600,000.

The car was of conventional design having a 16/20hp 2.8-litre four-cylinder engine with coil ignition, four-speed gearbox and overhead worm drive. Bodies were made in a separate factory across the road, formerly the body shop of the Iris Motor Co before World War I. The proposed price was £298, but by the time the first cars came on the market in 1920 this had risen to £442. The increase, combined with very slow deliveries through difficulties in obtaining proprietary components, did Cubitt's reputation much harm and sales never reached the hoped-for figures.

At best the factory turned out about 20 cars a day, but this figure was not maintained for long. The only year in which it showed a profit was 1919-20 with £13,340. Thereafter losses mounted alarmingly, to £63,609 in 1920-21 and £163,813 in 1921-22. Cubitt Engineering made further losses and was liquidated in 1925.

Car production dropped sharply after about 1923, despite the introduction of a new, lower model, and the works kept going with the manufacture of four-cylinder engines of Anzani design for use in AC cars. The body shops also produced coachwork for AC, whose managing director, S. F. Edge, had also become managing director of Cubitt. All production ceased at the end of 1925 and the machinery was sold off. The buildings remained, with various owners, and are today the home of the engineering division of Versatile Fittings Ltd. GNG

CUDELL
GERMANY 1897-1908

Paul Cudell was the German licensee of De Dion-Bouton, building engines and tricycles at Aix-la-Chapelle (Aachen) from 1897. Four-wheelers followed in 1899. In 1900 Cudell formed Die Gesellschaft für Motor und Motorfahrzeug Bau with a capital of 75,000 marks to make boat engines, cars and so on, and after the first year's trading shareholders received a 4 per cent dividend. Some Cudell-adapted

De Dion-Boutons were put on the market in Britain in 1904-5 under the name of Cudell-Krupcars.

Cudell lost money in the period 1902-4 and in the latter year a fire destroyed the Aachen factory, along with 25 cars, 10 motorcycles and all the company's drawings. Both Adler and Stoewer negotiated De Dion licences with Cudell.

In 1904 Cudell decided to move to Berlin and with Leo Koelbing set up Cudell Motoren GmbH with 100,000 marks capital and 26 workers. Vehicles were no longer De Dion-based. Karl Slevogt designed an overhead-valve Cudell-Phönix which was also made in Budapest from 1905 in the factory that later produced the Magomobil and Magosix. Cudell ceased vehicle production in 1908, although the Phönix lasted in Hungary until World War I. NB

CUNNINGHAM
USA 1907-1936

Founded in 1838 in Rochester, New York, James Cunningham's firm made high-quality horse-drawn vehicles. Cars were added in 1907 using Buffalo and Continental engines, and three years later the company produced the first model to have Cunningham's own 40hp four-cylinder engine. The works manager until 1913 was James Howe, who had gained engineering experience at E. R. Thomas, Selden and Studebaker. The company was registered as James Cunningham Son and Co Inc.

Carriages continued to be made until 1915. A one-model policy for car production was adopted in 1916. The engine used was a 7.2-litre pair-cast Lacey-designed V8. Well made and stylish, the car attracted the attention of wealthy sportsmen, including Ralph de Palma.

Cunningham never made more than 200 cars a year in the early 1920s and did not offer a down-market model, unlike so many of its contemporaries. Coachwork was traditional and the business was kept going largely by ambulance and funeral car bodywork. The company did little advertising and had few dealers, although Walter L. Elbe looked after sales in Hollywood, where Harold Lloyd, Mary Pickford and Universal Studios' William Seiter drove Cunningham cars.

The Depression eventually spelled the end of the archaic V8 in 1934, by which time power output had risen from under 100 to over 140bhp. Continental straight-eight-powered hearses and ambulances were built on bought-in chassis until 1936 and about 150 town cars built on Ford V8 running gear were sold for $2600 each. Ford trucks were converted to half-tracks for military purposes and similar machines were made with Cadillac engines. Cunningham continues in business today as a supplier of electrical switchgear. NB

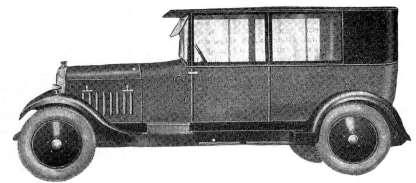
Cubitt Model K of 1925

Cunningham C4 coupé of 1952

CUNNINGHAM
USA 1950-1957

Briggs Swift Cunningham, born in 1907, was a wealthy American sportsman. The Cunningham family fortune came from Briggs's father's investments, principally in Procter and Gamble and his mother's railway and utility holdings. In 1928 Cunningham opted out of the US Olympic athletic squad in favour of another pursuit, sailing. A year later he gave up his education and turned his sporting interests to motor racing.

In 1940 he built a Mercedes-engined Buick special, which he raced as the Bu-Merc, and he became active in the Automobile Racing Club of America, later the Sports Car Club of America and the country's principal road race sanctioning body. After the war, in which he flew with the Civil Air Patrol, he raced Healeys, an MG and the first Ferrari imported into the USA. In 1950 he put the Cunningham name into the motor sport record books when he fulfilled an ambition to make the first American entry at Le Mans since 1935.

The Cunningham entries for the 24-hour classic were two Model 61 Cadillacs. One remained almost standard but the other was rebodied by the Grumman Aircraft Corporation, its angular streamlining earning it the nickname of 'Le Monstre'. The cars finished a creditable 11th and 12th, after endless dramas, which was enough to encourage Cunningham to establish the B. S. Cunningham Co in September 1950. He rented a factory in Palm Beach, California, and hired a staff of 40 to prepare an increased Le Mans effort for 1951.

He proposed a car suitable for road use as well as for racing and dubbed the prototype C1 and the 'production' cars C2. Four of the George Desler-designed cars were built in just three months; one was a Cadillac-engined road car and the other three were 180bhp Chrysler Hemi-engined cars for Le

Mans. In the race, two crashed but the third ran as high as second before falling back to 18th with fuel problems.

In November 1951 Cunningham advertised an $8000 sports roadster derivative of the C2 as 'the ultimate in sports cars', but only one was built, in 1952, before Cunningham reluctantly accepted that he needed a roadster *and* a racer. The racer would be the C4R, built in a new factory, and the road car, catalogued from February 1952, was the $9000 C3 Continental Coupé, bodied by Vignale to a Giovanni Michelotti design.

The C3 had a 210bhp, 331cu in Chrysler engine and most were automatics. It was extremely quick for its day and in its most powerful form would approach 140mph (225kph). In March 1953 a convertible version, priced at a hefty $11,422, was shown at the Geneva Show.

Eventually 18 coupés and nine convertibles were built, but the company failed to make a profit for five consecutive years, even enjoying 'hobby' status from the tax authorities. In 1955 the company was wound up, the plant was sold off and production was stopped.

The Cunningham racers had scored fourth place at Le Mans in 1952 (with the C4R) and a worthy third in 1953 (with the C5R). Cunningham kept trying until 1955, with the

Offenhauser-engined C6R, but had finally to admit that American power was not quite a match for European sophistication.

Having spent probably $1 million on his patriotic efforts, Cunningham joined Jaguar Cars Ltd in 1956 as distributor for New England and the company's American racing representative. The 1957 Jaguar-engined C6RD was the last Cunningham and the beginning of a long association with racing Jaguars. BL

CWS BELL
see Bell (GB)

CYKLON
GERMANY 1902-1931

The Cyklon Maschinenfabrik GmbH made motorcycles in Berlin before showing its first car, a three-wheeler, at the Leipzig Motor Show in 1902. Like the company's earlier motorcycles, and its better-known compatriot, the Phänomobil, the three-wheeler had its motor mounted above the single front wheel and drove it by chain. The first model, a two-seater, had a 3½PS 450cc single-cylinder engine and tiller steering. In 1904 Cyklon introduced the 10PS 1290cc twin-cylinder Cyklonette, which sold well in various versions including light vans until 1922.

In 1919 Cyklon merged with the Schebera Karosseriewerken, part of financier Jacob Schapiro's group of companies, which included several car manufacturers. Schapiro was a major shareholder in Benz, Eisenach and NSU among others.

In 1922 the company became Cyklon Automobilwerke AG and from 1923 it produced a 5/20PS 1.3-litre two-seater car for Schebera. The 1926 six-cylinder Cyklon 9/40PS was the identical forerunner of the 9/40PS Dixi, and from 1927 to 1929 it was produced under that name but only in limited numbers in spite of being the cheapest German six-cylinder car.

Cyklon's last model was the 1.8-litre 7/40PS Type D. It was built under licence from the French Donnet-Zédel company until Cyklon ceased trading in 1931. BL

Cyklon 9/40PS of 1929

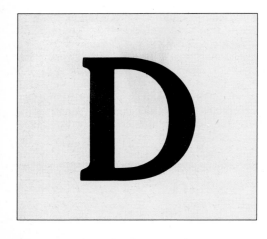

DAF
HOLLAND 1959-1981

This was the first Dutch company to build cars in volume since Spyker in the mid-1920s and was set up by the Van Doorne brothers, Hubert Jozef and Wim, sons of a blacksmith from Deurne. Wim, born in 1906, became the businessman of the two and Hubert, born on the first day of the 20th century, became the inventor and the power behind their companies.

In the early 1920s Hubert, or Hub, worked as a labourer, a chauffeur and a mechanic. A local businessman whose car he repaired lent money to form the engineering company Commanitaire Vernootschap Hub Van Doorne's Machinefabriek. In the late 1920s the company employed about 30 people, making truck and trailer parts for the growing truck industry. It expanded to build railway containers and military vehicles, including amphibians, artillery tractors and the six-wheel Trado.

Recovering after the German occupation with the help of Marshal Plan funds, Van Doorne progressed from military to commercial vehicle production, making truck and bus chassis – at first with Leyland and Perkins engines. The army was still a major customer and the company expanded rapidly during the 1950s. In 1955 Van Doorne employed some 6000 people in 1 million square feet (93,000sq m) of plant.

The prolifically inventive Hub devised an infinitely variable, belt-drive automatic transmission, which he called Variomatic and which was tested *in extremis* by towing trailers in severe conditions, up mountains and across deserts. In February 1958 at the Amsterdam Show Hub exhibited a car using his transmission and on 23 March 1959 it was launched as the production DAF 600, built by Van Doornes Automobielfabriek NV in Eindhoven.

In 1961, with a workforce of almost 6000, DAF produced some 15,000 cars and 5000 trucks, and even boasted a German assembly plant. By 1962 60,000 cars had been sold and in 1964 production reached 20,000 a year.

In 1965 DAF demonstrated the versatility of Variomatic on vehicles ranging from a 4×4 military truck to rally cars and an F3 single-seater racing car. That year, Hub Van Doorne retired (in line with Dutch law) as head of DAF, Wim taking over briefly as president.

In 1971 Hub also left the administrative board and formed Van Doorne BV Transmissie in Tilburg to develop a fully automatic transmission, the Transmatic, one of his 170 or so patented inventions. Hub was also a director of many other companies and was lavishly honoured for his work, as a Knight of the Order of the Netherlands Lion among others. He died in May 1979, Wim having died in 1978.

By the time of Hub's retirement, DAF was attracting outside backing. In 1967 the Dutch State Mines acquired a 10 per cent interest which financed a plant at Dorn, creating 3500 jobs by 1970 in the dying Limburg coalfield. In 1971 DAF built 50,000 cars and 12,000 trucks with a workforce of 12,000. In 1972 International Harvester bought 33 per cent of DAF's truck division and in 1973 introduced the World Utility Transporter, based on DAF mechanicals.

In the early 1970s, as DAF experienced continuing financial problems, International Harvester was one of the firms approached for assistance. DAF also approached the Dutch government but the government declined to make loans directly to DAF, preferring to support a takeover by the Swedish firm, Volvo, which acquired a one-third interest in the DAF car side in 1973, increasing to 75 per cent by 1975.

The Volvo takeover was largely engineered by Hub's son Martin, and government reluctance to support DAF may have reflected the fact that the make was never really a domestic success, over 65 per cent of sales being for export. By 1980 the Dutch government was supporting assembly by Volvo in 19 countries on the strength of an export market of almost 90 per cent.

After 1975 the DAF name was dropped and the range was gradually rationalized as small Volvos, such as the 343 and the 345. The last true DAF, the 66, was dropped in 1981, which also marked the last year of the DAF hallmark, Variomatic. Although the DAF name disappeared from the car market, it is still used by the highly successful truck-building side, which acquired control of the Leyland Truck and Freight Rover operations of the British Rover group in 1987. BL

DAGMAR
USA 1922-1927

The Dagmar was originally a radically restyled version of the homely six-cylinder Crawford, both being made by Mathias P. Möller, a Danish-born organ manufacturer of Hagerstown, Maryland. Named after Möller's daughter, the Dagmar featured rakish, angular-style wings and a radiator which has been described as a surrealist imitation of a Packard. The engine was a 70bhp six-cylinder Continental which was made until the end of production, although joined for 1925 by a

DAF Daffodil of 1966

DAF 33 of 1967

Daihatsu Fellow Max GHL of 1972

smaller 6-60 with a 60hp Continental engine.

The stylish Dagmars attracted a lot of attention, being photographed frequently with beauty queens, although they probably never had more than one distributor, in Philadelphia, all other cars being sold direct from the factory. Later models abandoned the angular wings, and the 6-60 never had them.

In December 1923 Möller transferred production to a larger factory in Hagerstown, which had been the original Crawford bicycle plant and where Pope Tribune light cars had been made from 1904 to 1907. In 1924 he added taxicabs to his line, the four-cylinder Luxor cab being assembled on the third floor while Dagmars were assembled on the ground floor, before both chassis went to the first floor for body mounting.

Taxicabs, which were built for sale by New York taxi tycoons Ally Freed and Mickey Heidt, proved more profitable than cars, and from 1926 car production tapered off, ceasing in 1927 with a final enormous nine-passenger limousine built for a European tour by Mathias P. Möller and daughter Dagmar. Like all its predecessors, it had no brakes on the front wheels. Production figures for Dagmar have not survived, but a carefully calculated estimate would be 300 cars.

The cabs were sold under a variety of names, including Astor, Blue Light, Five-Boro and Paramount and were so successful that the workforce went up from between 50 and 75 in the mid-1920s to 275 by 1928, when production was 125 a week. Cab production continued until about 1931, but the factory kept going, building cab and light van bodies on Ford V8, International and Diamond T chassis. Mathias P. Möller died in 1937 and this seems to have brought about the closure of the company. GNG

DAIHATSU
JAPAN 1930 to date

Founded in March 1907 as Hatsudoki Seizo Kaisha (Engine Manufacturing Co Ltd) the company's first complete vehicles were three-wheelers built in 1930, sold sometimes under the name Tsubasa. As Japan's total output of this type of vehicle was only 300 that year, Daihatsu's production would have been small. Light military 4×4s were made in 1937, along with pickups, but three-wheelers were the principal output when the company changed its name to Daihatsu Kogyo Kabushiki Kaisha in 1951.

Products that year included air-cooled 736cc single-cylinder and 1005cc vee-twin handlebar-steered chassis. They were available with commercial bodywork or with an open-sided driver's compartment and enclosed four passenger compartment over the rear wheels.

A four-door Bee car with 540cc twin soon followed and in 1957 the Osaka plant was expanded and new facilities opened at Ikeda. Within two years the company was employing 4000 men, had 3 million yen capital and was producing 45,500 Daihatsu and Midget three-wheelers a year, 1150 Vesta four-wheelers plus 40,000hp worth of diesel engines. In 1960 the Vesta received a four-cylinder water-cooled engine.

In 1963 the Compagno 797cc four-cylinder four-wheel passenger range was launched, followed in 1966 by the Fellow 360cc minicar. Toyota bought an interest in the firm in 1966 and took complete control two years later. In 1966 the Daihatsu became one of the first Japanese cars to be sold in Europe.

By 1970 annual output was 300,000 vehicles from 8800 employees. This included 275 electric cars for Expo 70. The company also had a foundry at Itami, near the main components and assembly plants at Ikeda.

In 1972 the three millionth vehicle was made and the 968,000sq ft (90,000sq m) Kyoto plant was built for the Charmant and Charade ranges. Two years later the company adopted the name Daihatsu Motor Co Ltd.

The Compagno gave way in time to Consorte versions of the Toyota Corolla, and the Charmant was similarly Toyota-based. Light 4×4 leisure vehicles were introduced in 1974; in 958cc then 1.6-litre form and from 1978 in 2.2-litre diesel form, these became important Daihatsu products. A new engine plant was built at Shiga in 1974.

In 1978 came the front-wheel-drive, trans-verse 550cc engined Max Cuore, which was sold in some markets as the Domino. The 993cc Charade had similar layout and three-cylinder engine and became capable of 100mpg (35km per litre) for the first time in its diesel form of 1983. Electric versions had been offered in 1980, followed by export versions of the popular 850cc forward-control minivan.

The Charmant LGX was introduced in 1984. This was a semi-luxury medium sized conventional four-door saloon powered by a new 1.6-litre engine. The same year a new improved range of four-wheel-drive vehicles known by the name Fourtrak was offered. These were available with petrol and diesel engines, the latter also with a turbocharger.

In 1985 Daihatsu announced a range of re-styled Charades with improved aerodynamics resulting in better fuel economy. The Charade Turbo Diesel was claimed to be the world's first turbocharged diesel of under 1 litre combining the performance advantages of turbocharging with the economy and reliability of diesels. An eight-year rust warranty was introduced for all models. The Cuore was given new 3-cylinder engines of 548 or 847cc in 1986. NB

DAIMLER/DAIMLER-BENZ,
MERCEDES-BENZ
GERMANY 1886 to date

It is a curious irony that the two pioneers of the motor car, Karl Benz and Gottlieb Daimler, whose companies were eventually to merge to form one of the largest automotive empires in the world, lived and worked within 60 miles (96 kilometres) of each other and yet never met.

Gottlieb Daimler was born in Schorndorf in 1834, and after four years' apprenticeship to a gunsmith he worked for various engineering firms including Armstrong-Whitworth in England. In 1872 he was appointed technical director of the Deutz Gas Engine Works run by Gustav Otto and Eugen Langen. His chief designer was his friend Wilhelm Maybach, and between them they increased production from one engine a day to three.

However, Daimler's interest in petrol engines – as opposed to the gas engines which were the bread and butter of the firm – led to increasing friction with Otto, and in 1881 Langen tried to solve the problem by sending Daimler to a branch factory in St Petersburg. Daimler preferred to strike out on his own, and taking Maybach with him, moved to Cannstatt where he set up a workshop.

There he developed a series of single-cylinder petrol engines, which he used to power a motorcycle (the world's first), a motor boat and, in 1886, a motor car which consisted of a four-seater horsedrawn carriage with strengthened frame, which the engine drove via belt and jockey pulley to an internally toothed ring attached to the rear wheels. This car made its first runs in the autumn of 1886.

Three years passed before another Daimler car was built, for Gottlieb Daimler was primarily interested in engines rather than complete cars. In the years 1886 to 1890 he built a number of engines to drive tramcars, fire engines, dirigible balloons, electric lighting plants and tugboats. Finding that no shipbuilder was prepared to buy his engines, he proceeded to manufacture the whole boat, and by 1890 hundreds of his tugboats were in use all over the world.

In 1889 Daimler and Maybach built a complete car with their own vee-twin engine, and steel frame and wheels made by NSU. This was known as the Stahlradwagen (steel wheel car). It was shown at the 1889 Paris World's Fair, and the engine was later manufactured in France by Panhard and Levassor and used in Panhard and Peugeot cars. In 1888 the piano manufacturer, William Steinway, had obtained US manufacturing rights to the Daimler engine, and production began at Hartford, Connecticut, in 1891.

The Daimler Motorengesellschaft was founded in 1890 but, soon afterwards, Daimler again quarrelled with his partners and in 1893 left the company to carry on private research with Maybach in the empty Hotel Herrmann in Cannstatt. There Maybach invented the atomizing, or spray, carburettor and Daimler continued the development of engines.

In 1895 there was a reconciliation, and Daimler and Maybach returned to the Daimler Motorengesellschaft. The company had made about 12 cars during Daimler's absence; contrary to his hopes, no complete cars were made at the Hotel Herrmann. The vehicles had rear-mounted two-cylinder in-line engines of 1060cc and 4hp, driven by belt. The first Daimler truck was completed in 1896 and in 1897 came the Phönix car, with front-mounted engine, four-speed sliding gearbox and chain drive. The first bus followed in 1898 and a four-cylinder car in 1899.

The company was still making engines for other purposes, including railcars and the first Zeppelin airship. The marine department made boats, from a light excursion craft with 2hp engine up to a 20hp cabin cruiser. In 1900 a new 1760-acre (710-hectare) site was acquired at Untertürkheim, which is still the headquarters of Daimler-Benz today.

One of the customers for the Phönix car in 1897 was Emil Jellinek, an Austrian banker and his country's consul-general at Nice. On the strength of this purchase he became an unofficial agent for Daimlers on the French Riviera and sold a number to wealthy friends and business associates. By 1900 he was encountering some sales resistance due to the short wheelbase and top heavy appearance of the cars, aggravated by a fatal accident to the driver of one in the Nice-La Turbie hillclimb. He told his fellow-Daimler directors that a lower, more modern design would sell much better, and he promised to take the first 36 cars off the line but on two conditions: the first was that he should have the sole agency for France, Belgium, Austro-Hungary and the USA; the second was that the new cars should bear the name of his 10-year-old elder daughter, Mercédès.

The new cars were designed by Maybach and Paul Daimler, son of Gottlieb who had died in March 1900. Among the car's modern features were a honeycomb radiator, gatechange gearbox, mechanically operated inlet valves and a pressed steel frame, as well as a low appearance. In one step it had moved from being a rather old-fashioned and ungainly design to the most up-to-date car on the market, soon to displace Panhard from its position as the acknowledged leader in car technology.

The name Mercédès was at first unofficial, but mandatory in France where Panhard still laid claim to the Daimler title. By 1902 it was generally used for the cars, although commercial vehicles retained the Daimler name until the merger with Benz in 1926. All heavy commercials were made in the Berlin-Marienfelde factory of the Motorfahrzeug-und-Motorenfabrik Berlin AG, a company set up by Daimler directors in 1900 and completely integrated in 1902.

The original 5.9-litre 35hp Mercédès was followed by both larger and smaller models, the former including the famous 9.2-litre 60hp and the latter the 3-litre 18/22 and 4-litre 18/28. Three privately owned 60hp cars were borrowed by the company for the 1903 Gordon Bennett Cup race after the 90hp team cars were destroyed in a fire at the Cannstatt factory, and Camille Jenatzy's victory in this important event set the seal on the Mercédès' position.

Henceforth, for many years, it was the car to beat – or to copy. Among well-known firms who based their 1904-5 models on Mercédès' patterns were Fiat and Itala in Italy, Berliet and Rochet-Schneider in France, Ariel in England and Locomobile in the United States. Several models of Mercédès were assembled at the Steinway factory at Long Island City from 1904 to 1907, and they were also made at the Austro-Daimler works in Vienna.

In 1907 Jellinek retired and Maybach left the Daimler company to found his own concern, which made airship engines and luxury cars. His last designs for Daimler were the large, chain-drive 37/70 and 39/80PS six-cylinder cars.

Design was now in the hands of Paul Daimler and Wilhelm Lorenz, who brought in a

Paul and Gottlieb Daimler in the first car, 1886   *Camille Jenatzy in 60hp Mercédès of 1903*

Mercedes-Benz SSK of 1928

Mercédès 24/100/140PS of 1924

range of shaft-driven cars from 1908 onwards. These varied in size from the 1.6-litre 6/18PS to the 7.2-litre 28/95PS, the latter remaining on the programme until 1924. There were also three chain-driven monsters, the 8.9-litre 38/70PS, 9.5-litre 37/90PS and 9.6-litre 38/95PS. Two models, a 16/45PS and 22/65PS, used the Knight sleeve-valve engine.

Since the turn of the century the Daimler Motorengesellschaft had been active in the aero engine field, at first for the airships of Count Zeppelin and later for powering heavier-than-air machines. By 1914 Daimler-powered aeroplanes had set distance records of 24hr 12min and a world altitude record of 26,575ft (8100m).

World War I saw great strides in aero engine development. In 1914 Daimler was making a 160hp in-line six-cylinder engine, but four years later it had started production of a 500hp eighteen-cylinder unit. A new factory was erected at Sindelfingen for the manufacture of complete aircraft and this later became the main centre for bodywork.

Daimler and its successor Daimler-Benz has not been a consistent supporter of motor sport at the top level, but has tended to make brief and highly successful appearances before dropping out for a few years. Such were its entries in the Grands Prix of 1908 and 1914. Christian Lautenschlager won the for-

mer (Benz was second and third) while the 1914 event saw the new 4½-litre Mercédès finish first, second and third. Their teamwork and careful preparation foreshadowed those of the 1934-39 Mercedes-Benz era.

Although the German economy was very shaky after World War I, German factories had not suffered from bombing as they would in World War II so that Daimler was able to get cars into production before the end of 1919. These were the 4-litre sleeve-valve 16/45PS and the 7.2-litre 28/95PS, both pre-war designs. They were joined in 1923 by two models which were the first production cars to offer superchargers, the 1.6-litre 6/25/40PS and the 2.6-litre 10/40/65PS. The supercharger was first seen (and heard) in action on a Mercédès in 1921 when Max Sailer won the Coppa Florio in Sicily on a 28/95, which he had driven all the way from Untertürkheim.

Paul Daimler retired from his firm in 1922, and was replaced as chief engineer by Ferdinand Porsche – who came from Austro-Daimler, where Daimler himself had worked from 1902 to 1905. Porsche set to work to design a new range of up-to-date six-cylinder cars with single-overhead cam engines and front-wheel brakes. These were the 4-litre 15/70/100PS and 6.2-litre 24/100/140PS. As with the earlier supercharged cars, the first figure represented the taxable horsepower, the second

the unblown bhp, and the third the bhp when the blower was in action. Although introduced as Mercédès models, these cars survived the merger with Benz, and were made until 1929.

Daimler and Benz had started negotiations in 1923, and in May 1924 the two firms signed an Agreement of Mutual Interest. The full merger was completed on 1 July 1926, giving the new company, Daimler-Benz AG, a capital of 36.36 million marks. The head of the company was Wilhelm Kissel, and at the time of the merger there were about 14,000 employees. Since 1909 Mercédès had used the three pointed star as its trade mark, while Benz had favoured a laurel wreath, so the two were combined in the familiar badge still used today. As Mercedes-Benz, Mercédès shed its accents.

Under the new regime, car and commercial vehicle ranges were rationalized; only two models of Benz car were continued, and those only until 1927. The truck ranges, which included diesels by both companies, were merged, and the Benz lines disappeared.

The Benz factory at Gaggenau became the headquarters of heavy vehicle production and the Marienfelde factory was reduced in status to a supplier of components. Sindelfingen became the chief body plant, and was also used for aero engine manufacture once this was again permitted. From a 20bhp flat-twin in 1925, the aero engine division progressed in 10 years to the 1050bhp inverted V12 DB600. Diesel engines were made for boats and airships; the *Hindenburg* and *Graf Zeppelin* both used 1200bhp sixteen-cylinder Daimler-Benz engines.

Car development in the late 1920s followed two lines, the glamorous six-cylinder Porsche-designed machines, which culminated in the SSK and SSKL sports cars, and the bread-and-butter line of six-cylinder side-valve Stuttgart and Mannheim models, joined in 1928 by the touring straight-eight Nürburg. The Porsche cars all had vee radiators while the Hans Nibel-designed touring models had flat radiators.

Far more of the latter were made, more than 16,000 of the 2-litre Stuttgart (1926-33), 6807 of the 2.6-litre Stuttgart 260 (1928-35), 2439 of the 3- and 3.4-litre 16/55 and Mannheim series (1926-30) and 2893 of the 4.6-litre Nürburg (1928-33).

By contrast, the big sixes accounted for only 671 units between 1926 and 1934. Most of these were the high chassis and poorly-braked Typ K (276 units), and as the cars became lower and more sporting, Mercedes-Benz sold progressively fewer of them; the 6.8-litre Typ S found only 170 buyers in four years (1927-30), the 7.1-litre Typ SS sold 173 units in eight years (1927-34), and the 7.1-litre short-chassis SSK only 45 between 1928 and 1934. The fastest of the whole series, the SSKL, was never sold to the public, only seven being made, purely for works use.

They were all very expensive, prices running from 30,000 marks for a four-seater sports S to 44,000 marks for a cabriolet C on the SS chassis; these prices were for factory bodies, but custom coachwork obviously cost more still. By contrast, a straight-eight Nürburg cost between 15,000 and 17,500 marks. The company probably made no profit from the K and S series, but its sporting successes such as Rudi Caracciola's victory in the 1929 Tourist Trophy, 1930 Irish Grand Prix and 1931 German Grand Prix, brought immensely valuable publicity.

Porsche resigned in 1928 and was replaced by Hans Nibel as chief designer. This ex-Benz engineer deserves far more credit than he has generally received, for his work ranged from the 1908 Grand Prix Benz and 1911 'Blitzen' Benz through to the SSKL Mercedes-Benz, the

Mercedes-Benz W125 of 1937

Mercedes-Benz 170V of 1936

Mercedes-Benz W154 of 1939

side-valve six-cylinder models and the successful 170 series, to the first of the all-conquering Grand Prix cars of the 1930s.

At the beginning of the decade he produced two contrasting designs, the 1.7-litre four-cylinder Typ 170, which was the smallest Mercedes-Benz yet made, and the 7.6-litre straight-eight Typ 770, aptly nicknamed 'der Grosser Mercedes'. The 170 broke new ground in having all-round independent suspension, and with prices starting at 4150 marks was aimed at the same market as the Adler Trumpf. It sold 13,775 units from 1931 to 1936, when it was replaced by the 170V with tubular backbone frame. This was the best-selling Mercedes-Benz of the pre-war era, with 71,973 delivered between December 1935 and October 1942, and a further 49,367 between June 1946 and August 1953. The next most popular model was the 2.3-litre Typ 230, of which 24,600 were made between 1936 and 1943.

Two unusual lines of development for their day were the 130H/170H rear-engined cars and the 260D, the world's first series production diesel-engined passenger car. The H series (for *Heckmotor* or rear engine) had tubular backbone frames and swing axle rear suspension. The 1.3-litre 130H was underpowered but a reasonable price of 3425 marks for a two-door saloon enabled 4298 to be sold between 1934 and 1936. The 170H (1936-39) was more powerful but was up against the more conventional 170V with the

same engine at 600 marks less, and sold just 2507 units.

There was also a 150H sports model (25 sold) and the 130H also appeared, as did practically every other small German car, in military *Kubelwagen* form. The 260D used a 2.6-litre diesel engine in the body and chassis of the 230, and although slow (59mph or 95kph maximum) it pioneered the way for post-war diesel cars from Mercedes-Benz, Fiat and others, leading up to the wide range of diesels made today. A total of 1967 260Ds were made, together with a few experimental 190Ds and 290Ds.

Hans Nibel died suddenly in 1934, his place being taken by Max Sailer who had driven in the 1914 Grand Prix team and had won the 1921 Coppa Florio, with Fritz Nallinger as his deputy. Nibel had been largely responsible for the first of the new generation of Grand Prix cars, the W25 of 1934, but it was Sailer who developed the all-conquering cars of the next five years. These included the 646bhp 5.6-litre W125 of 1937, the 420bhp 3-litre V12 W154 of 1938, and the W163 of 1939, which developed 480bhp from only 1½ litres.

The development cost of these cars was enormous, as was the salary bill for the team of talented drivers, and neither could have been maintained simply from company profits. However, under the Nazi regime the government was prepared to pay a handsome annual subsidy as well as prize money to

German makers of Grand Prix cars. The other recipient of this largesse was Auto Union; its rear-engined cars were designed by former Mercedes-Benz designer Ferdinand Porsche, but they never matched the success of the cars from Stuttgart.

At the top of the Mercedes-Benz range in the 1930s were the 380K, 500K and 540K series and the 'Grosser'; the former were *grands routiers* for high speed touring on the new *autobahnen* rather than out-and-out sports cars. They had overhead-valve supercharged straight-eight engines of 3.8, 5, or 5.4 litres, all-round independent suspension and servo-assisted hydraulic brakes. Production figures for these models were 154, 354 and 444 respectively. An enlarged straight-eight, the 580K, and a completely new V12, the 600, were in the development stage when war broke out, but not more than a dozen of each were made.

The 770 Grosser survived until 1938 in its original form, and was then replaced by a new model using the same engine in a lengthened version of the 540K chassis. Some of the 117 first series of Grossers were sold to anyone who could afford them (at 38,000 to 47,000 marks) but the 88 second series cars went entirely to the Nazi hierarchy or to foreign rulers such as Josef Stalin, Finland's Field Marshal von Mannerheim, Spain's General Franco and Antonio Salazar of Portugal. The old Nürburg side-valve straight-eight was made until December

1939, complete with wooden spoked wheels, surely the last survivor of this feature.

Apart from passenger cars, Daimler-Benz was very active in the commercial vehicle, aero engine and diesel engine fields. Commercials ranged from vans on the 170V chassis to 15-ton 6×4 trucks, buses and high speed *autobahn* coaches, the larger vehicles mostly diesel-powered. In the aero engine field the most successful unit was the inverted V12 DB600 which was to the Luftwaffe what the Rolls-Royce Merlin was to the RAF. In its final form it developed 2400bhp from 44.7 litres with methanol/water fuel-injection. Diesel engines were used in aircraft and also in railway locomotives and boats.

Cars were continued into the war years, 34 Typ 230s being delivered as late as 1943. In addition a wide variety of military equipment was made, from *Kubelwagen* on the 170V chassis to heavy half-track trucks and tractors, some of the latter powered by Maybach V12 engines.

These activities naturally attracted a lot of attention from British and American bombers, and by 1945 the Daimler-Benz factories had suffered very severe damage. Marienfelde was completely demolished and rebuilt, but the other factories at Untertürkheim, Sindelfingen, Gaggenau and Mannheim were gradually restored and were functioning well enough to start turning out cars from Untertürkheim and trucks from Mannheim by June 1946.

In 1946, 214 cars, all 170Vs, were built; 1047 followed in 1947 and 5116 in 1948. The figures contrasted with a pre-war peak of 28,039 in 1937. This was exceeded in 1950, however, when 33,906 cars were sold, and since then Mercedes-Benz production has seen a spectacular rise. The six-figure barrier was crossed for the first time in 1959, when 108,440 cars were sold; present-day production is more than four times this figure.

The 170V was joined by the more luxurious 170S and diesel-powered 170D in 1949. These two remained in production until 1955, although by that time several more modern designs were offered as well. They included the 220S and 300 with six-cylinder overhead-cam engines and the 180 with unitary construction and slab-sided body, which set the pattern for Mercedes-Benz saloon bodies for the next 30 years. Design changes have been gradual rather than spectacular, and there is more of a resemblance between the 180 of 1953 and today's 190 than between cars of any other make over a span of more than 30 years.

In the commercial vehicle field the most significant post-war product was the Unimog. This was a 4×4 multi-purpose vehicle which could be used as an agricultural tractor, road tractor or for a wide variety of specialized jobs. It was first made by the Bohringer brothers of Goppingen, but Daimler-Benz took it over in 1951 and put it into production at Gaggenau, where it is still made today. Gaggenau was used for the heavier trucks

Mercedes-Benz W121 190 of 1959

and Mannheim for the lighter, but in 1963 a new truck plant was opened at Wörth which took over much of the production of the older factories. In 1969 the company acquired another commercial vehicle factory at Bremen when it purchased Hanomag-Henschel. This is used today for manufacture of the 207/208/307/308 series of light vans, and also estate cars and the 190 saloon.

Mercedes-Benz made a dramatic return to motor sport in 1952 when the brand-new 300SL sports cars finished first, second and third at Le Mans. This began a very successful era for the company, with the 300SL, its even faster sports racing derivative the 300SLR, and the W196 Grand Prix cars. In 1955 it achieved the triple crown of World Formula 1 Constructors' Championship, World Sports Car Constructors' Championship and World Drivers' Championship (won by Fangio).

Unfortunately 1955 was also the year of the Le Mans tragedy, when Mercedes' driver Pierre Levegh and 82 spectators died in motor racing's worst-ever accident. The company withdrew from racing thereafter, although 300SLs and other models had considerable success in rallies for several years.

The 300SL was put into production in 1954; with its inclined six-cylinder single-overhead cam fuel-injected engine and gullwing doors

it was one of the most exciting cars of the 1950s. Production of the coupé was 1400 (1954-57) and of the convertible, 1858 (1957-63). There was also a smaller sports model, the 190SL, which never achieved the critical acclaim of the 300SL, but sold in far greater numbers, 25,881 between 1955 and 1963.

In 1958 Daimler-Benz acquired a controlling interest in Auto Union, which was making DKW three-cylinder cars, and helped in the development of the restyled DKW F102 of 1963. Two years later it put a newly-designed four-cylinder engine in the F102 body shell, the result being christened the Audi 60/70/90 range.

This gave Daimler-Benz access to a completely fresh market for smaller cars, but it decided not to continue the association. In 1964 the company went into joint ownership of Audi with Volkswagen and in 1968 sold its holdings to Volkswagen. It did acquire a factory out of the episode, though, as it kept the Auto Union car plant at Düsseldorf, while Volkswagen retained the former light truck plant at Ingolstadt.

Max Sailer had retired as chief designer in 1940, being replaced by his deputy Fritz Nallinger who had presided over the first postwar cars, although diesel engine development was the work of Max Wagner. In 1963

Mercedes-Benz W196 (Stirling Moss driving) of 1955

Nallinger in turn gave way to Hans Scherenberg, who supervised the new generation of saloons and coupés that were to appear in the late 1960s.

There was considerable overlap, and the 230/250/280SL sports car series introduced in 1963 was undoubtedly largely Nallinger's creation. Also in 1963 came the post-war equivalent of the Grosser Mercedes, the 6.3-litre V8 Typ 600. The engine was the first V8 to come from Stuttgart. The car was available in two wheelbases, the standard limousine at 126in (320cm) and the Pullman limousine at 153.5in (390cm). With an overall length of 20ft 6in (6.24m), the latter was the longest standard production car made since the war, and seemed even larger in its six-door form. A landaulette version was available from 1965, but this was bought almost entirely by heads of state. The 600 remained in production until June 1981, by which time 2190 of the short wheelbase limousines and 487 of the Pullmans had been sold. From 1968 to 1972 the big V8 engine was available in the 300SEL body shell, the model being known as the 300SEL/6.3.

In January 1968 came the 'new generation' of saloons, with smaller body shells and all-new suspension. There were seven different engines, including two sizes of diesel, from 1988 to 2788cc, joined in 1969 by a 3½-litre V8. Parallel with these was a new series of roadsters, the 350SL, and the longer wheelbase coupé versions, the 350SLC and 450SLC with 3½-litre and 4½-litre V8 engines.

By 1975 Mercedes-Benz covered a wide market range from the medium sized and priced 2-litre Type 200 to the luxurious and very fast 450SEL/6.9 with a 285bhp 6834cc V8 engine, which was an enlarged and improved

Mercedes-Benz 300SL coupé of 1955

Mercedes-Benz 300SL roadster of 1959

version of the 6.3-litre unit. With this car, the makers had no fears about challenging Rolls-Royce as the 'Best Car in the World'. A total of 7380 were made to 1980, when it was replaced by the 500SEL.

Despite the 1973 oil crisis, which hit so many manufacturers, particularly those making large and thirsty cars, Mercedes-Benz sales have increased in every year but one

(1978) from 1954 to the present, with the 1970s seeing a particularly dramatic increase, from 280,419 at the beginning of the decade to 429,078 10 years later. In 1979 Scherenberg was succeeded by Werner Breitschwerdt (chairman from December 1983) as chief engineer.

In December 1982 the company entered a new market with the 190. This had a new and smaller four-door saloon body, but it used the same 1997cc four-cylinder engine as the 200. The first 100,000 Model 190s came off the line in just under 12 months, and the rate of production was stepped up in 1984 with the opening of a new factory at Bremen.

The current range consists of the 190, 200, 230, 260, 300, 420, 500 and 560, with coupé versions of most models, and an open roadster in the 300, 420 and 500SL series. There are 190, 200, 250 and 300 diesel engines. In addition to these regular cars, there is the 4×4 G range, which is made for Daimler-Benz by

Mercedes-Benz 500SE of 1980

Mercedes-Benz 560SEC coupé of 1986

Mercedes-Benz 190E 2.3-16 of 1984

Steyr-Daimler-Puch in Austria. These come in open and closed, short- and long-wheelbase versions.

Despite the success of its car sales – more than 475,000 in 1983 – these represent less than 50 per cent of Daimler-Benz turnover. The balance comes from commercial vehicles, which unlike the cars are made in foreign countries, and diesel engines from 20 to over 3000bhp. The latter are used for stationary power plants of all kinds and for driving excavators in addition to railway locomotives.

Daimler-Benz is the world's largest producer of heavy trucks, and its engines are used in a number of other makes such as Kaelble in Germany and Nicolas in France. In 1977 Daimler-Benz bought the American dumptruck maker Euclid (sold to Clark Equipment Co in 1984) and in 1982 acquired a controlling interest in the Swiss heavy vehicle makers, FBW and Saurer. In 1984 Daimler-Benz owned eight factories in Germany, five of which were specially devoted to the production of trucks. In 1985 it acquired AEG and so became Germany's largest industrial company.

Daimler-Benz has overseas plants in Argentina (since 1951), Brazil (since 1953), Saudi Arabia (since 1978), and the USA (since 1980). In 1954 it set up an Indian manufacturing plant at the Tata Locomotive Works in Bombay, but since 1971 this has been operating independently. GNG

DAIMLER
GB 1896 to date

In 1888 Frederick Richard Simms met Gottlieb Daimler and was much impressed by the high-speed engines he was producing. Simms acquired British rights and his Simms & Co consulting engineering business did a good trade fitting Daimler engines to boats.

In 1893 Simms created the Daimler Motor Syndicate, with a capital of £6000, to take over his own firm and in 1896 he sold it to Lawson, Hooley and Rucker's British Motor Syndicate Ltd for £35,000. They managed to publicly float it for £100,000. Directors included Gottlieb Daimler (until 1898), pioneer motorist the Hon Evelyn Ellis, and Henry Sturmey of the world's earliest surviving motoring publication, *The Autocar*. Works manager was J. S. Critchley, who oversaw production of the first all-British Daimler in Coventry in 1897. It was built in the Motor Mills in Coventry, a former cloth factory that had become 'the world's largest autocar factory'. Lawson used the Motor Mills for another of his rather risky financial enterprises, the Great Horseless Carriage Company, which made MMC cars and bought many components from Daimler.

Sales in that first year totalled £13,822 and rose to almost £50,000 in 1898. Cars as well as launch engines were being produced, but profitability was marginal. Between 1899 and 1901 Sidney Straker of Straker-Squire was consulting engineer and the company achieved many trials successes and gained the privilege of royal patronage in 1900. That year there was a profit of £4430 on production of about 150 vehicles. Technical advances were also made, including the début of Britain's first four-cylinder car in 1899; one of these, driven by the Hon John Scott Montagu, was the first British car to race abroad.

Despite the standing of the firm, a £60,000 debenture issue flopped in 1902. The following year new 12 and 22hp models were designed by Percy Martin under the supervision of chief engineer E. W. Lewis, who left for Rover in 1903, a year in which Daimler earned

profits of £13,000. In 1904 a £200,000 flotation was favourably received and the Daimler Motor Company (1904) Ltd was created.

From 1905 an Italian company, SA Officine de Luca Daimler, assembled some of the British range, which became extensive in the years to 1910 and included 17 to 58hp models. Coachwork in the main was made by Daimler itself.

The company quickly performed well under chairman Percy Martin and general manager Ernest Instone. Gross profits quadrupled to £106,000 in 1905 and doubled again the following year when the workforce numbered 2000. Over-production in the slump years of 1907-8, however, produced a £50,000 loss. A new factory was built at Sandy Lane, Radford, Coventry, in 1908-9 for expansion into component manufacture, which among other products today includes the Jaguar V12 engine.

Daimler provided an excellent training ground for motor industry engineers; through its apprentice scheme passed hundreds of men who became prominent at many different motor factories in Coventry and farther afield. A notable early recruit was racing driver and journalist S. C. H. (Sammy) Davis, and in 1909 F. W. Lanchester became consulting engineer, a position he was to hold for the next 20 years.

In its effort to diversify, Daimler had bought the licence to make French Renard road trains and started making large engines for

Daimler twin-cylinder phaeton of 1898

power boats. In 1909 Charles Yale Knight's double-sleeve-valve engine was adopted and some were used throughout the range of cars and commercials.

The armaments and vehicle firm Birmingham Small Arms Co purchased Daimler in 1910. E. Manville was chairman of the enlarged board, a position he held until 1930, and for 10 years from 1913 the future prime minister Neville Chamberlain had a seat on the board, as did F. D. Docker of BSA.

Commercial vehicles became increasingly important to Daimler, which cast a covetous eye on the London bus market. However, the London General Omnibus Co had started its

Daimler limousine of 1913

own bus factory – soon known as AEC – so in 1912 Daimler lured away that company's chief engineer, Frank Searle. His new CC vehicle was based closely on the AEC B-Type, but had a sleeve-valve engine. It was ordered in large numbers.

In December 1912 an agreement was reached whereby Daimler would supply 10 per cent of the LGOC's vehicle requirements for 1914, would provide components for AEC and would be AEC's exclusive agent in the provinces and overseas. Daimler commercial vehicle capacity was then about 30 a week.

Daimler made a significant contribution to Britain's war effort between 1914 and 1918. It built 1000 ambulances in the first 18 months alone, produced 2000 heavy shells a week, vehicle production reached a weekly plateau of 55 to 60, and more than 4000 commercials were built. Thousands of aero engines were produced and dozens of aircraft were built at Radford. There were also components and engines made for AEC, 105hp tank engines, and heavy gun tractors evolved from the agricultural machines that Daimler had put on the market in 1911. At the peak of World War I the workforce numbered 6500. Assistant chief engineer was G. T. Smith-Clarke, who went to Alvis as chief engineer in 1922.

After 1918 AEC made its own sales arrangements and Daimler ended the exclusively factory-owned outlets for its cars and commercials, appointing agents instead. Daimler Hire was created with a pool of 250 vehicles in London.

Refined, silent and beautifully-made cars were produced in the 1920s. The high point was L. H. Pomeroy's sleeve-valve V12s, introduced in 1926. Annual car production was about 3000 but few commercials were now being sold.

In order to develop the commercial vehicle business Daimler entered into an arrangement with AEC and in 1926 the Associated Daimler Co Ltd was formed with Pomeroy as chief engineer. Commercial vehicles were to be made by AEC and fitted with Daimler engines. Few operators expressed interest, and in 1928 the association was dissolved.

Daimler Double-Six sports of 1931

Pomeroy took the first complete vehicle that he had designed, a high-speed, lightweight six-cylinder coach, to Daimler, where he became managing director in 1929. This coach provided the basis for Daimler's successful public service vehicle programme, which led to the formation of a separate company in 1936, Transport Vehicles (Daimler) Ltd. Its sales manager was a member of the Crouch car-making family, John Crouch.

In 1930 Daimler adopted the Armstrong-Siddeley type 'self-changing' Wilson gearbox, which was standard on all cars from 1932 to 1956. In 1931 Lanchester joined the group, making cheaper variations on the Daimler theme, extending the range into the family car market that had never been satisfactorily tapped. Poppet valves (now overhead) crept back with Pomeroy's 15 in 1933 and replaced sleeve valves three years later. Independent front suspension came to the 15 in 1938, two years after Pomeroy had departed for De Havilland.

The marque acquired greater glamour in the 1930s through sustained royal patronage and the addition of dramatic sporting models having double-six or Pomeroy-designed straight-eight engines which were occasionally fitted with striking coachwork. The new managing director, Edward Cooke, who

followed Pomeroy in 1937, encouraged innovation.

During World War II 55 factories and 17,000 workers came under Daimler control, many being scattered throughout the country to reduce the disruption caused by air raids on Coventry. Its principal 'shadow' factory was on 62 acres (25 hectares) at Browns Lane, Allesley, near Birmingham, and this became the home of Jaguar in 1961. Seventy per cent of the Radford factory was destroyed by bombing.

Daimler had been a principal subcontractor to Bristol Aero Engines since 1929 and built more than 50,000 Bristol engines during the war. An advanced scout car had been developed in 1938 with 4×4 and preselector/fluid flywheel giving five speeds both forward and back. A total of 6665 of these and 2764 armoured cars were made between 1939 and 1945. (Armoured cars would become a staple Daimler product from 1951, when the famous Rolls-Royce-powered Ferret first appeared.) Other wartime products included Bren and Browning gun components, millions of items for the motor industry and 1083 buses. Total value of Daimler's wartime output was £62.2 million at 1946 values.

Bernard Docker joined the board in 1940 and became chairman a year later. After the war he introduced a more flamboyant regime, which gave rise to the flashy Daimlers with gold plate and lurid paintwork that attracted much comment at post-war motor shows. Much more prosaic were the 500 ambulances built from 1949. These had bodies by Barker, which had gone into liquidation in 1938 and been bought by the group, as well as Hooper. Daimler's first home-produced diesel bus engine had made its début in 1946.

The straight-eight cars were dropped in 1953 and although limited production of ceremonial and formal cars continued, the range in general became slightly less rarefied. The DB18, a descendant of the 15, was revived after the war and more than 8000 were built until 1953, when it was succeeded by the Conquest.

Daimler Consort of 1950

In 1951 BSA had bought the makers of Triumph motorcycles for almost £2.5 million and so acquired Edward Turner, designer of the Ariel Square-four and Triumph twin. Turner became technical director of the automotive group and was responsible for the 2½-litre V8 Dart sports car of 1959 which would soon be known as the SP250. With sales of only 2650 in five years it was not a commercial success, but it had an excellent engine, almost 17,000 of which were used in the Daimler 250, with Jaguar bodyshell, to 1969. In 1962-63 Ogle styled some versions of the SP250 and the resulting body shape was adopted by Reliant for its Scimitar GTE.

Jack Sangster became chairman of the BSA group in 1956, when profits were £1.6 million; in 1960 it recorded a record profit of £3.4 million. But the picture was not so rosy at Daimler, where military contracts for the Ferret had dwindled, bus production was down to three a week and none of the car models was thriving. BSA decided to divest itself of Daimler, selling the division to Jaguar for £3.4 million in 1960.

Traditional big limousines like the Majestic Major and DR450 continued to be built until 1968 when a new car, utilizing the Jaguar MkX floorpan and mechanical elements, was produced; this was still in production 17 years later. Other Daimlers have been straightforward versions of Jaguars with more luxurious trim and stylized versions of the famous fluted radiator that had first appeared in 1904.

Daimler buses were gradually phased out as Jaguar placed most of its commercial vehicle emphasis on its Guy division, bought in 1961. The last Daimler bus was the well-known Fleetline, new in 1960, which was made at Leyland from 1973 following Jaguar-Daimler's absorption in British Motor Holdings in December 1966.

In 1983 the Daimler name was dropped from all markets other than the UK. Possible confusion with Daimler-Benz and the difficulty of establishing two names in foreign markets persuaded Jaguar to reach this decision. The Daimler badge and famous fluted grille continued to adorn versions of the XJ range in Britain. The Limousine is still manufactured and is now the only model unique to the Daimler marque. Production of cars bearing the Daimler name averaged about 3500 a month in 1984. NB

DANIELS
USA 1915-1927

N. E. Parish was a member of the railway equipment firm Parish Manufacturing Co of Reading, Pennsylvania, which was also a major supplier of vehicle frames. In June 1915 he formed the Daniels Motor Car Co Inc of Reading, with lawyer George E. Daniels as president. Parish was vice-president and backer; the designer was Charles Lufts. Production took place in a former stove works in Reading, with bodies coming from Fleetwood until some of that company's personnel were hired and installed in Daniels' own body plant.

Large, custom-built, luxury cars with Herschell-Spillman V8s were made at the rate of up to 300 a year until Daniels' V8 engine became available in 1919. Yet fewer than 200 of these were made before engine manufacture was subcontracted in 1920 to the Light Manufacturing Co of Pottstown. Plans were made to increase output to more than 1000 a year to keep pace with demand for the cars, particularly from the wealthy Hollywood set.

The firm became Daniels Motor Co in 1920, with increased capital, but financial disagreements caused a rift between Parish and Daniels, with the result that Parish left and the company collapsed in 1923.

Levene Motors of Philadelphia bought the company and closed the Reading factory in February 1924. A few more Daniels were subsequently built from spares in Philadelphia and the marque was still listed in 1927. Total production was 1500-2000 cars. NB

D'AOUST
BELGIUM 1912-1927

Jules d'Aoust opened a repair shop in the Brussels suburb of Anderlecht in 1908 and, aided by a colleague named Lamacq, began the production of cars in 1912. These were assembled machines powered by a variety of engines including Aster, Chapuis-Dornier and Decolonge.

Two years later he brought out a car powered by a 10/14CV four-cylinder engine of his own manufacture. This was revived after the war and continued until production ended in 1927. A sporting model of the 10/14CV with larger bore and lighter chassis had a number of successes. There was also a 3-litre single-overhead cam four-cylinder car named the 'Circuit de Corse' because it was built for the Corsican sports car race.

In 1923 two smaller D'Aousts were made, a 6/8CV with 1095cc overhead-valve Chapuis-Dornier engine and an 8CV with 1100cc SCAP side-valve engine; there were also two commercial models, a 1653lb (750kg) van and a 2-ton truck. As with so many firms, D'Aoust could not compete with cheaper mass production cars, and closed down in 1927. GNG

Daniels saloon of 1919

DARRACQ/TALBOT-DARRACQ
FRANCE 1896-1959

Alexandre Darracq was one of Europe's most successful promoters of the motor car, yet he never drove one, and was not even happy as a passenger. He was born in Bordeaux in 1855 and worked first of all in an arsenal, followed by several years with Hurtu and Hautin, a sewing machine and cycle-making firm which was later to manufacture cars.

In 1891 he went into partnership with a M. Aucocq to make bicycles under the name Gladiator. By undercutting the prices of the English bicycles which were selling in large numbers in France, Aucocq and Darracq made a great deal of money – but they displeased the English cycle interests led by Harvey DuCros (head of Dunlop) who bought them out in 1896 on the understanding that they would not engage further in cycle manufacture. DuCros and his associates also purchased Adolphe Clément's cycle business, and for a while Darracq joined the board of the new Clément Gladiator company.

In February 1897 he left to form Alexandre Darracq et Cie with a capital of 2 million francs and built a new factory, the Usines Perfecta, at Suresnes. He made bicycle components, motorcycles, tricycles and quadricycles with De Dion engines which he sold under the name Perfecta.

In 1896 he made a few electric cars, and then took out a licence to make Léon Bollée's four-wheel car, as the Le Mans manufacturer was too busy making his three-wheeler voiturettes. Darracq paid £10,000 for this licence, but the Bollée four-wheeler was not nearly as good a car as the three-wheeler, and very few were made.

Darracq's next car was much more successful, an up-to-date single-cylinder 6½hp light car with three-speed gearbox and shaft drive, designed by Paul Ribeyrolles. By the end of 1900 60 had been sold, and during 1901 more than 1000 found customers. Larger models followed, including 12 and 16CV twins by 1902. Profits grew too, from £75,000 in 1901 to £110,000 in 1903 and £112,000 in 1904, when 1200 cars were made. In 1902 he sold a licence for the manufacture of his cars in Germany by Opel, an agreement which lasted until 1907.

Early in 1903 an English group headed by Birmingham scales manufacturer W. B. Avery purchased Alexandre Darracq et Cie, capitalizing the new concern at £375,000 and paying Darracq and his associates £100,000 in 6 per cent preferred shares plus £71,109 in ordinary shares. Alexandre Darracq remained in charge of operations as managing director. In late 1905 a new company, Alexandre Darracq and Co (1905) Ltd was formed with capital of £650,000, over 80 per cent of the shares being held in Britain. About three-quarters of Darracq's output went for export,

Darracq tonneau of 1902

profits reaching a peak of £194,470 in 1907, when 2200 cars were made.

In 1906 an assembly plant and bodybuilding works was set up at Kennington, south-east London. The following year Darracq tried to break into the Italian market with the ALFA factory in Milan, which assembled mainly the smaller cars until 1910, when the Italian company engaged Giuseppi Merosi to design new cars that in due course became Alfa Romeos.

A sideline which proved much less successful was Alexandre Darracq's venture into commercial vehicles with the Darracq-Serpollet steam bus, for which he formed a new company, Darracq-Serpollet Omnibus Co Ltd, in May 1906 with a capital of £500,000. Although the steam bus chassis was to Léon Serpollet's design, it was to be built in new premises that were erected next to Darracq's existing factories at Suresnes. Two chassis were planned, a 25hp for single-decker bodies and a 40hp for double-deckers, and the Metropolitan Steam Omnibus Co of London intended to equip its fleet solely with Darracq-Serpollets.

Léon Serpollet's death in 1907 dealt a serious blow to the project; but steam was on the way out anyway, and the buses had no particular advantage over their petrol rivals. They sold in small numbers – the Metropolitan Steam Omnibus Co bought 20 – and there was even a short-lived two-cylinder steam car offered in 1907, but by 1910 Darracq was making petrol-engined buses and in 1912 the Darracq-Serpollet works was idle. The Darracq-Serpollet Omnibus Co went into voluntary liquidation in August 1912 and the directors of the parent company had to write off their £156,000 investment.

By 1912 Alexandre Darracq had also burnt his fingers with the money-losing Henriod rotary-valve engine. Retooling for large scale production of this new design consumed a lot of time and capital, and then the cars did

not sell well, as they were less powerful than the poppet-valve engine which Darracq had almost completely abandoned.

In 1911 the company had made a profit of £112,969 but the following year it was only £732 11s 8d. No dividend was paid on the ordinary shares, and in June 1912 Alexandre Darracq resigned, presumably not without some pressure from the English board. He played no further part in the motor industry and died in 1931.

For 1913 the rotary-valve engine was hastily dropped and a new designer was brought in: Owen Clegg, a Yorkshireman, had previously been with Wolseley, Siddeley and Rover, for which he designed the successful 12hp monobloc four. His 16hp Darracq resembled this and soon put the company back into good profits, 60 cars a week being made in early 1914. On the eve of World War I the factory employed 12,000 men who were turning out 14 chassis a day. During the war Darracq made Sopwith and Breguet aeroplanes, and the company paid a dividend of 20 per cent towards the end of the war.

In 1918 it took over Heenan and Froude, maker of dynamometers and other engineering products, and in October 1919 it acquired Clément-Talbot of London. For both these takeovers the company had to make big issues of shares, bringing its capital to more than £1.5 million. In June 1920 its empire building went still further with the acquisition of the Sunbeam Motor Co Ltd of Wolverhampton and W & G DuCros Ltd, London-based commercial vehicle maker. The new holding company was called STD Motors Ltd.

Post-war production at Suresnes was concentrated on a modernized version of Clegg's 16hp and a new 4½-litre V8 with coil ignition and a central gearchange. From October 1919 they bore the name Talbot Darracq, but in 1920 the French company was renamed Automobiles Talbot, and the name of Darracq was gradually forgotten. In England, however, they were still called Darracq to avoid confusion with the British-built Talbots from north Kensington. There was a lot of duplication of models between the three factories at Wolverhampton, north Kensington and Suresnes, and the eventual collapse of the STD combine owed much to fruitless competition between the models.

The most obvious duplication was the little Talbot 8/18 which was made at Suresnes as the 8hp Talbot-Darracq and differed mainly in the absence of a differential on the French product. The 3-litre straight-eight Grand Prix cars of 1921 bore the name Sunbeam when driven by British drivers K. Lee Guinness and Henry Segrave, and Talbot-Darracq when in the hands of Frenchman André Boillot. The 1½-litre four-cylinder Talbot racing voiturettes of 1921-25 were extremely successful, but unfortunately the 1½-litre straight-eight Grand Prix Talbots of 1926 were less so and money for competition work was running out.

although this never had any official blessing. The new cars had six-cylinder pushrod overhead-valve engines in three sizes, the 15CV 2.7-litre Baby, the 17CV 3-litre and the 23CV 4-litre, joined in 1938 by a 13CV 2.3-litre four-cylinder car. There was a plan to revive the Invicta, using Lago-Talbot chassis and Coachcraft bodies, but beyond one prototype this idea came to nothing. Sports and racing versions of the 4-litre car were made and in 1938 the latter were enlarged to 4½ litres for competition work. The cars were still called Darracqs in England, although few crossed the Channel.

Talbots returned to Grand Prix racing after the war, the big 4½-litre cars having at least some advantage over the 1½-litre supercharged Alfa Romeos and Maseratis as they could go a whole race without a refuelling stop. The largest of the post-war touring cars also used Becchia's 4½-litre 170bhp six-cylinder engine which had Riley-type high-set, but not overhead, camshafts. In 1949 it

One car was made with a 2.3-litre Simca V8 engine and in 1959 there was an extraordinary egg-shaped coupé made by Simca apprentices, powered by an Aronde engine.

These were sad and unworthy climaxes to the 60-year history of the cars from Suresnes. Tony Lago died in 1961, and the factory is now part of Automobiles Talbot SA, the name which was revived in 1979 for cars made in Chrysler's European plants. GNG

DASSE
BELGIUM 1896-1930

Gérard Dasse was born in Hodimont in 1842 and began his working life as a plumber. Around 1882 he moved to Verviers and set up a company in the Rue de Dison making plumbing and electrical fittings, domestic electricity having just been introduced. As the company prospered he began to think of building cars, and in 1894 he finished a tiller-steered three-wheeler with a horizontal single-cylinder 2½hp engine and belt-drive to the single front wheel.

This Benz-like device remained a prototype only, as Dasse moved his expanding business to larger premises in the Rue David. There he repaired or modified a three-wheeled Léon Bollée for a prominent local citizen Maitre Terfve, and shortly afterwards built his second three-wheeler as a close copy of the French car – this time with two wheels in front.

A third three-wheeler was followed in 1896 by the first four-wheel Dasse, and on its twin-cylinder engine Dasse introduced his own electrical ignition system to replace the earlier hot-tube. This was also the first Dasse intended for production and it appeared in several versions with both front and rear engines. At the 1904 Brussels Salon he showed two- and four-cylinder shaft-drive models, followed in 1905 by a 15hp three-cylinder which was built under licence by Durkopp until 1907 as the Durkopp-Dasse.

By 1911 Automobiles Gérard Dasse employed about 100 people and built 100 cars a year. By 1913 Dasse could boast that he built virtually every component of his cars except the tyres and magneto.

When Verviers was occupied during World War I, Dasse refused to work for the Germans and did not go back into business until the beginning of the 1920s when he opened a new factory in the Rue de Battice, joined by his sons Armand and Iwan. They built a few more cars, beginning with two 1921 models and continuing until the end of the 1920s. The small production included a very few sixes, introduced in 1925.

By 1924, however, Dasse production was switching to trucks, and later to buses. In 1927 Dasse's sons formed Automobiles Dasse SA and in the 1930s built vehicles for the Belgian forces, but in March 1956 the company went into liquidation. BL

Darracq four-seat tourer of 1914

In 1923 the design team was reinforced by Vincent Bertarione, Edmond Moglia and Walter Becchia, all of whom were lured away from Fiat. Bertarione designed the 1923 Grand Prix-winning Sunbeam and went on to produce some fine cars for Talbot, including the 1926 15CV 2½-litre six which formed the basis for all Talbots up to 1935. Variations included the 2.9-litre TL, sold as the Darracq 20/98 in England, and the 3.8-litre 22CV straight-eight Pacific with its companion smaller eight, the 3.4-litre 19CV Atlantic. Very few of these came to England.

The fortunes of the STD group declined sadly during the early 1930s, and in 1935 it collapsed. Sunbeam and the English Talbot were acquired by the Rootes group, while Talbot at Suresnes was taken over by Antoine Lago, who had been manager there for several years. He initially made do with modernized cars from the old regime, including a 10CV Six and the Atlantic straight-eight.

Then Becchia designed a new range of Lago-Talbots as they were soon nicknamed,

was joined by the 2.7-litre four-cylinder Baby, which was not a success; it was underpowered and the engine was rough and noisy. It did Talbot a lot of harm, just when the company could have done with a good, cheaper car to back up the very costly Lago Record. As with other French *grands routiers* in the post-war years, sales dropped alarmingly, from 433 in 1950 to 80 in 1951, and around one car a week thereafter.

In 1955 the Record and Baby were dropped in favour of a pretty and modern-looking GT coupé powered by a new 2½-litre 120bhp four-cylinder engine. About 70 of these were made up to 1957, by which time much of the Talbot factory had been leased to other firms.

Seeking more power, and quite unable to finance the development of a new engine, Lago went shopping to other manufacturers, including Ford in Britain and BMW in Germany. The 1958 Lago America had a 2½-litre BMW V8 engine, but very few were made; and in 1959 Simca took over the Usines Perfecta which Alexandre Darracq had built in 1898.

DATSUN
see Nissan

DAVID
SPAIN 1914-1922; 1950-1957

Probably the best-known Spanish cyclecar, the David had a very curious origin. A group of young sportsmen, led by José María Armangué and his three brothers, used to compete on the steep streets of Barcelona with wheeled bobsleighs which they called 'downcars'. To avoid having to push them back up the hills they fitted small motorcycle engines to power them, and in 1914 decided to put a light car into production. The name David was probably chosen by association with David and Goliath, and the Fabrica Nacional de Cyclecars David was founded in July 1914 with capital of 65,000 pesetas.

David Minicar of 1957

The cars had belt drive and were powered at first by vee-twin MAG or JAP engines and later by four-cylinder Ballots. About 100 cars were made in the first year, and more than 1500 left the factory in nine years. David cyclecars had many sporting successes and were also made with closed bodies, most of which were used as taxicabs. The company suffered a severe blow in 1917 with the death in a flying accident of José María Armangué, although two brothers continued under a new name, David SA, with capital increased to 1 million pesetas.

Encouraged by the success of the David taxicabs, the company branched out into cab operation on a large scale, using Citroëns and Berliets, and abandoned car production in 1922. It became one of Barcelona's largest garages for sales and service, especially of Citroëns, and had its own bodybuilding plant which made delivery vans and ambulances.

During the Spanish Civil War the company made a few electric cars, and in 1950 it launched a three-wheeler with 345cc single-cylinder two-stroke engine driving the front wheel. A curious variant of this was a five-wheeler light pick-up truck with tandem axles at the rear. About 600 single-cylinder Davids were made between 1950 and 1957. GNG

DAVIS
USA 1908-1930

The George W. Davis Carriage Co, founded in 1902, began producing cars in 1908-9 at its horse-wagon plant at Richmond, Indiana. G. W. Davis was assisted in running the company by his brother, Walter. It changed its name to the George W. Davis Motor Car Co and after making four-cylinder models concentrated on a 4655cc Continental-engined six after World War I. Chassis numbers suggest that a maximum of 600 cars were made in 1920, earlier production probably being on a smaller scale. A straight-eight came in 1927, and Davis bodies had unusual names such as Man o' War and Fleetaway.

The Automotive Corporation of America, based in Baltimore, Maryland, acquired the company in 1928 and ceased production in 1930, but not before the New York 6 had been equipped with its Parkmobile device which enabled it to enter parking spaces sideways. The Richmond plant concentrated on aero and general engineering and became an important producer of motor mowers. NB

DAVRIAN
GB 1965 to date

The glassfibre monocoque Davrian sports car was created by Adrian Evans around the excellent mechanical elements of the Hillman Imp. Unlike many short-lived kit cars, the Davrian went on to find both sales and competition success.

Evans, formerly a structural engineer in the building trade, first thought of building his own sports car in 1963 after he had seen a pre-production version of the rear-engined Imp. He started to build his car in 1965 and the first two, open cars were built that year in his house in Grove Park, London.

In 1967 Evans formed Davrian Developments Ltd and moved to a small factory in Clapham to start production. The prototype cars, dubbed Mark I, used plywood bodywork and superstructure on the Imp floorpan, but the production cars were to use the all-alloy, Coventry-Climax-designed Imp engine in a glassfibre monocoque body/chassis unit.

The first production cars, like the prototypes, were open-topped and a small number were built during 1968 before a fixed-head prototype called the Demon was shown at the London Racing Car Show in early 1969, originally offering the option of Ford or Leyland power as well as the Imp unit.

The Davrian was sold as a bare shell or as an almost complete car, lacking only an engine and wheels. Road and racing versions were available, both with only minimal equipment, the seats actually being moulded into the monocoque. The shells as sold were not even painted.

All the Davrians were very light, the road cars being perhaps 10cwt (508kg) and the lighter-bodied racers only 8½cwt (431kg). Even with the standard 875cc engine this gave 95mph (153kph) performance; the Imp Sport-engined car was good for 110mph (177kph) and 60mph (96kph) in 10 seconds and a typical racer would beat 130mph (209kph) with 0-60mph (0-96kph) in 7½ seconds.

The company had very little working capital, but early and continuing racing successes encouraged sales. In 1970 a Davrian could be built for under £500, the basic shell costing £350. Although its appeal as a road car was limited by its very basic nature, some 200 cars had been sold by August 1972, including several exports. A four-valve twin-cam Fiat 128-engined prototype, intended to sell in Italy, was shown at the 1971 Racing Car Show, but neither this nor a rumoured V8-engined car went into production.

In 1973 the Demon coupés were available with Volkswagen or Mini power, although the Imp unit was the popular choice. That year's

Davrian-Imp of 1972

Mark 6 had twin, foam-protected rear fuel tanks and pop-up headlamps, operated by cable. The car was still available as a kit, selling at £505 in February 1973, or £1400 for a complete car. Shells were delivered in four to six weeks and complete cars in three months. In 1974 Davrian won the British Mod-sports Championship outright, the start of a remarkable record of successes.

In 1976 Davrian, with 10 employees, moved to Tregaron, Dyfed, and built some 60 cars. In 1980 the company moved again, to nearby Lampeter, and in 1981 introduced a new model, the Dragon, which had a trans-verse, mid-mounted 1.3-litre Ford Fiesta engine and disc brakes all round.

In 1982 Davrian, with £51,000 from the Welsh Development Agency in a total investment of £100,000, moved into further new premises and planned increased production. Early in 1983, however, the company, which by then employed about 20 staff in its 7000sq ft (650sq m) factory, went into liquidation, the assets being acquired by an Ulster businessman, Will Corry. Corry set up the Corry Car Co in Ballynahinch, Co Down, and began production of a new Ford-engined car as the Corry Cultura. BL

DAY-LEEDS
GB 1913-1924

Day-Leeds 10hp of 1914

Job Day & Sons Ltd of Leeds, Yorkshire, was a company well established in the field of packaging machinery before it became interested in road vehicles. In 1912 it produced the world's first bacon slicing machine and also launched a conventional 500cc single-cylinder motorcycle. William Henry Day, son of the founder, was attracted by the cyclecar boom, and in 1913 he built a light vehicle powered by a 999cc vee-twin engine, with belt final-drive.

It was planned to sell this cyclecar at £120, but before production started Day decided to move upmarket with a proper four-cylinder light car, powered by a 1286cc Turner engine. This sold for £150 in 1914 and was replaced for 1915 by a similar light car powered now by a 1130cc engine made by Day.

DB Formula 1 car of 1954

Pre-war Day-Leeds production amounted to about 100 vehicles, including a few 5-7cwt (254-395kg) trucks with the charming name of 'lurry', a word normally reserved for really heavy steam or horse-drawn vehicles. The cars were revived in 1920, with little change in the design, although the price had jumped to £500. They were high-quality light cars with well-made bodies supplied by Lockwood & Clarkson of Leeds.

Prices were reduced each year in an attempt to keep down to the level of rivals like Morris, so that by 1924 the cheapest Day-Leeds cost only half the 1920 price. Even so, the company was forced to abandon car production at the end of that year, after about 300 post-war cars had been made. Day-Leeds was absorbed by the Baker-Perkins group which later acquired control of another packaging machinery and car making firm, Rose Brothers of Gainsborough. GNG

DAYTONA
USA 1976 to date

Daytona Automotive Fiberglass Inc was founded in Holly Hill, Florida, in 1976 with LaVerne Martincic as president. Daytona's first car was the Migi, a glassfibre-bodied replica of the MG TD, based on a VW Beetle floorpan and running gear. So like the real thing was the Migi that many of the fibreglass panels were allegedly interchangeable with MG metal.

In 1980 Daytona had 15 employees and built 360 cars, mainly the Migi II which was distributed by Fiberfab Inc of Pittsburgh, itself famous for kit cars with VW, Porsche and Chevrolet engines. In autumn 1980 Daytona advertised the Migi as 'the most popular kit-car in the USA'. In 1982 the 90mph (145kph) Migi, which then sold for $10,500, was joined by the two-door Moya roadster, both cars being available with optional luxury trim and wire wheels. These two models continued to be the company's joint main lines and by 1985 prices had risen to $17,500 for the Migi and $11,500 for the Moya. BL

DB/RENÉ BONNET
FRANCE 1938-1965

The DB, or Deutsch Bonnet, was one of France's most successful small sports racing cars and precursor of the Matra. It took its name from the somewhat loose association of Charles Deutsch and René Bonnet, who became friends when Bonnet bought Deutsch's garage business.

Deutsch, born in 1911, was the son of a cartwright who also built racing gigs and 'aerodynamic' car bodies to order. In 1929, when his father died, Charles took over the business and learned the trade. He also studied civil engineering, turning to that profession in the mid-1930s and continuing his associations throughout his time as a car builder.

He sold the original business to Bonnet in October 1932 and Bonnet used the premises as a garage and Citroën agency. Bonnet, born in 1904, had been invalided out of the navy and hospitalized for over two years before deciding he was not as ill as the doctors thought he was and setting up in business on his own.

In 1929 his sister, who lived in Deutsch's home town, Champigny-sur-Marne, asked him to take over her late husband's small garage. He expanded the business and bought Deutsch's premises in partnership with another brother.

Bonnet had a longstanding interest in motor sport, starting with rallying in 1932 and progressing to racing. Deutsch and Bonnet soon decided to build their own competition special, based on a wrecked Citroën 11CV *traction avant*. A wooden model was made in 1936, with streamlining copied from George Eyston's Thunderbolt record breaker, and DB1 was completed in March 1938. Bonnet eventually claimed DB1 and a smaller development, DB2, was built for Deutsch. World War II stopped the completion of a coupé, but the car was finished after the war and sold.

DB3 was designed but never built,

131

although many of the parts intended for it were used for Deutsch's DB4, which was finished in July 1945 and copied as the 2-litre DB5 for Bonnet. The cars won their respective classes in the first post-war race, the Grand Prix de Paris. The next car, the open-wheeled DB7, built from 1946 to 1951, was financed by selling the first two.

In 1947 the friends formed Automobiles DB, with Bonnet as the sole director and Deutsch apparently as an ordinary shareholder. Bonnet set up a separate company in which Deutsch held a small stake, to make DB parts and performance equipment, under an informal licence from the main company. DB8 was completed in 1948, with bodywork designed by the man who designed the aforementioned Thunderbolt, whom Deutsch met on a civil engineering business trip to New York.

DB also designed a Dyna-Panhard based racer, with co-operation from Panhard, and sold the first car, unveiled at the 1949 Paris Salon, to a club racer. DB strengthened its ties with Panhard after Citroën proved unhelpful (and after experiments in 1952 with Renault power were dropped). Some 15 copies of the first Dyna-Panhard car were subsequently built, marking DB's real arrival as a manufacturer. From the 1950s, production DBs used Panhard running gear in alloy bodies (glassfibre from 1955) with capacities from 610 to 1300cc, some with the option of supercharging.

DB also continued its highly successful competition career with numerous Le Mans successes, including the first of several Index of Performance wins in 1954. In 1953 the cars broke several international records and a series of glassfibre coupés was introduced. The racing programme costs were shared by Panhard, the Bonnet company and by customers, but not, so it would seem, by Deutsch.

Although Panhard became part-owned by Citroën from 1955, DB continued to rely on Panhard parts. It was disagreement over Bonnet's plans to use Renault engines at Le Mans in 1962 that caused Deutsch and Bonnet to split in January of that year, Deutsch continuing an illustrious career as a consulting engineer and Bonnet continuing to manufacture cars as René Bonnets, notably the Renault-engined Djet. Ironically, Panhard's car for the 1962 Le Mans won the Index of Performance and some 150 of them were built in 1963.

In 1964 Bonnet sold out to the Matra Sports division of the Matra aerospace company. The René Bonnet Djet became the Matra-Bonnet Djet and continued until 1968. In 1967 Matra closed the Bonnet factory and its new car, the Ford-engined MS530A, was simply called a Matra. BL

Decauville 3½hp of 1898

DE BAZELAIRE
FRANCE 1908-1928

F. de Bazelaire SA of Paris was perhaps better known for its modest racing efforts than as a manufacturer, but the company began production in Rue Gager-Gabillot in 1908, a year after its racing début in the 1907 Coupe des Voiturettes. Drivers of the team of 1100cc twin-cylinder cars in that race were de Bazelaire himself (a French nobleman), de Saint Didier and de Croizière. The 1908 cars had gearboxes in unit with the back axle and either 1100 or 1690cc twin-cylinder proprietary engines. A 2-litre four was also offered.

In 1910 De Bazelaire was back at the Coupe des Voiturettes with what was described as 'a four-cylinder touring car of standard design', but the team had to change the engine at the last moment following an accident on the road, and the car made no impression in the race. It is uncertain what De Bazelaire actually raced in 1910 as its 'Type Sport' was apparently over the capacity limit and the other models were even larger. The production cars that year included a 2½-litre six.

In 1913 De Bazelaire showed a six-cylinder Fischer-engined car but did not put it into production, instead offering five versions of its four-cylinder Ballot- or Janvier-engined models up to the outbreak of World War I. After the war, De Bazelaire continued with Janvier- and SCAP-engined assembled cars until 1928 when the company closed. BL

DECAUVILLE
FRANCE 1898-1910

Famed for its small locomotives and distillation equipment, Decauville of Petit-Bourg near Paris was founded in 1854 and reformed in 1893 with a capital of 7 million francs. It diversified into many types of metal work, including bicycles and trams. It made tricycle frames for De Dion and components for Serpollet.

In 1898 Louis Ravenez formed a subsidiary firm, Société des Voitures Automobiles des Ets Decauville Aîné, with a capital of 1 million francs. A car design was bought from Joseph Guedon and the firm's chief engineer was Pierre Cornilleau.

A total of 600 Decauville cars were planned for 1898, but only about 100 were actually produced. They had De Dion two-cylinder engines and marked the first use of independent front suspension in series production. Orio and Marchand built copies in Italy, as did Lux later; Fahrzeugfabrik Eisenach held the German licence; and there was a Standard-Decauville in America in 1903, offered by the Standard Auto Co.

A fire at Decauville put an end to the De Dion frame contract in 1899 and led to financial and production problems aggravated by the death of Louis Ravenez in 1901. Larger, front-engined cars had arrived in 1900 and in 1903 the parent firm took over the ailing car subisidiary and boosted production to 350 cars and about 20 commercial vehicles in 1904. The cars all had four cylinders from 1905, although a five had been intended in 1904. Some Cohendet engines were used.

In 1906 1600 men were employed at Petit-

DEASY
see Siddeley

DE BRUYNE
see Gordon-Keeble

Bourg, Corbeil, Dunkirk and Liège on the entire range of Decauville's activities, which included the building of motorboat engines, car frames and all sorts of railway equipment. Serious losses in 1908 led to the appointment of new management, which closed the car department in 1910. NB

DE DIETRICH/LORRAINE, LORRAINE-DIETRICH
FRANCE 1897-1934

The De Dietrich ironworking interests dated from 1684, and by 1770 the family had three large factories in lower Alsace as well as extensive banking interests. In the French Revolution the grandson of the founder was guillotined, and his father died soon afterwards.

In 1800 when a limited liability company was formed, there were more than 1200 De Dietrich employees. The prominent de Türckheim family entered the picture six years later when Baron de Dietrich died and his widow carried on the firm.

Alsace and part of adjoining Lorraine were transferred from France to Germany in 1871 and, with the De Dietrich factories now in Germany with headquarters at Niederbronn, a new factory was opened in Lunéville, towards Paris, to cater for France and her railway industry's need for wheels, carriages, axles and wagons.

Adrien, son of Baron Edouard de Türckheim, worked at Lunéville and was instrumental in gaining a licence to make Amédée Bollée cars in March 1897. Later that year the French operation became the Société de Dietrich et Cie de Lunéville, although the board members on both sides of the border were the same and Bollée cars were made by De Dietrich in both France and Germany.

In 1898 Lunéville made 72 cars, the figure rising to 107 in 1900 and 253 in 1902, the year in which it adopted designs by Léon Turcat and Simon Méry. Its German associates had already replaced Bollée cars with the Belgian Vivinus and French Georges Richard designs. In 1902 the German branch hired the Italian Ettore Bugatti, having acquired a licence to build his 1901 prototype. Alsace was henceforth to be Bugatti's home.

In 1904 Adrien de Türckheim fell out with Eugène de Dietrich of the Niederbronn factories, which halted car production that year. With financial backing from his father, his brother Eugène and Turcat-Méry chairman H. Estier, among others, he formed Société Lorraine d'Anciens Etablissements de Dietrich et Cie to continue making cars. He called them Lorraine-Dietrich, to highlight their French pedigree.

In the first financial year 430 cars were made as well as much railway rolling stock, which soon was concentrated at Lunéville. In 1906 a new car factory with the latest individually electric-powered machine tools was commissioned at Argenteuil to be near the Parisian market. Until it came on stream batches of cars built by the Société Alsacienne des Constructions Mécaniques in German Alsace, while Turcat-Méry probably also helped out. Cars were offered in the United States, but without much success. Commercial vehicles had been made from the outset and in 1906 a separate company was formed to promote this business. The group also made speedboat engines.

Share capital rose from 5 million francs in 1905 to three times that in 1907 in order to finance the acquisition of Ariel's factory in England, where Charles Jarrott and William Letts had sold many (Lorraine-) Dietrich cars since 1903 and where Ariel was said to be making three a week in 1908. The bulk of the Isotta-Fraschini business in Italy was acquired for 2 million francs.

Some 650 cars had been made in 1906 but over-expansion, followed by an acute recession which seriously affected the market for the high-priced cars that were Lorraine-Dietrich's speciality, brought serious problems. A loss of 10 million francs was announced in 1909 and in 1910 share capital was reduced from 15 million to 3.75 million francs, mostly held by Belgian investors.

In an effort to assist matters, some smaller cars were introduced, a railway locomotive division started, the English factory and Italian business disposed of and the commercial vehicle firm closed. Turcat and Méry left the company and Marius Barbarou joined as the car division's technical director. He was soon having to produce light lorries and aero engines for the war effort. Aero engines remained an important Lorraine-Dietrich product after the war, being licence-produced in a number of countries.

Barbarou's first car of 1919 was a 30CV pair-cast six, which echoed the marque's prewar designs. Slightly more promising was the American-influenced overhead-valve 15CV, known as the 'Silken Six' in Britain, which was made from 1921 at the rate of 500 to 1000 a year. The model disappeared in 1932, but not before sports versions had scored fine victories in the 1925 and 1926 Le Mans events. A four-cylinder car was also made until the late 1920s, by which time all models were known simply as Lorraines.

A Parisian coachbuilder named Gaston Grummer had by then become commercial director. Allied with the more sporting image came more stylish bodies by his firm and attractive advertising to match.

Lorraine's last new model was a refined and attractive 20CV six in 1932, which lasted until car production was ended in 1934. Argenteuil then made Tatra commercial vehicle chassis and aero engines. After World War II it made a few rail and dockyard tugs as a sideline to the great railway rolling stock business that continues at Lunéville to this day. NB

DE DION-BOUTON
FRANCE 1895-1932

The two partners in this pioneering company were Count Albert de Dion, born in 1856, and Georges Bouton, born in 1847. Bouton was known to de Dion as a maker of steam-driven toys, a business he had begun with his brother-in-law Trépardoux in 1869.

De Dion built a steam engine in 1876 and the three men produced experimental steam vehicles from 1883. These vehicles went on sale from 1885, when about 15 men were being employed. Steam launches were built from 1888 and a year later petrol engine experiments began, followed in 1892 by the first trial of Michelin tyres.

Trépardoux resigned from the enterprise in 1894 because of his lack of faith in internal combustion. He it was who had developed

De Dion-Bouton vis-à-vis of 1899

the famous De Dion axle with separate drive and load-carrying elements, and upon his departure the De Dion-Bouton partnership was formalized.

That year, 1894, De Dion's first articulated vehicle was built, one of the earliest ever made. Georges Bouton meanwhile developed the first high-speed small petrol engine, for which he had to develop special accumulator ignition to cope with 1500 to 2000rpm when less than 1000rpm was the norm. By late 1895 complete vehicles were sold; 1bhp was developed from only 198cc in the three-wheelers, the frames for which were bought from Decauville.

Count de Dion founded the Automobile Club de France in 1895 and was an articulate and influential promoter of the automobile. By 1897 his factory at Puteaux employed 250, a figure which grew to 950 in 1899, when a new factory had been opened. After a fire that year at Decauville, Clément supplied frames. The production of a quad led to the phasing out of trikes in 1901, after 15,000 had been sold. In the first 12 months alone, 1500 four-wheelers were sold.

Among the first car firms to conduct scientific research into materials, De Dion-Bouton had its own metallurgical laboratory before the turn of the century. Their sturdiness is borne out by the fact that in the annual London to Brighton run De Dion-Boutons regularly outnumber all other makes.

In 1898 Baron van Zuylen, an early automobile promoter, provided half of the 800,000-franc capital required to reorganize the company. Engines and patent rights were sold to numerous other companies. By 1914 more than 160 vehicle firms worldwide had used De Dion-Bouton engines, including Adler, Alldays, Argyll, Bianchi, Ceirano, Dennis, Hansa, Humber,, Peerless (which had previously made parts for a De Dion plant in Brooklyn), Pierce-Arrow, Star and Sunbeam – as well as over 70 French companies. At least 5000 engines were made in 1900 and about 1200 vehicles. The workforce numbered 1300.

In 1901 de Dion became a marquis on the death of his father. During that year the workforce swelled to 2000, the first front-engined models were produced in October and cars were built at the rate of 200 a month. Some 33,000 engines had been built by the end of 1902, when 2000 cars were sold.

Electric cars were made for three years from 1900, while steam commercials ended soon after the first petrol-engined heavy vehicles were produced in 1903. More than 300 buses were in service by 1910 in both Paris and London. In 1906 Marta acquired a De Dion licence and made 150 taxis.

A fervent patriot, de Dion was distressed by the number of American machine tools bought by French car firms, so with backing from Mors and other companies he started a machine-tool factory at St Ouen in 1907. It was never very successful, however, and was sold in 1913.

134

In 1908 the De Dion-Bouton company was restructured with a capital of 15 million francs. The workforce remained at 3000 and a chassis was completed every working hour. Bicycles were made for five years from 1909.

In 1910 the first production V8 engines were applied to cars and, in the following year, to experimental aircraft. The little CD single-cylinder model was the first car to appear, in 1910, without the special De Dion axle – which disappeared from other types in World War I. Single-cylinder cars were discontinued in 1912 and twin-cylinder models a year later.

Commercial vehicles were becoming increasingly important. In 1913 just 2800 vehicles were built, by which time more than 50,000 cars and 200,000 engines had been sold; 1000 buses and 2000 taxis were at work around the world.

During World War I employment peaked at 6000. Production included Hispano-Suiza and De Dion aero engines, lorries and staff cars.

The V8s were made until 1923 but the cars of the 1920s survived largely on past reputation. The company was stagnating, although its commercial vehicles showed some enterprising features and the low-level safety

De Dion single-cylinder of 1902

De Dion four-cylinder DK of 1912

coaches made from 1925 sold well in both France and Britain. A 1.3-litre JP model light car and van of 1926 came too late to save the firm, which closed for a time in 1927.

The French government prevented a putative takeover by Daimler-Benz but, although new capital was raised and production continued, the respite was brief. Car production ceased in 1932, a 2½-litre straight-eight having been made from 1929. Motorcycles using the De Dion-Bouton name were made in Amiens between 1926 and 1930. Commercial vehicles were built in limited quantities dur-

ing the 1930s, some from 1937 using Deutz diesels. Georges Bouton died at the age of 91 in 1938 and the Marquis at 90 eight years later in 1946.

In 1947 there was a brief revival of the firm, but vehicle output ceased in 1950. Part of the Puteaux factory became Rover's Paris headquarters. In the 1960s forward control Land Rover fire engines were badged De Dion-Bouton and the name was also used by A. Chichery for a range of scooters, mopeds and bicycles, made for about 10 years from 1955. NB

DEEMSTER/WILKINSON
GB 1914-1924

The Deemster light car had its origins in a four-cylinder light car built in 1912 by the Wilkinson TMC Co Ltd of Acton, west London, a subsidiary of the celebrated Wilkinson Sword Co which is well known for the manufacture of garden tools, razor blades and ceremonial swords. Few cars were made under the Wilkinson name, but in January 1914 a new company was formed to take over Wilkinson TMC after its four-cylinder motorcycle had gone out of production.

The new company was the Ogston Motor Co Ltd, headed by a Scotsman, J. N. Ogston, who had been with Napier; several other former Napier personnel were also on the staff. The car was originally called the Ogston, but the name was changed to Deemster during 1914. It was a conventional four-cylinder light car, with the company's own make of 9.5hp 1086cc engine. About 25 cars were made before the outbreak of war in August 1914.

After the war the company was recapitalized at £75,000, later raised to £250,000. A new factory in Victoria Road, Acton, was acquired for assembling and testing, while the original works was used for machining; cylinder block castings came from Qualcast, the lawnmower-makers. Bodies were made by the Victoria and Albert Metal Works in Shepherds Bush. Production ran at about 15 cars a week.

There was little change in the design, apart from the adoption of a 1½-litre Anzani engine in place of Deemster's own in 1922. The cars had handsome vee-radiators. An unusual feature was a mechanical starter operated from the driver's seat. In 1924 finance ran out and production of the Deemster ended. GNG

Deep Sanderson coupé of 1962

DEEP SANDERSON
GB 1961-1969

Chris Lawrence was a Morgan enthusiast and successful racing driver whose results included a class win for Morgan at Le Mans in 1962. He also raced motorcycles, MGs and even a Bugatti. Lawrence set up Lawrencetune Engines Ltd with four friends in London in 1959, tuning Triumph engines and race-preparing Morgans.

In 1960 Lawrencetune designed a Volkswagen-based Formula Junior car, which was redesigned in 1961 and raced as the Deep Sanderson – named after the music of Deep Henderson and one of Lawrence's backers by the name of Sanderson. The FJ car was not a success and Lawrence returned his attention to sports cars, with a variety of Deep Sandersons.

The high-backed rear-engined 997cc Mini Cooper-powered prototype was shown in December 1961. It was said to weigh less than 8cwt (406kg) and accelerate from 0-60mph (0-96kph) in just nine seconds. It used the 'Lawrence link' trailing arm rear suspension and was intended to sell at £610 in kit form or £951 fully built. By June 1962 it was being shown in the American press in aluminium-bodied form with a claimed top speed of 107mph (172kph).

The cars were widely used in competition, including the Nürburgring 1000 kilometre race, and by 1963 Lawrencetune had developed the much prettier two-seater 301 GT Coupé. The prototype aluminium body, by Williams and Pritchard of London, was used as a mould for the glassfibre production bodies; and 14 301s were eventually built, kits selling for £750. 301s were raced at Le Mans in 1963 and 1964 and Lawrence also built the fearsome 501, with two linked Downton-tuned Cooper S engines, one at each end of the car.

The Deep Sanderson 303 coupé was designed for Ford 1600 GT power, but later adapted for the Martin V8 engine. This was a project in which Lawrence had become involved through John Pearce's Pearce-Martin Formula 1 efforts.

After Deep Sanderson's last Le Mans appearance, in 1968, Lawrence concentrated on prototype design, his most important project being the development of the Martin-engined car into the French Monica. The Monica project began when French industrialist Jean Tastevin commissioned the new Christopher J. Lawrence & Co to develop first an engine and then a car for his company. Lawrence obliged by developing a car that might once have been another Deep Sanderson. BL

Deemster 10hp two-seater of 1921

DELAGE
FRANCE 1905-1953

'One drives an Alfa, one is driven in a Rolls – and one buys the girlfriend a Delage.' So car connoisseur David Scott-Moncrieff once summed up this celebrated French marque. Like all generalizations it by no means tells the whole story, although there is no doubt that the Delages of the 1930s seemed eminently at home in the grander Concours d'Elegance, complete with Dior-garbed lady and fashionably clipped poodle.

Louis Delage was born in Cognac in 1874 and began his career in the motor industry with Turgan-Foy, followed by Peugeot. In 1905 he and a fellow Peugeot employee, Augustine Legros, set up a small workshop in Levallois where they carried out general engineering for other firms while they worked on the design of their own car.

This had a single-cylinder De Dion-Bouton engine of either 496 or 1059cc, Malicet et Blin frame, and a light two-seater body. A later model with 696cc engine became more popular; after a racing model had finished second in the 1906 Coupe des Voiturettes, orders poured in, and Delage was able to move to a new site in Levallois in 1907.

Later that year Henri Davène de Roberval, a director of Malicet et Blin, joined Delage with a substantial injection of cash, enabling further expansion to take place. He also assured a regular supply of frames, gearboxes and axles at advantageous prices, and remained a director of Automobiles Delage until 1935.

In 1909 Delage took a step towards being a manufacturer rather than an assembler when he entered into an agreement with Ballot whereby the engine-maker would supply 50 per cent of Delage's needs and the drawings for Delage to make the other 50 per cent himself. Under the rather one-sided terms of this deal, all the engines were to bear the Delage name. These engines were small four-cylinder units, although singles featured in the Delage catalogue up to 1910.

Hard bargains were very much Louis Delage's style, and the contract he made with François Repusseau for the supply of bodies from 1909 to 1914 left the coachbuilder with no profit at all; Repusseau nevertheless went on to be a successful manufacturer of shock absorbers and servo brakes, and died a much wealthier man than Delage.

Delage began making his own gearboxes and rear axles in 1910, and two years later he bought an 11-acre (4-hectare) site at Courbevoie on which he erected a new factory where engines were made as well as transmissions. In 1913 came the first six-cylinder engine, a 2½-litre designed by Arthur-Léon Michelat, who was Delage's chief engineer from 1910 to 1919 and returned in 1934 to design the D6 and D8 series.

During World War I the company prospered greatly through munitions manufacture, and Louis Delage ended the war a very wealthy man. Not so fortunate was engineer Maurice Gaultier who had to take the blame for the supply of faulty munitions and was sent to prison. He later worked for Georges Irat and returned to Delage in about 1925, designing the straight-eight D8 of 1929.

The first post-war car was the Type CO, a 4½-litre six with front-wheel brakes, which did not sell in sufficiently large numbers; Louis Delage expected 3000 a year, but in fact it sold only 1390 in three years. It was replaced by the 2-litre four-cylinder DE, which became the most successful Delage ever made. With its more sporting variations, the DI, DIS, and DISS, the D series remained in production until 1928 and sold 14,309 cars. It was designed by Charles Planchon, Louis Delage's cousin, but a new designer was brought in for the next and most ambitious Delage yet. Intended to rival the Hispano

Delage saloon of c.1928

Delage D8 convertible of 1929

Suiza, the 100bhp single-overhead cam 6-litre GL was the work of Maurice Sainturat who had designed a somewhat similar prototype for Hotchkiss. Exactly 200 GLs were made from 1925 to 1927, after which Sainturat left to join Donnet.

In October 1923 Automobiles Delage became a public company with a capital of 1 million francs, increased during 1924 to 5 million and then to 25 million. It was in 1923 that Delage returned to racing, fielding a 2-litre V12 Grand Prix car designed by Planchon. The car was too hurriedly prepared and retired from the French Grand Prix, for which Planchon was dismissed by Louis Delage on the spot.

A team of three cars ran in 1924 and 1925, winning the French and Spanish Grands Prix, while for 1926 Albert Lory designed a beautiful little supercharged 1½-litre straight-eight car which won the 1926 British Grand Prix and the British, French, Spanish and Italian

Grands Prix in 1927. Glorious though these victories were, they were extremely expensive, and coupled with Louis Delage's own extravagant lifestyle initiated the downfall of the company. Racing ended abruptly at the end of 1927.

After the end of DI production in 1928, there were several small sixes designed by Gaultier, who had returned to the fold. Indeed, the best year ever for Delage production was 1928, when 3600 cars were sold, having been made by 2000 employees.

His greatest achievement, however, was the 4-litre overhead-valve D8, launched at the 1929 Paris Salon. The D8 and its sporting version, the 118bhp D8S, were among the most handsome cars of their day and carried the finest coachwork by such firms as Saoutchik, Letourneur et Marchand and Chapron. Unfortunately, like so many beautiful cars, their introduction coincided with the Depression and neither they nor their smaller, six-cylinder sisters sold very well. A total of 2002 eight-cylinder cars were built in four years, from 1929 to 1933, of which 99 were the low chassis D8S model. The sixes accounted for only a further 2300 sales.

By 1934 the Delage company was in dire straits. Gaultier designed some smaller sixes and eights with almost square cylinder dimension (75×75.5cm) and even a 1½-litre four-cylinder car, the D4, but they were put into production without sufficient testing and earned a bad reputation. Gaultier moved to Renault and was replaced by Michelat who proceeded to bring out new six- and eight-cylinder designs, but in April 1935 Delage went into receivership.

The company's assets were bought by Walter Watney, the Paris Delage agent, who sold off the factory to a machine tool manufacturer and made an agreement with Delahaye whereby they would assemble cars of Delahaye design but with Delage radiators. In fact one model, the D6-60, had a Michelat-designed engine, but other subsequent cars carrying the Delage name were basically Delahayes. The straight-eight D8-120 introduced in 1938 used the six-cylinder Delahaye 135 engine with two extra cylinders, and was the prestige model of the combine, as there was no straight-eight Delahaye. A few Delages were made with Citroën saloon or roadster bodies on the D1-12 and D6-60 chassis.

In September 1936 it was announced that the D6-70 would be built in England, at Slough, but nothing came of this. After World War II the only Delage to be revived was the D6-70, which was a bored out version of Michelat's D6-60, so the last true Delage outlived the crypto-Delahayes. Assembly was still undertaken in the Delahaye factory, however, and only 250 were made after the war, compared with about 2000 Delahayes. The final Delage was built in 1953.

Louis Delage remained nominally on the board as a tribute to his name, but he had lost all his fortune in the 1935 collapse of his own company. He died a poor man in 1947. GNG

DELAHAYE
FRANCE 1894-1954

The origins of Delahaye date back to 1845, when M. Brethon set up a brick-making factory at Tours. About 20 years later he was joined by a young engineer, Emile Delahaye, who had worked for the Belgian locomotive-makers Cail and who changed the direction of the firm towards steam engines followed by gas and petrol engines. In 1894 he built his first car, with rear-mounted horizontal engine, belt drive and tubular frame. He exhibited this at the 1895 Paris Salon, and the following year entered his first race, Paris-Marseilles-Paris.

For the next four years Delahayes featured regularly in most of the major town-to-town races, using their rather ponderous-looking breaks and wagonettes. Emile Delahaye did not think that two-seater cars would sell very well and he was not prepared to build machines specially for racing, so the company abandoned competitions once specialized racing cars became *de rigueur* after 1900.

Production at Tours was limited, with only 75 employees, but in 1898 Emile Delahaye joined forces with a firm of Parisian coppersmiths, Desmarais et Morane, to build his cars in the factory in Rue Banquier. This was greatly extended, first in 1898 and again in 1906, when it became one of the finest motor factories in Europe. By 1899 production was running at 20 cars a month. The chief engineer was 28-year-old Charles Weiffenbach, who was to remain with Delahaye until 1954.

In 1901 Emile Delahaye resigned because of ill health – he died in 1905 – and the company name was changed to Société des Automobiles Delahaye, Léo Desmarais et Georges Morane, successeurs. Commercial vehicles, first made in 1898, became an increasingly important part of Delahaye's production, and by 1906 included two-cylinder vans and four-cylinder chain-drive chassis for buses and trucks of 5-ton capacity. Two fields in which the firm became highly respected were those of postal delivery vans and fire

engines. The latter was a Delahaye speciality until after World War II.

The cars grew in size and price. The largest model in 1905 was an 8-litre T-head four with two hand- and two foot-brakes; one of these was bought by that connoisseur among monarchs, King Alfonso XIII of Spain.

Motorboat engines were also made from 1903 to about 1906, and a boat powered by a 350hp Delahaye engine took the world water speed record at Monaco in 1905. The department was very expensive to run, however, and brought few customers so Weiffenbach closed it down.

Delahayes were made under licence in Germany by Presto of Chemnitz in 1907, and a monobloc four-cylinder engine was used by White in America as the basis for its first petrol engines. By 1914 the company was the eighth largest French vehicle manufacturer, with annual production of about 1500 cars. The cars included an unusual 3.2-litre V6, and in-line fours from 1.6- to 5.7-litres capacity.

Delahaye made an important contribution to the war effort, producing army trucks, shells and guns, and also Hispano-Suiza V8 aero engines. After the war the company settled down to a range of conventional middle-class cars in the 2.6- to 4-litre range, and trucks up to 4-ton capacity.

Weiffenbach was attracted by mergers, hoping to form a French equivalent of General Motors. In 1919 he had hopes of an agree-

Delahaye carriage of 1898

Delahaye doctor's coupé of c.1911

ment with Berliet but this came to nothing. He tried again in 1927, bringing into his group Chenard-Walcker, Donnet and Unic. The last two companies soon left but the Chenard-Walcker's influence on Delahaye was seen in the adoption of ribbon radiators in place of the more handsome vee-type and a great similarity of engine and body design. By 1930 it was hard to tell the two products apart; this did no good to either, and in 1932 the agreement was ended. Two years later there arrived a new Delahaye model, which was completely to change the image and direction of the company.

A young designer named Jean François had joined the firm. Using as his starting point a 3.2-litre overhead-valve six-cylinder engine introduced in 1932 for a 3-4-ton truck, he proceeded to develop a sporting car of the *grand routier* type to rival those being made by Bugatti, Delage and Talbot-Darracq. This was the Type 135, made in either 3.2-litre (110bhp) or 3.5-litre (120bhp) forms. They had transverse leaf independent front suspension and either synchromesh or Cotal gearboxes. At last Delahaye had a chassis worthy of the best coachwork, and all the top French *carrossiers* went to work on the new chassis.

In 1935 Delahaye absorbed the Delage company, so acquiring Delage's expertise in racing, which led Delahaye to an active competition career in the five years up to World War II. From 1935 all Delages except for the D6-60 were, in effect, Delahaye-based and made in the Delahaye factory, although some such as the straight-eight D8-120 had no Delahaye equivalent.

Apart from a very small number of V12s based on a Grand Prix car, no Delahaye ever had more than six cylinders. The smaller fours were continued and some 2.2-litre four-cylinder engines were supplied to Amilcar for its Pégase model. A curiosity of the late 1930s was the Type 168, a Type 135 carrying four-door Renault Viva Grand Sport saloon body. This came about because Delahaye complained that Renault had 'trespassed' on Delahaye's long-held position as the major supplier of fire engines to the French government. Renault agreed to withdraw, but only on condition that Delahaye bought a certain number of Viva Grand Sports bodies. About 30 were built before World War II gave Delahaye a convenient escape from this unpopular agreement.

Delahaye was also still active with commercial vehicles, having built its first diesel truck in 1931. It offered Gardner diesel engines on all its large truck and bus chassis by 1939.

Towards the end of World War II Weiffenbach again went empire-building. This time he acquired Baron Petiet's GFA (Groupe Française Automobile), which included Simca and the truck-makers Bernard, Laffly and Unic.

Post-war Delahayes included the 2.2-litre Type 134, 3½-litre 135 and a new 4½-litre the

Delahaye 3500cc six of 1938

175 (178 and 180 with long wheelbase); the last-named had left-hand drive and was aimed at the American market. A two-door sports saloon body was built in series for Delahaye by Guilloré and the chassis was also available for specialist coachbuilders. The 134 was dropped in 1948, and from 1951 the only model was the 235, an updated 135 with 152bhp and up-to-date slab-sided bodywork made by Antem and Letourneur et Marchand. Car sales dropped drastically because of the French government's punitive taxation against large engines – from 483 in 1950 to 77 in 1951, and only three in 1953.

Commercial vehicles were still being made, and Delahaye tried to find another product in the form of the VLR, a 4×4 Jeep-type vehicle. Almost 10,000 were built for the French Army between 1951 and 1955, but it was then dropped in favour of the less complex Hotchkiss-built Jeep. In 1954 Delahaye merged with Hotchkiss and the last Delahaye trucks were made two years later. The 84-year-old Charles Weiffenbach only retired from Delahaye at the time of the merger, and he died in 1959. GNG

DELAUGÈRE/DELAUGÈRE et CLAYETTE
FRANCE 1898-1926

This was a typical French regional firm, with sales largely made in the district around Orléans. Jean-Pierre Delaugère (1810-68) established a carriage works in the middle of the 19th century, and his son Émile and great nephew Félix built a three-wheeler car in 1898, followed by a De Dion powered four-wheeler in 1900. Twins came in 1901 and fours in 1902, the engines being of Delaugère's own manufacture. In 1904 Maurice Clayette joined the company, which became known as E. et F. Delaugère et M. Clayette; two years later it was reformed as the SA des

Ets Delaugère, Clayette Frères et Cie, with a capital of 1.5 million francs.

A wide range of cars from an 8/10hp twin to a monstrous 80/100hp four of 15 litres was made, as well as taxicabs and trucks. Some vehicles were sold as far afield as Romania, the United States and Mexico, although the Delaugère never became well known, even in France, and the company's products were seldom written up in the press. In 1909 there were 350 workers, and production ran at an average of two cars a day. In 1913 came a sleeve-valve 15hp model using the patents of the Swiss designer Martin Fischer.

During World War I Delaugère-Clayette made army trucks and shells, and in 1920 returned to car production with a range of conventional side-valve designs, a 2.2-litre four and a 4.8-litre six. Overhead valves came in 1923, and front-wheel brakes in 1925, but the Orléans company could not compete with the big battalions such as Citroën and Renault.

In 1926 the factory was bought by Panhard for body manufacture, although Pierre Delaugère stayed on as a director. Spare parts for

Delaugère single-cylinder of c.1900

Delaugère cars were made until 1931. The works later passed into the hands of Citroën when it purchased Panhard, and were demolished in 1973 to make way for a large block of flats. GNG

DELAUNAY-BELLEVILLE
FRANCE 1904-1948

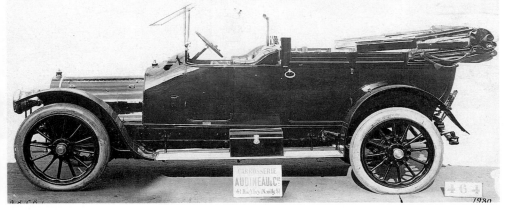

Delaunay-Belleville tourer of 1910

Louis Delaunay obtained a naval engineering training and in the late 1860s joined Belleville of St Denis, which had been formed in 1864 to make ship and locomotive boilers. He married the owner's daughter and both he and the firm changed their name to Delaunay-Belleville. The British Navy bought its Dreadnought boilers, the first being fitted to HMS *Terrible*, and by about 1900 some 1000 men were employed making boilers and steam engines.

A separate car firm was formed in September 1903 as the Société des Automobiles Delaunay-Belleville. Marius Barbarou from Benz and Clément was hired to design high-grade 16, 24 and 40hp four-cylinder cars which appeared towards the end of 1904.

Six-cylinder models were introduced in 1907, followed two years later by an unusually small six-cylinder 10CV version. A familiar feature was the rounded radiator and bonnet, similar to those of Hotchkiss.

From 1910 well into the 1920s these vehicles, usually chauffeur-driven, were advertised as 'The Car Magnificent'. Tsar Nicholas II of Russia was a regular customer and after the Revolution both Lenin and Trotsky drove Delaunay-Belleville cars.

In 1912 Louis Delaunay died at the age of 68, and Marius Barbarou departed for Lorraine-Dietrich soon afterwards. Robert and Pierre, sons of Louis, then ran the firm and introduced commercial vehicles. All pre-1914 cars had the firm's own carburettors and from 1909 several were equipped with air starters, tyre inflators and jacks.

In the first decade 7576 cars were made, about half being six-cylinder models. In peak years in Britain about 100 were sold annually, a number being assembled in Maida Vale, London. Hispano-Suiza aero engines and

army lorries of up to 5-ton capacity were made during World War I, and afterwards both 4×4 and light crawler machines were tried. Ships' boilers remained the parent firm's speciality, however.

The circular frontal styling of the cars continued in less pronounced form in the 1920s. Cars of 10 to 50hp were made, including an overhead-cam model from 1922, as well as an assortment of commercials, but output was small and the marque had lost much of its cachet by 1931 when American Continental straight-eight engines were offered. In the mid-1930s Delaunay-Bellevilles assumed a Mercedes-Benz-like appearance with the 2.3-litre six-cylinder R1.6, which was revived after World War II with Americanized frontal styling.

Fourteen post-war cars, one of them a coupé, were made, the last in 1948. Commercials, which had been produced in small quantities throughout the 1930s, were listed until 1949. One factory survives, having started in the days before cars had boots by making metal trunks and then specializing in radiators. NB

DELFOSSE
FRANCE 1922-1926

The Delfosse was a small, sporty car built from 1922 to 1926 with a variety of four-cylinder proprietary engines. The company's founder, C. Delfosse, was a motorcycle racer and distributor who bought a factory in Cambrai, Nord, towards the end of 1921 and began to assemble cars at that site under his own name.

Initially, Delfosse used chassis from Morain-Sylvestre of Courbevoie, makers of MS cars. The first Delfosse was completed in early 1922; this was the DS11, with a 1-litre twin-cylinder engine. Four-cylinder Chapuis-Dornier engines were also used from 1922.

The first models continued into 1923 and about 12 two-cylinder and six four-cylinder cars were sold before Delfosse decided to change from assembly to manufacture. The 1924 cars, shown at the Brussels Salon, were

all sporting two- or four-seaters of 1100 or 1500cc, with CIME engines. They were conventional except for their patented lever-and-spring rear suspensions, and continued in production until 1925, in which year the company moved to another factory, in Marly-les-Valenciennes.

The company entered competitions, with some success, almost from the start, and in 1925 built three racing cars with very low, streamlined bodies and supercharged 1500cc engines, for the Grand Prix de Boulogne. These Grand Prix cars first appeared in April and scored several class wins, usually driven by Delfosse himself, before finishing fourth in class in the Grand Prix in August. One of the racers was timed at over 100mph (160kph).

Delfosse stopped racing after the death of a Belgian customer, M. Lippens, and a proposed run of customer racing cars was not finished. Production of the sporting road cars continued until 1926, by which time some 160 cars had been built, mostly the 1924 and later CD6. Delfosse returned to the business of selling motorcycles and agricultural machinery. BL

DELLOW
GB 1949-1959

Dellow Mark III of 1954

The Dellow, built in Birmingham from 1949 to 1959, was the archetypal British trials car, which also happened to be quite usable as a sporty, 70mph (112kph) road car. In this guise it was enormously popular and highly successful, but the company was eventually killed by an attempt to turn the Dellow into something slightly more sophisticated, which was not what the customers wanted.

The alloy-bodied production Dellow was built by Dellow Motors Ltd of Alvechurch and was based on an 1172cc Ford 10-engined trials car built in 1947 by Kenneth C. Delingpole and Ron C. Lowe. It used an A-shaped tubular chassis, originally with quarter elliptic rear springs but later with coils, and an ingenious two-way handbrake for individual rear-wheel control – one of the skills of trials driving.

Originally, customers for Dellows provided their own parts, which were reconditioned and used as required. Ford subsequently agreed to supply new parts directly and by 1950 Dellows were being built from scratch, with options including a Wade-supercharged engine. By the end of 1949 the original batch of a dozen cars had collected more than 100 awards, and in 1950 Gordon Garage (Dulwich) Ltd acquired a dealership for London and the south-east.

In 1952 a four-seater version, the Mark III, was introduced on a lengthened chassis, and that year a firm of agricultural engineers bought a fleet of two-seaters for use by its sales reps. In 1952 the two-seater sold for £774 and the Mark III for £841. The last trials car was the ultra-light, coil front suspension Mark V of 1954, but by this time the car was meeting much tougher trials competition and sales, which had reached 500, were falling.

In 1956 the company was reorganized as Dellow Engineering Ltd, in Oldbury, Birmingham. It introduced the Ford 1172-engined Mark VI, with all-enveloping glassfibre bodywork, split windscreen and full weather equipment, but seemingly no-one wanted the non-trials Dellow and the car was dropped in 1959. BL

DeLoreans stockpiled in 1982

DELOREAN
NORTHERN IRELAND, USA 1976-1982

John Zachary DeLorean was born in 1925. His Romanian father went to America as a teenager and worked in the Ford foundries in Detroit. John studied law at night school but planned to be a motor engineer. He graduated in 1948, having spent part of the war in the army in the USA.

In 1950, after a period as an insurance salesman, he went to the Chrysler Institute and gained a degree in Automotive Engineering. After working briefly for Chrysler he joined the struggling Packard company, which he left in 1956 with several patents in his name and a fairly senior engineering title.

He joined Pontiac as head of its new advanced engineering department and revitalized the General Motors' division's dowdy image with a new emphasis on performance and style. By 1960 Pontiac was GM's second best seller and in 1962 DeLorean became the division's youngest ever chief engineer. In 1965 he became general manager.

In January 1969 he was appointed general manager at Chevrolet, becoming a group executive for the car and truck divisions in August 1972 in what seemed an inevitable path to the GM presidency. Although he reorganized Chevrolet when the company badly needed it, he left GM in 1973, frustrated by the unwieldy management, although there were suggestions that he had been dismissed because of his autonomous style.

In January 1974 the John Z. DeLorean Corporation was registered in Detroit as en-

gineering consultants. All the stock was held by Cristina, a Nevada company named after DeLorean's third wife. Although DeLorean was restricted by his GM severance terms, he was already talking about his own sports car project. He planned limited production and high price and saw the car as technically advanced and safety conscious.

In October 1974 Bill Collins joined DeLorean from GM as designer. A DeLorean subsidiary, Composite Technology Corporation, bought the manufacturing rights to a lightweight composite moulded material, known as ERM, which was to be used for the chassis. The body would be of unpainted stainless steel, as ERM itself could not be painted. Mock-ups were completed in mid-1975. Styling was by Giugiaro, based on his Porsche Tapiro exercise of 1970, the main feature being gullwing doors.

In October 1975 the DeLorean Motor Co was registered in Michigan, DeLorean's own shares being held by the John Z. DeLorean Corporation. Several subsidiaries were set up and allocated functions, among them the DeLorean Sports Car Partnership, the purpose of which was to raise capital. Helped by tax allowances as a research company, the Partnership offered 35 $100,000 units with options to convert to DeLorean Motor Co stock. There was little interest in this scheme. DeLorean also sought funds through a limited share offer to dealers of up to 400 $25,000 blocks, each to include a sales franchise. The dealers would thus contribute 75 per cent of the finance but own only 13 per cent of the equity, DeLorean himself retaining over 65 per cent. In August 1977 the offer was floated and although the expected number of shares

had been sold by the October deadline, the $3.4 million raised was still insufficient for the company's needs. The first running prototype had been completed in October 1976, and work on a second immediately followed.

The company was living on a shoestring while seeking $90 million for final development and production. In April 1977 DeLorean had entered an agreement with Puerto Rico but this depended on the company raising $30 million and guaranteeing 40,000 orders. The deal should have been finalized in July 1978 but in August DeLorean rejected Puerto Rico – and other possibilities including Spain, the Irish Republic, Detroit and several American states – and agreed terms with the British government to build his factory in Northern Ireland, creating jobs in a troubled area.

The package, arranged through the Northern Ireland Development Agency (NIDA), was worth $97 million: one third as an outright grant, $20 million in loans (convertible if job creation targets were met), one third as NIDA equity and a $12.3 million factory loan. DeLorean's only liability was for half the factory mortgage; building started at Dunmurry, Belfast, in October 1978. To satisfy British law, DeLorean set up a British company, DeLorean Motor Cars Ltd, with NIDA holding a controlling interest, but headquarters remained in New York, at great expense and with little direct role.

Production was planned for early 1980 but was delayed by factory building problems and car redesign. In October 1978 the DeLorean Research Ltd partnership, set up to raise the $30 million Puerto Rican requirement, paid $12.5 million to Geneva-based

GPD Services for 'engineering development'.

GPD was newly registered in Panama, had only one employee and used a post office box address. DeLorean eventually paid almost $18 million – including more than $5 million from the British company – to GPD, which claimed it paid Lotus Cars Ltd for rights to the Lotus vacuum moulding process that replaced ERM, and for other redesign work. Lotus was paid $24 million directly by DeLorean but apparently nothing by the mysterious GPD.

Pilot production should have started in May 1980 but was delayed by the redesign and approval testing. A Conservative government was elected in Britain in May 1979 but, in spite of doubts, continued to provide finance. When cars were available in the summer, DeLorean had trouble arranging bridging finance for their delivery, but in October he raised a $33 million government loan over the heads of NIDA.

In December 1980 DeLorean was pressing NIDA for $28 million as 'inflation adjustment' but the government now called a halt, there would be no more government help beyond $40 million in guarantees from the Northern Ireland Department of Commerce. DeLorean now employed over 1000 people and there were serious quality problems with the sluggish, overweight, overpriced cars; it was obvious that US sales alone could not support the company.

The first 500 production cars were due for shipment in April 1981, but there were still type approval problems and DeLorean even considered shipping via Canada. By August only 10 cars a week were being released to dealers, each after a virtual rebuild on arrival at a cost of up to $2000.

In July 1981 DeLorean tried to float the DeLorean Motors Holding Co, to exchange stock one-for-one with the Belfast company; this would have given John DeLorean around $120 million and NIDA less than $8.5 million for its near $150 million investment. In October, car sales (some at a premium) peaked at over 700, which was still only half the output of the workforce which now stood at 3000. After initial optimism it became apparent that the stock offering had failed.

From November, sales slumped and DeLorean was forced to seek credit extensions. In January 1982 the factory went on short time and DeLorean asked the government Export Credit Guarantee Department for $65 million credit. The American company was reorganized as DeLorean Motor Cars of America, with the possibility of becoming the marketing division of the British company. The government, already investigating DeLorean finances after allegations by a former employee, refused further support and in February 1982 a receiver took over the factory. In total a little over 5000 cars were built; some 4000 eventually found their way to the USA, selling at anything from below cost to as much as $32,000.

By March DeLorean was claiming that the government would write off its $170 million investment against a personal injection of $5 million and he cited several private investors willing to save the company. In reality, DeLorean's only assets were some 2000 unsold cars, worth $40 million; debts were $43 million, plus $22.5 million owed to the Belfast company for cars shipped but not paid for. The Bank of America refused to reschedule its crucial credit and in March won a court order impounding the unsold cars.

In April 1982 the cars were bought by liquidators, Consolidated International, with DeLorean retaining an option to buy back and sell exclusively, but on Consolidated's stringent terms. An attempt by a group of dealer enthusiasts to buy the Belfast factory in which to resurrect limited production of the TR7 sports car ground to nothing in the face of government reticence at funding another motor car venture. The factory was later taken over by the aircraft maker, Short Brothers.

All attempts at raising finance failed and in one final twist, John DeLorean was arrested by the FBI on 19 October 1982, the day after the British government's refinancing deadline expired, on charges of possessing more than $16 million worth of cocaine. In 1984 he went for trial on charges of drug-trafficking and was acquitted.

In February 1985 the British government sued the DeLorean accountants, Arthur Andersen, for $245 million for their negligence – and in April the 'born again' John DeLorean, who still intended to resurrect his sports car ideas, signed a deal to film his life story. BL

DENNIS
GB 1900-1915

John Dennis, born in 1871, was apprenticed to an ironmonger in Bideford, Devon, and in 1894 joined the Guildford ironmongers Filmer and Masons. In his spare time he built a bicycle from parts sold by his employers and, needing some ready cash, he advertised it for sale in the window of a shop. This and all the other bicycles he could produce sold readily but the retail price of parts was too much to make a worthwhile profit. He visited Brown Brothers, important component factors, then as now, and worked with that firm for a time.

In January 1895 Dennis returned to Guildford and started Universal Athletic Stores, which sold sports goods and his own Speed King and Queen bicycles, made on the premises. Business prospered and John's 17-year-old brother Raymond came up from Devon to assist. He was an enthusiastic cyclist who did much to promote their products, and in time he became sales manager.

By mid-1899 a De Dion-engined tricycle was running successfully – so successfully in fact that Dennis was stopped for 'riding furiously' and the £1 fine turned to good advantage in an advertisement that stated that the Dennis could ascend Guildford's steep High Street at 16mph (25kph) 'on the sworn testimony of a constable of the law'. Examples of these and similar four-wheelers were probably available in 1900, when the workforce numbered about 20 in a 1000sq ft (90sq m) workshop in the former garden of Universal Athletics.

Dennis Brothers Ltd was formed in 1901 with £30,000 capital, which rose to £100,000 by 1910. Cycle-derived motor vehicles were joined in 1901 by a shaft-drive model with front-mounted De Dion 8hp engine and using the Speed King name. About 200 vehicles were sold in 1902.

Larger models followed, with Aster, Simms

Dennis four-seat tourer of 1909

and White and Poppe engines. Tylor engines were also used in the commercial vehicles made from 1904, in which year the patent worm-drive Dennis back axle was adopted on all models.

In 1908 production began of what was to become a Dennis speciality – fire engines. In that year, too, 17 cars were sold to the Russian government. There were by then two factories employing 400 men, one in Onslow Street and one at Woodbridge Hill that was soon expanded to become the principal plant and is the present-day home of Dennis. In the first eight years 2000 commercial vehicles were made.

During World War I 7000 lorries were made, but car production ceased in 1915. In 1919 there were 14,000 Dennis employees, including those at recently acquired White and Poppe. Some 40 commercial vehicles were being made each week. Good profits were earned into the 1930s.

The transition from petrol to diesel engines proved painful for the company, but after five years of problems a satisfactory engine was built in 1936 for general haulage and passenger transport vehicles. Three years later both John and Raymond Dennis died.

World War II kept Dennis busy with vehicles and thousands of trailer fire pumps, but afterwards it failed to win back customers and was forced to concentrate increasingly on municipal vehicles, fire engines (many with Rolls-Royce engines) and ambulances (some of which had De Dion axles and Jaguar XK engines). In the 1960s the company got into financial difficulties and was rescued by the Hestair group in 1972.

Since the mid-1970s Dennis has again become strong in the bus and coach field as well as holding about 50 per cent of the British municipal vehicle market and selling a small number of goods vehicles each year. Exports have played an important part in the company's revival.

In 1985 a major reorganization saw just fire and bus chassis manufacture at Guildford. Fire appliance bodywork was then subcontracted to Carmichael of Worcester. Municipal chassis were henceforth made at Hestair Eagle in Warwick whilst all cabs came from another Hestair subsidiary, the Duple bus body firm. Some 450 jobs were lost at Guildford in the changeover but 250 created at the other sites. NB

DENZEL
AUSTRIA 1948-1960

Like the pioneering Bollées of Le Mans, Wolfgang Denzel came from a family of bell founders. Before World War II he was a keen, all-round sportsman, with a special regard for skiing – and for rally driving in a BMW 328. In Vienna after the war, Denzel began to build cars of his own that were based on Volkswagen running gear.

Denzel's first cars were built in 1948, using plentiful and cheap war surplus VW *Kubelwagen* chassis, the German equivalent of the Jeep. The first, four-seater sports cars were given wooden bodies and were sold as WDs. Denzel soon changed to using good-looking metal bodies and the cars became known as Denzels.

With the metal bodies the Denzels were also given more power, from larger engines, including 1300 and 1500 Porsche units. Denzel supplied his own increased capacity conversions and tuning equipment such as twin-carb manifolds for the VW Beetle – and, of course, these were also used on his own cars.

In 1955 a Denzel-prepared 1300 engine gave 65bhp and the 1500 gave 86bhp. The two-seater Denzel with all the tuning options would reach 105mph (170kph) and 0-60mph (0-96kph) in 11 seconds. The best known of the Denzels was the open, three-seater Seriensuper, with a tubular reinforced frame, standard VW suspension and welded-on aluminium body.

Denzel also prepared engines and complete cars for competition, some examples going to the United States. The out-and-out competition cars used shorter, wider chassis than standard, and Denzels scored several class wins in European rallies, including the 1300 class of the 1954 Alpine Rally, driven by Denzel and Stroinnig. The Denzel was a good car of its type but ultimately could not compete with the Porsche. The last cars were made in 1960. BL

DERBY
FRANCE 1921-1936

Bertrand Montet and Georges Goëtt formed the Montet company in Courbevoie in 1902. It was a general engineering firm that came to specialize in tow hooks and couplings. After World War I it dealt in ex-military Harley-Davidson motorcycles and used vee-twin engines from them to make cyclecars in 1921. It

Derby two-seat sports of 1928

chose the name Derby because of its aristocratic sound and associations with the turf. Engine vibration was considered excessive so four-cylinder water-cooled Chapuis-Dornier 4CV and larger units were soon adopted. About 300 cyclecars were made until 1926, when they were discontinued.

Fabbrica Automobili Officine Trubetzkoy of Turin made them under licence in Italy for two years from 1924 with the name Fadin. Then l'Autommerciale Italiana de Milano acquired the licence and made what was called the Derby-Talbot.

The Derby had numerous racing successes with Anzani 1100cc, Chapuis-Dornier 12-valve, Ruby and SCAP engines. Goëtt's design of Chapuis-Dornier-engined roadgoing sports models sold 200 in 1926, 150 a year to 1928 and 100 a year into the 1930s. Vernon Balls sold them in England from 1927 as Vernon-Derbys.

In 1928 Goëtt's six-cylinder CIME 1200 and 1300cc touring models were unveiled. Bertrand Montet died that year and his widow ran the company while Goëtt concentrated on the towing hitch side of the business, which is still controlled by his son Christian.

Denzel two-seater of 1957

In 1930 French-domiciled English racing drivers Wallace Douglas Hawkes and Gwenda Stewart (later Gwenda Hawkes) acquired Derby with money from Hawkes's stepfather, Charles Kinisson of London motor dealer Morgan Hastings Ltd. The CIME-engined six grew to 1850cc and a front-wheel-drive and independently-sprung Ruby-engined sports car was introduced in 1931.

Hawkes's team by then included Fred Cann and Robert Thiery, plus technical director Etienne Lépicard, formerly of Donnet, who had joined Marcel Violet's consultancy in 1928 and made a front-wheel-drive experimental V8. This was adopted as the TAV-Derby of 1933 with 2-litre overhead-exhausts, side-inlet-valve engine.

Derby bodies were made by Macquet et Galvier of Courbevoie until the company became insolvent in 1933, when Duval of Boulogne took over this work. The front-wheel-drive cars had complete wheel-out mechanical units, with radiator; some were built for racing with Miller and Salmson engines. There was also a 1-ton front-wheel-drive commercial offered from 1932 with Ruby or Meadows engines.

In October 1932 the company moved to the former Gillotte body factory in Courbevoie and used modern machinery to produce a forecast minimum of 12 cars a month, plus towing hitches. Only about 50 of the four-cylinder front-wheel-drive cars were sold in 1933-34 and sales of V8s probably did not exceed 30 up to the end of car production in 1936. Total Derby output was probably under 1400. NB

DE TOMASO
ITALY 1961 to date

Alejandro de Tomaso was born in Buenos Aires in July 1928, the son of a former Prime Minister of Argentina who died when Alejandro was only five. The family had extensive estates, which Alejandro was supposed to manage; but, against his mother's wishes, he took up motor racing from about 1951. He also became an active anti-Perónist and numbered Che Guevara among his friends. Under political pressure he planned to move to Italy, whence came two of his grandparents, and in 1955 he fled – although he retained his Argentine citizenship.

Through his racing contacts he met the Maserati brothers and drove their OSCA cars in 1957 and 1959. In 1957 he married an American, Elizabeth Haskell, herself a racing driver with a family fortune derived from auto finance in the early days of the industry.

In 1959, after he had fallen out with the Maserati brothers, de Tomaso decided to build his own cars, but not using his wife's money. He founded De Tomaso Automobili SpA in Moderna with $11,000 savings and two OSCA engines, around which he built his first racing cars. He built six Formula 1 cars in 1961, including the two OSCA-powered cars and two Alfa-powered machines for Serenissima. In 1968 de Tomaso built a flat-eight Grand Prix engine, but it only raced once; he also built an unsuccessful Indy car.

In 1963 he started work on a De Tomaso road car, the four-cylinder, Ford-engined Vallelunga, a Ghia-bodied GT version of which sold just over 50 between 1963 and 1965. The De Tomaso badge was a stylised 'T', from Isabel, the Latinized version of his wife's name. From 1964 he planned a V8 sports car and, having been turned away by General Motors, he approached Ford through racing contact Carroll Shelby. The outcome was the Mangusta, launched in 1969.

Meanwhile, De Tomaso was undergoing a reorganization. In May 1967 Alejandro persuaded Rowan Industries of New Jersey to take over the coachbuilder Ghia. Rowan's president and chairman were both related to de Tomaso's wife and Alejandro became president of Ghia. Rowan also bought the majority of De Tomaso stock in 1967, providing finance for expansion.

The 155mph (250kph) Mangusta – meaning mongoose or, fancifully, 'cobra-eater' – was imported into America at $11,150 with low-volume exemption from type regulations. In 1968 sales rose from $885,000 to $1.8 million, but the expense of launching the Mangusta caused profits to slump to around $25,000.

In 1969 Rowan bought 70 per cent of Vignale, which De Tomaso had owned since the recent death of Alfredo Vignale. Having expanded Ghia in anticipation of being adopted as Ford's official prototype builder, De Tomaso planned production of up to 20 cars a day at Ghia and began to plan a successor to the Mangusta, the Pantera.

The Pantera was to be built essentially for Ford, to link Ford in the showroom with European performance and coachbuilding. Ford guaranteed $2 million credit for tooling and guaranteed engine supplies.

De Tomaso Vallelunga of 1965

Ford originally intended to sell Panteras through Shelby's network, although De Tomaso wanted to market only through Lincoln dealers. Ford, in fact, set up Autosports Products Incorporated to sell the car. Compounding the corporate complexity, Rowan acquired 80 per cent of Autosports Products but sold its De Tomaso holdings to Ford in 1970 for some $2.8 million after Rowan's chairman and president were killed in a plane crash.

Ford installed Lee Iacocca as chairman of De Tomaso and left Alejandro with the Euro-

De Tomaso Longchamp of 1980

pean sales rights to the Pantera, launched in 1971. Alejandro never really got along with Ford management and in 1972 he was bought out, also selling his remaining Ghia stock. He retained the De Tomaso Automobili name and the Pantera later resumed production, although the Ford connection ended in 1974.

As well as the Pantera, de Tomaso built a few examples of the V6 Mustela in 1969, the front-engined, four-door Deauville from 1970 and a two-door variant, the Longchamp, from 1973 into the 1980s. He also made other acquisitions. He began managing the Benelli motorcycle company, turning its losses into profit until Rowan bought two-thirds of Benelli in December 1972 and used the holding to buy control of Moto Guzzi.

In 1976 Alejandro bought control of Maserati from Peugeot, which had acquired the company in its Citroën takeover and virtually closed it as unprofitable. De Tomaso's purchase was largely financed by the government-backed Gestione e Participazione SpA. In 1979 De Tomaso also nominally took control of the US branch of Maserati.

In 1976 Alejandro began managing Innocenti Mini sales and in September 1979, through Moto Guzzi, bought a majority holding as Nuova Innocenti. De Tomaso's other interests included boatbuilding and hotels, and in 1979 he worked on the design of the new Omni for Chrysler where Iacocca had moved from Ford. Although De Tomaso production *per se* remained small, in the region of 100 cars a year, the combined outputs of Innocenti and Maserati made the De Tomaso combine Italy's fifth biggest car producer in the early 1980s. In early 1985, De Tomaso's chairman, Aurelio Bertocchi, was killed in a car accident as a passenger in an Innocenti.

In 1985 the De Tomaso range comprised four versions of the Pantera, three of the Longchamp and the Deauville. Production was due to start in 1987 of a Pantera replacement, to be built by De Tomaso in collaboration with Chrysler and possibly using the superb Lotus V8 'Etna' engine – although probably using the Maserati name! BL

DETROIT ELECTRIC
USA 1907-1938

The Anderson Carriage Manufacturing Co had turned out as many as 15,000 horse-drawn vehicles a year until hit by the growing popularity of the motor car. The model name for the quality end of its range of wagons, surreys, buggies and carriages was High School.

In 1907 its factory in Detroit was reorganized to make Detroit Electric vehicles, which had a very simple control that made them especially popular with lady drivers. Indeed, they became the smart thing in which to be seen in town. Production in 1909 was 650, which rose to almost 1500 a year later. Models with artificial radiators looking like petrol cars were made from 1909 and in 1911 there was even a sporty-looking Model P roadster with underslung frame.

Soon after launching the Detroit, Anderson Carriages acquired the American branch of Elwell-Parker. This was the British electrical equipment company that supplied motors to makers of electric cars.

The Anderson factory was said to be the largest in the world producing electric carriages. For most models there was a choice of chain or shaft drive. Henry Ford had a Detroit Electric as did Charles Edison, whose nickel-steel batteries were available at extra cost. In 1911 when the firm became Anderson Electric Car Co with backing from the prominent Book family of Detroit, an advertisement stated that 14 makers of petrol-engined cars also owned Detroits. In Scotland, Arrol-Johnston made a batch of modified Detroits in 1913 to keep its Paisley factory occupied while the company moved to Heathhall, Dumfries.

Sales dwindled after World War I. In 1919 the company became known as the Detroit Electric Car Co and milk and bakery floats were offered, with some success. In 1922 a delivery vehicle was altered so as to have driving positions at the front, the rear and on either running board. Three years later this vehicle was put on the market with a petrol engine as the successful Divco.

Commercial Detroits ceased production in 1927 but cars continued to be built to special order. Town carriage styling similar to the 1910 pattern was still being offered in 1930, but thereafter stock Willys-Overland sheet metal was used and ownership of the company passed to Jamieson Handy. Very few cars were made after 1935, and four years later the firm turned down a Spanish order for several hundred electric vehicles because of lack of capacity. NB

DETROITER/BRIGGS
DETROITER
USA 1912-1917

The Detroiter was a popular light car sold from 1912 to 1917 by the Briggs-Detroiter Motor Car Co and its successors of Detroit. Claude Strait Briggs, born in 1872, moved to Detroit in about 1891 and founded the Briggs Dental Co in 1902 before forming the Krit Motor Car Co with four others in 1909. A year later he sold his interest in Krit to become manager of the Brush Runabout Co before setting up the Briggs-Detroiter Motor Car Co in September 1911 with several prominent Detroit businessmen.

In November the company commissioned William S. Lee to design a four-cylinder, 25hp touring car and another four-cylinder car to be sold as the Detroiter. Lee was paid $150,000 – exactly the taken-up share value of the company's nominal $200,000 capital, of which Briggs owned $40,000.

The car had been announced in October 1911, as a five-seater or a two-seater, and eventually went on sale in April 1912 after delays with engine problems. The first cars sold for $850 and $700, a little more than originally intended, but they sold well. Briggs planned to build some 500 cars in 1912 and

De Tomaso Pantera of 1980

Detroit Electric brougham of c.1909

soon announced that the majority were already ordered. In September the company announced that it was moving to a much larger factory, which it bought for $50,000, and raising its production target to 5000. About 1100 cars were actually built in the first year.

In 1913 Detroiter advertising claimed a network of more than 400 dealers, and 2750 cars were built in this the company's best year. Some cars were sold in Britain as Royal Detroiters and in 1914, when exports were reckoned at 20 per cent, Detroiters were even sold to Russia. The 1914 range included the $900 Kangaroo speedster, for which a run of only 150 was planned. In December 1914 the company announced a V8-engined five-seater for 1915, to sell at $1295.

There were financial problems, however, and production stopped in June 1915, when just over 6000 Detroiters had been built in all. Bankruptcy proceedings showed the company had little more than $110 in cash of its $750,000 assets, against liabilities that were in excess of $550,000.

The company was rescued, briefly, by Alfred Owen Dunk, who had already bought several struggling motor companies. Dunk bought the fixed assets and set up the Detroiter Motor Car Co in July. Detroiters were built in the original works until this was sold in January 1916 to the Denby Truck Co. The 1916 models were announced, with new backing, in August 1915 and four-, six- and eight-cylinder cars were made until the company was reorganized again in November 1916 as the United Detroiter Corporation, with Dunk as president.

In March 1917 a final reorganization was announced, with the former companies

being taken over by the Detroiter Motors Co of Delaware, a new company with $4 million nominal capital. This company planned to increase output to 5000 cars a year and tried to sell stock, but it still had insuperable cash problems and was declared bankrupt in December 1917. BL

DEUTZ
GERMANY 1909-1911

In 1862, in the workshop of Michael Zons in Cologne, a 30-year-old commercial traveller named Nikolaus August Otto made the first engine to work on the four-stroke principle. With the financial backing of Eugen Langen, who had made a fortune from a new type of boiler grate, N. A. Otto and Co was formed in March 1864 at Deutz near Cologne. In 1868 it was building gas engines at the rate of one a week, and four a week two years later. In 1869 Crossley acquired the British rights to the engine.

In 1872 the Otto firm became known as Gasmotoren-Fabrik Deutz AG, where Gottlieb Daimler was technical director and his friend Wilhelm Maybach chief designer for a time. It employed 240 men in 1875 and made 634 motors. In 1876, when Panhard et Levassor built some under licence in Paris, a way of running Deutz engines on benzin (petrol) was perfected, allowing them to be independent of town gas. In the years 1876 to 1895 8321 of the new type were produced.

Daimler and Maybach left the company in 1882 to develop their ideas for petrol engines and powered vehicles. Otto, by contrast, remained committed to the gas engine and its

stationary applications right up to his death in 1891.

Deutz did not enter the vehicle business for several years, although an American licensee made a tractor under the Deutz name in 1894. In 1907, however, Deutz built a motor plough and employed the independent consulting engineer Ettore Bugatti to design an advanced monobloc four-cylinder car, which entered production in 1909. Deutz changed its policy in 1911 and discontinued cars. Meanwhile Bugatti took away one of the cars that he had been working on as the basis for his Type 13 Bugatti.

Heavy tractors were made by Deutz in World War I, followed by lighter farm and industrial machines from 1929. The use of diesels dated from 1926.

In 1930 Humboldt and the engine firm of Oberussel merged with Deutz. They were joined by the Magirus commercial vehicle and fire engine firm in 1938. Air-cooled diesels were developed in 1942 and were used in Magirus-Deutz commercial vehicles, Deutz tractors and as proprietary power units after the war. NB

DE VAUX/CONTINENTAL, DE-VO
USA 1931-1932; 1932-1934; 1936-1937

Norman de Vaux earned a formidable reputation as a salesman. He sold Buicks from 1903 and then Auburn and Reo cars. In 1914 he took on the north Californian Chevrolet territory and pushed sales to first or second place in most west coast states. He was half-owner of the Chevrolet assembly plant opened in 1921 in Oakland but soon sold his interest to General Motors for $4 million.

He then took Star sales to third place in California, its best performance anywhere. In 1925 the Star and Durant sales operations in California were merged, with de Vaux at the helm. When it became obvious that W. C. Durant's luck had run out, de Vaux decided to produce his own car in a new factory in Oakland and sell it through his sales network.

The De Vaux-Hall Motor Corporation was a private company incorporated in December 1930, the Hall referring to Colonel Elbert J. Hall, vice-president of proprietary engine maker Hall-Scott Motor Corporation and designer of the Liberty aero engine. Hall designed a sound six-cylinder engine for the De Vaux, although Continental Red Seal engines were also used along with Warner transmissions.

To cater for the north and east coast a factory was opened near the Continental plant and adjacent to the Hayes Body Corporation at Grand Rapids, Michigan. It had a potential output of 200 a day, but daily production in April 1931 was just 65 – and about a dozen fewer at the Oakland plant.

The stylist at Hayes, Count Alexis de Sakhnoffsky revised redundant Durant bodies for De Vaux, and for 1932 a New Process gearbox with freewheel was adopted. Sales in 1931 totalled about 4600 but in mid-February 1932 De Vaux went into receivership with assets of $2 million, balanced by liabilities of a similar amount. Norman de Vaux was reputed to have personally lost $17 million.

Continental Motors, a substantial creditor, bought the Grand Rapids factory for a modest sum and formed the Continental Automobile Co, with W. R. Angell as president of both firms. They made the Continental car and chose model names such as Ace, Beacon and Flyer. Total sales reached 6500, including versions sold in Canada by Frontenac. This firm had been the last outpost of the Durant empire until separating as Dominion Motors Ltd of Leaside, Ontario, in 1931. It had then bolstered its range with De Vaux designs and had adopted Continentals before going out of business in 1933.

Continental was making no money from car manufacture and in 1934 it decided to abandon the venture. Norman de Vaux, meanwhile, had conceived the idea of a cheap and basic car suitable for export markets. The De-Vo Motor Car Corporation was therefore formed in Hagerstown, Maryland, in 1936 by de Vaux, F. F. Belle, a former vice-president of Packard, and G. R. Scott.

A four-cylinder Continental Red Seal engine was used and bodywork had a suspiciously Reo air about it, the Reo's makers having recently decided to concentrate on trucks. When De-Vo production commenced in January 1937 it was announced that the first few months' output had already been sold. That was about the last to be heard of the project. Assembly was almost certainly entrusted to M. P. Möller of Hagerstown, an organ builder of Danish extraction who had made batches of cars under numerous names, including his own.

Norman de Vaux's subsequent career is uncertain, but he was reported to have mining interests in Arizona in the 1950s. Continental later merged with Ryan Aeronautical and both are now a part of Teledyne, making aero engines and complete aircraft. NB

DE VECCHI
ITALY 1905-1917

This Milanese car-maker started production of a 10/12hp pair-cast four-cylinder chain-drive car in 1905. The partners were de Vecchi and Stradea, with technical help being provided by former racing bicyclist F. Momo. In 1908 the firm was liquidated and re-formed, without Stradea, as De Vecchi & Cia. A 16/20hp car with shaft drive was introduced and a larger 20/30 started life in 1909 with chains. Monobloc engines came on most models from 1911, when all cars had shaft drive.

From 1913 only 25hp four-cylinder chassis were made and between 1914 and 1917 most of these were fitted with lorry or ambulance

DFP 2-litre 12/15 sports of 1913

bodywork. From 1917 aero engines only were made, and the firm was re-formed as Officine Meccaniche de Vecchi. At the end of the war there was a fall in demand for aero engines, the company got into financial difficulties and was taken over by the CMN group in 1920, although cars were not revived. NB

DEVIN
USA, NORTHERN IRELAND 1958-1964

Former racing driver Bill Devin of El Monte, California, was a pioneer of bolt-on glassfibre body kits for production chassis, and he later branched out into producing complete Devin cars. Through his reputation for supplying high quality kits in the early 1950s, Devin was approached in 1957 by an Irish special-builder looking for a body for his car. Devin was impressed by the concept of the car and, after long negotiations, agreement was reached for Devin chassis to be built in Belfast by Devonshire Engineering and shipped to California to be bodied and trimmed.

The car used a substantial tubular frame, the 283cu in, 290bhp Chevrolet Corvette engine and De Dion rear suspension. It was well reviewed by the American specialist press, which was impressed by its 130mph (209kph) performance, 0-60mph (0-96kph) acceleration in under five seconds and 0-100mph (0-160kph) in only 12 seconds.

The handsome, fully-equipped Devin SS was offered at a very competitive $5950 but surprisingly few were sold, probably only 15 in all. The original plan had been to build 150 cars to gain approval for Sports Car Club of

America racing, when the Devin might have showed its mettle against Corvettes, Ferraris and others. The cars were offered for competition in various stages of completion and with engine options to order.

In 1962 Devin designed a Corvair-powered car, the model C, and a GT coupé, but very few were made. Devin reverted to offering bolt-on body kits for VWs and the like, including the Volkswagen chassised Type D, from 1959 to 1964, the final year of production. BL

DE-VO
see De Vaux

DFP
FRANCE 1906-1926

While a foreman at Peugeot in the early 1890s, Auguste Doriot met Ludovic Flandrin. The two worked for a time with Clément Bayard then started in business in 1906 as Doriot et Flandrin, making single-cylinder voiturettes. Two years later they were joined by Alexandre and Jules-René Parant who formed Doriot, Flandrin et Parant with 600,000 francs capital, the two founders receiving nearly 500,000 francs for their factory and the facilities in Courbevoie.

Chapuis-Dornier-engined fours were introduced in 1908 and an 18hp six in 1910. Production ran at about 500 a year, of which perhaps a dozen were sold every year in England until 1912 when Bentley and Bentley Ltd acquired the British Empire concession.

That year DFP began to make its own engines. Although DFPs were regarded primarily as touring cars in France, the Bentley brothers in England pushed the sporting image of the 2-litre 12/15 DFP, tuning it and fitting attractive bodywork. In 1914, when the firm was re-formed with capital of 1.5 million francs, aluminium pistons increased its race-winning potential. The original French aluminium pistons were replaced by a new design by Ward which was to achieve fame under the name of Aerolite.

The post-war chassis were dated in appearance and less well made. W. O. Bentley was by now more concerned with the car soon to bear his own name and in Britain Bentley and Bentley sold their concession, and went into liquidation. Although Tim Birkin attempted to uphold the prowess of DFP on the race-track, the cars were uncompetitive. Proprietary Altos and Sergant engines were used, but the 1923 14/50 had DFP's own pushrod unit as did the 1100cc DF Petite sports car, the engine of which was also sold to GN. Production came to an end in 1926, when the factory was acquired by Lafitte, the maker of a short-lived three-cylinder friction-drive light car. NB

DIATTO/FRÉJUS, NB, TORINO
ITALY 1905-1927

The Diatto brothers were carriage-makers in Turin before 1834, in which year they produced 15 horsedrawn vehicles and added an iron foundry. They later produced trams and from 1874 also built trains. They supplied funiculars to Switzerland and complete trains to Egypt, Italy and other countries. In 1906 they collaborated with Fiat in supplying petrol trams to the Milan Fair, and finally sold the railway side of their business to Fiat in 1918.

From 1905 Vittorio and Pietro Diatto made Clément-Bayard cars under licence and per-suaded Adolphe Clément to become president of their subsidiary company, Diatto, A Clément Vetture Marca Torino, with 1.5 million lire capital. Their cars were initially called Torino. The death of Clément's son in 1907 led him to withdraw and connections were severed two years later, when the first Diatto design, a monobloc 16/20, appeared.

The factory covered 269,000sq ft (25,000sq m) and employed 500 men who produced about 250 cars a year. In 1910-11 blocks of 300 chassis numbers were issued each year but probably not matched in production. In 1912 a one model policy was adopted with the 2.2-litre Tipo Unico. Three years later Diatto acquired Scacchi, which had made cars since 1911, mostly for sale under the Storero name, and Newton which had made about 1000 English-designed cars since 1913 for sale in Britain under the name NB. The machinery from both companies was moved to Diatto, which had its own Fréjus foundry and body works as well as a private test-track.

In 1916 the Italian branch of Gnome et Rhône was also acquired, and in addition to aero engines of this company's type Diatto made Bugatti eight-cylinder designs under licence and a variety of airframes. Trucks including chain-drive 3½ tonners were produced for the Italian Army, and other products included generators, pumps and compressors.

In 1919 both the Brescia Bugatti and Gnome et Rhône 10CV economy cars were in production at Diatto but losses increased, and the position was not helped by slow government payment for 6 million lire worth of war materials. The firm was reorganized twice soon after World War I and combined capital stood at 10 million lire in 1921, by which time the Diatto family had sold out to the Gussi brothers, who owned the Pomilio aircraft factory.

In 1922 a 2-litre overhead-cam car, designed by Giuseppe Coda, was adopted and this had the unusual features of gasketless cylinder-head joint and a wooden fan driven direct from the front of the camshaft. This car was improved by Diatto's development engineer, Alfieri Maserati, to produce 70 instead of 40bhp and was the basis for Diatto racing types. In 1926 when Diatto abandoned racing he departed with the double overhead-cam supercharged straight-eights he had produced for the company and these soon bore the famous Maserati name.

In November 1923 Diatto had gone into liquidation upon the collapse of its bank but had been re-formed in 1924 as SA Autocostruzione Diatto with 3.5 million lire capital. Directors were members of the Musso family and engineers Panetti, Prandi and Cornetti. Giuseppe Coda left to run Citroën's Italian factory.

In 1926 the Musso textile interests hit difficulties and Diatto suffered, its capital being reduced to 1.29 million lire in 1927, when car production was discontinued. Carlino Sasso rescued the firm in 1931 and continued to make spares for the former cars. Plans, discussed in 1945, for a return to production with a prototype for the Galileo Co came to nothing. Diatto ceased trading in 1955 and its factory was acquired by Beglio SpA. NB

DINOS
GERMANY 1921-1926

Loeb & Cie Automobilfabrik GmbH of Berlin-Charlottenburg began to build cars in 1909, as Lucs, after acting as agent for several other well-known marques. From 1911 the company imported British Daimler chassis fitted with Knight engines and German coachwork and sold them as Luc-Knights. During World War I the Loeb factory was given over to truck manufacture and soon after the war, in 1920, the works were taken over by Dinos, as Dinos Automobilwerke AG, and began to manufacture Dinos cars in 1921.

Dinos built four-cylinder 8/35PS and six-cylinder 16/72PS overhead-cam models, the latter only in very small numbers. After 1922 Dinos belonged to the Stinnes corporation, which also included the AGA and Rabag makes.

In 1924 a 15 per cent luxury tax was imposed on German cars, but import duties were cut, which resulted in imports doubling between 1925 and 1927. Most of the imports, over 80 per cent, came from the United States. Big, cheap American cars effectively killed many smaller German makers of small cars – or at best forced them into mergers.

Dinos was one of the victims, production being stopped in 1926 to allow additional AGA production in the Dinos works. AGA too was closed down late in 1926, although production rights were sold and cars were built in the original works until 1928, by which time Germany had a mere 23 car-makers, compared to more than 80 just two years before. BL

Diatto-Clément racer of 1907

Diva GT of 1966

DIVA
GB 1962-1968

The earliest Diva was a small, attractive, GT coupé designed by A. J. D. Sim and built from 1962 by Tunex Conversions Ltd of south-east London. Sim had previously built the Yimkin two-seater and Formula Junior racing cars, the first in 1959, and the first Diva was based largely on the 1172cc, Ford 10-engined Yimkin two-seater.

The Diva GT had a multi-tubular space frame, all-round independent suspension by spring/damper units and used the engine as a stressed component. Both aluminium and glassfibre bodies were fitted. Engine options included the BMC A-series or Fords of up to 1500cc, but the popular and highly tunable Ford 105E was the common choice, especially for racing. Diva achieved many competition successes, scoring over 50 wins in 1964; drivers included later Grand Prix drivers John Miles and Jackie Oliver.

In 1966 the company became Diva Cars Ltd. The following year the mid-engined Valkyr was introduced; it was designed to comply with the international Appendix J racing regulations and to accept a variety of engines including Lotus and Coventry-Climax units. The Climax-designed, all-alloy Imp engine was used in a few of the coupés. At the other end of the scale a 2.7-litre, 265bhp, Climax-engined racing version could reach 180mph (290kph).

Late in 1967, production rights were sold to Skodek Engineering Ltd of south-west London. This company continued to build Divas only until 1968. BL

DIXI
see Eisenach

DIXIE/DIXIE FLYER
USA 1915-1923

The Kentucky Wagon Manufacturing Co, founded in 1878, began to make electric trucks in 1911 under the name Urban at its plant at Louisville, Kentucky. It was involved with the shortlived Hercules Motor Car Co of New Albany and the Dixie Manufacturing Co of Vincennes, both in Indiana, and acquired the former's tooling when production ceased in 1915.

Dixie had introduced an assembled car in 1915 and this became the competitively-priced, Lycoming-engined Dixie Flyer when production transferred to Louisville. Despite its name it had a cruising speed of just 40mph (64kph). Another product was the Old Hickory Lycoming-powered truck from 1915, which received a Continental engine in 1919. The cars were revised in 1919, when there was an improvement in specification, Herschell-Spillman engines were used and prices increased.

Chassis numbers of the time suggest that 400 Dixie Flyers were made in 1916, 1300 in 1917, 1500 in 1918, 2000 in both 1919 and 1920, 1300 in 1921 and 1700 in 1922. Production ceased in 1923 when the car was taken over by National Motor Car and Vehicle Corporation of Indianapolis. It lived on until 1924 as the National 6-31, but then the company collapsed. Kentucky Wagon Manufacturing lasted until 1931 when it closed its doors, a victim of the Depression. NB

DKW
GERMANY 1928-1966

In 1907 J. S. Rasmussen, a Dane, started a workshop in Zschopau (now Karl-Marx-Stadt in East Germany) to make boiler and heater fittings. Another Dane, Mathiessen, joined him and they experimented with steam cars which they called Dampf-Kraft-Wagen (hence DKW) in 1916-19. However, their principal business during the period was making detonators.

Hugo Rappe had meanwhile designed and made engines that were bought by Slaby-Beringer of Berlin for use in its light cars from 1923. Slaby-Beringer was bought by Rasmussen a year later and subsequently made DEW electric cars and taxis until 1927 to designs by Rudolf Slaby.

In 1922 Rasmussen had formed Metallwerke Frankenberg (later to become Framo) to make components for DKW's growing range of motorcycles, which were commonly known as *Das Kleine Wunder* (The Little Wonder). DKW engines were also supplied to numerous other motorcycle manufacturers. By 1927 DKW was the world's largest manufacturer of motorcycles, 40,000 being produced in 1928 alone.

Rasmussen's motor company was known as Zschopauer Motoren-Werke J. S. Rasmussen AG from 1923 and produced its first DKW cars in 1928 in the former D-Wagen works. Rasmussen also acquired the Moll light car factory in Chemnitz, another user of DKW engines, which continued until 1925. The DKW had a two-stroke two-cylinder engine and wooden chassis-less construction by Rudolf Slaby.

The company was also making pumps, refrigerators, safes, generators, boat engines and components for other motor firms, including Audi, in which Rasmussen had become principal shareholder in 1928. He also acquired manufacturing rights to Rickenbacker engines and purchased the machine tool and motorcycle-maker Schuttoff in Chemnitz that year as part of an industrial empire that on 29 June 1932, with Wanderer and Horch, became Auto Union.

The Bank of Saxony was the largest shareholder in the group, which employed 20,000 men. Dr Richard Bruhn headed the company, Rasmussen was technical director and Carl Hahn was in charge of sales.

DKW's first front-wheel-drive F1 and F2, from Audi's design department, appeared in 1931 and their transmission was soon used by several other firms, including Audi and Tornax. Larger V4 DKWs were made in Berlin-Spandau (the D-Wagen factory) and smaller ones at Zwickau (Audi). Zschopau concentrated on engines and motorcycles. Some rear-wheel-drive cars and commercials were also built, including the F8 for export in 1939 and earlier Sonderklasse and Schwebeklasse. Rasmussen retired in 1934 at a time when DKW held about 15 per cent of the German car market, second only to Opel.

DKWs were made in Switzerland from 1934 to 1939 as Holka-DKWs and immediately after the war in Sweden as Philipsson-DKWs; they were produced later in Brazil by Vemag. The Spanish Eucort car was also DKW-based.

In 1948 some DKWs appeared in East Germany from the former Audi factory and two years later were joined by versions based on a pre-war three-cylinder F9 prototype. These cars were known as IFAs, and production ended in 1956.

Auto Union was reconstituted in Düsseldorf, West Germany, in 1949. Versions of the two-cylinder Meisterklasse were followed by the F9. Production later moved to Ingolstadt. Two-stroke cars continued to be made until the end of DKW production in 1966.

The motorcycle factory in East Germany also took the name IFA after nationalization and then MZ (Motorradwerke Zschopau) in 1946. Production of DKW motorcycles was resumed in the Western zone at Ingolstadt in

DKW two-stroke cabriolet of c.1928

DKW front-drive cabriolet of 1937

1949 but the company was acquired by Zweirad Union in 1957. In 1966 Fichtel and Sachs acquired Zweirad Union. Most of the machines now carry the Hercules name, although DKW continues to be used in some export markets. NB

DOBLE
USA 1914-1931

Born in San Francisco in 1895, Abner Doble grew up with a mechanical background, becoming a part-time apprentice in the family waterwheel factory at the age of eight. He built his first steam car at the age of 16 and from then on was totally committed to motor cars.

In 1914 while studying at the Massachusetts Institute of Technology he built another car, and then set up the Abner Doble Motor Vehicle Co of Waltham, Massachusetts, with a capital of $500,000 largely provided by his wealthy father. He built five of his Model A, selling four and retaining the fifth for further experiments. They had two-cylinder double acting engines mounted horizontally on the rear axle.

Seeking further finance to produce his improved Models B and C, he went to Detroit where he formed the General Engineering Co with C. L. Lewis, formerly head of the Consolidated Car Co which had built the Abbott-Detroit. The Doble-Detroit, or GEC Doble, was ready for production by mid-1917, with 11,000 orders placed, but the US government refused to allow the necessary steel for quantity production and only 40 or 50 were built.

Doble's next venture came from Emeryville, California, where he set up a new plant and built his most ambitious car yet. The Model E was intended to rival the world's best internal combustion cars, to be more flexible than a Packard twin six, quieter than a Rolls-Royce, more powerful than an Hispano-Suiza.

It had a 125bhp four-cylinder compound engine mounted on the rear axle, which gave the car a top speed of 95mph (153kph). Most important, it could move off in less than 40 seconds from a cold start, thanks to its electric firing and flash boiler, whereas a Stanley required 30 minutes. Eight body styles were offered, all made by Walter Murphy of Pasadena. Prices ranged from $8800 to $11,200, making the Doble Model E one of the most expensive cars in America.

The Model E was announced at the 1923 San Francisco Auto Show, with production plans for 300 cars a year to start with. Unfortunately Abner Doble was soon a victim of unscrupulous stock manipulations, which left him facing enormous claims. To meet these the factory had to be mortgaged and land earmarked for expansion had to be sold. Those customers who had not taken action against the company received their cars, but only 45 of the Model E and its improved successor the Model F were built between 1924 and 1931. A proposed cheaper car, the Doble-Simplex, was never built.

In April 1931 Doble Steam Motors went into liquidation; the factory was taken over by the Besler brothers, sons of the chairman of the New Jersey Central Railroad. They made a number of experiments including a steam powered aeroplane. Meanwhile, Abner Doble travelled to Europe where he worked with Sentinel in England and Henschel in Germany, developing advanced steam trucks and railcars. After World War II he was a consultant on two abortive steam car projects, the 1950 Paxton Phoenix and the 1956 Keen. He died in July 1961. GNG

DODGE
USA 1914 to date

John and Horace Dodge were born in 1864 and 1868 respectively in Niles, Michigan. They trained as machinists and later developed a ballbearing bicycle. They were shareholders in the Evans and Dodge Bicycle Co and in 1900 with the National Cycle and Automobile Co. After being bought out by Canadian interests they opened a machine shop, with nine employees, in Detroit and made transmissions for Olds in 1901-2.

In 1903 they obtained a contract to make engines for Henry Ford, which cost them more than $60,000 in tooling. They received 10 per cent of Ford stock in lieu of profit on the first 650 engines and other parts they produced; when this interest was sold back to Ford in 1920 it realized $20 million. Components were also made for many other firms and in 1910 a 24-acre (10-hectare) factory was bought at Hamtramck, Detroit.

Ford's strategy was to build his cars from Dodge components and then cut the price to shift them fast. At one point he refused to take more Dodge components unless the price was reduced, and threatened to make his

Dodge 3½-litre tourer of 1914

own parts. In case this should happen, Dodge began to develop its own car in 1911. When a number of Ford contracts were not renewed, the car was put into production in November 1914. As Dodge Brothers Corporation already possessed the tools and equipment, the car cost just $5 million to make ready – little more than the dividend earned in the previous three years on the brothers' Ford stock.

The first cars were 3½-litre monobloc side-valve fours that were tough and basic and served as staff cars and ambulances in World War I, when guns were also produced. From 1916 Budd all-steel tourer bodywork was used but some steel sedans were also made and these had wooden roof framing. From 1917 to 1919 a total of 1800 centre door sedans, nicknamed Pumpkins, were produced. In 1923 Dodge adopted sedans wholeheartedly.

Dodge was third behind Ford and Willys-Overland in 1915 with 45,000 cars produced. In 1920, however, its annual sales of 141,000 were second only to Ford's 419,500.

Both Dodge brothers died in 1920, John of influenza and Horace of pneumonia. Half a million Dodge cars had been sold in their lifetime; their company now employed 17,000 men and their factory had grown to 120 acres (48 hectares). They left estates with a combined value of $106 million.

Fred J. Haynes took over as president of the company in 1920. He persuaded the three Graham brothers who had been making trucks since 1919 at Evansville, Indiana, to build them in future in Detroit from Dodge components. This arrangement worked well and as many as 60,000 Graham Brothers vehicles were being made annually. In 1927 Dodge bought outright the Graham truck business.

Two years before, the Dodge family sold the Dodge Brothers company to investment bankers Dillon, Read & Co for $146 million. Output was climbing steadily – from 142,000 units in 1922 to 265,000 in 1926 – and in 1928 the bank sold the firm to Walter P. Chrysler for $170 million. Haynes was replaced as president by K. T. Keller.

In 1927 a 3.7-litre six with four-wheel hyd-

raulic brakes became available in the Dodge Brothers Senior Line. An assembly operation for trucks began in Britain that year, and from 1933 the Kew-Dodges and Kew-Fargos – made in Kew, Surrey, in a plant also assembling Chrysler cars – had a largely British content. There were Canadian and Australian Dodge factories also making Fargos.

Dodge car sales slipped to 67,000 and 13th position in 1928, largely as a result of competition from the companion Chrysler marques of De Soto and Plymouth. Although Dodge rallied to 124,500 and seventh position in 1929 the company had a lean time throughout the Depression.

A straight-eight-engined model was available for three years from 1930, and from 1931, when the Ram mascot arrived, there was general parts interchangeability with the Chrysler range. The three millionth Dodge was made in 1935 and the following year sales beat all previous records at 275,000.

Some of Chrysler's excesses like the Airflow had been avoided by Dodge, but for 1937 there was a strong family resemblance which, by the 1940s, made them hard to distinguish from De Sotos or the more expensive Plymouths. In 1940 Dodge sold 225,600 cars and only slightly fewer in 1941 before switching to war production.

Commercial vehicle sales had run at over

Dodge coupé of 1946

Dodge Charger of 1977

50,000 a year during the late 1930s and increasingly heavy models had been added in both America and Britain. The US truck operation was based at Warren, Detroit, from 1938, where a wide assortment of military vehicles was soon in production along with gyro compasses, tank transmissions and ammunition; the complete 450-acre (182-hectare) plant went on to build B-29 Super Fortresses. The well-known Dodge 4×4 'Beep' continued after the war as the Power Wagon, which changed little in 20 years.

The cars received the Red Ram overhead-valve V8 in 1953, just as more eights than sixes were being sold in America for the first time. The side-valve six finally disappeared from Dodge cars in 1959, although it was still to be seen in light trucks five years later.

In 1966, the first year of the Charger fastback coupé, Hamtramck had grown to 5.1 million sq ft (474,000sq m) of assembly area and a new truck factory was opened at Kenton, Missouri. Overseas factories had been started in Argentina in 1962 and in Brazil in 1969. Both of these were ultimately bought by Volkswagen after building an assortment of American and British (Hillman) designs.

The 1960 Dart took Dodge into a lower priced field. The 1961 Lancer was sister car to the Plymouth Valiant and in 1967 Chrysler's unitary construction was used for many Dodge models. A new trend in sports pickups was catered for in 1968 and from 1970 Mitsubishis were sold as Dodge Colts in the subcompact range, to be joined by former Simcas called Omnis in 1978.

The growing financial problems at Chrysler caused it to shed many subsidiaries in the late 1970s. One of these was British Dodge, which had joined with Commer at Dunstable in 1967 and become the sole marketing name from 1976. It and the Spanish Dodge (Barreiros) plant were sold to PSA Peugeot-Citroën in 1978. Renault bought a half share in the two European Dodge firms in 1981 and took over management control. The Spanish factory became Hispano Francesca de Vehicules Industriales SA in 1982, and a year later its products were badged as Renaults. In Britain, Renault trucks were assembled alongside Dodges from 1984.

Dodge car sales had averaged about 500,000 a year during the 1960s for seventh place in the market and Dodge remained in a similar position in the 1970s, reaching total sales of almost 1 million in 1973 with the inclusion of commercial vehicles. Dodge trucks had latterly included a wide range of light-to-heavy models, but production of heavy trucks was discontinued in 1975. Concentration on vans and pickups swelled commercial vehicle production to 470,000 two years later.

Early 1980s cars were similar to those of Plymouth, including the transverse-engined front-wheel-drive Aries and the 600 of 1983 with transverse four-cylinder overhead-cam 2.2- or 2.6-litre engines. Larger and more conventional V8s were also being offered. NB

DOLPHIN
GB 1908-1909

The Dolphin car was built between 1908 and 1909 by The Two-Stroke Engine Co Ltd, of Shoreham, Sussex, a company set up by Ralph Ricardo, a cousin of Harry (later Sir Harry) Ricardo. Sir Harry, the son of a London architect but with a family background in civil engineering, was one of the great creative talents in internal combustion engine design.

Ralph, formerly manager of the Glasgow salesrooms of the Arrol-Johnston company, took Harry's design for a 28-30hp four-cylinder two-stroke engine and persuaded associates Harry Hetherington and Michael Thornycroft Sassoon to put it into a car for commercial production. Harry Ricardo designed the engine while at Cambridge studying for a degree in mechanical engineering, and after he had become involved in the design of a light petrol engine for aircraft use.

Ricardo bought an old shipyard at Shoreham early in 1907 and the Two-Stroke Engine Co was registered the following year. Engines and gearboxes were initially built by Lloyd & Plaister of London, with chassis from Thornycroft, thanks to the family ties with Michael Sassoon, brother of the poet, Siegfried. The Dolphin was exhibited at the Olympia Shows in 1908 and 1909, but although it was a good car and reasonably priced at around £500, very few were sold, probably no more than a dozen.

Although all the principals came from fairly wealthy backgrounds, the company always lacked capital and bought-in components were an expensive burden. The company was out of business by early 1910. Harry Ricardo later sold manufacturing rights to a 750cc, two-cylinder version of his two-stroke engine to Lloyd & Plaister. It was used by this company in its own Vox car until about 1915. BL

DONNET-ZÉDEL/DONNET, ZÉDEL, ZL
FRANCE 1906-1933

Ernest Zürcher made the first motorcycle engines in Switzerland in 1896 at Neuchâtel. He was joined in 1899 by Hermann Lüthi and they opened works at St Aubin under the name Zürcher, Lüthi et Cie. The company supplied engines to several firms, including Alcyon and Minerva. In 1901 the name was changed to Société Zédel.

In 1902 a factory was opened at Pontarlier, just over the border, to cater for the French market and it was there that a four-cylinder monobloc 1128cc car was introduced in 1906. Models of up to 3563cc were added. Some of the smaller models were also made in Switzerland until 1908.

Ernest Zürcher left the company in 1907, when control of ZL – as its cars were known in

Britain – passed to Swiss citizen Samuel Graf. Martini's technical director in 1910, Fochier, had previously been with Zédel.

Production was 98 in 1907 but rose to between 200 and 300 in the next two years and 150 annually thereafter until 1912, when 452 cars were made. During World War I a total of 151 were produced.

The post-war cars consisted of side-valve 10 and 15hp fours. In 1923, when 1555 cars were made, the firm was bought by Jerome Donnet who had helped create Donnet-Leveque, which had made large numbers of aircraft to Denhaut designs in the war.

Donnet-Zédel Type G of 1924

Zédels became Donnet-Zédels and in 1924 production amounted to 3800. Ernest Henry was hired to design a side-valve 7.5hp G4 that year, which was made in the Donnet aircraft factory at Gennevilliers and achieved sales of 6000 until the end of 1926. Henry was also responsible for a number of sports versions; Etienne Lépicard made others with sixteen-valve engines.

Vinot et Deguingand of Nanterre was taken over by Donnet in 1926, when a six-cylinder 2½-litre car was designed by Saintaurat for the 1927 season. There were also 1.3 and 1.8 sixes, a licence for the latter being sold to Cyklon. Engines by Continental were used. To gain the benefits of bulk component buying, Donnet, Chenard-Walcker and Unic formed a loose consortium in 1927. Donnet production at the Zédel factory at Pontarlier ceased at the end of 1928.

The slump reduced sales markedly. A Violet-designed two-stroke car sold perhaps 100 in the early 1930s. By 1933 the firm was effectively insolvent but managed to produce some attractive Citroën-like saloons with such names as Donnette, Donnarex, Donnastar, Donnaquatre, Donnasuper and Donnamagna. At the end of 1934 the works closed and Henri T. Pigozzi acquired it for Simca. Donnet spares were bought by Contin-Souza, which sold a few complete cars for about two years. In all, about 100,000 Donnets and Donnet-Zédels were produced. NB

Dorris Six of 1923

DORRIS
USA 1905-1926

George Presson Dorris was born in Nashville, Tennessee, and built his first experimental car there in 1897. Two years later he moved to St Louis, Missouri, and began making one- and two-cylinder cars under the name St Louis. He advertised them as 'Rigs that Run', and this phrase has been listed as the make of car. A four-cylinder model came in 1904 and the following year he adopted his own name for the cars, the Dorris Motor Car Co being formed in 1906. Financial backing came from St Louis businessman H. B. Krenning, and was originally $50,000 but was later increased to $1 million.

Trucks were added to the range in 1911 and became an important part of the Dorris output. Like the cars, Dorris trucks used the company's own overhead-valve engine and transmission although in the 1920s they changed to Muncie gearboxes and Timken axles. The cars were in the upper-middle price bracket and sold steadily from 1910 to 1920, at between 180 and 274 a year, reaching a peak in 1921 when about 1000 cars and trucks were made. A six-cylinder engine was introduced in 1916. Prices were now as high as $6800 for a sedan.

In 1920 Astra Motors Corporation was formed to make a small touring car powered by a four-cylinder Le Roi engine and to merge with the Dorris Motor Co to create the Dorris Motors Corporation. Planned production was 2000 Astras a year, while Associated Motors Corporation of New York was to make a further 3000 for export. In fact only one prototype was made, and the reorganization into Dorris Motors Corporation never took place.

Dorris lost money every year from 1917 to 1922, by which year sales had fallen to less than 400, and in 1923 Krenning decided he

had had enough. The company was liquidated in December 1923 but was revived for the manufacture of trucks the following year. Unsold Dorris cars could still be bought as late as 1926, and trucks and buses were made in small numbers until 1928. The company is still in business under the name Dorris Speed Reduction Co making gear reduction units for grain elevators and is still run by the Dorris family. George P. Dorris himself died in 1968 at the age of 94. GNG

DORT/GRAY-DORT
USA, CANADA 1915-1925

Joshua Dallas Dort was a very successful carriage and wagon maker at Flint, Michigan, from the 1890s, being for a while a partner of Billy Durant, who later founded General Motors. For a time, Thomas Jeffery, maker of the Rambler car, worked for the Durant-Dort

Carriage Co. In 1915 Dort decided to enter the car business with a modestly-priced touring car with a four-cylinder Lycoming engine.

The Dort Motor Co had only been in production for a few months when it was approached by another carriage builder from north of the border, William Gray Sons, Campbell Ltd of Chatham, Ontario. This company had supplied wheels and bodies for Canadian-built Fords. Gray-Dort Motors Ltd was formed in October 1915, Grays putting up all the $300,000 capital and Dort receiving a quarter of the shares and a royalty on each Gray-Dort car built.

For 1917 a roadster and a sedan were added to the Dort range, with US prices running from $695 to $1065. Generally, Gray-Dorts paralleled the Flint-built models, but in 1918 some De Luxe models with additional equipment were sold for $150 more than the standard cars. About 300 of these were exported to the USA. In 1922 Gray-Dort made another special, the Model 19B Special, which included among its features an automatic reversing light, the first in the world to be fitted as part of the standard equipment. This was another Gray-Dort that had no Dort equivalent.

Both makes sold well for a number of years, their best year being 1920 with 23,853 Dorts sold and 5420 Gray-Dorts. Only one size of engine was used until 1922 when a 45hp Falls six was added to the 32hp Lycoming four. A ¾-ton delivery van was made at Flint from 1921 to 1924, but there was no Canadian equivalent.

For 1924 Dallas Dort wanted to make only six-cylinder cars, a decision that alarmed Gray which felt that the four was its bread and butter line, backed by years of good service. The company decided to continue the fours, buying engines direct from Lycoming. Shortly afterwards Dallas Dort announced that he was tired of the car business and was closing down. Although the Canadian content of the Gray-Dort was about 60 per cent, Gray relied on Flint for its engineering expertise and

Dort four coupé of 1922

Douglas of 1919

could not keep going alone. The company tried to find another US car-maker to work with and was on the point of signing agreement with the Gray Motor Corporation of Detroit when that company itself went out of business.

Dort production at Flint ceased abruptly in 1924. Gray was taken over by a bank (to whom the Gray family owed over $1 million), and which liquidated the company in the summer, although some cars continued to be sold until 1925. Joshua Dallas Dort died suddenly a few months after his retirement, but Bill Gray formed a new company to make and distribute components and this continued successfully into the 1940s. Total production of Dorts was about 107,000 and of Gray-Dorts 26,000. GNG

DOUGLAS
GB 1913-1922; 1932

Scots brothers William and Edward Douglas moved to the Kingswood area of Bristol from their native Greenock and in 1882, with borrowed capital of £10, founded the Douglas Engineering Co. The company prospered, its small foundry supplying, among other things, lasts for the shoe industry.

The company, without expressing great enthusiasm, began building motorcycles, having already started making castings for the car and motorcycle industries, by employing the designer of the Fairy motorcycle, Joseph Barter, after his own company, Light Motors Ltd, failed. The first Douglas flat-twin motorcycles were shown at the 1907 Stanley Show.

Production began slowly but in 1910 Douglas began a sudden expansion, employing 200 extra workers in an enlarged factory. In 1913 the company began to consider using its larger 8hp 1070cc air-cooled flat-twin in a cyclecar. William Douglas Sr insisted the car should be properly developed and sell for under £100, which dictated mass production.

Several prototypes, largely designed by William's son, also William, were built and the open two-seater car as finalized was more a fully equipped light car than a cyclecar. It actually sold for £160 and used a pressed chassis, Riley wire wheels and a metal body on an ash frame. A sports model was also listed and the 50mph (80kph) car was soon being used in competition.

Initial sales were good but were interrupted by World War I, during which Douglas made more than 25,000 motorcycles as well as munitions. Production of a revised, heavier version of the car resumed in 1919, in works formerly used by the Williamson motorcycle company. Douglas had mysterious pre-war connections with this company, there being some suggestion that Williamson actually referred to William's son. This car used a new, water-cooled 1224cc 10½hp twin and sold for about £500 in three versions. Few cars were made after the war, when competition was fierce, and production stopped in 1922, the company being happy to concentrate on motorcycles. William Sr died in the following year when the company was faced with tax problems in spite of nominally large profits.

In the late 1920s Douglas diversified into trucks, stationary engines and aero engines, but by the time it considered building another car the company was in decline. In 1931 Douglas was sold to a group of London businessmen and was reorganized as a public company, Douglas Motors (1932) Ltd.

In 1932 Douglas proposed another car, to a strange design by Cyril Pullin. This was a four-wheeler but with the rear wheels set so close together that it should have been taxable as a three-wheeler and saleable for under £100. Most authorities agreed, but the London County Council refused and so the project, including a proposed light commercial version, was abandoned.

Douglas also experimented with a peculiar, powered-wheel, all-terrain vehicle, the Dynasphere, in which the driver sat inside the large single wheel. It was originally intended for an Arctic expedition but was never fully developed.

In 1933 the company was in further financial trouble and a receiver was appointed, whereupon William Douglas bought back the £300,000 or so of unissued stock and formed William Douglas (Bristol) Ltd. After another reorganization in 1935 and a subsequent collapse, the company was bought by the British Aircraft Corporation to manufacture aero engines, although it never did. The company continued to build motorcycles and some electric vehicles after William's death in 1937.

During World War II Douglas manufactured aircraft components and some motorcycles but in October 1948 the receiver was back. Yet another new company, Douglas (Kingswood) Ltd, was set up – only to be taken over in 1956 by Westinghouse Brake & Signal Co, which stopped motorcycle production in March 1957. Thereafter, Douglas assembled Vespa scooters. The last Douglas four-wheel connection was the use of a Douglas flat-twin engine in the short-lived, Bristol-built Iota car in 1951. BL

DOWNSHIRE
see Chambers

DUAL-GHIA
USA, ITALY 1956-1958; 1960-1963

Virgil Exner's styling exercises for Chrysler around 1950 bred the Ghia-built Firearrow mock-up. Sales potential for this 'dream car' was limited and in 1955 Chrysler sold the rights to Gene Casaroll, who owned Automobile Shippers Inc and Dual Motors Corporation of Detroit. Using a Dodge Firebomb V8 engine and Dodge chassis, a prototype was shown in June 1955 and this entered production in 1956 as the Dual-Ghia Firebomb, the standard 220bhp being increased to 260bhp in the Super Firebomb.

Dodge chassis were shipped to Italy to be shortened and fitted with Ghia drop-head bodywork in steel. The power train was installed on completion in Detroit, with the engine set back for improved handling. Although the marque acquired early patronage from film stars, only 104 plus 13 prototypes were built before production ended in 1958.

Another Exner design exercise, the Dart, gave Dual-Ghia a hardtop car, which entered production after a gap of two years in August 1960 with 325bhp Chrysler V8 and air conditioning. It was planned to build one a week, and complete production took place in Italy under the name Ghia 6.4-L. Dual was now simply the component supplier and exclusive American agent, having sold all design and manufacturing rights to Ghia.

Frank Sinatra bought the first, but the project collapsed in 1963 after just 26 had been made. Any hope of reviving the marque using later Chrysler cast-offs was dashed when Gene Casaroll died in the mid-1960s. NB

DUESENBERG
USA 1920-1937

The Duesenberg brothers, Fred and August, had experience in many fields of motor engineering before they built the first passenger car bearing their name. From 1906 to 1913 they were associated with the Mason car from Des Moines, Iowa, for which Fred Duesenberg designed his famous 'walking beam' horizontal overhead-valve engine which was fitted to Mason racing cars. In 1913 the brothers set up a small plant of their own in part of the L. C. Erbes factory in St Paul, Minnesota, later moving to larger premises in the same city.

There they built four-cylinder 'walking beam' engines for racing cars which ran sometimes under the Duesenberg name, and at others under names including Crawford, Braender Bulldog and others, according to who was financing the car. They also built two 800hp in-line twelve-cylinder engines for a racing hydroplane, *Disturber IV*, which led to six- and eight-cylinder marine engines of

Duesenberg design being made in considerable numbers by the Loew-Victor Manufacturing Co of Chicago.

In 1916 they joined J. R. Harbeck, managing director of Loew-Victor, in a new company, Duesenberg Motors Corporation. It is a tribute to the brothers' reputation that the new company was named after them, for they had no financial stake in it. A new factory was erected at Elizabeth, New Jersey, for the manufacture of aircraft engines and was completed six months after the United States entered World War I. Here the sixteen-cylinder Bugatti-designed aero engines went into production, but not more than 60 were made before the end of the war, and the contract for 2000 engines was immediately cancelled.

The Duesenbergs had already supplied a few four-cylinder engines to car-makers such as Biddle, Roamer and Revere, but they felt that the four was outdated for luxury cars so in 1919 they severed their connection with Duesenberg Motors Corporation and turned to developing a straight-eight engine. The rights to the 'walking beam' engines were sold to Rochester Motors Co which made it as the Rochester-Duesenberg, selling engines to

a number of car manufacturers including Argonne, Meteor, Revere, Richlieu and Roamer.

In March 1920 the Duesenberg Automobile and Motors Co Inc was formed, and later in the year a 17-acre (7-hectare) site was bought at Indianapolis. The first Duesenberg passenger car, called the Model A, had a 100hp 4.2-litre straight-eight engine with single overhead cam and hydraulic front-wheel brakes. In both these respects it was a pioneer among US production cars, for although claims have been made for the Kenworthy's straight-eight engine and Heine-Velox's hydraulic front-wheel brakes, neither of these cars saw serious production.

Manufacture of the Model A was slow to start, and the first cars did not reach dealers until December 1921. About 150 cars were made in 1922, of which 110 were delivered complete and the others sold as bare chassis. Duesenberg did not make its own bodies, but ordered various styles in batches from Fleetwood, Rubay and especially Millspaugh and Irish. Custom coachwork was also built on the Model A chassis by Brunn, Judkins, Murphy and others. Prices for cars with 'standard'

Duesenberg Model J of 1932

bodies began at $6500, reduced to $5500 for a few months in 1923.

Poor management led to reduced production in 1923 and receivership early in 1924. Only 25 cars were built that year, but in 1925 Duesenberg Motor Co was formed with Fred Duesenberg as president and fresh financial backing. About 100 cars a year were delivered during 1925 and 1926, but the Model A was an ageing design, its straight-eight engine no longer unique, and the small company did not have the capital required to develop a new model.

Duesenberg Motor Co would almost certainly have gone under had not a rescuer appeared in the person of Errett Lobban Cord, who had already taken control of the Auburn Automobile Co. Cord had ambitions to build a 'supercar' to rival the world's best. He saw in Duesenberg a name that carried high prestige because of the cars' continuing race successes – they won the Indianapolis 500 in 1924 and 1925 – and a company that could be acquired fairly cheaply.

In the autumn of 1926 Auburn Automobile Co purchased the capital stock of Duesenberg for about $1 million. A new company, Duesenberg Inc, was formed as a wholly-owned subsidiary of Auburn, and Cord gave the Duesenbergs a clean sheet on which to design a new car which would be a world beater. While they were at work on this, the factory built a few of the Model X, an improved Model A, and these were displayed in order to keep the Duesenberg name in the public eye.

The new car, known as the Model J, was announced in the autumn of 1928. It had a 6882cc twin-overhead cam straight-eight engine built by Lycoming, another Cord-owned company, to the Duesenbergs' design. The claimed output of 265bhp has recently been disputed, but it was certainly around the 250bhp mark, which made it by far the most powerful car in the world at the time. The chassis price was $8500, and complete cars ranged from $11,000 to about $14,000 initially, although prices rose and fell over the nine years that the Model J was on the market.

Duesenberg had no bodybuilding plant, and the nearest thing to a standard body was a car styled by Gordon Buehrig, who worked for Duesenberg, and built by companies such as Murphy, Derham or Brunn. There were, of course, also custom bodies built by practically every American coachbuilder and many Europeans as well, with prices running as high as $25,000.

Cord's plan for the Model J was a batch of 500 cars, to be built at whatever rate the market could absorb, followed by another batch in due course. In fact, even the first batch was never completed, and it took 10 years to sell some 480 cars. About three-quarters of these were delivered in the first three years before the Depression reached its bottom.

From 1932 a supercharger was available, the cars so equipped being known as the SJ. Only 36 of these were made, but a number of Js were retrospectively supercharged or simply fitted with outside exhaust pipes to make them look like SJs. The last Duesenberg to be completed was a Model J with Rollson body for the German artist Rudolf Bauer, and this was not delivered from the coachbuilder until early 1940.

In 1937 the Cord empire collapsed, and the Cord-owned companies were sold off. The Duesenberg factory became the home of Marmon-Herrington trucks at least into the mid-1950s. Fred Duesenberg had died in 1932 after a road accident, but Augie formed the A. Duesenberg Marine Motor Co of Indianapolis, and advertised a range of four-, six, and eight-cylinder flathead engines, few of which were made. In 1947 he was associated with a proposed Duesenberg revival to be made by Indianapolis businessman Marshall Merkes, but not even a prototype was built. Eight years later Augie Duesenberg died at the age of 76.

There have been four revivals of the Duesenberg name during the past 20 years, two by members of the Duesenberg family. In 1966 Fritz Duesenberg, Augie's son, launched a four-door sedan powered by a 430bhp Chrysler V8 engine, with body styled by Virgil Exner and built in Italy by Ghia. Duesenberg and his associates hoped to sell 150 cars, priced at $19,500, in the first year, but the money ran out and only one prototype was ever made. The same fate awaited the Cadillac-based limousine proposed by Kenneth and Harlan Duesenberg, sons of Fred, and Augie's brother Wesley C. Duesenberg in 1979. This was priced at $100,000 and again, only one car was built.

Ironically, greater success came to the replicas of classic Duesenbergs built by outsiders. From 1971 to 1978 the Duesenberg Motor Corporation of Gardena, California, made about a dozen replicas of the 1936 short-chassis SSJ roadster, powered by a 6.3-litre Chrysler V8 engine and using a modified Dodge truck chassis. In 1980 Richard Braun's Elite Heritage Motors Corporation of Elroy, Wisconsin, launched the Duesenberg II, a Lincoln-powered replica of the 1933 SJ speedster, with fibreglass body. GNG

DUFAUX
see Marchand

DU PONT
USA 1920-1932

Du Pont Motors Inc was formed by E. Paul du Pont, a member of the famous family which had widespread interests in munitions and textiles. The motor company had no connection with any other du Pont enterprises. It grew out of the Delaware Marine Motors Co of Wilmington, which Paul du Pont started in early 1917 and which supplied engines to the US Navy during the war. With the coming of peace, du Pont turned his attentions to the building of a high quality car. He gathered a good team of men – general manager Arthur Maris, formerly with Biddle, chief engineer John A. Pierson from the Wright-Martin Aircraft Corporation, and sales manager William A. Smith who came from Mercer.

The 1920 Du Pont Model A had, surprisingly for a car of its size and quality, an engine of only four cylinders (4.1 litres) with a Brown-Lipe gearbox and bodies made in a branch factory at Springfield, Massachusetts. The engines were made in the former marine motor plant at Wilmington and final assembly took place in another factory at Moore, Pennsylvania. The new make was well received, but production was limited, only 118 four-cylinder cars being made in the five years from 1920 to 1924.

These Models A and B were the only Du Ponts to use the company's own engines: when it was decided that a six was essential to the company's image, Du Pont turned to a Herschell-Spillman Model 90. This powered the Model C, of which 47 were made between July 1923 and the end of 1924. Du Pont's own engine no longer featured in the 1925 catalogue, in which there was only one model, the six-cylinder overhead-valve Wisconsin-powered Model D.

The mid-1920s was a lean era for Du Pont: the Moore plant was given up and production concentrated at Wilmington. Only 27 Model Ds were made in two years, hardly more than one car a month, and sales were restricted largely to the east coast.

In July 1928 came the final flowering of Du Pont with the 5.3-litre straight-eight Continental-powered Model G, offered in 12 body styles at prices from $4360 to $5750. Bodies were now provided by such prestigious firms as Merrimac, Waterhouse and Derham. Encouraged by its New York distributor A. J. Miranda, Du Pont entered two cars at Le Mans in 1929, but only one started, and that retired on the 20th lap. No better success attended the Du Pont entry in the 1930 Indianapolis 500.

In 1930 the Indian Motorcycle Co of Springfield, Massachusetts, was acquired by Du Pont, and all production was transferred to Springfield. The first and second floors of the motorcycle plant were adapted for car production, and Model Gs were made until January 1932.

In the autumn of 1930 came the Model H. This had a longer chassis – 146in (370cm) compared with 141in (358cm) for the Model G – and in order to cut development costs Du Pont used the frame of the recently defunct Stearns-Knight car. Only three Model Hs were made, and the last Du Pont made was a Model G sedan. Almost 200 Model Gs were made out of a total production of 547 for all Du Pont cars. E. Paul du Pont had become president of Indian, and remained in this post until he sold the company in 1945. He died five years later. GNG

DURANT/EAGLE, FLINT, STAR
USA 1921-1932

William Crapo Durant was born in 1861 and grew up in Flint, Michigan, where his father owned a lumber mill. With C. W. Nash and J. D. Dort he made Durant-Dort horsedrawn vehicles and in 1904 bought a controlling interest in Buick, which had entered the motor field a year previously. By 1908 he had turned it into a major car producer and in September that year he created General Motors Co, soon acquiring Oakland, Oldsmobile, Cadillac and other car-makers as well as Rapid trucks, although he failed to raise the $8 million required to purchase Ford.

After a banking group took over GM in 1910 Durant backed William H. Little, whose Little car was made in Flint from 1912 to 1915, and Louis Chevrolet, with whom he created a new and successful marque. By exchanging Chevrolet for GM shares he was back in control of GM in 1916; but in 1920 he was replaced at General Motors and was paid off in shares worth $3 million.

Soft-spoken, persuasive, impulsive and disorganized, Durant made a third attempt to form an automotive giant and in January 1921 created Durant Motors Inc of New York, which readily attracted funds of $7 million from 67 friends. The main factory was at Lansing, Michigan, where engines and the Durant car were made from 1921. Another factory on Long Island was bought for $2 million from Goodyear. The company's chief engineer and production director were from Chevrolet.

The early sales slogan was 'Just a Real Good Car'. Some 55,000 Durants were sold in 1922, the year in which a cheaper Star line having Continental engine was added. Overseas the Star was known as the Rugby. The Star competed with the Ford T and achieved seventh highest sales in America in 1923, when 130,000 were sold. In all, 1.5 million Durants, Stars and Rugbys were probably built; other estimates of 900,000 may not have included all names.

A new $15 million factory at Flint was begun in 1922 to make a Continental-engined six called the Flint, designed by a team from Chrysler and produced initially by Locomobile, which Durant bought in 1922. It was made from 1923 to 1927 and gave Durant a higher-priced range that sold as many as 3000 a year. A Continental-engined Eagle in 1923-24 filled the gap between the Star and Durant. The Princeton was intended to be a luxury car with Ansted motor but it never got off the ground. The Eagle then quickly became the Flint 40. Light commercials were based on many Star/Durant models but heavier vehicles were made under the name Mason Road King at Flint between 1922 and 1925.

In California Norman de Vaux was doing an excellent job selling Durant products and in 1925 merged the Star and Durant operations in a plant at Oakland. Some 200 Stars a day were made and in 1928 the group as a whole produced nearly 44,000 cars.

Durant had left the running of his factories in the hands of his managers and from the mid-1920s things started to go wrong. The plant in Flint was sold in 1926 to GM for a quarter of its construction cost, although the Flint car was offered for another year. In April 1927 Durant announced that he had assumed direct control of the company, but production was at a standstill for much of the year, though abortive plans were made to buy Amilcar in 1928. As a result of sweeping reorganization just the Durant and Locomobile names remained in 1929. In the first three months of that year 21,075 Durants were produced.

W. C. Durant spent an estimated $40 million in attempting to prop up the company's shares, but lost it all with the Wall Street crash and pulled out of the firm in 1929. He bought Locomobile from Durant but was compelled to close it down within a year.

Under the new management of A. I. Philp, Fred J. Haynes and other former Dodge staff, the Durant company made 20,200 mostly Continental-engined cars in 1930 and cut the range from five to two models. In 1931 only 7270 cars were sold, and they included the fastest car for its price – the 619, capable of 80mph (128kph), which carried a price of $695. The company came to an end in 1932.

A Canadian Durant factory at Leaside, Ontario, became independent in 1931 as Dominion Motors and lasted for a couple more years, buying some of its designs from De Vaux and selling its cars under the name Frontenac. W. C. Durant filed for bankruptcy in 1936. In his old age he ran a diner and bowling alley. He died in 1947. NB

DÜRKOPP
GERMANY, AUSTRIA 1898-1927

This famous sewing machine company was founded by Nikolaus Dürkopp in 1867. It had branches in Graz, Austria, and Bielefeld, Germany. Both soon produced bicycles and had a combined workforce of 1700 in 1892. Johann Puch made bicycles at Graz and sold out to Dürkopp in 1897 before starting his own motor firm there. Motorcycles were added at the turn of the century under the name Dürkopp in Germany and Styria in Austria. Engines were applied to experimental vehicles as early as 1894.

In 1899 the German company, Bielefelder Maschinenfabrik, introduced cars built on what was described as the Canello-Dürkopp system and which actually resembled contemporary Panhards and German Daimlers. A French factory at Courbevoie built Canello-Dürkopps from 1899.

A pioneer six-cylinder car was developed for 1903 and twins were sold in France as well as England, where they were called Watsonia. Commercial vehicles, mainly buses, were sold in London by the Motor Car Emporium, the name of which they usually bore.

An extensive range of cars and commercials was offered in the early years and profits averaged the equivalent of about $250,000 a year between 1906 and 1914. In about 1909 Oryx, which had made both cars and commercials, was acquired. Under the control of a ballbearing magnate named Barthel, the group became Dürkoppwerke AG in 1913; some of its lighter cars were sold under the name Knipperdolling. The Austrian factory did not enter the four-wheel market and discontinued its Styria motorcycles in about 1908, the name reverting to Puch which still uses it for freewheel and geared bicycle hubs.

Various commercial vehicles were made during World War I, including massive artillery tractors. Commercials and light cars were revived after the war. The 2-litre P8A was developed into a car for racing by Kurt Volkhart, and in 1925 a sports car evolved from the P8A which could be supplied with supercharged 60bhp engine. Car production ended in 1927, but commercials lasted for another three years and included low-frame six-cylinder bus chassis in 1928 and six-wheelers

Durant four-seat tourer of c.1924

Dürkopp two-cylinder of 1901

that were produced in 1929.

Motorcycle manufacture had ended before the war, but textile machinery, components and power and pedal cycles were made in the 1930s. Dürkopp became an important producer of bearings, which remain a speciality. Sachs and Ilo-engined motorcycles were produced from 1949, followed by machines with Dürkopp's own engines in 1951, including the Diana scooter, which was made from 1953 until vehicle production finally came to an end in 1959. NB

DURYEA
USA 1893-1916

The Duryea was one of the first ever cars in America, and certainly the first to be produced commercially. It was built by brothers Charles E. and J. Frank Duryea, whose volatile relationship soon resulted in them going their own ways and Duryea having a relatively short existence.

Charles was born in Illinois in 1861 and Frank was eight years his junior. Frank worked as a toolmaker for the Ames Manufacturing Co and Charles sold and repaired bicycles in Peoria, Illinois. In 1891, while working on bicycles for Ames, Charles began to work on his petrol-engined car, which was really a powered horse buggy with a single-cylinder 4hp two-stroke engine.

A local businessman, Erwin F. Markham, put up $1000 for an interest in Duryea's cars. Although the original idea was Charles's he soon called on Frank, a trained machinist, for help. Charles went back to his business and Frank finished the first prototype in Russel's Machine Shop in Springfield, Massachusetts, starting long-running animosity between the

Duryea advertising, 1896

brothers over just who invented the Duryea.

The first car ran on 21 September 1893 and the second, four-stroke, prototype, built entirely by Frank, won America's first motor race, the *Chicago Times Herald* race from Chicago to Evanston, run on Thanksgiving Day 1895, after an earlier postponement. Frank drove the 50 miles (80km) in just over nine hours, beating the only other finisher, a Benz. The first Duryea is now in the Smithsonian Institution in Washington.

The Duryea Motor Wagon Co, the first American company formed specifically to build petrol-engined cars, was established in 1895 in Springfield. There were four local investors, George H. Hewitt as president, David A. Reed as treasurer, T. W. Leete and

Theodore Haynes. The Duryeas each held a one-third stake, although Charles believed he should have held more – in spite of still working from distant Peoria, where cars were also built by the Duryea Manufacturing Co.

In 1896 Duryea built 13 cars having horizontal engines and three-speed belt drive. Two took part in the Emancipation Day Run in Britain in November – the event commemorated by the annual London to Brighton Run – and in April 1896 a Duryea appeared with other assorted freaks in a Barnum and Bailey Circus parade.

In 1898 the original company was wound up, after Frank left for the projected Automobile Co of America, which eventually built just one car. Charles then founded the Duryea Power Co in Reading, Pennsylvania. All subsequent Duryeas were purely Charles's work and included various three- and four-wheeled, three-cylinder cars with much vaunted single-lever control, the steering tiller also operating the gears and throttle.

A British Duryea Co was formed in 1902 by Henry Sturmey, editor of *The Autocar*, with capital of £25,000. The company made Duryeas under licence in Coventry until 1906, after which it became the Sturmey Motor Co.

In 1907 Duryea built a three-cylinder rotary-valve model, followed in 1908 by the high-wheeled twin-cylinder Buggyaut, which sold for $750 and was listed until 1913, built by the latest Duryea company, the Duryea Motor Co, formed in Saginaw, Michigan, in 1908.

Charles went on to design a short-lived cyclecar called the Duryea, which was built in 1914 and 1915 by the Cresson-Morris Co of Philadelphia, and a three-wheeler cyclecar, the 1916 Duryea-Gem, built by Duryea Motors Inc also of Philadelphia. He later became the mechanical editor of *Automobile Trade Journal* and then a consulting engineer until his death in 1939.

Frank, meanwhile, left the Automobile Co of America and founded the Hampden Automobile & Launch Co, intending to build the Hampden car. In 1901, in need of funds, he began work on a car for the Stevens Arms and Tool Co of Chicopee Falls, Massachusetts, the Hampden becoming a 6hp twin-cylinder two-seater, known as the Stevens-Duryea. In 1905 the company added a four-cylinder and in 1906 a six, claimed to be the first American six. In 1906 a separate company, the Stevens-Duryea Motor Car Co, was formed to build the cars.

Frank left in 1909, following a nervous breakdown, but returned briefly in 1915 after Stevens had withdrawn the previous year. The plant was sold to Westinghouse for war production but the Stevens-Duryea was built in small numbers after World War I as the six-cylinder Model E.

In 1923 the company was taken over by Ray M. Owen of Owen Magnetic, and traded as Stevens-Duryea Motors Inc until 1927. Ownership then passed to Baker, Rauch and Lang and the company's final product was Raulang electric cars and taxis. BL

DUTTON
GB 1970 to date

Tim Dutton-Woolley was an apprentice tool-maker living in a pub in Sussex when he built a car which he called the Mantis coupé, using an unlikely mixture of Lotus 11 and Sunbeam Alpine parts. He sold it to a cousin. In 1969 he built a Lotus 7 for a friend and decided that he could build his own cheaper version of the 7.

Early in 1970 Dutton-Woolley, then aged 21, completed the first Dutton, the P1. It was based on a Mark 1 Austin-Healey Sprite but also borrowed from the Alpine, a Ford Zephyr and from Lotus. It cost £100, mostly in secondhand parts, and it seemed that there might be a market for similar cars.

In August 1970 Dutton Cars moved into 700sq ft (65sq m) of workshop, which was once a pig pen, in Fontwell, Sussex. The first customer car was sold for £190; weather equipment, hand-made by the boss, cost £25. Nine P1s were sold, the last in late 1971.

Dutton Sports Ltd was formed in 1971 and moved to a neighbouring factory. In October 1971 Dutton launched the B-Type, which used Triumph suspension and other parts, with the option of Triumph, Ford or BMC engines. Dutton also built an Alfa-powered version of the B until 1973.

In December 1972 the company moved once again, to a 3000sq ft (280sq m) factory in Tangmere, Sussex. A further 700sq ft (65sq m) was added shortly after for use as a glass-fibre moulding shop. Dutton made its first show appearance at the London Racing Car Show in January 1973, displaying a modified B-Type and a short-lived clubman's racing version of the B, of which only six were sold.

With the introduction of value added tax imminent, 36 cars were sold in the first six weeks of 1973, at which stage six staff were building five cars a week. Demand fell to about three a week when the new tax was levied in April. Between mid-1973 and December the B chassis was redesigned as the B-plus, partly to accommodate larger engines (particularly for American sales) and partly for use in the forthcoming Malaga, which started life as a B-plus with a different nose.

Some 250 Bs were sold and the Malaga was introduced in October 1973. Although Dutton planned to build 100 in the first year, half of them for export, just one was sold in December 1973 and no more were made until the summer. The oil crisis and short-time working in January 1974 slowed sales to the point where Dutton-Woolley was the only remaining worker, building just 10 cars in the first half of the year. The Malaga was at this stage sold as a body option on the B-plus, but became a separate model in January 1975.

Exports stopped completely in 1975 and only two Duttons were exported in 1976, from production running at four cars a week. The 500th kit was built in May 1977 and Dutton introduced the Phaeton, which could use

Ford, Leyland, Fiat, Chrysler, Vauxhall, Datsun or even Polski-Fiat engines.

Production rose to 500 a year in 1980, when Dutton introduced the Sierra estate car, with Ford Escort running gear, at £950. In 1981, when Sierra production had reached 10 a week, Dutton was involved in legal problems with Ford, just about to launch *its* Sierra, but the company kept the right to use the name.

In January 1982 the Escort-based Melos 2+2 was added to the varied and successful Dutton range, which in the mid-1980s had made Dutton Europe's biggest kit-car manufacturer by quite a margin. As well as the familiar Phaeton, now in S3 specification, the Melos and the Sierra, the 1986 range included a Cortina 1600 based sporty two-door saloon, the Rico Sports. New for 1987 was the Legerra two-seater for 1.4, 1.6 or 2-litre Ford engines. BL

DUX/POLYMOBIL
GERMANY 1904-1926

The Polyphon-Musikwerke AG, founded in Leipzig in 1895, was famous for both its mechanical music devices and for machine tools. From 1904 it made its own version of the Curved Dash Oldsmobile, which had additional seating in place of the dash. To begin with it was called the Gazelle and then the Polymobil. In 1907 indigenous 8 and 16hp two- and four-cylinder Polymobils appeared and in 1909 the motor department and its cars changed their name to Dux.

Polyphon had been losing money heavily until 1909 but thereafter Dux made profits of $190,000 over the next four years and employed 1000 men at the outbreak of World War I. During the war it made heavy trucks.

Afterwards the car range ran from 1.5 to 4.5 litres, the latter a luxurious six introduced in 1924. The company became part of the Deutsche Automobil Conzern GmbH, which also controlled the Magirus and Vomag truck firms and Presto. This last firm took over the Dux works in 1926, but the Dux name was soon dropped and Presto was acquired by NAG. The Polyphon company changed its name to Deutsche Grammophon in 1932. NB

D-WAGEN
GERMANY 1924-1927

Deutsche Industrie Werke AG was an ordnance factory located in Berlin from 1901. In 1920 its name changed to Deutsche Werke AG and it became a major supplier to the motor industry of pressings, bodies and machinery. It had 4500 employees in 1926, when its directors were Henry Jaime, Walther Kunze and Immo Zitlaff.

In 1921 the firm had taken over H. F. Gunther's Star motorcycle design and produced it as the D-Rad. Chief designer Christiansen developed a new machine and in 1927 Martin Stolle joined the firm from BMW. From 1924 a 1.3-litre four-cylinder car was mass-produced but failed to sell in adequate numbers, being discontinued after three years. The factory then assembled Durants for the German market before being taken over by DKW. Rights to the motorcycles were acquired by NSU, which discontinued them in 1933. NB

D'YRSAN
FRANCE 1923-1931

In 1923 Raymond Siran worked with Stewart Sandford on the carburation of Sandford's reworked Morgans before setting up Cyclecars D'Yrsan at Asnières later in the year with a partner by the name of Dondelinger. The two men made a three-wheeler with Ruby four-cylinder engine and independent front suspension, and D'Yrsan became the French agent for Blackburne engines, although these do not seem to have been used in the cars. In 1925 972cc and 1100cc Ruby versions, some with superchargers, were offered and an English company was formed in an effort to find a more receptive clientele.

In 1927 four-wheelers with independent front suspension or beam front axle and similar engines were produced, displacing the three-wheelers the following year. In 1929 plans were made to use the 1100cc Michel desmodromic-valve six-cylinder engine but in 1931 the firm went out of business. NB

D'Yrsan sport of 1929

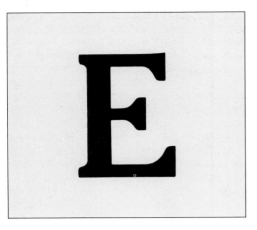

EAGLE (GB)
see Century

EAGLE (USA)
see Durant

EARL
see Briscoe

EDSEL
USA 1957-1959

The Edsel was the result of a marketing exercise by the Ford Motor Co to gain a better coverage of the middle price market than it had enjoyed with the Mercury. A separate Edsel division was set up, although much of the original planning was done by Ford's Special Products Division.

Originally the E-car (E for Experimental) was to be all new, with its own engines and body shell, but this would have been much too expensive, so it shared Ford and Mercury body shells – Ford in the lower priced Ranger/Pacer series, and Mercury in the bigger Corsair/Citation series. The two engine options were Ford, slightly bored out to give 5.9 litres, and the Lincoln/Mercury reduced to 6.7 litres.

The most distinctive feature of the car was its vertical 'horsecollar' grille which became the source of a great many jokes. Prices ran from $2519 to $3801, bracketing those of Mercury at both ends.

Ford planned to build the Edsel in five of its assembly plants, but within a few weeks of its launch in September 1957 it was apparent that sales were disappointing and most of the plants were hurriedly switched to other Ford products. Only Louisville, Kentucky, continued with Edsel to the end.

Sales of 1958 models were 60,120, compared with an anticipated 100,000, and the 1959s sold only 39,771. The range was drastically pruned for 1960 when a 3.7-litre six-cylinder engine, optional on the cheapest 1959 models, was made available on all models. The horsecollar grille was dropped in favour of a horizontal design. The 1960 Edsels were launched on 15 October 1959 and production ended on 19 November after only 2846 had been made.

Many explanations have been given over the years for the Edsel's failure. The fact that 1958 was a recession year for the motor manufacturing industry undoubtedly harmed it, but the car was simply an anticlimax after all the pre-release publicity that had surrounded it. Americans found that this was not the car of their dreams; it was just a Ford/Mercury with a funny front. GNG

EGO
GERMANY 1921-1927

Mercur Flugzeugbau GmbH of Berlin, which built the Ego light car, was founded in 1910 and originally built Rumpler aircraft engines under licence. During World War I the company manufactured the Albatross aero engine, but when the war ended German firms were banned from making machinery, including aero engines, with military connotations. Mercur therefore turned its production capacity to building the Ego car.

The first Ego was built in 1921, the four-cylinder 1040cc 15PS MKA. It was available as a four-seater torpedo or a two-seater sports model, with top speeds of 46 and 50mph (75 and 80kph). It had a fairly advanced engine design and soon developed a reputation for reliability.

In 1923 Rudi Caracciola, soon to become known as one of the all time great racing drivers, won his first race, the Berlin Stadium Race at Avus, driving a 4/14PS sports Ego with Ego works driver Fritz Schulz. It was one of 10 wins that year for Ego in the 4hp class.

The 24hp 1035cc four-cylinder sports model of 1924 was probably derived directly from the 1923 competition cars. It had a detachable alloy cylinder head and twin carbs, and in 1924 Egos scored 24 race wins. The company also built some light vans that year.

In 1925 the Mercur company was taken over by Hiller Automobilfabrik, but continued to build Ego cars, including the 1925 MKC with a choice of 1307 or 1336cc engines and four-wheel brakes. Rampant inflation in Germany in the early 1920s threw the industry into chaos and Ego was forced out of business by the start of 1927. BL

EHP/LORYC
FRANCE 1921-1929

Henri Précloux introduced a Ruby 900cc-engined sports car in 1921 which he named EHP after his Etablissements H. Précloux. It had transverse front and cantilever rear springs and its gearbox was attached to the front of a torque tube.

In 1922 a licence was sold to Loryc of Palma, Majorca, where more than 100 cars were made in the next four years. They were renamed Loryc or Loryc-EHP and had Talleres Darder or Ruby motors.

Bodies for EHPs were made by Comp. Gen. Automobile de Courbevoie which also worked for Bignan. EHP built several chassis for miniature fire appliances made by CGA in 1922 and was very soon taken over by that company.

In 1923 Bignan developed a D4 model EHP for CGA and also sold it with a Bignan radiator. CIME and SCAP engines were used by EHP in addition to Rubys. Various racing types were built and there was a small 1.3-litre six-cylinder sports touring car in 1928, a year before production of EHP ceased. NB

EHRHARDT/EHRHARDT-SZAWE
GERMANY 1899-1924

Heinrich Ehrhardt's famous German armaments factory began making cars at its Fahrzeugfabrik Eisenach factory in 1899. It built electric cars and petrol-engined Decauvilles, using the trade name Wartburg for both.

In 1904 Ehrhardt sold his interest in his company and returned to his home town of Zella St Blasii, where vehicle production con-

Edsel Ranger of 1959

tinued. The motor department was under the control of the founder's son Gustav, and for the first two years he made Ehrhardt-Decauvilles. Then in 1905 Ehrhardt developed its own two-cylinder 1.25-litre Fidelio model. It soon had a range of cars and commercials that included Germany's first four-wheel-braked car of 1913, which had a 50hp 8-litre engine.

During World War I Ehrhardt ranked second only to Krupp in munitions output and made large 4×4 lorries and tractors with unusual four-abreast rear driving wheels. After the war a range of two-, four- and six-cylinder cars and commercials of 6 to 60hp was made until 1922.

In that year Ehrhardt's motor department merged with coachbuilder Szabo and Wechselmann of Berlin, which had introduced its own luxurious Szawe cars in 1920. Production of Ehrhardt-Szawe cars continued at Zella St Blasii until 1924, commercial vehicles having been phased out in 1922. NB

EISENACH/DIXI
GERMANY 1899-1928

Eisenach in the Kaiserpreis of 1907

The Fahrzeugfabrik Eisenach was founded in the town of Eisenach in 1896 by Heinrich Ehrhardt who, at the age of 56, already had a considerable list of inventions to his credit, including the bell corkscrew, a scale for weighing locomotives, and a process for making seamless containers. The factory began by making munition wagons and bicycles, and added cars to its products in 1899, when Ehrhardt took out a licence to manufacture the French Decauville 3½hp *voiturelle* under licence. About 85 of these were made, and they were followed by larger, front-engined cars of Decauville design, made up to 1903.

Ehrhardt also made a small number of electric cars of his own design from 1899 to

160

1902, total production being 197. Both petrol-engined and electric cars were sold under the trade name Wartburg.

By the end of 1900 the financial position became worrying and in 1903 a loss of 1.3 million marks was recorded. Heinrich Ehrhardt and his son Gustav sold out and returned to their home town of Zella St Blasii where they had other interests and where they later made the Ehrhardt-Decauville and Ehrhardt cars. Fahrzeugfabrik Eisenach acquired the services of Willi Seck, who had designed the Aachen-built Scheibler friction-drive car, and in 1904 a completely new range was announced under the name Dixi (Latin for 'I have spoken' or 'the last word').

The Seck-designed cars, initially a two-cylinder 6hp and four-cylinder 12hp, made their appearance at the 1904 Frankfurt Motor Show and were soon being made under licence in France under the name Regina. As well as a growing range of Dixis, Eisenach made the Curved Dash Oldsmobile under licence for Ultramobil of Berlin from 1904 to 1906. Seck left to design the Liliput car for Bergmann's Industriewerke of Gaggenau, and was replaced by Georg Schwartz.

By 1908 the number of employees had risen to 1112; trucks were added to the company's products, followed in 1910 by aircraft engines, which were used by Dornier and the airship makers Flick and Heinig. Eisenach also made bicycles, bobsleighs, firefighting equipment and locomotive components. A wide variety of cars was made up to 1914, from 1.2 to 7.3-litres; the most popular was the 1.6-litre R8, of which 650 were made between 1908 and 1914.

During World War I the factory produced more than 10,000 military trucks and also trailers, anti-aircraft cannon chassis and field kitchens. In 1916 the Frankfurter Maschinenfabrik GmbH of Gross-Auheim, manufacturer of cannon barrels and truck chassis, was acquired by Eisenach.

In 1919 the manufacture of bicycles, cars and trucks was resumed. Three years later Eisenach merged with the Gothaer Waggonfabrik AG, both firms being controlled by financier Jacob Schapiro, who was also a major stockholder in Benz and NSU. Gothaer was a major manufacturer of railway wagons, and Eisenach became very much the junior partner.

Schapiro also owned the Cyklon Automobilwerke and in 1926 he put the 2.3-litre six-cylinder Cyklon into production at Eisenach, selling it as the Dixi 9/40PS from 1927 to 1929. Despite the fact that it was the cheapest German six-cylinder car it did not sell well, and Schapiro turned to another design as the saviour of his firm.

This was the Austin Seven, which went into production as the Dixi 3/15 at the end of 1927. In fact the first 100 cars came to Eisenach complete from Longbridge, and had their Dixi badges fitted on before they went to customers. By the end of the year 42 had been assembled in Germany; 12 months later the total was 6162. By the time the 3/15 was dropped in 1932 it had changed its name to BMW and a grand total of 25,156 had been made.

In October 1928 Dixi-Werke, as the company was now called, was purchased by the Munich-based Bayerische Motoren Werke AG, and from January 1929 the cars carried the name BMW. Only the 3/15 was made by BMW, although apparently a few 9/40PS Cyklon-type cars were sold by Dixi as 1929 models. GNG

ELCAR
see Pratt-Elkhart

ELECTRA KING
USA 1961 to date

The Electra King is a small and extremely basic electric car, built since 1961 by the B and Z Electric Car Co of Long Beach, California. Three- and four-wheeled versions of the tiny, angular-bodied car are available, with very limited weather protection and few other comforts. The Electra King is intended primarily as a shopping car or for use by the handicapped and various models offer ranges of between 25 and 40 miles (40 and 65km) on a single battery charge.

Performance is very limited, even for an electric car, with basic power being a 1hp DC motor running off four or five 6-volt batteries. The 1975 PFS121 to 128 range included Electra King's 'performance' option of a 3½hp motor at an extra $50, optional bigger battery packs and a variety of body types, at prices from $2270 to $2900. The four-wheel version was dropped between 1967 and 1971, but was then reintroduced alongside the three-wheeler, both cars being available with wheel or tiller steering. BL

Electromobile brougham of c.1907

ELECTROMOBILE
GB 1902-1920

The Electromobile was the most popular of the electric cars that flourished in Edwardian London. Their silence and cleanliness were preferred to petrol cars by many owners. The British and Foreign Electric Vehicle Co Ltd was established in 1900, and started selling imported French cars under the names BEC and Powerful.

In 1902 the name was changed to British Electromobile Co Ltd, and the cars were marketed as Electromobiles. They were now of British manufacture, the chassis coming from Greenwood and Batley Ltd of Leeds, while the bodies were made by a variety of firms, including the Gloucester Railway Carriage and Waggon Co Ltd, which had made bodies for the Bersey electric cabs a few years earlier. There was no connection between the British Electromobile Co and Electromobile Ltd of Otley, Yorkshire, which was an importer of American electric trucks.

The first order to Greenwood and Batley for 50 chassis was placed in October 1902, and they were delivered over the next six months. Most Electromobiles were broughams, with the driver sitting high up above the front axle, but they also made some lower open victorias, and in 1908 a number of taxicabs, which were operated by a subsidiary company, the Electromobile Taxicab Co. It was announced that 500 of these taxis were to go into service, but in fact not more than 20 did. Some were still in use in the early 1920s.

The total number of Electromobiles made was 303, and most of these had been supplied before 1910. They were long-lived vehicles and did not change in appearance, so owners had little incentive to buy new ones.

As well as selling cars, the company hired them out, and offered a contract maintenance service, under which an annual payment of £325 covered everything except the drivers' wages. It also hedged its bets by selling Napier petrol broughams, and by having the British concession for Opel cars. In 1907

the company moved from Lambeth to a garage at Hertford Street, Mayfair, which had accommodation for 300 cars. Because of its Napier connections, one of the directors was S. F. Edge.

In March 1914 the British Electromobile Co Ltd went into voluntary liquidation, selling the business to its hire department, the Hertford Street Hiring Co Ltd. However, a further attempt at manufacture was made in 1919 with a limousine called the Elmo. It had a body by T. H. Gill of Paddington and cost £1050; probably only one was made. GNG

ELITE/ELITE-DIAMANT
GERMANY 1920-1928

The firm of Elite Motorenwerke AG of Brand-Erbisdorf was founded in February 1914 as a continuation of the small marine engine builder Luders KG. In 1916 Elitewerke AG was also set up, with 80 per cent of its capital owned by George Gunther, a councillor to the local chamber of commerce.

At the end of World War I the company had some 1300 workers, although it did not originally build cars. In 1917 Elite took over the works of Elektromobilfabrik Gebhardt & Harborn in Berlin, and continued production of that company's Geha three-wheel electric car until 1923; four-wheel electric cars, used mainly as taxis, were also built in Berlin as Elites.

The first petrol-engined Elites were introduced in 1920. The company built four-cylinder 12/40PS and six-cylinder 10/50, 12/55, 14/60 and 18/70PS models, the last-named also being available as a 90hp sports model.

In 1921 Elite took over the Rex-Simplex marque, which had existed since 1901 and was currently built by Automobilwerke Richard & Hering AG in Ronneburg. Elite built the 13/40PS Rex-Simplex from 1921 to 1923 as the Elitewagen, in the original Rex-Simplex works.

By 1925 Elite employed about 3500 workers, but like most German manufacturers was hit very hard by the Depression. In 1927 Elite amalgamated with the Diamant company to become Elite-Diamant-Werke AG, still based in Brand-Erbisdorf. Subsequent models were known as Elite-Diamants, but the amalgamation could not save Elite and production stopped in 1928.

The company was subsequently acquired by Opel, then Germany's biggest car manufacturer with well over one-third of all sales. The works continued to make parts, but the workforce fell to only 450 in 1929 and the factory succumbed to the inevitable and was finally closed in 1935. BL

ELIZALDE
SPAIN 1914-1928

Arturo Elizalde Rouvier set up in business in 1909 as a manufacturer of car components such as valves, clutches, differential gears and shock absorbers. In 1910 he took over the Delahaye agency for the Barcelona district, and set up his company under the name Biada, Elizalde y Cia, with his brothers-in-law, the Biadas.

In 1914 they built their first car, a 15/20CV four-cylinder model which, the following year, attracted the attention and approval of King Alfonso XIII. They planned to import frames and possibly other components from Belgium, but World War I put a stop to this and forced Elizalde to make the whole car

Elizalde Tipo 26 racer of 1920

itself. Arturo Elizalde died in December 1914, but the business was carried on by his widow Carmen and his two sons Salvador and Arturo-Luis.

The 2.3-litre 15/20CV was made until 1917 when it was enlarged to 2.7 litres; commercial vehicles were also being made. In 1918 the company built a 150CV V8 aero engine, which was tested by the French Air Force and would have been ordered in large numbers had it not been for the Armistice. However, aero engines were made later, and kept Elizalde going after car production had been discontinued.

During the 1920s Elizalde widened its range in both directions. There were two small four-cylinder cars, the Tipo 513 of 6/8CV and 1195cc and the 1460cc Tipo 51 8/10CV. At the other end of the scale was the vast Tipo 48, with straight-eight engine of 8140cc, which was the largest car at the 1921 Paris Salon. The engine had four valves per cylinder, and among its features was a tyre pump operated by the engine, which could also work a vacuum cleaner for the car's interior. The Tipo 48 was catalogued from 1921 until at least 1924.

There was also a small straight-eight, the 3.4-litre Tipo 518. A sporting version of this, the Tipo 5181, had a guaranteed top speed of 100mph (160kph) and won a number of races and hillclimbs. Competition versions of the smaller Elizaldes also did well in Spanish events during the 1920s.

A variety of commercial vehicles was made at the same time as the cars. These ranged from a ½-ton van on the Tipo 51 chassis and a 2-tonner Tipo 23/26, which could be used for bus bodies, up to the Tipo 30C for 5-ton loads or 45 passengers.

In 1928 competition from cheaper imported vehicles forced Elizalde to cease car and truck production. It carried on with the aero engine work, however, after a change of name to Elizalde SA. Most of its work lay in the licence production of foreign engines such as the 450hp Lorraine (1928-36) or 110hp Walter J-4 (1934-35), but the company was also experimenting with its own design of radial air-cooled engines at the outbreak of the Spanish Civil War. The Elizalde factory did not survive the conflict. GNG

ELMORE
USA 1900-1912

James H. Becker and his brother were bicycle manufacturers before they formed the Elmore Manufacturing Co early in 1900 in Clyde, Ohio. The Elmore would be one of several cars built in Ohio just after the turn of the century, but it would be remembered mainly for its unflinching reliance on two-stroke engines. From 1900 to 1904 Elmore built a 5hp, single-cylinder light runabout, with three speeds and tiller steering. In 1903, when Elmore was one of the 28 members of the

Elva Courier Mark 4 of 1962

Elmore runabout of 1904

Association of Licensed Automobile Manufacturers, it introduced a twin-cylinder model which was given a dummy bonnet in 1904, even though the engine remained where it had always been, under the seats.

In 1905 Elmore advertising claimed that the cars would run on 'gasoline, kerosene or alcohol'. In 1906 the company moved to a larger factory, still in Clyde, and introduced a new range of cars with front-mounted two- and four-cylinder engines and side-entrance tourer bodies. Self-starters were also introduced on the 1906 cars.

In 1907 the company began production of a three-cylinder 24hp model which was built for several years. An Elmore was one of the few finishers from 70 starters in the 1907 Glidden Tour. In 1907 the Beckers sold out, very profitably, to E. A. Goss, who already controlled the E. R. Thomas Co of Detroit, manufacturer of the Thomas Flyer.

In 1909 Elmore was absorbed by General Motors as part of William Durant's doomed scheme for acquiring companies with what he saw as valuable patents. Goss received $600,000 in General Motors preferred stock for Elmore and for Thomas, which he sold at the same time. He went to work for General Motors.

Like many of Durant's other buys, Elmore – 'The Car that has no Valves' – failed as part of GM. When GM's bankers forced the sale of most of the non-Detroit companies, Elmore was closed down, in 1912, and the factories were sold off in 1917. BL

ELVA
GB 1955-1973

'Elle va' ('she goes') was how Frank Nichols came to name his Elva sports cars. Nichols ran the London Road Garage in Bexhill, Sussex, and raced a CSM Ford special and a Lotus 6 before deciding to build his own sports racing car. In March 1955 he completed the first Elva.

The chassis was built without the aid of drawings and it used Standard front suspension with a live rear axle. The Ford 1072cc engine used the overhead-inlet-valve head conversion devised by Nichols' mechanic, made by Birmingham Aluminium Castings and sold mainly to earn money for Nichols' racing activities. At one of the car's first races, at Brands Hatch, Nichols was asked to build a copy. Early in 1955 he formed the Elva Engineering Co Ltd, at the London Road Garage, and took his first orders for the Elva Mk1.

The early cars were all sports racers; the Mk1b had wishbone front suspension and the Mk2 had a De Dion rear end. The Ford 10 engine was soon replaced by a Coventry-Climax FWA. One Mk2 was sold in the United States where it was raced with great success, helping to establish a valuable export market.

Cars worth £15,000 were ordered in 1956 and £60,000 worth were sold in 1957, the majority in America. By 1958 Elva, now quite a major racing car producer, had moved to a larger factory, in Hastings, where it made almost all its own components.

Also in 1958, at the suggestion of the American importer, Elva introduced its first road car, the Courier, originally intended to have a BMC 948cc engine, but introduced with a BMC 1489cc unit. Most Couriers were exported and kits were not available in Britain until 1960, but by the end of 1961 400 had been built.

In 1961 production began at nine Couriers and two to three racers a week, but Elva encountered financial problems when the American importer was jailed, without paying for most of his sales. In spite of Elva's £250,000 export performance in 1960, the government refused to support the company, which went into voluntary liquidation.

A new company, Elva Cars (1961) Ltd, continued racing-car production on a reduced scale, moving to Rye, Sussex, in December 1962. More than 1000 racing Elvas had been built by November 1965, by which time Elva had racing connections with McLaren.

After a nine month gap Courier production was resumed by Trojan Ltd of Croydon, Surrey, builder of the Trojan three-wheeler and importer of the Lambretta scooter. A Mk3 version was launched in October 1962 and the independent rear suspension Mk4 followed in 1962.

At the London Racing Car Show in 1964, Trojan announced that it had taken over Elva, including racing-car production. Trojan retained Frank Nichols as a consultant until he retired through ill-health in 1965, later returning to his garage and engineering business. In August 1965 Elva announced plans for the pretty, BMW-engined GT160 coupé, designed by Fiore and to be built by Fissore, but only three were built.

In 1965, as demand for Couriers declined, Trojan sold the project to Ken Sheppard Customised Sports Cars Ltd, of Shenley, Hertfordshire, which continued production until 1969. The remaining parts were then sold to Tony Ellis in Windsor. He had no success in launching the Ford V6-engined Cougar and concentrated instead on supplying parts and service until the Elva name finally disappeared in 1973. BL

EMF/FLANDERS
USA 1909-1912

The EMF, variously and unkindly dubbed 'Every Morning Fix it', 'Every Mechanical Failure' and other epithets, was the product of three men, all whiz-kids of the American scene. Barney Everitt had a background in carriage and car coachbuilding which made him rich, and he built the Wayne car in Detroit from 1904 to 1908. William E. Metzger was a brilliant salesman who was one of the prime movers of the Cadillac Co, and Walter E. Flanders had manufactured crankshafts for Henry Ford.

Their car was a conventional four-cylinder 30hp machine with three-speed gearbox on the rear axle. The latter gave a lot of trouble, possibly showing that the rude nicknames were not entirely undeserved. The EMF 30 was priced at a modest $1250 and quickly attracted the attention of Studebaker which was looking for a reasonably-priced car that would sell in larger numbers than the expensive Garford it was offering at the time. Studebaker agreed to take half of EMF's production for 1909; planned for 12,000, the actual figure was 8132, including 172 cars made in 1908.

Everitt and Metzger, who had never been happy with the Studebaker agreement, left EMF in May 1909 to make a shortlived car called the Everitt. Flanders remained in uneasy alliance with the South Bend company.

In July 1909, with Studebaker help, he purchased the Detroit factory of the defunct De Luxe car, and used it for the manufacture of a four-cylinder car, smaller than the EMF, which he named after himself. The Flanders 20 sold for $1050 and in 1911 there was a five-passenger tourer for only $800, cheaper than an equivalent Model T Ford until Henry dropped his price to $700. Like the EMF, the Flanders was sold by Studebaker, which bought out Flanders' holdings in EMF in March 1910, thereby gaining complete control of the company.

Walter Flanders remained as a Studebaker employee until March 1912, when his employer tired of his devoting so much time to projects of his own, including a four-cylinder motorcycle and an electric car, and they parted. Studebaker retained the brand names Flanders and EMF for the 1912 season, but for 1913 they were renamed the Studebaker 20 and 30. Total production of EMFs was 47,619 and of the Flanders 30,707.

Flanders returned to his former partners in the Metzger Motor Co and the name of the Everitt Six car was changed to Flanders. The company also made about 2500 of the Bimobile four-cylinder motorcycle and 100 Flanders Electrics. Receivership followed in December 1912. Flanders then took over the foundering US Motor Co, scrapping such cars as the Brush and Columbia and renaming the Flanders Six the Maxwell. The unsuccessful electric car was renamed Tiffany for the 1913 season but sold no better with its jewellery connotations so the name was changed back to Flanders for its final year. Everitt, Metzger and Flanders teamed up again in 1921 for the manufacture of the Rickenbacker car. GNG

EMPIRE
USA 1909-1918

The Empire Motor Co was founded in the summer of 1909 and moved into the former Mohawk Cycle works in Indianapolis. It planned to produce up to 2000 Empire cars in 1910, selling at $800.

The company was set up by Arthur C. Newby, formerly president of the National Motor Vehicle Co; Carl G. Fisher, a racing enthusiast and founder of the Prest-O-Lite company; James A. Allison, another racing enthusiast; and Robert Hasler, a friend of Fisher and mechanical engineer for National.

The first Empire was the four-cylinder Twenty, introduced in 1909 and available as the Model A runabout for $800 or the more sporting B at $850. The cars were advertised as 'The Little Aristocrat'.

An Empire was the first car to run on the newly brick-paved Indianapolis Motor Speedway in December 1909. This was not because of its performance, which was strictly limited, but because Allison, Fisher and Newby were members of the original board of the Speedway, founded in February 1909. Empires ran in several other minor events at Indy but always without distinction.

EMF 30 of c.1911

Empire 31 two-seater of c.1912

For 1911 there was only one model, the well-built, well-equipped, two-seater C roadster priced at $950. Unfortunately, the company was neglected by its principals in favour of the Speedway, in spite of a brief appearance around March 1911 of Harry Stutz as designer. Stutz left shortly after to launch his own, more famous marque.

At the end of 1911, the Empire Motor Co stopped building cars and just made Fisher's Prest-O-Lite starters until March 1912, when the Empire Automobile Co was organized with $100,000 capital, of which $80,000 was apparently paid to the original company. Planning an immediate resumption of production, Empire sought a factory and reached agreement with a former parts manufacturer, the Greenville Metal Products Co of Greenville, Pennsylvania, to assemble cars. The Greenville-assembled Twenties were sold for 1912 only as Fays, named after Greenville's president. The Model 25, a larger car using Teetor and Continental proprietary engines and other bought-in parts, revived the Empire name.

In August 1912 Empire bought the Connersville Wheel Co of Indiana, intending to transfer production there as Greenville had switched to building railway carriages. In 1913 Empire offered only one model, the four-cylinder $950 Model 31 tourer and in 1915 the company moved to a new plant in Indianapolis, with around 250 workers. A planned doubling of production to 5000 a year, of a varied model range, was never even approached and the company ceased trading in the middle of 1918. BL

EMW
EAST GERMANY 1945-1955

In May 1945 the BMW factory at Eisenach in Germany was occupied by the invading Soviet Army, which ordered it to be dismantled in the same way that the Americans did at BMW's Munich factory. However, the workers gained a reprieve by assembling some BMW 321 saloons for the Russians, and by the end of the year 68 cars had been completed. The following year 1439 cars were made and in 1947 2035. Many went for export, particularly to Denmark, Holland and Switzerland, being sold under their pre-war name of BMW.

A total of 5940 Type 321s were made until the middle of 1948, when it was replaced by another pre-war design, the Type 327 cabriolet, which remained in production until 1955. In 1949 came a new model, the Type 340, which was basically the pre-war Type 326 with modernized styling. This was made as a four-door saloon, ambulance and delivery van and, like the 327, continued until 1955. About 15,000 were made.

Strictly speaking all the cars made until 1952 were sold as BMWs, despite protests by the West German company. At its request importers of the cars in West European coun-

tries filed the curves off the 'B' on the engine blocks to make the name EMW. BMW did not officially dissolve its Eisenach branch until October 1949. In 1952 the name was changed to Volkseigne Betriebe IFA-Werk Eisenach (People's Own Works Industrial Association for Vehicles, Eisenach) and the name EMW was henceforth used in all markets.

A number of prototypes of updated 340s were made and also some sports and racing cars under the name AWE, but the only serious production vehicles to come from Eisenach were the 340s. In 1953 the factory began to make the three-cylinder two-stroke-engined IFA F-9 and the 340 was phased out in 1955. The following year the F-9 was replaced by the similar-engined but totally restyled Wartburg, and updated versions of this are still made there today. GNG

ENFIELD/ROYAL ENFIELD
GB 1903-1915

The origins of this famous name can be traced to George Townsend, a maker of sewing and machine needles in the Worcestershire village of Hunt End near Redditch, in 1851. By 1882 his son, also George, was making rear forks, saddles and springs for bicycles as well as parts for sewing machines, and in 1886 they were building complete bicycles which they sold under the name Townsend. Later came bicycles and tricycles under the trade name Ecossais.

In 1892 the company name was changed to the Eadie Manufacturing Co, which began to make bicycles under the names Enfield and Royal Enfield. Albert Eadie formed the selling company for these bicycles which he named the Enfield Manufacturing Co Ltd and in 1897 the companies were renamed the New Eadie Manufacturing Co Ltd and the Enfield Cycle Co Ltd. By this time the business had expanded greatly, and the companies owned several factories in the Redditch area.

In 1899 Royal Enfield motor tricycles and quadricycles with De Dion-Bouton engines began to be advertised, probably made in the Eadie factory, and a few were actually marketed under the name Eadie. In 1900 came the first Royal Enfield motorcycles, Minerva-powered.

In 1903 light cars powered by 6hp single-cylinder De Dion-Bouton or 10hp vee-twin Ader engines were introduced. Prior to this, a few Vinot cars had been imported from France and the name Enfield substituted. From 1904 the Ader engine was replaced by a vertical twin of Enfield's own manufacture.

In March 1906 a new company was formed to look after car manufacture, named the Enfield Autocar Co Ltd. The Enfield Cycle Co Ltd continued to make Royal Enfield motorcycles and the Eadie Manufacturing Co was acquired by BSA in July 1907. Among the directors of Enfield Autocar were Albert Eadie and E. H. Lancaster, who had built up the

Enfield Nimble Nine of 1913

Clément car business in Britain, and who was responsible for the design of the new 15hp Enfield. A larger 25hp four-cylinder car was also made, but within two years the company had suffered a severe setback and was in the hands of a receiver.

A new company was formed, with a completely fresh board of directors, but they put it up for auction and it was acquired by Alldays and Onions Ltd for £10,000. Considering that the assets included 93 finished cars and 10 partly finished chassis, as well as the works and machinery, it would seem that Alldays got a bargain.

Manufacture was resumed in the Redditch factory but Enfield designs were gradually replaced by those of Alldays, which used the Enfield name to market the more expensive versions of its own cars. Alldays made a single-cylinder three-wheeler under the name Autorette in 1912, but this was replaced by the Nimble Nine four-wheeled light car, which was almost identical to the Alldays Midget. In 1918 the motor interests of the two companies were merged to form Enfield-Alldays Motors Ltd, and cars were made under this name until 1924. GNG

ENFIELD
GB, GREECE 1969-1976

Enfield Automotive Ltd, a member of the Enfield group of companies, the products of which included industrial power units and marine equipment, was announced in November 1969. It was in turn a part of the Greek shipping group of N. J. Goulandris and later Enfield cars were built on the island of Syros and finished at their port of arrival, Cowes, in the Isle of Wight. At the same time as the company launch, a pilot production run of Enfield electric vehicles for industrial and commercial use was started.

The Enfield 465 city car, a 2+2 saloon with sliding doors and a hatchback, was also revealed in November 1969 at the International Electric Vehicle Symposium in Phoenix, Arizona. The car was designed by former Diva sports car designer Sir Jon Samuel and bodied in 'Royalex', a plastic laminate developed by Uniroyal.

It used a CAV 48-volt motor, developing 4.65hp at 2200rpm, and seven-stage, fully-automatic control. Four special batteries in series supplied the power and the car had a built-in charger, so that it only needed to be plugged into a domestic supply for recharging – at an off-peak cost of only a few pence.

The Enfield had some plastic gears in its final drive and a friction-type torque limiter to cope with the large instantaneous torques of an electric motor. With independent front suspension, a live rear axle and Dunlop De-novo safety tyres, it coped well with a 40mph (64kph) top speed. On a full charge it had a range of some 30 to 40 miles (48 to 64km).

The British Electricity Council bought 61 of the total production of 108 Enfield 465s for long-term evaluation, but the car was too expensive to be a big seller. In 1975 the 8hp Model 8000 sold for a hefty £2808. This car had a ladder chassis with an alloy body on a steel frame, and a mixture of Hillman Imp and Reliant suspension parts. It was nominally a two-seater, with a range of 40 miles (64km) and a top speed of 40mph (64kph) – or considerably more downhill, with an all-up weight, including its eight 12-volt batteries, of over a ton. The Enfield eventually went the way of most electric cars, however good, and no more were built after 1976. BL

ENFIELD-ALLDAY
GB 1918-1924

Alldays and Onions had acquired the Enfield Autocar Co in 1908, but cars continued to be made under both names up to World War I. In 1918 a new company was formed to take over the car interests of both companies, named Enfield-Alldays Motors Ltd. The directors were William Allday and Edmund Tailby, both previously with Alldays and Onions and a later director was Hyam Marks, who was also chairman of the reconstituted Alldays-Onions Ltd.

The first Enfield-Allday car was a revolutionary machine named the Bullet. Designed by A. W. Reeves, it had a 1½-litre five-cylinder air-cooled sleeve-valve engine and tubular backbone frame. A. C. Bertelli, who had been with the Grahame-White Aviation Co, was invited to assess the design and pronounced against it as he thought it needed a great deal of development and would be uneconomical to produce.

Reeves left with the intention of building a car himself under the name Reeves Radial (he never did), and Bertelli was made general manager and asked to bring out a replacement design as quickly as possible. This was a conventional four-cylinder light car and was ready in time for the 1921 London Motor Show. Bodywork was made by Bertelli's brother Harry.

Some racing successes were achieved at Brooklands, but the car was very expensive at £525 for a 10hp sports model and in April 1923 Enfield-Alldays Motors Ltd went into liquidation, only to be revived eight months later. A larger model with 12/30hp engine was introduced, but few were made. The collapse of the parent company Alldays and Onions in 1924 pulled down Enfield-Allday with it, which was re-formed as Alldays Motor Repair Ltd in June 1924. About 100 cars were made altogether. Bertelli became a freelance consultant, then joined Woolf Barnato for whom he designed three sleeve-valve racing cars, and afterwards Aston Martin. GNG

ENFIELD
see also Alldays

ENGLISH MECHANIC
GB 1900-1909

The English Mechanic was not a true make of car but the name given to a small car that could be built from plans published in the magazine *The English Mechanic and World of Science and Art*. There were actually several English Mechanic designs between 1900 and 1905 and the first was described in a series of 56 weekly articles headed 'a small car and how to build it', which began in January 1900. The articles were written by an engineer, T. Hyler White, and the instructions and plans were very clear and easy to follow, but as few parts other than the cylinder head and block castings were available commercially, assembling an English Mechanic could take a very long time.

The first model described used a 3hp single-cylinder Singleton engine, rear-mounted. In 1903 a revised, front-engined model was detailed, with a two-cylinder 1200cc engine, three-speed gearbox and a top speed of 35mph (56kph). Other English Mechanic plans included a two-cylinder double-acting steam-engined car, a light two-cylinder, three-wheeler steam car and a 5hp petrol-engined runabout, the last plans appearing in July 1905.

After a break of several years, Hyler White started another series in 1909 on building a single-cylinder belt-drive English Mechanic runabout. It seems that a surprising number of enthusiasts actually completed English Mechanic cars. Three survive to the present day, a Benz-based two-seater of 1900, a 1903 steam dogcart and a 1904 8hp tonneau. BL

ENKA
see Aero

ENSIGN
see British Ensign

ERDMANN
see Oryx

ERIC-CAMPBELL
GB 1919-1926

Enfield-Allday racer of 1922

Eric-Campbell 10hp of 1919

Eucort 1-litre three-cylinder saloon of 1949

The name of this light car was derived from the middle names of its two sponsors, Hugh Eric Orr-Ewing and Noel Campbell Macklin. Eric, Campbell and Co was formed in 1918 and the cars were built in part of the Handley-Page aircraft works at Cricklewood, north-west London.

They used a 1½-litre Coventry-Simplex four-cylinder engine, and the polished aluminium bodies gave them a more sporting appearance than many of their contemporaries. They were, in fact, among the first postwar sports cars to become available and the makers gave notice of their sporting ambitions by entering two cars in the 1919 Targa Florio. British cars were rare enough anyway in this gruelling Sicilian event, but for a hitherto unknown small make to take part was quite exceptional. In the event only one car, driven by Jack Scales, started and he retired with a broken steering gear.

In the spring of 1920 Macklin left the company to concentrate on a high-performance sporting version, which he called the Silver Hawk and which he made in workshops attached to his house at Cobham, Surrey. Only a dozen of these were made. Macklin's next, and more successful, car venture was the Invicta.

Production of the Eric-Campbell continued at Cricklewood until 1921 when the company closed down and the unsold stock was cleared at bargain prices. Rights to the name and design were bought by the Vulcan Iron and Metal Works of Southall, Middlesex, which made it with little change in design until 1926 when the firm went into receivership. The last models had four-cylinder Anzani engines. GNG

ESSEX
see Hudson

EUCORT
SPAIN 1946-1951

Eugenio Cortés Cherto was acutely aware of the lack of Spanish-built utility vehicles and so, after a successful business career in Tarragona, started Automóviles Eucort SA, based in Barcelona, in June 1945. The name was a contraction of his christian name and his father's family name (which in Spain comes before the maternal name).

Scale models and plans were displayed at the Barcelona Fair in June 1946 and included saloons, pickups, estate cars and light commercials. Engines were DKW-inspired two-strokes, initially with two cylinders and then with three. There was a central tube chassis and independent suspension.

Production was planned at 150 a day but

shortages of materials and tools and problems over credit led to the firm's demise in 1951, after more than 1500 Eucorts had been produced. The last models were the Victoria, built in 1949, and the Avión of 1950 which had a circular chromed radiator shell. NB

EXCALIBUR
USA 1964 to date

The first and most successful of the American replicars, the SSK Mercedes-like Excalibur, was planned by Brooks Stevens as a 1964 model of Studebaker to liven up that company's image. Using a Paxton-supercharged Daytona engine and chassis, it was to have been the star of Studebaker's display at the 1964 New York Auto Show, but Studebaker ended production in the United States in December 1963.

Stevens and his sons managed to get the car, renamed Excalibur, onto a small stand of their own, where it generated great interest. A Chevrolet dealer ordered one, with a Chevrolet engine, and this led to a change of power unit, as the Daytona engine was in any case no longer available. The Studebaker Daytona chassis was used until 1969.

In 1964 Stevens and his sons set up SS Automobiles Incorporated in Milwaukee, Wisconsin, with a capital of $40,000, $25,000 in advance orders and $15,000 borrowed from the bank. By the beginning of 1966 they had sold 100 cars at $7250 each. All were two-seater roadsters styled after the famous Mercedes-Benz SSK, without attempting to be exact replicas. The flexible tubing for the outside exhausts came from the same German firm that had supplied it to Mercedes-Benz in the 1920s.

In 1967 a four-seater phaeton was added to the range, and a supercharger was an optional extra until 1970. There have been few major changes since then, although the Chevrolet

Excalibur Phaeton of 1984

Corvette engine was increased to 5.7 litres in 1970 and 7.4 litres in 1972, being reduced to 5 litres from 1980. Automatic transmission was standardized after 1974.

In 1976 the company name was changed to Excalibur Automobile Corporation, and the current president is David Stevens with his brother William as vice-president. There are 125 employees. Production has varied between 250 and 375 cars a year with 258 delivered in 1984 (213 phaetons and 45 roadsters). Prices in 1985 were $59,500 for the phaeton and $62,000 for the roadster. Excalibur has 28 dealers in the United States, and distributors in Canada and Japan as well as Monaco GNG

EXCELSIOR
BELGIUM 1904-1930

At the end of 1903 an engineer called Arthur de Coninck set up a small workshop in a Brussels garage to which he gave the grand title Compagnie Nationale Excelsior. His products would eventually live up to their title, but not at first. In January 1904 he began to build light cars powered by single or two-cylinder Aster engines and with armoured wood frames. He was also an agent for these well-known French engines, which he sold for marine and industrial use. For a while he represented the French maker Cornilleau-Sainte Beuve in Belgium.

Four-cylinder cars, still Aster powered, of 16, 22 and 30CV were made from 1905, now with Arbel steel frames and Malicet et Blin gearboxes. In 1907 the company became La Société Arthur de Coninck et Compagnie, with a capital of 12,500 Belgian francs, and larger premises were found. This enabled de Coninck to make his own engines and transmissions. The best-known model was the four-cylinder side-valve 14/20CV, which was made until 1914.

In 1909 further expansion took place with the acquisition of the Belgica factory at Saventhem, and the company name was changed once more to Société des Automobiles Excelsior. The first six-cylinder model, the 4.9-litre D6, came in 1910 and was joined in 1912 by the 5.3-litre Type F Roi des Belges.

De Coninck was active in motor sport at this time and entered a car in the 1912 French Grand Prix. This was the first six-cylinder car seen in Grand Prix racing. It was driven by Joseph Christiaens, who finished sixth. He was also sixth in the 1914 Indianapolis 500-Mile Race.

By 1914 Excelsior was established as a high-quality car, popular in export markets such as France and Britain as well as at home. The range consisted of the four-cylinder monobloc 14/20CV and two twin-bloc sixes, the D6 18/24CV and the F 30CV. Production for 1913 was 250 cars.

The factory was occupied by the Germans during World War I and all the machinery confiscated, so de Coninck had to design a completely new car. In fact the 1919 Adex – the name stood for Arthur de Coninck Excelsior, and was also used for patent designs – used the pre-war Type D6 engine with a longer stroke, but was distinguished by front-wheel brakes. In 1922 the engine dimensions were enlarged to those of the pre-war Type F, 90×140mm, or 5332 cc, and an overhead camshaft was used. This Adex C, later known as the Albert I after the Belgian king who owned several, was the only model of Excelsior for the rest of the marque's life.

A three-carburettor sporting model was offered and the cars were entered in the major sports car races such as Le Mans, the Georges Boillot Cup and the Belgian 24-Hour Race. They finished second in the last named in 1926, in which year Caerels won the Circuit des Routes Pavées for Excelsior. In 1927 Caerels and Sénéchal won the Belgian 24-Hour Race.

Production during the 1920s did not exceed 150 chassis a year, but the make had an excellent reputation as it was the only Belgian car, together with Minerva, which could be compared with Hispano-Suiza or Rolls-Royce. At £1150 to £1300 in 1928 it was somewhat cheaper than either.

In 1927 falling sales led to Excelsior joining Mathieu Van Roggen's Impéria empire, which also absorbed Métallurgique and Nagant. From 1929 Excelsior parts were sent to one of Impéria's car factories at Liège and some chassis were assembled there.

The last appearance of an Excelsior at the Brussels Salon was in December 1930, and production must have ended very shortly afterwards. The Saventhem factory was used for the manufacture of Impéria bodies until 1933, then sold. GNG

EYSINK
HOLLAND 1899-1920

D. H. Eysink's machine shop, opened at Amersfoort in Holland in 1886, built a prototype car in 1897 with front-mounted Benz engine. Cars and motorcycles were offered from 1899, the former having Eysink's own engines and the latter equipped with Minerva and Fafnir units. Serious production began in 1905, when a new factory was built. A range of four- and six-cylinder cars was made until World War I.

A light four-cylinder car using Malicet et Blin components was added in 1912, which was revived briefly after the war by Eysink Fabricken of Amersfoort. A total of about 400 cars were made until 1920, when production ceased.

Motorcycles were by then the firm's main business. British components from Villiers, Sunbeam, Rudge, JAP and New Hudson were widely used in the motorcycles during the 1930s, and Villiers, Sachs and Ilo engines, until production ended in 1956. NB

Eysink two-seat tourer of 1912

Excelsior 14/20 four of 1911

167

FACEL VEGA
FRANCE 1954-1964

Forges et Ateliers de Construction d'Eure et de Loire SA, or Facel, was founded in Paris in 1938 by Jean Daninos. The company made machine tools for the aircraft industry. During World War II, under German occupation, it made gas generators for cars but returned to aircraft-related production in 1946, making de Havilland gas turbine parts under licence. The company diversified, building office equipment, kitchen furniture (much of it in stainless steel) and car bodies, principally for Simca and Panhard.

By 1950 Facel had 2000 workers and several plants, which reached a peak car body output of more than 100 a day in 1952. Panhard stopped using Facel in 1953 but Simca bodies were built until 1961. Facel also designed and built bodies for Ford and Bentley; and the sporty Ford Comète was designed by Facel stylist Brasseur and built in quantity by Facel.

Daninos introduced his own first car, called simply the Vega, at the Paris Salon in July 1954. It followed an unshown prototype based on the Ford Vendôme, but used a 180bhp, 4.5-litre De Soto Firedome V8 (a version of the Chrysler Hemi) in a drum-braked tubular chassis. Two-speed Torque-Flite automatic transmission was standard, with the Pont-à-Mousson four-speed manual a desirable, if expensive, option. The elegant and superbly trimmed four-seater coupé body was welded to the chassis and the car was very expensive in all its markets, which were mostly export. A total of 46 Vegas were sold in 1954 and 1955.

By 1956 the car was designated Facel Vega and 227 FVS models were sold in 1956 and 1957, mostly to the United States. Engine size had grown to 5.4 litres and the HK500 boasted 6.4 litres and 350bhp. A convertible model was built in 1955 but rigidity problems kept production down to about six. The pillarless, four-door Excellence, introduced in 1957, sold more than 150 examples in spite of similar faults. It might have sold more as a Facel-Packard but the link was killed by struggling Packard's Mercedes connections.

The potent Facel II, derived from the HK500, was Daninos' last Facel. By 1962 the company was in serious financial trouble. The smaller Facellia, launched in 1960 with a planned output of 5000 a year, was a disaster; its Facel-built 1.6-litre twin-cam four, designed by former Talbot designer Carlo Marchetti, was noisy and unreliable. The company could not afford to solve the problems and only 500 Facellias were built.

Towards the end of 1962, in spite of support from Mobil, Pont-à-Mousson and Hispano-Suiza, a receiver was appointed. In the spring of 1963 the Volvo-engined Facel III offered unfulfilled hopes of a revival, but later in the year SFERMA, a subsidiary of Sud-Aviation, was given a one-year management contract, under Paul Badré, to save Facel.

Early plans for a new Facel engine were dropped and the FV6 was introduced with the six-cylinder Healey 3000 unit, linered down to fall within the domestic 15hp tax cut-off. A possible BMW engine deal came to naught and, after producing fewer than 30 cars, SFERMA declined to renew its options, although it still holds title to the Facel Vega name. The original company was declared bankrupt in 1965. BL

FAFNIR
GERMANY 1908-1926

Fafnir Type 471 racer of 1922

Carl Schwanemeyer founded his Aachen steel company Aachener Stahlwarenfabrik Fafnir Werke AG in the 1880s and soon became Germany's largest manufacturer of bicycle components. With the coming of the motorcycle and the motor car, the company began to build bolt-on, air-cooled engines, similar to the French Werner, and later built single-, twin- and four-cylinder water-cooled engines, all sold under the name Fafnir. The engines were widely used by makes including Falke, Horst, the British Phoenix, Rex-Simplex and Steudel.

In 1904 Fafnir began to sell the Omnimobil, a kit which comprised all the parts and instructions necessary to build complete cars. The first and best known had 6PS two-cylinder engines, but in 1908 there was a four-cylinder 16PS model in the range. A large number of companies, including Hartmann from Eisenach and Schilling of Suhl, used Omnimobil kits as the basis for their own car production.

In 1908 Fafnir began to sell assembled cars under its own name, with a range of four-cylinder models such as the 6/14PS Type 274 and the 8/16PS 284, which continued virtually unchanged until 1912. That year Fafnir introduced the advanced 8/22PS 472, which sold for 5425 marks and had a top speed of 46mph (75kph). The updated 472 was also built after World War I, when it was in production alongside the 10/25PS 384 and a new model, the 9/35PS 476.

Car production had become more important than engine production but Fafnir, like so many German firms, was a victim of the massive inflation of the early 1920s and production of cars was forced to a stop in 1926. BL

Facel Vega HK500 of 1960

FAGEOL
USA 1916-1917

The Fageol brothers, Frank and William, of Oakland, California, built a factory and made a few trucks before setting up Fageol Motors Co in November 1916. Finance came from local businessmen and car salesmen; Louis H. Bill was president. At the end of the year a 13½-litre Hall-Scott powered luxury car was produced. A series of 50 was planned in 1917 and a four-cylinder version was intended; but Hall-Scott, where Elbert J. Hall had helped to design the Liberty aero engine with Henry Leland from Cadillac, gave priority to producing plane and truck engines for the war effort so that fewer than 20 Fageol cars were made.

Front-wheel-drive orchard tractors with centre-pivot steering were made by Fageol at the same time and were joined by conventional Lycoming-powered tractors in 1918. Neither was produced for long.

In 1921 the firm's famous Safety Coach appeared, with four-cylinder Hall-Scott motor. It had 22 seats and a very low centre of gravity with powerful brakes to cope with California's long inclines. The plant of the defunct Thomart Motor Co in Kent, Ohio, was acquired for expansion and 260 coaches were sold in 1923 and 503 in 1924.

In 1925 the American Car and Foundry Co, a railway rolling-stock maker later known for ACF buses, bought Fageol's Ohio operation, although the Fageol brothers remained vice-presidents of this as well as of their independent Oakland plant, which made both trucks and coaches. After production of the Ohio range was moved to Detroit, the Fageols started up the Twin Coach Co back at Kent. There in 1933 a small experimental rear-engined four-door car was made, but did not enter production.

In the 1930s the Fageol business became unprofitable. The company was taken over in 1938 and the Oakland plant sold to T. A. Peterman, who built Peterbilt trucks there from 1939. NB

Fageol experimental tourer of c.1917

FAIRTHORPE
GB 1954-1978

Fairthorpe Ltd of Chalfont St Peter, Buckinghamshire, was founded in 1954 by Air Vice-Marshal Donald 'Pathfinder' Bennett, a wartime Mosquito pilot and officer commanding the Pathfinder section of RAF Bomber Command. Fairthorpe's first car was the quick but crude glassfibre-bodied Atom, a two- or four-seater coupé with rear-mounted 250, 350 or 650cc BSA motorcycle engines. It was followed by a front-engined 650cc derivative, the Atomota, but it was not until 1956 that Fairthorpe offered a more conventional car, the Electron.

This open two-seater used an 1100cc

Fairthorpe TXGT of 1968

Coventry-Climax engine, and an unsuccessful saloon version, the Electrina, was also designed. The smaller-engined Electron Minor followed and, latterly with a 1296cc Triumph Spitfire engine, was available until 1974, production having peaked at around five a week.

In 1959 Fairthorpe built the 130mph (210kph) Ford Zephyr-powered Zeta, based on a modified Electron chassis and offered with a number of tuning options, but only 14 were built. The Rockette was a more successful model which used the 1600 Triumph Vitesse engine.

In 1961 Fairthorpe moved to Gerards Cross and in 1964 moved again, to Denham and an airfield site alongside another Bennett company, Dart Aircraft Ltd. By then Donald Bennett's son Torix was becoming more involved in the company, which had become Fairthorpe Technical Exponents Ltd.

Torix developed the first of a more sophisticated breed of Fairthorpe, the TX1 of 1965. This used an ingenious cross-link rear suspension of Torix's own design. In 1968 the TX1 was given the 2-litre Triumph GT6 engine and renamed the TXGT, while the Electron Minor adopted the smaller Spitfire engine.

In 1971 the lighter, better-equipped TXS

was introduced. This was followed by the 130mph (210kph) fuel-injected TXSS which, strangely, only offered Torix's excellent suspension as an optional extra.

While the TXs continued as Fairthorpes, the Technical Exponents side of the company launched the TX Tripper in 1970. This was a distinctive convertible four-seater, not unlike a large buggy, and was available fully-built or as a kit. It offered a choice of Triumph 1300, 2-litre or 2.5-litre injected engines and the Torix Bennett suspension, but it was not available after 1978. BL

FARMAN
FRANCE 1921-1931

The three Farman brothers, Dick, Maurice and Henry, were of English extraction, their father being Paris correspondent for the *Standard* newspaper of London. In the 1890s they became famous racing cyclists and balloonists. Dick published a book in 1896 promoting automobiles and the family sold cars in London and Paris. Early attempts to build their own vehicles failed and from 1907 they took more interest in aviation. Henry flew a Voisin aircraft over a circular course of 1km in 1908 and the brothers opened aircraft factories. They later opened another factory in Billancourt to make aero engines and the engine building works prospered during World War I.

With the reversion to peace, Farman decided to enter the luxury car market with a 6694cc 40hp machine developed by Charles Waseige and using the latest in aero engineering practice. It had six welded steel cylinders surrounded by a steel water jacket and single overhead camshaft. Although it was shown in 1919, production did not start until 1921, when modifications were made. The cone clutch was replaced with a multiplate variety and the gearbox was now in unit with the engine. There was also a steering wheel lock and the price was in line with Hispano-Suiza. Actress Pearl White, the Shah of Iran and the Sultan of Morocco were among Farman's wealthy clientele.

Farman 6½-litre tourer of 1925

From 1923 blocks cast in Alpax alloy gradually ousted the earlier engine construction. In 1926 a very complex compound suspension system was developed employing transverse leaf springs at both front and rear with radius rods and four semi-elliptic helper springs. Separate steering mechanisms by worm and sector on each stub axle were introduced.

The 7-litre Farman NF of 1929 acquired a ribbon radiator shell and other transatlantic features, although the classic A6B continued. After building only about 100 cars, Farman stopped production in 1931. Plans to build a further car, V8-powered and styled by George Ham, were laid in the late 1930s but were ended by the onset of World War II. NB

FAUN/ANSBACH, BRAUN, OD
GERMANY 1909-1914; 1924-1927

Justus Christian Braun started a fire apparatus factory in Nuremberg in 1845 and built the first of 500 steam fire pumps in 1890. A workforce of 300 was employed by 1900 and battery and petrol-electric fire engines followed with other commercial vehicles.

In 1909 the friction-drive cars that had been produced since 1900 by Maurer-Union of Nuremberg were adopted and made in small numbers. In 1911 they were joined by a Kaiser-Wagen range of two-, four- and six-seaters and then by a 4/12hp model, but production ended with the coming of World War I.

In 1918 Braun merged with Fahrzeugfabrik Ansbach, which had been making commercial vehicles since 1906. In 1910 Ansbach had briefly offered a four-cylinder 6/14hp Kauz car, without much success. The joint firm

was called Fahrzeugwerke Ansbach und Nürnberg AG, or Faun for short.

Its speciality was municipal vehicles, including buses, but from 1924 to 1927 a series of Faun K1, K2 and K3 light cars with four-cylinder engine and in-unit gearbox was made. There was a 1½-litre overhead-cam sports model and several were available with detachable hard tops. Some time between 1926 and 1930 Ansbach withdrew from the company.

In 1939 Faun produced Germany's first rigid four-axle truck and after the war made many different types of specialized vehicle, including dumptrucks, military vehicles and crane-carriers. Rotating drum compression refuse collectors and motorized streetsweepers were first produced in the 1920s.

During 1955 Faun acquired Ostner-Fahrzeugwerke of Sulzbach-Rosenberg, which made light commercial vehicles and had produced a few OD three-wheel dual-purpose cars/commercials in the 1930s. Faun bought Frisch of Augsburg in 1977 and two years later acquired Eaton's Trojan loader division. Recent expansion has been in the area of earthmoving equipment. NB

FEG
see Oryx

FERGUS/OD
NORTHERN IRELAND, USA 1915-1916; 1921-1922

The Belfast firm of J. B. Ferguson Ltd, formerly a machine-tool manufacturer, became involved in the motor industry in the early 1900s, as a bodybuilder, as Irish agent for quality cars and, within a few years, as the largest car repair works in Ireland. When repairing other people's cars, Ferguson kept meticulous records of their faults and probable causes – in the majority of cases lubrication problems through neglect. In 1915 Ferguson introduced its own first car, the 2.6-litre four-cylinder Fergus 14/20hp, designed by J. A. McKee, with fellow directors R. Chilton and F. Eves, working from a new department set up solely to work on the car design.

The Fergus was described in the motoring press as 'undoubtedly the most interesting chassis that has been designed of late years' and it was indeed a highly advanced and beautifully made car. Where a typical car of the period had about 80 lubrication points, many requiring daily attention, the Fergus had only 11, almost all to be tended only six-monthly.

Oil circulated under pressure to all parts of the cantilever-sprung chassis, which was entirely built in the Ferguson works on presses designed and built by the company. The compact, overhead cam engine was mounted on rubber strips – perhaps the first use of rubber

engine mounts – and fuel tank pressure was created by an ingenious, variable, exhaust gas heat exchanger.

World War I stopped production in Ireland along with plans for a larger factory near Belfast. By March 1920 the car was being built in limited numbers at the 'development factory' of Fergus Motors of America Inc in Newark, New Jersey. It sold for $7500, and a six-cylinder 4078cc model was added.

The American-built Fergus was exhibited at the New York Show in January 1921, where it was described as 'the biggest attraction'. Assembly did return to Ireland, briefly, in 1921, when the company was renamed OD Cars Ltd of Belfast, and the cars OD – for Owner Driver.

The car was listed until 1922, at £1875, but it was too expensive to sell in quantity and OD had disappeared by 1923. Ferguson survived it as one of the world's major tractor producers, a result of brother Harry's far-reaching patents. In 1949 the still extant American company announced its intention of building an Austin A40 Sports-based sports car, a two-door two-seater Fergus roadster, but only one was ever built. BL

FERRARI
ITALY 1940 to date

Enzo Ferrari was born in February 1898 in Modena, northern Italy, and lived, with his elder brother Alfredo, above their father's workshop, which made railway equipment. In 1908 Enzo saw his first motor race and by 1911 he could drive the family car, one of the first in Modena. The family business expanded into motor repairs and Ferrari added motor racing to opera and sports journalism as possible careers.

In 1916 Alfredo was killed and their father died. In 1917 Enzo joined the artillery, first as a farrier and later as a mechanic working on aero engines, but he was invalided out of the army in the winter of 1918. He was turned down for a job with Fiat early in 1919 and went to work for a Bolognese engineer by the name of Giovanni who was rebodying small trucks as saloons, and even sports cars, for the starved market. Ferrari drove bare chassis to Milan where the bodies were fitted. Through a friend, racing driver Ugo Sivocci, Ferrari became a test driver for Construzione Meccaniche Nazionali in Milan and had his first race for CMN in October 1919 at the Parma Poggio di Berceto hillclimb.

In 1920 Enzo joined Alfa Romeo as a test driver and attracted engineers Luigi Bazzi and Vittorio Jano from Fiat. In October he finished second for Alfa in the Targa Florio. His racing career lasted until 1931 but it was dogged by illness, including a nervous breakdown in 1924. He finally retired after the birth of his only son, Dino, in January 1932.

After one of several wins in minor events, at the 1923 Circuit of Savio, Ferrari was congratulated by Count Enrico Baracca, father of the flying ace Françesco Baracca. Baracca was killed in 1918 after shooting down 34 enemy aircraft; his mother, the Countess Paolina, dedicated her son's prancing horse emblem to Ferrari, who adopted it as his badge on a yellow shield in honour of Modena.

In 1928, for his racing successes, Ferrari was given the title Commendatore, but when titles bestowed by the Fascists were reviewed after World War II Enzo happily reverted to being just Ferrari, or Ingeniere Ferrari.

In 1929 he left Alfa and in December formed Societa Anonima Scuderia Ferrari as a limited company in partnership with Mario Tadini and the Caniato brothers, in Modena. Officially an independent Alfa agent, the Scuderia looked after Alfa's racing customers

Auto Avio Costruzioni (Ferrari) 815 of 1940

Ferrari 500 (Alberto Ascari driving) of 1952

and ran its own racing activities, principally with Alfas. Since Antonio Ascari's death in 1925 Alfa had limited its direct involvement in racing but from 1930 Scuderia Ferrari was in effect the works Alfa team. In 1932 Alfa went into state ownership but Ferrari continued independently, also racing motorcycles for several years.

In 1938 Alfa formed Alfa Corse, with Ferrari as manager, in Milan, but he left in 1939, accompanied by Bazzi and others, after arguments with a Spanish engineer, Wilfredo Ricart. With his Alfa pay-off and the remaining assets of Scuderia Ferrari, Enzo formed Societa Anonima Auto Avio Construzioni Ferrari and took over the Scuderia's old premises, initially as a machine tool manufacturer but soon, prompted by a request from Alberto Ascari, as a racing car manufacturer.

His first car, the 815 (not called a Ferrari because of Enzo's four-year Alfa severance conditions), was designed by Alberto Massimino and built between December 1939 and April 1940, when two cars appeared in (and retired from) the Brescia Grand Prix. The straight-eight engine used some Fiat 1100 parts and the body was by Touring of Milan.

Production was stopped by World War II, during which Ferrari made aircraft parts and machine tools. Towards the end of 1943, under decentralization laws, Ferrari moved to nearby Maranello. The large new factory was bombed twice but was rebuilt in 1946, when

plus the larger capacity 342s and 375s specifically for the American market – although road cars were still really only a sideline. Milanese businessmen Franco Cornacchia and Luigi Chinetti provided working capital, the later becoming the longstanding Ferrari connection in America, where Briggs Cunningham imported the first of the marque, a 1949 Spider.

Subsequent American cars were almost invariably the largest-engined and most powerful derivatives. They included the 400 and 410 Superamerica types of the mid-1950s, the rapid lightweight 410 Superfast and, ultimately, the 400bhp 4.9-litre 500 Superfast.

Ferrari 500 Superfast of 1964

Ferrari announced that he would build road and racing cars – which could now be called Ferraris.

The first was the Colombo designed 1½-litre V12 125C racing sports car, announced in November 1946 and first seen in a sports car race at Piacenza in May 1947. Three 125s were built, followed by the larger engined 159 and 166. The latter was the basis of the first road car, the 166 Inter of 1947, the first 'customer' version of which was sold in January 1948. It was followed by the 195 Inter of 1951 and by the 212.

Ferrari sold more than 250 of these series –

From 1964 to 1966 the 500 represented the last of the big but relatively crude cars specifically for the American market. Later exports were essentially European models adapted to comply with local legislation and sales requirements.

Ferrari's success was still based on racing. In September 1948 the marque made its first Formula 1 appearance, in the Italian Grand Prix at Valentino Park where Raymond Sommer, one of a three-car team, finished third. Farina scored the first Formula 1 win at Lake Garda in 1948 and Gonzalez took the first Grand Prix win, in Britain in 1951 in a car

Ferrari 250GTO of 1962

designed by Aurelio Lampredi, who had rejoined Ferrari in 1949. In June 1949 Ferrari scored its first Le Mans win, with the 166MM. Ferrari won the Mille Miglia in 1951 and began a series of Formula 1 world championship victories in 1952 when Ascari won the drivers' championship.

Ferrari drivers have won the world championship nine times, and although Ferrari has a record of near misses in recent drivers' championships it maintains an outstanding record in the constructors' championship, which Ferrari himself undoubtedly considers more significant and which the company has won an unequalled eight times since its inception in 1958. In sports car racing Ferrari has won Le Mans nine times (beaten only by Porsche's 1985 win) and regularly dominated the sports car championship in its various guises until effectively giving up sports car competition in 1974. Although Ferrari has more than once withdrawn his cars from competition to make a point of principle he remains utterly dedicated to the sport and it has been fundamental in the company's technical and commercial development.

The other great influence was Dino's death in 1956, at the age of 24. While Dino was alive – and already proving his worth as an engineer with his part in the development of the V6 racing engine which bore his name – Enzo had a natural successor and it was logical for Ferrari to remain under family control. After Dino's death it became less important to Enzo that he retained total control of the production side, which was still of only limited interest to him.

In the early 1960s, Ford of America, keen to win Le Mans as part of the promotion of a new sporting image, came very close to buying Ferrari as a means to that end, but the deal foundered when Enzo realized that it would cost him control of his own racing operations – and anyway he had a more acceptable alternative. In 1955, when Ferrari had been asked by the national sporting authority to take over the struggling Lancia Grand Prix team, Fiat agreed to support Ferrari's racing team for five years, to the tune of 50 million lire a year. In 1960 the company

Ferrari Dino 308GT of 1973

became Societa per Azioni Esercizo Fabriche Automobili e Corse Ferrari, or SEFAC Ferrari, formally combining the production and racing activities.

In mid-1969 Ferrari relinquished a 50 per cent holding in his company to Fiat, which would take charge of road car production. In return Fiat guaranteed substantial and continued financial support for Ferrari's racing operations, which Enzo would continue to control with absolute autonomy for as long as he wished, which obviously meant until his death. All parties were thus more than happy.

In the mid-1960s production capacity was greatly increased and the Fiat connection was used to great advantage, but there was one stillborn Ferrari project at the beginning of the 1960s which gave rise to another marque, ASA. Between 1957 and 1963 Ferrari developed a four-cylinder engine intended for a small capacity touring car. It was tried in a Fiat 1100 chassis but pursued no further as Ferrari did not yet have the production capacity. The engine design was eventually sold to the De Nora family who began building the ASA Mille in 1964 in 1-litre guise, but the car struggled to find a market and lasted only until 1967.

From the beginning Ferrari's own road cars were essentially the means to his sporting ends, but in 1954 the 250 Europa, a true GT car, really committed Ferrari to road car manufacture. Variations of the 250 were Ferrari's staple European road car for many years, properly productionized with the 1956

3-litre 250GT. In 1961 the 250 range included the Lusso (literally 'luxury') and the 250GT 2+2, the first Ferrari with more than two seats. The 250s also gave rise to the larger-engined 330GT in the American series.

Ferrari also offered lightweight versions of his coupés, principally for racing, generically dubbed Berlinetta (literally 'little saloon'). In 1962 he introduced the ultimate short chassis racing derivative of the 250 series, the 250GTO – for Gran Turismo Omologato – of which some 45 were built until 1964.

With the 275GTB of the same year, Ferrari offered a standard body style on a chassis at last designed specifically for road use, with independent rear suspension. It was succeeded a couple of years later by the four-cam 275GTB4, following the Ferrari type numbering pattern which used the capacity of a single cylinder, an abbreviation for the body type and (where appropriate for distinction) the number of camshafts.

The last front-engined V12 Ferrari was the 175mph (280kph) Pininfarina-styled 365GTB4 Daytona, introduced in 1968 and still one of the fastest road cars ever made. It was joined later by the drophead 365GTS4 (the S signifying Spider).

At the other end of the scale in 1968, and reflecting the Fiat connection, Ferrari introduced the mid-engined Dino 206GT, developed from the 1965 206GTS racing sports car and a prototype shown at that year's Paris Salon. Aimed at a much larger market and competing directly with the Porsche 911, the

Dino used a Ferrari-designed Fiat-built engine and was badged not with the ubiquitous Prancing Horse but with the name of Dino, whose grave Ferrari still visited daily to confide his problems and plans.

Fiat itself used a de-tuned version of the V6 engine in its own front-engined Dino model, and the engine also found its way into the mid-engined Lancia Stratos, developed primarily for rallying, after Fiat had taken over Lancia in 1969. Ferrari's own Dinos developed with the larger-engined 246GT and 246GTS Spider of 1972.

In the Bertone-styled 308GT4 of 1973, Ferrari introduced his first roadgoing V8 engine, but the styling was not popular and so Ferrari returned to Pininfarina for the 1975 308GTB, which was built with glassfibre bodywork until 1977, when the 308GTS Spider version was added. Pininfarina also styled the largest Ferrari, the elegant four-seater 400, which developed from the 365GT4 2+2 and in 1976 offered the first automatic transmission option to Ferrari customers.

Following Grand Prix racing practice, Ferrari's next big car adopted a mid-engined layout with a power unit following the flat-12 format of the contemporaneous Formula 1 cars. This was the spectacular 365GT4BB Berlinetta Boxer, first seen as a prototype in 1971 and put into production in 4.4-litre form in 1973, followed shortly, as ever, by a Spider version. In 1976 the Boxer was given a full 5-litre engine as the 512BB (later type numbers signify capacity and the number of cylinders), keeping Ferrari among the fastest cars in the world.

Also underlying the company's continuing commitment to racing, in 1984 Ferrari introduced a new homologation special, built ostensibly as a road car but only in sufficient numbers to satisfy the requirements of racing

regulations. This was the 189mph (302kph) GTO, developed from the 308 series in much the same way as the original GTO developed from the 250s – and for much the same reason. Another name reappeared from Ferrari's past when the 180mph (290kph) Testarossa (meaning Red Head, after the colour of the cam covers) replaced the Boxer.

As well as constantly uprating its own cars, with larger engines for the 308 and Mondial types and more power for the 400i, which became known as the 412 in early 1985, Ferrari also became involved in developing four-wheel-drive systems for Fiat and a new V8 engine for Lancia. BL

FIAT
BRAZIL 1976 to date

The Brazilian Fiat operation was set up in 1973 under the name Fiat Automoveis SA, with works at Betim. The first distinctive cars were made in 1976. Known as the 147 they were based on the Italian 127 but had the larger engine of 1089cc. Various models were made, including an estate car, the Panorama, which had no Italian equivalent. In 1981 came the Spazio, a more expensive version of the 147 with a grille reminiscent of the Fiat Uno.

The Brazilian Fiat plant also makes an Alfa Romeo model, the 2.3-litre Ti-4 four-door saloon. Until 1978 this was made by FNM of Rio de Janeiro, in which Alfa Romeo had an 85 per cent holding, but when Fiat Automoveis bought FNM it acquired the Alfa design which is still marketed as an Alfa Romeo. Like many Brazilian cars, all these models are available with engines designed to run on alcohol fuel. GNG

FIAT
ITALY 1899 to date

It has been said that the French government owns Renault, nobody knows who owns Volkswagen, but Fiat owns Italy. While this last is an obvious exaggeration there is no doubt that the Fiat empire plays an enormous part in the Italian economy, and an even more dominant role in the life of its home city of Turin. As well as cars and commercial vehicles, Fiat makes ball-bearings, ships, aero engines and complete aircraft, marine engines and railway rolling stock, and has interests in paint and plastics, typewriters (Olivetti) and newspapers (La Stampa).

This enormous and diverse empire had its origins in the summer of 1899, when three wealthy young men met in Turin to discuss the formation of a new car company. They were Emanuele di Bricherasio, Giovanni Agnelli, a cavalry officer turned engineer, and Count Roberto Biscaretti di Ruffia, who was later to found the Turin Motor Museum.

They chose the name for their new company, Fabbrica Italiana Automobili Torino (Italian Motorcar Works, Turin), before they had any idea of what they were going to make, but their problem was solved when they bought up Giovanni-Battista Ceirano's small works and his prototype car. This had a 697cc rear-mounted flat-twin engine, with belt drive; Agnelli replaced the latter with chain drive, but otherwise the design went into production unchanged as the FIAT Tipo A. Eight of these were made in 1899-1900.

As well as the design, FIAT acquired the services of the engineer responsible for it, Aristide Faccioli, and about 50 employees, including two who were to become celebrated racing drivers for FIAT, Vincenzo Lancia and Felice Nazzaro. Faccioli left in 1901, by which time the company was making front-engined 8 and 12hp cars on Panhard lines. It had no body shop, and coachwork was obtained from Alessio or Locati e Torretta. Exports began in 1901, when 20 cars were sold abroad, rising to 52 in 1903 and 257 in 1905. The small factory in the Corso Dante trebled in size between 1901 and 1904.

Faccioli's place was taken by Giovanni Enrico, a civil engineer who had installed electric light at the 1884 Turin Exhibition. Under Enrico, FIAT blossomed out with large four-cylinder cars on Mercédès lines and engines up to 60hp (10,597cc), although the 24/32hp (6391cc and 6902cc) was the most popular. The 6.4-litre engine went into FIAT's first purpose-built commercial vehicles, a forward-control 4-ton chassis which was later used to carry double-decker bus bodies.

Although he retired in 1906, Enrico was responsible for the line of FIAT racing cars from 1904 to 1908, with which drivers such as Lancia, Nazzaro, Cagno and Wagner achieved numerous successes including the 1904 and 1908 Coppa Florio, 1907 Targa Flor-

Ferrari GTO of 1984

Ferrari 400i of 1984

io, Grand Prix and Kaiserpreis, and the 1908 American Grand Prize.

In 1905 and 1906 FIAT made a car jointly with machine-tool manufacturer Michele Ansaldi; smaller than the Enrico-designed cars, it had a 3-litre four-cylinder engine and chain drive. In 1906 FIAT bought out Ansaldi's holding in the FIAT-Ansaldi company, and henceforth the cars were made under the name Fiat Brevetti, with shaft drive from 1907 onwards.

At the end of 1906 the capital initials were dispensed with and the cars became Fiats, although the company name was not to be changed to Fiat SpA until 1918. Already Agnelli was beginning to diversify into other fields; he founded the RVI ball-bearing firm in 1905, and in the following year went into ship-building, when he bought a stake in the San Giorgio yard at Genoa, which built merchant ships and also made Napier cars under licence from 1906 to 1909. Fiat had made marine engines from 1903, and entered the aero engine field in 1908. From 1909 to 1912 it made bicycles, but a motorcycle was never offered.

Enrico's successor as chief engineer was Guido Fornaca, who gave the firm a new direction with his Tipo 1 of 1908. This was a smaller car than any since the pioneers of 1899-1900, with a monobloc four-cylinder engine of just over 2 litres capacity. It was Fiat's first monobloc engine, first L-head, and apart from the Brevetti which was not really a Fiat design at all, the first to use shaft drive.

The Tipo 1 led to the 1 *bis* of 1910 to 1915, joined by the Tipo Zero with shorter wheelbase. A total of 7192 of these small four-cylinder cars had been made by 1915, many of them seeing service as taxicabs in London and other cities. Indeed the Tipo 1 was revived for taxi use only, from 1919 to 1922.

Although Fiat was not neglecting the luxury market, it was firmly set on the path of providing middle-class cars, a policy reinforced after Agnelli's visit to the United States in 1912, when he was deeply impressed and not a little alarmed by the mass production might of Ford. In 1914 Fiat made 4644 cars, putting the company among the top five European car-makers (in America Ford made 308,162).

Fiats were represented in most important markets throughout the world, and had two foreign factories, Austro-Fiat in Vienna and American Fiat in Poughkeepsie, New York. These are covered separately as they had independent financial structures.

As might be expected, Fiat factories were extremely busy during World War I. Road vehicles ranged from 2.8-litre Tipo 2 staff cars through various sizes of army trucks to a vast artillery tractor powered by a 70bhp 10.6-litre engine, capable of pulling 100 tons. In 1918 Fiat built two prototypes of Italy's first tank. For the Italian Air Force, Fiat's subsidiary SIA (Societa Italiana Aeronautica) made 1336 complete aircraft and 15,830 aero engines, some of the latter being supplied to France for the Bréguet XIV and Britain for the Vickers

174

Fiat Tipo 1 landaulette limousine of 1908

Fiat 519 coupé de ville of c.1922

Vimy and De Havilland DH4 and DH9. As a result of all this activity Fiat assets quadrupled in the four years of the war to more than 100 million lire.

The profits made during the war enabled Fiat to expand its peacetime production greatly, and this expansion was symbolized in the building of the new factory at Lingotto, completed in 1922. This five-storey building was Italy's first reinforced concrete structure and incorporated a test-track on the roof. Fiat now had its own generating station in the Alps, producing electricity for all its plants, including Lingotto.

The effect of this expansion was a great increase in production, from 1973 in 1917 to 8988 in 1921, and 13,629 in 1923. Most of these figures were accounted for by the Tipo 501, a new 1½-litre car with four-cylinder detachable head engine and a pear-shaped radiator, which characterized nearly all Fiat cars until 1925. It also ushered in a new system of numbering, whereby 500s were reserved for passenger cars, 600s for commercial vehicles, 700s for tractors and 800s for racing cars. This lasted until the late 1930s, and in the case of commercial vehicles well into the 1950s.

The 501 was Fiat's first mass-produced car and more than 80,000 were made until 1926. It was joined by the 2.3-litre Tipo 505, 3½-litre Tipo 510, 4.8-litre Tipo 519, and a short-lived

6.8-litre V12, the 520, of which no more than five were made. As well as a wide range of commercial vehicles, Fiat was now making agricultural tractors, the first of which appeared in 1919.

The Fiat design team in the early 1920s was a galaxy of talent. Fornaca was still there, and there was also Carlo Cavalli who was responsible for the 501, Guilio Cesare Cappa who had used aluminium pistons as early as 1906 at Aquila-Italiana, Vittorio Jano who earned most of his fame with Alfa-Romeo and Lancia, and Vincent Bertarione who later designed racing cars for the Sunbeam-Talbot-Darracq group (the 1923 Grand Prix Sunbeams being called 'Fiats in green paint' by some). Finally there was Tranquillo Zerbi, who designed the double-twelve aircraft engines of 1931, and the 508 light car of 1932-48.

Fiat's aviation department became increasingly important during the 1920s, with its first complete commercial aircraft, the four-passsenger A1, appearing in 1923, and military aircraft and engines being sold to many countries including Czechoslovakia, Poland, Turkey and Yugoslavia. In 1922 the Argentinian and Ecuadorian air forces were said to be 'under Italian management', and almost exclusively Fiat-equipped.

In 1925 came a new and smaller light car, the 990cc Tipo 509 with 22bhp four-cylinder single-overhead cam engine. It outdid the 501 in production, more than 92,000 being made in under five years. It was the best-selling Fiat until the famous 500 'Topolino' of 1936-48, and even that needed 12 years to sell 122,000. To help sales of the 509, Fiat set up a hire purchase company and it also offered a low price insurance scheme.

At the other end of the scale was the 519, a 4.8-litre six-cylinder car which was made from 1922 to 1927. The sports model had a very Germanic vee-radiator, although the ordinary 519s had square Rolls-Royce type radiators which were also found on the 509 and intermediate Fiats. A total of 2411 519s were made, quite a respectable figure for an expensive car which was Fiat's last serious attempt to cater for the top end of the market. (The nearest subsequent offering was the 130 of 1969-73, but this offered more competition to Rover than to Rolls-Royce.) In 1928 Fiat

Fiat 500 'Topolino' of c.1936

delivered 44,404 cars, or 88 per cent of the national total.

Fiat's first diesel-electric railcar was made in 1925, the same year that it acquired the aircraft side of Ansaldo, and two years later the company bought up SPA, a Turin firm which was making aero engines, trucks and a limited number of high-quality six-cylinder cars. Trucks continued to be sold by Fiat under the SPA name until 1947.

In 1933 Fiat purchased another company which was becoming more famous for its trucks, although cars were still made. This was OM (Officine Meccaniche) of Brescia. The cars were soon dropped under Fiat ownership but trucks were continued until the late 1970s, when the name disappeared as Fiat-made trucks were marketed under the Iveco name.

By 1930 Fiat employed 35,000 people; as well as its own Alpine hydroelectric generating plant it owned two foundries and three steel works. The company was beginning to extend foreign activities beyond mere selling: there were two short-lived attempts at assembly in Britain, at the Vickers works at Crayford, Kent, in 1928 and at Acton, west London, in 1930.

Of much greater significance was the German operation, whereby NSU of Heilbronn made the six-cylinder Fiat 521 from 1930, and Walter of Czechoslovakia made the new four-

cylinder 514 as well as the 521. In fact Fiat bought NSU's new Heilbronn factory, which was used exclusively for the manufacture of Fiat cars and light commercials from 1930 to 1966.

Fiat also opened a Spanish factory at Barcelona in 1931 for the assembly of 514s; this led to the Spanish make SEAT in later years. Other foreign ventures which led to national production were Polski-Fiat at Warsaw from 1932, and Simca at Nanterre from 1935.

The 1.4-litre 514, made from 1929 to 1932, was a rather uninspiring small car, but its successor, the 508 or Balilla, was quite the reverse. Its 995cc engine had almost square cylinder dimensions (65×75mm), making it suitable for cruising at 55mph (88kph) on the new *autostrade* which Mussolini was building with gusto, while the basic 22bhp side-valve engine was tuned to give over 50bhp in overhead-valve form in the hands of Amedée Gordini. Fiat's own 36bhp 508S of 1934 to 1937 also had overhead valves and carried very attractive two-seater sports bodywork. All models received overhead valves on the 1937 508C, and this design, later known as the 1100, was made until 1948. Total production of the Balilla/1100 family, not including the French, German, Czech or Polish varieties, was more than 237,000.

Other Fiat cars of the mid-1930s included the four-cylinder 2-litre Ardita, six-cylinder 2½-litre Tipo 527 and six-cylinder 1½-litre 1500. This last was a thoroughly modern design with short-stroke engine of the same cylinder dimensions as the Balilla and an

Fiat 508S spider (Felice Nazzaro driving) of 1934

aerodynamic body with headlamps recessed into the wings.

Most important, however, was the 569cc four-cylinder 500, nicknamed 'Topolino' (Italian for Mickey Mouse). With a synchromesh four-speed gearbox and excellent hydraulic brakes, it set new standards for small cars and was arguably, with the Austin Seven, the most significant light car made in the inter-war period. It was also very good value, costing the equivalent of less than £100 in 1936 in Italy and France, where it was assembled and sold as the Simca Cinq. Its British price was £120.

A tuned 500 was the basis for the Siata Amica, the first complete car offered by the Turin firm that was to become famous for its sports cars after World War II. Tuned and re-bodied 500s were also offered by NSU in Germany. Production of the 500 was revived after the war and continued until 1948, by which time 122,016 had been made. It was replaced by the generally similar 500C with overhead valve engine and post-war styling, of which a further 376,368 examples were made until 1954.

At the outbreak of World War II, which for Italy was not until May 1940, Fiat was making the 500, 1100, 1500 and a new 2.8-litre six-cylinder car, the 2800. This was an attempt to cover the upper-middle price bracket, but only 620 were made, many of them as army staff cars. Because of Italy's late entry into the war, car production continued until surprisingly late: 23,502 cars were made in 1940, 13,799 in 1941, and 11,236 in 1942. In 1939 a new factory was opened at Mirafiori, on land which Agnelli had bought as a flying field during World War I.

Fiat's contribution to the war effort was wide, ranging from staff cars on the 1100 and 2800 chassis, light, medium and heavy trucks, to aero engines and complete fighter and passenger aircraft. After the collapse of the Fascist government in 1943, all Italian production was directed towards supplying the German forces.

Fiat workers were very reluctant to do this. There were many strikes, go-slows and sabotage, so that of the 180 aircraft which Fiat was supposed to supply each month, not more than 10 per cent were actually delivered. The German response, in January 1944, was to order that all Fiat tooling should be transferred to Germany, but this brought about an immediate general strike, so Fiat stayed where it was.

Post-war production was initially confined to trucks, some of which were produced as early as June 1945; Mirafiori had escaped with relatively little damage, but Lingotto was virtually destroyed. By mid-1946, however, cars were coming off the lines again, initially the pre-war trio of 500, 1100 and 1500. The

Fiat 1400 saloon of c.1950

of manufacture, formerly Stavropol, was renamed in honour of the Italian communist leader Palmiro Togliatti. The VAZ-2101, known in the West as the Lada, was a Fiat 124 with single overhead cam engine and is still made today.

In addition to these foreign makes, Fiat had assembly plants in many countries, notably Argentina and New Zealand, where there were stringent restrictions on the importation of complete cars. Export of complete cars to other markets flourished, France, Portugal and Switzerland proving very good customers. Fiat began to ship cars to the USA in 1956, selling 38,468 cars there in 1959.

The commercial vehicle and aircraft departments also flourished in the 1960s, although there were fewer new aircraft designs because of the massive cost of develop-

500 gained overhead valves in 1948, becoming the 500C.

For 1950 came Fiat's first all-new model for many years, the 1395cc overhead-valve short-stroke (82×66mm) 1400, with unitary construction four-door saloon body. A car for world markets, in the Standard Vanguard/Renault Frégate class, the 1400 was available with a diesel engine in 1953 and was widely used as a taxi. It was the first design to be made by the new Spanish firm, SEAT (Sociedad Española de Automoviles de Turismo), which put it into production in Barcelona in 1953. It was joined by the 1900 with 1.9-litre engine in the same body shell, and from 1953 the new 1100, using the old engine in a modern unitary construction body.

This new generation of Fiats was the work of Dante Giacosa, who had first come to notice when he helped Fessia in the design of the original 500. He was also responsible for the new 600 which replaced the 500C in 1955. It had a rear-mounted 633cc four-cylinder engine and two-door unitary construction saloon body, and was later made as a six-seater forward-control estate car/taxi, the Multipla.

The 600 was followed in 1957 by a new 500, again rear-engined but with a vertical twin engine of 479cc, the smallest engine Fiat had ever used. It formed the basis of the Bianchina, a two-seater coupé made by Autobianchi SpA, a company founded in 1955 by Ferrucio Quintavalle, involving Fiat, the Pirelli tyre company and the old-established firm of Bianchi, which had made cars up to 1939 and was still active in truck and motorcycle manufacture. In 1963 Autobianchi became wholly Fiat-owned, and since 1968 it has been merely a division of Fiat, yet still making its own designs of car.

These new models greatly boosted Fiat production. The 1100 became the first model to top a million, with 1,019,778 delivered between 1953 and 1962, while sales of the 500 and improved 500D had exceeded the 3 million mark by 1973. Fiat's first year to exceed 1 million sales was 1966.

A new six-cylinder model, the 1800 (later 2300) catered for the upper-middle class mar-

Fiat 130 coupé of 1969

ket, while from 1959 the sporting enthusiast could buy the 1500S, with engine designed by the tuning specialist OSCA. Fiat tended to rely on outside firms to make its high-performance variants. The best-known of these was Abarth, which made Fiat-based cars under its own name and also sporting models of Fiat such as the 600 and 850. In the late 1970s Abarth was responsible for preparing the works rally team of 131s. Thus Fiat was broadening its range, and apart from the top of the market limousine or GT class it could truly be said to be a general provider.

Its foreign operations did well in the 1960s, too. The Spanish (SEAT) and German (NSU) concerns had been joined by Zastava in Yugoslavia from 1954 and Premier in India from 1955, while the Austrian firm of Steyr-Puch made the 500 with its own two-cylinder engine. Polski-Fiat production was resumed in 1968.

The following year the first cars emerged from the new VAZ factory at Togliattigrad on the Volga. This marked the first successful collaboration between the Soviet government and the West in car manufacture since the Ford-based GAZ of 1932. Fiat provided the technical expertise, with Russian engineers being trained at Mirafiori and Italians supervising the building of the factory. In return Fiat received around £21 million, and the city

ment. The G-91 tactical fighter was Fiat's most important aeroplane, being made in Germany by Dornier, Heinkel and Messerschmitt.

Towards the end of the 1960s, Gianni Agnelli (grandson of founder Giovanni) added to the Fiat empire by buying Lancia, and purchasing a 50 per cent stake in Ferrari and a 15 per cent stake in Citroën, although the last was relinquished in 1974. Fiat had already collaborated with Ferrari in the Fiat Dino of 1967, which used a 2-litre V6 Ferrari engine and was the fastest and most expensive Fiat of the decade.

On the commercial vehicle front in 1975 Fiat formed the Iveco (Industrial Vehicle Corporation) consortium with Klockner-Humboldt-Deutz of Germany, maker of Magirus-Deutz trucks. The two ranges have since been rationalised.

Fiat returned to officially-sponsored competitions in 1969 when it ran a works-backed team of 124 spyder sports cars. It was fourth in the 1971 Acropolis Rally, and seventh in the Monte Carlo, but in 1972 the Fiat team won the Acropolis. The more recent team of Abarth-tuned 131 saloons has won the World Rally Championship in 1977, 1978 and 1980. In 1978 Marku Alen won the World Rally Drivers' Championship, a feat repeated in 1980 by Walter Rohrl.

Fiat's first front-wheel-drive car was the 128 of 1969. A replacement for the long-running 1100, it had transverse 1116cc engine, all-independent springing and front disc brakes. Fiat had used its Autobianchi division to try out front-wheel drive in the 1965 Primula, and when it planned to enter the 'super mini' class, followed the same course. The Autobianchi A112 was launched in 1969 and paved the way for the Fiat 127 of 1971.

Other important models of the 1970s were the 130 saloons and coupé of 1969-73, a move up-market with 2.8-litre V6 engine and automatic transmission (a first for Fiat, although a five-speed ZF manual box was an option), and the XI/9 (1973 to date), a mid-engined sports car powered by a 1.3-litre 128 engine. The cheapest model was the 126, a rear-engined 594cc successor to the 500.

In 1978 the 128 was replaced by the Ritmo (Strada in English-speaking markets), also a front-wheel-drive saloon with 1.1- and 1.3- or 1.5-litre engines which became available with a 1.7-litre diesel engine from 1980. For 1984 the Ritmo was joined by a notchback version, the Regata.

The 1987 range was concentrated on the popular end of the market, starting with the 126 and the Panda, a somewhat larger front-engined hatchback with 770 or 999cc petrol engines, or a 1.3 litre diesel, followed by the Uno three- or five-door hatchbacks with 999, 1116 or 1301cc engines, and the Ritmo/Regata with seven engine options from 1116 to 1995cc, including diesels. The range is completed by the Croma, Fiat's version of the up-market saloon also made by Alfa Romeo, Lancia and Saab, with 2-litre petrol or 2.4 litre diesel engines, and the XI/9 sports car, now sold under the Bertone name. Thus Fiat is quite unusual in being a manufacturer of the first rank with no model over 2½ litres capacity.

Production in 1985 was 1,422,000 cars and over 80,000 commercial vehicles, the latter running from light vans on the 127 chassis to articulated trucks with a gross combination weight of up to 44 tonnes. The large trucks now carry Iveco badges rather than Fiat.

Foreign production falls into two classes, local assembly of models basically similar to those made in Italy, and local manufacture of cars which differ more and are badged under separate names. In the former category are assembly plants in Argentina, Chile, Columbia, Egypt, Eire, Indonesia, Malaysia, Morocco, New Zealand, Portugal, Thailand, Venezuela and Zambia.

In some of these countries models no longer current in Italy are still made. Thus the Argentine factory was still making the 600 and 128 in 1983, and the Egyptian company El Nasr was making the 128. In addition the 131 is manufactured in Turkey under the name Tofas Murat. More distinctive foreign makes are described under their own headings: Fiat (Brazil), Premier (India), Polski-Fiat, SEAT, VAZ, and Zastava.

The workforce at Fiat's Italian car plants was 107,681 in 1984, while an additional 36,263 worked on commercial vehicles. This is only a small part of Fiat's overall activities, however, which include affiliated companies engaged in the manufacture of railway rolling stock, civil engineering and nuclear power plants. In 1983 the Lingotto factory was sold and became the site of the 1984 Turin Motor Show. GNG

FIAT
USA 1910-1918

The United States had been a good customer for Fiats, especially the larger models, since the first one crossed the Atlantic in 1902. The New York distributors, Hollander and Tangeman, sold 181 cars in 1908, which encouraged the setting up of an American factory.

A separate company, the Fiat Motor Co, was formed with financial backing from New York diamond importer Ben J. Eichberg and a factory erected at Poughkeepsie, New York. This was entirely self contained – the whole car was made on the premises, apart from ball-bearings and axle casings which were imported from Italy. Nevertheless, Fiat engineers paid regular visits to Poughkeepsie to ensure that high standards were maintained.

Only the larger Fiats were made in America, where there was little demand for anything under 4 litres capacity, although these could be imported by the Fiat Motor Co if a customer asked for one. First Poughkeepsie built model was the 5.7-litre four-cylinder Tipo 4, sold as the Type 54. Other models included the Light Thirty, a 4.4-litre Tipo 3A, and the large Type 55 (Italian Tipo 5) with 9-litre four-cylinder engine. One model which had no Italian counterpart was the 8½-litre six-cylinder Type 56.

From 1914 most American Fiats had pear-shape radiators. Production continued at the rate of 200 to 400 cars a year until March 1918, when the factory was sold to Duesenberg Motor Corporation for aero engine manufacture. Fiat cars were offered on the American market in the 1920s, but were either too dear or too small and few were sold. GNG

Fiat (Bertone) XI/9s of c.1974

Fiat Uno of 1984

FIBERFAB
USA, GERMANY 1965 to date

Bud Goodwin set up Fiberfab early in 1965 as a division of Velocidad Inc of Santa Clara, California, to manufacture bolt-on glassfibre body kits for Volkswagen Beetle chassis. The first Fiberfab kit was the Aztec, available in April 1965 as a $795 body kit, with optional extras offering the possibility of a complete car on a scrap VW base for under $1500.

No chassis cutting or welding was necessary and it was claimed that the car could be easily built with only spanners, a screwdriver and a drill. The whole top hinged upwards on a hydraulic strut for passenger access, and with an all-up weight of only 1300lb (590kg) performance was quite good. It could be further improved by using a Corvair engine.

In November 1966 Fiberfab was building its first complete car, the potent, mid-engined Valkyrie GT, designed for Ford 427cu in or Chevrolet 428 V8s, with five-speed ZF gearbox. It had all-round independent coil spring suspension and disc brakes, rather fancifully supplemented by a Simpson parachute 'for speeds over 140mph'. Top speed of the 1600lb (725kg) car was claimed to be 180mph (290kph) but a meeker, Corvair-based kit was also available.

Fiberfab built a GT40 look-alike, the Avenger GT, from mid-1967, as an $895 kit suitable for Porsche or Corvair engines, and later added the front-engined, MGA-chassised Jamaican. With a 3.5-litre Buick V8 the Jamaican went better than it stopped.

By late 1967 Fiberfab had sold more than 2000 kits. From 1969, Fiberfab kits were also built and sold by an associate company in Germany, Fiberfab-Karosserie, first in Stuttgart and after 1974 in Heilbronn. As well as the usual Fiberfab offerings they introduced the Citroën 2CV-based, Jeep-style Sherpa in 1975 and in the late 1970s were building about 120 cars a year.

In America, Fiberfab became Fiberfab Inc and moved to Pittsburgh. In December 1973 the range included a Ford Mustang-powered copy of the 1936 Aston Martin Ulster, known as the Liberty SLR. Other models included the Bonito and Bonanza coupés and in the early 1980s Fiberfab also sold Daytona's Migi II MG TD replica. BL

FIRESTONE-COLUMBUS
USA 1903-1915

The Columbus Buggy Co of Columbus, Ohio, had built horse buggies since the 1870s. In 1903 it offered electric power in place of the horse in the Columbus or Columbus-Electric car. In 1906 the company built a petrol-engined high-wheeler which was sold as the Firestone-Columbus, after Clinton D. Firestone, who had been a partner in the Col-umbus company since 1875.

For the next few years the company offered both petrol and electric vehicles. The Columbus was one of 54 electrics at the 1907 New York Garden Show. In Victoria or coupé models it offered a 21mph (34kph) top speed and a 75-mile (120-km) range at about 12mph (19kph). The high-wheeled, two-cylinder petrol-engined Firestone Motor Buggy, advertised as 'A Vehicle for the Masses, not a Toy for the Classes', was built until 1908 at $750 and was particularly aimed at farmers and rural doctors.

From 1909 the company built more conventional, and very sporting, roadsters, known until 1912 as the 'Mechanical Greyhound'. In 1910 Firestone-Columbus cars won several races, held a number of records and were very much in demand for competition.

In 1911, when 10 models were offered for the road, a Firestone-Columbus driven by Frayer and Rickerstacker was one of the finishers in the first Indianapolis 500, after an uneventful run with just a single tyre change. Sales fell, however, and only eight models, fours and sixes, were offered in 1913, which was also the last year of the electric cars.

Firestone-Columbus Motor Buggy of 1908

In 1914 the company merged with Thomas Auto Co of Buffalo, New York, builder of the Thomas Flyer. Plans to develop Firestone-Columbus production faltered, with only five models in 1914. These cars were designed by C. C. Bramwell, who had previously built the Bramwell-Robinson car, with engines under Bramwell patents. Only four models were offered for 1915 because of worsening financial problems, and Firestone-Columbus production stopped completely in May 1915. BL

FISCHER/BRUNAU
SWITZERLAND 1908-1922

Martin Fischer, born in 1866, invented an electric 'magneta' clock in about 1900 and in 1904 made a tiny single-cylinder go-kart-like car. This became the Turicum, with magneto lighting. In 1908 Fischer formed Fischer Wagen AG in a former tinsmith's premises in Zurich. His car featured a four-cylinder engine and friction drive, as had the Turicum.

In 1909 Fischer expanded into the J. Weidmann factory. Weidmann had been a general engineer who had turned to making Brunau cars and trucks in small numbers between 1905 and 1908. He stayed on to help Fischer and about 90 men were employed. The friction system was replaced by outwardly similar concentric drums which now contained gear teeth meshing with a pinion on the drive shaft, which could be moved laterally as well as forwards and backwards to mesh.

About 180 cars were made until 1913, followed by perhaps 100 more. They were exported in considerable numbers, notably to South America.

Fischer had introduced single-sleeve-valve four-cylinder 16/22hp engines in 1911 and a six-cylinder version in 1914. Delaugère & Clayette acquired a licence to make similar

Fischer four-seat tourer of 1913

FN Herstal of 1901

engines, which were also produced in the United States after successful trials by both Mondex-Magic and Palmer-Singer.

After World War I Fischer developed a friction-drive MAG-engined cyclecar and sold rights to the SIG metalworking firm of Neuhausen, which made a few in 1921. The following year the sleeve-valve engine rights were sold to a German firm and nothing more was heard of them. Fischer's car factory was said to have been taken over, but its fate is uncertain. Martin Fischer died in 1947. NB

FJTA
see Otav

FLANDERS
see EMF

FLINT
see Durant

FN
BELGIUM 1899-1936

The Fabrique National d'Armes de Guerre was founded in Herstal, Belgium, in 1889 by a syndicate of arms manufacturers to fulfil an order for 200,000 Mauser rifles for the Belgian government. Not long afterwards they obtained the Browning machine gun licence. FN soon added bicycles – hence the trade mark of a rifle crossed with a bicycle pedal

crank – and started motorcycle experiments possibly as early as 1894.

J. de Cosmo, an Italian, moved from Delahaye to design the first voiturettes of 1899. Some 280 of these were built in the first two years. Motorcycles entered series production in 1901. For 20 years from 1903 they featured shaft drive and, from 1904, diminutive four-cylinder engines.

Car production was always of secondary interest, especially when de Cosmo left in 1903 to make a few cars under his own name. In 1908 FN made 1700 guns, 400,000 cartridges, 1500 bicycles, 50 motorcycles but only five cars.

In 1909 car production sometimes reached 15 a week, and an assortment of models was offered. From 1906 to 1912 a 6.9-litre FNRS was in fact a Rochet-Schneider built under licence by FN. A true FN was the Type 2000, a four-cylinder 2-litre car typical of the modest types usually produced by the firm.

By 1914 about 3600 cars had been built. That year the factories covered a total of 31 acres (12.5 hectares) and employed 5000 men. As well as armaments, five cars, 100 bicycles and 20 motorcycles were made daily until the Germans overran Herstal and removed most of the machinery. The workforce was also dispersed, some escaping to make munitions in France.

Peacetime vehicle production began slowly and included commercial derivatives of several models. The most popular car was the Type 1300, of which almost 3000 were sold in the five years from 1923. There was also a Type 1250 which was also produced in Germany by Aga. The 1300 grew into the 1400 – the numbers indicating capacity – and 2000 of these were sold. A straight-eight 3252cc model was tried for five years from 1930 but

only 370 were sold, although in 1932 this engine helped boost commercial vehicle sales when installed in a 2½-tonner.

Trolley buses were made from 1933 but growing emphasis was placed on military vehicles, including 4×4s and FN and Minerva engined half-tracks. The motorcycle side was also busy with two- and three-wheelers. The final car models, named Baudouin (2100cc) and Albert (2260cc) after members of the Belgian royal family, achieved fewer than 1800 sales in three seasons and were discontinued in 1936.

After World War II motorcycles were again made until production ended in 1957. More trolley buses were built as well as a few civilian-type lorries and buses which continued to 1965. Military vehicles and weapons accounted for the bulk of production, however. FN also made Rolls-Royce and General Electric jet engines, had a licence to produce the Hawk missile and was involved in the development of Belgium's nuclear power station programme. NB

FNM
BRAZIL 1957 to date

Fabrica Nacional de Motores SA of Rio de Janeiro was established as the Brazilian state car manufacturing company in 1942 and remains the oldest motor manufacturer in Brazil. In 1956 FNM began manufacture of Alfa Romeo commercial vehicles under licence, followed by a Brazilian version of the four-cylinder twin-cam Alfa Romeo 2000 saloon from 1957. The saloon initially had the standard 1975cc engine but later a more powerful 2132cc, 118bhp version was offered as an alternative option.

In October 1968 Alfa Romeo aquired an 85 per cent shareholding in FNM. In April 1967 FNM had shown the first examples of a specially bodied 110mph (177kph) coupé version of the Alfa, known as the Onca. This car used a 131bhp version of the twin-cam engine, with a five-speed gearbox. It looked very similar to the early Ford Mustangs and was named after a variety of South American tiger, but it was extremely expensive and few were sold.

In 1971 the company had 3000 employees and built 1650 cars, almost all the basic 2150 Alfa saloon. In 1973, following Alfa's own reorganization, 51 per cent of FNM stock was owned by Alfa, 6 per cent by the Federal Union and others, and 43 per cent by Fiat. By 1977 the Alfa Romeo shareholding had fallen to only 6 per cent, the Brazilian government owned a minority 2.5 per cent and Fiat, through Fiat Automoveis SA of Betim, the Brazilian Fiat company, owned the rest. Fiat took over production in 1978, since when all FNM cars have been sold simply as Alfa Romeos, the 1987 model being a four-door 2.3-litre saloon known as the Fiat Alfa Romeo Ti-4. BL

FONDU
BELGIUM 1906-1912

The Usines Fondu engineering company was set up by Jean-Baptiste Fondu in Vilvorde on the outskirts of Brussels and originally supplied materials and equipment to the national railway company. In 1896 Charles Fondu took over the company from his father and in the early 1900s began to plan a Fondu car.

Automobiles Charles Fondu, also of Vilvorde, produced its first car, the four-cylinder 20/24hp Type 1 CHF, in 1906. It was designed by a 23-year-old Swiss engineer, Julien Potterat, who became a director of the company's car division. The large, well-built Fondu was soon seen in competition, with the 1907 24/30hp and 50hp six-cylinder models. Fondus took first, second and fourth places in the Ostend races of 1907 and a Fondu won the Boulogne speed trial.

In 1908 Fondu granted a licence for the 24/30 model to the Riga steelworks of Russko Baltiskij Vagonnij Zavod, which had affinities with Fondu as a railway constructor. Potterat went to supervise work at Riga in the autumn of 1908 and the first Fondu-based 24/30hp Russo-Baltique car appeared in May 1909. It was produced until 1915 alongside other models built under licence from Rex-Simplex of Germany.

Charles Fondu died in 1912, when his company was also offering smaller four-cylinder cars of 1131, 1690 and 2120cc. For some time Fondu had supplied engines to other carmakers and after 1912 the company did only that, building no more complete cars but supplying proprietary engines at the rate of about 50 a month.

A Fondu engine and gearbox assembly was shown at the Agricultural Hall Show in London in November 1910 priced at £84, and in 1911 three Fondu engine types were offered by the British agents TB André and Co of London. The engines were available throughout the 1920s and 1930s. BL

FORD
AUSTRALIA 1925 to date

Fords arrived in Australia in 1908, the year of the introduction of the Model T. Being part of the British Empire, Australia came within the selling territory of Ford of Canada. All Australian-sold Fords were Canadian-made until the local plant started up in 1925. The business was under the direction of H. C. French, an American-born Ford of Canada executive, who took a team of 16 Canadians with him to Australia.

Assembly began in an old wool-store in Geelong, Victoria, while the 100-acre (40-hectare) site at Geelong Harbour was being prepared. The original payroll was just 100 men. Engines were assembled from Can-

Australian Ford V8, Falcon and Fairlane

adian-made components, and chassis shipped direct, but bodies were locally built by the Ford Manufacturing Co of Australia.

Assembly and sales came under a separate company, Ford Motor Co of Australia Pty Ltd, which set up assembly plants in Granville (Sydney), Brisbane, Adelaide and Freemantle. All these plants were located on the coast, so that bodies could be shipped from Geelong while chassis came direct from Canada.

The beginning of Australian assembly coincided with a drop in the Model T's popularity: only 12,251 were sold in 1925-26 compared with the 22,951 Fords imported in 1922-23. In 1927 Ford lagged way behind General Motors in sales, with only 9.6 per cent of new registrations compared with General Motors' 35.1 per cent. The arrival of the Model A helped matters a bit and sales went up to over 16,000. Thereafter they dropped alarmingly with the coming of the Depression, and 1932 saw a record low of only 2590 sales, despite the arrival of the V8, which Australians would have loved to own if only they could have afforded it.

In 1930 Ford reverted to wooden-frame coach construction for closed cars in place of steel, which had been used since 1925. In 1935, however, all-steel construction was reintroduced. By this time Ford was making bodies for the small 10hp English Ford as well as for the V8.

Up to 1934 the Australian Ford line had been identical to the Canadian, apart from the frame construction, but in that year the company brought out a model which was to become typically Australian and would later be made by firms other than Ford. This was the coupé utility, familiarly called the 'ute', a closed coupé with comfortable seating for two ahead of a useful pick-up body of about

¾-ton load capacity.

The Tudor sedans of the late 1930s had a greater slope to the roof than their Canadian or American equivalents, but otherwise Australian Fords were identical, although the range of bodies available was smaller. Sales picked up from 1934, from 7477 that year to a peak of 14,584 in 1938. For 1939 the Mercury was added to the range.

In 1942 only 15 passenger cars were made for the civilian market as Ford Australia turned to war work. This included the manufacture of 35,146 trucks, mostly 4×4s of the Canadian Military Pattern, and also 4×4 and 6×6 armoured vehicles, mines, fuel tanks for aircraft and ammunition.

After the war the proportion of Australian-made components rose to 54 per cent of the cars and 48 per cent of trucks by 1950, the year in which H. C. French retired. His successor, C. A. Smith, authorized a massive expansion of the Geelong plant to include the manufacture of such formerly imported components as engines, gearboxes and rear axles. When his plans were completed the Australian content reached 93 per cent.

British Fords were made as well as Canadian, but these were assembled rather than manufactured, even the body panels of the Anglia and Prefect being imported. Trucks of both British and Canadian design were assembled in Australia from 1946. The cars followed the pattern of those of their mother countries, and it was not until 1972 that distinctly Australian models appeared.

In 1957 Ford spent $A28 million in extending the production line at Geelong, and in 1960 put up a new plant at Broadmeadows, Victoria, at a cost of $A27 million, for the building of the newly introduced Falcon. This American compact was directly aimed at the Holden, which had consistently outsold Ford in Australia. The Falcon was available with 90bhp six-cylinder engine, or a V8 option from 1966. It was the most successful Australian Ford yet. The English Zephyr was dropped in 1964 as being too close in size to the Falcon; but the Cortina was assembled in Australia, as was the Escort from 1974.

Styling that marked out the Falcon and Fairlane from their American counterparts was evident in 1972 and has been continued since with the Fairmont, Fairlane and LTD series of V8s. The 1979 XD-series Falcons and Fairmonts resembled European Granadas. They were made with six- and eight-cylinder engines until 1982, but the V8s were dropped for 1983 when the largest Australian Ford engine was a 4072cc six, in 133 or 150bhp versions.

The line-up started with the Escort-like Laser which was based on the Mazda 323 (1296 and 1480cc), followed by the 1490cc Meteor with in-line engine and front drive, the Mazda Capella-based Telstar, and Falcon, Fairmont and LTD, with rear drive and 3272 or 4072cc six-cylinder engines.

Ford overtook Holden to become the best-selling Australian car in 1982. In 1984 Ford held 23.9 per cent of the market compared with Holden's 18.07 per cent. The company currently runs two factories, Geelong and Broadmeadows, with assembly plants in Brisbane and Sydney. In 1985 more than 12,000 employees made 144,405 cars. GNG

FORD
BRAZIL 1967 to date

Ford's Brazilian company, Ford Brasil SA, was formed in 1919 and by 1930 had assembly plants at Rio de Janeiro and Sao Paulo. Cars of American design were assembled until the mid-1960s, with no particular local characteristics.

In 1967 Ford Brasil merged with Willys Overland do Brasil SA, which was making not only Jeeps and the Willys Aero 2600 sedan, but Renault Dauphines and the Alpine-based Interlagos sports car. All these were taken over by the new company and made for a while alongside the Ford Galaxie, but the Renaults were replaced in 1969 by a new four-cylinder car, the Corcel. This was styled by Ford's Roberto Aranjo and used Ford engines of 1289 or 1400cc, with front-wheel drive and coil and wishbone suspension.

The Willys 2600 was dropped in 1972, to be replaced by a Brazilian-built Ford Maverick, powered by a Willys Six or Ford V8 engine. This, together with the Jeeps and Corcels, was made until 1979, latterly with a 2.3-litre single-overhead cam four-cylinder engine. The Maverick was dropped in 1979, a year after its American cousin.

Subsequent production was devoted to the 1372cc Corcel II in two-door saloon or station wagon models, the 1555cc Del Rey two- or four-door hatchback saloon, the American-based Landau V8, several models of Escort,

and the simple Jeep CJ5. With the exception of the V8 these were still made in 1987. As with most current Brazilian made cars, all these models are available with engines adapted to burn alcohol fuel. In 1985 Ford do Brasil turned out a total of 164,563 cars and trucks. GNG

FORD
CANADA 1904 to date

The Ford Motor Co of Canada Ltd was formed in August 1904 by Gordon M. McGregor of the Walkerville Wagon Co, with Detroit banker John Gray as president and Henry Ford as vice-president. In 1906 Ford stepped up to the presidency and remained there until 1927 when he was succeeded by his son Edsel. Total capital of the company was $125,000, of which $55,000 was raised in Canada.

The first car which emerged from the Walkerville Wagon works in October 1904 was a two-cylinder Model C. The first year's production was 117 cars, of which seven were four-cylinder Model Bs, and the balance Model Cs. In the first four years of business, Ford of Canada grew only slowly, with 667 cars delivered to the middle of 1908. During this period, cars were assembled from US components rather than manufactured, although bodies were bought from William Gray and Sons of Chatham, Ontario, which later made the Gray-Dort car.

The arrival of the Model T boosted production to 486 cars in 1908-9, and 1280 in 1909-10. In 1911 capital stock was increased to $1 million and a new 55-acre (22-hectare) factory was built. Annual production then rose to 11,600 in 1912-13 and 15,675 in 1913-14. By 1927 a total of 757,888 Canadian Model Ts had been made. Generally they followed American designs, although Canada introduced the one-man top and swing-out two-piece windscreen in 1920, three years before Detroit.

An interesting sideline was the Ford boat, built from 1922 in co-operation with the Gidley Boat Co of Penetang, Ontario. This not

only used a Model T engine, but had the windscreens, sidescreens and hood from the Ford car.

The original agreement gave Ford of Canada sales rights in all countries of the British Empire, but Henry Ford took away the concession for Britain in 1907 and four years later set up a British Ford factory at Manchester. Ford of Canada set up branch assembly plants in South Africa and Australia, and distribution branches in Singapore, Malaya and Bombay.

In December 1927 Ford of Canada began production of the Model A, one month later than Detroit. The millionth Canadian Ford was a Model A sedan delivered in 1931. Like its parent, Ford of Canada launched the V8 in 1932 and the Mercury in 1938, but it never built Lincolns or Lincoln-Zephyrs.

During the 1930s an $11 million building programme was started, to enlarge both the Walkerville plant and a machine shop at Windsor which had been built after World War I. These expanded facilities enabled Ford of Canada to make a major contribution to the war effort from 1939 to 1945, particularly with production of the family of Canadian Military Pattern trucks. These 4×2 and 4×4 vehicles had distinctive angular cabs and were also made by Chevrolet.

Post-war Canadian Fords carried their own brand names and some differed in trim from their US counterparts. The Meteor was a 1949 Ford with a Mercury grille, and there was also the Monarch (1946-61), a slightly restyled Mercury, and the Frontenac (1960) based on the Ford Falcon. In 1962 the name Meteor Montcalm was used for a Canadian styled Mercury, and this name was continued until 1979. There was also the Meteor Niagara (1954-59 Ford Custom), Meteor Rideau (1954-59 Ford Fairlane) and Rideau Victoria (1955-56 Ford Victoria). Familiar Fords made in Canada under their own names included the Mustang, Maverick and Pinto.

In 1953 all Canadian Ford production was transferred to a new plant at Oakville, Ontario, and in 1968 another plant for compacts was opened at St Thomas. The current range is similar to that made in US factories. GNG

Canadian Ford Model A of 1929, with Australian body

FORD
FRANCE 1916-1954

The first French Ford agency was established in 1907, but sales were not particularly encouraging in the years up to 1914, because tariffs made the Model T more expensive than it was in Britain or the United States. In 1913 only 676 Fords were sold in France, compared with more than 5000 in Britain. Local assembly was the only way around the tariff problem and this began at Bordeaux in 1916. Automobiles Ford was in fact set up by Sir Percival Perry of the British company and the shares were held by nine Englishmen. In 1925 operations were transferred to Asnières, near Paris. As in other countries, the Model T was succeeded by the Model A during 1927.

An interesting sideline to French Ford production was the series of Montier Specials, tuned and lowered Model Ts and As which Paris distributor Charles Montier sold under his own name between 1923 and 1932. These never received the blessing of Automobiles Ford, but were tolerated until 1934, when new management cancelled Montier's agency.

In 1930 the USA introduced tariffs against imported goods, which brought corresponding retaliation from many European countries. France was among them, but Maurice Dollfuss, head of Automobiles Ford, gained breathing space by ordering a shipment of nine months' supply of cars and components before the law came into effect. The episode underlined the need for greater local control over the company's affairs.

Assembly of the Model Y began at Asnières in 1932 but the car never sold as well in France as in Britain or Germany, only 2839 finding buyers in 1932 and 1933. The V8 was imported from the US and cost the equivalent of $1484, compared with $550 in its native country.

In order to obtain manufacturing capacity, Dollfuss proposed a merger with the old-established Mathis company of Strasbourg. In September 1934 a new company was set up in which Ford held 60 per cent of the shares and Mathis held the balance. SA Française Matford rented the factories of Mathis at Strasbourg and Ford at Asnières. At first Mathis continued to make its own cars alongside Matfords at Strasbourg – there was a short-lived hybrid called the 'Quadriflex' with Ford V8 engine in an all-independent suspension Mathis chassis – but by 1936 only Matfords were being made.

The first Matfords barely differed from their American cousins, but in 1937 came the Series 72 and 76 with saloon bodies very like those of the small British V8. These bodies were made by Chausson and were available with either the 2.2-litre or 3.6-litre V8 engines. Saloons and cabriolets were available, also a hatchback 'commerciale' for commercial travellers, and from 1938 an estate car. Production rose from 1049 in 1935 to 8898 in 1938, but dropped to 4294 in 1939 as Matford devoted more of its resources to making trucks for the French Army.

The threat of war led the government to urge Dollfuss to find a factory further from the German frontier than Strasbourg. He decided to build from scratch, on a 60-acre (24-hectare) site at Poissy, on the Seine about 15 miles (24km) from Paris. The factory opened in 1939. With finance from the government and encouragement from Edsel Ford, Dollfuss also set up a new company called Fordair, with a factory at Bordeaux, to make aero engines. Mathis was bought out in 1938, and on the eve of war Dollfuss formed a new company, Ford SAF.

Like most other French car factories, the Poissy plant was in German occupied France from 1940 to 1944 and its production was devoted to the German war effort. Its output consisted mostly of 5- to 6-ton trucks, although 148 cars were made from 1940 to 1942. Despite regular visits from RAF bombers, Poissy recovered quickly after the war and delivered 900 units, cars and trucks, by January 1946.

The post-war Model F-472 was very similar in appearance to the pre-war small V8 and was offered only with the 2.2-litre engine. No open cars were catalogued, although some cabriolets were made for Ford by coachbuilders such as Antem and Guilloré. The F-472 was made until the autumn of 1948, when it was replaced by the Vedette, with coil and wishbone independent front suspension, hydraulic brakes and a completely new body similar to that of the 1949 Mercury.

This was no coincidence, for in 1945 Dollfuss had seen and liked the proposed small American Ford, and when Dearborn decided against making it in America, the whole project fell conveniently into Dollfuss' lap. The only unchanged part of the Vedette was the engine, which was continued without major change until the end of Ford SAF in 1954. A 3.9-litre V8 was offered in the larger Vendôme saloon of 1953-54. There were also some attractive coupés, bodied by Facel Métallon, with 2.2-litre (Comète) and 3.9-litre (Monte Carlo) engines.

None of these Fords sold as well as the management at Poissy or Dearborn had hoped, because the bulk of the French market lay in smaller cars of the Citroën 11CV/ Peugeot 203 size; anything over 15CV, as the Vendôme and Monte Carlo were, suffered a crippling tax surcharge.

Dollfuss retired in 1949, to be succeeded by François Lehideaux (Louis Renault's nephew) and then by an American, Jack Reith, who took the company into profit. A new small car seemed to be the only long term answer, however, and the cost of developing this was estimated at $50-100 million. Dearborn instructed Reith to find a buyer for Ford SAF, and in 1954 the company was acquired by Simca. Ford of America retained 15.2 per cent of the equity, but even this was sold off in 1958.

Just before the sale, Ford had brought out a new Vedette with updated styling, unitary construction, and the McPherson strut independent front suspension already employed on British and German Fords. This was continued as the Simca Vedette until 1962, production being stepped up from 150 to 200 units a day.

No more Fords were manufactured in France until 1975 when another Bordeaux factory was opened to make transaxles for the Fiesta and automatic transmissions for all the European Fords. Another French Ford enterprise lies in the field of construction equipment. This dates from 1972 when Ford purchased the old-established Paulin Richier of Charleville in the Ardennes. The range now includes wheeled and tracked excavators, shovel loaders and ancillary equipment of all kinds. GNG

FORD
GERMANY 1926 to date

Compared to other European countries, Germany proved to be stony ground for Ford at first. As the *Ford Times* commented rather sourly in 1912, 'The use of home products is regarded as a duty almost amounting to a religion.' Nevertheless, a parts depot was set up in Hamburg in 1912, and the Ford Motor Co AG was incorporated with capital of 5 million marks on 5 January 1925 with an assembly plant at Plotzensee, Berlin.

Ford Model T of 1912

Assembly of Model TT trucks began in April 1925, and of cars in June 1926. A total of 3771 cars were made until August 1927. The Model A took over in August 1928. As in Britain this was made in 3.3- and 2-litre (A or AF) forms. It was followed in 1932 by the B and BF four-cylinder models, and by the 3.6-litre V8. The last named was imported from 1932 to 1935, then became German-made.

In 1929 Ford was offered a 52-acre (21-hectare) site at Cologne by the Mayor, Konrad Adenauer, and the factory there went into production in May 1931. Unlike Berlin, it was a proper manufacturing plant with a growing proportion of German-made components being employed in the cars. This was vital because the Nazis, who came to power in 1933, insisted that no foreign materials be used in German-made cars. By 1937 the four-cylinder Eifel was totally German-made. The Berlin plant was closed in April 1931, after a total of 44,209 cars and trucks had been assembled there in seven years.

In 1933 the 933cc four-cylinder Model Y, known in Germany as the Köln (Cologne), went into production. The two-door saloon was almost identical to the British Model Y; although there were no German-built four-door models, convertibles were catalogued, made by Deutsch, which produced open conversions of German Fords until 1971. It is probable that there was some interchange of body pressings and engine components between Dagenham and Cologne during the mid-1930s.

A total of 11,121 Kölns were made until 1936, by which time they had been joined by the 1172cc Eifel, initially very similar to the Model C from Dagenham, although from 1937 it acquired more individual lines. Stoewer of Stettin made 200 roadster bodies for the Eifel, but a plan by Ford to buy Stoewer in order to gain extra manufacturing capacity was soon dropped. Ford returned to Berlin with a new assembly plant, but this was used only for making military equipment.

The Eifel was the most successful pre-war German Ford, selling 61,594 units until 1940. Together with the V8 it took Ford into fourth place in the sales league in 1937 behind Opel, Adler and Mercedes-Benz. In the commercial vehicle sales league Ford was in second position.

More than 15,000 V8s were made in the 1930s, most of them the 'full size' 3.6-litre versions, although the small 2.2-litre was also available. About 150 V8s were made under licence in Austria by Gräf & Stift, as the Gräfford; in Hungary, Eifels and V8s were made by Mavag in Budapest. There was also an assembly plant in Romania which built about 2500 cars annually between 1936 and 1940.

The last pre-war German Ford was the Taunus, which retained the Eifel's 1172cc engine but had a new streamlined body on the lines of the 1939 American Ford V8, and hydraulic brakes, which no British Ford would achieve until the 1951 season. Only 7100 Taunus were made until 1941 but they were revived after the war, when a further 62,828 were built.

Car production continued into the first four years of the war, with 41 Taunus being made in 1942. Ford also made 1961 4×4 heavy personnel cars, of Horch design but with Ford V8 engines, and more than 25,000 3-ton trucks. About 1000 of these trucks were made in half-track form, not only at Cologne but in Ford plants in Holland and France as well.

The Cologne factory did not suffer as much war damage as many other German plants and was able to resume production of trucks in May 1945. In 1948 Henry Ford II visited Cologne and discussed plans to buy Volkswagen, but little progress could be made because of the complexity of the ownership of the Volkswagen company.

The pre-war Taunus was back in production by 1948, but in 1952 it was replaced by a new model, the Taunus 12M, an integral construction two-door saloon with McPherson strut independent front suspension and the same 1172cc engine, which was given overhead valves in 1955. The success of this model enabled Ford to beat its prewar sales record for the first time in 1952 when 40,344 vehicles were delivered, including trucks.

The energetic Ehrhart Vitger, who had been put in charge of Ford in 1946, built up the dealer network so that the 236 dealers lost to East Germany were all but replaced by others in the Federal Republic by 1951. Between 1950 and 1960 Ford of Germany multiplied its production eight fold. It overtook

Ford of Canada in 1958 and built twice as many cars as the Canadian company in 1962.

The Taunus was gradually developed during this period. A four-door saloon was available for the first time in 1955, and engine capacity increased to 1½ litres in 1955 and 1.7 litres in 1957.

In 1958 an American, John Andrews, became general manager of Ford of Germany, and this marked a reversal of the pre-war American policy that overseas operations should be managed by local staff. By 1962 eight of the 12 Ford European branches would have American managers.

In 1962 came a brand new Taunus. Also called the 12M, it had a V4 engine driving the front wheels, and had started life as a subcompact, called the Cardinal, which was built in Ford's Louisville, Kentucky, plant. This was the first of a family of vee-engined cars. The 1½-litre and 1.7-litre rear-wheel-drive Taunus 17M were introduced in 1964, followed by the Taunus 20M 2-litre V6.

During the 1950s Ford of Germany had made some medium-sized trucks with capacities up to 4 tons, but these were discontinued in 1961 so that the Cologne factory could concentrate on lighter commercials. The best known of these was the Transit, introduced in 1965 and still going strong. The Transit was the first Ford vehicle to be made in Britain and Germany in similar form, the next 'international Ford' being the Escort car, launched in January 1968. The Escort was produced under the control of a new company, Ford of Europe, headed by John

Ford Köln of 1932

Ford Escort 1.6i cabriolet of 1983

Ford Taunus 15M of c.1955

Ford Sierra XR4i of c.1983

Andrews, and was followed by the equally international Capri coupé.

It was only a matter of time before the ranges of the two countries were almost completely integrated, with the British Cortina Mark III and German Taunus sharing the same body and engine options (1971) and the British Granada and German Consul being similarly integrated. In 1976 the Consul name was dropped, and all Granadas were made in Germany. The Fiesta, introduced in 1976, is even more of an international car, with examples being assembled in Spain and Germany from components made in these countries and also in Britain and Belgium.

In order to reach the potential market offered by the EEC, Ford of Germany opened a new factory in Belgium in 1964. Located at Genk on the Albert Canal, it was to become the biggest Ford plant in the world, with a site of 440 acres (178 hectares). This was followed by a second plant in Germany, at Saarlouis near the Franco-German border. It opened in 1968, making body stampings, and the first complete car, an Escort, left the production lines in January 1970. During the 1970s Saarlouis was responsible for the bulk of Capri production, taking over entirely after the last British Capri was made in 1977.

Today Ford has five plants in Germany, in Cologne which has multiple manufacturing facilities and is responsible for final assembly of the Capri, Scorpio (new model of Granada) and Fiesta; in Saarlouis (Escorts and body panels for other models); Wülfrath (transmissions, steering and suspension components); Berlin (plastic components); and Duren (axles for the Escort, Taunus, Capri, Scorpio and Transit). A design centre at Merkenich, near Cologne, concentrates on body and chassis design, while engine design is carried out at Dunton in England. The main proving ground for European Fords is at Lommel in Belgium. In 1985 Ford's German and Belgian plants produced 734,711 cars. Models offered for 1987 are the Fiesta, Escort, Orion, Sierra, Scorpio and Capri. GNG

FORD
GB 1911 to date

The first Ford to be sold in England was shipped over in 1903. Various companies held the Ford agency until 1911, when assembly of the Model T began in a former tramcar factory on the Trafford Park Industrial Estate, Manchester. The choice of Trafford Park was made by the most energetic British agent, Percival Perry, who was to become head of the Ford Motor Co Ltd and a baron in future years. The great advantage of the site was that crated Model Ts could come direct from the United States up the Manchester Ship Canal.

The Ford Motor Co (England) Ltd was formed in March 1911, Henry Ford personally owning 117 of the 200 shares. By 1914 Ford had 1000 British agents and Trafford Park 184

Ford Model T four-seat tourer of 1913

turned out 7310 cars. This was almost 29 per cent of total British car production and made Ford the largest car-makers in Europe.

In 1916 Perry formed a new French company, Automobiles Ford, with headquarters at Bordeaux. The following year, encouraged by Prime Minister Lloyd George, he purchased a 136-acre (55-hectare) site at Cork in Ireland and put up a factory for the manufacture of the newly introduced Fordson tractor. This concentrated on tractor production until 1921 and then on making Model T components for assembly at Trafford Park. Cork was used for assembly of many different Fords until its closure in July 1984.

Sir Percival Perry, knighted for his war services, resigned in 1919, partly for health reasons, although he returned to Ford nine years later. His place was taken by an American, Warren G. Anderson, who stayed less than a year, and he was followed by a succession of managers while Ford's policy for Europe was being hammered out.

British sales were disappointing and fell to second place behind Morris in 1922 for the first time since British operations began, yet Ford saw England as supplier to the entire European market and envisaged building the Detroit of Europe, a smaller River Rouge. The site for this was chosen by Ernest C. Kanzler, Edsel Ford's brother-in-law, in an area of unpromising marshland at Dagenham in Essex.

The site of 300 acres (120 hectares) was purchased in 1924 but building did not begin until May 1929. Ford used only 71 acres (28 hectares) for its own factories, the rest being let out as an industrial estate. One of the first firms to rent space was Briggs Manufacturing Co, the bodybuilders that had supplied Ford in Detroit with coachwork. A labour force was provided by the London County Council, which built housing for 25,000 families.

Two important events of 1928 were the resumption of tractor manufacture at Cork and the return of Sir Percival Perry at the

personal invitation of Henry Ford. The first specifically European Ford appeared in the form of the Cork-built Model AF, a Model A with smaller (2-litre) engine of 14.9hp which was fitted to the majority of the 14,516 Model As delivered between 1928 and 1931. Trafford Park was closed in 1932 after production of 250,000 Model Ts and 14,000 Model As. Dagenham turned out its first vehicle on 1 October 1931 – a Model AA 1½-ton truck.

The car which really set the Ford Motor Co Ltd on the road to success was the 8hp Model Y, announced in February 1932 and in production by July. It had an 833cc four-cylinder side-valve engine and was priced initially at £120 for a Tudor (two-door) saloon. This was cheaper than the equivalent Morris or Austin, yet in 1935 Perry managed to cut the Tudor price to £100 – the first time a four-seater saloon had been marketed in Britain for this figure. This car helped Ford's share of the 8hp-and-under market to rise from 22 per cent in 1935 to 41 per cent in 1936.

The original Model Y had boxy lines, but was redesigned by E. T. Gregorie of the Dearborn design staff, its curved radiator being adopted for the 1933 and 1934 American Fords as well. Although Britons tend to think of the Y as a British car, it was made in considerable numbers in Ireland, France, Spain, Germany and New Zealand. A total of 157,688 had been made in Britain when it was replaced by the Eight in 1937.

Up to 1935 all V8s sold in Britain were imported from Canada, but production then began at Dagenham, both of the standard 3.6-litre and the small 2.2-litre engines. From 1937 to 1939 the latter was offered in a car peculiar to the British market, the 22hp V8 with four-light saloon body similar to that used for the French Matford.

New four-cylinder models of this period included the 1172cc Model C of 1934-37 (96,533 built), the Ten De Luxe of 1937-38 (41,665 built) and the Prefect, launched in

October 1938 and made, with wartime interruption, until 1953 (379,339 built). The 933cc Model Y became the Eight in 1937 and the Anglia in 1940.

Dagenham also made tractors, vans on the car chassis and a range of V8 powered forward control trucks, quite different from their American counterparts. These, like the tractors, were known as Fordsons.

Dagenham made a very important contribution to the war effort, building 4×2 and 4×4 trucks from 15cwt (762kg) to 3 tons capacity, fire engines and tracked Bren Gun Carriers. They also made 262,000 V8 engines which were used to power personnel landing craft and fast launches, the latter using two or three engines.

Ford of Dagenham was quick to get civilian cars into production again after World War II. The first Anglia came off the lines in May 1945, and the Prefect a month later. By the end of the year 2324 cars and 26,266 commercial vehicles had been built. In 1947 a total of

the Pilot saloon (1947-50), but the first all new post-war Fords were the 1½-litre four-cylinder Consul and 2¼-litre six-cylinder Zephyr introduced for 1951. They had all-enveloping integral construction, McPherson-strut independent front suspension and brand new oversquare engines. They were followed by Mark II versions in 1956 and Mark IIIs in 1962. The line was continued until 1966, when they were replaced by the Zephyr Mark IV with V4 and V6 engines.

The small four-cylinder Anglia and Prefect gained Consul-style unitary bodies and McPherson strut suspension in 1954, but the old pre-war styled Anglia was continued under the name Popular until 1959. When the Anglia gained a new body and 997cc overhead-valve engine, the 1954-styled Anglia with side-valve engine was given the name Popular and another three years of life.

Ford expanded greatly in the 1950s, opening a product engineering division at Rainham, Essex, and a new commercial vehi-

troduction in January 1968 of the Escort, a conventional rear-drive saloon offered initially with 1100 or 1300cc engines, and made at Halewood, Genk in Belgium and Saarlouis in Germany. The first European Ford vehicle had been the Transit van, launched in 1965.

The Escort was the first fruit of a new company, Ford of Europe, which was founded in 1967 under the direction of Ford of Germany's head, John Andrews. The next international car was the Capri, a 2+2 coupé which could be thought of as a European Mustang. At first available with 1300 or 1600cc engines, later versions were much more powerful, with 2000, 2600 and 3000cc engines giving up to 175bhp. The Capri was made at Dagenham and Saarlouis.

Meanwhile there were two distinct medium-sized family cars, the rear-wheel-drive Dagenham-made Cortina and the front-wheel-drive Cologne-made Taunus. In 1971 came the Cortina Mark III and the new Taunus, now with rear-drive and sharing the

Ford Anglia of c.1950

Ford Cortina Mark I GT of 1964

Ford Escort Mark I of 1968

Ford Fiesta Popular Plus of 1982

114,812 vehicles were made including tractors, and in 1954 the total had climbed to 297,768, three times the 1939 figure.

Lord Perry, as he had become, retired as chairman in 1948 and was succeeded by Sir Patrick Hennessy, who had started in the Cork factory in the 1920s. Henry Ford II took a keen interest in his European operations, and at his suggestion Ford of Britain pulled out of its pre-war role as continental overlord. The shares in the European companies were bought by Ford America and the proceeds used for expansion at Dagenham.

The V8 was briefly revived in the shape of

cle plant at Langley, Buckinghamshire. It also bought Briggs Car Bodies and in 1963 completed a factory at Halewood, near Liverpool, with a capacity of 200,000 vehicles a year. In 1961 Ford of Britain became a wholly-owned subsidiary of the American parent company, which paid a $368 million purchase price. This was part of a general policy whereby Dearborn pushed towards total ownership of the European subsidiaries.

Despite the fact that they were producing cars for much the same markets, none of the parts for British or German Fords were interchangeable. This was to change with the in-

Cortina's engine options. These were very similar in design. A fastback coupé was also produced for the German market.

In motor sport, Ford of Europe played a bigger part than any other firm from the mid-1960s. The 3-litre V8 DFV engine developed by Cosworth Engineering has been the most successful Grand Prix engine ever, with 154 Grand Prix victories since Jim Clark's win in the 1967 Dutch Grand Prix. The engine has been used by most major names in the sport, including Lotus, Brabham, Matra, McLaren, Tyrrell, Hesketh, March and Williams.

At a lower level of racing, Formula Ford has

185

provided an excellent training ground for future Grand Prix stars, as well as giving relatively cheap sport to countless other drivers. The Lotus-Cortina of 1963 to 1970 was the first of the high performance versions of family saloons which are so familiar today, and was followed by the phenomenally successful Escort Twin Cam and RS1800 as well as competition versions of the Capri. There was also the GT40 programme referred to in the entry on American Ford.

The most important Ford of the 1970s was the front-drive Fiesta, a family saloon a size down from the Escort, and a competitor in the 'super mini' class, dominated by the Renault 5, Volkswagen Golf and Fiat 127. In order to be close to the southern European market, and to find an area of plentiful labour, Ford acquired land in Spain, near Valencia, and erected two factories for bodies and for engines. The transaxles were to be made at a new factory at Bordeaux, cylinder blocks, radiators and carburettors at Dagenham, and bodies and final assembly divided between Valencia and Saarlouis.

The Fiesta, in 950 and 1100cc versions, was launched in September 1976 and the 500,000th car was delivered a year later. The basic models were later joined by 1300 and 1600 XR-2 high performance versions.

In 1980 came the front-drive Escorts with all-round independent suspension, and in 1982 the Cortina-replacement Sierras. These were both international cars with vast development programmes behind them; the Escort cost £500 million and the Sierra £600 million, of which £100 million went on modernization of the Dagenham body plant. Both cars are built in Britain, Belgium and Germany. Like the Fiesta, they have high performance versions, the RS Turbo (Escort) and RS Cosworth (Sierra). Two older models formerly made in Britain, the Capri coupé and Granada luxury saloon, are now made only in Germany but are sold on the UK market.

Car production at Dagenham and Halewood in 1984 was 273,767. That year, Ford sold more than 475,000 cars in Britain. Despite a record turnover of £3752 million, Ford of Britain suffered an operating loss of £14 million; this was turned into an overall profit of £37 million thanks to interest payments on loans to the parent company in the USA. Ford was the UK market leader in cars, commercial vehicles and tractors for the eighth year running.

Ford has eight main plants in Britain, at Dagenham (foundry and general manufacturing facilities); Basildon, Essex (tractors, engine parts, radiators, suspensions); Halewood (Escorts, body panels, transmissions); Southampton (Transits); Swansea (rear axles for car and commercial vehicles, heavy truck gearboxes); Bridgend (Escort engines); Langley (A Series and Cargo trucks); and Belfast (carburettors). The European engine design centre is at Dunton, Essex, and administrative headquarters for Ford of Europe are at Warley, Essex. GNG

The first Ford factory, with three cars built there

FORD
USA 1903 to date

Born in Springfield, Michigan, on 30 July 1863, Henry Ford grew up as a farm boy who didn't like farming. Out of his preference for mechanical things grew one of the largest industrial empires in the world, and the car which brought motoring for the first time to the mass market. At the age of 16 he moved to Detroit where he had a number of engineering jobs; by the time he built his first car, in 1896, he was chief engineer at the Edison Illuminating Co, forming a friendship with Thomas Alva Edison that was to last until Edison's death in 1931.

Ford's first car had a two-cylinder horizontal engine and many bicycle components, including the seat and wheels, although these were later replaced. After he had worked on it until it could be improved no further, he sold it, and the $200 he received went towards his second car, completed probably in early 1898.

A demonstration run on this car persuaded a wealthy Detroiter, Thomas H. Murphy, to back Ford in starting a company, and in July 1899 the Detroit Automobile Co was formed. Ford resigned from Edison and threw himself into his new work. He was a small stockholder in the company, although he did not invest any money.

The Detroit Automobile Co was less than a success. Only one vehicle, a 1200lb (545kg) delivery van, was made and it performed so badly that it could not be sold. Most of the investors withdrew their backing, and the company was wound up in January 1901.

Some backers, including Thomas Murphy, continued to have faith in Ford, but their enthusiasm waned when he decided to build

The first Ford (Henry Ford driving), 1896

racing cars. Although these were successful there was a fundamental conflict between the backers and Ford, who was more interested in the publicity that would accrue from racing than in getting down to producing saleable cars.

A new firm, the Henry Ford Co, was formed in November 1901, but Ford himself left four months later. Murphy and his fellow directors agreed to drop the name Ford from their company title. They acquired the services of the celebrated engineer Henry M. Leland who brought with him a new design of engine, and in August 1902 the company was reorganized under the name Cadillac Automobile Co.

Meanwhile Ford built two enormous and crude racing cars, the 999 and Arrow, with four-cylinder engines of 18.9 litres capacity which took a number of records, including a mile at 91.37mph (147kph) on frozen Lake St Clair in January 1904, with Henry Ford at the tiller. Ford also turned again to the idea of producing cars for sale, encouraged by a prosperous coal merchant, Alexander Malcolmson. In October 1902 they formed the

Ford and Malcolmson Co, which was reorganized with additional capital in June 1903 as the Ford Motor Co.

The first production Ford car, appropriately called the Model A, had an 8hp horizontally opposed two-cylinder engine, two-speed epicyclic transmission and single-chain final drive. It was available as a two-seater runabout at $750 or a four-seater rear entrance tonneau at $850. The small factory at Mack Avenue, Detroit, was mainly an assembly plant, for all components were bought-in: chassis and running gear came from the Dodge brothers, who would later be famous car makers themselves, bodies from the C. R. Wilson Carriage Co, tyres and wheels from other suppliers. The first customer placed his order on 15 July 1903, and 1708 Model As were sold between then and October 1904.

Two new models were announced in 1904: the Model C, which was essentially an A with a frontal bonnet even though the engine was still under the seat, and the Model B, which was a much larger car with a 5.2-litre four-cylinder engine and shaft drive. This was

new factory was needed little over two years after the move to Piquette Avenue. This time Ford moved outside the city, buying a 57-acre (23-hectare) plot of land at Highland Park. Work began on the new factory in April 1907 and production started there in January 1910. The Piquette Avenue plant was sold to Studebaker the following year.

The formation of the short-lived Ford Manufacturing Co in 1905 signalled the move away from dependence on outside suppliers, and soon Ford was making all its own engines, chassis and bodies. Tyres were still bought in, from Firestone, whose chief, Harvey S. Firestone, became one of Henry Ford's closest friends and, with Thomas Edison, travelling companion on the famous Ford camping trips. In 1906 Ford jumped from fourth place in the American production league to first, which the company held for the next 21 years.

In 1907 Ford made 14,887 cars, the next largest manufacturer being Buick with 4641; these were the Models N, R and S, basically similar four-cylinder machines with 15hp en-

September, a year after its introduction, 10,607 had been made. After that there was no stopping the T: in the calendar year 1910 sales were 32,053, in 1911 69,762 and in 1912 170,211. All this was before the proper mass production lines were set up at Highland Park; these went into action in August 1913, raising production that year to 202,667, and to 308,162 in 1914. This was the year when it was said that you could have a Ford in any colour so long as it was black: this was not for penny-pinching but because only black Japan enamel would dry quickly enough to keep pace with the assembly line.

Because of increased production Ford could drop prices – from the original $850 of 1908, to $440 for a tourer in 1915, despite paying the highest wages in the industry. The $5 a day wage, introduced in January 1914, shocked Ford's competitors but brought workers flocking to Detroit from all over the country. Many of these were immigrants, and one of the lesser known activities of the company was the Ford English School, which in 1915 issued its first diplomas to workers who

Ford Model N of 1907

Ford Model T production line, Highland Park, 1914

priced at $2000 and went against Ford's aim of providing cars for the widest possible market. It was Malcolmson's idea, and one of the factors that led to the coal merchant's departure in July 1906.

In December 1904 the Ford Motor Co moved into a new factory on Piquette Avenue, Detroit, 10 times the size of the Mack Avenue premises. By April 1905 300 men were turning out 25 cars a day. Fifteen months later production was up to 100 cars a day.

These were mostly the two-cylinder Model F and four-cylinder Model N, but the company was also making a large six-cylinder car, the 6-litre 40hp Model K. Like the B, this was a pet of Malcolmson's rather than Ford's, and never sold well. To move stocks of the K, Henry Ford told dealers that for every 10 of the popular Model N they were allocated, they must take one Model K. It was dropped in 1907 after 584 had been made. Henry abandoned the expensive car market until he acquired Lincoln in 1922, and was not to make another six-cylinder car until 1941.

Production was expanding so fast that a

gines and two-speed epicyclic transmissions. At $600 the N was the cheapest model, with the better equipped R and S costing up to $750. These cars kept Ford going until the introduction in October of the Model T.

This epoch-making car had an engine slightly larger than that of the Model S, at 2.9 litres and 20bhp, but incorporating two important improvements – monobloc casting and a detachable cylinder head. It shared with its predecessors the two-speed epicyclic transmission and was available initially as a two-seater runabout, four- or five-seater touring car, town car and delivery van.

The earlier Fords were dropped and for the next 19 years the Model T was Ford's sole model. Although it was very much Henry's 'baby', credit should be given to Childe Harold Wills who was responsible for the metallurgy and supervising the team of draughtsmen. Wills had been with Ford since 1902, and later manufactured his own car, the Wills Sainte Claire.

Volume production of the Model T did not begin until the spring of 1909, yet by 30

had mastered the language. Also in 1915 Ford opened its own hospital, and Henry's 'peace ship' *Oscar II* sailed to Europe in a vain attempt to bring a halt to World War I.

Although Ford was a pacifist he could not avoid contributing to the Allied cause. The factory turned out thousands of Model Ts for use as staff cars and ambulances, as well as Liberty aero engines, Eagle boats, tanks, shells and helmets. Ford wanted to forego the profits on this war production, but the shareholders did not share his views. Ford then suggested returning the profits on his own Ford stock to the US government and the complications following this resolution were not settled until 1924.

In 1915 Ford bought 2000 acres (810 hectares) of open land on the River Rouge near Dearborn, and began construction of what became the River Rouge plant, Ford's biggest factory. Main operations were moved to the Rouge from Highland Park in 1927. Model T production reached a new peak of 734,811 units in 1916, then dropped somewhat because of the demands of war production. No

Ford Model T speedster of 1914

Ford Model A roadster of 1929

cars at all were made for domestic use from the middle to the end of 1918.

Meanwhile a new and highly significant Ford product appeared. This was the Fordson tractor. Because some shareholders objected to the manufacture of tractors at Highland Park, Ford set up a separate company, Henry Ford and Son, with a new plant at Dearborn. Production began in 1917. After Ford had bought out his minority shareholders in 1918, the tractor company was brought back into the Ford Motor Co, but the name Fordson was retained for the tractors, and was later applied to British Ford commercial vehicles.

In 1919 Ford overtook International Harvester to become America's largest producer of tractors, a position it held until 1926 when International regained its lead. Two years later Ford abandoned tractor production in the USA, concentrating on its Irish factory at Cork, and later the English Dagenham factory. Tractors of Fordson design were also made in the Putilov Iron Works in Leningrad.

Also new in 1917 was Ford's first purpose-built commercial vehicle chassis, the 1-ton worm-drive Model TT. It used the same power unit and transmission as the Model T car and more than a million were made in the next 10 years.

Car production picked up rapidly after the war, reaching 820,445 in 1919, 1,173,745 in 1922 and a peak of 1,817,891 in 1923. The following year prices reached an all-time low, starting at $290 (£58 at the prevailing exchange rate) for a roadster. The Ford was outselling its nearest competitor, Chevrolet, by six to one. The Model T virtually sold itself, and from 1917 to 1923 all advertising was suspended, apart from that by local dealers.

Although sales remained well over the million mark until 1926, the Ford's advantage dropped to two to one, and apprehension spread throughout the company, reaching all but Henry Ford himself. It was with great reluctance that he agreed to a replacement for his beloved 'Lizzie', the last of which came off the production line in June 1927. A total of 15,007,033 had been made in the USA and Canada, not counting those from overseas

plants which had been set up in England, France, Belgium, Denmark, Italy, Germany, Spain, Brazil, Argentina and Japan.

During the 1920s Ford had acquired more and more facilities for producing complete cars; bodies were made from wood grown in Ford-owned forests in Michigan and Wisconsin, and garnet for grinding and polishing plate glass came from Ford-owned mines in New Hampshire so that by 1924 the company was independent of former lamp suppliers. From 1920 to 1929 Ford owned the Detroit, Toledo and Ironton Railroad, some of whose locomotives were Ford-built, including, in 1924, the world's largest electric locomotive.

In 1922 Ford purchased the Lincoln Motor Co, the makers of a high-priced V8 car, and in 1924 the Stout Metal Airplane Co. This company made single-engine commercial aircraft, but under Ford control it introduced the famous Ford Trimotor in 1926, a twelve-passenger airliner of which 196 were made between 1927 and 1933. Ford built Detroit's first airport and operated a daily service to Buffalo and other places.

Ford plants turned out no cars from early June to mid-October 1927, when the new Model A was launched. To those who had been expecting a radically new car, with six-cylinder or even a rumoured X8 engine, it was something of a disappointment, but at least it was up to date in having a conventional three-speed gearbox and four-wheel brakes. The 3285cc four-cylinder side-valve engine developed 40bhp and gave the Model A a top speed in the region of 60mph (95kph). Prices ran from $385 for a roadster to $570 for a four-door sedan. These undercut the A's chief rivals, Chevrolet and the Willys Whippet, by a satisfactory margin.

Ford sales, which had dropped to little over 356,000 in 1927, rose to 888,050 in 1928, and topped the million mark again in 1929, when they once more beat Chevrolet into first place. Prices went up a bit in 1929, when a roadster cost $450, and there was a top-of-the-line town car at $1200, the most expensive Ford since the 1906 Model K.

By 1930 Ford had 32 assembly plants in the USA, three in Canada and 10 in the rest of the

world, not counting service plants in many other countries. Ford had been assembling in Italy since 1923, but an attempt in 1930 to strengthen its Italian base by having Isotta Fraschini assemble cars in Milan was foiled by a combination of Fiat and the Italian government.

The Depression affected Ford severely. The company's worst year was 1932, when it made only 232,125 cars and registered a loss of more than $74 million, although this was partly due to the massive capital investment required for the new V8. The last Model A left the production line in April 1932, after a little over 5 million cars and trucks had been made in the USA.

The Model A was replaced by the short-lived Model B, which used the A's four-cylinder engine in the V8's chassis and body, but this was only made officially from March to September 1932. The four-cylinder engine was an option until 1934 on passenger cars and light commercials, and was continued much longer by the British plant at Dagenham.

The V8, which was also launched in March 1932, was Henry Ford's reply to the six-cylinder Chevrolet; characteristically he went straight from four to eight cylinders with the world's first mass produced popular market V8 car. Its 3622cc engine developed 65bhp, and with a car weighing less than virtually any of its rivals, a top speed of 75-80mph (120-128kph) was easily reached. Its short wheelbase of 106in (2.7m), only 2½in (63mm) longer than the Model A, and continued use of transverse leaf suspension made handling exciting and sometimes dangerous, but the glamour of the V8 engine – which Chevrolet were not to introduce until 1955 – helped sales throughout the 1930s.

From 1933 a 112in (2.8m) wheelbase and double-drop frame were used, giving the car a lower and more modern appearance. Edsel Ford's influence on styling was increasingly evident, some compensation for the fact that although he was nominally president of the company, his father gave him little overall responsibility. Despite the increased size and power, the Ford V8 cost barely more than the

Model A, 1933 prices running from $410 for a roadster to $610 for a Fordor sedan.

As America climbed out of the Depression, so Ford sales picked up. In 1935 the company was once more at the top of the league, selling 942,439 cars. The two millionth V8 was built on 2 June that year, and 1936 saw the production of the three millionth Ford truck.

The years from 1936 to the outbreak of World War II were not very happy ones for Ford. It lost its lead to Chevrolet in 1936, and apart from the unrepresentative year 1945, when the industry was just recovering from war, did not beat its rivals again until 1959.

Although good-looking, Fords suffered from their old-fashioned suspension and lack of hydraulic brakes; the latter was not rectified until 1939, while the old transverse leaf springs soldiered on until 1949. From being the best in the industry, Ford's pay rates dropped until they were 10 cents an hour less than Chrysler's by 1938. Henry's refusal to accept the unions provoked bitterness and even bloodshed, and his henchman Harry Bennett's opposition to the liberal Edsel contributed to the latter's death in 1943, at the age of 49. There were two attempts at making a cheaper car, the 2.2-litre V8-60 of 1937-40 and the 3.7-litre six of 1941, but the former was particularly lacking in performance, and neither sold well.

A move in a different direction was signalled by the introduction for the 1939 season of the Mercury V8; this was aimed at the middle section of the market, between the Ford V8 and the Lincoln V12. Generally similar to the

to the British war effort. Only gradually did he realize that the two might be linked, but once he became convinced that America would be drawn into the conflict, and before the Japanese attack on Pearl Harbor in December 1941, he ordered the production of Pratt and Whitney aircraft engines, tanks and reconnaissance cars.

During 1941 construction began at the Willow Run plant which was to be devoted to the manufacture of Liberator bombers. With an area of 67 acres (27 hectares) Willow Run was the largest factory under one roof in the world and by 1944 was capable of turning out a Liberator every hour. Total Liberator production at Willow Run was 8686. Other wartime products of Ford factories included Jeeps, both land-going and amphibious, gun carriers, M-4 medium tanks and CG-4 heavy gliders.

With the death of Edsel Ford in May 1943, his 80-year-old father resumed command of the company, with his 25-year-old grandson, Henry Ford II, as vice-president. Another vice-president who had played a major role in the company, Charles E. Sorensen, resigned in 1944, and in September 1945 Henry II became president.

Production of private cars, which had been suspended on 10 February 1942, was resumed on 3 July 1945, with cars which were slightly face-lifted 1942 models. The Willow Run plant, which was surplus to peacetime requirements, was sold to Henry J. Kaiser for the production of Kaiser and Frazer cars and subsequently passed into the hands of Gener-

al Motors, which still uses it today for transmission production. Also disposed of were most of Ford's fleet of cargo ships, the wood distillation plant at Iron Mountain, Michigan, and the plate glass plant at River Rouge. Henry Ford II was worried about increased costs resulting from post-war shortages and low productivity; 128 man hours were required in 1945 to produce a car which took 87 man hours in 1941.

On 7 April 1947 Henry Ford died at Dearborn aged 83. Company policies remained unchanged, as he had played no active part for the last two years of his life. Henry II brought in a new team nicknamed 'the Whiz Kids', among whom was Robert McNamara, who later became President Kennedy's Secretary of Defence. They swept away the old regime's rough-and-ready cost accounting and put the company on a sounder footing for the post-war years of tough competition.

In June 1948 came the brand new post-war Ford, with all-enveloping bodies and coil independent front suspension to replace the transverse leaves which had survived from Model T days. Only the engine remained unchanged. Also new in 1948 was a truck range which included heavier models up to a 5-ton 6×4 powered by a 135bhp V8.

Ford was again making tractors, too, after reaching agreement with Harry Ferguson whose three point hitch was employed on the 9N tractor made since 1939. Ferguson sued Ford for breach of the agreement, which had only been a verbal one, claiming $251 million damages. After four years of litigation he eventually settled for $9.25 million.

Ford held second place behind Chevrolet during the 1950s, with sales edging above the million mark in 1953 for the first time since 1930. Design changed only gradually, important milestones being the option of automatic transmission in 1950, a 'square' 3½-litre overhead-valve six in 1952 and a brand new 3.9-litre overhead-valve V8 developing 130bhp in 1954. An enlarged version of this engine (4.8 litres, 198bhp) powered the Thunderbird two-seater introduced for the 1955 season.

The Thunderbird was Ford's answer to the Chevrolet Corvette, and it was a more sporting package, with greater power and the option of a manual gearbox; it outsold its rival by more than 4½ to one in its first three years.

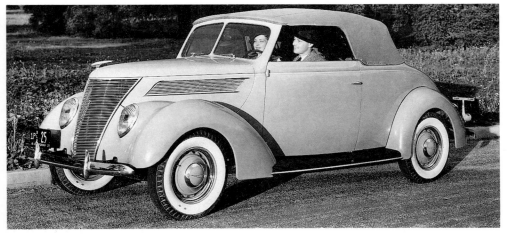

Ford V8 Club Cabriolet of 1937

Ford V8, apart from a larger engine, of 3.9 litres, and 116in (2.9m) wheelbase, the Mercury was priced from $916 to $1018. Ford products now covered 90 per cent of the market, from the $640 V8-60 coupé to the luxury Series K Lincoln, for which prices ranged from $4800 to more than $7000. The Mercury was, and is, a product of Ford's Lincoln division, and their histories are covered in the Lincoln entry.

As World War II approached, Henry Ford was no longer a pacifist but he was very much of an isolationist, believing in arming America for her own defence but not contributing

Ford Thunderbird of 1956

Ford Mustang fastback of 1966

Ford decided that a four-passenger version would sell better, and the company was correct, as the 1958 four-seater sold nearly twice as many units, and the 1959 more than three times the 1957 figure. Enthusiasts, however, regretted the loss of the crisply-styled sporty two-passenger model.

In 1955 Ford decided to offer company stock to the public. Up to 1919 Henry had shared ownership with five other people, but he then bought them out and the family became sole owners. By the mid-1950s about 90 per cent of their stock had been passed to the Ford Foundation, established in 1936, and it was the Foundation which offered equity of $22.4 million at $64 a share. Old Henry would have been aghast at the thought of sharing power with 350,000 investors, but the move brought a great deal of goodwill to Ford.

In 1959, the year in which it built its 50 millionth car, Ford beat Chevrolet into first place. Since the end of the war Ford had built 22 new manufacturing plants in the US and 21 new parts depots.

Ford joined its rivals in producing a compact car for 1960, the 2.3-litre six-cylinder Falcon. More conventional than the inclined-engined Plymouth Valiant or rear-engined Chevrolet Corvair, it easily outsold these in its first years.

In 1964 came one of the most important Fords since the Model T. The Mustang was planned as a 'personal' car for the young or young-at-heart driver, and was a close-coupled four-seater convertible or coupé. It was the brainchild of Lee A. Iacocca, who had worked his way from the showroom floor to vice-president of Ford in five years and would become president in 1970. Within five months of its launch the Mustang was the third most popular car in America, and sales to September 1965 exceeded 680,000. It was soon developed into a high performance sports car, reaching its fastest form in the Shelby GT 500 which was largely rebuilt by Carroll Shelby in his plant near Los Angeles airport.

This was only part of Ford's involvement in motor sport in the 1960s, when the company campaigned on four major fronts: stock, drag, track and international sports/prototype racing. These programmes cost millions of dollars but brought high rewards in the shape of victory at Le Mans for the GT40s in 1966 and 1967 – the 1968 and 1969 winning cars were not Ford-entered but clearly benefited from Ford's development programme – and domination of the Indianapolis 500 by Ford-powered racing cars from 1965 to 1969.

Ford entered the 1970s with a wide line up of cars, very different from the one-model days of the T, A, or V8. Smallest of the range was the sub-compact Pinto, with a choice of British-built 1.6-litre pushrod engine or German-built 2-litre overhead-cam engine. Next came the compact Maverick, a replacement for the Falcon, followed by the intermediate Torino and full-sized Galaxie, XL and LTD, as well as the Mustang and Thunderbird. Neither of the last two retained the individuality and charisma of the earlier models; from 1974 onwards the Mustang was a much smaller car, 19in (48cm) shorter and with 2.3- or 2.8-litre engines, the latter a German-built V6. The Pinto had a very successful run until replaced in 1980 by the new front-wheel-drive Escort which was imported from Germany. This had a purely American sports coupé version known as the EXP.

On 15 November 1977 Ford produced its 100 millionth vehicle built in the United States. Worldwide production approached the 150 million mark during 1978, which marked Ford's 75th birthday as a manufacturer. The euphoria generated by these celebrations was somewhat dampened by the slump the following year. Between June 1979 and the end of 1981 Ford cut its white collar workforce by a quarter and reduced the blue collar payroll from 190,000 to 115,000.

In 1980 Henry Ford II stepped down from the three-man 'office of chief executives' who ran the company and Lee Iacocca moved to Chrysler. Their places were taken by Henry's brother William Clay Ford and Donald E. Peterson; Philip Caldwell remained as the third member of the team.

In 1985 a total of 1,636,150 Ford cars, in-

Ford two-door coupé of 1978

Ford Thunderbird Turbo coupé of 1985

cluding Lincoln and Mercury models, were made in the United States. The previous year, after three years of losses, Ford had made a record profit of $187 million.

The 1987 Ford line up consisted of the sub-compact Escort and EXP, the compact front-drive Tempo sedan and rear-drive Mustang coupé, the intermediate Taurus with body similar to the European Scorpio (Granada in the UK), the standard LTD Crown Victoria and Thunderbird luxury coupé. There were also two 4×4 vehicles, the V8 Bronco and V6 Bronco II. Ford had 16 assembly plants in the USA, including truck plants. The truck factory at Louisville, Kentucky, was responsible for the L and CL series of heavy trucks, powered by Cummins, Caterpillar or Detroit Diesel engines.

Apart from the major foreign Ford companies making cars of their own design, such as those in Britain, Germany, and Australia, Ford has numerous operations overseas. They include assembly or manufacturing plants in Argentina, Mexico, New Zealand, Portugal, the Philippines, Spain, South Africa, Taiwan, Uruguay and Venezuela. Most of these make versions of either American or European Fords, but the Philippines factory builds the Fiera, a very simple light truck for Asian markets. GNG

FOUILLARON
FRANCE 1900-1914

Gustave Fouillaron opened a bicycle shop in Angers, Marne et Loire, in 1899 and began to build motor bicycles, tricycles and quads in 1900. That year he patented a variable transmission with expandable pulleys and belts of chrome leather and cat gut. To keep the belts out of the way of grit and water, final drive was by chains. From 1902 the factory and office was at Levallois-Perret. De Dion engines, vehicles and other components were offered for sale.

In 1906 the original Angers business was listed as a garage, hiring Peugeot and Fouillaron cars. In 1908 the Levallois range ran from 6 to 25hp and was said to include lorries. The belt transmission arrangement lasted to the end of Fouillaron production in 1914, engines by Buchet, De Dion and others having been used, including a 15/18hp six. NB

FRAMO/BARKAS
GERMANY 1932-1937

J. S. Rasmussen, the founder of DKW, formed Metallwerke Frankenberg in the town of that name in 1922 to make bicycle and motor components. From 1927, under the name Framo, it made commercial vehicles using DKW motorcycle components and engines mounted above the single front wheel. In 1930 the engine was enclosed and in 1932 four-wheelers were produced as well. The first cars of 1932 were front-engined, single-front-wheel-drive three-wheelers but for 1933 the Stromer three-wheeler had two driven front wheels and DKW engines of 200 to 600cc.

A diminutive rear-engined four-wheel car was also made and an additional factory was opened at Hainichen. Car production ceased in 1937, by which time about 1000 had been made. From 1937 to 1942 only commercial vehicles were produced.

Following nationalization by the East Ger-

man government the company made vans and pickups from 1949 to 1954, when its name was changed to Barkas. A four-wheel 1-tonner was added in 1961, with Wartburg engine, and that model was still in production in the early 1980s. NB

Fouillaron 10hp tonneau of 1902

Franklin six-cylinder tourer of 1912

FRANKLIN
USA 1902-1934

Born in 1866 on a farm near Syracuse, New York, Herbert H. Franklin went to work for a local newspaper, which he ended up buying, and then in 1895 founded the H. H. Franklin Manufacturing Co of Syracuse. The company was a pioneer specialist in diecasting. The transmission specialists of later renown, A. T. Brown and C. A. Lipe, introduced Franklin to John Wilkinson, a Cornell graduate and former bicycle draughtsman, who had made three experimental air-cooled cars between 1897 and 1901. Franklin commissioned Wilkinson to build a four-cylinder car in 1901. Following successful trials, Brown and Lipe organized a production and marketing department in the Franklin plant and sold the first car in June 1902.

Thirteen Franklins were made that year, followed by 184 in 1903. All cars until 1928 had laminated wooden chassis and very supple full elliptic springs, and all had air-cooling until production ended in 1934. The early cars were successful in endurance trials and bottom-gear stunts and could, it was said, 'withstand heat and drought like a camel'.

Possibly America's first successful six was

produced in the Franklin works in 1905, when the early transverse-engined models were discontinued and a barrel-shaped bonnet adopted. In 1907 Franklin pioneered automatic spark advance and from 1910 used forced-draught cooling with vertical cylinder fins and flywheel fan. In 1912 came recirculating pressure-fed lubrication. In 1913 four-cylinder engines were discontinued.

In 1917 3200 men were employed at the Franklin factory and that year the car division became the Franklin Automobile Co. A car came off the production line every 13 minutes. Annual sales in 1920 had reached 8648 and the sales total in the first 20 years was reputedly 70,000.

'Scientific Light Weight' was a favoured Franklin slogan from the earliest days, and among the features of the 1920s cars were aluminium pistons. Head of sales was R. A. Rawson, who left for Stutz in 1924 and thence for Elcar and Moon.

The series 10 of 1922 had dual con-rods and front-mounted compressor-fan behind a dummy radiator shell instead of the Renault-type used for the past 10 years. The series 11 for 1926 had body styling by J. F. de Causse and plated 'radiator' so as to be less conspicuously unconventional. De Causse had formerly been in charge of Locomobile's custom body department after gaining experience at Kellner. The ending of the front-hinged bonnet caused John Wilkinson, who had been vice-president and chief engineer from the outset, to resign. Chief experimental engineer at that time was John Burns, who had helped Wilkinson with his first experimental car.

Franklins were moderately powered, expensive and very well made, and they evoked great customer loyalty. Production for most of the 1920s exceeded 10,000 a year– and reached almost 15,000 in 1929. Dietrich styled and produced many of their later vintage bodies after the death of de Causse in 1927. They were built, in most cases, by the Walker Co of Amesbury, Massachusetts.

Hydraulic four-wheel brakes were intro-

191

Franklin Airman Six speedster of 1932

duced in 1927 on the Airman range, a name chosen to go with a marketing strategy that linked the cars to successful air-cooled engined planes and to such pilot/owners as Charles Lindbergh and Amelia Earhart. Steel chassis came to some models in 1928, but all still retained the excellent full elliptic suspension designed by chief engineer Edward Marks and his assistant Carl Doman.

They had a $750,000 engineering budget in 1929 with which to keep the car ahead of competition and they adopted side-blast cooling, which reduced the horsepower absorbed by the fan by 50 per cent. A 40 per cent increase in engine horsepower gave 95bhp and impressive performance owing to low weight. Because of their comparative lightness Franklin engines were used in aircraft from the late 1920s.

During the Depression sales slumped to 7511 in 1930 and 3881 in 1931. Franklin responded by cutting prices and boosting horsepower by ducting slightly pressurized cooling air to the carburettor. The more expensive models were faring better than the cheap ones and so a 6.8-litre V12 that had been under development since 1927 by Glen Shoemaker and by Doman and Marks was launched in 1932. It went on to sell between 200 and 300. Cars were being sold in Japan, Holland, Hungary, Britain, France, Argentina, India, Uruguay, Venezuela, Mexico and Chile.

Some $5 million had been borrowed for expansion, but reduced sales made repayment impossible. The banks appointed a manager who insisted on greater use of cheaper (and heavier) proprietary components, semi-elliptic springs and Le Baron styled bodywork to be built by Franklin for the V12 – all of which added over a ton in weight to the cars. Fred Haynes, who had once worked for Franklin and then risen to head Dodge, returned as general manager but did not like the atmosphere and soon quit.

The sixes were supplemented by a cheaper Olympic line for 1933, based on Reo bodies

and chassis bought for $525 each, but in 1934 Franklin went bankrupt. Sales continued, rather dismally, into 1935: 1577 in 1932, 1180 in 1933 and fewer than 1000 in 1934-35.

Doman and Marks had departed early in 1933 and formed Aircooled Motors Corporation, which acquired the Franklin name and many personnel. Republic Aviation bought this company then sold it to the Tucker Corporation for $1.8 million. When the water-cooled Tucker car failed, Doman left for Ford at the end of 1949. His company was later reorganized as the Franklin Engine Co in Syracuse and continues to serve the aircraft industry. Herbert H. Franklin died in 1956. NB

FRAYER-MILLER
USA 1904-1909

The Buckeye Motor Co made engines, including an opposed-piston air-cooled twin, and also produced a sliding-gear transmission invented by Lee A. Frayer, the foreman of a Locomobile distributor, the Oscar Lear Automobile Co of Columbus, Ohio. William J. Miller was a gas engine designer for Buckeye and in 1904 Lear put a forced-draught, air-cooled four-cylinder car, designed by Frayer and Miller, into production.

It was an expensive, high-quality car, joined by an even better 6½-litre six in 1906. Lee Frayer drove one in 1906 Vanderbilt Cup events with teenage E. V. Rickenbacker as his mechanic.

Frayer-Miller began to offer air-cooled trucks at this time, selling some to the Seagrave fire appliance firm, but in 1909 their venture was in liquidation. E. S Kelly bought Oscar Lear's shareholding and created the Kelly Motor Truck Co. Its products resembled Frayer-Millers until 1912, when water-cooled engines were adopted and they became Kelly-Springfields. This name lived on with a brand of tyre when truck production ended in the late 1920s. NB

FRAZER-NASH
GB 1924-1957

Archie Frazer-Nash had built the GN cyclecar with his friend Ron Godfrey, but both left the company in September 1922 in protest at the introduction of four-cylinder shaft-drive cars by the other directors. Frazer-Nash founded Frazer-Nash Ltd in November 1922 with £6000 capital and opened negotiations with GN Ltd in order to buy the parts for chain-drive cars which GN no longer wanted.

About a dozen GN chassis were modified and sold as Frazer-Nash-GNs. Two other stop gaps were a Ruby-engined GN chassis and a shaft-driven Frazer-Nash which was in fact an Anzani-engined Deemster on which Frazer-Nash put his own bodies and badge. Not more than six of these were made.

The Frazer-Nash factory was in Kingston, Surrey. It had a staff of about 10 men in 1924, including several ex-GN employees. The first Frazer-Nash car proper was announced in July 1924 with 1½-litre overhead-valve Plus-Power engine, but this company was soon in difficulties and Frazer-Nash turned to Anzani for their power units.

In October 1925 Frazer-Nash merged with William G. Thomas, converters of former War Department lorries, which had larger premises across the road. The new company was known as William G. Thomas and Frazer-Nash Ltd. This arrangement lasted only for two years, when a new saviour appeared in the shape of Richard Plunkett-Greene who put several thousand pounds into the company and gained control at the end of 1928, when Archibald Frazer-Nash became seriously ill. From 1927 the company was known as AFN Ltd. Control later passed to H. J. Aldington, who had been with Frazer-Nash in its earliest days and who, with his brother Bill, was to control Frazer-Nash until the end of its life.

Frazer-Nash himself had little to do with the cars thereafter, concerning himself with the Frazer-Nash gun turret which was used on many famous aircraft of World War II, including the Whitley, Stirling, Lancaster and Wellington bombers, and the Sunderland flying boat.

The Frazer-Nash, with its outmoded transmission by chains and dog clutches, had a small but extremely loyal following and its design changed little during the 15 years it was in production. The main changes were in the power unit; the Anzani engine was supplemented by a Meadows 4ED in 1929, the last Anzani being used in 1932. Other power units included the Gough, designed by Albert Gough and made by Frazer-Nash, and the six-cylinder Blackburne.

Peak years for production were 1925 and 1926, with one car a week leaving the factory. During the Aldington regime the company's finances were in better shape, but production was very small, only 14 cars in 1930, 24 in

Frazer-Nash 11.5hp three-seater of 1925

1931, 33 in 1932, 32 in 1933 and 39 in 1934. In 1930 the factory moved to new premises at Isleworth, Middlesex. The following year H. J. Aldington purchased Aston Martin from A. C. Bertelli, but though sales and advertising were handled jointly, there was no tie up in the design of the two cars. In 1932 he sold Aston Martin to Lance Prideaux-Brune.

In 1934 Aldington obtained the sales and manufacturing rights to the BMW from Franz-Joseph Popp. He never took up the manufacture, but he held discussions with Alvis and Riley concerning the possibility of selling such rights to them. Most Frazer-Nash-BMWs came into England complete, although some were imported in ckd form and assembled at Isleworth.

Models sold in England included the Type 34 (BMW 315), Type 40 (BMW 315 or 319), Type 55 (315 sports), and Type 326, 327 and 328 which used the same nomenclature as the BMWs sold in Germany. The Frazer-Nash-BMW had a dual appeal, that of the sporting connotations of the Frazer-Nash and the advanced design, appearance and comfort of the BMW. Some BMWs had British carriage work by Abbott.

Although the chain-drive cars were occasionally advertised alongside the Frazer-Nash-BMWs, they were given little priority from 1935 onwards, and sales dropped to 14 in 1935 and 11 in 1936. Figures for 1937, 1938 and 1939 were two, one and one respectively. By contrast AFN sold some 707 Frazer-Nash-BMWs between December 1934 and September 1939.

During the war all three Aldington brothers served in the army. 'D.A.' was transferred to the Ministry of Supply, which brought him into contact with the Bristol Aeroplane Co and led to the adoption of the BMW engine in the new car which Bristol were to produce after the war. 'H.J.' became a director of Bristol, and was instrumental in bringing to England the drawings for the BMW 328 and some engines and parts. He also hired Fritz Fiedler, who was responsible for the ingenious horizontal pushrod design of the 328 engine.

The new car was originally to have been called the Frazer-Nash-Bristol, but the aeroplane company decided this was too clumsy and preferred the straight name Bristol. It was agreed that the two-door saloon would be built by Bristol, but the sports models would be built by Frazer-Nash at Isleworth and would carry the Frazer-Nash name.

They were designed by Fiedler and used engines and gearboxes made by Bristol. A variety of models was offered, of which the Le Mans replica was the most successful in competitions and in sales. Even so, only 34 were sold between 1948 and 1953. Other models included the Mille Miglia and Sebring with all-enveloping coachwork, and a fixed head coupé.

With some encouragement from Leonard Lord of Austin, H. J. Aldington prepared an Austin A90-engined roadster with Targa Florio type body, and showed it at the 1952 Earls Court Show, but at the same show Donald Healey showed his Healey Hundred, which Lord quickly chose as Austin's sports car. He was suitably apologetic to Aldington and refunded Frazer-Nash's involvement in the abortive project.

The Frazer-Nash car now began to go the way of the pre-war chain-drive version, but the foreign cuckoo in the Isleworth nest was no longer BMW but Porsche. Annual production dwindled to single figures by 1956. The last new model was the Continental coupé with 3.2-litre BMW V8 engine. It was intro-

Frazer-Nash, Alpine Cup, 1951

duced in 1956, but at a price of £3751 it was hardly competitive with the DB2/4 Aston Martin at £3076, still less so with the Jaguar XK140 coupé at £1711.

Only two Continentals were made; the last one in 1957 was also the last car to bear the Frazer-Nash name, although the make lingered on in magazine price lists until 1960. Total production of the post-war cars was 84; added to the 323 pre-war models, the grand total barely exceeds 400, less than a morning's output from a major manufacturer, yet the Frazer-Nash has an almost fanatical following all over the world.

AFN Ltd flourishes to the present day as the UK Porsche concessionaires, but it has also handled sales of BMW cars and motorcycles, DKW cars and Steib sidecars. H. J. Aldington died in 1976 but the business is carried on by his son, John. GNG

FRÉJUS
see Diatto

FRISKY
GB 1957-1964

Among the crop of minicars which flourished in Britain in the 1950s the Frisky was unusual in being made as a sideline by a major engineering company, Henry Meadows Ltd of Wolverhampton. This company was founded in 1919 by an ex-Clyno employee and soon became one of Britain's leading suppliers of proprietary engines to a large number of firms, including Invicta, Lagonda, Lea-Francis and Phoenix.

The Frisky car had its origin in Egypt, where Raymond Flower had designed a minicar for production by the Cairo Motor Co Ltd. Bad feeling between Britain and Egypt because of the Suez crisis in 1956 put an end to this project and Flower took the design to Meadows.

The Frisky was a four-wheeler with close-set rear wheels that dispensed with the need for a differential. It was powered by a rear-mounted 249cc Villiers two-stroke engine. The prototype had a Michelotti-styled metal body with gullwing doors, but production cars had simpler glassfibre bodies made by the Guy factory, Meadows' close neighbours. Later cars used the 324cc Villiers engine.

There was a Frisky Sprint powered by a 30bhp 492cc Excelsior engine but this never got beyond the prototype stage. A three-wheeler Family Three had accommodation for two adults and two children, and was powered by a 197cc Villiers single or 250cc Excelsior twin.

Meadows' production of Friskys lasted little over a year, until the company was taken over by Guy; in 1961 production was switched to Sandwich, Kent. The Sandwich works concentrated on three-wheelers, with 197, 250 or 324cc engines, but relatively few were made. The Meadows factory was bought by Jaguar in 1960 and was later used for licensed production of American Cummins diesel engines. GNG

FSO
see Polski-Fiat

FULDAMOBIL
GERMANY 1950-1969

In the 1940s Norbert Stevenson was an unemployed former student looking for a backer for his idea for a very small car. After World War II Stevenson had worked briefly as a journalist for *Rhein-Zeitung* whose publisher, Herr Stein, provided him with limited funds to build a prototype three-wheeler. Stein, whose newspaper was in financial trouble, ran out of money before Stevenson had acquired all the necessary parts and what he had bought had to be sold again.

Stevenson approached several other businessmen for backing but with no success until he met Karl Schmitt, an electrical wholesaler who also ran an electrical engineering firm, Elektromaschinenbau Fulda GmbH, in the town of Fulda. Schmitt was already interested in building a car roughly in line with Stevenson's ideas and in October 1949 he paid Stevenson to start building his first chassis, with a single rear wheel driven by a 200cc Zundapp engine.

It was tested, without a body, in late December. A body was designed in January 1950 and the Fuldamobil, as it was now named, was first shown in public in March, when the engine overheated due to lack of proper cooling. Nevertheless, there was enough interest to prompt Schmitt and Stevenson to plan production. They received valuable help from engine builders Baker & Polling, who adapted one of their chainsaw engines to give Stevenson a 250cc 8hp single-cylinder unit with fan cooling.

This was used towards the end of 1950 in the production prototype, which would reach about 45mph (72kph), and Schmitt ordered lightweight bodies, of alloy panels

on a wooden frame, from a former glider manufacturer, Schleicher. Production started in early 1951 and about 50 two-seater cars were built in the first six months before demand suddenly dropped.

In August 1951 Stevenson restyled the car, with a rounded nose in place of the former flat front, and a body made of plywood – but production was now hampered by a batch of faulty engines. With the Type N, which followed, Fuldamobil reverted to a metal body of unpainted, hammer-finished alloy, and production reached a peak of about 20 cars a week in 1953. This heady output allowed Fulda to win a medal at an exhibition in Dusseldorf for bringing motoring to the people!

Fuldamobil Type N of c.1953

In February 1954 the restyled Fuldamobil S was introduced with a Fichtel & Sachs engine and a steel body. In August the engineering company Nordwestdeutsche Fahrzeugbau GmbH of Willeshaven began building the Fuldamobil under licence, as the NWF 200, with an ILO 200cc motor. This car was sold exclusively in Germany and Fulda's own output was now all sold elsewhere in Europe. Nordwestdeutsche Fahrzeugbau, however, only continued production until 1955, in the face of growing competition.

In the same year Schmitt almost sold a production licence to Zundapp, but Zundapp then adopted the rather larger Dornier four-seater design which it sold with some success. Schmitt was more successful in selling rights to build the Fuldamobil abroad, particularly after the adoption of glassfibre bodies, in 1957.

From September 1955 Fuldamobils were imported to Britain by the Beauship Trading and Shipping Co of London, which offered a closed three-seater and a sunshine-roofed four-seater, both with ILO engines of 200cc. In March 1958 York Nobel Industries took out a licence to build the Fuldamobil in Britain as the Nobel 200, although it was actually built for the company by various contractors, including the shipbuilder Harland & Wolfe and car-maker Lea-Francis, but only until 1961.

The Fuldamobil was also built under licence in South Africa, in Chile as the Bambi, in Holland as the Bambino, in Greece as the Attica, in India as the Hans Vahaar and in Sweden as the King. In Germany, production of the three-wheeler virtually stopped in 1960 but Schmitt went on to build a number of small, Heinkel-engined four-wheelers, the last of them in 1969. BL

Frisky Sprint of c.1959

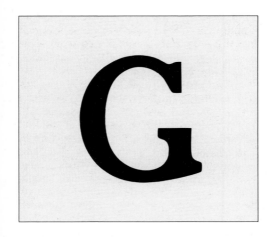

G

GAETH
USA 1902-1911

Paul Gaeth was a German immigrant to Cleveland, Ohio, who built experimental cars, one steam-powered and one internal combustion in 1898, followed by another internal combustion car in 1899 which he sold for $500. He then became chief engineer of the People's Automobile Co of Cleveland, making buses and passenger cars from 1900 to 1901, before setting up his own shop and forming the Gaeth Automobile Co in 1902. Finance came from a number of local businessmen including an undertaker and a wholesale meat dealer.

Over the next two years Gaeth built about 24 cars, mostly to special order, with single- or two-cylinder engines under the seat, two-speed planetary transmissions and two- or four-seat bodies. In this they were not unlike many other American light cars of the period, but in 1904 Gaeth became more innovative with the Gaeth Triplex which had a large three-cylinder engine mounted horizontally under the seat. This was followed by a range of conventional cars with front-mounted four-cylinder vertical engines. The Gaeth company also produced a number of light vans with single- or four-cylinder engines from 1906 to 1910.

Production expanded slowly, and agents were appointed as far afield as Chicago, New York, Milwaukee and Denver. All cars were hand-made, design changed little and the cars were not promoted well, all factors which led to receivership in 1910 and purchase of the assets by the Stuyvesant Motor Car Co.

Stuyvesant made a few more four-cylinder Gaeths at Cleveland, as well as its new Stuyvesant Six at Sandusky, Ohio, but production did not last long and the last Stuyvesant was made in 1912. Total production of Gaeth was about 300 cars. Paul Gaeth ran a small garage and workshop in Cleveland and continued to work on cars old and new, but preferably old, until his death in 1952 at the age of 79. GNG

GAGGENAU/LILIPUT
GERMANY 1904-1911

Building cars named after the German town where they were made, the Gaggenau factory was a continuation of Bergmann's Industriewerke, which had built the Orient Express from 1895 to 1903 and made Liliput cars from 1904. It had also manufactured Badenia bicycles to meet the need for this form of transport.

In 1905 the motor department of Bergmann was re-formed and given a separate identity as Suddeutsche Automobil-Fabrik GmbH. Suddeutsche continued to manufacture the friction-drive Liliput until 1907. Other Suddeutsche versions of the car were called Libelle and Bergmann, and a version produced by a licensee in Suhl was called Schilling. The Gaggenau name was reserved for Suddeutsche's larger cars and commercials, both of which were also sometimes known as SAG, SAF or Safe.

Buses, lorries and fire engines were also produced. In October 1907 Benz acquired Suddeutsche, taking over complete control in late 1910. The company was renamed Benzwerke Gaggenau GmbH. Gaggenau cars were discontinued in 1911 and the factory became the headquarters for Benz commercials. It continued in use after the merger of Daimler and Benz and is now devoted to the production of Unimogs. NB

GALBA/HUASCAR
FRANCE 1929-1931

The two-stroke light cars of Marcel Violet entered production with Vinot et Deguingand and then, in 1929, a Deguingand-like machine – but with two instead of four cylinders – cropped up in Courbevoie made by the Société Sylla. It was named Galba after a Roman emperor. For the 1930 Paris Salon the car was renamed Huascar, and production ended in 1931.

Marcel Violet then turned his attention to light military vehicles and aircraft, making the Ava engine for the SFAN. He was a consultant to SOMUA, Simca, for which he designed a four-cylinder, oil-cooled motorcycle in 1938 for military use, Daimler-Benz and Peugeot's motorcycle division. He designed 500cc racing cars and remained a freelance designer into the 1960s. NB

GALLOWAY
see Arrol-Johnston

GAMAGE
GB 1903-1905; 1914

Gamages, a large London department store, was founded in Holborn by A. W. Gamage in 1878 and remained in business for almost 100 years. It made a particular speciality of sporting requisites and into this category came motor vehicles. From 1903 the company sold cars and motorcycles under its own name.

The provenance of the machines remains in doubt, although the cars were probably by Lacoste et Battmann as well as Mass, in addition to the Renaults and De Dions sold in 1903. The motorcycles included Omega and Radco. A tandem tricar in 1904 was probably British as it had a Hubbard engine.

The motorcycles were sold until 1924 but the cars faded away in about 1905. However, a Chapuis-Dornier engined 1½-litre four was

Gaggenau Liliput runabout of 1906

Gaggenau Kaiserpreis racer of 1907

offered in 1914 for less than £200, An interesting feature was the starting lever, which was positioned by the driver's seat and worked a cable and ratchet arrangement on the front of the engine. In 1920 Gamages tried to market the Slaby-Beringer car, but with little success. NB

GAR
FRANCE 1922-1931

M. Gardahaut's company was set up in 1919 and three years later was offering two-cylinder GAR cyclecars from a factory on a new industrial estate at Clichy. GAR soon progressed to CIME and Chapuis-Dornier engined four-cylinder sports cars which were sometimes raced with success in twelve-valve (twin-inlet) form. A SCAP-engined 1500cc straight-eight was also offered.

For two years from 1927 GARs were built under licence in Milan by Costruzioni Automobile Riuniti, as GARs then CARs. GARs were also sold in Spain, Belgium, Poland, Czechoslovakia, Holland and Germany. In 1927, 898 and 1094cc cars with Chapuis-Dornier engines and gearboxes were sold in Britain.

Gardahaut moved his factory to Asnières in about 1926. Three years later a 770cc four-cylinder car with transverse front leaf spring suspension appeared, using a GAR motor. The price was just 11,600 francs – but 900 francs more for front-wheel brakes and electric lighting. There was also a 1375cc straight-eight version, of which only about a dozen were made. These, and many of the fours, were available with superchargers.

Production probably ended in 1931, although the cars may have been offered for two more years. In 1934 a handful were built by J. Pipault under the name JP, using straight-eight components and with bodywork by Bellon Frères. NB

GARDNER
USA 1919-1931

Brothers Russell E. and Fred W. Gardner started up in business making spokes in Galion, Ohio, before founding the Banner Buggy Co in 1882 in Columbus. Production moved to St Louis, Missouri, where Russell E. Gardner called himself 'the buggy king' and claimed to make more buggies than any other firm in the world.

In 1910 a motor department was set up but the Banner motor buggy was not a success and so, from 1915, Chevrolet cars were assembled in the three-storey buggy factory. Russell Gardner, who was president of the Chevrolet Motor Co of St Louis, sold out to General Motors in 1919 having produced 60,000 cars for the local market.

In place of the Chevrolet in 1919 came the

assembled Gardner car. It had a two-bearing 3.4-litre four-cylinder Lycoming engine, Spicer transmission, Timken axles, Borg and Beck clutch, and Westinghouse electrics. Five bearings were adopted for 1922, when the cars were available in Britain for £395. That year 12,000 cars were made. Output fell to 8000 in 1923.

In 1924 additional Lycoming six and straight-eight models were offered. The four was soon discontinued, followed by the six, so that from 1926 to 1929 only eights were made. Twin Schebler carburettors were used on some models. In August 1929 six cylinders returned, on cars having Lockheed internal expanding hydraulic brakes. Like all Gardners, these cars displayed the flying griffon mascot.

In January 1930 came a low-slung front-wheel-drive Continental six-cylinder powered Gardner with Warner gearbox and Baker-Raulang body. Lycoming engines were also quoted for this model, few of which were built. Car production came to a halt in 1931, although some V8 powered ambulances and hearses were made for another year. Russell Gardner died in 1938. NB

GARFORD
USA 1904-1913

Garford 30 two-seat tourer of 1910

Arthur L. Garford was president of the Cleveland Automatic Machine Co and of the Federal Manufacturing Co of Elyria, Ohio. The last-named was a $5 million corporation which owned a Chicago steel plant and was a large producer of bicycles, chassis and components for the motor industry including Rainier and Cleveland. In 1904 Garford was approached by Frederick S. Fish of Studebaker to supply chassis to enable Studebaker to enter the petrol car business, as the company did not have the facilities itself, despite being the world's largest maker of horse drawn carriages and wagons.

Garford began with a 16hp two-cylinder chassis, following this with 20, 28 and 30hp fours. The cars were called Studebaker-Garford at first, then simply Studebaker.

In 1907 Garford launched two cars under its own name, the 30hp Model A and 40hp Model B, priced from $3500 and $4000 respectively. It continued to supply chassis to

Studebaker as well. In 1907 the workforce totalled 600. Garford discontinued its own brand cars in 1909, but the following year Studebaker cancelled the agreement as it was now buying cheaper cars elsewhere.

Garford produced a wide range of cars for 1912, two fours and a six, with 19 body styles. In that year the business came under the control of John N. Willys, who bought all the Garford stock held by Studebaker. Arthur Garford then retired.

Although the company under Willys built a new Six in 1913, with 'cyclops eye' single headlamp, Willys's main intention was to use the Elyria factory for production of the new Willys-Knight car with sleeve-valve engine. This began in 1914 and no more Garford cars were made. From 1915 the factory was used for making Knight engines, the rest of the cars being built at Toledo. Garford trucks were made at Lima, Ohio, until 1933, from 1927 under the control of Relay Motors. GNG

GAUTIER-WEHRLÉ
FRANCE 1894-1900

Starting as Rossel, Gautier et Wehrlé in 1894, this company built steam cars in Paris and from 1896 petrol types were offered. Rossel was dropped from the company name in 1897. In 1898 electric cars were added to the range and bodywork was undertaken for a number of firms. Jobs were also subcontracted from Serpollet. In 1897 the company came under the control of Société Continentale and production ended in 1900. NB

GAYLORD
USA 1955-1957

The Gaylord brothers, Jim and Edward, came from an Illinois family which had made a vast fortune in property and the beauty industry, their father being credited with inventing the 'bobby-pin'. They grew up in Chicago, surrounded by many of the finest cars in the world, for which they formed a deep respect. Jim, as engineering vice-president of the family business, studied motor engineering and as a member of the Society of Automotive Engineers numbered several major motor industry executives among his friends.

In the early 1950s he committed himself to designing and building the 'ultimate' personal car, blending performance, style and luxury. The Gaylord would be a money-no-object project with a target of selling about 25 cars a year at upwards of $10,000 each.

On his way to designing the tubular, semi-backbone, spaceframe chassis, Jim dismantled and studied cars such as Rolls-Royce, Cadillac and Mercedes. After Alex Tremulis had declined to style the Gaylord because of his Ford contract, Brooks Stevens was set to work in late 1954 to produce a modern de-

Gaylord Gentleman of 1955

sign which would also evoke the classic era.

To exhibit the car at the Paris Show in October 1955, Stevens built a quarter-scale model. The prototype was built directly from full-size drawings, with no intermediate mock-up. The first car, with retractable hard-top, was built by the German coachbuilder Hermann Spohn of Ravensburg, supervised by Gaylord and Stevens.

The first car used a 365cu in Chrysler V8 but later versions used a blueprinted Cadillac V8; a supercharged version was planned but never built. The Gaylord certainly met its quality aspirations, with meticulous attention to vibration suppression, driver-controlled variable weight power steering, an automatically presented spare wheel and excellent performance.

Jim Gaylord was not totally happy with the body style and a revised version was shown at the 1956 New York Show. This and the original chassis were subsequently destroyed and the first four-headlamp, Cadillac-engined car built. Several cars were ordered after the shows and for 1957 production of up to 300 was planned at a price which eventually reached $17,500.

Gaylord saw quality problems in the few bodies built by Spohn, and two chassis and one body were built by Luftschiffbau Zeppelin before legal problems sent Gaylord looking for another coachbuilder – which he never found. The pressures of the project eventually put Jim Gaylord in hospital with total exhaustion and no more of his 'ultimate' cars were built. BL

GAZ
SOVIET UNION 1932 to date

The Gorkovsky Avtomobilni Zavod (Gorki Automobile Works) was the first factory in the Soviet Union to build passenger cars in large quantities. With a site area of 256 acres (103 hectares) and a workforce of more than 12,000, it was billed as the biggest automobile factory in Europe. The buildings were designed by Ford architect Albert Kahn and built with advice from the Cleveland-based construction engineers, Austin and Co. (This gave rise to the quite unfounded suggestion that the British Austin Motor Co was connected with GAZ.) Thirty Russian engineers spent some time at Ford's River Rouge plant, and quantities of parts (initially) and machine tools went to Gorki from Ford.

The first vehicle, a Model AA truck, came off the lines in January 1932, and passenger cars followed soon afterwards. The main product of the plant was commercial vehicles.

Cars and trucks were very close to Ford in design. The GAZ-A continued in production until 1936, four years later than its American counterpart, while Model A-based trucks were made as late as 1948. A total of 41,917 GAZ-As were made, nearly all of them tourers; the dies for closed cars were never acquired by GAZ, but a few saloon bodies were made by Aremkuzov in Moscow.

The GAZ-A's replacement was the M-1, made from 1936 to 1940. It used the same 3.2-litre four-cylinder engine as its predecessor, but had a more modern body, reminiscent of the 1934 Ford V8. It was available as a saloon, tourer or pick-up. It was replaced by the GAZ 11-40 and 11-73 with generally similar bodies but six-cylinder engines of 3483cc. These cars were produced until 1948. Although these models, including a 4×4 version, were made in small numbers during World War II, the expanded Gorki factory was mostly occupied making a Jeep-type vehicle, the 4×4 GAZ-67B, and a variety of trucks.

The first post-war car from the Gorki works, now generally known as the Zavod Imieni Molotova (Works named for Molotov), was the GAZ M-20 or Pobieda (Victory). This was a 2.1-litre four-cylinder saloon with up-to-date styling somewhat reminiscent of the Standard Vanguard. It was made from 1946 to 1958, mainly as a saloon, although there were a few tourers, and a 4×4 version, the M-72, was introduced in 1955.

The Pobieda was widely used as a taxi, and a total of 247,172 were made. It was also built in Poland as the Warszawa, originally with a Polish chassis and suspension and Russian-made engine and body, but later built entirely in Poland. The Warszawa long out-lived the Pobieda, about 253,000 being made until 1972.

The Pobieda was designed by Andrei Lipgart, who was also responsible for the larger Z1M or GAZ M-12, made from 1951 to 1960. This was a largish seven-passenger saloon with 95bhp 3½-litre overhead-valve six-cylinder engine and was not for general sale, although some were exported to Sweden and Finland. In all 21,546 were made before it was replaced in 1959 by the Chaika (Seagull), which was the same class of car but was powered by a 195bhp 5½-litre V8 engine. Like the Z1M, the Chaika was not available to the average Soviet citizen, but could be acquired by more important professional people, and state officials who did not qualify for the top-ranking Z1S or Z1L limousines.

In 1965 there was an interruption in Chaika production, but the name reappeared in 1977 on another limousine with similar sized V8 engine and updated body design. Equipped

GAZ-A tourer of c.1932

GAZ-69 four-wheel drive of c.1953

with push-button automatic transmission and power steering, this was still being made in the mid-1980s.

The Pobieda was joined in 1955 by a more modern saloon with 70bhp 2½-litre engine. Known as the Volga, this took over as the sole middle-sized Russian car after the Pobieda was phased out in 1958. It has been gradually developed over the years, with new body styles coming out in 1968 and 1982 and is still made today.

Unlike the Pobieda, which was only offered abroad briefly, on the Belgian market, the Volga has been exported to many countries including Britain. A 65bhp Land Rover diesel engine was offered on the Belgian market cars for a while, and the current Volga 3102 is made with two sizes of Indenor diesel, 2 and 2.3 litres, as well as the 2½-litre petrol engine. Car production at the GAZ factory was quoted as 145,000 in 1981, of which the great majority were Volgas. GNG

GENERAL MOTORS
USA 1908 to date

The General Motors Co was created by William Crapo Durant on 16 September 1908 and promptly embarked on a buying spree. It acquired Buick in October and Olds in November, followed in 1909 by Oakland (later Pontiac), Cadillac, Welch, Cartercar, Elmore, Ewing, Randolph and Rapid/Reliance. In most cases the companies were bought by the issue of GM shares, but the purchase of Cadillac was made largely with cash. The more significant makes are listed separately.

In 1911 the General Motors Truck Co was created to run Rapid/Reliance and the initials GMC were used on many General Motors commercials thereafter. Through Buick, GM gained an interest in the Canadian firm McLaughlin, which assembled group cars and became General Motors of Canada after being purchased by GM in 1918.

In 1910 GM accounted for 20 per cent of US vehicle output, with 40,000 sales, but that year a bankers' trust took over management of the firm, closing or selling off many of the fringe companies Durant had bought. Durant himself left the company and founded Chevrolet. C. W. Nash was president of GM from 1912 until buying the Thomas B. Jeffery Co in 1916 and creating Nash.

In 1915 GM group sales rose to 100,000 vehicles, now just 10 per cent of the market. Principal shareholders at about this time included the du Pont chemical family, who owned 26.4 per cent in 1918 and 36 per cent in 1921.

Chevrolet, which had risen meteorically under Durant, took control of GM in a complex share exchange in 1916 which saw capital grow by $40 million to $100 million and the formation of General Motors Corporation. In 1918, however, the roles were reversed and GM acquired Chevrolet.

General Motors' former headquarters in New York

Some 20,000 trucks and 5000 ambulances were made in World War I, along with aero engines and other products. Durant, like Ford, was a pacifist who initially would not allow war materials to be made in GM factories, although he tempered his views after Henry M. Leland left to develop Liberty engines.

The Samson tractor line, bought in 1917, failed in the face of Fordson competition. Other purchases were more successful, however, and included Northway Motors; Champion Ignition; Guardian Frigerator, which cost $56,000 and became Frigidaire; Hyatt Bearings, which brought A. P. Sloan, later GM president, into the group; Dayton Engineering Laboratories, run by C. F. Kettering, who headed GM research for many years and originated anti-knock petrol and octane rating; and Fisher Body.

Assets leapt from $135 million to $575 million as a result of this buying flurry but sales of $270 million in 1918 were savaged in the 1920 slump. Only Buick and Cadillac were paying their way and Chevrolet was nearly wound up. W. C. Durant was bought out by the bankers with $3 million worth of shares and Pierre S. du Pont was put in charge. Walter P. Chrysler, who had come into GM via Buick, later recruited K. T. Keller from GM to head his own motor empire.

A clear policy was now devised to tackle different segments of the market with different makes of car. The Sheridan and Scripps-Booth overlapped other makes so were discontinued. All cars were to be priced at the top of their market sector and were to be quality products. Chevrolet would cater for the bottom end, Cadillac for the top, with Oakland, Oldsmobile and Buick in-between. In the mid-1920s Pontiac was added as a closed car and ranked above Chevrolet while La Salle was added below Cadillac. Annual model changes, with the model year starting in August, became GM policy.

From 1923 corporate financial control, forecasting, buying, advertising and research were instituted. A central department organizing credit sales to the trade and customers had existed since 1919. An Art and Colour section was created in 1927 under Harley J. Earl to promote corporate identity in styling and design.

A range of 'copper-cooled' engines introduced in 1923 was quickly stopped when fewer than 800 cars had reached the public. Later in the year the industry's first fully balanced (and, on the Cadillac V8, compensated) crankshafts were introduced on GM-designed machines. GM held 17 per cent of the market but was overproducing drastically, so reports were requested from dealers every 10 days to help forecast requirements more accurately.

In 1928 GM exported an all-time peak of almost 300,000 vehicles, but as protectionism was growing in many overseas markets it also began assembly operations in such centres as London, Antwerp and Copenhagen. In 1925 it bought the then financially precarious Vauxhall for $2.6 million and in 1929 the somewhat healthier Opel for $33 million. In 1925 it started assembly in Brazil and two years later began an assembly operation in Japan. Its original British assembly operation at Hendon employed 1000 in 1929.

At home, GM Truck merged with Yellow Cab Manufacturing of Chicago in 1925 and

GMC manufacturing was then undertaken until 1943 by Yellow Truck and Coach Co. In 1926 GM exceeded 1.25 million vehicle sales, and in 1927 Chevrolet alone exceeded 1 million and overtook Ford. GM sales quadrupled in the 1920s.

At the end of the decade it diversified into engines and equipment for railways when it acquired the Winton Engine Co and Electro-Motive Engineering. Complete two-stroke diesel locos were mass-produced to standard designs from 1938 and 4000 were exported in the next 25 years.

In 1919 40 per cent of US Fokker – which became General Aviation – and the Dayton Wright Aircraft Co had been bought. Allison, a specialist workshop for Indianapolis Speedway, was purchased in 1929 and is nowadays in the Detroit Diesel-Allison division, making automatic transmissions and aero components.

Detroit was the name given to the division making smaller two-stroke diesels from 1938, which are still in production for trucks, earthmovers and similar vehicles. Detroit also developed torque converter transmissions for buses in the mid-1930s.

In the car division, steel 'turret tops' were introduced in 1934; independent suspension had come the previous autumn. In 1938 Buick and Oldsmobile tried semi-automatic transmission that led to Harley Thompson's successful Hydramatic system in 1939. Thompson had been responsible for pioneering synchromesh in 1928. In 1940 Harley J. Earl became the first stylist to reach vice-president level in the US motor industry and was responsible for the look of more than 50 million cars by 1960.

Some $350 million was spent on plant and equipment expansion and renewal in the 1930s, which stood GM in good stead as a supplier of defence material during World War II. Up to 1945 Allison made 70,000 aero engines, which it had first developed in the 1930s. Several divisions, including Cadillac, made tanks and tank gearboxes/engines, and $2 billion worth of trucks and DUKWs were supplied. Total value of wartime production was $12.5 billion.

After the war Holden, an Australian body-builder which had been purchased in 1931, became a car manufacturer and other overseas plants were acquired. The Euclid construction machinery firm was bought in 1953 but later sold because of anti-trust laws and the GM Terex division was formed in its place. Gas turbine manufacture began in 1954.

Some 30 million GM vehicles are in current use around the world. The company employs more than 500,000 people, including about 20,000 scientists and engineers at the Detroit research centre. General Motors is America's largest manufacturer and the world's largest maker of vehicles. Chevrolet alone, GM's largest division, had made 50 million vehicles by June 1963. In 1975 GM produced 7 million vehicles in the USA and Canada.

GM makes special local models in many countries including Belgium (the Ranger since 1970), Canada (the Acadian since 1962) and South America. It was a pioneer of diesel cars in the USA in the late 1970s and imported smaller diesels from Isuzu, in which it took a 34.2 per cent stake in 1971 and whose products it markets under GM brand names in the USA and other countries.

In 1982 GM acquired a 5 per cent stake in Suzuki and the following year announced a joint venture with Toyota. In 1985 GM bought the Mexican company Diesel Nacional SA which makes Dina commercial vehicles, and was said to be interested in acquiring ENASA (Pegaso) and Leyland in Britain.

In 1984 General Motors had worldwide sales and revenue of $83.9 billion. Worldwide sales equalled 8.3 million vehicles out of an estimated world market of 37.7 million, representing 22 per cent of all vehicle sales. The same year a joint venture was set up with Toyota to utilize an idle plant in California to produce a new subcompact model entitled the Chevrolet Nova. This new operation was formally named the New United Motor Manufacturing Inc.

At the beginning of 1985 GM announced the formation of another subsidiary, thereby adding a sixth North American nameplate. The Saturn Corporation, as the new venture was entitled, was formed as a 'clean sheet' operation to develop and manufacture a new range of small cars principally to compete with Japanese and European products. GM sales worldwide rose to 9.3 million vehicles in 1985, at a value of $96.4 billion. NB

GEORGES IRAT
FRANCE 1921-1948

Using a four-cylinder 2-litre overhead-valve engine designed by Maurice Gaultier from Delage, Georges Irat began building fast touring cars at Châtou, Seine et Oise, in 1921. The company was also responsible for production of the Majola and may have intended to build its own cars as early as 1914, when Automobiles Irat was listed in Blvd Pereire, Paris.

In 1922 output was 150 cars from a well-equipped factory of 377,000sq ft (35,000sq m). All but the body was built in-house and there were extensive test facilities. In 1923 100 cars were made, followed by 200 in 1924 and the first of many competition successes. Although Maurice Gaultier had returned to Delage, Irat produced in 1927 a 3-litre six of identical bore and stroke to Gaultier's four, which remained in production.

In 1928 Georges' son Michel introduced a little 1086cc CB2 sports model. This Michel Irat was sold from his father's showrooms in Paris but was probably made initially by Chaigneau-Brasier. The Michel Irat became a Georges Irat model in 1930, the year after Irat had moved to a new factory at Neuilly.

The six had grown to 3.6 litres by 1929 and in 1930-31 came 4- and 5-litre Lycoming straight-eights, installed in long, low Saoutchik-bodied cars. These models were ended in 1933. In 1934 there was a six, with freewheel, that may well have been Chenard et Walcker based.

Following near financial collapse, the firm moved to Levallois-Perret in 1935 with new backing from Godefroy et Leveque, which needed a tied customer for its Ruby engines. About 1500 front-wheel-drive 1100cc sports cars were made in the next three years.

In 1938 was introduced an additional front-wheel-drive car with 11CV Citroën running gear and all rubber suspension. Some 40 to 50 were made. In 1939 the company was known as Etablissements Irat, Godefroy et Leveque.

During World War II, fully independently sprung cars and vans were made having electric rear-mounted motors and batteries under their bonnets. The early post-war years saw the adoption of Grégoire-like construction on a single prototype which used magnesium alloy bodywork and a flat-four 1100cc engine. A double overhead-cam, rear-wheel-drive companion model also failed to progress as far as production.

Georges Irat 1086cc two-seater of 1935

In 1948, when cars were discontinued, the new firm of Irat et Cie was created at Begles-Tartifume, Gironde, to make DOG diesel engines, some of which appeared in Field Farmer tractors while others were sold to Isobloc the bus-maker. Irat trucks were made for several years in Bordeaux, and included a remarkable DOG-powered frameless front-wheel-drive oil tanker with independent rear suspension and Cotal gearbox which was displayed at the 1949 Paris Salon. The Bordeaux truck venture came to an end in the early 1950s. The Société Cherifienne d'Etudes des Automobiles Georges Irat developed a Dyna-Panhard engined utility car in Casablanca in 1951 with help from Emile Petit, but few were built. NB.

GEORGES RICHARD
see Brasier

GEORGES ROY
FRANCE 1906-1928

This Bordeaux manufacturer was little-known outside its immediate region. Starting in 1906 it made one-, two- and four-cylinder cars, although only the latter was made in 1909. In 1910 monobloc 12 and 16hp fours were joined by a pair-cast six. A road test on the round-radiatored 12 in 1912 commented on the remarkable absence of vibration and stated that it performed well on hills.

Old fashioned but well made cars with Georges Roy-built bodywork were produced after World War I. From 1922 to 1925 bullnose cars with either 1-litre or 2-litre engines, but otherwise of similar specification, were offered. A 1½-litre model was being made when production ceased in 1928, although the chassis was available for light commercial vehicles until the early 1930s. NB

GERMAIN
BELGIUM 1898-1914

The Ateliers Germain of Monceau-sur-Sambre were established in 1873 to manufacture railway carriages and, later, tramcars. In November 1897 the company acquired from Madame Emile Levassor the Belgian rights for the manufacture of the Daimler-Phoenix engine and the Panhard car which used it. The first cars emerged from the factory in June 1898; called either Panhard Belge or Daimler Belge, they had 6hp two-cylinder engines and looked almost identical to the contemporary Panhard.

The extensive Germain works enabled production to get under way quickly, and by October 1899 the company was making 10 examples a month of the 6hp as well as the French designed Elan voiturette, for which it had also acquired a licence. A Panhard-derived 12hp four-cylinder car was added in April 1900, and the 1901 range consisted of 6 and 8hp twins and a 12hp four, now with lower and longer chassis and equal sized wheels. Production was running at three cars a week.

In 1902 Germain acquired the licence for the manufacture of Renault light cars, replacing the now defunct Elan, but the Renault frames had to be strengthened to cope with Belgian streets. The larger cars continued to be built on Panhard lines until 1903 and were joined by commercial vehicles from 1100lb (500kg) to 5 tons capacity. At least one Germain 32-seater double-decker bus ran in London in 1904.

For the 1904 season Germain broke away from the *système Panhard*, introducing three four-cylinder cars, 16/22, 24/32 and 35/40CV, with side-valve engines, chain drive and armoured wood frames. They were known as Germain-Standards. In mid-season the company delivered its 1000th car. The workforce

totalled 650 men, of whom about half were working on vehicles, the others on railway equipment. Germain also began to manufacture motorboats in conjunction with the Cockerill steel works.

For the 1906 season came the Germain-Chainless, with shaft drive and steel frames.

Germain 30hp Grand Prix car of 1907

Teams were entered in the 1907 and 1908 Grands Prix, but they did not distinguish themselves, and Germain abandoned competition after that. It also abandoned commercial vehicles around this time as it felt that the heavier commercial chassis needed chain drive but the engineering department was firmly orientated towards the shaft-drive Chainless range.

A fairly wide range of Chainless models was made until 1914 with four- and six-cylinder engines. From 1912 to 1914 two models had sleeve-valve engines imported from Daimler of Coventry. Car production was not resumed after World War I, although a few cars were assembled from pre-war components and Germain lingered on some lists until as late as 1922.

The company continued with its railway work and exhibited a 5-ton truck powered by a CLM three-cylinder opposed-piston diesel engine at the 1937 Brussels Salon. Neither this nor a similarly powered agricultural tractor went into production. After a merger with the Société Anglo-Franco-Belge de la Croyère, the company name was changed to Anglo-Germain, and as such survived until 1967. Among its last products were rotary discharge bodies for refuse trucks. GNG

GIBBONS
GB 1921-1926

Built by Gibbons & Moore of Chadwell Heath, Essex, between 1921 and 1926, the Gibbons was an extremely basic, plywood-bodied two-seater with an air-cooled engine hung outside the offside of the body. Three engines were available, a single-cylinder 349cc Precision, a single-cylinder 488cc Blackburne and a 688cc flat-twin Coventry-Victor. Power was transmitted by twin belts, one running to

Georges Roy two-seat tourer of 1910

each rear wheel. The belt to the offside wheel ran over a pulley arrangement which offered a clutch of sorts and the low ratio, and the belt to the nearside wheel was engaged by a lever to give high gear.

Even with the largest engine, performance was strictly limited and hills were an embarrassment. The lack of performance was probably a good thing, as the Gibbons' brakes were simple rubbing blocks on the belt pulley rims and steering was by wire and pulley to the centre-pivoted solid front axle.

The smallest car had tandem seating, the others side-by-side, and the largest engined model was the most popular. £140 plus taxes in 1922 was very expensive for a car which counted a spare wheel, wipers, lights, a horn and a speedometer as extras and, not surprisingly, very few Gibbons were sold. BL

GILBERN
GB 1959-1974

Gilbern Invader of 1970

One of the few companies ever to build cars in Wales, Gilbern was set up in the small village of Llantwit Fadre near Pontypridd, Glamorgan, by a former German prisoner of war and a local butcher. German-born Bernard Friese used his experience with a glassfibre manufacturer to build a glassfibre-bodied special, which attracted the attention of Giles Smith; the two formed Gilbern Sports Cars (Components) Ltd in a workshop behind Smith's butcher's shop in 1959, forming the name from their own christian names.

Gilbern's first production car, the GT Mk1, used a spaceframe chassis and an unstressed body, with BMC A-series suspension and running gear. Three choices of engine were offered, the 948cc A-series (with optional supercharging), the 1558cc B-series or the 1098cc Coventry-Climax. The popular choice was the reliable B-series, which gave the lightweight four-seater 100mph (160kph) performance, matched by good roadholding.

Early production ran at about 10 days per

car and Gilberns were distributed by hill-climber Peter Cottrell. Eleven were built in the first year, mostly as £978 kits.

Gilbern showed its cars at the 1961 London Racing Car Show and later that year adopted the new 1622cc MGA engine, giving performance on a par with the Austin-Healey 3000. Production reached 83 cars for the year. In 1962 production was a steady one car a week; by then a small dealer network had been started, although the delivery time was still about a year.

Towards the end of 1962 the two directors and three employees moved to a slightly larger factory. They added extra staff to increase production and in 1963 the 1798cc MGB engine updated the car as the 1800GT.

After negotiations with a German MG distributor, Gilbern planned export of about 100 cars a year to Germany. The modestly priced four-seater was selling well at home. In 1965 production was three to four cars a week, for a total of 157, and Gilbern was recognized by the Society of Motor Manufacturers and Traders, elevating its status from a kit builder to a true manufacturer.

In 1966 Gilbern introduced the restyled two-door Genie coupé, with 3-litre Ford V6 engine and BMC running gear. The 120mph (193kph) Genie sold for about £1500 in kit form or £2000 fully built and sold quite well. A further 100 or so GTs brought the total for that model to over 500.

Seeking money for expansion, Gilbern was taken over in April 1968 by Ace Holdings Ltd of Cardiff, Britain's biggest slot-machine manufacturer. Giles Smith left but Friese stayed, as development director alongside new managing director Michael Leather, formerly a brewery manager. In 1969 Ace itself was taken over by the Clubman's Club, part of the Mecca leisure group, and Friese resigned.

In 1968 Gilbern offered a fuel-injected Genie, the PI 130, but few were sold. Genie production continued until 1970, when it was replaced by the very similar Invader, first seen

in July 1969. In 1970 Gilbern planned to increase its four dealers to 10, selling complete cars, and boost production to 10 a week. However 99 per cent of cars were being sold as kits, and these were delivered direct to customers by trailer.

In spite of plans for overseas manufacture under licence, Gilbern was hit by increased competition from mass produced sports cars and in April 1973 by the introduction of value added tax. Production stopped in mid-year and a receiver was appointed in September. A brief takeover by a Welsh property developer failed to revive Gilbern, which finally ceased trading in 1974. BL

GILLET-FOREST
FRANCE 1900-1907

Société Gillet-Forest began building cars at St Cloud, Seine, in 1900. The first, three-seater cars, which appeared at the Paris Salon in August 1900, resembled a miniature Amédée Bollée and were powered by a 5hp single-cylinder horizontal engine. They had band brakes, a three-speed gearbox and direct drive – fully enclosed in an aluminium-cased oil bath which gave the car a very neat appearance.

Gillet-Forest delivery van of 1903

At the 1901 Paris Show, Gillet-Forest claimed that its car was the most economical on the market and in the consumption trials the car apparently used so little fuel that the judges refused to accept the results. A second, observed test persuaded them to accept the figures. In December 1901 *The Autocar* noted that Gillet-Forest cars were doing remarkably well in alcohol and other trials. The Gillet-Forest engine produced between 2hp at 100rpm and 7hp at 1200rpm and the reason claimed for its outstanding economy was that the exhaust was regulated to leave some burnt gas in the combustion chamber, thereby limiting the incoming charge.

Larger versions of the horizontal single engine were offered between 1902 and 1905, after which two- and four-cylinder vertical engines, built under Métallurgique licence, were used – except on Gillet-Forest light commercials. The company built cars from 8 to 40hp until 1907. BL

GINETTA
GB 1958 to date

Racing enthusiasts Bob, Douglas, Ivor and Trevor Walklett ran an agricultural and construction engineering business, Walklett Bros, in Woodbridge, Suffolk. In the early 1950s Ivor built a modified and rebodied Wolseley Hornet sports car which would retrospectively be named the Ginetta G1.

The G1 prompted a low-cost production version of the Ginetta and early in 1958 the Walkletts formed Ginetta Cars Ltd. The G2 was launched in the same year, the alloy bodied two-seater being sold in kit form and having a multi-tubular chassis and Ford running gear. About 100 G2s were built between 1958 and 1960. There followed the glassfibre bodied G3, which could take the new Ford 105E engine as well as the earlier side-valve units; about 60 were sold.

At the 1961 Racing Car Show Ginetta introduced the G4, which could be used as a two-seater road car or as a club racer. It was designed by Ivor – Bob was the administrative talent, Douglas the general manager and Trevor the stylist – and used mainly Ford running gear. The G4 was very successful in competition and in sales, more than 500 having been built between 1961 and 1969.

A year after the G4 was launched, Ginetta

Ginetta G15 of 1973

Ginetta G21 of c.1972

Ginetta G4 of 1965

moved to a larger works in Witham, Essex, and the Walklett brothers gave up their other business. A Series II G4 was introduced in 1963, followed by a Ford 1500 engined version, directly derived from racing experience. This was originally known as the G5 but was popularly, and later properly, known as the G41500. In 1964 Ginetta built three examples of a glassfibre-monocoque Formula 3 single-seater, the G8.

The next road car was the larger, two-seater G10, powered by an American 4.7-litre Ford V8 in an attempt to broaden Ginetta's markets. It was introduced at the 1965 Racing Car Show but only six were built. The similar G11, with milder MGB power, was launched in 1966 but only 12 were built.

More than 50 of the mid-engined G12 were built and continued the G4's competition successes, but Ginetta's best known model was the Hillman Imp powered G15 coupé, introduced in 1967 at the London Motor Show. Series production started in 1968.

Ginetta grew with the success of the G15; in 1970 the company had 20 staff building three G15s a week alongside the latest run of racing cars. In March 1972 it moved to a new, fully-equipped, 40,000sq ft (3700sq m) factory at Sudbury, Suffolk, but the introduction of value added tax in 1973 stopped production of the G15 by April 1974 after over 800 had been built. The company returned to Witham.

In 1970 Ginetta had launched the 3-litre Ford V6 or 1725 Sunbeam powered G21, a pretty, two-seater coupé, but production did not start until September 1973. After the G15 was dropped this was the sole production model until 1981. G23 and G24 models were built in 1980 but never went into production and instead, in 1981, Ginetta launched a modern version of the G4, the Series 1V, later renamed the G27.

At the 1982 London Motor Show the Walkletts showed a five-seater leisure vehicle, the GRS Tora, which they subsequently sold as a kit. They also planned to revive the G15 theme with the mid-engined, Fiesta-powered G25, but stopped work on that car to launch the very pretty Cortina-based G26 saloon for 1985, either fully built or as a kit. Ginetta saw in the G26 a real opportunity to expand production perhaps even past the six a week peak achieved by the G15 and to as many as 50 cars a week – given sufficient finance. A new model for 1987 was the mid-engined G32 for XR3i or RS Turbo engines. This was available complete except for the engine, while the G26 and G27 could still be had in kit form. BL

GLADIATOR
FRANCE 1896-1920

The Société Gladiator was founded in 1891 by Aucoc and Darracq to make bicycles. They were very successful, but their price-cutting methods attracted the displeasure of the British cycle manufacturers to whom the French market was very important. In 1896 Aucoc and Darracq were bought out by a syndicate led by Harvey DuCros, head of Dunlop, and company promoter Ernest Hooley. The new company was called Clément, Gladiator and Humber (France) Ltd, and added motorcycles and cars to its products in 1896.

The cars were light voiturettes powered by rear-mounted 4hp single-cylinder horizontal engines, followed by front-engined cars with Aster power units. These were sold under the name Clément as well as Gladiator, because Adolphe Clément was on the board of Gladiator and remained there until 1903. Even after that Gladiator continued to use the Clément name, which is why Adolphe Clément called his own products Clément-Bayard from 1903.

In 1903 Gladiator's works at Pré St Gervais employed 800 men making more than 1000 cars a year, of which four-fifths were sold in Britain. The Cléments, which were handled in Britain by E. H. Lancaster, had live axles, while the otherwise similar Gladiators used chain drive and were handled by S. F. Edge until he became too busy with Napiers.

By 1907 quite large Gladiators up to 5.5 litres were being made, but soon afterwards car production at Pré St Gervais was run down. Cléments were made in England by Swift of Coventry from 1908 to 1914. It was also announced that certain Gladiator models would be made by Austin, but this did not come about. Harvey DuCros had interests in both these English companies.

In 1910 production of Gladiator cars was transferred to the Vinot et Deguingand works at Puteaux, and the Pré St Gervais factory was devoted solely to bicycles. Subsequent Gladiators were almost identical to Vinots, except that the six-cylinder Gladiators had no Vinot equivalent. By 1914 the sixes had been dropped and the range consisted of four four-cylinder models, from 1.7 to 4.1 litres. Two of these were revived in 1919, but after 1920 the Gladiator name was dropped. GNG

GLAS/GOGGOMOBIL
GERMANY 1955-1969

The Hans Glas Isaria Maschinenfabrik was an agricultural machinery business established in 1883 at Pilsting, Bavaria, later renamed Dingolfing. In 1951 it began to make the Goggo motor scooter and four years later entered the minicar market with the 246cc rear-engined Goggomobil.

This was more car-like than its rivals, the Isetta and Messerschmitt, having four wheels, side doors and a small bonnet which accommodated luggage. It was a great success and although it was the first car to be made by Glas it outlived all its successors, remaining in production until June 1969, by which date 280,739 had been made, including forward control vans for the German Post Office.

From 1962 to 1966 6100 Goggomobil cars and vans were built in Spain by Munguia Industrial of Bilbao. Plans to make the 1700 saloon there came to nothing.

In 1957 a larger car with 584cc engine was announced. Called the Isar, after the river that runs through Dingolfing, it was also made with 688cc engine and featured an American-styled wrap around windscreen. More signi-

ficant was the 1004 front-engined four-cylinder coupé, which pioneered the use of a toothed belt instead of a chain for the camshaft drive. Introduced in 1962 it was followed by even more ambitious cars, the 1700 four-door saloon, 1300 GT coupé, with body designed and built by Frua, and finally the 1965 2.6-litre V8 coupé with twin overhead camshafts and again a Frua body. This was nicknamed the 'Glaserati' and was pitched between the Porsche 912 and 911 in price.

These were all good cars but the relatively small Glas firm was competing directly with BMW and Porsche and in addition was making too many models. The only one to make a profit in the mid-1960s was the hardy Goggomobil and this was not sufficient to keep the company afloat.

In 1966 BMW purchased Glas for 91 million marks and proceeded to whittle down the range, which still consisted of eight models. The body presses for the 1700 saloon went to South Africa where they were used, with BMW engines and radiator grilles, as the basis of a locally made range that lasted to 1975. The profit making Goggomobil was continued until 1969, and the Frua-bodied coupés were integrated into the BMW range, the 1300 with a BMW 1600 engine and the V8 with a slightly larger engine and, of course, BMW badging. About 400 of these were made.

The real value of the acquisition to BMW was the factory. After a 453 million mark modernization programme it has become BMW's most up to date plant, with much greater room for expansion than at Munich. It currently employs more than 10,000 workers and builds the 5, 6, and 7 Series BMW cars. GNG

GLASSIC
USA 1965 to date

The idea for the Glassic Ford Model A replica came from Jack Faircloth, a successful, semi-retired International-Harvester dealer, and Frank Taylor, an imported-car dealer, both of West Palm Beach, Florida. In 1963 Faircloth and three partners put up backing for Glassic Industries Inc to be formed in 1964 and to produce the first Glassic Phaeton in 1965.

This first car was moulded from a genuine 1930 Model A, albeit somewhat modified. It used the 93hp four-cylinder engine and three-speed manual gearbox of the International-Harvester Scout, which gave it a top speed of over 90mph (145kph).

Faircloth's partners left soon after the prototype was completed but Jack and his son Joel put the Glassic into production in 1966, showing it at that year's New York Auto Show and offering options such as four-wheel drive, limited slip differential and even power take-offs. Thus equipped, the car was eligible for International-Harvester service and warranty terms through their 4700 dealers.

In 1966 production reached two cars a week, fell back to a total of 50 in 1969 and then rose to four a week by 1972, even that being some way short of demand. By 1971 the Fairclouths had built some 300 cars.

In August 1972 the company was taken over by Fred Pro, president of Parker-West, who saw a chance to expand production to a fully commercial scale. Seeking more performance and without Fairclouths's I-H ties, Parker-West gave the Glassic a handbuilt chassis and 200bhp, 302cu in Ford V8, to put performance into the Corvette class. Parts and service were available through any Ford or Lincoln-Mercury dealer.

Parker-West opened a showroom in Beverly Hills in March 1973 but almost all cars were ordered by mail. In their first year the new owners built 250 cars. In 1975 they introduced the Romulus II, a Ford-powered Auburn speedster replica which was a continuation of the Auburn built by Pro's company the Auburn Motor Car Corporation.

In 1976 production was taken over by Total Performance Inc of Wallingford, Connecticut. Total revised the car with Chevrolet V8 engines and offered the original A replica and other replicas based on the Ford Model B. BL

GLIDE
USA 1903-1919

The Glide was built by the Bartholomew Co of Peoria, Illinois, which had worked on a Bartholomew car briefly between 1901 and 1903, although it did not apparently go into produc-

Glas Goggomobil minicar of 1955

Glas V8 coupé of 1966

tion. The first Glide was built in 1903. It had an 8hp horizontal single-cylinder engine, mounted under the seat and driving by chain. It was sold until 1907 as the Glidemobile and contemporary advertising urged potential customers to 'Ride in a Glide and Then Decide'.

In 1905 Glide introduced the Glideabout, a 14hp twin-cylinder model. This was supplemented by a 30hp Rutenber vertical four-cylinder model with shaft drive replacing the earlier models' chains.

In 1910 Glide listed the Special, a seven-passenger 45hp touring car, at $2500, the similarly priced 45hp Scout and a Special roadster at $2400 – all with twin-plug ignition. The 1910 advertising assured customers that 'Glides are licensed under the Selden Patents', and compared the cars with the best competitors, saying 'Forget Price'.

From 1911 to 1913 the company also listed trucks. From 1915 until production stopped in 1919 the cars were fitted with 40hp six-cylinder Rutenber engines in very ordinary chassis. BL

GN
GB 1910-1925

Undoubtedly the most successful of the cyclecars, the GN was the product of two engineers, H. R. Godfrey and Archibald Frazer-Nash, who had both worked at Willans and Robinson (now English Electric) at Rugby. Together they built a number of purely experimental cars while still in their teens, and in December 1910 launched a vee-twin cyclecar with belt drive. *Motorcycle* observed: 'All parts except the engines (JAP or Peugeot) and magnetos (Bosch) and minor fittings, are made at the works of Godfrey and Nash.'

The first six cars were made in the stables of the Frazer-Nash family home. 'The Elms', Golders Green Road, Hendon, but they then moved to The Burroughs, Hendon, a series of sheds occupied by several small businesses. In 1911 Godfrey and Frazer-Nash started manufacturing their own 90 degree vee-twin using Peugeot cylinders and valves and in 1912 they made their own inlet-over-exhaust design cylinder heads. The pre-war GN cars used a variety of transmissions incorporating belts and chains. Production at Hendon did not exceed two cars a week up to 1916.

In 1919 British Grégoire bought GN for £70,000. The company restarted production at East Hill, Wandsworth, in 1919 and before long was employing 500 men. The maximum output was 58 cars a week and during the best month 220 cars were built. Two travelling service representatives inspected owners' cars. GN was only the second firm to do this, the first being Rolls-Royce.

In 1919 GN established a connection with the French Salmson company because Marcel Lourde was a director of British Grégoire and a personal friend of Salmsons. He negotiated for Salmson to manufacture GNs under licence and sell them under the name GN. Six cars had been built by the time of the 1919 Paris Salon and about 1600 were made until 1922, when Salmson built its first four-cylinder car. Salmson paid GN £15,500 in royalties over the three years.

GN sales began to fall in 1921 at the end of the post-war car boom, a receiver was appointed and the company was bought by a Mr Black who wanted to go for mass production of touring models while Godfrey and Frazer-Nash preferred to continue with sports cars. A water-cooled four-cylinder shaft-drive model was announced for 1922 powered by a DFP engine. Godfrey and Frazer-Nash left in October 1922 and the four-cylinder car was in production by December.

The 1923 models both had shaft drive, one with a vee-twin GN engine and the other with a four-cylinder Chapuis-Dornier engine, chosen because it was cheaper than the DFP. Production ended in May 1923: there was a deficit on manufacture of more than £84,000, but on the spares and repairs side a small profit of £6950.

A new company, GN Ltd, was formed by two employees to provide service and spares for the older models. This company assembled a few chain-drive chassis with Anzani 11.9hp four-cylinder engines in 1924-25. In 1928 an unsuccessful attempt was made to market a single-cylinder three-wheeled delivery van. The following year GN Ltd became a garage selling General Motors products and the East Hill factory was occupied by the Clayton Mineral Water Co.

Godfrey founded his own company to service GNs, later joining Stuart Proctor to manufacture the Godfrey Proctor car and later still joined Halford and Robins to make the HRG. Archie Frazer-Nash formed Frazer-Nash Ltd in 1922. GNG

GOBRON-BRILLIÉ/GOBRON
FRANCE 1898-1930

Gustave Gobron was born in Ardennes in 1846 and became a politician and businessman. During the Franco-Prussian war he achieved a measure of fame by fleeing besieged Paris in a balloon in order to continue the fight against the enemy. Eugene Brillié, born in 1863, was a talented student of the Ecole Centrale des Arts et Manufactures who developed an opposed-piston 'vibrationless' motor.

The two men formed Société des Moteurs Gobron-Brillié in Paris in November 1898. It had a capital of 500,000 francs and made two-cylinder four-piston cars with, for the first five years, an ingenious metering device in place of a carburettor.

The firm became a limited company in 1900, and increased its capital to 1 million francs and moved to Boulogne-sur-Seine on the edge of Paris. Gobron-Brillié production

GN touring model of 1921

ran at 75 to 150 a year. Cars were sold in Britain by Botwoods of Ipswich under the name Teras.

Eugene Brillié struck out on his own in 1903 by which time four-cylinder cars were being offered. Brillié's name was not finally dropped until the 1920s, although it was often placed in brackets after about 1912 when the cars were mentioned in the press.

In 1904 a 13½-litre four-cylinder car became the first officially to exceed 100mph (160kph), but competition success largely eluded this and other models. Most pre-war Gobrons were monstrous luxury cars, some retaining chain drive into the 1910s. Production also included some cheap taxi chassis with two-cylinder engines and modest touring chassis.

In late 1908 an X-layout, eight-cylinder, sixteen-piston aero engine developing 80hp, yet weighing only 330lb (150kg), was announced. Little more was heard of this or the cars until 1919, when the firm became

Gobron-Brillié double phaeton of 1898

Automobiles Gobron and moved to Levallois-Perret. There it continued producing its opposed-piston cars, reviving a 35 and bringing out a final 25 in 1922 which had the added complexity of sleeve valves. Also in 1922 there was a conventional Chapuis-Dornier engined 10hp light car, some of which were also made for sale by Stabilia under its own name in the mid-1920s.

Sales were poor throughout the 1920s and Gobron's swansong proved to be the 1928 Cozette supercharged CA 4 Turbo-Sport. It was largely the work of M. Chabreiron of EHP and had a 1½-litre side-valve engine said to be able to propel the car at more than 100mph (160kph). In 1930 Gobron gave up the unequal struggle. NB

GOGGOMOBIL
see Glas

GOLIATH
GERMANY 1928-1963

Goliath GP700 sports coupé of 1951

The Goliath was Carl Borgward's first entry into motor manufacturing. Born in 1909, the son of a Hamburg merchant, Borgward set up a tyre factoring business in Bremen in 1919 and two years later formed Bremer Kuhlerfabrik Borgward & Co to make radiators, principally for Hansa and Hansa-Lloyd. In 1924 he set up Goliath-Werke and built a prototype four-wheel car, but the first production Goliaths were 200cc Ilo-powered three-wheel vans, the Blitzkarre. They were widely used by the German Post Office and a four-wheel version was also made.

At the 1928 Berlin Show, Goliath presented the 198cc Pionier car, a well-made three-wheeler with independent suspension and electric starting. Its small size exempted it from tax and the need for a full driving licence. A fastback version of the Pionier was offered in 1933 but in 1934 Goliath returned to building only commercials, namely the Hansa-powered Rekord light truck, Borgward having bought Hansa between 1929 and 1932.

The Borgward works, including those of Goliath, suffered badly during World War II, being almost 80 per cent destroyed. Although demand for Goliath trucks was strong, production was not resumed until 1948.

In 1950 Goliath returned to car building with the 24bhp 688cc two-stroke twin, front-wheel-drive GP700. The little car was quick

and handled well; the engine took several records in a special three-wheeler chassis, but it also proved terribly unreliable, particularly with the optional Bosch fuel injection offered from 1951. A coupé, the GP700E, was built in very small numbers in 1952 and in 1953 a synchromesh gearbox replaced the former four-speed crash unit.

In 1955 the 40bhp 886cc GP900 was introduced, this with the troublesome fuel injection as standard, although the GP700 now offered only carburettors. In 1956, the last full year of two-stroke sales, Goliath claimed a quarter of its sales were exports to 70 countries – but sales were down to only 8125.

The flat-four, four-stroke 1100 was introduced in 1957, again with front-wheel drive but having scrapped fuel injection completely. Versions of 40 and 55hp were offered, sold in the United States and Australia as the Borgward Tiger, and were known for very sporty performance. The 1100 suffered from the reputation of the 700 and 900 and fewer than 15,000 were sold before mid-1958 when it was renamed the Hansa 1100.

The Goliath name was dropped on all but commercial vehicles and on the limited production, Jeep-style, four-wheel-drive Jagdwagen. The Borgward empire failed in 1961, effectively ending Goliath, but some production continued until 1963, the year in which Carl Borgward himself died. BL

Goliath 1100 coupé of c.1957

Gobron-Brillié 40/60hp of 1906

GORDON-KEEBLE/
DE BRUYNE, GORDON
GB 1959-1961; 1964-1968

When Ipswich garage proprietor Jim Keeble uprated a customer's Peerless with a Chevrolet Corvette power train and showed the car to John Gordon of Peerless Cars, Slough, both men were sufficiently impressed by its performance to set up the Gordon Automobile Co in 1959. The Peerless features of De Dion axle and tubular frame were used in the new car they built, together with a Bertone four-seat steel body styled by the 21-year-old Giugiaro, and a 300bhp Chevrolet V8. Gordon Keeble Ltd was formed with financial backing from George Wansborough, a former Jowett chairman, and his son David.

Production versions, with Williams and Pritchard fibreglass bodies, plastic trim and

Gordon-Keeble of c.1964

Chevrolet 5.4-litre engine, were made in a factory at Eastleigh, beside Southampton Airport, in 1964. The idea was to produce a car which could do all a Ferrari four-seater could for half the price, and to make 250 of them a year.

Finance and production were limited, however, and in March 1965 the firm failed. Keeble left after about 93 cars had been made. The original factory is now used by Air UK as a freight forwarding department.

Fresh backing came from motor dealer Harold Smith, who had a dozen orders outstanding; but, although Keeble and sales director Sir Richard Blake were persuaded to return, the firm collapsed again in 1966 after a further six cars had been built.

Its designs were acquired by an American, John de Bruyne, who showed a modified type at New York in 1968 but only two De Bruynes of Gordon-Keeble type were made. Jim Keeble formed KeeWest Developments Ltd at Totton, Southampton, where some of the former Gordon-Keeble production staff continued to service and restore the cars, and to produce the last batch of Winchester taxi chassis. NB

GOTTSCHALK
see Oryx

GP
GB 1968 to date

GP Speed Shop Ltd of Feltham, Middlesex, was one of the first British companies to build American-style beach buggies in the buggy boom years of 1968 to the early 1970s. The buggies were based on shortened Volkswagen Beetle chassis, for which GP supplied simple, bolt-on body tubs.

In 1970 GP introduced a glassfibre coupé with lift-up roof sections, the Centron, also to be used on a Beetle chassis. The four-seater

Alpine buggy, on a full length Beetle floorpan, was derived from the Super buggy.

The LDV, a hardtop buggy with a pick-up back, initially envisaged as a utility vehicle for developing countries, was shown at the 1971 London Racing Car Show. It soon became popular as another fun-car and more than 200 were sold before the end of 1979.

A hardtop buggy kit, the £395 Ranchero, was shown in 1975 at the Racing Car Show. That same year the company, which had moved to Isleworth in 1972, became GP Concessionaires Ltd.

The gullwing doored Talon, for VW or Porsche engines, was launched in 1979. In 1981 GP introduced the 1939 Packard inspired Madison roadster, still VW-powered and rear-engined in spite of its long-bonneted look. These cars continued to be the mainstay of the range which, in 1987, also included the Turbo Style Beetle and an excellent replica of the early Porsche Speedster, sold as the Spyder. BL

GRÄF & STIFT
AUSTRIA 1907-1938

The Gräf brothers, Karl (a bicycle repairer), Franz (a coachbuilder) and Heinrich (a mechanical engineer) built a one-off car in Vienna in 1895-97 with front-mounted De Dion engine driving the front wheels. They knew about, and were probably involved with, car importer Wilhelm Stift's car experiments, which culminated in the Braun of 1899 and the Buchet-engined Celeritas of 1901.

In 1902 Stift joined the Gräf brothers in making Spitzwagens for another Viennese importer, Arnold Spitz. These came with one, two or four cylinders and were designed by racing driver Otto Hieronymous.

In 1907 Spitz went into liquidation, whereupon Gräf & Stift produced its own range of substantial cars, in 1908 forming Wiener

Automobilfabrik AG. Luxury models, some using De Dion licence axles from 1912, and some reputedly based on Rolls-Royce Silver Ghost ideas, were produced by the company. Commercial vehicles were made from 1909. Bodies were made in the firm's own factory at Liesing and output was 250 to 500 vehicles a year.

The assassination in 1914 of Archduke Franz Ferdinand, who happened to be riding in a 1910 Gräf & Stift 28/32, precipitated World War I, during which lorries and heavy tractors were made. After the war commercials and a new series of four and six-cylinder cars were made, followed in 1930 by a

Gräf of 1897

straight-eight. In 1928 an ingenious opposed-piston engine had been tried in which power was transmitted by rockers, the axis of which could be altered to keep the compression constant despite differing fuel charges.

The workforce totalled 1300 in the mid-1920s and the Automobilfabrik Perl was acquired in 1926 to increase space for body production. J. Gräf ran the factories at this time while financial control was in the hands of A. Dubsky.

Alongside the luxury cars, six-cylinder Citroëns (Gräf-Citroëns) were assembled from 1935 and German Ford V8s (Gräfford) from 1937. A 3.9-litre V12 and 4.7-litre overhead-cam straight-eight appeared in 1938 but were not pursued after Germany overran Austria. The chief engineer, Siegfried Sperling, fled to England and joined Maudslay.

Having built about 3500 cars, the Gräf & Stift factory then concentrated on commercial vehicles with Mercedes-licence engines, although Czech Aero Minors were assembled briefly in 1949-50. The firm's own vee-configuration two-stroke diesels were used for a time in the 1950s before being largely replaced by Henschel and Büssing engines.

In 1970 Gräf & Stift merged with OAF (formerly Austro-Fiat), which was soon taken over by MAN. Gräf & Stift thereafter specialized in making trolley buses and MAN-engined buses, which still carry the name Gräf & Stift and bear the I emblem, signifying First, in place of the silver lion that had adorned the company's vehicles between the two world wars. NB

Graham-Paige (for Pope Pius XI) of 1930

Graham-Paige 3½-litre convertible of 1938

GRAHAM-PAIGE/GRAHAM
USA 1927-1940

The Graham brothers, Joseph, Robert and Ray, started in business making bottles in Indiana and Oklahoma, but in 1916 they sold out and began building truck bodies in Evansville, Indiana. They also made conversion sets for turning cars into light trucks, and from this it was only a step towards building complete trucks, which they began in 1919.

Soon afterwards they attracted the attention of Frederick Haynes, of Dodge Brothers, who wanted to get his company into the trucking business without disrupting passenger car production. In April 1921 there began an agreement whereby Graham Brothers would supply trucks with Dodge engines and transmissions for sale solely through Dodge dealers.

This agreement was so successful that Graham Brothers soon opened factories in Detroit, Stockton, California, and Toronto, Canada. By 1926 they were making more than 37,000 trucks a year, but in that year the brothers resigned from Dodge, which purchased the balance of Graham Brothers shares to add to its existing 51 per cent.

On their own again, the Grahams formed the New York-based Graham Brothers Corporation to handle their non-automotive interests and a few months later bought the Paige-Detroit Motor Car Co for $4 million, with the promise of a further $4 million to improve plant facilities. Paige-Detroit had a new 45-acre (18-hectare) factory in Dearborn, Michigan, where production of the existing Paige six- and eight-cylinder cars was continued in 1927 while the Grahams prepared their own products.

The 1928 Graham-Paige lineup was announced in January 1928; it was ambitious, with four six-cylinder models and a straight-eight, each aimed at the sector of the market already held by a popular car. Thus the $875 Model 610 rivalled the Dodge Four, the $1295 Model 614 met the Buick Standard Six head on, the $1595 Model 619 vied with the Chrysler 72. The $1985 Model 629 was aimed at the Studebaker President Eight, and the $2285 straight-eight Model 835 was priced to rival the series 526 Packard. All Graham-Paiges were above average performers, and the brothers' aggressive self-confidence was rewarded with sales of 73,195 cars in 1928, a record for a new make in its first year.

To meet the expanded demand, Graham-Paige acquired the old Harroun Motor Car Co factory in Wayne, Michigan, as a body plant, built another in Evansville, Indiana, and bought a lumber mill in Florida to supply wood for body frames. By the end of 1928 the workforce had grown from 2840 to 7200, plant capacity from 300 to 700 cars a day, and world wide distributors from 832 to 2270.

Through their charitable work the Grahams had received Papal honours, and in return presented Pope Pius XI with a Le Baron-bodied Series 835 town car. Graham-Paige seemed set to become one of the great success stories of the US motor business, but its prosperity was shortlived: in 1929 the company made more cars – over 77,000 – but profits were more than offset by losses at the retail end of the trade.

Gräf & Stift SP8 sports coupé of 1932

Sales in 1930, now that the Depression was beginning to bite, were down to 33,560 and for 1931 Graham-Paige offered its cheapest car yet, ironically named the Prosperity Six. This cost only $785, although the company was still making the Custom Eight, priced at $2095 for a seven passenger limousine.

The cars were called Graham from 1931, even though the company name remained Graham-Paige Corporation. Sales were down to 20,428 in 1931 and the Evansville body plant and Florida lumber mill were gradually phased out, being leased to other companies.

The 1932 Blue Streak models were radically new with their sloping radiator grilles and fender skirts, and set trends that the whole industry was to follow. They were styled by Amos Northrup of the Murray Corporation. Unfortunately 1932 was the worst year of the Depression, and only 12,969 cars were sold. Business picked up a little the following year, when the Blue Streak was largely unchanged, and 10,967 were sold to earn a small profit of $67,000.

In 1934 a supercharger was offered on the Custom Eight, giving 135bhp. Apart from the Auburn 851 Speedster, Graham was the only American car to feature a supercharger, which remained in the range until 1939.

From 1935 onwards only six-cylinder cars were offered, and Graham lost the styling lead it had gained with the Blue Streak. The 1936 models used bodies of Reo Flying Cloud design for which a royalty of $7.50 per body was paid to Reo. Sales were picking up again as America climbed out of the Depression, with 19,205 recorded for 1936.

Graham made several agreements with foreign manufacturers in the late 1930s, including Lammas Ltd in England for engines and chassis, and Voisin in France for engines. Very few units were supplied to either company, probably 30 to Lammas and 12 to Voisin. More profitable was the sale of 1935 body dies and engine tooling to Nissan of Japan for $390,000. Graham entered a new field in 1937 with the Graham-Bradley farm tractor, powered by a six-cylinder car engine. This was made only until 1939.

For 1938 Graham was again a styling innovator, although the bodies were controversial, and did not begin trends as the Blue Streak had done. Nicknamed 'the Sharknose', they had forward leaning grilles, square headlamps faired into the wings and spats on the rear wheels. The public did not take to them, and only 8800 were made in the three years from 1938 to 1940.

Graham was now in serious trouble, having recorded losses every year since 1933. The company had a final throw with the Hollywood, which used the Cord 810 body dies with the six-cylinder Continental engine used in 'the Sharknose'. These dies were shared with Hupmobile, another company in dire straits; in fact Hupp Skylarks were made alongside Graham Hollywoods in the Graham-Paige factory. Only 859 Hollywoods

were made between April and September 1940, when the Graham-Paige factory ceased car production for ever.

During World War II Graham-Paige made a variety of aircraft and marine engine parts, and also the amphibious tractor nicknamed 'The Alligator'. In 1944 Joseph W. Frazer took control, later making cars with Henry Kaiser in the Kaiser-Frazer Corporation. From June 1946 to February 1947 Graham-Paige made Frazer cars but could not finance its one-third share of the vast Willow Run plant and withdrew from car production altogether.

Graham continued to make farm machinery for a while at York, Pennsylvania, then went into real estate. In 1962 it changed its name to Madison Square Garden Corporation after the New York sporting centre it had acquired.

Joe Graham retired in 1942 and died in 1970 at the age of 87. His sons now run Graham Farms Inc and the family has returned to agriculture, which the three brothers abandoned for bottle making at the turn of the century. GNG

GRAHAME-WHITE/G-W
GB 1920-1924

In 1901 Claude Grahame-White, the brother of wealthy pioneer motorist Montague Grahame-White, was owner of the Reyrol Motor Car Co Ltd, importers of the Passe Partout car, and later ran an automobile and marine engineering firm in London that supplied foreign taxis. In 1909 he bought a Blériot monoplane and a year later set up a flying school at Pau, France. In 1913 he was making Grahame-White biplanes and running the 300-acre (120-hectare) aerodrome at Hendon, near London, having formed the Grahame-White Co with £200,000 capital.

After World War I the firm listed its products as aeroplanes, cyclecars, coachwork, bedroom suites and office furniture. The cyclecars included the minuscule G-W Buckboard, with 3hp air-cooled single and two-speed gearbox, priced at 95 guineas, and a friction-drive 7hp twin using Coventry-Victor engines. A larger Dorman-engined car probably never entered production and the last cyclecar was made in 1924. For a time after the end of production of the Angus-Sanderson at Birtley, these cars were assembled in the Grahame-White factory. The aerodrome is now the home of the RAF museum. NB

GRANT
USA 1913-1922

Brothers George D. and Charles A. Grant, who ran a car sales firm in Detroit, developed in 1913 an unusually small car by American standards that had a four-cylinder, 12hp engine and was to be sold for $500. James Howe, who had worked for E. R. Thomas, James Cunningham, Selden and Studebaker, was chief engineer; factory manager was George Sulzman, who had worked for Simplex. All the components were bought-in and assembly started in 1914 at Findlay, Ohio. The gearbox was in-unit with the back axle; an Allis-Chalmers dynostart was an option. In Britain the cars were sold as Whiting-Grants by the London department store Whitings.

In 1915 an $800 Falls-engined six replaced the original model and an output of 20,000 a year was announced, although at most it probably reached only a quarter of that figure. In 1921 the Falls engine was replaced by a Walker. The addition of trucks with Continental engines and Torbenson drive axles did little for sales. The cars used Durston gearboxes, and in 1920 Columbia axles replaced the Peru type on earlier sixes. Cantilever suspension also gave way to semi-elliptics.

Gray 2.7-litre tourer of 1924

208

In 1916 the original Grant Motor Co had been reorganized as Grant Motor Car Corporation and moved to Cleveland after the Denmo truck plant had been acquired, although the Findlay factory was retained to make shells. Despite the financial skills of the company's new president, David Shaw, Grant just could not compete with the larger firms and a receiver was appointed in October 1922. NB

GRAY
USA 1922-1926

Lumberman's son O. J. Mulford was a printer and boat-builder before forming the Gray Motor Co with banker John S. Gray to make boat engines. Gray was Ford's largest shareholder early on, and was briefly president of the company before his death.

The Gray company was for a time owned by the United States Motor Co, but when that firm collapsed Mulford bought back Gray for a reputed $160,000. Gray made proprietary car and truck engines, but when F. F. Beall joined the firm from Packard after World War I a complete car was developed.

This project was taken over by Saxon, but when Frank L. Klingensmith left Ford in 1921 he was persuaded to become president of the newly formed Gray Motor Corporation and take control of work on a 2.7-litre Gray light car, which was launched in 1922. It competed with Ford, Chevrolet and Star and met with an encouraging response. Eighty a day were soon being produced, and 23,000 were sold until early in 1924.

Under the slogan 'The Aristocrat of Small Cars' an improved version, with bodywork by the American Motor Body Co, was produced in 1924. About 14,000 of these and an S model, as well as 2500 trucks, were made before the firm collapsed in 1926, a year after Klingensmith had resigned. In 1924 the Canadian Gray-Dort company, which had no existing connection save the name, had sought a liaison with Gray but this did not have time to materialize. NB

GRAY-DORT
see Dort

GRÉGOIRE
FRANCE 1904-1924

Emile Ouzou et Cie was registered in Paris in 1899 with 60,000 francs capital and made Cyklone and Soncin motors, the latter named after their inventor, Louis Soncin. In 1900 the company introduced Soncin-engined Soncin and Ouzou voiturettes, made at Poissy and engineered by J.-P. Grégoire. When Emile Ouzou went out of business in 1901 the car

Grégoire 14/20hp sports model of 1908

firm was reorganized as Soncin, Grégoire et Cie. Emile Ouzou then started a garage in Paris and this lasted until 1908.

In October 1902 the car company became Grégoire et Cie and Louis Soncin built his engines at a separate firm for two years, supplying diminutive units for Darracq's Perfecta tricycles and, at the opposite extreme, 38-litre straight-eights. In 1904 Grégoire launched its own range of one-, two- and four-cylinder cars which were light, well engineered and competitively priced.

Xavier Civelli de Bosch raced and had exclusive sales rights to Grégoires, which sometimes went under his own name until he became insolvent in 1907. Grégoire had increased its capital to 1.2 million francs by then and it rode out the recession by making monobloc 9 and 15hp fours followed by a new twin in 1909, when 40hp Grégoire-Gyp aero engines were also offered. From 1906 royalties of 1 per cent were paid to Renault for use of its direct-drive system.

Some extraordinary streamlined torpedo and submarine body-shapes were offered, with round side windows and curved glass windscreens from 1910, and the marque became a favourite with aviators, including Claude Grahame-White in England. British sales were handled by Captain Theo Masui under the name Grégoire-Gordon from 1908. In 1910 he advertised 'A four-cylinder for the price of a two' and 'A six-cylinder for the price of a four'.

There was a brief flirtation with Knight engines before they were dropped in 1913. Output that year was about 500 cars and a few commercials in addition to aero and racing boat engines. In 1912 the Dumont friction-drive system was tried and in 1913-14 single-cylinder Dumont cars were sold. A new 20hp T-head four sports model was introduced just

before World War I. Delco lighting was a novel feature for early post-war French cars.

By 1919 Grégoire had come under the control of Forges et Ateliers de la Fournaise and was making the 17 Bignan in the Poissy factory. These Bignans were sold in England by Malcolm Campbell as Grégoire-Campbells. A light 1100cc CIME-engined car, known as the Little Greg in Britain in 1921-22, was made by J. Hinstin, a former Grégoire employee. The Grégoire name disappeared in 1924. NB

GRÉGOIRE
FRANCE 1942-1970

During World War II Jean-Albert Grégoire, previously associated with his own make, the Tracta, and the Amilcar Compound, worked on the design of a small front-wheel-drive family car powered by a 610cc 15bhp flat-twin engine, with a frame of Alpax light alloy castings. This was made by l'Aluminium Français, and the car was generally known as the Aluminium Français Grégoire, or AFG.

The first prototype ran in 1942, and well before the Liberation of France the design was offered to major French car manufacturers. After being rejected by Citroën, Renault, Peugeot and Simca, it was taken up by Panhard, which marketed it as the Dyna-Panhard from 1946. Grégoire also tried to sell licences for manufacture in England as the Kendall, and in Australia as the Hartnett, but he had no success with the former and only limited success with the latter.

Meanwhile he had designed a 2.2-litre flat-four front-wheel-drive car which was to have been made in an idle Blériot aircraft factory at Suresnes, but the design was taken up by Hotchkiss and sold as the Hotchkiss-Gré-

Grégoire 2.2-litre convertible of 1959

goire from 1951 to 1953. After the demise of Hotchkiss, Grégoire attempted to continue the design under the name Grégoire Sport.

Assembled in his Asnières factory where the Tractas had been made, the new cars used Chapron cabriolet bodies and a 130hp supercharged version of the Hotchkiss engine. Production did not start until 1956, and Grégoire wisely limited himself to an initial batch of 15 cars. In fact, only 10 were ever made, and the last of these was not sold until 1962. Grégoire himself admitted that he had made a loss of 1.5 million francs per car.

In 1970 he built four prototypes of an electric car powered by a UNELEC motor and, as always, using front-wheel drive. The frame was a cast light alloy structure harking back to the AFG days, but much more solid in appearance. This design was never commercialized. GNG

GRICE
see GWK

GRIFFITH
see TVR

GSM
SOUTH AFRICA, GB 1958-1966

Bob van Niekerk and Willie Meissner met as students at Stellenbosch University and through a mutual interest in motor racing they began to plan their own racing car. Meissner raced the first prototype, impressively, in January 1958 and in March the partners announced a company, Glassport Motor Co Pty Ltd of Bottlecary, Cape Town. They planned to build one GSM car a week.

The first model was known as the Dart and used an 1172cc Ford engine, in three stages of tune, and a three-speed gearbox. It had a tubular chassis and glassfibre body with a removable hard top. For competition use 1100 and 1500 Coventry-Climax versions were offered. The company announced that if it was still in production after one year it

would treble production and consider export sales.

In October 1960 GSM Cars Ltd was set up in West Malling, Kent, to build the Ford 105E engined two-seater Delta coupé in Britain. Bob van Niekerk came to Britain with the project and continued GSM's impressive competition performance. Delta kit prices ranged from £666 to £1189 and by October 1961 four or five a week were being sold – mostly to the United States and Canada.

Only five cars were built in South Africa in 1960, but late in the year van Niekerk returned to South Africa to negotiate a deal intended to allow GSM to expand and ultimately build a family car. An investment company, Bowiscore, bought a controlling interest in GSM, which was re-registered as GSM Pty Ltd in Paarden Eiland, Cape Province, on 1 January 1963. Van Niekerk stayed on the board under Managing Director J. A. Goodall.

Development of the family car, with a projected price of £750 to £850, and a ¾-ton pickup were expected to take up to two years. In the meantime the new management saw a sports car market of around 30 cars a year. With the introduction of the Taunus-powered Flamingo 2+2 sports car, designed by Verster de Witt and engineered by van Niekerk, production reached 250 cars a year. The 120mph (193kph) Flamingo was another excellent car, luxuriously trimmed in leather and with tinted laminated glass and stainless steel trim. It sold for about £1425 in kit form in January 1963, compared to £944 for the latest Dart.

The Flamingo claimed some 70 per cent local content and Willie Meissner was designing a twin-cam head for the Taunus engine which would make the Flamingo an even quicker car. The planned saloon was never built, however, and no more of the promising GSMs were made after 1966. BL

GTM
GB 1966 to date

In 1966 Bernard Cox's garage business, Cox & Co (Manchester) Ltd of Hazel Grove, Cheshire, built its first Mini-based, mid-engined kit car, which was launched at the

January 1967 London Racing Car Show as the Cox GTM. It used a semi-monocoque steel box chassis, plus much modified Mini suspension subframes, braced by tubular spaceframes. The unstressed glassfibre body was riveted and bonded to the chassis.

The Cox car was an excellent car but difficult to build well, and that limited sales. In 1969 the company became GTM Kit Cars, still in Hazel Grove, and between 1971 and 1972 it was taken over briefly by Howard Heerey Engineering Ltd, makers of Heglass glassfibre materials.

Later in 1972, as GTM Cars Ltd, the company was moved to the Lundberg Engineering company's works in Hartlepool, County Durham, where GTMs were made in very small numbers until 1977. Mike Smith, a director of KMB Autosports Ltd of Wellingborough, Northamptonshire, then bought the production rights and resumed production at a projected rate of two cars a week.

KMB also worked on promoting the GTM and claimed that one advertisement alone prompted more than 1400 enquiries. Demand soon exceeded producton. By mid-1978 KMB had built 70 cars, helped by a major chassis redesign which made the car considerably easier to build.

In 1979 the GTM was available as a complete kit, less engine, for £2055 plus taxes, or as a complete car for £4815 plus tax. In 1981 the company changed identities once again, to become GTM Engineering, and moved first to Nottingham and later to Loughborough, where production continued. By 1986 prices started from as low as £1480 for a basic body kit. With a 1275cc engine the GTM had a claimed top speed of about 120mph (193kph). BL

GUTBROD/BUTZ, RAPID, STANDARD, TROLL
GERMANY, SWITZERLAND, NORWAY
1933-1954

Born in 1890, Wilhelm Gutbrod worked for Robert Bosch in Stuttgart as a lathe operator and toolmaker. In 1920 he became works manager at the steamroller factory at Karl Kaelble, which nowadays makes trucks and construction machinery. In 1923 he joined the Eugen Klotz motorcycle factory in Stuttgart and when this closed in 1926 he set up his own company, Standard-Fahrzeugfabrik GmbH, at Ludwigsburg. He later bought the Zehnder motorcycle factory in Switzerland.

From 1930 Gutbrod's company made motorcycle-based commercials and in 1933, when a move was made to Feuerbach near Stuttgart, Standard-Superior two-cylinder, two-stroke light cars designed by Joseph Ganz were introduced. Gutbrod moved to a former jam factory in Plochingen on the Neckar in 1937 and because of Hitler's policy of 'type limitation' abandoned car production in favour of three-wheel commercials.

Ganz went to Bungartz and Co of Munich in 1934 where he developed another batch of economy cars, known as Butz, with 200 or 396cc engines. As the political situation worsened, Ganz moved to Switzerland where Rapid of Dietikon made prototypes of similar Ganz-designed cars in 1938, producing them briefly in 1946. Ganz later worked for Holden and died in Australia in 1967.

After World War II Gutbrod's company was restyled as Motostandard GmbH. It produced Farmax tractors/load carriers from 1946, Atlas forward-control four-wheel trucks from 1948 and Gutbrod-Superior cars from 1949. Motor vehicle production in 1946-47 had been just 200 but this reached 750 in 1948. From 1952 the cars could be equipped with what Gutbrod proclaimed to be the world's first fuel-injected two-stroke petrol engines.

In 1954 cars, commercials and probably motorcycles as well were all discontinued as production was concentrated on agricultural and garden machinery. The remnants of the cars went to Norway, where they were called Trolls, but only five were produced.

In 1962 the company produced Europe's first gear-driven four-wheel light tractor. Engines, power sweepers and tillers were also made. Motostandard became Gutbrod-Werke GmbH in 1959 and in 1971 launched the Gutbrod 3000 utility vehicles. In 1974 the Bungartz and Peschke tractor factory at Hornbach was acquired and from there Kommutrac 4×4 utility vehicles are still made for snow clearance, towing and load carrying. NB

GUY/LE GUI
FRANCE 1904-1916

These cars, made at Courbevoie, Seine, took their name from their maker, H. Guillemin. The first car appeared in 1904 and a variety of names came to be used, including Guy, Guillemin Le Gui, and Le Gui. In England they were known as Millard Le Gui, after their importer.

Buchet and Barriquand et Marré engines were mostly used in the early range, which ran from 7 to 30hp. In 1909 the Société H. Guillemin et Cie went into liquidation but was replaced by H. Nicolas et Cie; share

capital was a tiny 59,000 francs.

The new firm concentrated on the smaller Le Guis, which ultimately used Chapuis-Dornier engines. Production ended in about 1916. NB

GUY
GB 1919-1925

Sidney Guy was works manager of Sunbeam before founding Guy Motors Ltd of Wolverhampton in 1914. The company was established with a capital of £30,000 as a maker of commercial vehicles. Truck production soon gave way to the building of Wasp and Dragonfly aero engines and Tylor truck engines, as well as of gearboxes for Maudslay.

After the war the company returned to making commercial vehicles, and in 1919 developed a Cadillac-inspired 4072cc V8 car with inclined heads and side valves. It had automatic chassis lubrication that was activated by turning the steering to full right-hand lock. Orders worth £2¼ million for the car were placed at the 1919 Olympia Show, but only 25 at most were ultimately sold.

Various prototype cars of 12 to 17hp were developed, some with Coventry-Simplex or Climax engines in Rubery Owen chassis, but few went into production. The entire car programme was discontinued in 1925 after a total of about 130 cars had been sold. In 1927 Guy returned to car-making when it acquired Star through an exchange of shares.

During World War II the company produced thousands of military vehicles and 3000 buses. It also invented a process for welding armour plate which speeded armoured car production. In 1948 it acquired Sunbeam Commercial Vehicles.

Guy was compulsorily wound up in November 1961 after years of unprofitable trading. Jaguar acquired the factory for £800,000, together with the Guy name and the well-known 'Feathers in our Cap' Indian head emblem, which was used on commercial vehicles until the late 1970s. After the Leyland takeover of Jaguar, the Guy division became surplus to requirements and was closed in 1983. NB

GUYOT SPÉCIALE
FRANCE 1925-1931

Born in 1882, Albert Guyot owned a garage in Orléans and from 1908 was a motor racing enthusiast. After World War I he worked with Rolland-Pilain making racing cars and in 1923 installed an eight-cylinder Duesenberg engine in one at premises in Levallois. Burt-McCollum licence sleeve-valve six-cylinder engines were then tried. Three racers were sold to Albert Schmidt, president of Continental engines, to run in the Indianapolis 500 as Schmidt Specials.

Schmidt appointed Guyot as the French and Belgian agent for Continental engines, which came to be sold to Tracta, Georges Irat, Delaunay-Belleville, Rolland-Pilain, Mathis and others. (Continental also acquired world rights to the Burt-McCollum design, which it relinquished in the 1930s to Bristol Aircraft.)

From 1926 Guyot offered two-seater 1.5-litre sports/racers; touring cars using Continental 3.45-litre sixes had fake overhead-valve covers to disguise the use of side valves but the Lockheed hydraulic brakes were genuine. About 70 cars were made, probably at Clichy, from 1923 to 1930 in addition to a few Continental 5.2-litre eight-cylinder versions. Production ended in 1931. NB

G-W
see Grahame-White

GWK/GRICE, UNIT
GB 1910-1931

In 1910 in Beckenham, Arthur G. Grice, J. Talfourd Wood and C. M. Keiller developed a light car. Grice had worked for a crane company and Wood and Keiller had worked for the Great Western Railway at Swindon. Grice developed the car's variable transmission after watching a lens grinder in action.

GWK production, using rear-mounted two-cylinder Coventry-Simplex engines, totalled 52 in 1911. The work transferred to Datchet in 1912, when 150 were sold. By the time Admiralty contracts had taken precedence in 1915, 1069 cars had been built and many had performed with credit in sporting events.

Grice formed Rotary Units Ltd in 1912 to make a five-cylinder pumping engine. With M. A. Van Roggen, a wealthy Belgian marble merchant, he then started G&VR Ltd at the Cordwalles works in Maidenhead and before World War I planned to make cars there. GWK moved to Maidenhead in 1914 after Wood and Keiller were enlisted.

After the war G&VR Ltd was incorporated in GWK (1919) Ltd. Coventry-Simplex four-cylinder front-engined GWKs were then produced as were 82 of the old twins. Production

Guy V8 tourer of c.1919

of the new F model totalled 86 in 1919, 450 in 1920 and 438 in 1921, but many teething problems were encountered and these were not fully resolved when Grice returned to Rotary Units in 1920.

Grice had a couple of former army sheds erected at Wooburn in Buckinghamshire and with Van Roggen's backing made the rear vee-twin air-cooled Bovier-engined Unit No 1 car. This had friction drive and received a front engine in 1921, unitary construction in 1922 and a Coventry-Climax four in 1923, the year in which production ended after about 50 had been made.

GWK had gone into liquidation in 1922 and Wood and Keiller departed. Percy Richardson, formerly of Daimler and Sheffield-Simplex, became managing director and Grice and Van Roggen joined him upon the demise of Unit. £10,000 extra capital was provided by T. Warwick of Bal-Lon-Ette tyres.

GWK output thereafter was small. A three-wheel, £90 JAP-engined prototype of 1927 failed to go into production and nothing came of Grice's interest in the Galba (a Violet design) and the radial-engined Lafitte. In December 1926 GWK was renamed Impéria Motors Ltd, signalling its intention to build the Belgian Impéria, but little came of this other than the importation of fewer than 50 cars.

GWK spares and a few cars continued to be offered until 1931. A final rear-engined GWK, designed by Grice, was still-born. NB

GWK 8hp two-seater of c.1914

GWYNNE/ALBERT
GB 1922-1929

Founded in 1849, Gwynne achieved particular fame as a pump maker, especially centrifugal fire pumps in the 20th century. It also made Clerget aero engines, with help from W. O. Bentley, and machine tools in a large works at Church Wharf, Chiswick, west London, during World War I.

The company then decided to produce a light 950cc overhead-valve car based on a design bought from Arturo Elizalde in Spain by Neville Gwynne. A similar 8hp vehicle was made in Madrid as the Victoria between 1919 and 1923. A strike by moulders delayed its introduction at Gwynne until 1922.

Meanwhile the firm had been making engines for the A. O. Lord-designed Albert car, and bought its makers Adam, Grimaldi & Co Ltd in 1920. From then Gwynne made the complete chassis for the 12hp Albert, which was bodied by Adam, Grimaldi and had a Rolls-Royce shaped radiator. Harry Lancaster's Service Motor Co contracted to take the 3000 to be produced in the first year, but parts for 700 sat for almost a year without cylinder blocks and only about 250 cars were actually made in 1920, rising to an estimated 850 in 1921.

In 1922 the Albert was joined by Gwynne Cars' Model 8. Until 1924 the final Alberts were known as Gwynne-Alberts and were increased to 14hp; otherwise they were simply Albert-radiatored Gwynne 8s.

Virtually all parts were made in-house, where the latest machines could bore a complete block in one operation and make 12 steering worms simultaneously. The little Gwynne missed the immediate post-war boom, however, and its sales prospects were dashed by the collapse of Service Motors. Cheap and economical, and well made to aero engine quality, it was competing with Morris and Austin. Despite an increase to 10hp, production ended in 1925. Gwynne Engineering Ltd continued to assemble a few cars until 1929, when Gwynne Cars Ltd was finally wound up. NB

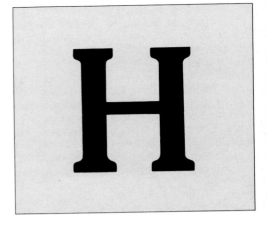

HAG/HAG-GASTELL
GERMANY 1922-1927

The Hessische Automobil AG of Darmstadt began production of the HAG car in 1922 with a well designed 5/18PS touring model. By 1925 this had been uprated as the four-cylinder 1305cc 5/25PS, with gear-driven overhead camshaft, and this continued as the only HAG model. Also in 1925 the company was taken over by Waggonfabrik Gebrüder Gastell GmbH of Mainz Mombach, formerly a railway carriage maker. The cars now became known as HAG-Gastell but were otherwise unchanged, although a 1.5-litre sporting two-seater was also offered.

Car manufacture stopped in 1927 when the company was reorganized as Westwaggon AG and continued to build carriages. The Mainz Mombach works were later taken over by Magirus Deutz, the truck manufacturer whose Deutz origins commemorate founder Nikolaus August Otto and which is now part of IVECO, the giant Industrial Vehicles Corporation combine. BL

HAL TWELVE
USA 1916-1918

Like the Chandler, the Hal was built in Cleveland by former Lozier men, in this case led by the president, Harry A. Lozier Jr. In 1912 he resigned from his company when it planned to enter the popular-price market and three years later he announced a 12-cylinder car in two or five passenger form, for the very modest price of $1750 f.o.b. Detroit. The car was named from his initials the Hal Twelve.

It is not certain that any cars were built in Detroit, but in 1916 the H. A. Lozier Co was established at Cleveland and a Weidely-powered V12 was marketed. The price was now $2100, still quite a reasonable price when compared with Packard's Twin Six, which cost from $2750 to $4800. H. A. Lozier resigned in September 1916 'because of continued ill-health' (which may or may not have been the true reason) and the company name

Gwynne 8 tourer of c.1922 (foreground)

was changed to the Hal Motor Car Co.

During the latter half of 1916 production of Hal Twelves was running at 10 a day, and dealerships were opened in a number of states including California. Prices rose steadily, reaching $3600 to $6000 by the end of 1917, and sales were badly hit by America's entry into World War I. A merger with the Abbott Corporation was mooted, but Abbott went bankrupt in January 1918 and Hal did likewise a month later. The last 10 cars were auctioned in April 1918.

In November 1916 H. A. Lozier formed a new company in Philadelphia to make cars, but few if any were produced. He died in 1925. GNG

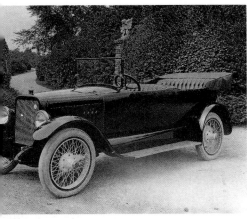

Hal Twelve roadster of 1916

HALLADAY
USA 1905-1922

As a young man Lou P. Halladay worked in Marion, Indiana, for his father's Marion Cycle Works. In his mid-20s he moved to Streator, Illinois, and, with two partners, set up the Streator Metal Stamping Works, whose main product was pressed-out music stands.

Halladay had several patents granted, most with motoring connections, and he eventually designed a complete Halladay car. It first appeared in 1905 as the Type A, with four-cylinder 30hp Oswald engine. Five were built in 1905 and 15 in 1906 before it was updated as the Rutenber engined Type B in 1907. To the end of 1908, 85 of this model were built.

In 1909 Halladay sold his share in the stamping company to his partners and formed the Streator Motor Car Co, making cars and accessories. Halladay cars were quite well received – a Type D was used as a Press car on the 1910 Glidden Tour – but the undercapitalized company was almost bankrupt by September 1911. It was bailed out temporarily by the two main backers, both local landowners, and in 1912 added a 50hp six to its range, which by the following year would be exclusively sixes.

In January 1913 all Streator's assets were sold for $56,000 to a company liquidator who resold them in March to Albert C. Barley, a director of the Western Motor Co, makers of

Rutenber engines. In 1914 Barley also took over the Nyberg Automobile Works and the Wahl Motor Co after proprietor George Wahl had committed suicide.

He continued Halladay and Nyberg production separately for a year before combining the companies as the Barley Manufacturing Co in Streator. He sold the Nyberg works and from 1915, as the Barley Motor Co, concentrated on his new Halladay Light Six. In February 1916 Barley showed a new sports model which he called the Roamer and which quickly began to sell well.

In March, after a long strike at Streator, he sold rights to the Halladay to a group of Ohio businessmen, who formed the Halladay Motor Car Co and announced that production would resume in Mansfield, Ohio. As Halladay sales revived, production moved to larger works in Lexington and then to the former Cameron Car Co works in Attica.

In January 1920 Halladay announced that a new plant was to be built in Newark, financed by a stock issue. Although Halladay moved in in June 1920 its activities were now in a decline and only one model was offered for 1921. The range was expanded later and a new four was shown in 1922 as the Falcon, but all Halladay production stopped in March 1922.

Barley and the Roamer meanwhile were doing rather better. Towards the end of 1917, prompted by a $5000 grant from Kalamazoo Chamber of Commerce, he moved Roamer to the former Michigan Buggy Co works and continued production. The Barley Motor Car Co became the Roamer Motor Car Co in 1923. BL

HAMARD
see Buckingham

HAMPTON
GB 1911-1933

The Hampton car took its name from the Warwickshire village of Hampton-in-Arden, where Walter Paddon built his first prototype in 1911. The following year he started the Hampton Engineering Co Ltd at Kings Norton, Birmingham, making a conventional car powered by a 12/16hp four-cylinder Chapuis-Dornier engine selling at £295. Very few of these were made, and before the outbreak of war in 1914 Paddon had brought out three more designs, a cyclecar with 8hp two-cylinder Precision engine, a cyclecar with two-cylinder two-stroke engine, and a light car with four-cylinder 10hp Chapuis-Dornier engine.

In 1919 the Hampton Engineering Co moved south, taking over part of an ironworks at Dudbridge, Stroud, Gloucestershire, where a 10/16hp light car was made, powered by a 1496cc four-cylinder Dorman KNO en-

Hampton 12hp of c.1926

gine. This was soon joined by a 1795cc car, also Dorman-powered. Bodies were mostly made in-house and production reached six cars a week by the middle of 1920. The company underwent the first of its many reorganizations during the year, emerging as the Hampton Engineering Co (1920) Ltd. For 1923 Meadows engines were used, in two sizes, 9/21hp and 11/35hp.

For four years the company struggled to keep afloat, but towards the end of 1924 it went into receivership before being rescued by Major Griffith Jones, who acquired the company for about £13,000. He was helped by W. F. Milward, the works manager, Gerald Dixon and J. W. Leno. Milward and Dixon had been with the Charron-Laycock company.

The new company was called the Stroud Motor Manufacturing Co Ltd but lasted less than 15 months, becoming bankrupt in January 1926. Another company was formed, Hampton Cars (London) Ltd, with finance from the capital and an office in Westminster, although the factory remained at Stroud.

The 11/35hp became the 12/40 and was joined by a 1247cc 9hp and a 1683cc 15hp six-cylinder model. The latter was very short-lived, being replaced for 1929 by a larger six with 2931cc Meadows engine, a handful of which were produced. The most popular model was the 12/40, which made up the bulk of the 300 cars made each year at this time. For 1930 Hampton offered a supercharged sports version of the 12/40, while some models were offered with the Cowburn coned roller gearbox, made by Kitson Components Ltd of Stroud.

In 1930 Hampton's credit with Meadows ran out, and as the Wolverhampton company was its main supplier of engines, Hampton was faced with a serious problem. A small four-cylinder engine of 1196cc was offered, possibly of Hampton's own manufacture, while for its larger model it went to the German Röhr company, from which it ordered 100 2262cc straight-eight engines, and 50 chassis with independent suspension by double transverse half-elliptic springs. The discrepancy in numbers was presumably because Hampton had a number of its own chassis that it wanted to use up, and could sell the result at a lower price than for the more sophisticated Röhr chassis.

However, the company failed again before many of the German components reached Stroud. It was reorganized by the receiver, Thomas Godman, as the Safety Suspension Car Co Ltd at new premises at Cainscross, near Stroud. Although Godman offered the Röhr chassis with a choice of a 2.4-litre six-cylinder engine or the Röhr straight-eight, now enlarged to 2736cc, it is unlikely that any were made. The last Hampton was probably the Röhr-engined car constructed by Milward from parts acquired at the Dudbridge sale. GNG

HANDS
see Calthorpe

HANOMAG
GERMANY 1924-1951

Hannoversche Maschinenbau AG vorm Georg Eggerstorff was founded in Hanover-Linden in 1835 to build railway locomotives, but around the turn of the century, suffering a slump in business after the cancellation of several foreign orders, the company began efforts to diversify. In 1905 it began to build steam lorries under Stolz patents, but what it really needed was a cheap mass-market product, ideally a small car.

The first Hanomag car, however, did not appear until 1924 when the company offered a very basic two-seater, widely and affectionately known as the *Kommisbrot* or Army Loaf, because of its unusual shape. Emphasizing its background it was advertised as 'cheaper than a 3rd class railway ticket'.

This side-by-side two-seater 2/10PS model used a rear-mounted overhead-valve 499cc single, with chain drive and no differential – rendered unnecessary by a very narrow rear track. The car was offered in open or closed versions, the latter unusual for what was essentially a cyclecar, with a single side door, a single 'cyclops' headlight and sliding windows. Body construction was largely of wood and canvas. The little car would just exceed 40mph (64kph).

Up to 1928 15,775 were built – paving the way for more conventional Hanomag models. The first was the 776cc side-valve four-cylinder 3/16PS, a 745cc version of which was available for competition in the 750cc class. Works drivers Karl Haeberle and von Buthenuth had several rally and trials successes and in 1929 Hanomag also ran a supercharged racing model. Larger models followed, the Garant and Kurier, both of 1089cc, and the Hanomag team filed three joint winners in the 1100 class of the 1931 Alpine Trial, through a carefully contrived 'photo-finish'.

The 1494cc Rekord and six-cylinder 2250cc Sturm which followed were both available as open two-seaters and the Rekord name was also used on a 35hp 1910cc diesel-engined model, introduced at the 1936 Berlin Motor Show. Hanomag was among the first to offer small diesels in private cars, mainly using designs by Joseph Vollmer. Vollmer, who was also involved in designing the first German tanks, worked through his own design bureau, Deutsche Automobil Konstruktion GmbH. Hanomag set a world record for diesel engined cars in 1939 when an aerodynamic version of the Rekord achieved 95mph (152kph) and a more streamlined production saloon version would top 70mph (112kph).

A six-cylinder diesel engine was designed for car use but its introduction was prevented by the outbreak of war, during which Hanomag built trucks, as it had already done for some years. In the commercial field, Hanomag had pioneered the German introduction of forward control cabs in the 1930s but its wartime output was mostly of more traditional, bonneted types as required by the Schell Programme's specification standardization.

Hanomag emerged very healthy from the war and showed a new car design, the Partner, at the 1951 Frankfurt Motor Show, but the two-stroke three-cylinder 697cc front-wheel-drive three-seater was not put into production and Hanomag made no further cars. The company's total output was 94,897 cars, of which the biggest-selling model was the Rekord, which sold 18,114 units between 1934 and 1938.

The Hanomag name continued on commercial models and the company later merged with Henschel as Hanomag-Henschel. When Borgward failed in 1961, Hanomag was one of several companies interested in taking over production; but although it eventually bought most of the Borgward factories, subsequent output was all of commercials.

In the 1960s, as part of the Rheinstal group, Hanomag-Henschel built Vidal and Tempo vans. Mercedes-Benz took over Hanomag's truck operation and the Hanomag-Henschel name was dropped in 1975. BL

Hanomag 2/10hp Kommisbrot two-seater of c.1925

Hanomag Sturm coupé of 1938

Hansa Type B sports model of 1912

builder of NAG cars since 1902) and Brennabor (Gebr Reichstein Brennabor-Werke of Brandenburg, maker of the Brennabor since 1908) formed a joint dealership arrangement as GDA, or Gemeinschaft Deutscher Automobilfabriken. The idea was to improve bank confidence in the individual partners, but the group split up in 1927.

In 1929 Hansa and Hansa-Lloyd were taken over by Carl Borgward's Goliath-Werke Borgward & Tecklenborg GmbH of Bremen. Hansa stopped production at Varel, but Hansa cars continued to be built at Bremen, while Hansa-Lloyd stopped private car production altogether to concentrate on building commercial vehicles, after 1930 in association once again with NAG. In 1931, when Hansa was effectively bankrupt, Borgward acquired

HANSA/HANSA-LLOYD
GERMANY 1906-1939

Hansa Automobil-Gesellschaft mbH was founded in the town of Varel in December 1905 by engineer August Sporkhorst and a doctor, Robert Allmers, with capital of 30,000 marks and the intention of producing small cars. It began to do so in 1906 with a 720cc single-cylinder De Dion-engined 7/9PS car, based on the French Alcyon and sold under the name HAG (not to be confused with the HAG made later in Darmstadt). This was followed by two four-cylinder models, a 9PS and a 12PS, with proprietary engines, and in 1907 Hansa introduced its own four-cylinder engine in the 6/14PS.

The company continued to produce progressively bigger models up to World War I. These ranged from the sporty 1.8-litre Type B, through the 2.5-litre Type F and the 2.6-litre Type D to the 3.8-litre 15/50PS Type E, introduced in 1911 and usually fitted with substantial limousine bodies.

Hansa also built the large RAF cars for the German market for the Austrian company Reichenberger Automobilfabrik of Reichenberg. This company, founded by Baron von Liebieg – who in 1894 had made the first ever long-distance car journey, in a Benz Victoria from Reichenberg to Mannheim – in turn built the small Hansas under licence, until RAF merged with Laurin and Klement in 1913.

In 1913 Hansa took over the Bielefelde factory of Ramesöhl & Schmidt AG, which had built the Westfalia car since 1906 and continued to do so in its factory at Oelde until 1914, and started to build Hansa cars there, but only from 1914. That year, the Type F was very successful in the Austrian Alpine Trial and was known thereafter as the Alpine.

In May 1914 Hansa merged with Norddeutsche Automobil und Motoren AG, maker of the Lloyd car, to become Hansa-Lloyd Werke AG of Varel. NAMAG had been founded in 1906 in a move towards diversification by the Norddeutscher Lloyd shipping company. It had initially built Krieger electric cars

Hansa 2-litre saloon of 1937

under licence but introduced a petrol model in 1908, the large but not very successful 3.7-litre 15/35. The company lost money consistently from 1907 to 1912 and the 1914 merger was in reality a takeover by Hansa.

The Lloyd name was dropped, although it reappeared in 1950 after Hansa-Lloyd had been taken over by Borgward, but new models appeared under both the Hansa and Hansa-Lloyd names. The Hansa factory continued to produce its original models until World War I, while the Lloyd works built mainly commercial vehicles.

After the war, the Lloyd factory also built two excellent luxury cars, the 4-litre four-cylinder Treff As, or Ace of Clubs, introduced in 1923, and the Trumpf As, or Ace of Trumps, with 4.6- or 5.2-litre straight-eight engines of up to 100bhp. This was the first German eight-cylinder car engine and gave the large and generally heavy bodied Trumpf a top speed of 75mph (120kph).

Hansa-Lloyd had worked throughout the war, building many trucks and increasing its workforce to more than 2000. The post-war Hansa models, as that name continued, were mostly light and medium models, such as the 2-litre four-cylinder 8/36PS Type P, also available as a short wheelbase sports model, the six-cylinder 13/60PS and the eight-cylinder 16/70PS, with Continental engines.

In 1919 Hansa, Hansa-Lloyd, NAG (Nationale Automobil-Gesellschaft of Berlin,

the remaining shares and the company became Hansa-Lloyd und Goliath-Werke Borgward & Tecklenborg, of Bremen.

Hansa continued to build four- six- and eight-cylinder models with a mixture of its own and proprietary engines of up to 5.8 litres, but in 1933 it took an important and successful new direction with the introduction of the small Hansa 400, a rear-engined twin-cylinder two-stroke, which was available until 1935, latterly increased in capacity to become the Hansa 500.

In 1934 the company produced 856 of these cars and introduced the four- and six-cylinder 1100 and 1700 models at the Berlin Show. They stayed in production until mid-1939, the 1700 also being offered in twin-carburettor sports form, alongside two larger cars, the 2000 and 3500 Privat. Between 4000 and 6000 1100s were made each year and around 1000 1700s. The 1100 was continued as a Hansa until June 1939 and the 1700, redesigned as the six-cylinder 2300, became the first car to bear the name Borgward under the Nazi rationalization laws of 1939.

Thereafter Hansa was used only as a Borgward model name, starting with the first post-war Borgward, the Hansa 1500 of 1949, until it was used again from 1958 on a flat-four engined Goliath front-wheel-drive car, which became the Hansa 1100. The name disappeared when the Borgward group of companies went bankrupt in 1961. BL

HANSON
USA 1917-1925

The Hanson was a very conventional car in its design, but was unusual in that it was built far from the centres of the American car industry, in the city of Atlanta, Georgia, but sold well outside its home state. It was produced by George Washington Hanson, a successful motor dealer selling Franklin, EMF and Saxon cars. He assembled the prototype Hanson car in Detroit in 1917 but later that year erected a factory in Atlanta with a capacity for producing 100 cars a day.

After delays caused by the government requisitioning this factory for war work, he finally delivered his first Hansons in June 1918. It was a thoroughly conventional car of the period, with Continental Red Seal six-cylinder engine, Borg and Beck clutch, Covert gearbox, Timken rear axle and other proprietary components. Bodies were by the Murray Body and Fender Co, supplemented by the Budd Body Co of Cincinnati, which Hanson bought and moved to Atlanta.

Production did not get under way until 1920, when 32 cars were delivered. Despite ambitious plans to build a super sports car powered by the Duesenberg straight-eight engine (one prototype was assembled) and a small car based on the Moller, the Hanson remained a conventional medium sized six, always a bit too expensive to compete successfully with makes like Maxwell, Studebaker and Jewett.

Some Hansons were sold as far from home as Florida, Philadelphia and Boston, and there were even plans to manufacture in Florida, but these came to nothing. The best year for Hanson production was 1921, when 375 cars were delivered, followed by 240 in 1922 and 193 in 1923. No figures were published after that but it is believed that a few cars made in 1923 were still being sold off in 1924 and even 1925.

George Washington Hanson later manufactured baby feeding bottles and then became an insurance salesman. He died in 1940 at the age of 65. GNG

HARRIS-LÉON LAISNÉ
see Léon Laisné

HARTFORD
see Pope

HARTNETT
AUSTRALIA 1951-1952

Sir Lawrence J. Hartnett was general manager of General Motors' Australian subsidiary,

Holden, from 1934 to 1947, and was one of the men responsible for Holden launching a car of its own make in 1948. After he left the company he looked around for a smaller car which could become an Australian 'people's car' and chose the Aluminium Français Grégoire, which he actually saw in its English manifestation, the Kendall-Grégoire. He was promised £750,000 by the state government of Victoria, to which was added £250,000 by public subscription, so that Hartnett Motors Co of Melbourne started off with a theoretical capital of £1 million.

Unfortunately a change in the federal government in Canberra led to withdrawal of the promised backing, and Hartnett was forced to use more than £100,000 of his own money to get production going. Components were ordered from various firms in Great Britain and France, but the bodies had by law to be built in Australia.

Most body plants were taken up with work on the new Holden, but Hartnett managed to secure a contract with Commonwealth Engineering of Sydney for the supply of open four seater bodies. Orders for the little car poured in, not only from Australia, but from New Zealand, South Africa and India.

Commonwealth never came up with any bodies, however, so Hartnett was forced to have them hand-made at great expense by a number of small firms. This eliminated any chance of profit, and after 120 cars had been completed Lawrence Hartnett was forced to liquidate his company. The consequent lawsuit against Commonwealth Engineering lasted for four years, but eventually Hartnett won, and was awarded £37,228 in damages. He subsequently went on to be a successful importer of Datsun cars. GNG

HAUTIER
FRANCE 1899-1905

Etablissements d'Exploitation des Brevets Hautier of Auteuil, Paris, began to exploit Hautier patents in 1899 when the company started building electric cabs, just a little too late for the big city electric cab boom which was already beginning to wane. Accordingly, in 1900 Hautier built a petrol-engined voiturette, which used a single-cylinder Soncin proprietary engine. The basic model used a water-cooled 4hp motor but a 7hp version was also available.

With a Hautier patented three-speed constant-mesh gearbox and all foot controls, the little 5cwt (254kg) car could exceed 25mph (40kph). It was also regarded as a very neat design, with the motor, gearbox, tanks and ancillaries all mounted on an independent frame. The maker advertised that any type of body could be fitted and that the body was easily removable within three minutes.

At the 1901 Paris Show, Hautier exhibited a single-cylinder 5hp model. By now, however, the company also offered two- and four-cylin-

der cars, the four-cylinder engine being listed as an Espérance.

One of Hautier's patented technical features was a unique hot tube ignition with variable timing, introduced when electrics were beginning to take over and the hot tube's main drawback was its inflexibility. The Hautier system was intended to vary the timing by changing the compression ratio through a split combustion chamber arrangement. The system was optional and claimed to allow a speed range from 1000 to 1500rpm – corresponding to an output of 4½ to 7hp.

The Hautier chassis was a channel section frame designed to be pressed, bent and welded quickly and cheaply and the complete frame weighed only 83lb (37kg). Single-, twin- and four-cylinder models with chain or shaft drive and 7, 13 or 18hp engines were available in 1902 and similar models were available until the make went out of production three years later in 1905. BL

HAYNES-APPERSON/
HAYNES
USA 1894-1925

Elwood Haynes was born in Portland, Indiana, in 1857, the son of a lawyer who later became a circuit court judge and founder of the People's Bank of Portland. After a spell as a schoolteacher Haynes studied metallurgy and in 1887 became field superintendent of the newly formed Indiana Natural Gas and Oil Co at Greentown. In 1893 he met the Apperson brothers, Elmer and Edgar, who were running a small engineering company, the Riverside Machine Works at Kokomo.

Haynes provided a single-cylinder two-stroke Sintz marine engine which the Appersons installed in a buggy-like car with chain drive. From conflicting evidence it seems that the car was Haynes designed and Apperson built, apart from the engine, but Haynes was the more astute publicist and in later years always referred to this first car simply as a Haynes. He even claimed that it was America's first car and used the words 'Haynes – America's First Car' from 1912 onwards, although he was personally acquainted with John William Lambert who had built a car in 1891.

The car ran for the first time on 4 July 1894 and soon attracted requests for replicas. For the next four years the Appersons turned out a very limited number of cars, devoting most of their time to the repair of bicycles, threshing and other machinery. Haynes supervised the work, although he kept on his job at the gas company until 1901.

In 1898 the Riverside Machine Works became the Haynes-Apperson Automobile Co, with a capital of $25,000. Production began at the rate of one car every two or three weeks, but by September 1898 they were making two each week, and in June 1899 an enlarged factory was working two shifts, 24 hours a day, to turn out more than one car daily. The cars were made in two-, four- or six-passenger models, all powered by a rear-mounted 3120cc flat twin engine.

In 1901 the Apperson brothers left the firm, setting up on their own as the Apperson Brothers Automobile Co, although the Haynes-Apperson name survived for another four years. There was little change in design for several years, although wheel steering replaced the tiller in 1903, and in 1904 the engine was moved to the front, under a conventional bonnet.

From June 1904 the cars came to be more generally known simply as Haynes, and on 1 September 1905 the company name was officially changed to the Haynes Automobile Co. Elwood Haynes was president and general manager at the time, but stepped down from the latter post to give himself greater opportunity for design work.

The horizontally-opposed twin engine was dropped for 1905, and thereafter Haynes cars had conventional vertical four-cylinder engines, which grew in size and price. By 1908 the 60hp with landaulette body cost $5000. In that year capital was increased from $300,000 to $600,000. The business prospered over the next few years, and by 1916 capital was at its peak of $4 million. A six was introduced in 1913, and three years later came a twelve, with Haynes's own 5.8-litre V12 power unit.

A new addition was made to the factory for V12 production, this being the fifth extension made during that fiscal year. Elwood Haynes continued his outside work, forming in 1912 the Haynes Stellite Works to make his patent alloy, 'Stellite', which retained its hardness even when heated to a very high temperature.

Haynes's best year for production was 1916, when more than 7500 cars were delivered, and in 1920 the company still made 5900, putting it well ahead of its rival, Apperson, which was making much the same class of car. However, as with so many medium sized firms, Haynes lost out to the big battalions as the 1920s progressed. It dropped the V12 in 1922 and thereafter made two sixes, the 55bhp 4.7-litre Model 55 and the 70bhp 4.9-litre Model 75. Production in 1923 was only about 2000 units, with even fewer deli-

vered in 1924, when only one model was listed, the 4½-litre Model 60.

The company failed in the winter of 1924, although 1925 models were announced, being similar to the previous year's but with balloon tyres. A planned rescue through a merger with Apperson failed to come off, and the Haynes Automobile Co was auctioned in March 1925. Elwood Haynes died in April. His name survives, not on motor cars but in the Haynes Stellite Division of the Union Carbide Corporation, which makes special heat- and corrosion-resistant alloys. GNG

HCS
USA 1919-1925

Harry C. Stutz ran the Marion Motor Car Co for J. N. Willys before leaving in 1910 and designing a proprietary transmission and drive axle that the Stutz Auto Parts Co sold to several firms. He also produced a Stutz car for the 1911 Indianapolis 500 and this was billed as 'The Car That Made Good in a Day'. He formed the Stutz Motor Car Co and remained president for three years.

He and his partner Henry Campbell sold their Stutz shares in 1916 and with a group of stockholders formed the HCS Motor Car Co in 1919. Although some cheaper Stutz models had been known by his initials, Harry C. Stutz had no further connection with the Stutz Motor Car Co, but he did help to run the separate Stutz Fire Engine Co of Indianapolis, formed in 1916.

HCS built a new plant in Indianapolis and began production of a stylish and expensive sports tourer with four-cylinder Weidely or, from 1923, six-cylinder Midwest engine. An eight-cylinder Miller was raced as an HCS Special to publicize the marque but the firm could not compete with the 'genuine' Stutz and car production was discontinued in 1925. The company then became the HCS Cab Manufacturing Co and sold Waukesha-engined taxis until 1927.

Harry Stutz retained an interest in the Stutz Fire Engine Co until his death in 1930. That company lasted another 10 years. NB

HE
GB 1920-1931

The Herbert Engineering Co Ltd of Caversham, near Reading, Berkshire, was run by Herbert Merton with financial backing from his mother. During World War I the company repaired and serviced aero engines, but when the war ended it was looking for work. In 1919 it agreed to build a car designed by Roland J. Sully, who had established one of the earliest motor cab businesses in Wales in about 1906.

The car was announced in 1920 as the HE and was a handsome, modern fast tourer. It used a 1795cc four-cylinder proprietary engine and a separate four-speed gearbox. The same year the company added the 14/20 tourer and in 1921 Sully, the designer, used a special two-seater model to establish records at up to 87mph (140kph) at Brooklands.

A 1921 chassis cost £720, the production two-seater was £910 and the tourer was £955 – all fairly high prices but reflecting excellent quality. HE continued with the introduction in 1922 of the 14/40 model, available as a 67mph (107kph) tourer or in tuned, short chassis form with close ratio gears. It was advertised as 'tHE Car of Character' and production reached about 14 cars a week.

HE 14/40hp sports model of 1922

Herbert Engineering had a foundry at Caversham and now made its own cylinder blocks, gearbox casings, frames and so on, although bodywork was still bought-in. Up to 1924 production demands were such that the factory could work 24 hours a day with its 500 or so employees on shifts.

Nevertheless, the company experienced constant financial problems, partly because its over-generous guarantee cost it dearly in repair work, but it also aggravated its problems in 1924 by building two racing cars, a short chassis sprint car and a Brooklands single-seater. A 16-valve experimental engine for the latter proved unreliable and very costly and in the end the racers used modified 2-litre road car engines.

HE 16/65hp tourer of 1927

Having built only a few 1924 cars, HE suspended production just before the 1924 Motor Show; but a few key staff continued servicing work and reorganized the company in 1925. Apparently learning little from its earlier problems the company now offered a *five-year* guarantee on a new model (much as the old) which was being turned out at the rate of three a week by the summer of that year.

In 1927 the four was supplemented by a 2.3-litre side-valve six, again with a sports option, and in 1928 the four was replaced by a new 1½-litre HE Six, still with side-valves and relatively sluggish. It was improved in 1930 as the 16/60 and frames were now bought-in from Rubery Owen.

The final HE model was a smaller six, the 12/35, launched with a capacity of only 1419cc but enlarged in 1931 to 1622cc. A dozen of these were built, including one supercharged two-door fabric saloon for racer and record breaker George Eyston. Some 64 Sixes were sold in all, but the company's finances never paralleled its reputation for quality and HE went out of business in 1931. BL

End Trial. In 1929 he had his first overseas outing, with a Triumph in the Monte Carlo Rally. In 1930 he joined the sports car manufacturer Invicta at Cobham, Surrey, where he helped design the classic 4½-litre low-chassis model. Having been the first British finisher, in seventh place, in the 1930 Monte, he won in 1931 for Invicta.

In 1933 he joined Riley, but a year later he moved again, and moved house to Warwick to work for Triumph, where he became technical director in 1937. In the 1935 Monte Carlo Rally he survived his Triumph Dolomite being hit by a train on a Danish level crossing – only to be held by the local police until he could guarantee repair costs for the train.

During World War II Healey worked with Triumph's Coventry neighbour, Humber, and planned a car which he originally intended for Triumph. When Triumph declined to pursue the design, Healey formed the Donald Healey Motor Co in Warwick in 1945 and became a manufacturer.

The first Healey, an open four-seater tourer with a Riley 2.4-litre four-cylinder twin-cam engine, had a chassis designed by A. C. Sampietro and a body by Ben Bowden, built by

Humber distributor Westland Motors of Hereford. The first example was completed in January 1946 in part of the Benford works in Warwick and a saloon version, bodied by Elliots of Reading, followed very soon on the open car. The new company moved shortly afterwards to its own larger workshops nearby and started production proper in the autumn of 1946 with almost 40 staff and initial production of five cars a week, to sell at £1598.

Predictably the cars were soon seen in competition, and in 1948 Count Johnny Lurani won the touring car class of the Mille Miglia. In October Healey introduced the four-seater drophead Sportmobile at £2879. A much cheaper car followed in July 1949, the spartan £1250 Healey Silverstone, principally intended for competition.

Briggs Cunningham imported the first Silverstone to the United States and gave it a 5½-litre Cadillac V8, but in December 1949, while travelling to America, Healey met George Mason, president of the Nash Motor Co, and from October 1950 the American company marketed the 3.8-litre (later 4.2-litre) six-cylinder Nash-Healey exclusively in

Healey 2.4-litre four-seat tourer of 1946

Austin-Healey 3000 of 1968

HEALEY/AUSTIN-HEALEY
GB 1946-1971

Donald Mitchell Healey was born in 1898, the son of a Cornish builder and early local motorist. He was apprenticed to the aircraft builder Sopwith at Brooklands, where the racetrack opened in 1907, and he saw a good many motor races. During World War I Healey served with the Royal Flying Corps until he was invalided out after crashing in 1917. He returned to his native Perranporth and opened a small garage. He also ran the Perraphone Radio Co for a while, making radio sets.

In the early 1920s he became involved in motor sport through local hillclimbs, mostly using Buick and ABC cars, and from 1923 he competed regularly in the London to Lands

Healey Silverstone of 1949

the USA. In 1952 the Nash-Healey was re-styled by Pininfarina and was produced until 1954. The car took fourth place at Le Mans in 1950 and a remarkable third in 1952.

A 3-litre Alvis six-cylinder engined two-seater convertible version, bodied by Panelcraft of Birmingham, was available in Britain from October 1951 and this was the last Warwick-built production model. An overall total of 1185 chassis were built there until the end of production in 1954.

By 1952 Healey was looking for an engine supplier capable of offering better volume supplies at reasonable cost. He built a prototype car around the 2.6-litre Austin A90 engine, had it bodied by Tickford and put it on display at the London Motor Show as the Healey 100. Leonard Lord, boss of the newly formed British Motor Corporation, liked the car sufficiently to adopt it virtually on the spot, arranging production at Longbridge as the Austin-Healey 100 and immediately cutting the price by £100 as a consequence of volume production that Healey could never hope to achieve at Warwick.

Jensen, whose own prototype was narrowly beaten by Healey for Austin's favour, built the production bodies, as Tickford did not have the capacity for the planned output of 150 cars a week. The first 25 bodies were hand-built between October 1952 and February 1953, and production began in May.

Healey continued its competition interests with the 100S, of which 50 were built from 1954, a supercharged streamlined version achieving over 192mph (309kph) at Bonneville with Donald Healey himself driving. A similarly tuned version of the later 2.6-litre six-cylinder 100-6, the production version of which was introduced in September 1956, reached over 203mph (326kph).

In January 1958 another Healey model was launched, quite literally. This was the Healey Sports Boat, designed by Donald with sons Geoffrey and Brian, with an MGA engine, re-dubbed the Austin-Healey 55, and built by the newly formed Healey Marine Ltd at the rate of about 20 a week.

In 1957 car production moved from Long-bridge to Abingdon and Donald Healey produced plans, which he sold to Austin in return for a royalty, for a new, smaller, 948cc popular sports car. This went into production as the 'frog-eye' Austin-Healey Sprite in May 1958, later restyled with conventional head-lights and joined in May 1961 by the similar MG Midget.

By July 1959 the big Healey had become the 2.9-litre 124bhp 3000, available in Mark II guise from 1961. All the big Healeys had considerable competition success, especially in international rallying, but the car was effectively killed in December 1967 by problems in meeting new regulations in the USA – to where some 80 per cent of output was exported. Neither a Healey-styled MGC nor a rather attractive 4-litre Rolls-Royce engined car went into production. The Austin-Healey link ended in mid-1971 when the Sprite was

phased out in favour of the Midget, Healey's royalty arrangement also coming to an end.

In April 1970 when American Kjell Qvale became president of Jensen, which built the big Healey bodies right up to the end of production, Healey became chairman and at Geneva in March 1972 Jensen launched the Jensen-Healey as a replacement for the 3000. In 1974 Healey Automobile Consultants Ltd (which held the agreement with Jensen) and Healey Cars Ltd were separated from the Healey group of companies, and the Donald Healey Motor Co Ltd was sold to the Hamblin group. After the Jensen-Healey went down with Jensen in May 1976, the family-owned Consultants Ltd continued to work on various design projects, including a wind-powered generator and a car based on the American spec Ford Fiesta. BL

HEINKEL
GERMANY 1955-1958

The Heinkel car was a post-war product of a German company far better known for its aeroplanes. Heinkel's founder, Professor Ernst Heinkel, was born near Stuttgart in 1888, the son of a metalsmith, and he trained in engineering at the Stuttgart Technical College from 1907 to 1911. In 1909 he developed an interest in aircraft after the Frankfurt exposition and in 1911 he built his own aeroplane, based on a Farman design. He was badly injured later when he crashed the machine.

During World War I Heinkel worked with the LGV and Hansa und Brandenburgische aircraft companies as technical director and designed several fighter aircraft. In December 1922 he founded Ernst Heinkel Flugzeugwerke at Warnemunde and, as a way of getting round the ban on German military aviation, built a series of biplane fighters for export, notably to SAAB, another aircraft builder who would turn to cars.

In mid-1935 the He51A-1 biplane became the newly formed Luftwaffe's first fighter and Heinkel moved to a larger factory, at Rostock-Marienhe, and then to an ultra modern factory at Oranienburg, near Berlin. Heinkel built all types of aircraft for the Luftwaffe throughout World War II, notably the twin-engined He111, more than 7300 of which were built, as bombers, transports, torpedo carriers and glider tugs. Having worked with Wehrner von Braun to build the rocket powered He112 in 1937, Heinkel built the world's first turbojet aircraft, the He178, which first flew in August 1939, some two years before the British Gloster Whittle.

In 1942 Heinkel's design staff was transferred to Vienna-Schwechat for the duration of the war and one of their last projects was a piggy-back jet-engined 'People's Fighter', designed to be produced at a rate of up to 2000 a month by May 1945 as a last ditch effort at saving the war. It did not, and the German

aircraft industry was again put out of business by Allied legislation.

Ernst Heinkel was tried for war crimes, in common with most military manufacturers, but was acquitted. In fact his outspoken criticism of many of Hitler's social policies had probably cost his firm many contracts.

Like fellow aircraft-builders Messerschmitt and Dornier (in association with Zündapp), Heinkel turned to cars as an alternative product. He founded Ernst-Heinkel AG in Stuttgart-Zuffenhausen and in 1955 launched a bubble car called the Cabin Cruiser. It was a short, high, egg-shaped device which closely resembled the Italian Isetta, introduced in 1953. The first model was a three-wheeler, with two front wheels and a single rear wheel driven by an air-cooled overhead-valve single-cylinder 174cc engine of Heinkel's own design and manufacture. In 1957 a 198cc version with twin rear wheels was offered, but the Heinkel was never very successful and only some 6000 were built in Germany before production was stopped in 1958, Ernst Heinkel having died in January of that year.

The production rights were sold in 1958 to Dundalk Engineering in the Republic of Ireland, which then apparently sold them again to Trojan Ltd of Croydon, Surrey. This company relaunched the car in 1961 as the Trojan 200, which was also available as a light van, but production stopped in 1965. BL

Trojan (Heinkel) 200 'bubble car' of 1962

HENNEY/STAVER
USA 1907-1914; 1921-1931

John W. Henney started the Henney Buggy Co in Cedarville, Illinois, in 1868 and received backing from the Stover Engine Works. When the railway bypassed Cedarville he moved to nearby Freeport. In 1895 bicycles were made. The Stephens family, owners of the Moline Plow Co, acquired Henney in 1902 and then, in 1908, Henney's Freeport Carriage Co.

Following the Moline takeover, Henney formed the Staver Auto Manufacturing Co and made Staver and Staver-Chicago cars from 1907 to 1914. These started as high-wheelers but later grew into four- and finally six-cylinder conventional cars.

Some prototype cars were built for Henney by Alanson P. Brush in Detroit in 1915 and these materialized as the Stephens when Henney ceased wagon-building in 1915. The Henney-Buggy factory then assisted production.

In 1916 J. W. Henney Jr started building motor hearse bodies in east Freeport. Five years later Continental-engined six-cylinder passenger cars of Kissel or Cunningham-like appearance were marketed and proved particularly popular with funeral directors. In 1925 factories were acquired from Moline Plow and in 1928 the firm became the Henney Motor Co, making vehicles that looked like Lincolns.

Having made small batches of cars throughout the 1920s and even an aeroplane ambulance in 1929, in association with the Great Lakes Co, four convertibles were made with Lycoming engines and Detroit transmissions in 1930-31 and some funeral types, with potential pleasure roles, were made until 1942. Total American ambulance-funeral car production averaged 3000 a year in the 1930s and Henney's share was quite substantial, sufficient to keep 312 employees busy in 1939.

In 1946 John Henney sold his company, and Russell Feldmann became president and Preston A. Boyd general manager. Advertising was by C. Roy Clough, who had run the sales side since 1930 and started his career with Buick in 1905 followed by Oakland. Henney used Packard chassis and running gear for its post-war vehicles – and indeed for most of its cars from 1938 – and also built some custom car bodies for Packard in 1953-54. The company closed its doors and went out of business in 1955.

In 1960 prototypes of an electric version of the Renault Dauphine were exhibited as the Henney Kilowatt by the Henney Motor Co of Canastota, New York, and a modernized form was offered 20 years later by R. S. Witkoff of Glen Cove, New York. NB

HENRIOD
SWITZERLAND, FRANCE 1896-1913

Born in 1865, Fritz Henriod of Bienne was a pioneer Swiss car-maker. He built a three-wheeled steam car in 1886 and a four-wheeled petrol car in 1893, but production did not start until 1896, when he was joined by his younger brother Charles-Edouard. With financial and technical aid from the Baehni brothers, makers of springs at Bienne, the Henriods founded Henriod Frères and made a small number of cars powered by horizontally-opposed two-cylinder engines, both air- and water-cooled, with three-speed gearboxes and direct drive to the rear wheels.

In 1898 they made a smaller model with single-cylinder engine and chain drive. Later that year the engines were moved to the front. Charles-Edouard set up a French factory at Neuilly towards the end of 1898, but planned to continue car production at the Baehnis'

factory at Bienne. Fritz left the company and later set up his own Société Neuchâteloise d'Automobiles at Neuchâtel.

Swiss production of Henriods seems to have come to an end in 1899, but the French factory turned out a number of designs during the early 1900s. These included the Simplon 6hp voiturette and some larger cars of 12 and 24hp, all with gearboxes incorporated in the rear axles. Henriod also experimented with alcohol-fuelled engines.

Meanwhile, Fritz's company began to build cars with air-cooled engines in 1903, selling them under the name SNA. In 1907 Fritz introduced a large four-cylinder car with laterally mounted fans; this 25/30CV was made in small numbers until 1913 and was sold by Charles-Edouard in France. Some were equipped with a steering column gearchange invented by Charles-Edouard, so the brothers obviously maintained good relations across the Franco-Swiss frontier. In 1912 Fritz made a 75hp aero engine.

In 1911 Charles-Edouard designed a four-cylinder rotary valve engine which he sold to Darracq, although that company had little success with it. He continued with design work, particularly in the field of trouble-free transmissions, up to his death in 1942. GNG

HERMES/HISA
ITALY, BELGIUM 1906-1909

Hermes Italiana SA, or HISA, was founded in Naples on 10 July 1906 with capital, mostly from Belgium, of 2 million francs. The organizers were the Belgian racing driver Baron Pierre de Caters, an Italian, Alberto Manzi-Fe, and Edmond Tart of the Liège company Société Mécanique et Moteurs, maker of the car of the same name. Early in 1906 Mécanique et Moteurs, which was founded in 1903, was in financial difficulties and, through de Caters, showed its 12/14hp car to Manzi-Fe who wanted to develop it as a 16/18hp model for HISA. Meanwhile, Tart and the engineer Paul Hutinel, late of Rochet-Schneider and Clément-Bayard, designed a 20/24hp four-cylinder car.

The first Hermes was shown at the Paris Salon in December 1906, but Hutinel died during the same month and was replaced as technical director by Paul Moulin. In 1907 the company – whose Italian factory was mainly dependent on Belgian parts and materials – opened a new factory at Bressoux, Liège, with a planned capacity of 600 cars a year.

In July 1907 Hermes entered two short chassis cars in the Coupe de l'ACF, but de Caters and Moulin retired by half distance and the company was little more successful on other competitive outings. A 40hp sporting model was added to the range in 1908 but Hermes in Belgium and HISA in Italy both struggled vainly against the general economic recession and the company was wound up in August 1909. BL

HERON
see Westcar

HERTZ
USA 1925-1928

John D. Hertz set up a taxi business in Chicago in 1910 and in 1915 he began the manufacture of cabs which were sold under the name Yellow Cab. In 1920 he launched an expensive passenger car which he named Ambassador. This had been made under previous ownership under the names Shaw and Colonial, with V12 engines, but Hertz's car had a six-cylinder 5.3-litre Continental 6-T engine. Fewer than 100 were made between early 1921 and the end of 1923, and production was suspended in 1924.

Although continuing his cab manufacture, Hertz realized that there was a growing market for self-drive hire, and for 1925 he launched a new Ambassador aimed specifically at this trade. The Model D-1 was smaller and cheaper than its predecessor, with a 3.2-litre Continental 7-U engine and a price of $1695 for a sedan.

In 1925 Yellow Cab was taken over by General Motors. Hertz remained as president and the Ambassador D-1 became the Hertz. Apart from a larger engine in 1927, this was made with little change until 1928. Most were sedans, although a tourer was available, and few, if any, were bought by private owners.

After 1928 Hertz found it cheaper to use other makes for his growing car hire business, which has been for many years the largest in the world. The current worldwide Hertz fleet is about 400,000 cars, and a car is rented somewhere in the world every 2.5 seconds. Since 1967 Hertz has been a wholly-owned subsidiary of RCA. GNG

HEWITT
see Adams

HILLMAN
GB 1907-1978

Like so many makes of car from the English Midlands, Hillman had its origins in the cycle industry. Its founder, William Hillman, was born in 1849 and began his career with the Coventry Machinists Co, which later became the Swift Cycle Co. In the early 1870s he went into partnership with W. H. Herbert to found the Hillman and Herbert Cycle Co. This later became the Premier Cycle Co, Hillman being responsible for setting up the German branch at Nuremberg. Hillman's other ventures included the Sparkbrook Manufacturing Co of Birmingham and the Auto Machinery Co of

Hillman 25hp tourer of 1907

Hillman Minx saloon of 1938

Coventry which he founded in 1886.

In 1907 Hillman secured the services of the French-born designer Louis Hervé Coatalen, who had been with Humber since 1901. Near Coventry they acquired premises on a small estate, the Pinley Estate, of which the former mansion house became the social club of the Hillman-Coatalen Motor Car Co Ltd.

Coatalen's first design was a large 25hp four-cylinder car with 'square' cylinder dimensions of 127×127mm (5×5in) giving a capacity of 6.4 litres. The prototype was driven in the 1907 Tourist Trophy by Coatalen, and the following year two cars took part, driven by Coatalen and Kenelm Lee Guinness, although without great success.

Meanwhile the 25hp was put into small-scale production, joined in the catalogue by a monstrous 9.7-litre six of which hardly any were made. These engines were also offered for marine use. In 1908 a smaller Hillman-Coatalen appeared, the 2.3-litre 12/16hp, which was made in slightly larger numbers, but production was still very modest. Not more than 300 cars were turned out between 1907 and 1913, an average of 50 a year.

It seems that Coatalen practically ran the Hillman works as well as the drawing office, and it was a severe blow to the little company when he left in 1909 to join Sunbeam, for which he did his most famous work. (It is intriguing to note that the three British companies that employed Coatalen – Humber, Hillman and Sunbeam – all ended up as part of the Rootes group.)

In 1910 the name was changed to Hillman Motor Car Co Ltd. The company attempted to market a taxi based on the 12/16hp chassis and also brought out a little-known 10hp two-cylinder car, but the make remained very obscure and would almost certainly have disappeared had the company not engaged a new designer called A. J. Dawson.

Arriving in mid-1913, Dawson scrapped all the Coatalen T-head designs and introduced a one-model policy with an attractive small four-cylinder car, the 1357cc L-head monobloc 9hp. Despite the fact that it had several rivals such as the Standard Nine, Singer Ten and Enfield Nimble Nine, the Hillman sold

well: 65 in the latter part of 1913, 450 in 1914 and 244 in 1915, when the company was already turning over to war work.

A handful of cars was made until 1917, these having a bored-out engine giving 1593cc and a Royal Automobile Club rating of 11hp. This was the basis of Dawson's post-war Hillman, although he left the company in June 1918 to make a car under his own name which was built in small numbers in Coventry from 1919 to 1921.

Dawson's successor was Hillman's son-in-law, John Black, who was in charge of the factory until 1930 when he joined Standard. The 11hp Peace model was in production early in 1919. It was offered as a two- or four-seater tourer or two-seater drophead coupé.

The bodies were supposed to be made by Vanden Plas, but although the London firm received an initial order for 1000 two-seaters, no more than 12 were delivered. Further orders for 200 four-seaters and 300 coupés were placed in April 1919, but only one of each was supplied. Presumably Hillman obtained cheaper bodies locally, although Vanden Plas prices do not seem excessive at £30 for a two-seater and £55 for a four-seater. A total of 1466 Hillmans were made in 1919 and 1920 and 644 in 1921, a year in which many car firms were badly hit by strikes.

From 1920 to 1922 Hillman produced an attractive little sports car with pointed radiator and polished aluminium body, one of which gave Raymond Mays his introduction to motor sport. Because of its high price of £620 – a Model AL Salmson cost only £265 – not more than 120 Super Sports Hillmans were sold in three years.

The company ran a 'works car' in various events in 1920 and 1921, the driver being George Bedford who finished seventh in the 1921 Brooklands 200 Mile Race. A racing department was an expensive luxury for a small firm, however, and it was abandoned after 1921, the year William Hillman died.

The 11hp remained in production until 1925 when it was replaced by the Fourteen, a 1954cc four-cylinder family car in the tradition of the Austin Heavy Twelve Four. This sold well, with about 11,000 finding buyers

between autumn 1925 and the end of 1930.

The factory was considerably enlarged in 1927, by which date Hillman was making all its own bodies. At the same time the Rootes brothers became sole distributors at home and abroad, a prelude to the fusion between Hillman and Humber at the end of 1928, which led to both makes, together with Commer commercial vehicles, already owned by Humber, coming under the control of the Rootes family.

Rationalization began as early as 1931, when the Hillman Vortic used the 2.6-litre straight-eight engine in a Humber chassis and body. This straight-eight had been introduced for 1929 as a companion to the Fourteen which it resembled externally, apart from a longer wheelbase. The 58bhp overhead-valve engine gave the car a 70mph (112kph) top speed, but it developed a very bad reputation for big end failure which damaged the image of all the larger Hillmans. Nevertheless it sold 2795 units between 1929 and 1932, making it the best-seller of any British straight-eight. (Daimler, for whom the title is sometimes claimed, did not sell more than 1230 straight-eights in the years between 1934 and 1953.)

A 2.8-litre side-valve six called the Wizard appeared in 1931, ancestor of a line of sixes made until 1938, but much more important was the introduction at the 1931 Olympia Motor Show of the Minx, a four-door family saloon with 1185cc four-cylinder side-valve engine selling for £159. By the outbreak of war eight years later the Minx had become a British institution, more luxurious and refined than equivalent Tens from Austin, Morris or Ford, and quintessential transport for the younger element of the English upper middle class.

The Minx also embodied some important improvements, including the first example of a factory fitted radio on a small British car (the 'Melody Minx' of 1934) and, more important, an all-synchromesh four-speed gearbox from 1935. From 1933 to 1935 there was a sports model with underslung frame, the Aero Minx, which formed the basis of the Talbot Ten when the Rootes brothers acquired the Sunbeam-Talbot-Darracq concern in 1935, and for the New Zealand market Rootes made a Minx-based Humber Ten. The Minx lost its synchronized bottom gear, due to cost cutting, on the 1939 models and it was not restored until 1965, but otherwise it followed, or sometimes set, prevailing fashions, with pressed steel wheels from 1936 (in which year running boards were dropped), external access boots in 1938, and integral construction on the 1940 models.

Minx production rose from 16,671 in the 1932-33 season to more than 55,000 in 1938-39, which put Hillman in fourth place among British car-makers. Total pre-war Minx production exceeded 152,000 and the 1940 models stayed in limited production for the armed forces and essential civilian use until 1944.

The larger Hillmans were the 2.6-litre Sixteen and 3.2-litre Hawk and Eighty sixes, the latter with transverse leaf independent front suspension designed by the American Barney Roos during his brief sojourn with Rootes in 1937. Last of the pre-war Hillmans was the 1938-40 Fourteen, which looked like an enlarged Minx with 1944cc four-cylinder engine. It shared the six-light saloon body with the Humber Snipe and was the ancestor of the post-war Humber Hawk. About 14,800 Hillman Sixes of all types were made from 1931 to 1938, and 4600 Fourteens.

Wartime production was devoted to Minx

gine was enlarged to 1265cc for 1950. The Minx was developed steadily through the 1950s and 1960s, receiving a 1390cc overhead-valve engine in 1955, a new Sunbeam Rapier-inspired body in 1956, optional automatic transmission in 1958 and front disc brakes in 1964. Variations included a short wheelbase estate car called the Husky (1955-65) and the Super Minx (1962-66), an elongated Minx with 1592cc and later 1725cc engines. The Minx was made under licence in Japan by Isuzu from 1953 to 1961.

In 1963 Hillman broke new ground, literally and figuratively, with the Imp, a rear-engined saloon built to challenge the Mini. Made in a new factory at Linwood, near Glasgow, it was the first Scottish-built car since the 1920s. The factory was intended to employ 5000 people and build 150,000 cars a year.

The 875cc single-overhead cam, aluminium four-cylinder engine was based on a Coventry-Climax design and was mounted in-line (and canted at 45°) at the rear of an integral two-door saloon with all round independent suspension. Later variants included a fastback coupé, which was also badged as the Singer Chamois and Sunbeam Stiletto, and an estate car for which the Husky name was revived. The Imp was a good design, although the rear-engined layout had been rendered old-fashioned with the advent of the

front-wheel-drive Minis, but suffered from a variety of teething problems which persisted for several years.

By 1968 most of the design and development faults had been put right, but the damage to its reputation had been done and the Imp never achieved the hoped-for sales figures. A total of 440,000 were made in 13 years until it was dropped in 1976. The engine, sometimes enlarged to 998cc, was used in a number of sports cars including the Clan Crusader, Davrian and Ginetta G15.

Development work on the Imp proved so costly that Rootes was forced to seek outside financial aid from the American Chrysler Corporation. In 1964 Chrysler took a 46 per cent stake in the Rootes Group ordinary shares and 65 per cent in non-voting shares increasing this in 1967 to give it total control. In 1970 Rootes became Chrysler UK Ltd.

The first product of the Chrysler era was the Hillman Hunter, a five to six seater saloon with 1725cc alloy head engine from the Super Minx and Ford-like strut front suspension. Launched in 1966 the Hunter was joined the following year by a cheaper version with 1496cc engine, which was the last Hillman to bear the name Minx; it was made until 1970. From 1967 Hunters were exported to Iran where they were assembled under the name Peykan but the loss of this business in 1978 as a result of the Iranian revolution was a serious blow to the finances of Chrysler UK Ltd.

The last model to be made under the Hillman name was the Avenger, a four-door saloon with all-coil independent suspension and a choice of 1248cc or 1498cc four-cylinder engines. It was launched in 1970, became a Chrysler in 1976 and a Talbot in 1979 before being dropped in 1981. The Avenger was sold in the United States for a few years as the Plymouth Cricket, and with Dodge badging in other countries. South African Avengers used Peugeot engines. The Hillman name disappeared completely after 1978.

After the demise of the Imp, the Linwood factory was used for the production of Avengers. Despite hopes that the Chrysler Horizon might be made there, the end of the Avenger in the summer of 1981 also saw the closure of the Scottish factory with the loss of more than 5000 jobs. GNG

Hillman Avenger GT of 1974

saloons and 10cwt (508kg) utilities; some of the latter were made as estate cars, and this became a catalogued model in the post-war Minx range. Some of these were badged as Commers, as were all the Minx-based delivery vans made from 1935 onwards. Otherwise the 1946 Minxes were virtually identical to the 1940s, and were only slightly changed in 1948 when recessed headlamps and steering column gearchange were adopted. From 1946 Hillmans were made in a new factory, shared with Humber and Sunbeam-Talbot, at Ryton-on-Dunsmore, outside Coventry.

A completely new all-enveloping body came on the 1949 models, together with coil independent front suspension, and the en-

Hillman Imp saloon of c.1970

HINDUSTAN
INDIA 1946 to date

Hindustan Motors Ltd of Uttarpara in West Bengal was founded by the Birla brothers, successful Calcutta industrialists, in 1942 with capital of £3.5 million and plans to build cars in association with Morris Motors of Cowley, Great Britain. Morris's parent, the Nuffield Organisation, had been widening its overseas interests since the formation in 1933 of Morris Industries Exports Ltd (which later became Nuffield Exports) and saw post-war India as a growing market.

ris-based production continued with the side-valve Series II Oxford and in 1957 Hindustan gave the car overhead valves and its own model name, the Ambassador. It evolved through the 1963 Mark II and 1975 Mark III to the current Mark IV, introduced in 1979. Available engines are 1489 and 1760cc four-cylinder petrol units and, since 1978, a 40hp diesel.

An experimental glassfibre-bodied front-wheel-drive two-cylinder two-stroke mini car designed in 1960 by Hindustan itself never reached production, but a Jeep-type vehicle called the Trekker and with Ambassador engine options was introduced in 1977. In 1982, with some 16,000 employees, Hindustan

improvement on the typical dowdy Japanese cars of the time and in 1965 the Contessa won the Alassio Concorso di Eleganza in Italy.

In October 1965 Toyota acquired Hino and car production ended in 1967. At that time Hino had a workforce of about 6000, capital of 12,500 million yen and annual sales worth 73,500 million yen. In 1980 these figures had risen to 8000, 14,850 million and 365,000 million. Its commercial vehicles are now built in two factories in Tokyo and a new complex at Nitta in Japan, and they are assembled in 38 overseas plants.

In 1981 Hino was second only to Mercedes-Benz in terms of heavy commercial vehicles sold worldwide, when its output reached

Hindustan Trekker diesel of c.1977

Hino Contessa saloon of 1965

Prior to World War II India had extremely poor roads, very few cars and highly restrictive legislation on private motoring. There was no domestic manufacturer and most of the imports were from Britain, with American cars next in popularity and Fiat and Opel just beginning to show some interest in the market. The popularity of British cars was not only a result of India's place in the British empire and the number of ex-patriate Britons in the country, but also because British cars attracted an import tariff of only 30 per cent compared to the otherwise standard 37½ per cent.

During the war India had developed dramatically industrially, with several companies making bodies for military vehicles, but there had been little progress in light, precision engineering so India still needed to import its motor industry. High distribution costs favoured small local plants. Hindustan located its first in Bombay province, which had new US Ford and Chevrolet assembly plants but was starved of British cars.

The first Hindustan, the Hindustan Ten, built in 1946, was a version of the 1140cc Series M Morris, the first integral construction car from Cowley. It was followed by the Morris Oxford-based Hindustan 14 and the Baby Hindustan, 803cc and 948cc copies of the Minor.

During the 1950s Hindustan also built cars under licence from Studebaker, mainly the six-cylinder side-valve Champion, which was introduced in the United States in 1939. Mor-

built 25,079 cars and Trekkers. In 1983 it advanced firmly into the late 1960s with the introduction of the Vauxhall Victor lookalike Contessa, which used the same Morris engine as the Ambassador Mark IV.

Since 1980 the Indian government has relaxed its restrictions on imported engines, which has given Hindustan some competition from cars such as the Suzuki-based Maruti 800, but the big, rugged Ambassador and Contessa are still well-suited to the country's needs. With an output of just over 24,200 cars in 1984, Hindustan's biggest problem nowadays is that the old Morris body dies will probably wear out before demand does. For 1987 the Contessa will be re-engined with an Isuzu unit. BL

HINO
JAPAN 1953-1967

This well-known commercial vehicle builder was created in 1942 in a break away from Diesel Jidosha, a firm that had grown out of Jidosha KK. Hino Motors Ltd made the Renault 4CV in Tokyo from 1953 as a sideline to trucks and buses, and from 1961 evolved its own Contessa models with quasi-Detroit styling.

In a complete redesign in 1964 the cars lost most vestiges of their Renault ancestry, although they were still rear-engined, and received Michelotti styling. This was a great

63,000 trucks and 5000 buses. It has a factory in Jacksonville, Florida, making 2000 trucks a year. In New Zealand its products are marketed as Fords. In 1984 its diesel engines were reported to be based on MAN designs from Germany. NB

HINSTIN/SUP
FRANCE 1921-1929

Jacques Hinstin was something of an adventurer and playboy, but he was also a serious and talented engineer. From about 1900 he was involved with André Citroën and André Boas in Engrenages Citroën, the gear cutting business which gave the later Citroën car company its double-chevron badge and the *Titanic* its steering gear. In 1905 the firm worked from an old mill at Essonne. When the gear cutting business was slow it contracted to build 500 car engines for Sizaire et Naudin, the first car connection for either Hinstin or Citroën.

In 1919 Hinstin met Adolphe Kégresse, a French-born engineer who had once overseen the Russian imperial car fleet and had designed on behalf of the tsar, with Russian winter conditions in mind, a light flexible halftrack system which was granted a French patent in 1913. Hinstin acquired four of the early Citroën chassis for the now French-based Kégresse and, working in premises provided by the car-maker Grégoire, built a halftrack vehicle which was demonstrated to André Citroën early in 1920.

Citroën immediately adopted the vehicle for production and Hinstin and Kégresse were put in charge of Citroën's new halftrack department. The Citroën-Kégresse went on to make a historic first motorized crossing of the Sahara in 1922-23, and was built in some numbers for military and commercial use.

Hinstin, meanwhile, through Etablissements Jacques Hinstin in Paris, had his own car interests and in 1921 at the Paris Salon showed a well made cyclecar with two side-by-side seats and a 1099cc overhead-valve four-cylinder engine, designed by an engineer called Picker. In standard form the engine gave 17hp but a 20hp 62mph (100kph) sports version of the car was also available.

Early in 1921 this car was marketed as the Hinstin-SUP, built now by Hinstin for Société des Usines Paquis of Cons-la-Granville, Ardennes. This firm was founded in 1908 by Albert Henon, first to produce components and accessories and later to produce complete but unlabelled chassis around which several makers based their own cars.

SUP had several factories by 1919 and also produced a car under its own name, a four-cylinder 11CV model, alongside the Hinstin-SUP. Henon had originally intended SUP to build its own cyclecar and had built a single prototype, with an engine by Picker, but was content to order 700 cars from Hinstin.

The cars entered various competitions, including Le Mans in 1921, with mixed results caused by marginal reliability. They were built until late 1923 or early 1924, when the Lequeaux brothers, engineers at SUP, bought the unassembled parts and set up a small workshop repairing old cars and even assembling a very few new ones, perhaps until as late as 1928. Henon left SUP for Le Zèbre, but SUP itself continued to be a major parts supplier to the motor industry.

Hinstin continued to build cars for others; they included, up to 1924, a small number of 1100cc 10hp voiturettes for the Grégoire company of Poissy, in effect that company's last car, and the Guillick – built for the Belgian company G. Guillick et Cie until 1929, after which Hinstin built no more cars. BL

HISA
see Hermes

HISPANO-SUIZA
FRANCE 1911-1938

Although Hispano-Suiza originated in 1904 as a Spanish company, following on from the Swiss engineer Marc Birkigt's involvements with the short-lived La Cuadra and Castro makes in Barcelona, it is widely thought of as being a French make. In fact the French branch of the company was not founded until some seven years after Hispano-Suiza's first appearance, but such was the style and quality of the French-made cars that the relatively downmarket if much more numerous Spanish cars were soon at least partly eclipsed.

The Hispano-Suiza made its first appearance in France in 1906, when two four-cylinder models, a 3.8- and a 7.4-litre, were shown at the Paris Salon. The car was marketed in France from then on and, as elsewhere, achieved some sales success.

It was Hispano-Suiza's win in the Coupe de l'Auto Grand Prix des Voiturettes at Boulogne in September 1910, however, that really established the marque in the French market. Engineer-cum-works driver Paolo Zuccarelli

won the race with an extremely long stroke 2646cc four-cylinder model which effectively spelled the end for the more outrageous single- and twin-cylinder designs in voiturette racing but also, surprisingly, marked Hispano-Suiza's last official racing involvement. Zuccarelli was later implicated in the alleged pirating of Birkigt's pioneering twin overhead cam design by Ernest Henry, but his involvement remains in doubt.

The Société Française Hispano-Suiza was founded in 1911 and the first French factory was in an old tramcar depot at Levallois-Perret, Seine. At first, and until after World War I, it was in reality only an assembly plant for the Spanish models, notably the 3.6-litre Alfonso sports car – derived from the 1910 race winner and a great sales success throughout Europe.

In 1913 the French factory produced 150 cars and in 1914 the company moved into larger works at nearby Bois-Colombes. The company's capital was still only 1.5 million francs, a relatively modest figure, but Hispano-Suiza's forthcoming wartime role as an aero-engine manufacturer meant that the company would always be financially secure and always have enough resources for developing fine cars.

Although the Spanish company continued to produce cars throughout World War I French production was switched to aero engines. Birkigt had developed his water

Hispano-Suiza Alfonso of 1912

cooled V8 in Barcelona shortly before the war and it was ready for production in 1915. Of the 21 plants throughout the world which built almost 50,000 of these engines, 14 were in France and the engine was built under licence by Peugeot – beneficiaries of the alleged Henry copying of the Birkigt twin-cam design.

The French company put its wartime earnings and engineering lessons to superb use with the first all-French model, launched in 1919 at the Paris Salon, the magnificent H6B. It had a 6.6-litre six-cylinder engine in light alloy with steel cylinder liners and a single overhead camshaft. It also had a light but beautifully engineered chassis with excellent four-wheel brakes at a time when these were

Hispano-Suiza H6B of 1929

still far from the norm, and was the first to introduce mechanical servo assistance. Rolls-Royce later used the system under licence from Hispano-Suiza into the 1960s.

It was intended unequivocally as a luxury car par excellence and with coachwork from the very best houses it was exactly that. It also drew almost universal critical acclaim for its behaviour on the road. It stayed in production with little major change until 1934 and was a worldwide success.

In 1924 it was joined by a sportier 8-litre model, the H6C, named the Boulogne after André Dubonnet's success with a prototype in the Coupe Boillot race at Boulogne. Dubonnet, of the drinks family, also owned the spectacular tulip-wood bodied car, clad in riveted tulip-wood planking by the aeroplane-builder Nieuport. In 1928 a Boulogne handsomely beat a Stutz Black Hawk whose makers had challenged the Hispano-Suiza to a 24-hour speed and reliability contest at the Indianapolis Speedway. A less exotic version of the H6B was also built in Spain in very small numbers, and Skoda in Czechoslovakia built the car under licence from 1923 for some six years.

In 1930 Hispano-Suiza took over the Ballot company and by now Hispano-Suiza capital stood at some 42 million francs. From 1931 the 4.6-litre six-cylinder Hispano Junior, a very mundane car by former standards, with Ballot chassis, was built in the former Ballot works, but only until 1932.

Also in 1931, however, Hispano-Suiza introduced its largest and most complex model ever, the 9.4-litre V12 Type 68, followed in 1934 by the 11.3-litre 68bis. Both models would exceed 100mph (160kph), the quickest open short chassis cars with the large engine being capable of perhaps 115mph (185kph) – and in this case in rather more silence than Hispano-Suiza had previously offered, as these cars used pushrod operated valve gear. It was verging on the impractical and hugely expensive at a time when depression was almost universal but it still sold 76 examples up to 1938.

That was the year in which Hispano-Suiza, in France at least, decided to stop car production, having built an estimated 2614 units. The company then concentrated exclusively on aero engines, perhaps not a difficult decision in the political climate of that year. When the war ended Hispano-Suiza would make a half-hearted foray into the car world with a prototype Ford V8-engined front-wheel-drive car, but it never saw production.

After the war Birkigt retired to his native Geneva where he died in March 1953. His company continued as world leaders in aero engine and weapons technology and in 1963 Hispano-Suiza acquired what remained of Automobiles Bugatti after that great company's final decline. Hispano was finally absorbed into the French national aerospace industries combine, SNECMA, and as part of that organization continues to build aircraft components. BL

HISPANO-SUIZA/CASTRO, LA CUADRA
SPAIN 1903-1944

The brilliant Swiss engineer Marc Birkigt was born in Geneva in 1878. At the age of 11 he was orphaned and passed into the care of his grandmother who sent him to the Ecole des Arts et Métiers in Geneva, from where he graduated with distinction in 1898. He had trained principally in railway and electrical engineering. From college he began his compulsory period of national military service,

Hispano-Suiza sports tourer of c.1914

serving with the artillery, where he learned much about materials and precision engineering through his enthusiastic involvements with the ordnance factories.

From the artillery he left Switzerland, at the suggestion of a Spanish friend he had met in Paris, and went to Barcelona to work for a company which built electric locomotives. In 1899 he built an electric bus for E. de La Cuadra y Cia, a company owned by Emilio La Cuadra which also made electric batteries. In 1901 Birkigt designed a four-seater petrol car for La Cuadra, an 1100cc 4½hp vertical twin with chain final drive. It was Spain's first petrol car but its rather ordinary specification gave little indication of Birkigt's potential and only six were built before La Cuadra, crippled by strikes, went bankrupt in 1901.

The company was taken over by one of its principal creditors, Sr J. Castro, and renamed J. Castro Sociedad en Comandita. Castro resumed car production under his own name with the Birkigt/La Cuadra design. Birkigt stayed with the company to design a new 10hp twin-cylinder car for 1902, now with shaft drive, and then a 2.2-litre 14hp four-cylinder model which was put into limited production in 1903.

Like La Cuadra, Castro was hit by labour problems and by 1904 production had been stopped through lack of finance. The company was taken over by a group of businessmen headed by Don Damien Mateu and on 14 June 1904 became Sociedad Hispano-Suiza

Fabrica de Automoviles, with capital of 250,000 pesetas and obviously named on the assumption that Birkigt's role as technical director was to be a long term one. Mateu remained with the company and contributed greatly towards its success and stability up to his death in 1929.

The car was now renamed Hispano-Suiza, but the first models were 12-15 and 20-24hp fours based on the Castro design. In 1906 Birkigt designed 20-24 and 35-40hp cars for the Société des Automobiles à Genève, which were built as SAGs until 1910 when the company was renamed Piccard-Pictet et Cie, still in Geneva, and the cars became Pic-Pics.

Although Hispano-Suiza would later be widely thought of as a French company, after the formation of Société Française Hispano-Suiza at Levallois-Perret in 1911, it was virtually unknown outside Spain until about 1907. Two four-cylinder cars, a 3.8 and a 7.4-litre, were exhibited at the Paris Salon in 1906 and the marque made its British debut at the Birmingham Show in January 1907, by which year the company had gained the patronage of the royal motoring and motor racing enthusiast King Alfonso XIII of Spain, who would subsequently own many Hispano-Suizas and become a good friend of Birkigt's.

The company introduced its first six, the 6.2-litre 30-40hp, in 1906, joined by a similar 10.4-litre 60-65hp model. By 1908 there was a choice of five chassis types.

In 1909 Birkigt designed a team of voiturette racers to contest the Catalan Cup race, whose trophy was donated by King Alfonso, and he took what he saw as best advantage of the complicated technical regulations with an 1852cc side-valve four-cylinder engine. Paolo Zuccarelli led the race with this car for three of its 13 laps but retired with a broken clutch – clutches would always be the Achilles' heel of Birkigt's otherwise formidable designs. Zuccarelli won the Coupe de l'Auto Grand Prix des Voiturettes in 1910 with a long stroke development of the car, but that was the end of Hispano-Suiza's official racing involvement.

It is often alleged that in 1911 Birkigt designed a twin-overhead camshaft 16-valve 2.6-litre four-cylinder engine, which was tried in prototype form by King Alfonso, but whose design was appropriated by Ernest Henry, then working for Hispano-Suiza as an engineer, and later presented as his own milestone design for the racing Peugeot.

The first car known as the Alfonso evolved from the Coupe de l'Auto winner, the best known of several versions being the 3.6-litre, with engine and gearbox in unit and a top speed of around 75mph (120kph). It was one of the first true popular sports cars and sold well throughout Europe. There was even a plan to build Hispano-Suizas in Russia, where they were also well known, at the Russo-Baltique works in Riga where copies of cars such as the Rex-Simplex and the Fondu were built. Coincidentally, Russo-Baltique also had a Swiss engineer, Julien Potterat, but the outbreak of World War I prevented production.

One notable Hispano-Suiza copy which did go into production was the Abadal, built from 1912 to 1914 in Barcelona by Francisco Abadal, who had been Hispano-Suiza's agent in Madrid from the company's beginnings.

With the approach of World War I, Birkigt had developed an aero engine for the Spanish government, a water-cooled V8 with shaft and bevel gear driven overhead camshafts, as first seen on his pre-war cars. The engine went into production in 1915 and 49,893 were eventually built in Spain, France, Britain, the United States and Italy, playing a significant part in winning the war and in founding a reputation for superb aero engines which was underlined in World War II and beyond.

The aviation connection also gave Hispano-Suiza its famous flying stork mascot, sculpted by François Bazin, from 1918. It commemorated the squadron badge of French flying ace Georges Guynemer, a friend of Birkigt's who disappeared behind enemy lines in 1917 after scoring over 50 kills with his Hispano-Suiza engined SPAD fighters.

The new French Hispano-Suiza company had in effect been only an assembly plant before World War I and the specifically French models did not appear until after 1919, at which point they largely began to eclipse the cars built for the less prosperous Spanish market. Overhead cam 16 and 30hp fours were built in Barcelona up to 1924 and the Spanish company also built a 3.7-litre 'economy' version of the glorious French H6B.

In 1930 Barcelona introduced a 3-litre pushrod overhead-valve six-cylinder model whose engine was also to have been used by Hudson in the USA but never was because of the Depression. Larger versions of this six were made by the Barcelona company until it stopped car production in 1944 and other sixes of up to 8 litres completed the range.

The Barcelona operation in fact made far more cars than the French, a total of some 19,000 vehicles between 1904 and 1944 – although more than half of these were com-

mercial or utility, built in a factory near Madrid and including fire engines and road rollers. Barcelona built many 2½-litre four-cylinder cars for the Spanish army, government and civil service, and production continued in spite of the Civil War, World War II and the French factory's demise in 1938. From 1931 to 1943 alone Barcelona built over 3000 cars – more than the total French output of 2614.

Car production had ended in Barcelona by 1944, however, as Hispano-Suiza decided to concentrate on aero engines and armaments, which it does to the present day. In late 1946 the Barcelona works were partially nationalized as Empresa Nacional de Autocamiones SA, which in 1951 introduced another rather fine Spanish car, the Pegaso. BL

HOLDEN
AUSTRALIA 1948 to date

Holden is General Motors' Australian operation and had a 34-year history of bodybuilding before the appearance of the first Holden car. The company began in 1885 as Holden and Frost of Adelaide, making horse carriages, and built its first car body, on a Lancia, in 1914. It expanded over the next six years, becoming Holden's Motor Body Builders Ltd in 1920, although Holden and Frost continued as a separate business engaged solely in leather trimming.

They closed in 1925, by which time Holden had acquired a new 22 acre (9 hectare) site at Woodville, South Australia, and had been appointed sole body supplier to General

Motors Export Co. Founded in 1918, this changed its name to General Motors (Australia) Pty Ltd in 1926 and five years later bought Holden for £1,111,600.

As would be expected, the bulk of Holden's work was on General Motors cars, especially Chevrolet and Buick, but it also made bodies for a number of other American makes such as Hudson, Essex, Chrysler, De Soto, Plymouth, Willys, Graham, Reo and Studebaker. Holden's first closed body was built on an Essex chassis in 1924. A distinctive Holden style was the two-door fast back coupé, nicknamed the Sloper, which was built on Buick, Chevrolet, Oldsmobile, Pontiac and Vauxhall chassis from 1935 to 1941. This anticipated the fast back coupés made by General Motors' American divisions in the early post-war years.

Holden also built on a number of European chassis, particularly Vauxhalls, for which it created a number of styles not seen in Britain, and also on Austin, Morris, Singer, Clyno and Fiat. In 1936 Holden opened a new plant at Fisherman's Bend near Melbourne to make bodies for Bedford, Chevrolet and General Motors trucks.

During World War II Holden built more than 30,000 bodies for the war effort, ranging from Chevrolet sedans to ambulances, tankers and gun tractors, mostly on the Chevrolet CMP (Canadian Military Pattern) chassis that was also made by Ford. After the war production of bodies was resumed on Chevrolet and Vauxhall chassis, but Holden was already working on the idea of an all-Australian car which would be more suited to the local market than the over-large American products and the too-small British ones.

Holdens old and new

Holden Torana 6 GTR of 1971

Monaro was being equipped with the Chevrolet 454 (7.4 litres), and outperformed Ford's 289 Falcon in stock car racing. A machine in the tradition of the American muscle cars, the Monaro was made from 1968 to 1976, a total of nearly 41,000 being built. The Torana range was widened, and in 1974 on the LH series, Toranas could be had with four-, six- or eight-cylinder engines, from a 1.9-litre Opel four to a 5-litre V8.

Torana production ended in December 1979, their place at the lower end of the market having been taken by the Gemini, which had been introduced four and a half years earlier. The Gemini marked the end of the 'Australian car for Australian markets' philosophy, for it was the Isuzu version of Gener-

The man behind this was Sir Lawrence Hartnett, Holden's managing director from 1934 to 1947, who not only secured the backing of General Motors management in Detroit but also obtained a £3 million loan from Australian banks, with the support of the government. The first prototypes, built in America and Australia, were tested in both countries between 1946 and 1948, and the first production Holden car left the line in November 1948.

Known as the 48/215, it was a four-door unitary construction sedan powered by a 2.2-litre six-cylinder overhead-valve engine and owed a lot to pre-war Chevrolet plans for a smaller car which had never materialized. Hartnett had planned for an advanced, slab-sided design, but General Motors in Detroit opted for a more conventional body with separate wings, and the ensuing disagreement led to Hartnett's resignation to set up his own company under his own name.

The new Holden was enthusiastically received by patriotic Australians, who for the first time had a mass-produced local car to buy. It was particularly welcome to the Holden workforce, who had turned to a variety of products to keep the five plants busy once war contracts were completed. These included stainless steel sinks, carpet sweepers and filing cabinets.

Production of bodies on Buick, Chevrolet, Oldsmobile, Pontiac and Vauxhall chassis was revived, but sales were disappointing because the imported chassis cost 100 per cent more than in pre-war days. The last bodies on American chassis were made in 1948 and on Vauxhall in 1952, although cabs and bodies were built on Bedford truck chassis up to the late 1950s.

Sold through 600 dealers the 48/215 was an immediate success, with 30,00 finding buyers between November 1948 and February 1951. That popular Australian design, the coupé utility or 'ute', joined the sedan in January 1951. The 60,000 mark was reached in April 1952, and 100,000 had been sold by May 1953.

Later that year came a slightly restyled model called the FJ215, but the first major changes did not come until July 1956 with the

Holden Statesman Series II Caprice of 1983

FE, a full width six-seater sedan, still with the same engine and transmission. Basically Holdens worked on a three year body programme, with minor restyling every 18 months. Engine capacity went up to 2.3 litres (75bhp) on the 1960 FB series and automatic transmission was offered for the first time on the 1961 EK models.

The first Holden exports went to New Zealand in 1954, and by the early 1960s the cars had found markets in several countries of South East Asia, Africa and Hawaii. They have never been sold in countries with a strong General Motors industry, such as the United States, Great Britain or western Europe.

Holden gained first place in the Australian sales league in 1950 and held it every year until 1982 when it was displaced by Ford. The millionth Holden was made in October 1962, and the two millionth in March 1969.

Fisherman's Bend was the main plant, but the original Woodville factory was the main supplier of bodies. There were also assembly plants at Pagewood in New South Wales, The Valley in Brisbane, Mosman Park in Perth, and Birkenhead in South Australia. A new body plant was opened at Elizabeth, South Australia, in 1962-63, and another factory at Acacia Ridge, Queensland, in 1964.

In 1967 Holden offered a small car in the shape of the Torana HB, a restyled Vauxhall Viva, and the following year extended the range at the other end with a 5-litre Chevrolet V8 option in the HK series. All-Australian V8s in 4.1- and 5-litre sizes came in 1969 in sedans, and there was also the Monaro coupé with the locally made V8 and with a Chevrolet 327 (5.3-litre) unit. Within a few years, the

al Motors' T-car, alias Vauxhall Chevette/ Opel Kadett.

The second non-Australian Holden was the Commodore, introduced for 1979, which was an Opel Commodore with some styling features from the Senator, and four-, six- or eight-cylinder engines from 1.9 to 4.1 litres. It quickly became Australia's top-selling car and remained so for three years until displaced by the Ford Falcon.

The older American-styled Holden theme was continued in the Statesman. From 1974 some of these were sold without engines to Mazda, which fitted them with Wankel rotary engines for the Japanese home market. Holden affirmed its faith in the larger car by bringing out a revised Series II Statesman in 1983, with 5-litre V8 engine and three-speed automatic transmission.

More important, though, was the Camira, a version of the J-car (Chevrolet/Vauxhall Cavalier, Opel Ascona) with Isuzu front end panels, made in sedan and station wagon form. The panels of the latter are also exported to the United Kingdom for the Vauxhall Cavalier station wagon, as are engines for British, German and South African-built J-cars. In particular, the Opel engines for the Swedish market all come from Holden, as Swedish and Australian emission regulations are similar. Engines for both markets use a Pulse Air Injection system.

The 1987 Holden line-up consisted of the 1.3-litre Barina (Suzuki Swift imported from Japan), 1½-litre Astra (Australian-assembled Nissan Cherry), the Gemini in petrol or diesel form, the Camira and the Commodore with 3-litre ohc Nissan or 5-litre GM V8 engines.

Holden Commodore of 1984

Holden also sell under its name the W.F.R. Shuttle, a forward-control petrol van/minibus which it imports from Isuzu.

The loss of the sales lead to Ford in 1982 was a blow to Holden's pride, even though the margin was a mere 137 units. More than pride was dented in 1983, when Holden's sales were some 31,000 below Ford's, at 102,634 with only 18.07 per cent of the market, compared with 22.6 per cent in 1982 and a high of 45 to 50 per cent in the early 1960s. However, despite the reduced market share for Holden, the Commodore and Camira were the second and third best-selling Australian-built cars. As well as the Australian plants which employ nearly 18,000 people, Holden has a New Zealand assembly plant at Upper Hutt near Wellington. GNG

HOLMES
USA 1918-1923

Arthur Holmes, a former vice-president and chief engineer of Franklin, was joined by another Franklin man, C. H. Rockwell, to form the Holmes Automobile Co at Canton, Ohio, in 1917. The company had a capital of $2.5 million. Holmes and Rockwell spent $300,000 on a 23-acre (9-hectare) site belonging to Republic Stamping and Enamelling Co, whose president, R. E. Bebb, joined the Holmes board.

The first of some 2700 six-cylinder air-cooled 30hp models appeared in 1918. They had forced draught flywheel-fan cooling and were similar to Franklins, although less attractive. A four-cylinder version was also intended but financial difficulties halted production in 1922 and the firm went out of business in May 1923. NB

HOLSMAN
USA 1902-1911

Regarded as the pioneer of the high-wheeler, architect Henry K. and J. A. Holsman developed an air-cooled opposed-twin with rope drive in 1902 that became one of the best known buggies of the day. It is believed to have been based on a McCormick prototype shown in 1898 and revised two years later.

The Holsman Automobile Co of Chicago started production in 1902 of a buggy which had wheels 4ft (1.2m) in diameter. The slogan was 'Tried – safest, simplest, strongest, cheapest, proven', and soon the buggy encouraged many imitators.

In the boom period for these curious American vehicles about 1000 Holsmans were sold a year. They were built mainly during the winter for sale when the snows cleared in the spring. This led to cash-flow problems for the company and in 1909 it moved to Plano, Illinois, probably by now with financial backing from International Harvester – which may have retained an involvement from the McCormick days, and certainly held some of their patent rights.

Flat fours were introduced in 1910 and cars were exported to Australia and India. However, as American roads improved and more conventional cars made high-wheelers seem outdated, Holsman failed to graduate. No further news of the company appeared after 1911. NB

HONDA
JAPAN 1948 to date

Soichiro Honda was born in 1906 in the small town of Hamamatsu in central Japan, the son of a blacksmith. In his teens he was apprenticed to the Art Trading Co, a Tokyo garage which specialized in car repairs. In September 1923 the Art Trading Co was one of the many victims of the great Tokyo earthquake and was virtually burned out in the ensuing fire. Honda stayed on, gaining valuable mechanical experience through rebuilding fire-damaged cars. He stayed in Tokyo until 1928 then returned to Hamamatsu and started his own garage, also called Art Trading, with the former owner's approval.

During this period, with his brother, Soichiro also built several racing cars, including one with a 90hp Curtiss aero engine. He won a few races in the All Japan Automobile Speed Championship but retired from racing after almost killing himself in an accident with a supercharged Ford-engined racer and thereafter concentrated on his business.

In the late 1930s he began to manufacture piston rings but scrapped most of the first batch which, because of his lack of metallurgical knowledge, had turned out to be near useless. He learned quickly, however,

through evening classes at the local technical college, and by the outbreak of World War II his revitalized piston ring company supplied most of the domestic engine manufacturers – until his works were bombed.

Honda sold the piston ring company after the war and, ever interested in invention, worked on the commercial extraction of salt from seawater and on designing a rotary weaving machine. He also acquired a batch of 500 small military surplus generator engines and built himself a motorized bicycle as a first step to producing such machines.

Production of the motorcycles was started in October 1946 with 12 workers and a single machine tool in a 12ft by 18ft (3.6m by 5.5m) shed on a convenient bomb site. Honda soon used up his stock of surplus engines, building his machines at the rate of around one a day. Well aware that he had found a steady market, he began to make his own 50cc two-stroke engines – to run on the then enforced post-war raw pine resin fuel.

The clip-on engined bike was refined as the ½hp Honda A Type, the first Japanese motorcycle made entirely, frame and engine, by one maker. As business boomed Honda formalized the operation in September 1948 as the Honda Motor Co with capital equivalent to £900 and 34 employees in slightly more spacious works in Hamamatsu. In March 1950 Honda opened a Tokyo office and in 1953 a new factory at Saitama.

In 1951 he switched from two-stroke to four-stroke engines for his motorcycles and in 1954 established the Hamamatsu factory in its modern form, buying in over $1.1 million worth of machine tools from the United States, Germany and Switzerland at a time when the actual capital of the company represented only $166,000. This rapid and costly expansion coincided with a severe national recession, in addition to which Honda suffered cash flow problems as retailers defaulted on payments and the banks refused to provide bridging finance. Honda's own workers saved the company by working through their holidays to complete the new plant and build enough motorcycles to cover urgent debts.

In 1957 Honda sold his first exports, two

Curtiss aero-engined Honda racer of c.1925

machines to Okinawa! After the 1958 introduction of the C-100 'step-through' moped, Honda sales boomed and the company became the first ever to sell over 1 million motorcycles in a year. In 1958 Honda exported two bikes to the USA and in 1959 established the American Honda Motor Co Inc as its sales organization there. In rapid succession companies were also set up in Germany, Belgium, Thailand and elsewhere.

In 1960 Honda opened the Honda Research and Development Co, initially to build the racing motorcycles in which Honda was just developing an interest and which would soon totally dominate the sport in all classes. The R and D company's lessons were rapidly adapted to production designs and Honda has remained a greatly respected technical innovator.

In 1962 Honda, now the world's largest manufacturer of motorcycles, made the progression to cars. At the Tokyo Show it introduced the four-cylinder S500 sports car, initially shown with 356 or 492cc twin-overhead cam engines and double chain final drive, but put into production with first 531cc, later 606cc and eventually 791cc engines – launched in Britain and elsewhere as the shaft-drive S800.

In August 1964 Honda entered a car in the German Grand Prix to begin a rather patchy Formula 1 racing episode. A Honda, driven by Richie Ginther, won the 1965 Mexican Grand Prix, the last run to the 1½-litre formula, and John Surtees won the 1967 Italian Grand Prix to the new 3-litre formula.

become a Grand Prix winner in 1985 but was too inconsistent to be a serious championship contender until too late.

Honda's major four-wheel racing success has been in Formula 2, first in 1966 when Honda-powered Brabhams won each of the 11 championship races. In the 1980s the Ralt-Honda, introduced in 1980, took over BMW's former domination of the category.

The first Honda sports car was built until 1969 and in 1966 the tiny front-wheel-drive N360 saloon, with air-cooled twin-cylinder 354cc engine, was launched, to instant success. It remained in production until 1974.

In 1968 Honda moved towards full-size cars with the front-wheel-drive 1298cc air-cooled four-cylinder 77 saloon, introduced at the Tokyo Show and joined by a coupé in 1970. In 1973 the water-cooled 1169cc Civic saloon was launched and the model name has continued to the present through numer-

Honda N360 saloon of 1966

ous new versions. The three millionth Civic was built during 1982.

From 1974 the Civic was offered with Honda's stratified charge CVCC (Compound Vortex Controlled Combustion) engine, offering low fuel consumption and very low emissions, which had been announced in 1971. The CVCC engine was also used in the hatchback Accord, launched in 1976, and in its sporting derivative the Prelude coupé from 1978. From 1983 the handsomely restyled Prelude was also offered with anti-lock brakes, another remarkable Honda development for a car in the Prelude price range.

In 1979 Honda signed an agreement on technical co-operation with British Leyland. The 1981 Triumph Acclaim was Leyland's version of Honda's own Ballade, introduced in the same year with the same engine range as the Civic. The Quintet, also launched in 1981, was a larger luxury derivative of the Accord, while at the other end of the scale Honda offered the diminutive City, which had a turbo option from 1982.

Also in 1982 Honda formalized technical ties with Peugeot in France, pursued plans to build cars in South Africa in co-operation with Mercedes-Benz and began to build the Accord in the USA, in Ohio, where Honda motorcycles had been assembled since 1979. In the early 1980s domestic production was approximately 911,000 cars and worldwide production almost 1.1 million. In 1984 the fruits of the Honda-Leyland collaboration were seen in the form of a new small Rover, the 213, followed in 1986 by the Rover 800,

Honda S800 coupé of c.1965

Honda Civic saloon of 1973

Even Surtees' acknowledged brilliance as a development driver, however, never really solved Honda's problems of prodigious power squandered on overweight chassis engineering.

Honda retired from Grand Prix racing after Jo Schlesser was killed in an experimental air-cooled V8 Grand Prix car at Rouen in 1968 – although it did make a tentative and inconclusive return in 1983 by supplying turbocharged engines to the Spirit Grand Prix team, themselves Grand Prix newcomers. In 1984 Honda began to supply Grand Prix engines to former constructors' champion Frank Williams, but the engines' obvious power was wasted on an uncharacteristically poor Williams chassis. The combination did

Honda Prelude coupé of 1983

another example of Honda's continuing technical excellence which now encompasses manufacture and assembly in New Zealand, South Africa, Portugal, Costa Rica, Malaysia, Taiwan, Indonesia and the USA as well as in Japan.

By 1984 American Honda was vying with American Motors for fourth place in the American manufacturers' league table and was planning to open a further North American assembly plant in Canada in 1987. There, Honda would initially assemble Accords and then a version of the Sterling V6 executive saloon which it has developed jointly with Austin-Rover.

The 1987 range comprised the 550cc 2-cylinder Today sold only on the domestic market, several versions each of the small 1.2 litre City (called the Jazz in some markets), the Civic (Ballade), the four-wheel-drive Shuttle, the Accord (Vigor) and the Quint (Integra) medium-sized saloons, and the Legend, a luxury saloon powered by 2- or 2½-litre V6 engines also used in the Rover 800 series. The Legend is also made in the Austin-Rover factory at Cowley, Oxfordshire. BL

HORBICK
GB 1902-1909

At the turn of the century Horsfall and Bickham had a large factory at Pendleton, Manchester, making textile machinery. The company was then taken over by H. Worthington and his brother-in-law George Kennedy, who experimented with a 6hp MMC-engined prototype in 1900 and displayed a car in Manchester in February 1902.

In 1903 Horbick cars were using Forman engines and would later employ Johnson, Hurley and Martin of Coventry's Alpha engines. From 1905 White and Poppe three- and four-cylinder engines were used, joined in 1907 by a 2.7-litre six. Horsfall and Bickham also made some of its own engines, notably a 1907 5.9-litre four and 8.1-litre six, and used the boring machinery for reconditioning engines long after car production ceased. The two-cylinder Minor of 1904 was billed as 'Absolutely the Simplest Little Car in the World, YOU Can Know All About it in 10 Minutes'.

William Senior, who was later to become a Leyland truck dealer, was the engineer in charge of the car department. Most Horbicks were sold locally to business associates of the firm and a 1906 brochure contains 12 testimonials, all from the north-west of England.

Dozens of Horbicks were reputedly sold in India and there was talk of an order for 2000 London taxis. As room was lacking for expansion, the firm decided to keep to the business it knew best. H. W. 'Doc' Cranham, the sales manager, resigned as a result and was not replaced. The company pulled out of car manufacture in 1909. NB

HORCH
GERMANY 1899-1940

August Horch was born in 1868, the son of a blacksmith, in Winningen, Mosel. He began his technical career in a wagon-building works in Heidelberg and then moved to a railway company on the Serbo-Hungarian border. From 1896 to 1899 he was manager of the Benz works at Mannheim. Then he left to form his own company in small premises in Ehrenfeld, Cologne, with finance from a local cloth merchant.

August Horch and Co was founded in the spring of 1899 and the first Horch car was ready the following year. It was of modern design, with a front-mounted 5PS two-cylinder engine and shaft drive. About 10 of these first Horchs were made, with bodies supplied by Utermöhle of Cologne, and were sold for 2300 marks each. Horch found the Cologne premises too small, and in 1902 he moved to Reichenbach in Vogtland, where he began to build larger cars of 10/12PS (two-cylinders) and 16/20PS (four-cylinders). Production was still very small, less than 50 cars a year, but in 1903 he moved to his third and last factory, at Zwickau in Saxony. Here much larger premises with 300 employees enabled output to increase, as did the size of the cars he now produced.

The twins were continued to 1907, but the best-known model was the 2.7-litre 18/22PS four-cylinder car with overhead inlet and side exhaust valves, made from 1904 to 1909. One of these won the 1906 Herkomer Trophy. Encouraged by this sporting success August Horch entered a team of cars in the first Prince Henry Trial, held in 1908. These had streamlined torpedo bodies and are considered to be among the earliest ancestors of the sports car. Horch himself was a keen competition driver and was partnered by Dr Rudolf Stöss, who later became a director of the company. Horch also offered a larger four-cylinder car, the 5.8-litre 23/40PS made from 1905 to 1911, and tried a 60PS six in 1907 which was not a success.

In 1909 Horch disagreed with his fellow directors and left to form a new company in the same town. He was prevented from using his own name, so he chose the Latin word Audi, which has the same meaning as Horch has in German (hark or listen). His new company flourished as did the one he left, and both eventually became part of the Auto-Union combine.

After Horch's departure the directors appointed Georg Paulmann as technical director and Seidel as chief engineer, both men being long-standing Horch employees. Between 1909 and 1914 the range was extended, with two small four-cylinder cars, the 1.6-litre 6/18PS and the 2.1-litre 8/24PS at one end, and the 6.4-litre 25/55PS at the other. Horch made steady profits each year from 1904 to 1914, and by the eve of war had

capital of £150,000 and a workforce of 800.

During World War I Horch made staff cars and also 3-ton trucks and heavy artillery tractors. In 1920 the company was taken over by the engine-maker Argus Motoren Gesellschaft of Berlin which controlled Horch for 11 years. During this period the managing director was Dr Moritz Straus; there were two chief engineers, Arnold Zoller (1920-22) of supercharger fame and Paul Daimler (1922-29), son of Gottlieb. Zoller was responsible for the four-cylinder side-valve 2.6-litre 10/35PS, improved by Daimler in 1924 as the single-overhead cam 10/50PS.

In 1926 came Daimler's most important contribution to Horch, the twin-overhead cam straight-eight made in various sizes from 3.1 (12/60PS) to 3.9 litres (16/80PS). A total of about 8000 of these straight-eights were made for Horch between 1926 and 1931 in the Argus factory. In 1925 a workforce of 1500 was making between eight and 10 cars a day, and in 1929 the workforce had risen to 2500 and daily output to 14 or 16. The twin-over-

Horch twin-cylinder tourer of 1900

head cam Horchs were not exported in large numbers so were little known outside Germany, but they had an excellent reputation in their own country.

The Depression hit sales of Horch cars and this factor, combined with the increasing demand for aero engines, led Argus to sell Horch in 1931 to the newly-formed Auto Union AG, a combine that also included Audi, DKW and Wanderer. The Porsche-designed Auto Union Grand Prix cars were made in the Horch works. Dr Richard Bruhn, formerly with the State Bank of Saxony, became managing director, and the chief engineer was J. S. Rasmussen, best known for his two-stroke DKW design. He was followed in 1935 by William Werner.

Horchs of the 1930s were nearly all eights, apart from a short-lived luxury 6-litre V12, of which about 80 were built from 1931 to 1934. The straight-eights had single-overhead cam engines designed by Fritz Fiedler during his short stay with Horch in 1931 between working for Stoewer and BMW. They were made in

Horch 18hp Herkomer Trial car of 1906

Horch 5-litre sports cabriolet of 1939

various sizes, from 3 to 4.9 litres up to 1935, but from then until 1939 there was only one straight-eight, with 4.9-litre engine and all-round independent suspension.

The V8s were smaller and cheaper, running from 3 to 3.8 litres and 7500 to 14,000 marks compared with 13,900 to 23,500 marks for the straight-eights. Total production of V8s for the civilian markets was 11,730 and of straight-eights 6300. In addition 4200 4×4 command cars were made for the Wehrmacht, using the 3.8-litre V8 engine.

The larger Horchs of the 1930s were very elegant cars, selling for rather lower prices than the equivalent straight-eight Mercedes-Benz, particularly in export markets when they were subsidized, as were the cheaper Auto Union cars. In 1938 a 4.9-litre Horch cost £985 in England and a Mercedes-Benz 540K £1890. Passenger car production came to an end in 1940, but the 4×4 command cars were made throughout the war, some being built by Ford with Ford V8 engines.

The Zwickau factory came under East German control after the war and the Horch line was not revived, although the name was used briefly for a 2.4-litre six-cylinder car made at Zwickau from 1956 to 1959. After objections from the West German-based Auto Union AG, these cars were renamed Sachsenring in 1957. August Horch, who had had no connection with the Audi company since 1931, died in 1951 at the age of 83. GNG

HORSTMAN(N)
GB 1914-1929

Gustav Horstmann was born in Westphalia in 1829 and after being apprenticed to a horologist he moved to Britain and set up a clock business in Bath in 1854. He had four sons, one of whom, Sidney, born in 1881, built an engine at the turn of the century and then invented a variable transmission with expanding pinion, some of which were fitted to FN motorcycles.

The Horstmann Gear Co was formed in 1904, and in the absence of orders made timers for gas lamps using clock techniques. The mass-production of small and complex mechanisms became its speciality.

Sidney Horstmann developed a light car in 1912 and in 1914 rented an old cinema and skating rink in Bath in which to produce it. Unusual features included his own four-cylinder 1-litre engine with detachable head and horizontal overhead valves worked by rockers on the side of the block. Starting was by foot pedal working an Archimedes' screw on the prop shaft, the gearbox being in the rear axle. Listers of Dursley provided some parts for the engine.

In deference to anti-German feeling after World War I, the second 'n' was dropped from

Horstman 11hp Super Sports of 1921

231

Horstmann two-seat convertible of 1914

the name and the cars reappeared as Horst-mans in 1919. These soon adopted Coventry-Simplex and then Coventry-Climax engines. There were also sports and racing models with British Anzani engines.

Financial difficulties beset the firm despite frequent loans from brothers Otto (also known as Fred), Hermann and Albert who ran the successful timer factory. A receiver was appointed in December 1921 and in 1925 Horstman Cars Ltd was compulsorily wound up with assets of £1746 and liabilities of £26,324.

A new company, Horstman Ltd, made a few more cars up to 1929, the last six or so having Hayes engines. So frequent were detail changes that Sidney Horstman declared that his cars could be dated by the hour rather than the year. Estimates of production range from 1500 to 4000, the former probably being more accurate.

The make was credited with the first British use of Lockheed hydraulic brakes in 1924 and the first cellulose spray paint in 1925. A mid-engined prototype was made, and this was followed in 1928 by a four wheel independently sprung car by Sidney Horstman's friend and business partner for 30 years, Captain Rooke. It covered 250,000 miles (402,000km) and encouraged them to form Slow Motion Suspensions Ltd, which did much to improve the ride and speed of tracked military vehicles.

Horstman Ltd went on to make camshafts and motor components, precision gauges and an unsuccessful swashplate engine. By 1940 the Horstman factories employed 700. The Simms company took over various parts of the Horstman empire in 1954. Sidney Horstman died in 1962, but many items are still produced bearing his family name. NB

HOTCHKISS
FRANCE 1903-1954

Although the Hotchkiss was in many ways a typical French car, its manufacturer was founded by an American, was managed for many years by an Englishman, and some of the company's greatest designs were the work of an Italian.

Benjamin Berkeley Hotchkiss (1826-1885) was born in Watertown, Connecticut, of a family which had settled in the state in 1641 and were active in hardware manufacture. He began munitions manufacture in his parental factory, and later set up his own shell factory in New York City. The Civil War broke out soon afterwards, and the Hotchkiss brothers Benjamin and Andrew supplied more shells to the Union army than all the other manufacturers combined. In 1870 Benjamin moved to France and set up a factory at St Denis where his famous machine guns and cannons were made from 1875.

Laurence Vincent Binet, an American of Minorcan extraction, joined the company as chief engineer in 1884, and would remain with Hotchkiss for 52 years. He took over control on Benjamin Hotchkiss' death in 1885, but two years later the company was reorganized, with largely British capital and several British directors, as a subsidiary of Hotchkiss Ordnance Co Ltd.

In the late 1890s falling munitions orders led the company to diversify into making car components for Panhard and De Dietrich. The next step was to hire a talented designer, Georges Terrasse, who had worked for Mors, and who produced the first Hotchkiss car in time for the Paris Salon of December 1903. It

had an 18/22hp four-cylinder T-head engine with ball bearing crankshaft, a round honey-comb radiator that was to distinguish the make for many years, and shaft drive. Racing driver Henri Fournier was the Paris agent, and 32 cars were sold during 1904.

The following year sales rose to 169, and a British agency was set up by John James Mann of Mann & Overton, which was later to become famous as agent for Unic and Austin taxicabs. Racing cars were entered in the 1904 and 1905 Gordon Bennett Eliminating Trials, and the 1905 models featured the famous Hotchkiss drive – an open propeller shaft driving a live axle whose torque reaction was controlled through its suspension.

Sales dropped to 125 in 1907, which was a poor year for the whole European motor industry. The Hotchkiss models were large and expensive – 4.6- and 7.2-litre T-head fours and a 9.5-litre six – but from 1908 American-born managing director Charles Parsons introduced smaller monobloc L-head models of 2.4 and 3.1 litres. The expensive ball bearing crankshafts gave way to plain bearings.

These monobloc fours were designed by Harry M. Ainsworth, a nephew of Daimler dealer J. J. Mann who had joined the Hotchkiss drawing office in 1904. By 1914 he was works manager, and from 1928 to 1950 he was chief administrator.

In 1911 the French subsidiary acquired the British holding company, which was liquidated, and capital was reduced from 6 million to 4 million francs. Output that year was up to 427 cars, from 189 only three years earlier, and climbed to between 550 and 600 in 1913 and 1914. Hotchkiss now had agents in 16 countries. It earned a reputation for using the best possible materials and achieving high standards of precision engineering, as befitted cars bearing a crossed gun trade mark.

Soon after World War I broke out Paris was threatened with occupation by the German army, and Hotchkiss rapidly transferred 400 men and the necessary tooling to the Pilain

Hotchkiss 20hp Targa Florio car of 1904

factory at Lyons. Within a short time this plant was making 4000 machine guns a month.

The St Denis factory made staff cars, and Ainsworth went to Coventry where he set up a machine gun factory to supply the British War Office. This factory made 40,000 weapons and was used after the war for the manufacture of engines for Morris, which bought the factory in 1923. Ainsworth then returned to France and took over as chief designer from the ageing Georges Terrasse.

Ainsworth's manager at Coventry, Hans Lanstad, joined him at Hotchkiss where he became manager of a new factory on Boulevard Ornano, St Denis, which remained the Hotchkiss home until the company's closure. In 1926 Lanstad returned to England where he became a director of Morris.

For its post-war offerings Hotchkiss revived the 4-litre AF of 1914, the round radiator replaced with one of horseshoe shape. This was continued until 1924, but a better selling car was the 2.4-litre 12CV AM made at the new Boulevard Ornano factory from 1924 to 1928. This, and a prototype 6.6-litre luxury car, the single-overhead cam AK, were designed by Maurice Sainturat who had been with Hotchkiss on and off since 1904, but who left for Delage in 1924.

Production rose from 451 in the first full peacetime season (1919-20) to 2000 annually after Ornano came on stream in 1925-26. The vehicle workforce stood at about 1200 at this time, when Hotchkiss was also making engines of AM type but with overhead valves for Morris Léon Bollée. About 12,000 of these engines were supplied between 1924 and 1928, and in 1926 the AM received overhead valves as well, the new model being designated AM2.

The firm's slogan from the early 1920s onwards was 'Le juste milieu', and its policy of catering to the middle class market was continued in the 3-litre six-cylinder AM80. Introduced for 1929 and largely the work of former Talbot-Darracq designer Vincent Bertarione, this was the ancestor of the famous 3½-litre Hotchkiss, which was made until the early 1950s and which earned the company six Monte Carlo Rally victories, in 1932, 1933, 1934, 1939, 1949 and 1950.

Smaller cars with four-cylinder engines were also made, and contributed greatly to Hotchkiss' record sales of 7642 units in 1934. Thereafter they dropped to 4213 in 1936, and around 2500 a year in 1937 to 1939. Trucks powered by the 13CV four-cylinder engine were introduced in 1936, and their descendants were still being made in 1964, long after cars had become only a memory at the Boulevard Ornano.

Hotchkiss also supplied engines for trucks made by Laffly and La Licorne, particularly the 6×4 and 6×6 military models. Some field cars and trucks of Laffly design were made by Hotchkiss. Tanks designed by Edmond Moglia were also made in the 1930s.

In 1937 Hotchkiss took over its neighbour at St Denis, Amilcar, and the following year

Hotchkiss Type 686GS of 1948

Hotchkiss four-cylinder side-valve engine of c.1913

entered the small car market with the J. A. Grégoire-designed Amilcar Compound, an advanced design with integral construction in Alpax aluminium alloy, all-independent springing and front-wheel drive. It handled well but the 33bhp 1185cc side-valve engine failed to give it the performance it deserved. For 1940 Bertarione designed an overhead-valve 1340cc engine for the Compound, but only 120 of these were made before the war stopped production. A total of 696 Compounds were made, those on the UK market being called Hotchkiss Tens.

Hotchkiss finances suffered a severe blow when the French armaments industry was nationalized in 1936, for the company lost important contracts and did not receive full compensation until 1944. By then the works had been badly damaged by RAF bombs, but even so Hotchkiss was accused of not going slowly enough in the repairing of German tanks. Because of this it received no government assistance after the war, and sales of the 3½-litre were badly hit by the tax which charged a car over 3 litres capacity four times as much as one just under.

Only 143 cars were sold in 1947, in which year Peugeot acquired a 12 per cent stake in the company. In late 1948 Hotchkiss received government approval to reintroduce the 2.3-litre four, and sales rose to 1787 in 1950 and 2705 in 1951. Of these only 429 were sixes.

In 1949 Hotchkiss took up another Grégoire design, a 2-litre flat-four front-wheel-drive six-passenger saloon. It did not go into production until 1951, when it received a more powerful 2.2-litre engine and Hotchkiss never had the capital to develop it properly. Also, its controversial looks hindered sales, and only 180 found customers.

Hotchkiss sales slumped badly in the 1950s – 910 in 1952 (95 Grégoires), 237 in 1953 (36 Grégoires), and just 5 in 1954. A merger with Delahaye in July 1954 helped neither concern. However, a licence to manufacture Jeeps had been acquired, resulting from a wartime meeting in Canada between Harry Ainsworth and Ward Canaday of Willys-Overland. Production of trucks and Jeeps continued until 1970, after which only ordnance was made.

In 1964 Hotchkiss made the first French truck with tilt cab, and amongst its last vehicles was a tracked amphibian with Hotchkiss petrol or diesel engines. It had briefly marketed Leyland commercials in France in the 1960s to augment its own limited range.

Hotchkiss merged with metal products company Brandt SA in 1957, and Hotchkiss-Brandt was subsequently taken over by the Compagnie Française Thompson-Houston, manufacturer of compressors and refrigerators, in 1966. In the mid-1960s the Boulevard Ornano factory was demolished to make way for a housing development, and a factory was acquired in Boulevard Anatole France, St Denis. GNG/NB

233

HRG
GB 1935-1965

The HRG Engineering Co Ltd of Tolworth, Surrey, was founded in November 1935 and took its name from the initials of its three partners, E. A. Halford, Guy H. Robins and H. R. Godfrey (formerly the 'G' of GN, which was wound up in 1925). HRG originally set up its works in part of the Mid-Surrey Gear Works factory, in Norbiton, Surrey, and its first car was a traditionally styled 1½-litre two-seater sports model with a four-cylinder overhead-valve Meadows engine.

Five of the 90mph (145kph) cars were built until the end of 1936, selling at £395, and then the company moved into a new factory at Tolworth, near Kingston-on-Thames. The new factory was next to works used by Nash & Thomson Ltd, maker of gun turrets, the Nash of which was Archie Frazer-Nash, Godfrey's old partner at GN and founder of the Frazer-Nash car company.

HRGs soon began to appear in competition and achieve successes which helped to establish the name. In 1937 HRG took second place in the 1½-litre class at Le Mans.

Up to the outbreak of World War II, HRG made 25 of the Meadows-engined 1½-litre cars and before the war also built an 1100 model with an engine based on the 1074cc overhead-cam Singer 9 unit. The first was offered in 1938 at £275 and eight were built until 1939. In September of that year HRG also completed a prototype using a modified version of the larger overhead-cam Singer 12 engine – with Singer's co-operation. Halford also designed a very quick 1½-litre Triumph engined two-seater coupé which was listed at £475 for the 1938 Motor Show, but only one example was built.

After the war HRG resumed production in 1946 with basically unchanged 1100 and 1500 models. It also made perhaps the first British production car with a full width body, the Aerodynamic 1500, designed by Marcus Chambers and R. de Yarburgh-Bateson. The bodies were built by Fox and Nichols and the car was some £100 more than the standard model, at £991, but it was only made until 1950.

Chambers also designed an HRG-based Formula 2 car in 1948 but it was easily outclassed and was dropped in 1949. Elsewhere, HRG fared better, with a fine Le Mans 1½-litre class win in 1949 and good performances in major rallies.

Sales fell badly after the war, however, from 40 in 1948 to only 11 in 1950. The Singer-based 1100 survived until 1953 and in 1955 a new tubular-framed model with independent suspension, cast alloy wheels and an alloy body was introduced. It used a Singer Hunter-based 1500 engine with an HRG twin-cam alloy head conversion, giving 108bhp compared to the Singer's 55. Singer became interested in a production version of this car

HRG Meadows-engined prototype of 1935

HRG racing lightweights of 1949

and showed a prototype Hunter saloon at the 1955 Motor Show with an iron-headed version of the engine, but the 1956 takeover of Singer by the Rootes group stopped further production.

In 1956 the traditional two-seater HRG was finally dropped and only a few of the newer model were made until all car production stopped later in the year. The company continued, specializing in cylinder-head conversions and other light engineering. Towards the end, HRG was run by Grace Leather, who had started work as a secretary in 1936, became a director and finally the sole proprietor.

In 1965 HRG built one last car, an experimental spaceframe sports car, first with a Cortina engine and later with a Vauxhall VX4/90 unit but the project was abandoned when the company was wound up in 1966. Godfrey died two years later, after a long illness. BL

HUASCAR
see Galba

HUDSON/ESSEX, TERRAPLANE
USA 1909-1957

Howard Earle Coffin and Roy Dikeman Chapin, both born in 1873, had been chief engineer and sales manager respectively at Olds before founding Thomas-Detroit (later known as Chalmers-Detroit) with other former Olds employees in 1906. Three years later they started a subsidiary line of cheaper cars named Hudson after the Detroit tycoon who owned the largest department store in the world and gave financial backing to the company. Capital was $100,000 and stockholders were Chapin, Coffin, Fred Bezner, J. L. Hudson, Roscoe Jackson and Hugh Chalmers. Chalmers sold his interests before the end of 1909 to the first three for $80,000 and bought out their holding in Chalmers.

In the first year 1000 high quality, small 20hp four-cylinder cars were made in a two-storey 80,000sq ft (7400sq m) factory in Detroit by 500 employees. A new 223,000sq ft (20,700sq m) factory was built in 1910 and output grew to 4556 cars.

For 1911 came the Model 33 with in-unit monobloc engine, clutch and gearbox and, according to the company, '900 less parts than rival cars'. Some 6500 cars were sold in 1911 and 5700 in 1912, when J. L. Hudson died. In 1912 a six-cylinder Model 54 with Delco electric starting, lighting and ignition was launched.

In 1914 America's lightest six-cylinder car, the 6-40, helped to cut prices and give Hudson its lasting reputation for good performance. That year 10,260 Hudsons were sold, rising to 12,864 in 1915. Hudson was then the world's largest maker of six-cylinder cars and had 26 acres (10 hectares) of factories, but it earned only modest profits. The Metal Products Co had supplied many components but Chapin then took over most of this work in-house. Hudson began to produce more enclosed sedans than its rivals and over the next 10 years bought most of its special bodies from Biddle and Smart of Amesbury, Massachusetts.

In 1916 Stephen Fekete perfected a monobloc side-valve six of the same capacity as the 6-40 yet with dynamically balanced crankshaft and 76bhp output. This engine went in the Super Six, of which more than 50,000 had been sold two years later and the first of many competition successes achieved.

In January 1919 a four-cylinder car went on sale after about 100 had been built in 1918. It came from a separately financed subsidiary, the Essex Motor Car Co, which had been formed in September 1917 and was run by W. J. McAneeny, formerly of Pope-Hartford and Hudson. A former Hudson shell factory was utilized and about 20,000 of each brand of car was made in 1919.

In 1922 28,242 Hudsons and 36,222 Essex cars were sold, including a higher proportion of enclosed sedans than any other mass producer. Enclosed sedans, also known as Coaches, were offered on the Essex from late 1921 and soon accounted for over 50 per cent of sales.

The Hudson and Essex companies were combined in 1922 and the first small public stock flotation left the founders in control and the beneficiaries of $7 million cash and $16 million worth of stock. A 1923 $20 shareholding was worth $12,000 three years later. The man responsible for this financial wizardry was Chapin.

Roscoe Jackson, Chapin's founding colleague, became president of the company in 1923 but died of influenza at the age of 50 in 1929, when he was succeeded by McAneeny. Coffin remained as an adviser until 1930, concentrating increasingly on outside aeronautical interests and leaving Fekete in charge of engineering.

The price of Coaches was progressively reduced to the point, in 1925, when they were cheaper than the open Hudson or Essex. Coach bodies were now being bought-in from Briggs, Fisher and Budd until Hudson opened a $10 million factory in 1926 to make 1500 a day.

Six cylinders were introduced on the Essex range in 1924. The following year combined Hudson-Essex production was 270,000 – 160,000 of which were Essex – and in 1929 output had risen to 301,000. This combined production put Hudson-Essex in third place in the sales league behind Ford and Chevrolet. Exports played a big part in the company's success and accounted for more than 40,000 units in 1928. A light commercial line, the Dover, existed briefly in 1929-30.

Sales slumped to 114,000 in 1930 and even this figure was subsequently halved and led to losses of $2 million in 1931, $5.5 million in 1932 and $3 million in 1933. In 1932 the Essex name on cars and commercials was superseded by Essex Terraplane and soon became just Terraplane.

A straight-eight from new chief engineer S. G. Baits was offered by Hudson in 1930. It was initially of 3½ litres and remained in production in enlarged form until 1952. This engine was soon adopted in Britain by Brough Superior and Railton, which also used Hudson sixes. Hudsons were popular in Britain and a large assembly plant in west London sold about 2000 cars a year, some being given 'small' engines to reduce horsepower tax.

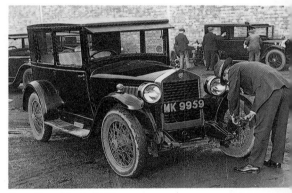

Essex Super Six of c.1925

Hudson Super Six of 1922

AMERICA'S LOWEST PRICED FINE CARS...
NEW HUDSON COMMODORE SERIES

Here, Symphonic Styling reaches its richest beauty, in a wide range of superb exterior-interior color harmonies, one of which is pictured in the accompanying illustrations. These are cars of superlative luxury . . . including the 128-horsepower, 121-inch wheelbase Eight shown here; a companion Six; a Custom Club Coupe; and lavishly equipped Custom Sedans on 128-inch wheelbase. Airfoam Seat Cushions are standard in all Commodore models, and available at small cost in all other 1941 Hudsons.

(Two-tone exteriors available without added cost in Hudson Commodore Custom models; optional at moderate extra cost in other 1941 Hudsons. White sidewall tires extra.)

Hudson Commodore of 1941

The last Hudson, a Hornet, 1957

After World War II this factory assembled the final Railtons.

A design by Birkigt was to have been used in Detroit by Hudson but the Depression intervened and instead it became a utility model produced by Hispano-Suiza in Spain from 1932. Also in 1932 a Canadian plant was opened at Tilbury, Ontario, and that year a form of independent front suspension with leaf springs and divided front beam axle was offered.

Both the Terraplane and Hudson exploited their fine performance record in numerous competitions, having gained all the important American Automobile Association stock car hillclimb records by the end of 1933. A vacuum operated gear shift was introduced in 1935, the year in which H. M. Northrup became chief engineer on the elevation of Baits to the vice-presidency.

Profitability returned to the company in 1934 and sales slowly recovered to over 100,000 annually from 1935 to 1937, but they then dropped sharply to 51,000 in 1938 and did not reach six figures again until 1947, when the three millionth car was produced.

The Terraplane name was discontinued in 1938. By then McAneeny had departed to run Hupp, and Chapin had assumed control of the company in 1933 before dying prematurely in 1936. A. E. Barit, who had been with Hudson since 1910, took over the reins.

Coil spring independent front suspension was introduced in 1940, when 88,000 vehicles, including about 1000 commercials (some of them forward control vans), were produced. The cars were billed as 'America's

safest'. War production included aircraft components and sections, Invader marine engines and Oerlikon guns made under licence in the vast new Hudson Arsenal in Detroit.

Frank Spring, head of design since joining from the Walter Murphy coachworks in 1931, introduced the Step-Down series in 1948; chief engineer Sam Frahm and Reid Railton assisted him on the project. The bodies and chassis were welded together to give semi-unitary construction and the rear of the chassis continued on the outside of the wheel arches with the floor pan below the chassis. The straight-eight engine was used, although a version of the Super Six was standard in the later Pacemaker. Record post-war profits of $13.25 million were achieved in 1948.

Chief engineer T. Toncray and chassis engineer N. Bodischer designed the 145bhp

side-valve Hornet in 1951 with its new six-cylinder engine, which phased out the old eight and brought the marque many sporting successes. Unfortunately for Hudson the rest of the motor industry was favouring V8s, while its own six was the last with a capacity of over 5 litres to be built after the 1930s.

From 1948 to 1950 annual sales reached almost 150,000 but by 1951 they had declined to 93,000 and dropped to 76,000 two years later, when the company lost $10 million. In 1954 the figure sagged to 33,000. A compact 3.3-litre Jet model, introduced in 1953, failed to make much impact.

In 1954 Hudson merged with Nash in the new $200 million American Motors Corporation. In the following two seasons Hudsons were almost pure Nash, made at Kenosha in Wisconsin, although they were given Jet or Hornet engines. Hudson sales in 1955 were up to almost 53,000. The top model used a Packard V8 and there were small Ramblers available with both Nash and Hudson badges as well as versions of Austin's Metropolitan. From 1958 the cars were known as Ramblers. Chapin's son, also named Roy, was then running the automotive side of American Motors.

Although car production had ended in Detroit, the Hudson factory, with about 3000 employees there, continued fulfilling military contracts, including the 4×4 Mighty Mite. It eventually became part of the AM General armaments firm. NB

HUMBER
GB 1901-1976

Humber was one of the best-known names in the cycle industry for many years before cars were thought of. Born in Sheffield in 1842, Thomas Humber began to make copies of French velocipedes in Nottingham in about 1870, moving to nearby Beeston two years later. Financial backing from T. H. Lambert in 1885 led to expansion, with the acquisition of factories in Wolverhampton and Coventry in 1887, the year in which Humber & Co Ltd was formed.

Tricycles were added to the range, and experiments were made with one of these driven by compressed air, but most of the business was devoted to the new safety bicycle which had been pioneered in 1885 by John Kemp Starley. Among the draughtsmen employed by Humber in the 1890s were the racing cyclist John Davenport Siddeley, who would later achieve fame as a car manufacturer in his own right, and G. H. Wait, who made bicycles, motorcycles and cars in Leicester, under the name Clyde.

An American factory was opened at Westboro, Massachusetts, which was turning out 150 bicycles a week in 1894, and five years later was taken over by Locomobile for the manufacture of steam cars.

Thomas Humber retired in 1892, and experiments with cars were stimulated by works manager Walter Phillips. A prototype electric car was built in 1895, and some examples of the French Léon Bollée three-wheeler were built in 1896, and sold under the name Coventry Bollée. These were to have been made in Humber's factory, but when this was badly damaged by fire in July 1896, Humber were given space in the ground floor of the Motor Mills, owned by the Great Horseless Carriage Co. Coventry Bollées were made under Humber auspices from about November 1896 to early 1897, when Humber vacated the Motor Mills.

Motorcycle production began when Humber bought engines from Phelan & Moore of Cleckheaton, Yorkshire, fitting them in Humber cycle frames, but from 1900 complete motorcycles were made. Forecars and quads were added, and in 1901 voiturettes powered by Aster and De Dion engines were offered for sale. They had single-spoked steering wheels, a Humber hallmark in the early years, and shaft drive. In 1902 and 1903 respectively came 12 and 20hp four-cylinder cars, but the most important arrival in 1903 was the 5hp single cylinder Humberette, the first really popular British light car. This was on the lines of the De Dion with a front-mounted engine of 613cc, two steering column levers controlling the two-speed gearbox, tubular frame and shaft drive. It was made at the Beeston and Coventry factories, costing £147 from the former and £125 from the latter. Beeston-built cars always had a better reputation for quality which justified their higher prices.

The leading designer at Humber between 1901 and 1908 was the French-born Louis Coatalen (1880-1962), who later helped Hillman and won his greatest fame as a designer with Sunbeam. One of his contemporaries was T. C. Pullinger who had been with Sunbeam before joining Humber, and was works manager at Beeston from 1905 to 1909 when he moved to Scotland to join Arrol-Johnston.

The Humberettes were dropped in 1905 and a wider range adopted, which ran from 8/10hp to 20/25hp. In 1906 1500 men were employed in car manufacture out of a total workforce of 2000, and weekly production was sometimes as high as 75 cars, 50 from Coventry and 25 from Beeston. Profits rose from £6500 in 1905 to £154,000 in 1907; the last figure was not exceeded for 30 years.

Expansion in Coventry led to the purchase of the Progress Cycle Works and the old factory of Bayliss-Thomas. In 1908 a new Humber factory was built at Stoke on the outskirts of Coventry. It covered 22½ acres (9 hectares) and employed 5000 men, with a prospective output of 150 cars and 1500 bicycles a week. Unfortunately this coincided with a slump in the motor industry, leading to heavy losses in the motor department and the closure of the Beeston factory.

Humber Forecar of 1896

Humber 8hp two-seater of 1909

A new board was appointed, with Earl Russell as chairman and J. A. Cole as managing director. From 1909 to 1913 the works manager was H. G. Burford, who had been with British Mercedes and Milnes-Daimler and later made commercial vehicles under his own name. Like Daimler, Humber was a great breeding ground for motor industry men, and in addition to those already mentioned who worked there can be added R. H. Rose, later with Belsize, Sunbeam, Riley and Lea-Francis; W. O. Bentley; F. T. Burgess who left to join Bentley in 1920; and later (1933-36) Alec Issigonis of Morris Minor and Mini fame.

Between 1909 and 1914 car production ran at about 2000 a year, reaching 2500 in 1913 when Humber was the third largest British car company, after Ford and Wolseley. T-head engines were employed up to 1911, after which came a range of L-heads from an 11hp monobloc four to a substantial 28hp selling for up to £630.

In 1913 Humber entered the cyclecar market, being one of the few major manufacturers to do so, with the V-twin Humberette in air-cooled or water-cooled form. Car production was suspended in 1916, but motorcycles were made throughout World War I, and up to 1930, gaining overhead camshafts from 1928. Bicycle production continued until 1932, when Humber's rights were sold to Raleigh.

An aeroplane department in the charge of Captain Lovelace and a Frenchman named Le Blon was opened in 1910. A Humber aeroplane carried the first official air mail in India, but the department was not a commercial success until World War I, when production

A 3-litre six, the 20/55, joined the range in 1926, and by the end of the decade there were two sixes, the 2.1-litre 16/50 and the 16/55, as well as two fours, the 1057cc 9/28 and 2050cc 14/40. Production rose steadily, from 1750 in 1920 to about 3000 a year until 1927, when 3500 cars were made; in 1930 the figure reached 6110.

Humber had avoided involvement with commercial vehicles, apart from a few light vans on car chassis, but in 1925 the company snapped up Commercial Cars Ltd of Luton, manufacturer of Commer trucks, whose depressed state made it a cheap purchase. Then in 1928 Humber bought up its Coventry neighbour Hillman.

Meanwhile Rootes Motors Ltd, the retail motor business run by the Rootes brothers, William and Reginald, had been buying up Humber shares and by 1931 they held 60 per cent. They took over management of Humber in July 1932, and replaced the inlet-over-exhaust engines with cheaper to build side valves for the 1933 season. On the financial side, the owners of £1 ordinary shares saw them split in two, of which half was surrendered to the company to be used to pacify the preference holders who had not seen dividends for several years.

During the 1930s Humbers became rationalized in the new Rootes empire, their role being to cater for the upper middle class market and the cheaper end of the chauffeur driven trade. They featured Bendix brakes, downdraft carburettors and, from 1934, synchromesh gearboxes, free wheels and automatic clutches.

The smallest model was a four-cylinder Twelve of 1669cc, but the classic Humbers were the 3498cc Snipe saloon and Pullman limousine which received 4086cc engine from 1936. In 1932 Rootes had acquired the old-established London coachbuilder Thrupp & Maberly, which became responsible for Pullman bodywork.

A luxury Sunbeam that used a Georges Roesch-designed straight-eight engine in a Humber chassis and shown at the 1936 Olympia Show never got beyond the prototype stage, but the Humber Snipe was the basis for the 4.1-litre Sunbeam-Talbot made from 1938 to 1939. One of the best Humbers of the 1930s was the 1938-39 Super Snipe, which used the larger 4.1-litre engine in the shorter chassis, giving an 85mph (136kph) top speed which was effectively curbed by the new hydraulic brakes.

The Super Snipe was one of the leading staff cars of World War II, being made as an open tourer as well as a saloon. Viscount Montgomery's tourer, 'Old Faithful', carried the Field Marshal for thousands of miles in North Africa and Italy.

Another important Humber military vehicle was the Super Snipe-based 4×4 Heavy Utility, of which about 6500 were produced between 1940 and 1944. Had it been continued after the war it would have given the Rootes group several years' lead over the Land Rover, and indeed with its four-door bodywork and 100bhp engine, it was more in the Range Rover class.

Humber also made some 3600 light 4×2 armoured cars (Ironsides) and 4300 rear-en-

Humber doctor's coupé, with dickey, of 1927

reached 25 planes a week. These were mostly Avros, in addition to Bentley's rotary aero engines. Some vehicles were also made, notably ambulances.

The first post-war offerings were revivals of the pre-war 10 and 14, the latter increased to 15.9hp. They were well made and well-equipped but not very exciting, and were joined in 1923 by the 985cc 8/18 which had inlet-over-exhaust valves. This layout was extended to the whole range for 1923, but front wheel brakes were delayed for as long as possible (in some models to 1927), because J. A. Cole distrusted them.

Field Marshal Montgomery's Humber Super Snipe staff car of 1941

Humber Pullman saloon of 1952

gined 4×4 scout cars, as well as tank engines and trucks, and aero engines which were built at the Rootes No 1 Shadow Factory at Stoke Aldermoor near Coventry.

Post-war production concentrated on three models, the 1944cc 14hp Hawk which was a re-styled 1940 Hillman Fourteen, the 2731cc 18hp Snipe which was derived from the 1936 Humber 18, and the 4086cc Super Snipe with its companion long wheelbase limousine, still called the Pullman. Styling was updated for 1949 when steering column gearchange was introduced, and overhead valves arrived in 1953.

Production was running at about 13,000 a year in 1951, made up of 8000 Hawks, 4400 Super Snipes and 800 Pullmans, and annual profits were around £500,000. Humbers were sold in the United States where their size and luxurious interiors, if not their lack of automatic transmission, made them relatively popular (800 were sold between 1948 and 1953); these vehicles were also assembled in Eire.

The later 1950s were not so good for Humber, whose image of dignity and craftsmanship was not well served by the new transatlantic styling of the 1957 Hawk. The Super Snipe's 113bhp 4138cc overhead-valve engine, borrowed from the Commer truck range was too thirsty for British motorists, and the model discontinued in 1957. The Super Snipe name was continued on a smaller car, with 2651cc 'square' engine, and unitary construction body shared with the four-cylinder Hawk, and these, together with an upmarket model called the Imperial, lasted until 1967. The Hawk lasted for one further season, but thereafter the Humber name was carried only by the Sceptre, a luxurious version of the Hillman Super Minx which had first appeared in 1963.

The Rootes group was fully acquired by Chrysler in 1967, and the larger Humbers were, in theory, replaced on the UK market by Australian-made Chrysler Valiants, although very few of these were sold. The French-built 180 might have carried the Humber name, but this was thought to lack international appeal, and it was called the Chrysler 180 instead.

The Sceptre, which was dropped in 1976, came off the same production lines as the Minx, and Humber's Stoke plant had for a number of years been used for engine manufacture for the rest of the group. It is now also used for the preparation of Hillman Hunter ckd kits sold to Iran where they are marketed under the name Peykan. GNG/NB

HUPMOBILE
USA 1909-1940

Robert Craig Hupp was born in 1876 and had worked for the Olds, Ford and Regal motor companies before he launched his own car in 1909. The Hupp Motor Car Co was formed in

Hupmobile runabout of 1910

Detroit in November 1908 with a working capital of $3500, soon increased to $11,000. Company president was a former lawyer, J. Walter Drake, and Hupp's right hand man was another ex-Olds employee, Charles D. Hastings.

The first car was shown at the Detroit Auto Show in February 1909. It was a small car by contemporary American standards, with a 2.8-litre four-cylinder engine, 86in (2.18m) wheelbase and two-seater runabout body. Priced at $750 it sold well, 1618 cars being delivered between March and December 1909, 5340 in 1910, and 6079 in 1911, in which year a larger four-seater model on a 100in (2.54m) wheelbase was introduced.

In May 1910 Robert Hupp formed the Hupp Corporation with a diversity of activities including the Hupp-Yeats Electric Car Co, Hupp-Turner Machine Co, Hupp-Johnson Forge Co and several other firms. He was president, Hastings vice-president and his brother Louis was secretary/treasurer. His concentration on the Hupp Corporation led to disagreement with his partners in the Hupp Motor Car Co, and in September 1911 he sold his shares in the latter and left.

The name of the Hupp Corporation was changed to the RCH Corporation and Hupp made under its name a light car which was very like the original Hupmobile 20. It survived until 1916, but before then Hupp had left, to be associated with two other unsuccessful car companies, the Monarch of Detroit and the Emerson of Kingston, New York. He died in 1931.

Meanwhile the Hupp Motor Car Co was forging ahead under Hastings and Drake, adding for 1912 a larger touring car, the Model 32, with 2980cc engine and 106in (2.69m) wheelbase. This took the company's sales up to 7640 in 1912 and 12,543 in 1913, the last year of the original Model 20. A new designer joined the company in 1912, Frank E. Watts,

who was to remain with Hupp for 26 years.

More conventional looking cars were now being made, the Models K, N and R all with side-valve four-cylinder engines, with electric lighting and starting from 1914 onwards. The R survived until 1925. In 1916 the company name was changed to Hupp Motor Car Corporation, which was capitalized at $8 million. Annual production rose to 12,055 in 1916 but dropped thereafter because of war work. This included manufacture of trucks under contract to Denby, a Detroit company of which Drake was vice-president.

The 3-litre Model R was the sole Hupmobile from 1918 to 1924, during which time it sold more than 124,000 units. By the mid-1920s Hupmobile had more than 5000 employees and 1,570,000sq ft (145,000sq m) of factory area. Bodies were mostly made by the H and M Body Corporation of Racine, Wisconsin, which had been formed in 1919 by Hupp and Mitchell and became solely a Hupp supplier after Mitchell went out of business in 1923. In the production league Hupp's position was quite significant, varying between seventh and thirteenth during the 1920s.

In 1925 the R was joined by the straight-eight Model E and for 1926 was replaced by the six-cylinder Model A. Hupp was unusual in making an eight before a six. In the later 1920s Hupp progressed upmarket with Ray Dietrich-styled 'custom' bodies on the 'Distinguished Eight' chassis and prices as high as $5795, compared with $1295 for the cheapest six. In 1927 the eight-cylinder cars made up less than 16 per cent of production. The H and M Body Corporation was now owned by Murray, one of the major body suppliers in America, whose stylist Amos Northrup was responsible for the 1928 Hupmobiles and also the striking 1932 and 1934 models.

Hupp's record year for sales and profits

was 1928, when 65,862 cars were made and profits totalled $8,790,000. An eight-storey building was added to the Detroit plant and in November 1928 Hupp bought the Chandler-Cleveland Corporation of Cleveland, Ohio. The company continued the manufacture of Chandler cars for six months and then started making the Hupmobile Century Six in the Chandler factory and bodies in the Cleveland factory. This lasted for three years, after which falling sales caused by the Depression prompted Hupmobile to move production of the Six back to Detroit, although it continued to use the Cleveland body plant until 1934.

Sales dropped alarmingly in 1930 to 22,183, and still further to 17,481 in 1931. The 1932 models were striking in appearance, with cycle-type wings and stylized 'H' bonnet-mascot designed by Northrup and Raymond Loewy, but only 10,467 cars were sold. The 1934 Hupmobiles were even more unusual, with aerodynamic bodies tested in a wind tunnel, and headlamps faired into the bonnet sides. Production in 1934 was 9420 cars, a slight improvement on 1933's 7316, but only 3218 of them were the aerodynamic models, the balance being the conventional-looking six-cylinder Model 417-W. From 1933 to 1936 Hupmobiles were assembled in Canada, as they had also been from 1911 to 1914.

In October 1934 company promoter Archie M. Andrews, who had been involved in the debacle of New Era Motors which led to the collapse of Kissel and Moon, became president of Hupp. He had ambitious plans for a front-wheel-drive Hupmobile, also hoping to sell Willys and Citroën cars through Hupp dealers. He also hoped for a Willys-Hupp merger, with a new small Hupmobile which would have been a restyled Willys 77, but nothing came of this. Andrews' reign, which lasted just 12 months, did Hupp a lot of harm, as he ran foul of the Securities and Exchange Commission and his reputation prevented some potential rescuers, notably Charles Nash, coming to help Hupp.

The company ended 1935 with debts of over $1 million and no credit. Only 74 of the 1936 models were made before the directors suspended production; the plant did not reopen until July 1937, when some 1936 models were assembled to use up left over parts before the new 1938 models were ready.

These were more conservatively styled than the aerodynamic cars and were not very different from many other 1938 American cars. Engines were the 4-litre six and 4.9-litre eight used in the earlier Hupps. The car might have succeeded in a good year, but 1938 brought a small recession in the American car industry and only 3483 Hupmobile 'Seniors' were made between September 1937 and May 1939. Of these only 397 were eights.

In July 1938 Hupp bought the dies and tools for the Cord 810 from the defunct Auburn Automobile Co for $45,000, planning to make a low-priced car, the Skylark, using the Cord bodies with a six-cylinder Hupp engine.

Hupmobile eight-cylinder saloon of 1939

Hupp could not afford to get it into production, however, and it was eventually built by Graham Paige. Production lasted only from May to July 1940, with 319 Skylarks delivered.

The Hupmobile car was finished, but the company survived receivership and concentrated on contract machining and stamping. In July 1946 the name was changed to the Hupp Corporation and headquarters were moved to Cleveland. The Detroit factory was razed in 1956 to make a parking lot. Hupp prospered in Cleveland, making heating and air conditioning equipment, and in 1967 became part of White Consolidated Industries. As the Hupp Division of White – which has no connection with Volvo-White Truck Co – it still exists today. GNG

HURST/HURMID, HURST & LLOYD, LLOYD & PLAISTER, VOX
GB 1897-1915

George Hurst was a London model-maker with workshops in High Holborn and who, in the 1890s, became involved with Lewis A. Lloyd in building a number of small petrol engines. In 1897 they put one of their engines, a horizontal two-cylinder type, under the floorboards of a belt-drive car which became known as the Hurst & Lloyd. In 1898 they moved into a small workshop in Wood Green, north London, where they assembled a few of these cars, essentially as a series of one-offs, until 1900.

Hurst then left the company and W. E. Plaister took his place. A few unsold Hurst &

Lloyd cars were sold as Lloyd & Plaisters and the new partners then introduced their own models, all vertical four-cylinder models of 10, 16, 20 and 40hp, the smaller ones with shaft drive and the 40hp with double chain drive.

In 1909 Lloyd & Plaister became Lloyd & Plaister Ltd, staying in Wood Green. They continued to build Lloyd & Plaister cars until 1911, completing about 50 in all, of which only six were the large chain-drive model. They also made the Allen-Liversidge four-wheel brake system, as fitted to several makes including their own, and they made fire engines and railway inspection cars.

Having dropped the Lloyd & Plaister car, the firm built the Vox light car from 1912 to 1915, this using a 750cc, two-cylinder, two-stroke engine with one pumping cylinder and one working cylinder, of the type designed by (Sir) Harry Ricardo for his Dolphin car. The Dolphin had been built from 1906 to 1909, with Lloyd and Plaister supplying engine and gearbox parts. Ricardo then sold the manufacturing rights for his engine to them for the original Vox.

George Hurst, meanwhile, had set up a workshop in north London where he built a few 12hp two-cylinder and 24hp four-cylinder cars which he claimed were made entirely in his own works. In 1906 he launched a 30/40 and a 60hp six, the former of 5560cc, the latter 8601cc, a 3295cc four-cylinder 15/18hp and a 10hp twin. In the same year he was joined by R. E. Middleton to form Hurst & Middleton Ltd of Holloway, and as such they continued to build the same models until 1907 as Hurmids. BL

HURTU
FRANCE 1896-1930

The firm Hurtu, Hautin et Diligeon was established in 1880 at Albert, Somme, to manufacture sewing machines, but it soon added bicycles, grinders and machine tools to its products, under the brand name Hurtu. In 1895 E. Diligeon bought out the interests of the other partners to form Société Diligeon et Cie, but he still called his products Hurtu.

At this time the company had some 500 employees and was one of the largest metalworking companies in France. Between 1896 and 1897 Hurtu became a motor manufacturer by building several hundred Léon Bollée tricycles for Bollée and followed this with its own first model in 1897, a small single-cylinder copy of a Benz, with belt drive.

By 1898 Hurtu could offer three models and the company was also building bicycles, typewriters, sewing machines and tools. In 1899 it was reorganized as the Compagnie des Automobiles et Cycles Hurtu, registered in Paris, although manufacture was still based at Albert. The new company's nominal capital was 1.5 million francs, but by 1902 apparently only 237,000 francs was paid up.

In 1900 Hurtu introduced a 3½hp single-cylinder De Dion-engined voiturette with shaft drive, and also various twin- and four-cylinder Aster-engined models. In 1901 Hurtu's Benz-copy chassis were being fitted under licence with English bodies made by Marshall & Co of Manchester and sold in Britain as the Marshall-Benz, forerunner of the Belsize.

In 1907 Hurtu offered three models, an 8hp single and 14 and 24hp fours. It continued to market single-cylinder cars as late as 1912 but all subsequent models were fours. The cars were only ever seen as a minor part of the manufacturing range of Hurtu, and the company never went into competition or made anything larger than 2 litres. In 1913 it sold around 600 cars, perhaps 10 per cent of the then total French market for low-priced cars, costing less than 5000 francs, in which Hurtu competed with only six or seven makes.

After World War I Hurtu resumed production with a 12hp 2-litre model with pushrod overhead-valves and front-wheel brakes. This was advertised in Britain by the sole British agent, Ariel Motor & General Repairs Ltd of south-east London, with the chassis at £400 and with a 'London-built' cabriolet body for £650. A complete range of 12 models was in fact offered, ranging from £525 to £695 for a sporting four-seater.

Hurtu's last new model was a 1328cc four, introduced in 1925, but fast tourers such as the Hurtu were already losing favour to the small cheap models pioneered by Citroën, and Hurtu had neither a model to fill that gap nor the inclination to make one. The company made no more cars after 1930 but continued with other profitable lines. BL

Hyundai Pony 1400GLS of 1985

HYUNDAI
SOUTH KOREA 1968 to date

Hyundai, the largest industrial corporation in Korea, with interests mainly in shipping and civil engineering, was one of four Korean companies – the others were Asia Motors, Shinjin Motors and Kia Industrial – which began to assemble foreign cars under licence in the 1960s. At the time Korean sales were confined entirely to assembled imports, mainly of Ford Cortinas, Opel Rekords and smaller Chevrolets, with a local content of about 60 per cent; some 40 per cent of all car sales were for use as taxis.

Hyundai Motor Co's plant at Ulsan in South Korea started assembling British Ford cars and trucks in 1968, and in 1973 built about 7000 of the total Korean vehicle market of 17,750 units. It was a natural step for Hyundai to move from assembly to production, encouraged by a government which actively sought American and European investment as an alternative to Japanese domination. In fact, most of the backing for Hyundai came from Barclays Bank in Britain and from other City of London financial houses.

The task of creating a new car (and in effect a new manufacturing company) was also entrusted to a Briton, George Turnbull. Turnbull was born in 1926 and apprenticed to the Standard Motor Co Ltd, later becoming deputy chairman of Standard Triumph and managing director of the Austin Morris division of what was then the British Leyland Motor Corporation. He went to Korea and took just three years to create the Hyundai car, overseeing the local engineering and co-ordinating a complex international chain of design and pre-production engineering.

The new car was styled by Giugiaro and engineered by Ital Design in Turin, although bodies were partly built in France and most of the dies came from British Leyland. The engine was to be the 1238cc four-cylinder 70hp Mitsubishi Saturn unit, with Mitsubishi gearbox, rear axle and suspension units – all built under licence in Korea to give an overall local content on production cars of around 90 per cent.

In London in November 1974 Turnbull announced that the Hyundai Pony would be in production by 1976, with a production target of 56,000 cars a year by the end of 1976, initially for home and local markets only. A new £35 million manufacturing site was also under development near the existing plant and the first pilot production was planned for December 1975, although prototype cars were to be run on Hyundai's own test-track some time before that.

Turnbull succeeded in meeting this difficult schedule largely because of the skill and enthusiasm of his local staff and genuine co-operation from Hyundai's corporate management in allowing him total control. A prototype of the four-door Pony saloon was shown at Turin in October 1974 (as was a dramatic two-door coupé which did not go into production) and the Pony was indeed in production by late 1975. Output was planned to rise to 120,000 by 1979 and actually reached 103,000; in 1982, when Hyundai had 12,000 employees, production was 91,000 cars.

The New Pony, a slightly revised version of the original, still with Mitsubishi running gear but now with an optional 92bhp 1439cc engine, was introduced in 1982. In 1983 Hyundai extended the range further with the Stellar, a booted saloon with the 1439cc engine or optional Mitsubishi 1597cc unit.

Output continued to hover around the 90,000 mark up to 1984 by which time Hyundai was expanding its export markets quite dramatically. The company had started selling cars in Canada and planned to enter the American market in 1986. British sales rose by over 70 per cent during 1984.

A further revised Pony model, known as the Pony Excel in Korea, was introduced, with Mitsubishi Colt running gear, early in 1985. This was being built on newly expanded production lines aimed at providing 200,000 cars initially, half of them for export, and an ambitious annual target of 400,000 by 1987. BL

IFA/TRABANT
GERMANY 1945 to date

IFA, although occasionally used as a marque name on both cars and motorcycles, was not actually a manufacturing company but an administrative association of several nationalized East German makes, including Audi, DKW, Framo and Phänomen. It was formed in 1945, when these and all the remaining East German car companies were nationalized, and it had its manufacturing base at the former Audi works at Zwickau. The initials derived from the full name of the organization, Industrie-Vereinigung Volkseigner Fahrzeugwerke, Zwickau.

The first car to use the IFA name was the F8, which was built as an IFA from 1948 to 1955. It was a small front-wheel-drive saloon, based on the DKW Meisterklasse which was introduced before World War II, and it was propelled by a similar 684cc twin-cylinder two-stroke engine.

Another model, the F9, was introduced in 1950 and this was also based on a pre-war DKW design – although in this case one which had only previously been seen as a prototype. It used the same 896cc three-cylinder engine and front-wheel drive as contemporary DKWs, and very similar body styles, but it was sold as a separate make until 1956. It was latterly made at Eisenach, at VEB Automobilwerke Eisenach, and after 1956 it was rebodied as the post-war Wartburg. This make has continued, with gradual but minor mechanical changes and one major restyling (in 1967) until the present day.

In 1955 the IFA F8 was also renamed, as the Zwickau P70, and was thereafter built by VEB Automobilwerke Zwickau. It retained the same 684cc engine and front-wheel-drive running gear but gained a new body, in glassfibre – one of the first German mass production cars to use the material.

In 1959, after about 25,000 Zwickau P70s had been built, the car underwent further minor changes to become the Trabant P50, built by VEB Sachsenring Automobilwerke in Zwickau. It should have become the Trabant (which, like the Russian 'Sputnik', means fellow traveller) in early 1958, but production did not start until very late that year, largely due to raw material shortages, particularly of sheet metal. For the same reason the early Trabant bodies were not actually of glassfibre but of resin-reinforced papier mâché. The P50 had a smaller, 500cc twin-cylinder 18hp two-stroke engine, based on the earlier unit, but was otherwise very much the recipe which dated right back to the pre-war DKW.

By 1960 the related Trabant and Wartburg cars were the only passenger cars being made in East Germany, after the recent demise of Sachsenring as a marque in its own right. This had been made since 1956, as a successor to the Horch, by the company which now built the Trabant.

Trabant built about 20,000 cars in 1959 and expected to increase output to 65,000 a year by the mid-1960s. An estate car version of the P50, the Kombiwagen, was shown at the Leipzig Fair in 1960 and in 1962 the P50's engine size was increased to 594cc, with an output of 26bhp. This car was shown at the 1963 London Motor Show as the Trabant 600, but most sales were still on the home market.

Another development, the two-cylinder two-stroke 601, was launched in 1964 and the Tramp, an open four-seater resembling a Mini Moke, was introduced in 1979. In October 1983 the range was uprated with 12-volt electrics and in 1985 comprised saloon, estate car and the open top models. Trabant built about 120,000 cars in 1982 and the workforce of the company is currently about 9000 people BL

IKA Torino saloon of c.1966

IKA/RENAULT-ARGENTINA
ARGENTINA 1955 to date

Industries Kaiser Argentina was formed in January 1955 to produce Jeeps and Kaiser sedans of the 1954-55 pattern in Buenos Aires using predominantly Argentine assembly and a high proportion of local material. President of IKA was Jim McCloud, brother-in-law of Henry Kaiser's son, Edgar. The dies were removed from Toledo and production eventually started in 1958. The cars were named Carabela (Caravel, a sailing vessel) and were very similar to the United States product, with stiffer suspension and manual transmission but without the supercharger.

About 3000 Carabelas a year were made from 1958 to 1962. They accounted for less than 10 per cent of IKA production, the balance being made up of Jeeps. In 1962 a smaller car was introduced under the name

IFA F8 saloon of 1950

Impéria four-seat tourer of 1911

Bergentin (another sailing ship, the Brigantine). This used body dies for the Alfa Romeo 1900 with a new grille, and four- or six-cylinder Jeep engines. It was made until 1964, but the bulk of the manufacturing capacity was taken up with licence production of Renaults (Dauphine and the R4), Jeeps and Rambler. In November 1966 appeared the Torino, based on the Rambler American but with locally designed bodywork, and a year later Kaiser Jeep sold its share to local interests and the direction came increasingly under Renault influence.

The company name was changed to IKA-Renault in 1968 and to its current title, Renault-Argentina SA, in 1975. The Torino was dropped for 1983, and the current range consists of Renault 4, 11, 12, 18 and Fuego. Production in 1982 was 34,278 cars. GNG

IMP
see Kiblinger

IMPÉRIA
BELGIUM 1906-1949

Automobiles Impéria of Liège was founded by Adrien G. Piedboeuf, who began his career selling Métallurgique cars in Aachen. In 1904 he began to build motorcycles under the name Piedboeuf at Liège, following with cars two years later. He gave these the name Impéria and chose as trade mark a crown, both recalling the empire of Charlemagne. In vari-

ous forms the crown remained part of the Impéria badge for the rest of the make's life.

At first production was very small and sales were limited to Piedboeuf's family and friends, but in 1908 he acquired the Pieper factory at Nessonvaux, near Liège, and in the same year he was joined by the German engineer Paul Henze, who was later responsible for Steiger and Simson Supra cars in his homeland.

The original 4.9-litre 24/30CV four-cylinder car was joined by a 3.3-litre 16/20 and a 9.9-litre 50/60CV, the two larger models having chain drive. A smaller car with 1764cc monobloc four-cylinder engine was introduced for 1909 and remained in production until 1914. Impéria were quite active in sport, and in 1908 Edith Paterson put 53 miles (85km) into the hour at Brooklands on a 16/20, at a time when women were not permitted to take part in ordinary races.

In 1912 Impéria merged with Automobiles Springuel, a small Liège firm which had been making four-cylinder cars since 1907. Its proprietor, Jules Springuel, became managing director of Impéria. Up to 1914 parallel ranges were made, that of Impéria running from 8/10 to 14/16CV, and of Springuel from 12/14 to 28/35CV. Some models were sold under the name Springuel-Impéria.

Quite distinct from these were two sporting models designed by a Spaniard, Francisco Abadal, who had formerly been a sales agent for Hispano-Suiza at Barcelona. In 1913 he asked Impéria to provide components for two models, a 15/22 and a 20/26CV, which he would assemble at Barcelona. The larger was very similar to the Hispano-Suiza Alfonso

XIII, with the same long stroke engine (80×180mm) with unit construction of engine and gearbox. Bodies were fitted in Spain, the main difference in appearance between the two cars being that the Abadal design featured a handsome V-radiator.

As well as the cars sent to Spain to be sold under the Abadal name, some were sold in Belgium as Impérias. To complicate matters further, a French dealer, Monsieur Magne, sold them in Paris as French cars.

In 1920 both factories were acquired by a young businessman, Mathieu Van Roggen, who continued the Abadal designs for a few years. These included a magnificent 5.6-litre single-overhead cam straight-eight, of which only three or four were made, and a 3-litre twin-overhead cam sports car, one of which won the 1922 Belgian Grand Prix at Spa.

Fewer than 200 cars were made between the end of 1919 and the middle of 1923, and Van Roggen soon realized that building expensive cars in small quantities was no way to make money. He hired Arnold Couchard, who had been with FN since 1905, to design a new small car, the 1-litre (1094cc from 1924) 6CV with slide-valve four-cylinder engine.

This has been described, rather unkindly, by Lord Montagu as a slightly down at heel Panhard-Levassor in miniature. It was often asked to carry bodywork too heavy for it, but with light coachwork it was a reasonable performer, with a top speed of 60mph (96kph). Van Roggen won the 1100cc category of the 1925 Monte Carlo Rally in one; the next two places also went to 6CVs. An unusual feature was a servo assisted transmission brake; front wheel brakes were available from 1926.

Impéria 11/24hp of c.1925

There were plans to make the 6CV in England at the GWK works in Maidenhead, but they came to nothing, and a proposed tie up with Voisin in France did not eventuate either. To pave the way for this proposed development Impéria bought a considerable quantity of Voisin stock, but all that resulted was that a few Impérias received Voisin bodies.

The 6CV did enable production to grow, but not dramatically. In 1925, 250 cars were made, in 1926, 420 and in 1927, 504. A 1650cc six was added in 1927, enlarged to 1800cc two years later.

In 1929 Van Roggen acquired four other Belgian firms in order to combat imported cars from a broader base. These were Excelsior, Métallurgique, Nagant and the coachbuilder Mathys et Osy. He also diversified into the manufacture of motor boats. Unfortunately the Depression hit Europe soon after Van Roggen's mergers, and none of the three car-making companies he acquired survived beyond 1932.

The old Couchard designs were modernized, but what Impéria needed was a new and up to date small car, and this Van Roggen could not afford to develop. His solution was to negotiate with Adler to make its newly-introduced front-wheel-drive Trumpf under licence. In fact Van Roggen imported the engines and transmissions from Germany but chassis, suspension and bodies were made in Belgium.

Impéria's version of the Trumpf was known as the TA-9 (*Traction Avant* 9CV) and was made from early 1934 until 1940. It was joined by the 995cc TA-7, based on the Adler Trumpf Junior, and the 1910cc TA-11, based on the 1938 Adler 2-litre. These were the only Impéria models made during this period, although a few TA-9s were fitted with slide-valve engines in 1934 and four of these ran unsuccessfully in the 1936 Spa 24 Hour Race.

In 1935 Van Roggen bought the moribund

Minerva company, and a few TA-9s were sold in France under the Minerva name. There was also an experimental front-wheel-drive car powered by a transverse mounted Ford V8 engine, of which three were made in 1937. The Adler agreement proved very satisfactory for Impéria, which registered a profit of 739,831 francs in 1936, compared with a loss of 1,422,012 francs that was incurred three years before.

Towards the end of the 1930s it proved increasingly difficult to trade in the normal way with the Nazi regime in Germany, and Van Roggen was forced to barter Belgian textiles for Adler engines. This put him in debt to the textile company Gerard-Hauzeur, which took control of Impéria in 1940, but Van Roggen retained Minerva.

Production of Impéria cars continued for a while after the German occupation of Belgium in 1940, and they could be bought by Belgian subjects provided they had an authorization from the occupying forces and promised to equip them with producer gas fuel systems. Later in 1940 the German army took over the factory and car production ceased.

In 1947 a new Impéria came out, the TA-8, which used a 1340cc Hotchkiss-Amilcar engine bought from Hotchkiss, which had discontinued the model. Bodies were a two-door saloon, drophead coupé or roadster. About 1000 TA-8s were made between 1947 and 1949.

Thereafter Impéria assembled Standard Vanguards, including a roadster model not made in England. In 1950 the company was making 300 Vanguards a month. Later in the 1950s it assembled Adler scooters, Alfa Romeo cars and Büssing trucks, and also made a large number of machine tools, a side of the business which dated back to 1934. Standard-Triumph ended its agreement with Impéria in 1958, and the company was liquidated soon afterwards. GNG

INNOCENTI
ITALY 1961 to date

When he was 16 Ferdinand Innocenti was employed in a small workshop in northern Italy. By the time he was 18 he had his own workshop and in 1922 he moved to Rome where he began to develop improved methods of making steel tubing, which then became his main product. In 1931 he moved to the Milanese industrial zone, Lambrate, and in 1933 founded SA Fratelli Innocenti, which soon became Innocenti Anonima per Applicazioni Tubolari Acciaio, making steel tube products of which scaffolding was the most profitable and led to production of a virtually universally used scaffold clip which would provide the company with much of its later finance.

Innocenti prospered up to the outbreak of World War II, during which its operations were moved to Rome. Its factories were so badly damaged during the war, however, that Innocenti virtually had to start again after the end of hostilities.

In Italy, as elsewhere, after the war there was a huge demand for cheap, economical transport, catered for by a sudden proliferation of small motorcycle manufacturers – in both senses. Innocenti decided to build slightly more civilized scooters and in 1946 introduced the Lambretta, which also became available in a small three-wheel delivery van version. The Lambretta quickly dominated the market and production reached the rate of a machine a minute.

By the mid-1950s Innocenti had three divisions, one building the scooters, one making mainly tubing and a third making specialized machinery, presses and machine tools. Around 40 per cent of Lambrettas were exported and they were also made under licence in South America and the Far East, while up to 80 per cent of the heavy machinery, including presses for motor industry customers such as Alfa Romeo, Fiat, Lancia, Ford and Volkswagen, went abroad, making Innocenti a very wealthy company.

In 1961 Innocenti, trading as Innocenti Societa Generale per l'Industrie Metallurgica e Meccanica, moved into car production, something he had planned to do since immediately after the war, building versions of the Austin A40 saloon under licence from knocked down kits. Next the company added an Austin-Healey Sprite, rebodied by Ghia, for which it gradually began to build more parts and import fewer until it was only importing the engines.

In 1963 Innocenti moved into the BMC front-wheel-drive range with its version of the Morris 1100, the Innocenti IM3, and in 1965 began to build the Innocenti Mini, which would also be available in Traveller guise from 1967. By the mid-1960s Innocenti had some 7000 employees.

Ferdinando Innocenti died in June 1966, by

which time his company had sold almost 150,000 cars. His son Luigi, who had been working for the company since 1958, then took control.

In May 1972 British Leyland, looking for a larger share in the Italian market, purchased Innocenti's car-making operation as the company was split up. Lambretta production transferred to a Spanish subsidiary and the machine tool side, which made all the machinery for the new Lada plant at Togliatti, passed into government control. BL also transferred its Jaguar, Rover and Triumph marketing operations from BL Italia to Innocenti, although the cars were imported from Britain.

By 1974 Innocenti had added the Regent, a version of the Allegro and, late in the year, the Bertone-styled New Mini, with hatchback. By this time the cars had returned to using up to 60 per cent imported parts.

By 1975 the company was in deep financial trouble, having shown a £10 million loss for

1983 2280 employees built 22,578 cars.

In 1980 the Mini Mille was introduced, followed by the Mini 90LS in 1981 and the Mini 90SL in 1982. By this time de Tomaso had already reached an agreement with Daihatsu for future supplies of its three-cylinder engine after BL engine supplies had been threatened from February 1981, and in 1987 the range comprised three-cylinder front-wheel-drive Tre saloons with or without turbocharging or even with a diesel engine, plus a twin-cylinder Daihatsu-powered 650 version of the same car. The 72bhp turbo Tre, introduced in 1983, is known as the Turbo De Tomaso.

Early in 1985 plans were in hand for Innocenti, which built 16,873 cars in the previous year, to merge with De Tomaso's Maserati interests, under the auspices of the government organization GEPI. This, it seems, was primarily intended to raise finance for Maserati's joint sports car project with Chrysler. De Tomaso himself will retain a 14 per cent shareholding in Innocenti. BL

tacts with cars through working in the paint industry. In 1958, just married, he returned to Europe with no specific plans but then became involved in designing racing chassis for Giannini Automobili SpA in Rome. From there he moved to Turin and founded Costruzione Automobili Intermeccanica in mid-1959 as a subsidiary of the North East Engineering Co of Canada.

His first car, which appeared in 1960, was called the IMP, for Intermeccanica-Puch, and was a rear-engined two-seater GT coupé powered by a modified 645cc two-cylinder Puch engine. Only 21 were built after Reisner ran into problems in getting engines and other running gear from Puch in Austria. The new company also made tuning kits for cars including Renault and Peugeot and built a moderately successful Peugeot-engined Formula Junior car.

In the 1960s and 1970s Intermeccanica built larger cars, around American V8 engines and hand-built chassis, starting in 1963 by building 69 bodies for the Buick-engined Apollo 3500GT for International Motor Cars of Oakland, California. In 1964 International sold production rights to Vanguard Inc of Dallas, Texas, and Intermeccanica supplied a further 19 bodies for assembly as the Vetta Ventura before that company went bankrupt, the last of that batch of bodies being assembled by Precision Motors in 1971.

In 1965 Intermeccanica also began supplying convertible Apollo bodies to Long Island Ford dealer Jack Griffith, who assembled TVRs for the American market. In 1966 these went on sale in the USA as the Ford-powered Griffith GT – but only until Griffith, too, went out of business.

Further shells were completed as the Omega by Suspension International Corporation of Charlotte, before Intermeccanica itself took over production in 1967 as the Intermeccanica Torino, with 4.7-litre Ford V8. The Torino was renamed the Italia in 1968 and was later available with 5.4- and 5.7-litre engines and as a coupé. A one-off special version, the IMX, was available in 1969. Intermeccanica also built a few examples of a 7-litre station wagon, the Murena.

By the end of 1970 Intermeccanica had

Innocenti (Austin) A40 of 1962

Innocenti Tre of 1985

that year alone. Fiat, Honda and Alejandro de Tomaso all approached BL with deals but in December 1975 BL closed the company down and left it in the hands of the Italian government.

In 1976 de Tomaso finally beat Fiat to joint ownership of Innocenti with the government rescue agency GEPI, BL retaining a 5 per cent holding. The company was renamed Nuova Innocenti SpA, resuming production in May 1976 with the Innocenti Mini de Tomaso, the Bertone type.

In September 1979, de Tomaso increased his holding when his company Seimm Moto Guzzi bought 76.7 per cent of Nuova Innocenti, and with sales that year reaching $175 million it became his most profitable asset. In

INTERMECCANICA
ITALY, USA 1959-1980

Intermeccanica's history is nothing if not cosmopolitan. Its founder, Frank Reisner, was born in Hungary in 1932 and fled with his parents before World War II to Canada and thence to the United States. He was trained as a chemical engineer and had his first con-

Intermeccanica Italia IMX of 1968

built some 500 cars. In 1972 it introduced a new model, the Indra, with a choice of Opel engines, including two Chevrolet-derived V8s. This car was built at the instigation of Opel itself.

In 1974 Intermeccanica had about 20 workers in Turin and a host of outside contractors, but in 1975 the Italian operation was closed and the Intermeccanica name taken over by Automobili Intermeccanica, a new company that had been founded in Los Angeles by Tony Baumgartner.

The new company took a totally different line from 1977 with a $7000 glassfibre replica of a Porsche Speedster on Volkswagen Beetle platform chassis and running gear. It was a very faithful replica, down to the use of appropriately narrow wheels, but it and the 1980 La Crosse, a Ford-based 'nostalgia' model, were a long way from Frank Reisner's original models. By the end of 1980 some 600 Speedsters had been built and production was stopped as Intermeccanica, now relocated in Fountain Valley, California, began marketing a soft top conversion for the Ford Mustang and Mercury Capri range, selling them through Ford dealerships for about $16,000. BL

INTERNATIONAL
USA 1906-1912; 1960-1980

The International Harvester Co was founded in August 1902 with a capital of $120 million. It consisted of five major farm machinery makers: Plano Manufacturing Co, McCormick Harvesting Machine Co, Deering Harvester Co, Milwaukee Harvester Co, and Warden, Bushnell & Glessner Co, the manufacturer of Champion machines. Of these firms the oldest was McCormick, which had been founded by Cyrus Hall McCormick, who was born in 1809 of Scottish-Irish descent in Virginia. In 1831 he perfected a mechanical reaper that was to revolutionize farming.

Unlike many other American agricultural pioneers, International Harvester eschewed steam power, although internal combustion had been used on Deering and McCormick self-propelled mowers in the 1890s and for barn engines. The production of tractors began in 1906, when 14 were built, followed by 153 in 1907 and nearly 600 in 1908. By 1922 over 150,000 had been sold. Between 1924 and 1932 some 134,000 of the Farmall line alone were produced.

IHC engines were also developed to power high-wheelers for farming customers. E. A. Johnston, who had joined McCormick in 1894 and had experimented with cars from 1898, shortly after Deering's George Ellis, produced a high-wheeler design that was ready in October 1906. A total of 99 were made in the McCormick works in Chicago in 1907. Production moved to Akron, Ohio, where a large series of air-cooled horizontally-opposed twin-cylinder Auto-Buggy models

International Harvester Auto-Buggy of 1910

were made. They were joined in 1909 by the similar, but load-carrying, Auto-Wagon.

In 1910 and 1911 four-cylinder autos were made with either International air-cooled or British-American water-cooled engines. Up to 1912 a total of 4100 Wagons and more than 6000 Buggies – including 1100 of the J-30 four-cylinder water-cooled models and 2700 of the 1907-10 Buggies – were sold, after which high-wheeler motor trucks were made. These trucks carried an International rather than an IHC badge from 1914 until production ended in 1916.

From 1915 conventional trucks were produced, but these had radiators at the back of coal-scuttle bonnets, just like the 8-16 Junior tractor. In 1921 several front-radiator models were introduced, including a ¾-ton Speed model with Lycoming engine. This was made in a new vehicle plant at Springfield, Ohio. Truck production in 1921 reached 7000.

Trucks have subsequently been the company's most important product alongside farm equipment, and the firm has regularly been America's largest producer of heavy trucks. From 1964 it made an indigenous Australian range. In 1974 it bought Seddon-Atkinson in Britain after taking a minority stake in DAF two years before. These European interests were sold in the early 1980s.

Pickup trucks have been a regular sideline since the earliest days and station wagons have been produced at various times since the C-I model of 1936. In late 1960 came the Scout utility range, initially with either 4×2 or 4×4, of which 200,000 had been made by 1968 in Fort Wayne, Indiana. The Scout chassis was also used by Glassic for replicars.

The oil crisis and slump of the mid-1970s seriously affected International, and its last year of profits was 1979, when it made the equivalent of £162 million. By 1982 it owed its banks $2.4 billion and had cut its work-

force by 52 per cent to 44,800. A rescue plan was then begun, involving the sale of many of its divisions and interests which reduced its gross assets to $8 billion and its annual sales to about $5 billion. Plans to make a 'world truck' fell through after £106 million had been spent on the project and IHC's attempts to market IVECO vehicles in America also came to nought in 1982.

In its efforts to regain liquidity IHC sold its axle section to Rockwell, its construction machinery division to Dresser Industries for $100 million and in 1985 its farm tractor and implement side to Tenneco (which already controlled Case and David Brown).

Despite its difficulties International truck sales are America's highest in the heavyweight class and in 1985 accounted for a quarter of the market. It also builds a 6.9-litre diesel engine for use by Ford. NB

INTER-STATE
USA 1909-1918

The Inter-State Automobile Co was founded in Muncie, Indiana, in February 1909 with nominal capital of $300,000, two-thirds of which was common stock and the balance preferred stock. The company was formed by three businessmen, T. F. Hart, Otto Holden and J. M. Maring, and the first Inter-State car, the four-cylinder 4.7-litre Model 28 roadster, was designed by Claude E. Cox and introduced in 1909 at a price of $1750.

In 1911 Inter-State launched the 40hp Model 34, known as the Bulldog, which had electric lighting and was available as a five-passenger Torpedo for $2000. That year also included the 50hp 5- to 7-passenger Model 35 Torpedo tourer at $2700.

By 1912 eight models were available, with

both four- and six-cylinder engines. In 1913 the new six-cylinder Model 45 sold for a substantial $2750, but in October of that year Hart, the president of the company, faced with continuing financial problems, put Inter-State into the hands of the receiver. It was originally intended only to use up old stock to fulfil remaining orders, but the company was instead reorganized as the Inter-State Motor Co, still based in Muncie.

In 1914 Inter-State introduced the much cheaper four-cylinder Model T, which initially sold for $1000 but by 1916 was available for only $850, that year's range also introducing a light delivery van. The cars were now little more than assembled models using the 19.6hp Beaver proprietary engine until production stopped again early in 1918, ostensibly because of World War I but in reality because of continuing financial problems.

Production was never resumed and in March 1919 Inter-State sold its plant and site to General Motors, which intended to use it for parts manufacture but between 1920 and 1921 built the short-lived Sheridan car, a low-

Inter-State four-seat tourer of 1914

priced four-cylinder model. In 1922 GM sold the factory to William Crapo Durant's new Durant Motors Inc, which had works all round the country building the various cars in Durant's ill-starred empire. At Muncie, Durant would build the six-cylinder Durant during 1922 and 1923 but then car production stopped there for good. BL

INVICTA
GB 1925-1950

Invicta Cars Ltd was formed by Noel Macklin, who had previously been associated with the Eric Campbell and Silver Hawk cars. He was encouraged by the brothers Oliver and Philip Lyle of the Tate & Lyle sugar company. His aim was to make a car with a very flexible top gear performance, and many of the company's publicity demonstrations were made to exhibit this feature.

In 1924 a prototype was built in the three-car garage in the grounds of Macklin's house at Cobham, Surrey, using a 2-litre six-cylinder Coventry-Simplex engine and gearbox, Marles steering and other proprietary components in a Bayliss-Thomas frame; the designer was W. G. J. Watson. Five further cars were made on these lines, but all the engines were ruined when they were left outside on a cold night without benefit of anti-freeze, so Macklin started again in 1925 in new premises at the Fairmile, Cobham, with a 2½-litre six-cylinder Meadows engine, Thompson frame, Moss or ENV gearbox and Alford and Alder front axle.

The Invicta was always an assembled car, for the little works at Cobham had no facilities for manufacture apart from finned brake drums and cast aluminium dashboards. Initially, bodies were made by Gordon England, which held the London agency for the first year, but in 1926 Invicta opened its own showroom in Curzon Street and thereafter practically all sales were direct. Invicta recommended various coachbuilders to customers, but from the early 1930s tended to standardize on Cadogan, Carbodies, Mulliner and Vanden Plas.

The initial 2½-litre Invicta was priced at £594 for the chassis, and 147 were sold from early 1925 to 1927. It was always a handsome car, characterized by a square cut radiator

and rivets down the bonnet, although the artillery wheels of the early models gave them a rather staid appearance. By 1927, when the 2½-litre engine was replaced by a 3-litre, also by Meadows, wire wheels were almost always used. The hoped-for top gear flexibility was there from the start, with acceleration from walking speed to over 60mph (96kph).

In July 1927 Violet Cordery, Macklin's sister-in-law, won the Royal Automobile Club's Dewar Trophy for Invicta with a supervised run at Brooklands covering 5000 miles (8046km) at an average of more than 70mph (112kph). Two years later, partnered by her sister Evelyn, Miss Cordery again won the Dewar Trophy for Invicta by covering 30,000 miles (48,280km) in 30,000 minutes (500 hours) at Brooklands.

In the meantime the indefatigable Violet, aged only 25, drove a 3-litre Invicta round the world at an average running speed of 24.6mph (39.6kph). In 1930 she drove from London to Monte Carlo and back in third gear, from London to Edinburgh and back in bottom, and 11 times round the RAC's London traffic route in top. It was only consideration for her sanity rather than for the car that prevented her from driving nine laps (25 miles or 40km) round Brooklands in reverse!

In the summer of 1928 came the most famous Invicta, the 4½-litre, powered by a 4467cc six-cylinder engine evolved by Meadows. Macklin and Watson worked very closely with the Wolverhampton engine manufacturer, and the 4½-litre unit was exclusive to Invicta until the end of 1933, when it was taken up by Lagonda.

The smaller cars were dropped after 1929, and the 4½-litre A Type was joined the following year by the much lower S Type. The frame was underslung at the rear and swept up over the front axle, the wheelbase being shortened from 126 to 118in (3.2 to 2.9m). The radiator was lowered and the rectangular Invicta badge was replaced by a winged motif, used only on the S Type. The engine gave 115bhp,

Invicta 4½-litre two-seater of 1928

increased later to 140bhp, which conferred a top speed of over 100mph (160kph) on the S Type. Donald Healey won the 1931 Monte Carlo Rally in one of these cars and was second in 1932.

Out of approximately 500 4½-litre Invictas made, not more than 75 or so were S Types. A figure of 77 has been quoted, based on serial numbers, but this was then revised to 'around 50'. However, a long time Invicta employee has stated that the actual figure was more likely to have been over 70. Most were made at Cobham, with about a dozen being assembled at Invicta's Chelsea service depot after manufacture at Cobham ended in 1933. A similar number of 4½-litre chassis were made for Invicta by Lenaerts & Dolphens of Barnes, who had made the Beverley-Barnes.

Although he was justifiably proud of the 4½-litre Invicta, Macklin was as aware as anyone else of the effects of the Depression, and in order to cater for a cheaper market he brought out a 1½-litre six-cylinder car for the 1932 season. This used a single-overhead cam engine made by Gillett and Stevens and was made mostly with tourer or four-door saloon coachwork by Carbodies. It was an attractive little car, and not overpriced at £399 – £575 with supercharger – but it was heavy and performance was not sparkling. Not more than 50 to 60 were made.

For 1933 an exciting twin-overhead cam 1½-litre called the 12/100 was announced, but only one chassis was ever made. There was also to be a 5-litre twin-overhead cam super sports car, but this never got off the drawing board.

By the autumn of 1933 the small company could no longer carry on and on 'black Friday', 13 October, most of the staff were dismissed. The stock of components was taken over by the Earl Fitzwilliam who had been running the London sales department and who was one of Macklin's backers. As already mentioned, a few 4½-litre Invictas were assembled at Chelsea until the stock was used up, while the Cobham works soon became home to another car, the Railton.

There were two attempted revivals of the Invicta name. In 1937 it was announced that Invicta Cars of Alpha Place, Chelsea, would market for the next season three cars, of 2½, 3 and 4½ litres, all with six-cylinder overhead-valve engines and all-synchromesh gearboxes. The word 'market' indicates that manufacture was probably never intended, and the only 1938 Invicta made was in fact a 2½-litre Talbot-Darracq, with a different radiator.

After World War II a new company was formed called the Invicta Car Development Co Ltd. Nominal capital was £50,000, later increased to £100,000, and Watson was brought back from Lagonda where he had done some preliminary work on the 2.6-litre.

Another link with the past was the choice of a 3-litre twin-overhead cam engine from Meadows for the Invicta Black Prince. The most unusual feature was the Brockhouse

turbo transmitter which gave an infinite variety of ratios selected automatically. A prototype was completed by the middle of 1946 and production was due to start at a Virginia Water, Surrey, factory no later than October 1947, with a target of 250 cars a year. However, the chosen bodybuilders, Charlesworth, went out of business in September 1947 after they had made just two bodies, a saloon and a drophead coupé. By the time new bodybuilders had been found, Airflow Streamlines, the price had risen from a planned £2940 to £3890.

Not more than 20 Black Prince Byfleet dropheads were made, mostly bodied by Airflow with a few by Jensen, before the company was wound up in February 1950. The assets were acquired by AFN Ltd, but this company did not make any cars. GNG

IRIS
GB 1905-1915

Lucien Alphonse Legros, born in 1864, worked for British Gas Traction Ltd laying tramways before going into partnership in 1904 with wealthy Guy Knowles, then in his mid-20s and an experienced driver of French cars, to form Legros and Knowles Ltd. The company had a capital of £20,000 and specialized in gear cutting and car repairs.

Their first batch of cars was not a success, but in 1905 Ivon M. de Havilland designed 15, 25 and 35hp four-cylinder cars for them that carried the name of Iris, the mythological speedy messenger of the gods. They were produced in the company's small factory at Willesden, north-west London. In about 1908 the firm also made the first aero engines designed by Ivon's brother Geoffrey de Havilland. A draughtsman at Legros and Knowles from 1906 was F. T. Burgess, who left to design the Valveless car and was then chief engineer of Humber until joining Bentley in 1920.

A six was developed for 1906, in which year a selling organization named Iris Cars Ltd was formed with £12,000 capital to market

the products of Legros and Knowles. It collapsed in 1908, however, and in the following year Iris Cars Ltd, with £30,000 capital, took over both Legros and Knowles and the sales company. Its managing director was G. A. Mower, who also ran the Bifurcated and Tubular Rivet Co in Aylesbury, Buckinghamshire. Two bays were hired from this company and Iris assembly was transferred there.

The workforce probably never exceeded 60 and output was small. C. K. Edwards was designer for about three years before joining the bus firm AEC in 1912. Legros himself left the company to start the successful Grant, Legros typecasting firm; he was killed in a motor accident in 1933.

During World War I Stokes mortar bombs were made by Iris at Aylesbury and afterwards partially completed cars and spares were prepared for sale. However, progress was too slow and the collapse of the post-war boom ended these plans and years later the stock was sold for scrap. The works then reverted to the rivet company and when G. A. Mower died in 1941 the Iris company name died with him. NB

ISETTA/ISO
ITALY 1953-1979

The Isetta and Iso were cars at totally opposite ends of the motoring market but both were built by the same Italian company, run by Renzo Rivolta. Rivolta founded Isothermos in Bresso in 1939 but all production plans were halted almost immediately by World War II. In 1948, as Iso Automotoveicoli SpA, he began to build mopeds and motor scooters.

Booming sales made the company very profitable and in April 1953 it progressed from scooters to bubble cars with the introduction of the air-cooled 236cc Isetta. It was a tiny rear-engined four-wheeler with very narrow rear track and a length of less than 90in (2.3m). Access was by a swing-up front door, to which the steering wheel and column were attached. The car went on sale in early 1954.

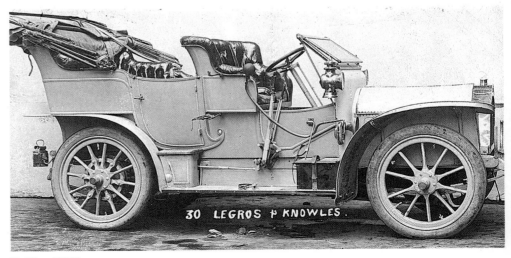

Iris 25hp of 1905

In offering economical closed motoring at the time of the Suez crisis it became an instant success; it was built under licence by VELAM in France, Borgward-Iso in Spain, Iso-Romi in Brazil and, most successfully, by BMW for the fuel conservative end of the German market. Production in Italy stopped in 1956, but BMW offered the car with its own 250cc single-cylinder four-stroke engine until 1963; and from 1957 to 1964 the BMW-engined type was built under licence by Isetta of Great Britain Ltd.

A total of some 36,000 Isettas was built and with the profits Renzo Rivolta looked towards the prestige GT market, planning from the start to build a relatively straightforward car with bought-in engines, initially Chevrolet V8s, for their ready availability. The car was to be built in a new factory on the family estate near Milan.

The first Iso-Rivolta, the 145mph (233kph) GT300, was shown at the Turin Show in late 1962 with a 5.3-litre 300bhp Corvette engine (with 350bhp option) and a four-seater body by Bertone. Although it was relatively expensive and obviously newly developed it sold

Isotta-Fraschini two-seater of 1902

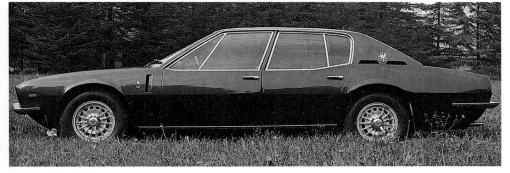
Iso Fidia S4 of c.1976

quite well, with early exports to Britain, the Middle East and the United States.

In 1963 Rivolta introduced the potent Grifo, engineered by Giotto Bizzarini, late of Ferrari and already involved in producing his own very similar car, the Bizzarini GT Strada 5300. The Grifo was again styled by Bertone and sold well from 1965 to 1974, with Chevrolet, and later Ford, V8s of up to 7 litres. A less successful four-door saloon, the Ghia-styled Fidia, was introduced in 1968 but was very badly timed for the straitened domestic market and the approaching fuel crisis of the early 1970s.

The original Rivolta was replaced in 1969 by the Bertone-styled Lele, a four-seater sporting saloon for which the 5.8-litre Ford V8 was standardized in 1973, giving near 150mph (241kph) performance and a degree of luxury at a reasonable price. In 1973 Iso offered a special version of the Lele known as the Marlboro, after the cigarette company sponsor which backed Iso's brief and none too successful entry into Grand Prix racing from 1973. The Formula 1 project eventually passed to Frank Williams who would later become World Constructors' Champion with his own Grand Prix cars, and began Iso's

involvement with Gianpaulo Dallara, the young designer of the classic Lamborghini Miura.

Dallara, however, was not to design a classic for Iso. The company was already faced with serious financial and labour problems and the price gap between the 'kit-car' Isos and the true exotics such as Ferrari and Lamborghini was narrowing, to Iso's cost. Under acute stress from these problems, Renzo Rivolta died and the company was taken over by his son.

Bizzarini was engaged again to design a mid-engined two-seater replacement for the Grifo. As the Varedo, it appeared in prototype form at the 1972 Turin Show but it did not go into production.

Faced with continuing financial problems Rivolta sold Iso to an American refrigerator manufacturer, Dr Iro Pera, who put his Brazilian son-in-law, Carlo Beltiore, in charge. Things did not improve and in 1975 production stopped when Iso was declared bankrupt. A new company, Ennezeta sdf, was formed and resumed production briefly in Milan between 1976 and 1979, building only the automatic Lele and the Fidia. Production stopped again for good in 1979. BL

ISOTTA-FRASCHINI
ITALY 1900-1949

Italy's greatest make of luxury car began with the partnership of lawyer Cesare Isotta and car enthusiast Vincenzo Fraschini who set up a business in 1898 to import Renault and De Dion cars and Aster engines into Italy. In 1900 they founded the Societa Milanese d'Automobili Isotta, Fraschini and Cia, and built their first car in the same year. It bore a close resemblance to the contemporary single-cylinder Renault and had an Aster engine. These small cars were made in limited numbers until 1903 when a line of Mercédès-like four-cylinder cars of 12, 16 and 24hp were introduced.

In November 1904 the company name was changed to Fabbrica Automobili Isotta-Fraschini; the new firm was capitalized at 2.5 million lire. At the same time the company moved from the Via Melzi in Milan to new premises at Via Monterosa.

In April 1905 there arrived a new chief engineer in the person of Giustino Cattaneo, who was responsible for all Isotta designs up to 1935. He introduced bi-bloc construction on the four-cylinder engines, which were made in nine different models for 1905 from a 2-litre light car to the 17-litre Tipo D racing car, of which only two were made. In 1906 Isotta-Fraschini made about 300 cars, which put them in second place among Italian manufacturers, although admittedly a good way behind FIAT's 1800 cars.

In 1907 the Italian industry suffered a severe recession and many companies went under. Isotta needed a partner, and found one in the French Lorraine Dietrich company which bought 50 per cent of the shares of the

Isotta-Fraschini 8A landaulette-limousine of c.1925

and publisher William Randolph Hearst. Elsewhere, owners included the Queen of Romania, the King of Egypt, the Aga Khan, several maharajahs, Pope Pius XI and Benito Mussolini. Seven were sold simply to 'Moscow, USSR', individual owners unknown.

In 1924 came the Tipo 8A with enlarged engine of 7370cc (110-120bhp) and servo brakes. In its six years of production it sold more than twice as many as its predecessor, but from 1928 production was curtailed to make way for aero and marine engines.

Aero engines included the Asso (ace), a 500bhp V12 that weighed only 9cwt (502kg) which powered, among other aircraft, the Macchi M67 Schneider Trophy seaplane of

Italian company. The relationship was short-lived, however, due to personality clashes. Cattaneo, in particular, resented Lorraine's unwarranted claim for the success of his racing cars, although some good ideas did come from Lorraine including a six-cylinder car designed expressly for the French market, and a lowered chassis for town work. In 1909 the agreement came to an end, and Isotta sold a manufacturing licence to Praga in Austria. This, too, was short-lived, as Praga soon adopted its own designs.

The years 1906 to 1908 saw active participation in racing, with Minoia winning the 1907 Coppa Florio and Trucco the 1908 Targa Florio. In the United States Isotta scored some notable victories in races such as the Savannah and Briarcliff Trophies, and the Long Island Motor Parkway Sweepstake of 1908. These successes gave Isotta a useful foothold in the American market, which it continued to enjoy right up to the Great Depression.

All the victories were achieved with large cars of 8 litres or more capacity, but in 1908 Cattaneo produced a little gem of a car powered by a 1.3-litre single-overhead cam engine. A team of three ran in the Coupe des Voiturettes that year and although the best place was only eighth, the company put a modified version into production, and they were made until 1911. Lionel Martin used the chassis of one of these cars as the basis for his first Aston Martin.

In 1910 Cattaneo and Oreste Fraschini, a brother of Vincenzo, designed a front wheel braking system that was featured on some Isottas at that year's Paris Salon. This feature was offered on production cars in 1911 and by 1914 was standardized on larger models; Isotta was the world's first company to make a commercial success of four wheel braking.

In the years leading up to World War I Isotta made a wide range of cars, from a 2.3-litre up to two large sporting cars with 16-valve overhead-cam engines and chain drive, the 6.2-litre TM and 10.6-litre KM. Some of them sported very Mercédès-like radiators. They were made only in small numbers, 20 TMs and 50 KMs. Total output in 1914 was 125 cars.

During World War I Isotta made about 1250

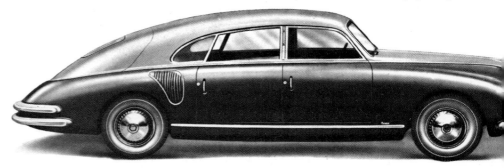

Zagato-bodied Isotta-Fraschini 8C Monterosa of 1947

trucks for the Italian army, some in armoured car form, and also aero engines and power units for torpedo boats and the assembly of fuselages for trimotor hydroplanes. The aero and marine division continued to be active after the war ended and assumed increasing importance as the years passed. Trucks were not revived (until 1934), nor was the pre-war multiplicity of models.

Instead, Oreste Fraschini planned a one-model policy aimed directly at the luxury market of Rolls-Royce and Hispano-Suiza. His answer to those was the Tipo 8, a 5880cc straight-eight with alloy cylinder block, three-speed unit gearbox and, of course, four wheel brakes. It developed a conservative 80bhp and gave a top speed of 70 to 80mph (112 to 128kph), depending on the body. As with other cars of its class, the Tipo 8 was supplied as a chassis only. Italy's leading coachbuilders of the day, especially Castagna and Sala, made many of the bodies, as did foreign firms such as Barker in England and Fleetwood and Le Baron in the USA.

Oreste Fraschini died in 1921 and the following year his brother Vincenzo and Cesare Isotta left the company they had founded. The new owner was Count Lodovico Mazzotti, the great sporting enthusiast who was later to be one of the founders of the Mille Miglia.

Company policy continued without change, and the Tipo 8 soon assumed the position that Oreste had hoped for it, as the leading Italian luxury car, and one of the three or four top cars in the world. It became particularly popular in the USA. About 450 cars were sold there between 1919 and 1932 and owners included film stars Clara Bow and Rudolph Valentino, boxer Jack Dempsey

1929. Asso engines sold in large numbers to American aircraft-makers. The New York to Boston line was served exclusively by Isotta-Fraschini-engined planes in the late 1920s and early 1930s. Isotta-Fraschini aero engines were made under licence in Romania and Russia, where Cattaneo's son Guido supervised production. Unfortunately the company's best talent was taken from cars to aero engines, which was one reason for the company's failure in 1933; the other reason was the lack of a smaller car to back up the Tipo 8.

The Depression hit Isotta-Fraschini very hard, relying as it did so much on the American market, where it was the most expensive car available. There was no question of bringing out a cheaper model, and interest in cars was clearly running down anyway. For 1931 the company introduced an improved Tipo 8, the 8B, with more power (160bhp), coil ignition and a more massive frame. Production lasted until 1932, but a mere 30 were made.

In 1930 there was a proposed association with Ford. Ford Italiana SA, with headquarters at Trieste since 1923, had been limited to commercial transactions apart from assembly of a small number of tractors. In July 1930 Ford Italiana's capital was increased to 100 million lire, organized by Sir Percival Perry. Ten million lire were to be reserved for Isotta-Fraschini shareholders. In exchange Ford would purchase 100,000 shares in Isotta-Fraschini at a higher than market rate, giving a 23 million lire boost to Isotta's finances. Isotta was to erect a new factory to produce a guaranteed 5000 Ford Model A chassis per year. These numbers caused Fiat serious alarm, and combined pressure by Fiat and the government brought an end to the project.

This proved to be the final straw for Isotta-Fraschini, which by November 1932 could barely pay wages or fuel bills. No cars were manufactured after 1931 and only 11 of those assembled in 1932 were sold. Stocktaking in June 1932 revealed 19 Tipo 8s still unsold plus 52 new Tipo 8B chassis and unassembled components for 48 more Tipo 8Bs. Few of these were sold and most were scrapped immediately after World War II.

In 1933 the company changed hands again, the new owner being aircraft-maker Count Caproni di Taliedo, who made widespread use of Isotta engines in his planes. Cattaneo resigned and began a new career in marine engineering; he lived until 1973.

As might be expected, Caproni concentrated on aero engines but also revived commercial vehicle production with 4- and 7-ton trucks, the engines for which were made under licence from the German firm MAN. They had Isotta-Fraschini chassis and Zagato cabs. During the late 1930s Isotta became part of a Caproni-directed conglomeration of firms engaged in aero and marine engines, ordnance and aluminium manufacture.

Unfortunately the company's efficiency in providing material for the Axis war effort put it in bad favour with the post-war Italian government. A promising link with Fabrica Nacional de Motores in Brazil to make commercial vehicles was blocked and the contract awarded to government-owned Alfa Romeo. A merger between Isotta-Fraschini and the Cemsa Caproni company was also stopped.

While these attempts to broaden its base went on, Isotta continued to make trucks and buses and also brought out a completely new car. Known as the 8C Monterosa, it had a rear-mounted overhead-cam V8 engine, a platform frame and independent front suspension by rubber in compression. It was designed by Fabio Rapi and bodies were by Zagato and Touring (saloons) or Boneschi (convertible), but only six were made before the government liquidated Isotta-Fraschini to prevent it going bankrupt. The company was later acquired by the Breda engineering group.

Under Breda control Isotta made a few trolley buses in the 1950s and attempted a return to truck and bus production in 1958 with some advanced designs, but they came to nothing. The company still exists today under the name Fabbrica Automobili Isotta-Fraschini e Motore Breda, making a variety of engines and hydraulic torque converters.

Independent of Breda was Costruzioni Revisione Motori (CRM), which was set up in 1952 by former Isotta-Fraschini technician Cesare Bormioli, initially to service Isotta engines used in torpedo boats of the Swedish navy but later to manufacture marine engines. CRM operations began in part of the old Via Monterosa factory which Bormioli leased from Breda, but the company later moved into a new plant at Castellanza when the Monterosa factory was acquired by Siemens of Italy and demolished. GNG

ISUZU
JAPAN 1918-1937; 1953 to date

The Tokyo Ishikawajima Shipbuilding and Engineering Co started car experiments in 1916 and between 1918 and 1927 made Wolseleys under licence. It then made American-inspired vehicles, mostly for military purposes, under the name Sumida (Tokyo's main river) until 1937.

Ishikawajima and DAT merged in 1933 as Jidosha KK and were joined in 1937 by Tokyo Gas and Electric, which had made TGE trucks from 1917 and TGE-Chiyoda trucks from 1930. The joint firm was named Tokyo Jidosha Kogyo (Tokyo Automotive Industry). Vehicles named after the sacred Isuzu River had been made since 1933 by Jidosha KK and government-backed heavy vehicles, including diesels, were made at a new plant at Kawasaki from 1938. The group spawned Hino in 1942 and the remaining vehicle interests were renamed Isuzu Motors in 1949.

In February 1953 an agreement was reached with Rootes to make the Hillman Minx in Japan; the agreement would last until 1965. The first car was made in October 1953 and had 70 per cent local content, which rose to 100 per cent four years later. Orders were collected from a dealer network set up by the Rootes-controlled Yamata Motor Co, and 250 men were employed at Omori on assembly. Other components came from the main workforce of 2300 at Kawasaki, from the engine plant at Tsurumi that employed 1300 and from the foundry at Sueyoshi with 550 men. Mitsubishi made the bodies using Pressed Steel dies and these were painted with cellulose, as synthetics took too long to dry in Japan's dusty climate.

In 1959 the Elf 1-ton truck was the first Isuzu light commercial produced, and it used many Minx components; a small diesel was also offered. This diesel engine was offered in the first Isuzu-designed car, the Bellel of 1961, and in the following year was used in 30 per cent of all Bellels sold. Some 2300 men were employed at a new plant at Fujisawa making the Bellel and the Minx, and production averaged 1000 cars a month.

In 1968 Isuzu produced its 400,000th post-war truck, a number that included nearly 4000 US-pattern 6×6 military trucks for the US Army Procurement Agency, Japan. In 1960 Isuzu accounted for more than half the diesel vehicles made in Japan. Its domestic sales in 1970 exceeded 1 million for the first time.

In 1971 General Motors acquired a 34.2 per cent stake in Isuzu. One of the first outcomes of this was the LUV pickup, sold in America by Chevrolet from 1972. Then in 1974 came the joint Gemini project, this car being sold in America by Buick from 1976 and by Holden in Australia.

In 1978 the one millionth vehicle was exported and the one millionth Elf produced. New for 1981 was the Trooper light 4×4. In 1983 a joint project to make 4×4s was signed between General Motors, Suzuki and Isuzu, in which the latter two companies exchanged 10 million shares. A sister company in Thailand made its 100,000th Isuzu in 1980 and there is also a joint company with General Motors in the Philippines.

As well as the main plant in Kawasaki (producing trucks and engines) and Fujisawa (cars and light trucks), there are components factories in Tsurumi and Tochigi. A proving ground exists at Hokkaido and a factory is being built there to produce the Gemini saloon, introduced in 1984, for the North American market. In 1982 Isuzu launched its Aska version of the GM World J-car and a year before that the Piazza (also called Impulse) sports saloon and Trooper 4×4 estate car. The Piazza was based on a Giugiaro styling exercise shown at the 1979 Geneva Motor Show. As the Piazza Turbo launched in Britain in 1985, it had a turbocharged 2-litre engine and was capable of 130mph (210kph).

In 1984 Isuzu made 88,500 cars and about 350,000 commercial vehicles. Under the company's president, Kazuo Tobiyama, were 15,500 employees who contributed to total sales in 1984 worth 7691 million yen. The 1987 range consisted of the Gemini three- or four-door saloon (sold in the US as the Chevrolet Spectrum), Aska four-door saloon, Piazza coupé and Trooper estate car. NB

Isuzu Piazza Turbo of 1986

Itala 120hp Grand Prix car of 1907

ITALA
ITALY 1904-1934

Like many early Italian companies, Itala was founded by one of the Ceirano family. In July 1903 Matteo Ceirano left his brother Giovanni Battista and their company Fratelli Ceirano and in November set up Matteo Ceirano & Co SA in Turin in association with Guido Bigio, Grosso Campana, Giovanni Carenzi, Leone Fubini and Angelo Moriondo. They intended to build racing cars, for which Itala would be a type name.

Early in 1904 the company moved to a new 32,300sq ft (3000sq m) factory and became Matteo Ceirano & Co – Vetture Marca Itala. Nominal capital was 3 million lire (later increased to 5 million), of which 1.5 million was paid up. The workforce numbered 150.

In the same year, Matteo won the light car class at the Susa-Mont Cenisio hillclimb with one of the first Italas, a 4.5-litre 24hp four. Bigio and Giovanni Battista Raggio added more competition successes and success brought customers.

Needing to expand and buy new production machinery, the company was reorganized in September 1904 with additional backing from a Genoese financial group headed by banker G. B. Figari. It was now known as Itala SA Fabbrica Automobili Torino. Paid up capital was increased to 1.75 million lire and the company acquired a 750,000sq ft (70,000sq m) site in Orbassano, well served by road and rail, where a new 527,000sq ft (49,000sq m) factory for 400 workers was erected under the direction of the engineer Fenoglio.

Itala was now the marque name and not simply a Matteo Ceirano model. Bigio became managing director, and he, Ceirano and the other principals were joined by Figari, Albano, Cattaneo, Cortese, Florio and Pallavicini. The original intention remained only to build racing cars.

In 1905 Matteo Ceirano left Itala and with Michele Ansaldi founded Ceirano-Ansaldi, which went on to build the SPA from 1906. Alberto Balloco was employed as technical director from 1905 and Itala launched the 14-litre 100hp racer with which Raggio won that year's Coppa Florio. The following year Allesandro Cagno won the first Targa Florio for Itala; Graziani, Rigal and de Caters finished second, fourth and fifth.

Cagno won the Coppa Florio, run to the Grand Prix formula, in 1907 with the new 120hp model and between June and August Prince Scipione Borghese, co-driver Luigi Barzini and mechanic Ettore Guizzardi, covered 10,000 miles (16,100km) of often appalling roads to win the epic Peking to Paris race by no less than three weeks. Although racing car production continued, it was the last great Itala success.

Racing had certainly helped sales and Itala ended the depression years of 1906 and 1907 with a profit of almost 300,000 lire. From 1907 the company made an extraordinarily complicated range of four- and six-cylinder models, some of which stayed in production for several years. They included the 2610cc four-cylinder 14/20, the 7433cc 35/45 Peking to Paris type and an 11,148cc 35/40 six, the 5401cc 20/30 and 25/35 fours, a 10,604cc (later 9236cc) 50/65, the 120hp racer, a 75hp of 12,930cc and a profusion of smaller models of between 1944cc and 3308cc. By 1910 Itala employed some 780 people and produced 350 cars that year, doubling to 700 in 1911 from 1000 employees.

In 1911 Itala showed the first Balloco sleeve-valve design and a year later began to concentrate on Avalve rotary sleeve-valve types, beginning with the 3308cc 25hp 18/30 and continuing until 1922 through 25, 35 and 50hp models, ranging in capacity from under 4 to over 8 litres. From 1916 some models were also designated by number, both Avalve and conventional types, including the 2614cc Tipo 39, the 2813cc 50 and Sport 51, the 54 taxi, the valveless 55, the 56 and the six-cylinder 61. The last type listed was the 65, a six-cylinder overhead-valve twin-cam six.

Bigio was killed while testing one of the rotary-valve racers prepared for the 1913 French Grand Prix – Itala's last Grand Prix appearance – and the company experienced terrible problems during World War I, which almost ruined it. Itala began the war by building personnel carriers but in 1915 the factory was retooled to build Hispano-Suiza V8 aero engines under licence. By the time the engine had been found to lack power and Itala had retooled again for a bigger version, the war was over.

Itala and other companies had invested on the basis of building some 3000 engines but the virtual halving of the government order put the company in serious financial difficulties. Itala sold off as much of its wartime surplus as was feasible but, aggravated by post-war labour problems, ran its workforce down to just 180 by 1920.

Even a somewhat half-hearted post-war resumption of sporting activities did little to alleviate Itala's plight. Although Giulio Cesare Cappa was brought in from Fiat as chief designer there was not enough money and the best he could manage was the Tipo 61.

In 1925 a receiver was brought in by the government and by 1926 Itala was being run by the state Societa Finanziaria di Liquidazione, forerunner of the Istituto Recostruzione Industriale, which later saved Alfa Romeo among others. The SFL tried hard, and even supported one last racing effort with a proposed supercharged front-wheel-drive 1½-litre V12 Grand Prix car in 1926, also intended as the basis of an 1100cc road car which probably never ran in any form.

Still, in 1929 Itala lost some 21 million lire and amalgamated with the trailer manufacturer Officine Metallurgiche e Mechaniche di Tortona, under the new name Itala SA and supposedly with capital of 35 million lire. That lasted until 1931 when the company was liquidated. It reappeared in 1932 as Itala SA Costruzioni Auto but failed to make money out of a 2.3-litre redesign of the 61 as the Tipo 75, finally closing down at the start of 1935. BL

IVANHOE
see Russell

IVEL
GB 1899-1906

Ivel 8hp landaulette of 1900

Dan Albone, born in 1860, became a well known racing cyclist and owned a cycle workshop in Biggleswade, Bedfordshire, when he was still in his 20s. He called his machines Ivel after the local river and made one of the first safety bicycles for ladies.

In 1897 he began working on farm tractors and in 1898 built a light car with 3½hp Benz-type engine. Two-cylinder cars followed in 1900. It is known that Albone bought engines from Payne and Bates of Coventry and also from Aster, but these may have been for the three-wheel tractors that were produced from 1902 with the formation of Ivel Agricultural Motors Ltd.

Cars were made in small quantities until 1906 but it was the tractors that spread the name of Ivel. One that was sold to a buyer at that time replaced six horses and three men. The tractors featured opposed-twin engines with Renolds chain and gear drive. Hans Renolds was a friend of Albone from bicycling days as was S. F. Edge, who helped market the tractors through United Motor Industries, a company he had formed with Napier.

'Smiling Dan' Albone died in October 1906. His workshop manager, A. Hoffman, then worked for United Motor Industries before returning full time to the Ivel tractor business in 1911. This lasted for a further 10 years, but the product changed little in appearance or specification and could not compete with post-war American imports. NB

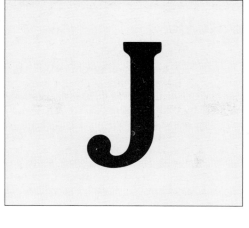

JACKSON/JAXON
USA 1902-1923

The Jackson Automobile Co was established in Jackson, Michigan, on 19 July 1902 by local businessmen Byron J. Carter, George A. Matthews and Charles Lewis. The company was founded with a total of $24,000 capital held in three equal blocks of 800 $10 shares by the three principals.

Carter was the original local man, born in Jackson county in 1863, the son of a farmer. He moved to Jackson city in 1885 and established the Steam Job Printing Co and also made rubber stamps, running this business until 1901. In 1894 he opened a bicycle store with his father, and in 1896 added another printing company, the US Tag Co.

Carter was also an inventor; through the steam printing company he worked on steam engines and patented a three-cylinder engine which later became the basis of the Jaxon car. In 1903 he also patented a friction drive system which ultimately led to his later Cartercar company being absorbed by General Motors in Billy Durant's patent-buying spree.

Lewis was born near Leeds in England in 1853. He went to the United States in 1867, moving to Jackson to establish a carriage

spring manufacturing company, Lewis & Allen, which became the Lewis Spring & Axle Co in 1897 when he bought out his partner.

Matthews, like Carter, was a farmer's son, born in Ohio in 1852. He studied business formally before working for a carriage wheel maker and then, with borrowed money, set up on his own. In 1891 he bought shares in the Fuller Buggy Co in Jackson and took over the company when Fuller died in 1892.

Lewis and Matthews were both directors of local banks, the Union Bank and Jackson City Bank respectively, but Carter was the engineer. He had built himself a petrol-engined car in 1899 but Jackson began production in 1902 with the steam-engined Jaxon – based on one of two steam prototypes which Carter had built and exhibited in 1901. The 6hp three-cylinder engines were built for Jackson by a local company, Trask Field Gas Engine Co. The steamer was made until 1903, selling in that year for $975 for the Model A or $800 for the Model B.

Alongside the steam cars Jackson also offered a petrol model Jaxon from 1902. This was a 6hp single-cylinder which sold for $750 and was built at a rate of around four or six a week until replaced in 1904 by a twin-cylinder petrol model. After 1904 all the cars were known as Jacksons, rather than Jaxons. The two-cylinder 1904 petrol model was known as the Orlo; Jackson made twins until 1909.

In 1905 the company introduced its first four-cylinder car and in 1910 Jackson offered only fours, some with overhead valves. The fours were built until 1916, a six-cylinder range being started in 1913 with the Northway-engined Sultanic. In 1908 Jackson changed its advertising slogan from 'Sturdy as Old Hickory' (an allusion to the eponymous President Jackson's nickname) to 'No hill too steep, no sand too deep'.

By then Byron J. Carter had left Jackson to found The Motorcar Co. This company paid him $35,000 for his 1903 friction drive patent, $15,000 for his drawings and patterns and a further $25,000 for goodwill, all of which led to the Cartercar.

Jackson four-seat tourer of c.1914

Jackson had moved to a new, larger factory in 1908 and in 1910 George Matthews became the sole owner until his death in 1914, when Jackson took over the remains of the Fuller Buggy Co. The Jackson company was then controlled by the Matthews family until it ceased to be a car-maker in 1923. Lewis had left to return to the Lewis Spring & Axle Co; he was also involved with Briscoe and the Clark Motor Car Co before his death in 1912.

A rather strange 1913 model called the Duck, with rear seat steering, not surprisingly sold very few copies and in 1916 the six and larger fours were replaced by two V8 models. For 1917 and 1918 the Wolverine 8, an assembled car with Ferro V8 engine, was the only model.

In 1919 the company was reorganized as the Jackson Motor Corporation and introduced the Continental-engined 6-38 for 1920, selling at $1185 for an open tourer or $2850 for a sedan. In 1923 Jackson, with Dixie Flyer and National, was absorbed into the new Associated Motor Industries Inc and the last Jackson model, a 1923 six, was sold as the National Model 6-51. BL

JAGUAR/SS
GB 1927 to date

Jaguar as a make dates only from 1945 but the company's history begins with the Swallow Sidecar Co in the early 1920s, a company founded by William, later Sir William, Lyons, who was born in Blackpool, Lancashire, in September 1901. On leaving school he was almost apprenticed to Vickers shipyards before his father steered him, in 1918, into a job as a trainee with Crossley Motors in Manchester and an evening engineering course at Manchester Technical College. Lyons, however, soon returned to Blackpool to help in his father's piano restoration business.

For some years he had been a motorcycle enthusiast, owning and racing several machines, and now he went as a junior salesman to a local Sunbeam dealer, continuing to buy and sell machines himself at the same time. In June 1921 William Walmsley, the son of a coal merchant from Cheshire, moved into a house near Lyons' home, from the gar-

age of which he continued his business of building aluminium sports sidecars at the rate of around one a week.

Lyons bought one of Walmsley's Swallow sidecars and suggested that the two work together to expand the business. After some resistance from Walmsley, 10 years Lyons' senior, and with help from their respective fathers, who guaranteed a £1000 overdraft facility, they formed the Swallow Sidecar Co. With Lyons doing most of the organization they began to work from premises on the top floor of an electrical equipment factory in Blackpool. The company was officially registered some time later, in September 1922, on Lyons' 21st birthday.

The business did well and in 1926 moved to larger premises in Blackpool as the Swallow Sidecar and Coachbuilding Co, intending to develop the latter service. In 1927 Swallow designed a special body for an Austin Seven owned by Lyons. This car was first shown in May of that year as the two-seater Austin Swallow, with optional hinged hard top, and soon went into production. In August the Morris-based Cowley Swallow was announced, while Swallow also built one-off bodies on chassis including Alvis and Clyno.

By 1928 Swallow had some 50 workers but needed more space to meet growing demand, the works only being able to build two cars a day alongside approximately 100 sidecars a week. In November the business moved to a former shell works in Coventry where the production target was 50 cars a week, now including larger models on Fiat chassis. In 1929 the company made its first appearance at the Motor Show.

By February 1931 Swallow was making 30 cars a day. In October 1931 the SSI, the first to use a purpose made chassis (made by Rubery Owen) as well as Swallow body, but with Standard 16hp running gear, was introduced at a remarkably low £310. In 1932 the company sold 776 cars. The smaller SSII, based

Austin Swallow Mark II of 1929

Jaguar XK120 roadster of 1949

on the 1052cc Standard Little Nine, was introduced at the same time as the SSI. In March 1935 Swallow introduced its first true sports model, the 2663cc 20hp two-seater SS90, of which 23 examples were built, although there had already been drophead versions of the four-seater cars.

Although the company built sidecars until 1939, it had become simply the Swallow Coachbuilding Co Ltd in 1930 and in October 1933 the car building operation was separated as SS Cars Ltd. Another new name appeared in September 1935 with the introduction of the 2663cc overhead-valve SS100 Jaguar. Thereafter all SS models would be suffixed Jaguar and very soon it would become the marque name.

In January 1935 SS Cars Ltd was floated as a public company. Walmsley, who had been increasingly at odds with Lyons, left to join the caravan company Airlite Trailer Co and he died in 1961. William Lyons became the major shareholder when 140,000 ordinary five shilling shares and 100,000 £1 preference shares were offered at 10s 6d and 21s 6d respectively in SS Cars Ltd, a nominal subsidiary of the Swallow Coachbuilding Co at this time. Lyons put the Swallow Coachbuilding Co Ltd into voluntary liquidation and set up a separate private company, Swallow Coachbuilding Co (1935) Ltd, with £10,000

age, SS survived the war relatively unscathed.

After the war the company began a major reorganization, beginning in March 1945 with the creation of Jaguar Cars Ltd and the sale of Swallow to the Helliwell group. In 1946 Tube Investments Ltd bought the rights to the Swallow name and continued sidecar production. In 1954-55 Swallow built a few examples of the Swallow Doretti, an open two-seater touring car based on the Triumph TR2 with special body, but in 1956 the Swallow Coachbuilding Co (1935) Ltd was sold again, this time to sidecar-maker Watsonian and the name is still registered, if not used.

Jaguar resumed production in July 1945 and the first post-war car was completed in October. In February 1947 the company suffered a major setback when fire destroyed part of the factory, causing £100,000 worth of damage.

Until 1948 Jaguar built what were essentially pre-war models, with 1.8-litre four-cylinder engines and 2.7- or 3.5-litre sixes. All the sixes were Jaguar's own, and after 1949 the old Standard-based four was completely dropped.

Engineering was in the hands of William M. Heynes, formerly of Humber, who had joined SS as chief engineer in 1934 and, with Harry Weslake, had first redesigned the Standard engines and later created the classic Jaguar

the company moved gradually into the Brown's Lane factory which had formerly been occupied by Daimler and now gave Jaguar 1 million sq ft (93,000sq m) of production area.

In the early 1950s Jaguar went racing in earnest, first with the XK series and later with the purpose built C- and D-Type racing sports cars. The prime objective was to win the Le Mans 24-Hour classic, which it did five times, in 1951 with the C-Type and in 1953, 1955, 1956 and 1957 with the D-Type. Jaguar then retired from racing – at least partly as a result of its involvement in the 1955 Le Mans disaster – and the Competition Department, under 'Lofty' England, was closed in 1956.

Jaguars run by private owners remained hugely successful in sports car and saloon car racing, and in the 1980s Jaguar became officially involved in motor sport once more with a team of XJ-Ss in the European Touring Car Championship, which it won in 1984. Jaguar also returned to Le Mans in 1984 with a team of American built XJR-5s and it seems that the company is now more than interested in a sixth Le Mans win, having endorsed American-built entries at Le Mans in 1984 and then re-entered sports car racing officially in mid-1985 with the XJR-6, built by Tom Walkinshaw Racing.

One still-born Jaguar racing car was the

nominal capital, to continue sidecar production and sales.

At this time the company had some 600 employees and produced around 1500 cars a year. A possible takeover of the bankrupt Sunbeam Motor Car Co Ltd came to nought as Jaguar was beaten to the deal by Rootes.

The SSI and SSII models were dropped in 1936 but in late 1937 and early 1938 the company suffered a crisis while introducing new models with troublesome all-metal bodywork. SS had taken over Motor Panels (Coventry) Ltd but later sold that company to Rubery Owen. In spite of the problems, the company made a small profit and the final production year before World War II was the first to exceed 5000 cars.

During the war, SS built Meteor aircraft centre sections, repaired and serviced bombers, built some 10,000 sidecars and experimented with parachutable lightweight vehicles such as the JAP-engined VA. Unlike most of Coventry, which suffered massive bombing dam-

sixes and V12 with engineers including Walter Hassan and Claude Baily. Heynes joined the board of Jaguar in May 1946 and played a major part in shaping the company's future.

In October 1948 Jaguar announced the sensational XK120 sports car, with 160bhp 3.4-litre twin-overhead cam six-cylinder engine and a top speed of 120mph (193kph). Again it had a remarkably low price, £1273 in original open tourer form, and 12,055 were sold until its replacement in October 1954 by the 190bhp XK140. Remarkably, some 92 per cent of XK120s were exported and in 1952 96 per cent of *all* production was exported – over 60 per cent to the United States.

The XK's success was also image building for Jaguar's saloon cars, the latest of which was the Mark VII, introduced in 1951 with the twin-cam engine which then totally replaced the earlier pushrod units. More than 30,000 Mark VIIs were built until 1957 and these sales levels enabled Jaguar to expand considerably. From late 1950 to November 1952

mid-engined four-cam V12 engined XJ13. That was a technically advanced design from 1966 whose racing career was scotched by the British Motor Corporation amalgamation, but which has since become well known as a demonstration car and Jaguar's first ever mid-engine design. Racing lessons were applied to the road cars, the best known being the introduction in 1953 of disc brakes which reached the production cars in 1958.

Towards the end of 1955 the company announced the unit construction 2.4-litre saloon, retrospectively dubbed the Mark I, and by 1957 this was also available with a 3.4-litre option, to be joined by the 3.8 in 1959. The 3.8 engine also powered the top of the range XK150, introduced in May 1957, and of which 9398 were built before being replaced in March 1961 by the similarly powered E-Type, a direct descendant of the racing D-Type.

Jaguar was now undergoing further expansion and William Lyons had been knighted in 1956. In February 1957 another disastrous fire

Jaguar E-Type Series 2 of 1965

riolet was launched with an all-new, lightweight twin-overhead cam six-cylinder 3.6-litre engine, the AJ6; from July 1985 the cabriolet was available with the V12 HE engine. The new XJ6 retained the general lines of its predecessors, but had the new 2.9 and 3.6 litre 6-cylinder engines.

Sales improved dramatically through some 22,000 cars in 1982, more than 28,000 in 1983, to a record 38,500 (including Daimler limousines) in 1985. Productivity improved enormously from a smaller workforce and Jaguar planned an annual output of 60,000 cars within five years. Against this background Jaguar Cars Ltd stock was keenly sought when the company was privatized from the state-owned Leyland in August 1984. The issue was over-subscribed some eight times, putting a value of more than £300 mil-

destroyed almost a quarter of the factory, causing some £3.5 million worth of damage but, remarkably, production was back to normal by April. In 1959 Jaguar bought the factory from its erstwhile landlords, the Ministry of Supply, and planned more efficient production.

In June 1960 Jaguar bought the Daimler Co Ltd for £3.4 million from the BSA group, which had controlled it since 1910, continuing Daimler production before eventually turning the Daimler into a 'badge-engineered' Jaguar. The Daimler acquisition brought the Jaguar workforce up to some 8000. Jaguar also acquired Guy Motors Ltd, truck manufacturers since 1914, from the liquidator for £800,000 in 1961 and bought Coventry Climax Engines Ltd in March 1963. Guy introduced a new range of trucks in 1964 and the marque was in production up to 1979.

Jaguar introduced the Mark II saloon in October 1959 and the much larger Mark X in 1962, adding the hybrid S-Type, a long booted Mark II with the X's independent rear suspension, in 1964. A 4.2-litre twin-cam six extended the engine range in 1965 and was used in the 420 saloon of 1967, an uprated S-Type.

In July 1966, largely at the instigation of Sir George Harriman of BMC, Jaguar merged with the British Motor Corporation to form British Motor Holdings, with Sir William Lyons retaining control of Jaguar. In May 1968, through the merger of Leyland and BMH, Jaguar became part of the new British Leyland Motor Corporation.

Jaguar's first product as a part of BL was the XJ6 saloon, introduced in September 1968 and another instant success. In 1972 the XJ became available as the XJ12, with the superb 5.3-litre overhead-cam V12 engine as introduced in 1971 on the Series 3 E-Type. In 1975 the E-Type was replaced by the controversially styled V12 XJ-S, a luxury four-seater sporting car, but not a sports car. A total of 72,584 E-Types had been built.

In spite of Jaguar's sales success Leyland could never quite come to terms with its autonomy. From October 1972 Jaguar Cars

256

Jaguar XJ-S cabriolet of 1984

Ltd no longer existed as a separate entity and 'Lofty' England succeeded Sir William Lyons on his retirement as managing director, and later chairman.

In 1974 a new managing director, Geoffrey Robinson, newly returned from Leyland's Italian offshoot, Innocenti, planned further expansion but was denied by government pressure. In 1975 the government-commissioned Ryder Report on Leyland's problems decried Jaguar's independence and Robinson resigned. Under Sir Michael Edwardes' remarkable revival of Leyland, however, Jaguar regained its identity, to the extent of being known as Jaguar Cars from 1978, although Leyland's 'prestige' grouping of Jaguar-Rover-Triumph was short-lived.

In April 1980 John Egan, formerly of Massey-Ferguson, was appointed chairman of Jaguar and in the same year the company became Jaguar Cars Ltd once again, with Sir William Lyons continuing as honorary president until his death in 1985 at the age of 83.

Egan had much in common with Lyons in his positive personal approach to Jaguar as an individual marque and even the new racing involvements were an integral part of his image reinforcement programme. Under Egan, Jaguar began, particularly in America, to rebuild a reputation recently damaged by marginal quality control as just another part of Leyland. New models were planned, including a successor for the XJ6, which appeared in October 1986, and a successor for the E-Type. In October 1983 an XJ-S cab-

Jaguar Sovereign of 1986

lion on the company and suggesting a high degree of confidence in its future.

The confidence seems well founded, as Jaguar increased its profits by 83 per cent to £91.5 million in 1984, from £50 million in 1983. Well over 70 per cent of the turnover was in the reborn American market, where sales are expected to have increased sevenfold from 1980 to the end of 1985. Jaguar is also now making significant inroads in Germany, the home of its major rivals, Mercedes-Benz and BMW, and it is doing all this by adhering to the Lyons dictum of selling cars of exceptional quality at a reasonable price. BL

JAMES AND BROWNE
GB 1901-1910

James and Browne was founded by Tom Bousquet Browne, who had been branch manager of the electrical engineers New and Mayne, and Francis Leigh Martineau, who had been with the Premier and New Beeston cycle companies. The identity of James is unknown; he does not appear on any company records and members of the Browne family have no recollection of him. The partnership was originally concerned with 'repairs and experimental work' in 1900 and was registered as a limited company in January 1902 with a capital of £10,000 'to carry on the business of automobile, flying machine and submarine manufacturers'.

Premises were at Hammersmith, west London, and the company had already built its first car, a 9hp horizontal twin with transverse crankshaft and flywheel between the cylinders, when the company was registered. Later in 1902 it moved from Queen Street to King Street, still in Hammersmith, and soon added a four-cylinder model to the range, still with horizontal engine.

These early cars had conventional bonnets, but most James and Brownes sold were under-floor engined landaulettes or broughams, successful competitors for the electric broughams popular at the time. Martineau left in 1904 and later became chief engineer at the Pilgrims Way Motor Co at Farnham, Surrey, another company that was also in the business of making horizontal-engined cars.

Commercial vehicles were made from 1904, including a van on the 9hp two-cylinder chassis followed by a 5-ton lorry with 20hp four-cylinder engine which was under powered. In 1906 came the Vertex models with conventionally mounted vertical engines, a 20hp four and a 30/40hp six. Although more powerful and smoother than the under-floor engined cars, the Vertex was now competing with innumerable conventional cars, and few were sold.

A ban on the use of petrol-engined cars in Hyde Park damaged sales of the broughams, and the company's business dwindled from about 1906. The Lacre Motor Co was appointed sole agent in November 1906, and one of the truck models, a forward control 3-tonner, was sold under the name J and B Lacre.

One of the company's last ventures was the manufacture in 1909 of the chassis for Britain's first trolleybus. By the end of 1910 it had sold all its spare parts and castings to Rawlings Brothers, who also took on some James and Browne staff. T. B. Browne had a distinguished career in the Royal Army Service Corps in World War I and later in civilian life he founded an extremely successful advertising agency. He died in 1965 at the ripe age of 92. GNG

James and Browne Vertex limousine of 1906

JAWA
CZECHOSLOVAKIA 1933-1946

The Jawa name was always better known on motorcycles than on cars, and the company was set up in 1929 to build German Wanderer motorcycles in Czechoslovakia. The name derived from F. Janacek, the designer, and Wanderer. These were replaced by machines of Villiers and DKW design, and when car production began in 1933 Janacek again turned to DKW for inspiration. Apart from having all steel bodies in place of the DKW's wood and fabric, the early Jawas were identical to the German product. Just over 1000 of these were made in 1933 and 1934, after which only motorcycles were made for two years.

In 1937 the company produced a more interesting design, the Minor, with swinging-arm rear suspension. The bodies were original and attractively styled, but the 615cc engine, gearbox and front wheel drive were still derived from DKW. Car production was always secondary to motorcycles; total pre-war production of cars was 3200 compared with 59,385 two-wheelers.

After World War II a few Jawa Minors were made, followed in 1946 by the Aero Minor, a rather bulbous-looking saloon which used the same engine, front wheel drive and backbone frame. As the Jawa factory was entirely taken up with motorcycles, the Aero Minor was built in the Walter aero engine factory at Jinonice, bodies being made by another aircraft firm which made cars, Aero of Prague.

About 14,000 Aero Minors were made, and there was a short-lived plan for them to be built under licence by BSA in England. Jawa motorcycle production continues, and it is now Czechoslovakia's leading make of two-wheeler. GNG

JAXON
see Jackson

JEAN GRAS
FRANCE 1924-1930

Société Anonyme des Autos Jean Gras was founded in 1924 in Lyons-Montchat, Rhône. The company took over the former Philos works, where light cars with proprietary engines had been made from 1912 to 1923. Its offices were near those of Voisin, in Issy-les-Moulineaux, Paris, and capital was 1.8 million francs.

It had early success making Parisian taxis and also produced small-engined cars of high quality in small numbers, some of which had Sedbi brake servos. Most interesting was an overhead-cam 10CV Gran Sport, which was joined in 1926 by a 1500cc six 'in the price range of a four'. It is likely that production later moved to Issy-les-Moulineaux before ceasing entirely in 1930. NB

JEANTAUD
FRANCE 1894-1906

Charles Jeantaud was born in Limoges in 1843. He built an experimental electric carriage in 1881 and later did work for Serpollet's steam tricycles. He began to produce Jeantaud electric carriages on a commercial basis in 1894 and made cars with Fulmen electrical equipment from 1895. Two years later he began making taxis. By then he owned one of the most fashionable coach and carriage works in Paris. In 1898 a Jeantaud became the fastest road vehicle in the world at 39.24mph (63.16khp) in the hands of Count Chasseloup-Laubat and began a four year rivalry with Jenatzy for the land speed record.

Charles Jeantaud backed F. H. Gaillardet's Société Française d'Automobiles in 1897 which, with Bardon, was to be one of the cornerstones of the Georges Richard Unic business. In 1899 American rights to Jeantaud vehicles were acquired by Henderson Bros of Somerville, Massachusetts, who appear to have made little progress, however. A significant number of electric cabs were nevertheless sold in France, and in 1903 petrol-driven Jeantauds were added to the range. The firm collapsed in 1906 with the death of its founder, who was discovered asphyxiated in his apartment with the flue of his stove deliberately blocked. NB

JEEP
USA 1941 to date

The name Jeep was derived from GP (for General Purpose) and the 4×4 Jeep first appeared in 1940 as a Bantam prototype from consulting engineer Karl H. Probst. Although Bantam made 2675 of these vehicles in 1940-41, the US Army required volume production and eventually Willys made 360,000 and Ford 290,000 during World War II.

Willys registered Jeep as its own trade mark in the United States and 111 other countries. It launched the civilian Universal Jeep and then added the Jeepster roadster in the later 1940s. Willys made Jeeps on the same production line as the Aero car until 1955.

The Kaiser Corporation merged with Willys in 1954, changing the company's name to Willys Motors Inc. By January 1956 550,000 Jeeps had been made since the war. Tens of thousands were used as Jeepney taxis in the Far East. A Brazilian plant, acquired by Ford in 1968, produced Jeeps, which were also made elsewhere under licence by Hotchkiss (1954-69), Mitsubishi (from 1953), Mahindra, Ebro and IKA-Renault.

In 1960 the first of more than 14,000 4×2 US Mail vans were built and in 1963 the firm was renamed the Kaiser-Jeep Corporation. In 1964 the 1.4 million sq ft (130,000sq m) Studebaker factory at South Bend, Indiana, was acquired along with a contract to build 27,000 6×6 trucks for the US Army.

In 1970, when Jeeps were being produced or assembled in 29 countries, American Motors bought Kaiser-Jeep of Toledo, Ohio, and changed that company's name to the Jeep Corporation. The heavier vehicle and special products division became AM General Corporation the following year and began to produce transit buses at Mishawaka, Indiana, followed by 350 electric versions of the Jeep. Ownership of AM General changed in 1983 when it was acquired by the LTV Co of Texas for $170 million.

In 1973 Jeep sales in the USA totalled 67,000, or 17 per cent of the 4×4 market; almost the same number were exported. Two years later production totalled 140,000.

By the mid-1970s Renault owned 48 per cent of American Motors and the PRV engine used by Renault was adopted in a variety of Jeep models. It followed use of the Buick 'Dauntless' and Pontiac 'Iron Duke' units. In 1983 American Motors spent £32 million on a one-third share of a Chinese factory for producing 4×4s. The intention was to produce 20,000 vehicles a year and use various Jeep components in the products of the Beijing Jeep Corporation Ltd. In addition to its 'working vehicles', Jeep has expanded into the 'leisure 4×4' market and its designer in this field is a former Jowett and Ford employee, Roy Lunn. NB

Jeep Wagoneer 4×4 estate of 1985

JEFFERY
see Rambler

JENATZY
BELGIUM 1897-1904

Historian and racing driver S. C. H. 'Sammy' Davis once described Camille Jenatzy as 'that extraordinary man, Jenatzy, whose theatrical, forked red beard and excitable nature had made him a distinct character'. That was written of Jenatzy as a racing driver, nicknamed 'The Red Devil', but Jenatzy was also a pioneer manufacturer of electric cars and petrol-electrics.

He was born in 1868, the son of Belgium's first rubberized fabric manufacturer and tyre pioneer, who had founded his own company in 1865. Camille trained as a civil engineer, developed an interest in electricity and built his first car, a chain drive dos-à-dos electric, in late 1897.

In the autumn of 1898 he began to manufacture cars at Boulogne-sur-Seine, and Jenatzy cabs and light commercials were also made by Compagnie Internationale des Transports Automobiles in Paris. In January 1899 he began a great rivalry with another electric vehicle maker, Charles Jeantaud – or at any rate with his driver, the Count Chasseloup-Laubat – for outright speed. Jenatzy built a torpedo-shaped racer with a body by Rheims and Auscher, made of partinium, an early aluminium alloy, and known as *La Jamais Contente*. On 29 April 1899 at Achères he achieved almost 66mph (106kph) – the first time any car had exceeded 100kph (62.13mph). He also raced petrol-engined cars for Mors, Mercédès and others during his racing career.

Jenatzy made electric cabs and commercials until 1901, but from 1900 he was more interested in petrol electrics, driving a car of his own design (including his patent magnetic clutch) in the 1900 Gordon Bennett races. In January 1901 he showed a 6hp Mors-engined petrol-electric, manufactured under Pieper patents, at the Paris Salon.

World War II Jeep of 1944

Henry Pieper had founded an arms factory in Liège in 1866, began to make electrical equipment in 1883 and, like Jenatzy, made his first car in 1897. In 1903 Jenatzy made 12/15 and a few 20/28hp petrol-electric cars under the name Jenatzy-Martini in Pieper's Martini-Henry rifle factory in Liège.

In 1904 Jenatzy's son was killed and Camille stopped making cars in order to run the family rubber company, now one of Belgium's biggest tyre manufacturers. He continued racing, however, notably for Mercédès and Pipe (which also used his magnetic clutch under licence). Jenatzy, well known as a practical joker, was killed in a hunting accident in 1913; imitating the sound of a wild boar he was shot dead by a companion. BL

JENSEN/JENSEN-HEALEY
GB 1935-1976

They saw the opportunity in W. J. Smith & Sons, a small bodybuilding company in need of better management. They joined as joint managing directors and quickly reorganized the van and bodybuilding sides of the company before starting production of car bodies. So successful were their efforts that in 1934 they were able to take the company over as Jensen Motors Ltd, building bodies for a wide range of cars including Standard, Morris, Singer and Wolseley. They also started work on what would be the first car to carry the Jensen name, a 3.6-litre 120bhp Ford V8-engined four-seater tourer which was first seen in 1935. Clark Gable bought a Jensen-bodied Ford V8 tourer and copies of the car were soon in demand. They were luxurious and mechanically excellent, with a two-speed back axle giving six forward speeds, and they sold well.

Ford was initially reluctant to supply parts but changed its mind apparently after a

on its later Sheerline. Austin then supplied Jensen with a batch of 4-litre Sheerline engines for its saloon and the Interceptor cabriolet, and commissioned design proposals for a sports car, which became the 1950 Austin A40 sports, for which Jensen eventually built some 3500 bodies.

At the 1953 Motor Show Jensen launched an important new model, the glassfibre bodied 541, a 115mph (185kph) GT saloon. In 1956 on the de luxe version of this car, Jensen offered one of the first all-round disc brake systems.

The company was expanding now and in 1956 moved into a new and larger factory in West Bromwich, where it would also build bodies for vehicles as diverse as the Tempo front-wheel-drive commercial, the big Austin-Healey and the Volvo P1800 sports car. At the same time Jensen sought outside finance and found it in 1959 from the Norcross group, which installed Carl Duerr as a trouble shoot-

The Jensens in their Austin Seven special of c.1925

Jensen Interceptor cabriolet of 1949

Allan and Richard Jensen, the brothers who created the Jensen car, first made their names in the motor industry as body stylists and coachbuilders from the late 1920s. Richard, born in 1909, was apprenticed to Wolseley, and Allan, three years his senior, worked in the drawing office of Serck Radiators. When their father gave them a 1923 Austin Chummy they immediately stripped it of its body and set about building a more sporting two-seater.

They took the resulting car to a hillclimb at Shelsley Walsh where Arthur Wilde, chief engineer of the Standard Motor Co, saw it and was sufficiently impressed to ask the brothers to build a similar body on a Standard Nine chassis. The car was completed in 1928 and again very well received, which led to Allan being asked to work with Avon Bodies, a small specialist coachbuilder, and design a production version, the Avon Standard.

He then went to work for Edgbaston Garages Ltd, a successful general motor trade business, where he was soon joined by Richard, who came from Wolseley via a brief spell at Joseph Lucas. The brothers showed that they had management skills as well as engineering talent and eventually joined the board of the company, but they were already looking for a chance to create their own business.

chance meeting between the Jensens and Edsel Ford. The company agreed to supply sufficient parts for small series production.

In 1935 Jensen added a four-door saloon, the S-type, which stayed in production until 1939 in open and closed versions. In 1936 the Ford-engined car was offered at £645 for a sports tourer, £695 for the saloon and £765 for a drophead coupé.

Jensen built a Steyr-engined prototype for the 1938 Motor Show, but it did not reach production and the next car to do so was the Type H, a long wheelbase derivative of the S with a 4.2-litre straight-eight Nash engine, although a few were also built with the 4.3-litre Lincoln V12.

Car production was halted by World War II, during which Jensen built ambulances, fire engines, amphibian tank conversions and a high speed bulk carrier. The company resumed production very quickly after the war with work for Invicta and Lea-Francis, work for outside companies being an important adjunct to its own car-building.

The first post-war design was launched in 1946. This big PW saloon used a Nash engine (although the prototypes used the 3.8-litre Meadows straight-eight) as Jensen had abandoned plans to build its own. This model led to contacts with Austin, which it was suggested had come close to copying the design

Jensen CV8 saloon of 1963

ing consultant managing director.

The 541S offered automatic transmission from 1960 and in 1963 the 541 series was replaced by a new CV8, powered by a 305bhp 5.9-litre American Chrysler V8, with a choice of manual or automatic transmission and a top speed of over 130mph (209kph). In 1965 Jensen offered the CV8FF with Ferguson four-wheel-drive and Maxaret anti-lock brakes and by 1966 the CV8 offered up to 6.3 litres and 330bhp.

The Jensen brothers were by then approaching retirement. Allan retired as an executive director in 1963 but stayed on the board, and Richard resigned as chairman three years later, before leaving the board completely in 1967.

There were also changes coming for the cars. Kevin Beattie, formerly with Humber and with Rootes in Australia, had taken over from Richard Jensen as chief engineer in January 1960 and in 1965 he joined the Jensen board. He sought to modernize Jensen's image and consulted Touring, Vignale and Ghia on styling ideas before settling on a Touring design to be built by Vignale for the next generation Jensen.

Beattie eventually brought Vignale's body tooling to Britain and the new car was introduced in 1966 as the Interceptor, with 6.2-litre Chrysler V8 and 140mph (153kph) performance, plus the option of the Ferguson/Maxaret systems on the Interceptor FF, which sold for a hefty £5340. The FF would remain in production until 1972.

Jensen Interceptor Series III of c.1973

Coinciding with the new introductions were serious financial problems for the company. Jensen had been building bodies for Rootes (some 7500 for the Ford V8-powered Sunbeam Tiger), but the Chrysler takeover ended Alpine production in 1967, when the big Healey was also being phased out. The workforce was cut right back, from 1400 to 400, but car sales alone were not enough to support the company. A £183,000 profit from 1966 turned to a £52,000 loss in 1967. In June 1968 the merchant bank William Brandt bought all the shares in Jensen and appointed Alfred Vickers as general manager to seek new sales possibilities.

Vickers contacted Kjell Qvale, an American west coast car dealer who specialized in British quality and performance cars and who had previously sold the Austin-Healey; he too was looking for new possibilities and the tie up was logical. Qvale, with the co-operation of Brandt, bought a major shareholding and appointed Donald Healey and his son Geoffrey to the Jensen board. Healey was set to work to design an Austin-Healey replacement acceptable to both the American and home markets and to give Jensen a volume production car alongside the expensive Interceptor.

The Jensen-Healey was introduced at the Geneva Show in 1972, in which year Jensen profits had climbed back to £200,000. The
260

prototype had used a 2.3-litre overhead-cam four-cylinder Vauxhall engine but production cars used a Lotus developed 16-valve slant four. The engine was always problematic and tended to be noisy and unreliable. In any case the Jensen-Healey had an identity problem for it was hard to think of it as either a Jensen or a Healey. It was not the success that the company desperately needed with a projected output of 150 to 200 cars a week and the onset of the oil crisis was slowing Interceptor sales to a trickle. The Jensen-Healey GT Estate, introduced in 1975 at £4198, sold well initially but not for long.

On 15 September 1975, against a background of labour problems, the oil crisis, increasing US legislation but with a full order book, Jensen, vainly seeking £5 million for its

1976 programme, went into receivership and its 600 workers were laid off. Most of its assets were auctioned but made only £33,000 and the company was finally closed in May 1976 – but that was not quite the end.

In 1976 the receiver set up an independent company, Jensen Parts & Service Ltd, which evolved into International Motor Importers, which handled such imports as Subaru, Hyundai and Maserati. In 1981 this company moved out of the old works to new premises and in 1983 the original Jensen Parts & Services, which had hitherto been restoring and converting existing cars at the rate of around one a year, announced that it could also build 'new' Interceptors, precisely to the 1972 designs, to order for about £25,000. BL

JEWEL/JEWELL

see Croxton

JEWETT

see Paige-Detroit

JOMAR

see TVR

JORDAN
USA 1916-1931

'The legendary Jordan cars were never so much automobiles as they were a state of mind', wrote historian Tim Howley, encapsulating the make's appeal and its place in history. An assembled car of no great originality, the Jordan is remembered not for its engineering and only a little for its styling, but for its colour schemes and its advertising – both the work of its maker, Ned Jordan.

Edward S. Jordan was born in 1882 and worked his way through college as a reporter on the *Wisconsin State Journal*. His entry into the world of cars came in 1906 when he joined the Thomas B. Jeffery Co, rising to general manager and marrying one of the Jeffery daughters. In 1916 he left Jeffery taking two key men with him, and succeeded in raising $300,000 from bankers in Chicago and Cleveland, where he built a factory in four months.

The first Jordan cars left the assembly line in August 1916, and sales began in September. They were conventional tourers and roadsters powered by a 29.4hp six-cylinder Continental engine, with Brown-Lipe clutch, Gemmer steering and other components by well-known proprietary firms. The aluminium bodies were made by Jordan.

Ned Jordan's flair for words first became evident on the 1918 Sport Marine model, with colours of Briarcliff Green, Ascot Maroon or Liberty Blue, and in 1919 came the first Playboy, a pert two-seater roadster available in Copenhagen Blue, Burgundy Old Wine and other colourfully-named hues. Just about the only colour unobtainable was black.

Fancy names for colours are widespread today but they were an innovation in 1919, as were the beautifully-written atmospheric advertisements that Jordan composed in the 1920s: 'A Million Miles from Dull Care', 'The Port of Missing Men' and most famous of all, 'Somewhere West of Laramie'. They were not, as Jordan claimed, the first car advertisements 'to get away from nuts and bolts', for Cadillac had done the same thing in 1915, but they captured the public imagination and helped sales exceed 11,000 in 1926. Jordan was also a pioneer in labour relations, inviting all employees to own stock in the company and making cash gifts to their wives.

Profits and stock rose during the first half of the 1920s, and at the beginning of 1924 company assets were well over $3 million. The Continental six-cylinder engine was still used on all models, but in August 1924 Jordan announced its 'Model A Line Eight', powered by a 74bhp straight-eight engine. This was made by Continental but to Jordan's specifications, the jigs, dies and patterns belonging to Jordan.

For 1926 all models were straight-eights, but then came the Little Custom, an attempt to enter the quality small car market. Unfortu-

Jordan Series E six-cylinder saloon of 1929

nately, as Templar and others had found, there was little demand for this class of car, and the Continental six-powered Little Custom did not sell.

In 1927 Jordan made 10,527 cars but 4000 of these were unsold by the year's end. The company registered its first loss, nearly $1.5 million. It built some very handsome cars in its last three years, culminating in the 5.3-litre 115bhp Continental-powered Speedway Eight, with Woodlite headlights and aeroplane-type instrument panel. Priced from $5000, nearly double the figure for other Jordans, they were quite the wrong cars for 1930 and very few were sold.

For 1931 Jordan concentrated on the more modest straight-eights, priced between $1775 and $2795, but production ended in March 1931. A further 265 cars were assembled up to August 1931 and a year later the factory was sold to a company making vacuum cleaners.

Ned Jordan moved to New York and became involved in advertising and public relations. Perhaps his own epitaph on the Jordan Motor Car Co sums it up best: 'The answer is we were never automobile manufacturers. We were pioneers of a new technique in assembly production, custom, style, sales and advertising.' He died in 1958. GNG

JOWETT
GB 1906-1953

Ben and William Jowett were born in 1877 and 1880 respectively in Bradford, Yorkshire. Their father made gas engines. After working at a local mill, they set up in business as bicycle-makers in 1902 with £90 capital. From 1904 they made engines for cars and for Scott motorcycles.

In 1906 they registered their first complete car, which had the horizontally-opposed twin engine that was to be the Jowett hallmark. Their weekly wage bill in 1907 was £9 8s. Car production did not begin seriously until 1910, when the Jowett Motor Manufacturing Co was formed.

During World War I munitions, particularly fuses, were mass-produced. In 1920 the firm became Jowett Cars Ltd, a private company with £30,000 capital, and moved to Idle, near Bradford.

Jowetts were particularly popular in the north of England and attempts were made to limit production to 25 a week in the 1920s to keep the family firm to a manageable size. Actual production grew from 249 in 1921 to 2223 in 1925, at which average level it stayed until 1934. The Jowett factory was destroyed by fire in 1930, but rebuilt by early 1931. In the year September 1933 to August 1934 a pre-war peak of 3134 vehicles were made, including 1314 commercial derivatives. Production then fell back slowly to 1972 in 1939.

The works manager at this time was Harry Mitchell, who had come from the makers of ABC motorcycles. Gladney Haigh ran the

publicity side of the business with a series of famous advertisements making the most of the humble Jowett's homely qualities compared with its flashy competitors from the south – and omitting to mention that wages in Bradford were about half those of Coventry. S. C. Poole was chief designer from 1928, having spent eight years with Singer and gained earlier experience with Wolseley, Standard and Clyno since 1907.

In 1935 Jowett Cars Ltd was publicly floated and the Jowett brothers soon withdrew from the firm. William concentrated on the Jowett-engined Bristol crawler tractor, which was produced until the 1960s, in later years having Austin and Perkins engines.

Some £5 million worth of machine tools and munitions were produced by Jowett during World War II, and in 1942 Gerald Palmer joined to design the post-war Jowett Javelin with 1½-litre flat-four engine and streamlined body. Palmer had worked under O. D. North at Scammell and later on for the Nuffield Organization.

The workforce rose from 500 in 1939 to 2000 at the end of the war and then fell back to 1600 by 1951. The first all-new design, a fastback four-cylinder saloon, was ready in 1945, when Jowett was bought by financier Charles Clore, but he sold out to Lazards Bank two years later; the other principal shareholders were the Green family, well known light-engineers in Leeds. Lazards appointed as chairman George Wansborough, who would later give financial backing to the Gordon-Keeble project.

The Jupiter, a sports derivative of the Javelin, was developed from an ERA prototype produced by Dr Eberan von Eberhorst – formerly of Porsche, Auto-Union and Cisitalia – and was launched in 1950. This model was supposed to sell at half the volume of the Javelin to boost exports and also assure an adequate government steel quota. Yet profits fell by £200,000 to £128,000 in the year to March 1951 and Jupiter output in the company's entire life was just 902 cars. Javelin production reached a peak of 5500 in 1951 and in all 23,000 were built. The pre-war twin lived on in the Jowett Bradford van, which sold 43,000 in total to the end of production in 1953, when its little-changed engine had been in production for 50 years.

Jowett 'Long Four' of 1925

Jowett 907cc tourer of 1928

Joint managing director after William Jowett's retirement in 1939 was Calcott Reilly, who left for Cyclemaster in 1949. Roy Lunn from AC and Aston-Martin replaced Palmer as designer, Palmer returning to Nuffield and then moving on to Vauxhall.

In 1952 Lunn went to Ford, Dagenham, and then Detroit. He worked on the GT40 before switching to American Motors; in 1983 he was running the Renault-Jeep operation. Donald Bastow, who had worked for Daimler, Rolls-Royce, Armstrong-Siddeley and BSA, became chief engineer in 1952. Frank Salter, formerly of General Motors, Hendon, Standard and Rootes, was production director at Jowett after 1945 and on the board from 1952.

Pressings and bodywork for Jowett vehicles came from a Briggs factory in Doncaster, which also made parts for Lanchester, but following slow payment and stockpiled bodies, Briggs refused further orders from Jowett, which had tooled up for the first 5000 of a four-cylinder Bradford in December 1952. In February 1953 Ford bought Briggs, which was paid in full by Jowett in June – but no more orders were accepted.

A plastic-bodied R4 Jupiter was prepared in July, but Lazards then decided to cease all production. Donald Bastow left for Coventry-Climax, which considered buying Jowett for the R4 project. John Baldwin, the post-war publicity manager, moved to Rover, and many dealers switched allegiance to the newly imported Volkswagen.

The Jowett Cars factory passed to International Harvester and all debts were subsequently paid in full. The firm then made spares and in 1958 became Jowett Engineering Ltd, its workforce of 100 primarily involved in the manufacture of aircraft components for Blackburn and General, which acquired the remnants of the firm. By 1963 Jowett was part of the Hawker-Siddeley group and in 1983 the former Jowett factory was demolished. NB

JUNIOR
see OTAV

Jowett Jupiter sports two-seater of 1950

Jowett Javelin saloon of c.1947

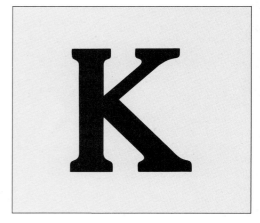

KAISER-FRAZER
USA 1946-1955

The title of Richard Langworth's history of Kaiser-Frazer, *Last Onslaught on Detroit*, says it all, for it was indeed the last time a new company attempted to challenge the automotive giants for a significant slice of the mass production popular car market. The founders were not complete strangers to car manufacture for one of the partners, Joseph W. Frazer, had been president of Willys-Overland and then Graham-Paige. He teamed up with Henry J. Kaiser, who had built 1490 Liberty, Victory and other ships during World War II, and they set up manufacture in Willow Run, the world's largest bomber factory which Henry Ford had built specifically for the production of Liberators.

The cars were to be built in two series, both powered by 3.7-litre six-cylinder Continental engines, the cheaper front-drive Kaiser and the more expensive rear-drive Frazer. In the event, only prototypes of the front-wheel-drive car were made, and when production began in October 1946 both cars had rear-wheel-drive and very similar bodies with slabsided styling by Howard 'Dutch' Darrin.

Kaiser prices ran from $1868 to $2301, and Frazer from $2053 to $2550, which put them in the same range as the Buick Super and Roadmaster and well above the low price three, Ford, Chevrolet and Plymouth. Nevertheless they sold well, totalling 144,490 in the calendar year 1947 and 181,316 in 1948. These figures put them eighth in the United States production league, the highest of any independent company. Profits were nearly $20 million in 1947 and $10 million in 1948.

Both makes were restyled in 1949, and two significant new body styles were introduced that year. One was the Kaiser Traveler and Vagabond hatchback sedan which gave the advantages of a station wagon without the need for expensive dies for a new body shape. (Kaiser-Frazer never offered a conventional station wagon.) The other was the four-door convertible, the first post-war American car of this pattern, sold as a Frazer Manhattan or Kaiser De Luxe. There was also the Kaiser

Virginian four-door hard top.

Unfortunately none of these sold very well, for 1949 was the year for which the Big Three brought out their all-new post-war cars, whereas the Kaiser-Frazers were only mildly restyled 48s. Sales dropped to 57,995, putting the group 17th in the production league. The company had to borrow $69 million from the Reconstruction Finance Corporation to keep moving with new models. Relations between Kaiser and Frazer, seldom very cordial, broke over the question of retrenchment – 'the Kaisers never retrench', said HJK – and Frazer stepped down, though for appearances' sake he remained with the company in the nominal position of vice-chairman.

Much of the Reconstruction Finance Corporation loan was earmarked for the development of a new, low price small car christened the Henry J and intended to fulfil the role of a latter day Model T Ford. It was a two-door sedan powered by a choice of four- or six-cylinder Willys engines; with the latter it had quite a lively performance but it was stark in specification, early models having no exterior access to the boot.

Despite a targeted price of $1000, it cost $1363 when it reached the showrooms for the 1951 season, less than $100 below the cheapest Chevrolet. A large market for a cheap compact car did not exist at the time, and in fact the De Luxe model at $1499 outsold the Standard sedan.

An interesting offshoot of the Henry J was the Allstate, built exclusively for sale by Sears Roebuck, the mammoth mail order company which was developing new car shops adjacent to its retail stores. The Allstate had different grille and more luxurious trim, with Sears' own brands of tyres, batteries and sparking plugs. Despite the extra quality the Allstate was very competitively priced, the cheapest Four costing $12 less than the equivalent Henry J.

Allstates were marketed for the 1952 and 1953 seasons, but sales were very disappointing, possibly because the promotion concentrated on south-eastern states, although it was available nationwide through the Sears Roebuck catalogue. Only 2363 had been sold when Sears cancelled the contract early in 1953.

Apart from the Henry J, Kaiser-Frazer had a brand new full size car for the 1951 season, with striking body styling that featured a greatly increased glass area compared to its nearest competitor and a lower belt line than any production US car made before 1956. This was the Kaiser, made in two- and four-door sedan versions; the Frazer was less extravagantly restyled but it did have a new grille. Unfortunately what neither car had was a new engine, although the old Continental six was now giving 115hp. The lack of a V8 in the range was an increasingly serious drawback for Kaiser-Frazer, which was competing against such makes as Buick, Olds and Mercury, all of which had V8 engines by 1952. The Frazer line was dropped after 1951.

The company struggled on with the Kaiser Manhattan and the Henry J through to 1954, when it merged with the Willys Overland Corporation of Toledo, Ohio, to form Kaiser-Willys. The Willow Run plant was sold to General Motors and Kaiser production transferred to Toledo. The only significant change was the adoption of a McCullough supercharger on the Manhattan, boosting power to 140bhp. The Henry J was dropped for 1955 after a total production of about 130,000.

A new model for 1954 was the Kaiser Darrin 161, a two-seater sports car with fibreglass body styled by Howard Darrin. Production began at Kaiser's Jackson, Michigan, warehouse and was then transferred to Toledo along with the other cars. The 161 was dropped at the end of 1954, after 435 units had been made, but Darrin purchased 50 bodies and chassis and fitted them with Cadillac engines. These were sold as Darrins from his Los Angeles premises from 1955 to 1958.

The move to Toledo only delayed the end for Kaiser-Frazer, and in the spring of 1955 the board announced the end of the Kaiser car in America (and also, incidentally, the end of Willys passenger car production). The last onslaught on Detroit had failed, as much as anything because of the greater unit cost of tooling and advertising a new model for a 100,000 car run compared to that for a million car run such as the Big Three were accustomed to. Kaiser-Frazer made no profit after 1948 and the company's losses over seven years amounted to more than $92 million.

Export activities had always played an important part of Kaiser-Frazer, which had assembly plants in Holland, Israel, India and Japan. In 1955 a contract was signed with the Argentine government to form Industrias Kaiser Argentina SA (IKA) to make Jeeps and Kaiser sedans in Buenos Aires. This gave the 1955 Kaiser design a further seven years' life. The Kaiser-Frazer Corporation name was changed to Kaiser Industries Corporation, which continued to be active in engineering and the sand and gravel industries. GNG

KEETON
see Croxton

KELLER/BOBBI-KAR, PLM
USA, BELGIUM 1945-1954

The Bobbi Motor Car Corporation was founded in San Diego, California, in 1945 by S. A. Williams with the oft expressed intention of building an economy car for the American market. Several prototype versions of the Bobbi-Kar were built, all with glassfibre bodies. The coupé had a removable steel hard top and a rear engine but the other models, a saloon and a station wagon (with real wood trim), were powered by front-mounted four-cylinder 25bhp engines. The Bobbi-Kar also featured a novel, all-independent suspension system of torsion bars bonded in rubber, developed by the B. F. Goodrich tyre company and known as Torsilastic.

Unfortunately the Bobbi-Kar did not make it into production before legal difficulties in California over the financing of the company forced Bobbi to relocate in Birmingham, Alabama, in 1947 as the Bobbi Motor Car Corporation (Dixie Motor Car Corporation). The company was then taken over in 1948 by George D. Keller, a former sales vice-president of Studebaker, as the George D. Keller Motors Corporation of Huntsville, Alabama.

Keller redesigned the Bobbi-Kar, retaining the basic concept but with more 'conventional' body styling and larger Continental engines, at first of 49bhp but later of 58bhp. The cars were available in two series, Chief and Super Chief, and three models, a convertible, saloon and station wagon, of which, again, only the convertible had a rear engine.

George Keller expected to build up to a production of 6000 cars a month. He quickly established a network of some 1500 dealers, but in October 1949 he died suddenly of a heart attack after only 18 Keller cars had been made.

The designs were briefly taken up by a Belgian industrialist called Poelemans, who founded Montages Automobiles PLM in Merksen, Antwerp, and in 1953 and 1954 assembled a few of the Keller-designed station wagons with 2650cc Continental engines and Borg-Warner gearboxes. Poelemans planned to build these and other Keller designs in volume and to sell the cars very cheaply, but he was no more successful than the two previous owners and production stopped for good in 1954. BL

KENDALL
GB 1945-1946

Formerly head of Citroën's body plant, Dennis Kendall was in charge of a factory at Grantham, Lincolnshire, making Hispano-Suiza 20mm cannon used in Hurricane and Spitfire fighters. He was elected as Independent MP for Grantham in 1943 and the town had high hopes of his plans to mass produce cars and tractors in the armaments factory.

His first project was designed by Horace Beaumont and was an unusual little car powered by a three-cylinder radial engine. In an attempt to keep the price down to the magical figure of £100 it dispensed with such features as a synchromesh gearbox and electric starter, and had only one headlamp. It seems to have been a very unsatisfactory performer, and Kendall never even managed to drive it to London to show to fellow MPs.

Having abandoned the Beaumont design – Horace Beaumont was later jailed for fraud in connection with an electric car – Kendall then took up the Aluminium Française Gré-

Kieft Formula 3 car (Stirling Moss driving) of 1951

goire, Jean Grégoire's flat twin front-wheel-drive car which eventually went into production as the Dyna-Panhard. For this project he claimed to have the backing of an Indian maharajah and the British government, but he could not obtain adequate supplies of steel or components and very few cars were made at Grantham.

In November 1946 the factory was closed with the loss of 1000 jobs, and despite rumours of a £300,000 rescue operation by a City group, it never reopened. The designs and some tools were acquired by the Australian Lawrence Hartnett, who made some cars of Grégoire design in Melbourne for a short period in the early 1950s. GNG

KIBLINGER/IMP, McINTYRE
USA 1906-1916

Founded towards the end of the 19th century, the W. H. Kiblinger Co of Auburn, Indiana, entered the motor field in 1906 with six different high-wheelers starting at a modest $250 for a 4hp single and going up to $450 for a 10hp twin. They had air-cooling and planetary transmission. In 1909 the motor buggies were renamed McIntyre after the wagon-builder W. H. McIntyre, established in 1880, had assumed control of Kiblinger.

McIntyre introduced a 32hp four-cylinder buggy followed by more conventional cars and commercial vehicles, the latter including models of up to 5 tons capacity in 1913. A Canadian associate named Tudhope-McIntyre Co of Orillia marketed the vehicles in Canada and the Auburn Motor Chassis Co of Auburn continued to make high-wheelers looking suspiciously like McIntyres for two years after they had disappeared from the McIntyre range in 1912.

From 1913 a six-cylinder car was offered, as was the V-twin air-cooled Imp cyclecar. The Imp was soon refined with a four-cylinder water-cooled unit and was joined by a 25hp Golden, Belknap and Swartz powered four. The six was by then known as the Hoosier, a nickname for Indiana. William H. Kiblinger was made personally bankrupt in 1915 and his firm followed suit in 1916. NB

264

KIEFT
GB 1950-1961

Cyril Kieft founded Kieft Cars Ltd in Bridgend, Glamorgan, in 1950 to build racing cars for the popular 500cc Formula 3 class. The first Formula 3 Kieft was designed by Ray Martin, Dean Delamont (later competitions director of the Royal Automobile Club) and John A. Cooper (technical editor of *The Autocar*). It had a Norton engine and swing axle suspension.

Stirling Moss, at the start of his career, scored many race wins for Kieft in 1950 and with a revised car in 1951, and racing success brought enough demand to turn Kieft into a commercial constructor. The company briefly tried a small rear-engined sports car in 1952, with a 650cc BSA engine, but demand for the JAP, Norton and Vincent engined racing and hillclimb cars prevented its development.

In 1953 Kieft Cars Ltd moved to new works in Wolverhampton and expanded its operations. These included a new sports racing model, designed for Kieft by Raymond Flower, who also designed the Egyptian-built Phoenix sports racing, sports and mini cars and the Meadows Frisky which evolved from the last of these. The sports racing Kieft had a multi-tubular spaceframe with removable alloy body, three seats (with the driver central) and, initially, a 1½-litre MG engine.

The car was not very successful and was soon replaced by a lighter and more conventional front-engined model in 1954 with 'right-hand drive' and the brand new Coventry-Climax 1100 four-cylinder engine. This was hardly more successful but was the basis of the only model offered specifically for the road, during 1955-56. It sold for about £1500 and was offered at $3250, ex-works, in the United States.

In fact the company ceased trading for much of 1955 but was reorganized in 1956 and moved into new premises in Birmingham, where the main work was tuning but where the 110mph (177kph) Climax-engined 1100 sports was revived. Another car, with aerodynamic body and tuned Austin A50 engine, was planned but never produced. Other stillborn Kieft projects included a Coventry-Climax engined Formula 1 car (dropped because the 2½-litre V8 Godiva engine was never fully developed) and a 2-litre flat-four engined sports car, the engine for which was designed by Ronald Mead using mostly Norton components.

Kieft was taken over by racing driver Lionel Mayman and his rally driver wife Pauline who in 1960 laid down a production line of 50 rear-engined FJ racing cars designed by Ron Timmins. In spite of some promising showings by the works cars, few were sold in a very competitive market. As a consequence of this lack of sales, the company was closed down in 1961. BL

KING
USA 1910-1924

Charles B. King, born in 1868 at Angel Island, California, attended Cornell University and then worked for railway wagon firms. He started his own business in 1894 in Detroit, having developed pneumatic hammers, railway brakes and a motorized tricycle with Sintz engine in 1893.

He rented facilities from an engineering company and made a four-cylinder engine with detachable head. In 1896 he drove a carriage equipped with this engine before selling the design of the engine to the Buffalo Gasoline Engine Co and a complete two-cylinder car to Byron J. Carter of Cartercar. He made gears, engines, wheels and many other parts for the Detroit pioneers, including Henry Ford.

King served with the USS *Yosemite* in the Spanish-American war and afterwards sold his marine engine business to Olds in 1900. He worked for Olds until 1902, when he became co-founder and chief designer at Northern, where he remained until 1908.

After two years studying European methods he started the King Motor Car Co in Detroit in 1909. From 1910 this company made cheap, four-cylinder cars with monobloc engines and in-unit gearboxes with centre change. It soon adopted the slogan 'The car of no regrets'.

In 1912 Charles B. King left the firm, with no regrets, and took with him his patents. These he proceeded to sell to numerous firms including General Motors and Reo. During World War I he designed and built aero engines – including 2000 under licence from Bugatti – and helped develop the Liberty engine, the name of which he is credited with coining. He later became one of the first automotive historians and built up an important archive.

King V8 tourer of c.1920

The King Motor Car Co adopted Park Leonard electric lighting and starting in 1914, the year it also produced America's second V8. Only V8 models were made from 1916, when production was planned at 10,000 for the year, although chassis numbers suggest that fewer than 4000 were actually made, the same as in 1914 and 1915. Artemas Ward was president by then, the vice-president being E. A. Barthel, who had started his career with Olds in 1902. Salmons, the British body-builders, sold Kings with their own coach-work before and after the war, including one to the Earl of Medina in 1920.

Chassis numbers ran from 16,001 at the start of 1917 to 50,000 by the end of 1919, but far fewer cars were actually built – and con-sisted of 26 and 29hp V8s. In 1923 King moved to a smaller factory in Buffalo, New York, and fewer than 250 cars were made that year. The final year of production was 1924, although old stock was sold in England until 1926. NB

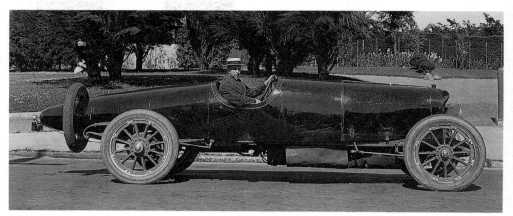

Kissel Kar torpedo racer of c.1915

KING MIDGET
USA 1947-1969

King Midget of c.1964

The early post-war years saw a large crop of American midget cars, most of which dis-appeared within a year or two. The one ex-ception was the King Midget, of which about 5000 were made in a 22-year life span. It was developed by Claude Dry and Dale Orcutt of Athens, Ohio, who leased a two-storey super-market which they furnished with war surplus machine tools. From 1945 to 1947 they made motor scooters and then launched the King Midget.

The first model was a single-seater which resembled a midget racing car, powered by a rear-mounted single cylinder 6hp Wisconsin engine. For the first year or two it was only available as a kit, at the very low price of $270. Dry was a Linotype mechanic and Orcutt a maintenance supervisor in a trouser factory, and the partners ran Midget Motors Corpora-tion in their spare time until 1949, when sales of the Midget justified their becoming full time car manufacturers.

In 1951 the car was completely redesigned with a two-seater body and cloth top and a larger Wisconsin engine of 7½hp (376cc). Kits were still available but a complete car cost $550. This model attracted more cus-tomers, and for a while production ran at 90 cars a month. Even so, the company was never in a position to employ more than 21 workers.

The only important changes beween 1951 and 1969 were the adoption in 1958 of a new body with doors, and in 1967 of a larger en-gine, a 476cc Kohler developing 12bhp. By this time kits were no longer offered and inflation had brought the price up to $1095. In 1961 a body-less version called the Driver Training Car was offered for driving instruc-tion in schools.

Dry and Orcutt sold out to a group of east coast businessmen in 1966, although they stayed on to give technical advice. The presi-dent put in by the new owners was Joseph C. Stehlin Jr, but he had little luck with the com-pany as the appeal of the crude, harsh-riding little car was running out. In 1969 Midget Motors was sold to Vernon Eaads who plan-ned to revive production in Hollywood, Florida. He went bankrupt before any cars were made there. GNG

KISSEL
USA 1906-1930

The Kissel family were well established in Hartford Plow Works and the Hartford Electric appeared in 1906. The father Louis Kissel was a German immigrant who had a prosperous hardware and grocery business, and with his four sons Adolph, Otto, William and George, controlled the Kissel Manufacturing Co, the Hartford Plow Works and the Hartford Electric Co. The two youngest brothers, Will and George, set up the Kissel Motor Car Co in 1906 after building an experimental car in the family farm implement factory the previous year.

The first model was a conventional shaft-driven machine powered by a 35hp Beaver engine, with bodies from Zimmerman Bros of Waupun, Wisconsin. The name Kisselkar was suggested by the wife of the Milwaukee distributor; this became Kissel Kar from 1908 to 1918, and thereafter plain Kissel.

In 1907 the new company received an order for 100 cars from a Chicago distributor, and during the next two years the team was reinforced by two gifted engineers, both of German origin. Herman Palmer came to Hart-ford as a cellist in a small orchestra, but he soon joined Kissel and remained with this and successor companies until 1956. J. Fried-rich Werner was a skilled carpenter who had

There is satisfaction in the ownership of a KisselKar

YOU'LL be proud to own a KisselKar—and your pride is justified in the knowledge that it is an automobile of consistent performance. Every tried and tested feature in automobile construction is embodied in it. The stand-up records of the thousands of KisselKars in use is a striking demon-stration of what can be accomplished by the right application of mechanics and skillful workmanship.

KisselKar

In appearance, comfort, silence and ability the KisselKar is unsurpassed—in innumerable details and refinements it is an immeasurably superior automobile. The liberal wheelbase, empha-sizing the long low effect of the body and unusually roomy tonneau and deep seats, give the KisselKar a distinction not surpassed

even by the highest priced automobiles. The KisselKar Catalog describes and illustrates the three models; 60 "Six" at $3150; 48 "Six" $2350; 40 "Four" $1850. Eleven types of bodies. All fully equipped, electric lighted and started, left hand drive, center control. If you are in-terested, write for this catalog.

Service Contract

The KisselKar is sold under a written guarantee of service to owners—a definite contract that plainly stipulates the scope of KisselKar service. The unusual facilities at the KisselKar Service Stations, at all principal points, are always at the disposal of owners of KisselKars and KisselKar Trucks.

KISSELKAR TRUCKS—six sizes—1500 lbs. 1—1½—2½ 3½—6 tons. Big illustrated portfolio sent on request.

Kissel Motor Car Company, 135 Kissel Ave., Hartford, Wis.

BOSTON, NEW YORK, CHICAGO, MILWAUKEE, KANSAS CITY, MINNEAPOLIS, ST. PAUL, DALLAS, SAN FRANCISCO, LOS ANGELES, OAKLAND, Philadelphia, Detroit, Houston, El Paso, New Orleans, Washington, Baltimore, Nashville, Louisville, Duluth, Buf-falo, Pittsburgh, Hartford, Conn.; New Haven, Albany, Troy, Rochester, Providence, St. Louis, Marshalltown, Iowa; Omaha, Hast-ings, Neb.; Madison, Montreal, Quebec, Toronto, Winnipeg, Calgary, and 800 other principal points throughout America.

Kissel Kar tourer of c.1909

worked for Opel and who was in charge of Kissel's body department for more than 20 years.

Commercial bodies were mounted on the car chassis from 1908, and in 1910 Kissel launched a line of purpose-built truck chas-sis up to 5 tons capacity, with chain drive on the larger models. These used Waukesha or Wisconsin engines, while most passenger car engines were made by Kissel itself, apart from a short-lived V12 by Weidely in 1917-1918. A 60hp Big Six joined the range in 1909, and in 1915 came the company's first mono-bloc six, the 6-38 or Hundred Point Six, promoted as 'The Car with a Hundred Quality Features'.

Kissel was a leader in body design, thanks to Friedrich Werner, offering an all-weather top which made a snug sedan in winter but could be removed to leave the car an open tourer in the summer. This 'All Year Gibraltar' body was available from 1915 to 1921. In 1918 a New York dealer named Conover T. Silver produced some exciting speedster designs for Kissel and Apperson cars. Four-seaters were built on both chassis, and in 1918 came the Silver Special Kissel, a rakish two-seater

Kissel White Eagle 8 of 1929

with wire wheels and auxiliary outrigger seats which could be folded out of drawers just behind the doors. This layout was later copied by Marmon and Paige. In 1919 a yellow coloured speedster was nicknamed the Gold Bug, and this stuck for all subsequent speedsters although it was always unofficial.

The Kissel factory was active in truck production during World War I, being given over entirely to manufacture of the FWD four-wheel-drive 3-tonner. Kissel engineers, like those from many other American vehicle builders, contributed to the design of the standardized Liberty trucks.

During the 1920s Kissels were among the most handsome of American cars, although they never sold in large numbers. From a very low figure of 506 units in 1920 sales rose to a peak of 2024 cars and 99 trucks in 1923. In 1921 a $750,000 mortgage had to be taken out against property and machinery.

Up to 1924 two sizes of Kissel-built six – 4.3 and 4.7 litres – were the only engines quoted, but for 1925 the company offered a 4.7-litre straight-eight which used a Lycoming block with Kissel's own aluminium head. This was available in three wheelbases and the same body styles as the sixes. Because of development work on the straight-eight, sales dropped in 1924 to only 803 units but they picked up again to 2122 in 1925. There were rumours of a merger between Kissel and its much larger Wisconsin neighbour, Nash of Kenosha, but nothing came of the scheme.

From 1926 sales dropped alarmingly, and even the introduction of new lines such as funeral cars and ambulances failed to stem the decline. From a total of 1972 vehicles in 1926, sales dropped to 889 three years later, of which 285 were taxicabs and 200 funeral cars. The taxis were sold under the name Bradfield and New Yorker, but the distributor for the latter never paid Kissel for them, which added to the company's problems.

The final line of cars was called White Eagle by Kissel and featured flat-topped La Salle-type radiators in place of the rounded design which had been an identifying mark of the Kissel since 1918. Palmer's 'Hundred Point Six' engine was dropped in favour of two sizes of Lycoming-based eights and a Lycoming six.

The last year of production was 1930, when just 221 vehicles were delivered comprising 93 passenger cars, 77 funeral cars, 49 taxicabs and 2 trucks. Of the cars about 20 were sixes and the balance eights. Kissel would probably not have survived for many years longer anyway, but an agreement in March 1930 with Archie Andrews' New Era Motors simply hastened the end.

Andrews was promoting the front-wheel-drive Ruxton car and persuaded George Kissel to agree to make 1500 Ruxtons annually, as well as five Kissel cars, one funeral car and one taxicab daily for the rest of 1930. In return he promised $250,000 in new finance, but only $100,000 ever materialized and Kissel could not meet its production commitments.

In September 1930, rather than come under the control of New Era Motors, George Kissel filed for voluntary receivership. He had never made any complete Ruxtons, although the Hartford factory turned out a number of final drive assemblies which were shipped to the Moon plant at St Louis where the Ruxton was being put together. A few Kissels were made under receivership, and models for 1931 were even announced, but no cars were built after December 1930. A few Bradfield cabs were made during the first months of 1931.

The company was reorganized as Kissel Industries and built some experimental Powell-Lever engines which were tested on Kissel cars. Thereafter Kissel Industries made chains, replacement cylinder heads for Fords and Chevrolets, outboard motors and, with the approach of World War II, torpedo parts.

George Kissel died in October 1942, and 16 months later Will sold the business to the West Bend Aluminium Co, which specialized in outboard motors. It retained the premises until 1965 when they were sold to the Chrysler Corporation's outboard division. GNG

KLINE KAR
USA 1910-1923

James A. Kline was born in Pennsylvania in 1877 and brought up on a farm. He worked briefly as an optician before opening a machine shop in Harrisburg in 1899. That year he saw a Locomobile steam car demonstrated in New York and ordered one, finally taking delivery after a long wait.

Kline serviced and modified the Locomobile himself and learned much about motor engineering from it. Some of the suggestions for improvements which he passed on to Locomobile were actually taken up by the company and in 1901 Kline obtained the Locomobile dealership for Harrisburg. He sold several cars and at the same time built four steam cars to his own designs, apparently almost entirely in-house.

In 1902, after Locomobile had stopped steam car production, he took an agency to sell the popular Oldsmobile runabout and he sold some 200 in the next two years. He also sold Franklins but gave up his agencies in about 1904.

In 1905, backed by a group of local businessmen, Broomell, Schmidt and Steacy (who had built a rather impractical six-wheeled car called the Pullman since 1903) Kline formed the York Motor Car Co in York, Pennsylvania. He designed a four-wheel four-cylinder five-seater surrey, which was in production by the end of the year as the York but which had reverted to being called a Pullman by 1907.

Kline sold his own interest in Pullman in 1909 and with Samuel E. Bailey and Joseph C. Carrell formed the BCK Motor Co in York, based in what had once been Bailey's carriage works. He designed a six-cylinder 40hp car which was launched in 1910 as the Kline Kar which sold well and scored several wins in dirt track races.

In April 1911 the thriving company was bought by a group of businessmen from Richmond, Virginia, and reorganized as the Kline Motor Car Corporation with capital of $200,000. An 80,000sq ft (7400sq m) factory was completed in Richmond in November 1912 and production was transferred, although engines to Kline's designs were now built by the Kirkham Machine Co of Bath, New York, rather than in-house.

In 1912 Kline advertised four- and six-cylinder models from 30 to 60hp as tourers and speedsters and these conventional models continued until World War I. The Kline factory was taken over by the American Locomotive Co during the war to make war materials, which forced Kline to move to a temporary factory.

The company resumed production with models ranging in price from $1095 to $3500 but efforts to break into the low-cost market failed as only about 600 of the cheapest 6-36 model were sold. As sales went down Kline, without the reserves of the bigger companies, was compelled to increase prices rather than cut them.

By 1921 the Kline was little more than an assembled car, the 6-55 for instance using a Continental engine, and by 1922 the financial problems were so bad that the decision was taken to close the factory. The company was not officially wound up until 1924 and it continued to provide parts and service for a while, but there was no effort to resume production. James Kline died in 1944. BL

R & V KNIGHT
see Moline

KNOX/ATLAS, LYONS
USA 1899-1914

Harry A. Knox built experimental four-cylinder opposed internal combustion engines from 1895 and in 1896 developed a car for the Overman Wheel Co, a bicycle-maker of Chicopee Falls, Massachusetts. Overman soon settled for steam, however, the Victor being a short-lived venture that was sold to Locomobile in 1902. Knox, who assisted with the construction of the first batch of Duryeas, formed the Knox Automobile Co in Springfield, Massachusetts, in 1898. His backer was Harry Fisk, who started the tyre firm bearing his name in Chicopee Falls that year.

In 1899 Knox developed an unusual air-cooled car using planetary transmission and screwed-in brass tubes rather than fins to dissipate heat. A total of 12 were made that year and about 100 in 1900. They were initially three-wheelers, but four wheels were adopted in 1901 having single springs on each side, the outer ends being attached to the axles.

By early 1902 output was three to five a week from a new 156,000sq ft (14,500sq m) factory. This expansion was financed by a $1 million share flotation in 1901, when C. L. Goodhue was company president. The car was known as the Waterless Knox or, more familiarly, Old Porcupine but the company rather undermined its credibility when it adopted water-cooling on some models in 1908.

This about-turn followed serious financial difficulties in 1907, when the workforce totalled 600 men, although the firm lasted until 1914 making mostly large and expensive models. A feature was an in-unit engine-gearbox mounted low and in direct line with the back axle, which was claimed to reduce power loss through the universal joints.

Commercial versions of the cars had been built since 1901 and in 1904 Harry A. Knox founded the Knox Motor Truck Co. Although involved in the car firm, he had not been on its board and was in fact employed by Overman Wheel up to 1908.

In 1907 Knox Motor Truck became the Atlas Motor Car Co of Springfield, making two-stroke-engined chassis for use as cars, vans and taxis. It also made proprietary engines which Hudson used in 1909-10. In 1911 the two-strokes were replaced by Knight engines and the resulting Atlas-Knights were built as large touring cars for two years. In 1912-13 James W. Lyons purchased Atlas and Harry A. Knox continued to manage the car business, producing Lyons-Atlas and Lyons-Knight cars. Lyons-Atlas later became the Midwest proprietary engine company.

Charles Hay Martin, who had built a few cars for another Springfield engineer in 1900, had joined the Knox Automobile Co in 1903 to design a 1-ton truck and, after taking time off to develop an articulated coupling, returned to Knox to produce three-wheel tractors incorporating the feature in 1909. These, as well as ordinary trucks and fire engines, sold well and production in 1911 reached about 750. In March 1913 he set up the Martin Tractor Co.

With the winding up of the Knox car firm in 1914 Martin moved to Chicopee Falls and, with help from Harry Fisk, formed Knox Motors Co in 1914 and then the Martin Rocking Fifth Wheel Co in 1916, this latter company named after the peculiar direct coupling system which it developed. There he made four-wheel versions of the tractor, now known as the Knox-Martin, which had hand-hydraulic braking to the trailer. Output in 1914 was quoted as three tractors, 15 traction units and three engines a day.

In 1919 Martin merged with Militor Motors Co, which made Militair pressed-frame motorcycles, in a $2.5 million transaction. N. R. Sinclair was president of the new company, which was known as Knox Motors Associates of Springfield. It built winch tractors and articulated vehicles carrying the Knox-Martin name, but faced increasing competition from better-known truck makers that forced it to cease trading in the mid-1920s. Harry A. Knox had stopped building vehicles in World War I and joined the US Army Ordnance Department. Part of the former Knox works was taken over by American Rolls-Royce to serve as its bodywork drawing office. NB

KOMNICK
GERMANY 1907-1927

The Elbinger Maschinenfabrik at Elbing, formerly in Germany but now in Poland, set up a motor department in 1907 named after the firm's founder, Franz Komnick. Its cars had scuttle-mounted radiators and came in a variety of sizes up to 5.5 litres. The company added heavy lorries in 1913, when the works employed 2000 men, and lorries and army cars were built throughout World War I.

After the war just a 2.1-litre four-cylinder overhead-cam car with front-mounted radiator was produced; but there followed later an assortment of commercial vehicles and motor ploughs produced by the motor department, which in 1922 became Automobilfabrik F. Komnick AG. The motor ploughs were an important sideline and could be bought with Benz diesel engines. Indeed, the Benz and Komnick agricultural machine departments are believed to have merged in the 1920s.

Car production ended in 1927, but lorries, buses and road tractors continued to be made until 1930, when the firm was bought by Büssing. The Komnick name then disappeared from vehicles. NB

Knox twin-cylinder tourer of 1904

KRIÉGER
FRANCE 1897-1909

Louis Antoine Kriéger was an electrical engineering graduate from the École Centrale des Arts et Métiers in 1891 and lived, appropriately, in the Rue Ampère in Paris. In 1895 he formed the Société Civile des Voitures Electriques, Système Kriéger, in partnership with Severiano de Heredia, a wealthy Cubanborn, French-naturalized politician.

The company's first car, built in 1897, was a modified horse carriage with a forecarriage power pack and drive through separate motors in each front wheel. In 1898 the company was reorganized as Société des Voitures Electriques, Système Kriéger, with 4 million francs capital – most shares going to existing stockholders and the rest being offered to the public.

Kriéger established works at Courbevoie in 1898 and went into production with town carriages and electric cabs, which performed well in the 1898 Paris Motor Cab Trials. Kriéger sold licences to the British and Foreign

Kriéger electric two-seater of c.1900

Electrical Co, which sold imported cars as Electromobiles.

The company struggled, however, and was dissolved in February 1900, but was reorganized in July as the Compagnie Parisienne des Voitures Electriques (Système Kriéger) with capital reduced to 2 million francs. Kriéger's saviour was the Société Française pour l'Industrie et les Mines, the first French bank to provide motor company finance.

The bank was represented on the Kriéger board and Kriéger himself was technical director. The hundred or so employees built 43 cars in 1900 and 1901, electrics using Postel-Vinay motors and having six forward speeds and two coasting gears in which the motors were used as generators to recharge the batteries. Range was typically around 45 miles (72km) but in 1901 a Kriéger electric was demonstrated for 192 miles (309km) on a single charge.

Kriéger, recognizing the move away from electrics, built an 'alcohol-electric' car for a 1902 trial but its 4hp De Dion engine was effectively an auxiliary and in any case the car did not compete. In 1903 the company built a true petrol-electric, with 24hp Richard-Brasier engine, and this was put into limited production in 1904.

Expecting expansion the company bought large and expensive premises for a service base and leased them to a new company, founded in 1905 in association with Henri Brasier, the Société des Garages Kriéger et Brasier, which bought rights to the Kriéger name. Kriéger electrics were also built in Italy by STAE and in mid-1905 the French Army Corps tested a Kriéger-powered searchlight trailer, probably the first of its type. In 1906 another licence was sold in Germany and some electrics were built as Lloyds.

The company was under-capitalized, however, and that year offered another 2 million francs in bonds. Another company, Compagnie Parisienne des Taxautos, was set up and ordered 150 cabs from the ailing parent, which was now supporting its bank which had its own problems.

The bank failed first, in March 1907, and although Kriéger moved to Colombes in 1907 the end was near. The company patented a gas turbine electric in 1908 but in February the firm failed.

A few Brasier-engined front-wheel-drive cabs were built in 1909 but production then ceased entirely. The name reappeared briefly in World War II on electric conversions of La Licorne and Chenard-Walcker vans, but the company did not. BL

KRIT
USA 1909-1916

Krit tourer of c.1914

The Krit Motor Co was founded in Detroit in 1909 by Kenneth Krittenden, from which it obviously took its name, but there is no explanation for how the name came to appear as initials with full points as used on the car. Cynics have suggested the letters may have stood for Keep Right In Town, but the KRIT was really not such a bad car.

The first models were small four-cylinder three- and four-seater tourers, all of very similar design. The cars were badged with a black swastika – of the Greek style, betokening good luck, as opposed to the later more sinister reversal – in a red border.

Krit built 936 of the conventional cars in 1910, and in 1911 introduced a two-seater with an underslung chassis and sports body. In 1913 Krit offered the 25/30hp four-cylinder five-passenger model KT tourer. The cars were now apparently exported fairly widely. Charles Mackintosh of Hamburg, the German and Swiss agent, advertised a 10/24PS four-cylinder Tourer at 4950 marks, as made by the Krit Motor Co Ltd of Detroit and London, and the make was indeed listed as an import to Britain from 1913 to 1917.

By that time the company was actually out of business, the last cars being 3.6-litre four-cylinder light cars, available as tourers or roadsters, both at $850, which were made until 1916. When the company was wound up, in April of that year, the works were bought by Packard. BL

Kriéger petrol-electric taxi of 1907

KURTIS/MUNTZ
USA 1949-1955

Frank Kurtis, born in Colorado in 1908, began to build midget racing cars in the 1930s and after World War II moved, with great success, into the larger Indianapolis racing classes. Kurtis-Kraft Inc, originally based in Glendale, California, built more than 900 racing cars including the 1950, 1951, 1953, 1954 and 1955 Indy 500 winners, the Novi specials and the Cummins diesel-engined Indy cars.

In 1949 Kurtis branched into building sports cars for the road. His 1950 model was available as a kit with a simple, attractive glassfibre body and torsion bar suspension, but the choice of engine and other components was left to the customer. Depending on the completeness of the kit, prices ranged from $1495 to $3495; most customers used a side-valve Ford V8 engine.

Kurtis built 36 of his 1950 model but then sold the sports car operation to Earl Muntz, a wealthy TV and radio manufacturer, also based in Glendale. The new Muntz Car Co redesigned the cars on a longer wheelbase as four-seaters with Kurtis-like bodies (but now in aluminium) and Cadillac engines. In what was left of 1950 it sold 28 cars as the Muntz Jet California.

Late in the year Muntz moved to Evanston, Illinois, and for the 1951-52 model years lengthened the wheelbase still further, made the bodies of steel, offered a removable hard top, and replaced the Cadillac engine by a big Lincoln V8. In 1951 and 1952 Muntz sold 230 of the 108mph (174kph) $4450 car, then for 1953 and 1954 developed it again with power increased from 154 to 218bhp and top speed up to 120mph (193kph). Muntz sold 136 of this model to bring total production under his name to 394.

In 1954 production passed back to Kurtis himself, who established the Kurtis Sports Car Corporation in Glendale. His 1954 model had a tubular frame based on Bill Vukovich's 1953 Indy winner and was dubbed the 500-KK. Fifty chassis were built; 30 were sold as kits, leaving engine choice to the customer as before, and the remainder were sold as complete cars, usually with stock Cadillac V8 engines at $5800. Kurtis also built some 30 competition sports models, the 500-S, with Mercury and Hudson engines and not for road use.

The final 18 supercharged 500-M models with glassfibre bodies were sold as 1955 models. Kurtis aggressively advertised his 135mph (217kph) car as 'guaranteed to outperform any other sports car or stock car on the road'.

Kurtis returned to building Indianapolis cars until the European type rear-engined cars began to dominate oval racing in the early 1960s. The company also built special purpose vehicles including rocket sleds for space research. BL

LA BUIRE
FRANCE 1904-1930

The Chantiers de la Buire was an old established Lyons engineering firm founded in 1847. Under the name Les Chantiers de l'Horme et de la Buire it achieved considerable fame as a maker of railway and tramway rolling stock. The company's first link with motor vehicles came in the 1890s when it built some of Léon Serpollet's steam cars under contract. It also made the steam-powered road trains sold by Scotte between 1897 and about 1910. In 1903 the firm was listed as a maker of electric vehicles, but nothing is known of these. Among the staff in these pre-petrol car days was François Pilain, who was an associate of Serpollet and worked for La Buire from 1890 to 1894; later he would make cars under his own name.

In 1904 came the first car to bear the name La Buire. It was a conventional four-cylinder T-head design made in 16 and 30hp sizes, with four-speed gearboxes and chain drive. The following year a new company was formed specifically for car manufacture, the Société Anonyme de la Buire. The commercial director was Maurice Audibert, who had made Audibert-Lavirotte cars until being bought out by Berliet in 1901, after which he worked for Rochet-Schneider for a number of years.

By 1906 La Buire was making three fours, of 4.9, 7.5 and 13.6 litres, the last of these one of the largest four-cylinder touring cars ever made. One was used by Joseph Higginson in English hillclimbs for several years, and it was to replace this that its owner suggested to Vauxhall that they make a more powerful Prince Henry, the first 30/98. Shaft drive appeared on the smaller La Buires in 1907, and L-head monobloc engines in 1910.

In September 1909 La Buire went bankrupt and was taken over by the technical director, M. Berthier, who remodelled the cars slightly, helped by Barron, later of Barron-Viale. Three four-cylinder chassis and one six carried the Berthier name for one season, then he was joined by a group of industrialists to form the Société Nouvelle de la Buire Automobiles,

with capital of 800,000 francs, compared with the 2.4 million francs under M. Berthier.

For 1911 the name La Buire was resumed and a series of medium-sized long-stroke fours was made. By 1913 the range consisted of four four-cylinder and two six-cylinder models, some with mechanical starters. Production was quite modest, running at about 200 a year in the period 1911-14. Commercial vehicles up to 4-tons capacity were also made from 1907 onwards, some of the larger ones being sold to the Russian government.

During the 1920s La Buire tended to rest on its laurels, as did so many French manufacturers of medium sized, undistinguished cars. Only one model was offered immediately after World War I, the 2650cc 12/14CV with fixed head, side-valve engine. It acquired front wheel brakes in 1922 and overhead valves in 1923, when a Speed Model was offered on the British market. A team of streamlined saloons on this chassis ran in the 1924 French Touring Car Grand Prix, but without success.

In the mid-1920s La Buire blossomed out with a wide range of five models, from a 1323cc 8CV to a 2860cc 15CV, all except the smallest with overhead valves. A 3-ton truck chassis was also listed, with a 4.1-litre engine. Unfortunately the market for a regional make of no particular distinction was shrinking rapidly as the big makes like Renault and Peugeot extended nationwide marketing.

By the late 1920s La Buire was down to two models, 10 and 12CV (1.8 and 2 litres) and a light truck based on the latter. Production slowly dwindled and the last cars left the factory in 1930. The building was subsequently used as a spare parts depot by the French army. GNG

LACOSTE et BATTMANN/
SIMPLICIA
FRANCE 1896-1913

Lacoste et Battmann (Imperial) 6hp of 1904

This obscure Paris firm specialized in making kits of parts or complete chassis for sale under its own or other companies' names. Commencing in 1896 as J. Lacoste et Cie, it tended to make small cars that had Aster, Clément, Prunel, Buchet, Gnôme or De Dion engines. Larger Mutel-engined 24hp fours were available in 1903 and heavy commercials, including London buses, appeared in 1906. Battmann joined the company in 1901 and the firm became British registered the following year.

From 1903 Oscar Selbach sold Lacoste cars in England as Regals, and some Gamage models were from the same source. Other makes that were either pure Lacoste, or models probably based on Lacoste parts, included Imperial of Manchester, Speedwell, Highgate, Napoleon, Mass, Waddington, Achilles, Mohawk-Manon, British Lion, Mobile, Jackson of Britain, B&L, Horley, Leonard, Elswick, Martin, Cupelle, Lacoba, Anglian, Wesley, Horse-Shoe, Hexe and possibly Canterbury and l'Elegante. One way of identifying a complete Lacoste chassis was by the rear springs, which were splayed outwards nearer the back.

In 1908 the firm went into liquidation but was re-formed and apparently reverted to French registration. It produced cars for its own retail sales as Simplicias until the end in 1913. These cars had a backbone chassis and Aster 1.8-litre monobloc fours. NB

LAFER
BRAZIL 1972 to date

Lafer Sa Industria e Comercio of São Paulo is one of Brazil's largest furniture makers and is controlled by the Lafer brothers, Samuel, Oscar and Percival. In October 1972 the corporation introduced a glassfibre-bodied replica of the 1952 MG TD, based on the standard Volkswagen Beetle platform chassis and running gear, as still manufactured locally. The prototype car was shown at the 1972 Brazilian Auto Show.

The first 40 cars used the 1500 Beetle engine but all later models had the 1600 unit as standard, with a wide choice of states of tune. In 1976 Lafer built a few examples of another model, the 4.1-litre six-cylinder LL coupé, using Brazilian Chevrolet engines, but all production quickly reverted to the MG replica. Also in 1976 the Lafer was being imported into the United States by International Development Service Inc of Cherry Hill, New Jersey, where it was sold as the Spinnaker, selling at $5000 for a kit or $8000 for a fully built car – twice the cost of the real MG.

By 1980 Lafers had been exported to 17 countries, with most sales going to Italy. In 1981 Lafer sold 312 cars and in 1982 252 cars, contributing to total sales by 1983 of over 3500 cars. By 1984, however, sales of only about 90 were claimed.

The latest TI model with slightly different nose treatment and a smoother body, introduced in November 1978 and virtually unchanged since, still uses the 65bhp 1584cc VW engine to give a claimed top speed of 86mph (138kph). In 1985 it was available alongside the broadly similar MP, which remained closer to the original MG's looks, with a conventional radiator grille. BL

LAGONDA
GB 1908 to date

Ohio-born Wilbur Gunn began building motorcycles in a small workshop at the bottom of his garden in Staines, Middlesex, in about 1900. For his company he chose the name Lagonda Engineering Co after Lagonda Creek near his home town of Springfield. The creek was originally called Ough Ohonda (Bucks' Horns) by the Shawnee Indians and the name was contracted by French settlers to La Ohonda, and then Lagonda.

The early days of Lagonda Engineering are poorly documented. Gunn may have built a prototype front-wheel-drive motorcycle as early as 1898, and he also dabbled in steam launches.

By May 1904 he was advertising 3½ and 4½hp motorcycles, and a limited company, the Lagonda Motor Cycle Co Ltd, was formed with nominal capital of £10,000. Tricars were also made from 1904, and two-wheelers were dropped after 1905. As with their contemporaries, the tricars gradually became more car-like, adopting wheel steering in 1906, in which year six box van tricars were sold to the Post Office.

Tricar production ceased in 1907 after 69 had been made. Sales were very seasonal and in April 1907 a receiver was called in and set about winding up the company, although this process was not completed until January 1910.

Meanwhile Gunn turned to four-wheelers, starting with a shaft-driven 10hp V-twin and following this with larger cars using 14/16hp and 16/18hp four-cylinder Coventry-Simplex engines. Very few of these were made and they were never advertised.

In fact the financing of the company during the years 1907 to 1913 is a mystery, as officially the firm did not exist and no backers can be traced. It is unlikely that Gunn had sufficient private funds to keep the company going, yet there was quite a lot of activity, including some racing successes at Brooklands in 1909

and the establishment of a Russian agent at St Petersburg in 1910. Indeed it seems that most of the cars made until 1913 were sold in Russia, although a London agency existed in the form of the Burlington Motor Co of Piccadilly.

For 1911 the Coventry-Simplex powered cars were replaced by a 20hp four and 30hp six with Lagonda-built engines, both having a bore of 90mm (3½in), which was dictated by the size of machines in the Lagonda factory. The largest of the V-twin tricar engines also had a 90mm bore.

In 1913 a new company, Lagonda Ltd, was formed, finance coming from Henry Tollemache of the brewing family, and Harry Griffin, a motor engineer. All Gunn's property including his house was made over to the new company, but he remained in charge and soon introduced a completely new design, smaller than previous Lagondas and with the very advanced feature of integral construction. The engine was a monobloc four in unit with clutch and gearbox of 1099cc capacity and 11.1hp. About 200 were made until 1916, including some delivery vans. By this time the Lagonda factory was quite substantial, making some of the machine tools as well as most components of the cars.

War work took over in 1916, the factory being engaged in the manufacture of shells. Like many firms, Lagonda made more money from armaments than from cars and it ended the war on a sounder financial basis than it had started. The company had extended the

Lagonda 14/60 tourer of 1926

Lagonda tricar of 1906

factory premises at Staines and had an office and sales department at 195 Hammersmith Road, London, which had been the premises of Tollemache and Griffin, now no longer connected with Lagonda. The 11.1hp was revived in 1919 and increased in size to 1420cc and 11.9hp in 1921. Gunn died in 1920 at the age of 61, largely through overwork during the war, and he was succeeded by Colin Parbury, a director and substantial shareholder.

Finances remained sound for several years during which the 11.9 grew into the 12/24, a heavier car with the same engine as the later 11.9. When production ended in 1926 a total of about 6000 of the little cars had been made in a 12-year run, almost equal to all other pre-1939 models put together.

The new model for 1926 was the 14/60 which was to bring about a complete change of direction for Lagonda, although this was not particularly evident in the first examples, which did not look very different from a later 12/24. It had a new four-cylinder twin-camshaft engine of just under 2 litres capacity, conventional chassis and powerful Rubury brakes. At £430 for a chassis it cost nearly twice as much as a 12/24, which was listed at £230 for the chassis, although nearly all 12/24s and their predecessors were sold complete with factory-built bodies, necessitated by the integral construction. A new £50,000 debenture was issued in February 1926 to raise finance for the new model.

Because they were moving into a higher

Lagonda V12 Le Mans racer of 1939

price bracket, Lagonda sales dropped after the introduction of the 14/60 from about 700 a year to 400, but profit margins on each car were presumably higher and the company continued to flourish. For 1928 the 14/60 was renamed the 2-litre, and a speed model signalled the emergence of Lagonda as a sports car. This perhaps reflected the growing influence of Brigadier-General Francis Metcalfe who joined in 1926, later becoming managing director.

A 3-litre six-cylinder also came in 1928 and a supercharged 2-litre in 1930. An ambitious racing programme was undertaken with entries in the 1928 Le Mans race and from 1929 onwards in conjunction with the well-known distributors Fox and Nicholl.

An admitted drawback of the 3-litre was its tricky gearchange. To overcome this, design-

er Alf Cranmer incorporated the Maybach *doppelschnellgang* vacuum-operated eight-speed preselector gearbox in a new model of 3-litre known as the Selector Special. The chassis had to be stiffened to carry the enormous and heavy gearbox, which Lagonda made under licence from Maybach, and the model was not a great success.

The Depression took its toll of Lagonda sales and not more than 170 cars were sold between November 1931 and July 1932, less than half the rate of the late 1920s. A six-cylinder 2-litre was introduced in August 1932 using a bought-in engine for the first time since the Coventry-Simplex-powered cars of 1909. The unit chosen was the six-

Lagonda M45 drophead coupé of 1935

cylinder Crossley that had powered that company's Shelsley model. The chassis was generally similar to the old 2-litre, the car being known, however, as the 16/80. The engine, although made by Crossley, was completely dismantled and rebuilt by Lagonda. ENV preselector gearboxes were offered optionally from 1933.

Up to the early 1930s nearly all Lagondas had been made with factory bodywork, some of the 2-litre and 3-litre saloons being made under Weymann patents. With the moves up-market, more chassis were supplied for the mounting of special coachwork by such firms as Vanden Plas and Gurney Nutting. This trend went further with two new models introduced in 1933, the 9hp Rapier and the 4½-litre six-cylinder Meadows' engined chassis.

The Rapier had a completely new 1104cc twin-overhead cam four-cylinder engine designed by Tim Ashcroft and a preselector ENV gearbox; the chassis cost £270 and all bodies were made by outside firms, notably Abbott, Maltby, Newns, Ranalah and Whittingham and Mitchel. Early engines were Lagonda-built but later ones were made by Coventry-Climax to Ashcroft's design.

The 4½-litre M45 used the overhead-valve Meadows engine which had powered the 4½-litre Invicta; with the demise of that company Meadows was glad to find a new customer. This car took Lagonda into the Bentley class, although it cost £795 for a chassis compared with £1100 for the 3½-litre Bentley. Factory-built four-door saloons and tourers were available, but drophead coupés were made by such firms as Freestone and Webb, Carlton and Lancefield, while Vanden Plas also made saloons and tourers.

Sales of Lagondas were very seasonal, and in the spring of 1935 they failed to pick up from the winter slack so that the works were cluttered with unsold chassis, especially

Rapiers. Cash flow problems arose at once and a receiver was called in. Financing had always been largely in the hands of the banks, which were unwilling to advance any further money, while the number of models must have been a severe liability. At the time of the receivership, seven models were nominally in production – the Rapier, 2-litre, 3-litre, 16/80, 3½-litre and two kinds of 4½-litre.

The receiver invited tenders for the company, and the successful bidder was a young solicitor, Alan Good, who paid £67,000 plus £4000 for the stores, just beating Rolls-Royce, which would clearly like to have eliminated a rival to the Bentley. Third was Alvis with a £35,000 bid. Ironically, Good had just secured the services of W. O. Bentley as his designer, although he lost several old Lagonda hands including Cranmer who went to Maybach, and Bert Hammond who had been at Staines since 1904 and now left to join Lammas-Graham at nearby Sunbury. Just before the company had been put up for sale, a 4½-litre had won at Le Mans, the only British victory between the Bentley era of 1927-30 and the Jaguar era of the 1950s.

The new company was called Lagonda

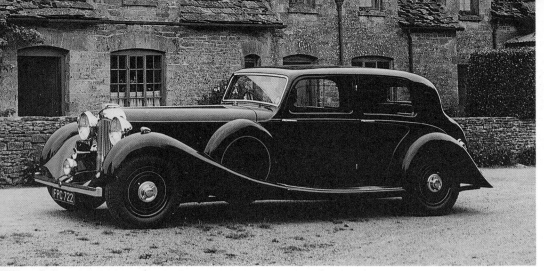

Lagonda LG45 saloon of 1937

Motors (Staines) Ltd as Lagonda Ltd was still theoretically in existence, and its first act was to discontinue the Rapier. However, Ashcroft together with Bill Oates, who had raced Lagondas since before World War I, and financier Nevil Brocklebank raised enough money to buy the stock of parts and set up their own Rapier Cars Ltd in the old Lagonda sales depot at 195 Hammersmith Road. Factory space was acquired at Wylers the coachbuilders at Kew, and there they continued to make Rapiers until the end of 1937.

The company was wound up in 1938 and finally dissolved in 1943, although Ashcroft had hopes of reviving the make after the war. A few Rapiers were built by private enthusiasts from pre-war parts up to about 1950. Total production was around 300.

The first signs of W. O. Bentley's influence appeared on the 4½-litre LG45, a modified M45, but the Sanction III Meadows engine of 1937 showed further improvements, followed by the LG6 with Meadows engine and a new chassis with independent front suspension, and finally an all-new 4½-litre V12 engine in this new chassis. The very handsome bodies for these cars were again made by Lagonda, although a few outside coachbuilders made the occasional example, including Freestone and Webb, Gurney Nutting, Hooper and James Young. Total production was 82 LG6s and 187 V12s.

The factory concentrated on making flame throwers during World War II, but from 1944 on W. O. Bentley and a small team were working quietly on the post-war Lagonda. Finally unveiled in September 1945 it had a 2½-litre twin-overhead cam six-cylinder engine in a cruciform chassis – but was never built by Lagonda.

Alan Good had lost interest in the cars, the company could not secure adequate supplies of steel and the new design might well have been stillborn had not tractor-maker David Brown stepped in. He had recently acquired Aston Martin and was interested in Lagonda mainly for the engine, which he saw as a good power unit for the future Aston Martin.

In 1947 he bought Lagonda for £52,500 and formed a new company, Aston Martin Lagonda Ltd, as a subsidiary of David Brown & Sons

Ltd. Both new cars were to be made at the Aston Martin factory at Feltham; the Staines plant was sold to Petters, the oil engine makers. W. O. Bentley chose this moment to retire from the motor industry.

The new 2½-litre Lagonda eventually went into production in 1949 and a total of 550 saloons and drophead coupés were made until 1954, when it was replaced by a 3-litre which was made until 1958. Subsequently there have been three revivals of the Lagonda name, one still current, and these are described in the Aston Martin entry. GNG

LA LICORNE
FRANCE 1901-1950

In 1895 a 25-year-old cycling enthusiast and holder of many records, J. Corre, set up a small bicycle factory at Levallois-Perret. In 1899 he began to manufacture motor tricycles and quadricycles powered by De Dion-Bouton engines, and also to sell De Dion, Peugeot and Renault cars.

Two years later he began to make a car under his own name. This was a De Dion-powered voiturette very similar to the contemporary Renault, one of which finished third in the voiturette section of the 1901 Paris-Berlin race. A delivery van was offered on this chassis, but there were no purpose-built commercial vehicles until 1912.

Corre used De Dion engines at least until 1910, introducing a 10hp twin in 1902 and an 18hp four in 1905. He also used four-cylinder Aster and Mutel engines. Up to 1904 Corre cars carried their radiators on each side of the bonnet, but from then until 1907 they were in the dashboard position, à la Renault, after which they were moved to a conventional frontal position.

In 1905 an English company, Automobiles Corre Ltd, was founded with capital of £40,000 to acquire Corre et Cie. A year later it set up a French company, the Compagnie Française des Automobiles Corre, with new premises at Neuilly.

In 1907 the name La Licorne (The Unicorn) was used on the radiators for the first time, and from then on the cars were always called La Licornes although the company name remained Corre for many years. In 1921 it was sometimes rendered as Compagnie Française des Automobiles Corre-La Licorne but by the 1930s the name Corre had been dropped.

In 1908 J. Corre himself left the business he had founded and began to make four-cylinder light cars at Rueil under the name Corre, Le Cor or JC. This lasted until 1914.

Meanwhile the range of La Licornes was expanded, with some largish four-cylinder cars up to 25hp and even a 35hp V8 in 1910, which presumably used De Dion's recently introduced V8 engine. The 2-litre Model DX was the first to use an engine of La Licorne manufacture, although the company con-

Corre (La Licorne) four-cylinder racer of 1906

tinued to employ proprietary units, now by Chapuis-Dornier and Ballot. The first purpose-built La Licorne truck, which appeared in 1912, was Ballot-powered.

The company continued a modest but steady course in the 1920s, making conventional touring cars with engines in the 1.3 to 2.3-litre range by Ballot, Chapuis-Dornier, SCAP and itself. Vans were available on most of the car chassis and a few trucks were produced to 3½ tons. Production seldom exceeded 1500 vehicles a year.

In 1927 La Licorne took a new direction with the introduction of the 5CV, a 900cc four-cylinder light car of superior quality, despite its small size. This set the pattern for the next 10 years, in which La Licornes were fitted with attractive coachwork and often appeared successfully at Concours d'Elegance. This coachwork was contracted out, to Duval or several other small Parisian firms, and featured pillarless saloons from 1932 onwards.

The 5CV grew up into an 1129cc 6/8CV in

For 1939 La Licorne brought out a new and more original car, the 6/8CV. This was a two-door saloon with double forked backbone frame and the choice of a 1125cc La Licorne or 1628cc Citroën engine. The former was quite reasonable at 23,700 francs, although more expensive than the Renault Juvaquatre or Peugeot 202. In addition, the complicated 1939 range included two Citroën engined and bodied models and four with La Licorne engines and Citroën bodies, as well as cabriolets with La Licorne bodies on all the chassis, and a Labourdette-bodied limousine on the 14CV chassis.

During World War II a number of 6/8CVs were converted to electric propulsion and sold under the name Aeric or Mildé-Kriéger. A small number were made after the war, together with light vans and a prototype of a handsome cabriolet powered by the 2.4-litre 14CV engine. Only one of these was built.

The final La Licorne design was a sporty coupé to be powered by a 1½-litre Bugatti Type 73 engine developed in the La Licorne

1931, but four years later *The Light Car* reported that, after several years of experiments, Lambert had decided to put his car into commercial production. His catalogue illustrated two styles of coupé and an open sports car, but the only known photographs show a low coupé, and this may have been the only 'Sans-Choc' made. He also advertised a single-cylinder voiturette, but his small company ceased production in 1936.

During World War II he made a few electrically powered versions of his voiturette, subsequently moving again to Giromagny, near Belfort. There he began to make small sports cars which did, at least, see limited production. They were powered by 1100cc four-cylinder engines described as 'Lambert Ruby'; he claimed to have obtained the manufacturing rights to the Ruby engine, but it is more likely that they were part of the stock that he had built up before the war.

On his post-war cars, which appeared in 1948, Lambert forsook his pre-war originality and employed a beam front axle with semi-

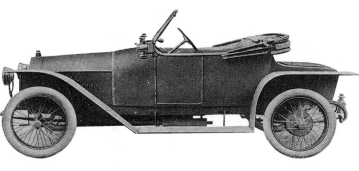

La Licorne 5CV BV two-seater of 1914

La Licorne 11/14CV saloon of 1938

1931, but a new small car, the 935cc L610 arrived in 1934. All engines were La Licorne-made at this time, the largest being the 2.1-litre DR4. Overhead valves and transverse independent front suspension made their appearance in 1934. By 1936 the largest model was a 14CV 2438cc four.

Production continued at around the 1000 to 1200 units a year mark during the 1930s and in 1939 the factory employed 450 men. This was clearly too small in the days of increasing mass-production, for the La Licorne was competing with Renault and Citroën, yet the limited numbers meant that they were inevitably more expensive.

For 1938 La Licorne bought saloon bodies from Citroën and used these either with its own engines in 8, 10, 11 and 14CV models or with the 9 or 11CV Citroën engine. In the latter case the only difference from a genuine Citroën lay in the radiator grille and the fact that the engine and gearbox were turned round to drive the rear wheels. Even so, they cost 28,500 to 29,500 francs compared with 24,700 to 27,700 francs for the equivalent Citroëns.

factory which Ettore Bugatti had bought at the beginning of the war. This never saw the light of day, however, and in 1950 the factory was closed, subsequently being acquired by Renault. GNG

LAMBERT
FRANCE 1926-1952

Born in 1904, Germain Lambert served in the French air force in Morocco in 1925 and then worked at the La Buire factory in Lyons. In 1926 he set up on his own as a maker of sports cars at Macon. The first Lambert had a Ruby engine and all round independent suspension by transverse leaves. Very few were made. In 1929 he moved to Reims where two years later he produced a front-wheel-drive car powered by Ruby or Chapuis-Dornier engines of 1100cc. The suspension was similar to his first car, and Lambert gave his machines the name 'Sans-Choc'.

It was announced in the French press in

Lambert 6CV coupé of 1932

elliptic springs and rear wheel drive. He finished third in his class in the 1949 Bol d'Or, second in 1951 and first in 1952, but these successes failed to generate enough sales to keep the small company solvent. The last Lambert had a stylish Ferrari-like coupé body by Schmitt, but it was too expensive to compete and only one was made.

Lambert closed down during the summer of 1952 and everything was sold at auction the following year. Germain Lambert took one or two of his cars and retired to Petit Arran, Parly, where he ran a small café until his death in 1981. GNG

LAMBERT
USA 1891-1917

Among the many claimants to the title of America's first petrol-engined car, the 1891 Lambert had a very strong case which was never fully pursued because of its maker's genuine modesty and his friendship with another of the pioneer claimants, Elwood Haynes. It is virtually certain, however, that the first Lambert car ran in February 1891, some 18 months before the Duryeas who are more generally accepted as America's first motorists.

John William Lambert, the car's designer and builder, was born in 1860 and began to take an interest in engines after he had seen a stationary gas engine in the rubble of a burned out tannery in December 1876, apparently being aware of the work of Benz and Otto at a time when few Americans were. In 1885 he moved to Ohio City where he became a successful businessman and local property owner, with shops, grain stores, a timber yard, the local opera house and even the town hall belonging to him.

Around 1890 Lambert began to finance John B. Hicks of Cleveland who was developing a stationary petrol engine. Towards the end of 1890, having paid Hicks some $3300 – far more than originally intended – Lambert entered a licensing agreement with Hicks to use the engine in a car. Hicks patented his three-cylinder engine in December 1890.

By this time Lambert himself was already working on a lightweight single-cylinder ver-

Lambert phaeton of 1908

sion for his proposed car and he took a part-finished engine from the Lowell Machine Works in Cleveland, where the parts were being made, and finished it in Ohio City. At the same time he built a three-wheel vehicle to take the engine and it may have run first in January 1891 before having its inadequate steering modified and being run on the road in February 1891.

In the same month, Lambert confidently advertised copies of his vehicle for sale in a mailed brochure. He received several enquiries but no orders and, disheartened, he turned to stationary engine manufacture. What was quite possibly America's first petrol

car was destroyed by fire later in the year.

In 1892 Lambert moved his stationary engine business into space in the family's Pioneer Pole & Shaft Co works in Union City, Ohio. Two years later he opened a new factory in Anderson, Indiana, as the Buckeye Manufacturing Co.

In 1895, partly because of his friendship with Haynes, whose pioneer car had now also run, Lambert planned a car to be powered by one of his Buckeye engines and by 1898 he had put an engine into a four-wheeled buggy. Around 1900-02 Lambert also experimented with a friction drive system which became one of his 600 or so patents and was used on every subsequent Lambert car.

In 1902 he formed the Union Automobile Co in Union City and from 1902 to 1905 built a small twin-cylinder car known as the Union, production of which reached about 10 a month. The first, an 8hp model, was shown at the Cleveland Auto Show in February 1903 priced at $1250. In 1904 he moved into a new 300,000sq ft (28,000sq m) factory in Anderson and in 1905 founded the Lambert Automobile Co there, apparently just allowing the Union company to fade away.

Lambert designed his own engines but had them built outside and the first car was completed in 1905, a twin-cylinder model. Eight models were available in 1906, costing from $800 to $3000, and by now Lambert was also building tractors, fire engines and trucks. By 1910 he had more than 1000 employees and was producing up to 3000 cars and commercials a year. The cars now included four- and six-cylinder models with Buda, Continental and Rutenber engines and all used the Lambert friction drive – at first with chains, later with shaft final drive.

The cars were popular and the company prospered and expanded until World War I, when Lambert began manufacturing shells, wheels and vehicles for military use but, after 1917, no more cars. He was not interested in competing with the larger manufacturers, which he accurately foresaw as dominating the industry in the future, and he transferred his efforts, with huge success, to making components and machine tools for the motor and other industries, latterly under the name of Lambert Inc. BL

LAMBORGHINI
ITALY 1963 to date

Ferrucio Lamborghini was born into a farming family in Ferrara, north of Bologna, in 1916 and he gained his first knowledge of mechanics and engineering from working on the farm. He was trained formally at a nearby industrial training college and graduated in industrial technology before joining the Italian air force, in which he served during World War II. He learned much more about engineering, especially about improvization,

while trying to keep aircraft operational. He spent much of the war on Rhodes, latterly as a British prisoner of war, but he returned to northern Italy in 1946.

There he started a business converting military surplus vehicles, which were plentiful and cheap, into agricultural vehicles, which were not. Having found this eager market he began expanding his business to keep pace with orders, taking on skilled labour where possible with an eye to the future.

Alongside his new business, Lamborghini loved fast cars and in 1947 he finished building a modified Fiat Topolino with an engine increased in size from 500 to 750cc. He raced this Mark I as he called it in the 1948 Mille Miglia, with Baglioni as co-driver. They failed to finish but the car attracted a lot of attention and several requests for copies. For the moment, however, Lamborghini was not very interested in building cars as he concentrated on expanding the tractor business.

In 1949 he formalized his efforts by forming Lamborghini Trattici and built his own new factory where he now started building purpose-designed tractors as opposed to surplus conversions. By 1959 Lamborghini was building 10 tractors a day.

That year he expanded the company's interests by starting to manufacture domestic and industrial heating and air-conditioning systems through a new branch of the company, Lamborghini Bruciatori. It was already a well subscribed market in Italy but Lamborghini succeeded in breaking into it by offering particularly good after sales service.

By 1962 tractor output had reached 20 a day and the healthy profits generated by his two businesses allowed Lamborghini to think of building a very high-quality GT car. His enthusiasm for fast cars continued and he had owned some of the fastest, but found faults with most – and, according to legend, with the treatment handed out to customers, even those of Lamborghini's financial stature, by Ferrari.

He set out to build a car good enough for himself, eliminating the shortcomings he saw in others. In 1963 he founded Automobili Ferrucio Lamborghini SpA and built a new factory, specifically for cars, at Sant'Agata Bolognese, between Modena and Bologna. By the time the factory was complete at the end of the year the first car had already been designed and built at the tractor works.

It was the 350GTV. Its 3.5-litre V12 engine was designed by Giotto Bizzarini, formerly of Ferrari and also working at this time on Renzo Rivolta's Iso car. Bizzarini's V12 was scaled up from a putative design for a 1½-litre Formula 1 engine which had not been built, and had four overhead camshafts and 360bhp. The chassis was designed by Gianpaolo Dallara – also later involved with Iso in the design of GP cars – and the two-seater coupé body was by Touring, a Zagato berlinetta also being designed.

The car was first exhibited at the Turin Show in 1963 and went into production in

Lamborghini 400GT (foreground) and Miura of 1967

Lamborghini Countach of 1985

1964 with a slightly detuned engine and the Touring body. Virtually everything was made at Sant'Agata except the five-speed ZF gearbox. The 160mph (257kph) car was widely acclaimed. In 1964 150 were built, rising to 250 the following year when Lamborghini also began making his own gearboxes and final drives.

In 1966 the 4-litre 400GT, a marginal 2+2, was introduced alongside the dramatic Miura P400 which had first been seen at Turin in November 1965. This mid-engined coupé, reminiscent of the Ford GT40, used the 4-litre V12 mounted transversely and it gave this altogether superb car a claimed top speed of 180mph (290kph). Lamborghini was now a genuine challenger to Ferrari in spite of the fact that he adamantly rejected going racing.

Lamborghini showed the rather flashy Marzal as a prototype in 1967; it had a 2-litre six-cylinder engine derived from one bank of the V12 but did not go into production. It did, however, give its basic shape to the front-engined four-seater Espada, powered by a whole V12, which was launched in 1968 and was joined later in the year by the Islero, a pretty 2+2 successor to the 400GT, which itself gave way to the Jarama in 1970.

In 1971 Lamborghini made a bid for the smaller sports car market with the 2½-litre 220bhp V8 Urraco. This was mid-engined like the Miura but, except perhaps in pseudo-racing Silhouette guise as added in 1976, it

Lamborghini Jalpa of 1985

was never a car with the same charisma.

The Miura was named after a fighting bull, and Lamborghini's badge, a bull, is Ferrucio's birth sign. The Miura's successor, the very dramatic Countach, took its name from the local dialect expression for 'that's it!' (or words to that effect) – and it certainly was. It was originally intended to use a 5-litre V12, promising 200mph (321kph), but the Countach was launched with the familiar 4-litre unit, the full 5-litre unit emerging in 1982.

The company, meanwhile, had been through enormous changes and very hard times. Around 1970 Ferrucio Lamborghini decided to retire, prompted by a serious downturn in the Italian agricultural industry which was affecting the tractor company badly. He sold control of the car company to a Swiss, Georges-Henri Rosetti, whose family had

made a fortune as clockmakers; but with problems arising in the clockmaking industry from Japanese quartz products, Rosetti quickly sold part of his holding to a property developer friend called Leimer.

Lamborghini was suffering badly at this time of general Italian industrial unrest, with regular strikes and quality control problems due to uncertainty over the future of the company. Leimer's problems were compounded by a proposed collaboration between Lamborghini and BMW, whereby Lamborghini would build the production versions of the BMW M1 sports car, falling through.

Possible takeovers of the company by Grand Prix team sponsors Walter Wolf and David Thieme also eventually failed and Rosetti and Leimer sold out to a German, Dr Neumann and the former racing driver Hubert Hahne. They in turn sold the company to a Hungarian-born American, Zoltan Reti.

It was Reti who finally decided that the company had failed and put it into receivership. It was bought at auction by the Mimram family in June 1981 as Nuova Automobili Ferrucio Lamborghini SpA and 25-year-old Patrick Mimram, whose family had leased the factory for almost a year before the final sale, just to keep the business going, took control.

Lamborghini launched a new, smaller sports car, the 3.5-litre V8 Jalpa, in 1982 and began work on a new off-road vehicle, the LMA, following an earlier off-road vehicle, the Chrysler 5.9-litre V8-engined Cheetah. Like the Cheetah, the LMA, which was to have a

new 7-litre Lamborghini V12, was meant largely for the Saudi Arabian market. The prototype had a claimed top speed of over 125mph (200kph). Early in 1985 Lamborghini announced a four-valve-per-cylinder version of the Countach, with capacity increased to 5167cc. This Countach qv had a claimed top speed of 183mph (300kph). A four-valve engine was also imminent for the smaller Jalpa.

Under Mimram the company has diversified into building powerboat engines, making Swiss watches and even running a record company. Car production in 1985 totalled about 250 units. Mimram, whose family made their fortune in business in Senegal, lives in Switzerland. For his part Ferrucio Lamborghini returned to his farming roots and became a wine grower, offering a wine, predictably perhaps, called 'Bull's Blood'. BL

LANCHESTER
GB 1895-1956

The Lanchester was unique among early British cars in that it owed nothing to foreign designs such as Benz or Panhard but was designed from first principles by a brilliant engineer. Frederick William Lanchester was born in 1868, and at the age of 20 joined a small Birmingham firm making gas engines under the name Forward. He was joined in 1889 by his 15-year-old brother George, who four years later became works manager at Forward when Frederick left to pursue experimental work.

This resulted in England's first motor boat, launched in 1894, and first successful car, which was built slowly during 1895 and made its first trials in February or March 1896. It was powered by a single-cylinder horizontal engine of $4\frac{3}{4}\times4\frac{1}{2}$in (120×114mm) with two overhanging balanced cranks, each with its own flywheel and connecting rod. The cranks revolved in opposite directions, giving a smoothness of running unknown to Lanchester's contemporaries. Other features of this remarkable car included an epicyclic gearchange, tubular frame and full-width body.

This car was built in a workshop rented from the Forward Gas Engine Co, but Frederick Lanchester and some associates soon took larger premises, also in Birmingham, and gathered a staff of 10 skilled men. A new two-cylinder engine was fitted to the car in 1897, in which year George Lanchester joined his brothers Fred and Frank. A second complete car was built in the same year.

Experimental work, financed by Fred's royalties from the Clerk-Lanchester gas-engine starter, occupied the next two years, and it was not until December 1899 that the Lanchester Gas Engine Co was formed, with £45,525 paid up capital. Fred was general manager and chief designer, George his assistant and Frank company secretary with particular responsibility for publicity and seeking financial backing. Despite Frank's charm, shortage of capital was always a problem, and after a new factory at Sparkbrook, Birmingham, had been bought and equipped, there was little money left for production.

Six cars were completed during 1900, all being set aside as director's and demonstration vehicles, so no revenue came to the company until 1901. The cars were similar to the second prototype of 1897, with mid-mounted horizontally-opposed two-cylinder engines driving through three-speed epicyclic transmissions and worm rear axles. Steering was by side tiller, or lever as the Lanchesters preferred to call it, a feature that characterized the cars until 1911, long after all other car manufacturers had gone over to steering wheels.

In the autumn of 1901 Max Lawrence joined the firm as works manager. His sisters were the founders of Roedean girls' public school, and through them the Lanchesters found their first celebrated customer, Rudyard Kipling, who owned a number of the cars. Another literary owner in later years was George Bernard Shaw.

At the insistence of the directors, the early Lanchesters had bodies by outside firms, but Fred was dissatisfied as they were not interchangeable and involved expensive chassis alterations, so in 1903 he was given permission to set up his own body department. In 1906 a new factory was set up next to the main works which accommodated the coach-building, upholstery and paint divisions.

Four models of two-cylinder car were offered up to 1904. The 10 and 12hp engines were of the same size but the former was air-cooled, and it was reckoned that the fans

Lanchester 'Gold Medal' phaeton of 1897

Lanchester Forty limousine of c.1925

absorbed 2hp at maximum speed, hence the difference in quoted power. The 16 and 18hp cars were made in very small numbers, only 20 of the former and six of the latter. By 1904 customers were expecting four cylinders for an engine of this size (4.9 litres), and Fred was in the process of designing a four when the company ran out of cash. Even though they had a full order book, the directors decided to liquidate the firm.

Later in 1904 it was reorganized as the Lanchester Motor Co Ltd and run by a receiver for nearly a year. During this time Fred retained his position of general manager, but when the directors took over he was demoted to 'designer and consultant' with a reduction in salary from £350 to £250 a year. This reinforced Fred's distrust of men of business, and the next 10 years saw increasing disagreement leading to his virtual resignation in favour of his brother George.

The first four-cylinder Lanchester, a 20hp, appeared at the end of 1904. The engine was now front-mounted and vertical but the bonnetless appearance was retained by locating the engine between the driver and front passenger. This layout was more or less followed on all Lanchesters made until 1914. Engine, clutch and epicyclic gearbox were in one unit, and Lanchester was a pioneer of pressure lubrication, at 30lb per sq in. One lever was used to operate the clutch, gear selection and main brake.

In 1906 the four-cylinder 20hp was joined by a six-cylinder 28hp with the same cylinder dimensions (4×3in or 101×76mm), and these two models were continued with little change until 1910 when the six became a 38hp (4×4in or 101×101mm). The following year came the four-cylinder 25hp with the same dimensions. This was the last of Fred Lanchester's designs as the later, more conventional cars were the work of George.

Wheel steering was optional from 1907 and standard from 1911, and a further concession to convention was the abandonment of the lever brake. Yet Lanchesters still looked distinctive and were appreciated for their exceptionally comfortable ride, thanks to their long wheelbase. Customers included several Indian princes, the most loyal being Prince Ranjitsinhji, the Jam Sahib of Nawanagar, better known as Ranji the cricketer who bought his first Lanchester in 1902 and his last in 1947.

The Lanchester company made steady profits after its re-formation in 1905, but the directors paid out too much in dividends and put too little back into the firm, so the shortage of cash for development of new models was still evident. Although still paid a meagre salary, Fred was able to supplement his income from patent rights, particularly the torsional vibration damper for six-cylinder engines and the harmonic balancer for four-cylinder engines, rights for which were sold to Aster, Daimler and Vauxhall as well as to several American companies.

Such innovations as there were on the 25 and 38hp Lanchesters of 1911 to 1914 were the work of George rather than Fred, while Frank was now in the London sales office where his tact and charm were of immense value to the company. The next design was entirely George's work, Fred having resigned in 1913 to become technical adviser to Daimler. Known as the Sporting Forty, it was much more conventional, with a side-valve six-cylinder engine mounted under a long bonnet, semi-elliptic springs and a bevel driven rear axle. This design was forced on George by the directors. Although a better car than he admitted, it never pleased him and he was relieved that the outbreak of war prevented more than half a dozen being made.

In the early years of the war the Lanchester factory made shells, but Frank was soon able to secure orders for armoured cars and searchlight tenders built on the 38hp six-cylinder chassis. A total of 42 armoured cars were supplied to the Royal Naval Air Service and gave invaluable service in Russia. Other activities included making RAF 1A and Sunbeam Arab aero engines, and the Constan-

Royal customers were the Duke of York, later King George VI; the present Queen's first public appearance was in a Lanchester Forty at the age of six weeks.

The Forty's engine was used in the second series of Lanchester armoured cars. These were six-wheelers with steering columns at both ends, of which 39 were made and supplied to the 11th Hussars and 12th Lancers between 1927 and 1931.

In 1928 came the last of George Lanchester's designs for his own firm, the 30hp Straight-8. This had an 82bhp 4½-litre monobloc engine with single-overhead cam which shared many components with the 21, or 23 as it had become in 1926 when capacity went up to 3.3 litres. The Straight-8 was probably the finest Lanchester ever made, but the Depression shortened its life so that only 126 were built.

In January 1931 the bank called in Lanchester's overdraft, although it was not exceptionally large at £38,000, and gave the directors the ultimatum to amalgamate or go bankrupt. They chose amalgamation with the Daimler Co Ltd which was looking for the opportunity to expand into a cheaper market. They were also happy to acquire a modern poppet-valve engine design to replace their ageing sleeve-valve units. Daimler was owned by BSA, which transferred the Lanchester plant to the Daimler works at Coventry and

der Roadrider and Roadrider De Luxe (1937-39). Some of these, such as the Ten and Light Six, had equivalents in the BSA range, while the Roadrider De Luxe was a cheaper version of the Daimler DB18, with the surprising option of synchromesh in place of the fluid flywheel of other Daimler/Lanchesters of the period.

George Lanchester had left the company in 1936 and moved to Alvis, for whom he designed the 12/70 car and supervised the development of Alvis-Straussler armoured cars. Frank remained in the sales department until his retirement just before World War II while 'Dr Fred', who had been given an Honorary LL.D. by Birmingham University in 1919, although he had no connection with the Lanchester company after 1913, continued to produce a wide variety of inventions and patents in electrical and mechanical engineering, almost up to his death in March 1946.

The post-war Lanchester Ten was a refined little car with a 1287cc pushrod overhead valve four-cylinder engine, fluid flywheel and coil independent front suspension. The only body style offered was a six-light saloon made by Briggs of Dagenham, which was replaced in 1949 by a more expensive four-light saloon by Barker. The Ten sold quite well – 3050 in five years – but the price rose even more rapidly than the rate of inflation,

Lanchester 15/18 saloon of 1931

Lanchester Fourteen cabriolet of 1952

tinesco interrupter mechanism for synchronizing the firing of a machine gun through the propeller arc of fighter planes.

For their post-war car the directors decided on a single model, the Forty. This had a new 6.2-litre six-cylinder single-overhead cam engine in a chassis based on that of the pre-war Sporting Forty. It was a luxury car with a chassis price in 1920 of £2200, or £100 more than the Rolls-Royce Silver Ghost. Like the Rolls it soon acquired a smaller sister in the shape of the 21hp, a 3-litre six-cylinder car which was the first Lanchester to have a detachable cylinder head and also the first to have a conventional gearbox and four wheel brakes.

To give it an adequate performance George Lanchester had decided that four speeds were essential, but a four-speed epicyclic box would have been very complex and expensive. The Forty continued to have a three-speed epicyclic box to the end of its life in 1929. About 500 were made, quite a number finding their way to the United States. Among

moved one of its subsidiaries, the Burton Griffiths Machine Tool Co, into the Lanchester works. Frank Lanchester became a sales director for the new Lanchester division of Daimler, and George a member of the senior design staff.

The Straight-8 was continued in small numbers up to 1932 and was joined by a 2½-litre six known as the 15/18. This was a compromise design bridging the two eras of Lanchester, as it had been planned by George but was cheapened at Daimler's insistence and the original overhead-cam engine was replaced by a pushrod unit. A modern feature was the fluid flywheel in conjunction with a Wilson pre-selector gearbox. Just over 2000 were made until 1935, latterly with a shorter stroke engine of 2390cc, while from 1936 to 1939 the name Lanchester Eighteen was carried by a variant of the Daimler Light Twenty.

Alongside these were several smaller models of Lanchester, the 1203cc Ten (1933-36), 1378cc Light Six (1935-36), 1444cc Eleven (1937-39) and the 1527cc or 1809cc six-cylin-

from £761 in 1946 to £1170 in 1951. It was replaced by the Fourteen, which was really a Daimler Conquest with two fewer cylinders and a Lanchester grille. About 2100 of these were made from 1951 to 1954, after which Lanchester brought out two oddities.

The Dauphin was a luxury two-door saloon powered by a 2½-litre Daimler engine with a Hooper body, priced unrealistically at £4010, while the Sprite had a 1.6-litre four-cylinder engine, a unitary construction saloon body and Hobbs automatic transmission. The Dauphin could never have been an economic proposition (only one or two were made), while it is doubtful if the Sprite could have sold the 5000 units annually required to make it viable. The new Edward Turner regime at Daimler killed the project after about 10 cars had been completed, and the once great Lanchester name faded from the scene.

Frank survived his company by a few years, dying in March 1960 when just short of his 90th birthday. George died in February 1970 at the age of 95. GNG

LANCIA
ITALY 1906 to date

It has been said of Vincenzo Lancia that he never made a bad car; and while some achieved more renown than others, this is certainly not an exaggeration. Lancia was born in 1881, the youngest child of a wealthy soup manufacturer. His first job was as bookkeeper to Giovanni Ceirano's bicycle import business in Turin.

When FIAT took over Ceirano in 1899 Lancia became chief inspector to the new company and began a successful racing career with a victory at the Padua meeting in July 1900. He continued to drive for FIAT until 1908, but two years before he set up as a manufacturer, forming Lancia & Cie, Fabbrica Automobili on 27 November 1906. He was encouraged, and doubtless aided financially by, among others, Count Carlo Biscaretti di Ruffia who was also a founder of FIAT. He acquired a factory from Itala in which he initially employed 20 men, a number of them former FIAT employees.

The first Lancia was destroyed by fire in February 1907, before it had ever run, and it was September before its successor was ready. This Alfa, as it was retrospectively named, was a conventional car with 2543cc 28hp bi-bloc four-cylinder engine, four speed gearbox and shaft drive.

It went into production in early 1908, and 108 Alfas were made before they were replaced by the slightly larger monobloc 3120cc 15hp Beta. There was also a 3815cc six-cylinder Dialfa, of which only 23 were made. The Beta was developed into the 3460cc Gamma in 1910 and the 4080cc Delta in 1911, while production climbed from 150 in 1909 to 303 two years later.

It was in 1911 that Lancia bought much larger premises, at Via Monginevro on the outskirts of Turin, where he had 107,000sq ft (10,000sq m) of factory on a 430,000sq ft (40,000sq m) site. This was Lancia's main base until the later 1930s though he kept the 17,050sq ft (1584sq m) Via Ormea factory for coachbuilding. Outside coachbuilders such as Locatti & Torretta, Stabilimente Farina and Garavini also did work for Lancia. By 1911 several export markets had been found, including Britain, Argentina and Russia.

Lancia's most important pre-war model, the 35hp 4940cc Theta, was made from 1913 to 1918. It featured full electric lighting and starting, the first standardized system by a European manufacturer. A total of 1696 Thetas were made. The engine was also used in Lancia's first commercial chassis, the 1¾-ton IZ/Iota, as well as subsequent commercial chassis made as late as 1929. About 2300 trucks were made during the war, some of which were fitted with armoured car bodywork.

Lancia's first post-war car was the Kappa, an updated Theta with detachable cylinder head and central gearchange. Only 188 were made in 1919 but the following year a record 1059 were produced.

A foretaste of the future appeared at the 1919 motor shows in the form of a narrow angle (22°) V12 with monobloc casting. Although this never went into production a 4594cc 22° V8 was made from 1922 to 1925 under the name Trikappa, and when Lancia's famous Lambda appeared in 1922, that had a V4 engine with an even narrower angle of 13°. The Trikappa used the same chassis as the Kappa, and was the last of the old generation of Lancia. A total of 847 were made, of which 347 had front wheel brakes, and a further 358 earlier cars were recalled to be fitted with front wheel brakes.

In September 1921 tests began of the prototype Lambda, and the design was ready for production a year later. It was one of the most innovative cars of the decade, with its single-overhead cam V4 engine, vertical coil independent front suspension, unitary construction of the chassis and lower half of the body, and four-wheel brakes.

The typical early Lambda was a low-built four-seater open tourer. It was made in nine series, up to 1931, by which time the engine capacity had grown from 2120 to 2570cc and a total of 13,000 had been made. A separate chassis was available as an alternative to the monocoque from 1926, so that outside coachbuilders could work on the Lambda, but the factory body styles of torpedo tourer or six-light saloon were the most popular.

Because of its excellent road-holding the Lambda was often thought of as a sports car in Britain, but in its native Italy it was merely a comfortable fast tourer, and the closed model was popular as a taxicab. A few special two-seater sports models were made, three being entered in the 1928 Mille Miglia, in which they finished third, seventh and ninth.

In 1926 Vincenzo Lancia was approached by an American called Flocker with the idea of forming an American company which would make a 4-litre car especially designed for the US market. The following year Lancia Motors of America Inc was formed with nominal capital of $1 million. Lancia was asked to supply 10 prototypes for exhibition at the New York Importers Car Show. Lancia learnt too late that this was a mere stock promotion scheme, and he was never paid for his 10 prototypes, but they did form the basis of his next model, the Dilambda.

Introduced in 1929, this had a 3960cc 22° V8 engine developing 100bhp, an electrically welded frame and centralized chassis lubrication. Open and closed factory bodies were offered, but the Dilambda chassis became very popular for custom coachbuilding. Some of the earliest work of Pinin Farina was on the Dilambda, and other coachbuilders included Castagna and Viotti in Italy; Weymann, James Young and Gurney Nutting in England; Kellner, De Viscaya and Labourdette in France; and Murphy in America.

A total of 1686 Dilambdas were made between 1929 and 1935, including 20 with left hand drive which probably all went to the United States, as Italian quality cars still

Lancia Alfa of 1908

favoured right hand drive. Lancia did not change until 1954.

The Lambda was replaced for 1932 by two models, the Artena and the Astura which at first shared the same bodies and differed only in their engines, a 1924cc V4 for the Artena and a 2604cc V8 for the Astura. They resembled scaled-down Dilambdas to start with, but soon adopted much more flowing lines, especially the fourth series Asturas of the late 1930s, which had 2972cc engines and hydraulic brakes and carried some of Pinin Farina's most extravagantly futuristic coachwork. By 1939 the Artena had been relegated to an army staff car or light van chassis, as it had been supplanted by two of Lancia's most famous small cars, the Augusta and the Aprilia. Total production of Artenas was 5072, and of Asturas 2946.

Introduced at the 1932 Paris Salon, the Augusta had the smallest engine of any Lancia yet, a V4 of 1194cc, with the single-overhead cam found on all its predecessors since the Lambda. The standard four-door saloons had unitary construction, but a separate chassis was available for custom coachbuilders.

From 1933 to 1937 Augustas were assembled in France by a French company capitalized at 10 million francs, with a factory at Bonneuil sur Marne. They were known as Belnas, and were succeeded by the Ardennes, which was the Aprilia imported com-

Giuseppe Baggi (mechanics).

Although he drove a prototype, Lancia never saw the Aprilia in production, for he died of a heart attack in February 1937 at the age of 56. His widow Adele became the symbolic president of the company, while management was taken over by Manlio Gracco. Soon afterwards Vincenzo's son Gianni Lancia took control, remaining at the head of the firm until 1955.

The Aprilia received a larger engine of 1486cc in 1939, and in the same year was joined by a smaller sister on similar lines, the 903cc Ardea. Both models were revived after the war. The Aprilia was dropped in 1949 after 14,704 had been made, but the Ardea continued to 1953 with more than 22,000 produced.

Commercial vehicles had been an important part of Lancia's business during the interwar years, and the 6½-ton 3RO with its five-cylinder diesel engine was made in large numbers for the army before and during World War II. More exciting was the Lince (Lynx) armoured car powered by a V8 Astura engine, with four wheel drive and steering, of which 250 were made. From 1937 onwards commercial vehicle production was concentrated at a factory in Bolzano.

The first new post-war Lancia was the Aurelia of 1950, designed by Gianni Lancia and former Alfa Romeo engineer Vittorio Jano. It

tions. The engine was increased to 2266 and finally to 2451cc and a De Dion rear axle appeared on the 1954 and later models. These Fourth Series B20s were also the first Lancias to have left hand drive as a standard item. The Aurelia saloons received the 2- and 2.3-litre engines in due course and were made until 1955, total production being 12,786. The coupés and a few convertibles were continued to 1958, with 3230 made.

The Aurelia B20 was very successful in racing and rallying between 1951 and 1955, and this encouraged Lancia to set up a competition department which fielded teams of sports/racing coupés and roadsters in the classic events such as Le Mans, Mille Miglia and Targa Florio. These D20, D24 and D25 cars had V6 engines of 2.6 to 3.7 litres and claimed many victories, including the 1953 Targa Florio and Carrera Panamericana, and 1954 Mille Miglia and Targa Florio.

In 1954 Lancia entered Formula 1 racing with the D50 2487cc four-overhead cam V8 Grand Prix car, which had pannier fuel tanks. Ascari won the 1955 Turin and Naples Grands Prix, and Lancia might have had a really successful season, but Ascari was killed testing a Ferrari at Monza in May. This tragedy, combined with the financial strain caused by the racing programme, led to the sale of the Grand Prix cars and their spares, tools and drawings to Ferrari. Jano, who had lost his

Lancia Dilambda coupé of c.1929

Lancia Augusta saloon of 1934

plete from Turin. About 2500 Belnas and 1600 Ardennes were sold before the French operation was closed down in 1938. More than 15,000 Augustas were built, making it the largest production Lancia of pre-World War II days.

Vincenzo Lancia's last design was the Aprilia, which has been described as the most advanced car built by a European firm in the 1930s. It had an all-new 1352cc V4 engine with single-overhead cam and hemispherical combustion chambers, all-round independent suspension and a fastback four-door unitary construction saloon body. A four-speed gearbox innocent of synchromesh might seem old-fashioned by 1937, but the Aprilia was intended for the keen driver and sold very well all over Europe. While the overall concept was Lancia's, the detail design fell to Battisto Falchetto (in charge of bodywork) and

Lancia Ardea saloon of c.1945

had a 1754cc overhead-valve V6 engine, and four-speed gearbox integral with the rear axle, of which the top three speeds now had synchromesh. The body was initially a four-door saloon, but in 1951 came the 1991cc B20 coupé which became one of the classic sports coupés of the 1950s and enabled Lancia to make a successful return to competi-

position as Lancia's chief designer, went to Ferrari as well. The cars appeared later in the season under the name Lancia-Ferrari. They had a very successful 1956 season, with Fangio winning the Drivers' Championship.

The competition cars brought a lot of fame to Lancia, but they did no good at all to the balance sheets, and in 1955 Gianni Lancia and his mother decided to sell their company. A buyer was found in millionaire Carlo Pesenti, who began a big modernization programme. This included the building of a 16-storey office block in Turin, which is still the company headquarters today, the street below it being renamed Via Vincenzo Lancia. Jano was replaced by Antonio Fessia who had been responsible for the Fiat Topolino and the Cemsa Caproni front-drive car.

The first product of the Pesenti regime was the Flaminia, a four-door saloon with all-enveloping styling by Pininfarina, 2458cc V6

Lancia Stratos rally car of c.1974

engine and De Dion transaxle. The traditional sliding pillar front suspension was abandoned after 35 years, being replaced by wishbones and coil springs. Launched in 1957, the Flaminia saloon sold well to start with, at the rate of about 650 a year until 1962, when engine capacity went up to 2775cc, but thereafter sales dropped to little more than 300 annually while the last 599 Flaminias took seven years to sell, from 1964 to 1970.

Pesenti's concentration on smaller cars meant that there was little money or manpower to spare for improving the Flaminia, and competition from Jaguar and Mercedes-Benz was too keen anyway. Flaminia coupés and convertibles by Pininfarina, Touring and Zagato sold better, with 8663 being made between 1959 and 1967.

The small Lancias of the period were the Appia, which was essentially a baby Aurelia with 1089cc V4 engine although later ones looked more like the Alfa Romeo Giulietta, the flat-four Flavia and the V4 Fulvia. The Flavia was a resurrection of Fessia's 1949 Cemsa Caproni design with 1488cc flat-four engine driving the front wheels and four-door integral construction saloon body. A total of 64,739 were made between 1961 and 1970, together with 19,293 Pininfarina coupés. From 1970 to 1974 a further 15,025 saloons and 6791 coupés were made with a 1991cc engine, making the Flavia the best-selling Lancia yet.

However, it was outsold by the smaller V4 Fulvia, with 1098cc (later 1216/1298cc) engine, which was also made as a four-door saloon and two-door coupé. The Fulvia was made from 1963 to 1976, during which time more than 359,000 found buyers. Most Flavias and all Fulvias were made at a new body and assembly factory at Chivasso.

Lancia sales dropped alarmingly in the late 1960s from a peak of 43,000 in 1967 to 37,000 the following year and still fewer in 1969. Pesenti was no longer interested in the company and looked around for a buyer. Ford was considered but the Italian government did not want control to go abroad, so an approach was made to Fiat. In October 1969 the 'colossus of Turin' took over Lancia, paying a nominal 1 lira per share, although it also acquired massive debts as well. Fulvia

production was streamlined and prices reduced, while the Flavia was renamed the Lancia 2000 and with its 1991cc engine was continued for a further four years.

A casualty of the Fiat takeover was Lancia's heavy vehicle department, whose products were too close to Fiat's. Truck production ceased in 1970, but buses were continued for two more years to allow for the completion of contracts. Since then the Bolzano factory has made Fiat's specialized 4×4 trucks, including those for the army.

Lancia's successful rally programme which centred on the purpose-built Stratos coupé was also run down, although Lancia Squadra Corse was not finally merged into Fiat's Squadra Corse Unificata until 1978. By that time the Stratos had won 14 World Championship Rallies and 68 other international events. The leading drivers were Bernard Darniche, Sandro Munari and Tony Carello.

The first fruits of the Fiat takeover appeared at the 1972 Turin Motor Show in the shape of the Beta, a six-light fastback saloon styled by Lancia but powered by Fiat engines of 1438, 1596 or 1756cc which drove the front wheels via a five-speed gearbox. Later variants included the coupé and HPE (High Performance Estate) models, while 1975 saw the Monte Carlo coupé with 1995cc engine mounted amidships and driving the rear wheels.

In 1976 came a replacement for the Fiat 130, the Lancia Gamma, powered by a 2484cc flat-four engine of entirely Lancia design and construction, with five-speed gearbox, front wheel drive and all independent suspension. The six-light body, though having some family resemblance to that of the Beta, was styled by Pininfarina and was joined by a coupé, also the work of Pininfarina.

Less original than the Gamma was the small car of the new regime, the Fiat Ritmo-based Delta, unveiled in 1978. Engine options were Fiat 1302 or 1499cc units and McPherson strut front and rear suspension also came from Fiat. The Delta's body was an original design by Giugiaro, but the car was, and is, built in the Fiat factory. In 1983 it was joined by a booted version, the Prisma, and a turbocharged 4×4 Delta was announced for limited production later in the year. It is likely that four-wheel drive will be extended to the whole Lancia range by 1990.

The Beta's replacement appeared in the shape of the Trevi, a four-door saloon with boot, and engine options of 1585 or 1995cc. The Volumex version of the larger Trevi was unusual in having an engine-driven Roots supercharger instead of the turbocharger so fashionable among rival manufacturers.

The 1984 Lancia range included, as well as Delta, Prisma and Trevi, the HPE and Beta coupés, Montecarlo coupé including the supercharged Rally version which cost nearly 44 million lire, compared with 18 million lire for the 'regular' Montecarlo, and Gamma sa-

Lancia Y10 of 1986

Lancia Thema V6 of 1986

loon and coupé. The 1985 range was slimmed down, with only the Delta and Prisma being carried on. A new model for 1985 was the Thema four-door saloon, a contender in the Peugeot 505/BMW 5 Series market, available with five different engines from a basic 1.6-litre through a PRV 2.7-litre V6 to a Ferrari 3-litre V6 developing 200bhp. Also new was the Y10, a stubby three-door hatchback with 999 or 1050cc four-cylinder engines in 45, 55 or 85bhp forms, built by Autobianchi and sold under either the Autobianchi or Lancia names. Although fully integrated into Fiat's financial structure, Lancia continues to make highly individual cars. In 1984 190,950 cars were made. GNG

LA NEF
FRANCE 1899-1921

La Nef three-wheeler of 1901

This obscure and primitive De Dion-engined and tiller-steered three-wheeler had a one-cylinder engine driving Bozier gearbox and side belts to the two rear wheels. It would hardly warrant a mention but for its long production life.

Lacroix, a photographer who made early experiments with colour, built a prototype in 1899 and formed Lacroix et de Laville at Agen, Aquitaine, to make the La Nef (a fanciful word for ship). Up to a dozen men were employed by the firm and about 200 vehicles had been made by 1914. The machines were especially popular with local doctors and vicars (to whom 'nef' meant 'nave').

The car was still listed in 1921 but under a new maker's name, that of René Augustin in Agen, but this may have been no more than a spares and servicing operation. Several La Nefs are still known to exist. NB

LA PERLE
FRANCE 1913-1927

Meaning both pearl and, by association, the best, the Perle was the work of Fernand Lefèvre of Boulogne-sur-Seine. It started in 1913 as a two-cylinder cyclecar but re-emerged after the war as a 9.5hp light car. The engines came from Jacques Bignan and the chassis from Malicet et Blin. Five were built for racing, production models becoming available for 1922. Bignan's freelance designer, Némorin Causan, produced for La Perle an overhead-valve, four-cylinder 1½-litre engine in 1921 followed by an over-

head-cam, 1½-litre six in 1924.

Franz Lefèvre joined the firm to give his brother freedom to promote the make in voiturette races and hillclimbs, and roughly 300 sales of four-cylinder cars and 75 sixes followed before the factory closed in 1927. Louis Lefèvre, another brother, who also raced, converted his 105mph (169kph) six into a sports car in 1931, one replica of which was built using spares. NB

La Perle voiturette racer of 1921

LA PONETTE
FRANCE 1909-1925

G. Granvaud's single-cylinder 7hp light car with planetary transmission was made at St Remy les Chevreuse, Seine et Oise, from 1909. It may have had some connection with the equally skittish La Trotteuse made in the town in 1913-14 which also used small singles.

The Ponette (Pony) was said to be the work of Englishman John Averies, who probably had a hand in Dupressoir's Rolling models, one of which became the Averies cyclecar in England in 1913-14. As Paul Dupressoir of Maubeuge made chassis for other firms the horsepower of Chevreuse may have owed something to him. Granvaud came out with a new line of Ballot-powered four-cylinder cars in 1912 and these quickly replaced the singles.

After World War I G. Granvaud (La Ponette) of Chevreuse gave way to Société Anonyme des Automobiles La Ponette at Clichy, Seine et Oise, by 1923. Chassis numbers then exceeded 700. The car range went up to 2.8 litres and used some home-built engines, although Ballot and SCAP units were still being offered. Production finally came to an end in 1925. NB

LA SALLE
see Cadillac

LAURIN AND KLEMENT
AUSTRIA, CZECHOSLOVAKIA 1905-1927

In the mid-1890s a mechanic named Vaclav Laurin and a bookseller named Vaclav Klement, both of Mlada Boleslav in what is now

Czechoslovakia but was then a province of the Austrian empire, set up a small workshop to make bicycles. At first they had only five employees and worked in a single rented room, but the cycles, which were named Slavia, sold well, and in 1898 they moved into a proper factory.

The following year they began manufacture of motorcycles, initially with Werner engines over the front wheel but later with conventionally-mounted single and V-twin engines of their own make. They were sold as Slavias in their homeland, as Germanias in Germany where they were made under licence by Seidel and Naumann of Dresden, and Republics elsewhere. The first V-twin was made in 1903, and the first four-cylinder motorcycle in 1905.

Car production began in 1905 with the Type A, a 7hp V-twin two-seater with shaft drive, followed by the larger 9hp Type B. The works expanded greatly over the next two years, and in 1907 the hitherto private concern became a joint-stock company.

Four-cylinder cars of 16 and 28hp appeared in 1907, as did the first commercial vehicles which were light vans on the small two- and four-cylinder chassis. A straight-eight touring car was built in 1907 using two 2.4-litre 16hp engines in line; it was probably a one-off, but the Austrians still deserve credit for a pioneering design.

In 1908 Otto Hieronymus joined the company as chief designer, although he also won fame as a competition driver. He was responsible for the Model GDV four-cylinder car, which was widely used as a taxicab in Prague, Vienna, Paris, Moscow and St Petersburg. Hieronymus designed a 50hp aero engine in 1909, which he installed in a Bleriot monoplane and flew himself in 1910.

Exports accounted for about 70 per cent of Laurin and Klement's output in the pre-1914 period. Military trucks were produced for the armies of Russia and Japan, as well as forward control trucks and buses for the post office of the kingdom of Montenegro, now part of Yugoslavia.

By 1911 Laurin and Klement was making road rollers, motor ploughs and stationary engines in addition to cars, trucks and motorcycles. Production that year was 800 cars, 300 motorcycles and 270 stationary engines. Exports to western Europe began to

Laurin and Klement Type A of 1905

dwindle in the last pre-war years, but this was compensated by other markets, particularly Russia, which took 30 per cent of Laurin and Klement's output, Mexico, Egypt and Japan. A few vehicles were also sold in Australia and New Zealand.

In 1912 there was further factory expansion at Mlada Boleslav, and in the same year the Reichenberger Automobil-Fabrik of Liberec was acquired. Founded in 1907 this German-owned company made sleeve-valve engines under Knight licence, so for 1913 Laurin and Klement was able to offer two large sleeve-valve cars, the 3.3-litre MK and 4.7-litre RK, in addition to its other models. In 1914 the Liberec factory was sold and its equipment moved to Mlada Boleslav.

During World War I the company kept going with the manufacture of trucks for the Austrian army; the commercial side of the business continued after the war. The market was much smaller after 1918, being virtually confined to the new republic of Czechoslovakia. Car models included the 2.4-litre S-Type and 4.7-litre Type 300, both with poppet valves, and the sleeve-valve 3.3-litre four-cylinder Type 400 and 5-litre six-cylinder Type 500. These were made in smaller numbers than before the war, not more than a few hundred a year, and the introduction of a new small car, the 1.8-litre four-cylinder Type 100, did not help sales much.

Laurin and Klement was at a disadvantage compared with its Czech rivals Praga and Tatra as it lacked alternative products (such as Tatra's railway rolling stock). Unable to carry on independently the company merged with the enormous armaments firm Skoda, although the name did not disappear immediately as for two years the new owner carried on with the old designs, which wore both names on their radiators. These were the 2-litre Type 110 and 3.7-litre Type 350, the latter being the first Laurin and Klement to have overhead valves. After 1927 these models became part of the Skoda range. Both Laurin and Klement continued to work for the new company right up until their deaths on 4 December 1930 and 13 August 1938 respectively. GNG

LEADER
GB 1905-1909

Charles Binks Ltd was a bicycle manufacturer in Apsley, Nottingham, from 1901 and in March 1905 introduced the Leader car. The first models were 10 and 14hp four-cylinders, the cylinders being cast separately. The 10hp offered a two-seater body and the 14hp was available as a tourer or a hansom. They were very cheap but quite well made, *The Car* remarking that a price of 200 guineas for the 10hp was a 'sensation' for an English-built four-cylinder car.

Among the features of the first models was a carburettor of Binks' own design and for

which he ultimately became much better known than as a car-maker. It had a jet adjustable from the steering wheel by way of turning one perforated nozzle over another, to give far better contol over engine speed than most contemporary arrangements.

At the Olympia Show in November 1905 Leader announced a large variety of models including two V8s, one of 30hp and another allegedly of up to 120hp, but these were too late for the show and only the smaller models were shown, the 8hp four-cylinder at £195 being probably the cheapest four-cylinder car on the market. The 10hp four was now £280, the 30hp V8 a very cheap £550 and the supposed 120hp V8 a somewhat more daunting £1500.

At that time the company was listed as Leader Motors Ltd of Nottingham, but in 1906 it became New Leader Motors Ltd, in time for the Olympia Show in April. One model, a 20/30hp four, was again late in arriving, but then proved very popular alongside the 10/12. At this show Leader also exhibited two launches, one of 24ft (7.3m) and one of 40ft (12.2m), powered by marinized versions of the car engines.

A six-cylinder Leader was introduced in 1906, joining a huge range of engine types and sizes from a 1225cc three-cylinder to a 15,934cc V8. Strangely, although the Binks carburettor was widely known, and used on other makes including Rover, the 10/12hp Leaders listed in 1907 used Brown and Barlow carburettors.

By 1907 Leader also offered a 15hp van, advertised as 'Absolutely the Best', but by 1909 car manufacture had stopped, the last models being 12/16hp fours, introduced in 1906 and continued through to the end. BL

LEA-FRANCIS
GB 1903-1960; 1980 to date

Like so many firms in Coventry and elsewhere, Lea-Francis had its origins in the cycle industry. In 1895 Richard Henry Lea and Graham Ingoldsby Francis formed a partnership in Day's Lane, Coventry, to manufacture bicycles. Lea had been with the Singer company since 1878, while Francis had worked for the woodworking machining company Ludwig Loewe Co in Berlin, for Pratt & Whitney (machine tools) in the United States, and the Auto Machinery Co of Coventry, a ball bearing manufacturer run by William Hillman.

In 1896 they formed a limited company, Lea and Francis Ltd, with issued share capital of £11,000, and bought a 2-acre (0.8 hectare) site from Lord Leigh in Lower Ford Street, Coventry, which was the home of Lea-Francis cycles, motorcycles and cars up to 1936. As well as cycles, components such as patented reflectors and geared hubs were made for sale to other firms.

Bicycles were made until World War I and motorcycles from 1911 to 1924, although not

more than 1500 of these were made. An early customer was George Bernard Shaw. In 1903 the partners hired an independent engineer, Alexander Craig, to design a car for them. To protect the cycle business a new company was formed purely for motor car development. The Lea & Francis Motor Syndicate Ltd was incorporated in June 1903 with authorized capital of £10,000, although only £3942 was ever taken up.

The car was an unusual design, with a horizontal three-cylinder engine of 3680cc mounted under the floorboards, very long connecting rods of 33in (838mm) and immense flywheels at each end of the crankshaft. It was overpriced, at £787 10s, later increased to £850, and although three cars were made, only two were sold. One went to Hans Renold, the famous chain maker and a personal friend of R. H. Lea.

Lea & Francis salvaged something of their investment by selling the licence to the Craig design to Singer, which made a few two-cylinder cars of similar layout. The Motor Syndicate was kept alive until 1909 but no further cars were built, and an overall loss of £3375 was made on the project. Craig's main interest was in the Maudslay company, of which he was chairman from 1910 to 1935, although he was also a director of Rover from 1926, and chairman from 1931 to 1933.

The company survived on the production of cycles and motorcycles until World War I, when it also undertook the production of range-finding gear and other instruments for the Admiralty. Motorcycles were made until 1916, and a number of second hand machines were bought by the Italian army.

In 1919 Lea-Francis returned to four wheels with a rather heavy 11.9hp four-cylinder car, whose 130mm stroke gave it a capacity of 1944cc. It was designed by Arthur Alderson who had previously worked for Singer and Calcott, but was not sufficiently different from the many other cars in its class on the market, and only 23 were sold.

The next three years saw some prototypes of two-cylinder light cars, one designed by R. H. Lea and another by Lea and Alderson, but the next car to see production was a light four-cylinder machine powered by a 1074cc Coventry-Simplex engine, with a Meadows three-speed gearbox.

This was designed by Alderson, but was considerably re-vamped for production by Dutch-born Charles Van Eugen, who joined the company in 1922 after working for Daimler, ABC, Briton, Royal Ruby (motorcycles), Clyno and Swift. His arrival coincided with a reorganization of the Lea-Francis board, under the chairmanship of C. B. Wardman who was also head of Vulcan Motors Ltd. This began links with the Southport firm which lasted for six years, and did little, if any, good to Lea-Francis.

Van Eugen's light car went into production in April 1923, and after 91 had been built in four months, a change was made to a 1247cc overhead-valve Meadows engine. Most of the bodies were made by Robinsons of Coventry, including the first aluminium sports body delivered in 1924, but Avon of Warwick also contributed some four-seaters.

The success of the 'C' and 'D' light cars gave Lea-Francis its first post-war profit in 1925 (£4150), when 750 cars were sold. In 1926 sales reached the 800 mark and profits were £11,700. Although the little Meadows-engined cars were made until 1928, they were eclipsed by the 12/22 and 12/40, touring and sports models powered by the new Meadows 4ED 1496cc engine.

If only Lea-Francis had kept to these three cars its future might have been assured for some time, but from 1927 the company embarked on a costly failure. This was the LFS 14/40, a 1696cc twin-overhead cam six designed by A. O. Lord and built by Vulcan, which used the engine in its own 14hp. On paper it sounded an exciting proposition, but it was very unreliable, in particular suffering bearing failures, and would not have been a blessing as a gift. In fact, Lea-Francis had to pay £20,000 to Vulcan for the privilege of

Eighteen in February 1932. The 2-litre car was known as the Ace of Spades, because of the resemblance of the engine seen end on to the playing card.

Only 29 cars were delivered in 1932, 12 in 1933 and three in 1934, when Van Eugen left in order to design the Autovia V8. Sales in 1935 were five cars, but there were 12 new cars unsold at the August 1935 stocktaking. No cars were made in 1936, but nine of the left overs were sold.

In 1935 a consortium called Leaf Engineering Co Ltd headed by George H. Leek, former general manager of Riley, tried to raise money to acquire the company but did not succeed, and in 1936 the Lower Ford Street works, together with the remaining machinery and plant, were sold for £22,000 to General Electric, which is still there today.

Meanwhile, Leek and his friend Hugh Rose were planning a new car with an engine of the latter's design. Rose had also been with Riley, for whom he designed the 12hp Lynx engine, and the design he produced for Leek was similar to the Riley, with high-mounted, but

Francis vehicles were built as estate cars to avoid purchase tax. Production in 1949 was about 500, in 1950 nearly 700 and in 1951 just under 600, but thereafter only about 170 before the last cars were sold in 1952. Assembly of the final chassis took place in 1952.

The market for the specialist hand-built car was a crowded one at the time, and Lea-Francis was competing with Alvis, Armstrong-Siddeley, Riley and above all Jaguar, whose excellent-value cars outsold all their rivals. From 1949 to 1953 some chassis and engines were supplied to the makers of Connaught sports cars, and there was also an unsuccessful attempt to sell engines for use in American midget dirt track racing cars.

Subcontracting work, including naval gun trolleys and jig and tool design, kept the company busy through much of the 1950s, but at the 1960 London Motor Show a new car appeared. This was a flamboyant 2/4 seater roadster on a tubular frame powered by a 2¼-litre Ford Zephyr engine. Known as the Lynx, it attracted more jokes than favourable publicity, and although three demonstrators

Lea-Francis 10hp G-Type of 1925

Lea-Francis sports two-seater of 1980

using it. At £550 for a saloon, it was the most expensive Lea-Francis yet made. A total of around 350 LFS models were sold.

The company became increasingly involved in competitions from 1924, winning 96 major trials awards in 1924 and 1925, and turning to racing from 1926. Its efforts were crowned by Kaye Don's victory in the 1928 Tourist Trophy with a supercharged Hyper sports, derived from the 12/40. However, the expenditure on racing and on the LFS brought about a loss of £17,200 for the year to mid-1928, and this led to the resignation of Wardman, followed soon afterwards by the other Vulcan directors. By 1930 production was down to 290 cars and losses amounted to more than £12,000.

A receiver was appointed in March 1931, the workforce was cut back, and the three Hyper team cars were put up for sale. Within two weeks R. H. Lea resigned, breaking the last tie with the original partners, as G. H. Francis had left in 1924 to concentrate on the Swedish Skefco Bearing Co.

Production of the 12/40 and the new 2-litre single-overhead cam six designed by Van Eugen continued in declining numbers until 1934, and was joined by a 2243cc six-cylinder

not overhead, twin camshafts.

A new company called Lea-Francis Engineering (1937) Ltd was formed in July 1937, and premises acquired from Triumph in Much Park Street, Coventry. Two sizes of engine were offered, a 1496cc Twelve and a 1629cc Fourteen, with attractive bodies by New Avon and Charlesworth. About 100 were made until the outbreak of World War II, but the new company lost £16,400 up to 31 January 1939, and £4000 in the next 12 months.

As with most engineering companies, the war was a financial godsend to Lea-Francis, which did subcontracting work for BSA, Shorts of Belfast and A. V. Roe. The company ended the war with a 1944 profit of £51,855, and launched its post-war cars in January 1946. Engines were similar to those in the pre-war models, but the bodies were now made by A. P. Aircraft Ltd in the former Cross & Ellis factory.

Lea-Francis sold 326 cars in 1946, 565 in 1947 and 551 in 1948, when it bought the Charlesworth body factory for the production of a new streamlined saloon powered by Rose's new 2½-litre four-cylinder engine. A two-seater sports car with 1.8 or 2½-litre engine was made from 1948, and many Lea-

were built, no orders were received and the project was abandoned.

Lea-Francis then dabbled in the making of go-karts, assembling Nobel 200 three-wheeled bubble cars, and making a garden tractor called the Unihorse, as well as starting work on another car, a large saloon to be powered by a Chrysler V8 engine. This was never completed, and after mounting losses the Lea-Francis assets and name were acquired in November 1962 by the replacement components firm Quinton Hazell Ltd for £55,000. This company formed a subsidiary, Lea-Francis Engineering Ltd, and used the name as a brand for certain replacement parts such as water pumps and clutches. This disappeared after Quinton Hazell was acquired by Burmah Castrol in 1972.

The assets and rights of the motor car division were bought in 1962 by Barrie Price of A. B. Price Ltd, which handled spares and service from Studley, Warwickshire. In 1977 he and Peter Engelbach decided to revive the marque using the Jaguar XJ6 engine in a sports car of traditional shape. The first car was completed in 1980, and since then four pre-production prototypes have been manufactured. GNG/NB

LEGROS
FRANCE 1900-1913

At the Paris Salon in 1900 René Legros of Fécamp, Seine-Inferieure, showed the Legros-Meynier electric car. It had five forward speeds and three braking speeds but was described as 'somewhat top-heavy'. Soon after, Legros introduced its first petrol car, with 4hp single-cylinder air-cooled engine mounted at the front and driving the rear wheels by way of two-speed gears and a belt final drive. They were known, appropriately, as 'La Plus Simple', a name which Legros used right up to the end of production.

By the end of 1901 Legros offered a 6hp model with a choice of its own, Aster or De Dion engines and this continued with few changes up to 1906. In 1902 8 and 12hp models were listed, and at the Paris Salon in 1904 Legros showed a two-stroke 10/12hp twin and a 15/20 twin.

In January 1905 the company showed a three-cylinder two-stroke model having a compound piston arrangement of one long, hollow working piston surrounding a fixed piston to pump mixture to the combustion chamber via a non-return valve system. A 12/15 model listed in December 1905 had a rotary inlet valve added to the design and all models used an ingenious tapered triangular section sliding drive-shaft design. The 18hp chassis was very reasonably priced in 1905 at only £350. In 1906 a 10hp twin-cylinder model with three passengers and their luggage averaged a creditable 20mph (33kph) in the Paris-Monte Carlo-Paris trial, but Legros did not really have any sporting aspirations.

By 1912 the range included two twins and four four-cylinder models, all with two-stroke engines very similar to those used since 1905. The range continued largely unchanged until production stopped in 1913. BL

LE GUI
see Guy (France)

LÉON BOLLÉE/MORRIS LÉON BOLLÉE
FRANCE 1895-1933

Léon Bollée was the son of Amédée Sr, the bell-founder and steam pioneer of Le Mans, and brother of Amédée Jr. At the age of 25 he made his first 3hp voiturette with single driven rear wheel in 1895. It was he who coined the term voiturette for this machine. H. J. Lawson acquired British rights for 500,000 francs and had some Coventry Motette versions built.

The French rights went to Gustave Chauveau's Société des Voiturettes Automobiles, which subcontracted manufacture

Leon Bollée double saloon of 1911

Leon Bollée design of 1898, constructed by Darracq

to sewing machine maker Diligeon et Cie. In 1896 Michelin ordered 200. Léon Bollée, who also developed a mechanical calculator, was left free to invent and produced a four-wheeler with independent front suspension in 1898, the rights of which were sold to Darracq for 250,000 francs.

After various experiments Bollée launched 28 and 45hp cars in 1902 from a factory provided by his father in Le Mans near Amédée Bollée's own car works. They were intended in particular for the American market and were joined by an 11.9-litre six in 1907. A 10/14hp four was added in 1909. Output ranged between 150 and 350 cars a year. Financial backing came from Vanderbilt interests. Orville and Wilbur Wright spent much time with Léon Bollée working on aero engine design.

Bollée died prematurely in 1913 and his widow took control of the business. In 1914 a total of 267 cars were built, and on the return of peace the figure rose to about 500 yearly until 1921. The firm and its products then stagnated and in late 1924 Automobiles Léon Bollée was acquired by Morris, having made 255 examples of its 10CV that year; about 400 were produced in 1925. The new 12CV Morris Léon Bollée of 1925 used French-built Hotchkiss engines and production ran at about

2500 in 1926. Later on a few carried six- and eight-cylinder Wolseley 15 and 18CV units.

The works manager was Harry Smith, who was brought in from Morris's engine branch, and design was by Van Vestrant and Hans Landstad. Formerly of Hotchkiss, Landstad later became technical director of Morris and a board member from 1926.

By October 1928 losses had reached the equivalent of £150,000 and sales that year sank to under 2000. In September 1931, after two years of selling only about 400 cars a year, Morris cut its losses by disposing of the factory to Société Nouvelle Léon Bollée, a company run by A. Dunlop Mackenzie, Harry Smith and a representative of a major supplier of components. This company lasted until 1933, making the 12CV and various commercial vehicles. NB

LÉON LAISNÉ/HARRIS-LÉON LAISNÉ
FRANCE 1913-1937

Léon Laisné was born in 1880 and went to work in a bronze foundry at the age of 13. Two years later he joined the Hurtu company which later made Benz-like cars but at that time were concentrating on sewing machines and bicycles. He then went to Léon Bollée at Le Mans. He built two cars for his own use in 1899 and 1901, and after military service started a small machine tool works at Douai. There he made one or two experimental cars with independent front suspension and in 1913 started to build cars, with Chapuis-Dornier engines and tubular chassis, to special order.

During World War I Douai was invaded by the German army; Laisné joined the air force but was invalided out in 1916. He then returned to machine toolwork, taking larger premises at Nantes, where he was kept very busy making shells.

In 1919 he began to make cars on a commercial basis; they had four-cylinder Ballot or Chapuis-Dornier engines and all-round independent suspension by vertical coils. They were made in small numbers, always as a sideline to the machine tool business; various other engines were used from time to time, including Decolonges and SCAP.

In the mid-1920s the total workforce was 100, fewer than half of whom worked on the cars. In 1926 Laisné obtained additional capital from an Englishman named Harris and a new range of cars was launched under the name Harris-Léon Laisné. These had tubular frames, in which were mounted coil springs which provided the suspension, and sliding pistons which acted as dampers. Low-slung saloon and tourer bodies were provided, somewhat reminiscent of the Lancia Lambda, and all seating was within the wheelbase.

A variety of engines was provided, to the customer's choice. They included 1.2-litre and 1½-litre four-cylinder SCAP, 1.2- and 1.4-litre six-cylinder CIME, and 1½- or 2-litre straight-eight SCAP. By 1930, when rubber suspension units had replaced the coil springs, larger engines were available including 3-litre six-cylinder Continental and Hotchkiss units. Some handsome two-door saloon bodies by Million-Guiet were mounted on these Type V chassis.

About 150 Harris-Léon Laisné cars were made between 1928 and 1932, of which more than half were acquired by the experimental departments of manufacturers in France and abroad. At least one Model A Ford was fitted with Harris-Léon Laisné rubber suspension. Harris and Laisné parted company in 1933, the Englishman later making a single example of a front-wheel-drive car with Laisné suspension and Standard 12 engine, which he called the Harris Six.

Production of Léon Laisné cars dwindled in the 1930s and finances were probably not helped by some experimental cars which were never sold to the public. These included a 1.2-litre front-drive saloon of 1930, and Type V chassis powered by a 4-litre D8 Delage engine (1934) and 3.6-litre Ford V8 engine (1935). The smaller cars were listed until 1937. Laisné retired three years later to run a garage in Toulouse. He died in about 1946. GNG

LE ROY
CANADA 1899-1904

Built by the brothers Milton and Nelson Good in Berlin (now Kitchener), Ontario, the Le Roy was Canada's first car to be made in series. They built an experimental car with single-cylinder engine in 1899, following it with a petrol-engined conversion of a Mobile

steamer in 1901, but neither of these was suitable for production.

The success of the Curved Dash Oldsmobile in America led the Good brothers to plan a car on these lines, and in 1902, aided by a nephew, I. G. Neuber, they formed the Le Roy Manufacturing Co to build cars which were closely patterned on the Olds, but which had a wavy front as they felt the curve would be difficult to steam and bend. This had the fortunate effect of giving the Le Roy a quite different appearance from its American prototype, because otherwise it was a very close (and unauthorised) copy. One other difference was that the Le Roy had no brakes, the driver relying on the reverse speed of the planetary transmission when he wanted to stop.

The first five cars were made in small rented premises, bodies being supplied by a neighbouring lumber merchant, Jacob Kaufman. Early in 1903 the Goods took larger premises and as Kaufman was unable to supply bodies in quantity they bought these from a carriage maker in Breslau. Some of these were dos-à-dos four seaters.

Lack of capital prevented the Goods from improving their car and production came to a standstill at the end of 1904, after 25 further cars had been made, though not all completed. The brothers made stationary engines for farm use for a few years and then gave up their partnership. Nelson took on the McLaughlin agency for the Berlin area but died young in 1914, while Milton became an osteopath and lived until 1955. GNG

LEWIS
AUSTRALIA 1900-1907

Australia was fairly slow to accept the car and up to the turn of the century was very much a horse dominated society, boasting around one horse per head of population. A few steam cars were built, but fuel was a problem, and the few petrol cars imported piecemeal were even less well catered for, with no garages as such and severe restrictions on the amount of fuel which could be stored.

In May 1898 Mlle Serpollet, of the French motoring family, visited Sydney and demonstrated a Gladiator tricycle, the first petrol car to be imported to South Australia and supplied by a local bicycle agent. After the machine had failed to run on a first attempt, it was serviced at the Lewis Cycle and Motor Works in Adelaide, prompting the proprietor of Lewis's, T. P. O'Grady, to plan a car of his own.

By the end of 1898 he had built and successfully run an engine, which he tested in a tandem. Lewis's began assembling cars for sale in about 1900; they were the first four-wheeled petrol-engined cars in South Australia and only two years behind the first import.

The Lewis car used a 4½hp single cylinder

engine and belt drive. Several were built over the next few years, although Lewis's main business continued to be servicing and repairing other makes and building bodies.

In 1902 a local newspaper hired a Lewis car to ferry copy from a murder trial to the nearby telegraph office, giving Lewis valuable publicity, but most Australian car buyers still settled for imports. Like Lewis, many cycle dealers gradually took up car agencies, mostly bringing in cars from the United States and often taking one third of the price as a deposit long before giving a delivery date.

Although Lewis continued to build cars until 1907 – and motorcycles until 1914 – the company could not compete. Its Victoria Square works stopped car production and were eventually demolished to make way for a new State Administration Centre. Lewis stayed in business until 1975, finally making invalid carriages. BL

LEWIS
USA 1913-1916

The Mitchell and Lewis Co of Racine, Wisconsin, from which had grown the Mitchell Motor Car Co, was run by William Mitchell Lewis. Following the reorganization of the family firm in 1910 into the $10 million capitalized Mitchell-Lewis Motor Co, Lewis formed a rival concern in 1913 called the Lewis Motor Co, also based in Racine. A long-stroke six-cylinder 5.5-litre model was designed for Lewis by René Petard, who had also worked on Mitchell models, and this was sold under the slogan 'Monarch of the Sixes'.

In 1914 William Mitchell Lewis retired from Mitchell-Lewis and his new firm was reformed as the LPC Motor Car Co. (The initials stood for Lewis, Petard, and James Cram from Mitchell's New York sales office.) World War I hampered sales of Lewis cars and Petard returned to his native France.

Another Mitchell-Lewis company, Corliss Steel, and the local J. I. Case engineering factory supplied creditors' representatives who liquidated LPC in March 1916. Spares were sold to the American Motor Co of Indianapolis and parts of the factory to Mitchell-Lewis. NB

LEXINGTON
USA 1909-1926

The Lexington was made for most of its life in Connersville, Indiana, but it first saw the light of day in Lexington, Kentucky, hence its name. The original company, capitalized at $50,000, was formed by a local horse race promoter, Kinsey Stone, and the first Lexingtons were conventional assembled cars with four-cylinder Rutenber engines.

In less than a year demand proved too great for the small building, and rather than ex-

Lexington roadster of 1910

pand, Stone sold his company to a group of Connersville businessmen who moved production to Indiana during 1910. With the company went its chief engineer, John C. Moore, who remained with Lexington until its demise. For 1911 the range was increased to eight models on two wheelbases, the top model being a limousine priced at $2500.

The Lexington Motor Co got into difficulties in 1913 through over-expansion which it could not finance, but a group of Connersville citizens came to the rescue and the company entered 1914 on a sounder footing. It brought out a larger car powered by a 6.9-litre six-cylinder Continental engine which was assembled for a Chicago distributing firm to be sold under the name Howard. The manufacturer's name was changed to Lexington-Howard, but the larger car failed to sell well and was dropped, although the new company name survived until 1918.

For 1915 Lexington had three models, the regular four, a light six ('Thoroughbred Six'), and a big six, all with John Moore's Multiple Exhaust System, which was claimed to give 30 per cent more power on less fuel. All engines were by Continental.

In 1916 came a cheaper six, the 'Minute Man Six', priced at $1350 for a convertible sedan which had a detachable hard top, giving the comfort of a conventional sedan at a time when such a body was rare on lower priced cars. Wartime production included the building of General Motors trucks for the army and hemp rope for the navy.

On 1 April 1918 Frank B. Ansted, who had controlled Lexington for five years, formed the Ansted Engineering Co which acquired the engine builder Teetor-Hartley of Hagerstown, Indiana, and in 1919 Ansted formed a larger group, the United States Automotive Group, which owned Lexington, Teetor-Hartley, Ansted Engineering, and the Connersville Foundry Corporation. A new factory to make Ansted engines was erected next door to the Lexington plant, and thenceforth all Lexingtons were Ansted-powered. Ansted engines were also used in Durant cars and in the last few Australian Sixes.

In 1920 Lexington production reached its peak of more than 6000 cars, which for a time were being made at the rate of nearly 1000 a month. The following year was not so good, with only 2080 sales, and thereafter production fell to under 1000 by 1923. As with so many smaller firms which had nothing particularly distinctive to offer, Lexington simply could not compete with the big battalions. Despite the use of names recalling the American Revolution such as Concord and Minute Man Six, the cars did not even sell well in New England.

The Ansted Engine Co flourished for a while with orders from Billy Durant, but in April 1923 both Lexington and Ansted were in the hands of the receiver. A few cars were made over the next three or four years, the final ones of 1926 being sold in the Chicago area under the name Ansted. The Ansted plant was bought by E. L. Cord in 1926 for $40,000 and the Lexington plant went to Auburn the same year for $35,000. GNG

LEYAT
FRANCE 1919-1927

Born in 1885, the son of a magistrate, Marcel Leyat became interested in aviation at an early age and while working for the hydroplane maker Astra he started experiments in propeller design. His particular interest from 1907 was economical, low-powered flight and he flew a machine with his own design of engine in 1910. He then began experiments with propeller-driven tricycles in 1911-12.

In 1918 he took out patents for his Hélica car. This machine had a two-cylinder 8hp ABC engine, independent suspension, mesh-covered front propeller and rear-wheel steering with front brakes. It was marketed for a time in the early 1920s and 600 orders were said to have been taken at a 1921 show. Manufacture took place in Paris.

A three-cylinder 16hp Anzani-engined Hélica was driven 348 miles (561km) on mixed roads in 12 hours in 1921 to prove the practi-

cality of the system. A similar vehicle was offered concurrently by the Traction Aérienne firm of Neuilly, which used the name Eolia, although Hélica was sometimes applied to it, perhaps erroneously, by magazines.

Few Leyats were sold. The last was apparently a very low-built model in 1927 which embodied Leyat's intention that his cars should be thought of as aeroplanes without wings rather than cars with propellers.

Various Leyat aeroplanes were built both during and after the 1920s, notably the Leyat-Jacquemin, Hélicat and Lioré et Olivier, some of which used Renault engines. In the 1930s it was musical instrument design that began to absorb Leyat and after World War II he developed the Maler teaching system for languages, elocution, writing, typewriting, shorthand and musical instruments. NB

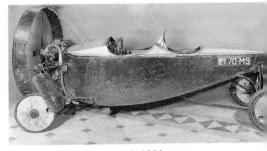

Leyat two-seat propeller car of c.1924

LEYLAND/BRITISH LEYLAND
GB 1918-1922; 1961 to date

British Leyland, which in 1975 effectively became the British national car producer after the government stepped in with a financial rescue, is an agglomeration, built throughout the 20th century, of many famous names in the motor industry, the central strand being the Leyland company.

Leyland was a Lancashire village where the Sumner family had run the blacksmith's forge for several generations. In the early 1880s the Sumners built a steam wagon, followed by a steam tricycle and then, in 1895, a steam tri-car for Theodore Carr, a well-known local biscuit-maker.

In 1892 James Sumner took charge of the family business and expanded it with financial backing from T. Coulthard and Co of Preston, which made steam wagons from the mid-1890s. In 1896 two brothers, George and Henry Spurrier, the latter a railway draughtsman recently returned from Florida, joined with Sumner and provided much of the money to form the Lancashire Steam Motor Co, with Henry on the board. The firm began to build steam wagons and steam lawnmowers and by 1902 it employed about 100 workers. A year later the workforce had grown to 160 and the company was reorganized with capital of £50,000.

In 1904 it started building trucks with Crossley internal combustion engines and in 1907 the Lancashire Steam Motor Co merged with its original backer, T. Coulthard and Co, to become Leyland Motors Ltd. By 1914 it was building 10 trucks a week, had an annual turnover of £500,000 and made a profit of £100,000.

The company expanded significantly during World War I, when it built as many as 40 trucks a week, plus ambulances and travelling workshops. Even before the war ended, Henry Spurrier had decided that the now financially secure company should build a luxury car.

The 7.3-litre Leyland Eight was designed by the company's chief engineer, John Godfrey Parry Thomas, and his assistant, Reid Railton, during 1917 and 1918. Thomas was a brilliant designer who had become a friend of Henry Spurrier Jr after a transmission to Thomas's designs was fitted to a Leyland-built railcar. He joined the company in 1917.

His Leyland Eight was planned as the world's finest luxury car, money no object. It was first shown (with a slightly smaller engine than subsequent production models) at the Olympia Motor Show in 1920. Its 40hp straight-eight engine had a single overhead cam and the chassis had servo brakes and torsion bar assisted rear suspension. It was a superb car, the most expensive British car of the time, at £3050, and the most powerful, with up to 145hp available. Unfortunately, its

involving the creation of £750,000 in new share capital. This was used to market refurbished ex-military vehicles but the post-war slump killed that market and by 1923 Leyland had a £1 million deficit.

From 1922 to 1928 Leyland built the spartan, low-cost Trojan car for Leslie Hounsfield until production passed to Trojan Ltd. Leyland's own output remained solely commercial vehicles. With the company revitalized by new management and with improving markets, Leyland was back in profit by 1929 and even managed to make about £500,000 a year during the Depression, helped by strong bus and truck sales.

The company continued to do well up to World War II, during which it made a wide range of military vehicles and equipment. After the war Leyland began a successful export programme, led by Donald Stokes who had joined the company as an apprentice in 1930. By 1954 this programme had created the first £1 million profit year and brought Stokes onto the Board.

Leyland continued to discuss mergers with sundry other commercial vehicle-builders and in 1951 paid almost £3 million for truck-builder Albion, itself a car-maker briefly before World War I. In 1955 it bought another truck-maker, Scammell, bringing group annual turnover to about £60 million.

Sir Henry Spurrier Jr, son of the joint founder, and Stokes now decided to re-enter the car market and did so through three more major company acquisitions, Standard-Triumph in 1961, ACV (which owned AEC, Thornycroft, Maudslay and Crossley) in 1962 and Rover (which had recently taken over Alvis) in 1967. At much the same time, encouraged by the government, Leyland was also discussing a takeover of the struggling Rootes group, but this was eventually dropped and Rootes was rescued by the American Chrysler Corporation. In 1962, after Spurrier had suffered a serious illness, Stokes became managing director.

While Leyland was growing, another major British conglomerate, the British Motor Corporation Ltd, was forming – largely engineered by Leonard Lord who later, ironically, caused BMC to have serious internal rifts. The main elements of BMC comprised the Austin, Morris, MG, Riley and Wolseley makes and several major component manufacturers. In July 1966 BMC, which had opened talks on a possible merger with Leyland as long ago as 1954 (with a view to surviving alongside other European giants), also acquired Jaguar, Daimler and Coventry-Climax, to become British Motor Holdings Ltd. Early in 1968, with much government manipulation, Leyland and British Motor Holdings finally combined, forming the British Leyland Motor Corporation with Stokes as chief executive on a joint board.

The new organization, with so many makes, had vast sales, amounting to about £907 million in 1968, rising to £1868 million in 1975 – and record profits of £58 million in 1973. It also had enormous duplication of resources, and management, re-equipment and new model development problems. These were made very much worse by rising oil prices, falling demand and serious industrial unrest in Britain in the early 1970s.

Lord Ryder, head of the government's National Enterprise Board, made an official report on the corporation which confirmed that without massive and immediate financial injections it was probably doomed. Accordingly, BMC was reorganized in 1975 as British Leyland Ltd, ostensibly a public company but with the government buying 95.1 per cent of the shares. Alex Park, formerly the Director of Finance, took over as chief execu-

Leyland Eight Vanden Plas of 1922

appearance coincided with major problems for Leyland over back taxes owed and only 18 cars were built before production stopped in late 1922.

Parry Thomas had raced the Eight successfully at Brooklands and subsequently built two 200bhp Leyland-Thomas racing cars. A third was built from spares in 1929, two years after Thomas had been killed during a land-speed record attempt.

Struggling to survive, Leyland considered mergers with other companies but tentative talks with Daimler failed and the company was expanded instead by a reorganization

Leyland-built Trojan 10hp RE saloon of 1931

tive and the company's operations were split into four major groups: Leyland Cars, Leyland Truck and Bus, Leyland International and Leyland Special Products. Each was largely autonomous.

The company launched new models in the Austin-Morris, Rover, Triumph and Jaguar ranges and attempted, not altogether successfully, to rationalize the existing ranges – resulting in the eventual disappearance of the Wolseley, Riley and Triumph names.

The unwieldy company continued to have massive problems however, and in 1978 Park was replaced by Michael Edwardes, seconded from the Chloride group. Edwardes spent the next four years completely restructuring BL, streamlining both production and management and undoubtedly saving it from extinction in the process. Under his regime individual marque names were given more prominence, groupings were changed from time to time and the Leyland name was consigned once again to the sphere of commercial vehicles only.

After Edwardes departed in 1983, the major vehicle groupings became Austin-Rover Group Ltd (which is now developing close ties with Honda), Land-Rover Group Ltd, Leyland Vehicles Ltd and Jaguar Cars Ltd – a profitable division which was floated as a public company in 1984. Leyland's truck division came under DAF control in 1987.

Although Austin-Rover has an increasingly well-respected product range, the company is still at a critical size, falling awkwardly between the real giants and the smaller specialists and its future, still relying heavily on government support, is by no means yet secure. It seems that the long list of Leyland mergers may still have further additions. BL

LEYLAND AUSTRALIA
AUSTRALIA 1948-1982

Of the dozens of overseas factories owned by the Leyland group or licensed to make its products, only one actually evolved an indigenous car called a Leyland. This took place in Australia, where both the British Motor Corporation and Standard-Triumph had factories.

The BMC factory stemmed from an Austin assembly plant opened in 1948 in the former Ruskin body plant in Melbourne and from a Morris one at Victoria Park, Sydney, which became the headquarters. Over the years BMC developed various local models of Austin and Morris, such as the Morris Marshall of 1957 (virtually an Austin Westminster), the Lancer and Major of 1958 (Wolseley 1500-based), the 1962 Austin Freeway Six, the Nomad of 1969 and the 1800-based Tasman and Kimberley of 1970.

By 1971 the Australian company held only 6.7 per cent of the market compared with more than 40 per cent in 1951 by the various marques that had later joined Leyland. Profits

in 1969 had slumped to a loss equivalent to more than £1 million in 1971, the year in which a completely individual large car was conceived.

It appeared in 1973 as the Leyland P76 with Michelotti styling and choice of 4.4-litre Rover V8 based engine or a 2.6-litre six also used in local Marinas. In that first year 8000 of the P76 were sold, but in 1974, with losses rumoured to be $50 million, the 64-acre (26-hectare) Sydney plant was closed before a coupé version could enter series production. Minis and Mokes were made at Enfield, near Sydney, for a time, the Mokes being transferred to Portugal in 1982. Selling, rather than making, cars in Australia brought profits once more and the firm continues to produce commercial vehicles there. NB

LE ZÈBRE
FRANCE 1908-1931

Le Zèbre 5hp tourer of 1909

Jules Salomon was an employee of the Bardon company which merged with Georges Richard et Cie to create Unic in 1906. Salomon, born in Cahors in 1870, had worked for numerous engineering firms including a brief spell with boilermaker Delaunay-Belleville. With his friend Jacques Bizet, son of the composer and a motor dealer and credit financier to car-buyers, he designed a small single-cylinder car which the two men used for personal transport. Unic agreed to make a batch of the cars in 1908-9 and named the vehicle after a horse called Zèbre (Zebra) in the company's transport stable.

These cars sold well at the equivalent of £100 and in 1910 Société Anonyme Le Zèbre was formed with a factory at Puteaux. Capital was 300,000 francs and directors included C. L. Baudry de Saunier, the motoring journalist. About 1000 of the 5CV cars were sold until 1912 and included some sold in Britain by F. B. Goodchild in London for £145. Four-cylinder cars of under 1 litre appeared in

1912. Capital was then increased to 650,000 francs in order to build a new factory at Suresnes, which opened in 1913.

Good profits were earned up to World War I but car production was curtailed in 1917. Salomon then joined Citroën in 1917 to design what was to become the very successful Citroën A. He later went to Rosengart. Another Le Zèbre designer, Lamy, left to join the Amilcar project, and several other colleagues joined him there. Jacques Bizet killed himself, reputedly over a lady, but the Zebra, as it was called in England, resumed production in the 1920s, initially with a 998cc four. In France Le Zèbre grew up to a 1974cc model in 1924 with Ricardo turbulent head and sleeve valves.

Like so many of its contemporaries, however, it succumbed to the slump. It made a last appearance at the 1931 Paris Salon with the sort of engine its founders would have approved of: it once more had only one cylinder, although this time it took the form of the much more sophisticated opposed-piston, two-stroke diesel made by Peugeot subsidiary CLM and was fitted in a 2-litre chassis. The last few chassis were acquired by Leon Max and sold under his name; he also sold CLM diesel chassis as the basis of light trucks. NB

LIBERTY
USA 1916-1924

The Liberty Motor Car Co was formed in Detroit in January 1916 with a capital of $400,000. The president was Percy H. Owen, formerly of Saxon and Chandler, and the vice-president James F. Bourquin, formerly Paige-Detroit general manager. Several other directors came from the Saxon company, and manufacture began in the Detroit plant formerly occupied by the RCH Corporation. The Liberty was a conventional medium sized car powered by a six-cylinder Continental engine and priced competitively at $1095 for a roadster.

Production began in July 1916 and rose rapidly, reaching a peak of 6000 cars in 1919. In that year the manufacturer discarded the Continental and brought out its own 3.8-litre six-cylinder engine. It has been suggested that this was the cause of the company's declining fortunes, but it is more likely that Liberty simply suffered the fate of so many of the smaller car-makers, being unable to compete once mass production by firms like Buick got going.

Sales for 1921 dropped to 1200 and by 1923, despite the slogan 'All the World Loves a Winner', only 80 motorists loved the Liberty sufficiently to buy one. In September 1923 the Liberty company was bought by the Columbia Motors Co, which planned to market the Liberty as an upmarket companion to its own cars. By the end of 1924, however, Columbia was in receivership, which marked the end of the road for Liberty too. GNG

Lifu 10hp steam phaeton of 1901

LIFU
GB 1899-1902

H. A. House Sr and Jr made a number of inventions associated with light steam engines and patented a steam tube boiler fired by liquid fuel (hence LIFU) in Bridgeport, Connecticut, in 1894. The following year a factory exploiting the House patents was making boat engines, launches and patent anchors in east Cowes on the Isle of Wight. It was financed by Sir Thomas Cassell and from 1897 made steam commercial vehicles, followed in 1899 by cars, all of which featured burners automatically regulated by the pressure in their copper boilers.

In 1899 200 workers at Cowes were making 30 wagons and 20 launches a year, but in 1900 the factory was sold to the Hiram S. Maxim Automobile Syndicate. The factory soon became the home of Saunders, a company that built boats and, later, aircraft.

The Liquid Fuel and Engineering Co appeared next on the mainland and by 1903 was in business at Hamworthy, Poole. It made commercial vehicles up to 1905 and boat engines until at least 1907. Some of the commercial vehicles were made under licence by Belhaven in Scotland.

The cars, which ceased around 1902, were probably all produced by licensees of the Steam Car Co, which held the rights to House's system and existed in London in 1902. A surviving 1901 car carries the plate of Thomas Noakes and Sons of London.

In the contemporary press there were references to ALFU (American Liquid Fuel) cars and a steam vehicle in 1899 in the United States with Malevez Frères chassis from St Servais-lez-Namur, Belgium, using House patents. The Malevez vehicles may have been imported to Britain for sale as LIFUs and are referred to as early as 1897 and as late as 1905. NB

LIGIER
FRANCE 1971 to date

As well as making highly successful Grand Prix racing cars, Automobiles Ligier of Vichy have sold road cars which doubled as racing cars for the World Championship of Makes sports car series, and typically French sub-50cc microcars. The company's founder, Guy Ligier, was born in 1927 and had little formal education before starting work as a butcher's boy when he was about 14.

A few years later, determined to create his own business, Ligier bought a large but cheap secondhand mechanical digger and set up as an earthmoving contractor. By virtue of sheer hard work and putting almost all his profits back into the business, Ligier eventually had a company employing over 1000 people, with some 500 machines and a turnover of several million pounds.

As well as a businessman, Ligier was a sportsman; he rowed, he played rugby for France and he raced motorcycles, before deciding in 1960 that he wanted to be a racing driver. He bought an Elva FJ car which he raced briefly without much success and then did slightly better with a Porsche Carrera.

Through his racing he met another driver, Jo Schlesser, and the two began to race together, winning the 1967 Sebring 12-hour race in a Ford GT40 Mark 2, after which they opened a garage in Paris selling imported Shelby cars. Ligier pursued an ambition to be a Grand Prix driver by buying a Cooper-Maserati, but wrote it off in an accident at the Nürburgring. He replaced it with a Brabham for 1967, but that too was uncompetitive.

Next, Ligier and Schlesser built an also-ran Formula 2 car before deciding to have a serious attempt at building a competitive racing sports car which could also be sold as a road car. By now Ligier had wound up his contracting business as the banks who supported him withdrew their support, and he began to build a factory for his planned cars. Schlesser was killed while racing the air-cooled experimental V8 Honda Grand Prix car at Rouen in 1968, but Ligier continued the project alone, commemorating his late friend in all subsequent Ligier type numbers, which always begin JS.

The first road car was a mid-engined coupé on a backbone chassis, designed by Michel Tetu and styled by Frua. The first used a 1.8-litre Cosworth engine and was in fact meant for racing, as the JS1, but the JS2 road cars at first used a 2.6-litre German Ford V6 and then the 2.7-litre Maserati V6 as used in the Citroën-Maserati SM. The car was launched at the 1971 Paris Show and from 1973 it had a full 3-litre version of the Maserati engine, but with carburettors instead of the injection used on the SM versions and a top speed of over 145mph (233kph).

In 1975 Ligier also built a Cosworth V8 engined version of this car for use in the World Championship of Makes but could not match the dominant Alfa Romeos or Alpines. Ligier also introduced his own, Matra-powered Grand Prix car in 1975, although the car did not race until the 1976 season, as the JS5, backed by the national tobacco company Gitanes.

In 1977 Jacques Laffite won the Swedish Grand Prix with the Matra powered JS7 and in 1979 Ligier won four Grands Prix with the Ford V8 powered JS11/15 and almost won the World Championship. The cars were again very competitive in 1980 and in 1981 reverted to Matra power as the Talbot-Ligier and won two more Grands Prix. Since then, with Ford and now Renault engines, they have scored no more wins although they finished the 1985 season with second and third places in the Australian Grand Prix.

When Ligier started his Grand Prix team his resources as a manufacturer had already been very stretched. Citroën began to distribute the JS2 and support Ligier, which in turn built the SM at Vichy, and Citroën virtually controlled Ligier by 1974. Up to mid-1975 some 125 JS2s had been built but SM engine supply was due to end late in the year and Ligier looked to Matra, Renault and Peugeot (Citroën's new owner) for a possible replacement but failed to find one and JS2 production ended in 1976.

In 1980 Ligier took a completely different path with the JS4 four-wheel microcar, with an all-steel body/chassis and a 49cc Motobecane two-stroke engine with centrifugal clutch and belt drive. At around £2000 the two-seater soon became the microcar market leader. The current model is powered by a 327cc diesel engine. BL

LILIPUT
see Gaggenau

Ligier JS2 of c.1971

LINCOLN/MERCURY
USA 1920 to date

The Lincoln Motor Co was founded in August 1917 by Henry M. Leland and his son Wilfrid. Henry was already 74 years old and the Grand Old Man of the American motor industry, having supplied engines to Oldsmobile at the turn of the century and having formed the Cadillac Automobile Co in 1902. His greatest contribution to Cadillac was the V8 engine of 1914, and although the first two years of his new company were devoted to production of the Liberty aero engine, he undoubtedly always had car manufacture in mind.

His war contract ended in January 1919, with 6500 engines delivered, and before the end of the year two prototypes of the first Lincoln car were running. Leland announced his car to the public in September 1920.

In essence the Lincoln V8 was an improved Cadillac, faster and more powerful, with the first use on a car of thermostatic radiator shutters. With a top speed of 80mph (128kph) it was good value at $4600 for a tourer, but the first Lincolns had an uninspired appearance, probably because neither Henry nor Wilfrid were stylists, being much too busy with engineering. Although 1500 orders had been placed before the car was shown to the public, a number of these were cancelled when the Lincolns reached the showrooms, and sales never reached the hoped-for 6000 during the first year.

By the end of 1921 Lincoln had 151 dealers in the USA, not bad going for a new company, but had sold only 3407 cars. A heavy tax bill forced the company into receivership, from which it was rescued by Henry Ford who paid $8 million to the receiver's court. By the time he had settled unpaid taxes and numerous creditors' claims, Ford's purchases cost him more than $12 million.

The 1922 Lincolns were the first made under Ford ownership and were virtually unchanged except for their prices, which were drastically cut. A five-passenger tourer now cost $3300 and the top price Judkins sedan $5200. While famous coachbuilders like Judkins and Brunn worked on the early Lincolns, most had 'factory' bodies which were in fact made either by the Towson Body Co or the Anderson Electric Car Co (maker of the Detroit Electric car) which together merged into the Mercury Corporation in 1926.

The Lelands were initially retained by Ford, but there was not room for two strong-minded Henrys in one firm and within five months the Lelands were gone. Henry, now 79, went into semi retirement although he continued to be active in local affairs, and died in 1932 at the age of 89. Wilfrid became a mining engineer.

During 1922 a total of 5512 Ford-built Lincolns were made, together with 255 from the Leland era. In fact for several months after the takeover Lincoln radiators still bore the words 'Lincoln, Leland-built'. Henry Ford cancelled most of the Lincoln dealerships and sold the cars through Ford agencies. This continued up to 1947, when the two sales forces were separated.

In June 1923 a new factory was opened, with a 3082ft (940m) test-track. Design was little changed, although quoted power output of the 5.8-litre engine was now 90hp and there was a growing emphasis on custom bodywork by such firms as Brunn, Fleetwood and Judkins. Edsel Ford became increasingly interested in styling and discussed body design with all the custom coachbuilders who worked on Lincolns.

The first year that the Lincoln Motor Co made a profit was 1923, when 7875 cars were sold. Also in 1923 President Calvin Coolidge took delivery of a Lincoln, establishing a connection with the White House which has lasted to the present.

The Leland-designed V8 engine continued with little change through the 1920s, being increased to 6.3 litres and 90bhp in 1928. Production grew steadily, to 8380 in 1925 and 8858 in 1926; by contrast, on 31 October 1925, Ford made more than 10,000 Model Ts in one *day*. Although Lincoln never officially made commercial vehicles, it introduced a long wheelbase chassis in 1925 especially designed for ambulance, funeral car or police wagon bodies. Both the latter and standard tourers and sedans were popular with police departments.

Edsel's interest in coachwork led to a number of coachbuilders making batches of popular designs for Lincoln, which could be sold at much lower prices than a one-off custom body. A good example was the Locke Dual Cowl Phaeton, which sold for $4700 in 1927. A total of 298 of these were made between 1927 and 1929. Lincoln had also set up its own body department which, with Murray, accounted for the more everyday body styles.

Sales dropped sharply with the Depression, and only 3515 cars were sold in 1930. This was the last year for the old Model L, which was replaced for 1931 by the Model K. This used the same size V8 engine, now giving 120bhp, but was a much lower and more elegant car, with a slight vee to the radiator and a longer wheelbase of 12ft 1in (3.6m), compared with 11ft 4in (3.4m). The gearbox had synchromesh on the upper two ratios. In 1932 this chassis received a brand new 150bhp 7.2-litre V12 engine, to make the Model KB.

The V8, now called the KA, was continued, and a wide range of custom and semi custom bodies were fitted to these models. Many

Lincoln Dual Cowl Phaeton of 1928

Lincoln 112 phaeton of 1921

Lincoln 139 saloon of 1924

Lincoln Continental cabriolet of c.1940

classic fanciers think they are the best looking of all Lincolns, for 1933 saw the arrival of
fender skirts and sloping radiator grilles
which detracted from the dignified appearance of the original KA and KB. KA prices
started at $2900 and KBs at $4300. Only 1765
of the former and 1623 of the latter were sold.
The V8 was dropped for 1933, and for the next
16 years Lincoln would make only 12-cylin-
der cars.

Somewhat confusingly, the designation KA
was applied to a smaller V12 of 6.2 litres,
1420 of which were sold in 1933. Production
of the KB ceased at the end of the year, with
only 587 sold. A new 6.8-litre aluminium
head V12 was the sole model of 1934 and
1935, but for 1936 Lincoln brought out a completely new low priced V12, the Zephyr.

A separate unit was formed by Edsel Ford
to handle the Zephyr, which had a streamlined integral construction body based on a
John Tjaarda design, and a 110bhp 4.4-litre
V12 engine. Prices started at $1275 for a two-
door sedan, and the first year's models sold
15,449 units, more than 10 times the figure for
the 'senior' Model K whose prices ran from
$4200 to over $8000.

Production of the big Lincolns declined
gently over the next four years, with only 120
cars being built in 1939, and a few of which
were sold as 1940 models. The Zephyr went
from strength to strength, with a coupé added
to the range for 1937 and a four-door convertible sedan for 1938. Prices were still very
reasonable, the latter being the most expensive Zephyr at only $1790.

In November 1938 the Lincoln division
brought out a new car, the concept and development of which were the work of Edsel
Ford. He even chose the name, Mercury, from
103 suggestions put to him.

In appearance the Mercury was very like
the Ford V8, but it had a longer wheelbase,
roomier body and a larger engine of 3.9 litres.
Edsel's aim was to fill the middle price gap in
the market, for, when Ford owners wanted to
trade up from the V8, they had nowhere to go

Lincoln Premiere coupé of 1957

in the Ford range, so were likely to buy a
Pontiac or Buick.

The Mercury was initially priced from $916
to $1018 and sold 76,198 units in its first
season. From the $640 V8-60 to the $7000
plus Model K Lincoln, Ford now covered over
90 per cent of the market, and even though
the big Lincolns were soon phased out, the
wisdom of the Mercury as a marketing exercise was never in doubt.

For 1940 Edsel produced another new design, which was destined to become one of
the greatest classic motor cars, the Lincoln
Continental. This was derived from a personal car which Edsel had ordered in 1939, a
four-passenger convertible, and was made in
convertible and club coupé form.

The first year's models were virtually hand-
made, yet cost just $2783-$2840. The engine
was the regular Zephyr V12, now enlarged to
4.8 litres. A total of 350 coupés and 54 convertibles were made in 1940. Figures for 1941
Continentals were 850 coupés and 400 convertibles, making them very rare cars compared with the 17,756 Zephyrs and 80,000
Mercurys delivered in that last full year of car
production before America entered World
War II.

The Continental was revived after the war,
but only for three seasons. Edsel Ford, the
driving force behind the car, had died in
1943, and Ford executives generally were not
in favour of such a small production run. It is
quite possible that Lincoln never made a

profit on any V12 Continental sold.

Henry Ford II became president of Ford
Motor Co in September 1945 and one of his
first decisions was to make the Lincoln-Mercury Division a separate entity, the reorganization being completed in 1947. This
meant that administration, engineering and
sales were separated from Ford, although
financially the two divisions were linked and
there was obviously a lot of exchange of engineering ideas. The sales force was independent, though, and Lincoln-Mercury dealers
no longer necessarily sold Fords as well.

In 1947 a new Lincoln-Mercury plant was
opened at Los Angeles, the first time Lincolns
were made outside the Detroit area. Later
another plant was built at Metuchen, New
Jersey, which still assembles Mercurys today.

The last Lincoln V12 engine was completed on 24 March 1948, and with it died the
Continental in its first and greatest form. The
new Lincoln had a 152bhp 5½-litre V8 engine
and a completely new all-enveloping body.
Mercury also had an all-new body, although it
retained its V8 engine. Like the 1947 Ford, it
abandoned the old transverse leaf front suspension in favour of coil independent front
suspension. The one millionth Mercury was
delivered in July 1950 when the division produced a record 334,081 Mercurys and 35,485
Lincolns. A fleet of 10 custom-built Lincoln
Cosmopolitans was delivered to the White
House; one remained in service until 1967.

Completely new Lincolns and Mercurys

were brought out for 1952, with a new overhead valve 160bhp V8 engine for the Lincoln and many styling similarities between the two makes. Mercury was now definitely a 'junior Lincoln' rather than a 'senior Ford'. In 1952 Lincoln entered the Mexican Carrera Panamericana, finished 1-2-3-4 that year and again in 1953, and 1-2 in 1954, although the 1954 winner was a private entrant.

For 1956 a new 285bhp 6-litre V8 made its appearance and went into the Lincoln Premiere and a revival of the Continental theme, the Continental Mark II. This was the responsibility of a separate Continental Division, and among those who contributed to its design were Gordon Buehrig of Auburn and Cord fame, Harley Copp and William Clay Ford, younger brother of Henry II.

Styling was quite distinct from the Lincolns; although it shared the same wheelbase it was 4in (101mm) longer and the only body style was a close-coupled four-passenger coupé. The price was $10,000 compared with $4747 for the most expensive Lincoln Premiere. Just over 3000 were made until the June 1957 season and it is probable that, as with its predecessor, no money was made on the Continental Mark II.

For 1958 came the Lincoln Continental Mark III which was merely the top of the line Lincoln, in sedan and convertible form, priced at about $6100. It was followed by the Lincoln Continental Mark IV for 1959 and Mark V for 1960, after which the marque numbers were given a rest until they were revived in 1968 for a new personal car, confusingly called the Continental Mark III. The Continental Division was merged with Lincoln-Mercury in 1959 and was not revived as a separate entity for the later cars. In 1958 Lincoln Mercury built the ill-starred Edsel but fortunately its disastrous reputation did not attach itself to its builders.

Mercury's offering in the compact car stakes appeared in 1960 as the Comet, a more expensive version of the Ford Falcon and using the same 2.4-litre six-cylinder engine. This was the first six ever offered by Mercury, although the regular cars were also available with a 3.6-litre six for 1961. The Comet was a great success, more than 178,000 being sold in the first year, together with 161,785 larger Mercurys.

The 1958 to 1960 Lincolns included the biggest American cars of the post-war era and came onto the market at a time when criticism of over-large cars was just beginning to surface. Sales dropped from 50,323 in 1956 to only 20,683 in 1960, and for 1961 Lincoln came up with a completely restyled machine advertised as 'America's only compact luxury car'. By any standards except Lincoln's own it was hardly a compact, but the wheelbase was cut by 8in (203mm) to 10ft 3in (3.1m) and overall length by 15in (381mm) to 17ft 6in (5.3m). The same 7-litre engine was used. An unusual body style was a four-door convertible, the only one on the American market. This was made until 1968. Sales rose to

Lincoln Continental saloon of 1982

33,180 in 1961 and 37,750 by 1964.

Mercurys of the early 1960s were closer to Ford than Lincoln in styling, but when Lee Iacocca was put in charge of the division he pushed them closer to Lincoln. In 1965 advertising proclaimed 'It's now in the Lincoln Continental tradition' and the biggest Mercurys used the 7-litre Lincoln engine. For the first time sales of the Comet were eclipsed by those of the regular Mercurys in 1965.

Two years later with the Cougar, Mercury entered the pony car market pioneered by the Ford Mustang. The Cougar was a sporty two-door hard top with 4.7-litre or 6.4-litre engine that was priced from $2851. The Cougar name has been continued to the present day, although the 1970s saw a decline in the performance image and it is today used for a four passenger coupé powered by a 3.8-litre V6 engine.

In 1968 Lincoln returned to the idea of the Continental as a distinctly separate prestige car, with the Continental Mark III. It was powered by its own 7½-litre V8 engine and had distinctive styling, although not so different from the regular Lincoln line as its predecessor. It was not so expensive either, costing $6585; first year sales were an encouraging 18,463.

Lincoln sold its one millionth car in 1968 and the marque's sales were climbing again, with 45,776 cars delivered, in addition to the Continental Mark IIIs. In 1969 they were down to 43,291, but obviously some of these customers had gone to Continental which sold 21,933 units.

For 1970 Lincoln abandoned unitary construction and reverted to a conventional chassis, which had been a feature of the Con-

Lincoln-Mercury Capri RS of 1979

tinental Mark III. This became the Mark IV from 1972 to 1976 and the Mark V from 1977 to 1979. The theme was continued on the 1980 Continental Mark VI, but this, like the other Lincolns, was a considerably smaller car, with wheelbase reduced by 10in (254mm) and weight by 900lb (408kg). Engines were 5- or 5.7-litre V8s and prices were between $12,000 and $14,000.

From 1982 only the smaller engine was available, and the distinction in appearance between the regular Lincoln and the Continental Mark VI became much less. Confusingly the 'regular Lincoln' became the Continental and Town Car models, while the Mark number cars were re-named Lincoln Mark VI, dropping the word Continental. A 3.8-litre V6 engine was available in 1982, but from 1983 only the 5-litre V8 was used.

The 1985 range included the Mark VII, Continental and Town Car sedans, all with the 5-litre petrol V8 or a 2.4-litre BMW turbocharged six-cylinder diesel engine. There was also the Merkur XR4 Ti which was similar to the European Ford Sierra XR4.

Lincoln Continental saloon of 1963

Lincoln production reached a peak of 191,355 in 1977, dropping to 157,434 in 1984. All Lincoln assembly is carried out at one plant in Wixom, Michigan.

The Mercury range became wider in the 1970s than it had ever been before. From the summer of 1970 the German-built Ford Capri was imported and sold by Lincoln-Mercury dealers. Another import handled was the De Tomaso Pantera, of which about 4000 were sold between 1970 and 1974. The Comet name was used on Mercury's version of the compact Ford Maverick from 1971, while the larger Mercurys, the Marquis series, were very Lincoln-like in appearance and used 7.4-litre V8 engines.

From the mid-1970s Mercury grew closer to the Ford range, with parallel versions of most Ford models. The 1976 Bobcat and 1978 Zephyr were upmarket versions of Ford's Pinto and Fairmount respectively, while the 1981 front-wheel-drive Lynx was a variant on the international Ford Escort. Ford's EXP coupé had its Mercury version in the LN7, but this was dropped for 1984, leaving a still considerable range sold with Mercury badging on the sub-compact Lynx, compact front-wheel-drive Topaz (Ford Tempo), compact coupé Capri (Ford Mustang), intermediate front-wheel-drive Sable (Ford Taurus), full-size (or Standard) Grand Marquis (Ford LTD Crown Victoria) and luxury coupé Cougar (Ford Thunderbird).

Mercury production reached a peak of 674,618 in 1979, dropping to 475,381 in 1984. Mercurys are currently assembled in nine different plants across the United States, from Metuchen, New Jersey, on the east coast to San Jose, California. GNG

LINON
BELGIUM 1897-1914

Louis Linon worked in the engineering trade in Aachen and Stolberg before joining Ateliers de Construction Vervietoise in about 1894. There he worked on a steam car before starting his own bicycle workshop in Ensival near Verviers in 1895 with his son André. They built a few Gautier-Wehrlé based steam cars from 1897 and then petrol-engined cars in 1900, including both Gautier-Wehrlé and genuine Linon types. Linon appears to have built some of its own engines and even supplied them for the Waddington. Other engines used in subsequent Linons were bought in from Fafnir, Vautour, Fondu and Ballot.

In 1905 a monoplane was built and flown with some success, and cars of up to 4.9 litres were soon offered, including Fafnir-engined sixes. By 1910 only Ballot engines were available and other parts, including transmission and steering gear, came from Malicet et Blin. Production ended with the outbreak of World War I, by which time 1500 to 2000 Linons had been sold. NB

LLOYD
GERMANY 1906-1914; 1950-1963

The Lloyd car was the result of efforts at diversification by the shipping line Norddeutscher Lloyd of Bremen, which at the turn of the century had financial problems. In 1902 a subsidiary, Norddeutscher Maschinen und Armaturenfabrik AG, was founded to make electric motors. Four years later Dr Heinrich Wiegand, Norddeutscher Lloyd's general manager, with backing from the company's bankers and in association with the Compagnie Parisienne des Voitures Electriques (Système Kriéger), maker of Kriéger electrics in Paris since 1897, founded Norddeutscher Automobil & Motoren Aktiengesellschaft (or NAMAG) in Bremen to build Kriéger designs under licence as Lloyds.

By the time the first Lloyd-Elektros appeared in 1907 the short-lived electric boom was all but over, and Kriéger itself would be out of business within two years. Lloyd knew it needed a petrol car and Wiegand approached the designer Joseph Vollmer, who had founded the industrial design bureau Deutsche Automobil Konstruktion GmbH in 1907.

Vollmer had been a designer since 1896 and in 1902 he was working as chief designer with Kuhlstein Wagenbau of Berlin-Charlottenburg, the maker of Kuhlstein electric cars since 1898 and then the Kuhlstein-Vollmer petrol car. Kuhlstein was taken over in 1902 by the large electrical company AEG, Allgemeine Elektrizitäts Gesellschaft, of Berlin.

In 1901 AEG had bought the Allgemeine Automobil-Gesellschaft company, maker of the 5PS AAG light car, designed by Professor Georg Klingenberg, since 1900, and set up the Neue Automobil-Gesellschaft company (or NAG) to sell the cars, first as AAGs, until 1902. They now had Vollmer design a two-cylinder car which became the first NAG, the Model A.

Vollmer's first design for Lloyd was the 3.7-litre four-cylinder 15/35PS, which was not a particular success, nor was another 2.3-litre four. Although Vollmer worked for Lloyd only on a consultancy basis he drove his own 15/35 car in the 1908 Prince Henry Trials. A 2.5-litre 10/25PS and 5.5-litre 22/50PS were also built between 1910 and 1914 but Lloyd lost money consistently throughout this period and in May 1914 was taken over by Hansa Automobil-Gesellschaft mbH of Varel, the maker of Hansa cars. The Lloyd electric cars had also continued in production until then, but the company was re-formed as Hansa-Lloyd Werke AG and the Lloyd name disappeared.

It reappeared, however, in 1950 as a product of the Borgward company. Borgward had taken over Hansa-Lloyd completely between 1929 and 1931, dropping the Hansa-Lloyd name from private cars in 1929 and the Hansa name in 1939, until the latter was used again as a Borgward model name from 1949 and briefly in its own right from 1958.

The 1950 Lloyd, built by Lloyd Motoren-Werke GmbH of Bremen, a part of Carl F. W. Borgward GmbH, also of Bremen, was a small car built to cater for the bubble car boom. It used a two-cylinder 293cc engine and at first had a wood-framed, leatherette-covered body, although a steel body was introduced in 1954. It was very successful and more than 45,000 were sold in 1955. In 1957 it was given a 596cc engine as the Alexander and a four-cylinder model, the 897cc Arabella, was also introduced that year. Lloyds continued to be successful, with over 40,000 cars sold in 1959, but ultimately the marque was a victim of the Borgward collapse of 1961.

Lloyd Arabella of 1961

A few Arabellas were built from the parts stock and were sold until 1963, the Arabella de luxe having been sold as a Borgward in 1960 and 1961. Like Borgward, Lloyd paid all its creditors in full after the bankruptcy, but there were to be no more cars. BL

LLOYD
GB 1936-1950

Lloyd Cars Ltd was formed in the rather unlikely location of the fishing port of Grimsby, Lincolnshire, by Roland Lloyd whose father had sold Crossley, Arrol-Johnston, Riley and Willys-Overland cars. The first Lloyd was an ultra-light two-seater, powered by a rear-mounted 347cc Villiers two-stroke engine, with single chain drive to the nearside rear wheel, backbone chassis and independent suspension all round. The price was a very low £75; the van which joined the range in 1939 cost £90. Ten of the cars were bought by the Gas Light & Coke Co for its inspectors, and about 250 were made until 1939. Some were exported to the Netherlands and South Africa.

War work led to considerable expansion of the factory, which produced components for Rolls-Royce aero engines and Mosquito fighter-bombers, and in 1945 Roland Lloyd built the prototype of his post-war car, which went into production the following year. It was a more ambitious design than the pre-war 350 and, given the climate of the times, was doomed to failure. He used virtually no proprietary parts, making his own 654cc two-cylinder two-stroke engine which was mounted transversely in the front of the frame and drove the front wheels. The Lloyd 650 had an all-synchromesh (including reverse) gearbox, double backbone frame and all-independent suspension.

The price was a hefty £480 for the two- to four-seater roadster – saloon and van versions never passed the prototype stage – and the power-to-weight ratio was such that 0 to 40mph (64kph) took 30.4 seconds. Top speed was 47mph (75kph). A production target of five cars a week was set but the average was usually two or three.

Exports took the Lloyd 650 to Belgium, Denmark, India and Australia, and a total of 350 to 400 were made in five years. Growing availability of mass-produced cars on the home market damaged Lloyd's sales and production ceased in May 1950, at which time the factory employed about 200 workers.

The name Lloyd Cars Ltd was retained by the company, which continued in precision engineering for Rolls-Royce, Gardner, Perkins, Aston Martin and Lotus among others until March 1983. Then the company was wound up and the premises sold to Birds Eye-Wall's, the frozen food manufacturer which was already established next door. GNG

LLOYD & PLAISTER
see Hurst

LOCOMOBILE/RIKER
USA 1899-1929

John Brisben Walker, the owner of *Cosmopolitan* magazine, bought rights to the steam cars of the Stanley twins for $250,000 with help from A. L. Barber of Barber Asphalt Co, and together they formed the Automobile Co of America in June 1899 with $2.5 million capital. Another firm of the same name turned out to have been registered already, so on 10 July 1899 the name was changed to the Locomobile Co of America. The Stanleys, who had made Stanley steam cars since 1897, handled engineering and production.

Walker soon left to make Mobile steamers but Barber made Locomobiles at Newton, Massachusetts, from July 1899 and took over the American Humber bicycle factory at Westboro. In 1900 a move was made to what was claimed to be the world's largest car plant at Bridgeport, Connecticut, and the Stanleys bought back their old factory to resume Stanley car production.

In 1900-1, 400 Locomobiles were sold in Britain, including one to Rudyard Kipling, and an additional factory was opened at Long Island Sound. In 1902 the Victor Steam Car business was acquired and A. L. Riker became vice-president and chief engineer.

Riker's career had begun in 1887 when he

built an electric version of a Coventry Lever trike. From this grew an electric car business that he sold in 1896 to Pope Columbia. He then developed Riker petrol cars, which Locomobile adopted in 1903 to replace its steamers, over 5000 of which had been sold.

The 1904 Locomobile models were Mercédès-inspired and henceforth the company concentrated on the luxury market with 'The Best Car in America' as its early slogan. Its first six-cylinder car, the 48, was introduced in 1911 and, gradually updated, it lasted until 1929. In 1915 a custom body department under J. F. de Causse was opened.

Mk VII tank engines, De Dion-like staff cars

Locomobile steam buggy of 1902

Locomobile saloon of c.1920

and trucks were made during World War I. Trucks had first appeared in 1912 as Locomobiles but were known as Rikers from 1916 until production ceased in 1921. Attractive graphics with few words characterized the advertising of post-war Locomobiles, which were promoted as the 'Finest and Most Expensive U.S. Cars'.

From 1920 Emlen Hare, a former Packard salesman who owned Hares Motors in New York City, took Locomobile under his wing, along with Mercer and Crane-Simplex. A. L. Riker was engineering consultant to the group, until it became insolvent in January 1922. Locomobile's assets and liabilities were each around $5 million, including new cars and trucks valued respectively at $800,000 and $200,000.

In September 1922 William Crapo Durant formed the Locomobile Company of American Inc to acquire its assets. Durant's Flint car was mass-produced in the Long Island Sound factory but actual Locomobile output ran at only 500 to 2000 a year between 1923 and 1927.

The cars received four wheel brakes and a major restyle from Le Baron Inc in 1924, and were joined in 1925 by a cheaper Junior Eight line which outsold the big cars by 8 to 1 and clocked up 3000 sales before being replaced by the Lycoming powered 8-70. These cars did much to undermine the glamour of the 48 and the new six-cylinder 90 of 1926.

From 1929 Durant concentrated all his

efforts on Locomobile, but his talents at reorganization had little time to succeed in the prevailing economic gloom. Sales in 1929 included just 53 in April, 29 in May, 28 in June and 8 in July. After unsuccessful attempts to rescue Locomobile the plant and contents were sold for $200,000 in February 1932. The only subsequent motor involvement was the abortive Dymaxion dream car, on which a few Locomobile men were briefly employed. NB

LOHNER
AUSTRIA 1896-1908

The Viennese coachbuilding company Hof-Wagenfabrik Jacob Lohner & Co was founded in 1832 and became carriage builders to the emperor of Austria. In 1896 it became the first company in Austria to start commercial production of motor cars, with a two-cylinder 6hp model powered by a French Pygmée engine.

This car was built until 1898, when Lohner introduced an electric car, the Egger-Lohner, powered by 3hp motors made by Vereinigte Bela Egger Elektrizitäts-AG, also of Vienna. In 1898, as well as the electric motors, Egger gave Lohner a new designer, Ferdinand Porsche, who from 1893 had been apprenticed to the company and had eventually been head of the test department.

Born in 1875 and the son of a tinsmith, Porsche was interested in electricity from an early age and installed various electrical systems in his father's workshops; his first motoring interests were not in the petrol cars for which he became famous but in electrics. He became chief engineer for Lohner in 1899, when the company had some 100 workers and a 410,000sq ft (38,000sq m) factory.

Having failed to negotiate a licence with Daimler to build petrol cars, Lohner became committed to electrics and at the 1900 Paris World Fair introduced the Lohner-Porsche Chaise, which Porsche had designed the previous year. The car had an electric motor in each front hub, of 2½ or 5hp, driving the wheels directly and independently.

The car was very successful and Porsche earned much publicity for Lohner. In 1900 he drove one from Paris to Versailles at an average speed of almost 20mph (32kph) and in September he drove a stripped chassis to a new outright record on the 6.2-mile (10km) Semmering Mountain course. In 1902 he also won his class in the Exel hillclimb.

Porsche's design was a commercial success as well as a competition winner and in 1901 the London Fire Brigade acquired engines fitted with the Porsche hub-drive system, several years before their Viennese counterparts. In fact Lohner built fire engines for many brigades to the Porsche system, and also made trucks.

In 1901 Porsche designed a hybrid-drive

Lohner-Porsche Chaise of 1900

car for Lohner, the Mixte, in which a 16hp petrol engine drove a generator which supplied the hub motors. These used Daimler and Panhard engines, but the rest of the car was built entirely in Vienna. They were very sporty, with a top speed of over 50mph (80kph), and Porsche demonstrated one for army personnel, who were very enthusiastic, at the Kaisermanoeuvres at Sasvar. Porsche, then an army reservist, actually chauffeured the Archduke Ferdinand, whose later assassination triggered World War I. By 1903, Lohner offered the Mixte with up to 80hp, but the cars were vastly overpriced, a 1902 tourer costing more than twice as much as a Mercédès.

Porsche left Lohner in 1904 to join Austro-Daimler, and in 1906 Lohner sold the electric patents to Emil Jellinek who built electric cars briefly from 1906 to 1907 as the Mercédès Electrique before continuing with his much more successful petrol models. Lohner continued to build electric cars, including the Cedes landaulette of 1907, but stopped building cars in 1908. Lohner-Stolle trolleybuses were produced until about 1920, and the Lohner-Porsche system was used by other makers on road trains as well as commercials.

After World War II a new company, Lohnerwerke GmbH, began building motor scooters in 1950 with 98cc Rotax or Sachs engines, adding a 125cc model in 1954. Production stopped in 1958. BL

LOMBARD
FRANCE 1927-1929

Lombard 1100cc sports two-seater of 1928

André Lombard came to fame as the competition manager for Salmson, but left the company in 1923. Four years later he was able to fulfil his ambition to have a car bearing his own name when he brought out an advanced sports car with 1093cc twin-overhead cam four-cylinder engine developing 49bhp, or 70bhp with supercharger. It was designed by E. Vareille and built by E. Brault of Courbevoie. The open two-seater and coupé bodies were made by Duval. Deliveries began in the summer of 1928, by which time production had been taken over by Salmson. Brault built only the 1927 Paris Salon cars.

The AL3, as it was called, did well in races from 1927 to 1929, coming fourth in the 1928 Spanish Grand Prix and winning the 1929 Bol d'Or. A total of 94 were made before Salmson's move away from sporting cars in 1929 brought production to an end. All parts and unfinished cars, together with a few complete ones, were bought by Charles de Ricou of BNC, which proceeded to sell them with BNC badges.

Lombard meanwhile formed another company, the Société des Automobiles Lombard, to manufacture a luxury car with a 3-litre overhead-cam straight-eight engine. Only one show chassis was completed. GNG

LORELEY
GERMANY 1906-1927

The Loreley was built by the Maschinenfabrik Rudolf Ley AG of Arnstadt, Thurigen, a company founded in 1856 which built shoemaking and other specialized machinery. The company introduced its first car, a 1559cc four-cylinder 6/10PS model with three-speed gearbox and shaft drive, in 1906, having started prototype production during 1905. The car was designed by Albert Ley, a brother of the firm's founder. It was built from 1906 to 1908, with a two-seater version priced at 3800 marks and a four-seater at 4900 marks. There was also a 1232cc four-cylinder 4/10PS model during 1906 which was actually the first to use the name Loreley, as opposed to Ley, and that name was then used for all the cars.

In 1907 Loreley introduced the 2599cc six-cylinder 10/25PS, certainly one of Germany's first sixes and probably *the* first. Up to World War I the firm offered various interesting and well-made four- and six-cylinder models, including the four-cylinder 1132cc 5/12PS from 1909 to 1911, the six-cylinder K6, with the same capacity as the earlier 10/25 but now rated as a 10/28PS from 1912, and the 1550cc six-cylinder Type 6A, introduced in 1912.

The smaller cars were Ley's speciality and sold well until the war, with four-cylinder cars of up to 2068cc being offered. After the war, Ley resumed production fairly quickly with various four-cylinder types following on from the pre-war models and a 3134cc six.

The four-cylinder 1530cc 6/20PS was built from 1920 to 1926 and two more fours, the 1990cc M8 and the 3070cc U12, were both built from 1921 to 1927. A four-cylinder 1498cc overhead-cam sports model, the TO, was introduced in 1924. In 1922 Ley also experimented with streamlined racing bodywork to Paul Jaray's designs on a 26PS chassis, capable of 80mph (128kph), Jaray himself testing the not particularly attractive but very effective cars with Ley's designer and director, Gockenbach.

The Jaray-bodied cars were never put into production, as Ley stopped building cars in 1927. The company continued briefly with small commercial vehicles until 1929 and then stopped production altogether. BL

LORRAINE
see De Dietrich

LORRAINE-DIETRICH
see De Dietrich

LORYC
see EHP

LOTIS
GB 1908-1912

Sturmey Motors Ltd, which made the Lotis car from 1908 to 1912, was directed by Henry Sturmey, who founded the world's oldest motoring magazine, *The Autocar*, in 1895 and dedicated it to 'the interests of the mechanically propelled road carriage'. In 1900 Sturmey attempted to design and build a '£100 motor car', which would have been a unique achievement. The one car that he built used a 2¾hp MMC motorcycle engine (the largest air-cooled engine then available to save the cost and complication of water-cooling), a three-speed epicyclic gearbox and a basketwork body, which was sprung to the chassis, although the back axle was not.

From 1902, having given up his efforts with the £100 car, Sturmey began building the American Duryea under licence in Coventry. For this purpose he set up the British Duryea Co, with capital of £25,000. Sturmey continued to build Duryeas until 1906 and also built the Parsons 15cwt (762kg) delivery van. On stopping building Duryeas, Sturmey changed his company to Sturmey Motors Ltd and set the original factory to building the Lotis car.

The first was a front-engined 22hp four-cylinder model of 1908, and built in that year only. It was followed by an 8hp single-cylinder, also just for that year; 10/12 and 12/18 Riley engined twins were produced from 1908 to 1911.

In 1910 Lotis introduced 16/20 and 20/25hp fours and thereafter production concentrated on fours, mostly with White & Poppe engines, the largest of which was a 4084cc 25/35. The range remained basically similar, with the addition of the Lotis-Parsons, a light car designed to run on paraffin, until production stopped in 1912. BL

LOTUS
GB 1948 to date

What became Lotus began life in the late 1940s as a one-man operation building Austin and Ford specials, but where most other special builders quickly faded, Lotus became a major group of automotive companies and six times world champion Grand Prix car constructors. Until his premature death in December 1982, Colin Chapman, the brilliant innovator who founded the company, *was* Lotus. At the time of his death Lotus was in serious financial trouble, but it was rescued and looks set to survive. It will probably always be thought of as Chapman's company.

Chapman was born in 1928 in Richmond, Surrey. From October 1945 he studied structural engineering at University College, London, graduating with a BSc degree. In

1949 he joined the Royal Air Force for two years' national service, having already had considerable flying training with the university air squadron.

For Christmas 1945, shortly after he had survived a motorcycle accident, his parents gave him a 1937 Morris Eight Tourer, and by the beginning of 1946 he was making spare time cash by buying and selling used cars. He modified some of these cars while he had them in stock, but with petrol rationing becoming even tighter he was out of business in 1947, which was when he decided to build a sporting special from an unsold 1930 Austin Seven fabric saloon.

He built this first car in the lock-up garage behind his girlfriend Hazel's house, completed it in early 1948 and used it very successfully in trials. He started his second car, first with a Ford 8 engine but then with a Ford 10 unit, in 1949, while he was still in the RAF. He left the RAF later that year and went to work as a constructional engineer with a London-based steel erecting company for a year before joining the British Aluminium Co as a development engineer.

In 1950 he sold his 'Mark 2' car and contested a few more trials with the much-modified Mark 1, then took a new step by building two cars specifically for sale. He started the Mark 3 on 1 January 1951 for the new 750 racing formula, building one for himself and two for the Allen brothers. To speed production he moved the cars into the brothers' larger workshop in Wood Green, north London, but in the end only his own car was completed and raced, and the other two were used for spares. The car was hugely successful, using a strengthened Austin Seven chas-

Lotus Mark 3 of 1951

Lotus Mark 6 of 1952

sis and a cleverly modified cylinder head which was a liberal interpretation of the rules, something for which Chapman would become very well known.

He eventually completed the other two chassis as Mark 3Bs. When the purchaser of the Mark 2 asked for a Mark 4, Chapman began to consider building cars for sale. He moved into an old stable in Hornsey, north London, adjoining property owned by his father, and went into partnership with one of the Allen brothers, Michael, forming the Lotus Engineering Co on 1 January 1952.

With the Mark 4 Chapman made two im-

portant moves: it was the first Lotus with a purpose built spaceframe chassis, as opposed to a modified Austin, and it was always intended to be roadworthy. This became the prototype of the first 'production' Lotus, which, because the 750 Mark 5 car was designed but not built, became the Lotus Mark 6. It used a multitubular chassis with stressed aluminium panels and additional bodywork by Williams & Pritchard, a local company. The usual engine choice was the Ford Consul unit but Ford would not supply engines direct.

In February 1953 Lotus became the Lotus Engineering Co Ltd, Michael Allen left and Hazel became the other director, lending the company £25, which was its total working capital. While Chapman was still working for British Aluminium, he was somehow also managing to build one car a fortnight.

Lotus now temporarily skipped another number, Mark 7 having originally been intended for an ERA-powered Formula 2 customer car which was never finished, but the number was kept for a planned revision of the Mark 6 which became one of the best known of all Lotuses, the Lotus 7. Meanwhile, work started in January 1954 on the Mark 8, a sports racing car with aerodynamic body designed by Frank Costin, brother of Mike Costin, a racing friend of Chapman and one of the first Mark 6 customers, who was gradually drifting into working for the company.

Both Frank Costin and Chapman began to work for the company full-time in January 1955, Chapman having married Hazel Williams in October 1954. Another company, Racing Engines Ltd, was set up to provide tuning services and equipment and in 1955 Lotus joined the Society of Motor Manufacturers and Traders, allowing it to exhibit at the

Lotus Mark 16 of 1958

Motor Show for the first time in October. A little more space was gained in Hornsey but the works were still very small.

In 1957 the company took over the small workshops previously used by the people who built Lotus bodies, to use as a racing department, as racing was becoming more and more serious. Chapman's reputation was already such that he had been used by the major British Grand Prix teams BRM and Vanwall to design suspension and chassis respectively.

In October 1957 the 7 was launched at the Motor Show. It was made by another company offshoot, Lotus Components Ltd, and was offered mostly in kit form to take advantage of prevailing British tax exemptions. The success of the 7 effectively established the Lotus name. Chapman now began building a dealer network and in June 1959 moved to larger premises at Cheshunt, Hertfordshire, as Lotus Cars Ltd and Lotus Components Ltd.

Most of the Lotus types at this time were still racing cars. The Mark 9 was offered as a complete car with Coventry-Climax engine in 1955 for £1150 plus tax and made Lotus's Le Mans début, running well but being disqualified for a driving infringement. The 9 was followed by the Costin classic, the Mark 11, which took a Le Mans class win and several speed records.

In 1957 Lotus built its first single-seater, the Formula 2 Lotus 12, introducing Chapman-strut rear suspension and the brilliantly simple but unreliable Lotus gearbox. The 16 was the first Formula 1 car, a beautiful front-engined model not unlike a small Vanwall, introduced in 1958.

Lotus became a Grand Prix winner in 1960 when Stirling Moss won the Monaco Grand Prix in Rob Walker's privately entered 18-

Lotus Mark 72 (Ronnie Peterson driving) of 1973

Climax. Innes Ireland scored Lotus's first 'works' win at the 1961 US Grand Prix. Up to the end of the 1984 season Lotus had scored 72 Grand Prix victories, six drivers' world championships and seven constructors' championships, as well as winning the Indianapolis 500 and starting a new 'European' design era there in the early 1960s.

Of the Grand Prix cars perhaps the most notable are the 25, which introduced monocoque construction in 1962, the 49, in which the Cosworth V8 engine made a winning début in 1967, and the 79, which made 'ground effect' aerodynamics a success in Formula 1 in 1978. The racing cars were Chapman's real love and his loss was a huge blow, although the team continued under the direction of long time team manager Peter Warr and French engineer Gerard Doucarouge, the Grand Prix car latterly using Renault turbocharged engines and returning to the winner's circle in 1985.

With the road cars, Chapman took a new direction in the Mark 14, the first Elite. It used a glassfibre monocoque shell with very little

metal stiffening and the Coventry-Climax 1216cc engine. Development started in 1956 and some 1000 examples were built between May 1958 and March 1964, by which time it had been joined in October 1962 by the open two-seater Elan, powered by Lotus's own Ford-based twin-overhead cam engine in a backbone chassis.

A fixed head coupé was added in 1965, a Plus 2 version from 1967 and the Sprint from 1971, with a 126bhp version of the originally 100bhp twin-cam. The twin-cam was also used in the Lotus Cortina, introduced in 1963 in collaboration with Ford and hugely successful as a road car, rally car and circuit racing car.

In December 1966 Lotus introduced the mid-engined Europa, initially with the four-cylinder Renault R16 engine and later with various Lotus twin-cam options. The Europa was also developed for racing, as the 47 and ultimately the 62.

Elan production continued until December 1974, latterly with the Plus 2 only, and approximately 13,250 of all types were built,

Lotus Mark 14 Elite of c.1959

From £1.16 million profits in 1973, Lotus plunged to a return of only £294,000 in 1974 and a £488,000 loss the following year. It made a modest £17,000 profit in 1976 and climbed steadily back to a new record £1.28 million profit in 1979 before slumping to only £461,000 in 1980 as the bottom fell out of the American market. In 1979 Lotus started a very short-lived joint marketing deal with Rolls-Royce in the USA which was terminated in 1982 when annual US sales had slumped to

Lotus Turbo Esprit of 1980

including some 4600 Plus 2s. The Europa was made until March 1975 as the Europa Special, and some 9000 were built in all.

The cars were becoming gradually more sophisticated and the company was changing, too. In 1966 Lotus moved to a new and much larger factory at Hethel, near Norwich, where it also began to build its own engines rather than buying in assemblies from JAP as previously. Hethel, formerly a World War II US Air Force base, also had perimeter roads and runways eminently suitable for a test-track and corporate airfield.

In October 1968 Lotus became a public company, with most of the 7.5 million ordinary shares controlled by the Chapman family. From January 1969 Group Lotus Car Companies Ltd was the holding company for subsidiaries including Lotus Cars Ltd and Lotus Components Ltd. From September 1968 Team Lotus International Ltd, the racing operation, had a special relationship with Group Lotus, of which it was legally independent, whereby the group could provide funds in some circumstances and did so.

Lotus Components moved from a financially unstable period back into profit by 1969, in which year total production was 4506 cars, not including 7s, of which Lotus itself built some 3000 (almost all as kits) from 1957 to 1973. In 1973 manufacturing rights to the 7 were sold to Caterham Car Sales of Caterham, Surrey, which had formerly marketed the car. This company has continued to build updated models as the Super 7 and Caterham 7 to the present.

In 1974 Lotus turned its attentions to 'executive' sports cars, having spent some £6 million since 1969 in creating this new generation of more up-market Lotuses. The first was the new Elite, a totally different car from the original, with a Lotus-developed 2-litre slant-four engine and four seats. At almost £5500 for the basic model it was expensive for a 2-litre car but sales were helped by the timely onset of the fuel crisis, which made the small engine suddenly attractive.

The Elite was introduced in May 1974 and sold 687 cars in its first, and best, season. Its worst year of full production was 1977, with just 210 sold, but by then Lotus had also introduced the fastback front-engined Eclat,

Lotus Elan Sprint prototype (Jochen Rindt driving) of 1970

in 1975, and the Giugiaro-styled mid-engined Esprit, in 1976. A total of 2398 Series 1 Elites were sold before it was replaced by the slow-selling S2.2 in 1980, alongside an S2.2 Eclat, S2.2 Esprit and the rapid Esprit Turbo.

During this period Lotus also supplied some 11,000 of the slant-four engines to Jensen-Healey between 1972 and 1976. It also produced the Talbot Sunbeam Lotus, a sort of latter-day Lotus Cortina, between 1979 and 1981, building a total of 2298 cars.

less than 50 cars. In 1981 the company lost again to the tune of £109,000.

Probably Lotus's only profitable venture in this troubled period was its controversial involvement with the doomed DeLorean project in re-engineering DeLorean's original design. From November 1979 Lotus redesigned the chassis and suspension and turned the car into a production design by the end of 1980, involving so many of its own top engineers that it delayed Lotus's own developments.

When Chapman died, of a heart attack in December 1982, the company was in serious trouble. Group Lotus had been forced to renegotiate an extension of its £1.7 million overdraft facility from its bankers, American Express, and to seek outside capital to de-

Lotus Etna prototype of 1985

velop the new small sports car on which its future depended. This was a Toyota-powered 'modern Elan', planned to sell up to 5000 cars a year.

In June 1983 David Wickins' British Car Auctions, a hugely profitable company, bought a large part of Lotus. New shares intended to inject £3.5 million into the company were issued. Existing shareholders were offered up to £2.3 million worth of shares and BCA acquired £1.2 million worth directly, while underwriting the unsold general issue. In July Toyota also gained a 16.5 per cent stake in Lotus by buying £1.6 million worth of shares, originally having discussed taking over Lotus *in toto* but being discouraged by government pressure.

A massive £2.1 million loss for 1982 had been Lotus's low spot, but things began to improve rapidly. A new American distributor, Lotus Performance Cars, re-opened that market and by the first half of 1983 Lotus was able to report a gross trading profit of £257,000.

As the company continued its return to profitability it introduced a new 4-litre V8 engine at the 1984 Motor Show and showed it in a handsome Giugiaro prototype, the ETNA. Lotus managing director Mike Kimberley suggested that this would be in production by 1988 alongside the smaller sports car, planned for 1986, and possibly a high performance, high security head of state limousine, the Eminence. Lotus also seemed likely to offer the 180mph (290kph) ETNA's new V8 to other manufacturers to take advantage of increased volume production. The future suddenly looked very much more promising.

Sales rose from 642 in 1983 to 837 in 1984, and although only 813 cars were produced in 1985, the company was further strengthened by its engineering developments for others, notably further work on 'active-ride' suspension (at least partly for General Motors) and on four-valve-per-cylinder heads for Chrysler USA. In March 1985, following the agreements to develop these heads, rumours that Chrysler was acquiring Lotus shares caused a quick rise in their value. What shares were available, however, were taken up by existing major shareholders, notably BCA, up to just over 29 per cent, Toyota (almost 21.5 per cent) and J. C. Bamford (JCB, the earthmover manufacturer, first involved early in 1985 and now with a near 16 per cent holding). Towards the end of 1985 Group Lotus was acquired by General Motors.

Meanwhile, the Chapman family interests were reduced as Hazel Chapman sold much of her holding and Fred Bushell resigned as deputy chairman in June 1985, coincidentally selling most of his holdings. With his retirement under the cloud of continued investigation, particularly into the DeLorean dealings, by the Inland Revenue, links between Group Lotus and the 'private' companies such as Team Lotus were formally tightened. Lotus seems suddenly to have found an identity more independent of Chapman than most people ever thought possible. BL

LOZIER
USA 1905-1917

Henry Abram Lozier made a fortune in the bicycle and sewing machine businesses, selling the former to the American Bicycle Co in 1897 for $4 million. He invested the proceeds in the Lozier Motor Co which made marine engines in Plattsburgh, New York, from 1900. The first year's production was 200 engines, which powered many high-class racing boats and cabin cruisers, and in 1901 there were rumours that the company would build steam cars.

Lozier died in May 1903 and was succeeded by his eldest son, H. A. Lozier Jr, known as Harry. He sent the company's chief engineer John G. Perrin, who had joined the old bicycle firm in 1893, to Europe to study the best in contemporary design, and at the end of 1904 Perrin came up with a beautifully built 30/35hp four-cylinder chain-drive car aimed at the Mercédès or Locomobile market. With an aluminium four-seater body this Lozier Type B was priced at $4500.

Prototypes were built by the Ball Manufacturing Co of Stanford, Connecticut. Production began at Plattsburgh in early 1905 and 25 cars were sold that year, followed by 56 of the slightly larger Model C, and larger engined Model D, in 1906. Perrin spent a year with the Pope-Waverly electric car company in Indianapolis, but returned to Lozier in time to design the 1907 models, including a new 60hp four-cylinder Model F priced at $8000 for a limousine. Among the features of these Loziers were water-cooled brakes.

About 60 cars were made in 1907, the workforce at Plattsburgh being now nearly 300. There were also about 100 men working at the Ball plant at Stanford, which was an experimental department supervised by Perrin to develop new ideas. Head of the sales department was Frederick Chandler, formerly in charge of the old company's bicycle business in Germany and later to become a successful car-builder in his own right.

Shaft drive and six-cylinder engines arrived with the 1908 models, although a 45hp four was still available and would subsequently be enlarged to 46hp (8.9 litres) in 1911. Between 1908 and 1911 Lozier ran a very successful works team, using mainly stripped touring cars to win several major races including the 1909 Brighton Beach and 1911 Vanderbilt Cup events. The leading driver was Ralph Mulford, who had joined the company in the marine engine days in 1900 and who won the 1911 drivers' championship despite missing several important events because his religious principles did not permit him to race on Sundays.

In 1908 Lozier began naming his models, using prestige titles associated with country clubs and exclusive hotels – such as Briarcliff, Meadowbrook and Lakewood. Production expanded rapidly so that by 1910 the

Lozier 51hp tourer of c.1911

Plattsburgh factory turned out 528 cars. The company hoped to make a somewhat cheaper car with 33hp six-cylinder L-head engine, the Type J, but the factory's annual capacity was no more than 600 cars.

Harry Lozier was persuaded to build an additional factory in Detroit, for which local financiers put up much of the money. Built on a 65-acre (26-hectare) site and costing over $1 million, the new factory was designed by Albert Kahn who was responsible for Ford's Highland Park and River Rouge plants and also the Ford-backed GAZ factory at Gorki. Annual capacity was 1200 cars. The plan was that a cheaper car costing about $3500 would be made there, and that Plattsburgh would concentrate on the traditional Loziers in the $6000 to $8000 range. The cheaper car, a development of the Type J called the Type 77 Light Six, made its appearance in September 1912.

Meanwhile, Harry Lozier, who had surrendered control of his company when he allowed Detroit investors to finance the new factory, was eased out of the presidency and replaced by one of the investors, Harry M. Jewett of the Paige-Detroit Motor Car Co. Lozier stock had been increased from $2 million to $3 million to finance the manufacture of a 5-ton truck at Detroit, but very few were made and the project was abandoned within a year.

Jewett claimed that 450 Type 77s had been sold before the first one left the factory in December 1912. This may have been true, but the staff lacked confidence in the new management and in January 1913 five leading men, including Frederick Chandler, left to form the Chandler Motor Car Co at Cleveland. Perrin would have joined them but his contract had two years to run.

Although a few of the old, large sixes were still made at Plattsburgh, the Detroit plant turned out a still smaller car in January 1914, the 29hp four-cylinder Type 82 selling for $2100. For a while production ran at four cars a day, but in August 1914 the Detroit plant closed down and five months later the company was put up for sale.

Harry Lozier and John Perrin both left, the former to make V12 cars in Cleveland under the name HAL, the latter to embark on a distinguished career with the Timken Axle Co, Willys-Overland and the aero engine maker Pratt and Whitney. Lozier died in 1925, Perrin in 1966.

The Lozier company had two sets of owners in its declining years, and one move from the spacious Mack Avenue plant to a more modest premises where the Warren car had been made. The Plattsburgh plant was sold in March 1915.

Production of the Four and Light Six lingered on into 1917, but without the glamour of the Big Sixes the make had no real identity. In March 1918 it was announced that the company was still making cars to order, but there is no evidence that orders were forthcoming. GNG

LUC
GERMANY 1909-1914

The Luc car took its name from its manufacturer, Loeb und Co GmBH of Berlin, a company founded in 1906 initially as a modern and very well equipped repair works for other makes of vehicle. Loeb also had a paintshop and filling station and opened a showroom selling several makes of car, including Benz, Fiat and Panhard et Levassor, and an agency for Körting proprietary engines, as used by several German makes.

Loeb probably always intended to build cars and in 1908 started work on prototypes, the first being finished in 1909. It was a 3-litre four-cylinder 12/36PS model designed by Reissig, who drove one of these cars in the 1910 Prince Henry Trials, finishing without penalties. These first models were mostly sold as taxis and were made until 1913.

In 1911 Loeb began to import Daimler chassis with Knight sleeve-valve engines from Britain which were fitted under licence with good quality German coachwork and sold as Luc-Knights. Two models were offered, an 8/22PS and a 16/40PS.

For 1913 Reissig designed a technically advanced 2.6-litre four-cylinder 10/30PS model with a complex rear suspension arrangement with double semi-elliptic springs and auxiliary coil springs. It was well received. At this time Loeb was beginning to expand its car manufacturing operation with the addition of a second factory in Berlin, started in 1913. Also that year, Loeb changed from a limited company to a joint stock company, Loeb und Co AG, but although it continued to make the 8/22 and 16/40PS Luc-Knights and the 10/30PS Luc until 1914, it stopped car production at the outbreak of World War I and concentrated on building trucks and aero engines.

Loeb did not resume car production after the war. In 1920 the company was taken over by Dinos Automobilwerke AG, which began car production under its own name in 1921 in the newer Loeb factory located at Hohenschönhausen, Berlin, BL

300

LUC COURT
FRANCE 1899-1936

Born in 1862 at Rives, Isère, Luc Court became an electrical engineer and set up his own business at Lyons in 1892, making electric motors and transformers. In 1899 he became attracted to the motor car and built a light voiturette powered by an 8hp two-cylinder engine with the unusual feature of a five-speed gearbox. It was followed by a 10hp twin, and in 1904 came a 20/24hp four which soon replaced the twins.

Some Luc Courts of this period had a two-part chassis which could be separated just behind the engine. This enabled alternative bodies to be used with the same engine, giving the advantage that an appropriate countershaft ratio could be provided to suit the body.

Luc Court advertising, 1923

Various four-cylinder models up to 40hp were made, but in 1910 Luc Court introduced the classic H4 and H6 engines, both with inlet over exhaust valves and dimensions of 70×140mm (2¾×5½in) giving capacities of 2154 and 3230cc respectively. The H4 was made until 1936.

Luc Court production was always limited, as the works at 88-90 Rue Robert at Lyons were too small to permit manufacture of more than two or three vehicles a week. Some of these were commercials on the H4 chassis, which retained chain drive for both passenger and goods versions, until 1915. Some larger cars were offered in the 1920s, including the 4.7-litre Type HR (1921-25), but this engine does not seem to have been used in goods vehicles. Most Luc Courts were sold locally, although they did have a Paris agent in the early 1920s. From 1925 the H4 was the only model made.

Car production dwindled until, by the early 1930s, they were said to be available to special order only. The only body offered was a classic *conduite intérieure avec malle* (saloon with luggage boot) unchanged from 1932 to 1935, but for 1936 the company produced a modernized version not unlike the contemporary Peugeot 301.

It is surprising that Luc Court went to the trouble of making a new model when so few cars were being sold. Perhaps it hoped to make a return to larger scale production, but no cars at all were made after 1936.

As the cars dwindled so the commercials grew, in size anyway, and the late 1930s saw a range of trucks up to 3 tons capacity and coaches for 18 to 22 passengers, powered by petrol or diesel engines. Luc Court himself died during the war, but commercial vehicle production survived in a very small way until 1950. GNG

LYONS
see Knox

Luc Court buggy of 1902

McFARLAN
USA 1910-1928

In 1856 English-born John B. McFarlan (1822-1909) merged several small carriage-building firms of Connersville, Indiana, into the McFarlan Carriage Co. This flourished over

ley, it was a monobloc T-head unit; this make was used exclusively by McFarlan until it brought out its own power unit in 1921. Carriages were dropped in 1914, by which date a wide variety of open and closed bodies was offered. A larger Teetor engine of 9374cc was adopted for 1915, when the rather staid artillery wheeled models were joined by a sporty 'submarine roadster' with wire wheels and a vee radiator which was very much in the German style.

In 1916 sales reached three figures for the first time, with 130 cars leaving the factory. Production dropped to 105 in 1918, but the factory was busy with war production for which it turned out, in 20 months, 6000 carpenters' chests and a large quantity of kapok-stuffed cushions. These were prosperous years for the company.

The 1920 McFarlan, called the Ninety from the horsepower developed by its enormous Teetor engine, was a high priced car, ranging from $4800 to $6500 according to body style. It was succeeded in 1921 by an even more expensive model, and the most famous of the McFarlans, the Twin Valve Six.

today's money.

Despite its high price, the TV McFarlan sold well to start with, and 1922 was the company's best year ever, with 235 cars sold. Perhaps profits per car were disappointing, for the following year McFarlan took on work for another customer, building sedan bodies for Auburn. These were made at the rate of 35 a day, and in 1925 Marmon and Locomobile became customers. This was now the firm's most important activity.

In November 1923 McFarlan added a smaller car, the SV (Single Valve) with 4.4-litre six-cylinder Wisconsin Y engine. It cost less than half the price of a TV, from $2500 to $3150. However, production fell to 170 in 1923 and 127 in 1924, as the factory was still devoting much of its capacity to building bodies.

Four wheel hydraulic brakes came in for 1925, and for 1926 a 4.9-litre Lycoming-powered straight-eight replaced the SV. Production climbed to around 180 thanks to the straight-eight, but Harry McFarlan became seriously ill and this resulted in a loss of dynamic leadership. Only 70 cars were made

McFarlan Knickerbocker Cabriolet of 1922

the next 50 years, becoming part of the Industrial Park which McFarlan established in 1886 and which succeeded to such an extent that it boasted eight different companies by the turn of the century.

In 1909 McFarlan's grandson Harry, born in 1881, decided to enter the automobile business, making a conventional car powered by a 35/40hp six-cylinder engine built by the F. A. Brownell Co of Rochester, New York. This went onto the market as a 1910 model priced at $2000. Production built up only slowly, with an estimated 25 cars sold in 1910, 35 in 1911 and 40 in 1912. Brownell, Buda and Wainwright engines were used in these early models.

For 1913 a new engine was chosen, the Teetor, built by the Light Inspection Car Co of Indianapolis. Also known as the Teetor-Hart-

Four valves and three sparking plugs per cylinder gave it a total of 24 valves and 18 plugs, the latter a record for the industry. The 9374cc engine had the same dimensions as the Teetor, but developed 120hp. It is generally thought of as McFarlan's own, but was designed for the company by Jesse Kepler and built by him in his Dayton, Ohio, workshop. Prices ranged from $6300 for a two-passenger roadster to $9000 for the Knickerbocker Cabriolet, which was a landaulette town car.

Most McFarlans had bodies made in-house, but a Brooks-Ostruk town car was sold in 1922 for $11,650. The most expensive McFarlan ever made was a 1923 Knickerbocker Cabriolet liberally covered with goldplate, even on the wheel rims and hubs, which sold for $25,000 – well in excess of $300,000 in

in 1927, and although 1928 models were announced it is possible that none were made during the calendar year. The enormous TV was listed until the end, together with the straight-eight.

The company was declared bankrupt in August 1928 and the machinery was sold soon afterwards. The factory was bought by Auburn in April 1929 for the storage of leather materials, small parts and Auburn and Cord cars awaiting dispatch to dealers. Part of it was demolished in 1939 and the rest in the early 1960s. Harry McFarlan died in 1937. GNG

McINTYRE
see Kiblinger

McLAUGHLIN/ACADIAN, BEAUMONT
CANADA 1908-1971

Established in the same year as the federation of Canada (1867), the McLaughlin company of Oshawa, Ontario, made about 25,000 high-quality sleighs and wheeled horse-drawn vehicles before R. Samuel McLaughlin, son of the founder Robert McLaughlin, formed the McLaughlin Motor Car Co Ltd in 1907. He attempted to develop a complete car, but from 1908 was forced to incorporate Buick mechanical items. Nearly 200 cars were built in the first year and about 1000 in 1914.

R. Samuel McLaughlin had had business dealings with W. C. Durant in 1908 and Durant's Chevrolet car was produced for the Canadian and British Empire markets at Oshawa from 1915, when the horse-wagon plant was sold. When Chevrolet was bought by General Motors in 1918, McLaughlin was also taken over and became General Motors of Canada.

A total of 15,000 cars were made in 1922, and from the following year, when the agreement with Durant ran out, cars under the name McLaughlin-Buick were produced, often with better quality coachwork than their American counterparts. A $2.5 million factory extension with four storey fireproof office was built in 1927.

R. S. McLaughlin rose high in General Motors management and the Canadian firm flourished, assembling a variety of models, although the McLaughlin name disappeared from cars in World War II. Some 5 million McLaughlins and Canadian GM vehicles had been made by the mid-1960s, when annual sales reached 35,000 cars and 70,000 commercials. By the mid-1970s annual car sales reached 444,000 and 137,000 commercials were sold.

In 1962 a special Canadian model, the Acadian, was produced at the plants in Oshawa, Windsor and St Catharines. It was based on the Chevy II. The following year the Chevelle-based Acadian Beaumont was introduced. For three years from 1966 it was called simply the Beaumont. From 1968, with a reduction in tariff restrictions, Acadians were brought in from the United States instead of being assembled in Canada. The name was discontinued in 1971. R. Samuel McLaughlin died in January 1972, in his 101st year, just four years after retiring from the board of GM of Canada. NB

MAF
GERMANY 1908-1921

The MAF car was built in Markranstädt, near Leipzig, by Markranstädter Automobil-Fabrik Hugo Ruppe, founded in 1908. Ruppe was the son of Arthur Ruppe who had founded the

MAF F6 tourer of 1913

firm of A. Ruppe & Sohn in Apolda in 1854 as an iron foundry and agricultural machinery manufacturer. From 1902 Ruppe had also made motorcycles under the name Apoldania, and in 1904 introduced the popular, low-priced Piccolo car, which was made until 1912.

Hugo Ruppe left his father's company in 1908, when it became the joint stock A. Ruppe & Sohn AG, to form MAF. The original company introduced the Piccolo-Apollo car in 1910 and from 1912, when the firm was renamed Apollo-Werke AG, built cars known simply as Apollos.

The first MAF car, which appeared in 1908, was an air-cooled four-cylinder model, very similar in basic design to the Piccolo; up to 1914 MAF built variations on this model ranging from 1192 to 1910cc. Although the cars were well made and sold quite widely, the company had serious financial problems and in 1911 was forced to declare itself bankrupt.

It was taken over, however, by a finance house which bought the works and resumed production. Ruppe, who had originally been the sole proprietor, now became technical director for the new company, Markranstädter Automobil-Fabrik vorm Hugo Ruppe GmbH.

The MAF continued to sell well until the outbreak of World War I and the company became more successful financially. It set up an agency in England and raced cars with minor success.

After the war, production resumed with the pre-war 6/18PS model and a new 8/24PS model. MAF also built a small number of air-cooled 3483cc four-cylinder overhead-cam 14/38PS tourers, but in 1921 Hugo's company was bought out by his father's Apollo-Werke and MAF production stopped. Apollo built the small 4/20PS sports car until 1925 before stopping production itself in 1926.

Hugo Ruppe did not stay on with Apollo

but went to motorcycle builders DKW, there to design two-stroke engines. He later set up his own company, Berliner Kleinmotoren AG, building a very good 174cc two-stroke engine called the Bekamo, which was widely used as a proprietary engine in motorcycles. Bekamo also experimented unsuccessfully with complete motorcycles with reinforced wooden frames during the 1920s. BL

MAG
HUNGARY 1910-1935

The company which went on to make the MAG car was founded in Budapest in 1886 by engineers Podvinecz and Heisler. From 1905 to 1915, first as the Phönix Automobile Works and from 1911 as the Machinery, Mill and Automobile Works, it built cars and buses based on the technically advanced Cudell-Phönix. This was designed by Karl Slevogt for the Cudell Motoren-Compagnie mbH of Aachen, but it was not produced in Germany as that company virtually ceased production shortly after the car's introduction in 1905.

In 1910, the Hungarian Phönix company opened a new factory at Matyasfold near Budapest which became Magyar Altalanos Gepgyar Reszvenytarsasag, or MAG. The new company bought manufacturing rights to various Austro-Daimler models from Österreichische Daimler Motoren AG of Vienna and up to the outbreak of World War I built Porsche-designed four-cylinder models of 25 and 35hp as MAGs.

Recovering after the war, during which it made vehicles and aircraft components, the company was reorganized in 1920 and began to build smaller cars to its own designs. The first was the 1.8-litre side-valve four-cylinder Magomobil, introduced in 1922. This was followed in 1925 by the Magomobil-Lex, also a four-cylinder model with four-wheel brakes, widely used as a taxi.

In the same year MAG introduced the side-valve six-cylinder Magosix, first with a 1.6-litre engine and later with 2.1- and 2.4-litre developments – latterly as the Supermagosix, introduced in 1929. All the sixes used four-wheel hydraulic brakes.

MAG was the first car-maker in Hungary to use assembly line production methods and in 1930 built some 2000 cars, 140 trucks, 1200 automobile engines, 800 aero engines and 350 complete aircraft. In spite of this prolific output, MAG production was apparently not profitable and was stopped in 1935. BL

MAJA
see Austro-Daimler

MAJOLA
FRANCE 1911-1928

The Majola was a quality light car with some unusual features, particularly the single-overhead cam engine with inclined valves and hemispherical combustion chambers which was used on all four-cylinder models made by the company. This was designed by M. Doutré and offered as a proprietary unit from 1908, three years before complete cars were made.

In 1911 came a 1300cc four-cylinder car, the Type A, joined by the 1000cc Type B, described by *The Motor* as 'a vigorous four-cylinder'. The main difference in design was that the Type A's camshaft was driven by helical gearing while the Type B used chain drive. A small number of these cars was made in J. Majola's St Denis works up to 1914, with two or four seater open bodies.

A team of four was constructed for the 1914 Grand Prix des Voiturettes, which was cancelled because of the war, but they turned up undeterred when the race was eventually held in 1920. Three retired but Rost managed fourth place.

In 1920 Majola was taken over by Georges Irat, who was about to launch his own 2-litre touring car. The Majola formed a useful line of smaller cars, production taking place in the Georges Irat factory at Châtou, Seine et Oise. Two models, the Type A enlarged to 1390cc (the DT), and the Type B enlarged to 1100cc (the F), were the only Majolas made in the 1920s until the introduction of a cyclecar powered by an air-cooled flat twin engine in 1927. Few of these were made, and in 1928 all production ceased with the reorganization and change of factory of Automobiles Georges Irat. GNG

MAJOR
see Violet

MALICET & BLIN
see Marlborough

MANNESMANN
GERMANY 1923-1930

The origins of this motor firm stem from the Scheibler commercial vehicles made in Aix-la-Chapelle (Aachen) on the German-Belgian-Dutch border from 1899. The vehicles became known as Mulags after about 10 years and the firm belonged to Carl Mannesmann from 1911. Two years later Mannesmann-Mulag became Mannesmann-Mulag Motoren und Lastwagen AG with branch works at Westhofen. Mannesmann was a major engineering group that had made profits worth $120,750 in 1913. Its capital in 1914 was the equivalent of $500,000 and output was about 1000 heavy vehicles a year.

In 1923 light cars were produced from a factory in Remscheid where the Mannesmann Motorenwerke subsidiary had been formed in 1920. The 1300cc four-cylinder light cars were accompanied by sports versions, but financial difficulties were an inhibiting factor. In 1926 a loss of 10 million marks was declared. The car business was re-formed in 1927 as Mannesmann Automobilwerke and in 1928 lorry production at Aachen was discontinued, the factory being sold to Büssing.

The car factory added small, overhead-valve 55bhp straight-eights in 1927 built under licence from SCAP. These could be bought with Zoller superchargers and were then capable of 90mph (145kph). In 1929 came a 5.2-litre 100bhp straight-eight Mb model which, like the 55bhp Ma, could have Maybach overdrive transmission. The engine was the Rickenbacker design by J. S. Rasmussen, of Audi. Most coachwork was by Karmann of Osnabrück. About 2000 Mannesmann cars had been made when family finances ran out in mid-1930 and the Remscheid factory was closed. NB

MARCHAND/DUFAUX
ITALY 1898-1909

Orio and Marchand started out as a bicycle and sewing machine manufacturer in Musocco, Milan, run by the Marchand brothers, Paul and Lesne, and Stefano Orio. In 1898 Orio and Marchand moved from Musocco to Piacenza, south-west of Milan, and began to produce Marchand cars. The first Marchands were small, rear-engined models built under licence from Decauville, but with assistance from engineer Giuseppe Merosi, who went on to achieve fame as a designer for Fiat, Bianchi and Alfa Romeo.

Stefano Orio died in 1899 and the company became known as Fratelli Marchand, which continued to build two- and four-cylinder models. By 1902 all Marchands were front-engined and the range included 8, 10, 12, 16 and 20hp models, all with chain drive. Mar-

Majola four-cylinder tourer of c.1919

Marchand 10hp tonneau of 1902

chand also built some motorcycles and in 1904 Tamagni used one to win a long distance trial from Milan to Nice organized by the newspaper *Gazzetta dello Sport*.

In 1905 the company became Anonima Marchand, registered in Genoa, but this version of the company did not last long before another reorganization took place in 1906, when that company went into liquidation and the remains were taken over by Swiss brothers Charles and Frederic Dufaux, who built Dufaux cars in Geneva. The Italian company became Marchand & Dufaux, still in Piacenza, with the intention of building Dufaux designs in Italy.

In 1906 the range included three four-cylinder models, a 10/14, an 18/22 and a 28/35hp, plus a 50/60hp six, all with chain drive. Dufaux at this time was building two four-cylinder models and a straight-eight, but it ceased production in 1907. Marchand continued production of its own models until late 1909 when that marque too disappeared. BL

MARCOS/MIDAS
GB 1959 to date

The name Marcos is derived from Jem Marsh and Frank Costin, two brilliant designers with extremely original ideas.

Jeremy George Weston Marsh was born in 1930, served in the Royal Navy and sold cars briefly before joining Firestone's technical department.

Francis Costin was born in 1920 and worked with numerous aircraft companies as fitter, designer and technical director, finally working as aerodynamic flight test engineer in charge of the experimental department of De Havilland from 1951 to 1953. He stayed with De Havilland until 1958, during which time he also transferred his skill in aerodynamic design to many cars, including several Lotuses, the 1957 Maserati coupé and the Grand Prix Vanwall. His brother, Mike, was the 'Cos' of Cosworth Engineering, builder of racing engines.

In 1959 Marsh founded Speedex Castings and Accessories Ltd in Luton, Bedfordshire, to supply fibreglass shells and mechanical components to special builders. As well as aeroplanes and cars, Costin was interested in boats, which he built in his spare time, learning all about plywood construction. Combining this and his aerodyamic ideas he designed a lightweight high-performance two-seater, with integral body and chassis in marine ply and glassfibre; it had Triumph Herald front suspension and Nash Metropolitan rear. Marsh built the car.

This hunchbacked gullwing-door coupé with cycle wings and a 1-litre Ford engine had a top speed of 120mph (193kph) and was very successful in sports car races, usually driven by Marsh. Customer versions of the car, already called a Marcos, soon followed, these having full wings.

In 1962 Marcos Cars Ltd was formed to sell the cars as kits. Marsh was the main partner and Costin primarily the designer. In 1963 the

Marcos gullwing coupé of 1961

company moved to Bradford-on-Avon, Wiltshire, and Denis Adams styled a prettier, if no more efficient car, still with the strong wooden chassis but now with a one-piece body and four-cylinder Volvo 1800 engine. It went on sale in 1964 as the Marcos GT.

The well-equipped Volvo-engined car was too expensive to sell in large numbers and Marcos quickly introduced a 1.6-litre Ford-engined version, the 1600GT. In later years the highly respected coupé was offered with 2-litre V4 and 3-litre V6 Ford engines, latterly with a steel chassis, the use of which was dictated by cost, not efficiency.

In 1970 Marcos established dealerships in the United States, but cars shipped there did not meet new regulations and were effectively a total loss financially. At the same time the company was moving to larger premises in Westbury, Wiltshire, and trying to introduce a four-seater model, the Triumph 2.5PI powered Mantis, a 140mph (225kph) coupé styled by Adams.

Only 32 Mantises were built before Marcos succumbed to its financial problems. Production of the Mantis and the GT stopped in 1972, a year after the company had been sold to racing team proprietor Rob Walker.

Marcos continued to build the Mini-Marcos, a small GT with a glassfibre shell and tubular frame that could accept any kind of Mini running gear. Introduced in 1965, it sold from as little as £200 and was very successful.

In 1975 the Mini-Marcos was taken over by D & H Fibreglass Techniques Ltd of Oldham, Lancashire, a company run by former Jaguar development engineer Harold Dermott. Production of the Mini-Marcos continued until 1981 and alongside it Dermott worked on a completely revised and very pretty modern version, the Midas. This 2+2 with a glassfibre reinforced plastic monocoque shell was styled by Richard Oakes and was introduced in 1978 to general acclaim.

In 1979 the Midas kit sold for £2495 plus value added tax compared to £695 plus tax for the much less comprehensive Mini-Marcos kit. One enthusiastic Midas owner was Gordon Murray, designer of the world championship winning Brabham Grand Prix cars.

In 1981 the company became Midas Cars and moved to a new 4000sq ft (370sq m) factory in a former sawmill in Corby, Northamptonshire, where from late 1983 it began to offer fully-built Midas cars as well as the kits, a turbocharged version being added in 1984. An improved model, the Metro-based Midas Gold, was announced in July 1985, at a basic kit price of £2750 plus tax.

Nor were the other Marcos models quite dead. In 1977 the Mantis moulds had been sold to three enthusiasts who planned to build cars with Triumph TR6 engines and GT6 chassis, but at some £10,000 these were far too expensive and apparently only two

were made. In 1980 the moulds were sold again, to Colin Carter of Eastdean, Sussex, who planned to offer a much more basic kit for less than £1500.

In 1981 Jem Marsh himself formed Jem Marsh Performance Cars in the old works in Westbury and put the Marcos GT back into production, the project being managed by his son Chris but with most manufacture done by sub-contractors. By 1986 the car was being built at a rate of about two a week. Current models take Ford engines, or in the Marcos Mantula, the 3½-litre Rover V8. The Mantula is available as a coupé or convertible. BL

Midas Gold of 1986

Marcos 3-litre coupé of 1970

MARENDAZ/MARSEAL
GB 1920-1937

Captain D. M. K. Marendaz was an enthusiastic Brooklands competitor and from 1919 was one half of the Marseel Engineering Co Ltd of Coventry, the other half being a man by the name of Seelhaft. The Marseel was a conventional assembled light car and evidence suggests that the company also built the unsuccessful Marseel motor scooter.

The first four-wheeled Marseel appeared in September 1920 and was a light car with a 1½-litre 10.5hp four-cylinder Coventry-Simplex engine and a three-speed gearbox, built in Coventry. The announcement of its introduction stated that 'its manufacturers have considerable experience in the production of car components'.

The car as introduced sold for £450. The design was very simple, with a flat-sided body eliminating the need for expensive panel beating. By the following April the body had been simplified still further, with two doors instead of three, and the price reduced to a very low £393. At the beginning of 1922 the sole concessionaire for the Marseel was the GNU Motor and Accessories Co of London.

In March 1922 the company, which Marendaz had renamed Marseal Motors Ltd as Seelhaft had now left, showed an oil-cooled four-cylinder engine of 1018cc, of which two prototypes had been made. The cars were also renamed Marseal.

When the next model appeared, in October

Mini-Marcos of 1966

1922, although its capacity was 1018cc it used a conventional water-cooled Coventry-Climax engine. As a four-seater it sold for just £255. There was also a sports model, with Anzani 1505cc side-valve engine, at £400.

In February 1923 the car was given improved suspension and more power. A contemporary reviewer remarked that it was one of the lightest cars built, with a power to weight ratio approaching that of a racing car.

Captain Marendaz did indeed use the Marseals to some effect at Brooklands for racing and record breaking, including one example nicknamed 'Blancmange' which he drove in 1923, but he also drove many other makes including Amilcar and Graham-Paige. There was also, briefly, a 1750cc six-cylinder Marseal, but the marque name was dropped in 1925 when Captain Marendaz began to call his cars Marendaz Specials, used principally for racing. The company was renamed D. M. K. Marendaz Ltd and moved into works in London which had once been a Bugatti service station.

In November 1927 Captain Marendaz used a 1096cc four-cylinder model to set new G-class 3-hour and 500km records at up to 71.13mph (114.42kph). Early models included this 1100 type and supercharged and

Marendaz Special sports two-seater of c.1926

unsupercharged 1½-litre Anzani-powered cars, all on the same low slung chassis and looking very like a small Bentley.

In October 1931 a 13/70hp Marendaz Special was announced and it was 'understood that production is going ahead'. This was a six-cylinder side-valve of 1869cc, available as a two-door coupé or an open two- or four-seater, and designed by *The Autocar*'s artist, Max Millar. It was also available in supercharged form and the engine was a joint British/American production, offered later in a larger, 1991cc form, with three carburettors and 90bhp.

In 1932 Marendaz moved to Maidenhead, Berkshire. The company reduced the chassis price of the 13/70 to £375 for the following year, when the supercharged 17/97 model was the most expensive variant at £675.

When the next model appeared, in 1934, with a side-valve six-cylinder engine, using some Erskine/Continental components, it was more properly known as a Marendaz

306

than a Marendaz Special and was followed in 1935 by a 2-litre six-cylinder Coventry-Climax powered model, the 15/90, which was again highly successful in competition. Marendaz also thought of introducing a straight-eight model and it seems that one Miller-engined car was built, but it did not go into production. Marendaz stopped building cars in 1937. BL

MARION/MARION-HANDLEY
USA 1904-1919

The Marion Motor Car Co of Indianapolis started building air-cooled cars, very similar to the air-cooled Franklin from Syracuse, New York, in 1904. The first model, introduced in 1905, used a transversely mounted 16hp four-cylinder Reeves engine and chain drive, but by 1906 the engines, 16 and 28hp Reeves fours, were placed longitudinally.

Shortly after this change Marion abandoned air-cooled engines and adopted water-cooled Continentals and other proprietary makes, and in 1908 built a prototype 9½-litre V12 car. The production models, however, were mainly straightforward fours and sixes, and sold well.

By 1913 Marions were being built in the former Willys-Overland factory, which even worked a night shift to keep up with full order books. Marion had been associated earlier with Overland through the American Motor Sales Co, whose president, John North Willys, a former car dealer from Elmira, New York, had rescued Overland in 1907. Willys, who had sold Marions in his original dealership, now took over distribution.

In May 1912 J. I. Handley, who was president of the American Motor Sales Co from its reorganization the previous year, bought control of the Marion Motor Car Co, which continued to build cars simply known as Marions

until 1915. In 1914 Marion offered a four-cylinder four-passenger coupé and sporty two-passenger roadster, and larger six-cylinder models in similar body types, at prices from $2150 to $2950. Advertising proclaimed 'The Marion is built expressly for those who value absolute reliability, comfort and style'.

In 1916 the car became known as the Marion-Handley, being produced by the Mutual Motors Co in Jackson, Michigan. As the Marion-Handley it was built for only a few years and was a typical assembled car with six-cylinder Continental engine and available as a tourer or four-seater roadster, each on a choice of two chassis lengths.

The Marion-Handley was built until 1919, and in 1921 Handley became involved with Handley Motors Inc of Kalamazoo, Michigan, building the Handley-Knight, which used the four-cylinder Knight sleeve-valve engine. The company also built models with conventional engines, mostly sixes, and these were known simply as Handleys. Production of both Handley and Handley-Knight continued only until May 1923 when the factory was taken over by the newly formed Checker company, also of Kalamazoo, which was just beginning to build taxicabs. BL

MARLBOROUGH/ANDRÉ, MALICET & BLIN, MARLBOROUGH-THOMAS
GB, FRANCE 1906-1925; 1933-1934

The French bicycle and motor components firm of Malicet & Blin of Aubervilliers, Seine, supplied individual parts and sometimes virtually complete cars to the fledgling motor industry. It employed 400 men in 1905 and almost the only item it did not then make was engines.

A Marlborough made from Malicet & Blin parts was shown in London in 1906 by the

Marion 30hp roadster of 1910

Chassis Construction Co of Taunton, England. By 1909 it had been taken up by T. B. André and Co Ltd, a London components firm that held the agencies for Malicet & Blin, Ballot engines and Hartford shock absorbers. Assembly took place at a garage in Lorn Gardens, Regent's Park, and then in Notting Hill Gate from about 1911. Fivet engines were mostly used, although it is likely that Ballot units were also featured. André and Co was also sales agent for the London Waverley made by the carburettor firm Trier and Martin, which was also involved in the construction of the Marlborough.

An 18hp six joined smaller fours in 1910 and from 1912 the firm concentrated on 8/10hp four-cylinder cyclecars. Car production ceased from 1916 to 1919 but then resumed with more cars being built from French components, some of the sportier ones using British-built examples of Anzani engines.

A racing programme using Parry Thomas engines in six Marlborough-Thomas cars helped foster the sports image from 1923, although in the range at that time was also a very basic 8hp CIME-engined light car. Indeed, nothing larger than 12hp was ever available until the demise of the Marlborough in 1925, although a 2-litre Coventry-Climax engined 15.7hp sports model was then being considered. About 2000 Marlboroughs are believed to have been sold.

In 1933-34 T. B. André and Co built half a dozen little V-twin JAP-engined sports cars under its own name. Vernon Trier, who had worked on the early Marlboroughs, became managing director of the motor components firm Silentbloc and then ran the André company after World War II. NB

MARMON
USA 1902-1933

Howard Carpenter Marmon was born in Richmond, Indiana, in May 1876, and after gaining an engineering degree at the University of California he joined the family firm of Nordyke and Marmon at Indianapolis. By the turn of the century this company, established in 1851, had become the world's largest maker of milling machinery, but Howard Marmon's interests were more car orientated, and between 1898 and 1902 he worked on a design of his own which had a number of advanced features. The engine was an air-cooled overhead-valve V-twin with pressure lubrication, mounted on a sub-frame suspended from the main chassis frame. The body was a side-entrance tonneau at a time when most two-cylinder cars still had rear-entrance tonneaus.

The V-twin was not produced for sale but its successor, the 24hp V4 Model A with aluminium front seat structure, went into production in 1904, when six cars were sold. In 1905 Marmon sold 25 of the generally similar Model B at $2500 each, and the air-cooled V4

Marmon Model 34 roadster of 1919

theme was continued for the next four years. Soon the entire body was made of aluminium, as well as some of the running gear, Marmon operating its own foundry.

Howard Marmon experimented with a V6 engine, and a complete 65hp V8 car was shown at the New York Motor Show in December 1906. Its price of $5000 was probably more of a deterrent to customers than its novelty, and there were no takers.

The early air-cooled V-engined Marmons were made in very small numbers, fewer than 100 a year at best, and in 1909 Howard Marmon turned to a conventional in-line four-cylinder water-cooled design which would lend itself to quantity production. His father, Daniel W. Marmon, died that year and it may be that Howard now felt more free to expand the car side of the business at the expense of the milling machinery.

Production of the new Model 32 grew slowly until the company received a wonderful boost with Ray Harroun's victory in the first Indianapolis 500-Mile Race. Marmon took away $16,000 in prize money and more orders than he could cope with. In 1913 he built his first in-line six, the Model 48, which was a slow seller because of its high price of $5000 to $6250, compared with $2850 to $4100 for the Model 32.

In 1913 Marmon took on two men who were to father an important new car; Frederick E. Moskovics joined as commercial manager, and Alanson P. Brush, designer of the Brush Runabout, as chief engineer. They produced a brand new, advanced design which came on the market as the Model 34 for 1916.

It had a six-cylinder monobloc engine of 5½ litres capacity with a high proportion of aluminium alloy components – cylinder block, crankcase, pistons, water pump, inlet manifold and pushrods. With 74bhp available the Marmon 34 could easily reach 70mph (112kph) with a four-seater body, also of aluminium. At $2700 it was not overpriced, but it had little time to become accepted before America's entry into World War I made Marmon turn over to war production, particularly making the Liberty V12 aero engine.

The Model 34 helped Marmon production

into four figures, but even so the 1500 output in 1916 was less than 10 per cent of Cadillac's. The aluminium block caused a number of problems, and when the 34 came back on the market in 1919 it had a bi-bloc cast-iron engine, and cost almost double the previous figure because of low volume production. Brush left Marmon in 1919 to join Hale and Kilburn, the Philadelphia chassis-maker, while Moskovics left in 1923 for Franklin and later Stutz, where he achieved his greatest fame.

During the early 1920s prices of the Model 34 were cut back and sales gradually improved. By 1923 nearly 3000 found buyers at prices starting at $3185 for a touring car. Front wheel brakes were now optional.

Marmon was only just keeping its head above water and the Model 34 was a nine-year-old design when George M. Williams, formerly of the Dayton Wright Airplane Co and Buffalo Wire Wheel Corporation, was hired in 1924 to revive the company's fortunes. He believed that success lay in the straight-eight rather than the six, but as an eight would take some years to develop he revamped the Model 34 as the 74, with balloon tyres and restyled bodies. By pricing the closed models at only $100 or so above the open ones he took advantage of the burgeoning popularity of closed cars, and increased sales from 2597 cars in 1924 to 4352 in 1925 and 4462 in 1926.

Williams then reorganized the company, forming the Marmon Motor Car Co as a separate entity from Nordyke and Marmon. At this point Howard Marmon became disenchanted with what he saw as the abandonment of quality in search of higher sales and went into semi-retirement. His place as engineering vice-president was taken by Barney Roos, who had designed the Locomobile Junior Eight and now proceeded to provide Marmon with a similar small overhead-valve straight-eight.

This appeared in 1927 as the Little Eight of 3.1 litres capacity, developing 64bhp. Whatever Howard Marmon may have felt about it, the new eight-cylinder policy worked wonders for the company's sales graph. Production jumped from 4462 in 1926 to 10,489 in

MARMON'S Year !

8 FIRING IN LINE

MARMON'S year ! 1928—the year of 8-cylinder motoring, established by MARMON . . . the car which made even experienced owners stand bewildered by its unparalleled performance — and delighted them by its beautiful design . . . its colour-scheme . . . its luxurious comfort and general refinement. "A year ahead of all other cars "—that's what you'll say when you see the new series of "78" and "68" MARMON models at Olympia.

NEW PRICES:

Model "68" - - from **£565**
Model "78" - - from **£695**

(Including complete equipment, six wire wheels, luggage carrier and bumpers.)

POINTS.

More impressive body lines.
More interesting interiors.
UNTARNISHABLE CHRO-
MIUM PLATING ON
EXTERNAL FITTINGS.
More power—improved accelera-
tion.
More massive front appearance.
DUPLEX TRANSMISSION
AND IGNITION LOCK.
Even, smoother and quieter
travel.
Theft - proof spare wheel
mounting.
Vibration absorbing clutch.
SIX WIRE WHEELS, LUG-
GAGE CARRIER, AND
BUMPERS INCLUDED
WITH EVERY MODEL.

MARMON
EIGHT CYLINDERS IN LINE
Sole Concessionaires:

PASS AND JOYCE LTD.
MARMON CAR SHOWROOMS:
24-27, ORCHARD STREET, LONDON, W.1
(At the Marble Arch end of Oxford Street.) Telephone: Mayfair 5140

STAND **42**
MAIN HALL
MOTOR
EXHIBITION
OLYMPIA
OCT. 11—20.

A.J.W.

F31 MENTION OF "THE AUTOCAR," WHEN WRITING TO ADVERTISERS, WILL ENSURE PROMPT ATTENTION.

Marmon advertisement, 1928

1927, 15,753 in 1928 and 22,300 in 1929. By the end of the decade there were several lines of Eight, from the 3.3-litre Roosevelt (often listed as a separate make), through the 3½-litre New 68 to the 5.2-litre Big 8. Prices ranged from $995 for the Roosevelt to nearly $5000 for custom models of the Big 8.

Named after Theodore Roosevelt, President of the United States from 1901 to 1909, the Roosevelt was marketed as a semi-independent make – as was Buick's Marquette, Cadillac's La Salle and Oldsmobile's Viking – so as not to dilute the quality image of the larger Marmons. Not that the Roosevelt was a bad car, although Ken Gross, Feature Editor of *Special-Interest Autos*, summed it up as 'an honest but relatively undistinguished offering'.

In fact the $995 price was something of a delusion, as this bought you the car less bumpers and shock absorbers, the price of which was another $45. Four body styles were avail-able, sedan, victoria, standard coupé and 'collapsible', i.e. drophead, coupé, all made by Hayes.

For 1930 the Roosevelt was renamed Marmon-Roosevelt. Teddy's head disappeared from the nameplate and was replaced by a rectangular Marmon-Roosevelt emblem. Other models continued as before, but the Depression had the effect of forcing sales down to 12,300.

For 1931 the eights were joined by the magnificent Sixteen. This brought Howard Marmon back into the fold, for he had been working quietly on his own on the Sixteen for five years, even forming a dummy company, the Midwest Aviation Co, to cloak his activities. He had originally planned to use two Little Eight engines in V-formation, but their combined capacity of 6.2 litres he deemed too small for a luxury car, so he designed an all-new aluminium alloy V-6 engine of 8.1 litres developing 200bhp.

The car was styled by Marmon's friend Walter Darwin Teague Jr, eight bodies being listed at prices from $5200 to $5500. These were about $150 lower than the Cadillac V16, added to which the Marmon was 10mph (16kph) faster and of at least comparable quality. Unfortunately production was delayed until April 1931, by which time the Cadillac was well established.

Prices of the Sixteen were reduced to $4825 in 1932, which eliminated any profit that might have been made on the cars. The eights were abandoned during 1932, leaving the Sixteen as the only offering for 1933, but hardly any were made that year. Total sales for 1932 were just 1365 cars. The Sixteen sold 390 units during the course of its three-year production life.

In May 1933 Marmon went into receivership, and in January 1934 the assets were taken over by the American Automotive Corporation, headed by Harry Miller of racing car renown and Preston Tucker who would launch his own radical car after World War II. They attempted to keep the Sixteen in production, but it is probable that no cars at all were made in 1934.

The last Marmon design was an advanced two-door sedan with tubular backbone frame, all-round independent suspension and a 6-litre V12 engine, built at Howard Marmon's own expense (estimated at over $160,000). Also styled by Teague, but in a much more modern way than the Sixteen, the car was built during 1933 largely outside the Marmon factory. Howard Marmon tried unsuccessfully to interest various Detroit firms in its manufacture. He then retired to his home at Pineola, North Carolina, where he died in 1943.

The Marmon name has survived on vehicles in a roundabout way up to the present. In 1931 Howard's elder brother Walter went into partnership with Colonel Arthur Herrington to make all-wheel-drive trucks under the name Marmon-Herrington. This business continued until 1963, when the company was broken up and the highway tractor division sold to Adrian Roop, who changed the name to Marmon Motor Co and began limited production of highway tractors at Garland, Texas. Despite changes of ownership, Marmon trucks are still made at Garland and Dallas today. GNG

MARQUETTE
see Buick

MARSEAL
see Marendaz

MARSH
see Metz

MARSHALL
see Belsize

MARTA
see Westinghouse

MARTIN
see Knox

MARTINI
SWITZERLAND 1897-1934

Friedrich von Martini founded a textile machinery factory in 1860 and in 1869 perfected his famous repeater rifle that was to become standard issue to the armies of Britain, Turkey and Portugal. Gas engines were made from 1880 and in 1889 the firm produced its first petrol engines.

Friedrich's son Adolf built the first of several prototype cars at the works in Frauenfeld in 1897. Series production began in 1902 under Rochet-Schneider licence and about 30 were made that year, all with V4 engines. In 1903 one of these cars climbed a funicular railway track to 2235ft (2045m) and gained an altitude record for cars in the hands of Captain Harry Deasy.

Although engines were made at Frauenfeld until 1917, chassis were produced at a new factory at Saint Blaise by Lake Neuchâtel from 1903. The factory had been established by Adolf's brother Max. About 100 Martinis were made in 1903, when the two Martini factories employed 500 men. In the following year car output totalled 130. Commercial vehicles had been made following trials of a 4-tonner in 1901 and included models from 1540lb (700kg) to 22,050lb (10,000kg) in 1905.

Production of the Martini Automobile Co in 1906 was 220, the majority of which were exported. Switzerland at that time imposed severe restrictions on car usage and local motorists tended to favour imports, despite the high quality of Martini cars. The Martini factories came under British financial control, headed by Captain Deasy of Siddeley-Deasy, in 1906 and the following year an international racing programme helped improve export prospects even further.

In January 1908 ownership of both Martini factories passed to the locally funded Société Nouvelle des Automobiles Martini, capitalized at 2 million Swiss francs, which made 260 cars in 1909. Designs, including some four-valve-per-cylinder sports models, were undertaken by technical director Charles Baehni, who in 1912-14 would be responsible for about 100 of his own YAXA cars.

In 1910 the car division was re-formed after more financial difficulties; E. Lambelet was president and Fochier from Zedel was technical director. Its products by then accounted for 13 per cent of cars on Swiss roads and modest profits were earned from 1912. (By

this Adolf von Martini was involved in the production of the Adem car of uncertain origin that was offered on the British market in 1912.)

Sales in 1913 of 197 leapt to 385 in 1914, when Switzerland was cut off from the outside world. Some 265 men at Saint Blaise produced 276 vehicles in 1916 and 325 in 1917. That year the Frauenfeld engine division came under the joint control of Martini and Berna.

In 1919 a one model policy with a 3.8-litre four-cylinder car (plus commercials using the same engine) was adopted, but sales were disappointing and the entire board of directors resigned in 1920. After further management changes the firm was rescued in 1924 by Walter Steiger, a Swiss-born engineer who had made Steiger sports cars in Germany from 1920. The first six-cylinder types appeared in 1925. Some 300 were sold in 1928, about half the works' potential, but only 750 Martinis were on Swiss roads the following year out of total registrations of 55,150.

A cheaper line was needed and so a Wanderer licence was acquired in 1929, most parts coming from Germany. The resulting Helvetia 2½-litre six-cylinder model was not very popular and losses in 1930 totalled 940,000 Swiss francs. A 4.38-litre six-cylinder NF model was offered in 1931, although production stopped for a time that year.

Only 60 cars were made in 1933 and liquidation followed in 1934, by which time a total of about 2000 Martini cars had been made. The once affiliated machinery company at Frauenfeld is still in existence. NB

Martini 'racer' (Max von Martini driving) of 1906

MASERATI
ITALY 1926 to date

Of the six Maserati brothers, sons of a railway engineer from Voghera, south of Milan, one, Marco, became a painter while the other five, Alfieri, Bindo, Carlo, Ernesto and Ettore, became engineers. Carlo, the eldest, raced motorcycles and won several races in 1899 and 1900 on a Carcano machine, which he designed, built and rode himself for the Marquis Carcano de Anzano del Parco. He also raced cars and worked as an engineer for Fiat, Bianchi and the Torinese firm Junior, but he died in 1911.

Alfieri worked as a test driver for Isotta-Fraschini and raced for the marque from 1908. Bindo also worked for Isotta and from 1910 to 1913 Alfieri and Ettore worked in Isotta's Argentine factory. Having returned to Italy, Alfieri, with Bindo and Ettore, set up Officine Alfieri Maserati SpA in December 1914 in Bologna. It was essentially a small tuning shop and worked closely with Isotta-Fraschini, particularly on racing cars.

During World War I the Maseratis made sparking plugs and also worked on Isotta aero engines. In 1919 Ernesto, the youngest brother, also joined the firm. After the war the Maseratis built a four-cylinder racer, based on a shortened Isotta chassis and one bank of a V8 aero engine. From 1921 they also began to race Diatto cars, from Turin, and Alfieri acted as that firm's development engineer,

Maserati Type V4 (Ernesto Maserati driving) of 1930

being one of the few to dare challenge Fiat, in spite of the latter's obvious superiority.

In 1924 Diatto asked the Maseratis to design a new supercharged 2-litre twin-overhead cam straight-eight Grand Prix car, which was completed in 1925 but raced only once, Alfieri retiring it from that year's Italian Grand Prix. Shortly after, Diatto withdrew from racing due to financial problems and went out of business completely in 1927. The Maseratis inherited the Grand Prix car, probably in part payment of debts, and out of Diatto's demise came the first Maserati.

In 1926 the brothers introduced their own Grand Prix car, based on the Diatto design but with capacity reduced to 1½ litres in line with the new Grand Prix formula. It was designated the Maserati Tipo 26 and made its début in April, when Alfieri won the 1½-litre class of the Targa Florio and finished ninth overall. It was badged with a Neptune's trident, the badge of the city of Bologna, and Alfieri won the Italian racing championship in 1927.

Until the late 1940s virtually all Maseratis were racing models, although there was the occasional dual purpose racing sports car that could, with a bit of imagination, double as a road car. The 26 was followed by the 2-litre 26B and in 1929 Maserati produced a monstrous *formula libre* car, the V4 or *Sedici Cilindri*, with two of the 2-litre straight-eights in a vee on a common crankcase. In racing trim it would exceed 155mph (250kph) and was all but undriveable in anything but a straight line, yet one roadgoing version was built which had a Zagato two-seater body.

Slightly more suitable as road cars were the other racing derived models, such as the 4CS-1100 and 4CS-1500, from 1932 and 1933, of which about 12 were made; a 1½-litre six based on the 6CM single seater; the one-off 8C-2500 saloon of 1938, bodied by Castagna; and other straight-eights of up to 3 litres.

In March 1932 Alfieri died, aged only 44, after an operation for a recurrence of problems from a racing accident as long ago as 1927, and control of the company passed to Ernesto. Alfieri's death was a serious blow at a time when the German national teams were

beginning to move into motor racing. Maserati's 3.3- and 3.7-litre developments of the 8C-3000 Grand Prix car and the 4.8-litre V8 R1 of 1935 could only achieve occasional success, and this was extremely damaging for a company which relied heavily on sales of customer racing and sports cars.

By the late 1930s the surviving Maseratis were forced to look for outside backers and in 1937 they found them in Modenese industrialist Adolfo Orsi, whose group Orsi SAS made machine tools, controlled several railway and bus systems and made sparking plugs, which may have been his first interest in Maserati. Orsi took over the company and appointed his son, Omer, as managing director. He retained the Maserati brothers under a 10-year contract and made it clear that he still intended to pursue a racing programme.

In 1938 Maserati moved from Bologna to Modena and because of Italy's late entry into World War II continued to race into 1940. When the war ended, Maserati – still a very small company with only just 30 employees in 1947, when battery and plug production were the main money making operations – was quick to restart car production. A revised 4CL racing car won the first post-war Grand Prix at Nice in April 1946, and at the Geneva Show in 1947 Maserati displayed a Farina-bodied derivative of the A6-1500 racing sports car. This was the last design by the Maserati brothers before their 10-year agreement ended in 1947 and they left to form Officine Specializzata Costruzione Automobili, or OSCA, back in Bologna.

Several versions of the car were built but only in very small numbers, leading to the first real production car, the A6G-1500, which was first shown at Turin in 1948. This was developed through the A6GC-2000 and A6GCS-2000 which were built until 1957 with bodies by Pininfarina, Frua, Zagato and various others on a total of approximately 65 cars. The highest total production of all types of Maserati up to then was some 34 cars in 1956, but in 1958, having launched a serious effort at road car production with the six-cylinder 3500GT, production reached three figures for the first time.

Maserati 8CM of 1934

Maserati 250F (Juan Fangio driving) of 1957

The year 1957 was one of mixed blessings for Maserati in racing. It won the World Championship, with Fangio driving, and might have won the sports car championship but for a disastrous last race in the Venezuelan Sports Car Grand Prix at Caracas, where the entire team of four cars were destroyed within minutes of each other in a series of accidents. The financial effect of this one race and problems for Orsi's parent company with defaults on payments by Argentine creditors ended Maserati's official racing programme. Customer cars continued to be built, however, especially sports cars – and there was even a Grand Prix engine built for Cooper at the beginning of the 3-litre Grand Prix formula.

Maserati Bora of 1978

Maserati Biturbo Spyder of 1984

This left Orsi free to concentrate on road cars, although Maserati had numerous other interests. A division, Fabbrica Candele Accumulatori Maserati SpA, still made plugs and batteries, and from 1953 to 1960 made about 50 two- and four-stroke motorcycles ranging from 123 to 246cc. In the mid-1950s the company also built light lorries, hydroplanes and machine tools, and between 1957 and 1959 built several electric models of the racing cars, some for the Orsi family and a few apparently for sale.

In 1959 the 3500GT, of which about 2000 would be built from 1958 to 1964, including, later, Spiders and the fuel-injected second series, was joined by the 160mph (258kph) V8 5000GT, which was also built until 1964 but to a total of only 36 cars. At Turin in 1963

Maserati introduced the four-door Quattroporte and by 1964 this was in production with the 3.7-litre (4-litre from 1966) Mistral and the Sebring 2+2 coupé, both six-cylinder models. They were followed in 1966 by the 4.7-litre V8 Ghibli and Mexico, the Ghibli proving particularly successful with more than 1250 being built.

In January 1968 Maserati concluded an agreement with Citroën to co-operate on design and manufacture, specifically developing the new V6 engine for the projected Citroën SM luxury car. In March 1968 Citroën acquired a majority shareholding in Maserati, although the company retained its own identity within Citroën. In 1971 Adolfo Orsi sold his remaining interest in the company to Citroën after policy disagreements, but Omer remained with the company.

From 1946 to 1968, under Orsi's control, Maserati had built just over 5500 cars, the last year being the peak, at 675 built, a figure which Citroën never quite matched in seven years of control up to 1975. Its best figure was 670 cars in 1973, although total output exceeded 8500 in that period.

New cars introduced under the Citroën management included the 1968 4.2-litre V8 Indy (commemorating two Maserati wins at Indianapolis, as the Boyle Special, in 1939 and 1940); the 4.7-litre V8 Bora, styled by Ital Design and introduced at Geneva in 1971; the V6 SM-engined Merak (and later the lightweight and more potent Merak SS); and the Bertone-styled front-engined 4.9-litre V8 Khamsin introduced in 1974.

A large and elegant Bertone Quattroporte II was shown at Turin in 1974 and scheduled for production from January 1975, but by then the Citroën-Maserati alliance was in trouble, Maserati's losses in 1974 amounting to more than the total capital value of the company. The SM never sold in sufficient numbers to make it viable and Maserati's total output was running at only some dozen cars and 120 engines a month, a cripplingly low output for a 700-strong workforce, which was put on short time working from early 1975.

In May, after being taken over by Peugeot, Citroën intended putting Maserati into liquidation, but in June began talks with Allesandro de Tomaso as a possible purchaser of the company. In December de Tomaso and the government-sponsored company rescue organization, Gestione e Participazione Industriali SpA (or GEPI), concluded a deal which gave de Tomaso a 30 per cent holding and GEPI the balance. Ernesto Maserati died that same month at the age of 78.

Maserati resumed production in early 1976 with a workforce now trimmed to a more realistic 200. Omer Orsi continued as commercial director until he retired from the board in 1977, and de Tomaso's manager Aurelio Bertocchi became Maserati's general manager.

Production continued with the Bora, Merak and Khamsin – although the Bora was dropped in 1980 – and in 1976 de Tomaso introduced the luxurious two-door Frua-bodied Kyalami, with 4.1- or 4.7-litre V8, a new Quattroporte and a 2-litre version of the Merak. Total production in 1976 when de Tomaso took over had been about 35 cars but it quickly climbed back to about 300 by 1978.

In 1982 Maserati introduced a somewhat different car, the compact, high performance Biturbo saloon, powered by a twin turbocharged 2-litre V6 engine giving 180bhp. It was a highly successful introduction, especially in Italy, and Maserati produced some 6000 examples in 1983, contributing to a doubling in overall turnover for the company to give it its best sales year ever.

In December 1983 Maserati announced a four-door Biturbo, the 425, with capacity increased to 2.5 litres and a top speed of over 130mph (210kph). The company expected to sell a total of some 10,000 Biturbos in both models in 1984, making it by far its biggest seller. In fact, total 1984 sales were 6365 cars but even that was an achievement.

Also in mid-1984 Chrysler in the United States acquired a 5 per cent interest in de Tomaso in exchange for some £600 million worth of design and building contracts to be spread over six years. This arrangement involved Maserati to quite a degree, principally in development of a two-seater Chrysler-Maserati sports car, expected to use the Lotus-developed four-cylinder 16-valve 2.2-litre twin-cam engine in the USA and possibly even the potent Lotus ETNA V8 in Europe. Ironically, this replacement for the de Tomaso Pantera largely owed its existence to Lee Iacocca, now at Chrysler but formerly the man who put Ford into the Pantera project.

Although Maserati was becoming increasingly profitable, helped by new models in 1985 including the 420 (a 2-litre version of the 425) and the 228 (falling between the Biturbos and the Quattroporte), it still sought extra money for its planned expansion. By late 1985 it seemed that a government-backed merger with de Tomaso's other major company, Innocenti, was the most likely source. BL

MASON/MAYTAG
USA 1906-1914

The Mason was a fairly ordinary Midwest American car made famous because it was designed by Fred Duesenberg, who later made magnificent cars under his own name. In 1905 Duesenberg was working in a garage in Des Moines, Iowa, when he was approached by a local attorney, Edward R. Mason, to go into the automobile business.

Mason purchased a blacksmith's shop in Des Moines and the first Mason car emerged in February 1906. It had a 24hp flat-twin engine under the driver's seat, planetary transmission and chain drive. In its design it differed little from hundreds of other American makes of the period, but an advanced aspect was the casting of the inlet manifold integrally with the cylinder block, a feature found on almost every Duesenberg-designed engine. Production began in August 1906, most mechanical parts being made in the Mason factory and bodies coming from the Des Moines Cabinet Co.

At the end of 1908 the Mason Motor Car Co was succeeded by the Mason Automobile Co with capital of $250,000, 10 times that of the original company. In 1909 Senator F. L. Maytag, a farm machinery manufacturer from Newton, Iowa, invested in the Mason company, which changed its name to Maytag-Mason Motor Co. Capital was increased to $1 million and the cars were renamed Maytag, while in 1910 production was moved to a factory in Waterloo, Iowa, where the Galloway high-wheeler truck had previously been made.

The range now consisted of 16hp two-cylinder and 30hp four-cylinder cars, but Maytag withdrew his money before the end of 1910 and the name Mason was revived for both company and cars. These continued to be made in small numbers, but a receiver was appointed in 1913 and the last Mason cars were delivered about a year later.

During the Maytag era Fred Duesenberg was selling Reo and Mitchell cars, but he rejoined Mason in 1912. His side rocker arm engines were installed in Mason touring and racing cars, and from 1914 onwards the racers were campaigned under the name Duesenberg. GNG

MASS/PIERRON
FRANCE 1903-1923

This Courbevoie-based factory started in 1903 by making Aster and De Dion-engined cars which used other components either copied or bought from Lacoste et Battmann. The principal was Léon Pierron, formerly designer and technical director of Motobloc. The British importer was J. R. Richardson and Co of Lincoln, which possibly supplied cars for Gamages in London to sell under their own name. In 1907 J. R. Richardson was recorded as being in charge of Mass production in France.

The Mass name came from W. J. Masser-Horniman, who in 1904 was described as proprietor of the marque and was based in Ladbroke Road, west London. De Dion engines of up to 3.92 litres were used in 1904-5, although there was also an electric model, and Gnôme engines then predominated for a couple of years until Ballot units of up to 8 litres were adopted. In 1907, when Richardson was running the French works, production was taking place at both Courbevoie and Levallois-Perret.

A. F. King, who had formerly worked for De Dion-Bouton and been an aircraft engineer at Blériot, was manager of the principal sales outlet in London, Lancaster Motor Garage of Lancaster Gate. This firm had handled the Mass for J. R. Richardson from the beginning, despite the existence nearby of Masser-Horniman's Mass Car Co.

Very cheap single- and twin-cylinder models gave way in 1910 to an up-to-date 2-litre monobloc four-cylinder car. Motor boats were also offered by Mass Cars in the Isle of Wight. In France from 1912, Mass cars went under the name of Pierron. In 1913 the Mass Car Co in London began to sell the smaller models of Paige from America as Mass-Paiges, and also handled the American RCH.

A six-cylinder 5.43-litre Mass car was introduced in 1913 to a range of vehicles that included a four-cylinder tractor and a variety of Richard Brasier-engined commercials. In 1914 all Mass cars had Ballot four-cylinder engines, including one of 5.34 litres. Both the Mass and the Pierron 15.9hp types were revived after World War I, but production ceased in 1923. NB

MATHESON
USA 1903-1912

The Matheson Motor Car Co, initially of Grand Rapids, Michigan, was founded in April 1903 with capital of $600,000 by the brothers Charles Walter and Frank F. Matheson. Frank, born in 1871, and Charles, born 1876, became interested in cars while they were working for a mail order office equipment supply company in Grand Rapids and they bought a Stanley steamer. They then purchased the assets of the defunct Holyoke Automobile Co in Holyoke, Massachusetts, which had been incorporated in April 1900 but had built very few cars.

The Holyoke's designer, a young Swiss engineer named Charles R. Greuter, became Matheson's chief engineer. Greuter had produced a car under his own name as early as 1898 and that car led to the first Holyoke, a two-cylinder tourer of 1900.

In fact, by the time the Mathesons moved into the Holyoke factory in August 1903 they had already built a pilot model Matheson car in Grand Rapids, which went on sale in July. It was a 24hp four-cylinder with shaft drive, known as the Style A and designed by an Englishman called Hedges, but only about six were made.

The first production car, designed by Greuter, was also a 24hp four-cylinder tourer, but with chain drive. It was extremely expensive at some $5000 and was joined in 1905 by an even more expensive 40hp model. Nevertheless, Matheson sold some 60 cars up to 1905 and began to expand.

In March 1906 the company moved to a large new purpose-built factory at Wilkes Barre, Pennsylvania, helped by the local chamber of commerce and with capital increased by $200,000 through investment by New York financiers Charles A. Singer and Henry U. Palmer, who set up the Matheson Co of New York to buy all Matheson's output in chassis

Mass four-seat tourer of c.1905

form. In 1907 this company became known as the Palmer & Singer Manufacturing Co of Long Island and sold four- and six-cylinder Palmer-Singer cars which were actually built at first by Matheson.

Up to 1907 Matheson's success continued, helped by cheaper but improved models, of which some 300 were sold that year alongside even more expensive 40/45 and 60/65hp cars. Palmer & Singer's independent operation caused it to break its agreement to take all Matheson production, which led to serious financial problems which Matheson only survived, albeit on a reduced scale, with the co-operation of its creditors.

Greuter left in 1908 to design another car of his own, which never went into production, and the new six-cylinder Matheson 17 of that year was designed by L. C. Kenan. Kenan was in turn replaced in 1908 by A. M. Dean, who designed the excellent 'Silent Six' which was built until the company stopped production.

Some 300 model 17 sixes were sold in 1908 and 1909, but the company's financial problems continued and in July 1910 Matheson went into receivership, to be reorganized in November as the Matheson Automobile Co, with paid up capital of $2,160,000, and the Matheson brothers still in control. They continued to sell the improved six and made about 700 in the next two years, but it was not enough and production stopped towards the end of 1912 after a total of about 800 four-cylinder and 1000 six-cylinder Mathesons had been built.

In 1914 the factory was bought by the International Fabricating Co, which used it to make shells during World War I and later built the Owen Magnetic under licence until 1922, when Frank Matheson bought the plant back as a distribution base for various makes. Charles Matheson became a vice-president of Dodge in 1921, held the same position at Oakland, Kelvinator and Chrysler, and by 1938 was president and general manager of the Graham company until he was killed in a road accident in 1940. Frank died in 1967. BL

MATHIS
GERMANY, FRANCE 1910-1950

Emile Mathis was born in 1880 of French stock but with German nationality as a result of the German occupation of Alsace and Lorraine after the Franco-Prussian war of 1870. His father was a hotelier and he trained in this business before building an experimental car in 1898.

He later became an agent in Strasbourg for a variety of makes, including Panhard, De Dietrich, Rochet-Schneider, Fiat and Minerva, and by 1905 his Auto-Mathis-Palace was the largest sales organization in Germany and the third largest in the world. He also had his own coachbuilding works for bodying these cars, most of which were sold as chassis only. He drove a De Dietrich in the 1902 Paris-

Vienna race and came to know Ettore Bugatti at about this time.

In 1904 he set up the Mathis Société Alsacienne de Constructions Mécaniques at Graffenstaden, near Strasbourg, engaging Bugatti as his designer. The cars, which were called Hermes, were large four-cylinder chain-drive machines, advertised in six sizes from 28 to 98hp, although it is possible that the larger models existed only on paper. According to Ernest Friderich, who worked at the factory and later became a leading driver for Bugatti, 25 Hermes chassis were made, after which Mathis and Bugatti quarrelled and Bugatti joined Deutz.

Mathis assembled 40 Lorraine-Dietrich chassis, but up to 1910 most of his income came from the cars he sold. Customers included the Kaiser, who bought two Fiats – which were the only foreign-made cars in the Imperial garages.

In 1910 Mathis began to manufacture a conventional 2-litre four-cylinder car, supplementing this by a 2.8-litre model which he bought complete from Stoewer of Stettin. These were sold in Germany under the name Stoewer-Mathis, but in France the name Stoewer was omitted from the badging. Mathis was good at forgetting the origin of cars he was connected with. By the mid-1920s he was describing the Type 13 Bugatti,

Mathis part-wood tourer of 1922

which he had sold, as a Mathis, while his personal Fiat racing car, which he sold to Sir Frederick Richmond in 1913, he described as a 100-120hp Mathis! Production was limited, with just 75 cars being made in 1911.

The following year Mathis brought out a smaller car, the 952cc Babylette, and this was joined in 1913 by the 1327cc Baby, which was probably the Type 13 Bugatti. There were five larger models, from 1460 to 3434cc, the larger ones having Knight sleeve-valve engines. It is likely that these were Minervas with Mathis radiators or possibly Fiats with Minerva engines and Mathis radiators. Apart from the Babylette it is difficult to decide exactly what was a genuine Mathis-built car at this period.

Production was certainly up, with 200 cars promised for the UK market alone in 1912, and 600 in 1913. The British agent, Gordon Marshall, cannot have been pleased by a 1913 deal between Emile Mathis and Harrods, whereby the London store would take 175 cars direct from Strasbourg, by-passing Marshall altogether.

By 1914 Mathis was deputy chairman of the DAHV, the German motor trade association, similar to Britain's Society of Motor Manufacturers and Traders, and a substantial figure in the trade although still only 34 years old. During the war he was sent to neutral countries such as Switzerland to try to purchase desperately needed tyres for the German war effort. On one of these journeys he slipped into France and never returned to Germany, which he probably regarded with the ambivalence of all Alsatians.

In 1918 Alsace became French once more, and he was able to return to his factories. These were completely rebuilt in the early 1920s, and during the decade Mathis became a leading manufacturer of popular cars. Production rose from a thousand or two in 1920 to over 20,000 in 1927, putting Mathis in fourth place behind Citroën, Renault and Peugeot.

The Babylette was revived in 1919, enlarged to 1131cc, and in 1923 there was a tiny four-cylinder T-type of only 628cc. In 1923 also came the first small six, the 1.2-litre L-Type with single-overhead cam which made quite an attractive sports car. Mathis competed in the French Touring Car Grand Prix from 1923 to 1925, finishing 1-2-3 in its class in 1923; but Emile was more of a businessman than a sportsman, and when he saw that racing brought no profit he abruptly closed the competition department at the end of 1925.

The small six was discontinued in 1926, but the previous year had seen the appearance of one of the best-selling Mathis cars, the 1.6-litre GM family saloon aimed at the Citroën market. This was replaced in 1927 by

313

the 1.2-litre MY fabric saloon; a Mathis slogan at this time was 'Le Poids – voila l'Ennemi' (Weight is the Enemy). The MY was good value at 15,950 francs compared with 17,450 for the comparable Renault NN.

It was joined in 1928 by the 1.8-litre EMY-6 six-cylinder car, a competitor for the Citroën C6, followed in 1930 by the 3-litre FOH straight-eight. Two larger eights were listed in 1932, of 4.6 and 5.4 litres, both made by Continental, but very few were sold. Only six of the 5.4-litre models were made, and one became the personal property of Madame Mathis.

Mathis was a great admirer of American mass-production methods and in 1930 he planned a deal with Billy Durant whereby a slightly enlarged version of the 1.2-litre PY would be made in Durant's Lansing, Michigan, factory. Prototypes were shown at the 1931 New York and Chicago Shows, and there was talk of 100,000 cars a year being produced to sell at $455 each. In fact the project never got off the ground, but if it had it would probably have met with no more success than the American Austin. American motorists were just not interested in small cars at that time.

Mathis was never famous as a truck builder, but from 1929 to 1933 made a few 3- and 4-tonners, including a six-wheeler, powered by side-valve six-cylinder engines, while vans were offered on most of the car chassis. Car sales slipped in the early 1930s, despite such advances as hydraulic brakes in 1931, synchromesh in 1932 (a year before Citroën and Renault) and transverse independent front suspension on the 1933 1½-litre EMY-4. This and companion 2.1-litre EMY-6 and 3-litre EMY-8 made up the range until 1935, when Fords began to invade the production lines at Strasbourg.

This was the result of a new company, SA Française Matford, in which Ford held 60 per cent of the shares and Mathis the balance. It was expected that both makes of car would be made side by side, but the less popular Mathis models were soon ousted after the appearance of a short-lived hybrid called the Quadriflex with Ford V8 engine in an all-independent suspension Mathis chassis. From 1936 to 1938 the Strasbourg factory

made only Matfords, and in 1938 Emile Mathis sold all his shares to Ford but retained his factory.

Mindful of German feelings about him as a result of his World War I defection – his friend Jean Grégoire said that he would have been shot without trial had he been caught – Mathis went to the United States in 1940. He spent the war years running a small marine engine factory under the name Matam (Mathis-America) which he had planned to use for his Durant-built car of 1931.

In 1945 he returned to Strasbourg and at the next year's Paris Salon exhibited a curious egg-shaped three-wheeler based on a pre-war design by Jean Andreau. Named the VL333 (for voiture legère, 3 litres to 100km fuel consumption, 3 seats, 3 wheels) it was powered by a 700cc flat-twin engine. Several prototypes were built but the French government would not give Mathis a permit for quantity production. In 1948 he tried again, with the 666 (6 seats, 6 cylinders, 6 speeds), a 2.8-litre six-cylinder saloon with *avant-garde* lines, panoramic windscreen and all-round independent suspension. This was still around in 1950, but production never started.

Mathis kept his factory going by making light aero engines, and components for Renault, and in 1954 he sold out to Citroën, which still uses the factory for the manufacture of engines. Mathis was still designing cars at the time of his accidental death in 1956. GNG

MATRA
FRANCE 1965 to date

Matra as a car manufacturer grew from a massive French aerospace and armaments company, which only became involved in motoring in 1964 but which has since become a very successful road and racing car manufacturer. The company was founded before World War II by Marcel Chassagny as a small aeronautical engineering contractor known as CAPRA, but in 1941 the company name was changed to Mécanique Aviation Traction, or MATRA, offering a wide variety of development and manufacturing services to

the aeronautics industry.

In 1945, helped by a French government policy of backing new technology, Matra developed a rocket launcher and soon became the national market leader, moving to the manufacture of guided missiles in the early 1950s as Engins Matra. From the start of the 1960s Matra was the French member of the consortium MESH, which was developing the European satellite launcher, the other elements of the mnemonic representing the German company Erno, Saab of Sweden and Britain's Hawker Siddeley.

In 1964 Matra took over the René Bonnet sports car firm, run by the eponymous friend of Chassagny and in the past supported to some extent by Matra and by Chassagny personally. Bonnet had previously been associated with André Deutsch as manufacturer of the successful racing DB sports car, but had split with his former partner in 1962 over plans for the Le Mans race and had subsequently built a prototype René Bonnet called the Djet.

Chassagny created a new division of Matra, Matra Sports, in October 1964 under the direction of engineer Jean Luc Lagardere, formerly of Avions Marcel Dassault, and the René Bonnet Djet became Matra's first car, the Renault-engined Matra Djet. The Djet was built with various engine developments until 1968, but in 1967 Matra had closed the original Bonnet factory and opened its own facility at Romorantin to introduce the first true Matra road car, the Ford V4 engined M530 coupé.

Alongside establishing the road cars, Lagardere was given the task of organizing a racing and rallying programme for 1965. He soon increased his original competition staff of four to 12 and Matra made its racing début on schedule with two cars in the Formula 3 race supporting the 1965 Monaco Grand Prix. The MS5's chassis construction owed much to aerospace technology and ultimately the cars were very successful. In 1967 Matra moved into Formula 2 and dominated that formula for the next three years.

In January 1967 Matra reached agreement with the state-owned petrol company Elf for a four-year co-operation to develop an all-French Grand Prix car. Matra had asked the government to support this objective from

Mathis four-cylinder sports model of c.1913

Mathis EMY-4 of 1934

1966 and was chosen in preference to Renault because it already had an engine design staff under former Simca engineer Georges Martin. The government also saw a Matra Formula 1 car as a means to advertising a putative prestige sports car and in April 1967 entered a three-year agreement for backing worth some 6 million francs.

By early 1968 Matra had tested a 3-litre V12 Formula 1 engine which was potent but thirsty and, ironically, Matra's only win in the Formula 1 constructors' championship was gained in 1969 with the Ford-Cosworth engined MS80, driven by Jackie Stewart for Ken

Matra-Ford MS5 (Jean-Pierre Beltoise driving) of 1967

Matra 530 coupé of c.1969

Matra Rancho of c.1982

Tyrrell. Nevertheless, Matra has been involved with Grand Prix racing ever since, latterly as supplier of engines to Ligier, and has won many races. In sports car racing, with engines derived from the Grand Prix unit, Matra has had even greater success, winning the World Championship for Makes in 1973 and 1974 and Le Mans in 1972, 1973 and 1974.

Meanwhile, the first road cars were less successful. The mid-engined 530 failed because of a poor dealer network, Ford's co-operation ending with the supply of engines and Matra needing more marketing support from such a supplier. It found it in 1969 in a tie up with Simca, a part of Chrysler, France, whose new vice-president, Bill Reiber, had had earlier contact with Matra as president of Ford, France. Simca effectively took over Matra Sports and a new company, Matra-Simca Division Automobile, was formed within Engins Matra in 1969 operating from new works at Vélizy.

In 1973 Matra introduced the Simca-engined Baghera, a mid-engined coupé with a 1.3-litre engine mounted transversely. A 1.4-litre option was added in 1976 and in 1977 the company introduced a front-wheel-drive estate in the Range Rover idiom, the Rancho, helping the year's production to a healthy 12,000 cars.

In 1978 Matra became part of the giant Peugeot-dominated PSA grouping when PSA took over Chrysler in France (and England and Spain), and from 1980 the pretty replacement for the Baghera, the Murena, with steel body in place of the previous glassfibre and optional 2.2-litre Chrysler engine, was sold under the Talbot badge. In 1983 Matra split

with Peugeot Talbot and was absorbed into Renault, for which company it began to develop an eight-seater family vehicle, the Espace, based on Renault's front-wheel drive Trafic van and launched in 1984.

Unfortunately, the Espace failed to live up to its early promise and by mid-1985 production was running at 40 per cent below Matra's planned volumes. An experimental taxi based on the Espace has been built for the Paris authorities but pending its acceptance (and following Renault's own problems) Matra has been forced to seek an outside buyer for its car division, with Toyota and General Motors both in the forefront. BL

MAUDSLAY
GB 1902-1923

Henry Maudslay was born at Woolwich in 1771 and was to influence many aspects of Victorian engineering. He started as a cartridge filler at the local arsenal and helped Bramah perfect his patent lock. He also developed a hydraulic seal that made Bramah's press successful and invented the slide-rest, screw cutting lathe and micrometer. From a factory in Lambeth came the engine for the first Thames paddle steamer in 1812, followed by hundreds more for naval and merchant ships including HMS *Blake* and the *Great Western*. Soon after Henry Maudslay's death in 1831 his sons made improvements to Sir Charles Dance's steam carriage and built a steam drag for him in 1833.

With the rise of internal combustion, Maudslay opened a marine engine factory in Coventry in 1899 and, following the steam firm's liquidation, Cyril C. Maudslay registered the Maudslay Motor Co as a private company in 1901. His brother Reginald soon set up his own business, the Standard Motor Co.

Alexander Craig designed engines and cars for both firms, as well as for many other Coventry firms including Lea-Francis. Those for Maudslay had three cylinders and the pioneer features of pressure lubrication and overhead camshaft, both of which were retained on all subsequent Maudslay cars.

In 1903 a limited company was formed and commercial vehicles as well as cars were built alongside engines for many purposes, including marine and industrial use. A 200hp unit was exported to the United States and 80hp locomotive types were also being made.

In 1907 a £100,000 company was floated which took over the original firm for £34,000 and expanded the factory at Parkside, Coventry, to 86,000sq ft (8000sq m) and 200 employees. John Crouch worked there and J. K. Starley, the Rover founder, provided much early financial help. Alexander Craig joined the board in 1908.

Six-cylinder cars had been tried from 1904 and circular or horse-shoe radiators became a distinctive feature in 1906. Before long, 40 and 60hp sixes gave way to fours, and many of the commercials made do with two cylinders. In 1909 a four nicknamed the Sweet Seventeen appeared and gradually replaced all previous car models. Several were exported to the USA as well as to the colonies.

By the end of World War I more than 1700 Maudslay trucks were in military service, about 200 having been sub-contracted to Rover's adjoining Parkside factory. Maudslay itself did much sub-contract work on Le Rhône and other aero engines.

During the brief post-war demand for commercials Maudslay built 348 in 1919, 263 in 1920 but then just 35 in 1921, when the availability of secondhand vehicles and the effects of the recession affected sales. The downturn prompted a return to car production, but only prototypes of an interesting six-cylinder double-overhead-cam 2-litre sports model appeared in 1923. This was the work of Alexander Craig, J. A. Kemp (Albion's chief designer in the 1950s) and J. R. Hamilton, subsequently Maudslay's technical manager. The first British 'Low-Level Safety Coaches' appeared in 1924 and helped sales to exceed 100 in 1925 and 200 in 1926. In 1927 a six-cylinder version appeared and total sales of commercials that year were more than 300.

The Depression caused severe problems for the company. Craig died in 1935 and two years later Maudslay retired. Only about 100 vehicles a year were made in the depths of the slump and receivership followed, although a few vehicles and contract work kept Maudslay alive until refinanced in 1938 by timber merchant G. Tisdale and builder O. D. Smith. Chief engineer was Siegfried Sperling from Gräf & Stift.

Capital was reduced to £41,000, the range was simplified and profits returned. AEC diesel engines were adopted during World War II, after which Maudslay moved to a factory near Alcester, Warwickshire, where it continued to make commercial vehicles.

Maudslay merged with Crossley and AEC in 1948 and continued to make vehicles under the Maudslay name for 10 years. Its final products were dump trucks and axles for AEC. With a workforce of 1000 it was bought by the Rockwell axle and components firm in 1972 and still exists as Rockwell-Maudslay. NB

MAURER/MAURER-UNION
GERMANY 1900-1925

The Maurer-Union was introduced in 1900 by Nurnberger Motorfahrzeuge-Fabrik 'Union', a company set up in Nuremberg by an engineer, Ludwig Maurer. The first cars used an 1140cc 6hp single-cylinder engine, whose power output was later improved to 8hp. From 1902 the range was extended to include vee-twin models. All the engines were designed and built by Maurer, as were almost all other parts of the cars, but the main feature of the Maurer-Union was its pioneering use of variable friction drive by means of a disc and wheel.

Maurer's cars were very popular and, predictably, several other manufacturers copied the transmission system. They mostly did so illicitly, and Mars, which was also based in Nuremberg and started using the system in 1906, was one of the few to pay a licence fee.

Maudslay 17hp 'Sweet Seventeen' of 1913

Maurer-Union was also developing four-cylinder engines by 1905 but they never really went beyond the prototype stage as the company ran into financial problems in 1908 and Ludwig Maurer left. The bankrupt company was taken over by fire-engine builder Nurnberger Feuerloschgerate- und Maschinen-Fabrik vorm Justus Christian Braun AG.

Braun continued to build Maurer-Union cars until 1910, but in 1911 he merged his company with a local cycle-maker, Premier, to form Justus Christian Braun Premier-Werke AG. This company went on to build Kaiser and Premier cars in Nuremberg until 1914.

Ludwig Maurer meanwhile set up another car company in 1908, calling it Johanna Maurer – using his wife's name to get round a ban on his starting another car company for a fixed period after leaving Maurer-Union. He began to build Maurer cars in small numbers, with 1520cc twin-cylinder engines and, of course, friction drive, but he stopped production in 1909 and continued just to build engines for others, mainly four-cylinder types.

After World War I Maurer was able to use his own name again and he formed Automobilfabrik Ludwig Maurer. He began manufacturing motorcycles and in 1923 he used a flat-twin two-stroke engine from one of these in a small chain-drive car. He apparently built several prototype cars up to 1925 but the Maurer name never reappeared on a production model. BL

MAXIMAG
SWITZERLAND 1923-1928

In 1901 Henri Armand Dufaux of Geneva developed a small engine that could clip into a standard bicycle frame. He called it the Motosacoche (motor in a case) and formed Motosacoche SA to make a wide range of proprietary engines. These became known by the initials MAG (Moteurs à Genève) and

thousands were sold to numerous motorcycle manufacturers throughout Europe. Some 20,000 were exported to Britain alone, where sales were handled by former Rover employee and Australian racing bicyclist Osborne de Lissa.

Motosacoche also made complete motorcycles and by the early 1920s was turning out 5000 to 6000 a year as well as about 4000 engines. In 1914 the firm had developed an engine for voiturettes and in 1923 a complete Maximag 1.1-litre light car with four-wheel brakes was offered. Branch factories made MAG engines in several countries and the one in Lyons, France, is believed to have built a number of Maximags in the mid-1920s. Output in Switzerland must have been small because just 156 were recorded in Swiss registration records in 1929, the year after Maximag production ended.

In 1937 Ateliers des Charmilles, which had previously been involved with Picard Pictet, bought Motosacoche. Motorcycle production ended in 1957 but 10 years later 400 employees were making MAG engines. This business continues today together with the production of hydraulic and electro-pneumatic equipment for the aircraft and other industries. NB

MAXWELL-BRISCOE/
MAXWELL
USA 1904-1925

The Maxwell-Briscoe Motor Co was built on the familiar combination of one man's know-how and another's money. The design of the car, and indeed the idea of forming a company at all, came from Jonathan D. Maxwell (1864-1928) who had worked for Olds and Northern, while the money was put up by radiator manufacturer Benjamin Briscoe (1869-1945). In fact more than two thirds of the $162,000 provided by Briscoe came from the New York financier J. Pierpont Morgan.

For a factory they rented the plant at Tarrytown, New York, where John Brisben Walker had made the Mobile steam car. There during 1904 they began production of a two-seater runabout powered by a 15hp horizontally opposed twin engine with square cylinder dimensions (4×4in or 101×101mm) and mechanically operated inlet valves.

Because of planning problems only 10 Maxwell-Briscoe Model L runabouts were made in 1904, but the following year the company made 823 cars, Model Ls and the larger 5×5in (127×127mm) cylinder Model H five-passenger touring car. It also built a light truck on the Model H chassis until 1912. Business boomed in 1906 with nearly 2200 vehicles made, which put Maxwell-Briscoe in fifth place in the production league.

Briscoe felt insecure in a rented factory, and during 1906 he began construction of a large plant at Newcastle, Indiana, which

Maxwell 25 of c.1915

eventually cost over $1 million. To finance this Briscoe sought a merger, first with Billy Durant, Ransom Olds and Henry Ford. The last two were never very interested, and Durant eventually dropped the idea in favour of his own group of companies which he called General Motors.

Unfortunately the Morgan bank took umbrage at these merger plans and pulled out its money in 1909. Maxwell and Briscoe were fortunate that sales were so good that they were able to survive this event and to finance the Newcastle operation out of their own resources.

Maxwell's first four-cylinder car, the 30/40hp Model D, was launched in 1907 and priced at $3000. This was made at Tarrytown, production of the twins being transferred to Newcastle as soon as the factory was ready. Production climbed steadily to reach 10,000 in 1910, the year in which Briscoe merged the company with the Columbia Motor Car Co, which already owned Brush, Courier and Stoddard-Dayton, to form the United States Motor Corporation, capitalized at $16 million. Jonathan Maxwell, who was the better businessman of the two, was never keen on this unwieldy group, with far too many models made by companies which were not very sound anyway.

The new group found itself with seven marque names, 52 models, 18 factories and 14,000 employees. Within two years US Motor Corporation collapsed, Briscoe departed to make cars under his own name, and Jonathan Maxwell was left with the soundest of the companies and the only one to survive. Financier Eugene Myers brought in Walter Flanders from the Flanders Motor Co, and Maxwell soon quit.

Flanders, whose fee included $1 million in cash and $2.75 million in stock in the new company, reorganized production with the four-cylinder Maxwell 35 being made in the former Stoddard-Dayton plant in Dayton, Ohio, and the six-cylinder Maxwell 50-6 being made in the former Flanders plant in Detroit. New for 1914 was a low priced Maxwell 25, selling for $750, which became the staple Maxwell for the rest of the company's life. They sold very well, giving Maxwell sales of over 17,000 in 1914, rising to 75,000 three years later to which was added 25,000 1-ton trucks which used the same 21hp four-cylinder engine as the 25 passenger car.

From 1915 the 25 was the only Maxwell car made, and in 1918 production was transferred to the Chalmers plant in Detroit. Sales never reached the 1917 figure again, although Maxwell recorded a healthy 50,000 in 1919, the year in which it introduced its first four-door sedan, priced at $1095.

In 1920 the finances of Maxwell and Chalmers were merged, but they were no sounder combined than they had been separately. The post-war slump hit Maxwell very hard, and in June 1920 the company had debts of nearly $32 million and 26,000 unsold cars. In 1921 Maxwell sold only 16,000 cars, and Chalmers 3000. Maxwell ceased production for several months that year, and after a rift between the companies Maxwell purchased Chalmers outright.

The 1922 models were redesigned externally but they used the same old 21hp engine. Named 'The Good Maxwell' they sold about 40,000 units. (Combined Maxwell-Chalmers sales were 44,811 and although an individual breakdown is not known, Chalmers sales were not at all high.)

Maxwell-Chalmers came under the control of Walter P. Chrysler in November 1921, his committee outbidding Durant, Willys, White and Studebaker with an offer of $10.9 million. Walter Chrysler became president and continued the Maxwell through 1923 and 1924, but in the later year it was outsold by the new six-cylinder car sold under his own name. The 1925 Maxwells were the last, and for 1926 they appeared as the Chrysler 58 with the same engine but Chrysler styling. GNG

MAYBACH
GERMANY 1921-1941

The name of Maybach is one of the most respected in the history of the automobile, for Wilhelm Maybach, born in 1846, as Gottlieb Daimler's partner in the pioneering days of the Daimler Motoren-Gesellschaft and was responsible for such important developments as the spray carburettor and vertical twin engine. He was a close friend of the Daimlers, their wives having been acquainted since school days, and he remained with the company for seven years after Daimler's death in 1900.

Then he joined Graf Zeppelin in airship work, being responsible for the engines which were made by the Luftfahrzeug Motorenbau Gesellschaft of Bissingen, which Maybach founded in 1909. Increasingly helped by his son Karl, Maybach made engines for airships and also Gotha bombers up to 1918, moving his factory to Friedrichshafen in 1912 in order to be close to the Zeppelin factory.

After World War I the Maybachs were forbidden to make aero engines so they turned to making power units for cars and commercial vehicles, as Maybach Motoren-Werken. The only customer for their car engines was the Dutch firm of Spyker, which took about 150 of the W2 5.7-litre six-cylinder between 1920 and 1925. Commercial vehicle buyers included Faun of Nuremberg and ABOAG, the Berlin bus company, while Maybach also made flat-twin motorcycle engines for Mars of Nuremberg, and diesel railcar units from 1923 onwards. None of this activity generated sufficient orders to keep the factory fully em-

Maybach W5 limousine of 1925

Maybach SW38 drophead of 1936

ployed so the Maybachs decided to build cars to put their engines in.

Launched in 1921 the Maybach W3 used an improved version of the W2 engine in a conventional box section chassis which had Germany's first four-wheel brakes. Its most unconventional feature was its two-speed epicyclic gearbox, as used in the Model T Ford. Maybachs always had either fewer or more speeds than normal.

At 22,600 marks for a chassis, the W3 was the most expensive German car of its era, yet despite its price and despite the general poverty and rampant inflation in the country it sold creditably, 700 finding buyers between 1922 and 1928. Maybach supplied chassis only, bodies coming from Auer, Neuss, Papler, Kellner and others, although during the 1930s Maybach's preferred coachbuilder was Spohn.

In 1926 the W3 was joined by the larger W5 with 6995cc 120bhp six-cylinder engine. Initially it had the same two-speed transmission as its predecessor, of which bottom gear was only required for starting on hills, but in 1928 a separate overdrive was available, operable in either gear, giving four speeds.

This optional extra was called the *schnellgang* (fast speed), and when Maybach progressed later to an eight-speed system it was logically called the *doppelschnellgang*. The *schnellgang* was made for sale to other carmakers including Hansa, Hansa-Lloyd, Mannesmann, Opel and Wanderer, but nobody else except Lagonda in England wanted the complexity and expense of the *doppelschnellgang*.

In 1929, the year in which Wilhelm died and a Maybach-powered Zeppelin airship flew round the world, the company launched its grandest car yet, the 6962cc 150bhp V12 which employed a conventional three speed and reverse gearbox with overdrive on all ratios, giving six forward speeds and two reverse. The wheelbase was 12ft (3.6m) and a complete car weighed about 3¼ tons.

Even more elephantine was the DS-8 of 1930 onwards, the first Maybach to bear the name Zeppelin, which had a 200bhp 7977cc V12 engine and *doppelschnellgang* transmission. This involved two low gears and three high gears, each operable on two ratios, giv-

ing a total of eight forward speeds (and four in reverse if one wanted them). It was an unnecessary complexity in a car whose smooth and powerful V12 could move it from a standstill on a reasonable ratio of 3:1.

The Zeppelin and other Maybachs appealed to the conservative rich who thought a Mercedes too flashy and a Horch too middle class. About 30 a year were made until 1937, but thereafter only 25 were made altogether before production ceased in 1940.

For those who could not afford 36,000 marks for a Spohn-bodied Zeppelin seven-passenger cabriolet, there was the 5184cc W6 DSH or 6996cc W6, both six-cylinder cars on the same wheelbase, which looked very similar to the Zeppelin until one lifted the bonnet. About 150 of these were sold at prices that ranged from 22,000 to 26,500 marks for a complete car.

Maybach still had no body department, but by the mid-1930s most coachwork came in 'factory recommended' styles from Spohn. A number of bodies were also supplied by Erdmann and Rossi, including a seven-passenger cabriolet on a Zeppelin chassis for Dr Dorpmuller, Reichsminister of Transport, and a four-seater close-coupled cabriolet, also on a Zeppelin, for Prince Bernhard of the Netherlands.

In 1935 came a smaller Maybach, the six-cylinder SW35 with 3435cc square dimensions (90×90mm or 3½×3½in), single-overhead cam engine, and a modern chassis with coil and wishbone independent front suspension and swing axles at the rear. Although not as cheap as a Packard 120 or Lincoln Zephyr, the SW (standing for *schwing achse*) was definitely a junior series intended to widen Maybach's market coverage. The engine was enlarged to 3817cc (90×100mm or 3½×4in) in 1936 and to 4197cc (90×110mm or 3½×4⅓in) in 1939, these models being called the SW38 and SW42 respectively. Bodies were mostly by Spohn and prices ran from 18,000 to 23,700 marks. About 615 SW models were made from 1935 to 1941.

As well as cars Maybach made a range of six- and 12-cylinder diesel engines for railcars, and during World War II turned out 140,000 engines for tanks and half-track vehicles. The company continued with engine

manufacture after the war, but apart from two post-war bodied SW42s no cars were made. In 1960 it contracted to make Mercedes-Benz heavy diesel engines at Friedrichshafen, and the company is today known as MTU (Motoren-Turbinen-Union). GNG

MAYTAG
see Mason

MAZDA
JAPAN 1960 to date

The Toyo Cork Kogyo Co was founded in Hiroshima in 1920, originally making cork products, but in 1921 its president, Jujiro Matsudo, turned the company towards building machinery. In the wake of the disastrous Tokyo earthquake of 1923, which effectively crippled the city's transport system, Toyo Cork Kogyo began to build small motorcycles, copying British and German ideas but producing its own 250cc two-stroke engine, although only a small number were made.

In 1927, continuing the move into industrial products, the company was renamed Toyo Kogyo Co Ltd and in 1930 designed its first small three-wheel truck, which went into production in October 1931 as the 500cc Mazda DA. The name Mazda was derived from the good side of the oriental principle of the harmony of good and bad. The company made virtually all parts of the vehicle in its own new purpose-built factory in Hiroshima, where production and administration are still based.

By 1932 Toyo Kogyo had started to export the DA three-wheeler, production of which reached about 100 a month at its peak. In January 1934 came the 485cc DC three-wheeler, which grew to 654cc later in the year and set new production records. The company continued to develop its range of small trucks and by the middle of 1937 production had reached some 75 a week.

Toyo Kogyo was now planning to expand, but moves to import presses and other heavy machinery from overseas were stopped by the war in the Pacific. Three-wheeler production gradually gave way to rifles and by 1940 all production was of armaments, although a prototype saloon car, the company's first, was built in 1940 before the complete switch.

Almost half the factory and machinery were destroyed by the Hiroshima bomb and with huge numbers of the workforce also killed production stopped completely. It resumed, very slowly, in December 1945 with the three-wheel trucks and gradually built up again to allow a new expansion from 1948, by the end of which year production had risen to about 200 vehicles a week.

In 1950 the company started to build four-wheel trucks and fire engines, and with the outbreak of the Korean war in June demand increased dramatically. In 1958 a larger four-wheel truck, the Mazda Romper, went on sale and in May 1960 Toyo Kogyo finally made the move into car production with the R360 coupé, which had a rear-mounted air-cooled 356cc twin-cylinder engine.

In its first year of car production Toyo Kogyo actually produced more cars than trucks, 23,417 compared to 19,725. This balance would not be repeated until 1970, after which car production moved rapidly ahead of commercials.

At the 1961 Tokyo Motor Show the company showed a two-seater 700, but the next production model was the two-door four-seat Carol, introduced in 1962 with a water-cooled

Mazda 110S of 1967

Mazda R360 of 1960

Mazda RX-7 of 1986

358cc four-cylinder engine. It was followed in 1963 by the Mazda 800 Estate.

In March of that year the one millionth Mazda was built, but the next million would take only three more years and include new models such as the four-cylinder Familia series and the 1½-litre Luce, first seen at Tokyo in 1963 but not in full production until 1966 when the Japanese economy began to climb out of a two-year recession. In 1967 car production exceeded 100,000 for the first time, the actual total being 129,051.

Mazda was also making dramatic technical progress. In 1962 it signed design agreements with Bertone, and in 1965 opened a new test track at Miyoshi and signed agreements with Perkins in England to develop diesel truck engines by 1967. Most important, however, was a licence arrangement with NSU for the production of Wankel rotary engines, as designed by Dr Felix Wankel.

Company president Matsuda had visited NSU in Germany in October 1960, and in November 1961, with an agreement concluded, the first NSU engines were delivered to Toyo Kogyo's research department. A prototype Mazda rotary engine was tested in a car in 1962 and shown in Tokyo in 1963, but, like NSU, Mazda had serious problems with tip sealing on the engines' rotors and in April 1963 established the Rotary Engine Development Division.

By 1964 the division had concentrated its efforts on a twin-rotor design, having also tried three- and four-rotor types. The first rotary-engined car, the 110S coupé with two 491cc rotors, went on sale in May 1967, to be

Mazda 626 coupé of 1984

followed for 1968 by the R100 Familia coupé and in 1969 by the first rotary saloon, the R100 Sedan (or Familia SS, depending on market), plus the R130 coupé.

Mazda entered rotary-powered cars quite widely in competition, mostly to prove their stamina. In 1972 RX-2 models, as introduced in 1970, finished 1-2-3 in the Japanese sports car Grand Prix.

Mazda continued to build conventional reciprocating piston models alongside the rotaries, with capacities from 987cc to 1796cc. Production rose steadily, passing 300,000 a year in 1971, when total production passed 4 million; the 5 million mark was reached the following year.

In April 1970 the first Mazdas were exported to the United States and in May Mazda Motors of America (North West) Inc was

founded, the first of several American dealerships which merged to form Mazda Motors of America Inc in 1973. American sales nudged 120,000 that year, when the millionth Mazda was exported. Other developments in 1973 included the launch of the 1.3-litre 818 coupé and its RX-3 rotary derivative, plus the 359cc Chantez minicar.

In 1977 Mazda introduced the 323, with a hatchback model available and 982 or 1272cc engine options, but, unlike many competitors, with conventional front-engine rear-drive layout. Up to 1981 and the launch of a front-wheel-drive 323 all Mazdas were rear-wheel drive.

In 1978 Mazda launched the RX-7 sports car, with rotary engine, which won the Japanese Car of the Year Award, one of many for various Mazda models, and went on to develop a reputation around the world as one of the very best small sports cars. Rotary production reached a total of 1 million that year and in 1980 Mazda's total annual output, including commercials, passed 1 million.

A new car plant was completed at Hofu in 1982 and Mazda introduced turbocharged versions of its rotary engine, and front-wheel-drive versions of the larger 626 series cars, known variously elsewhere as the Capella or Montrose.

Ford USA has acquired a 25 per cent interest in Mazda and Ford's 1984 domestic minicar was assembled by Mazda in Japan and shipped to the United States, some Australian Ford cars being partly built by Mazda's operation there as the Laser. Small rear-wheel-drive models have also been built under licence in Korea since 1977.

In October 1985 the company had 27,609 employees and capital of almost 55,500 million yen. Apart from cars it was also building buses, commercial vehicles and machine tools. In May 1984 Toyo Kogyo Co Ltd became the Mazda Motor Corporation.

Domestic car production in 1985 totalled about 815,000 – a substantial fall from 1983 but not enough to slow new model development, including a proposed V6 executive saloon, a new supermini and a successor for the RX-7. Of these only the restyled RX-7 had appeared by late 1986. Technical investigations include four-wheel steering, three-rotor Wankel engines and four-valve-per-cylinder piston engines. Kenichi Yamamoto, who played a major role in developing the original Mazda Wankel engines, is now president of the company and started work on an American assembly plant near Detroit during 1985, while some of Ford's surplus European plant may also soon devolve to Mazda. BL

MBM
see Monteverdi

MEDEA/MEDIA
see Rhode

MENDIP
GB 1913-1922

Cutlers Green Ironworks at Chewton Mendip near Bristol was a small forge where swords had been made. In the early part of this century the business was run by C. W. Harris & Co, which repaired agricultural machines and replaced iron tyres. Named after the surrounding Mendip hills, a few steam wagons were built from 1908 and Aster-engined vans from 1911.

Mendip cars were introduced in 1913 with the firm's own 1092cc engines. Most parts

were made in the works, an exception being the Belgian nickel-steel frames. The manager from 1913 was G. R. Thatcher, formerly of Lagonda and Thornycroft. The firm, by then renamed Mendip Engineering Co, was acquired by W. H. Bateman Hope in 1914 and moved to premises in Bristol.

It concentrated initially on parts for locally produced Straker-Squire vehicles and Bristol aircraft as well as trenching equipment during World War I. Meanwhile, C. W. Harris of the original firm is believed to have assembled a few more cars from spares that he had taken to Weston-super-Mare. This project soon collapsed and Mendip Engineering then revived the cars after the war under chief designer W. L. Adams. Alpha engines were used and about 300 cars built.

Bateman Hope died in 1921 and the firm was liquidated. A. J. Thatcher, who had joined the company in 1917, then helped G. R. Thatcher form the New Mendip Engineering Co at Atworth, Melksham, in 1922. They used up the last few Belgian frames on a batch of cars that year and afterwards concentrated on aircraft components, their company ultimately joining the Dowty group. NB

MERCEDES-BENZ
see Daimler (Germany)

MERCER
USA 1910-1925; 1931

Mercer Type 35 Raceabout of 1913

Through one famous model, the Type 35 Raceabout of 1911, which was probably the nearest thing to a racing car on the roads of America, the Mercer became almost a cult car before World War I and the subject of numerous imitators. It grew out of the Roebling-Planche car built by the Walter Automobile Co of Trenton, New Jersey.

The Roebling family were steel rope makers who had engineered the Brooklyn bridge, and Etienne Planche was a French-born designer who later helped Louis Chevrolet to develop the first car to bear that name. The

Roebling-Planche models used four-cylinder engines and included a 20hp landaulet and a massive, 120hp two-seater racer priced at $12,000.

In 1909 the company changed its name to the Mercer Autocar Co, named after Mercer County where Trenton was situated, and the cars which followed were known as Mercers. The first, in 1910, used a four-cylinder Beaver proprietary engine and the fastest version was the $1950 Model 30 Speedster, a very quick, cycle-winged two-seater that looked very like a contemporary racer. There was also a Model 30 Tourer at $2085 which claimed a speed range from 4 to 60mph (6 to 96kph), all in high gear. Also in 1910 the company became the Mercer Automobile Co.

In 1911 Finlay Robertson Porter, a mechanical engineer who had previously dabbled in steam cars, joined Mercer as chief engineer and designed the Type 35 Raceabout. With a four-cylinder 55hp T-head engine, four wheels, two seats and little else, it went into production in 1911 as a road car which could double as a racer for the amateur sportsman.

Several professional drivers, including Barney Oldfield, Ralph de Palma and Eddie Pullen, also raced Mercers with great success. In 1912 a racing model driven by Hughie Hughes was third at Indianapolis, where it was the smallest car in the race, and in 1913 Spencer Wishart finished second at Indy in the Model F racing version of the 35. In 1914 Pullen, who had joined the company as a works driver in 1910, won the American Grand Prize race, the first all-American combination to do so. By 1913, with numerous other race wins, Mercer advertised the Raceabout as 'The Champion Light Car'.

Porter left the company in 1914 to build the FRP car, which he did in small numbers until 1918, after which his design was sold to the American & British Manufacturing Corporation of Bridgeport, Connecticut, which built a few more up to 1922. When Porter left, Mercer adopted a car designed in 1913 by Erik H. Delling, who later founded the Delling Steam Motor Co in West Collingwood, New Jersey, and built the Delling Steamer. His Deltal racer became the side-valve 22/70 Raceabout, with

L-head engine but more comprehensive bodywork than the 35 and not a fraction of the character, although it was still popular and also available as a touring model.

By 1917 a 22/73 Raceabout cost $3500, but Mercer was in financial trouble and in 1920 it became part of Hare's Motors Group of New York, with Locomobile and Crane-Simplex. This grouping lasted until 1922.

In 1919 A. C. Schultz replaced Delling as designer and produced the Series 4 and 5 Raceabouts, which were even further from the original idea. A Rochester six-cylinder engined model appeared in 1919 and from 1923 to 1925 was the only model made. When production stopped in 1925 some 25,000 Mercers had been built in all.

That was not quite the end. In November 1929 a new company, the Mercer Motors Corporation, was formed in Delaware by a group of businessmen who had bought the Mercer name. They were led by Harry M. Wahl, formerly of Chevrolet, and former Elcar designer M. J. Graffis was chief engineer.

Initial plans to produce up to 3000 cars in 1930 were soon dropped but some four or five Continental straight-eight engined prototypes were built in the former Elcar works in Elkhart, Indiana, and cars were shown at a New York hotel at the time of the New York Show in January 1931. Production of this car in several body styles and at prices from $2650 to $4000 was supposed to start in the old Elcar works in March, but it never did and the Mercer was no more. Finley Robertson Porter, designer of the legend, died in February 1964 at the age of 92. BL

MERCURY
see Lincoln

MERLIN
see Thoroughbred

MESSERSCHMITT
GERMANY 1953-1962

Professor Willy Messerschmitt had been one of Germany's leading aircraft makers in the inter-war years. Founded in 1923 at Bamberg, Flugzeugbau Messerschmitt's best known contribution to the war effort was the Me109 fighter, the German equivalent to the Spitfire, but the company also made a pioneer jet fighter, the Me262. By 1945 75 per cent of the Augsberg factory had been destroyed and the workforce was greatly depleted, but Messerschmitt was soon back in business in a small way, making sewing machines and car components.

At the same time an ex-Luftwaffe pilot, Fritz Fend, had started making invalid cars in a small factory at Rosenheim in Upper Bavaria.

At first hand-propelled, his tiny three-wheelers later had 38cc Victoria engines, and in 1948 he brought out an open-bodied single seater for general sale, powered by a 98cc Sachs engine and called the Fend Flitzer. A tandem two-seater and an enclosed single-seater followed in 1951, by which time Fend had made about 250 vehicles.

Needing larger production facilities if he was going to succeed commercially, Fend approached Messerschmitt with his design, and during 1952 the Fend Flitzer was remodelled into the Messerschmitt Kabinenroller (cabin scooter). This was put into production at Messerschmitt's Regensburg factory in 1953.

The original Kabinenroller, the KR175, was a tandem two-seater three-wheeler powered by a 173cc Sachs two-stroke engine. Steering was direct, by handlebar, with three-quarters of a turn from lock to lock. The KR175 had no reverse gear but this was provided on its successor, the 191cc KR200, which was made from 1955 to 1964.

The Messerschmitts sold well at first, for they answered a genuine need for cheap transport and also were seen as an amusing novelty in Britain and the United States. Despite this, however, sales suffered through competition from the Isetta and Heinkel bubble cars, which offered side-by-side seating, and the market for all these mini vehicles evaporated in the 1960s when growing prosperity led to a demand for larger cars. About 10,000 KR175s were sold, and nearly 40,000 KR200s, together with 250 of the 425cc four-wheeled version known as the Tiger, made from 1958 to 1961.

In 1956 the ban on German aircraft constructors was lifted, and now that Messerschmitt was able to return to its true *métier* it found the Kabinenroller a bit of an embarrassment. It therefore sold the Regensburg factory and the name to Fend, who reorganized his company under the title Fahrzeug-und Maschinenbau GmbH, Regensburg (FMR for short). This company continued with general engineering after Kabinenroller production ended in 1964, but Fend left the firm. GNG

MESSIER
FRANCE 1926-1931

Georges Messier of Montrouge, Seine, was described as a shock absorber maker in the early 1920s but in fact his 'sans ressorts' (without springs) experiments were more fundamental and consisted in 1921 of a Peugeot that rode on oleo-pneumatic cylinders pumped up to constant height, whatever the load, by a compressor. The idea was tried out by SLIM-Pilain in 1924.

Two years later, in 1926, Société Commerciale des Automobiles Messier (Sans Ressorts) began to produce complete cars with this suspension, the compressor of each

Messerschmitt KR200 Kabinenroller of c.1955

being driven off the overhead cam of the CIME 1.6-litre four-cylinder engine. Six- and eight-cylinder American engines – the latter, and probably the former too, by Lycoming – were soon adopted and went up to 4.85 litres. Few cars were built and production ended in 1931.

Georges Messier was killed in a riding accident in 1933. An aircraft he had designed flew in 1934 and was the first to have hydraulically retractable landing gear.

Citroën experimented with the Messier suspension in 1939 and adapted it for post-war use. However, it is aircraft landing gear and disc brakes – used at an early stage by Gordini – that have kept the firm busy to this day. The company has branches in Britain and India. NB

MÉTALLURGIQUE
BELGIUM 1901-1927

The Société Anonyme La Métallurgique was founded to manufacture railway rolling stock and tramcars, and by the 1890s had three factories at La Sambre, Nivelles and Tubize. In 1898 the branch at La Sambre was instructed to investigate the manufacture of motor cars, but as the necessary machine tools were lacking it was decided to build a new factory at Marchienne au Pont. This was completed at the end of 1900, and the first Métallurgique cars were exhibited at the 1901 Paris Salon alongside engines and other parts to be sold to outside manufacturers.

The cars were both four-seaters powered by 4CV two-cylinder engines, but one was a rear-engined *vis-à-vis* and the other a front-engined two-seater with spyder seat. The first year's production was 25 cars. Shortly afterwards a four-cylinder model was added, but manufacture was only on a small scale until the arrival during 1903 of the former German Daimler designer Ernst Lehmann.

For 1904 he designed a completely new range of modern four-cylinder cars, two twins and two fours from 7CV to 20CV, with mechanically operated inlet valves, steel frames and shaft drive. The twins were dropped in 1905.

Métallurgique soon had a flourishing export market, being represented in Germany by Piedboeuf et Compagnie – Adrien Piedboeuf later founded Impéria – and in Britain by Warwick Wright. In France Métallurgiques were made under licence by Gillet Forest from 1904 to 1907 after that company had given up its own horizontal-engined cars. In 1907 the car-making side was separated from the parent firm, and was given the new title L'Auto Métallurgique SA.

There were now seven four-cylinder cars from 20/24 to 70/80CV as well as a revived twin of 12/14CV. They had an excellent reputation for quality and reliability. In 1907 the author's grandfather took a tour from Sussex to the Scottish Highlands, over 2000 miles (3220km) in all, in a 26/32CV Métallurgique with no involuntary stops, even for punctures. The famous V-radiator which characterized the marque for the rest of its life was adopted on the larger models in 1908 and throughout the range in 1909.

Success in the 1907 Herkomer Trials led to the Bergmann electrical equipment firm taking an interest in Métallurgique, and from 1909 to 1915 and again from 1920 to 1922 the company made the Bergmann-Métallurgique under licence. There were strong German connections even before this, doubtless encouraged by Ernst Lehmann, for Métallurgique bought its radiators from NJW of Ulm, electrical equipment from Bosch, and bearings from DWF.

By 1914 Métallurgique was well established as one of the leading Belgian makes, but it was very badly hit by the war which robbed it of all machinery and also its designer, Lehmann, who returned to Germany and later worked for Selve. Lehmann was killed at the wheel of a Selve in the 1924 Teutoberger race.

The first post-war cars were assembled from pre-war stock and pre-war designs of 14, 18 and 26CV and subsequently built. In 1922 a new 2-litre single-overhead cam four-cylinder car which Paul Bastien had designed for Somea was put into production as the sole model. This was made in small numbers but was never profitable and suffered from competition from cheaper imported cars, as did all Belgian makes in the 1920s.

In 1927 the parent company decided to close down the Marchienne au Pont factory, which was sold to Impéria. Having removed the machinery to the Nessonvaux plant, Impéria resold it to Minerva. GNG

METZ/MARSH, ORIENT, WALTHAM
USA 1898-1922

Charles Henry Metz, born in Utica, New York, the son of a German immigrant, became an agent for Columbia bicycles and in 1886 began to make bicycle components, joining the Union Cycle Co three years later as a designer. In 1893 he formed the Waltham Manufacturing Co with $100,000 capital and produced Orient bicycles. Financial backing came from prominent members of General Electric and Thompson-Houston, and electric car experiments took place in 1898. Steam cars were also tried.

De Dion-engined quads and motorcycles were built at Metz's firm in 1898, at which time Albert Champion (the future spark plug manufacturer) was a test rider. Some 15,000 bicycles a year were made in the late 1890s, when De Dion and Aster licences were acquired. In 1900 Aster-engined Orient motorcycles and runabouts were displayed. In 1901 the company was reorganized; C. A. Coffin of General Electric took control, sales manager W. D. Gash left for Searchmont Motors and C. H. Metz departed to become editor of *Cycle and Automobile Trade Journal*.

From the makers of Tribune bicycles Coffin hired B. Gaylord, who produced the Orient Buckboard single-cylinder air-cooled rear-engined marginal motor car for 1903. A four-cylinder version of this engine was developed by J. C. Robbins and this was offered in a more substantial Waltham-Metz in 1905.

Meanwhile C. H. Metz had been building Thor-engined motorcycles and in late 1904 he joined forces with the Marsh brothers, who had made a steam car in 1898-99 and gone on to produce motorcycles. As the American Motor Co they made Marsh-Metz or M-M motorcycles at Brockton, Massachusetts, from 1905 as well as a short-lived two-cylinder light car.

Metz was then invited back to Waltham, which had got into difficulties under manager W. H. Little, who subsequently left the company and went on to make the Little car. In 1909 Metz conceived the ingenious idea of selling Metz Plan Cars in 14 packages at $25 a time for home assembly. The cars had friction drive and two-cylinder air-cooled 12hp engines. The scheme worked, and in August 1909 the firm became the Metz Co with capital of $500,000. The Waltham manufacturing title was sold to White along with its ALAM licence.

Plan Cars lasted until 1911. Complete cars followed, being built from about 1910 at the rate of 3000 a year, a figure that soon increased to 10,000. An attempt to sell Blériot-type planes as Metz Air Cars came to nothing in 1911, but a four-cylinder water-cooled car engine designed by J. C. Robbins was adopted that year.

Metz swept the board in the final Glidden Tour in 1913, and new factories with 12 acres (48 hectares) of floor space were ready at the outbreak of war. The nearby American Watch Tool factory was bought in 1916 to make the firm independent of outside suppliers of carburettors and electrical items. About 100 cars a week were made until the factory was requisitioned in 1917 to produce De Havilland aircraft parts.

Production of the friction-drive cars ended in 1919 after some had been built as light commercials. They were succeeded that year by a completely conventional assembled Metz Master Six car with Rutenber or Lycoming 45hp unit, Timken axles and Warner or Brown & Lipe gearbox. Custom bodies were also made for Ford Model Ts.

In 1922 the firm was reorganized as the Motor Manufacturers of Waltham Inc but production ceased that year and marked the end of what had been New England's largest maker of cars. In all some 40,000 to 45,000 Metz cars had been made. The plant was sold in 1923 for over $1 million.

Charles H. Metz went on to make ice-boxes and wooden items for house builders and had ideas of producing a three-wheel economy car and camping trailers in the early 1930s. He died in 1937. The original Orient bicycle factory was bought in 1927 by Perrine Quality Products Corporation, which continues to make storage batteries there. NB

Metz two-seater of 1913

MG
GB 1924-1980

In 1922 Cecil Kimber was manager of the Morris Garages in Oxford. Becoming tired of the everyday Cowley and Oxfords that he was selling, he ordered some Cowley chassis and mounted on them a close-coupled four-seater body made for him by Carbodies of Coventry. These he sold under the name Chummy, assembling them first at the Morris Garages in Longwall Street and later moving to a small workshop in Alfred Lane. The next special body was a two-seater by Raworth of Oxford, of which only six were made, followed by a four-door saloon on the Oxford chassis which Kimber advertised as 'the M.G. V-front saloon' in *The Morris Owner* magazine in March 1924.

This was the first use of the name MG in an advertisement, but it is a moot point whether the saloon or the Raworth two-seater should be considered as the first MG. The latter was advertised in May 1924 as 'The M.G. Super Sports Morris', complete with the famous Octagon surrounding the letters MG, yet the first Raworth car was sold in August 1923. Later in 1924 Kimber built a number of sporting four-seaters on the Oxford chassis, their appearance being considerably improved when the Oxford's wheelbase was increased.

The Alfred Lane workshop measured only 20×100ft (6×30m) and in September 1925 Kimber moved to one bay of Morris Motors' Radiator Branch. The next move took place in September 1927 to a new factory in Edmund Road financed by a £10,000 loan from William Morris. By this time Morris had replaced his 'bullnose' radiator with a flat one, and Kimber followed suit.

July 1927 had seen the first move to independence with the formation of Morris Garages as a limited company, followed in the spring of 1928 by the MG Car Co (Proprietors of the Morris Garages Ltd). The cars were now carrying MG car numbers as well as Morris chassis numbers. In November 1927 an MG secured the make's first race victory in Buenos Aires.

As the MG became more of an individual car Kimber ceased to buy complete rolling chassis from Morris and instead bought frames, engines and axles separately, the axles from Wolseley. In 1928 MG had its first stand at Olympia, where it exhibited two new and important models, the Morris Minor-derived Midget with 847cc overhead-cam engine, and the 18/80 Six also with an overhead-cam engine but with six cylinders and 2½ litres capacity.

These new models led to a trebling of production in 1929, from about 300 to 900, and in 1930 production was nearly 1900. Of the sales for 1929, about 12 per cent were the old 14/40, 30 per cent the 18/80 and the balance the Midget.

In 1929 MG moved again, for the last time

MG K3 Magnette of 1934

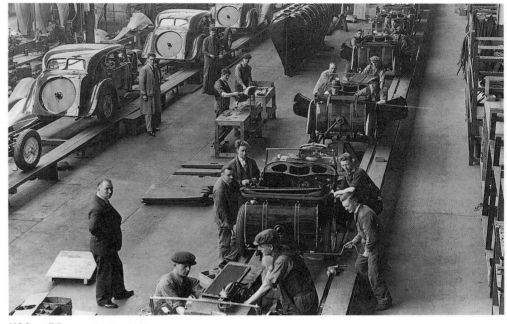

MG S and T-Type production, 1937

as it turned out. The site chosen was part of the Pavlova Leather Co's premises at Abingdon, 7 miles (11km) from Oxford. Production dropped below the 1500 mark in 1931, but this was a bad year for the industry generally, and rose to 2400 in 1932.

By now the company's racing programme was beginning to reap successes, although the really great years were 1933 to 1935 when the K3 Magnette in particular scored countless victories, including Nuvolari's outright win in the 1933 Ulster Tourist Trophy, and the team prize in the 1933 Mille Miglia. Yet Kimber was not alone among car-makers in discovering that glory on the racetrack does not always bring profit on the balance sheet, and he came under constant pressure from Morris to curb expenditure on racing and to buy as many components as possible from within the Morris empire. In 1933 he severed his connection with Carbodies and thenceforth bought his coachwork from Morris Bodies Branch.

In 1935 Lord Nuffield, as William Morris had become the previous year, sold the MG Car Co to Morris Motors. A tough Yorkshireman, Leonard Lord, later to become head of Austin, became managing director and one of his first moves was to close down the competition department.

The overhead-cam engines were dropped and replaced by pushrod units from the Morris-Wolseley range. The TA Midget received a 1292cc engine similar, though not identical, to that used in the Wolseley Ten, while a new model to rival William Lyons' recently introduced SS Jaguar was the SA 2-litre, powered by a Wolseley Super Six engine. The four-door saloon was Kimber-designed and Morris-built, but the drophead coupé and tourer bodies were bought in from Tickford and Charlesworth respectively.

Later came 1½-litre and 2.6-litre versions of the same theme, comfortable well-equipped touring cars with disappointing acceleration to the enthusiast yet good cruising

MGA twin-cam of 1959

speeds. Racing of various models continued, but only by private owners. Production reached its highest pre-war level in 1937, when 2850 cars were delivered.

As soon as World War II broke out in September 1939 the patriotic Kimber ceased car production to concentrate on war work, but it was some time before any contracts came his way and then it was not via Cowley but directly from various ministries. The company's biggest wartime achievement was the making of frontal sections for the Albemarle bomber, of which it made 653 and completed a further 285. It also produced engine mountings and other components for Lancaster, Typhoon and Tempest aircraft, and built Crusader tanks and Neptune amphibious tanks.

Cecil Kimber had incurred the displeasure of Miles Thomas, the new managing director of the Nuffield Organization, for accepting the Albemarle contract without consultation, and he was dismissed in 1941. He subsequently worked for Charlesworth and the Specialloid Piston Co and died in a railway accident in February 1945.

Like most other car-makers, MG entered the post-war market with a pre-war design, the TC Midget, which was a slightly modified version of the 1939 TB. The bigger cars were not revived.

MG was earlier into production than many firms, announcing the TC in October 1945 and building 81 of them by the end of the year. Exports to the United States began early in 1947 and the TC Midget soon became a cult car, sparking off a sports car boom which led Detroit to enter the market itself a decade later with the Chevrolet Corvette and Ford Thunderbird. Indeed the Sports Car Club of America grew from one US branch of the MG Car Club. By the time the TC was replaced in March 1950 a total of 10,000 had been made of which 6592 were exported, 2001 to the United States.

Its successor, the TD, was made in much larger numbers totalling 29,644 in four years, a high proportion of which went for export. In 1952 42 TDs were sold abroad for every one in Britain.

Sales dropped badly after the introduction of the Austin-Healey 100, however, and Leonard Lord turned down a proposal to

MG ZA Magnette of 1955

bring out a brand new Midget in 1953 on the grounds that the newly formed British Motor Corporation did not need two new sports car designs. This was just one of the many snubs that Abingdon had to suffer from top management at BMC and, later, British Leyland; for a number of years it felt very much the Cinderella of the organization.

Badge engineering began to creep in with the ZA Magnette saloon of 1954, which shared a body shell with the Wolseley 4/44 and the B-Type engine with the Wolseley and Austin Cambridge. More encouraging was the MGA sports car of 1955-62 with tuned version of the B-Type engine and streamlined two-seater body. This was made in larger numbers than any previous MG, a total of 101,181 being produced in seven years including about 2100 with twin-overhead cam engines.

It was replaced by the MGB unitary construction sports car which was an even better seller, totalling over 460,000 and lasting right up to the end of MG in 1980. In the same bodyshell there were also 9000 MGCs with six-cylinder ex-Austin-Healey 3000 engines and 2591 V8s with the Rover 3½-litre unit.

Meanwhile BMC was playing musical chairs with production of its various models. In 1957 Austin-Healey production was trans-

ferred to Abingdon, taking over the space occupied by Riley, which had been Abingdon-built since 1949 but was now merely a badge-engineered Wolseley. A new small sports car, the Austin-Healey Sprite joined the 100 in 1958 and an MG version of the Mark II Sprite came out in 1961, reviving the name Midget.

In 1959 the first MG to be made away from Abingdon appeared. This was the Cowley-built Magnette III, which was simply the BMC Farina-styled saloon with twin carburettors and MG radiator grille.

Sales of MG sports cars dropped in the early 1960s due to competition from such cars as the Triumph Spitfire and Mini Cooper,

MGB GT V8 of 1973

and Abingdon acquired a useful sideline in the assembly of Morris Minor estate cars and vans. In 20 years MG production never fell below 30,000 a year including Rileys and Austin-Healeys. The best year was 1972 when 55,639 sports cars were made, of which 39,393 were MGBs.

In 1968 BMC merged with Jaguar to form British Motor Holdings and the MG Car Co Ltd became the MG Division. Soon afterwards BMH merged with the Leyland group to form British Leyland. The rival sports car maker Triumph was now in the same group, although higher status was accorded Triumph as it came under the specialist car

MG Metro 6R4 Group B rally car of 1986

division – Standard-Triumph, Rover, Jaguar – while MG was illogically put into the Austin-Morris Division.

It became increasingly clear that Abingdon was not favoured by BL's bosses, Sir Donald Stokes and later Sir Michael Edwardes. At least two promising MG prototypes were scotched in favour of the Triumph TR7, but the ageing MGBs soldiered on, outselling the TR7 in the US market even when the price of the Triumph was substantially cut.

In December 1975 the millionth MG left the factory, but no new models were forthcoming. The Midget was discontinued in the spring of 1979 and early in 1980 the company announced the closure of the Abingdon factory. It marked the end of an era in British motoring history.

BL agreed to sell it to a consortium led by Alan Curtis of Aston Martin but it would not part with the MG name, which it wanted to keep for future models of BL cars. These later emerged as the MG Metro, Maestro and Montego. The latest car to bear the MG name is the EX-E prototype shown at the 1985 Frankfurt Motor Show. It is a sports car designed to take the 250bhp V6 engine used in the Metro 6R4 rally car, which should give it a potential top speed of 170mph (273kph). The factory without the name was of little interest to the consortium, however, and the Aston Martin deal came to nothing.

The last MGB was produced in the autumn of 1980, and the factory was sold the following year to the Standard Life Assurance Co for £5 million. The majority of the area was demolished in the autumn of 1981 and a new industrial estate has been built on the site. GNG

MICHEL IRAT
see Brasier

MIDAS
see Marcos

MIESSE
BELGIUM 1896-1926

Jules Miesse was a foreman in the steel stamping works SA Cartoucherie Belge in 1894 when he left to form his own general engineering company in Anderlecht, Brussels. His youthful aim to make a motor car was realized in 1896 when he built an armoured wood frame steam car powered by a paraffin-fired three-cylinder horizontal engine. He named it *La Torpille* (Torpedo) and tested it in a number of competitions before starting production of generally similar cars in 1898. By 1902 two types were being made, of 6 and 10CV, increased to 10 and 15CV in 1903 when the frames became of steel construction.

In the spring of 1902 an English company was formed, the Miesse Steam Motor Syndicate Ltd, to exploit Miesse patents in the British market, and later in the year licence manufacture of the steam cars was taken up by Turner's Motor Manufacturing Co of Wolverhampton. For two years the cars were sold under the name Miesse, but in 1904 the name was changed to Turner-Miesse. Turner's also built steam trucks, and continued to make steamers until 1913, seven years after the Belgian company had given them up.

In 1900 Jules Miesse began to hedge his bets by experimenting with petrol cars, the first of which was offered for sale two years later. The first taxicab chassis was made in 1904, and this became an important part of the business, with cabs being supplied to Brussels and a number of other cities.

Although Miesse exhibited a large car with Goldschmidt-Direct gearless transmission at the 1904 Brussels Show it seems that very few petrol cars were made until 1906, when the steamers were abandoned and a range of 24hp four-cylinder and 35hp six-cylinder cars were made. The works were more than doubled in area during 1906, enabling car production to exceed 200 a year within a short time.

In 1913 the former flat radiator was replaced by a handsome vee style, which was used for all Miesse passenger cars up to 1924. Three models were listed that year, 14/16, 15/18 and 22/24hp with monobloc engines and poppet valves, and a sleeve-valve 20hp. A further factory extension allowed Miesse to make its own coachwork.

In 1914 Miesse brought out an advanced 2-litre four-cylinder car with single-overhead cam, but the war prevented development. The overhead-cam principle was seen on several of the post-war cars, however.

In 1910 Miesse began to offer light commercial vehicles on car chassis and in 1916 brought out its first larger truck, a 3-tonner with four-cylinder single-overhead cam engine. In 1919 a large extension to the factory enabled commercial vehicle work to be increased, and this side of the business soon took precedence over passenger cars.

Two passenger cars were introduced in 1919, the Type H 2-litre four-cylinder, and the Type J 4-litre straight-eight, both with single-overhead cam engines and the same cylinder dimensions of $69 \times 130mm$ $(2.7 \times 5.1in)$. These were also used for a 3-litre six introduced in 1923 which was joined by a smaller six of 1356cc. A flat radiator replaced the vee in 1924 and front-wheel brakes arrived in 1925, when the Type J was increased to 4.6 litres.

By this time car production was down to fewer than 100 a year, and 1926 proved to be the final season. In 1923 there had been plans for Miesse to manufacture the 3.4-litre straight-eight Dunamis car sponsored by the tobacco maker Theo Verellen, but this never passed the prototype stage.

Commercial vehicles, on the other hand, flourished, with a wide range of trucks and buses being made. Notable developments were a 100CV straight-eight introduced in 1926, possibly the first use of this layout in a commercial vehicle, the adoption of the Bellay gas producer on some models in 1931, and Gardner diesel engines in 1932.

From 1949 to the mid-1950s Miesse assembled Nash cars and trucks and Mack trucks, in addition to its own trucks and buses which were made until 1974. In 1951 Jules Miesse, aged nearly 80, retook command of the company on the early death of his son Edmond, but soon handed over the reins to his granddaughters Yvonne and Renée. GNG

MILDÉ
FRANCE 1898-1909

Before the turn of the century Charles Mildé was already prominent in the new electrical business and from 1898 Mildé et Cie of Levallois-Perret, Seine, made a wide variety of electric vehicles and, later, petrol-electrics. Mildé's first offering was a bolt-on self contained 3hp electric power pack and drive system which could, he claimed, be fitted to any type of carriage. By November 1898 Mildé was advertising a light delivery van, powered by a Postel-Vinay motor and with a range of about 35 miles (56km) and a top speed of 9mph (14kph).

He continued to build various commercial types and at the Paris Show of October 1900 he displayed five vehicles, including an omnibus, a cab, a three-wheeled car and a rather strange forecarriage. Some of the Mildé cars looked like little more than a three-wheel basket chair with the batteries, exposed gear-drive and motor all hung around the tiller-steered front wheel on a system of rails and rollers.

In 1901 with Michel Ephrussi, who had connections with the Rothschild family, Mildé took over the assets of the struggling Société l'Electromotion in Paris, a company which had been formed to import Pope-Columbia electrics from America but which collapsed in 1901. Mildé and Ephrussi's support allowed the company to continue until 1907, making a wide variety of electric town cars.

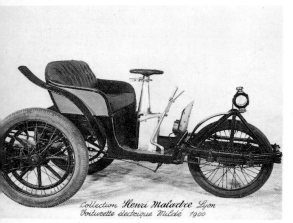

Mildé electric voiturette of 1900

Mildé also built a light three-wheeler, the Mildé et Mondos, with two motors on the rear axle. From 1903 the company concentrated on some much more conventional looking cars with single motors at the rear.

In 1904 Frederic Gaillardet joined Mildé from Société La Française, builder of the Diamant petrol car, having previously been chief engineer of Société Française d'Automobiles (Système Gaillardet), which built the Doctoresse car from 1899 to 1902. Under Gaillardet's supervision Mildé added a 6hp single-cylinder De Dion-engined petrol-electric to the range, and petrol electrics continued alongside the pure electric models as Mildé-Gaillardets from 1907.

At the Paris Show in November 1911, 18/20 and 35/40hp six-cylinder models appeared under the new name of Mildé-Gaillardet, but the company only continued production under the name Mildé until 1909. Thereafter Mildé built commercial vehicles up to World War I. In World War II the name reappeared briefly on the Mildé-Kriéger, electric conversions of Chenard-Walcker and La Licorne cars and vans. BL

326

MINERVA
BELGIUM 1899-1939

The famous Belgian make of Minerva was founded by a Dutchman, Sylvain de Jong, born in 1868. He began his working life as a journalist, and later settled in Antwerp where he made bicycles from 1897. The cycles were sold under the trade names of Minerva and Romania, although only the first name was ever used for motor vehicles. Motor tricycles followed in 1899, when de Jong moved to larger premises on the outskirts of Antwerp. This factory had 200 workers who turned out some 800 bicycles a month.

At the 1899 Antwerp Cycle Show de Jong exhibited a prototype voiturette and light van, but he was too busy with cycles and engines to bother with cars for several years. His motorcycle engines were used by 75 different European manufacturers in the first decade of the century, including Humber, Royal Enfield and Triumph of England, Cottereau in France, and Adler, Opel and Seidel & Naumann in Germany. There were also complete Minerva motorcycles made from 1901 to 1910.

In 1902 a Panhard-like car with 6hp four-cylinder engine was made, being followed by other two-, three- and four-cylinder machines, but the first serious four-wheeler was the 636cc single-cylinder Minervette voiturette introduced in 1904. Meanwhile de Jong had replaced his Sylvain de Jong et Cie with Minerva Motors SA, capitalized at £130,000. Joint managing directors were Sylvain de Jong himself and David Citroën, a cousin of car-maker André and founder of the London branch of Minerva which was set up, like the new Antwerp company, in 1903. Another director was de Jong's younger brother Jacques. Curiously, although David Citroën sold the Minervette in London, the larger Minervas were handled by C. S. Rolls before he went over to selling Rolls-Royce cars exclusively.

Larger Minervas, including a 6250cc 40hp six, had appeared by 1907, when the works employed 1200 people and turned out 600 cars and 1500 motorcycles. A customer for the 40hp was the famous comedian George Robey.

Minerva was never particularly known as a sporting make, but it built some 8-litre four-cylinder racing cars in 1907 which finished in the first three places in the Circuit des Ardennes, the winning car being driven by J. T. C. Moore-Brabazon. Three cars were entered in the 1914 Tourist Trophy and were among the six finishers of 23 competitors.

In 1909 Minerva became the second European firm, after Daimler of Coventry, to adopt the Knight sleeve-valve engine. Both sleeve and poppet valves were offered that year, but from 1910 only sleeve-valve units would power Minerva cars to the end of the make's life.

King Albert of the Belgians bought a 38hp

Minerva 3.3-litre racing car of 1914

tourer in 1910 and drove it himself on a tour of the Tyrol. By 1914, other royal owners included the Kings of Norway and Sweden, the latter having a striking limousine with non-standard vee-radiator and a wrap-around windscreen. Another famous Minerva owner in 1912 was Henry Ford.

In 1913, the last full year of peace-time production, Minerva built 3000 cars, making it the largest car manufacturer in Belgium. Four models of 14, 18, 26 and 38hp were listed. The company also began to make heavy commercial vehicles, a sideline which would become increasingly important in later years.

The factory kept going for as long as possible after the outbreak of war in August 1914, building armoured cars on 38hp chassis until Antwerp was overrun in October by the German army, which used the factory for the repair of vehicles. De Jong went back to Holland, where he rented a corner of the Spyker factory and began to design the post-war Minervas.

He visited the United States in 1919 to study the latest production methods and to restock with modern machine tools, and by the end of the year 20hp cars with four-cylinder monobloc engines were leaving the factory in respectable numbers. A six with the same cylinder dimensions (90×140mm or 3½×5½in) appeared in 1920, followed by a small 2-litre four in 1922.

Practically the whole car was made in-house at this time with the exception of chassis frames, magnetos, carburettors and tyres. Bodywork was made at a newly-acquired factory at Mortsel, an Antwerp suburb, although many of the larger Minervas carried custom coachwork by famous names such as d'Ieteren, Vanden Plas and Labourdette.

By the mid-1920s Minerva was one of the half dozen highest quality cars in Europe. It was becoming well thought of in the USA, too, where a number were imported – and sometimes bodied – by Paul Ostruk of New York.

In 1923 Minerva took over the Antwerp factory of the defunct SAVA company, using it for component manufacture. The following year, needing to expand further and finding an insufficient supply of labour in the Antwerp district, the company bought the Brussels factory of Pipe.

Commercial vehicles loomed larger with the purchase, also in 1924, of Auto Traction, which had made Chenard-Walcker road tractors for four years, powered by Minerva engines. The Auto Traction name was subsequently used for several years on other types of trucks and buses.

Minerva was riding high in the mid-1920s with car production at 2500 in 1925 and nearly 3000 in 1926. More than half went for export, and a good quantity of these to Britain, where in their declining years they became popular as hire cars. A 2-litre six, called in the catalogue *la fille de Minerva*, was made from 1926 to 1933 but was too heavy for its engine and was never as popular as the bigger cars. These were the 5.9-litre six-cylinder AK (1927-37) and the 6.6-litre straight-eight AL (1929-36), the latter designed by Alexis Vivinus who had been a car-maker in earlier years.

In 1927 de Jong began exploratory talks with FN about a possible fusion of interests, if

Minerva AP landaulette of 1937

not an outright merger, but his death in January 1928 ended these talks. It is likely they would have foundered anyway, as neither side was willing to give anything away.

De Jong's death marked the beginning of Minerva's decline: this was partly due to the loss of a dynamic boss, but also to the malaise which affected all Belgian makes, which were unable to compete with foreign-assembled cars on the home market and were losing exports because of the Depression. The straight-eight AL was a beautiful car but it was competing with new V12s from Maybach and Hispano-Suiza, and even V16s from Cadillac and Marmon, for a share of a shrinking market. Not more than 50 ALs were made, the last ones being laid down in 1933 although not sold until three years later. The last AK was also laid down in 1933, but a new one could still be bought in 1937.

To keep the company going Minerva moved to smaller cars, although the 4-litre straight-eight AP (1931-36) was an attractive car which sold well in England at £900 for a limousine. It had a 3-litre six-cylinder sister, the AR (1931-36), while Minerva's last offer-

ing was an uninspired 2-litre four-cylinder car, the M4, which was the first Minerva with synchromesh and was made from 1934 to 1936. It looked no more distinguished than a contemporary Citroën or Renault.

Despite support from banks and the Belgian government, Minerva steadily lost money in the early 1930s. In 1934 the company was reorganized as the Société Nouvelle Minerva, under whose direction the M4 was launched and production of the larger cars tapered off. About 250 M4s were made, but they could not keep the company afloat.

In October 1935 the Société Nouvelle was liquidated and Minerva became part of Mathieu Van Roggen's Impéria company. A handful of APs were assembled at Antwerp, where commercial vehicle production continued, but the rest of the pre-war Minerva-Impérias were no more than Adler Trumpf-based front-wheel-drive Impéria TA-9s. They were sold as Minervas in France and Britain to take advantage of the old name's prestige.

In 1937 Van Roggen displayed an advanced car with unitary construction, all independent suspension by torsion bars and automatic transmission. Just about the only conventional part of this Minerva TAM-18 was its Ford V8 engine, and even this was mounted transversely. Only three were made, in the Impéria factory at Nessonvaux, for the Antwerp factories were taken up with commercial vehicle production.

In 1939 Ettore Bugatti was considering transferring his works from Molsheim to one of the Minerva factories as a response to the strikes which were afflicting his own works. He was having talks with King Leopold of the Belgians when news of the death of his son Jean recalled him to Molsheim, and less than a month later World War II broke out.

After the war Minerva carried on with commercial vehicle production for several years, and from 1950 to 1953 made a number of Land Rovers under licence. Van Roggen made two more attempts at car production, in 1952 with the Italian Cemsa-Caproni design and the following year with a luxury car based on Armstrong-Siddeley Sapphire components. The latter was never built, although Minerva did assemble a few Sapphires.

In 1955 there was talk of a tie-up with Salmson, but the French company was on its last legs and nothing came of the idea. Minerva's final fling was with a Continental-powered Jeep, of which a small number were made from 1954 to 1956. The Mortsel factory was sold off in small lots during 1957, although the street that runs alongside it is still called Minervastraat. GNG

MINI
see Austin

MINI COOPER
see Cooper

MITCHELL
USA 1903-1923

Henry Mitchell established a wagon factory at Fort Dearborn, Chicago, in 1837. Eight years later his Mitchell Wagon Co moved to Kenosha, Wisconsin, and then to Racine, Wisconsin, in 1857. William T. Lewis, a telegraph operator born in 1840 in Utica, New York, married Mitchell's daughter Mary and joined the firm in 1864. The company's name was changed to the Mitchell and Lewis Co 20 years later.

Lewis and his son, William Mitchell Lewis, organized the Mitchell Motor Car Co in 1902 and produced a 7hp air-cooled twin the following year. Water-cooling and larger four-cylinder cars quickly followed. Output in 1904 was 80 cars.

The factory had grown to 3 acres (1¼ hectares) in 1908 and 6½ acres (2.6 hectares) in 1909. The company produced 666 cars in 1906 and 3000 in 1909. The 'car you ought to have at the price you ought to pay' had shaft drive from 1907. By 1910 the range included a 50hp six.

In January 1910 the wagon and car firms were consolidated as the Mitchell-Lewis Motor Corporation, which had capital of $10 million. There were 13 acres (5 hectares) of single-storey steel and concrete factory in Racine with a potential output of 10,000 to 15,000 cars a year and 2800 employees. Virtually everything but tyres and magnetos was made on the premises. Sales branches were formed in London (1911) and Paris (1912). The sales manager was J. W. Gilson, president was Captain William Mitchell Lewis, and vice-president until his death in 1916 was William T. Lewis. Captain Mitchell Lewis set up the rival Lewis Motor Co in 1913 with René Petard, Gilson and James Cram.

Output at Mitchell was 8000 cars in 1914, when 30,000 of its old speciality, horse-drawn wagons, were built. A total of 6186 cars were made in 1915.

The following year a new firm was formed

to take over the Mitchell-Lewis Motor Corporation. Mitchell Motors Co Inc had Otis C. Friend as general manager and among prominent members of its board were R. M. Owen, formerly of Reo sales and owner of Owen Magnetic, and A. P. Warner, whose name was better known as part of the famous transmission manufacturer, Borg-Warner. Chief engineer and vice-president was J. W. Bate. Some $100,000 was to be spent on the 45-acre (17-hectare) factory site to boost production to 30,000 a year. Bodies would be made in the wagon works and all models would have six cylinders, although a V8 was offered briefly in 1916.

A misjudged, but rapidly rectified, styling blunder in 1920 gave the cars a rearward-sloping radiator, which earned them the nickname 'drunken Mitchells'. Sales were damaged and the company soon collapsed. In 1923 its factory was acquired by Nash. NB

MITSUBISHI
JAPAN 1917-1921; 1959 to date

The Mitsubishi company's origins date back to the formation of the Tsukumo-Shokai shipping company in Osaka in 1870. In 1873 that company was renamed Mitsubishi Shokai, Mitsubishi being the Japanese word for 'three diamonds', the symbol on the company flag and the badge used on today's cars.

In 1874 the company moved its headquarters to Tokyo and in 1875 it merged with the government-backed mail-shipping organization to become the Mitsubishi Mail Steamship Co. In 1887 this company in turn took over the Nagasaki Iron Works and became Mitsubishi-Sha Ltd.

In 1907 the manufacturing and service sides of the company were separated and in 1917 the Mitsubishi Shipbuilding Co Ltd was formed, independent of the growing banking, insurance, warehousing and other interests of the main company. In 1917 the Shipbuilding Co, based in Kobe, built its first car, the Mitsubishi Model A, based on a Fiat design. About 20 of these were built until 1921, plus several experimental vehicles, but then the company switched to building trucks and

buses, which it continued to do in the 1930s and early 1940s with American style vehicles sold under the name Fuso.

In 1920 an engine building subsidiary, the Mitsubishi Internal Combustion Engine Manufacturing Co Ltd, was formed (and dropped the word 'Manufacturing' a year later). In 1928 this was reorganized as the Mitsubishi Aircraft Co Ltd and in 1934 re-merged with the original shipbuilding arm of the company to form Mitsubishi Heavy Industries Ltd, with wide manufacturing interests.

During World War II the company built tanks, ships and armaments and for that was split up under Allied control after the war. By 1952 Mitsubishi had been split into three parts, Mitsubishi Shipbuilding and Engineering Co Ltd, Mitsubishi Heavy Industries (Reorganized) Ltd (which made Mizushima three-wheelers and Silver Pigeon scooters), and Mitsubishi Nippon Heavy Industries Ltd (which continued to build Fuso trucks). From 1950, Heavy Industries (Reorganized) made Kaiser Henry J cars under licence and from 1953 made Jeeps under licence, but it was not until 1959 that Mitsubishi built cars of its

Mitsubishi coupé de ville Model A of 1917

own design.

These were the small, four-seater, rear-engined, twin-cylinder 20hp 500. In 1962 this became the Colt 600, introducing the name which was subsequently widely used as the type name, particularly for western markets.

In 1964 the separate companies were again amalgamated as Mitsubishi Heavy Industries Ltd, with a vast product range from beer, cameras, aircraft and computers to earth moving machinery, nuclear fuels, locomo-

tives and ships. It has become one of the largest companies in the world.

The car output included Colts and the larger Debonair saloons and, from 1966, the tiny 356cc Mitsubishi Minica 360. In 1969 the Colt Galant range was introduced, with four-cylinder overhead-cam engines, alongside the pushrod engined Colts.

In 1970 the fast growing motor interests were separated again as the Mitsubishi Motors Corporation, its present day identity. By June 1971 the American Chrysler Corporation had a 35 per cent stake in Mitsubishi Motors and Galants were subsequently sold under the Dodge badge in the United States. Both output and exports increased dramatically in the 1970s until Mitsubishi made a million vehicles a year for the first time in 1979 – about a quarter of them to be sold by Chrysler.

The four-cylinder overhead-cam Lancer series was introduced in 1973, in 1.2-, 1.4- and 1.6-litre models, and the Celeste first appeared in 1975, one of about 50 models in the whole range. From 1974 the cars were available in Britain under the Colt name.

Mitsubishi 500 of 1959

Mitsubishi Colt Sapporo of 1978

By 1977 the main series comprised the Minica, the small Colt Lancer and Colt Celeste saloons, the larger Colt Galant, the up-market Colt Sigma and the big six-cylinder Debonair. In 1978 the sporty Sapporo saloon was introduced and this was sold in America with both Dodge and Plymouth nameplates. Also in 1978, Mitsubishi built its first front-wheel-drive car, the Colt Mirage, which had a clever dual-range gearbox on the 1.4-litre model.

Mitsubishi Galant Turbo of 1986

MMC phaeton of c.1902

The range stayed basically the same for the next couple of years but engine sizes grew, with the largest reaching 2.6 litres by 1980 and a 2.3-litre diesel also appeared as an option, with or without turbocharging.

In 1980 Chrysler sold its South Australia plant to Mitsubishi to produce a Colt-clone which they called the Lonsdale and which was largely intended to circumvent British import restrictions on Japanese-built cars, but the idea was less than successful and by 1984 the Australian cars had been rebadged as Mitsubishi Sigmas.

The company also began to emphasize performance from the early 1980s, with more turbocharged options from 1982, on models which in 1986 included the 540cc Minica, the Colt 1600, the Tredia 1600, the Cordia 1600, the Galant 2000, the Sapporo 2000 and the Starion coupé. Non-turbocharged models included the Debonair luxury saloon with 3-litre V6 engine. The hugely diverse range also included the four-wheel-drive Shogun 'off-road' diesel vehicle, for which a petrol-engined option was added in 1985. Mitsubishi's expansion continues with plans to build an American assembly plant in association with Chrysler. BL

MMC
GB 1897-1908

The Motor Manufacturing Co had its origins in the Great Horseless Carriage Co, one of the creations of the celebrated company promoter Harry J. Lawson who had floated the English Daimler company in 1896. He found premises for Daimler manufacture in some disused cotton mills in Coventry, soon renamed the Motor Mills, and the Great Horseless Carriage Company, floated for £750,000, was set up in another part of the Motor Mills in the summer of 1896.

No cars emerged from either factory until the following year, but by June 1897 four or five chassis were under construction according to A. C. Brown, who joined the company as an apprentice fitter. They were similar to the Daimlers being made next door, with 4hp

vertical twin engines, tube ignition and tiller steering. Engines and gearboxes in fact came from Daimler, with the bodywork and wheels being made by the Great Horseless Carriage Co.

In 1898 the firm was reorganized as the Motor Manufacturing Co, which secured as its chief engineer George Iden, formerly with the London, Brighton and South Coast Railway. The company continued with the crypto-Daimlers and also made motorcycles and tricycles powered by MMC-De Dion engines until Iden's designs were ready. These were rear-engined vehicles ranging from the 4½hp Princess two-seater to the 11hp Balmoral charabanc. They were not an unqualified success: A. C. Brown said 'I worked on most of George Iden's "Flight of Fancy" designs. Some did not go at all and some went a bit, and most of them were flops.'

In 1898 75 cars and 31 engines were made, the figures for the first 10 months of 1899 being 163 cars and 92 engines. By now all engines were made in-house, whether of Daimler, De Dion-Bouton or Iden design, together with all other components except for tyres and chains. In 1901 Alfred Bradford Burgess became company secretary; he had joined the Great Horseless Carriage Co as a clerk in 1896 and was later to manage one of the re-formed MMC companies.

The first reorganization took place in June 1902 when the complex range was reduced to three models only, with one, two or four cylinders. The cylinders were of the same dimensions and a number of other components were interchangeable. All models were now front-engined. This policy must have paid off because in 1903 MMC announced a dividend for the first time. In that year the largest model was a substantial 20/25hp four-cylinder car, on which a particularly luxurious saloon body was mounted for exhibition at the Paris Salon.

George Iden resigned in December 1903, later making cars under his own name at Parkside, Coventry. The MMC range continued with little change for 1904, but at the end of that year the company was declared bankrupt. In August 1905 the MMC part of the Motor Mills was sold to Daimler by the

receiver and MMC moved to new premises at Parkside.

There it said it would supply from stock or make to order cars of 9hp single cylinder, 12/16hp two cylinders and 10, 14/18, 20/25 and 25/35hp four cylinders. The company also announced that 'a new heavy chassis for omnibuses, lorries and vans is in course of construction'. It is doubtful whether more than a prototype was made of this heavy chassis, and some of the car models existed on paper rather than in the metal.

In 1907 MMC announced that it had made more than 4000 cars in nine years, but these were mostly past glories. The company was reorganized yet again in February 1907 as the Motor Manufacturing Co (1907) Ltd. Alfred Burgess was now manager, and he moved right away from Coventry, taking a lease on a 20,000sq ft (1850sq m) factory at Clapham, south London. There he planned to make an annual minimum of 104 of a new six-cylinder 35/45hp car.

The new works were never completed and only one chassis was made. According to a company report the car was not a success, although an employee, writing many years later, said that it was a very satisfactory job. By December 1908 the company was in voluntary liquidation. The machinery at Clapham was sold the following year.

In 1910 Burgess was involved with a Mr Wellington in the Wellington Motor and Aerial Navigation Co Ltd, 'a car manufacturing concern with aerial aspirations as an extra object'. This was still located at the Clapham works, but not a single car, still less an aeroplane, was made there, and the flotation of the company was cancelled within a month of its formation.

The name Motor Manufacturing Co Ltd survived as a new venture by Burgess which he operated at Finchley, north London, from 1912. The company supplied spare parts for MMCs and sold, it said, 'all makes of new and second hand cars'. GNG

MOBILE (GB)
see Calthorpe

MOBILE
USA 1899-1903

John Brisben Walker, the owner of *Cosmopolitan* magazine, met the twins Francis E. and Freelan Ozro Stanley as a result of their dry photographic plate business, and with help from A. L. Barber of Barber Asphalt Co he bought rights to their steam cars for $250,000. Walker and Barber formed the Locomobile Co in 1899 but, after a disagreement, Walker left to make Mobile steamers in an enlarged former Stanley plant at Tarrytown on the Hudson River, New York. The Stanley twins handled engineering and production for the Mobile.

Looking similar to the Locomobile at first, the Mobile soon evolved numerous different body styles to give a vehicle in most price ranges. The firm soon had 10 branches and 58 agencies. It was later described as the only steam car to be 'fully automatic in every detail'. Some $500,000 was spent perfecting the cars, which were said to have a million miles of travel experience behind them.

With interest growing in internal combustion-engined cars, the few orders that were available for steamers tended to go to Stanley. Shortly before Mobile halted production in 1903 the firm claimed that it had built 6000 cars and there was 'never a single accident or explosion with the boiler'. NB

MOCHET
FRANCE 1924-1957

Mochet light two-seater of 1955

Charles Mochet's chief claim to fame lies in his persistent advocacy of the pedal car as a practical means of transport for adults. He began manufacture of these at Puteaux in 1918 under the name Vélocar and built them until the end of World War II. They came into their own during the war when, in the almost complete absence of petrol, they were widely used by businessmen, doctors and priests for their daily work.

From 1924 to 1930 Mochet built a light cyclecar powered by a 346cc single-cylinder

Monica pre-production 5.9-litre saloon of 1973

engine, with chain final drive and a plywood two-seater body. Top speed was 30mph (48kph). In 1929 he brought out an even smaller car, which was a powered version of the Vélocar: this had an engine of only 142cc capacity. Evidently these did not sell very well, and from 1930 until 1951 he concentrated on the Vélocar.

This was quite a substantial machine, with side-by-side seating for two adults and a boot said to be suitable for carrying luggage or children! Features included independent front suspension, four speeds by *derailleur* gear, and electric lighting. Empty weight of a Vélocar was about 110lb (50kg).

In 1951 Mochet returned to powered vehicles with the Vélocar Type K, a very simple two-seater powered by a 100cc single-cylinder Ydral engine. It rode on bicycle wheels, with brakes only at the rear. It grew into the Type CM Luxe with 125cc engine which in 1955 became the CM125Y, a four-seater rolltop convertible with top speed of 37mph (60kph).

For a while Mochet was able to sell these little cars at the rate of 40 a month, one of their attractions being that they required no driving licence. He also made a prototype sports car with 750cc CEME flat twin engine in 1953, and built a few lightweight motorcycles between 1950 and 1955. All production ended in 1957. GNG

MOLINE/MOLINE KNIGHT, R & V KNIGHT
USA 1904-1924

The Moline Automobile Co of East Moline, Illinois, was formed in 1903 and began to produce two- and four-cylinder high-wheelers a year later. Billed as 'the car of unfailing service' in 1912, when it had an unusually long-stroke engine but more conventional wheel size, the Moline began to use Knight sleeve-valve engines in 1914. By then the company was promoting its vehicles as 'cars for discriminating connoisseurs'. In 1914 one

ran continuously for a fortnight.

For 1919 the cars were renamed R & V Knight in recognition of Moline's partners, Root and Vandervoort Engineering Co, which had made engines since 1899 and whose speciality had become Knight-licensed engines. The company had supplied samples to AEC and Daimler for lorries in 1915 and subsequently built engines for the Chicago-built Highway Knight as well as overhead-valve units for Stephens.

Production of R & V's high-quality cars at East Moline reached a peak of 750 a year. In 1922 part of the works was leased to General Motors for Yellow engines. R & V cars were discontinued in 1924. The Moline name was also used for commercial vehicles by Moline Plow Co, which acquired Root and Vandervoort and the maker of Stephens cars in 1920. NB

MONICA
FRANCE 1973-1975

The French-built American-engined Monica started life as a prototype Deep Sanderson car, designed and built in Britain by Chris Lawrence and originally intended to use his development of the Martin V8 racing engine. French industrialist Jean Tastevin was the man who turned the Deep Sanderson into the Monica, which was named after his wife, Monique.

Tastevin ran the Compagnie Française des Produits Métallurgiques in Balbigny, Loire, which made rolling stock for the French railways. Tastevin planned a prestige car and in 1967 approached Lawrence with an interest in the twin-cam V8, which could be made to fall conveniently within the French 2.8-litre taxation class and which Lawrence had shown at the 1967 Racing Car Show in London. The engine was based on Ted Martin's earlier design for the Pearce-Martin Formula 1 car and was to be produced under licence by Coventry-Victor.

Initially Lawrence was to supply Tastevin

with engines for a car to be designed in France, but by late 1967 he had been commissioned to design a complete car. Dropping the V8 idea, it was originally to have been a Triumph-powered two-seater, but Lawrence then interested Tastevin in his four-door Deep Sanderson prototype which used a 3-litre version of the Martin V8.

Lawrence eventually built six prototypes using the Martin engines made by Coventry-Victor and five-speed ZF gearboxes, with several changes in body design. A batch of engines had already been ordered with a view to production by 1972 when Tastevin again changed his mind – this time in favour of a Chrysler V8 and Torqueflite automatic transmission.

The first cars were built by Lawrence in London. The prototype bodies were built mainly in aluminium but steel was specified for the production cars. Production was then moved to Balbigny. The car made its first public appearance at the Paris Salon in 1972 but the final version did not appear until the Geneva Show.

When pilot production began in 1973 the car had a 310bhp 5.9-litre Chrysler V8 with five-speed ZF gearbox. As the Monica 590 saloon it was in full production by 1974 at a rate of one or two cars a week and sold at almost £14,000. A Torqueflite automatic version was offered shortly after, with the option of a two-speed final drive, based on the Rover 3500 differential with an extra gear cluster on the nose and a second gear lever in the car.

The Monica was actually quite a good car but it was very badly timed for it coincided with the arrival of the mid-1970s oil crisis. Indeed, Tastevin may have been better sticking with his first thoughts. In 1975, after just

38 Monicas had been built, Tastevin abandoned the project. The chassis tooling is thought to have gone to Ligier and rumours that the Monica might be revived by Panther in Britain came to nothing as that company had enough problems of its own. BL

MONROE
USA 1915-1924

Founded in 1913 next to the Buick plant in Flint, Michigan, with $250,000 capital, the Monroe Motor Co began to deliver cheap, assembled cars in January 1915 that had Mason or Sterling engines. W. C. Durant was vice-president of the company and its cars were sold through Chevrolet outlets. Output for 1915 was planned at 3500. The firm had close ties with Chevrolet and built axles for that company and probably 490 bodywork too.

The payroll increased from 130 to 700 in 1916, when capital grew to $1 million and the Port Huron Construction Co was acquired so that the firm could make its own engines. In May 1916 land was bought in Pontiac for expansion and the adjoining former Welch factory utilized.

For 1916 sales independent of Chevrolet were handled by sales manager L. E. Haase. Output was planned at 2000 small cars and 5000 larger tourers, all of which could have cloverleaf seating. About 3500 were actually built that year. Sedans were added in 1917.

In 1917-18 the Monroe Motor Co was purchased by the William Small Co, the Chevrolet dealer of Indianapolis, Indiana, which had an interest in the Frontenac Motor Co that

had built racing cars for Louis Chevrolet since 1915. Monroe production was then switched to Indianapolis. Tourer and speedster Monroes were each offered at $1195. Most components were bought-in, but the four-cylinder engines were built by Small.

In 1923 the Stratton Motors Corporation of Indianapolis acquired control of Monroe. Frank B. Stratton had previously been sales manager of Grant and had raised finance to produce his own four-cylinder car that year. He was in difficulties almost immediately, however, and the Premier Motor Corporation of Indianapolis then stepped in. Premier gave the Monroe a new radiator shape and produced the cars until 1924; the final examples were known as Premier Model Bs. NB

MONTEVERDI/MBM
SWITZERLAND 1959-1984

Born in 1934, Peter Monteverdi was a former racing driver who ran a large BMW dealership in Basle which he had taken over after his father's death. He had been apprenticed as a mechanic to the Saurer company and when he was 17 he built a Fiat-engined racing special. From 1959 he built his own MBM racing cars, including about 12 DKW-engined FJ cars, two series of Ford-powered FJ cars, an OSCA-engined sports two-seater and, in 1962, a Ford-powered GT coupé.

He was forced to retire from racing after a bad accident and in 1967 he began to produce small numbers of a two-seater GT car built largely to his own designs by his own mechanics in his BMW workshops. The first car, the 375S, used mostly bought-in parts,

Monteverdi 375L of 1968

including a massive square-tube chassis built to Monteverdi's designs by a local contractor; a 375bhp 7.2-litre Chrysler V8 with Torqueflite automatic transmission was standard. The 375S and 400bhp 400SS variant had bodies designed by Frua and built by Fissore in Turin for assembly in Basle.

The long-wheelbase 2+2 375L was added in 1968 and Monteverdi's steady sales included some exports. In 1971 he introduced the ambitious mid-engined 450SS Hai, with the Chrysler engine and Fissore body format as before, but with a ZF manual gearbox. This 160mph (257kph) car was expensive and very short-lived, as was a four-door four-seat saloon, the 375/4, introduced in 1972 on a lengthened chassis.

Sales in general were slowed drastically by the early 1970s fuel crisis and as the company struggled to meet new American legislation, production virtually stopped in 1974 and 1975. During this time the company was heavily subsidized by the continuing BMW dealership and only thus did it survive to take a new direction from the late 1970s. It did so with the introduction in 1976 of the Safari, a luxurious four-wheel-drive Range Rover type vehicle, with a choice of Chrysler V8s of up to 7.2 litres and 120mph (193kph) performance.

In 1977 Monteverdi introduced the Chrysler-engined Sierra saloon, which was also available very briefly, and to special order only, in convertible form as the Palm Beach. The Sahara was another short-lived four-wheel-drive model, very similar to the Safari but with International Scout running gear. By 1981 only the standard Safari and the Sierra were listed and Monteverdi's 170 employees built just 350 cars.

In 1983 Monteverdi replaced the Sierra with the Mercedes-based Tiara, a super-luxury saloon with a choice of 3.8- or 4.9-litre V8s and a 145mph (233kph) top speed. By this time it was the only model offered but it was no longer built after 1984. BL

MOON
USA 1905-1930

The ancestor of the Moon Motor Car Co was the Moon Brothers Carriage Co, founded in St Louis, Missouri, in 1873. Twenty years later one of the brothers struck out on his own, making buggies which were cheaper and sold in larger quantities than carriages. He called his company the Joseph W. Moon Buggy Co, and as such it flourished well into the first decade of the 20th century. From 1899 to 1904 its sales manager was J. J. Cole, who later made buggies and cars under his own name.

In 1905 Joseph Moon erected a new factory to make motor cars, forming the Moon Motor Car Co. The buggy company was continued, but in a subsidiary role to the new firm.

The first Moon car was a conventional machine with a four-cylinder Rutenber engine and shaft drive. It was designed by Louis P. Mooers, who had been with Peerless at Cleveland and who was to be responsible for a number of improvements to Moon design over the next few years. These included an arched rear axle to provide better ground clearance, a shaft-driven overhead camshaft and a four-speed gearbox with direct drive in third, top being an overdrive. All these features appeared on 1907-9 Moons. In 1908 Moons were sold in the New York area by Hollander and Tangemann under the name Hol-Tan.

By 1912 Moon was established as a quality car in the upper middle price bracket, prices running as high as $3750. However, cheaper models were also offered.

From 1914 Moon ceased to make its own engines, buying instead from Continental, and by 1920 the former carriage building company was even buying its bodies from outside, chiefly from Ames and Central Manufacturing Co. Moon became increasingly an assembled car, with Borg and Beck clutch, Brown-Lipe or Warner transmissions, Parish and Bingham frames and so on.

Four-cylinder cars were no longer made after 1915, but Moon offered a 1½-ton chain-drive truck with four-cylinder engine and solid tyres from 1914 to 1917. This was built in a separate factory owned by the Joseph W. Moon Buggy Co.

In 1915 production was about 1000 cars, but this rose to 3195 in 1921. Joseph Moon died in 1919 and was replaced by his son-in-law Stewart McDonald, vice-president since 1907, who 'borrowed' the Rolls-Royce style of radiator for that season's Moons. Known as the Victory Six, the new Moon was made in a variety of attractive colours, and the sportier models featured step plates instead of running boards.

Under McDonald's leadership sales climbed dramatically to around 7500 in 1922, 10,000 in 1923 and 12,964 in 1925, the high water mark for Moon. Two sizes of Continental engine were used in the early 1920s Moons, the 3.2-litre 6Y and the 4.2-litre 8R.

Moon 30/35 roadster of 1911

Moretti coupé of 1976

In 1925 McDonald borrowed from Europe again, choosing the Belgian Minerva radiator design for his new straight-eight, which was marketed as a separate line under the name Diana (Goddess of the Moon). Appropriately for a car named after the Goddess of the Amazons, the Diana was particularly aimed at women motorists, whom McDonald claimed outnumbered men by 15 to four when it came to buying Dianas. Advertising stressed the easy steering and balloon tyres, as well as the car's fleet appearance.

It was powered by a 4-litre Continental 12-Z specially made for Moon, which gave it a top speed of 77mph (124kph). Prices were in the $1595 to $2895 bracket, with a seldom-seen town car costing $5000.

The Diana was introduced in June 1925 as a 1926 model. Early examples suffered from a number of problems, particularly in the cooling system, and a lot of engines had to be replaced, which cannot have helped Moon's already troubled finances.

Despite 1925's record sales, the modest 1926 profit of $125,421 was wiped out by the repayment to the government of an overdue war loan, and the company ended the year with a net loss of $496,638. It was never to make a profit again, and sales in 1927 slumped to 5276 for Moon and Diana combined. An economy model, the 3-litre Jubilee 6-60, was introduced for 1927 at $995.

In 1928 McDonald was succeeded as president by Carl W. Burst, who had started in the machine shop in 1909 and had risen to vice-president by 1925. His grandson, Carl W. Burst III, is one of the world's leading collectors of Moon cars.

The Diana was dropped for 1928 and the leftover engines were used in the first few Aerotype Eights, Moon's top of the line offering that year. Styled by Howard Darrin for a $3000 fee for three days' work the Aerotype was made in a variety of body styles. Once supplies of the Diana's engine had been used up a larger straight-eight Continental, the 4.4-litre 15-S, powered the Aerotype. This was

backed up by the Jubilee 6-60 and an intermediate 6-72, but Moon sales were flagging, in contrast to the industry as a whole.

A new name was launched in January 1929, the Windsor White Prince. Named after Britain's popular Prince of Wales, the Windsor was really no more than a re-badged and slightly restyled Aerotype Eight and did nothing to help Moon's sales. Nevertheless, Burst and his team had so much confidence in the name that in April 1929 they renamed the Moon 6-72 the Windsor 6-72, which marked the end of Moon as the name of a car. The first Windsor Eights carried the Prince of Wales' coat of arms of three white feathers on their radiator badges, but by mid-year these had been replaced as a result of protests from Buckingham Palace.

Total production for 1929 was only 1333 cars, but at the end of the year there came on the scene company promoter Archie M. Andrews who was looking for a factory to make his Ruxton front-wheel-drive car. Although fiercely opposed by Carl Burst and other Moon executives, Andrews gained control of Moon by April 1930 and put in the Ruxton's designer William Muller as president. The arrangement was that the Moon plant would assemble Ruxtons, using Continental engines, transmissions built by Kissel, and bodies from Kissel, Budd or Baker-Raulang.

Ruxton production began at St Louis in June 1930, and about 450 cars had been assembled when Kissel went into voluntary receivership in September. The supply of bodies and transmissions ceased and Moon went into receivership itself, closing its doors on 10 November 1930.

The receiver managed to assemble 15 more Ruxtons and the Moon plant was eventually sold for $86,000 in 1935. The final distribution of assets was delayed by legal wranglings until 1968, when $25,938 was paid against creditors' claims of $350,588. This represented a rate of just over seven cents in the dollar. GNG

MORETTI
ITALY 1945 to date

Giovanni Moretti was born in Reggio Emilia in 1904 and began work at the age of eight upon his father's death. When he was 16 he moved to Turin and got work with the makers of Ladetto & Blatto motorcycles, rising to be head mechanic.

In 1925 he started his own workshop in Turin and made racing motorcycle engines. He then produced more than 1000 three-wheeler vans and pickups, some with electric motors. A four-wheel car had been built in 1928 but serious production at Fabbrica Automobili Moretti did not begin until 1945. In that year a two-cylinder 250cc La Cita light car was developed and was soon uprated to 350cc. By 1950 four-cylinder 600cc and 750cc versions had been produced. Total sales of all models by then were 250.

There followed an extensive range of cars, including 750cc double-overhead cam racing/sports types and 1200cc GTs, and light commercials. Virtually all components were made in-house. Cars were sold in the United States against 50 per cent deposits and sales leaflets were printed in wonderfully confused English.

From the mid-1950s increasing emphasis was placed on coachwork. Just 116 complete cars were made in 1958, car production being phased out over the next three years.

Fiat gave Moretti contracts to build specials and conversions of existing cars and vans in its range. New 86,000sq ft (8000sq m) premises with 200 workers were occupied in 1958. The firm had Stablimenti Carrozzeria added to its title in 1962.

Standard productions currently include on/off road 'fun' cars sold through the Fiat dealer network. Most are drophead versions of Fiat saloons, particularly the Uno and Regata. The business is now run by Giovanni Moretti's sons, Gianny and Sergio. NB

MORGAN
GB 1910 to date

Although his grandfather, and his father, the Revd Prebendary H. G. Morgan, were both vicars in the village of Stoke Lacey in Herefordshire, H. F. S. Morgan chose not to work for the church but to design one of the most individual of all British cars, the Morgan.

H.F.S., as he was invariably known, was born in 1884 and from 1897 attended Marlborough public school. Soon after, he moved to Crystal Palace Engineering College, which was more appropriate to his mechanical bent. He was always encouraged by his father, who saw no harm in H.F.S. not becoming a preacher and in fact became a staunch supporter and advocate of his son's cars. His support continued undiminished until H.G's death in November 1936.

H.F.S. was apprenticed at Swindon to the chief engineer of the Great Western Railway, a position arranged by his father. At the end of his training as a mechanical engineer he declined a job with the railway in order to pursue his own interests, and in 1906 he opened a garage in Malvern Link, Worcestershire. He sold Darracqs and Wolseleys and briefly ran a public bus service between Malvern and nearby Worcester, with a Wolseley bus. He then started a hire-car service with a friend but he was already more interested in experimenting with vehicles to his own design.

In 1908 he built a motorcycle, with a 7hp vee-twin Peugeot engine, but apparently did not like two wheels and began to plan a car with three – although still taking advantage of the tax concessions for light weight. Between 1908 and 1909, working in the engineering shop at nearby Malvern College and with the help of Mr Stephenson-Peach, an engineering teacher at the college, H.F.S. built a light, single-seater three-wheeler around the Peugeot engine. It set the pattern for all later Morgans and some of its design features are recognizable in the Morgans of today.

The vee-twin engine was mounted at the front and drove the single rear wheel via a propshaft running through a large tube which was the main chassis element. Two-speed transmission, without reverse, was provided by dog clutches and two secondary chain drives of different ratios. The front suspension was independent, by sliding coil-sprung pillars on each end of a beam axle. It was one of the first independent front suspension systems to be used anywhere and a similar type is still used by Morgans today. Steering was by tiller and the car had no bodywork as such but it aroused sufficient interest for H.F.S. to think of building similar cars for sale.

In 1910, with £3000 from his father, he built and equipped a small factory in Malvern Link to start limited production as the Morgan Motor Co Ltd. He showed his first two 961cc JAP-engined production cars at the Olympia Motor Cycle Show in November 1910, but

334

their single seats limited their appeal and only four orders were taken. He developed a two-seater in 1911 and Harrods store became the first Morgan agency.

As demand increased, Morgan expanded the factory and gave up his garage business. In 1912 the company showed a small profit and continued to be increasingly profitable up to the outbreak of World War I, when production was approaching 1000 cars a year. Sales were helped by numerous successes in racing and trials, the most important being a win in the French Cyclecar Grand Prix at Amiens and a Gold Medal in the Six-Day Trial, both in 1913.

Just before the war Morgan launched a racing model based on the Grand Prix chassis with a MAG engine and other new models, including a four-seater in 1915, were even developed during the war. Also in 1915 Morgan built a prototype four-wheeler but only three-wheelers were sold. Limited production continued alongside war work, which mostly involved shells and munitions. Most wartime output was exported, a condition imposed on supply of raw materials.

The company grew during the war and was able to resume full production, at up to 15 cars a week, soon after, limited only by a shortage of engines. Morgan acquired additional assembly space in 1919 in Pickersleigh

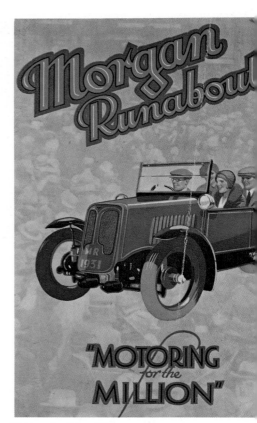

Morgan advertising, 1931

Morgan Plus 8 of 1983

Road; full production was moved there in 1923 and the factory is still in use.

A four-seater, later to be known as the Family model, was officially available from 1919. Later that year Morgan granted a licence to Darmont et Badelogue in Courbevoie, which began production of a French version as the Darmont with output of several hundred cars a year.

The three-wheelers continued to sell well and to win every kind of competition and while basically changing very little they gained more powerful vee-twin engines, neater bodywork, front-wheel brakes, electric starting, geared-down steering and other niceties. Engine options over the years included Anzani, Precision and Blackburne vee-twins as well as the popular JAP. Prices fell steadily, in line with the market in

Morgan Grand Prix of 1913

Morris Oxford 'Bullnose' two-seater of 1913

Morris Cowley convertible of 1928

general, until the cheapest Standard Family model was available for just £75 in 1931.

Three-wheelers were banned from racing after an accident in 1924, but in 1927 the Morgan Club was reorganized as the Cyclecar Club and by running competitions open to all cyclecars managed to re-establish the three-wheeler in racing – with endless successes for the marque. In 1929 Gwenda Hawkes set a kilometre class record of over 115mph (185kph) with her Morgan.

The three-wheeler range now covered everything from racing models to four-seater tourers. From November 1933 a three-wheeler was also available with a four-cylinder Ford 8hp engine, alongside the JAP and recently introduced Matchless twins. In 1935 Morgan reluctantly dropped the popular but short-supply JAP engine and thereafter the Matchless was the standard twin.

In December 1935 Morgan announced its first four-wheeler, and not a moment too soon as sales of three-wheelers had started a dramatic decline, partly because of ever-cheaper four-wheeled competition and partly because of the general state of the economy. The new 4/4 used an 1122cc Coventry-Climax engine and although not as fast as many of the three-wheelers it soon began to sell well. It too was built under licence in France, by Morgan agent Stewart Sandford in Paris.

A fire at the factory in October failed to stop production for very long but World War II did bring a halt, shortly after a 1267cc engine built specially for Morgan by Standard had been introduced in the 4/4. During the war, part of the factory was leased to Standard while Morgan mostly machined aircraft parts.

The factory ended the war undamaged and very well equipped. A few cars were built from spares in 1945 but production did not start properly until late 1946, and then almost entirely for export, especially to the United States. There was little export market for the three-wheelers, however, as other countries did not offer such tax concessions as Britain, and in February 1952 the Morgan three-wheeler era ended.

The staple was now the Plus 4, which had replaced the 4/4 in 1950 and used a 2088cc

Standard Vanguard engine, which gave excellent performance. The connection with Standard led to an offer from that company to buy Morgan in 1954, but it was resisted – as was a more tentative offer from Rover in 1966.

In 1955 Morgan reintroduced the 4/4, with a Ford 10 engine, as a cheaper but much slower alternative to the Plus 4, which now used Triumph TR2 engines but was usually in short supply. These two models, in two- and four-seater variants, were the basis of the range up to 1968, the Plus 4 moving through Triumph's TR3 to TR4 engines and the 4/4 keeping pace with Ford developments up to the 1600GT engine.

Sadly, H.F.S. died in June 1959, just before Morgan's 50th anniversary. The company was left in trust to his four daughters and son, Peter, who took over after some financial reorganization.

In 1962 Morgan scored perhaps the most prestigious of all its racing results when tuning specialist Chris Lawrence scored a remarkable class win at Le Mans. It was Morgan's last major international success and came at a time when the company was struggling somewhat, after American sales had slumped. In 1964 Morgan built the Plus 4 Plus, which had a modern coupé shell on a Plus 4 chassis. Only 50 were built, but they reminded the press that Morgan still existed.

From 1966 Morgan was unable to sell cars in the USA at all, because of legislation, and that as much as anything prompted the 125mph (200kph) Plus 8. This replaced the Plus 4 in August 1968 and its Buick-based 3.5-litre Rover V8 allowed Morgan to return, successfully, to the US market from 1969.

This model, which has used a fuel injected version of the engine since 1984 and offered the Vitesse engine as an option since late in that year, continues as top of the Morgan range, which still includes two- and four-seater versions of the 4/4 with the 1600 Ford engine, and the 2-litre Plus 4, again with Ford engine options. Fiat engines were used in the 4/4 and Plus 4 from 1982 to 1985. Morgan built 420 cars in 1985 and still has one of the longest waiting lists of any motor manufacturer in the world. BL

MORRIS
GB 1912-1983

William Richard Morris was born in Worcester in 1877. When he was three years old his family moved to Cowley, near Oxford, where his father became a farm bailiff. In 1893, at the age of 15½, he joined Parkers, a leading cycle agent in Oxford, but left nine months later because his employer refused to increase his wages from five to six shillings a week.

He then set up on his own as a cycle repairer and soon began to assemble bicycles from pieces provided by the many components suppliers who catered to the trade. His first machine was bought by the rector of St Clements, Oxford, and trade soon improved so much that Morris rented two premises in Oxford.

In 1900 he built a motorcycle, and three years later began production of these and forecars, with financial backing from a local businessman, F. G. Barton, and a wealthy undergraduate. The partnership was dissolved in 1905, and for the next seven years Morris earned his living by selling bicycles and cars, and operating a hire car and taxi service.

In 1910 he began to draw up plans for a light car which could be produced in quantity at a reasonable price by buying as many components as possible from well-known suppliers. He obtained financial support from the Earl of Macclesfield to the tune of £4000 and in August 1912 formed WRM Motors Ltd.

A factory was acquired at Cowley in an old military college which had formerly been Hurst's Grammar School, where Morris's father had been educated. The prototype Morris Oxford car was assembled in its maker's Oxford premises in Longwall Street, but all production cars were made at Cowley.

The Morris Oxford had a 1018cc four-cylinder T-head engine made by White & Poppe of Coventry to Morris's specifications. The gearbox was also by White & Poppe while the axles and steering came from E. G. Wrigley of

Birmingham. The two-seater bodies were made by Raworth of Oxford, wheels were from Sankey and lighting from Powell & Hanmer. The rounded radiator, originally nicknamed the 'Bulletnose' because of its resemblance to a 0.303 rifle bullet, and later modified to 'Bullnose', was made by Docherty of Coventry. It is hard to think of a single component that was not bought in, but this was Morris's way of doing things, an approach he shared with Henry Ford in his early days.

The Oxford was announced in the press in October 1912, but the first car was not ready until March 1913. By the end of the year 393 had been sold, and in 1914, when the range included drophead coupé, sports and delivery van bodies as well as the original two-seater, production reached 909.

The advent of World War I inevitably caused a drop in output, with the figures for 1915 being 159, for 1916 thirteen and for 1917 only one. Most of these were assembled from parts made before the war. The Morris factory was devoted mainly to the production of hand grenades, howitzer bomb cases and, from 1916, mine sinkers.

Just after war broke out Morris had travelled to the United States to seek cheaper components for a new four-seater car to supplement the Oxford. White & Poppe could not quote less than £50 each for a 1½-litre engine and gearbox, but the Continental Motor Manufacturing Co of Detroit quoted only £18 for such an engine. A gearbox could be obtained from the Detroit Gear & Machine Co for £8.50, and axles and steering gear for £16.25. Morris ordered 3000 engines and other components from Detroit, but half of the engines were lost at sea, and the necessity to devote most of the factory space to war production meant that not more than 1344 Cowleys were made between September 1915 and 1918.

After the war the supply of Continental engines ended, as the American company could find no customers among their own countrymen for such a small unit, and it was not economic to make it for Morris alone. Luckily an alternative engine-maker was soon found in the shape of Hotchkiss, the Coventry branch of the French armaments firm, which had a well equipped factory but no work at the end of hostilities. Hotchkiss agreed to make a copy of the Continental engine, and deliveries began in July 1919. Morris decided on a two-model policy, the basic Cowley and a better-equipped car to be called the Oxford and selling for £50 more.

In mid-1919 WRM Motors Ltd was liquidated as a means of ending two onerous agency contracts, and Morris Motors Ltd was formed in its place. The new company was capitalized at £150,000, with Morris being allotted £75,000 in consideration of the net assets of WRM Motors. Among other backers, the Earl of Macclesfield took £25,000 worth of shares.

Morris Motors lost £8000 in its first year of

Morris Eight saloon of c.1935

trading, and by February 1921 Morris was seriously alarmed at the large stockpile of unsold cars. This was due to rapidly escalating prices, from £295 for a Cowley two-seater in 1919 to £465 in October 1920. He then took the bold step of cutting prices even though costs were still rising. The two-seater's price tag went down to £385, and the four-seater from £525 to £425.

This strategy worked better than even Morris had hoped; sales shot up from 68 cars in January to 244 in February and 377 in March. Other manufacturers cut their prices by an average of 17 per cent at the 1921 Motor Show in October, but Morris cut still further, so that the Cowley was 35 per cent cheaper than it had been in February.

Total sales in 1921 were 3077 cars, rising to 6937 in 1922, 20,024 in 1923 and 32,939 in 1924. The best year for the 'Bullnose' cars was 1925, with 54,151 sales, which put Morris ahead of all other British manufacturers.

During the 1920s Morris followed the example of Ford and Buick in buying up his suppliers. Hollick and Pratt of Coventry, which had supplied bodywork, was acquired for £100,000 and moved to Cowley. L. W. Pratt became deputy managing director of Morris, followed by E. H. Blake from Dunlop. Other suppliers arrived to support Morris in his isolated position 50 miles (80km) from Coventry and Birmingham. They included Doherty (later Osberton) Radiators, which occupied a former skating rink bought by W. R. Morris in Oxford. Fisher and Ludlow handled pressings locally, although chassis, which had earlier arrived from Belgium, came from Rubery Owen in Darlaston. The SU carburettor firm was bought in 1926 for £100,000 and moved from London in the early 1930s to the new Morris-Commercial factory in part of the Wolseley works.

Morris bought the Hotchkiss engine firm in Coventry for £350,000 in 1923 as well as Wrigleys in Birmingham for £213,000, the latter becoming Morris-Commercial Cars Ltd in 1923 under managing director W. Cannell, and the first British owned mass-producer of trucks (2500 in 1924 and over 10,000 in 1928).

Morris Ten-Four Series M saloon of 1939

It remained in W. R. Morris's personal ownership until being bought by Morris Motors in 1936, as did Morris Industries Ltd, formed in 1927 to hold the component subsidiaries.

Few changes were made to the Cowleys and Oxfords up to 1926. The latter's engine was increased to 1802cc in 1923 when it was an optional alteration to the 1548cc unit; it was standardized in 1924. The Oxford acquired front wheel brakes in 1925, and these were optional on the Cowley a year later, and standardized on all models in 1929.

In September 1926 came the new models characterized by the flat radiator which has led them to be called the 'Flatnose' in contrast to the 'Bullnose'. They were considerably modified in frame and suspension, although the engine, gearbox and rear axle remained unchanged.

In 1927 Morris acquired the Wolseley company for £730,000, and the latter's overhead camshaft layout began to be seen on the Morris range, with the 2½-litre six-cylinder Six of 1928 and the 847cc four-cylinder Minor of 1929.

The Minor was Morris's long delayed answer to Herbert Austin's Seven. It never sold as well as its rival, and the basic £100 two-seater with side-valve engine introduced in 1931 lasted for only three seasons. Other side-valve Minors followed, and after 1932 they superseded the overhead-camshaft models. Total production of Minors between late 1928 and 1934 was 39,083 overhead-camshaft models and 47,227 with side-valve engines. In contrast the Minor's successor, the Morris Eight, sold 440,000 cars in four seasons.

In the early 1930s a bewildering variety of Morris cars was made, including the old 11.9hp Cowley (up to 1934), the 1938cc six-cylinder Morris Major, renamed Cowley Six in 1934 and Fifteen Six in 1935, the side-valve Oxford Six and overhead-cam Isis Six, a Ten-Four and Ten-Six, and the large 3486cc six-cylinder Twenty Five. Sales fell from 63,000 in 1929 to 44,000 in 1933.

A rescue came in the simplified range of 1935 onwards, made after a £300,000 modernization of the factory. The best-selling model was the 918cc side-valve Eight, which was made as a two- or four-door saloon or open tourer, and sold for between £118 and £142 10s.

The completely new engine was developed under the leadership of Leonard Lord who had been involved in the reorganization of Wolseley after 1927, and was made managing director of Morris in 1933. (Three years later he left when his request for a share of the profits was refused by Morris. In 1938 he joined Austin and in the post-war years he masterminded the merger of Austin and Morris into the British Motor Corporation, was knighted in 1954, and created Baron Lambury in 1962.)

The Morris Eight was to some extent modelled on the Model Y 8hp Ford, to which it was an obvious rival, and its lines were closely copied by Singer on the Bantam saloon.

The Series II 10 and 12hp models with fast-back bodies were launched in May 1935, soon followed by 16, 18, 21 and 25hp sixes with similar styling. Production for the year reached almost 100,000 and profits exceeded £1 million for the first time since 1930, although they had never fallen below £500,000 in the intervening years.

For 1938 came the Series III models, with pushrod overhead-valve engines and Easicleen wheels in place of the wire wheels of the Series II. The range was now smaller, Ten-Four, Twelve-Four, Fourteen-Six and Twenty-Five, as well as the side-valve Eight which had become a Series II.

Further new models came in the shape of the integral construction Series M Ten saloon in August 1938, followed two months later by the rebodied Series E Eight, with streamlined radiator grille, headlamps faired into the wings and no running boards. Both these models were revived in the post-war period and kept the company going until the arrival of the new Minor, Oxford and Six in 1948. The Series M Ten was built in India from 1946 as the Hindustan, and later Morris models are still produced there.

William Morris became a baronet in 1929, a Baron in 1934 and Viscount Nuffield in 1938. He had 'gone public' in 1926, when Morris Motors was quoted on the Stock Ex-change at £5 million, £2 million of which was held by Morris himself. Over the next 20 years he increased this many times, but he was a great philanthropist, and during his lifetime he is estimated to have given away £30 million, particularly to hospitals, higher education for the underprivileged, and servicemen's welfare.

The one millionth Morris car was made in May 1939, making Cowley the first British factory to build a million cars. Austin, although it started seven years before Morris, did not reach the magic figure until 1946.

The Nuffield Organization was a mass-producer of armaments during World War II, including trucks (military types made between 1934 and 1945 totalled 80,000), tanks, Bren gun carriers (22,000 made by Wolseley), aero engines, Bofors guns (appropriately made in the old Hotchkiss works) and aircraft, mostly under Vickers control at Castle Bromwich, which became the Fisher & Ludlow bodyworks after the war.

Post-war production of the Series E and M saloons (the Series E tourer was not revived) began in September 1945 and continued for three years until they were replaced by the Minor, Oxford and Six.

The best known and longest lived of these was the Minor, designed by Alec Issigonis, with detail transmission work by C. M. Van Eugen who had been with Lea-Francis. It had the familiar 918cc side-valve engine, but the integral construction body, rack-and-pinion steering and torsion bar independent front suspension were completely new, and provided handling previously unknown in a popular British light car. It was thought at Cowley that the Minor might run until 1952, but the last one was not delivered until April 1971, after more than 1.5 million had been made.

The 1½-litre side-valve Oxford and 2.2-litre overhead-cam Six were also of integral construction and with independent front suspension, and had their equivalent Wolseley models in the 4/50 and 6/80.

The two millionth Morris was delivered in October 1951, and in February 1952 the Nuffield Organization merged with the Austin Motor Co to form the British Motor Corporation. Lord Nuffield was the first chairman of the Corporation, but resigned after six months in favour of his old colleague and head of Austin, Leonard Lord.

Nuffield went into virtual retirement after that, and died in 1963. He left no children, but although his name is no longer perpetuated in the motor industry, it continues in Nuffield College, Oxford, and the Nuffield Nursing Homes run by the British United Provident Association which he helped to set up in 1947. Tractors made by Nuffield Mechanisation Ltd carried his name from 1948 to 1969, when they were renamed Leyland.

The most important result of the Austin merger was that Morris cars received Austin engines. In particular the 803cc overhead-valve Austin A30 unit powered the Minor from

Morris Minor 1000 saloon of 1956

Morris 1100 Mark II saloon of 1968

Morris Marina 1700HL saloon of 1979

1953 to 1956, when the 948cc Austin A35 engine was adopted on the Minor 1000. The Oxford's side-valve engine was replaced by a 1489cc overhead-valve Austin unit in 1954, and when the Pininfarina-styled Series V Oxford arrived in 1959 it shared a body and engine with the Austin Cambridge.

During the 1960s all new Morris models had their equivalents in the ranges of Austin and other BMC marques, MG, Riley and Wolseley. These included the Issigonis-designed Mini, which was launched as the Morris Mini Minor in 1959, the 1100, 1300 and 1800. Details of these cars and of the transition from BMC to BMH and then British Leyland can be found under Austin and Leyland.

The last specifically Morris car was the Marina, introduced in 1971. This was a conventional four-door saloon with rear wheel drive, Minor-type independent front suspension and leaf spring rear suspension. The head of British Leyland, Lord Stokes, had decided that the innovative front-wheel-drive cars should all be Austins, while the conventional Morris Marina would cater for the more conservative customer, especially fleet operators. The millionth Marina was delivered in October 1978, and a further 250,000 were built before it was succeeded in July 1980 by what was to be the last Morris car, the Ital.

This was a face-lifted Marina with styling by the Italian company Ital Design, and was made in saloon, coupé and estate forms until December 1983 when the Morris name was discontinued. Ironically the Itals were made at the Austin factory in Longbridge, whereas Cowley had become the base for Austin-Rover Ltd.

In 1984 the Ital dies and production line were sold to Pakistan, where the car is to have a new lease of life, although it will still be under the name Ital. GNG/NB

MORRIS LÉON BOLLÉE
see Léon Bollée

MORRISS-LONDON
see Crow-Elkhart

Mors tourer of c.1911

MORS
FRANCE 1895-1925

In 1851 a M. Mirand set up a company in Paris to make artificial flowers, with paper-wrapped wire stems. M. Mirand later adapted his wrapping machinery to make insulated electrical wiring and began to make other electrical equipment including telegraphs, railway signalling equipment, instruments and gauges. In 1874 the company was taken over by Louis Mors and in 1880 control passed to his sons, Louis and Émile, formerly electrical engineering students.

In 1886 they employed a 22-year-old draughtsman, Henri Brasier, who had previously worked for the Orléans railway company. In 1887 Mors began to build small boats and oil-fired steam tricycles to Brasier's designs.

From 1892 to 1893 Mors made small petrol-engined railway trucks then, in 1895, built a petrol-engined car distinguished by coil and dynamo electrical ignition developed by Émile. In 1897 the company began to produce the belt-drive V4 rear-engined cars in series and also started racing, with Émile finishing seventh in a two-seater in the Paris-Dieppe race. His own career ended with an accident the following year, but Mors cars continued to be one of the first serious challengers to the racing Panhards, winning such races as the 1901 Paris-Bordeaux and Paris-Berlin races and, most prestigious of all, the 1903 Paris-Madrid, driven by Gabriel. That, however, was the last big racing success and Mors gave up competing altogether in 1908.

The production cars developed alongside the racers. In January 1898 the company became known as the Société d'Électricité et d'Automobiles Mors, with works in Paris and capital of 2 million francs, a quarter of it held by Émile. That year the workforce numbered about 200 and the output was about 200 cars.

Around the turn of the century Mors experimented with petrol-electric cars and a magnetic clutch but continued to sell more conventional models, including a light flat-twin with low tension magneto ignition from 1899 and vertical four-cylinder models from the same year.

Mors also introduced several technical advances over the years, such as shock absorbers on the 1902 racers, a compressed air starter in 1906 and its own distinctive clutch design.

In 1901 Brasier was the first of several key personnel to leave Mors, when he went to Georges Richard where he later made cars under his own name. In 1902 his former colleague Georges Terrasse went to work for Hotchkiss and in 1904 another Mors designer, Charles Schmidt, joined Packard in the United States. Up to then Mors had enjoyed considerable commercial success, with peak profits of 2¼ million francs in 1902 but then, hit by these defections, frequent management changes and a suspected share fraud, the company went into a decline. Although the workforce had reached 1200 by 1904 and output was a steady two cars a day, Mors made almost continual losses thereafter.

All the 1905 cars were four-cylinder types, ranging from 2.3 to 8.1 litres. From 1906 to 1909 there was an American Mors, made under licence by a railway car builder, the St Louis Motor Car Co, but that company then turned its attentions to building its own car, the Standard.

In 1908 André Citroën, who was related to a major Mors shareholder and director, was brought in to run the company. He sold the electrical side back to Émile Mors and reformed the car side as the Société Nouvelle des Automobiles Mors, with capital of 4 million francs but a workforce reduced to about 350. With a range of cars from 10 to 50hp and also buses, taxis and lorries of up to 5 tons, sales improved, from 280 cars in 1908 to 650 in 1910, but profits did not follow suit.

By 1912 the company was in decline again and began to use Knight sleeve-valve engines from the Belgian manufacturer Minerva, for which Citroën's brother was the London agent. Mors also used the patented double-helical gears which were later stylized as the Citroën trade mark.

Citroën tried to introduce up to date production methods after his visit to America in 1912 and Théophile Schneider attempted to buy out the company but failed.

By 1914 Mors was building small side-valve cars, the larger sleeve-valve models and a 17/20hp sports car, but was almost bankrupt. It was saved by the coming of World War I, during which it built large numbers of aero engines and also munitions.

After the war Citroën took over the armaments factory to produce his own first car and Mors continued independently though in much reduced circumstances, dropping all its commercial vehicles and all the cars save some sleeve-valve models. The most noteworthy was the stylish 3.6-litre Sporting 20, which gained four wheel brakes in 1921 but could not stop the decline.

Production stopped in 1925, when Citroën took over the rest of the works. A subsidiary of Émile's electrical company built a few Mors electric cars during World War II and from 1951 to 1956 also made two-stroke motor scooters called the Speed, after which the marque finally disappeared. BL

V-twin engine. These were made in small numbers up to about 1918, when Moser brought out a three-wheeler powered by an air-cooled V-twin. This was rapidly replaced by a four-wheeler version which was made until about 1922.

Moser had meanwhile acquired the services of Rudolf Egg, who designed for him a four-cylinder light car powered at first by a Zürcher engine – Moser had worked for Zürcher as a young man – and later by a Moser-built 1100cc engine. The earlier cars bore the name Egg on the radiator, although they were made in the Moser factory.

Cars were little more than a sideline for Moser, who had a French factory for his proprietary engines at Pontarlier. After 1924 he concentrated on engines and motorcycles, which were made until 1932 when the factory was acquired by another Swiss motorcycle maker, Allegro. GNG

MOSKVICH
SOVIET UNION 1947 to date

The Moskvich was the standard small family car of Russia for nearly 30 years before being eclipsed recently by the Fiat-based VAZ or Lada. The ancestry of the Moskvich dates back to 1939, when the Soviet government recognized the need for a popular car smaller than the GAZ, and the MZMA (Moskowskii Zavod Malolitrajnikh Avtomobilei or Moscow Light Automobile Works) was set up.

It produced the KIM-10, which used an 1172cc four-cylinder side-valve engine, similar to that of the German Ford Eifel, in a two-door saloon body slightly reminiscent of the Opel Kadett. A prototype four-door model looked almost identical to the Kadett, and it was this car that was the basis for the postwar Moskvich. Production of the KIM-10 was halted by World War II after about 500 had been made.

The Moskvich 400 of 1947 was an almost exact copy of the 1939 Opel Kadett, for it had not only the Opel's body shell but also its 1074cc engine and its three-speed non-synchromesh gearbox. The dies and tools were

taken by the Russians as war reparations from Opel's factory at Brandenburg, near Berlin. Van and estate car versions were added to the range in 1948, and the Moskvich 400 was made with little change until 1956.

Quite a number of 400s were exported, at first to Finland, then to Belgium and Holland from 1949. The Norwegian market was opened up in 1953 when some Moskviches were bartered for a consignment of Norwegian herrings. Production rose from 1501 in 1947 to about 80,000 in 1955. Total production of the 400/401 series was 247,000.

In 1956 came a completely restyled car, designed by A. F. Andronov, with up-to-date all-enveloping saloon body and an engine enlarged to 1220cc. This was the Model 402, and the design was steadily updated through the 1360cc Model 407 of 1958 to the 1480cc single-overhead cam Model 412 of 1968. In the mid-1960s a number of Moskviches were sold in Belgium with British Perkins diesel engines under the name Scaldia (Latin for the Scheldt River).

The millionth Moskvich was made in 1967, and the following year saw a change in organization when MZMA altered its name to AZLK (Avtomobilei Zavod Lenin Komsomol or Lenin Collective Automobile Works). The factory was completely updated and largely automated. In 1969 a new factory at Izhvesk was opened, the cars made there bearing the name IZH.

Since then a number of differences have emerged between the products of Izhvesk and Moscow, the former having more luxurious trim and larger overhead-cam engines of 1478cc compared with 1357cc for the current Moskvich. Both cars are available with estate car and delivery van bodies as well as four-door saloons.

The two plants employ about 27,000 people, and in 1980 combined production was 235,000 cars. The Moskvich is currently the only car on sale in the Soviet Union for which there is no waiting list. In 1983 an agreement was signed between AZLK and Renault for the French firm to design and supervise the construction of a new front-wheel-drive saloon. A prototype, the IZH-2126 five-door hatchback, appeared in 1986. GNG

Moskvich 412 saloon of c.1968

MOSER
SWITZERLAND 1914-1924

In 1902 Fritz Moser began to make motorcycles in part of his father's watch-making factory at St Aubin on the shore of Lake Neuchâtel. After a few years he added proprietary engines to his products and built a new factory across the road from his father's premises. He soon became a major supplier of engines, the second most important in Switzerland after Motosacoche.

In 1914 the factory had over 100 employees and Moser embarked upon car production with a light car powered by a water-cooled

MOTOBLOC/SCHAUDEL
FRANCE 1901-1930

Charles Schaudel, a gunsmith of Bordeaux, made La Bordelaise bicycles from the mid-1890s and developed a 3hp two-cylinder car in 1898. An engine in-unit with gearbox, described as motobloc, was displayed at Paris in 1900 and in the following year a complete car with transverse engine was named the Motobloc. Design is credited to Schaudel's brother-in-law, Emile Dombret, although Léon Pierron, later of Mass, was designer and technical director. The cars were available in kit form and were also sold in Britain as the British Ideal in 1901. They had tubular frames and 6, 8 or 12hp engines.

The Ateliers Schaudel, with a small factory at La Bastide, Bordeaux, became Société Anonyme des Automobiles Motobloc in 1902 after Schaudel went to work for Manufacture Française des Armes et Cycles (et Automobiles) de St Etienne, maker of Hirondelle bicycles. There he produced about 100 more Schaudel cars.

Dombret took control at Motobloc, which had 600,000 francs capital and a growing range of one-, two- and four-cylinder cars plus a six by 1911. In 1907 the four-cylinder cars substituted shaft drive for chain drive and had central flywheels.

Motobloc racer (Charles Farous driving) of 1908

After years of inadequate profits capital was doubled to 1.2 million francs in 1909 and increased again to 2 million francs in 1913. Output grew to between 200 and 300 and included 2½-ton commercials from 1912. Most sales were to northern France and the UK. Some 400 vehicles were made in 1913.

During World War I 300 men were employed making shells and Salmson radial aero engines. The expanded and re-tooled factory had capacity for 1000 vehicles a year in 1919, when 2.4- and 3-litre four-cylinder cars were announced, but output probably never exceeded 300 a year, despite a 1.5-litre overhead-cam sports model and smaller cars being added.

By 1927 the workforce had dwindled to 90. Although new management introduced six-cylinder cars with all-round independent suspension the move was not successful. Car production ceased in 1930. NB

MUNTZ
see Kurtis

340

NACIONAL PESCARA
SPAIN 1929-1932

Intended as a high-quality touring and sports car, the Nacional Pescara was the product of the Marquis Raul Pateras Pescara, his brother Enrique and the Italian designer Edmond Moglia. The marquis, who had built a helicopter in 1923, was the guiding spirit behind the project and it was he who obtained the approval and moral support of King Alfonso XIII.

Finance, to the tune of 16 million pesetas, came from the Banca Garriga, while Enrique Pescara and Moglia were responsible for the design. It was said that this was worked out during a series of parties at the Ritz Hotel in Barcelona where the marquis had a permanent suite, and that instead of ink the finest champagne was used for the plans.

Parties notwithstanding, it was a very advanced design, a 2960cc straight-eight with twin-overhead cam aluminium block and head. American influence was seen in the Delco coil ignition and three-speed unit gearbox, and also in the Chrysler-like ribbon radiator. Two models were offered, a touring car with 16-valve engine, and a sports/racing model with 32 valves. Power output was 75/80bhp and top speed of a two-seater over 100mph (160kph). The cars were made in the Barcelona factory formerly occupied by Wilfredo Ricart, which gave rise to the story that the Nacional Pescara was a Ricart design.

Unfortunately the Nacional Pescara appeared at a very bad time, for in 1931 a republic was declared and Alfonso went into exile. This loss of royal patronage, combined with the deepening Depression, was too much for the little company and it went out of business in 1932.

Fourteen 32-valve cars were made, and probably about the same number of 16-valve tourers and saloons. The marque won the 1931 European Mountain Championship with drivers Juan Zanelli and Esteban Tort, and continued to excel at hillclimbs for several years after production ceased.

Raul Pescara moved to Switzerland, where in 1934 he designed a 3.6-litre V16 car for the locomotive builder SLM. Three engines were completed, but only one car. GNG

NACKE/COSWIGA
GERMANY 1901-1913

Emil Nacke ran an engineering workshop in the small town of Coswig, Saxony, which in 1901 began to produce vehicles under the name Coswiga. Nacke and August Horch became friends when Horch moved into the region and there were also technical links between their two firms.

In 1907 in London, 14hp 2½-ton vans were at work and these were known as Nackes; 24, 28 and 35hp chassis were also available. Six-cylinder cars were offered in 1908 and overhead inlet valves were introduced in 1909. Commercials and trailers replaced the cars after 1913. Five-ton subsidy-types with worm drive were made for the German army in World War I and 2½- and 5-tonners with four and six cylinders and worm drive were Automobilfabrik E. Nacke's output until the collapse of the firm in 1929. NB

Nacional Pescara hillclimb car of c.1933

NAG
GERMANY 1902-1934

The Neue Automobil-Gesellschaft of Berlin was the vehicle making division of the great electrical firm, founded in 1887, AEG (Allgemeinen Elektrizitäts-Gesellschaft). In 1900 Emil Rathenau, general director of AEG, acquired the rights to a small car designed by Professor Georg Klingenberg of the Technical High School in Berlin-Charlottenburg, of which a few had been made and sold under the names AAG or Klingenberg.

It was a conventional looking voiturette with single cylinder 5hp engine, but had the unusual feature of engine, gearbox and differential being mounted in one unit on the rear axle. By December 1901 this car was being made in AEG's Berlin factory. It was sold under the name NAG-Klingenberg and was followed by a larger five-seater rear entrance tonneau model.

In 1902 AEG acquired the Kuhlstein Waggenbau, also of Charlottenburg; this company mainly built bodies but had made a few *avant-train* attachments for horse drawn vehicles and electric and petrol cars designed by Joseph Vollmer, who now became chief designer for NAG. His cars were conventional T-head vertical-twins with shaft

more significant for NAG's fortunes was the K2, a 1.6-litre monobloc four made from 1908 to 1914. Initially it was called the Puck, but with a slight increase in output it became the Darling from 1911 onwards. The engine had the same dimensions as those of the Stoewer G4, and a batch of Stoewers was built for NAG which bodied them in Berlin and sold them as Pucks.

Electric cars were made from 1906 to 1914. They included a considerable number of taxicabs which were operated in Berlin by NAG's own cab company, ABG (Automobile Betriebs GmbH).

By 1914 there were five petrol-engined models from the 6/18PS Darling up to the 33/75PS 8½-litre K8. Although some airship engines were made with six cylinders, all NAG's cars were fours until 1926 when the company merged with Protos. For several years the company had been among Germany's leading vehicle makers with annual production in excess of 2000, including commercial vehicles.

Like most car firms the world over, NAG had a 'good war', producing large numbers of trucks and 200hp Benz aero engines. In 1917 the company paid a record dividend of 15 per cent.

The staple post-war model was the C4, a side-valve 2½-litre car of conventional design. It was the work of Christian Riecken,

who came to NAG from Minerva in 1914. The original C4 was a stodgy looking car whose heavy appearance and artillery wheels were not redeemed by the Delaunay-Belleville-like rounded vee radiator.

In 1922 came the C4b, a sporting tourer with wire wheels and much lighter lines. Riecken not only designed this car but also drove it in competitions, taking 78 first and second places between 1924 and 1926, and covering 1656 miles (2265km) in 24 hours at Monza for an average speed of 69mph (111kph). In 1926 Riecken finished second to Rudi Caracciola in a 2-litre straight-eight Mercedes. Alas, as so often happens, racing did not help finances and in 1923 NAG paid no dividend for the first time for years, although it was back on form three years later.

In 1919 NAG had joined with Brennabor, Hansa and Hansa-Lloyd in the GDA group, a loosely-knit sales organization which operated a joint dealer network. The GDA was disbanded in 1926, the year in which NAG bought the Protos company from another electrical giant, Siemens Schuckert. A year later it purchased Presto Werke AG of Chemnitz, which owned the moribund Dux Automobilwerke AG of Leipzig.

From all these acquisitions came a new range of cars which replaced the C4 and its successor the D4, after about 5000 had been made in seven years. The new NAG Protos

NAG-Klingenberg 5hp buggy of 1901

drive, followed by larger chain-driven four-cylinder cars.

More important numerically were NAG commercial vehicles, of which a wide variety were made, taxicabs, buses for Berlin and for export to Russia, municipal vehicles and enormous road tractors with iron shod wheels for colonial use. It was the commercials rather than the cars which fuelled NAG's expansion from 300,000 marks capital in 1901 to 1.5 million marks by 1906. Two years later AEG transferred operations to a wholly-owned subsidiary, the name of which became Nationale Automobile-Gesellschaft in 1915.

The Kaiser added an NAG to his stable in 1905 and bought one for his wife in 1907. Another royal customer was the King of Romania, who had several NAGs between 1905 and 1914. These were large cars, but

NAG 212 cabriolet of 1932

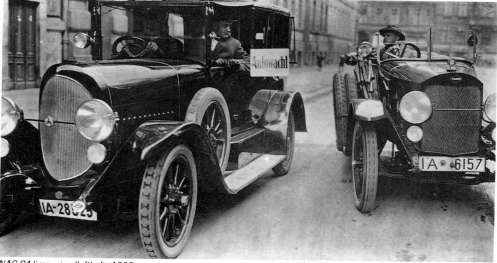

NAG C4 limousine (left) of c.1923

was a pushrod-overhead valve six made in several sizes, from 3075 to 3963cc, and lasted from 1927 to 1933. It now had a flat radiator and looked not unlike a Fiat 525, and in this it followed contemporary German fashion. There were also generally similar NAG-Prestos in 2613 and 3119cc versions, made from 1927 to 1928.

At the end of 1929 NAG acquired a new designer in Paul Henze, formerly with Impéria, Steiger, Simson and Selve. He designed the 4½-litre V8 Type 218, a 100bhp car with attractive cabriolet coachwork which competed head on with the Mercedes-Benz Mannheim but cost between 3000 and 4000 marks more. NAG had nothing like the cachet of Mercedes-Benz, and the company was lucky to sell about 50 V8s between 1931 and 1934.

Even fewer were sold of the Type 212 which used the V8 engine turned round to drive the front wheels. It was designed by the well-known front-drive specialist Richard Bussien, who was also responsible for the last NAG, the Type 220 Voran. This was a complete change from previous NAGs, harking back to the Puck in size although not in design. It had a 1484cc air-cooled flat-four engine with a steel-panelled wood-frame body and fabric roof. The standard body was a two-door saloon, but a four-door taxicab version was offered on a longer wheelbase. At 3300 marks it was more expensive than competitive cars like the 1.3-litre Opel, and only 133 were sold in 1933 followed by 250 in 1934.

In August of 1934 NAG abandoned car production, but the name survived on Büssing-NAG commercial vehicles, which were made from 1931 to 1949, during which time NAG was owned by the famous truck and bus manufacturer from Brunswick. Light trucks of 1½-ton capacity were made in the former Dux factory at Leipzig, but NAG's Berlin factory was used by the parent AEG company for its own purposes until 1945, when it was nationalized by the government of East Berlin. GNG

NAGANT
BELGIUM 1896-1929

Nagant Frères of Liège was established by the brothers Léon and Maurice Nagant and made armaments, machine tools and electrical equipment. Like many arms manufacturers around the turn of the century, Nagant was seeking alternative income and also like many they looked naturally to car production.

As early as 1896, designer and inventor Raoul de Meuse built a two-cylinder prototype for the company, but Nagant eventually went into production in 1899 with French Gobron-Brillié models built under licence. Nagant arranged the licence through a Belgian agent, Société Belge pour l'Exploitation en Belgique et en Holland des Moteurs Gobron-Brillié, run by Albert Roland from the same address as Nagant.

Nagant built the twin- and four-cylinder opposed-piston cars (and some commercials) from 1899 to 1904 as the Gobron-Nagant. In 1900 he organized a new company, the Fabrique d'Armes et d'Automobiles

Nagant Frères, directed by Maurice and with an impressive new three-storey factory. Nagant built about 150 a year of these models with almost no changes except to the engines, and then became briefly involved with another of Roland's licensing arrangements when, from 1905, it built Rochet-Schneider designs both as Nagants and on behalf of Locomotrice.

Nagant did not renew its Gobron-Brillié licence and instead employed the German Ernst Valentin to design a true Nagant car, surviving in the meantime on other interests which still included arms and now also motor components and engines. In 1906 Nagant moved into new works, still in Liège, with some 300 workers – of whom around three-quarters worked in the automobile side.

From 1906 Nagant cars were sold in Britain as the Nagant-Hobson through the London agent H. M. Hobson Ltd, the 35/40hp 6872cc chassis being listed at £700 for that year. In Germany the Nagant was marketed as the Hexe. The first Valentin-designed models, 24 and 40hp four-cylinder types, went on sale in 1907 and were also sold in France by Voiturettes Busson of Paris as the Busson-Dedyn.

In 1909 Valentin moved to Siemens-Schuckert in Berlin, which had just acquired his old employer Protos, and he was replaced by a new technical director, Dufresne. In 1911 Nagant introduced an excellent side-valve four-cylinder 14/16hp model with lively performance, followed in 1913 by an even livelier 1816cc four-cylinder light car.

Nagant underlined its new sporting bent in

Harry Lauder with 35/40hp Nagant-Hobson of c.1908

1914 with a surprise two-car entry in the Grand Prix de l'ACF at Lyons for Elskamp and Esser. The cars used twin-overhead cam four-valve 4433cc engines and five-speed gearboxes. Esser finished a splendid sixth, at 60.4mph (97.2kph) compared to Lautenschlager's Mercédès' winning average of 65.4mph (105.2kph).

Any publicity value was lost to the outbreak of World War I, during which the Nagant factory was occupied by the Germans and more or less left in ruins. Nagant's car output up to the war had been about 3000 units and the company was very quick to resume production afterwards, showing pre-war designs at the Paris Salon in October 1919.

By the first post-war Brussels Salon, in December 1920, Nagant had a new model, a 2996cc four-cylinder 16hp, initially with side-valves, later with overhead inlets. Sporting aspirations were revived with the overhead-valve 1954cc four, with four-wheel brakes. This grew to 2121cc in 1925 – in which year two of these cars finished first and second in the 3-litre class of the Spa 24-hour race.

It was the last competition success and the last car of any note. A supercharged version was shown at the 1927 Brussels Salon alongside a rather boring six-cylinder side-valve model which saw the company to its demise. Nagant was absorbed by Impéria into SA des Automobiles Impéria-Excelsior in 1928, and set to work as Impéria's six-cylinder engine supplier – the last Nagant being sold from stock in 1929. BL

Napier taxi of 1910

NAPIER
GB 1900-1924

The engineering firm of D. Napier and Son was founded in 1808 by David Napier and had an excellent reputation for high-grade machinery of all kinds. In 1841 the company made the first steam powered gun-finishing and bullet-making machinery, which was installed at Woolwich Arsenal. It later supplied similar machines to France, Spain and Egypt, and from 1854 made machines for printing postage stamps and banknotes, and also for minting coins. By the 1890s, under the direction of David's son James Murdoch Napier, the business had become very run-down and at his death in 1895 it employed seven men.

James's son Montague was a well known racing cyclist when he took over the business, and this activity brought him into contact with an even better known cyclist, Selwyn Francis Edge, who asked him to design a new engine for his 1896 Panhard. This was a 7hp vertical twin with coil ignition, completed by November 1899, and was followed by a complete Napier car the next year. Both the first engine and first car could be described as 'improved Panhards' but were none the worse for being so, and Edge was sufficiently impressed to contract with Napier to buy his complete output, as Rolls was to do with

Napier 60hp racer of 1907

Royce five years later.

Edge's company, in which he was partnered by Harvey DuCros of Dunlop, was formed in October 1899, before he had seen the Napier engine or car running. In 1900 the name was changed to S. F. Edge Ltd. At first he handled one or two other makes such as the French Gladiator, but from 1907 concentrated exclusively on Napier.

The first year's contract was for only six cars, three two-cylinder and three four-cylinder models. One of the twins was entered in the Thousand Miles Trial in which it was awarded a bronze medal, and one of the fours took part in the Paris-Toulouse race but retired. In both events the driver was Edge, who was to campaign the cars actively until the

end of the 1904 season.

Both the 8hp twin and 16hp four were made in 1901-2, customers including Prime Minister A. J. Balfour. There was also a monstrous 50hp four-cylinder racing car with capacity of 17 litres which ran unsuccessfully in the 1901 Paris-Bordeaux and Paris-Berlin races. Up to now all the cars had been made in the small premises at Lambeth, south London, which had housed the company for nearly 100 years, but the manufacture of 250 cars in 1902 strained the works to the seams and a larger factory was built at Acton, west London, to where all production was transferred during the summer of 1903.

In 1902 Edge drove a 30hp four-cylinder racing car to victory in the Gordon Bennett

John Cobb's Napier-Railton racer of 1933

Race, the first important win for a British car in international competition and one which brought to Britain the honour and task of organizing the following year's race. Although they continued for several years Napier cars were never so successful again internationally; but the win put the make firmly in the public eye.

For 1904 an 18/30hp six-cylinder car joined the range, and although it may not have been quite the first six in the world, as Edge later claimed, it was certainly the first to go into serious production. It joined chain-driven fours of 15 and 24hp, and a shaft-driven four-cylinder 30hp.

Commercial vehicles had been made since 1901, and from 1903 Napier combined with Yarrow the boatbuilders – whose founder, Alfred Yarrow, had built a steam carriage at the age of 21 in 1862 – to make a successful series of motor boats. Profits, which in 1900-1 amounted to £19, had reached £18,117 three years later.

In July 1907 S. F. Edge Ltd was reorganized as S. F. Edge (1907) Ltd, which agreed not to handle any other make of car so long as Napier provided them with at least £160,000 worth of vehicles a year. This worked for a while, but in 1911 Edge complained that the cars supplied were old-fashioned and of poorer quality than before. Napier retorted that Edge was not taking up the agreed minimum.

In 1912 Edge issued a writ against Napier claiming damages for sale of bad cars, and a series of actions followed, culminating in the

liquidation of S. F. Edge (1907) Ltd. Napier purchased Edge's holdings for £152,000 and the dealer undertook not to engage in the motor trade for seven years. He was later involved with AC cars from 1921 to 1929 and died in 1940.

If there was any truth in Edge's complaint that Napier's quality had declined it was relative to Rolls-Royce, whose star was in the ascendant with the growing success of the Silver Ghost. Compared with this the big Napiers seemed heavy and clumsy, but for a few years, between about 1906 and 1911, they were the leading British make. The 1910 catalogue listed over 160 prominent members of the aristocracy, army and church as Napier owners, and they were particularly favoured by Indian potentates. In 1906 the Viceroy of India ordered a Napier as the most suitable car in which to meet the Amir of Afghanistan.

Unlike Rolls-Royce, Napier made a wide range of cars, from a 10hp 1.3-litre two-cylinder which was mainly used as a taxicab, up to the vast 14-litre 90hp six which cost £2500 for a chassis in 1907. The taxi market proved very profitable during the boom years when London cabbies were abandoning their horses as rapidly as they could. In 1909 Napier sold 556 taxis, 10hp twins and 15hp fours, to 366 cars, and in 1910 562 taxis to 617 cars. The bulk of the demand for motorcabs had been satisfied for the time being, and 1911's sales figures were 135 cabs and 801 cars. This was the peak year for car sales, which dwindled to about 300 by 1914 despite the introduction of

a more modern 30/35hp worm drive six and a 15hp four which was also made in Colonial form with higher ground clearance.

Napier had two foreign operations at about this time. From 1904 to 1909 the Napier Motor Car Co of America built approximately 100 cars, both four- and six-cylinder models, at Boston and Jamaica Plains, Massachusetts, while 25, 40 and 60hp cars were made in Italy from 1906 to 1909 under the name San Giorgio. These Italian cars were made at Genoa by a shipbuilding firm in which Fiat had a stake, but the Turin firm apparently did not object to a subsidiary making small numbers of quasi-Napiers. The works were under the supervision of Arthur Macdonald, a well-known Napier racing driver.

Back in Britain, a commercial vehicle department was set up in 1912 to produce a range of trucks from 1½ to 3 tons, but these failed to sell in large numbers until 1914 brought War Department contracts. Production then amounted to about 2000 vehicles.

The most important effect of World War I on Napier, however, was to introduce the company to aircraft engines. It began by making the Sunbeam Arab V8 and RAF 3a V12 under licence, but from 1916 developed its own Napier Lion, a 500hp broad arrow 12-cylinder engine which was one of the best aero engines of the 1920s. It powered a number of Land Speed Record cars including Campbell's Bluebirds of 1927 to 1932, Segrave's 1931 Golden Arrow, and the 1938-47 Railton-Mobil of John Cobb.

In 1919 Montague Napier returned to car production, but only as a temporary measure to keep the factory going until the expected orders for peace-time aero engines materialized. Designed by A. J. Rowledge, the 1919 T75 was a luxury car in the Rolls-Royce class having a 6.2-litre single-overhead cam six-cylinder engine with aluminium cylinders and steel liners. A batch of 500 was planned but only 187 were made, the last cars being delivered in November 1924. Bodies came for the most part from the Cunard Motor and Carriage Co, which was controlled by Napier. A total of 4258 Napier cars were made, the peak years from 1909 to 1911 accounting for nearly 1800.

Montague Napier died in January 1931, and later in the year the company began negotiations to purchase the bankrupt Bentley concern. Plans for a 6¼-litre overhead camshaft Napier Bentley car were coming on, and it is said that the factory at Acton had been cleared for tooling up on the new car, but Napier was outbid by a mystery purchaser, which later on was revealed to be Rolls-Royce. Napier's other road vehicle of 1931 at least reached the prototype stage: this was a three-wheeled mechanical horse which was subsequently made in large numbers by Scammell.

Demand for the Lion aero engine fell off in the early 1930s, but Napier soon brought out a new range of H-formation engines with 16 and 24 cylinders. These were designed by Major F. B. Halford who had raced a 1½-litre Grand Prix car of his own design at Brooklands in 1926. The best known of these Halford-designed engines were the Rapier, Dagger and Sabre. In its 1944 form the Sabre was a 36.65-litre H-24 developing 2200bhp. In 1945 D. Napier and Son Ltd became part of the English Electric group. GNG

NARDI
ITALY 1932; 1947-1957

Enrico Nardi was a racing mechanic, engineer and racing driver who worked just before World War II for Enzo Ferrari's new Auto Avione Costruzione, forerunner of the Ferrari marque. He previously worked for Lancia and in 1932 he built a 998cc V-twin JAP-engined front-wheel-drive racer, called the Nardi-Monaco after Nardi and co-designer Augusto Monaco, and nicknamed *Chichibio*.

In 1947 Nardi established a partnership, Nardi-Danese, with Renato Danese in Turin. They built racing cars, mostly with motorcycle-derived engines, lightweight multitubular chassis and alloy bodies, but unlike *Chichibio*, with rear-wheel drive.

The 750cc BMW flat-twin powered 750ND, with cyclops headlight, was typical. Other engines used included Dyna Panhard and Universal twins, and Nardi even built 1½- and 2-litre racers with engines based on the original Ferrari straight-eight blocks which he had somehow acquired.

In 1951 the partnership was reorganized as Nardi & Co, although the cars were still identified as NDs. Crosley and Fiat engines were also used and the four-cylinder ND750 of 1956, available as a spyder or a coupé, would reach 87mph (140kph) in standard form or 100mph (160kph) with Nardi-tuned engine. A spectacular model in 1956 was the 118mph (190kph) 750cc Bisiluro, a twin-boom design for Le Mans with the 64bhp Giannini twin-cam engine in the left-hand pod and the driver in the right, the two joined by an aerofoil section spar.

Nardi built a Lancia-engined Formula 2 car and also built a one-off coupé for the Chrysler Corporation, based on the ND chassis but with Plymouth V8 power, and this car was seen at the Paris Show. A few Nardi competition cars were imported into the United States, but Nardi never really sold more than a few very specialized cars on either side of the Atlantic. By 1957 it had abandoned car manufacture completely for the more lucrative tuning and accessory business. BL

NASH
USA 1917-1957

Born in 1864, Charles W. Nash progressed from farm boy to vice-president of the Durant-Dort Carriage Co by the age of 31. In 1912 he became president of General Motors but disagreement with Billy Durant led to his resignation in 1916, followed by the purchase of the Thomas B. Jeffery Co for $9 million. Shortly afterwards the Nash Motor Co was incorporated for just under $25 million. It was nearly a year before the cars acquired Nash badges and the first Nashes were otherwise identical to the 1917 Jefferys, but 1918 models had a new overhead-valve engine.

By this time the United States had entered World War I and most of the company's output was devoted to the Quad 2-ton truck with four wheel drive and steering. In 1918 a total of 11,490 Quads were made, a record number of trucks built by one company in a year. The Quad remained in production, nominally until 1928, but Charlie Nash's heart was not in trucks and annual production in the 1920s did not exceed a few hundred.

Car production went from strength to strength, reaching 27,000 in 1919 and 35,000 in 1920. To ensure a satisfactory flow of bodies Nash bought a half interest in the

Nash six-cylinder tourer of 1918

Nash Palm Beach of 1956

Rambler Custom of 1960

Seaman Body Corporation of Milwaukee, which had supplied bodies to Jeffery and other middle sized makers such as Kissel, Mitchell and Velie. In 1936 Seaman became the body plant for Nash. A new factory was acquired in Milwaukee for the manufacture of the 1920 Nash Four and in 1923 production of the luxury Lafayette was transferred to a plant next door to this.

The Lafayette V8 was designed by D. McCall White, formerly of Cadillac, and bore quite a close resemblance to 'the Standard of the World'. It was first made by an independent company at Mars Hill, Indianapolis, but financial backing came from Nash and his associates, so it was a logical step to rationalize production by bringing the plants close together – not that there was much similarity between the $5500 Lafayette V8 and the $935 Nash Four.

The Lafayette did not sell as well as Nash hoped and in 1924, having poured more than $2 million into the project, he sold it to Ajax Motors for just $225,000. Ajax was in fact a wholly owned subsidiary of Nash Motors whose name was later given to a new six-cylinder car made in the former Mitchell plant at Racine, Wisconsin, which Nash bought in 1923.

Despite the unhappy affair of the Lafayette, Nash forged ahead in the 1920s, selling 41,652 cars in 1922 to net a profit of $7.6 million. The following year the figures were 56,677 and $9.3 million. The four-cylinder cars were dropped after 1924, and two lines of sixes saw the company through the decade to a record profit of $20 million and sales of 138,000 in 1928.

The Racine-built Ajax of 1925 did not sell particularly well under that name so Charlie changed it to the Nash Light Six for 1926. Exports accounted for 10.8 per cent of production in 1927, and Nashes found their way to several royal garages including those of King Carol of Romania, King Ghazi of Iraq, Prince Wilhelm of Sweden, and a number of maharajahs.

In October 1929 Nash launched his first eight-cylinder car, the 4.9-litre dual ignition Advanced Eight which sold at a remarkably low $1625 for the cheapest model. It was not

the best time to launch a new model, and Nash sales inevitably suffered from the Depression of the next few years. However, the cautious Nash had never gone wild with over-expansion in the lush years of the 1920s, and he made profits in 1930 and 1931 of $7.6 million and $4.8 million when other companies were losing anything between $2 million and $14 million. Nevertheless a loss of nearly $1.2 million was recorded – the first in Nash history – in 1933, when sales were down to 14,973.

For 1934 cars were styled by the Russian Count Alexis de Sakhnoffsky and included rear wheel spats and built-in luggage boots. Also in 1934 Nash revived the Lafayette name for a low-priced six-cylinder car selling for between $595 and $695. This was sold as an independent make until the 1936 season, after which it became simply a model of Nash. The loss for 1935 was down to $610,000, and from 1936 the company was back in profit with sales encouragingly up to 53,038 and then 85,949 in 1937.

A new era began in 1937 with the merger of Nash and the Kelvinator Corporation, the well known maker of refrigerators. This came about because Charlie Nash wanted George Mason as executive vice-president, and to get Mason he had to buy Kelvinator as well. Mason was no stranger to the auto business, having been with Studebaker, Dodge and Chrysler before becoming president of Kelvinator in 1928. With Mason's arrival Charlie Nash, now 73, went into semi-retirement, although he retained a keen interest in his company until his death in 1948.

During the 1930s Nash held a steady place in American car production, usually 12th or 13th, although it rose to 11th in 1941. Sales and profits dipped badly in 1938, but then so did everyone else's. Among innovations were 'weather eye' air conditioning in 1938 and integral construction on the 1941 600 sedan. This low priced model, so-called because it could run for 600 miles (965km) on its 20 gallon (75 litre) tank, helped Nash to sales of 80,408 in 1941.

Production of 1942 models ended in February after 5428 had been made, and the company began its contribution to the war effort

with the manufacture of Pratt and Whitney radial engines for naval aircraft. It expanded the Kenosha plant and bought 200 acres (80 hectares) of land for a proving ground.

Nash went quickly back into car production after the war and actually won third place in 1945 figures, behind Ford and Chevrolet. Needless to say, once the industry got back into full production Nash found itself in its customary 11th place for 1947 and 13th for 1948. Nevertheless the post-war years were good ones for Nash, which recorded an $18 million profit in 1947.

In June 1948 Charlie Nash died at the age of 84. The farm boy who had been abandoned by his parents at six years old without a cent to his name left an estate of $43 million.

Perhaps thinking of his own mortality, Mason recruited a new deputy, George Romney, who was to see Nash merged with Hudson to form American Motors. In later years he became Governor of Michigan.

Like most of the industry, Nash relied on restyled pre-war design to tide it over for the first few post-war years, but for 1949 it launched the revolutionary looking Airflyte, with fastback sedan body and all four wheels enclosed. Unkindly dubbed the 'Bathtub Nash', it brought integral construction to the whole Nash range and was made with two sizes of six-cylinder engine. The Ambassador 8 was not revived after the war. Sales for 1949 were a record 142,592 and profits $26 million, although this was greatly helped by the non-automotive Kelvinator Division.

George Mason's philosophy was that an independent car-maker had to be different, to offer products not obtainable from the Big Three, and in 1950 Nash broke new ground with the Rambler, a compact car on a 100in (2.5m) wheelbase powered by an 85bhp six-cylinder engine. Styling followed that of the larger Nashes and when these received Pininfarina-designed bodies for 1952, the Rambler followed suit for 1953.

Another link with Europe was provided by the Nash Healey sports car which used a chassis built by Donald Healey in England and a tuned Nash Ambassador 125hp engine. In 1952 these, too, received Pininfarina's attention, but this time the bodies were not only styled in Italy but also made there. This international cocktail of a car cost $6000 and only 504 were made between December 1950 and August 1954.

By early 1953 the market share of the independent car-makers had dropped from 18.6 per cent in 1946 to below 5 per cent and Mason realized that the only hope lay in a merger. After abortive talks with Packard, Nash merged with Hudson on 1 May 1954 to form American Motors Corporation.

It was the biggest merger yet in the American motor industry, giving the new group in 1954 combined sales figures of 95,198 cars. This was lower than 1954's other big merger, Studebaker and Packard, which had a combined figure of 112,845, and way below the smallest of the Big Three, the Chrysler group with 723,000. George Mason died suddenly in October 1954 and was succeeded by George Romney.

In 1955 Nash and Hudson dealerships were combined and at the same time the cars were rationalized so that Hudsons used Nash bodies with Hudson 6 or Packard V8 engines and different grilles and trim. These were continued into 1956, and in mid-season American Motors brought out its own 5.8-litre 255hp V8 for the Nash Ambassador Special and Hudson Hornet. The 1957 models were the last to bear the old names, and for 1958 all American Motors cars were badged as Ramblers or Metropolitan, the sub-compact powered by an Austin A40 engine. GNG

NATIONAL
GB 1902-1912

The National, or Rose National, was made by Rose Brothers, an old-established firm founded in 1895 to make packaging machinery, mainly for cigarettes but also for black lead, butterscotch and chocolate. The Albion works in Gainsborough, Lincolnshire, was already flourishing when, in about 1902, the Roses decided to add motor cars to their products.

These were designed by the Baines brothers, Edward and Frank, and were made originally in two models, a 10/12hp two-cylinder and an 18/22hp three-cylinder, both with shaft drive. They were followed in 1905 by a 20/24hp four-cylinder car, but a projected six announced in 1906 apparently never saw the light of day. All mechanical components of the National cars were made in the factory, but bodies came from outside, chiefly from Hamshaw of Leicester.

Paul Hasluck's *The Automobile* stated in 1909 that current National models were the 18/20hp three-cylinder, and 24 or 40hp fours, the latter 'built closely on Mercédès lines'. Company publicity claimed that cars were made until 1912, but there is a suspicious lack of press references to the National after 1906. It would seem that the majority of the 50 cars made were of the three-cylinder model.

Rose Brothers later became part of Rose Forgrove Ltd, itself now a division of the Baker Perkins group, which also absorbed another packaging machinery firm turned car-maker, Day-Leeds. GNG

NATIONAL
USA 1900-1923

The National Automobile and Electric Vehicle Co was formed in Indianapolis in 1900 to make a light electric runabout and horse-drawn carriages. Company president was Arthur C. Newby and other directors included W. Guy Wall, who remained with National as chief engineer throughout the company's life, and William E. Metzger, who joined Cadillac in 1903 and formed the EMF Co with Barney Everitt and Walter Flanders in 1908.

In 1901 Guy Wall began experiments with petrol cars, and the first of these came onto the market in 1903. It had a four-cylinder Rutenber engine and shaft drive. Apart from the engine nearly all components were made in the National factory. By 1905 National was making a 24/30hp car with a round radiator which was entirely swept by the fan, as well as a smaller four-cylinder car and 12 models of electrics. Carriages were abandoned after 1902 and electric cars after 1905.

National's first six, and one of the first in America, was announced for the 1906 season. In 1907 the company acquired its own engine plant, leased from the Indiana Chain Co, and that year offered two fours of 40 and 50hp and a 75hp six. In 1908 the round radiator was replaced by one of shield shape, which in various forms was continued for the rest of the make's life. Prices ranged from $2750 to $5000.

From 1909 to 1912 National had many sporting successes, including winning the 1911 Elgin and Illinois Trophies and the 1912 Indianapolis 500. The latter victory was very appropriate, as Arthur Newby was one of the Indianapolis businessmen who backed the building of the Speedway.

The big fours and sixes were continued with little change for several years. A monobloc six came in 1914, but in 1915 National broke new ground with the Highway Six and Twelve. The Six used a Continental Red Seal engine but the Twelve had National's own twin-camshaft V12 power unit, which was made until 1919. The old Newport Six was continued and in fact was higher priced than the Highway Twelve, at $2395 to $2850 compared with $1990 for the Twelve. By 1917 only the Highway models were offered, at $1850 and $2250.

In 1916 the National Motor Vehicle Co was purchased by a New York concern and was reorganized under the name National Motor Car and Vehicle Corporation. The new company offered 53,000 shares at $42.50 each. Despite the comprehensive name, no vehicles other than passenger cars were offered, although the firm made a considerable number of Jeffery Quad 4×4 trucks for the US Army in 1917-18.

The Highway Twelve was no longer made after 1920, but the six was continued under the name National Sextet and used the company's own 4.9-litre engine. About 600 cars were made in 1921 but sales dropped to fewer than 200 in 1923, and not all of these were of National manufacture.

In an attempt to extend market coverage, National formed a sales organization called Associated Motors in May 1922 which also represented Dixie Flyer and Jackson cars and Traffic trucks. For 1923 the four-cylinder Dixie Flyer was badged as a Model 6-31 National, and the Jackson Six as the Model 6-51 National, even though both cars were made in their respective factories at Louisville in Kentucky and Jackson, Michigan. National's own six was called the 6-71, the second figure indicating the brake horse power. Associated Motors was not a success, and all three makes were out of production by the end of the year. GNG

National tourer of 1922

NAZZARO
ITALY 1911-1923

Felice Nazzaro was born in 1880, the son of a wealthy Italian coal merchant. For a while he was apprenticed to Giovanni Battista Ceirano's Welleyes bicycle company, which in 1899 built a prototype single-cylinder car, also called a Welleyes, which shortly after became the first Fiat.

Besides acquiring the car, Fiat also spotted Nazzaro as a talented driver and in 1900, driving a 6hp Fiat, he finished second to his friend Vincenzo Lancia in the Padua-Vicenza-Padua race. He won the 1901 Giro d'Italia with a Fiat and finished fifth in the first Coppa Florio in 1904, driving an old Panhard for the race's founder Vincenzo Florio who employed Nazzaro as a chauffeur. He became a Fiat works driver in 1905, finishing second in that year's Gordon Bennett Cup.

In 1907 Felice won the season's three major races, the Targa Florio, the Kaiserpreis and the first French Grand Prix – all to different formulae but all for Fiat. It was the highlight of his racing career and although he continued to race he also turned his attention to manufacturing. Early in 1911, with Maurizio Fabry, Pilade Massuero and the engineer Arnaldo Zoller, he set up Nazzaro & C, Fabbrica di Automobili in Turin.

Within a year the company moved to larger works and in March 1912 the first Nazzaro car was shown. Known as the Tipo 2, the 4.4-litre four-cylinder side-valve car betrayed Felice's background by looking very like a Fiat, but contradicted it by looking anything but sporting.

Nevertheless, Catalano and Losa took 12th place in that year's Targa Florio for Nazzaro and in 1913 Felice won the race for his new marque – adding victory in the Coppa Florio in 1914, by which time the Tipo 3 had gone into production. Offsetting this success, Nazzaro suffered a very expensive failure of all three of his entries, specially built overhead-cam 16-valve 4½-litre racers, in the 1914 French Grand Prix.

Nor was Nazzaro doing very well commercially. In the four years up to 1916 the company produced around 230 cars and only 50 commercials and late that year went into liquidation. Felice left, eventually to return to Fiat, for whom he scored his last major race win – in the 1922 French Grand Prix – and whose competition department he went on to manage from 1925 until his death in 1940.

The factory meanwhile was acquired by Tosi of Legnano in 1917 and put to work building aero engines during World War I. After the war, in 1919, a new company, Automobili Nazzaro, was founded in Florence. The new cars, Tipo 5, were more sporty 3½-litre overhead-cam fours, the last versions of which, made in 1922, had two exhaust valves per cylinder. Some 210 were built before the new company closed down in 1923. BL

NB
see Diatto

NEC
GB 1905-1920

The New Engine Co Ltd of Willesden, north-west London, was founded in 1903 to manufacture two-stroke aero engines designed by G. F. Mort. These were made at least until 1913 and were supplied to A. V. Roe and Co in 1910. A Short-built Wright biplane, also made in 1910, used a 50hp V-4 NEC two-stroke engine.

The first NEC car was put on the market in 1905. Like all its successors it had a horizontal engine mounted under the floor and a flat front with no bonnet. The first model was a 24hp four-cylinder, but 15 and 20hp twins were made between 1906 and 1911 and 30 and 40hp fours from 1907 to 1914. Only two sizes of cylinder were used for all NECs, 114×114mm (3½×3½in) or 127×114mm (5×3½in). All seating was within the wheelbase, which was 11ft 6in (3.5m) on the largest models, giving a very comfortable ride.

Production of NECs was quite limited, not more than 100 a year at the most, and the majority had tourer or landaulette bodies, although a few two-seaters were made on the smaller chassis. G. F. Mort died in 1911 and the business was carried on by his brother J. C. Mort. The 30 and 40hp models were listed up to 1922, and a few may have been assembled after the war from pre-war stock.

By 1921 the company was involved in making drilling machine tables, general engineering and component manufacture. In 1938 the works were occupied by Norton and Gregory Ltd, which produced mathematical instruments. GNG

NESSELSDORF
see Tatra

NEW ORLEANS/ORLEANS
GB 1900-1910

In 1900 Burford, Van Toll and Co signed a two-year agreement with Vivinus to make 600 of the Belgian cars in Twickenham, Middlesex, for sale in Britain and the United States. The firm became the New Orleans Motor Co in 1901 with £20,000 capital; A. Vivinus and two Belgian counts were on the board. H. G. Burford had earlier been with LIFU and was works manager of Humber before making lorries under his own name.

Water-cooled two-cylinder cars supplemented the original air-cooled single-cylinder model in 1901. Larger models with four cylinders followed. In 1905 the company's name was changed to Orleans Motor Co Ltd, although the cars were still sometimes called New Orleans.

A six-cylinder 35hp car joined the range in

Nazzaro Tipo 2 roadster of 1912

1907, but none of the later large cars equalled the popularity of the earlier Vivinus types and production ended in 1910. In 1915 Straker-Squire bought the Twickenham factory, which still stands. NB

NEW PARRY
see Pathfinder

NG
GB 1979 to date

NCG Design Ltd was founded by Nick Green, an engineering graduate from Hatfield Polytechnic who had worked for John Britten Garages of Barnet building Arkley demonstrators. Initial capital was £7000 and premises were acquired at New Milton, Hampshire, behind the Ashley Post Office Stores owned by Green's parents.

The first NG kit car was the TA, the styling of which was inspired by the Aston Martin International of the early 1930s. The fibreglass open four-seater body came from John Ingram Fibreglass, alloy bonnet panels from Rod Jolly of East End near Beaulieu, and the box section cruciform chassis from Ian Terry of Lymington. The body and chassis were supplied to customers for £595, with most of the mechanical components coming from the MGB apart from Spridget fuel tank and Austin 1800 radiator.

At first Green and his wife Linda thought

NG TF sports four-seater of 1984

they would sell only a few cars, relying on their design consultancy for their bread and butter, but orders were so encouraging that they formed NG Cars Ltd to look after manufacture, keeping NCG Design Ltd for freelance consultancy work. By June 1981 they had sold 54 TAs.

In 1981 the TA was joined by the TC, a two-seater styled on the Aston Martin Ulster and intended for MGB V8 or Rover V8 power. The price was £1565 for the De Luxe kit. Two additional models are now also made, both four-seaters for MGB or Rover V8 running gear – the TD with cycle wings and the TF with flowing wings and running boards. The latest development is the option of Rover 2.3- or 2.6-litre six-cylinder engines.

In 1981 production was moved to a 15,000sq ft (1400sq m) factory to the west of New Milton where Nick and Linda Green and two staff turn out about three kits a week. In 1984 new premises were acquired at nearby Milford-on-Sea which now houses the showroom, design office, prototype shop and stores. As well as selling all over Britain, NG cars have been exported to several European countries, the USA, Australia, New Zealand and Kenya. By August 1985 a total of 500 had been delivered, consisting of 200 TAs, 178 TCs, 72 TDs and 48 TFs. GNG

NICLAUSSE
FRANCE 1906-1914

Like Delaunay-Belleville, the firm of J. and A. Niclausse was a well-known boilermaker, providing many boilers for the battleships of the French Navy. The company was founded by Jules and Albert Niclausse in 1890, and by the time car production began the works in the Rue des Ardennes, Paris, covered more than 10 acres (4 hectares) and employed about 1000 men. Cars were built in a separate factory adjoining the main boiler works.

Introduced at the 1906 Paris Salon, the first Niclausse car had a 30/40hp four-cylinder T-head engine with separately cast cylinders and shaft drive. This model was made throughout the make's life, although renamed a 35/50hp by 1913. For 1908 three models were offered, a 12hp at 10,800 francs, an 18hp at 18,000 francs and the 30/40hp at 25,000 francs, all with four speeds, four cylinders and shaft drive. The 12hp had a monobloc or pair-cast cylinders, the 18hp had pair cast only.

These three models were made in small numbers with little change until 1914. Niclausse expanded during World War I so that the workforce was doubled by the early 1920s, but motor cars were not revived at the end of hostilities. GNG

NISSAN/DATSUN
JAPAN 1933 to date

Japan's second largest motor manufacturer and the world's fourth largest, Nissan Motor Co Ltd was founded on 26 December 1933, but the history of its predecessor companies dates back to 1912. In that year an American-trained engineer, Masujiro Hashimoto, founded the Kwaishinsha Motor Works in Tokyo, and built a prototype light car.

Nothing is known of its design, but it was followed two years later by another car named the DAT, after the names of three men who financed Hashimoto's company. They were K. Den, R. Aoyama and A. Takeuchi. Dat is also the Japanese word for 'hare'. In 1915 came the DAT 31, with four-cylinder 2-litre engine enlarged to 2.3 litres on the 1916 Model 41. All components were made in Japan apart from the wheels, tyres and magnetos.

The DAT Model 41 was made in small numbers up to 1926, when production ceased in favour of trucks such as the 1½-ton Model 61. In 1925 Kwaishinsha had changed its name to DAT Motor Car Co and the following year moved to Osaka, merging with the Jitsuyo Jidosha Seizo Co.

This firm had been founded in 1920 to make three-wheeled cars designed by an American engineer resident in Japan, William R. Gorham, and had progressed to the four-wheeled Lila light car in 1921. Many of these were used as taxis in Japanese cities, where their narrow track of less than 40in (1m) suited the streets. They were made for a short period after the merger with DAT.

In 1931 DAT was acquired by a large industrial concern, Tobata Imono, whose president, Yoshisuke Ayukawa, was very keen to build a mass-produced Japanese car which could compete in export markets with American products. His dream began to become fact with the building in 1931 of a prototype DAT small car, named the Datson (son of Dat). This name was soon changed to Datsun, as the word 'son' in Japanese means 'loss', hardly an auspicious name for a car which was intended to gain worldwide favour.

Production began in 1932, when 150 Datsuns were made in roadster, tourer and saloon form. They had 495cc four-cylinder engines developing 10bhp, and a top speed of 35mph (56kph). A superficial resemblance to the Austin Seven has led to suggestions that the Datsun was a copy of the British car, but its engine was considerably smaller and it had semi elliptic rear suspension and worm drive as against the Austin's cantilever springs and bevel drive.

Jidosha Seizo changed its name to Nissan Motor Co Ltd, and production of Datsun cars was moved from Osaka to a new factory at Yokohama. The thousandth Datsun was made in mid-1934, in which year the first exports were recorded; 44 cars were shipped to Spain, India and the United States. In 1935 engine capacity went up to 722cc (16bhp), remaining at this size until after World War II.

Light commercial vehicles were made on the car chassis, but in 1937 Nissan brought out a range of 1½-ton trucks and buses using 3.7-litre six-cylinder engines, and with the approach of war these took precedence over the passenger cars. In 1939 Nissan made 17,781 vehicles, of which probably 75 per cent were commercials. The 3.7-litre engine was a Graham design, Nissan having bought engine tooling and body dies from the American company and using them in the Model 70 sedan (1937-40) as well as in the commercials. The Model 70 and the commercials carried the name Nissan, only the small four-cylinder vehicles being Datsuns.

The peak year for production before Japan entered World War II was 1941, when 19,668 vehicles were made; nearly all of these were commercial and military vehicles. During the war aero engines were built, for which a new plant was opened at Yoshiwara. It was from this factory that the first post-war cars were made in 1947, the Yokohama factory being reserved for truck production.

The Standard DA two-door saloon of 1947 used the same 722cc engine as its pre-war ancestor, and the body was more old-fashioned looking. Capacity went up to 860cc on the 1951 Thrift, which was the first Datsun four-door saloon. Various styles of full-width saloon bodies were tried in the early 1950s, but the only attractive Datsun was the DC-3 roadster in the style of a pre-war MG or Singer.

In 1952 Nissan signed an agreement with Austin to produce cars under licence, first the A40 Somerset and from 1955 the A40/A50 Cambridge. This lasted until 1959, but meanwhile the old Datsun 860cc engine soldiered on, with more modern bodywork, until 1958 when it was replaced by an Austin-based 1.2-litre overhead-valve unit on the first of the Bluebirds, a name that has survived in the Datsun/Nissan range up to the present day.

Nissan suffered a crippling, four month long strike in 1953, but as a result the All Nissan Motor Works Union was formed which has developed such good relations with management that the company has not had another strike since. Production rose steadily from 12,458 vehicles at the beginning of the 1950s to 77,822 at the end.

Datsun 240Z of 1971

Datsun's first international sporting success came in the 1958 Australian Mobilgas Trial, when Bluebirds took first and fourth places. This was followed by victories in saloon car racing in Australia and Macau, but it was not until the coming of the sports/racing programme of the late 1960s and the arrival of the 240Z sports coupé in 1969 that Datsun became a name to be respected in international motor sport. A Bluebird won the 1969 East African Safari and a 240Z won it in 1970.

The Austins were replaced in 1960 by the Cedric, a 2-litre family saloon with four-speed all-synchromesh gearbox that was sold as a Nissan up to 1966. A significant year for exports was 1960, when the Nissan Motor Cor-

Nissan March Turbo of 1985

Nissan Patrol 4×4 of 1986

Nissan Prairie Anniversary II of 1985

poration was formed as a sales organization in the USA and the first post-war Datsun was sold in Europe, going to Norway.

The first overseas manufacturing subsidiary, Nissan Mexicana SA de CV, was established in 1961 and began production in 1966. Today it has three factories employing 4400 people; it makes Violet and Silvia cars for the Mexican market, and several models of truck for both home and export markets, including the whole of South America. Capacity is 80,000 cars and 110,000 engines a year.

The Datsun range became increasingly complex during the 1960s when the Bluebird, Cedric and President saloons were joined by the Fairlady 2-litre sports car and two models from the Prince range, the Skyline and the

Gloria, after Nissan's takeover of Prince in 1966. The Fairlady was replaced in 1969 by the 240Z, a 2-seater coupé with 2.4-litre six-cylinder single-overhead cam engine. The 240Z became the best-selling sports car in the world, with sales of successive models nearing 723,000 by the end of 1980.

Notable models of the 1970s included the front-drive Cherry, launched in 1970 with 5 million having been made by 1977, and the 4×4 Patrol cross-country vehicle powered by a 4-litre overhead valve truck engine. The biggest car was the 4.4-litre V8 President, still made today.

Nissan's overseas operations have expanded greatly over the past 10 years. After Mexico, the next country to have its own

assembly plant was Australia; in 1976 Nissan took over the former Volkswagen factory at Dandenong, Victoria, where 2000 employees make around 50,000 Bluebirds and Pulsars a year. In January 1980 Nissan began to buy into the Spanish Motor Iberica SA which makes Ford-based trucks and tractors under the name Ebro. By May 1983 Nissan owned 65.52 per cent of Motor Iberica's shares, beginning production of Patrols in January of that year.

In June 1983 Nissan Motor Manufacturing Corporation USA began production of pickup trucks at its Smyrna, Tennessee, plant and a month later the first cars began to come off the lines at Pomigliano, near Naples. These were hybrid Nissan/Alfa Romeo cars which used Italian engines and transmissions (ex-Alfasud) in Nissan body shells assembled at the nearby Pratola Serra factory. The cars are called Arna after the joint company which makes them, Alfa Romeo e Nissan Autoveicoli SpA. Some Nissan models have been made in Taiwan since 1958 by the Yueloong Motor Co under the name YLN.

The most recent international ventures are the assembly of the Volkswagen Santana in Nissan's Zama factory, begun in February 1984, and the formation in April 1984 of Nissan Motor Manufacturing UK Ltd, which has acquired a 300-acre (120-hectare) site at Washington New Town, County Durham, with a potential capacity of 24,000 cars a year assembled from Japanese-supplied kits. Plant construction started in 1985, the first cars going on sale in 1986.

The Datsun name was officially dropped at the end of 1983, and all vehicles are now called Nissan. The 1987 range consisted of 15 basic passenger car models, from the 987cc Micra to the 4414cc V8 President, with several engine options within each range; all the smaller have front-wheel drive. In addition there is the rear-drive Z sports car range with 170bhp 2-litre or 230bhp 3-litre engines, the Sunny-based front-drive Prairie station wagon, and the 4×4 Patrol, as well as a wide range of small/medium commercial vehicles. A dramatic new model for production in 1987 is the Mid-4, a sports coupé with mid-mounted 3-litre V6 engine, four-wheel drive and steering.

Nissan currently operates seven factories devoted to motor vehicle production, including the original two at Yokohama and Yoshiwara. Two other factories produce textile machinery and aerospace equipment, while other activities in the car factories include making forklifts, industrial and marine engines, and motorboats. Nissan Diesel Motor Co Ltd is a separate organization, founded by Yoshisuke Ayukawa in 1935, which makes heavy trucks and buses.

At the end of 1985 Nissan Motor Co Ltd had a workforce of about 60,500 which produced 1,864,701 cars. The proportion of total production exported has risen from 38 per cent in 1972 to 55 per cent in 1985. The best export market is the United States, taking 47.8 per cent of the total in 1985, followed by the United Kingdom (7.7 per cent), Saudi Arabia (4.5 per cent) and West Germany (4.4 per cent).

In addition to the factories already mentioned, Nissan operates overseas assembly plants in Costa Rica, Ghana, Greece, Indonesia, Ireland, Malaysia, Mexico, New Zealand, Peru, the Philippines, South Africa, Thailand, Trinidad-Tobago and Zimbabwe. In 1985 a total of 304,612 Nissan vehicles were produced outside Japan. GNG

NORTHERN
USA 1902-1909

Jonathan D. Maxwell and Charles B. King founded the Northern Manufacturing Co in Detroit in 1902 and in October of that year introduced the Silent Northern, a 5hp single-cylinder two-seater designed by King and offered in three models from $800 to $890. From 1902 to 1906 it was also assembled under licence in Sweden by AB Södertälje Verkstäder, in Södertälje, as the Norden.

If the car looked like an Oldsmobile with a flat dash, that was perhaps not surprising, as both Maxwell and King had previously worked as engineers for that company. King had also built one of the first cars in Detroit, a four-cylinder model, in 1896. About the same time he also built engines for the Duryea

brothers, and a two-cylinder car for Byron J. Carter, later of Cartercar.

In 1904 Northern offered a single-cylinder runabout at $750 and a bonnetted 15hp twin-cylinder tourer at $1500. These continued, with improvements, in 1905 as 6½ and 17hp models and for 1906 King designed a four-cylinder car whose brakes and clutch were operated by air pressure – although there was a mechanical brake for emergencies. As well as the 30hp four, Northern also offered a 7hp single and 20hp twin in 1906, but that was the last year for the single.

Maxwell had left the company in 1904 and, backed by radiator manufacturer Benjamin Briscoe, had formed the Maxwell-Briscoe Motor Co and designed and built the first Maxwell-Briscoe car in the same year. In 1910 Maxwell-Briscoe became part of the new United States Motor Corporation, and upon that group's collapse two years later Maxwell and Briscoe resumed as separate marques, Maxwell being by far the more successful.

The Northern range by 1908 included twins up to 24hp and a 40hp four, but in that year King also left and in 1909 formed the King Motor Car Co, also in Detroit. This company built the King car from 1910 to 1924, latterly in Buffalo, New York, although King himself left in 1912 and went on to design and build aero engines, including development work on the Liberty.

In July 1908 Northern was merged with the Wayne Automobile Co, which had built the Wayne car in Detroit since 1904, and some smaller Detroit component manufacturers, to form the Everitt-Metzger-Flanders Co. Barney Everitt was the general manager, William E. Metzger had been part of the management at Northern (and previously with Cadillac), and Walter E. Flanders came from Wayne, which he had joined from Ford only shortly before the merger. Coincidentally, Flanders was eventually taken into the Maxwell Motor Corporation to reorganize it, and when he joined Maxwell left.

Everitt-Metzger-Flanders dropped both the Wayne and Northern makes and launched the EMF in 1908, alongside a smaller model, the Flanders. The company was taken over by Studebaker in 1912 for some $5 million. BL

NOVA
GB 1971 to date

Automotive Design and Development Ltd was founded in 1971 in Woolston, near Southampton, to build the Nova, a glassfibre body kit styled by Richard Oakes for fitting to a Volkswagen Beetle platform chassis and running gear. The Nova, Oakes' first car design, went into production in 1972 and was a worldwide success.

The design was very dramatic – a very low two-seater coupé with a huge steeply-raked windscreen, the whole of which lifted on struts with the roof to provide access. It was quickly adopted in the United States, where kits on Beetle chassis were already very popular, but because Chevrolet had a prior claim to the Nova name it was built under licence first as the Sterling. By 1975 it was also built in Australia as the Eureka.

In 1974 British production had moved to Accrington in Lancashire, but in spite of the Nova's apparent success production stopped in 1975 and the original company was wound up by June 1976. An independent operation run by Nigel Fox and Don Law from Cricklade, Wiltshire, began making Nova SSD kits using moulds taken from the original cars. In 1978 they formalized their operation as The Nova Shop, which also offered completely finished cars from about £3500, and Don Law even rallied a 2.2-litre turbocharged version of the car, but that operation too was soon closed down.

Also in 1978 another company, Nova Sports Cars Ltd, was established in Ravensthorpe, Yorkshire, and production officially resumed. Another Nova lookalike appeared in the USA in 1978 when Amore Cars Ltd in Milwaukee began building the gull-winged Cimbria, a car which could also use the Ford Pinto four or small block Oldsmobile or Chevrolet V8s. In 1981 this car found its way back to Britain as the Eagle, built by a subsidiary of the Dutton kit-car company in Sussex and available with Ford or VW engines.

The 'official' Nova company launched a series 2 car in 1981 with a slightly reshaped

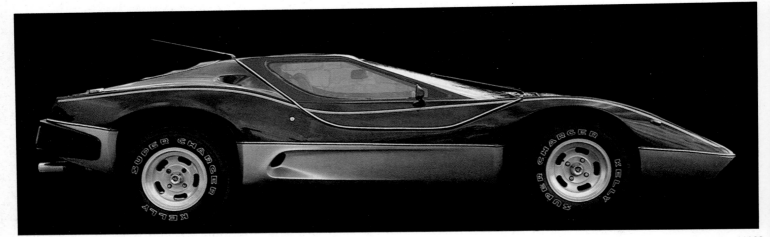

Nova sports two-seater of 1983

NSU Ro80 of 1974

front and engine cover and the option of an electrically operated roof. In 1982, Nova Sports Cars Ltd, with 34 employees, built some 340 kits. The price of a basic 1584cc Beetle-engined model, with a top speed of 110mph (177kph) was £4300 in 1983. In 1985 the cheapest kit retailed at £1600. The Nova has also been produced under licence in Italy and South Africa, as the Puma, and a special version even starred in a Walt Disney film. BL.

NSU
GERMANY 1905-1977

In 1873 two Swabian engineers, Christian Schmidt and Heinrich Stoll, set up a workshop at Reidlingen, on an island in the Danube, to manufacture knitting machines, part of the high technology of the day. The business did well but by 1876 there was no more room to expand and Schmidt left Stoll to run the works in Reidlingen while he went to establish a new factory at Neckarsulm. There, Schmidt branched out into building bicycles from the early 1880s and in 1886 he formed a new company, Neckarsulmer Fahrradwerke AG.

Like Neckarsulm, both Mannheim and Cannstatt (a suburb of Stuttgart) also stood on the river Neckar and in these towns, precisely at this time, Karl Daimler and Gottlieb Benz were bringing the motor car into the world. Very soon, Neckarsulmer Fahrradwerke became involved in this new field as a supplier of chassis to Daimler for the Stahlradwagen.

In 1892 the company adopted the initials NSU as a trade mark, although the name Neckarsulm was also used for several more years. In particular it was used in 1900 when the company began to manufacture motorcycles, which were in effect no more than motorized versions of the existing bicycles, but nonetheless popular. NSU went on to be one of the largest motorcycle producers in the world, with a reputation for technical innovation which was expressed through racing and record breaking until the late 1950s, when the company stopped building motorcycles.

NSU's first car was actually built under licence from the Belgian manufacturer Pipe in 1905. Pipe was already quite well known and had a reputation for quality, but the expensive luxury car had only a limited market and by 1906 NSU was ready to introduce smaller and less sybaritic models of its own making.

The first, not unlike a scaled-down Pipe, was a four-cylinder 6/10PS, followed shortly by a 15/24PS model and NSU built 20 of these in its first year as a manufacturer. NSU continued to offer well-equipped small cars and proved that it could compete with larger models by entering three cars in the 1908 Prince Henry Trial and finishing without penalty.

The company experimented briefly with an even smaller car in 1909, an 1100cc twin-cylinder, but it continued to concentrate on the successful fours, particularly the 1132cc 5/12PS of 1909, which gave rise to 5/15 and 5/20PS derivatives and was made up to and beyond World War I.

In 1910 the expanding company, now with over 1000 employees and an additional small plant at Heilbronn, was reorganized as Neckarsulmer Fahrzeugwerke AG. Larger cars, of up to 3.3 litres, and even lorries were added to the range before World War I and NSU continued to build cars, trucks and motorcycles through the hostilities.

After the war NSU developed its small four-cylinder cars and the 1.6-litre 6/30PS sports model into very successful competition machines but dropped the larger cars. In 1923 NSU 5/15s finished 1-2-3 in the Avusrennen race and in 1929 the six-cylinder cars (which were now available in supercharged form for the road) finished 1-2-3-4 in the smaller class at the German Grand Prix, also at Avus.

By 1922 the company had about 3500 employees but still relied on outside body suppliers, foremost among these being Schebera. NSU began to expand the factory at Heilbronn in the mid-1920s, with the intention of becoming self-sufficient there, and by 1927 the newly built works were in operation. The move was ill-timed, however, as NSU was suffering the effects of the Depression.

Since 1923 the majority of NSU shares had been held by speculator Jacob Schapiro, who also had interests in several other car companies, and in Schebera. In 1926, as Schapiro himself ran into financial trouble, NSU took control of Schebera but was hit badly by that company's losses, until in 1928 the Dresdner Bank, Schapiro's former backer, took control of 51 per cent of NSU.

NSU continued to build motorcycles at Neckarsulm but in 1929 was forced to abandon car manufacture on its own account at Heilbronn. Instead it sold a half share of the factory to Fiat and through a separate new company, NSU Automobil AG, built Fiats under licence there as NSU-Fiats. This name was used until 1966, after which NSU was able to reclaim the name solely for its own products.

After the 1929 hiatus Fiat sold its interest in the Neckarsulm parent company to the Dresdner Bank and by 1934 NSU had recovered sufficiently to commission Dr Ferdinand Porsche to develop a 'people's car' which they might build. Porsche designed the car and NSU built three prototypes before an upswing in the motorcycle market led them to shelve the project – which, nevertheless, was a significant step in the beginnings of the Volkswagen story.

The works at Neckarsulm, which had become NSU-Werke AG in 1937, were heavily damaged during World War II but production of lightweight motorcycles was resumed in 1949. In the 1950s NSU was again famous for its motorcycles and mopeds and also built Lambretta motor scooters under licence. In 1957, however, the company stopped motorcycle production – although it continued to make mopeds – and the following year made a return to car production.

NSU began a dispute with Fiat over the use of the NSU name on cars built at Heilbronn and in 1959 the company there was renamed as Neckar Automobilwerke AG and the Neckarsulm company became NSU Motorenwerke. Fiat used both Neckar and NSU-Fiat as brand names until 1966 when it relinquished its claim to the latter. The Neckar name lasted for one more year before Heilbronn-built cars became plain Fiats until production stopped in 1973.

The new NSU for 1958 was another light car, the Prinz, with an air-cooled 598cc twin-cylinder engine in the rear, owing a great deal to NSU's motorcycle expertise. The Prinz was an enormous success and with gradually more powerful engines and in sports and GT versions it stayed in production until the early 1970s. When the Prinz was launched NSU even built a holiday camp called the Lido, near Venice, solely for Prinz buyers – and early advertisements exhorted owners to 'Drive your Prinz to the Lido'.

The success of the Prinz and later 1000 and 110 models, with 500,000 NSU cars built by 1966, helped NSU to undertake a far-reaching development programme with a new engine, the Wankel rotary. NSU's first contact with Dr

Felix Wankel had been in 1951 when it had sealing problems with the rotary valves on its racing motorcycles. Wankel then developed extraordinarily efficient superchargers for NSU's 1956 record breakers and these were direct forebears of the rotary engine, which first ran at the factory in 1957.

NSU's rights to this engine led to a good deal of speculative investment in the company, which also sold a licence for its eventual use to Mazda. The Japanese firm almost beat NSU into production with the Wankel, which had been unexpectedly difficult to refine, but diplomatically held back for long enough to let NSU launch the first Wankel-engined car, the Wankel Spyder, in 1963. It went into production in 1964, with a 60bhp single rotor engine in a shell derived from the Sport Prinz, and proved itself to be very successful in a number of competitions, although still rather fragile and thirsty as a true road car.

In mid-1967 NSU showed the Ro80, a twin-rotor Wankel-powered front-wheel-drive sporting saloon which was immediately acclaimed but ultimately cost NSU a fortune in warranty claims on the engine, which still had a tendency to wear out quickly or, with hamfisted use, to seize completely. By the time the car was properly developed, not until the early 1970s, its other problem, a terrible thirst for fuel, had become too important and in 1977 it was dropped.

It was the last NSU; in 1969 NSU merged with Audi, which was part of the Volkswagen empire, to become part of Audi NSU Auto Union AG. NSU's design for a conventionally-engined partner for the Ro80 was taken over by Volkswagen and launched in 1971, disastrously, as its K70. With the successful smaller NSUs having already been phased out in late 1972, the Ro80 was the company's only product and good though it was now becoming it was too little and too late. When the Ro80 went, in 1977, the NSU name went with it. BL

NSU-FIAT
GERMANY 1930-1966

In 1929 the old-established NSU company entered into an agreement with Fiat whereby it would cease to make cars of its own design and instead build Fiats in its new factory at Heilbronn, while carrying on with motorcycles in its Neckarsulm factory. In fact Fiat bought a half share in the Heilbronn premises, the other half being taken up by the Dresdner Bank. The new company was managed by a Fiat appointee, Piero Bonelli.

The first cars to emerge from Heilbronn were called NSU-Fiat Standards, being 2½-litre Fiat 521s on the shorter wheelbase 522 chassis, with local bodywork. Production was modest to start with, and in 1932 only 548 NSU-Fiats were made, fewer than the 990 Fiats imported complete from Turin.

In 1934 the Balilla went into production at Heilbronn, and for the first time complete cars emerged from the factory. Bodies were built outside, mainly by two Heilbronn firms, Drauz and Weinsberg, and delivered to the NSU-Fiat factory to be mounted on the chassis. Production of the Balilla in 1934 was 1704, and more than 3000 were delivered in 1935.

It was followed by the Fiat 500 of which, about 7000 were made, 1100 (about 5000) and 1500 (about 4000), production of these models surviving into 1941. Bodies were mostly by Drauz or Weinsberg; the latter built about 300 two-seater sports bodies on the 500, which had no Italian equivalent. Otherwise styling followed Turin closely.

After World War II, production did not get under way until 1950, when the 500C in coupé and estate car form, and now like its Italian prototype with overhead valves, began to leave the production line. A total of 1047 were completed in the first year, together with two 1400s, but in 1952 Heilbronn made 4275 500s. By the time the car was replaced by the 600 in 1955, 11,974 had been made. Other Fiat models to emerge from Heilbronn included the 1100 in various forms from 1953 to 1968, and the 1400/1900 series.

In 1958 NSU of Neckarsulm returned to car manufacture, and a dispute arose over the use of the name by NSU-Fiat. As a result NSU-Fiat changed its name to Neckar Automobilwerke AG in 1959, although the cars often carried the NSU-Fiat name as well as the new one.

NSU-Fiat 500 Weinsberg of 1959

In 1959 Heilbronn produced a distinctive little coupé based on the two-cylinder 500 called the Weinsberg, of which 6190 were made until 1963. Heilbronn's most popular model was the 600 saloon. Peak production year was 1962, when a total of 50,297 cars were delivered.

After 1967 the Neckar name was dropped and cars were sold under the name Fiat up to 1973, when all production at Heilbronn ceased. The factory could not turn out more than 80 cars a day and it was more economical to import cars complete from Turin. The company name was changed to Deutsche Fiat AG, which had existed for a long time as a sales organization, and the Heilbronn factory was turned over to repair work. GNG

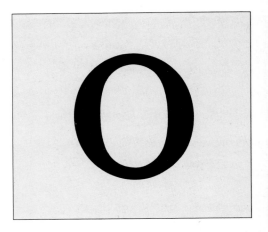

OAKLAND/PONTIAC
USA 1907 to date

Edward M. Murphy incorporated the Pontiac Buggy Co in 1891 in Pontiac, Michigan. From 1907 he produced cars having a two-cylinder, planetary transmission design from Alanson P. Brush, who had designed the first Cadillac and the Brush Runabout. As the rival Pontiac Spring and Wagon Works had just made a motorized high-wheeler a new name had to be chosen for Murphy's machine. The Oakland Motor Car Co was therefore formed in August.

Less than a year later Murphy died and the company was acquired by W. C. Durant's burgeoning General Motors Co, which in 1910 also purchased the remnants of the Buggy Co. Lee Dunlap was put in charge and he was followed in 1912 by George E. Daniels, who left after three years to make the Daniels 8 luxury car.

GMC had meanwhile bought Rapid and Reliance and consolidated them in the former Pontiac Spring and Wagon factory and had boosted sales of Oakland cars, which were promoted as 'cars with a conscience'. They had four cylinders and sliding mesh gears. A Northway-engined six was introduced in 1915 followed by a V8 and Oakland's own overhead-valve six in 1916, which became the marque's staple model in 1919.

Sales in 1917 were 35,000, reached 52,125 in 1919 but sagged to 11,852 in 1921. Oakland, however, proved useful to General Motors in other ways, supplying engines, bodies and chassis to Scripps-Booth and Oldsmobile in 1921 and acting as a test-bed for public reaction to new ideas.

The 'copper-cooled' engine tried by Chevrolet was supposed to be used by Oakland but was found to be unsatisfactory. Instead a cheap side-valve six was introduced in 1923. For the first time in the industry this new model was painted with Duco nitrocellulose produced by Du Pont, the financial backers of General Motors. This model was known as the 6-54 or 'True Blue' – the only colour produced – and was said to be the first car that could safely be left out in all weathers. The

6-54 used General Motors' Research Laboratory's first disc wheels.

Sales had been climbing steadily and reached 58,000 in 1926, the year General Motors' harmonic balancer was introduced by Oakland and a cheaper model called the Pontiac Six went on sale. This car was to be slotted just above the Chevrolet in price and specification and initially was offered only in closed models, a sedan and a coupé. It used many Chevrolet parts and was developed by Oakland, athough final engineeering work was undertaken by Chevrolet. The man in charge of development was Henry M. Crane, formerly of Crane-Simplex.

Despite being given an all new engine in 1928, the Oakland had slipped to 30,826 sales in 1929 and was losing ground to its own Pontiac. A V8 from the Oldsmobile Viking was used in the Oakland in 1930. Combined figures for Oakland and Pontiac showed sales of 86,000 in both 1930 and 1931, although Oakland's contribution was diminishing. The name was phased out in 1932, by which time just over 500,000 Oakland cars had been sold.

In 1932 the Pontiac Motor Co was formed. That year the cars used Cadillac's synchromesh and Oakland's V8 but then a straight-eight was introduced in 1933. Sales in 1932 were 46,594, but once the effects of the Depression receded this leapt to 80,000 in 1934 and 235,322 in 1937. The one millionth Pontiac was produced in 1935. Chevrolet and Pontiac were run together under William S. Knudsen, originally from Ford, through the worst of the Depression and then joined the Buick and Oldsmobile sales line-up.

General Motors' 'knee action' independent front suspension came to some Pontiacs in 1934, along with the all-steel 'turret-top' styling. That same year the model name Silver Streak was used for the first of many times. Hydraulic brakes spread to the entire range in 1936. There was a major redesign in the following year to give a longer, lower and wider look. A station wagon was also offered in 1937. Increased streamlining gave rise to Torpedo models from 1940.

In the last full year of pre-war car production, 282,000 sales were recorded, giving Pontiac fifth position in the sales league, a ranking it had held through much of the 1930s. During the war the Pontiac factory produced axles for Cadillac tanks, diesel engine parts, aircraft torpedos and Bofors and Oerlikon guns.

The first major post-war changes came in 1949 when X-frames and the option of Hydramatic transmission were adopted. In 1955 the straight-eights gave way to Pontiac's first V8 since 1932-33. Fuel injection was optional on some models in 1957.

The 1959 Pontiacs started a trend which has become widespread in General Motors – cross pollination between divisions, as they shared some inner body panels with Buick, Chevrolet and Oldsmobile. For 1961 Pontiac launched its contribution to the compact car race, the Tempest, in sedan, coupé and station wagon models. Like Oldsmobile's F-85, the Tempest had a unitary construction hull, but it was highly unusual in having a slightly curved propeller shaft whose action could be compared to that of a speedometer cable. The gearbox was in unit with the rear axle, and the power unit was a 3.2-litre four, with the option of a 3½-litre V8.

Pontiac GTO convertible of 1968

Pontiac Trans-Am Firebird of 1985

Oakland Model A runabout of 1911

During the 1960s Pontiac acquired a performance image in complete contrast to the rather staid family sedan character of the early 1950s. This was due to two models, the Tempest GTO introduced in 1964 and the Firebird introduced in 1967. In its most powerful models the GTO (Gran Turismo Omologato, a term originated by Ferrari) developed 370bhp from a 6½-litre V8 engine. It was made until 1972, by which time 444,441 had been delivered.

The Firebird coupé was based on the Chevrolet Camaro bodyshell but it came with engine options from a 165bhp 3½-litre six to the 345bhp 6½-litre V8 also seen in the GTO. In 1969 came the Trans-Am Firebird, whose engine was too large for the races after which it was named, but which was ideal for the 'traffic light grand prix'. The Firebird was still part of the Pontiac range in 1985, but since the mid-1970s power output has been greatly reduced, and current engine options run from 88 to 205bhp.

Pontiac's performance image was planned by Semon E. Knudsen, known as 'Bunkie', general manager from 1956 to 1961. Among his design team were Pete Estes who took his place from 1961 to 1964, and John DeLorean who held the same post from 1964 to 1969. Another engineer, F. James McDonald, succeeded DeLorean, but his place was taken in 1972 by Martin J. Caserio whose background was in marketing. He axed the GTO and came near to doing the same with the Firebird, but his marketing expertise was reflected in record sales in 1973 of 854,343 cars.

At the beginning of the 1970s Pontiac was making some of the largest engines of any American car, headed by the 7½-litre 370bhp V8 used in the Grand Prix, Bonneville and Catalina models, but like all other American makes they were drastically downsized towards the end of the decade. In 1979 came the Phoenix, Pontiac's version of the 2½-litre front-wheel-drive compact J-car, followed by the 1.8-litre subcompact J-2000 in 1981, and the 2½-litre intermediate A-car, the 6000, for 1982.

These were all continued for 1986, in addition to the larger-rear-wheel drive Bonneville, Grand Prix and Parisienne with engines of 3.8, 4.1 or 5.7 litres, the latter a diesel. As well as the Firebird, Pontiac makes a smaller mid-engined fibreglass sports coupé, the Fiero, powered by a 2½-litre four-cylinder or 2.6-litre V6 engine mounted transversely. Total car production in 1984 was 594,821, giving Pontiac 5th place in the US league. NB/GNG

OD (GERMANY)
see Faun

OD (NORTHERN IRELAND, USA)
see Fergus

OGLE
GB 1959 to date

Motor racing enthusiast and former Fleet Air Arm pilot David Ogle trained as an industrial designer and in 1954 founded David Ogle Associates at his home in Stevenage, Hertfordshire. He offered industrial and exhibition design and packaging and among his first customers were Bush Radio and Allied Ironfounders.

In 1959 he opened a proper office in Stevenage with four designers (including one Tom Karen) and a secretary. He started work on a car, a four-seater GT with a chassis designed by John Tojeiro and based on the Riley 1.5.

In 1960 David Ogle Ltd was set up with backing from saloon car champion Sir John Whitmore and millionaire racing enthusiast John Ogier, who continued to be involved after Whitmore's early withdrawal. Karen left, to work first for Hotpoint and then Phillips before his later return. Ogle designed a coach for an Irish company and started work on the

Ogle Mini SX1000 of 1962

Ogle Mini and on a special bodied Daimler SP2500. Six of these were to be built for a cosmetics manufacturer but only two were completed after he pulled out of the deal.

Sadly, David Ogle was killed in May 1962 while driving a long wheelbase prototype of the Ogle Mini to a Brands Hatch race meeting, but the company continued, reorganized as Ogle Design Ltd. Ogier became chairman and Karen returned as managing director and chief designer. There was a staff of two other designers and four assistants, and a new model-making shop.

Karen was born in Vienna, son of a wealthy brickworks owner and car enthusiast, and brought up in Czechoslovakia. He arrived in Britain, via Belgium, Spain and Portugal, in 1942 at the age of 16, his family having fled the Nazis. He studied aero engineering and worked in the aero industry for 10 years before studying industrial design. He then worked for Ford's design and styling department for four years before joining Ogle for the first time.

The Daimler was shown at the 1962 London Motor Show and the Ogle Mini launched. It was Ogle's only real production car, with some 80 examples built until 1964, but was dropped because the British Motor Corporation was reluctant to supply parts and sales could not justify the expensive alternative of cannibalizing whole cars.

Ogle switched from production to design and in 1964 styled the Reliant Scimitar coupé. A year later Ogle built the Triplex GTS, based on the Scimitar, to show the versatility of glass in car design. The car was bought by Prince Philip, but two years later was bought back by Ogle and later went to the National Motor Museum at Beaulieu.

Reliant remained one of Ogle's major clients, with Karen's Scimitar GTE launched in 1968 and his Robin – under development since 1964 – launched in 1973. Karen also designed the three-wheeled Bug, introduced in 1973 by Bond, by then a part of Reliant.

In January 1972 Ogle unveiled the Aston Martin based Sotheby Special. Two further examples were built, one for the Embassy

Grand Prix team and the other for a private owner, at a cost of approximately £30,000 in 1972.

By 1975 Ogle had expanded premises, with autonomous transport and other product design departments and a staff of over 40. Now the staff is around 80 and about half of Ogle's work is still transport-related. The company has designed and built bus, truck and ambulance bodies and prototype electric taxis, undertaken town car studies for the government, built Project 2000 (a small family car of the future), carried out styling exercises on cars such as the Astra and the Metro, made motorized toys and made crash test dummies for the motor industry – as well as making a huge range of non-motoring products from office equipment to knitting machines. BL

OHTA-KUROGANE
JAPAN 1934-1957

Ohta Jidosha Seizosho Co Ltd was founded in Tokyo in 1912. It produced a four-seat tourer prototype in 1922 but did not enter the vehicle market until 1934, when it made 736cc saloons, tourers, pickups and vans with financial backing from Mitsui.

From 1935 its manufacturing company was known as Kohsoku Engineering Co Ltd and output was said to be among the largest in Japan. In 1939 it switched to the manufacture of aircraft parts.

Post-war vehicle production was again of small types with 760 or 903cc engines. The range included a station wagon and, in the 1950s, a car with small pickup body at the rear.

In 1957 Ohta was acquired by Kurogane, which had made small cars and light 4×4s since the mid-1930s, initially under the name New Era. Ohta car production was brought to an end and although light commercials were produced for a while they were also soon discontinued. Kurogane went into liquidation in 1962, having most recently made forward control vans. NB

OLDSMOBILE
USA 1896 to date

Ransom Eli Olds (1864-1950) was born in Geneva, Ohio, the son of a locksmith of English extraction. In 1880 the family moved to Lansing, Michigan, which was to be the centre of Olds' two ventures into car manufacture. He built at least two experimental steam cars, one in 1887 and another in 1893, and also made several electric cars. In 1892 he took over the running of his father's firm, which was now a sizeable producer of steam and gas engines.

By 1896 P. F. Olds & Son was making petrol engines as well, and it is hardly surprising that Ransom Olds was attracted by the idea of the motor car. Wisely, he decided not to risk the success of the family firm in such a new venture, so he formed a separate company, the Olds Motor Vehicle Co, with $50,000 capital raised from Lansing businessmen.

The new company was established on 21 August 1897, although at least one petrol car was running towards the end of 1896. Only five or six cars were made over the next 21 months, and in May 1899 a new company with capital of $500,000 was formed, called the Olds Motor Works. Ransom Olds' stake in the new company was just $400. It was located in Detroit as it was felt that Lansing (population 2000) was too small to support a growing motor industry.

It was in the Detroit factory that the first production car, and the first to bear the name Oldsmobile, was developed. It had a single horizontal cylinder of 1565cc capacity, two-speed epicyclic transmission and single chain drive. The front of the body curved up to form the dash, hence the name Curved Dash Oldsmobile given it in later years. At the time it was generally called the Oldsmobile runabout.

In March 1901 the Detroit factory was almost completely destroyed by fire, but one runabout was saved, and this was the pattern for production models. A new factory was erected on a 52-acre (21-hectare) site at Lansing, where Olds had retained his engine works, and the first Curved Dash Runabouts emerged later in 1901. A total of 425 were made that year, rising to 2100 in 1902, 4000 in 1903, 5500 in 1904 and 6500 in 1905.

These figures put Olds way ahead of rival manufacturers, the Curved Dash being the biggest selling car in the world before the arrival of the Model T Ford. It gave rise to one of the first motoring songs – 'In My Merry Oldsmobile' (1905) – and was copied, or made under licence, in Canada (Le Roy) and Germany (Polymobil). Olds achieved some degree of line production, as the cars were pushed along on their wheels for components to be added by successive groups of workmen.

One of the attractions of the Curved Dash Runabout was its modest price of $650, which was maintained throughout its six year production run. However, Olds' board of directors wanted to make more elaborate and expensive cars, and rather than agree to this Ransom Olds left the company in January 1904 to set up the rival R. E. Olds Co (soon renamed Reo Motor Car Co). The Olds Motor Works continued under the direction of the Smith brothers, Frederick and Angus, whose father, lumber millionaire Samuel L. Smith,

Oldsmobile Curved Dash Runabout of 1901

had invested nearly $200,000 when the company was founded.

The Curved Dash (and a little-known companion with a straight vertical dashboard) continued until 1906, but bonnets and steering wheels made their appearance in 1904. Larger cars with four-cylinder engines came in 1906. Oldsmobile was trying to attract an entirely new type of customer; dealers who had had a ready market for the $650 Runabout now found that their standard offering was the Palace Touring Car at $2750.

Sales dropped to 1600 cars in 1906 and 1200 in 1907, and in November 1908 the company was acquired by William C. Durant for just over $3 million. This was Durant's first step towards forming his General Motors empire and despite the poor state of Oldsmobile at the time it turned out to be one of his wisest purchases. A $4500 six-cylinder model had joined the fours for 1908, and a small number of trucks were made as well.

Sales climbed to 1850 in 1910, when the massive Limited was introduced; this 11½-litre six rode on 42in (1066mm) wheels and cost between $4600 and $7000. A total of 325 Limiteds were sold in three seasons.

Production dropped to only 1075 vehicles in 1912, but thereafter business began to improve, with 1175 sales in 1913, 1400 in 1914 and a jump to 7696 in 1915. Delco electric lighting and starting were introduced in 1913 models, and the $1285 four of 1914 was the car which spearheaded Olds' climb back to success. The workforce grew from just 276 in 1913 to 2000 two years later.

Chief engineer from 1914 was Italian-born Fabio Segardi, who had worked for Darracq and Fiat. His main contribution to Oldsmobile was the 4.2-litre 40bhp side-valve V8 introduced for 1916 and made until 1923. Prices started at a modest $1195, and 13,440 V8s were sold in 1917 out of a total production of 22,613.

The V8 engines were built by Northway Motor & Manufacturing Co of Detroit, which had recently been acquired by General Motors. Northway also made some of Oldsmobile's fours and sixes, as well as supplying Oakland and Scripps-Booth within the GM empire, and Cole and Jackson outside it.

Sales in 1918 were down to 19,169 but this is hardly surprising as the United States was at war, and the Oldsmobile factory was busy making kitchen trailers and Liberty aero engines. 1919 was the best year yet for Oldsmobile, with about 4000 workers turning out 39,042 cars and 5617 of a new line of trucks which were to continue until 1924.

In November 1920 William Durant left General Motors for good, and shortly afterwards his manager at Oldsmobile, Edward Ver Linden, was asked to leave. His place was taken by another Durant protégé, A. B. C. Hardy, who phased out the V8s and initiated an all six-cylinder policy from 1924. This lasted until the arrival of a straight-eight in 1932.

Production boomed in the 1920s, reaching

Oldsmobile tourer of c.1920

Oldsmobile six-cylinder saloon of 1936

44,854 in 1924, 86,593 in 1928 and 101,579 in 1929. Even so, in that record-breaking year for the US car industry, Oldsmobile was ninth in the sales league and fourth among GM brands, behind Chevrolet, Pontiac/Oakland and Buick. Chromium plating was an Oldsmobile innovation in 1925, and four wheel brakes were available from 1927. Irving Reuter was general manager from 1925 to 1933, when he was succeeded by former engineer C. L. McCuen.

In April 1929 Oldsmobile launched a new car in a higher price bracket than its cars had occupied for many years. This was the Viking V8 which was marketed as a separate brand from Oldsmobile, although made in the same factory. The engine was a specially designed 4257cc side-valve V8 developing 81bhp and the Viking rode on a 10ft 5in (3.17m) wheelbase, compared with 9ft 5½in (2.88m) for the contemporary Oldsmobile.

Prices ran from $1695 to $1855, compared with $875 to $1165 for Oldsmobiles. The Depression dashed what hopes there might have been for the Viking's success, and it was dropped at the end of 1930 after just under 8000 had been made.

Overall Oldsmobile sales were down to 49,886 in 1930, and dropped to a miserable 21,933 in 1932, the worst year of the Depression. A 3930cc straight-eight was added in that year, and Oldsmobile offered parallel lines of sixes and eights up to 1948.

For nine years the GM-owned Fisher body plant was located at Oldsmobile's 87-acre (35-hectare) grounds at Lansing, but in 1933 Fisher moved to the premises of the defunct Durant company, and Oldsmobile was able to expand further. Sales rose encouragingly after 1932, reaching a pre-war peak of 230,701 in 1941.

Synchromesh arrived in 1931 and independent suspension in 1934, but Oldsmobile's most important innovation of the decade was in the field of transmissions. In June 1937 the company announced its Safety Automatic Transmission as an option on the eight-cylinder models. This was a semi-automatic system with steering column gearchange, while a clutch was still needed for starting. However, it paved the way for the genuine two-pedal Hydramatic automatic transmission, launched on the 1940 models. This was an option costing $57. Production of Hydramatic transmissions was slow to start, but in 1941 nearly 50 per cent of all Oldsmobiles sold were fitted with them.

Sherrod E. Skinner replaced C. L. McCuen as general manager in 1940, his first move being to open a new forgings plant which contributed 175 million pounds of material to the war effort, particularly axles for GMC 6×6 trucks. Other Oldsmobile factories produced aircraft cannon and aero engine components. On 1 January 1942 the name Olds Motor Works gave way to Oldsmobile Division, General Motors Corporation.

Oldsmobile was the first GM division to display its post-war models, in July 1945, but production was halted by a strike from November 1945 to April 1946. Up to 1948 Olds made face-lifted pre-war designs, but the restyled Futuramic models were announced in June of that year, and in September came the high compression Rocket V8 engine which developed 135bhp from 4.9 litres. Together with the slightly larger Cadillac V8, this began a trend towards powerful V8s which spread throughout the American industry. Sixes were dropped by Oldsmobile after the 1950 season and did not appear again until 1964, when the compact F85 made use of a Buick V6 engine.

Production rose during the 1950s to levels undreamed of before the war – 396,757 in 1950, 433,810 in 1954 and 643,460 in 1955. Oldsmobile, together with Buick, pioneered a new body style in 1954, the four-door hard top, which was adopted by other GM divisions two years later. Less successful was the New-Matic Ride air suspension of 1958, which was quietly dropped after one season, along with Buick's similar 'Air Poise' suspension.

A more important development of the 1959 season was the beginning of corporate cross-pollination, whereby the same pressings, and eventually the same complete body shapes, would be shared by the different GM divisions. Olds and Buick used the same inner panels.

For 1961 Oldsmobile joined the compact car club with the 3520cc aluminium block V8 F85. This featured unitary construction and independent coil springing all round, and used a 3684cc Buick V6 engine from 1964 onwards.

For the 1966 season Oldsmobile broke new ground with the front-wheel-drive 6960cc Toronado coupé. This was engineered by John Beltz who had joined the division in 1947 and was general manager from 1969 until his early death at the age of 46 in 1972. The Toronado was styled by David North, and once again showed that Oldsmobile was the pace setter among GM divisions, as it had been with automatic transmission and the overhead-valve V8 engine.

Cadillac brought out its front-wheel-drive coupé, the Eldorado, for 1967 and in the 1970s front drive spread to all marques in the GM empire, and indeed to the whole American industry.

There had long been an Oldsmobile tradition of putting chief engineers at the helm, and this was continued when Howard Kehrl succeeded John Beltz in 1972. The following year saw a record output of 918,120 cars, but this fell back to 654,490 two years later when the energy crisis bit into all car production, especially of larger models.

As with all other American makes, Oldsmobiles were downsized in the late 1970s as the industry became increasingly economy conscious. The Omega compact introduced in 1973 was a thinly disguised Chevrolet Nova, and 1975's Starfire hatchback coupé, the smallest Oldsmobile for many years, shared a body shell with the Chevrolet Monza/Buick Skyhawk.

Oldsmobile's last convertible came off the line in July 1975, and three years later came GM's first diesel engine, the 5731cc V8 used in the 88/98 standard sized cars. A year later the diesel was available in a smaller and lighter Toronado, and there was a 4257cc diesel option for the intermediate Cutlass range.

In 1976 Olds reached third place in the industry, with 874,618 cars sold, of which 515,000 were Cutlasses, making them America's best selling individual models that year. Sales topped the million mark for the first time in 1977, with 1,135,909 Oldsmobiles finding buyers. They remained over the million mark up to 1979, and although 1980's sales were 910,306, they were good enough to keep Olds in third place. This figure included 126,853 diesels, for over 30 per cent of the US diesel car market. Oldsmobile also made 152,000 diesel engines for other GM divisions in 1980.

Toronado production was moved to a new plant at Linden, New Jersey, in 1979, while the Cutlass was made at another brand new assembly plant at Lansing, and the 88/98 models at the older Lansing factory. The smaller Starfires and Omegas were manufactured at a number of different GM plants, where they came down the same production line as the equivalent Buicks, Chevrolets and Pontiacs.

This process was continued in the 1980s,

with several basic designs common to most, and sometimes all GM divisions. The Oldsmobile version of the front-wheel-drive subcompact J-car was the Firenza, of the compact X-car the Omega, and the intermediate A-car, the Cutlass Ciera. These were joined in the spring of 1984 by the New 98, one of the C-cars with a choice of 3, 3.8 or 4.3-litre (diesel) engines.

These made up the 1986 range, together with the Toronado. Now that the Delta 88 has become a front-drive car based on the 98, there are no rear-drive Oldsmobiles. Production in 1985 was 1,225,983 cars, which put Oldsmobile firmly in third place in the US league. GNG/NB

models were offered at first, a 28/45hp of 7.4 litres, and a 40/50hp of 11.3 litres, which was large even by the standards of the day. In 1906 smaller cars were made, one with 10hp three-cylinder monobloc engine of 1386cc and another 10/14hp four-cylinder of 3770cc. Both these models had shaft drive.

The three-cylinder car, and some of the larger ones, were made by an associated company at Brescia called Brixia-Züst SA – Brixia was the Latin name for Brescia – which was formed to look after the cheaper end of the market, while the big cars were made by Ing Roberto Züst Fabbrica Italiana di Automobili SA at Milan. The factory at Intra continued to make turbines, drills and lathes, the

The first OM car was the former Züst 25/35 Tipo S.305 which remained in production until 1923, but in 1921 came a completely new car designed by the Austrian engineer Barratouché. It had a 1327cc L-head four-cylinder engine developing only 18bhp, but was the ancestor of all the touring and sporting OMs, none of which used other than a side-valve engine. They did so well against more sophisticated cars that Lord Montagu of Beaulieu was prompted to entitle his chapter on the cars in *Lost Causes of Motoring* 'Why put the camshaft upstairs?'. Why indeed, when the marque took 118 first, second and third places in the 124 races entered between 1921 and 1931.

Oldsmobile 98 Holiday saloon of 1958

Oldsmobile Toronado saloon of 1966

OM 665S, Mille Miglia winner of 1927

OM/ZÜST
ITALY 1905-1934

Both these Italian makes had histories dating back to the middle of the 19th century, but they were not in any way linked until OM, which was the larger of the two, absorbed Züst in 1917. Roberto Züst was a Swiss-born engineer who in 1871 became a partner in the Güller and Groff engineering works at Intra on Lake Maggiore. Founded in 1850, this was a small concern with only 15 workmen making marine and stationary steam engines, but Züst extended its activities, adding turbines and machine tools to its products.

The company name was changed to Güller and Züst in 1888. Nine years later Roberto Züst died, and control of the firm passed to his five sons who opened a workshop in Milan in 1900 which began to manufacture car components. It is likely that experimental cars were being made by 1903, but the first Züsts only came on the market in 1905.

They were conventional cars on Mercédès lines, with four-cylinder pair-cast engines, honeycomb radiators and chain drive. Two

Swiss Railways being among its customers, but never manufactured cars.

By the end of 1906 Züst had representatives in France, Britain and the United States. A 28/45 took part in the 1908 New York-Paris race, finishing third. Trucks were added to Züst's output in 1910, while the three-cylinder chassis was popular as a taxicab. However, the Brescia factory made serious losses and in 1912 it was decided to merge the two companies into a new one, the Fabbrica Automobili Züst. The Milan factory was sold, and all production concentrated at Brescia.

The three-cylinder, which had been enlarged to 1500cc in 1910, was dropped, as was the 14/18, and for 1913 a new 25/35hp with pair cast L-head engine of 4712cc and all brakes on the rear wheels was introduced. A 2.8-litre 15/25hp and chain driven 7.4-litre 50/60hp were also listed up to 1915, together with three trucks from 2½ to 6-tons capacity and a 150hp aero engine.

On 1 October 1917 Züst was taken over by Officine Meccaniche SA, a Brescia-based company making railway locomotives. Founded as OM in 1899, its history could be traced back to a carriage and landau works set up by Felice Grondona in 1849.

The first of the Barratouché OMs was called the Tipo 465 (four cylinders, 65mm bore) and was followed by 467 and 469 variants, and in 1923 by OM's first six, the 665. These became very popular in Britain, where they were sold by L. C. Rawlence and Co whose engineer R. F. Oats tuned the competition cars, fitting them with Ricardo overhead-valve heads, stripped and rebuilt gearboxes and stronger crown wheels and pinions. Between 350 and 400 OMs were sold in Britain between 1923 and 1933.

Among the marque's competition successes were first, second and third in class in the 1923 Coppa delle Alpi; first and second in 1924; first in the 1926 San Sebastian Grand Prix; first, second and third in the 1927 Mille Miglia; a class win for Oats in the 1928 Essex Six Hours Race at Brooklands and Team Prize in the 1928 Coppa delle Alpi. All these victories were achieved with sporting tourers, for OM's only attempt at a Grand Prix car, the 1½-litre straight-eight of 1926, was not a success. A 3-litre straight-eight touring car of 1928 was only made as a single prototype.

OM was to have a much longer life as a maker of commercial vehicles than of private cars, and the first steps towards this were taken in 1925, when vans and taxicabs were offered on the 469 and 665 chassis. These outlived the cars, being made until 1935, but a more serious venture into heavy vehicles came in 1928 when OM acquired a licence from Saurer in Switzerland to make diesel trucks.

In 1930 capacity went up to 2.2 litres on the 667 series, sporting models which had sloping radiators and looked very like Alfa Romeos. The factory ran three supercharged four-seater team cars in 1930-31, but their best placings were only fifth in the 1930 Mille Miglia and third in 1931. Serious production seems to have ended in 1930, but OMs were still available in England a year or two later, assembled from a vast stockpile of parts at Rawlence's premises in the railway arches at Waterloo station in London. They were still exhibiting at Olympia in 1933 and 1934, although the cars were refurbished 1930 models.

The last OM car was a break with tradition. The 1934 Alcyone had a 2.3-litre exhaust-over-inlet valve engine, four speed synchromesh gearbox, and a sports saloon body not unlike a Fiat Ardita. Only one was made, not by OM but by two former employees, Augusto Coletta and Luigi Mangano, who bought up OM parts and formed a company called Esperia. They also planned a modern 1½-litre saloon with all-round independent suspension, but this never left the drawing board.

Fiat had taken a 50 per cent stake in OM in 1928 and increased this to 100 per cent in 1933. Saurer-based diesel trucks were made until the late 1940s, after which OM developed its own designs which came increasingly under Fiat influence after 1968. OM also made agricultural tractors (since 1929) electric and diesel-electric railway locomotives and rolling stock, forklifts and van bodies. Since 1978 the OM badge has been carried on certain Fiat trucks, but they are no longer of independent design. GNG

OMÉGA-SIX
FRANCE 1922-1930

The Oméga-Six was a high-quality sports car built without regard to commercial profit as the company was supported by the personal fortune of its founder. Jules Daubeck had made a great deal of money manufacturing railway sleepers for the Chemin de Fer du Nord, and he engaged the engineer Gadoux to design a 2-litre six-cylinder single-overhead cam engine which was mounted in a modern chassis with front wheel brakes.

Daubeck's aim was to provide the luxury and good looks of the Hispano-Suiza in a smaller car. As Gadoux had worked for Hispano, there was quite a resemblance between the two cars. The Oméga-Six was offered on two wheelbases, with tourer, saloon and coupé-de ville bodies. Production at the small factory at Boulogne-sur-Seine

was never great, not exceeding 50 cars a year at best.

Omégas ran at Le Mans in 1924 and 1925, without success, and also in the Circuit des Routes Pavées where their highest place was second in the 2-litre class in 1925. Engine capacity went up to 2667cc in 1926 and to 3 litres in 1928.

In 1928 Daubeck was joined by another rich industrialist, Boyriven, who provided the finance for two new models, a 3-litre twin-overhead cam six and a single-cam straight-eight in 3- and 4-litre sizes. Hardly any of the latter sold, and no Omégas at all found customers after 1930. Most Omégas were sold to Daubeck's friends or business associates, sometimes in payment for materials. The Depression brought ruin to all his enterprises and in 1932 he committed suicide. GNG

OPEL
GERMANY 1898 to date

Adam Opel was born in 1837 in Russelsheim, near Frankfurt, the son of a master locksmith. He trained as a mechanic and in 1857 set out to tour the world. In Paris he saw the latest sewing machines and in 1862, back in Russelsheim, he built his own first sewing machine in his uncle's cowshed and went into business as an engineer and manufacturer. By 1868 he had moved to a purpose built factory and soon dominated the German sewing machine market.

By now Opel had five sons and through their enthusiasm for bicycling he moved into bicycle manufacture in 1886, at first with high-wheelers. By the following year Opel had introduced a 'safety' type, which gained much publicity through the brothers' racing successes and like the sewing machines came to dominate the market.

When Adam Opel died, in 1895, control of the company passed to his widow, Sophie, and his elder sons Carl and Wilhelm, who began to look for further manufacturing areas as the dwindling bicycle market became oversubscribed. In 1897 they bought the rights to the Benz-like Lutzmann car, introduced in 1895 by Friederich Lutzmann, a locksmith from Dessau. Under the patronage of the Grand Duke of Hesse, Opel opened a car department, with Lutzmann, who had moved south to Russelsheim with all his machinery and workers, in charge.

In 1898 they showed their first car as the Opel-Lutzmann. It had a rear-mounted single-cylinder 4hp engine and was replaced by a twin-cylinder model in 1899. Neither was very successful; only 11 cars were built in 1899 and 24 in 1900, when losses on car-making wiped out the substantial profits from the sewing machines and bicycles. Lutzmann was dismissed and car production stopped.

In the same year, however, Opel arranged to become the sole agent for Darracq in Germany, Austria and Hungary, and began to

build the cars under licence with German bodies fitted to imported chassis as Opel-Darracqs. In 1901 the company also introduced a somewhat uninspired belt-drive single-cylinder motorcycle.

The Opel-Darracqs sold well, but in 1902, at the Hamburg Show, Opel showed its own 1884cc twin-cylinder 10/12PS model. Although it continued to sell the Opel-Darracqs until 1906 it now began to expand its own range, which included small commercials from 1905 and twin-cylinder motorcycles from 1906. Motorcycle manufacture continued, but only in small numbers, until 1925, latterly with simple, lightweight machines. From 1924 the Diamant motorcycle was sold as the EO, or Elite-Opel. Diamant amalgamated with the Elitewerke car company in 1927 as Elite-Diamant. This company was taken over by Opel in 1928 and continued to build the EO until 1930.

Up to 1910 one of Opel's more popular car lines was its 'doctor's car' in twin-cylinder 6/12 and 8/14PS models, but large expensive models, topped by a 6.9-litre 35/40PS, sold well on the strength of outstanding production quality. Sales were helped by extensive competition success; in 1905 Opels had recorded over 100 wins and in 1907 Opels finished third and fourth in the Kaiserpreis race, the first German finishers. Wilhelm Opel won the 1909 Prince Henry Trial and Opel's only real competition failures were in Grand Prix racing.

Opel-Lutzmann buggy of c.1898

Opel 4/8PS doctor's car of 1909

Opel racing car of 1913

Opel 4/12PS Laubfrosch of 1924

In 1911 the Opel works were almost entirely destroyed by fire, but Opel turned even this to advantage. Sewing machine manufacture was dropped, with exactly 1 million machines having been made, and the plant was completely rebuilt with the most modern production facilities for car-making.

Shortly after production resumed in 1912, the 10,000th Opel was built. During 1913 the company began to build heavier trucks and car production reached some 3200, putting Opel sixth in the European market, which was led by Ford. When Sophie died during that year, control passed completely to Adam Opel's sons.

Up to World War I the cars ranged from small 1-litre 5/12 and 6/16PS models through the 8/20, 10/25, 14/30, 24/50 and 34/65 to the 10.2-litre 40/100PS, with a chassis price of £800. During the war Opel built trucks and trailers, a few cars and BMW aero engines, but when the war ended Russelsheim was occupied by the French and the Opel works were under military control, adding to the problems of raw materials shortages and a virtually collapsed market.

Opel survived by producing a few old models until 1924, when it effectively started anew with a completely re-equipped plant which introduced moving assembly lines to the European motor industry with the most modern machinery available. It was from these new works that Opel introduced a small mass-produced car in 1924, copied from the Citroën 5CV and known as the 4/12PS *Laubfrosch* (Tree-frog) because of its standard bright green finish.

Sales were helped by a recovering economy and by import tariffs which lasted until 1925. By 1928 Opel's 8000 or so employees were building some 250 cars a day, of which about half were 4/12s, for a 37.5 per cent share of the German makes market. At that time Opel was also the world's biggest bicycle producer.

Aware of the strength of the American manufacturers in the German market, Opel styled its larger cars along American lines and then openly courted an association with General Motors, which already had an assembly plant in Berlin. In January 1929 the Opel family interests were reorganized into a joint stock company, Adam Opel AG. In March GM purchased 80 per cent of the stock and by October 1931 had acquired the remaining 20 per cent from the family to become sole owners, at a total cost of $66.7 million.

The first GM-inspired Opel, a 1.8-litre six, had already appeared in 1930, and this and a 1-litre four were the starting point for the ranges of the next few years, with gradual size increases. In 1935 Opel introduced the 1279cc Olympia, named for the Berlin Olympic Games, introducing unitary construction on a large scale to the German industry and helping Opel to achieve a 42 per cent share of

Opel Admiral four-door convertible of 1938

the market that year.

In 1936 Opel became Europe's largest car manufacturer and introduced a new car, for production the following year, the 1074cc 23bhp Kadett. At the same time it finally stopped building bicycles and sold the production rights to NSU, after more than 2.5 million had been built.

Some 107,000 Kadetts were built until 1940, by which time Nazi control of the industry was making GM's position as proprietor untenable, particularly when it was asked to turn the works to munitions production. Late in 1940 GM relinquished its control of Opel to the government and in October car production stopped, in favour of truck and engine production.

The works were heavily bombed during the war but what remained was taken over by the American military administration in May 1945 and set to work making spare parts. Vehicle production was resumed in July 1946, at first with trucks as all the tooling for the Kadett had been taken away by the Russians a month or so earlier. The Kadett subsequently re-emerged in Russia as the Moskvich 400.

Car production at Russelsheim was restarted in December 1947, with the Olympia – followed in 1948 by the larger 2473cc Kapitan. Just over 6000 cars were made in 1948 and GM formally resumed control of Opel in November.

These essentially pre-war models were built until 1953, when the first real post-war design was introduced with the 1488cc Rekord, which was descended from the Olympia. It was available in 1680cc form from 1959 and 1897cc from 1965, when it also gained an overhead-cam engine. The Kapitan was increased in capacity in the same years, going up to 2784cc, and the Kapitan engine was also used in the new Admiral when that name was revived in 1964. At the top of the range was the Diplomat, also introduced in 1964, with 4.6- or 5.3-litre Chevrolet V8s in a well engineered, thoroughly European chassis.

In 1962 Opel introduced a new 1-litre Kadett, built in a brand new plant at Bochum which had been started in 1960 and was now the most modern car plant in Europe. Another new generation of Kadett was introduced in September 1965, after 649,512 of the

Opel Kadett saloon of 1962

Opel Kadett City saloon of 1978

previous series had been built. In total in 1965, Opel built 623,989 cars, including its five millionth. By October 1966, Bochum had produced its own millionth car and by 1976 there were three manufacturing plants and an automated warehouse on the site. As part of this continued expansion Opel opened another new factory, for component manufacture, at Kaiserslauten in 1966, and in the same year completed a 640-acre (260-hectare) proving ground at Dudenhofen at a cost of some 30 million marks.

The new technical facilities were put to good use in developing sportier Opels for the 1970s. In 1969 the company began a rallying support programme and introduced the pretty GT coupé, based on Kadett running gear and with the option of a 1.9-litre overhead-cam engine. In 1970 it was joined by the Commodore, a high performance 2.8-litre six, with optional fuel injection. In 1971 Opel built its ten millionth car and in May 1972 the three millionth Kadett was made.

The sporty Manta was launched in 1971 with a choice of four-cylinder engines of 1.6 and 1.9 litres and in various degrees of tune. A few weeks later Opel announced the Ascona, a saloon based on the fastback Manta's mechanical elements.

During the 1970s Opel began to share more technical and styling features with Vauxhall, a trend which had already become apparent with the similar Viva/Kadett ranges in the early 1960s, even before Opel officially returned to the British market in 1967. Vauxhall, General Motors' other major European marque, became the corporation's first European acquisition in December 1925, some time before the Opel takeover, as a wholly owned subsidiary.

The sharing of designs continued with the 1974 Kadett City, Opel's first hatchback model; it closely resembled Vauxhall's Chevette which was launched a little later. Thereafter most models were available with minor variations as Opels or Vauxhalls, with some of the Vauxhalls actually built in Germany and exported to Britain, although no Opels made the opposite journey.

In 1981 Opel and Vauxhall formally combined their British marketing operations but remained responsible for different develop-

Opel Monza GSE coupé of 1985

ment areas. With the full backing of GM's American facilities, Opel now develops all the corporation's European cars and contributes greatly to the 'world-car' programme, while Vauxhall principally develops the European commercial ranges.

In 1978 Opel dropped its American inspired V8 engine in favour of new in-line overhead-cam sixes of up to 3 litres and these appeared first in the larger Commodore, Monza and Senator models. In 1980 the company launched a transverse-engined front-wheel-drive Kadett (which Vauxhall cloned as the Astra), and in 1982 the Ascona (the European version of the American J-car) also changed to front-wheel drive.

Opel continued its rallying activities with great success and launched a twin-cam 16-valve 2.4-litre four-cylinder engine in the 1979 Ascona Rallye. The engine was developed for the 1981 Manta 400, with a works-entered version of which Walter Rohrl won the 1982 drivers' and manufacturers' world rally championships for Opel. This was part of a clean sweep for the rally team in 1982, alongside the British Open and European championships (all with the Manta 400).

By 1982 Opel employed some 60,000 people in Germany. The company also has assembly plants in Antwerp, as GM Continental NV which employs some 12,000 workers and has also built cars for Vauxhall, and in Lisbon, as GM de Portugal Limitada. Daewoo

builds Kadetts in Korea for sale by GM in the United States.

In September 1983, at the Frankfurt Show, the company suggested a possible future direction with design studies for the Opel Junior, a very small, efficient and highly adaptable car using new materials and technologies, although not scheduled for production.

The smallest production Opel is the front-wheel-drive Corsa, introduced in 1982 and available in five-door form from 1985. The rest of the 1985 range comprised versions of the Kadett, Ascona, Manta, Omega (a Rekord replacement), Senator and Monza, giving Opel a comprehensive coverage of the market.

In spite of this, and although the latest aerodynamic Kadett became European Car of the Year, Opel made substantial losses in 1983 and 1984, almost $300 million for the European grouping including Vauxhall. Opel lost at least two months production in 1984 to a German metalworkers' strike and production fell by over 120,000 units, to 670,766 – and second to Volkswagen-Audi on the German market. The company also suffered badly from indecision over changes in engine emission regulations. Nevertheless, it has persevered with a £400 million a year investment programme which will include replacements for both the Manta and Ascona by 1988, and in 1985 production totalled 938,071. BL

OPPERMAN
GB 1956-1959

In October 1956 the well-established general engineering company S. E. Opperman Ltd of Borehamwood, Hertfordshire, announced that it had started limited production of a small rear-engined glassfibre-bodied car which was to be sold as the Unicar. Designed by Laurie Bond, designer of the Bond and Berkeley three-wheelers, the four-wheeled Unicar used a twin-cylinder 225cc or 322cc Anzani two-stroke engine in a semi-monocoque chassis that was made up of six mouldings bolted and bonded together and reinforced with a mixture of alloy pressings, tubular subframes and a glassfibre bulkhead. The rear track was 12in (0.3m) narrower than the front, at 3ft (0.9m), and independent suspension was used on the front only, the rear having a solid axle.

At a total price of £399 10s, cheaper than any car at the 1956 London Motor Show, the Unicar offered very basic transport for two adults and two children. The front seats were a hammock type and the very occasional rears were simply padded covers over the toolbox and battery box. Top speed of the very lightweight car with the larger engine was claimed to be 75mph (120kph). The car was sold either fully built or as a kit.

At the 1958 London Motor Show, Opperman introduced a rather stylish small coupé, the Stirling. It had a similar mechanical layout to the saloon, which remained in production, with a two-stroke Excelsior engine, motorcycle type gearbox and chain drive.

Opperman also intended to produce the Stirling in collaboration with Steyr-Puch, shipping cars less drive units to Austria to be fitted with a power pack comprising a fan-cooled flat-twin engine, gearbox and final drive. This version was intended mainly for local sale but might have been offered in Britain had there been sufficient demand. There was not, and Opperman ceased car production in 1959. BL

Opperman Unicar of c.1958

ORIENT
see Metz

ORLEANS
see New Orleans

ORYX/BMF, ERDMANN, FEG, GOTTSCHALK, TEMPELHOF
GERMANY 1900-1901; 1904-1922

The Berliner Motorwagen-Fabrik was founded in Berlin in 1898 by Kurt Bendix and Willi Seck with 198,000 marks capital. Within two years it was employing 115 men and had started to make Gottschalk private cars and commercials. From 1901 it concentrated on commercials, which bore the initials BMF.

In 1904 it resumed car production. These cars were based on the friction drive Erdmanns and were sometimes known as FEG after Friedrich Erdmann of Gera, who made cars using Horch and Fafnir engines between 1904 and 1908. They were unusual in using friction only for starting and for hills, otherwise there was direct drive. BMF also made these vehicles under the names Direkta and Berolina, and as such they were popular as taxis and vans. Also used were the names Oryx – from 1907, when Willi Seck designed the 10hp monobloc four-cylinder X Type – and Tempelhof.

In 1909 the name of the firm was changed to Oryx Motorenwerke when it was acquired by Dürkopp. An interesting feature in 1913 was that engine, gearbox, clutch and pedals were mounted on a detachable frame. Lord Kitchener used an Oryx in India at this time.

Car production ended in 1922, when the works at Berlin-Reinickendorf became a components supplier to Dürkopp. The British importer had been F. B. Goodchild, previously an agent for Le Zèbre. NB

OSCA
ITALY 1947-1967

In 1938 the Maserati brothers sold their interests in the firm bearing their own name to the industrialist Adolfo Orsi but stayed with the company under a 10-year arrangement, most of which was rendered fairly meaningless by World War II. In 1947 the three surviving brothers, Bindo, Ernesto and Ettore, left Orsi and returned to their native Bologna with plans to build racing cars for private owners.

In December 1947, unable to use their own name directly, they founded Officina Specializzata Costruzione Automobili Fratelli Maserati, or OSCA. The operation, with minimal capital or equipment, was based in the original Maserati works in the town; Bindo managed the business, while Ernesto became the designer and Ettore the works engineer.

The first OSCA car was an 1100cc four-cylinder sports car, which later doubled as a Formula 2 car, based on a tubular ladder chassis typical of the brothers' earlier designs. It was the first of only three distinct OSCA lines and was built for many years in sizes from 749cc to 1452cc, proving very successful in sports car racing.

In 1951 the Siamese driver Prince Bira asked OSCA to build a 4½-litre V12 Grand Prix engine which he could use in his Maser-

OSCA 4½-litre Grand Prix car of 1951

ati 4CLT/48 chassis and he won the Richmond Trophy race at Goodwood on the hybrid car's first appearance. In September 1951 a wholly OSCA-built Formula 1 car appeared in the Italian Grand Prix at Monza, but the car was never successful at this level and only four were built before OSCA moved back to Formula 2 and sports car racing.

In 1954 Stirling Moss and Bill Lloyd won their class and on handicap in the Sebring 12 Hour race with a 1500 Sport model and this helped the company to gain some orders in America. In 1955 it moved to a new factory at San Lazzaro di Savenna, just outside Bologna, and for 1956 the company offered a range of two-seaters, still intended mostly for competition, from 1.1 to 2 litres, the largest a six with a top speed of over 150mph (241kph).

Production was always very limited, with every car virtually hand built and bodywork bought-in. By 1958, with about 40 workers, OSCA was building only 20 or 30 cars a year, but these were technically interesting and included models with desmodromic valve gear, designed by Fabio Taglioni of the Ducati motorcycle company, which used the system with great success. OSCA used it on the 750 and 1500 models and on an ambitious but stillborn air-cooled flat-8 Grand Prix engine. Alejandro de Tomaso, at one time a works driver for OSCA who won the Index of Performance for the marque at Le Mans in 1958, used OSCA engines in two of his own new Grand Prix cars in 1961 and, coincidentally, went on to buy the Maserati company in 1976.

When Formula Junior was introduced in 1959, OSCA built a car with a modified Fiat 1100 engine and 'works' driver Colin Davis won the first FJ championship before the front-engined OSCA was outclassed by the new mid-engined cars.

OSCA 1600GTS coupé of 1962

Also in 1959 OSCA entered an agreement with Fiat whereby Fiat used a larger but detuned 1598cc version of the four-cylinder twin-cam OSCA sports car engine, which Fiat built itself, in its Farina-styled 1500S. OSCA then used a tuned version of the 'Fiat' engine in its own roadgoing GT cars, the first of the marque intended specifically for road use.

In 1963 the ageing brothers sold OSCA to Count Domenico Agusta's MV Agusta company, which manufactured the famous racing motorcycles and also helicopters, the latter mostly under licence from the American Bell company. In spite of his racing background Agusta decided to end OSCA's racing involvement and built rather bland cars from 1966 to 1967, based on the earlier chassis but with the twin-cam OSCA engines replaced by the 1.7-litre German Ford V4 engine. With these pale shadows, OSCA faded quietly away in 1967. BL

OTAV/FJTA, JUNIOR, TURKHEIMER
ITALY 1905-1910

Max Turkheimer, a German by birth, moved to Lombardy and began his business career in 1888, becoming a wholesaler and mail order supplier of bicycle components. He introduced his own bicycle range and imported Wolfmuller motorcycles in 1896 and made his own motorcycles from 1902.

In 1905 the Societa Anonima Officine Turkheimer per Automobili e Velocipedo (OTAV) was formed in Milan with 750,000 lire capital and an 86,100sq ft (8000sq m) factory. Before long an air-cooled single-cylinder car with two speed (no reverse) epicyclic gearing and belt drive appeared which was cheap, successful and very light at less than 560lb (254kg). The popularity of this car soon waned, however, and the financial losses accumulated by the company amounted to nearly 500,000 lire two years later, despite the adoption of a licence to build Turgan commercial vehicles in 1906.

OTAV 5½hp runabout of 1907

Temporary salvation came from Frederico Momo, an automobile dealer who had bought the Junior factory in Turin and then purchased shares in OTAV. Junior was the name given to Giovanni Ceirano Jr's car which had been introduced in 1905 at Fabbrica Junior Torinese Automobili (FJTA). Giovanni had previously worked for Fratelli Ceirano and had developed the new cars for 1904 at a company named Giovanni Ceirano Junior.

Juniors were initially De Dion one- or two-cylinder engined machines, although they became best known as fours, and these were the types, with engines of up to 8 litres, that

OTAV factory, c.1905

Momo retained alongside the little OTAVs in 1908. That year Carlo Maserati was working with Junior and the two factories in Milan and Turin were kept working separately, although finance, sales and advertising were handled on a common basis. Giovanni Ceirano left in 1906 to start SCAT.

Junior used Ford's London depot as its British sales headquarters and C. F. Bertelli, racing car designer, worked for OTAV's London importers.

Momo's plans did not prosper: OTAV is thought to have ceased car production at the end of 1908 and Junior was discontinued in 1910. Turkheimer regained control in Milan and continued to make industrial engines and accessories and components for two-wheelers. Until the 1950s his son and nephew were Italian concessionaires for Ariel motorcycles and their firm still exists. NB

OTOMO/ALES
JAPAN 1924-1927

Junya Toyokawa, the inventor of a gyro-compass, worked for Hakuyosha Ironworks in Tokyo and there developed small and medium Ales car prototypes in 1921. His colleague H. Ikenaga took up the idea in 1924 and made 30 production three-seat cars under the name Otomo. A study of American methods led him to believe that at least 1000 cars a year at the equivalent of $800 was necessary to undercut imports, and a four-cylinder air-cooled 944cc engine was tooled accordingly with all parts made by Hakuyosha.

A larger water-cooled four-cylinder model was introduced in 1926 but reliability and sales were both disappointing. After 270 Otomos had been sold, including the first Japanese car export, to Shanghai, production ended in 1927. NB

OTTO
FRANCE 1900-1914

The Société Générale des Voitures Automobiles Otto of Paris was the first company to import Otto engines to France, originally as stationary units. The first Otto free-piston engine was designed by self-taught inventor Nikolaus August Otto, from Cologne, based on Lenoir's earlier work, and the Otto engine was in production in a factory at Deutz, across the Rhine from Cologne, by 1872.

In 1875, under the direction of Gottlieb Daimler and Wilhelm Maybach, Otto's annual production exceeded 600 units. By 1876 Otto had turned to making a true four-stroke engine, although he ultimately failed to gain a patent on the principle, and by 1878 the engine had become a great commercial success.

By the time the Société Générale des Voi-

tures Automobiles Otto introduced its first cars at the Paris Show in August 1900, it had been building Otto engines under licence for over 20 years. Two models were shown, with front-mounted 7 and 12hp vertical twin engines (although another contemporary report lists them as 6 and 10hp models, respectively of horizontal and vertical type). The company announced that it did not intend only to build Otto-engined models but also planned to use the Diesel motor, for which it had secured the French manufacturing rights.

By February 1901 the company had moved from the Rue de la Convention to the Rue Lacourbe and in that month showed four cars in Paris, two horizontal twin-cylinder engined 10hp models and two vertical four-cylinder 20hp models, with steel reinforced wood frames. Electric ignition was standard, but with an Otto magnetic device as an option.

At the end of 1902 the company offered a much modified vertical single-cylinder 10hp model with engine speed regulated by a variable exhaust valve. This gave much more flexibility than was then common, with engine speeds from 250 to 2000rpm claimed.

In 1909, after several years of building models broadly similar to the earliest types, Otto introduced a model called the FL, phonetically after the French pronunciation of Eiffel, the engineer and his famous tower. The FL was a fairly ordinary four-cylinder 12/16hp model which was joined by a six-cylinder 18/24 in 1912 but few were made because of World War I and Otto stopped car production in 1914. BL

Otto 9hp doctor's coupé of 1909

OWEN MAGNETIC
USA 1915-1922

The Owen Magnetic was a high-quality car featuring an electric transmission developed by Justin B. Entz whose design had been incorporated in some Columbia cars and also in the battleship *New Mexico*. The R. M. Owen Co was founded to manufacture the Entz transmission for use in other makes of car, but at the end of 1914 the brothers Raymond and Ralph Owen launched their own car, the Owen Magnetic, to come on the market in 1915.

It was powered by a six-cylinder engine – said to be Owen's own, but possibly made by Weidely – which drove a generator, electric power being transmitted over an air gap to a motor which drove the propeller shaft. Advertised as the 'Car of a Thousand Speeds', it not only dispensed with clutch and gears but also with a starter motor, battery and magneto, all these functions being performed by parts of the transmission.

The Entz patents were owned by Walter Baker of the Baker Motor Vehicle Co and in 1915 the newly formed Baker, Rauch and Lang Co acquired the R. M. Owen Co and transferred production from New York City to Cleveland, Ohio. Engines and chassis were produced in the Baker plant, while bodies were manufactured in the Rauch and Lang plant.

The cars were expensive, prices rising as high as $6500 by 1918. Among famous owners were the operatic tenors John McCormack and Enrico Caruso.

In 1919 Baker, Rauch and Lang abandoned production of the Owen Magnetic as sales were disappointing. In their best year, they had managed to sell only about 250 cars in all. Raymond Owen acquired new premises at Wilkes Barre, Pennsylvania, where production continued on a small scale until 1921. The company was then acquired by J. L. Crown, who went on to manufacture a small number of cars under the name Crown Magnetic. GNG

Owen Magnetic tourer of c.1915

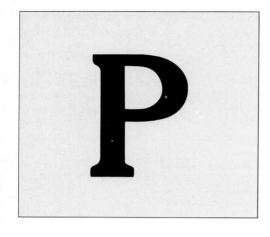

P

PACKARD
USA 1899-1958

The brothers James Ward and William Doud Packard founded their Packard Electrical Co in Warren, Ohio, in 1890 making, as was Henry Royce at the same time, electric bells, dynamos and lamps. The following year they established another electrical company, the New York & Ohio Co, and it was in the works of this company that the first Packard car was built in 1899.

It was designed by James aided by two ex-Winton employees, George Weiss and William A. Hatcher, who later went into partnership with Brew, to make the short-lived Brew-Hatcher car in Cleveland. A separate partnership was formed, Packard & Weiss, becoming the automobile department of the New York & Ohio Co on 30 December 1899, by which time at least six cars had been laid down.

In August 1900 the partnership was separated from the parent company by the formation of the Ohio Automobile Co, and production that year totalled 49 cars. The company exhibited at the first national automobile show in New York's Madison Square Gardens and sold two cars to William D. Rockefeller. The link between east coast conservative rich and the little firm from the Midwest had begun.

The Ohio Automobile Co still leased the buildings from Packard Electrical and the machinery from New York & Ohio Co, and in September 1901 it bought both these firms. Packard Electrical moved to new premises and flourished as a separate concern, being one of the leading suppliers of automotive wiring in the United States and becoming part of General Motors in the 1930s.

The famous slogan 'Ask the Man Who Owns One' was first used in a Packard advertisement in October 1901. Production that year was 81 cars, still basically the same single-cylinder gas buggy design as in 1899, but with wheel steering from early 1901.

James Ward Packard opposed an increase in the number of cylinders, saying 'more than one cylinder in a Packard would be like two

tails on a cat – you just don't need it', but like all conservative inventors he had to bow to progress in the end, and the Model G 24hp flat twin appeared in 1902, the same year that Henry B. Joy joined the company with very welcome finance from Detroit business interests. Another newcomer that year was Charles Schmidt, a French engineer who came from Mors.

The first front-engined four-cylinder Packard, the Model K, was introduced in 1903 and in October that year manufacture was moved to Detroit, where it was to remain until the end of production in 1958. The move marked the end of the role of the Packard brothers who stayed in Warren to supervise their electrical companies, although James Ward Packard remained in the nominal position of president until 1909. Henry Joy was now in charge of the Packard Motor Car Co.

Despite a $200,000 loss in the 1903-4 year, Packard recovered quickly and made profits each year for the next 18 years. Between 1903 and 1908 the factory on East Grand Boulevard grew in area from 100,000 to 580,000sq ft (9300 to 54,000sq m). By 1909 annual production was up to 3106 cars, giving Packard eighth place among US car-makers.

Truck manufacture began in 1905 and, although they were never as celebrated as the cars, more than 43,000 trucks were made until 1923. Exports began and flourished in this period, starting with an agency in Hawaii in 1908, followed by Britain, France, Spain, Cuba and several Latin American countries.

Two important events of 1911 were the introduction of Packard's first six-cylinder car and the arrival of Alvan Macauley who was to become president in 1916 and to remain in that post until 1938. A lawyer by training, Macauley was described as 'the only gentleman in the automotive business' and was the ideal man to head the dignified and aristocratic Packard company.

Unlike European luxury car-makers, Packard had its own bodyshop and listed a wide

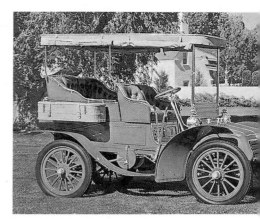

Packard Model F of 1903

range of 13 different styles on the new Six chassis. Prices ran from $5000 for a touring to $6550 for the Imperial landaulette, which put them near the top of the US price list, but still cheaper than Peerless, Pierce-Arrow or Stevens-Duryea. In fact the 1913 2-38 was offered with cheap bodies by Springfield or Fisher, but they were not successful. Packard customers preferred, and could afford, the best.

In 1912 Jesse Vincent came from Hudson to be chief engineer; he had worked with Macauley at the Burroughs adding machine company and was to remain with Packard for more than 40 years. In 1915 he brought out his first masterpiece, the Twin Six, which was the world's first series production car pow-

Packard Model 633 of 1929

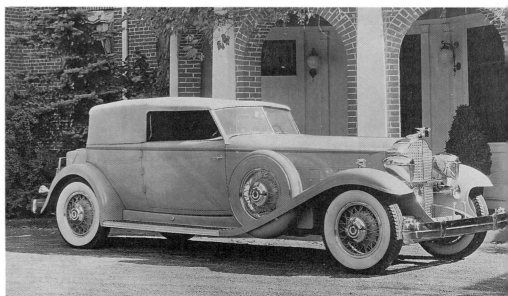

Packard Dietrich-bodied Twin Six of 1932

ered by a V12 engine. It was quite reasonably priced, from $2750 to $4800, and more than 35,000 were sold in an eight year production run. To meet demand the East Grand Boulevard works grew still further, so that by 1916 the area was over 100 acres (40 hectares).

Car production slowed after America's entry into World War I in April 1917 and ceased altogether in September 1918. The factory was now concentrating on manufacture of the Vincent-designed Liberty V8 and V12 aero engines, building 6500 of the V12.

After the war Macauley planned a great increase in production with a new six-cylinder car called the Single Six, which ultimately spelt *finis* for both the Twin Six and the trucks, whose department gave way to a completely new bodyplant. Both were phased out in 1923, the year that also saw the introduction of the new straight-eight, known as the Single Eight, and the ancestor of the whole line of 'senior' Packards up to 1942. The 1929 Eights were called the Sixth Series, after the model numbers, 626, 633, etc and this began a practice which continued until the 26th series of 1953.

Production rose dramatically, from 7684 in 1921 to 50,054 in 1928, enabling Packard to outsell Cadillac, which most people thought of as a cheaper car, although its single model was bracketed in price by Packard's six- and eight-cylinder cars. Although Packard still offered a wide range of factory built bodies, custom bodies now featured prominently in the catalogue from such firms as Holbrook, Judkins and Dietrich.

The Depression hit Packard as hard as most other car-makers, and sales dropped from over 50,000 in 1928 to a depressing 28,177 in 1930 and a terrifying low of only 6071 in 1934. Two contrasting models were introduced for 1932, the Light Eight aimed at the middle price market and priced between $1750 and $1795, and a new V12, the Twin Six, renamed Twelve from 1933. The Light Eight was dropped after one year as it was priced too close to the straight-eight, but the Twelve continued until 1939.

In October 1931 Packard opened a Canadian branch assembly plant at Windsor, Ontario, which operated until 1939. Apart from this, Packard had no regional or foreign assembly plants, all production being concentrated in Detroit.

The Light Eight had pointed the way towards a new, cheaper Packard, and in 1935 came the car which was to take the company into a new field, to boost production to new heights and in all probability to save the company from extinction. This was the 120, a 3.7-litre straight-eight priced at under $1000 for the business coupé and only $1095 for the top price touring sedan. Ten thousand orders were received before a single car was ready for delivery.

In the first nine months of 1935 Packard production totalled 31,987 cars, an increase of 760.75 per cent over the same period in 1934. The previous year's loss of $7.3 million

Packard Eight limousine of 1936

Packard Model 120 of 1940

was turned round to a $776,000 profit in the same nine months. The figures for 1936 were even better, with over $7 million profit and production at a record 83,226 cars.

In 1937 the 120 was joined by a similar looking six-cylinder car, for which prices began at $795, and sales totalled 109,518 cars. Of these more than 90 per cent were 'juniors' – that is, the Six or the 120 – yet half the workforce was engaged on building the remaining 8 per cent of 'senior' Packards, the big Eights and the Twelve. For the 1939 season Super Eight production was transferred to the 'junior' assembly line, a stockpile of Twelves was built up early in the season and then the Twelve line was closed down, to be replaced by a new assembly line for 'juniors'.

The strikingly styled Clipper series, introduced in April 1941, gave a boost to Packard's last full pre-war season with sales totalling 72,855, but all car production closed down on 9 February 1942 and the momentum generated by the Clipper was lost for ever. As in World War I, wartime production concentrated on aero engines, this time the Rolls-Royce-designed Merlin, of which 55,523 came from East Grand Boulevard between 1941 and 1945. The company also made V12 and V16 marine engines which continued in production after the war.

Post-war production concentrated on the Clipper, and the Senior Eight was not revived. The body dies for the latter were sold to the Soviet Union and the 180 reappeared in Rus-

sian guise in 1946 as the ZIS-110. The Clipper bodies came from Briggs, as they had done since 1941, and this dependence on an outside supplier caused Packard severe headaches in supply and quality control in the post-war years.

Sales were good to start with, reaching nearly 99,000 in 1948 and over 104,000 in 1949, but thereafter it was mostly downhill. Various factors can be blamed: the decision to abandon the top end of the market into which Cadillac promptly and successfully stepped, controversial styling, and the inability to match the giants with vital innovations such as the V8 engine. Packard did manage to launch its own automatic transmission, named Ultramatic, in 1950 and it was the only independent to do so without help from a transmission manufacturer.

In 1952 James J. Nance took over as president. Previously a salesman, Nance came from the General Electric's subsidiary, Hotpoint, and his sales skills were certainly needed at Packard where the plant was working at only 50 per cent of capacity. To retrieve the luxury car image Nance introduced long wheelbase sedans and limousines and the glamorous Caribbean convertible. At the same time the Clipper name was revived for the cheaper Packards, and for one season, 1955-56, this was listed as a separate make in order to isolate it from the up-market models.

In October 1954 Packard purchased Studebaker to form the Studebaker Packard

Corporation. The main idea was to broaden market coverage as Studebaker catered to the low and low-medium priced fields, and it also had a truck range to offer. Also Nash and Hudson had just merged to form American Motors Corporation and Nance thought that the future was not too bright for the independent makes with annual sales of only 100,000.

What he did not know, however, was that the Studebaker plant was operating at far below capacity and that its break even point was an annual sales figure of 250,000, although actual sales were only 186,484 in 1953. Studebaker had sunk from its position of style leader and profit maker in the years from 1946 to 1950 and now had a poor image, so Packard's reputation was not enhanced by the

Packard Electric set up a motor car department which produced various models of Oldsmobile up to 1907. It is possible that they differed somewhat from the American product, by using single-cylinder engines in the Model G chassis which in the United States always had a two-cylinder engine. They did not sell very well, and in December 1907 Packard Electric ceased manufacture of these disappointing machines and concentrated on its main business of making transformers and lamps.

In January 1909 it sold the motor car department to Reo, which made cars there until 1913. The Packard Electric Co has continued to exist at St Catharines and is now a part of the international Packard-Ferranti organization. GNG

Lakewood, Lenox, Larchmont, Montrose and Westbrook. In 1915 came the first six-cylinder model, the 6-46, priced from $1095 to $2250. The slogan 'The Standard of Value and Quality' was adopted, but two years later it gave way to 'The Most Beautiful Car in America'. This was a debatable claim, but Paiges of this era were above average in looks with slightly vee shaped radiators which, when combined with wire wheels on the sporting models, gave them some resemblance to the Bentley.

Authorized capital was increased to $1 million in 1915 and to $2 million in 1916. A stock dividend of 80 per cent was paid for the fiscal year 1915-16. At this period there were only about 18 shareholders. In 1917, when car production was running at 150 a day, the Detroit plant leased by Paige-Detroit was bought by the Pennsylvania Railroad and Paige acquired a 51-acre (20-hectare) site on which to build a new plant.

In 1918 the company began making trucks, producing a 2-tonner powered by a four-cylinder engine. This, like the passenger cars, was made by Continental, although later trucks, made until 1923, were Hinkley-powered.

Paige-Detroit began making its own engines in 1919; its 3.8-litre six was used in the 6-42 model but the larger 6-55 was powered by a 4.9-litre Continental. Production was down to 9900 in 1921, but it was soon to receive a tremendous boost with the introduction of the smaller and cheaper Jewett.

Before that came a handful of speedsters which earned the company more fame than any of the quantity-produced cars, although it is likely that it made no profit on them. The Paige Daytona Model 6-66, powered by a 5.4-litre 66bhp six-cylinder Continental engine, broke every stock car record in January 1922, including a mile at 102.8mph (1.6km at 165.4kph). The Daytonas had two-seater bodies but a third seat, with its accompanying foot rest, could be pulled out like a drawer from the side of the body. Whether any passenger braved this seat at anywhere near the car's maximum speed is not recorded.

The Daytona was priced at $3400 in 1922, and this was reduced to $2400 the following year, presumably because the speedsters were not selling. Only 56 Daytonas were made, and they were dropped at the end of the 1923 season.

For 1923 Paige-Detroit introduced the Jewett as a cheaper line, in the same way that Chandler brought out the Cleveland. Offered in seven models from $995 to $1665, the Jewett was powered by a development of the Paige 6-44 engine, the main improvement being the adoption of force-feed lubrication. The Jewett sold very well initially, bringing combined figures for the two makes to 44,000 for 1923, but this dropped to 39,380 in 1925 and 37,222 in 1926.

The larger Paiges continued to use the 5.4-litre Continental 10-A engine until 1925, then switched to smaller units for the 6-65 and 6-75 models of 1926-27. For the latter year the

Packard Caribbean convertible of 1959

acquisition of the Indiana company. Then other blows fell: Briggs now belonged to Chrysler and could no longer supply bodies to Packard, which had to set up a new body-shop in Detroit, while defence cutbacks hit Packard and Studebaker very badly as orders for aero engines and trucks were cancelled. Sales rallied slightly in 1955, which was a good year for the industry generally, but thereafter dropped badly.

In August 1956 Nance resigned and Studebaker-Packard was bought by Curtiss-Wright, primarily as a tax loss operation. The last genuine Packards were those of the 1956 season; thereafter all production was transferred to South Bend, and the 1957 and 1958 Packards were badge-engineered Studebakers with hints of Packard styling and, of course, higher prices. The last Packard left the production line in July 1958; Studebaker introduced the compact Lark for the 1959 season and began to make profits again, but only for a while. Curiously no-one has tried to market a Packard replica, as has been done with such marques as Auburn, Duesenberg and Stutz; perhaps it is an indication of the truth of the old company slogan, 'Only Packard can build a Packard'.

The Canadian branch of the Packard Electric Co also made cars, but they were Oldsmobiles, not Packards. The branch was formed in 1894 at St Catharines, Ontario, and five years later the Packard brothers severed their connection with the company. In 1905

PAIGE-DETROIT/PAIGE, JEWETT
USA 1909-1927

The Paige-Detroit Motor Car Co was formed in October 1909 by Frederick O. Paige, born in 1864, who had been with the Reliance Automobile Manufacturing Co of Detroit. Initial capital was $100,000, all of which was taken up by subscribers. The first cars, which were delivered in December 1909, used an unusual in-line three-cylinder two-stroke engine of 25hp and were made as roadsters selling for $800.

In 1910 the authorized capital was raised to $250,000, and in 1911 the company was taken over by a Detroit coal merchant, Harry M. Jewett, who had been born in 1870. A brother, Frederick, was vice-president, and another brother, Edward, was also a director. The cars became simply Paige, although the company name remained Paige-Detroit.

The Jewett brothers quickly discarded the two-stroke engine, replacing it with a conventional four-cylinder four-stroke unit of 20hp. By 1914 they were making two models of four-cylinder car, with 22 and 25hp engines and priced from $975 to $1850. Production that year was 4631 cars and two years later it had risen to 12,456.

Paige cars had attractive names for the different body styles, such as Brunswick,

Jewett was dropped, and sold as the Paige 6-45, powered by a 3-litre Continental engine. At the other end of the scale was the 8-85, a 4.9-litre Lycoming-powered straight-eight.

Although Paige-Detroit was completing a new, modern factory on a 45-acre (18-hectare) site in Dearborn, Michigan, which indicated confidence in the future, profitability was dropping and the Jewett brothers were anxious to sell. By coincidence the purchasers were also three brothers, Joe, Ray and Robert Graham, who acquired Paige-Detroit on 10 June 1927 for $4 million. Harry Jewett put some of his share into a laundry business.

The Paige line was continued for the rest of 1927, and for 1928 a new line of cars called Graham-Paige was announced. The cars were sold as Grahams from 1931 onwards, but in that year there was a short-lived express pickup on the Model 612 chassis marketed under the name Paige to distinguish it from the passenger cars. Frederick O. Paige died in 1935, just two years after Harry Jewett. GNG

1914. From 1915, when a six-cylinder car was offered briefly, 3- to 4-ton trucks were built, most having Dorman engines. The Palladium name is thought to have come from the former theatre where the cars were made.

In 1913 a move was made to Normand Road, Kensington, and then in 1914 to Felsham Road, Putney. Assembly of vehicles – and DH4 aircraft during World War I – took place at this address, although aero engines and parts replaced cars and commercials in 1917-18.

After the war the cars and commercials were all-British and were made on the modern machinery installed during the war years, with the exception of the Timken drive-axles and Continental engines from America that powered the 500 or so trucks sold until 1925. A cyclecar appeared in 1919, but more successful was a Dorman-powered 12 from 1922, versions of which had sporting pretensions and attractive styling.

The firm was by then called Palladium Autocars Ltd and was in financial difficulties.

Palmer-Singer roadster of 1909

PALMER-SINGER/SINGER
USA 1907-1920

The Palmer-Singer Co was formed in 1906 by H. U. Palmer and Charles A. Singer as a sales organization dealing in Simplex and Matheson cars, with branches in New York and Chicago. In 1907 they brought out a large sporting car advertised as 'The Third Oldest Six in America', which had a 60hp six-cylinder engine of 10 litres capacity and shaft drive. It had a three to one direct drive third speed, with a 2.1 to 1 overdrive top speed, giving 75mph (120kph). The first few cars were made to order only in the Matheson factory at Wilks Barre, Pennsylvania, and from 1909 to 1911 they were made in the New York City factory of the Hewitt Motor Co. Then William Metzger, formerly of EMF, gained control of Hewitt and discontinued car manufacture in order to concentrate on trucks, so Palmer and Singer were forced to make their own cars.

They leased a factory between Second and Third Avenues in Long Island City, and began to make a 28/30hp four-cylinder roadster called the Skimabout and the Town and Country landaulet with Renault-style dashboard radiator, also using the 28/30hp engine. At $3000 the Town and Country cost $150 more than the 6-60 roadster.

In 1913 came the Brighton Six tourer, named after the make's victory in the Brighton Beach, Long Island, Derby. Powered by a 50hp six-cylinder engine, the Brighton Six had a modern torpedo body with Mercédèslike vee radiator, wire wheels and the option of compressed air or electric starting. At $2575 it seemed an attractive proposition, one of the best-looking cars on the US market, but sales were slow and in a desperate attempt to gain publicity Palmer-Singer announced new cars in December 1913 which it called 1915 models. The only really new design was the Magic, which used a six-cylinder Fischer slide-valve engine in a body similar to the Brighton.

The old 6-60 was still listed, at $3525, but

Paige 6-70 tourer of 1923

PALLADIUM
GB 1912-1924

Dr J. Ross MacMahon's Motor Exchange car sales business became a limited company in December 1909 with £10,000 capital, later increased to £20,000. It had showrooms in Euston Road, London, but there is evidence that the cars it launched in 1912, made from high-grade French components including Chapuis-Dornier engines, were assembled for a time in Twickenham. Chassis numbers imply that 420 were made in 1913 and 240 in

A reconstruction scheme was organized in 1922, MacMahon continuing in business as the Palladium Engineering Co Ltd. In 1923 about 500 vehicles were built.

In 1924 the company went into voluntary liquidation and in May 1925 the factory in Putney became the place where Gordon England built his Brooklands Austin Sevens. In 1926 a few remaining Palladiums with British Anzani engines were sold. The spares were acquired by Jack McEwan in north London and passed from him to scrap dealer Bert Blower, who paid £100 for several truck loads that included some incomplete cars. These were all scrapped in 1940. NB by June 1914 the Palmer and Singer Manufacturing Co was out of business, the assets being acquired by William Wooster. It was rumoured that he would make a $500 car under the Palmer-Singer name, but instead he sold off the machinery in small lots.

Charles Singer purchased the name, patents, goodwill and parts, and set up a new business in the former Alco factory, also in Long Island City. In September 1914 he introduced his Singer Six, powered by a Herschell-Spillman engine and featuring a more sharply pointed vee radiator than the Palmer-Singer. Production of this model reached five a week for a while, with a variety of open and closed bodies offered at prices up to $5000. Production ceased with America's entry into World War I, and restarted in a new factory at Mount Vernon, New York, without Charles Singer at the helm. The pre-war Six and a Weidely-powered V12 were offered. Prices ran from $5800 to $7400. Very few post-war cars were made before the Singer Motor Car Co Inc closed down in 1920.

In 1913 there were plans for the Brighton Six to be assembled in Canada by the Maritime Motor Car Co Ltd of St John, New Brunswick, and sold under the name Maritime-Singer. Probably not more than six cars were completed, however, before Palmer-Singer went out of business. GNG

PAN
USA 1916-1922

Samuel Conner Pandolfo sought to make money out of the wartime bull market in motor shares. Formerly a schoolmaster and insurance salesman, in 1916 he began to promote the Pan Motor Co from Albuquerque, New Mexico, where he had been forced to move after insurance irregularities were uncovered in Texas.

Capital was to be $5 million. In the event, 50,000 people provided $6 million by 1918, when a factory with dormitory town for the workers was established at St Cloud, Minnesota. Unlike many similar promoters, Pandolfo at least intended to make something, although only one of his Pan Tank Tread tractors 'that will win the war' in fact materialized and, even then, it did not receive an engine until after the war had been won. His four-cylinder cars, including the Tourist Sleeper, which had seats that could convert into beds, were more numerous, 737 being made in all. Works manager was George Booth from Sheffield, England.

Pandolfo started a magazine, *Banker, Merchant and Manufacturer*, which published glowing accounts of Pan stock. The Minnesota State Securities Commission took a dim view of Pandolfo's self-endorsement and he was put on trial for 'using the US mails to defraud'. Samuel C. Pandolfo was sent to prison and his Pan Motor Co ceased trading in 1922. NB

PANHARD ET LEVASSOR
FRANCE 1891-1967

Perin and Pauwels were two carpenters who established a workshop in Paris in 1845 that became famous for its bandsaws and other woodworking tools. After Pauwels left the business 26-year-old René Panhard, a member of an old-established coachbuilding family, became Perin's partner in 1867.

In 1873 about 100 men were employed, larger premises in the Avenue d'Ivry were acquired and Panhard's friend, Emile Levassor, joined the company, purchasing 10 per cent of the equity for 50,000 francs. Panhard was also a friend of the Belgian engineer Edouard Sarazin, the French agent for the Gasmotorenfabrik Deutz, where Gottlieb Daimler was chief engineer, having worked briefly at Perin et Pauwels in the early 1860s.

In 1875 Perin et Panhard began to build the Deutz engines for the French market and production continued until Deutz established its own Paris factory in 1879. When Daimler, who had set up on his own in the 1880s, needed a French outlet Sarazin again approached Panhard, whose company agreed to produce Daimler engines. After Perin's death in 1886 the company was re-named Panhard et Levassor. Sarazin died in 1887 but his widow retained the Daimler licence and married Levassor in 1890.

Panhard et Levassor also built Benz engines for Emile Roger and assembled a few Benz tricycles for him as well. The company needed a major outlet for its Daimler engines, however. Accordingly it approached Peugeot in 1888 and began to supply that firm two years later.

Panhard's own rear and mid-engined car experiments began at the same time and resulted in the first two sales in 1891. The following year it produced a full colour sales catalogue and in 1893 commercials and motor boats were offered. A total of 294 Daimler engines had been sold by the end of 1893 as well as about 55 Panhard et Levassor cars. In 1894-95 the classic Panhard concept of wheel steering, front engine and rear wheel drive by chain – first tried in June 1890 – was established as the Système Panhard. In 1896 Emile Levassor was injured in the Paris-Marseilles race and died a year later.

The year 1897 was when the company was re-formed as Société Anonyme des Anciens Etablissements Panhard et Levassor with capital of 5 million francs. Board members included Gottlieb Daimler; René Panhard's son Hippolyte; Adolphe Clément, who had invested 1 million francs; Arthur Krebs, designer of submarine periscopes, balloons and carburettors; Léon Pierron; various machine tool magnates and sportsman René de Knyff. The company had 650 employees.

Production in 1898 was 336 vehicles and exceeded 1000 for the first time in 1902. Clément adopted the Krebs-designed Clément-Panhard light car, the prototype Napier of 1899 was a Panhard with Napier engine, and the Hon Charles S. Rolls raced Panhards with success and sold them in London from 1902. Germain, Dürkopp (which actually held a Panhard et Levassor licence), Star, Locomobile and MMC all made Panhard look-alikes and the Système Panhard was widely copied elsewhere. Hotchkiss made components for Panhard before starting car production on its own account.

In 1901 Panhard reputedly built three-wheelers for the short-lived De Boisse firm in Paris and commercial vehicles were by then in series production. It also acquired Löhner-Porsche French rights but apparently did not act on them.

Vehicle production reached 1127 in 1903, when 1500 men were employed. Adolphe Clément resigned that year to concentrate on his own vehicles. Production then slipped back despite the opening of an additional components works at Rheims employing 185

Panhard et Levassor 6hp tonneau of 1899

PARIS AMSTERDAM 1898

CHARRON sur PANHARD

Panhard et Levassor roadster of 1898

Panhard et Levassor 'skiff-torpedo' of 1912

Panhard Dyna saloon of c.1946

men. Just 788 cars were built in 1908 following massive layoffs the previous year because of falling demand, yet profits and dividends were maintained. Aero engines had been built from 1905, when Panhard's first six-cylinder car engine – of 11 litres capacity – appeared.

After René Panhard's death in 1908 his brother Léon and son Hippolyte took charge. Léon's son Paul had joined the company in 1906 and controlled the family's interests in the firm until the 1960s.

Sales recovered to 1038 in 1909, 1870 in 1910 and 2100 in 1913. Knight engines were mostly used from 1911 with design work being the responsibility of Dufresne, later of Voisin. In 1911 4×4 Châtillon-Panhard military vehicles with four wheel steering were developed and these, together with Dufresne's 15CV staff car and aero engines, were principal products in the war years. During this period Paul Panhard took full control and Krebs retired.

Pasquelin improved the Knight engines in the mid-1920s with lighter sleeves to allow higher revs. Poppet valves were ignored from 1923 to 1939. Four- and straight-eight cylinder sleeve-valve models were produced from 1923 and sixes from 1927. At the peak in 1928 there were no fewer than eight different sizes of Panhard engine in production. Two years earlier Delaugère et Clayette of Orléans had been acquired and henceforth made only bodywork and truck cabs.

As well as battery electrics, the commercial vehicle side in the 1920s made armoured cars, half-tracks, gazogenes, lorries and buses with sleeve-valve engines, and supplied the last named to Chenard et Walcker for heavy vehicles. Sleeve-valve diesels followed in the 1930s.

By then, however, the firm was stagnating and working at only about 60 per cent capacity, despite Alexis Kow's stylish advertising, successful railcar engines and, for 1937, the futuristic Dynamic car range. This had six-cylinder sleeve-valve engines of 2.5, 2.7 or 3.8 litres, synchromesh, centre steering wheel (left hand drive from 1939), hydraulic brakes, all-round independent torsion bar suspension and faired-in wheels and lamps. Tech-

nical director at the time was Paul Panhard's son, Jean.

During World War II the Rheims and Orléans plants were evacuated to Tarbes, although armoured cars were produced in Paris as slowly as possible for the German occupiers. A limited degree of integration between Panhard, SOMUA and Willème in the Union Française Automobile lasted until about 1950.

Louis Delagarde worked on post-war prototype commercials and Louis Bionnier on successors to the Dynamic. These were envisaged as being large cars, with Hotchkiss bodies and engines, but were never built. A small flat-twin front-wheel-drive car was tried in 1941. Features of the car were incorporated with the Aluminium Française Grégoire which, after a redesign, appeared in 1946 as the Dyna-Panhard. The Ivry, Paris, plant handled assembly and some manufacture, Rheims made components, Orléans body and trim and Tarbes produced gazogenes. The well-known Arbel chassis pressing firm made light alloy wings and Facel-Metallon helped produce the alloy bodywork.

Production in 1947 of 50 cars climbed to 1350 in 1948, 10,000 in 1950 and 14,220 in 1951. By then over a dozen specialist vehicle makers were using Dyna flat-twin air-cooled engines, units which achieved many successes at Le Mans. Output then slumped, due in part to high prices (more than a Morris Minor in Belgium).

From 1954 surplus capacity was used to make Citroën 2CV commercials. The new bulbous Dyna was introduced that year. It made even greater use of light alloys, had fewer castings, and was offered with a supercharged engine in sports versions.

Citroën purchased a 25 per cent holding in 1955. Car production that year climbed to 19,300 and to 38,000 in 1957. Cars received steel bodywork in 1958 and increasingly powerful engines, including a 60bhp unit in the Tigre of 1961. Trucks and buses had been phased out by the early 1960s.

Panhard was starved of money for its own future developments although it carried out major work on the Dyane for Citroën. In 1965 Citroën acquired full control and in July 1967

the last Panhard car was produced. Large parts of the Ivry factory were subsequently demolished.

In 1965 Jean Panhard, who had run the firm since 1950, acquired the armoured car business and formed Société de Constructions Mécaniques Panhard et Levassor, which retained offices at Ivry but concentrated production at Marolles. Among a variety of vehicles it makes an Alvis-like amphibious 6×6 armoured mortar gun carrier powered by a 140bhp Peugeot V6 petrol engine. Some were used by Argentina against British forces in the Falklands conflict of 1982 and Colonel Gaddafi's Libya is also known to possess a fleet of these vehicles. NB

PANTHER
GB, SOUTH KOREA 1972 to date

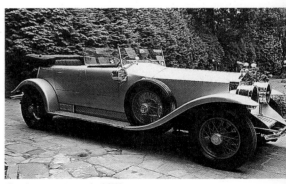

Panther prototype of c.1972

Bob Jankel was a racing enthusiast and engineer who worked for tuning specialist Superspeed Conversions in the 1960s and designed and built cars for his own use. He left Superspeed and went into the fashion trade, but continued to build his cars at the rate of about one a year. In 1971, prompted by being asked for replicas of his cars, he sold his fashion company shareholding and founded Panther West Winds Ltd, originally working from the garage of his home at Walton-on-Thames.

His first car, a four-seater reminiscent of a vintage Rolls-Royce, developed into the first production Panther, the Jaguar-powered J72, an SS100 look-alike introduced in 1972. The aluminium bodied car was entirely designed by Jankel and largely hand-made. In the first year 45 were made and Panther moved into the former Cooper Car Co works at Byfleet, Surrey.

Various subsidiary companies were set up to be responsible for different areas of manufacture. Panther's craftsmen also undertook restoration work and specialized coachbuilding for outside customers.

A 5.3-litre V12 version of the J72 was announced in·1973 but it was dropped after 1975 in favour of the 4.2-litre six. By 1973 Panther had some 80 employees and built 110 cars in that year.

Panther Kallista of 1986, and Panther De Ville production, 1975

At the Geneva Show in March 1974 it launched the Ferrari FF, based on modern Ferrari 330GTC running gear but styled after the 1947 125S. There was also a one-off version of a similar model with Lancia front-wheel-drive running gear. A car with modern buggy-type styling and a choice of six-cylinder or V12 engines, the Lazer, was offered in 1975 but never went into production.

In October 1974 Panther announced the V12-engined De Ville, evoking the Bugatti Royale and extremely expensive at an original price of £17,650. Nevertheless, it attracted more sales than the Lazer and a drophead version was offered from 1976. Also introduced that year, but only built in very small numbers, was the Rio, a Triumph Dolomite Sprint with hand-made aluminium body modifications and very up-market trim.

Much more successful was the same year's Lima, taking Panther in a new direction with glassfibre body and Vauxhall Magnum running gear. Sold through Vauxhall dealers at £4495 it was Panther's first effort at volume sales.

At the opposite end of the scale, at the 1977 London Motor Show Panther showed a modern open-topped car powered by a mid-mounted 8.2-litre turbocharged Cadillac V8 and with six wheels, including four small steerable fronts. This Super Six was offered at £39,950 but in spite of claims of numerous orders only two were built.

In August 1977 Panther's American importer became a public company as Buckingham Motor Imports Inc and planned to import about 20 Limas a week to the USA. The following year was Panther's best year to date with an output of 550 cars from 211 employees. A turbocharged Lima was added from 1979 but in spite of reasonable sales the

company ran into financial problems and went into receivership with debts of almost £1 million and staff reduced to just 23.

It was taken over in October 1980 for about £300,000 by a 41-year-old South Korean businessman, Young Chull Kim, on behalf of the family company Jindo Industries, a company with interests ranging from leather goods and clothing to shipping container manufacture. Jindo's annual turnover was some $150 million.

During its first year under Kim the new Panther Car Co Ltd dropped its entire range, Lima, J72 and De Ville. While plans were made for revised production Panther continued to produce conversions on other makes such as Mercedes and Range Rover, mostly for the Middle East, at the rate of about 20 a month.

In January 1982 the J72 was reintroduced as the Korean-built Brooklands; at £19,950 it was some £7000 cheaper than the earlier model. De Villes were also available, built in Byfleet but to special order only.

In 1980, its last full production year, the Lima had sold 141 units but now this most successful of Panthers was given a new chassis and an aluminium body built in Korea to very high standards and assembled in Britain with a choice of 1.6-litre four-cylinder or 2.8-litre V6 Ford engines. It was relaunched in October 1982 as the Kallista, with a large price reduction – to £5850 for the 1.6-litre – reflecting more efficient production. By the end of that year the workforce again exceeded 100 and Kallista production was about 30 a month, heading for an eventual target of 600 a year.

Early in 1984 Panther revealed plans to build an attractive modern mid-engined coupé, the Solo, in the medium price range. A

styling prototype was shown in September and production was planned for 1986 in Britain and the USA, where Jindo has a container assembly operation in Long Beach, California. The target was to produce up to 2000 cars a year.

The Solo was designed to use Ford XR3i power units and sell for less than £10,000 but when Toyota launched its mass-produced mid-engined MR-2 sports car Panther con-

Panther Solo prototype of 1985

sidered it necessary to move the Solo into a different class. Consequently its launch was delayed as various engine options were considered, including normal and turbocharged versions of the American 2.2-litre Chrysler four-cylinder and, for Europe only, the 2-litre turbocharged Cosworth engine from the Ford RS200 rally programme. This latter, in conjunction with four-wheel-drive from the Ford Sierra, would put the top of the range Solo into the £20,000 bracket, however.

Meanwhile, sales of the existing models totalled 447 cars in 1984, more than double the previous year's figure, and the Kallista was belatedly introduced in America in 1985 with the 2.3-litre four-cylinder Ford Mustang engine. BL

PARAMOUNT
GB 1949-1956

Paramount Cars (Derbyshire) Ltd was formed in May 1948 at Swadlincote by W. A. Hudson and S. Underwood as a motor engineering and garage business and built a much modified Alvis 14, the engine of which proved to be too expensive to use in the sports cars planned by the company. In 1949 the Paramount was officially unveiled in the *Daily Mail*. It had a four-seater wood-framed aluminium body and twin carburettor Ford 10 engine. It was reported to be built by 40 men at the rate of one a day.

In September 1951 the Meynell Motor Co Ltd with works at Melbourne, Derbyshire, took over the project and in March 1952 the original company was wound up with liabilities of £15,780 and assets of £4565. Despite earlier production forecasts the official receiver put the total figure built at 12, and Meynell possibly added a further six.

In the third move in its chequered career the Paramount went to Camden Wharf beside the Grand Union Canal at Linslade in 1953. There, Paramount Cars (Leighton Buzzard) Ltd was associated with the nearby motor dealer, Camden Motors Ltd. A pilot batch of 25 cars was laid down and possibly about 100 built in all. The cars featured Ford Consul engines from 1954 and were still full four-seaters.

The end came in 1956 when Welbeck Motors in London announced the 'breath-taking bulk purchase' of the last 26 Paramounts – 22 dropheads, 3 hard tops and one with a Ford 10 engine. A saving of more than £200 could be made on the list price of £1013, which was more than the cost of a TR2, MGA or a Ford Consul convertible. NB

PARRY
see Pathfinder

PATERSON
USA 1908-1923

The W. A. Paterson Co of Flint, Michigan, was founded in 1908 and grew out of the former W. A. Paterson Carriage Co. Its first solid-tyred buggy, the Model 14 with air-cooled twin-cylinder engine and chain drive, clearly showed Paterson's carriage building background.

In 1910 the company introduced a shaft-drive 30hp four-cylinder model, the Paterson 30, at $1400. From 1910 to 1914 it built only four-cylinder models, with four separate ranges on sale by 1913. In 1915 Paterson offered the four-cylinder 4-32 model but also expanded its range with the six-cylinder Continental-engined 6-32 and 6-48 models.

After 1915 the fours were dropped and very conventional cars were built, all with versions of the six-cylinder Continental engine. In 1922 Paterson advertised 'Your Idea of a

Beautiful Car' in three body styles – a tourer, a sedan and a coupé – with 'chassis built of the standard units of the industry', clear indication that the Paterson was now no more than an assembled car.

Also in 1922 Paterson announced that its plans for the year called for 'greater expansion'. Instead of growing, however, the company faded away and built no more cars after 1923. BL

PATHFINDER/NEW PARRY, PARRY
USA 1910-1916

D. M. Parry's Standard Wheel Co built wagons and the Overland car. When Willys bought Overland the firm became Parry Manufacturing Co and in 1910 it introduced 20 and 30hp four-cylinder Parry Tourist cars made in Indianapolis. Financial problems soon arose and the cars became known as New Parrys in 1911. Parry later achieved success as a body-builder for commercial vehicles and traded as the Martin Parry Co in 1919.

Parry's car interests were merged in 1912 with the Motor Car Manufacturing Co and production was discontinued. The Motor Car Manufacturing Co had been formed in Indianapolis in 1911 to make Pathfinder cars, which were initially four-cylinder machines but soon grew to sixes and, from 1916, included Weidely overhead-valve 6.4-litre powered V12s.

In Britain a monobloc 27.3hp six, chassis number 12B-579, with in-unit gearbox drove from Land's End to John O'Groats in top gear in 1912. That year also a four-cylinder car made five crossings of the United States driven by Walter Weidely, suggesting that the cars used Weidely motors.

Pathfinder is credited with producing the first fully retractable and enclosed hood, and it also helped to pioneer the enclosed spare wheel. Pathfinders had fancy model names such as Martha Washington, Daniel Boone and Leather Stocking. A quantity of ¾-ton trucks were built from 1913 to 1915 and in

1914 the company's president, W. C. Teasdale, announced that the factory was working 24 hours a day, seven days a week.

In late 1915 the firm became the Pathfinder Co with capital of $250,000; it was run by C. W. Richards, G. I. Lufkin and L. Kaminsky. In 1916 1000 cars were said to have been built (all with 12-cylinder engines after mid-year) and in 1917, when 2000 cars were planned, merger talks with the company's Indianapolis neighbour, Empire, were announced. The talks broke down and instead a $5 million stock flotation was organized and underwritten by the A. R. Scheffer Co. The assumption must be that this failed, for Pathfinder went out of business in 1918. NB

PEARSON-COX
GB 1909-1916

The steam car was never widely made in England, and 1909 was very late to launch a new make. Henry Pearson and Percy Cox opened a garage and repair works at Shortlands, near Bromley in Kent, in June 1908, and the following year they announced a steam car powered by a three-cylinder compound engine with semi-flash boiler and shaft drive. The original engine was rated at 12hp, but they later offered 8hp and 15hp cars, the latter with a five-seater body. They formed a private company with a capital of £2500 and even appointed a distributor for the northern counties at Gateshead, but production was always on a made-to-order basis and probably not more than 20 cars were built in all.

In 1913 they built a petrol-engined cyclecar with 8hp JAP engine and belt drive to a gearbox over the rear axle. From 1914 to 1917 they offered the ultimate eccentricity, a steam-powered motorcycle with single-cylinder 3hp engine. GNG

PEERLESS
USA, GB 1900-1933; 1958-1960

The Peerless Wringer and Manufacturing Co was formed in 1869 from the Peerless Wringer Co of Cincinnati and the Mercantile Manufacturing Co of Cleveland. The name was changed in 1891 to Peerless Manufacturing Co when the company began producing bicycles. Capacity was soon sufficient to produce up to 10,000 Peerless bicycles a year at Cleveland. Peerless also made parts for American assembled De Dion-Boutons and in 1900 acquired the licence to produce these cars.

Louis P. Mooers, who had developed a car at the New Haven Bicycle Co in 1897, joined Peerless in 1901. The following year Peerless built his shaft driven and wheel steered 8hp single-cylinder designs, but these were soon

Paramount Ten of 1950

Peerless 3.7-litre tourer of 1904

Peerless V8 tourer of c.1924

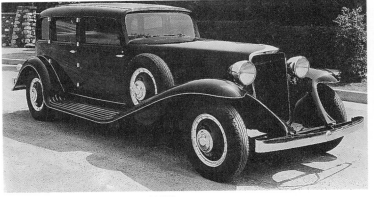

Peerless V16 aluminium prototype of 1932

for $500,000 and inherited a six-cylinder design for 1924. From 1925 the six used a Continental unit. Both this model and the better balanced 'equipoised eight' now had hydraulic four wheel brakes.

Collins was succeeded as president by D. A. Burke and then Edward Ver Linden, formerly of Buick, Oldsmobile and Durant, who returned Peerless to profitability. He resigned early in 1928, however, when Leon R. German took over. By using Baker-Raulang bodies, Columbia axles, and other locally produced components, Peerless claimed to be employing 10,000 Clevelanders.

In 1929 the ageing V8 was replaced by a Continental straight-eight, although one six-cylinder model still had a Peerless engine. James A. Bohannon from Marmon became president of the company that year at the age of only 33 and Count Alexis de Sakhnoffsky was hired to style a new range for 1930. In all, 3642 cars were sold in 1930, about half the previous year's total, yet a profit of $73,000 was achieved.

A 170hp V16 car with many lightweight features and Murphy body in aluminium was developed by Peerless and Alcoa in 1931 but it did not get beyond the prototype stage. This vehicle still exists. Peerless also acquired American rights to Bucciali designs at this time.

Car production fell victim to the Depression in 1931 after fewer than 1200 cars had been made that year. The board then looked for a more profitable product, and after the ending of Prohibition in 1933, the renamed Peerless Co and its vacant plant became a brewery. The Peerless name was discontinued in 1936, but the brewery still exists.

In Britain, Slough Lorries and Components Ltd had supplied spares for Peerless army trucks after World War I and in 1925 the company became Peerless Trading Co of Slough, which gradually added British components to its reconditioned Peerless trucks. The final vehicles were Gardner and Meadows engined Peerless Traders, which often had the chain drive that made them popular for off-road work in gravel pits. Production ended probably in 1933, although the make was listed until 1938 and a part of the business became Peerless Motors, which held the Hudson and

replaced by a 16hp twin. Four cylinders were used in the first of many famous Peerless racing cars in 1902, and in 1903 America's first standard models with enclosed coachwork were offered by the company. Pressed steel frames and four cylinders were used from 1903.

In 1902 the firm became known as the Peerless Motor Car Co. Production of 90 cars that year rose to 400 in 1903, when the Peerless was America's highest priced car.

In 1906 Mooers joined the Moon Motor Car Co and Charles Schmidt from Packard took his place at Peerless, where in 1907 he developed six-cylinder models. Another key engineer was Herbert C. Snow, who in 1912 went to work for Willys-Overland and was later at Winton, Velie and Auburn.

In 1909 capital was increased from $600,000 to $3 million and in the following year output reached 1500 cars. Trucks were added for 1911, when a further $1.5 million was raised from Cleveland millionaire J. Robert Crouse. Output in 1913 was 3000 but production fell to under 700 in 1914.

William Strickland, who had become chief engineer, developed a V8 for late 1915. This had separate carburettor jets for economical

'loafing' and maximum power, hence the slogan 'Two Power Range Eight'. After the war Strickland became vice-president of Peerless before leaving for General Motors in 1922, where he worked on the fully-balanced Cadillac V8.

In 1915, when it earned over $2.5 million net profit, Peerless merged with the General Vehicle Co of New York, best known for GV battery electric trucks. The resulting Peerless Truck & Motor Co had a capital of $20 million, the Peerless Motor Car Co remaining a separate subsidiary. Peerless production, by then mostly army trucks, ran at around 9000 a year until the end of the war.

In 1919 Peerless was re-formed and financial control reverted to Cleveland, although GV continued to be represented on the board. L. H. Kittredge, general manager from 1903, was president. Also on the board was Walter C. Baker of Baker Electric. About 1500 cars were made in 1920, by which time truck production had been discontinued.

Despite an output of 6000 vehicles in 1921 the firm recorded a loss that year and was purchased by Richard Collins for $4 million. As part of the deal Peerless bought the three-year-old and unsuccessful Collins Motor Co

Jaguar agencies.

In 1957 the Peerless garage at Slough was bought by James Byrnes, a Warwickshire hotelier who was financing a project to build a TR3 engined GT car with De Dion axle, the machine being assembled in London by John Gordon to designs by Bernard Rodger. Byrnes bought the garage for assembly purposes and got Whitsons in West Drayton – which built bodies for 250 of the contemporary Coronet three-wheelers – to make the fibreglass bodies. Wincanton Engineering produced the later Peerless bodies.

From 1958 to 1960 325 Peerless GTs were made and then Bernard Rodger transferred the project to Horton, Wraysbury. Some 20 to 50 more were made under the name Warwick until 1962, when a final nine cars were assembled by Chris Lawrence. The Peerless name now survives only on a pub on the Slough Trading Estate – a sad contrast to the time when the name was bracketed with Packard and Pierce-Arrow as one of the three most famous American luxury cars. NB

PEGASO
SPAIN 1951-1958

The Pegaso, whose emblem was the flying horse Pegasus, was made by the Empresa Nacional de Autocamiones SA. ENASA was one of the first results of a wartime plan to boost Spanish industry and it was created by the government in April 1946 with 240 million pesetas capital. Hispano-Suiza Fabrica de Automoviles SA was integrated with ENASA in November to give 538,000sq ft (50,000sq m) of factory space in Barcelona.

Pegaso Thrill (right) and Z103 of 1953

In 1946 38 commercial vehicles were made, followed by 119 in 1947 and rising to 179 in 1950. Capital was increased to 620 million pesetas in 1949, a further 1480 million being added in 1952, by which time the workforce totalled 3000. M. W. P. Ricart, born in Barcelona in 1897, was technical director. He had earlier worked on Perez and Ricart high performance cars at Nacional Pescara, and Alfa-Romeo. M. A. F. Avila was president.

At the Paris Show of 1951 the remarkable four-overhead cam V8 2½-litre Pegaso sports car was unveiled, being built in various forms and with engines of up to 4.7 litres until 1958,

when Ricart retired and production ceased. These cars were looked upon as a means of stimulating better design and were largely a prestige and publicity exercise. Just 125 were built. They had De Dion axles with integral gearboxes, semi monocoque construction, up to eight Webers, dry sump lubrication and the option of superchargers.

The main business of the company was aero engines, until Hispano separated from ENASA which concentrated on road vehicles from 1956. The commercials accounted for an average of 520 sales a year to the mid-1950s, 2000 on average annually until 1960, when Leyland took a major shareholding, and over 6000 a year thereafter. Leyland had collaborated in production since 1957. In 1961 the Leyland Comet was built in Spain along with a variety of engines at a factory that had been opened at Barajas in 1955.

Comercial Pegaso SA was formed in 1962. In 1966, when 8720 men were employed, it took over SAVA, which held the Austin licence for Spain – and still make J4-derived vans in the 1980s. Leyland ultimately withdrew and International Harvester acquired a 35 per cent stake in 1980, which it sold two years later. Pegaso has a current capacity of 70 vehicles a day. In 1984 ENASA acquired the Seddon-Atkinson truck firm in Britain and developed closer ties with DAF by sharing a £33 million cab development programme.

ENASA lost £14 million in 1984 despite an order for 12,000 vehicles to replace the Egyptian army's Russian truck fleet. It had about 10,000 employees making approximately 12,000 vehicles a year (including versions of the former BMC J4 van). In 1985 General Motors was rumoured to be acquiring ENASA from the Spanish government. NB

PEKING
see Beijing

PENNINGTON
USA, GB 1894-1902

As with many emergent industries, the early years of motor manufacture attracted a few less than totally reputable entrepreneurs. One of the most remarkable was Edward Joel

Pennington, a larger than life character aptly described by his own patent agent, Eric W. Walford, as a 'mechanical charlatan'.

Pennington was born in 1858 in Cincinnati, Ohio, and in 1871 he was apprenticed there to J. A. Fay & Co, where he trained for eight years as a machinist. In 1885 he set up the short-lived Pennington's Machine Shop in Fort Wayne, Indiana, and began to promote companies for making wooden machinery pulleys, raising a certain amount of money from gullible small town investors.

By 1890 he had extended his sales of stock to companies supposedly to build cars and even airships. He claimed himself to have built a three-wheeled electric car in 1887 and an airship in 1890 – earning him the popular nickname 'Airship' Pennington.

In 1894, backed by a cycle manufacturer named Hitchcock from New York and by Thomas Kane & Co of Racine, Wisconsin (which built office furniture and marine engines), he established the Racine Motor Vehicle Co to make the aptly named Kane-Pennington Hot Air Engine. It was an unorthodox design with long drawn-steel tube cylinders, devoid of additional cooling, a drip fuel feed and electric ignition giving what he called a 'long mingling spark'. It was fitted first to a motorcycle and then in 1894 he produced the four-wheeled Victoria, made from two cycle frames joined by tubular crossmembers and running on 'puncture-proof' balloon tyres – another Pennington 'invention'.

Four Pennington vehicles were entered for America's first 'race', the *Chicago Times-Herald* race of November 1895, but none started. In October an advertisement for the Victoria stated that in a demonstration by Pennington in Racine the four-wheeler had achieved 35mph (56kph) and the two-wheeler no less than 57mph (92kph). Enquiries regarding possible agencies were directed to a new company, the Pennington Motor Foreign Patents Syndicate Ltd in London – which was where Pennington himself had headed, as investors in the United States began to ask awkward questions.

He had sold his engine patents, allegedly for £100,000, to a British kindred spirit, Harry J. Lawson. Pennington thus became part of Lawson's ambitious £1 million Great Horseless Carriage Co, with one floor of the mysterious Motor Mills in Coventry as his works. From there emanated many announcements of war machines, fire engines and other inventions, but almost no vehicles.

Of the few vehicles that did emerge, probably five were Torpedoes, a balloon tyred three-wheeler with a very long stroke twin-cylinder engine in a frame made by the Humber company and supposedly capable of carrying nine passengers. Humber also supplied parts for a single-seater and a tandem motorcycle. A Torpedo entered in the 1896 Emancipation Day Run failed to make it from London to Brighton as one of its 'puncture-proof' tyres burst.

In March 1897 Pennington formed the Irish

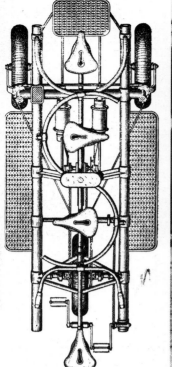

Pennington Torpedo of 1896, in theory and practice

Motor and Cycle Co in Dublin. He announced plans for a factory nearby to employ several thousand men but the company folded in August even before the factory was built, leaving yet more disillusioned investors.

He returned to England in 1898 and at that year's Crystal Palace Show introduced the Raft-Victoria. It had front-wheel drive, rear-wheel steering, a 3½-hp horizontal engine and rope drive. The announced price of £100 was increased to £115 10s after 400 had supposedly been ordered, but probably only three were built and none sold privately. One was built as the Stirling-Pennington in 1899. It had sprung bodywork by Stirling's Motor Carriages in Lanarkshire.

Probably taking with him some of the many deposits paid for Raft-Victorias, Pennington abandoned his latest company, the Pennington Motor Co Ltd, and in October 1899 returned to the United States. There he formed the Anglo-American Rapid Vehicle Co with Harry Lawson and, supposedly, control of 200 patents and $75 million capital. Pennington sold his own patents to the company for some $750,000 and was probably not too upset when that company also collapsed, in spite of alleged orders from the British army for 1000 four-wheeled Torpedoes for the Boer war.

While Lawson went briefly to jail Pennington returned to England late in 1900 to show another 'war-machine', based on the three-wheeler. It was another failure and by 1901 Pennington was back in America, where at the 1904 Cleveland Auto Show he exhibited a steam-powered front-wheel drive attachment for buggies, called the Tractobile.

He finally abandoned his car schemes to move into similar stock promotions in the new field of flying and actually opened a flying school at Springfield, Massachusetts. In total, Pennington had probably built no more than 20 vehicles by the time he died in 1911. BL

PERL
AUSTRIA 1921-1927

Gustav Rudolf Perl was the son of an Austrian haulage company proprietor but he studied first at technical college in Vienna and worked for some time as a civil engineer before joining the family firm. In 1907 he built his first twin-cylinder 2½-ton truck and then became an agent for Berna commercial vehicles from Joseph Wyss's Motorwerke Berna AG in Switzerland. In 1911 he became a partner in Berna Motorfahrzeuge Fabrik Ing Perl & Co in Vienna-Liesing, and in 1912, in a new factory, he began to build lorries under licence. He also went on to build electric lorries and tractor units.

In 1915 the company was reorganized as Motorlastwagen und Motorenfabrik Ing G. Rud. Perl and expanded considerably during World War I, supplying military vehicles. After the war, as Automobilfabrik Perl AG, Perl continued to build lorries and tractors and in 1921 introduced a 3/15PS small car, with a four-cylinder 898cc engine. Some were exported and it seems that a number of Perl cars were sold in Britain in 1922 by Captain L. G. Hornsted's Hornsted Motor Co, of central London, under the names Hornsted 12 or Summers.

Perl continued to build four-cylinder 898cc cars but with gradually improving power outputs, the 3/16PS Norma being introduced in 1925 and the 18PS Suprema in 1926. Perl stopped building cars in 1927 but continued to build commercial vehicles.

After World War II the company became known as Perl-Auhof Automobil Bestandteile- und Karosserie-Fabrik GmbH. From 1949 it concentrated most of its production facilities on buses, plus coachwork for other makers' bus chassis and for various makes of car.

In 1951 Perl experimented briefly with a very small car, the Perl-Champion, which had a motorcycle-type engine, but it was never put into production. Perl continued to build buses until 1968, when the company merged with another Austrian bus manufacturer, Gräf & Stift. BL

PERRY
GB 1913-1916

Perry 11.9hp two-seat tourer of c.1914

Begun as Perry and Co by James Perry and Sir J. Mason in 1823, the firm merged with a number of Birmingham pen and pencil case makers in 1876 with a combined capital of £500,000. In 1897 it was re-formed with a more realistic capital of £80,000 and by then had an important sideline in bicycle chains, free-wheel hubs, bells and components. It made motor tricycles in 1899 followed by forecars. At its peak the company had 2000 employees and 6 acres (2.4 hectares) of factory space.

In September 1912 the company formed a subsidiary with £60,000 capital called the Perry Motor Co Ltd, the directors including E. S. Perry and J. W. Bayliss. Designer was 20-year-old C. T. Bayliss, who professed to have been influenced by the Bedelia and Humberette – and his Triumph TT motorcycle. His first effort in 1913 was a two-cylinder, 8hp light car with in-unit gearbox.

A £60,000 factory was bought in Tyseley in October 1913 to build it but, although the parent company made a £65,000 profit in 1914, the Perry Motor Co made a loss. This state of affairs continued in 1915, despite the addition of an attractive 11.9hp four. Production ended in 1916 after fewer than 700 of each type had been made.

Bean acquired the design rights of the 11.9hp, on which it based its first cars, and Perry spares were sold to R. H. Collier & Co Ltd, where they were to be joined by those of Swift, Crouch, Clyno and many more defunct makes. Perry and Co carried on in business making pens and stationers' sundries. NB

PETTER/SEATON-PETTER
GB 1895-1898; 1925-1927

The Petter family owned a foundry in Yeovil that made Nautilus stoves and cream separators. Percival and Ernest Petter, together with Ben Jacobs, built a few steam engines and then a gas engine inspired by an article in the *Boy's Own Paper*. This gas engine was assembled in a garden shed and was tried in late 1895 in a phaeton built by Hill and Boll. (Hill and Boll made bodywork into the 1920s, having shown remarkable four wheel hydraulic brakes without much success at Olympia in 1909.)

In November 1896 the Yeovil Motor Car and Cycle Co was formed with a capital of £1000 to make Yeovil Autocars; perhaps a dozen were sold, including some electrics. Petter's horizontal lamp oil engines from the enlarged shed that became the Nautilus works achieved renown as stationary power plants and over 1000 had been sold by 1905. Tractors were also built. In 1912 there were 500

Petter 3hp dogcart of 1896

employees, and during World War I the company built 800 aircraft.

Douglas Seaton, apprenticed with Petters during the war, was responsible for the design of the Seaton-Petter two-stroke, two-cylinder light and cheap car developed by Percival Petter in 1925. The Petter Car Co was registered as a private company with £5000 capital that August. Its products were to be marketed by Seaton's British Dominions Car Co, which was formed in February 1926. Whether salesmanship or engineering was at fault is not recorded, but only about 70 cars were made until 1927.

In 1929 Seaton opened a modest garage in Yeovil, but the Petter company flourished,

Peugeot GP car (Georges Boillot driving) of 1913

making Westland aircraft and diesel engines. In 1938 the John Brown group bought the aircraft interests (now Bristol-Siddeley) and AEI the remnants, including the oil engine side, which was moved to Loughborough. H. O. Farmer, formerly of Crossley and Ricardo, was chief engineer. In 1947 the company settled in the old Lagonda factory at Staines, Middlesex. It became part of the Hawker-Siddeley group in 1957 and still manufactures engines as well as refrigeration plants. NB

PEUGEOT
FRANCE 1889 to date

Peugeot is the second oldest surviving car company in the world after Daimler-Benz and the oldest still in the hands of the same family. In fact the family had a manufacturing history dating back four generations before it became involved in motor cars.

Jean-Jacques Peugeot (1699-1741) was a cotton spinner at Hérimoncourt whose son Jean-Pierre (1734-1814) made hand tools. *His* sons, Jean-Pierre (1768-1852) and Jean-Frédéric (1770-1814), set up a foundry at Sous-Cratet in the north of the *département* of Doubs in eastern France and in 1810 invented the cold rolling mill. In 1832 they founded the Société Peugeot Frères Aînés, making watch springs, coffee mills, umbrella frames, saws, hammers and other hand tools. They had three factories, at Valentigney, Terre Blanche and Pont de Roide, all in the Doubs area.

The company was continued by the next generation, Jules (1811-89) and Emile (1815-74). It was renamed Les Fils des Peugeot Frères in 1876, by which time they had added to their range of products whalebone corsets and crinoline frames.

In about 1875 Emile's son Armand (1849-1915) joined the firm after spending some

Peugeot Quadrilette of 1891

time in England with a Leeds engineering company. He persuaded the company to add bicycles from 1885 and in 1888 he agreed to make a steam-driven three wheel car to the design of Léon Serpollet, using an engine made by La Buire of Lyons. Four were built during 1889 but Peugeot decided in favour of internal combustion, and called a meeting of Gottlieb Daimler and Emile Levassor at which it was decided that Peugeot would build cars powered by V-twin engines of Daimler design, made in France by Panhard et Levassor.

The first Panhard-built engines arrived at Valentigney in March 1890, and by the end of the year four cars had been built under the supervision of Louis Rigoulot. They had rear mounted engines. (Armand is reputed to have chosen a rear engine location because Emile Levassor told him that a front engine 'would stink', yet within a year Levassor was making front engined cars himself.) An unusual feature of the early Peugeots was that the cooling water circulated through the chassis tubes.

In 1891 Peugeot entered a car in the Paris-Brest-Paris bicycle race; before the event it was driven to Paris by Rigoulot and another employee, Auguste Doriot, who was later concerned with the DFP car. Although the Peugeot was slower than the winning cyclist it was the only car in the race and gained valuable publicity. Afterwards it was driven back to Valentigney and sold to a customer in Mulhouse.

Four other cars were sold in 1891, 29 in 1892, 24 in 1893 and 40 in 1894. They reached three figures for the first time in 1898, with 156 sales. Goods vehicles on the car chassis were offered from 1894, in which year a whip for chasing away dogs was a recognized extra, and quite possibly made by Peugeot itself.

The company involved itself in motor sport as early as it could and had five entries in the 1894 Paris-Rouen Trial and four in the 1895 Paris-Bordeaux-Paris race. Peugeot shared a prize with Panhard in 1894 and won in 1895, but only because the rules stipulated that cars must have four seats, and the Panhard which was the first car home had only two. More significant was the entry by the Michelin brothers of a Peugeot with pneumatic tyres, the first to be seen in a motor race.

Peugeot and Daimler had a rift in 1895, Daimler insisting that Alsace and Switzerland were German territories and that Peugeot could not sell his cars there. As a result Peugeot did not make use of the new Daimler Phoenix engine but used a new horizontal twin designed by Gratien Michaux. At the same time Armand took car production away from Valentigney, where his cousin Eugène (1844-1907) continued with the firm's traditional products, and set up a new factory at Audincourt a few miles away. In 1898 Armand opened another factory at Lille, employing 300 workers, with Audincourt accounting for 500.

Peugeot built its 500th car during 1899 and its one thousandth a year later, making it the biggest car producer in Europe. A total of 637 cars were turned out in 1902, by which time engines had moved to the front. The Bébé had a 785cc single-cylinder engine and shaft drive. Larger cars were on Mercédès lines, with two- and four-cylinder engines, pressed steel frames (the Baby's was still tubular), honeycomb radiators and chain drive. The first two- and four-cylinder Siddeleys were based on these Peugeots.

Shaft drive gradually took over throughout the range, although there was a monstrous chain drive six-cylinder with a capacity of 11,150cc in 1908. Between 1902 and 1914 Peugeot offered no fewer than 83 different models, not including the Lion-Peugeots.

The Lion-Peugeots were made at Valentigney, where Robert Peugeot (1873-1945), second son of Eugène, had been making motorcycles since 1903. The cars were called Lion-Peugeot to distinguish them from the Audincourt products of his uncle Armand. The Lion was the symbol of the city of Belfort, and had been used as a trade mark by the Peugeot family since 1858.

Designed by Michaux the Lion-Peugeots were singles at first, but mostly V-twins or V-fours. They were never very large, sizes running from the VA, a 785cc single made from 1906 to 1908, to the VD, an 1888cc V-four made from 1913 to 1915. The Lion-

Lion-Peugeot VC2 phaeton of 1909

Peugeot factory also made some remarkable long-stroke racing cars, including a 65×260mm V-four, and these were successful in voiturette racing for several years. In 1910 the two companies joined forces, although the distinctive Lion-Peugeot continued in production at Valentigney until 1915. The new company was called Société Anonyme des Automobiles et Cycles Peugeot.

In addition to those at Audincourt, Lille and Valentigney, Armand Peugeot opened a Paris factory in 1904 and another in the Doubs district, at Sochaux-Montbeliard, in 1912. He also formed a company with Tony Huber in 1905 to make two-stroke and marine engines, and another with his former partner F. Rossel in 1910 to make aero engines at Suresnes, near Paris. A small number of cars, the Bébé and Type 71, 2.2-litre chain drive four, were made under licence in Turin from 1905 to 1908 as Peugeot-Croizats.

Car production rose from 1261 in 1905, when Peugeot built its 5000th car, to over 5000 in 1913, when it built its 25,000th. (Other milestones were the 50,000th in 1922, 100,000th in 1925, half-millionth in 1937, millionth in 1952, five millionth in 1969 and ten millionth in 1977.)

The Bébé name was revived in 1912 for a tiny four-cylinder car designed by Ettore Bugatti and originally offered to Wanderer in Germany. It had an 856cc monobloc engine, and a curious two-speed transmission with two concentric propeller shafts providing the two forward speeds. A total of 3095 were made at Valentigney between 1912 and 1916.

One of these finished second in the 1913 Cyclecar Grand Prix, while a larger Peugeot with 7.6-litre twin-overhead cam engine designed by Ernest Henry won the 1912 French Grand Prix in the hands of Georges Boillot. Smaller engined Henry-designed cars won the Coupe de l'Auto and French Grand Prix in

Peugeot Bébé of 1913

1913. The 4½-litre cars had a successful career in the United States, Jules Goux winning at Indianapolis in 1913, Dario Resta in 1916 and Howard Wilcox in 1919.

Peugeot vehicles played an important part in World War I as staff cars, ambulances, trucks and armoured cars, including some half-track versions of the latter. The French army commissioned prototypes of a fully tracked light tractor, but neither this nor a proposed post-war agricultural version went into production. During the war Peugeot was run by Eugène's three sons, Robert, Eugène and Jules. Their father had died in 1907 and their uncle Armand in 1915.

Peugeot emerged from the war in a strong financial position. The company was back in production with the 2.8-litre four-cylinder Type 153, joined by the 1.4-litre four-cylinder Type 163, while in the commercial field it continued its wartime Type KM 4-tonner. Heavy vehicles were made until 1927, after which the only goods vehicles made were versions of Peugeot passenger cars. Engines for some of the trucks were supplied by Latil, which took over production of the Type 1543 low frame 2-tonner in 1926.

Peugeot began experiments in 1923 with diesel engines designed by Monsieur Tartrais but did not put a diesel into production until 1928 when a subsidiary firm, CLM (Compagnie Lilloise des Moteurs), began making opposed-piston Junkers diesels for use in commercial vehicles. CLM operated from the Lille factory, later becoming the Compagnie Générale des Moteurs and in 1958 Indénor, which still makes light diesels for Peugeot cars today. CLM engines were used in a number of trucks, including Laffly and Willème.

Peugeot 190S saloon of 1928

Peugeot team for the Belgian Grand Prix of 1926

In the early 1920s Peugeot brought out two new models at opposite ends of the price scale. The Quadrilette was a successor to the Bébé, with 688cc four-cylinder engine, three-speed gearbox in unit with the rear axle which had no differential, and a punt-type frame. It was very narrow, with a 30in (762mm) rear track, so seating was staggered or even tandem. About 3500 were made in 1921 and 1922, after which it grew up into the Type 172 with a wider, conventional chassis. This was much longer lived, being produced until 1929, by which time 47,932 had been made. It was succeeded by the Type 190, of which 33,677 were made from 1928 to 1931.

The other new direction for Peugeot was a line of expensive sleeve-valve-engined cars, all made in the Paris factory between 1922 and 1928. The best known was the six-cylinder 3.8-litre Type 174, of which 800 were made, together with a further 200 174S sports models, some of which were raced successfully in the French Touring Car Grands Prix (André Boillot won in 1925 with a streamlined saloon), Targa Florio, Coppa Florio, and Belgian 24 Hour race (which Boillot and Rigal won in 1926).

The big sleeve-valvers were in the same category as the six-cylinder Delage or Voisin,

but Peugeot's *métier* was the cheaper car, and in 1927 it brought out a small six, aimed at the Berliet, Mathis EMY and Donnet 14CV market. This was the Type 183, of which 12,636 were made from 1927 to 1931.

Although post-war production started hesitantly, with only 500 cars made in 1919 and 770 in 1920, it picked up quickly, reaching 20,724 in 1925 and 43,303 in 1930. Capacity was increased by the purchase of the Bellanger and De Dion-Bouton factories in 1927, although at least part of the latter was still used for De Dion's own cars up to 1930, and commercials later still. Peugeot also had a short-lived German factory at Mannheim in 1927.

From 1923 to 1928 Lucien Rosengart was in charge of publicity and sales. He wound up the racing department in 1926 and moved the commercial department from Sochaux to Paris before starting up his own successful car factory in 1928.

During 1928 Peugeot invested 125 million francs in the development of a new low-

Peugeot 402 saloon of 1937

priced model which was to replace the 172/190 series and 100 million francs went towards factory extensions at Sochaux. The Type 201 was a conventional 1100cc four-cylinder car with transverse front suspension and coil ignition. It gained independent suspension in 1932 and synchromesh in 1934. A total of 142,309 were made before it was replaced in 1938 by the 202. It started the Peugeot numbering system, still used today, whereby the first number is an indication of size, the second number is always 0, and the third the series. Thus the small 2 cars have passed through 201, 202, 203, 204 to the

recently-introduced 205, and the same system has applied to the 3, 4, 5 and 6 sizes.

The introduction of the 201 was the responsibility of André Boillot, who was killed in 1931 while testing a 201X which was powered by a 996cc overhead-cam engine that was half a Bugatti Type 35. Only 20 of these were made. Other models in the 01 series were the 1.5-litre 301, the 1.7-litre 401 and the 2.1-litre six-cylinder 601.

In 1934 the 401 and 601 were available with electrically operated convertible roofs, the first of their kind in the world. These bodies were designed by Emile Darl'mat and built by Pourtout. This combination was also responsible for some coupés and roadsters based on the 402, three of which ran at Le Mans in 1937.

The 02 series was dramatically styled, with an airflow grille behind which the headlamps were located, and streamlined bodies. It was Peugeot's answer to the *traction avant* Citroën, and although chassis and drive were more conventional, the Peugeot certainly gained on styling.

The 2-litre 402 was the first to appear, in October 1935, followed by the 1.7-litre 302 in October 1936 and the 1.1-litre 202 in October 1937. The 402 was offered with an automatic transmission designed by Gaston Fleischel, but only prototypes were made, and the nearest customers got to an automatic was the Cotal electro-magnetic pre-selector box. There were also experiments in 1937 with the Oberhansli diesel engine, but production never took place, and buyers had to wait another 22 years before they could buy a diesel-engined Peugeot.

During the 1930s car production was con-centrated on the Sochaux plant, with Audincourt run down, Lille devoted to CLM engines and Valentigney to motorcycles and bicycles which were made by a separate company, Motorcycles Peugeot. Car production fluctuated between a Depression-induced 28,317 in 1932 to a peak of 47,213 in 1938, when Peugeot beat Renault into second place in the French league. Car production continued well into the war, with 8211 being made in 1942. Peugeot also made 377 light electric two-seaters called the VLV, being the only major producer to do so.

France was liberated during 1944 and

Peugeot 504Ti of 1978

Peugeot was back in production with the 202 early in 1945. The larger models were not revived and Peugeot pursued a one model policy for 10 years. In 1948 there was the launch of the 1.3-litre unitary construction 203 four-door saloon, which was being made at the rate of 100 a day by April 1949. A year later the best pre-war production year had been easily surpassed, with 62,486 cars made, and in 1952 the millionth Peugeot left the factory at Sochaux. It had taken 65 years to make the first million, and only another seven years to make the second million. In 1950 Peugeot absorbed Chenard-Walcker, continuing its forward control van as part of the Peugeot range, and gained a controlling interest in Hotchkiss.

A win in the 1953 Australian Redex Trial led to an increasing involvement in tough, long-distance rallies. A 403 won the 1956 Ampol (Australia) Trial, and the fuel injection 404s won the East African Safari in 1963, 1966, 1967 and 1968.

The 203 was made until 1960, by which time 685,828 had been built, but it was joined in 1955 by the 403 saloon with 1½-litre engine and all-synchromesh gearbox. This was available with automatic transmission in 1958 and an Indénor diesel engine in 1959. The body was styled by Pininfarina, establishing a connection with the Italian firm which has continued to the present day. A South African assembly plant was set up in 1954, the first of many overseas operations, and in 1958 exports to the USA began.

New models of the 1960s were the 1.6-litre 404 saloon, introduced in 1960 and made until 1975, the 1.1-litre front-wheel-drive 204 saloon and coupé (1965-80) and the 1.8-litre 504 (from 1969). In 1964 Roland Peugeot took over as president, being the eighth generation to run the company since Jean-Jacques founded his cotton mill in the early 18th century. Peugeot now had eight factories, of

Peugeot 309SR of 1986

which five were making cars (Sochaux, Mulhouse, Vesoul, Lille and St Etienne), two were making components and tools (Audincourt and Pont de Roide), with Valentigney still devoted to bicycles, mopeds and motorcycles.

In 1973 came the smallest Peugeot for many years, the 993cc 104 in saloon and short wheelbase coupé form; this model was made at the Mulhouse factory only. By the mid-1970s Peugeots were being assembled in 14 foreign countries, but the number has been somewhat reduced since then due to closure of plants in Australia, Belgium, Eire and New Zealand.

In 1974 Peugeot acquired a 38.2 per cent holding in Citroën, gaining total control in May 1976. The first joint model was the Citroën LN, which used a Citroën two-cylinder engine in the short version of the Peugeot 104 body shell. In 1975 a new 2.7-litre V6 engine was jointly developed by Peugeot, Renault and Volvo, known as the PRV engine, and built in a joint factory at Douvrin. It was used in the Peugeot 504 coupé and cabriolet and from 1976 in the 604 four-door luxury saloon.

In 1980 the Peugeot empire expanded further with the acquisition of the Talbot organization which had taken over Chrysler's companies in Britain and France. Peugeot

Peugeot 205 Lacoste of 1986

now controlled all the major French car producers except Renault. It also merged its Argentine company with that of Fiat, forming Sevel Argentina SA. In September 1981 it withdrew from the agreement, although the Peugeot 505 continued in production in Buenos Aires until 1982. Other foreign plants currently operating include those in Chile, Italy, Nigeria, Paraguay, Portugal, South Africa, Spain, Taiwan, Turkey and Thailand.

The most important new model of the late 1970s was the 305, a four-door saloon with light alloy single-overhead cam, four-cylinder engine of 1.3 or 1.5 litres. Introduced in November 1977 the 305 reached the million sales mark by January 1983 and, like most other Peugeots, is available with a diesel engine. (Europe's first turbocharged diesel for cars was the 604 GRD introduced in 1980.) Other models in the 05 range are the 954/1124/1360/1580cc 205 saloons (made from 1983) and the 1971/2165/2498cc 505 saloons and estates (from 1979).

The current Peugeot range is a wide one, from the 104 two- and four-door models to the 205s, 305s and 505s. The big 604 was dropped in 1986. A new model for 1986 was the 309, a five-door hatchback to slot in between the 205 and 305, made in the French Talbot factory at Poissy and the British Talbot factory at Ryton. The introduction of a 1360cc rally version of the 104 in 1980 heralded a return to rallying, which became more serious in 1984 with the building of the 205-based Turbo 16, a 4×4 mid-engined coupé with 195bhp 1775cc engine.

Peugeot currently employs about 60,000 people, and has car factories at Sochaux, Dijon, Lille, Mulhouse, St Etienne, Vesoul, Bondy, La Rochelle, Sept Fons, Sully-Loire and Valenciennes. In 1985 European production totalled 936,100 cars. GNG

PHÄNOMEN
GERMANY 1907-1927

Phänomen Phänomobil 4/9PS of 1910

Gustav Hiller's bicycle works at Zittau in Saxony was founded in 1888 and in 1903 introduced its first Fafnir-engined motorcycles, named Phänomen (phenomenon). From 1907 the three-wheel Phänomobil was produced with V-twin, air-cooled engine mounted above the single front wheel, which it drove by chain. It was produced until 1927 in various forms, including military types and commercial vehicles.

The original V-twin soon gave way to transverse vertical twins and fours with tiller steering and epicyclic transmission. A London branch with £5000 capital was opened in 1909 and vans were sold to several newspaper firms. In 1911 more conventional four-wheelers with 2.58 and 4-litre engines were added. They were built in small numbers into the 1920s. In 1924 a new 3.13-litre overhead-cam sports and touring model was

introduced by the Phänomen Werke AG, so-named in 1917.

From 1927 only commercial vehicles were made, the forced-draft, air-cooled Granit four-wheelers being popular as ambulances, military vehicles and mail vans. These initially had 1.55-litre engines but soon grew to 2.5 and 3 litres, some of which were offered as proprietary units in the course of the later 1930s.

After World War II Phänomen found itself located in East Germany and in 1948 was combined with Auto-Union, Framo and other motor factories under the initials IFA. The Granit continued to be made by IFA-Phänomen in Zittau until 1956, when a similar vehicle made in the same factory was renamed the Robur Garant. Although usually diesel powered, the Robur is still produced with air-cooled engines. Its days may, however, be numbered as in the early 1980s Volvo and Renault were reported to be assisting in the modernization of East Germany's motor industry. NB

PHILOS
see Jean Gras

PHOENIX
GB 1903-1925

The mythological bird that rose from the ashes held considerable significance for J. Van Hooydonk, who in his youth was nearly killed by a fire in his native Belgium and was severely disfigured. He emigrated to Britain and obtained work as a marzipan maker for Pascalls in London. In his spare time he raced for the Phoenix Cycle Club.

In 1889 he started his own bicycle workshop in Islington and was joined by A. F. Ilsley, a racing cyclist who worked for A. J. Wilson and Co. Minerva-engined motorcycles were made from 1900 followed by Trimo tricars. In 1903, when Van Hooydonk patented a front wheel braking system, the Phoenix Motor Co was formed with £10,000 capital.

Four-wheelers were produced in 1904, the De Dion-engined Phoebus being succeeded in 1905 by the Quadcar, which had Fafnir or Minerva engines. In 1906 Albert Bowyer-Lowe joined as chief designer from JAP and was responsible for a two-cylinder Minerva or Impéria engined conventional light car launched in 1908 and for the scuttle radiatored four-cylinder car of late 1912. The four-cylinder had Phoenix's own 11.9hp engine, gearbox and back axle, the pressings for which came from Belgium although many castings were produced in Scotland.

In 1911 Phoenix moved to the new Garden City of Letchworth, Hertfordshire, where it employed about 105 men who produced seven cars a week. During World War I the

company made military equipment.

At this time Bowyer-Lowe designed a unitary construction 8hp car but the firm was not keen on the idea and went to the opposite extreme with a large 18hp car reputedly based on drawings of the Arrol-Johnston Victory. Bowyer-Lowe then left the company to make the Autogear cyclecar in Letchworth.

The 18hp Phoenix was a commercial disaster – some of its parts later cropped up in the Ascot – and the 11.9 was speedily revived, although now it had a front radiator. About 400 more were built. Capital leapt from £25,000 in early 1919 to £250,000.

In 1922 the 11.9 gave way to a Meadows-engined 12/25 and a total of 168 of these were made until 1925. Phoenix went into voluntary liquidation in April 1924 but managed to make six new six-cylinder Meadows-engined cars that year plus three in 1925. A solitary four-cylinder engine was bought in February 1926, after which the Phoenix disappeared, its factory giving rise to Ascot and Arab motor cars. NB

PICCOLO
see Apollo

PICK
GB 1898-1925

Pick 3.6-litre sports model of 1923

The son of a Lincolnshire publican and butcher, John (Jack) Henry Pick was trained as a blacksmith and then worked for the Blackstone agricultural equipment and engine firm in Stamford. He left to make hoes, needles for rug making and then bicycles with his brother Walter and C. Gray. They took premises in Blackfriars Street, Stamford, and employed 40 men.

In 1898 they built a French-engined dogcart and sold it to a doctor. Further dogcarts were bought by the local gentry, who financed the Pick Motor Co with £10,000 capital in 1901. The Marquess of Exeter from nearby Burghley Park was chairman. Everything for the cars, apart from wheels, Longuemare carburettor and engine castings, were made on the company's premises.

When a decision was taken to discontinue the Pick of All bicycle, Jack Pick left to set up

Pick's Motor Works opposite the George Hotel on the Great North Road in Stamford. Initially he intended just to undertake repairs, but after the collapse of the original firm he formed the New Pick Motor Co in 1908 and made cars, now called New Picks. Maximum output probably never exceeded one car a week but, unlike most other small makes, they were sold all over Britain and were even exported to Australia and New Zealand, where a few survive.

In 1915 the company's name was changed to the Pick Motor Co Ltd and machining and subcontracting jobs replaced car production. After the war a farm tractor with roller-drive and transverse 30hp engine appeared, followed by a more conventional four-wheeler in 1920.

Four-cylinder cars of similar specification to the pre-war types were revived in the early 1920s but production had ceased by August 1925, when a receiver gave up efforts to keep the company in business. Jack Pick then became a fruit and vegetable grower. He died towards the end of 1953, aged 87. NB

PIC-PIC
SWITZERLAND 1906-1924

Pic-Pic phaeton of c.1910

In December 1904 four Swiss industrialists founded the Société des Automobiles à Genève (SAG) to manufacture high-quality cars designed by Marc Birkigt who, although Swiss, was at that time working for Hispano-Suiza in Barcelona. They gave up the idea of building a factory of their own and instead arranged for the cars to be built in the works of the Société Piccard, Pictet et Cie of Geneva. This company was an old-established maker of turbines for hydroelectric power stations which had made the 1904 Dufaux racing cars. At first the cars were known as SAGs, but after a few years the name Piccard-Pictet, or Pic-Pic for short, was generally adopted.

The first SAG of 1906 had a conventional 24/30hp or 35/40hp four-cylinder T-head engine, leather cone clutch and shaft drive. It was joined by a 40hp six in 1907, and during the next four years several models were made, of 14/18 and 22/28hp.

In January 1910 the Société des Automobiles à Genève was wound up and the cars came directly under Piccard-Pictet control. Production was limited, seldom exceeding 100 a year. In 1912 a 30hp sleeve-valve model was introduced, although 16 and 20hp poppet valve engines continued to be used. Two cars with 4½-litre four-cylinder sleeve-valve engines were entered for the 1914 Grand Prix, but both retired. Pic-Pics were quite prominent in local hillclimbs and races, and one of them won a one-hour championship race at Buenos Aires in 1915.

Although Pic-Pic never made a commercial chassis as such, many ambulance bodies were built for the Swiss army on car chassis, some strengthened with twin rear wheels. This work kept the factory busy during the war with 7500 workers at its peak, but 1919 brought a disastrous slump and debts of 24 million francs by the end of the year. Two post-war models had been announced, both with sleeve-valve engines and handsome vee radiators, but sales were very poor.

Attempted negotiations with Vickers were unsuccessful, and the banks to whom most of the money was owed formed the Ateliers des Charmilles SA to take over the business. They were mainly interested in the turbine side of Piccard-Pictet. However, they made one model of car, with 2950cc sleeve-valve engine, at the rate of two a day up to 1922 when there was an attempted merger with the big French engineering firm, Schneider Le Creuzot. This failed and only one further car was made, which was shown at the 1924 Geneva Show. Ateliers des Charmilles continued in the turbine business in which it is still active. GNG

PIERCE-ARROW
USA 1901-1938

One of the most prestigious makes of American car, the Pierce-Arrow was made by George Norman Pierce, born in 1846, who set up in business in 1873 in the firm of Heintz, Pierce and Munschauer of Buffalo, New York. The company made birdcages (hence the nickname 'Fierce Sparrow' for the cars), ice-boxes, tinware and washing machines.

In 1878 he set up on his own with the George N. Pierce Co which also made birdcages and ice-boxes, adding the newly invented ammonia refrigerator and, in 1888, children's tricycles. Bicycles for adults were added in 1892, just as the bicycle craze was reaching the United States, and three years later all other products were discontinued. The precision-ground gears for Pierce bicycles were made by Leland & Faulconer of Detroit, whose director Henry Leland was later to found the Cadillac and Lincoln companies, both of which made cars to rival the Pierce-Arrow.

The George N. Pierce Co was incorporated in 1896, by which date it had a fine five-storey factory with 75,000sq ft (7000sq m) in Buffalo. Experiments with steam cars began in 1900, but George Pierce was more impressed with the single-cylinder De Dion-Bouton engine which he fitted to a light two-seater car in November 1900. This was followed in 1901 by the Motorette, also De Dion-powered, which was designed by Yorkshire-born David Fergusson who came to Pierce from the E. C. Stearns Co of Syracuse, New York. (Two later distinguished Pierce-Arrow engineers, H. Kerr Thomas, and John Younger, were also British-born.) During the first production year, June 1901 to May 1902, 25 Motorettes were sold at $650 each. A slightly larger De Dion engine was used in the 1902-3 Motorettes, of which 125 were made.

Pierce-built engines were used from early 1903, and in the same year a completely new car on Renault lines was introduced, called the Arrow. This led to the Great Arrow of 1904, a $4000 car which put Pierce among the leading makes of high-quality cars. It was made in three sizes, 24, 30 and 40hp, all with four-cylinder T-head engines and shaft drive.

About 300 Great Arrows were built in 1905 and 700 in 1906. The Glidden Tour, America's most important long distance trial, was won by Great Arrows every year from 1905 to 1909.

In April 1906 Pierce purchased a 16-acre (6-hectare) site on which the Elmwood plant was erected. This was enlarged to 44 acres (17 hectares) in 1916, and in 1975 was dedicated as a National Historical Site. All car production was transferred to Elmwood. The old factory was used for the manufacture of bicycles and, from 1909 to 1914, motorcycles. It was now a separate company, the Pierce Cycle Co, headed by George's son Percy Pierce.

Pierce-Arrow 66A series 5 tourer of 1918

Pierce-Arrow 38C series 3 coupé of 1915

The car company was renamed the Pierce-Arrow Motor Car Co in late 1908, and the following year two Pierce-Arrows became part of the new motor fleet at the White House in Washington DC (the other two were a Baker Electric and a White Steamer). The cars were personally selected by President Taft's chauffeur, George Robinson. George Pierce retired in 1909 and died the following year, to be succeeded as company president by George K. Birge, with Colonel Charles Clifton as treasurer.

By 1909 there were two four-cylinder and four six-cylinder models in the range, and production stood at 956 cars. Even so, the anticipated output was often sold before the year began, a happy situation which lasted up to 1918. Like Rolls-Royce, Pierce-Arrow ran a two-week training course for chauffeurs. In 1912 it adopted its characteristic fender-mounted headlights which were seen on practically all Pierces until the end of production. The aim was to give a higher and wider beam than conventionally mounted lights, and they were designed by Herbert M. Dawley, head of the art department, who later became a celebrated Broadway actor and theatrical director.

The classic Pierce-Arrows of the years 1912 to 1918 were the 38, 48 and 66, all of which had six-cylinder pair-cast engines. Capacities were 6.8 litres, 8.6 litres and 13.5 litres, this last being the largest production car engine ever made. The prototype Bugatti Royale engine displaced 14.7 litres, but the five 'production' Royales were only 12.7 litres, while the Hall Scott-powered Fageol of 1917 (only two or three made) had exactly the same dimensions as the Pierce Arrow 66, of which 1071 were sold in seven years. Prices of the 66 ran from $5850 to $8200.

In 1910 Pierce-Arrow entered the truck field with a 5-tonner designed by two Englishmen, John Younger who came from Dennis and H. Kerr Thomas from Hallford. They were fortunate in having a range of suitable trucks for military use, and with the outbreak of war in Europe truck production was greatly stepped up. Several thousand 2-, 3- and 5-tonners were made as well as 1000 of the standardized Liberty B trucks. This work gave Pierce-Arrow two of its best years in 1915 and 1916, with profits exceeding $4 million each year. In 1916 it became a public company with shares issued to a value of $10.7 million.

Profits fell in 1917 as a result of expensive factory extension, and once the war was over demand for trucks fell sharply. John Younger retired in 1918, and H. Kerr Thomas returned to England where he worked for AEC for five years and then became a director of Bean.

The 66 was no longer made after 1918, and the 48 was dropped after 1920, leaving the 38 as the sole model until 1925. Two developments of 1921 were the use of a monobloc engine, and the moving of the steering wheel to the left hand side. Pierce-Arrow was the last American firm to make this move; it is said that it retained right hand drive for so long to enable the chauffeur to leap nimbly onto the pavement to open the passenger's door.

Unfortunately these relatively small updatings were not enough to keep the company competitive in the 1920s. The 'old guard' of east coast conservative rich were not such a high proportion of buyers as they had been before the war, and the Pierce-Arrow found little favour among the new rich of Texas and Hollywood. What was needed was an eight- or twelve-cylinder engine, but Pierce did not offer them until 1929 and 1932 respectively.

There was a big shake up among personnel at Buffalo as policy became increasingly controlled by representatives of Seligmans, the merchant bank which had floated the share issue. Herbert Dawley left in 1917, Dave Fergusson and Colonel Clifton in 1921.

The recession of 1921 hit Pierce-Arrow badly: sales were down to 1000 compared with 2250 the previous year, and the company lost $8 million. A new president was brought in, Myron E. Forbes, who brought out the small 80 model in August 1924 to supplement the old T-head 38.

The 80 had a six-cylinder L-head engine of 4.7 litres and was priced at $2895 to $4000. At first it sold very well, boosting the 1925 total to 5654 units. By the time the Model 80 was phased out at the end of 1927 about 16,000

Pierce-Arrow 143 coupé of 1931

had been made, but it was outsold by rivals like the Packard Single Eight which had more modern styling. Pierce-Arrow had had its own coachworks since the earliest days, but from the 1920s onwards it also used well known firms such as Brunn, Le Baron and Judkins, and these were available on the 80 as well as on the larger cars.

In 1924 Pierce-Arrow made three 'all aluminium' cars designed by Laurence H. Pomeroy, in which about 85 per cent of the content was in fact aluminium, exceptions being items like gears, springs and cylinder block sleeves. The engines were four-cylinder units and the bodies in the style of the Model 80.

Commercial vehicle production continued in the 1920s, the best known model being the Model Z low frame bus chassis powered by the T-head passenger car engine, of which just under 1000 were made between 1924 and 1928. The smaller Fleet Arrow truck line used a reworked version of the Model 80 car engine, and was made from 1928 to May 1929.

Truck production was then suspended until a new six-cylinder engine could be developed, as the cars now used only eight-cylinder engines. A new truck line was announced in December 1930, but not more than 200 were made before production ended in December 1932. Later Pierce-Arrow trucks were made by White, and were mainly Whites with Pierce-Arrow badging.

In August 1928 Studebaker gained control of Pierce-Arrow through buying $5.7 million of the Buffalo company's stock. Studebaker President Albert R. Erskine became chairman of the board at Pierce-Arrow, although Myron Forbes remained as president until the end of 1929. The two companies remained separate, and although the cylinder blocks of the new Pierce Straight Eight were cast at South Bend, Indiana, they were in no way reworked Studebaker Presidents as has sometimes been claimed.

Known as the Series 133 and 143, the new cars had 6-litre L-head engines giving 125bhp and were priced from $2875 for a 133 roadster to $8200 for a 143 French brougham. They were very successful for a couple of years, selling 9840 units in 1929 and 6916 in 1930, but thereafter the Depression took its inevitable toll. Sales were down to 4500 in 1931 and 2692 in 1932, with a steady decline each year thereafter until production ended in 1938.

For 1932 Pierce-Arrow brought out a V12 at last; it came in two sizes, a 140bhp 6.5-litre or 150bhp 7-litre and took more than two years to develop. About $2 million had been spent on factory improvements, but 1932 was the rock bottom year of the Depression, and on sales of $8 million Pierce-Arrow made a loss of $3 million.

Probably the most dramatic Pierce-Arrow of all appeared in January 1933 – the streamlined Silver Arrow saloon built on a V12 chas-

following year they slipped into three figures (875) and thereafter it was downhill all the way, 787 in 1936, 167 in 1937 and a paltry 17 in 1938, these being assembled from parts made in 1937.

In August 1936 Pierce-Arrow brought out the Travelodge trailer caravan made in three sizes and priced from $784 to $1282, but it did not help the financial position and only 450 were made. In August 1937 Pierce-Arrow President Arthur Chanter announced that a new, medium priced car to sell for $1200 would be launched at the New York Automobile Show; this might have used a Hayes body as supplied to Graham and Reo, but the necessary $10.7 million to finance the new car could not be raised.

The company assets were sold off during 1938, the plant going to a newly formed group, the 1685 Elmwood Avenue Corporation, which continued to provide service and parts until 1942, when all remaining parts were scrapped for the war effort. Tooling and production rights on the engines were bought by the Seagrave Corporation of Columbus, Ohio, for use in fire engines. The last Seagrave using a Pierce type V12 engine was made in 1970. The name Pierce Arrow, without the hyphen, is currently used for a fire engine made by Pierce Manufacturing Co of Appleton, Wisconsin. GNG

PIERRON
see Mass

PILAIN
FRANCE 1895-1920

François Pilain was born the son of a miller in St Berain in 1859 and was apprenticed in his early teens to an engineer in Chalon-sur-Saône. In 1887 he was workshop manager for Serpollet and then in 1890 designer for La Buire, where parts for Serpollet were made as well as railway wagons and cars too, later.

Pilain started his own workshop in Lyons in 1894. Some cars were produced – they were listed in 1895 – and in 1897 the Société des Voitures Automobiles et Moteurs F. Pilain et Cie was formed with 380,000 francs capital. A year later Pilain was helping the engineering firm Vermorel, a few miles up the Rhône, to start a department building cars under the Système Pilain, although series car production at Vermorel was some years away. While there he was helped by his nephew Emile Pilain, who was soon to produce the Rolland-Pilain car.

In 1901 François Pilain concentrated on his own models once more, having set up Société des Automobiles Pilain with 1.5 million francs capital in Lyons. A feature of early Pilains was independent shaft drive to gearing in each rear wheel. This was retained in modified form into the 1920s.

A new factory enabled capacity to rise to about 300 cars a year from 1905, but losses were made and in 1907, when an 8.6-litre four was being developed, Pilain went into liquidation. François Pilain left the firm, which was now run by M. de Villeneuve.

With better management and less emphasis on experimentation the company recovered, producing smaller and cheaper cars such as a 1.9-litre four in 1909 and a 2.4-litre six in 1912. Profits in 1912 were about 4 million francs, roughly double the enlarged but

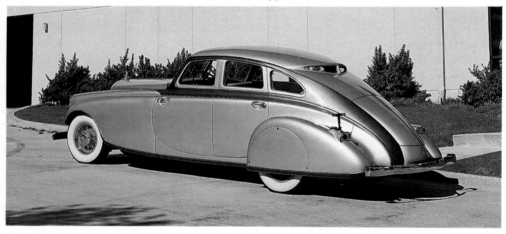

Pierce-Arrow Silver Arrow coupé of 1933

sis and priced at $10,000. They were made at South Bend and were publicity attractions rather than serious commercial propositions, although a modified version was made in small numbers in 1934. Only five of the original Silver Arrows were made.

In the spring of 1933 Studebaker went bankrupt, and in August the company was glad to unload Pierce-Arrow on to a group of Buffalo businessmen for $1 million. Although Pierce had borrowed from Studebaker during its five year association, the rest of the debt was cancelled.

The new owners estimated that they could make a profit on sales of 3000 cars a year, but they never reached that figure. In 1934 there were two series of eights and two twelves, the cut-price eight starting at only $2195, but the year's sales amounted to only 1740 cars. The

Pierce-Arrow 1701 Club saloon of 1937

Pilain four-cylinder torpedo of 1914

still modest capital. Cars sold in Britain usually had Vincent of Reading coachwork.

During World War I the firm's reputation for fine engineering prompted the government to requisition the factory for the manufacture of armaments under Hotchkiss control, and 400 Hotchkiss men were moved there. At the end of the war the Société Lyonnaise de l'Industrie Mécanique took over the factory, making Pilains until 1920 and then the SLIM-Pilain, an unusual 18/40hp four-cylinder overhead-cam car with compressor and tanks driving the air starter, jacks, horn, tyre pump and four wheel brakes. In 1924 Messier used a SLIM chassis for its car and suspension experiments.

François Pilain, who had attempted to start a company making front-wheel-drive cars in 1913, died in 1924, apparently unconnected with SLIM, which continued to make cars until 1929. The last cars lacked air suspension but had twin-cam 16-valve engines. NB

PILGRIM
GB 1906-1914

The picturesquely named Pilgrims' Way Motor Co Ltd was named after the ancient pilgrims' track running from Winchester to Canterbury, close to which the company's Farnham, Surrey, works were built. The company was registered in June 1905 with a capital of £10,000, and the first cars were built in 1906. They were of unusual design, having 5.6-litre 25/30hp four-cylinder engines mounted horizontally across the chassis, two-speed epicyclic gearboxes and final drive by single enclosed chain. The designer was F. Leigh Martineau who had formerly been with James and Browne. A total of 18 of

these large Pilgrims were made, mostly with landaulette bodies.

The Pilgrims' Way Motor Co went into receivership in March 1908, but was reorganized, and after a period when it was engaged on subcontract work for other companies it brought out a new design in 1911. This was a front-wheel-drive delivery van powered by a 1½-litre flat-twin engine, the work of C. T. Hulme who also designed for Straker-Squire and Swift. There was also a two-seater light car version of this, whose dashboard, radiator and coal-scuttle bonnet gave it a close resemblance to a Renault. These were listed until 1914 but production was small. The 30 or so workers were often kept busy with subcontracting work, such as making the Wall Auto Wheel and chassis parts for Vauxhall.

The cars were not revived after the war, but the company survived, and as the Pilgrims' Way Engineering Co Ltd it made precision tools and chassis lubrication systems from 1914 to 1939 followed by small aircraft components for Vickers during World War II, after which it returned to making precision tools until 1961. The last product was a thief-resistant messenger bag with built-in alarm system which was made from 1959 to 1962, when the company closed down. GNG

PILOT
USA 1909-1924

The Pilot Motor Car Co of Richmond, Indiana, was founded in 1909 to make large and expensive cars. It had a purpose-built factory and a capital of $100,000. Total output to 1915 was fewer than 1600 judging by the

chassis numbers. Using the slogan 'The Car Ahead', it offered sixes in 1913 and quickly discontinued production of fours. The Pilot 75 with 90bhp was described in factory literature as 'the most beautiful and most powerful pleasure car in America'.

After six years there was a complete change of policy. Henceforth a cheaper 6-45 with Teetor engine was made. Output appears to have been fewer than 1000 a year, despite the addition of Herschell-Spillman powered models in 1922. Production ended in 1924. NB

PIPE
BELGIUM 1898-1923

The Belgian Pipe, an expensive high-quality car, was named after its manufacturer's less glamorous earlier products, plumbing systems. In February 1898 Alfred and Victor Goldschmitt founded the Compagnie Belge de Construction d'Automobiles (Brevets Longtin et Mulders), in Brussels, with capital of 1 million francs. They started by designing a car and, although they acquired a small rented workshop in 1899, the first Pipe was built in Liège in 1898 by Usines des Moteurs à Grande Vitesse.

This was apparently a development model but at the Brussels Salon in March 1900, by which time it had moved to a larger factory at Ixelles, the company showed a two-cylinder chain-drive 6CV production model, designed by an engineer called Vignal and very like a Panhard-Levassor. Lucien Hautvast finished third in the Spa-Bastogne-Spa race with a two-cylinder car, while the first four-cylinder Pipe was driven in the 1901 Paris-Berlin race by Jean de Crawhez.

A 15CV four-cylinder production model joined the 6CV in 1902, by which time the company had a British distributor, the London Motor Garage Co Ltd. In later years, Pipes were even represented in Moscow.

The cars sold well and in 1902 the company bought land at Anderlecht for further expansion. In 1903 the name was changed to Société Anonyme des Usines Pipe and 65 cars were built. Annual production reached 100 in 1904, when four models were offered, all side-valve fours, of 12, 15, 20 and 30CV. These were chain drive, but the Jenatzy Magnetic clutch was also available as an option.

Pipe entered the Gordon Bennett races in 1904 and Hautvast finished sixth with a chain-drive 13.5-litre 60CV car. At the Paris Salon in December, Pipe showed its first 1905 model, designed by Otto Pfänder, a German who had previously worked for Mercédès and for Clément-Bayard. The 1905 range included 12/16, 18/24, 18/28 and 35/50CV models.

Pipe had now also begun to build trucks and buses, while NSU, already a major bicycle and motorcycle manufacturer, began car manufacture in Neckarsulm in 1905 by build-

Pipe 60hp Gordon Bennett racer of 1904

ing Pipes under licence. Pipe, now with some 300 workers, moved to a larger works near Mons as production continued to increase, passing 300 a year in 1907.

Hautvast scored Pipe's greatest competition success by finishing second to Nazzaro's Fiat in the 1907 Coupe de l'Empereur, but Pfänder was killed during testing for the event and his death caused Pipe to stop car production for almost two years, during which time it concentrated on building aero engines, including a 70hp V8. Another aero engine, introduced in 1910, used a hemispherical combustion chamber with combined concentric inlet and exhaust valves.

When car production resumed in 1909, with a four-cylinder 30CV model, the cars, except the chain-drive 80CV model which continued from 1907 until World War I, were less impressive, although they were equally well made. Two six-cylinder 30CV models were offered in 1911, but by 1913 all the cars had reverted to long-stroke side-valve fours, ranging from 12 to 80CV.

Production was stopped again by World War I, during which the factory was badly damaged. Although it was eventually rebuilt Pipe did not resume car production until 1921, when the company showed two four-cylinder models at the Brussels Salon, a 3-litre and a 9-litre. Although it built a few more cars until 1923, it had already started to concentrate on building trucks and tractors.

The Goldschmitts left the company in 1930 but commercial vehicles were made until 1932, when Pipe was taken over by another truck-maker, Brossel. Brossel had also taken over Atelier des Albert Bovy of Brussels, which had built commercial vehicles since 1902 and a few cars between 1904 and 1910, and it continued to build Bovy-Pipe trucks until 1950. BL

PIPER
GB 1967-1975

The Piper GT, which was built from 1967 to 1975, first as a kit and later as an assembled car, was a glassfibre-bodied sports car, initially designed to use a variety of engines including Hillman Imp, Ford and BMC A-series. It was designed by Tony Hilder and built first by Campbells Garages of Hayes, Kent. The name derived from Campbells' badge, a Scottish piper.

Campbells was owned by George Henrotte, a former refrigeration engineer who built and raced his own Ettorne 500cc Formula 3 car in the 1950s until he was seriously injured in a racing accident. For a while from 1963 he ran the Gemini Formula Junior racing team on behalf of The Chequered Flag, the cars' constructors, but the team was dogged by accidents and in 1965, Henrotte, having lost a good deal of money, returned to running the garage, mainly preparing racing cars and engines under the Piper name. He also planned to build a sports car with former Gemini driv-

er Ross Greenville. Late in 1965, however, Greenville returned to his native New Zealand and took the part-finished sports car project with him.

Henrotte then met Hilder, who had already designed a car and was looking for someone to build it. Their first open, spaceframed sports racing car was built early in 1966, purely for competition use, and several were sold with a variety of engines. There were also a couple of Piper single seaters around this time, but they had few successes.

Also in 1966, a group of club drivers asked Henrotte and Hilder to build a car to use Austin-Healey Sprite engine and running gear. After the original group had pulled out of the project Brian Sherwood, who owned one of the Piper sports racers, continued to back the idea and the first Piper GT, now with a tubular backbone chassis, was shown at the London Racing Car Show in January 1967, after which some six examples were built, with Ford and BMC engines. A much improved development of the design was then put into limited production, with 1600cc Ford engines as standard, as the Piper GTT.

In 1968 Henrotte separated the car building, which still included occasional racing models, from his tuning company and formed Piper Cars Ltd, run by Sherwood from a small new factory at Wokingham, Berkshire. Unfortunately, Sherwood was killed in a road accident in 1969, and Henrotte left the car company to concentrate on the engine and tuning business – which still flourishes as Piper FM Ltd in Ashford, Kent. In June 1971, after a Ford strike had caused parts supply problems, the firm was wound up.

Production, however, was resumed in 1971 by a new company, Emmbrook Engineering Ltd, formed by two former Piper managers, Bill Atkinson and Tony Waller. They launched a new car with similar body styling but heavily revised chassis as the Piper P2, later offered with a pop-up headlamp option.

In mid-1973 Emmbrook moved to a new works at South Willingham in Lincolnshire, but the business had suffered as the introduction of value added tax in Britain in April 1973 removed the tax concessions for kit cars. A few fully assembled and very well equipped Pipers were made in Lincolnshire, bringing the total built to 150 cars, but Emmbrook stopped building Pipers early in 1975. BL

Piper GTT sports coupé of c.1967

PLAYBOY
USA 1946-1950

The Playboy was one of many American attempts to make a compact car in the post-war period. It was the idea of three Buffalo businessmen, Packard dealer Louis Horwitz, Pontiac engineer Charles Thomas and garage owner Norman Richardson.

Designed by Thomas, the 1946 prototype featured a rear-mounted four-cylinder Continental engine and all independent suspension, but production models had front engines and conventional springs at the rear. The unit body was a three-seater coupé with retractable steel roof made by Federal Engineering in Detroit. Later cars had Hercules or Willys engines.

The promoters tried to finance the operation by selling franchises to potential dealers, as well as by a share issue. They began production in the former Brunn coachbuilding plant at Buffalo, but finding it too cramped they moved to a giant factory at North Tonawanda, New York, that had been used for wartime production of Pratt & Whitney aero engines. These premises proved to be much too large for the limited Playboy production.

The share issue, made in June 1948, was very disappointing, as it coincided with Preston Tucker's examination by the Securities Exchange Commission which became a nationwide scandal. The public got the message that new car companies were bad news, and it is surprising that Playboy sold even $2.5 million of the $10 million offered. Horwitz tried another share issue but it flopped completely and he filed for bankruptcy two weeks later.

There were numerous attempts to keep the Playboy alive, notably by a Connecticut dealer, Alvin Trumbull, but with no success. In February 1950 the contents of the North Tonawanda plant were auctioned off after 97 cars had been made. Nearly a quarter of these were still in the factory, and were sold off to the Lytemobile Corporation of New York City, owned by Chinese Nationalists. They encouraged Trumbull to start production at Meriden, Connecticut, but the Korean war stopped that.

Trumbull tried to sell the Playboy idea for the next 14 years, approaching among others Checker, International Harvester and Lance Reventlow, the maker of Scarab racing cars. His final plan, in 1964, was for a fibreglass-bodied sports car on a Saab chassis, but it did not even reach the prototype stage. GNG

PLM
see Keller

PLYMOUTH
see Chrysler

POLSKI-FIAT/FSO
POLAND 1932-1939; 1968 to date

The licence-built Fiat Balilla was the first serious attempt at quantity car manufacture in Poland, and was the result of an agreement between Fiat and the Polish government, which provided much of the finance for the Warsaw factory. Initially this assembled ckd kits, but with the arrival of the 508C in 1937 practically the whole car was Polish made, only the instruments coming from the NSU-Fiat factory in Germany. Production continued right up to the Nazi invasion of Poland in September 1939.

There was an attempt to revive the Polski-Fiat production in 1968 with the 125P; a hybrid not identical to any native Fiat model, it lian government were not good enough. The Fabryka Samochodow Osobowyc (FSO) factory therefore began making Russian Pobieda cars under the name Warszawa. It restarted Fiat production in 1968 with the 125P; a hybrid not identical to any native Fiat model, it had the engine, transmission and suspension of the superseded 1300/1500 series, with the body of the current 124. Some components for this car were made in the former Stoewer factory at Szczecin (Stettin).

In 1972 another factory was set up at Bielsko-Biala for the manufacture of the Fiat 126 and also the Polish-designed Syrena. This factory is still in operation and built about 175,000 126s and 10,000 Syrenas in 1981. The Warsaw plant still makes the 125P in 1300 and 1500 versions, and in 1979 brought out the Polonez, a three- or five-door hatchback powered by the 1500 engine. During 1981 the make name was officially changed from Polski-Fiat to FSO. In 1983 there were about 25,000 employees at FSO Warsaw who made 52,700 125s and 26,400 Polonez. For 1987 FSO plans to come up to date with the 1300 five-door hatchback. GNG

POLYMOBIL
see Dux

PONTIAC
see Oakland

POPE/COLUMBIA, HARTFORD, ROBINSON, TOLEDO, TRIBUNE, WAVERLEY
USA 1896-1914

One of the most complex stories of the early motor industry in the United States was the rise and fall of Colonel Albert A. Pope's empire. Pope was born in Boston in 1843, fought in the Civil War and in 1877 formed the Pope Manufacturing Co in Hartford, Connecticut. A year later the company began making bicycles.

One of the brand names was Columbia, for which Metz was an early agent. An automotive department was established in the 1890s, Hiram P. Maxim becoming engineer of the department in 1895 after having motorized a Columbia tricycle two years before. He was helped by Herbert Alden, who became chief engineer of Timken in 1906. The tricycle's engine was installed in a light Crawford four wheel carriage in 1896. The Crawford carriage was also made by one of Pope's companies, which together employed 3043 men that year and held a virtual monopoly on the sale of nickel steel.

In 1897 both petrol and electric vehicles were sold by Columbia, production taking place near the main bicycle plant in a factory later used by Underwood typewriters. A special line conceived by Colonel Pope were three-wheelers with a choice of delivery box or bench seat placed longitudinally in front of the driver.

Associated with Pope was the Electric Vehicle Co, registered in 1897 with $12 million capital. It was run by former US Naval Secretary W. C. Whitney, who used the Pope plants for most of his requirements, including an order for 1600 electric taxis in 1899. (By 1907 some 9000 of the taxis in the eastern states were Columbias.)

The Electric Vehicle Co had evolved from Morris and Salom, which made a few vehicles from 1895 and became the Electric Carriage and Wagon Co with the addition of a neighbouring accumulator firm in Philadelphia where Justus B. Entz, designer of a well-known magnetic transmission system, was chief engineer. The Electric Vehicle Co held the rights to the Selden patents, which it subcontracted to other ALAM members.

Columbia's car department joined the group in 1899, which then became the Columbia and Electric Vehicle Co. In December 1900 Riker was acquired, causing an increase in capital from $8 million to $20 million.

Colonel Pope's other bicycle firms were reorganized into the grossly over-capitalized $36 million American Bicycle Co in 1899. One of its many constituents was the Waverley Bicycle Co, which had made Waverley electric cars from 1898. The American Bicycle Co collapsed in 1902 but Waverley production carried on in Indianapolis, Indiana. The car was known as the Pope-Waverley from 1903 with the formation of the new Pope Motor Car Co. This company was a subsidiary of a re-formed Pope Manufacturing Co, which bought the remnants of the American Bicycle Co and the American Cycle Co for a modest $350,000, as well as International Motor Car Co, Federal Manufacturing and National Battery Co. The designer of the Pope-Waverley was Elmer Sperry, formerly of the Cleveland Automatic Machine Co.

The Pope-Waverley was sold in Britain in 1903 by the Locomobile Co of Great Britain,

Pope-Waverley electric buggy of 1907

while Columbias were sold by City and Suburban Electric Carriage Co, which had supplied one to Queen Alexandra in 1901.

The Toledo bicycle chain plant, which had made American Bicycle's Toledo steamers from 1900, turned to petrol-engined cars in 1903. These Pope-Toledos were expensive four-cylinder cars which, in 1905, were guaranteed to travel at 60mph (96kph). Production totalled about 400 a year. An early employee was Louis Chevrolet, who also worked on Pope's Rambler bicycles and the Waverley car.

Another new brand in 1903 was the Pope-Hartford, which was made in the company's original factories in Hartford, Connecticut. In 1901 an attempt had been made to obtain a Panhard et Levassor licence, but Hartford production cars were typically American and a little below the Pope-Toledo in price.

The cheapest car in the Pope range was the Tribune, made in Hagerstown, Maryland, from 1904 from parts made principally at Hartford and available in 6hp form in England for £131 in 1905. It was designed by Gilbert Loomis, who had supplied silencers and carburettors before joining Pope in 1903.

Another allied make, although actually controlled by Colonel Pope's nephew, Edward Pope, who had worked for Pope Manufacturing, was the Pope-Robinson. Starting out in 1899 as the Bramwell-Robinson, this car was made by a machinery company of Hyde Park, Massachusetts. When Bramwell left to make cars under his own name, a venture which quickly foundered, the vehicles were known as Robinsons. Edward Pope bought into the firm in 1902 and his name was added to the range of luxury cars produced in 1903 and 1904, after which the car division was said to have been absorbed by Buick, which may have supplied engines.

In 1907 the unmanageable Pope group was tottering and when its advertising agents pressed an overdue account the whole venture, capitalized at $22.5 million, collapsed. Colonel Pope managed to have himself

appointed receiver and various parts of his empire were separated and sold off, although the Tribune disappeared entirely.

Columbia became the Columbia Motor Car Co in 1909 and the following year became enmeshed in Benjamin Briscoe's US Motor Corporation, along with Sampson, Brush, Stoddard-Dayton and Maxwell-Briscoe. Columbia used Knight engines in 1911 but the marque was not revived after the collapse of Briscoe's business in 1912-13.

Waverley and Toledo had both been subsidiaries of Pope Motor Car Co. Waverley, which had lost its factory manager, J. S. Conwell, to the Marion Motor Car Co shortly before the collapse of Pope, was acquired by the new management and continued to make electric cars in Indianapolis until the war years. Toledo, however, lasted only until 1909, its factory being bought by Montrose Metal Gaskets and later used by Dagmar.

The only parts to remain under Pope family control were the bicycle factory at Westfield, Massachusetts, and the Hartford car plant. In December 1908, with assets of $5 million, these factories started trading again and were profitable for a time. Pope-Hartford employed 1000 men and intended to make 1000 cars in the 1909 season. It soon had an extensive range going up to 60hp including commercial vehicles of up to 5 tons capacity as well as fire appliances and ambulances. The Westfield plant built Pope motorcycles from 1911.

In late 1913 the parent firm was in trouble again. Colonel Pope had died in 1909 and management had been partially in the hands of other members of his family, although his youngest son, Harold, had left Pope-Toledo for Wright Aeronautical.

Car and commercial production ended in 1914 but the two-wheeler factory was reformed as Westfield Manufacturing Co and built Pope motorcycles until 1918, along with munitions. It also owned the rights to such famous bicycle names as Columbia, Rambler, Pope, Crescent, Stearns, Spalding and Cleveland. NB

PORSCHE
AUSTRIA, GERMANY 1948 to date

Ferdinand Porsche – the name was a corruption of the Slavic Borislav – was born in September 1875 in Maffersdorf, then in Bohemia, the third child of a tinsmith. After his elder brother Anton was killed in a working accident Ferdinand joined the family business. He became interested in electricity, although there was no supply in the village, and began to tinker in his spare time. His father disapproved but his mother privately encouraged him and he was eventually allowed to go to evening classes at the technical school in nearby Reichenberg. In 1890 he built a complete electrical system, including a generator and control board, for the house and workshop and in 1894 his father finally agreed to send him to college in Vienna.

He also had an apprenticeship arranged there with Bela Egger, who made electrical equipment and machinery. By 1898 he was manager of the test department and in 1899 joined the long established carriage builder Jacob Lohner to develop electric and petrol-electric cars, as the Lohner-Porsche. He often drove his own designs in competition, usually successfully, and in 1902, as a Reserve Infantryman, he drove the Archduke Franz Ferdinand during a demonstration of the Lohner-Porsche for military use.

In 1905 Porsche succeeded Paul Daimler as technical director of Austro-Daimler in Vienna Neustadt. From 1910, even before there was any Austrian aeroplane, Porsche designed aero engines and his air-cooled flat-four of 1912 is widely regarded as a direct ancestor of the Volkswagen and Porsche car engines. He continued his work on mixed drives at Austro-Daimler, including an 85hp racing car in 1907, which he drove himself. He was actually racing in September 1909 when his son Ferry, his worthy successor, was born.

Porsche Type 64 record-breaking coupé of 1938

During World War I Ferdinand designed a road train with hub motors on each wagon, and the C-train, carrying a huge Skoda mortar (Skoda was part of Austro-Daimler), the heaviest motorized gun ever built. In 1916 he became managing director of Austro-Daimler, was honoured by the emperor and received an honorary doctorate from the University of Vienna. He continued his aviation interests with plans for an electric quasi-helicopter, but it was never built.

After the war, with Austria's reorganization, Porsche became a Czech citizen, a status he retained until 1938 when the Nazi system forced him to become a German national.

In 1922 Count Sascha Kolowrat, head of Austria's largest film company and a close friend of Porsche, wanted a small sports car for hillclimbs and rallies. Porsche had long wanted to build a small car but Austro-Daimler always resisted. The nearest Porsche had built was an air-cooled two-cylinder two-seater as a Christmas present for 10-year-old Ferry in 1919. Financed by Kolowrat he designed a very quick four-cylinder 1100cc car which Austro-Daimler grudgingly built in small numbers as the Sascha — one of which won its class in the 1922 Targa Florio.

In April 1923 Porsche succeeded Paul Daimler in another post, this time at Daimler,

was ultimately dropped as too expensive, but Porsche carried on with a similar project for NSU using an air-cooled flat-four engine. This was completed in January 1934 but was again shelved as NSU's motorcycle sales boomed.

Coincidentally, early in 1934 Porsche was commissioned to design a 'people's car' and Project 60 eventually became the Volkswagen. Porsche signed the design agreement in June 1934 and the first three prototypes were completed in 1936, in Porsche's own garage.

In 1932 Porsche visited Russia at the invitation of the government and was offered what amounted to a blank cheque to develop his ideas and the title of 'State Designer'. He declined. In 1936 he visited the United States and Britain to look at their motor industries and in 1937 he returned to the USA with Ferry, meeting Henry Ford and discussing the 'people's car' concept.

At the opposite end of the scale from the VW, Porsche developed the awesome mid-engined V16 Auto Union P-wagen Grand Prix car and its record breaking derivatives. These racing designs were handled by a small independent company, Hochleistungs Fahrzeugbau GmbH, set up in November 1932. Porsche also planned a land speed record car, but the onset of World War II, for which

he designed the Tiger tank among other things, ended that project.

With the VW in limited production for the military by the outbreak of war, Hitler gave Porsche the title Professor. Porsche called Hitler Herr Hitler and never Führer and remained as distant from politics as his position allowed. He stayed in Stuttgart for the duration of the war, although his works moved to Gmünd in 1944.

In October 1945 he was arrested by the Americans then handed over to the French, who allowed Renault to consult with him, and was finally imprisoned for two years. He was released in August 1947, largely as a result of payments made in connection with his designing the Cisitalia Grand Prix car.

Late in 1947 Porsche took the decision to build a Porsche sports car, based very much on pre-war ideas for a VW sports car derivative. It was given the project number 356 and was to be a lightweight open two-seater with a tuned 1131cc VW engine and VW suspension all round. The first chassis was completed in March 1948 and the open bodywork, intended only for the prototype, was added in May, all at the small works in Gmünd. The prototype was sold to a Swiss in September for much needed foreign currency.

In August 1948 the first streamlined coupé

Porsche RS60 Spyder of 1959

where he worked for five years as a designer. In January 1929 he moved to Steyr, then Austria's biggest car-maker, as chief engineer and a member of the board. Later in the year, after the collapse of its bank, Steyr was absorbed by Austro-Daimler.

Porsche left the company and started his own design office in Stuttgart in December 1930 as Konstruktionsbüro für Motoren- und Fahrzeugbau Dr Ing hc Ferdinand Porsche GmbH. He took with him his protégé, the brilliant young engineer Karl Rabe whom he had first met at Austro-Daimler. Rabe would be Porsche's chief engineer until 1966. Ferry, now 21 and previously apprenticed to Bosch and Steyr, also joined the original staff of nine, which grew to 13 during 1931 and to some 115, including assembly workers, by 1938.

The bureau was officially registered in March 1931 and Porsche designated his projects by numbers, starting with Project 7 (a small car for Wanderer) so as not to appear totally inexperienced! Project 12, started in September 1931, on behalf of Zündapp, was a small car for which Zündapp wanted a five-cylinder water-cooled radial engine. The idea

Porsche Grand Prix car of 1962

Porsche 901 (known as the 911) of 1963, against a background of three 356 models

body, as intended for production, was completed and small scale production at the rate of about five a month, with hand-made bodies, began just before the end of 1948. The car was first shown at the Geneva Show early in 1949, and although it was advertised as having the 1131cc engine it actually used a 1086cc unit.

The first 50 cars were built at Gmünd, but the capacity there was obviously insufficient and Porsche began to negotiate with the military authorities for the return of the Stuttgart works. They began their return in July 1949 but did not complete it until September 1950 as the American military were reluctant to move out.

The company had 108 staff by 1950 and the planned production rate of up to 10 cars a week soon doubled until almost 300 cars were made during 1950. The 500th Porsche was built in March 1951 and in June Porsche made its first entry at Le Mans, finishing 20th. Porsche has been continuously involved in competition since, scoring a record 10th Le Mans victory in 1985, with the 956.

Porsche also built air-cooled Grand Prix cars under the 1½-litre formula in the 1960s which were never completely successful but did win the 1962 French Grand Prix, driven by Dan Gurney. More recently, Porsche returned to Grand Prix racing in 1983 as an engine supplier, developing and building a turbocharged 1½-litre engine on behalf of Techniques Avant Garde as the TAG Turbo, with which McLaren won the 1984 and 1985 Drivers' and Constructors' championships with a record number of Grand Prix wins in 1984.

Ferdinand Porsche did not live to see the competition success; he died after a stroke in January 1952. Ferry was his natural successor and had in effect been running the company since his father's wartime internment.

The basic 356 design continued with development and variations until its replacement in September 1964 by the 911 series. A 1500 model was introduced in 1951 (although the 1100 was available until 1954), a 1600 in 1955 and the final 356 series engine development was the 130hp 1996cc unit of the 1964 2000GS. The most radical of the 356 body styles was the cut-down-screen Speedster, introduced in the United States in 1954, but the design really changed very little. In 1955 some 75 per cent of the 3000 or so cars built by Porsche's 600-strong workforce went to the USA, mirroring the popularity of the VW. The 10,000th Porsche was built in March 1956 and by the end of the 1950s annual production was almost 8000 cars.

With the introduction of the 911, Porsche's success continued. It was launched in September 1964 with a 1991cc flat-six engine, initially of 130bhp. The 912 replaced the 356C in 1965, using the earlier car's 1582cc flat-four engine. The 911 gradually grew in capacity and power. Fuel injection was available from 1970, when capacity went up to 2195cc. In 1972 it was raised again, to 2343cc, and late in 1973 went up to 2687cc, after which

Porsche 956 winning Le Mans of 1985

injection became standard.

Also in 1973 Porsche introduced the very quick Carrera RS, following a model name already used on various racing models and a special version of the 356. The company built 15,415 cars that year and again almost 75 per cent were exported.

For 1975 Porsche introduced a turbocharged version of the 911, with 2994cc engine and type-numbered the 930. This gained a 3299cc engine with a full 300bhp late in 1977 and remains one of the fastest accelerating cars in the world.

The 930 developed for racing as the 934 and 935 and Porsche's own testing and development facilities at Weissach were dramatically improved from 1961 to 1974. During that period a basic test-track was transformed into a full technical centre.

In the late 1960s Porsche was set for partnership with Volkswagen, one of the few visible effects of which was the launch of the VW Porsche 914 in 1969. Porsche was also developing a Beetle replacement for VW and VW effectively took over Porsche distribution, particularly in the USA, through a new joint company, but in 1971 the VW project and most of the connections were cancelled in the face of mutual problems. Porsche AG eventually resumed its own distribution.

Also in 1971, Dr Ing hc Ferdinand Porsche

Porsche-engined McLaren MP4/2 of 1985

KG, a limited partnership controlled by the Porsche and Piëch families (connected to the marriage of Ferdinand's daughter Louise and Dr Anton Piëch), became Dr Ing hc Ferdinand Porsche AG, or a joint stock company. This was a deliberate attempt by Ferry, who resigned from active management to chair the overall board, to widen the company's management beyond the two owning families. It was also the beginning of a somewhat shaky period for the company which was affected by the general economic decline, with sales falling to only 9424 cars in 1975 before a dramatic recovery with the introduction of the low-priced 924 in 1975 and the luxurious 928 in 1977 – alongside the 911s, one of their most successful models of all time, and one which Porsche had no inten-

Porsche 930 (known as the 911 Turbo) of 1984

Porsche 928S of 1986

Porsche 944 of 1984

tion of dropping for many more years to come.

The 924 was a great departure, with a water-cooled 1984cc four-cylinder engine in the front and rear-wheel-drive. By 1981 over 100,000 had been sold, making Porsche a very different kind of manufacturer. The 928 was another departure, with front-mounted water-cooled 4474cc V8 engine and rear-wheel-drive, with a rear-mounted gearbox to balance the weight over the axles.

A turbocharged version of the 924 followed in 1979, joined later by a Carrera Turbo, and an S version of the 928 was added in 1980. The gap between the 924 and 928 was narrowed in 1982 by the 2479cc four-cylinder 944 and a cabriolet was added to the 911 range to give Porsche its most extensive range ever, with the addition in 1985 of the ultimate twin-turbocharged four-wheel drive development of the 911. This Group B 959 used a 450bhp version of the flat-six and had bodywork made in lightweight Kevlar material. Intended primarily for competition, a limited run of 250 cars was planned, and all were sold before they were built, at a price of £155,000 each.

As for its more mundane models, Porsche launched a turbocharged 944 in the spring of 1985, while a four-valve-per-cylinder version of the 928S, with slightly larger capacity, was available in America from mid-1985, just before its appearance in Europe. The 924S, with detuned 944 engine, replaced the 924, and in the longer term a small mid-engined two-seater, tentatively codenamed 984 was due in about 1989. Production in 1985/86 totalled 53,625 cars. BL

PORTHOS
FRANCE 1906-1914

The Société Générale des Automobiles Porthos started in business in 1906 by displaying a tricar at the Paris Salon and taking a stand at the British Stanley Show that year. As the company made three-wheelers it seemed appropriate to choose the name of one of the Three Musketeers. Production soon came to centre around larger four-wheelers, however, a 24/30hp four being followed in 1907 by a 50/60hp six. Porthos did not body its own cars.

A 10.86-litre straight-eight Grand Prix car was offered in 1908 and racing soon absorbed much of the firm's activity and finance. One of its drivers was Colin Defries, who obtained the exclusive British agency when he placed an order for six chassis at the 1906 Salon. He raised the necessary deposit with a Mr Herbert Hoover of the mine engineering firm Bewick Moreing in London. Hoover was later better known as President of the United States.

Porthos capital was increased to 1.5 million francs in 1907. The company made at most 250 cars a year and produced virtually everything apart from castings at its factory in Rue du Dôme, Billancourt, under the supervision of talented designer Kieffer. In 1910 the firm went into liquidation and in 1912 a new Porthos company began producing an assortment of more modest four- and six-cylinder machines which ended with the outbreak of World War I. NB

PRAGA
CZECHOSLOVAKIA 1907-1947

The origins of this Prague-based firm stem from 1871, when machinery for sugar refining was made. Railway locomotives were built later on, followed by motor vehicles from 1907. Initially based on popular French and German vehicles, they became Italian in design in 1909 when an Isotta-Fraschini licence was acquired, under which 3- and 8-litre cars were made. Lorries were added in 1910 and motor ploughs of typical Germanic type with two wheels plus a rear balance wheel.

From 1911 Frantisek Kec, chief designer, introduced his own ideas. These were generally conservative and included 1.13-, 2.8- and 3.8-litre fours under the model names Alfa, Mignon and Grand, and the Type V 4/5 tonner, widely used in World War I and later.

Motor ploughs continued to be built for a time in the 1920s and were sold to Western Europe from Paris showrooms. The cars and commercials were mostly for home consumption and included the baby Piccolo car from 1924. Later baby cars had independent suspension at front and rear and backbone chassis developed by Kec and Petranek.

In 1927 six and straight-eight cylinder models were introduced; the latter were known as Grands and had Kellner-designed bodywork produced by Praga. In 1928 a merger with Breitfeld and Danek brought motorcycles and aero engines to the range and in 1930 Deutz diesels were adopted in some of the commercial vehicles. Light planes were produced in the 1930s and were made under licence as Hillson-Pragas in Britain. In 1929 Ceskomoravska-Kolben, which had been involved with Mignon production, joined the group.

Thanks to the success of the Piccolo and related Baby cars, Praga production climbed from 500 in 1930 to 1000 in 1931. It was the most popular marque in Czechoslovakia in 1933 and 1934 with over 2200 sales annually, falling to third behind Tatra and Skoda with just under 2000 sales in 1935, when the 3.9-litre six-cylinder Golden replaced the Grand.

In the later 1930s commercials took precedence and were made in Yugoslavia, where they led to the post-war TAM, and in Slovakia province, under the name Orava. Pragas were widely used by the Germans in World War II.

Apart from a few Goldens produced for government leaders in 1946-47, trucks kept the name alive after the war. Since 1953 the speciality has been 6×6 normal control V3S models with air-cooled diesels. These are made in Avia's factory, an aircraft associate which produced some Pragas in the 1960s and obtained a licence to produce SAVIEM commercial vehicles in 1968. Praga also makes motor components, particularly axles. Frantisek Kec, who was responsible for Praga design at least until 1939, was killed in 1971 at the age of 90 in an accident with one of his own trucks. NB

PRATT-ELKHART/ELCAR, PRATT
USA 1909-1931

F. B. Pratt started the Elkhart Harness and Carriage Manufacturing Co in 1893 in Elkhart, Indiana, and with help from his sons made it the biggest mail order firm in its specialized lines in the world. They began motor buggy experiments in 1906 and started production of four-cylinder Pratt-Elkhart cars having constant mesh gearboxes in 1909. These cars were initially sold by mail order, but the firm was soon compelled to use agents. Some models had Brown-Lipe sliding mesh gearboxes.

Elkhart was dropped from the name in 1912, possibly to avoid confusion with a nearby competitor, Crow-Elkhart. Having made a variety of sizes the company offered only the Pratt-Fifty in 1914, but then came Continental six and Herschell-Spillman eight-cylinder engines.

The car firm was now the Pratt Motor Car Co, a subsidiary of the original company. In 1915 the parent became the Elkhart Carriage and Motor Car Co, signifying financial difficulties that were accompanying its transition from horses to horsepower.

The cars then became known as Elcars and had four-cylinder Continental engines and Gemco axles. These continued until 1917, when ambulance bodies were built. Horsedrawn equipment was not revived after World War I but in 1919 production began of Elcars with four-cylinder Lycoming and six-cylinder Continental engines. Production amounted to 4000 that year, a figure which was never again equalled.

The Pratt family sold out in 1921 to a group of former Auburn employees who continued the range and added a 90hp Lycoming eight-cylinder version in 1925. Some of the four-cylinder types were sold as taxis. In 1926 the British Isotta-Fraschini importer attempted to set up an Elcar agency in the UK. In 1927 Elcar's president, F. B. Sears, announced the cheapest straight-eight available, the 8-78, at $1395. For 1928 all engines were Lycomings.

A car with Powell Lever six-cylinder engine was exhibited in 1930 when different chassis and Elcar's own home-built body styles gave the range a total of 31 models. In 1931 the Lycoming eight-powered model developed 140bhp, but that was the end of the marque. The firm had merged with Lever Motors Corporation of Indiana in 1930 and its final task was making revived Mercers. This venture failed after very few had been made. NB

PREMIER/COVENTRY-PREMIER
GB 1912-1923

Premier was a well-known Coventry bicyclemaker which had been established in 1876 as Hillman and Herbert, later Hillman, Herbert and Cooper Ltd. By 1892 the company had assumed the title Premier Cycle Co Ltd, under which motorcycle production began in 1908 and cyclecars in 1912. The cyclecar was a conventional machine with transverse aircooled V-twin engine and chain drive.

The company also had branches, originally set up for bicycle manufacture, in Germany at Nuremberg, in Austria at Eger and in Japan. The German factory made cars under the name Kaiser and later Premier, while in Austria they were known as Omega. So far as is known the Japanese operation was confined to pedal cycles.

In November 1913 the company secured the services of G. W. A. Brown, who had worked for Talbot, and he designed for Premier a small car with 10.4hp four-cylinder engine and shaft drive. This was intended to replace both the cyclecar and the motorcycles, but as it was not ready until late 1914 the war prevented serious production. The last motorcycles were made in 1915.

Premier advertising, 1911

The company name had been changed to Coventry-Premier in October 1914 and it was under this name that a three-wheeler with an 8hp water-cooled V-twin engine was introduced in 1919. In July 1920 Coventry-Premier Ltd was sold to Singer & Co Ltd, but the three-wheeler was still marketed under its own name as was a four-wheeler version introduced for 1922. The last Coventry-Premier for 1923 was a 10hp four-cylinder car which was in fact a utility version of the Singer Ten, selling for £241 compared with £294 for the Singer. In 1924 Singer was able to reduce its own prices, so there was no point in continuing with the Coventry-Premier.

The German firm, Braun-Premier, did not survive World War I, but the Austrian branch at Eger – part of Czechoslovakia since 1918 – continued to make motorcycles under the name Premier until 1933. GNG

PREMIER
USA 1903-1924

The Premier was the creation of George A. Weidely, an Indianapolis engineer who built a home-made car in 1900 and sold it to a friend in 1902. The following year, with finance from several local businessmen, he set up the Premier Motor Manufacturing Co, capitalized at $50,000. The first Premier car had a front-mounted vertical twin engine with shaft drive, and was priced at $2500 for a five passenger rear-entrance tonneau.

After a small number had been sold it was decided to move into a cheaper market, so Weidely designed a light car with armoured wood frame, epicyclic transmission and single chain drive. The engine was a 16hp air-cooled four mounted transversely across the frame under a small bonnet. Priced from $1200 to $1500 it was made from 1904 to 1907, being joined in 1906 by a larger air-cooled model with conventionally located 20/24hp four-cylinder engine. For 1907 the company offered the choice of air or water cooling, and a customer could purchase both sets of cylinders and use air cooling in winter and water in summer if he wished.

A water-cooled six selling for $3750 joined the range for 1908. For the next few years Premier offered fours and sixes of conventional design, known as the 4-40 and 6-60.

In 1913 George Weidely left the company to form his own Weidely Motors Co which made proprietary engines in considerable numbers up to 1924. The company was particularly known for its V12, used by such makers as Hal, Austin, Pathfinder and Kissel. Curiously, only two models of Premier used a Weidely engine, in 1914 and 1915. A 40hp six-cylinder Herschell-Spillman engine was used in one 1913 Premier, but otherwise the Indianapolis company made its own power units, culminating in a fine 4.8-litre overhead-valve six with aluminium block, crankcase and pistons which powered all Premiers from 1916.

In December 1915 the Premier Motor Manufacturing Co was sold to a New York syndicate and was re-formed as the Premier Motor Co with capital of $2.5 million. At the same time the assets of the Mais Motor Truck Co of Indianapolis were acquired, and in April 1916 the Premier Motor Corporation was formed to control both companies.

The 1916 models featured the aluminium six engine designed by E. G. Gunn, formerly with the Northway Motor & Manufacturing Co, and also the Cutler-Hammer electric gearchange, an early form of pre-selector. A complete line of open and closed models was offered, open bodies by Fleetwood and closed by Central Body Co; prices started at $1685. Thanks to this model, 1917 was Premier's best year, when over 2000 cars were sold. However, wartime inflation pushed the price of the cheapest tourer up to $2285 in 1918 and $2585 in 1919.

Despite the fact that the 1920 models were said to be the most completely equipped cars in America, including such features as Pyrene fire extinguishers, Kellogg power tyre pump and electric cigarlighter as standard equipment, sales fell to only 540 that year. In 1921 the company was again reorganized as the Premier Motor Car Corporation, but it went into receivership in July 1922 when production was down to 20 cars a month.

In January 1923 it was announced that Premier would make a low priced four-cylinder touring car called the Stratton-Premier, after its designer Frank B. Stratton. Only a few prototypes emerged, but later in the year Stratton gained control of the William Small Co which had made the Monroe car for a number of years. A few Monroes, which were also low priced four-cylinder cars, were made in the Premier factory in 1924. That year also saw the end of Premier cars, the last of which had hydraulic four wheel brakes and balloon tyres. Production in 1923 was not more than 110 units, with a mere handful being delivered in 1924.

This was not quite the end of vehicle production at the Premier factory, for a taxicab powered by a four-cylinder Buda engine was made until 1928. George Weidely's engine company folded in 1924, but he was later involved in other non-automotive ventures and died in 1948 at the age of 77. GNG

PRESTO
GERMANY 1900-1927

Presto 8/25PS two-seater of 1913

George Günther made Presto bicycles in Chemnitz, Saxony, from 1898 and perhaps a little earlier. In 1900 a Presto car with the firm's own 5½hp water-cooled engine was exhibited at Britain's Stanley Show by Louis Bernstein; 3½ and 4½hp models were also offered by the company.

In 1906 Günther and Co Fahrradwerke became Prestowerke AG and the following year made profits equivalent to $33,300. By then it was probably producing Delahayes under licence. Motorcycles, but few cars, had been made from 1901. Early bikes had Zedel, Minerva and Fafnir engines. Profits continued to be made until 1911-12, and then two years of losses totalled $80,000. Car and light commercial vehicle production did not begin in

quantity until after 1910 and contributed to profits of $42,000 in 1913, when a 2.1-litre car was offered. Capital in 1914 stood at the equivalent of $375,000.

Production from 1921 concentrated on a 2.35-litre four-cylinder car model and on 200cc Alba-powered motorcycles as well as on motor components. In the early 1920s Presto was a member of the Deutsche Automobil Konzern with the Vomag and Magirus truck firms. The ailing Dux company of Leipzig was acquired in 1926 when Presto employed 2200. The electrical firm AEG is said to have held shares in both firms and is thought to have organized the takeover, which resulted in a joint capital of 3,045,000 marks.

Presto-Dux commercial vehicles were made briefly until 1927, when Presto was bought by NAG (which had itself been started by AEG). For a short time the Presto car was known as the NAG-Presto. The motorcycles kept the Presto name and were built until 1940, latterly with Sachs engines. NB

PRIAMUS
GERMANY 1901-1923

The Priamus car never achieved great fame outside the district of Cologne where it was made, although production lasted for more than 20 years. In 1901 the Kölner Motorwagenfabrik GmbH vorm Heinrich Brunthaler built a light car designed by Wilhelm Uren. It had a 6PS single-cylinder engine with two-speed belt drive and a tubular chassis. In 1903 Uren took over the management of the factory and the company name was changed to Motorfahrzeugfabrik Köln Uren, Kotthaus & Co.

The single-cylinder car was continued, now with pressed steel frame and shaft drive, and was joined by two-cylinder models of 10/12PS and 16/18PS, and a four-cylinder 18/20PS. All these cars had subframes carrying the engine and gearbox, a notable Priamus characteristic.

The single and two-cylinder cars were dropped in 1905, and small-scale production of 18/20PS and 24/30PS fours continued until 1908. Priamus cars took part in the Herkomer Trials of 1905, 1906 and 1907, although without great success.

In 1908 Uren, Kotthaus & Co went bankrupt as a result of overproduction of expensive cars and a general slump in demand. A finance group took over the factory and formed a new company, Priamus Automobilwerke GmbH. The new owners wisely introduced a range of smaller cars, 6/16PS, 9/22PS and 10/32PS, which achieved reasonable sales up to 1914, being joined by an 8/24PS in 1913. These cars were also known as PAGs.

After World War I the 8/24PS was revived, joined by a 9/30PS, and in 1921 the company was acquired by Mollenkamp of Dusseldorf, a coachbuilding firm. It launched a new 10/50PS six-cylinder car in 1923 which was sold

under the name Molkamp and was made in the former Priamus works at Cologne. Few of these were built. and in 1924 Mollenkamp turned to licence production of the Italian Ceirano 150S, which lasted until 1926. GNG

PRINCE
JAPAN 1952-1966

The Prince car was originally made by Tama Motors Co of Tachikawa, a former aircraft company which had made small Datsun-based electric cars from 1947 to 1951. It then turned to a conventional four-door saloon with 1½-litre four-cylinder engine, named the Prince with the permission of Crown Prince Akihito. In 1955 it became the Prince Skyline with styling similar to the contemporary American Ford Fairlane. A Prince Skyline was the first Japanese car to appear at a European motor show, the 1957 Paris Salon, but no sales resulted. In 1961 the Skyline was joined by the 2-litre Gloria, and the latter model received a single-overhead cam engine, also of 2 litres, in 1964.

In 1954 Prince Motors Co was bought by the Fuji Precision Machinery Co of Tokyo, which had made all Prince's engines since petrol cars were introduced and also manufactured aircraft engine components and rockets. Fuji Precision Machinery is closely linked to Fuji Heavy Industries, manufacturer of Subaru cars, as both companies were formed from the break up of Nakajima Aircraft Industry Ltd.

Fuji greatly increased production, which took place at two factories, the Ogikubo and Mitaka plants, both in Tokyo. Skyline and Gloria cars together with vans and minibuses were made by Fuji until 1966 when it sold Prince Motors to Nissan. The two lines of car were continued under the Nissan or Datsun names, varying according to overseas markets, for several years. GNG

PROSPER LAMBERT
FRANCE 1901-1907

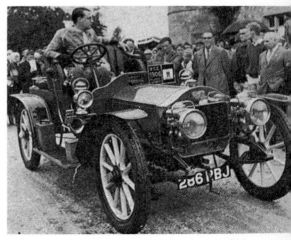

Prosper Lambert 16/20hp roadster of 1906 393

Founded at Nanterre in 1901 with a capital of 1 million francs, the Société Prosper Lambert first produced a shaft-driven, De Dion-powered single-cylinder light car. Its range then expanded to include twins and fours, many with Lambert's own engines.

Basic body styles were built in the factory, although Felber and Fils of Paris provided most of the others. A repair branch under director C. Hugot in Paris undertook repairs and sold cars and motor boats.

The range was extended to a 30hp in 1906, but by then financial difficulties were growing. The Société Française des Etablissements Prosper Lambert with 1.5 million francs capital took over from the old firm in September 1906, but to no avail. A further name change to Jean Bart Co in January 1907 preceded the firm's demise.

P. Lambert's PL Autos remained in car lists at least until 1913, although this may simply have been his garage at Nanterre. From 1917 P. Lambert was listed as a maker of speed boats and in 1924, in a different street to the old car firm, existed the Société Anonyme des Hydroglisseurs de Lambert. NB

PROTOS
GERMANY 1900-1926

The Motorenfabrik Protos was founded in Berlin by Dr Alfred Sternberg. His first cars were chain-driven voiturettes with his own make of single-cylinder engine in 3½hp and 8hp sizes. This was followed by a curious three-cylinder engine with two working cylinders and one, set at 180° to the others, with a freely operating piston whose purpose was said to be to combat vibration. Made from 1903 to 1905, this 'Kompensmotor' was replaced by a conventional four-cylinder T-head unit of 4.6 litres and 17/35PS rating. Like

all Protos cars since 1902, it had shaft drive.

Protos achieved international fame when a 17/35PS was driven into second place in the 1908 New York-Paris race, the journey taking 161 days. In the same year Sternberg's company was bought by Siemens-Schuckert, a large electrical engineering firm whose predecessor Siemens-Halske had built the world's first trolleybus in 1882 and made battery-electric cars and commercial vehicles from 1903 to 1913. It also made one model of petrol car, powered by a 6/10PS Korting engine, and this joined the Protos range after 1908, giving the company a light car with which to compete against the Puck from its Berlin rival (and eventually, partner) NAG.

From 1910 new Protos cars were designed by Dr Ernst Valentin who came from Nagant in Belgium and later worked for Rex-Simplex, designing both their own cars and the 40/60PS Russo-Baltic. For Protos he produced conventional L-head monobloc four-cylinder cars, initially in 6/18PS (1570cc) and 8/21PS (2190cc) sizes, but later joined by the 10/30PS (2614cc) and 14/38PS (3560cc). There was also a large six-cylinder 27/65PS (6840cc), descended from the old T-head designs, which was favoured by Crown Prince Wilhelm, the Kaiser's son. A 27/65PS limousine was also used by President Huerta of Mexico. In 1914 a modern-looking forward control truck was introduced, a number of which were exported to Germany's World War I ally, Turkey, up to 1918.

After World War I Protos cars concentrated on a single model, the 2614cc Typ C 10/30PS, similar to the pre-war model apart from its radiator which was not only pointed, like all contemporary German cars, but also continued the v motif on the header tank. In 1924 it became the C1 with overhead valves which boosted power from a feeble 30bhp to a rather more satisfactory 45bhp. It was offered as a light commercial vehicle as well as a

passenger car, which explains the high sales figure of around 10,000 – 50 per cent of all Protos production – between 1920 and 1926. At the end of 1926 Protos had 1110 workers.

In December 1926 Siemens-Schuckert decided to dispose of the car division, as to replace the ageing C1 would have been very costly. It found a buyer in NAG, which was making good profits and looking for ways to expand. The complete Protos operation was sold to NAG for 1.3 million marks. The C1 was continued for a short time as a light truck, but when the new NAG-Protos car appeared it was a completely new American-type six-cylinder model whose engine was designed by Christian Riecken before he left NAG. The rest of the car was the work of his successor, a Frenchman named Gabriel Lienard. This car and its descendants kept the Protos name alive until 1933. GNG

Protos 27/65PS tourer of 1911

PRUNEL
FRANCE 1900-1907

The Société des Usines Prunel was founded in Puteaux, Seine, in 1900 by J. Prunel. In May 1900 Prunel introduced his first car, a conventional chain-drive two-seater voiturette with a 3hp water-cooled De Dion engine and a top speed of about 18mph (30kph). Initially it was not sold as a Prunel but was marketed under the name of Atlas by E. J. Brierre of Paris. A 4½hp De Dion-powered four-wheeler made by Prunel was also sold as an Atlas. Between 1900 and 1901 Brierre also built a light voiturette with a 3½hp single-cylinder Morisse engine which he sold under his own name.

By 1902 Prunel was selling cars as Prunels and at the Paris Show the company exhibited a 6hp model called the Indispensable, with

Protos C1 ambulance of 1925

Aster or De Dion engines, plus a 9hp 1-ton van. In 1903 Prunel displayed the rather handsome wooden-panelled Apollo phaeton with 6hp single-cylinder De Dion engine, and other models with 9hp De Dion, 12hp twin-cylinder Aster and 16hp four-cylinder Aster engines. Other models used Herald or Pieper engines of up to 20hp.

By 1904 Prunel cars were available in Britain through the Normal Powder and Ammunition Co Ltd, which exhibited 12hp and chain-drive 24hp Mutel-engined cars at that year's Crystal Palace Show. In 1905 Prunel offered two twins and two fours, the largest a 4942cc 24/30hp model. The British cars were sold briefly as Gnomes by the short-lived Gnome Motor Car Co Ltd in 1905; this company then became known as the Gracile Motor Car Co and sold Prunel-built cars under the Gracile name until 1907.

From about 1904 to 1905 Boyer cars, as marketed by Boyer et Cie, were apparently made in Prunel's factory at Puteaux. The Prunel brothers were also responsible for the JP car made by J. Prunello et Cie, also of Puteaux, in a range very similar to Prunel's own. No more cars appeared under the Prunel name after 1907. BL

Prunel phaeton of 1903

PUCH
AUSTRIA 1900-1925

Johann Puch was born in Sakuschak, Lower Styria, in June 1862, the son of a farmer. He worked as a bicycle mechanic and in 1889 he set up his own workshop in Graz, with a view also to manufacturing. In 1891 he formed a new company, Johann Puch & Co Fabriksmassige Erzeugung von Fahrrädern, to build Styria bicycles. In 1897 he sold this successful company to Bielefelder Maschinenfabrik vorm Durkopp & Co AG, which made Durkopp cars from 1898 to 1927.

In September 1899 Puch founded a new company, Johann Puch Erste Steiermarkische Fahrrad-Fabriks AG, also in Graz. In 1900 he began to build De Dion-like single-cylinder three-wheelers, with a view to starting motorcycle production.

Early in 1900 he also built an experimental car, which ran successfully in March, but Puch did not yet have sufficient facilities to allow him to begin production. He built another prototype in 1903, this time after studying several makes of French car.

This second Puch was a 9/10PS voiturette, but again it failed to go into production, mainly because Puch had started making motorcycles – which went on sale from 1903 and soon became very popular, about 750 being sold up to the end of 1904. With the success of the motorcycles Puch also dropped an earlier plan to manufacture typewriters, but he kept in touch with cars by taking an agency for Dixi cars from Eisenach.

In 1906 he finally launched into car production with a very light, wooden-wheeled

Puch 70hp racer of 1909

904cc vee-twin-engined 8/9PS voiturette, which was intended to be built only in small numbers. As he had already done with bicycles and motorcycles, Puch attracted publicity for the cars through competition success, including first and second places in the touring class of the 1907 Semmering races.

By 1908 the cars were becoming at least as important as the motorcycles and Puch added a twin-cylinder 9/10PS sports model to its range. After 1908 the company built four-cylinder cars in increasing numbers and by 1910 the workforce in Graz had risen to about 800. Early in 1912 Puch obtained rights to use the Daimler-Knight sleeve-valve engine and in 1912 and 1913 built 16/40 and 27/60PS Puch-Knight cars with these engines.

In 1913 Puch introduced the conventionally-engined Type VIII Alpenwagen, with a 3560cc 14/38PS four-cylinder engine. It became the company's most successful model by far and stayed in production until 1923.

By the outbreak of World War I Puch was also building lorries – initially under licence from the German firm Mulag – and motorized railcars, and the workforce had risen to about 1200. After 1912 Johann Puch had effectively retired from direct control of the firm, which was renamed simply Puchwerke AG in May

1914. In July 1914, largely as a result of years of overwork, Puch died. His company continued, however, mainly working on military contracts during the war.

Private car and bicycle production were resumed in 1919 and Puch even offered a new model early that year, a smaller 6/20PS Alpenwagen, perversely dubbed the Type VII. It was not as well received as the earlier Type VIII and stayed in production only until 1920.

Motorcycle production was back in full swing by 1924 with a brilliant new 'split-single' two-stroke engine, which remained a Puch motorcycle feature for almost 50 years. The motorcycle interests soon overtook the now limited car production, which was mainly based on the 14/38PS Alpenwagen, and cars were finally dropped in 1925.

In December 1928 Puch amalgamated with Österreichische Daimler Motoren AG, maker of the Austro-Daimler car. In 1934 this group in turn was joined by the struggling Steyr-Werke AG, builder of the Steyr car from 1920, to form Steyr-Daimler-Puch AG, which remains one of the largest companies in Austria and still makes large numbers of bicycles, mopeds and small motorcycles under the Puch name. BL

PULLMAN/SPHINX, YORK
USA 1903-1917

Broomell, Schmidt and Steacy made boilers and radiators in York, Pennsylvania. There in 1903 Albert P. Broomell built a six wheel car having a driven centre axle with front and rear steering which he named Pullman after the luxurious railway carriages. The car was not a success, however, and so was rebuilt as a four-wheeler. Built in association with Samuel E. Baily of the York Carriage Co and engineer James Kline, the first 20 cars, renamed Yorks, were ready in late 1905.

In 1907 the cars had 20 or 40hp four-cylinder engines and became known as Pullmans again. The title of the production company changed from York Motor Car Co, which had been established with $100,000 capital and in which Ryan Schutte, Kline and Baily were officers, to Pullman Motor Car Co two years later. Kline and Baily then set up BCK and subsequently the Kline Car Co in one of Baily's carriage factories.

In 1910 when Thomas O'Connor became president, Pullman's four factories in York totalled 18,000sq ft (1670sq m) and made virtually all the company's own components, including engines. Production was said to be 1000 cars in 1909 and 2000 in 1910, when a surviving car (chassis number 4488) was built.

By 1912 an 8½-litre six was offered, but soon all was not well, judging by the departure of key personnel and the use of proprietary engines in some models, such as Lycoming in the 6-46A of 1915 which had push button magnetic gear shift. Herbert R. Averill, for seven years the sales manager, left in 1914 and started the Sphinx Motor Car Co in York, which had a very brief existence making Lycoming-engined cars. Charles Lufts, a designer who had also worked at SGV, left for Daniels in 1915 and W. G. Miller departed to make Niagara cars at Buffalo.

The Standard Chain Co had become involved with Pullman by 1915 and supplied the company's next two presidents. Some $100,000 was spent on modernizing the factory. In March 1916 900 cars were made and 600 men were on day and night shifts. W. F. Grove arrived from Bell to handle sales from a four-storey building that still stands in North George Street, York. In 1917 the New York sales branch, which had sold 677 cars in 1916, went into liquidation and Pullman itself was soon in the hands of receivers.

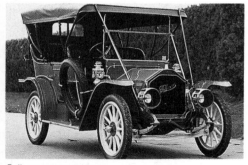
Pullman tourer of 1910

Production continued and ran at 80 to 100 a week in mid-1917. Several offers were made for the factories – $260,000 by National Products Co and $315,000 by Winterwitz and Co – and production ended that year. S. E. Baily's son, also named Samuel E. Baily, continued the original carriage tradition making truck bodies and in the 1950s became one of America's earliest professional restorers of old cars. NB

PUMA
BRAZIL 1962-1985

In 1962 Rino Malzoni designed a sports car based on the DKW front-wheel-drive three-cylinder car built in Brazil by Vemag. Milton Masteguin helped to put the car into limited production and about 50 were made. Malzoni and Masteguin were joined by Jorge Lettry from DKW's racing department and formed Soc de Automoveis Luninari Ltda at Sao Paulo in 1964 and then Puma Veiculos e Motores Ltda in 1966. The firm later became known as Puma Industria de Veiculos SA. The plant adjoined Vemag and output grew to 135 cars in 1967.

That year Vemag was bought by Volkswagen do Brasil which meant that Malzoni had to redesign the Puma to accept VW mechanical units and rear engine. Styling of the fibreglass body was handled by Anisio Campos. The new design was launched in November 1968 and 128 were made in the first six months before settling down to two a day. The workforce amounted to 111 in a 43,000sq ft (4000sq m) factory.

By 1977 production had reached 200 a month and then climbed to 300 with sales through VW dealers in Brazil and other South American countries. A few have also reached South Africa, Europe and North America.

Four- or six-cylinder front-mounted Chevrolet-engined GT models were introduced in 1973 and in 1975 Milton Masteguin designed a 760cc Puma city car. In 1976, with the ending of the Brazilian Karmann-Ghia which had provided many components, the sports Puma switched floor pan and engine to the VW Brasilia. The company ceased production in 1985. NB

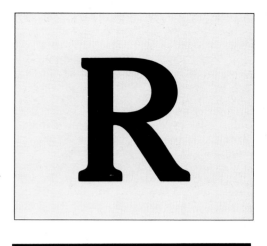

RAF
AUSTRIA 1908-1913

The Reichenberger Automobil Fabrik was located in the Bohemian town of Reichenberg, now part of Czechoslovakia and renamed Liberec. It was founded by textile magnate Baron Theodor von Liebig who made the first long distance car journey in 1894 when he drove a Benz 575 miles (925km) from Reichenberg to Mannheim. His partners were Oskar von Klinger and Manfred Ginskey.

The company was founded in June 1907, but a factory had to be built. Car production did not start until March 1908, when a conventional 25/30PS four-cylinder touring car was made. It was designed by Paul Henze who later worked for Impéria, NAG, Selve and Steiger, and was followed by a 10/12PS two-cylinder car, and in 1910 larger four-cylinder models of 30/35PS and 60PS. RAF also built commercial vehicles using the 25/30PS engines mounted under the driver's seat.

In 1912 RAF acquired a licence to make Knight sleeve-valve engines, building 40 and 70PS cars. Few were made under the RAF name as the company was taken over the following year by Laurin and Klement, which added the sleeve-valve cars to its own range. GNG

RAILTON
GB 1933-1949

The Railton was the fourth and last make of car to be created by Noel Campbell Macklin, who had previously been concerned with the Eric Campbell, Silver Hawk and Invicta. After Invicta production had come to an end at his factory in Cobham, Surrey, Macklin and his associate L. A. Cushman invited the designer Reid Railton to produce a car which would make use of American power in a typically British chassis and body.

Railton, who had previously been associated with J. G. Parry Thomas in the design of the Arab car, chose the 94hp 4-litre straight-eight Essex Terraplane engine for his power

Puma GTB-S2 coupé of 1981

unit, and used the Terraplane chassis as well. The radiator was reminiscent of the Invicta's, although with a slight vee, and the earlier car's bonnet rivets were retained. Bodies were supplied by outside firms, particularly Coachcraft of Hanwell and REAL of Ealing.

Only six cars were made in 1933, and for the following year the slightly larger 4168cc Hudson straight-eight engine was used. Railton quickly became popular on account of its classic British appearance, excellent acceleration as well as top gear flexibility, and reasonable price. A 1934 open tourer cost £535, compared with more than £700 for an Alvis Speed 20 or 3½-litre Lagonda. The 1935 Light Sports Railton had exceptional perform-

Railton drophead coupé of 1937

ance, with 0-50mph (0-80kph) in seven seconds, a better figure than the post-war Jaguar XK120.

In 1934 production was 224 cars, with 377 being delivered the following year. This was the Railton's peak. Production dropped to 308 in 1936 and little over 500 in the last three years of peace.

The cars became heavier in 1936, and in a misjudged attempt to compete with the SS Jaguar Macklin dropped the sporty tourers and concentrated on drophead coupés and saloons. They were very handsome but no longer so reasonably priced; a Cobham saloon cost £688 in 1936 and a University limousine £895.

In an attempt to widen the market Railtons were offered with smaller Hudson six-cylinder engines of 2723 or 3255cc but these lacked the traditional Railton performance. In 1938 Macklin brought out a 'baby Railton' on a virtually unmodified Standard Ten chassis, of which 50 were made.

With the inevitable approach of war Macklin and his team turned to the design and production of the Fairmile gunboat, which was planned for the Admiralty by the Fairmile Construction Co. Production rights of the Railton car were sold to Hudson Motors Ltd, the British concessionaire which assembled 14 cars after the war, the last two with independent front suspension and steering column gearchange. However, the weak pound made it quite uneconomic to import Hudson components and the last Railton was made in 1949.

Macklin, who was knighted for his contribution to the war effort, died in 1947. Reid Railton, who had also worked on the ERA and designed the Napier-Railton track car and Railton-Mobil land speed record car, went to the United States in 1939 as a consultant to the Hudson Motor Co. He died in California in 1977. GNG

RAINIER
USA 1905-1911

John T. Rainier, born in 1861, entered the automobile business in 1900 as one of the organizers of the Vehicle Equipment Co of Brooklyn, New York, maker of electric trucks and sightseeing charabancs. In June 1902 he formed the Rainier Co of New York City to make electric trucks and in the spring of 1905 he brought out his first passenger car, a 22/28hp model whose engine and chassis were manufactured for Rainier by Garford in Elyria, Ohio. This made the Rainier first cousin to the contemporary Studebaker, which was also Garford built.

The cars were assembled in John T's own factory at Flushing, New York. Quite large four-cylinder cars of 30/35hp selling for up to $5000 were made for 1906 and 1907. By the end of 1907 Rainier had built up a good distributor network from New York to California, and including Mexico, and in August 1907 he moved to new purpose-built premises at Saginaw, Michigan.

A new range of cars, no longer using Garford components but specially designed by former Garford engineer James G. Haeslet, was announced for 1908, based on a 45/50hp four-cylinder engine. Planned production for the 1907-8 year was 300 cars, but only 180 were completed before bankruptcy struck, caused by a general slump in the industry combined with mismanagement.

Rainier was operated for a short time by the receiver, but in March 1909 it was bought by William C. Durant who changed the company name to the Marquette Motor Co. It was now part of the infant General Motors Corporation. Cars were continued under the Rainier name in 1911, but that year the new company announced that it had also secured the exclusive right to manufacture the Marquette-Buick roadster, and for 1912 the Rainier was marketed as the Marquette Model 28 with a 45hp four-cylinder engine. Other Marquettes that year were the former Welch-Detroit models, but the name did not survive for more than a year.

The company name was changed again to Peninsular Motor Co in July 1912, but it is unlikely that any cars were made bearing the name Peninsular. The factory lay idle for five years, but was re-opened for wartime production of mortar shells and was subsequently used for making a variety of General Motors components such as Chevrolet and Oldsmobile engines, and spare parts. It was permanently closed in the summer of 1983.

John T. Rainier re-entered the motor business in 1916 when he began to make trucks in Flushing. A range from 1½ to 6 tons capacity was made until 1927. Rainier died in 1940. GNG

RALEIGH
GB 1903-1936

In 1877 Frank Bowden, the inventor of the rim-acting brake, retired from his business interests in Hong Kong seriously ill; according to his doctors he had only a few months to live. He returned to England and, on medical advice, took up cycling. Within six months he had overcome his illness and, not surprisingly, become a firm cycling enthusiast. The manufacturer of his bicycle was a small firm called Woodhead and Angois with premises in Raleigh Street, Nottingham, where about a dozen workers built three penny-farthing machines each week. Bowden bought a share in the company and soon reorganized it completely as the Raleigh Cycle Co.

By 1896 Raleigh was the biggest cycle producer in England with 850 workers and an output of about 30,000 machines a year – and it had become the second cycle company to be floated by the notorious company speculator Terah Hooley. In his early 20s, Hooley had received a £35,000 legacy from his mother's estate and established himself in Nottingham as a stockbroker and company financier. He specialized in attracting huge

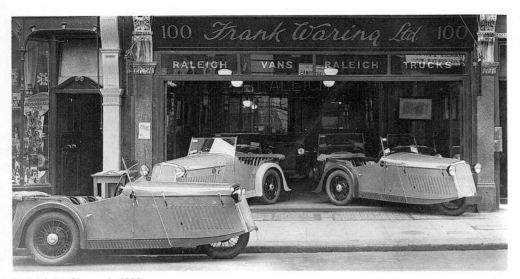

Raleigh Safety Sevens of c.1935

public investments in relatively small companies, often through the simple expedient of drafting distinguished names onto the board to lend respectability.

Several of his early flotations, including Bovril and Schweppes, were genuine successes and he continued to float several companies a year, becoming well respected and a millionaire. In 1895 he turned his attention to the booming cycle business and floated the Humber company, netting a substantial profit. In 1896 he turned Raleigh into the Raleigh Cycle Co Ltd, with capital of £250,000. In the same year he also floated the Singer and Swift companies. His biggest ever deal was buying the Dunlop patents for £3 million and floating the Dunlop Pneumatic Tyre Co with capital of £5 million.

Hooley's run came to an end in 1898 when the cycle boom ended and the collapse of several overcapitalized companies left him bankrupt. His association with the equally shadowy speculators Harry J. Lawson and Harvey DuCros led him to stand trial with the former in 1904 for conspiracy to defraud through the Electric Tramways Construction and Maintenance Co. Lawson went to jail, and although Hooley was found not guilty his financial career was effectively ended.

Raleigh fared better than many of Hooley's companies, extending its domination of the cycle industry with the introduction in 1901 of its first 'all-steel bicycle'. In 1899 the company started building motorcycles, which it did until 1906 and again from 1919 to the early 1930s. In 1903 it built a few examples of the Raleighette, a motorcycle-based 3½hp three-wheeler, some of which were made with commercial bodies.

In 1905 Raleigh built one experimental car powered by a four-cylinder 16hp Fafnir engine. It was designed by T. J. Biggs, who built the Eastmead-Biggs car in Somerset from 1901 to 1904. Raleigh also dabbled with cyclecars, rejecting a twin-cylinder design but eventually building a few 11hp models in 1915 which had four-cylinder side-valve Alpha engines. The limited production was brought to a halt by World War I.

In 1922 the company built another prototype, a low-cost light car with a flat-twin engine, but took the project no further. In September 1932 it showed a chain-drive single-cylinder light saloon or open tourer, based on its motorcycle derived 5cwt (254kg) light van. It was to sell at £89 15s but in 1933 – when bicycle production reached 200,000 – it was replaced by the more conventional Safety Seven, the only Raleigh car to reach anything like series production.

This three-wheeler was designed by Tom Lawrence Williams, who joined Raleigh in 1930 to run the Motor Department. It used a 17hp 742cc V-twin engine and shaft drive to the two rear wheels. About 3000 were built until 1936, when production was dropped. Williams bought the rights to the van which he had also designed and went off to build it himself as the first Reliant.

Raleigh built no more cars but continued to build bicycles and mopeds. In 1960 Raleigh Industries, which had acquired BSA and Triumph cycle interests between 1952 and 1957, merged with the British Cycle Corporation, a subsidiary of Tube Investments, which controlled most of Britain's other cycle companies. Raleigh became the cycle division of Tube Investments and remains Britain's largest cycle-maker. BL

RALLY
FRANCE 1921-1933

Among the numerous cyclecars shown at the 1921 Paris Salon, the Rally stood out because it was powered by an American motorcycle engine, a 989cc V-twin Harley-Davidson with overhead inlet and side exhaust valves. The clutch and gearbox was also by Harley-Davidson, while the light two-seater body was made by Carrosserie BG. Buyers had the option of a V-twin Indian or in-line four-cylinder Henderson or FN engines. The company was owned by Monsieur Rotschild, a businessman who had no connection with the bankers or coachbuilders.

The marque's first sporting appearance was in the 1922 Bol d'Or, by which time an 898cc four-cylinder Chapuis-Dornier engine was used, and it seems that the motorcycle units did not survive for 12 months. For 1923 an 1100cc CIME engine was featured, and four models were available, Tourisme, Sport, Grand Sport (with 30bhp CIME engine) and light van. For 1925 a larger touring model appeared, the Type PPR with 1202cc CIME engine and, for the first time, a differential. It was intended for four-door, four-seater bodies.

To back up this touring car Rally made two sports models, one with staggered seating and very narrow body, and one side-by-side version. Both had 1100cc CIME engines and did very well in competitions, especially hillclimbs, in France, Switzerland and Algeria. By 1925 production was running at about 100 cars a year.

A competition model with 1½-litre twin-overhead cam straight-eight engine made by Brault was planned for 1927, but the engine-makers (who also supplied to Lombard) did not have the capacity to furnish Rally as well, and only prototypes were made. The year 1927 was Rally's last for works-backed competition.

In 1928 came the Model ABC, a very attractive low car in cabriolet and fixed-head forms, together with a racing model with three valves per cylinder and the option of a supercharger. The engine was a 1095cc Cha-

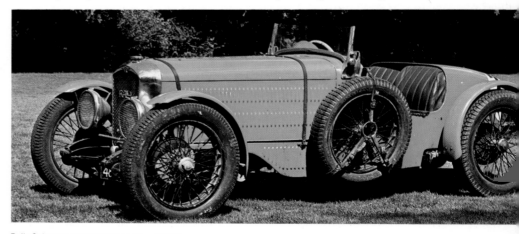

Rally Salmson-engined two-seater of 1933

puis-Dornier, replaced in 1929 by 1100 or 1170cc SCAP engines.

In 1930 SCAP and Chapuis-Dornier ceased making engines, so for 1931 Rotschild turned to the 1300cc Salmson S4. Salmson was no longer in competitions so it did not mind selling engines to a sporting manufacturer; in fact it was rather pleased that its engines would still be in action on the race tracks.

The Rallys of 1931 were the Models N and NC which used Salmson gearboxes and rear axles. There was a supercharged version but probably only 12 of these were made. The 1933 Rallys had the Salmson S4C 1500cc engine but production ceased in the middle of that year. GNG

RAMBLER/JEFFERY
USA 1902-1917

Like many successful car firms the Thomas B. Jeffery Co which made the Rambler grew out of the bicycle industry. Jeffery and his partner R. Philip Gormully, both English born, joined forces in 1881 to make bicycles in Chicago. They also made bicycle tyres – the Gormully and Jeffery Tire Co eventually became part of United States Rubber – and by the 1890s they were the second largest bicycle-makers in the United States after Colonel Pope.

In 1892 the name Rambler was adopted, and this was used for the first cars. Prototypes were built in Chicago and designed by Jeffery's son Charles with front mounted engines and wheel steering. Thomas Jeffery decided that they were too advanced for Midwestern tastes, and when production began at a newly acquired factory in Kenosha, Wisconsin, it was with a conventional motor buggy with engine under seat, tiller steering and single chain drive.

Although priced at a modest $750 the Rambler earned a net profit of $372 per car for the company, and business boomed. Fifteen hundred cars were made in 1902, making the Rambler the second best-selling American petrol-engined car; the Curved Dash Oldsmobile topped the list with 2500, but the Locomobile steamer beat them both with 2750.

Wheel steering came in 1903, and by 1905 the Rambler was a sizeable machine with front mounted two-cylinder engine. Sales that year were 3807 made in a factory area of over 14 acres (5 hectares), with another 33 acres (13 hectares) for testing. In 1906 Ned Jordan joined the company and his advertising style soon crept into Rambler's publicity with the slogan 'June Time is Rambler Time'.

Thomas Jeffery died suddenly in 1910 and under the terms of his will the company was incorporated with a capital of $3 million. Charles took over the helm and increased annual production from the 2500 or so which Thomas had deemed adequate to 4435 by 1913, to which was added 5578 trucks based on passenger car chassis.

For 1914, in honour of his father's memory,

Charles changed the name of the cars and trucks to Jeffery and built a total of 13,500 vehicles. The cars were conventional four- and six-cylinder machines selling for $1550 and $2550 respectively. More distinctive was the Jeffery Quad 2-ton truck with four wheel drive and steering. Powered by a four-cylinder Buda engine the Quad was supplied in large numbers to the United States, Russian and French armies and was one of the stalwart workhorses of World War I. So great was demand that they were built by Hudson, National and Paige as well as at Kenosha.

In July 1916 Charles Jeffery sold his company to Charles W. Nash, who had been president of General Motors. The purchase price was $9 million, and shortly afterwards Nash Motors Co was incorporated for nearly $25 million. By the summer of 1917 the cars were badged as Nashes, and a new major American marque was on its way. GNG

and these were sold in England from 1906 by Sidney Straker. In 1905 the designers were Bertoldo, formerly of Breda, and G. Coda, ex-Breda and Isotta-Fraschini. Coda later went on to Züst, Fiat and SCAT, and then designed the 1922 Diatto.

Giovanni Battista Ceirano soon left STAR because of ill health but his firm prospered and produced an extensive range of four-cylinder cars that spanned 12 to 50hp in 1910. The bulk of the output came to be provided by smaller cars and in 1915 there was just a 1.6-litre 10/12hp offered which had several modern features.

General engineering and repair work were carried out during World War I, after which Rapid cars were revived. They were unable to compete with Fiat, however, and STAR was liquidated in 1921, its assets going to another Ceirano-founded company, SPA, and to CIP, which briefly made light cars until 1924. NB

Rambler Cross Country tourer of 1912

RANGER
see General Motors

RAPID
ITALY 1905-1921

The Societa Torinese Automobili Rapid (STAR) was founded in Turin in 1905 by Giovanni Battista Ceirano who, with his brother Matteo, had set up Fratelli Ceirano. Matteo soon left the company to start ITALA and then SPA. His place at Fratelli Ceirano had been taken by another brother Giovanni, who left in 1904 to make the Junior car. Giovanni Battista then reorganized Fratelli Ceirano as STAR.

A few single- and twin-cylinder Rapids were made but the main products were fours,

RAPID (Switzerland)
see Gutbrod

RATIONAL
GB 1901-1906

Harry Heatly and Frank Gresham founded the Bassingbourn Iron Works, later the Heatly-Gresham Engineering Co, in the small Cambridgeshire village of Bassingbourn in 1901 to make a car of their own design called the Rational. It had a single-cylinder horizontal engine and unusual suspension in which the body was sprung on the chassis. Production cars had two-cylinder engines and most, if not all, had more conventional suspension. Transmission was by two-speed epicyclic gearbox and chain drive.

All the parts were made in the small iron works, which employed 20 men; the first two bodies were also made at Bassingbourn, but most came from Wilson of Royston. In 1904 Heatly and Gresham leased a factory at the new Letchworth Garden City, being the first business to set up there. They did not move until the spring of 1905, and their last work at Bassingbourn was to make a number of taxicabs which were operated in London by the London Motor Cab Co. Probably not more than 17 vehicles were made in all. Heatly-Gresham Engineering flourished in Letchworth, making vacuum exhausts, air compressors and other components, mainly for export. GNG

Ravel two-seat sports model (foreground) of 1926

RAUCH AND LANG
USA 1905-1928

The origins of the Rauch and Lang company date back to 1853 when German-born Jacob Rauch opened a wagon repair shop in Cleveland, Ohio. Carriage and wagon building was added in 1860, and the partnership of Rauch and his son Charles was joined by a real estate developer, Charles Lang. By 1900 Rauch and Lang were the leading carriage-builders in Ohio, but the partners decided that the horseless carriage was the coming thing and that the electric was likely to be the most favoured, certainly among the clientele that they were used to.

Rauch and Lang J5 electric coach of 1915

The first Rauch and Lang electric was completed in 1904, and production started in 1905 when 50 cars were completed. In 1907 the capital stock was increased from $75,000 to $250,000 and by 1909 to $1,000,000. The Hertner Electric Co, which supplied motors to Rauch and Lang, was bought in 1907 and John H. Hertner became the company's chief engineer. By 1909 production was running at 1000 cars a year and sales agencies had been appointed in 20 cities, some as far afield as Manchester in New Hampshire and Denver, Colorado.

Sales of electric cars generally began to fall from about 1912, and in 1915 Rauch and Lang merged with another leading Cleveland electric vehicle manufacturer, Baker Motor

400

Vehicle Co. Baker made trucks as well as passenger cars, which Rauch and Lang had never done, so the new company, with capital of $2.5 million and named the Baker, Rauch and Lang Co, had a wider range of products to offer. It also took over manufacture of the Owen Magnetic petrol-engined car.

Charles Lang left the company to form the Lang Body Co to make closed bodies for passenger cars and later, trucks. The last year for the Baker brand name on cars was 1916, although the following year the company began to make bomb handling trucks, the beginning of a new line of industrial trucks which has lasted up to the present day.

In 1919 a total of 700 electric cars were built, but in 1920 Baker, Rauch and Lang sold its passenger car business to the Stevens Duryea Co of Chicopee Falls, Massachusetts, which built a new factory adjacent to its existing plant. There, a dwindling number of electric passenger cars was built and also a line of taxicabs with petrol or electric engines, sold under the name Raulang. The final products were petrol-engined cabs and delivery vans powered by Willys-Knight engines with General Electric transmission, which were made from 1928 to 1935.

Meanwhile the Baker-Raulang Co, as it had been renamed in 1920, was operating in two divisions, one making Baker industrial trucks and the other car bodies, customers including Chandler, Franklin, Hupmobile, Packard, Peerless and Reo. In 1924 the company acquired the plant of another Cleveland body-building company, Rubay, and expanded production to 1000 bodies a month. There it built bus bodies for White, Reo and General Motors' Yellow Coach Division and from 1927 tourers for the Ford Model A. Passenger car bodies ceased in 1935, and the whole body-building plant was closed in 1948.

Industrial truck production continued, later expanding to include electric golf carts, postal delivery vans, in-plant buses and airport vehicles. The company name was changed from Baker-Raulang to Baker Industrial Trucks in 1954 when it became a subsidiary of the Otis Elevator Co. Since 1976 only forklift trucks have been made. In 1977 Otis sold Baker to the Linde Corporation of Wiesbaden, West Germany. GNG

RAVEL
FRANCE 1900-1909; 1923-1928

La Société des Automobiles Louis Ravel was formed in Neuilly in 1900 with a capital equivalent to £50,000. Earlier Ravels in the same town included Joseph, who made a steam vehicle in 1868 and, with Edward Ravel, went on to develop a petrol-engined two-stroke prototype vehicle. Joseph died in 1908.

Louis Ravel's firm made small V-twin cars for a few years from 1900. His factory became the home of Gentil bicycles whilst Ravel himself concentrated on making proprietary engines. Both Amstoutz et Ravel and Ravel et Homeyer were listed in the 1902-9 period, the former making Zénith engines from around 1907 in the ex-Chapuis-Dornier plant owned by Amstoutz in Besançon and the latter making cycles, cars and Hercule engines in St Etienne.

In 1909 Louis Ravel cropped up again as co-founder, with Théophile Schneider from Rochet-Schneider, of Automobiles Th Schneider at Besançon in the former Zénith engine factory. Soon afterwards Ravel registered Zénith Autos in Besançon, the Zénith name also being used for Rochet-Schneider's successful carburettor interests.

In 1923 Louis Ravel resumed car production in Besançon with Société Anonyme des Automobiles Ravel. The first cars had front wheel brakes and 2.1-litre overhead-valve engines on full width aluminium trays that could be slid out of the chassis. Smaller fours were introduced later on and then, in 1928, a 2.5-litre six. The cars appeared in some sales lists until 1930, although production probably ended in 1928. NB

REGAL
USA, CANADA 1907-1920

The Regal Motor Car Co of Detroit was founded in 1907 and built 50 four-cylinder cars during its first year. They were evidently not very satisfactory, for the following year the company took them all back and gave the customers a new 1908 model free of charge! These were conventional five-passenger touring cars powered by a 30hp four-cylinder engine and selling for $1250. In a 1909 advertisement Regal claimed that it would make 6500 cars in 1910, but it is not known if this figure was achieved. If it was, production would have been on a level with Reo and Chalmers, both substantial manufacturers at that time.

Early in 1910 Regal made the first of its ventures into Canada when it set up the Regal Motor Car Co at Walkerville, Ontario. The product was identical to the American-built car, but cost $200 more. Few were made, and production ended in 1911.

Regal's most distinctive car was launched in 1911. This was the Underslung which, like the American Underslung, had frame members which passed beneath the axles. A five-passenger tourer sold for only $950. They were sold in England by Seabrook of Great Eastern Street, London, under the name Seabrook-RMC.

By 1914 prices ranged from $1125 to $1600, and the second Canadian operation began. This was the work of Henry Nyberg, who had recently ceased making cars under his own name at Indianapolis. Canadian Regal Motors Ltd opened a new factory at Berlin (now Kitchener), Ontario, at the end of 1914 and began to turn out the Regal Underslung 30 for 1915. Major components, including Lycoming engines, were brought in from the United States, but many locally-built parts were used as well. A larger 1915 model used a 40bhp V8 engine, and there was also a 20hp Light Four.

The Canadian factory closed down at the end of 1916, due to the difficulty of obtaining components from the USA, after between 200 and 400 cars had been made. The Detroit operation was running down at this time as well, and although Regal brought out a six-cylinder post-war model in 1919, all production ended the following year. GNG

Regal Underslung roadster of 1911

RELIANT
GB 1934 to date

Tom Lawrence Williams was born in 1890 and after an early career working on heavy steam vehicles he joined the Triumph Cycle Co in 1916 to design motorcycles. In 1930 he moved to the Raleigh Cycle Co in Nottingham to take charge of the motor department. In 1932 he designed the company's first real production car, a 742cc three-wheeler known as the Safety Seven. In 1934 Raleigh dropped the light van versions of its three-wheelers and Williams acquired the rights to the design, with a view to producing the van himself.

With backing from his local branch of Barclays Bank he began work on his improved version in August 1934 from a small workshop in his garden in Tamworth, Staffordshire. He was joined in his work on an air-cooled single-cylinder chain-driven 7cwt (355kg) prototype by a colleague from Raleigh and the first example was finished in late 1934. It was registered on 1 January 1935 under the name Reliant.

The operation soon moved to larger premises on the site of a former bus garage at Two Gates, Tamworth, originally on a 14-year lease, where works and a wooden office were established. For a time Williams supplemented his income by selling petrol, having bought two pumps to take advantage of storage tanks which were already on the site. The first production van was delivered in June 1935 and in July the Reliant Engineering Co (Tamworth) Ltd was formed.

The first twin-cylinder model followed in March 1936, with a water-cooled JAP engine and shaft drive. At the 1937 Commercial Vehicle Show, Reliant came to an agreement with Austin and in March 1938 introduced an 8cwt (407kg) model with the four-cylinder Austin Seven engine, originally designed in 1922 but still a great improvement on the twins.

In June 1939 Reliant extended its factory and took over the freehold of the site and in September, just before the outbreak of World War II, produced its own, excellent, 747cc engine, based on the Austin design – thereby becoming independent.

Van production was halted by the war, during which about half the factory was requisitioned for war work. The first post-war Reliant was completed in March 1946 and in July additional workshop space was opened, leading to a completely new assembly shop in October 1947.

Reliant 10cwt delivery van of c.1955

Reliant Robin of 1973

In February 1950 Reliant launched the Regent van and in 1953 introduced the Regal, a slab-sided, drophead four-seater car, which sold for £352. In Britain a three-wheeler weighing less than 8cwt (407kg) was treated in law as a motorcycle, with attendant advantages of low tax rates and freedom to drive on a motorcycle licence. The car was an instant success and in 1956 Reliant switched from metal bodies to a one-piece glassfibre moulding over an ash frame as production continued to increase with the Regal Mk 3. By 1960 turnover had reached £700,000.

Production methods were vastly improved in 1962 by the introduction of a unitary body of bonded inner and outer mouldings. This construction, on a steel chassis, was introduced with the Regal 3/25 in October 1962. This car used a new Reliant engine, a 600cc overhead-valve four, which was Britain's first mass-produced all-alloy car engine. Its light weight allowed Reliant to improve other areas – notably trim, which was becoming more important in a competitive market – while still complying with the statutory weight limit.

In 1958 Reliant built its first four-wheeler, a station wagon called the Sussita and designed for Autocars Co Ltd of Haifa, Israel. It was the first of Reliant's 'package deals' for small or developing countries. It was followed for Autocars by the Ford-powered Sabra sports car and Carmel saloon, and these led directly to Reliant's first four-wheeler for the domestic market. This was the 1.7-litre Ford-powered Sabre 4, launched at the 1962 London Motor Show and followed soon after by the rather neater 2.7-litre six-cylinder Sabre 6 coupé.

T. L. Williams died in 1964 and was succeeded as managing director by Raymond Wiggin, who had joined Reliant in 1959 as Williams' assistant. Wiggin began a major expansion programme, developing existing models, introducing new ones and pursuing profitable 'package industry' deals. These packages were aimed at countries with a limited domestic market, typically fewer than 20,000 cars a year of a particular model. This made Reliant-developed glassfibre-bodied cars viable where the scale would be too small to support production in steel.

For a substantial fee, Reliant designs a car which meets all local legal and market needs, a factory in which to build it, trains local management and workforce and even produces the necessary literature and documentation in the appropriate language. After the Sabra scheme, Reliant developed the Anadol for Otosan Industries in Turkey in 1966, a pick-up and subsequently cars for Mebea in Greece between 1969 and 1975, and a version of the Kitten to be made by Sipani Automobiles Ltd in India as the Dolphin.

During 1963 the company became known as the Reliant Motor Co Ltd, part of the Reliant Motor group which was itself part of the Cardiff-based Hodge group which had acquired a controlling interest in Reliant in 1962.

Reliant Sabre Six GT of 1962

Hodge, whose founder and chairman Sir Julian Hodge became chairman of Reliant, had interests in engineering, insurance, credit finance, vehicle distribution and merchant banking – and was in turn part of the Standard and Chartered Banking group.

In November 1963 Reliant opened an additional 70,000sq ft (6500sq m) engine and gearbox factory at Shenstone, a few miles from Tamworth. Most components were made there for assembly at Two Gates. In 1966 the company was obliged to open a new body moulding plant, at Kettlebrook, after the original body shop was destroyed by fire.

In 1964 Reliant launched a small four-wheel saloon, the Rebel, which was offered at £525 with the 600 engine. This engine was enlarged to 700cc in 1967, 750cc in 1972 and eventually to 848cc in 1975. The year 1964 also saw the launch of a 2.6-litre Ford-powered coupé, the Scimitar GT, designed for Reliant by Ogle.

In April 1968 Reliant built its 50,000th 3/25 and later in the year introduced the trend-setting Ogle-designed Scimitar GTE, or Grand Touring Estate. This sporting estate car was very successful; it was given a 3-litre V6 Ford engine in 1980, in which year Reliant also introduced a drophead Scimitar.

In 1969 Reliant bought out rival three-wheeler manufacturer Bond Cars Ltd but retained the Bond name for the trendy Bug, introduced in 1970. With annual output boosted to 20,000 units Reliant became the second largest all-British manufacturer. By 1973 annual turnover exceeded £13 million.

The four-wheel Rebel was dropped in 1974 and a new three-wheeler, the Robin, was launched in 1973 as part of a £1.25 million expansion. A replacement for the Rebel, the Kitten, was launched in 1975 in saloon, estate and van versions. By 1976 turnover had reached about £20 million and as well as the three and four-wheel cars, Reliant manufactured the three-wheeled TW9 commercial chassis and cab unit and glassfibre cabs for larger commercial vehicles.

Success with economy cars started to slip, however, as increased competition from cheaper conventional cars hit sales. In 1982

Reliant Scimitar GTE of 1974

the Robin was replaced by the Rialto and the three-wheelers continued to be much more viable than the Kitten – which also gave rise to the Fox Basic Transport Vehicle, originally built in Greece and from October 1982 also built in Barbados by the Sapphire Motor Co Ltd of Bridgetown.

During 1984 Reliant showed pre-production versions of a new small sports car, to be known as the SS1, and in January 1985 in his annual statement Reliant's chairman said that the cost of launching the car would mean a loss in the first half of the year but that the company expected to be back in profit by the second half. The all-important popular sports car which joined the three-wheelers and hard- and soft-top Scimitars was officially launched in early 1985, with a 1.3-litre Ford engine at just under £7000 or a 1.6-litre Ford at just under £7800.

Reliant's future depended heavily on the SS1 succeeding. Target production for the first year was 800 cars, a substantial increase on 1984's four-wheeler output of just 135, and the Scimitar was even dropped from production in mid-1985 to concentrate Reliant's strained resources on the SS1. Sales, however, started slowly and the staple three-wheeler sales were badly hit by the British miners' strike of 1984-85. Reliant had a contract to build the 200 body shells necessary for Ford's RS 200 rally homologation car but that did little to alleviate losses in the first half of 1985 amounting to almost £600,000. In 1986 the SS1 was made more attractive by the option of a 1.8 litre 135bhp Nissan turbocharged engine. BL

RENAULT
FRANCE 1899 to date

Louis Renault was born in Paris in 1877, the fourth child of a moderately prosperous button manufacturer. After the death of his father in 1891 it was expected that he would enter the family business with his elder brothers Fernand and Marcel, but he preferred to tinker with machinery, and did not complete his studies. After a brief apprenticeship with the boilermakers Delaunay-Belleville, which was interrupted by two years of military service, he set up a small workshop in the grounds of the family home at Billancourt and built a light four-wheeled car powered by a single-cylinder De Dion engine which he had removed from a quadricycle.

Practically the whole car was made in the tiny workshop, including the body, although the gears were cut by a firm called Durand. The most unusual feature of the car was its transmission by propeller shaft to bevel gears on the rear axle, as opposed to chain or belt drive used on all contemporary vehicles. Another advanced feature was direct drive top gear in the three-speed gearbox.

Louis Renault made this little car, which was completed on Christmas Eve 1898, for

Renault 13/4hp buggy of 1899

his own amusement, but he soon received orders from friends for replicas, and in March 1899 he set up a company, Renault Frères, with 40,000 francs capital put up by his brothers. They took a stand at the Paris Automobile Salon in June, and by the end of the show they had taken orders for 60 cars.

A new factory was set up – in fact a disused boathouse, which was moved to the Renault garden. By the end of the year 60 workers had built 71 cars. During 1900, the first complete year of production, 179 cars were turned out.

The 270cc De Dion engine was replaced by one of 450cc, and a completely closed 'pillbox' coupé body was offered. This was made for Renault by Labourdette. The original round bonnet was replaced by one of coalscuttle shape, although the radiator was at the side. The classic coal-scuttle bonnet with dashboard radiator did not arrive until the 1904 models.

The Renault brothers were quickly aware

of the prestige value of racing, and entered their first event, the Paris-Trouville race in 1899, putting up the best performance for a light car. In the next three years they had many successes, capped by Marcel Renault's outright victory in the 1902 Paris-Vienna race when, with a 3.8-litre 30hp car, he defeated 70hp Panhards with capacities of 13.7 litres.

However, in the 1903 Paris-Madrid race Marcel was killed; Louis promptly withdrew all his cars, although the race was stopped at Bordeaux anyway, and never took the wheel of a racing car again. Although the company soon returned to racing, winning the first ever Grand Prix in 1906, competitions did not play an important part in Renault activities for many years.

In 1902 Renault began to make its own four-cylinder engines, and later singles and twins, but De Dion units were also used until the end of 1903. Production reached 1600 in 1903, and 2100 two years later, while the factory area grew annually, from 80,240sq ft (7455sq m) in 1902 to 298,480sq ft (27,730sq m) in 1905. The radiator moved to the dashboard in 1904, a trend followed by many imitators for a while, although none kept it up until 1928, as Renault did.

In 1905 came the first of the 1060cc two-cylinder cars whose most famous models were the AG and AX. These were the company's best sellers up to 1914 and were used widely as taxicabs and light commercial vehicles. The Compagnie Française de Fiacres Automobiles ordered 250 Renault taxis in 1905, following this with 500 in 1906, 750 in 1907 and 1500 in 1908-9. In London 1100 taxis were ordered in 1907 alone and important quantities of two-cylinder cabs were supplied to many cities round the world. Renault was also becoming known for heavier commercial vehicles including 3- and 5-ton trucks and a 21-seater Paris bus introduced in 1909.

In 1907 the passenger car range comprised six models, from 1060cc AG to 7429cc four-cylinder AI-C. Net profits rose from 10 million

francs in 1906 to nearly 22 million francs in 1910. Like many car-makers, Louis Renault entered the aero engine field when he felt the time was ripe, building his first unit, a 60hp air-cooled V8, in 1907. Mounted in a Maurice Farman it won the 1911 Michelin Cup for a non-stop flight from Paris to Clermont-Ferrand. By 1914 five French reconnaissance squadrons were equipped with Renault-powered Farman biplanes. The 80hp Renault V8 was the first aero engine to be made in the Rolls-Royce factory, although it was soon superseded by Royce's own Eagle.

By 1913 Renault was the largest motor vehicle producer in France, with an output of more than 10,000 units by a workforce of 3936. The range of cars consisted of 11 models from the 8hp two-cylinder AX to the 45hp six-cylinder ES.

Early in the year the factory was closed by a five week strike over time and motion study procedures, with automatic docking of pay for inferior work even if it was caused by faulty tools. Louis Renault won in the end, but he became increasingly isolated from his workforce as a result, which contributed not a little to his tragic end in 1944.

The outbreak of World War I in August 1914 resulted in a rapid growth of the Renault empire, the workforce growing to 12,800 in 1915, 20,157 in 1916 and 22,500 by 1918.

Louis Renault hears of Marcel's death, Paris-Madrid race, 1903

Renault AX roadster of 1910

Passenger car production dropped, but large numbers of military trucks, tanks and aero engines were turned out. However, Renault's most celebrated contribution to the war was performed by pre-war vehicles – the 600 taxis which were commandeered off the streets of Paris in September 1914 by General Gallieni and used to transport 6500 men (each cab made two journeys) to the front in what became the Battle of the Marne. This saved Paris from German invasion.

In anticipation of invasion, Louis Renault had evacuated his aero engine production to the Rochet-Schneider factory at Lyons, but other war material continued to be made at Billancourt. Over 3500 Renault-designed light tanks were made, 1850 at Billancourt and the others by Berliet, Delaunay-Belleville and Schneider. In aero engines Renault supplemented the V8 with a 300hp V12, which found particular fame as the power unit for the celebrated Breguet 14 biplane fighter.

As a result of wartime expansion the Renault works at Billancourt and nearby in 1919 consisted of 87 built up acres (35 hectares), including a steel foundry of 78,000sq ft (7250sq m), three iron foundries, one aluminium and one brass foundry, general machining shops and assembly shops for all components including bodywork. Billancourt even made its own tools, together with primary materials such as bricks, crucibles, moulds and coal briquettes.

In 1919 Renault acquired its own steel works at Hagondange in Alsace. Built by Thyssen in 1912 this was the most modern steel plant in Europe, and came to France as part of war reparations. The company also acquired the Ile de Seguin in the Seine opposite the Billancourt works, on which an enormous new factory was built but would not be completed until 1931.

The post-war Renault range consisted of three fours and a six. The latter became the famous 40CV (the 45 in Great Britain) in 1921.

It was an elephantine car with 9.1-litre fixed cylinder head engine, wooden wheels and two wheelbase lengths, 12ft 3in (3.7m) and 13ft 1in (4m). It acquired four wheel brakes in 1922 but was never renowned for its stopping power.

At the other end of the scale was the logical successor to the pre-war two-cylinder models, the 951cc four-cylinder Model KJ, made from 1922 to 1924, and continued as the NN to 1929. This was Renault's answer to André Citroën's 5CV and helped Renault car production to jump from 9500 in 1922 to 23,600 in 1923 and 46,000 in 1925.

Commercial vehicles were a significant part of Renault's activities, in many sizes from a 5cwt (254kg) van on the KJ chassis to 7½-ton trucks, long distance coaches and service buses for Paris and other cities. By the mid-1930s Renault had a virtual monopoly on the manufacture of Paris buses and also supplied a high proportion of the capital's taxicabs. Other products included wheeled and tracked agricultural tractors, railcars, tanks, marine, locomotive and aircraft engines.

Many of the best known French aircraft makes, including Breguet, Caudron, Farman and Potez, used Renault engines. In 1930 Renault was the largest aero engine manufacturer in the world, having built more than 40,000 in 23 years. In 1933 Renault bought the Société Caudron, and the following year a Caudron-Renault C460R monoplane took the world air speed record at 505.848kph (314.131mph).

Net profits rose from 15.5 million francs in 1922 to 85.5 million francs in 1928, although the Depression brought this down to 33 million in 1933. By 1929 the area of the Renault works was 250 acres (100 hectares), equivalent to the whole of the town of Chartres. This was to expand still further in the 1930s, with car production reaching a peak of 61,146 in 1936. This figure was reached despite a series of industrial troubles including a complete

shut down of the factories from 28 May to 14 June.

The enormous and old-fashioned 40CV was replaced in 1928 by the 7.1-litre straight-eight Reinastella, which was joined in 1930 by a smaller straight-eight, the 4.2-litre Nervastella, and in 1932 by the 4.8-litre Nervasport, a development of which won the 1935 Monte Carlo and Liège-Rome-Liège Rallies. At the other end of the range was a series of small fours, the Primaquatre, Monaquatre and Celtaquatre, and the intermediate Vivaquatre which was widely used as a taxi (the famous G7 series).

Renault also made a range of six-cylinder cars, all with the suffix 'stella'. These ran from the 1½-litre Monastella through the 3.1-litre Vivastella to the 4.1-litre Vivastella Grand Sport. The largest of the eights, the Reinastella, was dropped in 1935, but others were continued up to 1939, culminating in the 5.4-litre Suprastella which was the official vehicle for the French president and senior ministers. From 1935 some larger Renaults had streamlined bodies with wings and running boards joined into the coachwork, and headlamps set into the wings.

Renault NN1 saloon of 1927

Renault 4CV saloon of c.1950

Renault Dauphine of c.1960

Renault Argentina 4GTL of c.1984

The last pre-war model was one of the most important, the 1-litre 8CV Juvaquatre, a mass-market family saloon with integral construction. More than 27,000 were sold until the end of 1939, and several thousand more after the war. As a van the Juvaquatre was still available in 1959, latterly with the Dauphine engine.

Renault's only pre-war foreign assembly plant was at Acton, west London, where from 1927 to 1932 and from 1934 to 1939 French-built Renaults were finished with British wheels, lights, upholstery and paints. In 1938 a British version of the Celtaquatre was made with engine linered down to give a horsepower rating of below 12. After the war the 4CV and Dauphine were assembled at Acton from 1949 to 1960.

Commercial vehicles continued to be important to Renault in the 1930s; by the end of the decade the company was France's largest builder of commercials, with 15,613 delivered in 1939 compared with 9789 from Citroën and 4305 from Berliet. Renault's first diesel engine truck was made in 1930 and a new range of forward control trucks came in 1934.

For a few months after the outbreak of World War II the Renault factory continued to turn out Juvaquatres. Louis Renault thought the war would soon be over and was unwilling to disrupt production lines by turning over to military equipment. This decision was opposed by his 'number two', his nephew François Lehideux, and undoubtedly did him much harm later on, for he failed to contribute to the French war effort but was compelled to contribute to the German war effort once his factories were taken over in June 1940 after the fall of France.

Renault wanted to make gazogène-powered passenger cars, but the Germans insisted that he supply 3- and 5-ton trucks for the Wehrmacht. Production of these reached 70 a day by 1942. The works were badly damaged by air raids several times between 1942 and 1944 and on 23 July 1944 they closed indefinitely.

A month later Paris was liberated by the allies and soon afterwards Louis Renault was arrested by the French authorities and charged with collaborating with the Nazis.

Like many French industrialists he was only concerned with keeping his factories going, but his autocratic attitude towards the unions which he had displayed ever since the strike of 1913 served him ill now that he was at the mercy of largely communist ex-Resistance men. He was imprisoned in September 1944 and after a month of brutal ill treatment and denial of elementary medical care he died on 23 October.

Even before Renault's death a new boss had been appointed, 46-year-old former Resistance fighter Pierre Lefaucheux. He took charge on 6 October and four days later the first post-war truck left the factory. By the end of the year production had reached 30 a day, all destined for the French army.

In February 1945 the Société Anonyme des Usines Renault was nationalized, becoming the Regie Nationale des Usines Renault. Louis Renault's stake in the company, which amounted to 98 per cent, became government property, but his family retained their private assets which were very considerable, including three homes. His 25-year-old son Jean-Louis was financial manager, but François Lehideux left the organization and later joined Ford SAF.

During the war two prototype cars had been tested, a 4CV rear-engined saloon and an 11CV front-engined saloon. The former was chosen by Lefaucheux to be the spearhead of Renault's post-war attack on world markets. The production model of this 760cc four-cylinder four-door saloon with a wheelbase of only 6ft 10½in (2.1m) was shown at the 1946 Paris Salon, but it took some time for manufacture to build up, and the revived Juvaquatre was the mainstay of passenger car production until 1948.

By March 1949 300 4CVs were being made every day, rising to 500 a day by 1954. When the model was withdrawn in 1961, a total of 1,150,000 had been made, more than all Renault cars up to 1939. In addition about 37,500 were assembled in England at Acton, and the 4CV was also made under licence by Hino in Japan from 1953 to 1961. The 4CV was the basis for numerous sports cars, the best known being Jean Redélé's Alpine, which was first built in 1955 and was the ancestor of sports cars still made today.

Renault's second post-war design was the Frégate, a front-engined 2-litre saloon which, like the 4CV, had all round independent suspension. It was designed to compete with Citroën's 11CV front-wheel-drive saloons. Despite its modern specifications the Frégate was not a bestseller and was withdrawn in 1958 after 168,383 had been made.

During the 1950s several new Renault factories were opened to supplement Billancourt, which had expanded as far as it could. In 1952 a new automated plant at Flins near Mantes began making body pressings and final assembly of Frégates and some 4CVs, while plants at Le Mans and Choisy-le-Roi were making agricultural tractors and railcars respectively. The Cléon factory was opened for the manufacture of gearboxes and, later, engines.

In February 1955 Lefaucheux was killed at the wheel of his Frégate; he was succeeded as director-general by Pierre Dreyfus. In his first year of office Renault's commercial vehicle division merged with three other concerns, Floirat, Latil and Somua, to form SAVIEM (Société Anonyme de Véhicules Industriels et Equipements Mécaniques). The first trucks to carry this name appeared in 1957, and by 1973 they accounted for 32 per cent of France's medium and heavy trucks and 61 per cent of her buses.

In 1974 SAVIEM acquired its biggest rival, Berliet, and four years later a new single company was formed, Renault Véhicules Industriels. Nearly all trucks were badged as Renaults from 1980, exceptions being those sold in a few overseas markets where the Berliet name is better known. In 1979 Renault acquired a 20 per cent stake in Mack Trucks Inc of Allentown, Pennsylvania; Renault G series are assembled in the United States under the name Mack Midliner.

The 4CV was supplemented in 1956 by a larger rear-engined car, the 845cc Dauphine, of which 1 million had been made four years later. The Dauphine pioneered large scale sales of Renault cars in the USA, with more than 200,000 crossing the Atlantic in the model's first four years. It was made under licence in Italy by Alfa Romeo, and in Brazil by Willys-Overland. There was a high performance version, tuned by Amédée Gordini, and, for

1959, the Floride coupé and convertible.

The direct replacement for the 4CV in 1961 was the R4, which was planned as a more refined car than Citroën's evergreen 2CV, but in the same idiom. It had a 747cc front-mounted engine driving the front wheels, with sealed cooling system that was later featured on all Renaults.

In September 1963 work began on another new factory at Sandouville, near Le Havre, destined for production of a brand-new medium sized car, the 1½-litre front-wheel-drive 16 saloon. This went on sale in January 1965 and was supplemented by a higher performance TS version in 1968. Other models of the 1960s included the Dauphine's successors, the rear-engined 8 and 10 saloons, and a larger car in the shape of the American Rambler, which was assembled by Renault until 1968. The 8/10 series was supplanted by the front-engined front-wheel-drive 12 from 1969, and the last rear-engined Renault left the factory in 1972.

That year saw the introduction of one of Renault's most important models, the 845cc

and Volvo 264. Also employed in the ill-fated DeLorean coupé, this engine is known as the PRV (Peugeot-Renault-Volvo), although the organization that makes it is called Compagnie Franco-Suédoise de Mécanique. Other important plants are at Haren, Belgium, established before World War II, and in Mexico, Latin America, the Philippines, South Africa and Australia, giving truly worldwide production.

From the two-model range of the 1950s Renault has expanded its coverage of the market to include practically all categories of European car. The utilitarian 4 was still being made in 1987 together with various models of the 5, the 9 and 11 four-door saloons with petrol or diesel engines, the 21 four-door saloon and estate in 1721 to 1995cc form, and the 25 luxury saloon with 2-litre four-cylinder and 2.7-litre V6 engines. Turbocharged and diesel engines are available on many of these models. For the sports enthusiast there is the Alpine GT coupé which has been marketed by Renault since it acquired control of Automobiles Alpine in 1977.

In 1983 Renault had more than 32 per cent of the French passenger car market. Four of the five bestsellers were Renault models: the 5, 9, 11 and 18 were in first, second, fourth and fifth places respectively.

Renault made a spectacular return to Grand Prix racing, after a 71 year absence, in 1977 with a team of 1½-litre turbocharged cars which first appeared at that year's British Grand Prix. Success did not come at once, but Jean-Pierre Jabouille won the 1979 French Grand Prix and since then the team has won 15 Grands Prix in the hands of Jabouille, Alain Prost and René Arnoux. Jabouille also won the 1978 Le Mans race in a turbocharged sports/racing car.

The cars ran under the name Renault-Elf, their leading sponsor being the Elf petrol company, although they also receive substantial help from Longines (watches). However, the Formula 1 team was discontinued at the end of 1985 because of company losses and the team's indifferent performance in the 1985 season.

After some quiet years on the American

Renault 5TL of 1985

Renault Alliance DL of 1984

5 hatchback in the 'supermini' class. Designed by Michel Boue, who did not live to see his car in production, the 5 was aimed at a more youthful market than its predecessors, but soon had a worldwide appeal which made it the best-selling French car of all time. When it was replaced in September 1984 by the Supercinq, more than 5.4 million had been made, not only in France but in several of Renault's 25 assembly plants around the world. Larger engines were soon available in the 5, including 956, 1289 and Alpine-tuned 1397cc units, the ultimate development being the 160bhp mid-engined 5 Turbo, strictly a two-seater and the only rear-driven 5.

Renault's foreign operations expanded considerably in the 1970s. A Spanish plant had been opened at Valladolid in 1952, and in 1974 brought out its first distinctive model, a four-door notchback version of the 5 called the Siete (7), anticipating Renault's own four-door 5 by five years.

In Romania the state-owned Intreprinderea de Autoturisme Pitești began manufacture of the 12 under the name Dacia, and this continues today although the model was dropped in France in 1980. In 1975 a new factory was opened at Douvrin to make a 2.7-litre V6 engine for use in the Renault 30, Peugeot 504

Renault Grand Prix car (René Arnoux driving) of 1979

Renault 21 saloon of 1986

market Renault launched a new sales drive in January 1979 with an agreement with American Motors Corporation to market the 5, known in the USA as 'Le Car'. This was followed in October by a $150 million investment in AMC by Renault, and a year later by a further $200 million, giving Renault a 46.9 per cent stake.

The 18 and Fuego were added to the range, but a more important step was the decision to manufacture the 9 at American Motors Corporation's Kenosha plant, under the name Alliance. Introduced for 1983, the Alliance sold 140,000 units in its first year and was joined for 1984 by the Renault 11-based Encore. Renault's new director-general, Bernard Hanon, was on the board of AMC, which is chaired by another Renault executive, Jose Dedeurwaerder.

Renault is more heavily involved in American industry than any other European car firm, with a 45 per cent interest in Mack, a 49 per cent interest in the robot technology company, Cybotech, and a joint venture with Bendix to develop and build automotive electronic controls. Looking in the other direction, geographically and politically, Renault is co-operating with AZLK, maker of the Moskvitch, in the design and production of a new medium-sized Russian car to be launched in 1986. This will win the equivalent of £85 million worth of equipment orders from Renault, which will in addition receive a 'fee' of £25 million for engineering the car.

Renault ran into serious problems in 1984, losing its lead in the French market to PSA (Peugeot-Talbot-Citroën) and suffering an operating loss of nearly £1 billion. In January 1985 Bernard Hanon was replaced as president by Georges Besse who was brought in from Péchiney, a large state-owned chemical and iron industry group. GNG

RENAULT-ARGENTINA
see IKA

RENÉ BONNET
see DB

REO/WOLVERINE
USA 1904-1936

In January 1904 the Smith family, who controlled Olds Motor Works, parted company with Ransom Eli Olds because they believed that the future lay in cars and not his buggies. Horace T. Thomas, who had worked at Olds before moving to Columbia Electric, then joined R. E. Olds to design a new buggy.

In August 1904 Reuben Shettler, a car dealer who had earlier backed Olds Motor Works, helped form the R. E. Olds Co, capitalized at $1 million. Ransom Olds was allocated a

Reo buggy of 1906

quarter of the shares in exchange for use of his name, his patents and inventions. Not surprisingly Olds Motor Works objected to the company's name, so it was changed to Olds' initials as the REO Motor Car Co.

Richard Scott from the Olds Gasoline Engine Works, set up by R. E. Olds' father, was superintendent of the new factory in Lansing, Michigan. Ray Owen, a former Olds dealer who later made the Owen Magnetic, contracted to take the first 10 years' output. By 1909 the contract was worth $50 million but it was terminated because of production and management problems in 1910. For three years Reo also made cars to Owen's patents, which included centre gearchange.

Although early Reos were buggies, Olds soon showed that he was not averse to more conventional cars and by 1908 was outselling his old company four to one. Four-cylinder models were introduced in 1906. An unusual feature of some 1910 models was papier-mâché bodywork – examples still exist.

In 1905 production totalled 864 cars from a workforce of 304 and in 1906 Reo reached fourth position in the US sales league. In 1909 production was 6592 from 935 men.

R. E. Olds believed in making all the components for his vehicles and insisted on stringent quality control. This held back output, however, and led to boardroom rows that nearly caused him to sell out for $7 million in 1910 and join Benjamin Briscoe's abortive US Motor Corporation. Differences were resolved and in 1911 the quaintly named Reo The Fifth – 'The Car that Marks My Limit' – made its appearance. It was powered by a 3.7-litre four and featured Owen's patent centre change. Purpose-built trucks were added to the range that year, too.

Output moved up to 50 cars a day and in 1913 a profit of $2 million was earned; the company's 800 shareholders received a 50

per cent dividend that year. Capital grew to $10 million in 1915, when sales were almost 15,000 cars plus 1500 of the new Speed Wagon. Reo's first six-cylinder model was produced in 1916 and was named the Fashion Plate. A Speed Wagon six did not come along until 1922.

At the end of World War I Reo employed 4000 workers, had made 25,577 vehicles in 1917 – of which over a third were commercials – and had built a substantial number of Holt tractors for the government in 1918. In 1919 a total of 9185 trucks and 7303 cars were made. Profit was $10 million in 1920. That was the year of the six-cylinder T-6 car, with the unusual features of external engine bearing adjusters, no hand brake but a parking brake applied by full travel on the clutch pedal, and back-to-front gear-change.

In 1923 production consisted of 15,228 cars and 16,652 commercials. New Speed Wagons were designed by C. F. Magoffin after additional plant had been bought from the Duplex Truck Co in Lansing in 1925.

During the mid-1920s R. E. Olds sold his share and went into semi-retirement, putting into practice his lifelong fascination with rural subsistence living; his agricultural/industrial colony named Oldsmar exists to this day in Florida. In his place Richard Scott, once the factory superintendent, became president and introduced a cheaper line, the Continental 6 engined Wolverine in mid-1927. Earlier in the year there had been a replacement for the T-6 called the Flying Cloud, designed by Fabio Segardi, ex-Hudson and Olds.

The year 1927 was a successful one, 5000 workers producing 28,765 cars and profits of $4 million. In 1928 car and commercial sales were equally balanced at about 23,000 each and profits improved to $5 million. Yet sales of the Wolverine were disappointing and the model was dropped in 1929. This was the year in which herringbone gears gave a 'silent' second ratio until vacuum clutch and synchro were adopted.

A Continental 6 was used in the Reo 15, introduced in 1930. There were also larger cars with 5.9-litre straight-eight Reo engines, the Flying Cloud and Royale, the latter designed by Amos G. Northrup and Julio Andrade, and reputedly costing $6 million to develop. Both these models dated from 1931.

The Depression dragged car sales down to 11,500 in 1930 and 6026 in 1931, when losses totalled $2.7 million. In 1933 combined car and commercial production stood at nearly 10,000 and the company lost $2.5 million. Capital, which had increased in the 1920s, was halved to $10 million and R. E. Olds, then aged 70, returned to try to save the situation.

An Armstrong-Siddeley with Wilson preselective gearbox was acquired for examination and in 1933 Reo launched its similar 'self-shifter' that had cost the company $1.5 million to develop. A little over 3000 cars a year were sold in Reo's last three years of car making, the 1935 models having the appearance of subsequent Grahams as a consequence of the same body dies being used for both at the Hayes body plant. Reo cars, complete apart from engine, were supplied to Franklin and were marketed as inexpensive Airmans.

Car production ended in 1936 and R. E. Olds severed his links with the company the following year. He died in 1950, aged 86. In his final years he maintained an active interest in the Ideal Power Lawn Mower Co, the Reolds Farm Co and the First Bond and Mortgage Co.

Reo concentrated on trucks and buses – sometimes using the model name Flying Cloud – and built a Junior range for truckmaker Mack from 1936 to 1938; it also made lawn mowers. The firm became Reo Motors Inc in 1940 and became a major supplier of military trucks, including the Eager Beaver from 1950.

In 1957 White acquired Reo, followed by Diamond T, which was moved to Lansing in 1960. The trucks were known as Diamond-Reo from May 1967. Four years later the combined firm was sold by White to F. L. Cappaert, who revived the Royale name on some models. The Diamond-Reos sold well – more than 9000 in 1974 – but losses on the Eager Beaver contract and other problems led to bankruptcy in 1975.

Consolidated International of Columbus, Ohio, supplied spares for the 200,000 Reos, Diamond-Reos and Diamond Ts in use and bought rights that enabled it to grant a manufacturing licence and use of the name to truck dealer Osterlund Inc. Osterlund makes some Diamond-Reo Giants at Harrisburg, Pennsylvania, using proprietary components and, as a rule, Autocar cabs. NB

REVERE
USA 1917-1926

The Revere Motor Car Corporation was presumably named after the Revolutionary War hero Paul Revere, although company advertising did not make much of the connection. It was founded in Logansport, Indiana, early in 1917 by Newton Van Zandt, later to become first president of Duesenberg Automobile & Motor Co, aided by chief engineer Adolph Monsen and two former Stutz racing drivers, Gil Anderson and Tom Rooney.

August Duesenberg was on the first board of directors, so it is not surprising that the Revere was powered by a four-cylinder Duesenberg engine. The speedster used the big-bore version, with 5.9 litres and 103bhp, while touring models had the 'regular' engine of 5.6 litres and 81bhp. They were expensive high-quality cars priced at $4250.

Unfortunately, in their haste to get a factory built and cars into production, the directors set their capital requirements too low, and with only $25,000 asked for, they were always under financed. They announced a target of

2500 cars a year but, although a few pilot cars were running by the summer of 1917, production did not get going until early 1918.

By this time war demand for aero engines caused the supply of Rochester Duesenberg units to dry up, so Monsen designed his own modified Duesenberg engine, with higher mounted camshaft. A limited number of Reveres with these engines was made in 1918 and 1919, but in 1920 the company was reorganized as the Revere Motor Car Co.

The new company changed the name to ReVere and went back to using Rochester-Duesenberg engines, although the Monsen could be had as a more expensive alternative. About 200 cars were built during 1920 before bankruptcy occurred in December, and during 1921 not more than one car a week was made, under a receiver. Prices were high at $4850 for a speedster and $6500 for a sedan.

In 1923 a new company was formed, the ReVere Motor Co, with Monsen as vice-president and general manager. Prices were reduced to between $3200 and $4200, and about 100 cars were completed during the year.

In 1924 the four-cylinder Duesenberg engine was replaced by a 5.4-litre six-cylinder Continental 6J, although the Monsen unit was still listed until 1926. Styling remained much the same as it had been, but several interesting features were adopted over the next three years. These included small headlights placed above the regular ones, which could be turned by a lever on the dashboard, and two superimposed steering wheels, one for normal driving with a 7 to 1 ratio, and the other with a 14 to 1 ratio for parking. This was introduced in 1926 to ease parking with the new balloon tyres.

The 1926 models were the last, and the company quietly closed down at the end of the year. Total production has been estimated at 1000, less than half the predicted first year output. GNG

REX
GB 1901-1914

The Rex Motor Manufacturing Co Ltd of Coventry was founded by William Pilkington, who had begun in business by making weldless tubing in the 1880s at the beginning of the cycle boom. This concern merged with others to form Tubes Ltd, which led later to the present day Tube Investments Ltd.

Pilkington, however, left in 1899 and with his brother formed the Rex company which initially made bicycles and motorcycles. They absorbed another Coventry cycle-maker, Allard & Co Ltd, which also made cars from 1899 to 1902, and this launched them into motor car manufacture, although it was always a sideline to two-wheelers. Pedal cycles were given up in 1903, but motorcycle production was continued, with changes of ownership, up to 1933.

Rex Rexette forecar of 1906

A variety of car designs was made, from a 900cc single-cylinder voiturette to a 2.4-litre vertical twin. These were called Rex or Rex-Simplex, the latter name being used from 1904 to 1905. In 1906 came the Ast-Rex, a larger car with 3.7-litre four-cylinder Aster engine, followed by the Airex with 1.3-litre V-twin air-cooled engine. This constant change of name and designs indicate that Rex was not very happy with four-wheelers, but it had more success with the three-wheeled Rexette forecar, made from 1904 to 1906. These were nicknamed 'The King of Little Cars'.

In 1908 came the Rex-Remo, a conventional car with four-cylinder T-head engines of 2.6 or 2.8 litres capacity. Its only unusual feature was that its old-fashioned gilled-tube radiator was concealed by a honeycomb grille. These were made until 1911, when Rex abandoned cars, apart from a cyclecar of 1912 and a Dorman-powered light car of 1914, neither of which progressed beyond the prototype stage.

Motorcycles were much more successful and profitable for the company, which in 1922 merged with another Coventry firm, Acme, to make the Rex-Acme, powered by various proprietary engines. Production lasted until 1928. Four years later the Mills-Fulford sidecar business attempted a revival of the Rex-Acme but this lasted only a year. GNG

REX-SIMPLEX
GERMANY 1901-1923

The company Deutsche Automobil-Industrie Friedrich Hering of Ronnenburg was founded in the early 1890s to manufacture bicycle components but by the late 1890s it was also making proprietary car parts, including chassis, wheels and axles. In 1901 the company introduced a complete car, a De Dion-like model sold under the name of Rex. It used one of Hering's own chassis but with a De Dion engine, built under licence in Germany by Max Cudell of Aachen, one of Germany's pioneer car-builders. Hering also sold a 6hp single-cylinder De Dion-engined voiturette as the Rex-Simplex and all subsequent cars used this as the marque name.

By 1903 the company was offering a choice of De Dion or Fafnir engines and up to 1907 it built single-, twin- and four-cylinder models. In 1904 the company became known as Deutsche Automobil-Industrie Hering & Richard, which was reorganized again in 1908 as a limited company, Automobilwerke Richard & Hering AG.

All the early Rex-Simplex cars were fairly small models with a reputation for quality, and they sold well enough to prompt the company to develop its own engines from late 1907. Thereafter the cars were generally much larger, and among the most successful was the 4½-litre 17/38PS Type C, introduced in 1908 and built until the outbreak of World War I. Other early models with the company's own engines included the 9/16 and 10/28PS.

The four-cylinder 10/28 replaced the 9/16 and was designed by Dr Ernst Valentin, who joined the company in 1911 and helped Rex-Simplex acquire a reputation for very high technical standards. Valentin moved from Rex-Simplex to Russo-Baltic at Riga, where he developed two large four-cylinder cars for the Russian domestic market.

Before and during World War I, Richard & Hering also built a number of electric vehicles and lorries. After the war car production was resumed with updated versions of the pre-war 10/28 and 13/38PS types.

In 1921 the company was taken over as Elitewagen AG by Elite Motorenwerke AG of Brand-Erbisdorf, which had built petrol and electric cars since the end of the war. Elitewagen built the 13/38PS Rex-Simplex model in the Ronnenburg works from 1921 to 1923 under the name Elitewagen, after which the model was dropped. BL

Rex-Simplex 16PS landaulette of 1905

Rex-Simplex 17/30PS double phaeton of 1909

REYROL
FRANCE 1901-1930

Made by Automobiles Reyrol at Neuilly until 1907, and thereafter at Levallois-Perret, the Reyrol was often called by its alternative name of Passe Partout (Goes Everywhere). The first car was a single-cylinder voiturette powered by either a De Dion-Bouton or Aster 5hp engine, with belt and spur gear transmission. There were plans for it to be made in England by the Yorkshire Motor Vehicle Co, but that company went bankrupt before the end of 1901 so few, if any, were made.

The 1905 single-cylinder two-seater was available with 4½hp De Dion-Bouton or 6hp Buchet engines and was said to be France's cheapest car at 2700 francs. Larger Buchet engines were used in 1906-8 models, and Reyrol also offered a small monobloc four. Reyrols of this period had De Dion-type bonnets with the radiator mounted below, between the dumb irons, although the cars which ran in the 1907 Coupe des Voiturettes had Renault-type dashboard radiators.

Only four-cylinder cars were made after 1908, these being conventional small to medium sized machines from 1½ to 2.7 litres in capacity. Chapuis-Dornier engines were used almost exclusively in the 1920s, in sizes from 1.2 to 2.3 litres in thoroughly conventional touring cars. The exception was a front-wheel-drive sports car of 1926 for which the name Passe Partout was revived. Its lines were somewhat reminiscent of a Ballot 2 LTS, and it was powered by a 1½-litre single-overhead cam CIME engine. Few were made, Reyrol continuing with its rather pedestrian saloons and tourers up to 1930, when production ceased. As a garage and repair works, Reyrol survived until the early 1950s. GNG

RHODE/MEDEA, MEDIA
GB 1921-1929

F. W. Mead and T. W. Deakin made bicycle and motorcycle components in Sparkhill, Birmingham, and between 1904 and 1907 amalgamated their names in a prototype Medea car – sometimes spelled Media – which used a Fafnir engine bought from Swift. Their real money-spinner became Canoelet sidecars and then in 1912 they built two experimental Medea cyclecars with Salmon and Chapuis-Dornier four-cylinder engines.

In 1921 the Rhode Car Co, a subsidiary of Mead and Deakin, began to produce unusually lively small cars with overhead-cam engines. Nearly all parts, except the Wrigley gearboxes, were made in the company's new factory at Tyseley. They were initially of 1087cc and lacked a differential. They were rather stark Occasional Fours, although in

1924 came a full four-seater with 1232cc engine and differential.

The sporty image was lost in 1926 when quieter push-rod overhead-valve engines were used to broaden the appeal in an effort to reduce liabilities of £54,000 at Rhode and £20,000 at Mead and Deakin, which almost matched assets. The Rhode then became just another dull little car until for 1928 it returned to overhead-cam engines. M&D commercial vehicles were made from 1925 to 1927, but only about six were sold.

In July 1926 the two firms were amalgamated but financial difficulties continued despite Mead's attempts to market Trailavans. In 1929 Rhode was bought by McKenzie and

Rhode 10.8hp tourer of 1924

Denley, which was also to acquire the remains of Star of Wolverhampton. H. B. Denley, one of the partners, had been in charge of sales and testing at Rhode. After the purchase Mead worked for Morris-Commercial.

Rhodes were built from spares at Hall Green, Birmingham, in 1929 and then six Meadows 1.5-litre engines were bought. The Meadows-engined cars were listed until 1935 but there is no evidence that more engines were acquired or that any more Rhode-designed types were offered. Chassis numbers suggest that about 2000 cars were made until 1925, after which output was small.

The Rhode Motor Co Ltd brass plate remained on the door of Denley's garage at Kings Heath, Birmingham, up to the late 1960s. F. W. Mead's son, Richard, became a specialist coachbuilder responsible for bodying the Rover-based Marauder and other sports cars after World War II. NB

RICHARD-BRASIER
see Brasier

RIESS-ROYAL
see Bell (USA, Canada)

RIKER
see Locomobile

RILEY
GB 1898-1969

The Riley family of Coventry were master weavers and makers of weaving equipment who moved into the cycle business because of a decline in weaving in the last two decades of the 19th century. In 1890 they acquired the cycle-maker Bonnick & Co Ltd and in 1896 changed the name to the Riley Cycle Co Ltd.

In 1899 they built their first powered vehicles for sale, a tricycle and a quadricycle, but one of William Riley's sons, Percy, had made a light two-seater car three years earlier. This was remarkable for having mechanically operated inlet valves. When a continental firm tried to establish a patent for this design the British motor industry was able to point to Riley's precedent and avoid paying royalties.

Bicycles, motorcycles, tricycles and quadricycles kept the Riley Cycle Co busy in the first few years of the 20th century, but all engines were bought from such firms as De Dion-Bouton and MMC. In 1903 a new company, the Riley Engine Co, was launched by Percy and his brothers Victor and William to make engines for the Tricars built by the Riley Cycle Co. Between 1903 and 1907 these gradually grew more carlike, substituting seats for saddles and wheels for handlebar steering.

The first four-wheeled car appeared in 1907, powered by a 9hp V-twin engine which was also used for driving railcars in South Africa. One of these V-twins gave W. O. Bentley his first four-wheeled transport. The Riley Engine Co also made three-speed gearboxes.

Tricars were abandoned in 1908 and pedal cycles in 1911, but the Cycle Co acquired a new interest in the manufacture of detachable wire wheels which were made in a separate factory and which were supplied to 183 other car manufacturers including Hispano-Suiza, Mercédès, Rolls-Royce, Napier, Panhard and Renault.

Demand for these wheels was so great that in 1912 the Riley brothers formed a new company for the manufacture of cars, which might otherwise have come to an end. This was the Riley Motor Manufacturing Co Ltd with new premises near those of the Riley Engine Co. The Riley Cycle Co concentrated on the manufacture of wheels and in 1913 changed its name to Riley (Coventry) Ltd.

Production by the Riley Motor Manufacturing Co concentrated on the 12/18 V-twin and 17/30 four-cylinder cars, but in 1913 another brother, Stanley, took over the Nero Engine Co which had been founded by Victor Riley. He planned to build a completely new 10hp four-cylinder car which would fit into a gap in the market between those made by his brothers' concern. Prototypes were running by the summer of 1914 but the war prevented production. During the war the Nero Engine Co acquired land at Foleshill, Coventry, and

Riley two-seat 2-litre runabout of 1909

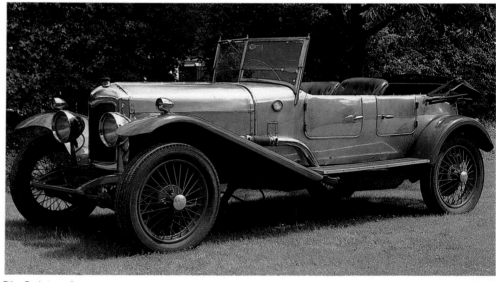

Riley Redwinger four-seat sports model of c.1925

Brooklands Riley of c.1929 (photo autographed by driver Freddie Dixon)

built a factory there for war production which became the main Riley works.

In 1919 a new 10.8hp four-cylinder car was launched, designed for the first time by someone outside the family, Harry Rush. This was made by Riley (Coventry) Ltd, which abandoned wheel production, absorbed the Nero Engine Co Ltd and moved into the Foleshill premises. The Riley Engine Co assembled a few of the 17/30 cars from pre-war stocks, probably no more than six, until 1922, after which the company made electric lighting and marine equipment up to 1926.

The 10.8hp became the 11.9hp for 1925 and these cars earned the company a good reputation, together with a number of sporting successes for the Redwinger model. However, they were overshadowed by the new Nine introduced in 1926.

This was once again a Riley design, being the work of Stanley and Percy working in the drawing offices of the Riley Engine Co, and featured inclined overhead valves operated by twin camshafts mounted half way up the block. This engine was the basis of all Riley power units up to 1957. Total production of the Nine until its demise in 1938 was over 10,000, of which 100 to 110 were the ultra low Brooklands version developed by the racing driver J. G. Parry Thomas. These cars were actually assembled by Thomson & Taylor Ltd at Brooklands track.

The standard Nines were built jointly by Riley (Coventry) Ltd and the Riley Engine Co Ltd but were always marketed by the former concern. Axles were made for Riley by Laycock Engineering of Sheffield. In 1929 sales exceeded £1 million for the first time and in 1931 profit was nearly £79,000.

In 1931 a new departure for the Riley Engine Co was the supply of a number of Nines or 14/6 engines to the boatbuilders J. W. Brooke & Co of Lowestoft, which had itself made cars from 1901 to 1913. The 18ft (5m) boat was known as the Brooke-Riley Runabout. Two years later Riley was supplying a Nine Marine Engine to another boatbuilder, Vospers of Southampton.

The Riley Motor Club was founded in 1925 with 30 members. Growth was rapid, however, and it had more than 2000 by 1933, making it the largest one make car club in the world. Sales boomed in the early 1930s. In 1933 output was up 138 per cent on 1932 and a new London Service Department opened at Hendon early in 1933.

Victor Riley was concerned with easy gearchanging and a Salernie fluid flywheel was offered on the 1933 14/6 Edinburgh saloon; Wilson preselectors were introduced on Nine and 14/6 models in 1934. These boxes were supplied by Armstrong-Siddeley, which made nearly 13,000 for Riley, 4240 for the Nine and 8373 for the 12/4, 14/6 and V8. Some Nines were fitted with ENV preselectors.

New 1496cc 12/4 engines were introduced for 1935 and were destined to continue basically unchanged for 20 years and to carry a wide variety of attractive bodywork including

Riley One-Point-Five saloon of 1959

the Merlin, Kestrel and Falcon saloons and the Lynx sports/tourer – as well as the Sprite two-seater sports, whose engine could be had in Kestrel and Lynx to provide a higher performance. About 40 to 50 Sprites were made. Some of the body styles, including Merlin, Kestrel and Lynx, could also be had with the Nine engine and almost any combination of engine, chassis and body could be obtained on special request.

A shortlived six-cylinder sports was the 1½-litre MPH derived from the 1933 Tourist Trophy cars; only 12 of these were made. Another low production model was the 8/90 with 2178cc 90° V8 engine with three camshafts. It was introduced for the 1936 season but only 37 were built.

For 1937 a new make appeared under the Riley auspices, Autovia Cars Ltd. This was formed to build a new luxury car, more expensive than any Riley, and powered by a development of the V8 engine, increased in size to 2849cc. A new factory was acquired, at Midland Road, Coventry; Victor Riley was among the directors and the chief engineer was Charles Van Eugen, formerly of Lea-Francis. Bodies were by Arthur Mulliner. Prices were £675 for the chassis, £975 for the saloon and £995 for the limousine, compared with £450 for the top priced Riley. Fewer than 40 were made. Production ended with the demise of the company, although the model was taken over briefly by the London Riley distributors.

Up to 1936 the company had been very profitable, paying dividends of 20 per cent less tax in 1933 and regularly carrying forward adequate funds for plant improvement and development of new models. Perhaps it was the wide variety of models which started the trouble. Indeed, in a 1936 advertisement the company declared: 'We make far too many models, of course. But then we have a pretty fertile design department, and we like making nice interesting cars.'

In 1937 it was admitted that a serious loss had been made over the previous year. The

reasons for this were complex, partly due to the fact that after the departure of George Leek in 1934 the company had no general manager for two and a half years, nor an overall designer after Hugh Rose left at the end of 1934 to join Leek at Lea-Francis. The 14/6 and the V8 were financial disasters, and only the 12/4 was earning money.

The market had been hit by the success of the SS Jaguar – and many Riley employees who lost their jobs in the cutbacks of 1937 went to work for SS. The uncertain prospects for car manufacture led the Riley family to withdraw some of their own capital and diversify their investments.

In January 1937 a new general manager appeared in the person of Lewis Ord, a Canadian organization and works study consultant who had worked successfully for the London Midland and Scottish Railway as well as Humber. Victor Riley gave him a free hand in all departments, but Ord concentrated on design, an area in which he had little experience, and his re-designed inlet manifolds for the new Nine were most unsatisfactory.

Public confidence was damaged at a critical time for Riley, and unsold cars piled up in the works, together with discarded 'Ord' manifolds. There was insufficient money for the development of the 2½-litre Big Four, and a merger with Triumph was mooted. In February 1938 a receiver was called in but production continued, although at a greatly reduced rate.

In September 1938 it was announced that both Riley companies had been acquired by Lord Nuffield for resale to Morris Motors Ltd, and that a new company would be formed, Riley (Coventry) Successors Ltd. Victor Riley was appointed managing director. A new range of cars was announced for 1939 using the 12/4 and 16/4 (Big Four) engines with new, rather bland, bodies. Few of these were made before the factory went over to war work in 1940, although in July 1939 a revised Kestrel was launched.

In 1945 the post-war Riley, known as the

RM series, was launched initially with the 12/4 engine only but was joined for 1947 by a model with the 2.4-litre Big Four. They shared the same body, which was much more handsome than the pre-war design and did a great deal to enhance the Riley name between 1946 and 1955. In 1948 Riley left Coventry after 50 years of vehicle-building and moved to Abingdon, where it shared the MG factory.

From the mid-1950s Riley cars progressively lost their individuality as they were merged into various slots in the British Motor Corporation range. The last RM, the 1½-litre RMF, was made in 1955. The previous year the 2.4-litre RM had been replaced by the slabsided Pathfinder, still using the familiar twin camshaft engine. This was followed in 1957 by the Two Point Six, which shared not only styling but engine with the Wolseley 6/90.

The Riley name survived until 1969, finding itself on such familiar BMC cars as the 1.5/Wolseley 1500, Farina-styled 1½-litre saloons, Mini and 1100. Indeed, the Mini and 1100 bore the time-honoured Riley names of Elf and Kestrel. GNG

RMB
GB 1973 to date

The RMB Gentry is a kit-type sports car closely modelled on the MG TF and using Triumph Herald or Vitesse running gear. Its originator, Roger Blockley, previously worked on the Triumph production line and saw Triumph's separate chassis as an ideal basis for a self-built car. He built his first as a hobby, stripping an old Vitesse chassis and fitting a very faithful copy of the MG TF body, using real MG wings, bumpers, radiator shell and wheels. This first replica was completed in 1973 after some 20 months of spare-time work.

Blockley thought it might be possible to build copies, advertised the car and received so many enquiries that he founded the RMB Motor Co Ltd in February 1974 and moved into a 900sq ft (83sq m) workshop, which had previously been used for growing mushrooms, at Barwell in Leicestershire.

He called his car the Gentry and he was the company's sole employee. In the first year he built 14 kits, comprising a primed aluminium shell with glassfibre wings and doors on a tubular frame with wooden bulkheads, at £295 plus tax. Weather equipment was available as an optional extra. A shorter version of the car was offered briefly for use on the Spitfire chassis, but only two were made and the option was dropped in mid-1975.

By 1975 Blockley had a six month waiting list for kits and even by working seven days a week could only hope to build one car every 10 days or so. In fact he built 40 kits in 1975 but the waiting list grew to nine months. In 1976 he added two part-time staff, including his father, to increase production to a car a

Roamer four-seat tourer of c.1923

week, now at £365 plus tax for a kit. He also offered more finished cars and a purpose made chassis using a mixture of Triumph and MGB suspension parts that could accept an MGB engine.

In July 1977 RMB moved into a larger workshop in Barwell, which helped increase production to two cars a week. It prompted a switch from the second hand MG radiator shells used previously to an RMB copy, but the Gentry remained one of the most faithful replicas available. In 1986 the basic kit price had risen to £895 plus tax, with weather equipment, windscreen assembly and a hard top available as optional extras. Visually the Triumph Herald/Vitesse based car was very little changed from the original. BL

ROAMER
USA 1916-1930

The Roamer was made by Albert C. Barley, who had run the Western Motor Co, maker of the Rutenber engine, and who had also acquired the Halladay, Nyberg and Wahl motor companies. In 1915 he formed the Barley Manufacturing Co to continue production of the Halladay at Streator, Illinois.

The following year he brought out a more expensive companion make which he called the Roamer. It is probable that he was inspired to do this by Clyde Y. Kenworthy, the New York agent for Rauch & Lang electric cars, who was looking for a good-quality petrol car to add to his line. It was an assembled car with a six-cylinder Rutenber engine and Warner gearbox. The aluminium bodies were made at the Barley works and the radiator was closely modelled on that of the Rolls-Royce. The Roamer's designer was Karl Martin, who was later responsible for the Deering Magnetic, Kenworthy and Wasp cars.

In 1917 Barley was lured to Kalamazoo, Michigan, where the Chamber of Commerce paid him $5000 to move into the empty fac-

tory where the Michigan cars had been made. The Halladay was sold to a group of Ohio businessmen, and Barley continued production of the Roamer.

The 1918 models were entirely new, featuring a six-cylinder Continental engine or a four-cylinder Duesenberg engine. The latter was the 5.6-litre 'walking-beam' unit used by Biddle, Revere and other cars; few were made, however, and an advertised 6.6-litre six-cylinder Duesenberg engine intended for use in the Roamer 6-90 was probably never built at all. The Duesenberg-powered Roamers cost $2950, compared with $2250 for the otherwise identical Continental-engined 6-54.

From 1919 onwards the Duesenberg engine was made at Rochester, New York, and known as the Rochester-Duesenberg. It also was available in the Roamer, up to 1925, but the majority of Roamers were Continental-powered until the introduction of the Lycoming straight-eight in 1926. Nevertheless, Roamer was Rochester-Duesenberg's best customer and took about 800 engines in seven years. Roamer's peak year was 1920 when 1620 cars were delivered, but from 1922 the annual average was between 400 and 500.

In 1922 Barley brought out a smaller six which he called the Barley. It had a 3.2-litre Continental 6Y six-cylinder engine and sold for $1850. Most seem to have been sold as taxicabs, the name of these being changed to Pennant from 1924. The company name was changed to Roamer Motor Car Co in 1923.

For 1925 a 5.1-litre Lycoming 3H straight-eight engine supplemented and later replaced the six, being joined in 1927 by a smaller eight, the 3.7-litre Lycoming GT. These eight-cylinder Roamers were known as the 8-78 and 8-88 respectively and were made in diminishing numbers until production ceased in 1930. The company was reorganized in 1928 as Roamer Consolidated Corporation, still under the leadership of Albert Barley, and for the last two years 1- and 2-ton trucks were made. GNG

ROBERT SERF
FRANCE 1925-1934

Robert Serf cars were designed by Monsieur Serf and built in the garage run by Georges Didier in the village of Colombey-les-Belles near Nancy in eastern France. They were mostly conventional small cars but, unusually for a regional make of this size, they used engines designed and built on the premises. These were 1100cc side-valve four-cylinder units. From 1925 to 1931 Didier turned out about 65 to 70 of these 7CV cars, manufacture doubtless being subsidized by Didier's Ford agency.

In 1932 came a smaller car, with 600cc vertical twin two-stroke engine, 10 of which were made in three years. Didier then moved his business to Nancy-Vendeuvre, where he built another two-stroke car, this time with front wheel drive. Only one was made.

Didier afterwards made cattle trailers, still under the name Robert Serf, until his works were requisitioned for military purposes in 1940. He died two years later, but Robert Serf was still running a garage in Nancy in the early 1980s. GNG

ROCHDALE
GB 1952-1972

Rochdale Olympic of c.1960

The bodywork repair company Rochdale Motor Panels Ltd was founded in Rochdale, Lancashire, in 1948 by panel beater Harry Smith and a partner, Frank Butterworth – both racing enthusiasts who also built several alloy-bodied Austin Seven based specials. Rochdale too built several one-off alloy bodies to customers' own designs before building its first glassfibre body in 1952, one of the first in the popular field of making sporty bodies for low-price Austin, Ford or other chassis. The first glassfibre shell was known as the Rochdale Mark 6 and sold in quite large numbers at £47 10s.

In 1954 Rochdale offered two new models, the F at £55 and the C at £75, and then introduced the ST, an open two-seater designed specifically for Ford chassis. This was followed in 1956 by a well equipped and easily fitted 2+2 GT shell, priced at £140, which was soon being turned out at the rate of up to four a week. Its success prompted the company to expand in 1957 as Rochdale Motor Panels and Engineering Ltd.

A drophead version of the GT, known as the Riviera, was also introduced, and up to September 1958 more than 400 of the two models had been built. About 750 were eventually completed before production stopped in 1961 and much of the profit was turned to developing a new car, the Olympic, the prototype of which was completed in 1959.

This was not just a glassfibre body but a complete tubular-reinforced monocoque body and chassis unit. It was launched in 1960, at a kit price of about £250, and took its name from that year's Rome Olympic Games. A Ford-based version was planned but all the cars sold were BMC based, with a mixture of Morris Minor and Riley 1.5 parts. Later, complete cars were offered at prices from just under £600.

The Olympic sold well at first, with production of up to three cars a week, but early in 1961 Rochdale's factory and almost all its equipment were destroyed by fire. New body moulds were made up from salvaged shells and the company moved to large new works in a former cotton mill in Rochdale.

At the 1963 London Racing Car Show a Mark 2 version was launched with the Ford 116E Classic engine as standard. Sales had fallen, however, typically to one or two a week up to 1965 – after which problems in buying-in parts for fully-built cars forced Rochdale to supply shells only.

With falling sales this soon became secondary to Rochdale's other activity since the early 1960s, making heating equipment. Production virtually stopped after 1967, but the car was still available until 1972 on a one-off basis. BL

ROCHET-SCHNEIDER
FRANCE 1894-1932

Edouard Rochet was born in 1866 and worked in his father's machine shop at Lyons from the age of 14. Father and son made bicycles from the late 1880s and in 1894 were joined by Théophile Schneider, who was distantly related to the armaments family of the same name. Single cylinder Benz-type cars were built from 1894 to 1901, serial numbers suggesting an output of about 240 small Rochet-Schneiders.

In 1896 the Société Lyonnaise de Vélocipèdes et Automobiles Rochet-Schneider was formed. Its 300,000 franc capital was increased to 1 million francs in March 1899 to finance a new factory that was opened in Lyons by 1901.

At the 1901 Paris Salon two- and four-cylinder cars were introduced with shaft drive and in 1903 these were redesigned along Mercédès lines. A total of 157 cars were sold that year and Rochet-Schneider soon became one of the most significant French makers of high-quality expensive cars.

At least 20 cars were sold to American customers and a licence to produce them in the United States was bought by the Sampson Machine Co, which probably did not act upon it. Martini from 1902, FN from 1906 and Florentia in Italy all produced versions of the Rochet-Schneider.

In 1904 the firm was sold for 4.5 million francs to British company promoters who formed a London-based company, Rochet-Schneider Ltd, with £300,000 capital. Production averaged fewer than 250 cars a year and by November 1907 Rochet-Schneider Ltd was

Rochet-Schneider 35hp of c.1906

Rochet-Schneider commercial vehicle advertisement, c.1950

in liquidation. Théophile Schneider soon started the car firm bearing his name, while Rochet and the Zafiropulo family (mostly of Turkish nationality) who had provided finance, created the French registered Etablissement Lyonnaise Rochet-Schneider in 1909 with capital of 2.5 million francs.

F. Baverey was general manager of this company, which did well with Rochet's automatic carburettor. In 1909 a subsidiary, Carburateurs Zénith, was formed which in some years was responsible for almost half the parent firm's profits. An extensive range of high-quality cars was produced and output averaged about 500 chassis a year, including commercials from 1906.

After World War I the market for luxury cars became much more competitive and affected sales of the company's 12, 18 and 30hp cars, which received new overhead-valve engines in 1923 and were promoted with the slogan 'Strength, Simplicity, Silence'. Increasingly it was commercials that provided the firm's regular earnings. Although merger talks

took place with Cottin-Desgouttes around 1930, both firms were in equally difficult straits and Rochet-Schneider decided to go its own way. It abandoned production of its handsome and long-lasting cars in 1932. Diesel lorries and buses were subsequently made with combustion systems built under

licence from Oberhaensli.

Rochet-Schneider was eventually bought by Berliet in 1951 and the name died two years later. Carburateurs Zénith had earlier been separated from Rochet-Schneider and this company nowadays has thriving factories in a number of countries. NB

RÖHR
GERMANY 1928-1935

H. G. Röhr, born in 1895, was a famed World War I fighter pilot and aero engine designer. In the early 1920s he modified existing cars to incorporate such advanced ideas as independent front suspension and in 1925 obtained financial backing and built a small factory at Darmstadt, Hessen, where he planned a six-cylinder car that he said would be 'the safest car in the world'.

After the Falcon light car of 1921-26 was discontinued its factory at Ober-Ramstadt became the home of Röhr. In 1928 there was produced a remarkable independently sprung straight-eight 8/40hp car with cold pressed steel stressed floor pan, David Brown worm axle and Lockheed brakes; total weight was just 2200lb (1000kg). A maximum of six a day were made until the firm collapsed in 1930 in the aftermath of the Wall Street crash. Total sales were 1300 at most. H. G. Röhr became technical director of Adler and then worked for Mercedes-Benz before his death in 1936.

The Röhr company was revived by new interests with largely Swiss capital as Neue Röhrwerke. The cars continued in updated form, Ferdinand Porsche designing an enlarged straight-eight that developed up to 140bhp when supercharged. A number of 2¼-litre engines and vestigial chassis were sold to Hampton in Britain.

More productive was a Tatra licence acquired in 1932, from which stemmed the Röhr Junior. This was produced until 1935 when Stoewer took over the licence and remaining cars. The Röhr name was then discontinued, although its Ober-Ramstadt factory continued in business making agricultural machinery. NB

Rohr eight-cylinder cabriolet of 1929

Rolland-Pilain 2.2-litre sports two-seater of 1909

ROLLAND-PILAIN
FRANCE 1906-1931

Emile Pilain was the nephew of François Pilain of Pilain cars and the two had worked together at the engineering company Vermorel. In 1905 Emile Pilain joined Rolland at Tours and in 1906 they introduced a 20hp vehicle that they claimed to be the first car with monobloc four-cylinder engine. That year a branch was opened in Levallois-Perret.

Despite being a very small firm Rolland-Pilain soon offered an extensive range and was experimenting with four wheel brakes and valveless engines in 1910. (The engines entered production and led to an unsuccessful patent infringement case being brought against Argyll.) In 1911 output was approximately 150 cars a year and in 1914 the range was pruned to just 1.9- and 4-litre fours, which continued to be produced after the war. In 1918 the company entered into an arrangement with the aero engine maker Gnome et Rhône, which in the following year built its own car with advanced overhead-cam 40 hp six, of which only three were completed.

In 1921 Rolland-Pilain introduced 2.2-litre overhead-valve cars with four wheel brakes hydraulically actuated at the front and revived the sleeve-valve RP model. In 1922 came a 2-litre straight-eight racer that at last gave the marque more than a regional reputation. In 1923 the firm's standing was enhanced by an overhead-cam four-cylinder 2-litre sports/touring chassis. The Paris sales and repair department was kept busy at that time.

Rolland-Pilains took part in the Le Mans 24 Hour and other events in the mid-1920s. In 1928 a new 2-litre model, now with six cylinders, was introduced but in 1929 came American Continental six and eight-cylinder units. In 1930 Rolland-Pilain shared a Paris

Show stand with BNC and BNC-Lombard, following the acquisition of all three firms by Charles de Ricou. Production ended in 1931, although spares were still being offered from the Paris depot, which also handled BNC parts, in the mid-1930s.

Emile Pilain, who had left the company, launched a Pilain 5CV four-cylinder car in 1930 that was intended for mass production at Levallois-Perret. Although a 1.2-litre version was also built, sales were disappointing and the firm ceased production in about 1932. Nothing more was heard of it after 1935. Rolland ran a Citroën agency in Paris in the 1940s. NB

ROLLIN
USA 1923-1925

Rollin Henry White designed the White steam car of 1900 but after his father's death he left the family firm, where he had been a vice-president, in order to make farm machinery. His Cleveland Motor Plow Co, formed in early 1916, produced a roller-wheeled machine with power-rotated cutter blade. This machine was not a success but after a year the company was reorganized as the Cleveland Tractor Co and made the very popular Cletrac crawler tractors.

A factory of almost 10 acres (4 hectares) under one roof was occupied at Euclid Avenue, Cleveland, and it was there that car production was intended to take place after World War I. The car was to have been known as the Allyne-Zeder, named after its financial backer and designer respectively, Fred M. Zeder later designing the first Chrysler engines. These plans were abandoned in 1922, and instead James G. Heaslet, a former vice-president of Studebaker, was brought in to organize the Rollin Motors Co with $2 million capital. Several other Studebaker personnel

held key positions.

In the autumn of 1923 the Rollin came onto the market. The car used a version of the Cletrac's four-cylinder 2.4-litre engine with Salisbury axle and Muncie gearbox. It had compact dimensions and four wheel brakes and was promoted as the 'Thoroughbred of the Thoroughfare'. Sales exceeded 6000 in 1924 but the car could not compete on price against mass-produced sixes and production ended in 1925, when sales were about 2400.

The Cleveland Tractor Co – whose products were sold as Burford-Cletracs in Britain by H. G. Burford – was acquired by the Oliver Corporation in 1944, when Rollin H. White retired. He died aged 90 in 1962, two years after White Motors Corporation purchased the Oliver Corporation. NB

ROLLS-ROYCE
GB 1904 to date

Frederick Henry Royce was born in 1863, and after a poverty-stricken childhood obtained an apprenticeship at the Great Northern Railway Locomotive Works at Peterborough. Although he never completed this due to lack of money, it gave early encouragement to his mechanical talent, which was backed up by a period with an electricity supply company in London and Liverpool.

In 1884 with a partner, Ernest Claremont, he set up a very small company in Manchester, making electric bells. Initial capital of Royce & Co was £70, and activities were later extended to the manufacture of dynamos and electric cranes. A limited company was formed in 1894 and by 1899 the share capital was £30,000. Competition from cheaper foreign made cranes hit sales, however, and stimulated a new field of activity.

It was inconceivable that a man of Royce's mechanical interests would have ignored the motor car, and in 1903 he acquired a second-hand Decauville. He tinkered with this until he could improve it no more, then set to making his ideal car, which in fact owed a lot in its basic layout to the Decauville.

The first Royce car left the works on 1 April 1904. It had a 1.8-litre two-cylinder inlet-over-exhaust engine of remarkable silence, but without an effective selling agent it would probably have had little future. That agent was found in the person of the Hon Charles Stewart Rolls, who was introduced to Royce by one of Royce's partners, Henry Edmunds. Rolls ran a successful sales company in London, specializing in expensive foreign cars, but he was so taken with the little Royce that he offered to take the entire output of the company on condition that they should bear the name Rolls-Royce.

The two companies, C. S. Rolls & Co and Royce & Co Ltd, remained independent until March 1906, when Rolls-Royce Ltd was formed with capital of £60,000. Royce & Co continued as a separate organization, making electrical equipment until its closure in 1933.

The first production two-cylinder car was delivered in September 1904, and during 1905 three more models were added to the range, with three-, four- and six-cylinder engines. The six was not very popular due to crankshaft vibration, but Royce completely redesigned the engine and at the end of 1906 brought out the 40/50hp model which came to be known as the Silver Ghost after the individual name given to the 13th car built, which had many silver-plated fitments.

This car was the idea of Claude Goodman Johnson, a partner of Rolls who played a tremendous part in the success of the company due to his flair for publicity and his tactful handling of that irascible genius Henry Royce. Through Johnson's well publicized runs and trials with the Silver Ghost, the name Rolls-Royce soon became famous – and it was the Silver Ghost which earned the title 'The Best Car in the World', a slogan first used in company advertising in 1911.

By the end of 1907 Silver Ghost production was running at four chassis a week. Order books were full and it was decided to expand to larger premises. These were found at Derby where a modern factory was built on a 12½-acre (5-hectare) site. To finance this, capital was increased to £200,000; a shortfall of £10,000 was met by Arthur Briggs, who had been a long time admirer of Rolls-Royces and who was rewarded for his generosity with a seat on the board. At Derby, production of the Silver Ghost rose to seven chassis a week and remained at this level until 1914. The smaller models were all dropped.

Rolls was killed in a flying accident in July 1910. Six months later Royce became seriously ill and was warned by doctors that he should never return to the factory. Johnson saved the day by organizing Royce's life so that he kept in constant touch with the works from his homes in Sussex and the south of France.

During World War I Silver Ghost armoured cars and tenders earned the company a new kind of fame, especially at the hands of T. E. Lawrence (Lawrence of Arabia), but the most important effect of the war on Rolls-Royce was the company's entry into the aero engine business. In 1914 Johnson obtained a government contract to build a V8 engine of Renault design, but Royce was not impressed with this and within 12 months produced the first Rolls-Royce aero engine, the 225hp V12 Eagle. More than 4000 of these were made in four years. They powered such famous aircraft as the FE2d fighter, Vickers Vimy and Handley-Page 0400 bombers and Fairey IIIb seaplane.

Net profits rose from £77,000 in 1914 to £153,000 four years later. Unlike many companies Rolls-Royce did not suffer a post-Armistice relapse but went on to record greater profits of £193,000 in 1919 and £203,000 in 1920. Although it suffered a little in the 1921 recession, the company never

Rolls-Royce 40/50hp tourer ('The Silver Ghost') of 1907

recorded a loss from the time it was founded until the crash of 1971.

The most significant development of the 1920s was the introduction of the 20hp, nicknamed the Baby Rolls. Although frowned on by the purists, as such innovations always are, it brought Rolls-Royce motoring to a new market, not only those who could not afford a Silver Ghost but those who did not want an enormous car, or those who preferred to drive themselves.

Sales soon exceeded those of the larger Rolls-Royce and it is possible that without the Twenty, and its successors, the company would not have survived the Depression as a car-maker. Certainly, without the smaller cars on which to build a new programme there would have been no post-World War II Rolls-Royces. Traces of the engine design of 1922 could still be found in the last six-cylinder design of 1959.

The Silver Ghost was replaced in 1925 by the overhead-valve Phantom I, which lasted until 1929, and then by the Phantom II. The last 'senior Rolls-Royce' made in any numbers was the V12 Phantom III of 1936-39, of which 710 were built. In the same period 1692 small sixes, 25/30s and Wraiths were made, as well as about 1260 Bentleys.

Two developments of 1933 were the death of Sir Henry Royce – he had received a Baronetcy for the contribution Rolls-Royce aero engines made to winning the Schneider Trophy – and the introduction of the new Bentley, the 3½-litre 'Silent Sports Car'. Rolls-Royce had acquired the Bentley company in 1931, largely to frustrate the production by Napier of a dangerous rival. The new car, inevitably christened the Rolls-Bentley by the popular press, used a more powerful version of the Rolls-Royce 20/25 engine in a chassis that had been intended for the small 2¾-litre Rolls that never went beyond the prototype stage.

Rolls-Royce 25/30hp sedanca de ville of 1937

When the 20/25 was replaced in 1936 by the larger 25/30, the latter's engine went into the new Bentley 4¼-litre, which carried the company through to the outbreak of World War II. Although Bentley Motors (1931) Ltd remained separate in name, it was in fact a wholly owned subsidiary of Rolls-Royce and its cars were built alongside the Rolls-Royces at Derby.

Throughout this period Rolls-Royce supplied chassis only, but from the days of the Twenty onwards there were 'recommended' bodies by firms such as Barker and Park Ward which were built in small series to keep the price down. Before 1914 most components such as carburettors, fuel pumps and electrical equipment had been made by Rolls-Royce itself, as Henry Royce could not find any proprietary brands of sufficiently good design and quality, but gradually components were bought-in, especially for the smaller models, including by the 1930s Zenith-Stromberg carburettors, SU fuel pumps, Bijur starters and Lucas electrics.

The aero engine business had suffered an eclipse after World War I, so much so that it might have been closed altogether, but Royce persevered with the Kestrel and this led to the R-type V12 with which the R. J. Mitchell-designed Supermarine S6 seaplanes took the

Schneider Trophy in 1929 and 1931 as well as the world air speed record at 407.5mph (655.6kph).

These successes encouraged Mitchell in the development of the Spitfire fighter, which first flew in 1936 powered by a Rolls-Royce Merlin engine. Rolls-Royce aero engines were used in several cars which gained the land speed record for Britain, including Malcolm Campbell's Bluebirds which took the record several times, the last at 301.13mph (484.51kph) in 1935, and George Eyston's Thunderbolt which used two R-type engines totalling over 4000hp and achieved 357.5mph (575.2kph) in 1938.

With the approach of war in 1939 Merlin production was accelerated, the Derby factory was increased by 50 per cent and new factories were built at Crewe and Glasgow. In 1940 2000 Merlins were built and in 1943 18,000. In addition Ford's Manchester factory built 3000 in five years and Packard built 55,523 at Detroit. The Merlin powered North American Mustangs as well as Spitfires and Hurricanes and was also used in Cromwell and Challenger tanks.

The post-war cars, named Rolls-Royce Silver Wraith and Bentley Mark VI, were announced in 1946 and used an inlet-over-exhaust version of the pre-war 4¼-litre engine. For the first time a 'factory' body was offered, on the Mark VI chassis. This was a four-door saloon built by Pressed Steel and finished at Crewe, and it was later offered with a Rolls-Royce radiator as the Silver Dawn. The Silver Wraith continued to be available as a chassis only.

Important changes of the 1950s included GM-designed Hydramatic transmission in 1952 (the last manual transmissions were on the 1957 Bentley Continentals), power assisted steering in 1956 and a completely new 6.2-litre V8 engine in 1959. The Silver Wraith was replaced in 1959 by the long wheelbase Phantom V, which used the same engine and transmission as the smaller Silver Cloud and carried special coachwork by such firms as survived of the British coach-building industry, notably H. J. Mulliner, Park Ward and James Young.

Meanwhile Rolls-Royce had diversified into a number of other fields apart from aero engines. It developed a series of engines known as the B series made in four-, six- and eight-cylinder forms with identical dimensions and many components in common. They went into such diverse vehicles as the Austin Champ military Jeep (four-cylinder B40), Daimler Ferret Scout car and Humber FV 160 4×4 army truck (six-cylinder B60) and Dennis fire engines (eight-cylinder B80). The eight-cylinder engine was also used in the very limited production Phantom IV car, of which only 18 were made, mainly for heads of state. The whole range of Alvis 6×6 military vehicles were B80 powered as were the Thornycroft Nubian airfield firetenders.

In the passenger car field Rolls-Royce supplied modified versions of the B60 to the British Motor Corporation, which installed them in the Austin A110 four-door bodyshell and sold them under the name Vanden Plas Princess R. Made from 1964 to 1968, about 7000 were sold; they were the only passenger cars other than Rolls-Royce to use a Rolls-Royce built engine.

Separate from the B series, which were petrol-fuelled, is the range of diesel engines made from 1952 to the present day, originally at Derby and since 1957 at Shrewsbury in the factory where Sentinel steam and diesel lorries had been made. These have powered many well known British lorries such as ERF, Foden, Seddon-Atkinson, the South African and Australian Atkinsons, Rotinoff heavy road tractors, Canadian Hayes logging trucks, and Finnish Sisu trucks, as well as heavy earthmoving equipment, shunting engines and a variety of boats. Current production of diesel engines is around 11,000 a year in sizes from 100 to 1500hp.

The aero engine division went from strength to strength in the post-war era due to pioneering work on the jet engine. The most significant engines were the Avon, Dart, Conway, Tyne and Spey, which powered at least 40 important aircraft including such household names as the Comet, Viscount, Boeing 707 and BAC One-Eleven.

Net profits climbed from £184,000 in 1947 to over £2 million in 1954 and remained around the £2 million mark until 1970. The best year was 1968 with a net profit of £8,793,000.

In 1969 Rolls-Royce entered into a contract with the American Lockheed Corporation to supply RB211 engines for the Lockheed air- bus. In order to secure the contract in the face of strong competition from American aero engine makers, Rolls-Royce quoted what turned out to be an unrealistically low figure. Inflation and technical problems quickly increased development costs and the discrepancy between these and the expected return was so great that in November 1970 the company approached the government for aid. Rolls-Royce was advanced £42 million, but even this was not sufficient. Rolls-Royce shares which had stood at 54s 10d dropped to the derisory figure of 4½d.

Bankruptcy was followed by the formation of a new, nationalized company, Rolls-Royce (1971) Ltd, set up in February 1971. A new public company, Rolls-Royce Motors Ltd, was floated to look after car manufacture. It was headed by David Plastow, the young and very successful director of the former car division.

The separate chassis Silver Cloud had been replaced in 1966 by the integral construction Silver Shadow. Custom coachwork was now ended, but there were hardly any firms to do the work anyway.

In fact, H. J. Mulliner/Park Ward built coupé and convertible versions, christened Corniche in 1971, and demand for these cars boomed in the 1970s to such an extent that there was a four year waiting list and impatient customers were prepared to pay a premium of several thousand above the already high list price of £16,000. The temptation to increase production was resisted. It would have been difficult to boost output to a great extent anyway, because of restricted factory space and the limited number of sufficiently

Rolls-Royce Phantom VI of c.1984

Rolls-Royce Corniche convertible of c.1980

$2 million from a 7 per cent 15-year sinking fund, and a factory was bought from the American Wire Wheel Co at Springfield, Massachusetts.

Production of the Silver Ghost began in 1920, but no complete cars were ready for sale until February 1921. The first 25 chassis were identical to the British product, but locally made components were then increasingly used, including American Bosch magnetos, Bijur starters and Buffalo wheels. Bodies came mostly from local firms such as Smith of Springfield, Merrimac of Merrimac, Massachusetts, and Biddle & Smart of Amesbury, Mass. They were easily the most expensive cars made in America, costing an average of $14,500 in 1921, compared with $11,000 for a Locomobile 48 and $8550 for a Pierce-Arrow.

In 1923 Rolls-Royce of America set up its own bodybuilding department in Springfield, as many American customers expected to be able to order a complete car off the showroom floor. Custom bodies from any of America's leading coachbuilders were available to special order. In January 1926 Rolls-Royce of America bought Brewster & Co, one of America's oldest and finest coachbuilders, and thereafter most Springfield-built cars were bodied by Brewster.

Production at Springfield was slow to start, with only 135 chassis delivered in 1921 and

Rolls-Royce Camargue of c.1978

skilled craftsmen. Production did creep up in the 1970s, from 2009 to 3347 in 1978.

A new, even more expensive model was the Camargue, with Pininfarina styled body built at Crewe, which cost £10,000 more than a Corniche when introduced in 1975. This and the Shadow's successor, the Silver Spirit, made up the 1985 range, together with the built-to-order Phantom VI. The Camargue was dropped in 1986 after a run of 530.

The Bentley image fell to a low ebb in the 1970s with only 10 per cent of the cars carrying the Bentley radiator. In recent years it has been given a new identity, however, with the Mulsanne Turbo and Turbo R, turbocharged versions of the Silver Spirit.

In August 1980 Rolls-Royce Motors became a part of Vickers Ltd. George Fenn became head of the motor car group, succeeding David Plastow who moved up to become managing director of Vickers. The diesel, specialist engines and precision components divisions were separated from the affairs of Rolls-Royce Motors, becoming part of Vickers Engineering Equipment group. In December 1983 Vickers sold the diesel division to the Canadian tractor group, Massey-Ferguson.

The 1970s recession hit Rolls-Royce as it did other car manufacturers, and the workforce was trimmed by 10 per cent. Nevertheless, production was 3175 in 1981. The figure for 1984 was 2238, of which 279 were Bentleys. In August 1985 Rolls-Royce delivered its 100,000th car and in that year a total of 2551 cars were produced. GNG

418

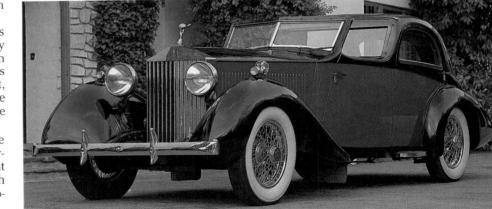

Rolls-Royce Phantom II coupé de ville (USA) of c.1930

ROLLS-ROYCE
USA 1919-1931

Rolls-Royce's American operation was the result of Claude Johnson's initiative and desire to expand the market for the Silver Ghost without incurring the penalty of heavy import duties. As the British government forbade the transfer of assets abroad, finance had to be raised in the United States, and this was provided by three wealthy individuals, investment bankers J. E. Aldred and Henry J. Fuller, the former being heir to the Gillette Razor fortune, and L. J. Belknap, a Canadian who had made a fortune building power stations. A total capital of nearly $6 million was raised,

230 in 1922. From 1923 to 1926 was the best period, deliveries averaging 325 to 365 each year. Profits were made every year from 1923 to 1928, although the purchase of Brewster for $202,500 was a strain on the 1926 balance sheet. Belknap resigned in April 1925 to become the successful head of Canadian Pulp & Paper Co, and his place as chairman was taken by Henry Fuller.

The Phantom I was introduced in England in May 1925, but it was a full year before retooling at Springfield was completed for production of the new model. Meanwhile, to keep customers happy, the company had to import Phantom I chassis from England on which it made little, if any, profit.

This marked the beginning of serious trouble for Rolls-Royce of America, but a much greater problem was presented by the Phantom II, introduced in England in September 1929. Springfield could not afford to retool for this substantially changed car, so it persuaded Derby to make 116 left hand drive Phantom II chassis, which were fitted with American bodywork. At the same time Springfield continued to assemble Phantom Is from existing stocks of components, this practice continuing until 1935, a year after the last left hand drive Phantom II had been shipped across the Atlantic.

In August 1934 Rolls-Royce of America, faced with bankruptcy, changed its name to the Springfield Manufacturing Corporation under pressure from Derby, which did not want to see the Rolls-Royce name tarnished by financial failure. In 1936 the assets of the company, apart from the Springfield plant, were sold to the Pierce-Arrow Sales Co of New York. The Springfield plant was divided into lots and sold in 1939. They realized $65,000 from a property whose original cost was $440,000. GNG

ROLUX
FRANCE 1938-1952

The Rolux minicar was made by P. Martin of Lyons, who was better known as the maker of New Map motorcycles. The New Map two-wheelers had been introduced in the early 1920s and were mostly assembled machines using JAP, Zürcher and several other makes of proprietary engines, ranging in size from 98 to 998cc. Martin also built 48cc New Map mopeds at this time, but the first Rolux car did not appear until 1938.

It was one of the first of the really small French minicars and had a rear-mounted air-cooled 125cc or 175cc single-cylinder engine in a very basic, doorless two-seater body. Commercial versions of the car were also made and Martin also offered three-wheeled light commercials.

The cars were sold under both the Rolux and New Map names and about 1000 were made, with peak sales in the austere years immediately after World War II. Car production was dropped in 1952 but Martin continued to build two-wheelers – a range of two- and four-stroke motorcycles mainly ranging from 98 to 248cc, plus a fully-enclosed scooter – and three-wheeled commercials until the late 1950s. BL

ROM CARMEL/SABRA
ISRAEL 1959-1981

The Israeli-built Rom Carmel was a continuation of the Sabra, Israel's first ever production car which was itself the first example of Reliant's 'package' motor industry for industrially developing countries. Autocars Co Ltd of Haifa was established in 1954 and ordered

100 three-wheeled vans in kit form from Reliant to assess the feasibility of local assembly and to test the durability of the design and materials, particularly the glassfibre body, under local conditions. The Reliant performed well and in 1959 Autocars ordered 500 kits for a new four-wheeled estate car, the Sussita, again to be assembled in Haifa, but now intended as the first stage in establishing a more permanent manufacturing operation.

This was Reliant's first four-wheeler design and used Ford Anglia engine and running gear in a Reliant-designed chassis and shell. As with later packages such as the Turkish Anadol, Reliant also helped to establish manufacturing, marketing and service operations while Autocars developed the local content.

Reliant delivered two more sets of 1000 kits each in 1960 and 1961 and Autocars even exported some station-wagon, pickup and van variants to the United States in 1960 although, predictably, very few were sold. In July 1960 Reliant offered Autocars an entirely different type of car, the Ford-powered Sabra sports car. Autocars, on behalf of Reliant, acquired licences from LMB and Ashley Laminates, which supplied the original chassis and bodies respectively, and the first Sabra was shown at the 1961 New York show. It went into production in Haifa shortly after, with a change from leaf to coil spring rear suspension – and gradually increasing local content. Reliant also introduced the car in Britain in 1962 as the Sabre.

Early in 1963 Autocars ordered 2800 further parts sets for various models (all of which now used Sabra as a marque name), worth about £575,000. These included the first 500 sets for a new saloon, based on the Sussita and called the Sabra Carmel FW3. The Carmel was also assembled in Greece as the Attica Carmel.

Reliant continued to supply components to Autocars until 1966, by which time production had reached about 60 cars a week, but ended its direct association in that year when Autocars signed an agreement with Leyland for supply of Triumph engines. Both Ford and Triumph engines were used until 1969, when the Triumph 1296cc unit became standard in the Carmel. In 1967 a new saloon, the Sabra Gilboa, was added to the range.

In 1974, when the workforce was about 600 and output was 1600 cars a year, Sabra production was taken over by Rom Carmel Industries, a member of the CLAL group, and the car became known as the Rom Carmel. In October 1977 Rom Carmel amalgamated with Urdan Industries Ltd, a private company founded in 1958 by L. Schindler and Y. Shubinski, but the cars continued to use the Rom name, on Triumph powered models, the Rom 1300 and Rom 1301 saloons.

By 1979 the workforce had been reduced to 400, although output was the same as in 1974. In 1980, however, it fell to only 540 cars and production stopped completely in 1981. BL

ROOTS & VENABLES
GB 1896-1904

Roots 5hp buggy of c.1900

James Dennis Roots was an inventor who started internal combustion engine experiments in 1884 and is said to have had an oil engine running in 1886-87. One was installed in a boat in 1890 and Roots subsequently made engines for H. E. Vosper, later associated with Thornycroft's marine business. In 1896 a Petrocar took to the road after a motor tricycle had been built which the inventor claimed to have run as early as 1892; engines are said to have been supplied to other car manufacturers from 1894.

Cuthbert Edward Venables helped Roots and was a fellow director of the Roots Oil Motor and Motor Car Co Ltd, formed in London in 1897 with a capital of £30,000. Roots was by then experimenting with model planes and helicopters and relied on BSA for many parts for the cars, which were assembled in London. His foreman in 1899, F. Hall Bramley, went on to a successful career in motor journalism, being technical editor of first *Cycle Trader* and then *The Auto*.

In October 1902 an agreement was reached for Sir W. G. Armstrong, Whitworth & Co to build the cars. Commander E. W. Lloyd, manager of Armstrong-Whitworth, joined the founders on the board of directors. C. R. F. Englebach, later a director of Austin, helped set up the Armstrong-Whitworth motor department, which in 1904 changed allegiance to the Wilson-Pilcher car, production of the Roots car being discontinued.

Much emphasis had been placed on the reduced risk of explosion from running the four-stroke Roots engine on lamp oil, and cars achieved success in reliability trials. J. D. Roots worked as a consulting engineer and patent specialist in London after halting car production. NB

ROSENGART
FRANCE 1928-1955

Born in 1881, Lucien Rosengart was a first rate publicist as well as engineer, and had a successful career in the motor industry long before he began to make cars under his own name. In 1909 he set up in Paris as a maker of screws and nuts, specifically for the motor

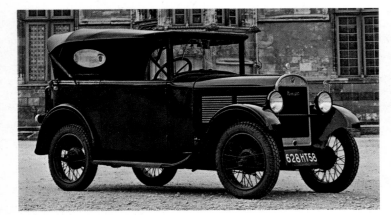

Rosengart LR5 torpedo of 1928

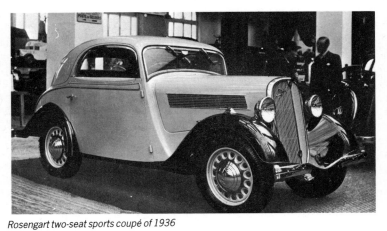

Rosengart two-seat sports coupé of 1936

industry, with a factory employing 60 workers. He was called up for military service in 1914 but was hastily demobilized so that he could supervise his factory on war work. Working closely with André Citroën he developed and manufactured a patent shell fuse; by 1918 his workforce numbered 4500.

After World War I Rosengart returned to making screws and bolts, but also pocket torches, assorted electrical gadgets and, in 1923, a motor attachment for bicycles. He helped Citroën over a financial crisis in 1919, forming the SADIF group to raise 20 million francs, and was rewarded with a seat on the Citroën board for several years.

From 1923 to 1926 he was 'commercial consultant' to Peugeot, while still running his screw factory. During his time at Peugeot he organized the purchase of the Bellanger and De Dion-Bouton factories, which led to a customized De Dion Model JP being sold briefly under the Bellanger name.

In 1928 Rosengart began making cars under his own name. His consulting engineer, Jules Salomon, who had designed the original Citroëns and the Le Zèbre, recommended a car the size of the Austin Seven, which would fill a gap recently vacated by Citroën and Peugeot. Rosengart therefore negotiated a licence agreement with Herbert Austin whereby the Seven would be manufactured in Rosengart's Paris factory. Initial capital was 10 million francs. Herbert Austin had a seat on the board as did representatives of Chenard-Walcker, with which Rosengart had a marketing agreement.

The first 100 cars were assembled from British parts, but thereafter they were 100 per cent French. The main differences were in styling; the Rosengarts had ribbon radiators from the start, and could never be confused with their British counterparts, as could the Dixi 3/15PS. The bodies were fabric or semi-panelled saloons and tourers, with a delivery van added in October 1928 and sports models offered from 1929.

Production began in March 1928 with optimistic forecasts of an output of 60,000 a year, but in fact it took two years for 11,000 to be made. In June 1930 production was running at 28 cars a day, probably the highest figure Rosengart ever reached. In 1931 he was said

to have 1500 agents throughout France, 250 in the Paris area alone.

In 1932 came a pint-sized six which bore the same relationship to the four as did the Wolseley Hornet to the Morris Minor – a lengthened bonnet and chassis but similar bodies. The engine of this LR6 was a 1097cc 25bhp side-valve unit. Rosengart is said to have got the idea because he saw a woman friend struggling with a Packard Eight, and could not understand why she should need such a monstrosity.

Also in 1932 Rosengart became attracted by front wheel drive, but as his factory was not suited to the production of a completely new design he went shopping across the Rhine and bought the rights to make the Adler Trumpf and Primus. These were made in small numbers up to 1935, with either German Ambi-Budd or French bodies. In 1935 only 167 front-drive cars were made out of a total of several thousand Rosengarts.

A new model for 1935 was the LR145 Dilux which used the 1645cc Adler engine driving the rear wheels, and French built bodies by SICAL which were close to the Adler's in appearance. The front-drive cars were given the name Supertraction, which was continued for the later Citroën-powered cars of 1938-39.

Rosengart continued with his 5CV Austin Seven based cars, which became increasingly Gallic in appearance, with pointed radiator grilles from 1936 and some quite elegant cabriolet bodies which figured in concours d'elegance. In 1939 it was the smallest and cheapest French car in regular production. Prices ran from 13,950 to 18,530 francs, compared with 20,900 francs for the Peugeot 202 or Renault Juvaquatre.

The small six with similar styling to the four was still available, and at the top of the range was the new Supertraction, a handsome saloon or cabriolet based on Citroën 11CV running gear. About 200 of these were made in 1939 out of a total of 5650 Rosengarts. Just before the outbreak of World War II, Lucien Rosengart acquired a licence to manufacture the German-designed Ganz minicar, but this came to nothing.

During the war Rosengart made some electric conversions of the 5CV which he called

the Electrirod, and at the 1946 Paris Salon he was back with a restyled version of the 5CV. He also showed an enlarged Supertraction powered by a 3.9-litre Mercury V8 and called the Super Trahuit, but only two of these were ever made. Like the pre-war versions they used a Citroën chassis and one was reputed to be powered by a 1934 Citroën 3.8-litre V8 engine.

Rosengart sold his company at the end of 1946 to a group called SIOP (Société Industrielle de l'Ouest Parisien) and retired to concentrate on inventions and painting. He died in 1976 at the age of 95.

SIOP brought out a new version of the 5CV in 1951. The Ariette had a modern-looking slabsided two-door saloon body and hydraulic brakes (at last), but it was still powered by the old 747cc side-valve engine whose 21bhp did not give it a very electrifying performance. At nearly twice the price of a 2CV Citroën it was no bargain either, and only 237 were sold in 1953.

For 1954 SIOP came up with the Sagaie, a slightly restyled Ariette now in fibreglass powered by a 748cc overhead-valve flat-twin CEME engine which was used in police motorcycles. This gave 40bhp and 74mph (119kph), but the sands had run out for the Rosengart and nobody wanted it. Some 200 Ariette bodies were sold to Panhard which fitted its own 850cc flat-twin engine and sold the result as the Panhard Starlet.

The final venture by SIOP was the Marathon coupé of 1954; this was the German Trippel with fibreglass body and rear-mounted 850cc Panhard engine. At most 50 were sold in 1954 and 1955. GNG

ROSSEL
FRANCE 1903-1926

F. Rossel was a director of Peugeot who struck out on his own in 1903, although he retained links with the company and entered into a joint venture to make aero engines in 1909. He acquired a factory in Sochaux, Doubs, where Peugeot was later to have one of its most important factories, and began production of a 22hp four-cylinder car with 'square' cylinder dimensions of 108×108mm (4¼×4¼in). This was followed in 1904 by a 22/26hp and 28/35hp, and by 1907 Rossel was listing five models from the 22/26 to a monstrous 60/80hp of 12 litres capacity.

Thoroughly conventional in layout, Rossel cars never became well-known, although in 1908 the business boasted agencies in Paris, Mulhouse, Lucerne and New York. The make was not introduced to the United Kingdom market until 1913, when Oylers Ltd of London advertised two small models of 8 and 12hp.

In 1909 Rossel went into partnership with a Monsieur Verdet, who had been both a designer and a racing driver for Lion-Peugeot, to make aero engines under the name Rossel-

Rossel coupé de ville of c.1915

Peugeot. The factory was in the Paris suburb of Suresnes. In 1910 it was announced that the famous Peugeot driver Jules Goux was testing a new aeroplane built by Rossel, but he seems generally to have been better-known for engines than complete aircraft. At the end of 1910 Rossel was making a seven-cylinder rotary radial engine developing 48hp.

The large chain-driven Rossels gave way to smaller shaft drive models in the years up to World War I, although the 7.4-litre 40hp chain-drive car was still listed in 1913. No fewer than seven models, from 1690 to 5516cc, were listed in the early 1920s but few were made, and there was no attempt at innovation. By 1926 the factory had been sold to Peugeot, which was already well-established in Sochaux, but Rossel production may have ceased a few years earlier. GNG

ROTHWELL
GB 1901-1916

Rothwell was founded in 1872 as Shephard, Rothwell and Hough. Hough became manager of Edison, for which company the Rothwell brothers Fred and Tom, who took over the partnership, made phonograph parts. The Rothwells' other products were sewing machines, bicycles and ticket punches. They had worked for sewing machine makers Bradbury and Co, later well known for motorcycles, and held all 50,000 £1 shares in the Eclipse Machine Co Ltd of Oldham that replaced the original Rothwell partnership.

In 1896 a Benz was examined, although prototype Rothwells actually owed more to Pennington, one of whose designs was sold to the Rothwells by a company promoter. The same entrepreneur also formed the Rothwell Machine Co in 1899 with £10,000, but the company collapsed in 1904.

Cars were sold from 1901 and were robustly made for local conditions and hills. Motorcycles and cycles were also produced. The cycle department manager, R. R. Eglin, subsequently set up a Ford dealership in Oldham in 1911.

Three Royce engineers were reported to be responsible for the design of early cars, although the only name recorded is that of A. J. Adams, who was hired in 1905 as designer and was responsible for some high grade coachwork, including a Roi-des-Belges type, built on the premises. Aster engines were used for cheaper models but the usual engine installed was designed by Adams. Nearly all parts were produced in-house. Cars were exported to India and South Africa but most of the 600 or so vehicles built, including commercials, remained in industrial Lancashire and Yorkshire.

The founding brothers, Fred and Tom Rothwell, died in 1914 and 1916 respectively. The last vehicles, including ambulances, were made in 1916. Although the founders' sons fulfilled wartime armaments contracts, vehicle production was not revived after World War I. The Viscount Street factory in Oldham later became a Co-op bakery. NB

ROVER
GB 1904 to date

Like Humber, Rover was a prominent name in the cycle industry for many years before motor car production began. Its origins date back to the foundation in 1861 of the Coventry Sewing Machine Co by James Starley (1830-81) and his partner Josiah Turner. In 1868 the company name was changed to Coventry Machinists Co Ltd so that manufacture could be extended to products other than sewing machines. These included French-designed velocipedes, and Starley made a number of suggestions about the improvement of these which were not received favourably by the conservative management of the Coventry Machinists Co Ltd.

In 1870 Starley left, taking with him his foreman William Hillman, and they set up to manufacture the bicycles with 54in (1.37m) front wheels, familiarly called Penny Farthings but properly known, then and now, as Ordinary bicycles. In 1876 they progressed to the Coventry Lever Tricycle and then to the four-wheeled Sociable tandem.

Meanwhile, Starley's nephew John Kemp Starley (1854-1901), who had worked with his uncle, left in 1877 to form his own company, Starley and Sutton, at the Meteor Works, West Orchard, Coventry. It was the first factory in Coventry to concentrate solely on building pedal cycles, and in 1884 they used the name Rover for the first time for their products.

The following year they brought out their Safety cycle which was one of the most significant machines in the history of transportation. By 1888 it had been refined into something quite close to the modern bicycle, with wheels of almost equal diameter, a diamond frame and geared up chain drive to the rear wheel.

William Sutton left the partnership in 1888, and the company was re-established as J. K. Starley & Co Ltd. The cycle boom was soon in full swing, and Starley was the leading Coventry manufacturer. He went public in 1896 with the formation of the Rover Cycle Co Ltd capitalized at £150,000. Production that year was about 11,000 bicycles.

As early as 1888 he had built an experimental battery-powered tricycle, and in 1897 he imported some Peugeot motorcycles to study the feasibility of making powered two-wheelers.

In October 1901 Starley died at the early age of 46, but work on motorcycles was already well advanced. Under the new managing director Harry Smith, the first 2¾hp Rover motorcycles were launched in November 1902, and 1250 were made before production was suspended in late 1905.

Meanwhile it was decided that Rover should join the ranks of other Coventry firms making motor cars, which included Daimler, Humber, Lea-Francis and Singer. Smith hired Edmund Lewis from Daimler to design a light

Rothwell ambulance of c.1912

Rover 8hp runabout of 1910

Rover 16hp saloon of c.1940

Rover P4 convertible of c.1955

car, which emerged in 1904 as the 8hp Rover.

The first Rover car was quite conventional in appearance with a front-mounted vertical 1327cc 8hp single-cylinder engine, but the chassis was unusual in being a steel backbone frame which contained the three-speed gearbox and to which the rear axle was bolted up rigidly. It was soon joined by a cheaper and simpler 780cc 6hp model, with conventional wood and flitchplate chassis and a normally sprung axle.

This cost £105, compared with £200 for the 8hp, and was the ancestor of a range of Rovers, the four-cylinder 16/20hp of 1905-10 and the two-cylinder 12hp (1908-10), both of which shared the 6hp's bore and stroke (95×110mm, later 97×110mm) piston, connecting rods and valve gear. Lewis left Rover to join Deasy at the end of 1905, but his designs persisted without major change until the arrival of Owen Clegg from Wolseley-Siddeley in 1910.

In 1906 the Rover Motor Co Ltd was formed with capital of £100,000. Car production that year was 754, together with almost 16,000 bicycles. The following year when capital was doubled the figures were 1211 and 20,100, and for 1910 883 and 10,858, plus 480 of the reintroduced Rover motorcycle.

Rover supported the Tourist Trophy races from 1905 to 1907 and in the latter year a 16/20 driven by Ernest Courtis won by more than 12 minutes. However, the company felt that racing was an easy way to squander profits, and Rovers were not seen on the racetracks again until the 1960s.

A few 8hp singles and 12hp twins with Knight sleeve-valve engines were made from 1911 to 1912, but the next important design was the Clegg-designed Twelve, an L-head monobloc four which was made with little change from 1912 to 1924. There was also a less popular Eighteen on similar lines, 150 of which were made in 1912 and 1913. The Twelve was a resounding success, and boosted sales from 883 cars in 1911 to 1943 in 1914, and profits from £7100 to £137,000 over the same period. Unfortunately Clegg did not stay to follow up his success, as he was 'poached' by Darracq to design rather similar, and equally successful, 12 and 16hp cars.

Two-wheeler production was separated

from the cars in 1912, and continued until 1923 for bicycles and 1925 for motorcycles. By the time manufacture ceased Rover had made 426,530 bicycles since 1896 and 10,401 motorcycles.

Rover's wartime production was diverse, including Stokes mortars, gas shells, fuses and other items which were made until some satisfactory vehicle contracts could be secured. These included Maudslay 3-ton lorries, of which Rover built 200, and Sunbeam 16hp staff cars, of which 1781 were Rover made. The New Rover Cycle Co Ltd made over 3000 motorcycles during World War I, many of which went to Russia.

Clegg's successor was Mark Wild, who wisely made little change to the excellent Twelve, either before or after the war, although the cylinder head was detachable from 1919 onwards. Wild was more of an administrator than a designer, and when Rover's management decided to enter the light car market they acquired the design of an 8hp air-cooled flat twin which had been devised by Jack Sangster. For the manufacture of this they bought an ex-munitions factory at Tyseley, Birmingham, where the chassis were to be made and delivered to the Meteor Works at Coventry for bodies to be fitted.

The 998cc 14bhp Eight was made from 1920 to 1925 and sold about 17,000 in two-seater, four-seater, closed coupé and delivery van versions. Sangster left Rover in 1922 to become assistant managing director of Ariel motorcycles, and later became chairman of BSA. The following year Harry Smith resigned, to be replaced by J. K. Starley Jr.

Production fluctuated in the 1920s, from 1400 in 1920 to around 6000 for several years, dropping to 3766 in 1928. Two lines of development were followed, the light car typified by the Eight and its successors the water-cooled four-cylinder 9/20 (1924-27) and 10/25 (1928-33), and the solid, middle sized 14/45 (1925-27) and 16/50 (1926-28).

These were designed by Norwegian-born Peter Poppe of the White & Poppe engine company which supplied William Morris with his first power units. The engine was an interesting design with hemispherical combustion chambers, inclined overhead valves and a worm gear-driven overhead camshaft

mounted in the cylinder head. This should have been a recipe for high performance, but its 45bhp was disappointing and when mounted in a heavy chassis and body, performance was by no means exciting.

An increase of cylinder bore to give 2413cc in the 16/50 was little help, and the cars were dropped in 1928 after fewer than 2000 had been made. Poppe then designed a simpler side-valve six known as the 2-litre which was made from 1928 to 1934, but although it was an improvement on the overhead-cam fours it was not enough to save the company.

No dividends had been paid since 1923 and there were serious losses in 1925-26 (£123,450) and 1926-27 (£77,945). A shareholders' action committee was set up, and two of its members joined the board in 1928. They appointed Colonel Frank Searle as joint managing director (with J. K. Starley), and although Searle was without motor industry experience, he made a very wise decision in appointing as general manager Spencer B. Wilks who had run Hillman until the Rootes takeover in 1927.

Wilks joined Rover in September 1929, and became managing director in 1933. It is no exaggeration to say that Wilks saved Rover from the oblivion which was afflicting many old established British companies at this time.

Wilks's first act was to hire ex-Hillman engineer Major B. Thomas to design a new small six to come between the 10/25 and the 2-litre six. This was the 1410cc Pilot which only lasted for two years but which gave rise to a line of small six-cylinder Rovers made until 1938.

422

Wilks authorized a line of high-quality middle-class cars with such features as clutchless gearchange with a freewheel (from 1933) and luxurious leather and wood trimmed interiors. The expensive Weymann fabric bodies gave way to Pressed Steel coachwork, and one Rover, the 10 Special, shared body panels with the Hillman Minx. Spencer Wilks's brother Maurice was in charge of engineering from 1931 to 1957, and with Robert Boyle was responsible for the excellent 10, 12, 14, 16 and 20hp cars of the 1930s which established Rover's reputation for years to come.

The Frank Searle-inspired rear-engined two-cylinder Scarab of 1931 was quickly abandoned before it reached the market place, and sporting models received little attention although there were a few Speed Pilots and Speed Meteors which did well in rallies and concours d'elegance of period.

The Wilks era saw production rise from 4960 cars in 1933 to 11,103 in 1939; net profits over the same period went up from £7511 to £205,957. Factories were rationalized. The old Meteor Works, which John Starley had erected in 1877 but which had been seriously under utilized since two-wheeler production ceased, were sold in 1932 and production concentrated at the Helen Street, Coventry, premises which were renamed the New Meteor Works. Tyseley was retained for engine and gearbox manufacture.

In 1936 Rover was invited to join other manufacturers in the Air Ministry's shadow factory scheme. This involved the setting up

return the Meteor tank engine. Various eight-cylinder (Meteorite) and 12-cylinder (Meteor) versions of this were built until 1964 and were used in Conqueror and Centurion tanks as well as in the Thornycroft Mighty Antar heavy truck.

In 1945 the New Meteor Works were sold and car production concentrated at the Solihull shadow factory. The first post-war cars came off the line in December 1945; they were the pre-war P2 saloons in 10, 12, 14 and 16hp form, and were made until 1948 when they were replaced by the P3 'halfway modernized' cars.

These were similar in appearance to the P2s, but had new inlet-over-exhaust engines of 1595cc (four cylinders) or 2103cc (six cylinders), and coil independent front suspension. They were known as the 60 and 75, starting a tradition of numbering models by their approximate brake horsepower which lasted into the 1960s.

The same engines were used in the completely restyled P4 series of 1949, which owed much to Raymond Loewy's 1946 Studebaker, and which had a cyclop's eye central head-lamp on the early models. The P4's shape became known as the 'Auntie Rover' because it was thought to be the sort of car your maiden aunt drove, although far more must have been driven by doctors, solicitors and businessmen. The basic shape survived, with various engine changes, until 1964, by which date more than 130,000 had been made.

Meanwhile Rover entered a new field with the Land Rover 4×4 utility vehicle on Jeep lines, which was launched in April 1948. It

was thought up by Maurice Wilks, who was annoyed that he had to use a foreign made Jeep on his Anglesey estate, and was designed by Gordon Bashford.

The engine was the 1.6-litre P3 unit, and aluminium alloy was used for the simple panelling to get round Rover's small steel allocation. This was based on past export performance, a field which Rover had sadly neglected.

Although initially thought of as a stop gap to make use of idle factory space, the Land Rover proved very successful. In the year 1949-50 8000 were sold, compared with 5709 cars, and its sales continued to exceed those of the passenger cars up to the introduction of the 2000 in 1963. The half millionth Land Rover was built in April 1966, and the one millionth 10 years later. A diesel version came in 1957, and a forward control truck was made from 1962 to 1972 (military versions to 1977).

Rover's other pioneering post-war work was in the field of gas turbine engines. In 1950 it demonstrated the world's first gas turbine powered car, a two-seater based on the P4. Later versions included a P4 saloon (T2A), a purpose built 4×4 coupé of 1956 (T3), a front-wheel-drive saloon (T4) of 1962, and a competition car built in collaboration with BRM which ran at Le Mans in 1963 and 1965.

None of these was produced for sale, but a separate company, Rover Gas Turbines Ltd, was set up in 1953 to specialize in emergency generators, fire pumps etc. It was responsible for the later gas turbine cars and for the ex-

Rover 3-litre P5 of c.1962

Rover P6 2000 of c.1970

of large factories with experienced personnel to manufacture aero engines in the shadow of the existing aero engine industry, which did not have the facilities to cope with greatly increased production. Rover's contributions were the factories at Acocks Green near Tyseley (1936) and at Solihull (1939-40).

These made components for Bristol aero engines, but Rover was later involved in the development of Frank Whittle's jet engine. This and the manufacture of Armstrong-Siddeley Cheetah engines took place at Barnoldswick, Yorkshire, and Clitheroe, Lancashire, but in 1943 Rover swapped the jet engine project with Rolls-Royce, receiving in

Rover SD1 2600 of c.1984

Range Rover four-door of 1986

perimental turbine-powered Leyland trucks of 1968.

In 1959 the P4 was joined by the larger P5 with 3-litre engine and integral construction, and in 1963 Rover entered the 2-litre executive market with the P6 2000, designed by Maurice Wilks's nephew Peter. This had a unitary overall frame but unstressed panels and a De Dion rear axle. In 1968 it was made available with the Buick-designed 3½-litre aluminium alloy V8 engine as the P6 3500, and continued until 1976. Total production of all P6s was 327,208. The P6 was made in a new, highly automated factory at Solihull, and a new component factory was opened at Pengam, Cardiff, in 1962.

Spencer Wilks, who had been chairman since 1957, retired in 1962 in favour of his younger brother Maurice, but the latter's occupancy of the post was brief as he died suddenly in September 1963, to be succeeded by George Farmer. Spencer Wilks died in 1971. Engineering was in the hands of Peter Wilks from 1964 to 1971, when he was succeeded by Spencer King.

In July 1965 Rover bought the Alvis company for its military vehicles, and in March 1967 it was itself acquired by Leyland for £20 million. Less than a year later the Leyland group merged with the British Motor Corporation to form British Motor Holdings, later to become British Leyland.

In 1970 came the 4×4 Range Rover, a much more luxurious vehicle than the Land Rover, but still with excellent cross-country performance, powered by the 3½-litre V8 engine which had also been used in versions of the P5 and P6, and which would be an option in the Land Rover from 1979 onwards. It was also used by Morgan from 1968 and by TVR from 1983.

The current range of Rover cars emerged in 1976 with the David Bache-styled SD1 saloon

Land Rover short-wheelbase hard top of c.1980

powered by the V8 engine. It was built in a new 23-acre (9-hectare) £31 million factory at Solihull employing 3200 people and capable of building 240 cars a day. Total Rover workforce at that time was 10,600. All other Rover car models were dropped, but in 1978 six-cylinder engines of 2.3 or 2.6 litres became available in the SD1 body shell, joined in 1982 by a four-cylinder 2-litre Leyland O Series engine and an Italian-built VM 2.4-litre four-cylinder turbocharged diesel.

In 1981 car production left Solihull for the Morris plant at Cowley under the control of the newly formed BL subsidiary, Austin Rover Ltd. Two years later Land Rover Ltd, established in 1975, took over the entire Solihull site, closing most of its other sites in Birmingham and Wales.

The latest cars to bear the Rover names are the Honda Ballade-based 213/216, a 1.3 or 1.6-litre four-cylinder saloon which was introduced in 1984 to replace the Triumph Acclaim in the Austin Rover line-up, and the Honda-developed 800 series powered by a British-built 2-litre four or a Honda 2½-litre V6 engine. Introduced in the summer of 1986 these replaced the SD1 models.

The SD1 is now made in India by Standard Motor Products of Madras, using a locally built 2-litre four-cylinder engine. GNG/NB

ROVIN
FRANCE 1946-1954

The Rovin was the most successful of the crop of mini cars which appeared at the first post-war Paris Salon in 1946, and the only one to survive into the 1950s. It was built by Robert de Rovin who, with his brother Raoul, had made motorcycles from 1920 to 1932, and also a few cyclecars which they raced.

Made in the Delaunay-Belleville factory at St Denis, the first Rovin resembled a child's pedal car, with a rear-mounted single-cylinder 260cc engine and a single headlight. This model never went into production, but the following year's Salon saw a similar looking model with twin headlights and a 425cc flat-twin engine. About 380 of these were made during 1948.

In October of that year came the D3 with wider body that had lost the pedal car look. At 192,640 francs (about £200) it undercut the Citroën 2CV at 235,000 francs, but its 43mph (69kph) maximum was even slower than the Citroën and it was much less roomy. Nevertheless de Rovin sold 527 D3s in 1949, 395 in 1950, 387 in 1951, and 422 in 1952. Thereafter sales slumped, despite the attraction of an enlarged engine of 462cc and a 53mph (85kph) top speed. Only 115 cars were sold in 1953, and although the car was theoretically still available in 1959, it is doubtful if any were made after 1954. Unlike any of its rivals such as the Julien or Bernadet, Rovin did have an export market of sorts, with representatives in Belgium and Switzerland. GNG

ROYAL ENFIELD
see Enfield (GB)

ROYAL STAR
see Sava

ROYAL TOURIST
USA 1904-1911

In November 1903 the Cleveland-based Hoffman Automobile Co was purchased by Edward D. Shurmer, who reorganized it as the Royal Motor Car Co and launched a new car named the Royal Tourist. It was a two-cylinder 16-18hp with a rear entrance tonneau body and was joined soon afterwards by a four-cylinder 32-35hp car selling for $3000 to $3375.

The company built up a reputation for making one of the best quality cars in America and adopted the slogan 'The Good of the Old – the Best of the New'. Sporting ventures in the 1904 and 1905 Vanderbilt Cup races did not bring any glory, but sales held up,

Rover Sterling saloon of 1986

Rumpler 'tear drop' car of 1921

reaching 250 in 1905 and 500 the following year.

Only four-cylinder cars were made in 1906, when capital was increased from $200,000 to $500,000 and the company name was changed to Royal Motor Car and Manufacturing Co. A new factory, employing 400 men, was acquired in September 1907, but soon afterwards the recession hit Royal Tourist and the new company went into receivership. It bounced back with a new name, the Royal Tourist Car Co and a new president, George J. Denham, who had been the company's Boston agent. More luxurious cars priced at up to $5700 were built in 1909. During that year the company introduced a horn placed at the centre of the steering wheel, with the horn itself under the bonnet, said to be the first example of this layout in America.

In March 1911 Royal Tourist merged with the Croxton Motor Car Co of Cleveland and the Acme Body and Veneer Co of Rahway, New Jersey, to form the Consolidated Motor Car Co, but later in the year the merger was dissolved. Croxton remained in business for about 18 months in Washington, Pennsylvania, but the Royal Tourist was discontinued. GNG

RUMPLER
GERMANY 1921-1926

Dr Edmund Rumpler, born in 1872 in Vienna, was a consultant designer of petrol and electric cars and trucks in Berlin from about 1907. He also had an Austrian office in Vienna. He had worked on the first Nesselsdorfs and then for Allgemeine Motorwagen-Gesellschaft after 1898, where he assisted the Daimler partners. At Adler he invented swing-axle suspension in 1903 and in 1906 left to start a specialist welding company. From this in 1909 grew an aircraft firm, Rumpler Luftfahrzeugbau, which built aero engines and the Etrick Taube glider.

Rumpler's remarkable 'tear drop' car was patented in 1919 and built under his own name in Berlin for some five years from 1921. Its rear-mounted 2580cc engine, made by Siemens and Halske, had three banks of two cylinders with in-unit gearbox and swing axles. A perimeter frame of pressed steel fol-

lowed the shape of the bodywork, and the driving position was central. Later examples had four-cylinder 2.6-litre engines but the concept was too advanced to achieve commercial success and teething troubles abounded. Nevertheless, several were sold on hire purchase as eye-catching taxis in Berlin.

Benz used some of the patents for racing and sports cars, but the Rumpler was intended as a windcheating and efficient open or closed touring car. Final front-wheel-drive Rumplers in the mid-1920s did not get beyond the prototype stage.

Rumpler Vorntrieb GmbH made front-wheel-drive commercial vehicles with air brakes, all-round independent suspension and engine ahead of the front wheels. They were produced between 1926 and 1931 but few were sold. Henschel built a railcar using Rumpler patents. Dr Rumpler died in 1940. NB

RUSSELL/IVANHOE
CANADA 1903-1916

At the turn of the century, as the motor car swept America, over the border in Canada motoring was taking off rather more slowly. The first cars had not been seen until around 1897 and the first Canadian production did not begin until 1900. With dreadful roads, no garages for petrol supplies and an understandable shortage of practised motor mechanics, the car was a poor alternative to the horse. In Ontario in 1903 cars were still limited to 7mph (11kph) within 100 yards (90m) of a horse, and the few motorists who did appear on the streets were frequently attacked both verbally and physically by horse riders, but some companies already looked ahead.

The Canada Cycle and Motor Co Ltd was founded in Toronto in 1899. At first it built bicycles but by 1900 was also making a few De Dion-engined tricycles and quadricycles, and some early bicycle-frame type Locomobile steamers, through its subsidiary, the National Cycle Co.

From 1903 to 1905 the company also built the Ivanhoe electric car, designed by Hiram Percy Maxim, the inventor son of the man

who invented the machine gun. Maxim Jr had previously put both petrol and electric power into bicycle type frames for the Pope Manufacturing Co in the United States which were sold as the Waverley. The chain-drive Ivanhoe used a Westinghouse motor and batteries over the front and rear axles.

By 1905 the company had dropped the Ivanhoe and turned its attention to petrol cars with the first two-cylinder Russell model, which took its name from T. A. Russell, then Canada Cycle and Motor Co's general manager. The Russell established a reputation for quality and achieved considerable sales success. It was advertised as 'made up to a standard, not down to a price'.

In 1906, when a four-cylinder range was added, a Model A 12hp tourer cost $1300, a Model B 16hp tourer was $1500 and the Model C 24hp de luxe tourer was $2500. On the early cars a speedometer, obviously not a high priority on Canada's restricted roads, was a $22 option and for $3 the owner could have his monogram painted on the doors.

Russells gradually grew bigger and in 1909 the Canada Cycle and Motor Co Ltd obtained sole Canadian rights to the smooth and silent Knight sleeve-valve engine. The Knight, designed by Charles Yale Knight, had been used briefly and not very successfully in the Chicago-built Silent Knight, but Russell was the first North American make to use it in any numbers, in the same year that Daimler adopted it in England and prompted its future popularity.

The Knight-engined Russell was a very good car and in spite of a $5000 price tag sold very well for a couple of years. In 1912 the car side of the company became the Russell Motor Car Co Ltd, still in Toronto and with agents in Montreal, Hamilton, Calgary, Vancouver, Winnipeg and even Melbourne in Australia. In 1913, however, the company hit mechanical and production problems with a new four- and six-cylinder Knight-engined range and ran into financial difficulties.

Looking for volume sales Russell reverted in 1915 to a conventional six-cylinder model at $1750, having sold the Canadian rights to the Knight engine to Willys-Overland, which in 1914 had taken over the New York built Edwards-Knight as the Willys-Knight. Russell showed some signs of recovery but stopped production in 1916 and never restarted. BL

RUSSO-BALTIC
RUSSIA 1908-1915

Russo-Baltic Model K tourer of 1912

The Russko Baltiskij Vaggonij Zavod (Russo-Baltic Waggon Works) was an old established private company making railway rolling stock in Riga, today the capital of Latvia, one of the Soviet Socialist Republics, but then an integral part of Imperial Russia. In December 1905 the directors of Russo-Baltic decided to enter the motor industry and 'borrowed' a 23-year-old Swiss engineer, Julien Potterat, who was working for the Belgian Fondu company. Like Russo-Baltic, Fondu built railway waggons and had recently gone into car manufacture, making a 24/30hp four-cylinder car with pair-cast cylinders designed by Potterat.

It took three years to get a Russo-Baltic car into production, for Potterat had to find local sources of machine tools, material for chassis and bodies, and gather a suitably skilled team of workers. Although the design was Belgian, no part of the car was made outside Russia. Tyres were made by Provodnik, which was sufficiently well known to export tyres to Britain and the United States.

Production was very small at first, only 10 cars being made each year in 1909 and 1910, rising to 33 in 1911 and 78 in 1912. An improved version of the Potterat design was made until 1915, and Potterat also produced other cars for Russo-Baltic before leaving in 1912 to supervise the manufacture of an abortive car in Odessa. His later designs included a smaller car with L-head monobloc engine of 2.2 litres, the Model K 12/24hp made from 1911 to 1915, and a few heavy chain-driven trucks.

In 1911 the Russo-Baltic directors called in another foreign designer, Dr Ernst Valentin of the German Richard & Hering company, which made the highly regarded Rex-Simplex. His design was much larger than Potterat's, being a 40/60hp 7.2-litre T-head engine which powered a car often carrying six to eight seater bodywork. Not many were made and it did not survive the 1912 season.

Production of the smaller Russo-Baltics was building up, with 150 delivered in 1913 and the same number in 1914, while 90 were made in the first half of 1915 before Riga was evacuated in the face of the invading German army. Russo-Baltic also made aero engines for Sikorsky biplanes, and cars never occupied more than 10 per cent of the total workforce of 8000.

The make was quite successful in sport, winning the 1910 Czar's Cup against strong foreign opposition and gaining the Coupe d'Endurance in the 1912 Monte Carlo Rally. No Russo-Baltics as such were made after World War I, but the Moscow-built Prombron C-24/40 of 1922-23 used Russo-Baltic components, as did the Penza cars made at Serpukov in 1925. GNG

RUSTON-HORNSBY
GB 1919-1924

Ruston and Hornsby Ltd was created in September 1918 from Ruston Proctor and Richard Hornsby, agricultural engineering firms of Lincolnshire that had been founded in 1840 and 1815 respectively. By 1877 Hornsby had 17 acres (7 hectares) of factory at Grantham and a workforce of 1450 men. The company was a pioneer of oil engines in the 1890s – one lit the Statue of Liberty – and tracked vehicles in the early years of this century.

The Ruston company of Lincoln employed 2550 men in 1900 and by then had built 20,000 steam engines. Like Hornsby it was to become famous for oil engines. By 1911 Ruston had built a total of 37,000 boilers, 5500 pumps, 42,800 engines, 600 excavators and 24,000 threshers. During World War I the company built 2750 aircraft, 35,000 carts, 440 Holt crawler tractors and 3200 engines.

Under managing director George Ruston Sharpley, the combined Ruston and Hornsby had £2.1 million capital and a workforce of 13,000. As work was urgently needed to keep the aircraft carpenters busy the company mass-produced furniture and it also manufactured van bodies.

In 1919 the Ruston-Hornsby car was developed. This 2.5-litre four was a large American-inspired machine with centre gear change. In 1920 a 3.3-litre four was offered. Most British sales were handled by the London agency of C. B. Wardman, which had links with Bean and the British Motor Trading Corporation. Ruston-Hornsbys also found particular favour in Australia.

The post-war slump enforced drastic economies on the company. The workforce fell by nearly two thirds and car production was axed in 1924, the 16hp models having used Dorman engines.

More successful was its creation of the Aveling-Barford earthmoving machinery firm at Grantham from the previously separate companies Barford and Perkins and Aveling and Porter. Ruston and Hornsby took a 25-year controlling interest in the steam and agricultural engineering company Ransomes, Sims and Jefferies (for which it made boilers), and acquired the Bucyrus excavator licence from the United States in 1930.

Profits eventually returned in 1935. The Paxman engine firm was bought in 1940 and tanks, engines, generators and other equipment were produced during World War II. Work began on gas turbines in 1945. Generators, locomotives, excavators and diesels now account for most of the output of the company, which forms part of the GEC group. NB

RUXTON
USA 1929-1930

Considering its short life the Ruxton had a very complex history with production being divided between two old established car-makers, and involving the downfall of both. It was designed by William J. Muller, an engineer with the Edward G. Budd Co in Phila-

Ruston-Hornsby tourer of c.1920

Ruxton eight-cylinder saloon of 1929

delphia, a well-known bodybuilding firm. It was a strikingly low four-door sedan – the prototype had a Studebaker engine and front wheel drive – and when completed in the autumn of 1928 it had no name; indeed the radiator mascot carried a question mark.

One of the Budd directors was entrepreneur Archie M. Andrews, who formed New Era Motors Inc in April 1929 to manufacture the car. His partners included Muller, C. Harold Wills, who had recently made the Wills Sainte Claire car, Frederick W. Gardner of the Gardner Motor company, and stockbroker William V. C. Ruxton, from whom the car got its name.

New Era Motors had $5 million in preferred stock, but no factory, and there began a hunt for manufacturing premises which took more than a year to find. Approaches were made to Hupp, Peerless, Gardner and Marmon, with little or no response; there was talk of making Ruxtons at the Sunbeam factory in Wolverhampton, but this came to nothing.

In April 1930 New Era gained control of Moon, and two months later the Ruxton went into production in Moon's St Louis, Missouri, factory. The engine was now a 4.4-litre six-cylinder Continental 18S; transmission was built by Kissel, and bodies came from Budd (sedans), Baker-Raulang (roadsters) and Kissel (phaetons, of which only two were made).

About 450 Ruxtons were assembled by Moon before Kissel went into voluntary receivership in September 1930. This halted the supply of transmissions, which were the most complex part of the car, and the already shaky Moon company went into receivership itself, closing its doors on 10 November. The receiver assembled 15 more Ruxtons, but they did not sell easily and eventually went for $350 each, compared with a list price of $3195.

Andrews later became board chairman of the Hupp Corporation, but after being involved in a controversial and bitter wrangle with stockholders was forced to resign. He died in 1938 at the age of 59. Muller had a very successful career in aviation, railroads and marine landing craft. GNG

RYKNIELD/ACE, BAGULEY, SALMON
GB 1903-1906; 1911-1921

Ryknield 9hp tonneau of 1903

Named after the Roman Road that passes through the brewery town of Burton on Trent, the Ryknield Engine Co was formed on a 6½ acre (2.6 hectare) site in February 1902 with a capital of £30,000. The business was run by Ernest Edwin Baguley, born in 1863, who had been apprenticed at loco builder Hawthorne, Leslie and then moved to Bagnalls at Stafford in 1890; the chairman, A. Clay, was a director of the Bass brewery.

Most of the vehicles produced were heavy lorries for the brewery trade, but cars were also made. Car production did not reach the 150 a week initially forecast, and 100 at most were sold in the first year. When the firm collapsed in 1906 car production ceased, soon after two Belsize-Ryknield buses had been supplied to Leeds. Although the Ryknield Motor Co, also capitalized at £30,000, continued to make commercials, E. E. Baguley left the company and later designed BSA's first cars.

Financial disaster hit Ryknield again in 1910 when its 150 workforce was paid off by managing director W. H. Clay after about 350 Ryknields had been made, including the first of a batch of 40 buses for Brussels. Designer P. Salmon subsequently formed the Salmon Motor Co to make Ace light cars.

In March 1911 Baguley formed Baguley Cars Ltd with £30,000 capital to take over

Ryknield's works and hired about 200 men, including W. L. Fisher who was later to be editor of *Automobile Engineer*. In 1915 the Salmon Motor Co, which had gone into voluntary liquidation, was taken over.

Baguley made 15/20hp cars, including high-clearance models for the Argentine, plus a very few Salmons. Railcars and petrol locomotives soon became the main business. Just 88 Baguley cars were made in all, the final ones being built in 1921. Baguley, which later built Drewry railcars, exists today as Baguley-Drewry Ltd. NB

Rytecraft Scootacar of 1935

RYTECRAFT
GB 1934-1940

The Rytecraft Scootacar, the roadgoing version of which was introduced by the British Motor Boat Manufacturing Co Ltd of central London in 1934, was one of motoring's more bizarre creations. The tiny 15mph (24kph) single-seater came in many guises, as a runabout, a small delivery van (the Scootatruck), a shopping car, a children's toy and even as a fairground dodgem – in which role a fleet of 15 was said to be able to earn £90 a day in the 1930s, when the roadgoing Scootacar cost only £70.

The Scootacar was basic in the extreme. The first road cars used a 98cc Villiers two-stroke engine with a centrifugal clutch and single speed drive to one rear wheel. The chassis comprised two side rails and two cross-members held together with U-bolts. It eschewed suspension and made do with balloon tyres. The single control pedal was pushed down for the throttle and lifted for the single band brake on the undriven rear wheel.

A good number of Scootacars were used with special bodywork for advertising and promotion, and between 1965 and 1966 a 1935 model originally registered to the Carreras tobacco company as 'an open two-seater with cigarette-box attachment' was driven round the world. Later models were better equipped, some having two-seater bodies, electric lights and a 250cc Villiers engine with three-speed gearbox, but production stopped in 1940. BL

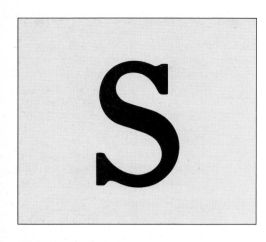

S & S
see Sayers

SAAB
SWEDEN 1950 to date

Svenska Aeroplan AB was incorporated in April 1937 as a state-backed national aircraft company to build aeroplanes for defence. Financial help also came from banker Marcus Wallenberg and refrigerator pioneer Axel Wennergren. A factory was built at Trollhattan on the west coast of Sweden, and in 1939 the company took over another aircraft plant at Linköping, 180 miles (290km) south of Stockholm.

After several years of licence production of American and German designs, Saab built its first independent design, the Model 17 two-seater dive bomber, in 1940. It later developed many other successful and pioneering aeroplanes, including western Europe's first swept wing jet fighter, the Saab 21.

At the end of World War II it was decided to diversify into other fields and a car department was set up under Gunnar Ljungstrom, who had worked in England for Standard and Rover before joining Saab in 1937. His car, called Project 92, had a 764cc vertical twin two-stroke engine driving the front wheels and was to some extent inspired by the pre-war DKW, which sold very well in Sweden. Ljungstrom insisted on an all-steel body, however, and stylist Sixten Sason came up with a streamlined design which resembled an aircraft wing in section.

The prototype 92 was running by June 1947 and differed only slightly from Sason's original design. Production began in 1950 and within two weeks a 25-year-old Saab engineer, Rolf Melde, won the Swedish Winter Rally in a 92 – the start of what was to become a tremendously successful rally career for the new make.

Only 1246 cars were made in 1950, but once the make became known sales grew, and by March 1954 some 10,000 Saabs had been sold. There was only one body style, the aerodynamic two-door saloon, until the appearance of the 95 estate car in 1959. A new factory was opened in 1954 at Gothenburg, where all engine and transmission assembly took place.

In 1956 the 92 was replaced by the 93, which had a three-cylinder two-stroke engine of 748cc in a similar body but now with a vertical radiator grille. This was the first Saab to be exported in any numbers, deliveries to the United States beginning in 1956. It was followed by the 96 with 841cc 42bhp engine, the car with which Erik Carlsson scored his great run of successes, including the 1960, 1961 and 1962 RAC, 1962 and 1963 Monte Carlo and 1964 San Remo Rallies.

Domestic sales climbed to 29,000 cars in 1964 but dropped to 26,000 in 1965 and only 19,000 in 1966. While the two-stroke Saab had a keen following among enthusiasts in Britain, the USA and elsewhere, the average Swedish motorist wanted a more trouble free four-stroke.

Saab chose the German 1½-litre Ford V4 engine, which was installed in the 96 bodyshell from 1967. Its success is shown by the fact that Swedish sales of the V4 in 1967 were 24,000, compared with a mere 500 two-strokes. In the USA, however, 6800 two-strokes were sold, compared with 3500 V4s. The last two-stroke Saab was made in 1968, and the Sason-designed two-door saloon finally disappeared in 1979.

As early as 1963 Saab's president, Tryggve Holm, was thinking about a completely new car to repace the Ljungstrom/Sason models, and when he learnt that Standard-Triumph was developing an inclined four-cylinder engine with Ricardo head he suggested a collaboration. The result was that Triumph built the engines to Saab's specifications, and these powered the all-new Model 99 which was launched at the end of 1969. The 87bhp 1.7-litre engine was mounted above the gearbox, driving the front wheels; the body was designed by Sason, who died seven months before the car was launched, and Björn Enwall. The engine was enlarged to 1854cc in 1971 and to 1985cc in 1972.

A new engine plant was opened at Södertalje in 1972 and pioneered group assembly, whereby small groups of workers are responsible for each engine and rotate jobs in order to reduce boredom. The practice was later taken up by Volvo. The new engine plant marked the end of collaboration between Saab and Triumph.

In 1968 Saab merged with the old-established truck maker Scania-Vabis, which also happened to be the Swedish importer of Volkswagen and Porsche cars. The new company became the fifth largest industrial enterprise in Sweden; today it is the second largest. Shortly after the merger a Finnish factory was opened at Nystad, jointly owned by Saab Scania and the Finnish engineering company Valmet OY. The advent of the Model 99 marked a move up-market for Saab, which has continued to the present day. In 1977 came the 99 Turbo, a 145bhp five-seater saloon with ample luggage capacity and a top speed of over 120mph (193kph). As Mark Chatterton, au-

Saab 92 of c.1950

Saab 93 of c.1956

Saab 99GL of c.1982

Saab 9000 of 1986

thor of *Saab – The Innovator* wrote: 'The 99 Turbo finally convinced both journalists and public that Saabs were no longer things which you overtook to get away from the trail of blue smoke – indeed they had become things that you simply could not overtake.' A year later came a move into the executive car class with the 900, a long wheelbase 99 which had a five-door body on the 900 GLS.

The 99 and 99 Turbo had a very successful career in rallying in the 1970s, leading drivers being Stig Blomqvist, Per Eklund, Simo Lampinen and Tapio Rainio. Victories included the 1971, 1972, 1973 and 1979 Swedish, 1971 RAC and the Arctic Rally from 1974 to 1977 inclusive.

Saab today is divided into four divisions: Aerospace, which builds one of the best combat aircraft in the world, the Viggen; Saab cars; Scania trucks; and Nordarmatur, which makes valves and piping systems. It also has a 50 per cent stake with the Swedish government in the computer concern Datasaab, markets American Sperry-Rand computers in Sweden, and has interests in machine tools,

textile process equipment, all-fuel boilers and solar heating systems. The company has a marketing agreement with Lancia, selling that company's Delta as the Saab 600.

The current range of Saab cars includes a modified 99 called the 90, available only as a two-door saloon, four models of the 900 including two with turbochargers, and the new top of the range 9000 saloon with 175bhp 16-valve twin-overhead cam turbo engine. Convertible versions of the 900 have recently been introduced, which are made in the Finnish factory, together with a long wheelbase 99 limousine, the first example of which was built for President Kekkonen. The Saab car division currently employs 7800 people; output in 1984 was 73,151 cars from the Swedish factories and about 28,867 in Finland. By 1985 production from both countries had reached 111,813. GNG

SABRA
see Rom Carmel

SAFIR
see Saurer

ST LOUIS/STANDARD
USA 1898-1909

The St Louis Gas Motor Co of Missouri, formed in 1898 with John L. French as president and George P. Dorris chief engineer, made single and twin-cylinder vehicles as well as sizeable commercial vehicles. Two cars a week was the planned output for 1900. The vehicles were promoted with the catching slogan 'Rigs that Run'.

French died in 1903 and the firm never really recovered from this loss. For a year from 1905 George Dorris made cars under his own name before establishing the Dorris Motor Car Co. In 1906 the original firm changed its name to St Louis Motor Car Co and transferred production to Peoria, Illinois. The move was not a success, however. The firm's liabilities stood at $150,000 in 1907 and in 1908 it was declared bankrupt. The plant was taken over by Bartholomew and Co, maker of the Glide car.

In St Louis, meanwhile, the St Louis Car Co, which had built rail wagons since 1887, had announced in December 1904 that it was to enter the road car business with the purchase of Whitaker-Weber to create 'the largest automobile factory in the West'. Whether it owned the St Louis Motor Car Co or simply adopted its name when that company switched production to Peoria is uncertain, but it soon acquired a licence to make Mors cars, which appear to have gone under the name American Mors or Standard. G. J. Kobusch, president of the St Louis Car Co, formed the Kobusch Automobile Co in 1906 but this was soon taken over by his parent firm. In 1907 it was certainly the St Louis Car Co, managed by T. H. Bailey, that held the American Mors patent rights. In 1909 Standard introduced its own design of car, a large 7.8-litre six-cylinder model.

The St Louis Car Co was refinanced in 1911 with $6 million capital but appears not to have re-entered the 'pleasure car' business, although in 1918 it still listed its automobile plant separately and may have used it to produce bus bodies. The company had 500 employees in 1925 and was offering buses, rail coaches, aircraft and elevators. Most of its subsequent production has been connected with railways. In 1956 the company devised an ingenious road train, which was produced for a time as the Wolfwagon, in which several complete trucks were linked and controlled by a single driver. NB

SALMON
see Ryknield

SALMSON
FRANCE 1921-1957

Born in 1859, Emile Salmson trained as a civil engineer and concentrated on building bridges and roads until he was nearly 50, when he was tempted into the air and built an unsuccessful helicopter. He realized that the weight of conventional car engines made them unsuitable for aircraft, and was attracted by the Swiss Canton-Unné seven-cylinder radial engine, for which he took out a licence to manufacture in France. This was the beginning of the Société des Moteurs Salmson, which was set up at Billancourt in 1912.

By 1914 he had a factory of 10,760sq ft (1000sq m) with 200 employees turning out 10 engines a month. World War I created an enormous demand for aero engines, and four years later the factory area had grown to 280,000sq ft (26,000sq m), the workforce to 9000 and engine output to 700 a month.

Salmson was also making magnetos and complete aircraft of British Sopwith and its own design at Billancourt and in another factory at Lyons. The end of the war brought a drastic cut in the aircraft business, although Salmson continued to make a variety of engines throughout the 1920s and 1930s.

Emile Salmson died in 1917 and control of the firm passed to M. Heinrich, director of the Lyons factory. He did not get on well with Salmson's sons and in 1922 they left to form the Société des Fils d'Emile Salmson, which made pumps and other machinery.

Heinrich then decided to diversify into car bodywork and complete cars. He chose to build under licence the British GN cyclecar to which he had been introduced by Marcel Lourde, a director of British Grégoire which owned GN. Six cars were ready for the 1919 Paris Salon, although quantity production did not start until mid-1920. The cars were identical to the British product, having 1100cc inlet over-exhaust V-twin engines and dog clutch and chain drive. Initial plans called for a series of 3000 to be made but only 1600 found buyers, including a number supplied to the Paris police force.

By 1921 Heinrich realized that if he was to remain in the car business he would have to find another product, and he turned to a 1087cc four-cylinder engine which had been designed by an independent consultant, Emile Petit. This had a curious valve operation whereby a single pushrod per cylinder also acted as a 'pull rod' for the inlet valve. The engine was set far back in the frame and the car had shaft drive with no differential. It was christened the Salmson AL after André Lombard, the Salmson employee who found Emile Petit for Heinrich. It was Lombard who introduced the St Andrews cross on the radiator, which characterized all Salmsons of the 1920s.

As well as the pushrod AL, Petit designed a twin-overhead cam engine for Salmson sports and racing cars, and the two models were produced side by side up to 1929. Fewer twin-overhead cam models were made, 2672 compared with 11,632 of the AL and its derivatives, but they earned Salmson an enviable reputation on the race track, which obviously helped sales of the touring cars. Sporting successes included wins in the 1921 French Cyclecar Grand Prix, 1922 French Grand Prix des Voiturettes, Tour de France and numerous other light car events. Twin-overhead cam engines were also used in a touring model, the D Type, which was the first twin-overhead cam touring car in the world.

In 1923 some AL3s were sold to the Bignan company, which fitted Bignan radiators and marketed the cars under its own name. This badge engineering was also used by Rally, whose sports car of the late 1920s was a disguised Salmson GS and whose touring cars of the early 1930s were shortened Salmson S4Cs.

The Petit era came to an end in 1929, when Heinrich decided to concentrate on touring cars rather than sports and racing cars. The new S4, although still a twin-overhead cam design, embodied features that Petit disapproved of, and the designer left to become chief engineer at Ariès.

The S4 had a 30bhp 1.3-litre engine and was usually fitted with four-door saloon bodies with which it could still achieve a respectable 65mph (104kph). A total of 3456 were made before it grew up into the S4C with a 1465cc engine, which was also made in England by British Salmson.

Salmson GS sports two-seater of 1926

Salmson Targa Florio racer of c.1927

Salmson S4C of 1932

Salmson 2.3-litre GT coupé of 1956

The early 1930s saw an increase in aero engine production to meet the new enthusiasm for private flying, and Salmson even built a few complete aircraft from 1933. This led to a corresponding reduction in car production, and only a little over 6000 S4s were made until 1939, compared with over 14,000 cars in the vintage period. The last pre-war Salmsons, the 1.6-litre S4.61 and the 2.3-litre S4E, were handsome saloons and coupés with torsion bar independent front suspension on the larger cars and the option of Cotal gearboxes on both.

After World War II the S4.61 and S4E were revived with little change. More than 2000 were sold from 1946 to 1950, when the G72 Randonée saloon was introduced. This was an S4E with a new, all enveloping body but only 630 were sold in two years.

In 1952 Salmson closed down for a few months. The aero engine business was almost dead, because radial engines were being replaced by horizontally-opposed designs, and Salmson could not afford to re-tool for production of these. In any case the company might have had problems with the patents established by the major producers such as Continental and Lycoming.

Salmson managed to open again for the 1953 Paris Salon, where it showed the 2300 GT coupé. This was an attractive car with a 105mph (169kph) top speed and it marked a return by Salmson to competitions, winning its class in the 1954 Tulip and Lyons-Charbonnières Rallies, and beating Stirling Moss's Sunbeam to achieve fifth place in the Alpine Rally of the same year. Unfortunately Salmson's finances were too frail to keep the 2300 going and for the first time the company had to go to outside suppliers for the bodies: Esclassan built the first 39 and Chapron the remaining 188. A few open two-seater and four-door saloons were built, but in February 1957 the last 2300 left Billancourt, and car production was at an end. GNG

SANDFORD
FRANCE 1922-1936

Malcolm Stuart Sandford, born in Birmingham, England, in 1889, lived in France with his widowed mother from the age of two. After World War I he became the Morgan agent in Paris but soon found himself losing sales to Darmont, which was assembling Morgan-based sports cars in Courbevoie.

Raymond Gueret left Darmont to become Sandford's foreman in 1921, remaining until 1934 when he established his own garage for servicing Sandford cars.

A prototype Ruby-engined sports car was built in 1921 followed by a second with Philos radiator and Morgan frame in 1922. That year a car based on a Darmont body and chassis was built for a customer and in 1923 regular production of three-wheelers and MS motorcycles began. The MS motorcycles replaced imported Metro-Tylers, but only about a dozen were made and then Dunelts were sold instead. The cars had four-cylinder Ruby engines and gearboxes and achieved many race victories, especially later in supercharged form.

In 1925 the firm moved to Levallois-Perret, where 12 men were employed. Output of Sandfords – sold with the slogan 'L'Avion de La Route' – soon ran at between one and two cars a fortnight. The aluminium bodies were bought-in from Lecanut. The vehicles were nearly twice as expensive as Darmonts.

In 1930 a prototype four-wheeler was built and in 1932 production versions with Ruby engines, tubular frames and all-round independent suspension were offered. Cheaper three-wheelers with flat-twin, air-cooled, Ruby 950cc engines were introduced in 1934, but sales were slow.

From 1936, after 250 to 300 Sandfords had been sold, the firm concentrated on its Morgan and Standard agencies. Subsequent Sandfords were in fact Morgans assembled by Sandford, but in 1939 a new prototype with Ruby engine was produced.

Malcolm Sandford sold Morgan, Standard, James and Velocette vehicles after World War II, as well as Singer sewing machines and Seagull outboards. These were mostly bought with currency raised by selling French alcoholic drinks in Britain. Plans to revive his own cars came to nothing. Sandford continued to sell British vehicles until his death in 1956. NB

Sandford three-wheeler of 1929

SAURER/BERNA, SAFIR, WYSS
SWITZERLAND 1896-1917

In 1853 Franz Saurer opened a foundry in St Georgen, near St Gall, Switzerland, then set up a factory at Arbon to make textile machinery. There Adolphe Saurer developed Helvetia bicycles and, from 1888, small engines for powering hosiery machines.

In 1896 a double phaeton with Saurer 5hp motor was built by the French carriage builder Koch of Neuilly. Several were sold in Switzerland and elsewhere until 1901. Adolphe's son Hippolyte then designed the first completely Arbon-built Saurers in 1902. A 5-ton truck was ready in 1903 and cars were in series production in 1904. All had four cylinders and most had patented engine brakes developed in 1903 for Alpine condi-

Saurer double phaeton of 1900

tions. Production of 30 and 50hp cars continued until 1917, and ambulance chassis were made into the 1920s, but most emphasis was on commercials.

Branches or licensees built Saurers in Britain (by Hall of Dartford), the United States (where American Saurer merged with Mack), Poland, Germany (at Lindau from 1910), Russia, Austria and France (Saurer France eventually merging with Simca-Unic in 1956). Spyker sold Saurer commercials in Holland from 1910. Saurer technology was of much wider significance than sales of 130 commercials and 56 cars in Switzerland in 1912 might suggest.

Automobilfabrik Safir built a factory in Zurich in 1907 to make Saurer-based cars and commercials. There the first Saurer compression-ignition experiments, supervised by Dr Rudolf Diesel, took place shortly before the factory got into financial difficulties and closed in 1908. Diesel Saurers were available from 1928 and a licence to build them in England was soon granted to Vickers-Armstrong. Shortly before World War II the licence was transferred to Morris-Commercial, which used Saurer-designed engines from 1948. OM sold Saurers in Italy from 1928 and was soon assembling them as well. It supplied lighter vehicles to the Swiss

market under a reciprocal arrangement that lasted until 1982.

In 1929 Saurer merged with Berna, a company whose origins went back to the cars built by Joseph Wyss in Berne from 1902 after a prototype had been made as early as 1897. Wyss's firm became the Schweizer Automobilfabrik Berna of Olten in 1904 and in 1906 a limited company with a capital of 3 million Swiss francs was created under the name Berna Motorwerke.

Berna cars featured integral gear drive in the wheels perfected by chief engineer Ernst Marti and patented by him in 1912. Commercial vehicles usurped the cars from 1905 until a final batch of six was made in 1907. Berna then produced only commercials, which were licence-built in England during World War I by Watson of Newcastle on Tyne, near where Armstrong-Saurers were later made. From 1915 Berna and the Martini automobile firm jointly owned the original Martini Engine Co.

The combined Saurer-Berna group, which continued to make textile and other types of machine, including Muller photocopiers and vibrating motor rollers, had a capital of 15 million francs in 1950 and employed 3000 men in 893,000sq ft (83,000sq m) of factories. Through the OM link the group acted as engineering consultant to Fiat and Iveco and had business links with Leyland.

With just 1000 vehicles being produced annually in the early 1980s by almost one third of the group's total workforce of 6500, the division became uneconomic. Accordingly a joint vehicle firm was formed on 1 January 1983 with a workforce of 350. The partners were Saurer (which held 45 per cent equity), Mercedes-Benz (40 per cent) and Oerlikon-Buhrle (15 per cent). The Oerlikon-Buhrle FBW commercial vehicle company was included in the £5 million capitalized consortium. Saurer assembled Mercedes-Benz vehicles for the Swiss and export markets from 1983, when Saurer ceased production of its own civilian vehicles, although military types continued to be built for two more years. In 1985 output ran at 140 to 150 chassis a month, of which 75 per cent were exported. NB

SAVA/ROYAL STAR
BELGIUM 1903-1923

Royal Star was founded in Berchem, Antwerp, in 1902 by M. Dodelinger to make motorcycles, cars and industrial engines. Two- and four-cylinder cars were developed in 1903 and three years later came a 25hp six as well as a 7hp single that was said to have parts interchangeable with those of De Dion-Bouton.

In 1907 the 107,000sq ft (10,000sq m) factory was listed as having a production capacity of 300 chassis and 1500 motorcycles a year. A total of 300 men were employed at that

time. In 1910, with backing from the British gear manufacturer David Brown, the firm was reorganized as the Société Anversois pour la Fabrication de Voitures Automobiles (SAVA).

The smallest monobloc four now had a Fondu engine and in others the side valves were displaced by an overhead exhaust and side inlet arrangement. David Brown worm gears were used in the rear axle for possibly the first time on the Continent. SAVAs, which were sold in Britain by David Brown, enjoyed some success in European sporting events.

During World War I SAVA concentrated on producing machine guns and afterwards made signalling equipment for Lahy et Stifkens. A 20hp car was then revived with the option of four wheel brakes, and in late 1921 a 15hp 2-litre overhead-valve model was announced. SAVA collapsed in 1923 and became the repair and spares department for Minerva. NB

SAXON
USA 1913-1923

The Saxon Motor Co of Detroit was formed by three former Chalmers men, Hugh Chalmers, H. W. Dunham and Harry Ford. The prototype was developed in the Chalmers plant and the first Saxon Fours reached the market early in 1914. They were aimed at the buyer who wanted a light car of reasonable quality, well above the cyclecar level but not necessarily a full size tourer.

Women were frequently featured at the wheel in Saxon advertising, as were travelling salesmen, and apart from a few delivery vans, all Saxon Fours were two-seater roadsters. The were powered by a Continental engine of only 1.4 litres and had a two-speed gearbox on the rear axle. The chassis members tapered towards the front, in the manner of the Austin Seven, and there were two substantial floorpans, one beneath the engine and the other beneath the body.

The price was $395, well below all other American cars apart from a few 'plywood and wire' cyclecars. Saxon advertising stressed 'The Saxon is *not* a cyclecar', adding 'Everybody *Ought* to Own a Car, now Everybody *Can* own a Car'.

The Saxon team certainly found a gap in the market. Sales were an encouraging 7500 in the first year, rising to 19,000 in 1915, and a peak of 27,800 in 1916, by which time Hugh Chalmers had left and a Continental-powered six at $785 joined the range. The latter was a full size five-passenger tourer aimed at the Ford Model T market, but by 1916 Henry had drastically reduced his tourer in price and the Saxon didn't have a chance.

The rapid increase in production necessitated a new factory, and Saxon suddenly found itself drastically under-capitalized. It unwisely dropped the Four for the 1918 season, and saw sales fall from 21,000 to 7200. Harry Ford died in the influenza epidemic

Saxon Four two-seat roadster of 1913

that year. The new factory, still uncompleted, was bought by the Industrial Terminal Corporation, which completed it and sold it to General Motors. It later became a Chevrolet assembly plant.

Saxon acquired more modest premises at Ypsilanti, Michigan, where it continued to make the six in declining numbers, 2500 in 1919 and 700 in 1920. In 1920 it reverted to four cylinders, this time using a 3.1-litre overhead valve Gray engine, but to no avail. Sales dropped to 500 in 1921 and 250 in 1922. Those listed as 1923 cars were probably left-over 1922 models sold off early in the new year. The last models were known as Saxon-Duplex. GNG

SAYERS/S & S
USA 1917-1930

The Sayers & Scovill Co of Cincinnati, Ohio, was established in 1876 as a maker of horse-drawn carriages, which it continued producing for many years. The company came to specialize in hearses and made its first motor hearse body in 1907, the year in which it also made a forward-control 2-ton truck. In 1913 it began to make its own hearse and ambulance chassis, sold under the name S & S and powered by Lycoming or Continental engines.

Four years later the company began to offer passenger cars, which were called Sayers Six to distinguish them from the professional cars. They were very conventional assembled machines and the company made no attempt to disguise this in its advertising: 'The mechanical parts bear names that stand for quality and service – Continental, Delco, Borg & Beck, Willard, Stewart, Hotchkiss, Fedders and a host of others.' Its price of $1695, later reduced to $1645, put it right in the middle bracket, slightly above the Maxwell and slightly below the Buick, where it had many competitors.

Sales were never very high, being limited by the size of the factory and the maker's wish not to lose sight of the main trade of ambulance and hearse manufacture. The peak year for the Sayers Six was 1921, when 650 cars were sold, falling to 312 in 1923, the last full year in which they were marketed under the Sayers name.

In 1924 they were reissued as the S & S, the name by which the professional cars had always been known, and production was carried on in a very limited way. Carrying the name Brighton (1924), Elmwood (1925-26), Gotham (1927-28) and Lakewood (1929-30), S & S were mainly sold to undertakers who used them as mourners' cars to follow the hearse, although private buyers could order one if they wanted to.

Continental engines were used, being straight-eights from 1928. Only closed bodies were offered, and they were by no means cheap: the 1929 Lakewood eight-passenger sedan cost $4275, more than the equivalent Cadillac or Pierce-Arrow.

After 1930 S & S cars were available to special order only, but the hearses were continued to 1935, after which they were built on Buick chassis although still carrying the S & S name. In 1938 they turned to Cadillac chassis. In 1942 Sayers & Scovill was reorganized under the name Hess & Eisenhardt, which still makes ambulances and hearses to this day. GNG

SB
GERMANY 1919-1924

In 1919 Dr Rudolph Slaby developed a diminutive battery-powered chain-driven car in Charlottenberg, Berlin, which he hoped would ease the plight of war cripples. Factory space and financial support were provided by A. Beringer. The bath-shaped single-seat body was made of wood and was sufficiently strong to require no chassis. A trailer could be towed to provide another seat or luggage space, and a longer wheelbase goods version was offered.

This ugly utilitarian vehicle was not well received, although one big order was placed by a firm 'in the East' and a photograph exists showing at least 50 SBs together. Examples were sold on the British market by Gamages in 1920. In an attempt to broaden the appeal DKW petrol-engined versions were offered in 1923, and these more attractive cars seem to have had tubular metal space frames.

In 1924 SB Automobilgesellschaft was bought by J. S. Rasmussen of DKW and production of SB cars was discontinued that year. Dr Slaby later developed electric taxis and cars with chassis-less wooden bodies. These were made in Berlin for Rasmussen and were sold under the name DEW until 1927. Similar constructional features were found on the first DKW cars of 1928. NB

SBARRO
SWITZERLAND 1967 to date

Born in Lecce, Italy, in 1939, Franco Sbarro emigrated to Switzerland at the age of 18 and two years later set up a small workshop for the repair of bicycles and farm tractors. In the mid-1960s he became manager of Georges Filipinetti's racing team, preparing Ferraris, a Cobra, Ford GT40 and Porsche 906, the latter winning the 1967 Targa Florio.

In that year he took over an abandoned cigarette factory at Grandson on Lake Neuchâtel, not far from Filipinetti's premises, and made his first car, a street version of the GT40. He formed a company called ACA (Ateliers de Construction Automobile) and made a few more street GT40s, followed in 1971 by a Chevrolet-powered replica of the Lola T70, one of the GT40's great rivals. Then, as later, cars were built to order only, against a written contract and 30 per cent deposit.

In 1973 Sbarro brought out a replica of the pre-war BMW 328 powered by a modern 3-litre BMW engine, which has proved to be his best seller, accounting for about half of the 315 cars made until the spring of 1985. Other replicas have included the Mercedes-Benz 540K and Bugatti Royale, the latter powered by two 3½-litre Rover V8 engines in tandem.

More original designs have been the Stash, a GT coupé powered by a supercharged Volkswagen K80 or 2-litre BMW engine, of which five had been made up to 1983, the Windhound 4×4 and Windhawk 6×6 cross country vehicles (15 and 1 respectively) and some astonishing 'hot' saloons. These have included a 345bhp Porsche Turbo powered VW Golf, and the Super Twelve, which had two 1.3-litre Kawasaki six-cylinder motorcycle engines in a Golf-like fibreglass body. The latest version of the Super Twelve has a Ferrari V8 engine.

Other Sbarro projects have included the TAG Cadillac-based six-wheeled Function

Car, the Carville (née Pilcar) battery electric saloon with all-coil independent suspension, and a series of coupés based on the Mercedes-Benz 500 SEC, powered by either 5- or 6.9-litre V8 engines. Some of these have gull-wing doors, and the Bi-Turbo has a 350bhp twin-turbocharged 5-litre V8 engine. Like all Sbarro's cars, the Mercedes-Benz coupés have fibreglass bodies. Sbarro employs 20 workers who turn out about 30 cars a year.

The Middle East provides the best market (the 6×6 Windhawk was a special order from King Khaled of Saudi Arabia), followed by Japan and Germany. In 1983 a licence to manufacture the BMW 328 replica was taken out by A. C. A. Podvin of St Loup Dordan, France, though production also continues at Grandson.

The current range of cars from Sbarro includes the 328, the Bi-Turbo and other Mercedes-derived coupés, the Windhound and the latest offering from Franco Sbarro's fertile brain, the Challenge. This is a very low, wedge-shaped coupé with an extremely low drag coefficient of only 0.22, powered by a 380bhp twin-turbocharged Mercedes-Benz V8 engine driving all four wheels. A production run of 10 is envisaged, and two had already been sold before manufacture began, at a price of £71,500 each. A 2×2 version was introduced in 1986. In theory most of the 50-odd designs that Sbarro has built are available to special order.

In a separate factory Sbarro makes children's versions of the BMW 328 and Mercedes-Benz 540K, powered by 47cc Sachs engines. The latter is a two-seater equipped with a radio, and costs over £5000. GNG

SCANIA/SCANIA-VABIS
SWEDEN 1902-1929

Maskinfabriks AB Scania was founded in 1900 in the southern Swedish town of Malmö to make Humber bicycles. It began experiments with motor vehicles the following year and in 1902 built six cars powered by two-cylinder Kamper engines made in Germany. Car production then lapsed until 1905, when Scania began to make its own four-cylinder overhead-valve engines designed by the German engineer G. Wentzel. Commercial vehicles up to 2 tons were also made, probably in greater numbers than the passenger cars. Between 1908 and 1912 only 31 Scania cars were delivered, all with four-cylinder engines ranging from 12 to 30/36hp.

In 1911 Scania merged with its rival Swedish firm of Vabis, and from 1914 vehicles were sold under the name Scania-Vabis. Scania's Per Nordeman became managing director and its designer Anton Svenson became chief engineer. The veteran Vabis designer, Gustaf Erikson, had left his company a year before the merger. Production of cars and engines was carried on at the Vabis factory at Södertalje, commercials coming from Malmö

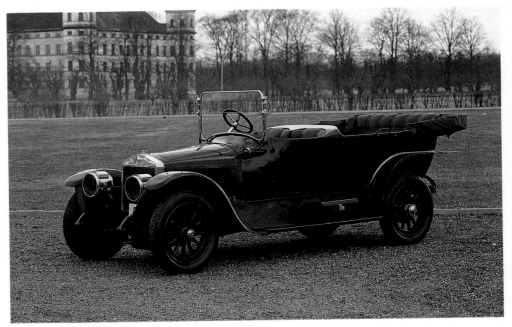
Scania-Vabis four-cylinder tourer of 1912

until 1924 when the latter factory was closed.

Commercial vehicles soon came to dominate Scania-Vabis production, although passenger cars were made in three models, 20, 30/36 and 50hp, until 1924. They were well built, conservative machines with Germanic vee radiators. A total of 351 cars were made until 1924, after which regular production was devoted to commercial vehicles. In fact four more cars were made to the special order of former customers, the last one being completed in 1929. Total combined production of Scania, Scania-Vabis and Vabis cars did not exceed 500.

Scania-Vabis flourished as a commercial vehicle-builder, becoming a major exporter during the 1950s and setting up assembly plants in Holland, Iraq, Brazil and Argentina. In 1968 it dropped the name Vabis from its vehicles and merged with Saab to form Saab-Scania AB. This put Scania back in the passenger car business, although it had kept a useful foothold there since it had acquired the Volkswagen agency for Sweden in 1948. Today the Saab group is the second largest industrial combine in Sweden. GNG

SCAP
FRANCE 1912-1929

The Société des Constructions Automobiles Parisienne of Billancourt, Seine, was better known in its later days as a supplier of proprietary engines; but from 1912 to 1929, as SA des Automobiles SCAP, run by Launay and Margaria, it also built complete SCAP cars. The first SCAP range comprised five four-cylinder models, using Ballot engines ranging from 8 to 15CV, and the 1913 12/16 and 14/16CV models also used Ballot engines and some very sporting body styles.

During World War I SCAP built aero engines and after the war introduced its own engines in its cars. The company also became one of the most popular sources of engines for voiturette makers, especially those of a sporting bent. In 1920 SCAP was supplying very highly regarded engines of up to 2359cc capacity, plus engines for marine and stationary use.

In 1923 Bollack Netter et Cie introduced the sporting BNC voiturette with an 895cc SCAP engine and in 1925 offered the only supercharged French production car of the time, with a Cozette supercharged 1097cc overhead-valve SCAP engine giving an impressive 53bhp. A Cozette supercharged 1099cc SCAP engine, with three valves per cylinder, was also used in the very quick Derby Special of 1927. Others to use SCAP engines, some as late as 1930, included Benova, Bignan, De Bazelaire, GAR and Turcat-Méry.

In 1921 SCAP's own four-cylinder side-valve 12CV Type L car used a strange rear suspension comprising a transverse cantilever spring pivoted on the chassis at its centre and with two linked semi-elliptic springs. It was followed in 1923 by the more conventional Type M, a small car with 1097cc engine, a sporting version of which was added in 1924.

From 1923 to 1929 all SCAP's own cars were of less than 1½ litres. From 1926 to 1927 SCAP built 4 and 6CV 1100 and 1200cc models, an 8CV two-door tourer with Weymann bodies, plus a three-seater cabriolet and a sports model. The most sporting SCAP of all was a supercharged short-chassis 1100 model with a claimed top speed of over 105mph (169kph).

The last SCAP car was a 1995cc overhead-valve straight-eight, built very briefly in 1929, but from 1923 the cars had been ever more secondary to the proprietary engines, which included several versions of the small capacity straight-eights. BL

SCAR
FRANCE 1906-1915

The Société de Construction Automobile de Reims was set up in the village of Witry, 4 miles (6km) from Reims by Messieurs Rayet and Lienart in 1906. Their first product was a conventional 18/20hp T-head four-cylinder tourer with shaft drive. One of these ran in the 1906 Tourist Trophy Race, finishing eighth. A year later the 18/20 was joined by a 20/30 and a 30/40, both also shaft driven.

By 1910 the engines were of L-head layout, the heads being detachable, and the cars had dashboard radiators with bonnets very similar to those of the Renault. Models included a 10/12hp twin, a 15.9hp four and a 20.1hp six. The twin and the six had both been dropped by 1914, when the range consisted of 11.9, 15.9 and 17.9hp fours.

A British company was founded in 1912, SCAR (London) Ltd, and a number were sold

SCAR 11.9hp roadster of 1911

on the UK market. Head of the London company was Sydney Cummings, who also sold the Ronteix cyclecar in England under the name Cummikar.

The village of Witry was in the front line during World War I and the SCAR factory was completely destroyed by enemy action. The company survived the war and operated a Mathis agency until 1925. Thereafter it was simply a garage and repair business until it closed down completely in 1933. GNG

SCARAB
USA 1932-1946

William Bushnell Stout, designer of the Stout Scarab, was born in Quincy, Illinois, in 1880. He was a prolific inventor in aviation and motoring, pioneer of the all-metal aeroplane and once credited with 'more technical innovation than any man since Edison'.

Around 1910 Stout built himself a motorcycle which he called the Bi-Car, and he worked for several magazines as a technical writer on aviation and motoring. From 1914 to 1916 he was chief engineer for the Scripps-Booth company in Detroit, then making cyclecars, and in 1916 he joined Packard's aero engine division as an engineer on the Liberty engine, becoming chief engineer in 1917.

He left Packard after the war but continued his work on aircraft design, founding Stout Engineering Laboratories in 1919 and pro-

Scarab seven-seater of c.1935

ducing the first American monoplane. Stout then began to build all-metal aircraft, first for the US Navy and then, backed by a syndicate of businessmen, for passenger carrying.

In 1926 he sold the Stout Metal Aeroplane Co to Henry Ford and, staying on as general manager, designed and built the Ford Tri-Motor aeroplane. Ford also backed Stout Air Services, one of America's first scheduled passenger carriers.

After leaving Ford, Stout designed various aircraft, including in 1931 a proposed two-seater, the Skycar. He also began to work on car design and built his first Scarab in 1932. It was based on the Sterkenburg, a streamlined rear-engined experimental car designed in 1931 by Dutch-born Detroit engineer John Tjaarda (who also designed the Lincoln-Zephyr). Tjaarda costed this car for production and even developed a high speed multiple welding process for the pressed steel frame, but his backers were over cautious and only one car was actually built.

The first seven-seater Scarab, radically streamlined, had a rigid tubular alloy frame panelled in Duralumin alloy, a rear-mounted 90hp Ford V8 engine, a large low floor with moveable seats and a table, and suspension by coil springs and adjustable aircraft type dampers. It was intended primarily as a design exercise and only one was built.

In November 1935 Stout announced a second Scarab, developed from the first. He planned to build 100 of these cars at a price of $5000 – to selected customers. The main differences were steel instead of Duralumin for the body panels, redesigned suspension and a restyled streamlined body, featuring headlights covered by metal grilles.

Ultimately, Stout sold only nine Scarabs and even these were very much experimental models which were apparently regularly returned to Stout for updating with his latest ideas. More successful, at least commercially, were his high-speed train and bus designs, although further proposals for his car/aircraft hybrid Skycar and Skycar II up to late 1945 came to nothing.

Also in 1945, backed by Graham-Paige shortly before its change of identity to Kaiser-Frazer, Stout produced one more development of the Scarab, as the Stout 46. The body was again redesigned and made by Owens-Corning Fiberglass Corporation as a large one-piece moulding, one of the first in the industry, and this car used a rear-mounted six-cylinder engine and independent suspension all round. Again, only one was built. It was Stout's last car and he died in 1956. BL

SCAT
see Ceirano

SCHACHT
USA 1904-1913

G. A. Schacht, a manufacturer of bicycles, carriages and car parts in Cincinnati, Ohio, developed what he called a 'clutchless and gearless' vehicle in 1904. It was in fact an epicyclic high-wheeler, two-cylinder buggy with engine under the seat. His company, G. A. Schacht Manufacturing Co, built this vehicle at the Cook Carriage plant and proclaimed it to be the most talked-of car since the advent of the automobile.

Rather more conventional 40hp four-cylinder cars were produced in 1909, when the company became the Schacht Motor Car Co. This firm collapsed in 1913 and 36 vehicles in various stages of assembly, plus parts and equipment, were sold for $35,000.

The company was re-started as the G. A. Schacht Motor Truck Co with financial help from R. K. LeBlond of the R. K LeBlond Machine Tool Co. Schacht's 'ten speed trucks' sold well, most of the components, apart from engines, being made in-house on LeBlond machines. Safety coaches followed in 1924 and in 1927 the company's name, though not that of its vehicles, was changed to LeBlond-Schacht Truck Co. G. A. Schacht was still active in the company although W. S. Schacht was president.

In 1928 a local rival, the Armleder Truck Co, was acquired. Output of Armleder was fewer than 100 a year compared with Schacht's average of more than 300 in about 1930. Another Cincinnati firm, the Ahrens-Fox Fire Engine Co, founded in 1911, was taken over in 1936, when Armleder production ceased. Schacht ended production early in World War II. Ahrens-Fox was sold in 1951 and after various changes of owner the name was discontinued in about 1956 when its parent, the C. D. Beck Co, joined commercial vehicle-maker Mack. NB

SCHAUDEL
see Motobloc

SCOTSMAN
GB 1922-1923

The Scotsman car, made by the Scotsman Motor Car Co Ltd, was first shown in January 1922 at the Scottish Motor Exhibition in Glasgow, where the car was built. It had been under development for about 11 months and was designed by J. Hall Nicol, a Scottish motoring enthusiast who had owned and driven various cars himself since 1898. A fellow director on the Scotsman board was the well-known Scottish comedian Sir Harry Lauder.

Three four-cylinder models were shown in Glasgow, all with proprietary engines and with a distinctive radiator whose surround gave the centre the shape of a thistle. The range comprised a 1460cc 10/20hp utility model at £495, a 1492cc 11hp at £425, and a 2354cc overhead-cam 14/40hp model known as the Flying Scotsman; this last was priced at £475 for the chassis only or £550 with four-seater tourer body and electric starting.

The cars were well built and comparatively cheap, but sold only in limited numbers until production stopped in 1923. The Scotsman name reappeared on another Scottish car, a version of the air-cooled French SARA, made by Scotsman Motors Ltd in Edinburgh from 1929 to 1930, but the Scotsman companies were totally unconnected. BL

SCOTT SOCIABLE
GB 1916-1924

Alfred Angas Scott began motorcycle manufacture in Bradford, Yorkshire, in 1909 in the Jowett factory, moving to his own premises in Shipley soon afterwards. He quickly built up an excellent reputation for his two-stroke engined machines.

In 1914 he began work on a three-wheeled machine gun car as a replacement for the sidecar machine gun carrier which his company was already making. The new design was quite unconventional, with two wheels in line and the third to the side of the rear wheel, which gave it the superficial appearance of a motorcycle and sidecar, but it had wheel steering. The engine was a 578cc two-stroke twin and final drive was by shaft.

Scott acquired a new factory to make this machine, but the hoped-for War Office contract never materialized so he decided to make a civilian version that he called the Sociable, and this was announced in June 1916. Body panels were in fibreboard. War work prevented it from going into production until 1919, when Scott left Scott Engineering Co and founded a new company, the Scott Autocar Co Ltd with capital of £30,000, specifically for the manufacture of the Sociable.

Yet another new factory was bought, at Lidgett Green, Bradford, and the Sociable made its début at the 1920 Olympia Motorcycle Show. Priced originally at £273, it was reduced to £215 in 1921 and to £135 in 1923. By this time it was facing strong competition from the Austin Seven, priced at £165, and Scott's death in August 1923 removed the driving force behind the car. Production ceased in 1924, after a run of about 200.

The Scott Autocar Co was wound up, but Scott motorcycles continued in production, latterly by Matt Houlder in Birmingham, until the early 1970s. GNG

SCOUT
GB 1904-1923

The Burden family were clockmakers in Salisbury, Wiltshire, from 1881, supplying clients as far away as Fort Salisbury in Africa. From about 1902 Albert T. Burden devised petrol engines for boats and other purposes and these were built at the Excelsior Works in the town. In 1904, with finance from a local landowner named Percy Dean, the firm of Dean and Burden Bros Ltd of Scout Motor Works, Salisbury, was established with £3800 capital. It produced cars for local customers and then made substantial commercial vehicles from 1909.

A new factory had been built near the London and South West Railway Station by 1907. The company employed about 80 men and each vehicle took six to eight weeks to produce. Only in about 1912 did output reach the hoped-for level of two a week.

Chassis and other items were bought initially from E. J. West and Co Ltd of Coventry, but once the new factory had been opened the company became almost self-sufficient, building its own two-, four- and six-cylinder engines. Percy Dean departed for Canada in 1911 and his successor on the board, named Radcliffe, was killed in an accident at the factory in 1920.

Sixes were no longer being built by 1912 and in the following year monobloc fours were offered in the smallest 10/12hp models. Munitions, including bombs and magnetic mine parts, were made during World War I. The company folded in the post-war slump, a winding-up order being issued in June 1921. Capital was then £30,000 and the workforce numbered 150.

Whatley and Co of Avonside, Pewsey, bought the spares and patterns in 1922 and produced a few more vehicles until 1923. The Burden brothers returned to clockmaking. Albert Burden died in 1960 at the age of 88 and the Scout factory is now a British Telecom depot. NB

Scripps-Booth 13.2hp two-seater of 1916

SCRIPPS-BOOTH
USA 1914-1923

James Scripps-Booth experimented with the Biautogo two-wheel car from 1908 but after five years accepted that it was not a viable machine and formed the Scripps-Booth Cyclecar Co in Detroit. The idea was to make the cheapest possible car for the working man to keep in his back porch.

Although 1000 Spacke air-cooled V-twin engined cyclecars, sometimes called Rockets, were planned from a modern factory in 1914, only about 400 were sold. In October 1914 the word Cyclecar was dropped from the firm's name and more substantial 25hp Sterling-engined four-cylinder 'luxurious light cars' were developed. The designer of these was William B. Stout, who had worked on the cyclecars and become sales manager. He later went to Packard and subsequently achieved fame with the Scarab car. His assistant at Scripps-Booth was W. I. Brown from Dodge.

A Ferro V8-engined model was introduced in 1916, the year the firm was reorganized with $1 million capital. Winston Churchill was on the list of prominent owners. Cars using Mason engines and other stock (but disguised) Chevrolet components from W. C. Durant followed.

In July 1918 Durant persuaded the General

Scout 11.9hp tourer of 1909

Motors board to purchase Scripps-Booth and from 1919 Oakland chassis and bodies were often used with overhead-valve Northway engines. General Motors discontinued the marque in 1923 and the plant was later used by De Soto. The firm's first president, William E. Scripps, ran the Scripps Marine Engine Co in the 1950s as well as the *Detroit News*. NB

SEABROOK
GB 1911-1926

Seabrook tourer of c.1924

Seabrook Brothers were cycle component factors in Great Eastern Street, London EC1, from 1895. The company was run by Herbert and Percy Seabrook. It had branches in Berlin and New York by 1901 and bought many of its lines in the United States, although a geared hub was made for the company by Kynoch in Birmingham. Bells and electric horns were a speciality.

The company imported the Regal car from the United States and called it the RMC or Seabrook-RMC from 1911. During World War I a variety of American lorries, notably Napoleons, were sold in Britain as Seabrooks. In 1917 there was talk of a British-made Seabrook car.

The RMC reappeared briefly after the war, but from 1920 an advanced 11.9hp 1800cc four-cylinder car with aluminium head and pistons was built in London. The producer of the engine was not divulged, but in 1921 a 9.8hp Dorman was substituted. In 1923 an 11.9hp Meadows-powered car was introduced; the Dorman version continued until 1925. About 160 Meadows engines were supplied, half of them in 1924.

In early 1926 Herbert and Percy Seabrook retired and Frank Burgess took over, the premises then being located in Chelsea. Only three Meadows engines were bought that year and none thereafter, although Seabrooks existed in buyers' guides until 1928. NB

SEARS
USA 1908-1912

Sears Roebuck, the most famous mail order company in the United States, was formed by Richard Warren Sears and Alvah Curtis Roebuck in 1887. By the early 20th century farmers and other folk living a long way from the cities could practically furnish a house from the Sears Roebuck catalogue, as well as buying the house itself in portable form. Sears also sold a variety of carriages and buggies, so when the motor car had become sufficiently well established it was logical that it would find its way into the catalogue as well.

Rather than sell an existing make of car, Sears chose to build its own, and as its customers were mostly country people the high-wheel buggy seemed the best idea. The company took on Alvaro S. Krotz as designer and acquired a factory in Chicago which employed 50 people by 1909.

The Sears Motor Buggy had a 10/12hp horizontally-opposed twin engine made by a small Ohio engineering firm named Somers. The engine was mounted under the seat and drove via friction disc transmission and double chain drive. The wooden wheels wore solid rubber tyres, 36×1⅜in (914×35mm). Fuel consumption was 25mpg (9km per litre) and top speed 25mph (40kph). 'The Sears will do everything that a $5000 car will do except travel faster than 25mph', company advertising claimed.

The price of the first Sears buggy from the autumn 1908 catalogue was $395, and by 1911 six models were being offered from $325 to $485. Variants on the basic two passenger buggy included a 'cosy coupé', and a Light Delivery Car, while for city and interurban customers pneumatic tyres could be provided.

The Sears was as good as any of the 75 makes of high-wheeler that jostled for a share of the rural market, and better than most, but by 1912 few motorists were happy with 25mph (40kph) and the horseless carriage appearance. Sears was selling many other makes of car now and its Motor Buggy department registered an $80,000 net loss in 1911-12. After building about 3500 vehicles the company ceased to offer cars by mail order, although the works turned out a few vehicles (mostly commercials) of similar design for general sale under the name Lincoln.

In 1927 Sears contemplated selling a small car of Austin Seven size. Gardner of St Louis was to build the chassis and Budd of Philadelphia the bodies. Gardner bought some Austin Sevens to study but Sears decided that the idea would not be profitable – a wise decision in view of the relative lack of success of the American Austin a few years later. Sears' next venture with mail order cars was the Henry J-based Allstate, built by Kaiser-Frazer. GNG

Sears Motor Buggy of c.1908

SEAT
SPAIN 1953 to date

Fiat's first involvement in Spain occurred in 1931, when a factory was opened in Barcelona to make 514s under the name Hispano-Fiat. The Civil War put an end to this, and although Fiat provided rolling stock and diesel locomotives for Spain's railways, and also Madrid's trams, no more Fiat-based cars were produced until the 1950s.

The Sociedad Española de Automóviles de Turismo SA was founded on 7 June 1949, financed jointly by the state-owned Instituto Nacional de Industria (INI), a consortium of six private banks, and by Fiat. Factory construction in Barcelona began in 1950, and the first SEAT 1400s, identical to the Turin product, left the plant in 1953. By the end of the year output reached 20 a day, and total production in 1953 was 1345 cars.

The 1400 was the only SEAT made until 1957, when it was joined by the rear-engined 600, followed in 1959 by the first local model, a saloon which combined the angular Pininfarina lines of the six-cylinder 1800 with the 1400 engine. By 1962 daily output had risen to 160 cars, reaching 350 in 1965, when 91,006 cars were made. SEAT models not part of the regular Fiat range were four-door versions of the 600D and 850, while some Siata-modified sports cars with Spanish bodywork were also made.

By the end of the 1960s SEAT was the largest car-maker in Spain, and the only one making local designs. Output in 1970 was 283,678 cars. During the next decade Fiat used its Spanish operation as a supplier of models which had been replaced at Turin but for which there was still a demand in some markets. Thus the 600D, dropped in Italy in 1970, was made in Barcelona until 1973, and the 850 until 1974, although the last Italian 850 was delivered in 1971.

The 127 went into production at Barcelona in 1973, together with the typically Spanish four-door version which was exported to Italy. Another Spanish model was the 133, a rear-engined 843cc saloon with 127 styling. A version of the Fiat 132 with 2-litre Mercedes-Benz diesel engine appeared in 1975, and Lancia Beta assembly began in 1976. The Fiat

Seat 600 saloon of c.1960

Seat Malaga saloon of 1986

Panda and Ritmo (Ronda in Spain) were introduced in Barcelona in the later 1970s.

In 1979 INI signed over direct management control to Fiat, but the following year the Italian company pulled out, largely because the Spanish government would not allow it to cut back on overmanning at the SEAT factory. The government then invested heavily in the company, leading to new models, still Fiat-based, such as the Trans, a delivery van version of the Panda, and the 127-based Fura. In 1982 SEAT began collaboration with Volkswagen, which led to assembly of the Polo, Passat and Santana at Barcelona. It is expected that SEAT will be part of VW by 1990.

For 1985 SEAT brought out two new models, the Ibiza three-door hatchback and the Malaga four-door saloon, powered by Porsche-designed overhead-cam four-cylinder engines of 1193 or 1461cc, with bodies styled by Giugiaro of Ital Design. These enines are also used in the Ronda which is otherwise similar to the Fiat Ritmo. Production in 1984 was 278,855 cars from three factories employing 22,875 people. GNG

SEATON-PETTER
see Petter

SECQUEVILLE-HOYAU
FRANCE 1919-1924

Alfred Secqueville and Gaston Hoyau founded an aero engine, propeller and component firm at Asnières-Naz in 1911. It had a capital of 20,000 francs. During World War I a well-equipped modern factory was in use at Gennevilliers, Seine, producing Hispano-Suiza and Bugatti aero engines.

In 1919 Secqueville-Hoyau produced a high-grade 1244cc four-cylinder car with inclined valves, central spark plugs and much use of aluminium. A Rolls-Royce shaped radiator completed the design, but the car was too expensive for such a small vehicle without sporting pretensions. By 1922 some 330 had been built but sales tailed off. About 500 cars were sold, the last in 1924. NB

SELDEN
USA 1906-1914

George Baldwin Selden founded the Selden Motor Vehicle Co in Rochester, New York, in 1906 and although Selden only survived as a vehicle maker for eight years, the early years of the American industry were virtually dominated by the Selden name, through his 1895 patent.

Selden was born in Clarkson, New York, in 1846. He served in the cavalry during the Civil War and was educated at Yale, becoming a patent attorney with a special interest in mechanical patents in 1871.

During the 1870s he developed at least one gas engine and outlined a vehicle to use it. The engine was an improved version of the two-stroke Brayton type, patented by George Brayton in 1872. Selden modified the excessively heavy Brayton engine to be practicable for road use, but he never actually used it – simply because he could neither afford to himself nor find backers to help.

In May 1879 Selden filed for wide ranging patents on a 'road locomotive' based on the Brayton engine, then, shrewdly aware of the 17-year patent life, he kept his pending – through constant amendments – until he felt he could gain greatest effect. His supposed 'master patent', US No 549,160, was granted on 5 November 1895. Selden planned to exploit it by licensing arrangements, but even to do this he needed backing.

One of the few industry figures to react to Selden's patent was Herman F. Cuntz, a mechanical engineer who was in charge of the Pope Manufacturing Co's patent interests. Cuntz advised Pope that the Selden patent was valid, and although the company did not take his advice to stop petrol car manufacture, it did become a fundamental part of the Selden affair.

In April 1899 Pope's motor carriage department became the Columbia Automobile Co, and two weeks later Columbia became joint owner, with William C. Whitney's Electric Vehicle Co (for which it built electric cabs), of the Columbia and Electric Vehicle Co. With the electric market faltering, Whitney

was looking for alternative income and on 4 November 1899 the Electric Vehicle Co bought the Selden Patent, giving Selden $10,000 and 20 per cent of future royalties.

In June 1900 the Electric Vehicle Co became sole owner of the Columbia and Electric Vehicle Co and that year made the first move to enforce the patent, against Winton – then the largest US maker of petrol cars. At first the royalty was set at 5 per cent but Olds and others resisted and forced the figure down.

In 1903 representatives of Olds, Pierce-Arrow, Locomobile, Knox and others joined Whitney to form the Association of Licensed Automobile Manufacturers (ALAM), recognizing the patent, formalizing its administration and now demanding a royalty reduced to 1¼ per cent. Of this, 20 per cent went to Selden and 40 per cent each to the Electric Vehicle Co and to ALAM as owners and administrators.

By 1904 ALAM had some 30 members but others fought, among them Henry Ford who founded his own company in 1903. He fought ALAM in the courts and in 1905, with Reo, Marmon, Maxwell-Briscoe and others, formed the American Motor Car Manufacturers Association (AMCMA) as a protective alternative to ALAM.

In 1907 Ford had a car built using a Lenoir-type, non-compressing engine to show that Selden's patent could have been pre-dated and the car made one run of some 8 miles (13km). Two cars were also built *to* the patent, one by Selden and his sons and the other by Henry Cave, an engineer for Riker, a company owned by the Electric Vehicle Co. Apparently neither Selden car could run for more than a few hundred yards.

In December 1907 the Electric Vehicle Co, having failed as a manufacturer, went into receivership, with liabilities of $3.6 million and notional assets of $14.2 million, $11.4 million of which represented patents – including Selden's. Since 1903 the total income from the Selden patent had been only $682,000. The Electric Vehicle Co was later reorganized as the Columbia Motor Car Co, became part of the US Motor Car Co and finally went down with that venture.

In spite of the Selden cars' dubious worth

and the Electric Vehicle Co's demise, ALAM continued and in 1909 the patent was declared legally valid by a New York court. AMCMA was disbanded and most members were accepted into ALAM, on payment of arrears and recognition of the current royalty of 0.8 per cent – bringing ALAM's membership to 83 companies.

Ford refused to join on any terms, even though he would have been gladly received. Instead, he continued to fight, supported by bicycle patent fighter turned Ford dealer, John Wanamaker. ALAM warned the public not to buy Ford cars; Ford put up a surety to protect his customers and agents and openly advertised his defiance of ALAM.

On 11 January 1911 a court upheld Ford's latest appeal and declared the Selden patent 'valid but not infringed', observing that Ford and all others involved were using Otto and not Brayton engines. Ford was seen as a hero and ALAM lost its control of the industry, a control which had been restrictive but also to an extent constructive, encouraging standardization and fair trading for instance. The patent would in any case have expired in November 1912.

As for Selden the manufacturer, he suffered the ignominy in 1905 – by which time he had found a backer, still a necessity as he made very little personally from the patent – of being refused a licence by ALAM because he had not proved his company's ability to build a car to ALAM's standards. In 1906 the Selden Motor Vehicle Co gained its manufacturing licence by taking over an existing ALAM member, the Buffalo Gasoline Engine Co – coincidentally, one of the first companies ever sued over the patent – and set up works in Rochester.

Selden first made a car with a four-cylinder Continental engine and then a larger four-cylinder model. In 1911 Selden advertised roadster, touring and torpedo models priced from $2250 to $2600 as 'Made by the father of them all'. The company stopped car manufacture in 1914 but continued to make commercial vehicles up to 1932, the year in which George Baldwin Selden died. BL

SELVE/COLIBRI, SPERBER
GERMANY 1908-1929

The Norddeutsche Automobilwerke at Hameln made light cars under the name Colibri from 1908, later using the name Sperber or the company's initials NAW. In 1913 15PS four-cylinder models were introduced. Army versions were produced following the takeover of the works by aluminium specialists Basse & Selve. The repair of Selve aero engines was then undertaken by NAW.

After World War I Dr Ing Walter von Selve reorganized NAW and made a variety of 1.5 to 2.35-litre four-cylinder cars and commercial derivatives all with the name Selve. Ernst Lehmann, who had started his career with

Daimler and then worked with Métallurgique for 10 years from 1903, was technical director but died in a car accident in 1924. A respected Selve designer was Karl Slevogt, whose work was also used by Puch, Laurin and Klement, and Apollo. Six-cylinder models were added to the range in 1925. Basse & Selve was still offering 5-15PS proprietary engines from its original Altena, Westphalia, factory in 1927.

A 3075cc Selecta six-cylinder car was introduced in 1927 which lasted until the end of production in 1929. A front-wheel-drive car designed by Henze using Voran transmission was exhibited in 1928 but not pursued, and neither was a 6×6 military version. NB

racing driver by the middle of the decade; in 1926 he was a member of the Delage team, buying his own 1500 Grand Prix Delage the following year. From 1928 he ran a garage in Paris that had Delage, Chenard and Ford agencies as well as a Bugatti service department. He organized the Motorcycle Club de France and after retiring from racing in 1931 became an airborne reporter of sporting events.

The final Sénéchal cars would seem to have been made in 1929, by which time the engines, of up to 1500cc, were being made in the Chenard factory. During World War II Robert Sénéchal trained pilots. He died in July 1985 at the age of 94. NB

Sénéchal Sport of 1924

SÉNÉCHAL
FRANCE 1921-1929

Robert Sénéchal, born in 1891, worked at a garage in Levallois-Perret before World War I, during which he served as a pilot. After the war he made a fortune with Louis Delage's son Pierre selling ex-army vehicles. In 1920 he joined his friends Cordier and Lebeau to make Eclair cyclecars, but their firm was liquidated before long.

In 1921 Sénéchal was making light sports cars under his own name in Courbevoie and employing 25 to 30 men. Most cars had Ruby four-cylinder engines, although a few used Chapuis-Dornier or vee-twin Train units. The Solex carburettor firm backed his company.

Robert Sénéchal raced his cars with success, scoring 51 victories in 56 races in 1922-23. Chenard et Walcker used Sénéchal as a sort of competitions department in 1923 and Chenard 'tanks' sometimes competed under the Sénéchal name.

A Chenard subsidiary named Société Industrielle et Commerciale de Gennevilliers obtained a five year contract to build Sénéchals from 1923, and by the end of 1927 4000 to 5000 had been produced. The workforce reputedly numbered 4000 at that time. During 1927 50 small chassis, 30 of which were Sénéchals, were made each week; 40 per cent were exported. Sénéchal sales in London were handled by Waverley Cars Ltd. Robert Sénéchal was probably a full-time

SERENISSIMA
see ATS

SERPOLLET
FRANCE 1887-1907

The leading proponent of the steam car in France, and indeed in all Europe, Léon Serpollet was born in 1858 in Culloz, a village between Lyons and Geneva, the son of a carpenter. In 1880 he went to Paris where he worked as a carpenter and pattern maker, spending his evenings on the invention of a flash-boiler for steam vehicles. In 1887 he built his first experimental steam tricycle, which he followed two years later with four more tricycles of heavier construction. These were made for him by Armand Peugeot at Montbeliard, with boilers and engines of Serpollet design made by La Buire at Lyons.

When Peugeot decided against going into production with steam cars Serpollet looked for backing to the wealthy sportsman Ernest Archdeacon, who was later to be an important figure in the development of aviation in France. With Archdeacon's help he commissioned several more tricycles of the Peugeot pattern from the Parisian coachbuilder Jeantaud, which later made electric cars, but by 1892 he realized that the tricycle was too unstable a vehicle for steam power and he turned to four-wheeled commercial vehicles.

Léon Serpollet on his steam tricycle of 1887　　　　　　　　*Serpollet roadster of 1901*

Between 1894 and 1897 about 80 steam trams and buses of Serpollet design, built for him by Decauville, were sold to operators mainly in Paris, but also in Geneva, Berlin and Vienna. However, the gradual turn-over to electric traction for trams forced Serpollet to look elsewhere for business.

He made a few steam cars during the 1890s and was fortunate in finding another backer in the person of the American Frank L. Gardner, who had made a fortune in Australian gold mines. He had also invested in the Anglo-French Motor Carriage Co, successor to Emile Roger the French agent for Benz, and when Anglo-French failed Gardner took over the works in the Rue Stendhal and made a number of single-cylinder cars designed by the English works manager, Charles W. James. Unlike Peugeot, Gardner had plenty of faith in steam and in June 1899 he installed Serpollet in the Rue Stendhal.

The new Serpollet cars, or Gardner Serpollets as they are often called, were a great advance on earlier designs, with paraffin-fired four-cylinder horizontally-opposed engines. Ordinary road cars were capable of 50mph (80kph), and in a specially geared and streamlined model called Easter Egg Léon Serpollet set a new world record for the flying kilometre at 75.06mph (120kph) at Nice in 1902. He fielded teams of racing cars in the 1903 Paris-Madrid Race and in the 1904 Gordon Bennett Trials.

Between 1900 and 1904 the workforce in the Rue Stendhal rose from about 60 to 140, and production was in the region of 100 cars a year. On the 1903 models the water tank was moved to the front, under a conventional-looking bonnet, and in 1904 the engine and boiler were also moved to the front.

Up to 1904 demand for steam passenger cars was sufficient to keep Serpollet going without making other vehicles, but then came a drop in the popularity of the steamer

and Serpollet turned increasingly to commercial vehicles. Having parted company with Frank Gardner, in May 1906 he signed an agreement with Alexandre Darracq whereby steam buses of Serpollet design would be made in a new Darracq-financed factory at Suresnes.

Serpollet's death from tuberculosis in February 1907 dealt a severe blow to the Darracq project, and although a few buses were built they never made a profit. Steam was on the way out anyway, and the last Serpollet cars were delivered in 1907. Although the lives of Serpollet and his company were short, he was recognized as an important pioneer and in 1911 a statue was erected to him in the Place St Ferdinand des Ternes in Paris.

There were two foreign ventures concerning Serpollet vehicles, neither of them successful. From 1900 to 1903 the British Power Traction & Lighting Co of Leeds made a few cars under licence, sold under the name PTL, while from 1906 to 1908 Serpollet Italiana SA made a few cars and commercial vehicles in the old Ricordi e Molinari factory in Milan. GNG

SGV
USA 1912-1915

In 1911 Herbert M. Sternbergh, president of the Acme Motor Car Co of Reading, Pennsylvania, sold his interest in the company to his father, J. Harvey Sternbergh, who took over as president. Herbert remained a vice-president and Robert E. Graham became treasurer. The Acme company had built two-, four- and six-cylinder models from 1903 to 1910 and had itself grown out of the earlier Reber Manufacturing Co, which built Reber cars in Reading from 1902 to 1903.

Later in 1911, the Sternberghs and Graham were joined by an engineer from New York, Fred Van Tine, who became works director. In July a new company, the SGV Co, was formed, taking its name from the directors' initials and taking over all Acme's assets and its works.

Van Tine also became SGV's designer and for 1912, with only about six months' development time, produced a design for a high-quality luxury car in three four-cylinder variants, a 25hp runabout and 25 and 30hp tourers. Van Tine's SGV was widely recognized as a blatant copy of the 1908 Lancia, although the company never admitted the fact.

Van Tine had previously worked for the Hol-Tan Co, a New York dealership which as well as selling a few cars under its own name in 1908 (built for Hol-Tan by the Moon Motor Car Co in St Louis, Missouri) had also imported European cars since before 1906 – including Lancias. Hol-Tan was run by E. R. Hollander and C. H. Tangeman, and in 1912 Tangeman became president of SGV, rather confirming the source of the SGV design.

All the SGV cars were four-cylinder models, luxurious and well-built but suitably expensive. In 1913 they offered a four-speed Vulcan electric gearchange, controlled by buttons on the steering wheels.

The directors never really agreed on many aspects of running SGV and late in 1914 Graham, who apparently had a substantial personal investment in the company, filed for its bankruptcy. The assets were subsequently bought by John A. Bell, under whose control the last SGV car was assembled in 1915. Bell then reorganized SGV again as the Phianna Motors Co in Newark, New Jersey, and in 1916 launched the Phianna, another superior, luxury car built in small numbers, latterly by M. H. Carpenter of Long Island City, New York, until 1922. BL

SHAMROCK

see Straker-Squire

SHANGHAI
CHINA 1965 to date

The factory had its origin in a small repair shop formerly run by members of Chiang Kai-shek's Kuomintang or Nationalist Party. After the communists took over in China in 1949, this repair shop was combined with two others, confiscated from foreign owners, and moved to a new location amid ricefields just outside Shanghai.

In 1958 the factory was renamed Shanghai Automobile Assembly Factory, and in 1960 it became the Shanghai Automobile Factory. A Jeep-type vehicle was produced in 1957, and a 1-ton three-wheeled delivery truck, Shanghai 58-1, and a 27hp tractor in 1958.

The first car built by the Shanghai Motor Vehicle Plant was the Feng-Huang (Phoenix), a 2.2-litre six-cylinder four-door saloon. It was introduced in 1958 and two more prototypes were made in the next two years. In 1965 the name was changed to Shanghai. As the SH-760 the design was continued, and production was increased in the 1970s. It is still made today, known as the SH-760A since 1974. The SH-760A is widely used as a taxi. About 3000 to 6000 are made each year, but production is expected to end in 1987 in favour of the Volkswagen Santana.

In 1967 a VIP-convertible was produced in very small quantities. This vehicle, using the same engine as the SH-760, was a very large underpowered prestige product named Shanghai SH-761. From 1970 to 1983 this factory built together with the SH-760 a 2-ton pickup truck named Shanghai SH-130, using a smaller four-cylinder 2.3-litre engine.

In 1982 an agreement was signed with Volkswagen whereby the VW Santana will be built in Shanghai. A pre-production batch of 100 has already been completed, and output from 1988 onwards is planned to be 20,000 cars and 100,000 engines annually. VW will have a 50 per cent interest in the enterprise, the balance being held by the Shanghai Tractor and Automobile Corporation (35 per cent) and the Bank of China (15 per cent). GNG

SHEFFIELD-SIMPLEX/
BROTHERHOOD
GB 1904-1926

Peter Brotherhood founded the famous engineering firm that bears his name in 1867. In 1904 an associate company, Brotherhood-Crocker Motors Ltd of West Norwood, produced a four-cylinder 12/16hp car that had been designed by former Daimler employee Percy Richardson.

Brotherhood's main factory was acquired to become the site of London County Hall in 1906 and the firm moved to Peterborough, where it still exists today under American ownership. It built aero engines in World War I and farm tractors and a few transverse boilered steam wagons in the 1920s.

In 1906 Brotherhood-Crocker production moved to premises costing £11,000 and purpose built for the company by one of the directors, the Earl Fitzwilliam, in Sheffield. Brotherhood-Crocker went out of business in 1907, although production of its 20hp model continued for two years under the name of Sheffield-Simplex. Earl Fitzwilliam, a wealthy coal magnate, supplied the finance and Percy Richardson drew up new designs based on Renaults. In 1909 there appeared a 45hp competitor for Napier and Rolls-Royce which had one gear forwards and backwards plus emergency low. A rear axle mounted gearbox was substituted in 1911 to allow a better speed range. Works manager was C. R. Garrard from Clément-Talbot. In 1912 a 30hp six and a similar 25hp replaced the 45hp and its smaller sisters. Electric starting was optional. Peak output was 25 chassis a month.

Cecil Kimber, later of MG, worked for the firm briefly during World War I, when shells, mines, armoured car chassis for Russia and ABC aero engines were produced. Commer's smaller truck models were subcontracted to Sheffield-Simplex, the two firms sharing several directors at that time.

An all-new 50hp 7778cc six-cylinder luxury car with six separate cylinders joined the 30 in 1920. It was meant to have compressed paper gears in the gearbox for silence, but it was found that the teeth disintegrated when grease reached them from the bearings so the idea was abandoned.

The market for a chassis costing £2250 – compared with £1850 for a Rolls-Royce 40/50 – was extremely limited and few were built. The Earl reputedly lost £250,000 in the final years of car production and the last chassis is thought to have been sold in 1925. Earl Fitzwilliam later gave financial support to Invicta cars.

In an attempt to diversify after the war, Sheffield-Simplex had built the Ner-a-Car two-wheeler, designed in the United States, at the former Sopwith factory at Kingston-on-Thames where prototype work on the 50hp had been carried out. The Ner-a-Car shared the factory with the ABC and Hawker motorcycles and the ending of production in 1926 coincided with an upturn in orders for Sopwith and Hawker aircraft. Up to 1500 Ner-a-Cars a year were built, many with engines produced by Sheffield-Simplex.

The slump in demand for lorries after 1919 led Commer to cancel its contract for 2-tonners and Sheffield-Simplex attempted to sell the remaining unsold lorries under the name Shefflex. The final batch was disposed of to the garage and haulage firm R. A. Johnstone Ltd of Sheffield, which sold them rapidly at half the price of comparable Commers and then started assembling more from spares in 1923. The fixed head, ball bearing crankshaft, Commer-type engine was used until 1930, from which time a variety of proprietary types was offered until the last Shefflex vehicle was built in 1937. Total production numbered about 200.

In 1938 the company became Shefflex Ltd, and still exists as a bodybuilder. The Sheffield-Simplex works was first bought by a razor blade manufacturer and then by the steel firm Darwins. As Fitzwilliam Works it now makes magnets. NB

Brotherhood 20hp tourer of 1905

SHELBY
USA 1962-1969

Carroll Shelby, the creator, with AC Cars Ltd and Ford, of the AC Shelby Cobra, was born in Leesburg, Texas, in 1923. He was the son of a mailman and grew up in Dallas. When he was 10 Shelby was found to have heart trouble; he gradually overcame it but its recurrence later ended his racing career. In his teens he developed an interest in cars and racing but could not yet afford to compete. He left high school and went into the Army Air Force where he qualified as a pilot in September 1942, spending World War II in the United States as a flying instructor.

He left the forces when the war ended and tried several business ventures, including hauling timber, running a truck company and, from 1948 to 1949, working for his father-in-law as an oil-field labourer. He then borrowed money and set up as a chicken farmer, making a profit with his first batch but going broke when disease killed the second.

He turned to helping a friend on his cars and in January 1952 had his first competition outing, winning a Texas drag race in the friend's MG special. In May he drove an MG TC in his first circuit race, and won again, after which his career as an amateur driver took off rapidly, with Jaguar XK120s and then Cadillac-Allards. He became as famous for racing in striped farm-boy dungarees as for his many wins, and continued to scrape a living through a little buying and selling and raising pheasants on his former chicken farm.

In January 1954 he won the amateur division of the Buenos Aires 1000km race and Aston Martin team manager John Wyer offered him a works drive in Europe if he paid his own expenses, plus a drive at Sebring, where he retired after going well. He went to Europe in April 1954, having turned down a deal with Texan oil millionaire Guy Mabee to join forces in building an American racing sports car.

He entered several races in Europe, including Le Mans, drove the Austin-Healey record breakers at Utah, broke his arm practising for the 1954 Carrera Panamericana then resumed a successful racing career, the highlight of which was victory at Le Mans in 1959 with Roy Salvadori for Aston Martin. He was less successful in Formula 1 with indifferent machinery and eventually retired in October 1960 when his heart trouble recurred.

In 1956 he had opened a dealership, Carroll Shelby Sports Cars, in Dallas, with Dick Hall, brother of Jim who created the racing Chaparral. Shelby had little to do with the company because of his racing and pulled out in 1958. He was already thinking of an inexpensive American sports car to compete with European cars and during 1957 discussed the idea with General Motors, which ultimately rejected it. He also talked to Aston

Martin, De Tomaso, Jensen and Maserati, with similar results.

When he stopped racing he opened a racing school, the Carroll Shelby School of High Performance Driving, at Riverside, and started a racing tyre distributorship, working from Dean Moon's Speed Shop in Santa Fe Springs.

In September 1961 he heard that Bristol would no longer supply engines to AC for its Ace and wrote to the company with his ideas for a lightweight V8 engined car. He originally intended to use an alloy Buick or Oldsmobile V8 but GM was still not interested. Ford, however, offered Shelby two examples of its new lightweight, cast iron 221cu in V8, intended for the Fairlane.

With the promise of an engine and financial support from Ford, AC agreed to develop a chassis, which would be fitted with engines in the USA in production. One 221cu in V8 was delivered to AC and used in developing the prototype, helped by Shelby who arrived shortly after the engine, but in January 1962 Ford delivered the first 260cu in version of the engine to AC and this was used in the first

completed car. This had inboard rear brakes and was used as a development car but all subsequent cars had outboard discs, and considerable chassis strengthening.

The first car was flown to California in February 1962, minus engine, and Shelby fitted a high compression version of the 260 V8. It was fortuitously timed for Ford's new interest in a younger image and received the company's full support, mainly in the form of engine supplies on extended credit and use of its dealer network. Shelby actually dreamed of the name Cobra, and the car was officially a Shelby-AC Cobra powered by Ford.

Final assembly of cars shipped from England began in Shelby-American Inc's Santa Fe Springs works at the rate of two a week and by June 1962 the first 30 had been built, prompting Shelby to move to much larger premises previously used by Lance Reventlow to build Scarab racing cars in Venice, California. Eventually 75 of the 260cu in cars were built and then Ford offered a 289cu in version which became the standard equipment. From 1962 to 1965 580 cars were built with

Shelby-AC Cobra (Phil Hill driving) of c.1964

Shelby GT350 Mustang of 1966

this engine. In November 1963 AC began building complete cars with right hand drive but only 127 Cobras were actually built outside the USA.

The 100th Cobra was completed in April 1963, making the car officially eligible for international racing, although its racing career had already started in October 1962 and its first race win came in January 1963, at Riverside. Thereafter the Cobra dominated production sports car racing for many years. Shelby won the World Sportscar Manufacturers Championship in 1965 with specially bodied racing derivatives, although winning at Le Mans eluded the special Daytona coupés.

Most Cobra development was prompted by competition considerations, especially the introduction of the 427cu in version in 1965, under development since October 1964. From 1965 to 1966 356 of the 427 cars were built, although from 1966 the model known as the 427 actually used Ford's new 428cu in motor. The last Cobra 427 was built in March 1967, by which time Shelby was also building derivatives of the Ford Mustang, known as the GT350 and GT500. Total Cobra production was 1140.

The GT350 was introduced in 1965 and was intended to be built in much larger numbers than the Cobra. In its original form it was very like a production bodied Cobra, but it generally became rather softer and more of a compromise for the road. Shelby built six convertible Mustangs in 1966 and built a fleet of special black and gold GT350s for Hertz as the GT350H.

In 1967 he introduced the GT500 with the 428 engine, and the following year a very few with the even more potent 427 were built. From 1968 production was transferred to Iona, Michigan, where Shelby parts were fitted to Mustang shells and Ford gradually took control of the whole operation, which now built both hard tops and convertibles of both GT350 and GT500 models. The last were sold as 1970 models, but all production had ended in 1969 by mutual agreement between Ford and Shelby.

Shelby was also deeply involved in the birth of Ford's GT40 and the Ford V8 engined Sunbeam Tiger, plus Dan Gurney's All-American Racers team from 1964 to 1967, building Eagle Formula 1 and Indianapolis cars. He retired from racing involvement in 1970 as a millionaire, but retained many business interests, including some in the motor industry, making wheels and other accessories. In 1981 he built a dozen further examples of the GT350 convertible from second hand basic cars and he also began to work on development models for Chrysler, including a possible Chrysler engined relaunch of AC's troubled ME3000 model in America. BL

SHERET
see Carden

Siata 208S America coupé of 1952

SIATA
ITALY 1926-1970

Societa Italiana Applicazione Transformazione Automobilistiche, or Siata, was founded in Turin in 1926 by Giorgio Ambrosini, an enthusiastic amateur racing driver. The company was set up mainly to offer tuning equipment and performance conversions for various makes, but principally for Fiat – and especially for the 508 Balilla after its introduction in 1932.

By 1933, when a Fiat 508S Balilla Super Sports ran in the Mille Miglia with Siata gearbox and overhead-valve conversions, Siata had raised the 508's output from 22 to 48bhp. In 1934 it built a supercharged 55bhp conversion and this engine was also used in a 95mph (153kph) single-seater racing Balilla.

In 1936 Siata offered a very popular overhead-valve conversion for the Fiat 500 Topolino and built Topolino based cars in many versions for road and racing use, including a spyder. Engine options went up to 596cc and 30bhp. Siata also built an aerodynamic coupé with faired rear wheels which could reach 75mph (120kph) and in 1938 set a 24-hour class record at 70mph (112kph).

After World War II, in 1948, Siata introduced a model called the Bersaglieri. This had a rear-mounted all aluminium four-cylinder twin-cam engine in a tubular chassis with all-independent coil spring suspension. It was a three-seater, in which the driver sat in the centre.

The next model, and the first which could really be called a production Siata, was the rather more conventional Amica. This was available as a two-seater spyder or coupé with independent front suspension and standard Fiat rear suspension on a Siata tubular frame. Engine options were based on the Fiat 500B/C and went up to a 25bhp 750cc Siata conversion. A very special 42bhp racing Amica with a Siata five-speed gearbox won the Italian racing championship in 1948.

In 1950 Siata modified the 1400 Fiat as the Daina, again available in open or closed forms and with a top speed of over 90mph

Siata Amica convertible of 1949

(145kph). Also based on the 1400 was Siata's 1951 Rallye tourer, which looked very like an MG TD and also offered a five-speed gearbox. The 1400 based models were offered up to 1958.

In 1952, alongside the popular Fiat based models, Siata began to build some cars with American engines, ranging from the 720cc Crosley to large Chrysler V8s. The Chrysler-engined car had independent torsion bar front suspension and a De Dion rear.

The company also offered Fiat-engined cars in the United States, mainly with the 2-litre V8 engine which was launched at the Geneva Show in 1952 in a limited edition sports car, the Fiat 8V, developed in collaboration with Siata. Among Siata's variations on the V8 theme was the 208S America coupé, with retractable headlights and a claimed top speed of over 120mph (193kph). A two-seater spyder version was also available and a Siata was entered in the 1953 Carrera Panamericana road race by the company's US importer, Ernie McAfee.

In 1954 Siata approached a different market with the Mitzi minicar, powered by a rear-mounted 328cc 12bhp twin-cylinder engine and with all round independent suspension by torsion bars. Fiat derivatives remained the main output, however.

In 1959 Siata joined forces with Abarth, as Siata-Abarth, although the union was purely administrative and each company continued to make its own models, virtually all Fiat-based. The arrangement lasted only until 1961, when Siata became independent again as Siata-Auto.

From 1962 Siata's main output was based on the Fiat 1300 and 1500 models and by 1964 94bhp twin carburettor conversions on the Fiat 1500 formed the bulk of the 1400 or so cars to pass through the Siata works during the year. Top of the 1500-based range was the TS1500 coupé of 1966, with a 1600cc conversion.

The last and possibly most popular Siata was the Spring, another 1930s MG lookalike, this time an open two-seater based on the rear-engined Fiat 850. It was built until 1970, when Siata production stopped. BL

SICAM/SIMA
FRANCE 1919-1922; 1924-1932

In 1919 Marcel Violet, who had already built his first Violet cyclecar in 1908, sold a cyclecar design to the engine manufacturer Société Industrielle d'Automobile et de Moteur (SICAM) of Pantin, Seine, a company that built motors for Violet's Mourre and Weler cyclecars and had Griffon and Motobecane among other customers. The SICAM, with 500cc two-cylinder two stroke, continued to be produced until 1922.

For two more years 98cc engines suitable for attaching to bicycles were also made. These were mostly used on machines built by Lucifer, a firm that soon developed its own motorcycle range which was produced until 1956. Violet also made a racing motor scooter that he used with success in the 1923 Bol d'Or, averaging 37mph (60kph) for 24 hours.

In 1924 a SICAM prototype became the SIMA-Violet. (SIMA stood for Société Industrielle de Materiel Automobile of Paris and Courbevoie, a company that was probably a re-formed SICAM.) The SIMA-Violet had the same flat-twin engine as its predecessor mounted at the front under an attractive streamlined bonnet.

As many as 5000 were built in four seasons, and versions were also marketed with Alcyon and Armor badges from 1925 to 1927. They had two forward gears, tubular backbone chassis and plywood bodies. Some, including a few with 750cc twins, were raced with success and in 1927 flat-four 1½-litre water-cooled Grand Prix examples were built.

Cyclecars were almost obsolete by then, so Sima – which had dropped the use of capitals – hired E. Dombret to design a more conventional car. This was probably Emile Dombret, born in 1874 and original designer of the Motobloc.

The result of his efforts in 1929 was the Sima-Standard, which was intended to carry on where 120,000 Citroën 5CVs had left off in 1926. It used the same engine, front axle and suspension, plus the transmission of a 6CV Amilcar with other components reputedly from Renault. In 1932 it was replaced by a longer wheelbase 1.3-litre version which failed to sell in the depths of the Depression. Production ceased that year. NB

444

SIDDELEY/DEASY
GB 1902-1904; 1910-1919

John Davenport Siddeley was born in Cheadle Hulme in 1866 and, like so many keen cyclists of his generation, sought work in Coventry. He was a draughtsman at Humber from 1892 and went to work at Rover in 1896. He then worked for the DuCros family, who owned the Dunlop patents, and started his own Clipper tyre firm. He became a motorist in 1899.

With financial backing from Lionel de Rothschild, J. D. Siddeley began to import Peugeots in 1901. The following year he began selling them under his own name from premises in London adjoining the Wolseley showrooms owned by Vickers. From 1903 Vickers built some of Siddeley's vehicles at Crayford and a year later appointed Siddeley as London manager of Wolseley.

Siddeley became general manager at Wolseley's Birmingham factory in 1905 when Herbert Austin left to set up his own firm. Several models of car and commercial vehicle were produced as Wolseley-Siddeleys.

As Siddeley had imported Peugeot cars so Captain H. H. P. Deasy, born in 1866 to wealthy Irish landowners, had been importing Martini cars, having briefly run the Swiss firm. In 1906 he took over the defunct Iden car factory in Coventry and in February that year formed the Deasy Motor Car Manufacturing Co Ltd, which had Australian sheep farmer Sir Waldie Griffiths as chairman.

E. W. Lewis from Rover designed a monobloc 4½-litre four-cylinder car and the range soon included models of up to 12 litres. Two to three cars a week were produced by a workforce of 100 men. Deasy then fell out with his board over competition policy and returned to Ireland, where much later he became Lord Justice Baron Deasy of the Irish Court of Appeal.

His place was taken in 1909 by J. D. Siddeley, who had had his own policy disagreements with Douglas Vickers. Along with Siddeley came A. G. Asbury, formerly of Swift and Vickers Crayford, as works manager. Siddeley became managing director at Deasy in 1910 and introduced his own JDS models with scuttle-mounted radiators and 2.9 and 4.1-litre engines – probably by Aster, which certainly supplied some models.

Smaller cars were then produced and in 1912 the firm became the Siddeley-Deasy Motor Manufacturing Co Ltd. D. M. K. Marendaz was apprenticed to this firm and Calcott was the exclusive subcontractor. J. D. Siddeley also formed Stoneleigh Motors Ltd in 1912 in order to make cars and commercial vehicles that would not compromise the quality image of the parent firm.

After 1911 Knight sleeve-valve engines were used in several models, including a 6.3-litre six that remained in production until 1919. The sarcophagus-like bonnet and silence of the engines, which were dismantled and re-built on arrival from Daimler, earned the cars the slogan 'As silent as the Sphinx'. An appropriate mascot was adopted, which was later used by Armstrong-Siddeley.

During World War I the firm did subcontract work for Standard, Maudslay and Rover,

Siddeley 6hp two-seater of 1904

Deasy 'rotund phaeton' of 1907

Simca Aronde Grand Large of 1957

made ambulances and field kitchens. Perhaps its most famous achievement was in perfecting the Beardmore-Halford-Pullinger aero engine for Arrol-Johnston. This became the Puma, of which 3225 were in use by October 1918.

Siddeley-Deasy worked with Austin, Wolseley, Daimler and Lanchester on the RAF1 engine and also built complete aircraft. Unlike most of its contemporaries, the company successfully kept its aircraft and aero engine business in operation after the war, when factory space totalled 25 acres (10 hectares).

In 1918 work was well advanced on a 30hp Marmon-inspired car with Deasy's own overhead-valve six-cylinder engine. It was about this time that Daimler, knowing it would soon lose the Knight engine contract, held merger talks with Siddeley. These came to nothing, however, and neither did Straker-Squire's attempts to sell Cosmos Engineering to Siddeley-Deasy.

Instead, Sir W. G. Armstrong, Whitworth and Co, which had resumed car manufacture at Scotswood on the Tyne, bought Siddeley-Deasy for £419,750 in May 1919 to create Armstrong-Whitworth Development Co. Armstrong-Siddeley Motors was then established as a subsidiary company. NB

SIGMA
FRANCE 1913-1928

Made by the Société des Automobiles Sigma of Levallois-Perret, Seine, the Sigma was always an assembled car of no great originality, although it survived for longer than many of its kind. Its greatest claim to fame is that one was owned by the famous World War I fighter pilot Georges Guynemer, whose 'flying stork' mascot was adapted by Hispano-Suiza.

The first Sigmas, of which Guynemer's was one, had four-cylinder Ballot engines in Malicet et Blin chassis. Ballot power was used again after the war, as well as SCAP in various sizes from 894cc to 1610cc.

The most sporting Sigma was the Model W of 1925, which used a 1494cc single-overhead cam CIME engine. A very staid-looking tourer, which could quite easily be mistaken for a Citroën B2, took part in the 1925 Circuit des Routes Pavées. It had claimed a top speed of 75mph (120kph), compared with 40-45mph (65-72kph) for the average Sigma.

Production was never large, seldom exceeding 200 cars a year. Although just viable in the early 1920s, figures like this for an undistinguished touring car were hopelessly uneconomic by the end of the decade, and Sigma closed its doors in 1928. GNG

SIMA
see Sicam

SIMA
FRANCE 1934-1981

Henri-Theodore Pigozzi took over from Ernest Lost as the French Fiat importer and in November 1934 he founded the Société Industrielle de Mécanique et de Carrosserie Automobile, or Simca, to build the 6CV Fiat under licence for the French market. Early in 1935 Simca took over a factory in Nanterre, Seine, recently vacated by SA des Automobiles Donnet. This company had built Donnet and Donnet-Zédel cars since 1924, when it was formed from the remains of two earlier manufacturers, Vinot et Deguingand and Zédel, but had gone out of business in 1934.

From 1935 to 1940 Simcas were essentially no more than French-built Fiats. The first was the 995cc 508 Balilla, and Simca also started to build a version of the 1.9-litre 518 during 1935. In 1936 the company introduced the Simca Cinq, a fabric-topped two-seater based on the Fiat 500 Topolino and with a 570cc four-cylinder side-valve engine.

The 1937 Simca Huit was based on the new Fiat 508C Millecento, with its excellent 1089cc overhead-valve engine. Some versions of this already sporty car were also substantially improved by Simca tuning specialist Amédée Gordini, who used one himself to win the Index of Performance at Le Mans in 1939.

It was one of many competition successes for this and other Gordini-prepared Simcas and gave the company some very valuable publicity in France and abroad. By 1937 Simca was already among the five largest French car-makers. In 1938, in spite of a six-week strike which closed the factory completely and even threatened bankruptcy, production reached a pre-war peak of almost 21,000 cars, about two-thirds Cinqs and the rest Huits.

The company began to recover in the first half of 1939 but production fell drastically with the approach of World War II. Although the factory was taken over by the German forces after France's occupation in 1940, Simca continued to build small numbers of cars throughout the war and in 1942 joined Baron Charles Petiet's joint sales organization, Groupe Française Automobile, which also

Simca Six of 1949

included Delage and Delahaye.

After the war French production in general was very slow to revive, hampered by heavy wartime damage, the removal of much machinery by the Germans, by materials and labour shortages, and, for the motor industry, punitive taxation on any but the smallest cars. Although production resumed in 1946 it reached only about one-third of the government's projections for 1947 and was still only about three-quarters of the target by the early 1950s.

Simca, which left the Groupe Française Automobile at the end of the war, resumed production with the pre-war Cinq and Huit models and recovered much more quickly than most manufacturers. In 1947 it introduced the Simca Six and in 1949, the last year of the Cinq, produced a pretty sports coupé version of the Huit, as one of a six-model Huit range which included a light commercial model. Production overtook the pre-war record with a total of more than 26,000 cars and in 1950 it passed 30,000 for the first time.

Sporting successes continued, with class wins in the Alpine and Monte Carlo rallies and the Spa 24-hour race, plus an outright win for Robert Manzon in the Bol d'Or race – all with due credit to Gordini, who eventually stopped working directly for Simca in 1951, to create his own marque.

In June 1951 Simca started production of the Aronde, a small saloon which was all-new except for its Huit-derived engine. It was enormously successful and stayed in production, with constant development and in a wide range of models, until 1964 – having passed the 1 million production mark in

445

February 1960.

By 1957 about one-fifth of the daily output of 600 Arondes was for export. The Aronde was introduced in Britain in 1952, originally imported by Fiat, and many cars were sold in the United States, particularly on the west coast where the sports version of the Aronde, introduced in 1953, was very popular. Since 1954 Simca had been building about one-sixth of France's total car output.

Simca's expansion included taking over the commercial vehicle-maker (and former car-maker) Unic in 1951, Ford's French subsidiary in November 1954, the French branch of the Swiss commercial vehicle-builder Saurer in 1956 and the ailing French Talbot company of Suresnes in 1959. The Ford company in particular was a very important acquisition and provided Simca with a large factory at Poissy, which gradually took over the majority of production and eventually allowed Simca to sell its Nanterre works to Citroën in 1961.

new companies, Simca Automobiles, which took over all the car manufacturing facilities, and Simca Industries, but late in 1965 these two factories recombined their interests in another new company, Société des Automobiles Simca. Chrysler had become the majority shareholder in the company in 1963, with a 64 per cent holding. Pigozzi, Simca's founder, died in 1964.

A completely new Simca model was introduced in 1962, the Simca 1000, a rear-engined 944cc saloon priced to undercut Citroën's popular Ami 6 and cheaper than the cheapest Aronde. Not surprisingly it sold very well; by 1963 it was the top-selling French export and the total produced passed 1 million in 1966. A coupé version was added in 1963 and Simca began an association with another tuning specialist, Carlo Abarth, with the twin-cam 1300cc Simca-Abarth in the same year.

In 1967 Chrysler increased its holding to 77

per cent and from that year all Simcas carried the Chrysler logo. In 1968 Simca launched its first front-wheel-drive car, the 1100 saloon, alongside two new versions of the 1100 for the home market, the sporting GLS and the economical 777cc Simca 4.

In 1969 Simca took over the racing and sports car manufacturer Matra Sports and formed a new company, Matra-Simca Division Automobile, within the parent aerospace engineering company Engins Matra. From 1973 Matra offered the Simca-engined Matra-Simca Baghera coupé and in 1977 added the front-wheel-drive Matra-Simca Rancho estate.

In July 1970, by which time Chrysler held over 99 per cent of Simca's shares, the company was renamed Chrysler France SA and a major investment programme was started, expanding existing plants and adding new facilities. This enabled Simca to build additional models under the Chrysler name, the

Chrysler (Simca) Horizon of c.1978

Simca 1100 of 1972

From 1955 it also provided Simca with a larger car, the Simca Vedette, based on the 2.3-litre side-valve V8-engined Ford Vedette. (This engine dated back to the same year as Simca itself, 1935!) The Ariane saloon, introduced in 1957, used the smaller Aronde engine in the Vedette body and was built until 1963. Limited production of the Vedette continued in Brazil as the Chambord or Presidence until 1967, although French production stopped in 1961.

In 1959 the side-valve Vedette engine replaced the BMW V8 in the Talbot Lago coupé and a smaller, Aronde-engined Talbot prototype was shown in Paris in 1960 in a last ditch effort to save this other Simca acquisition, but neither could save the Suresnes marque and no more true Talbots were made, although the name would reappear.

The changes which led to that began in 1958, when the Chrysler Corporation acquired an initial 15 per cent shareholding in Simca and announced that it would build Arondes under licence for Australia in the Chrysler factory in Adelaide. Chrysler took over Simca distribution in Britain in 1959 and continued as the British importer until the formation of Simca Motors (Great Britain) Ltd in May 1962.

In 1960 the Simca group was split into two

Simca 1307/1308 saloons of 1975

first of them being the four-cylinder Chrysler 160 saloon which started as a 1.6-litre model and evolved through 1.8 to 2 litres before its production was transferred to Chrysler's Spanish works in 1977.

Under its own name Simca added a 1.2-litre version of the front-wheel-drive 1100 in 1971, which helped the model to be the best-selling French car by the beginning of 1972, and the sporting 1294cc Rallye 1 version of the 1100. In 1973 the range comprised various versions of the 1000, front-wheel-drive 1100, 1301 and 1501 saloons and the larger Chryslers. The 1301/1501 range was dropped in 1976 while the 1000 survived until 1979, after which all Simcas had front-wheel drive.

Alongside the continuing Simca 1100 range, the British-designed Chrysler Alpine was built and sold in France from 1975 as the Simca 1307 and 1308. In 1978 the new Horizon, using a mixture of Alpine and Simca 1100 parts, was sold in France under the Simca name, in Britain as a Chrysler and in the USA as either a Dodge or a Plymouth.

In 1978 Chrysler France SA, suffering from the parent Chrysler Corporation's serious financial problems, was sold to the Peugeot-Citroën combine together with the rest of Chrysler's European car-making operation. In August 1979 Peugeot revived the Talbot name for all the European Chrysler models by reforming Chrysler France as Automobiles Talbot. The Talbot name was first revived on a car in January 1980 on British-built Alpines. Although the Simca name was used on the 1100 and on other models as Talbot-Simca until late 1981, it was dropped at the end of that year. BL

SIMMS
GB 1901-1908

Frederick Richard Simms was brought up in Hamburg where his father, originally from Birmingham, had a firm that supplied the local trawler fleet. Simms displayed an aerial cableway at Bremen in 1888 and met Gottlieb Daimler that year. He acquired the Daimler patent rights for the British colonies, excluding Canada, and helped to form the Daimler company in Coventry. It was Simms who coined the term 'motor car'.

He and Robert Bosch worked together to develop their famous magneto in 1895 and Simms founded what became the Royal Automobile Club two years later. In 1899 Simms was making proprietary engines, motor quads and his Motor Scout military vehicle.

In 1901 he helped form the Society of Motor Manufacturers and Traders and became its first president. He had severed his ties with Coventry Daimler in 1896-97 but remained on the board of German Daimler until 1902. He produced a four-cylinder overhead-valve engine in 1900 and then in December of that year created the Simms Manufacturing Co.

The initial premises were in Bermondsey,

Simms-Welbeck phaetons of 1905

London, adjoining Bryan Donkin and Clinch Ltd. E. B. Donkin joined the Simms board and his firm built chassis for the Simms cars which appeared in 1901. Donkin and Clinch moved to Chesterfield in 1902, which delayed Simms production and held profits back to £2350, so Simms moved to premises where all production could be under one roof.

His Welbeck works in Willesden Lane, north-west London, initially produced fours followed by some twins in 1904, various models with pioneer pneumatic bumpers in 1905, and a 30/35hp six in 1907, when the Panhard depot in Willesden was acquired for expansion. The cars and light commercials were often called Simms-Welbecks.

In 1908 car and engine production was stopped in order to enable the company to satisfy the strong demand for magnetos, which became a principal line. In 1909 Simms became agent for Voisin's aircraft and Friswells took over Simms' car repair, personnel and spares.

An American magneto factory was set up in East Orange, New Jersey, in 1910 and three years later Simms Motor Units Ltd was registered. During World War I the British company made and also imported from the United States many thousands of magnetos as well as making 2500 sparking plugs a week. By 1918 300 workers were employed.

In 1930 diesel engine components and injection equipment were added to the range of products produced by Simms. F. R. Simms retired in 1935 and died in 1944 in his 80th year. His firm made 40,000 magnetos for Bristol and Rolls-Royce alone in World War II. It took over Horstman in 1954 and Crosland Filters in 1961, and continues to be a major supplier to the motor and aero industries as a member of the Lucas group. NB

SIMPLEX
USA 1904-1917

The origins of this famous American make lay in the import business operated in New York City by A. D. Proctor Smith and Carlton R. Mabley. They sold Fiat, Panhard, Renault and Mercédès cars, and it was from the Mercédès Simplex that they chose the name for their own car when they decided to turn to manufacture in 1904. They bought a seven-storey factory, five above ground and two below, at West 83rd Street in New York and engaged as a designer Edward Franquist. Almost the whole chassis was made in this factory, exceptions being coils, tyres and wheels.

The first Smith and Mabley Simplex owed a good deal to Mercédès practice, with four-

Simplex racer (Ralph de Palma driving) of c.1910

cylinder pair cast T-head engines and chain drive. Most were of 30/35hp, although there was also a short-lived 18hp, and a single example of an unsuccessful 70hp racing car, both made in 1904.

About 120 cars were made before Smith and Mabley Inc went out of business in 1907, to be bought by one of its customers, textile importer Herman Broesel. He and his two sons, Herman Jr and Carl, renamed the company the Simplex Automobile Co and continued with production of the 30/35hp. It was soon replaced by a 50hp with 9.8-litre engine and a 90hp of 11 litres. Both had chain drive with a choice of driving sprockets according to the type of roads to be covered. A 38hp 7.8-litre shaft-drive model was introduced in 1911.

Herman Broesel Sr died in 1912 and the following year his sons sold the company to Goodrich, Lockhart and Smith of New York. The Goodrich brothers were sons of tyre manufacturer B. F. Goodrich.

The Broesels and Edward Franquist remained with the company and production was moved to a Broesel-owned foundry at New Brunswick, New Jersey. Output during the Broesel era was about 235 to 250 cars a year.

In September 1914 Simplex purchased the small Crane Motor Car Co of Bayonne, New Jersey, which was making a very high quality six-cylinder car of considerably more refinement than the Simplexes. It also acquired the services of its designer, Henry M. Crane, who replaced Edward Franquist.

A few of the old four-cylinder Simplexes continued to be made, but production at New Brunswick was mainly of the Simplex, Crane Model 5, or Crane-Simplex as it soon became known. About 500 chassis were made between August 1915 and July 1917, when the factory turned to manufacture of Hispano-Suiza V8 aero engines. The company never resumed car production as it became part of the Wright-Martin Aircraft Corporation. GNG

SIMPLICIA
see Lacoste et Battmann

SIMSON
GERMANY 1911-1932

In 1856 the Simson brothers took over a long-established arms manufacturing factory, dating from about 1741, in the German town of Suhl, and formed the company Waffenfabrik Suhl & Co. This continued as an arms manufacturer but in 1911 it also began to build cars.

The first were conventional 6/18 and 10/30PS models, which were quite well received and stayed in production until the outbreak of World War I, when the Simsons' attentions were diverted back to full-scale armament

Simson Supra 2-litre tourer of 1924

production. After the war, with a complete ban on arms manufacture in Germany, Simson quickly returned to building cars, starting in 1919 with updated versions of the pre-war models.

The first new post-war Simsons, introduced in 1920, were three very ordinary four-cylinder types, the 1.6-litre BO, 2.6-litre CO and the 3.5-litre DO. At the 1924 Berlin show, however, Simson introduced a much more interesting sports car, known as the S-Type, or Simson Supra. It was designed by Paul Henze, who had joined Simson as technical director in 1922. Henze was a talented young German designer who had worked for Cudell in Germany then, from 1908, for Impéria in Belgium. He worked for Steiger during World War I and he designed that company's first cars for production after the war.

His first Simson Supra was a sensation. Its 1950cc four-cylinder engine had twin-overhead camshafts and four valves per cylinder, which offered 60bhp and a top speed of about 75mph (120kph). It was widely acknowledged as the most advanced German design of its day and stayed in production until 1928, although it was extremely expensive and only about 30 examples were built.

All the company's subsequent models were called Simson-Supra but none was so spectacular as the first. A single-overhead cam version with two valves per cylinder and 40bhp was offered alongside the S-Type from 1924 to 1928, as the SO, and about 750 were made. Two other types were made between 1925 and 1926, one with a 40bhp 1.5-litre Knight sleeve-valve engine and the other a 3.1-litre overhead-cam six.

A new six, the 3.1-litre pushrod R-Type, was built from 1926 to 1932 and from 1929 it was joined by the more powerful 3.4-litre six-cylinder RJ. With the 4.7-litre straight-eight A-Type, introduced in 1931, the R and RJ continued until Simson-Supra production stopped in 1932.

With German rearmament Simson re-turned to arms production and in 1935 was nationalized. From 1949, in what was now East Germany, it built motorcycles, starting with a shaft-drive 246cc model known as the AWO and later using the Simson name on a variety of models which are still built, latterly mostly as 49cc mopeds and 74cc light-weights. BL

SINGER
GB 1905-1970

Born in 1847, George Singer worked with other motor industry pioneers at Coventry Machinists before branching out on his own in 1876 and making Xtraordinary cycles and tricycles. Terah Hooley used Singer for one of his stock market manipulations and created a £600,000 Singer limited company which made motorcycles and trikes from 1900, some of which employed the Perks Auto Wheel.

The first true cars to be produced were the underfloor 8 and 12hp engined models of 1905 built under licence from Lea-Francis and designed by Alex Craig. From 1906 more conventional two-, three- and four-cylinder White and Poppe engined cars were added, while some had Aster four-cylinder engines in 1907.

The company went into receivership in 1908 and the following year, when George Singer died, it was re-formed as Singer and Co (1909) Ltd. Capital stood at £50,500. The date was dropped from the company's name three years later.

Singer built some of its own engines, like the 14hp for 1913, but relied mostly on White and Poppe units. Singer was the engine firm's best customer, often taking a dozen a week, until Morris became a client. A 4.1-litre Singer was at the top of an extensive range when World War I began and this was the largest Singer car ever offered. The company subsequently made nothing over 2.4 litres and most of its cars were under 2 litres.

Singer had tackled the cyclecar boom with a true car in miniature in 1912, the 1.1-litre Ten. This car continued in production for military purposes during the war and afterwards became the company's principal offering, selling at the rate of 50 to 60 a week. It was priced about the same as a Citroën A.

After designer A. Alderson departed for Calcott, S. C. Poole joined Singer from Clyno as chief designer in 1920. H. C. M. Stephens, a protégé of Louis Coatalen, worked for Singer until returning to Sunbeam in 1932 to design the Dawn. William Rootes, born in 1894, was apprenticed at Singer before joining the family garage business and selling Singers with success – and later buying the company.

In 1922 Singer introduced a 2-litre six and bought the motorcycle firm Coventry Premier, briefly marketing a cheaper version of the Ten under this name. In 1926 the Calcott factory was acquired and output stood at 100 a week that year.

The range then included the Senior (formerly the Ten) and from 1926 the 848cc Junior, the first cheap British car with an overhead-cam engine. This feature had spread to all cars by 1936 and lasted for a further 20 years. At least 25,000 Juniors were sold from 1927 to 1930. Output of all models in 1927 and 1929 was reported to be 11,000 and 8000 respectively, putting Singer third in the British sales league. A licence was negotiated for Singers to be made in Germany by AGA, though nothing came of this.

In 1927 Singer moved into an additional multistorey factory in Birmingham which it had bought from BSA. The firm was unusual in making virtually all its own components, including bodies, radiators and castings. Capital in 1931 stood at £2 million, factory space totalled 44 acres (18 hectares) and there were 8000 employees on the payroll.

Rudolph Fane de Salis was chairman and W. E. Bullock managing director. Bullock was reported to have bought a number of designs from an Italian engineer, which might help to explain the multitude of engine types used until 1935.

An Industrial Motors section run by Les Perks, a relative of the designer of the original Auto Wheel, functioned from 1929, Singer having previously offered a few vans, but despite a sizeable commercial vehicle range the division did not enjoy success and was closed after three years. A subsidiary named Motor Units Ltd subsequently made small motor rollers and in the 1950s the OTA agricultural tractor was adopted by Singer as the Monarch.

Despite these attempts at diversification

Singer tricar of 1905

car production remained the basis of the Singer company. In the difficult year of 1930 cars and van derivatives achieved sales of 7650 and enabled the company to report a profit of £144,000. Two years later the Junior was replaced by the Nine, production of which was 1600 in 1932, rising to 4640 in 1933.

Charles Beauvais was hired as stylist from Standard and initially devised Kay Don specials, named after a famous racing driver. A. G. Booth from Clyno was responsible for designing Singer's chassis, H. M. Kesterton designed the transmission and L. J. Shorter, formerly of Humber and Calcott, worked on the engines. Shorter would become chief designer in 1935. In 1932 13 per cent of sales were exported and left hand drive was

Singer Nines in the Tourist Trophy of 1935

Singer Nine coupé of 1932

offered, Singers becoming the most popular British cars in Spain. The quality of workmanship was high, and final inspection was by a former Daimler employee.

In 1933 sports versions of the Nine opened up a new market to Singer and about 7000 sports cars were made until 1940. In 1934 some Singers were given clutchless gearchange while the new overhead-cam Eleven, which replaced the side-valve Twelve, had

Singer SM1500 of 1953

Singer Gazelle convertible of c.1958

independent front suspension. Sports car sales fell after the debacle of the 1935 Tourist Trophy race when Singers suffered much publicized steering failures.

An effort to fill the gap between the Junior/Nine and the larger six-cylinder models led to the introduction of the Ten, but only 800 were sold of this side-valve model. A 1476cc side-valve six for this chassis had equally disappointing sales. The Eleven could be had in a luxurious Airstream form styled by Fitzmaurice, who had been inspired by a Tatra, although many of the 750 laid down had to be fitted with conventional bodies to overcome sales resistance.

Following a profit of £104,000 in 1934 things deteriorated rapidly. Two Coventry plants were closed in 1935 and the £1 shares were written down to 12s 6d in a reconstruction scheme that brought in H. M. Emery (ex-Hudson) and resulted in a company name change in 1937 to Singer Motors Ltd. Charles Latham, later Lord Latham of Hendon, had been appointed a director in 1936 to represent the unsecured creditors.

About 5000 Singers were made in 1936 including the 9hp Bantam, which was cribbed from the Morris Eight and was given an all steel body made by former Fisher and Ludlow employees. In 1937 5150 Bantams and 1750 Super Nines were made but the six-cylinder models were no longer produced. Singer had now fallen behind the British 'big six' manufacturers.

From late 1938 HRG used Singer engines in its cars, although purchases totalled only about 200 in 14 years. Nicholas Straussler used Singer engines for his military vehicles.

During World War II Singer's five factories made shell cases, pumps, parts for Spitfire, Wellington and Halifax aircraft, and a few vehicles. In 1939 the company had introduced its Nine Roadster and made about 800 before the outbreak of hostilities. From 1946 to late 1949 some 2500 were produced while production of two revised models between 1949 and 1952 totalled 4400.

The pre-war Ten and Twelve were both revived after the war and continued to be built until 1949, by which time about 10,000 and 1000 had been made respectively. All production now took place in Birmingham. In 1948

L. J. Shorter's SM1500 model with American-inspired styling made its début. It had a cruciform-braced chassis and cost more than most rivals. Only 428 were made in 1949, the peak production year being 1952 when 6358 were made. Total sales of this model and the similarly shaped late 1954-56 Hunter were 24,000. Additionally there were 3450 SM Roadsters produced with the same engine. Some so-called Family Tourers were also assembled in Australia until 1953. A glass-fibre-bodied SMX roadster in 1954 did not enter production and nothing more was heard of earlier steam car experiments.

At the end of 1955 Singer was bought by William Rootes' company. Singer's gross assets were then £2 million, for which Rootes paid £235,000 cash plus shares. This takeover put an end to plans for a twin-overhead cam Hunter 75. Instead in 1957 a version of the unitary construction Hillman Minx Super de Luxe was offered as a Singer Gazelle with Singer engine, nearly 6000 being sold until 1958. Long-serving directors such as Shorter were replaced by Rootes family members.

Singers then became badge-engineered versions of other Rootes marques; there was the Gazelle, the Humber-like Vogue and the Hillman Imp-based Chamois, about 9000 of this rear-engined Singer being built. In 1961 production was 13,272 Singers to 140,000 Hillmans. The marque limped along until February 1970, receiving no further encouragement from Rootes' new owner, Chrysler, despite a 1250 per cent increased output of cars with Singer badges in 10 years of Rootes ownership. NB

SINGER (USA)
see Palmer-Singer

SIVA
GB 1969-1976

Neville Trickett was an automotive designer who came to prominence with his low roofline Mini conversion, the Minisprint, in the mid-1960s and later with the Ford-based Opus HRF hot-rod kit. In April 1967 he set up Neville Trickett (Design) Ltd, with assistant Nick Jenke and 2500sq ft (230sq m) of workshops in an old sawmill on a rural estate at Bryanston, near Blandford Forum in Dorset. Trickett's main work was in making small-run designs for individuals, including several Bentley conversions, a Hillman Imp-based rear-engined GT and a three-wheel cross-country vehicle. The company also made various non-motoring glassfibre products.

The first Siva was built in Trickett's usual way, to a customer's requirements and basic plan. Michael Saunders, who ran Siva Engineering in Bournemouth, wanted something resembling an Edwardian body to fit onto a Ford Popular chassis. Trickett and Saunders finished the first car in May 1969 and Saunders decided to market the car as the Siva. Kits were built under subcontract by Trickett and sold at £125 for the basic body, wings and wheel covers, or a complete car was available from about £350.

Siva Saluki coupé of 1973

A few cars were sold in 1969 and Siva moved to Poole, Dorset, early in 1970. Up to late 1972 about 100 cars were sold but then Saunders withdrew, although production continued through the newly formed Siva Motor Car Co Ltd in Aylesbury, Buckinghamshire, until Saunders reclaimed the chassis moulds towards the end of 1974.

Production of other designs continued only in Aylesbury after 1974, including cars such as the Volkswagen-engined Raceabout, introduced in May 1970, a slightly longer version called the San Remo, and a Citroën 2CV-engined Edwardian type called, appropriately, the Parisienne. None of these achieved double figure production runs up to the company's demise.

As well as the replica and fun type cars Trickett built some quite pretty kit sports cars. The VW-based gullwinged S160GT was first developed in 1971 and was followed by the Chevrolet V8-engined S530GT in 1972. In 1973 he produced the VW-powered Saluki coupé and in 1974 the open, Imp-powered Llama, but the company closed down in 1976. BL

SIZAIRE-BERWICK
FRANCE, GB 1913-1927

After the brothers Maurice and Georges Sizaire had been forced out of the Sizaire-Naudin car company in 1912 they were put in touch with a London car dealer, F. W. Berwick, by the Paris-based motoring journalist W. F. Bradley. Berwick was keen to get into car manufacture and had found financial backing from the Scottish marmalade-maker, Alexander Keiller.

A factory was obtained at Courbevoie, on the western outskirts of Paris, and Maurice Sizaire produced a design for a conventional high-quality car powered by a 4-litre four-cylinder side-valve engine, with four-speed gearbox and a Rolls-Royce shaped radiator. It has been said that Sizaire was aiming to make a visual replica of the Silver Ghost at less than half the price.

The company was registered in London as Sizaire-Berwick (France) Ltd in June 1913, with offices at 18 Berkeley Street, and work went ahead in Courbevoie to get the cars ready for the autumn's Paris and London Motor Shows. Production rose to five cars a week, of which four went to the UK market, the chassis being driven from Courbevoie to Le Havre to be shipped to England.

Bodies were mostly made at Berwick's Highgate factory, although some were provided by well-known coachbuilders such as H. J. Mulliner. However, this added considerably to the price of £745 for a Berwick-bodied tourer.

About 130 cars had been made by the end of June 1914, when the Courbevoie factory was taken over by the French government for war work. The last few chassis to be shipped

to England received armoured car bodies for the Royal Naval Air Service. The Highgate premises turned over to making a variety of bodies on Leyland chassis, such as living wagons for anti-aircraft crews, searchlight trucks and mobile photographic darkrooms.

In 1915 Berwick built a large factory at Park Royal, north-west London, which produced Le Rhône aircraft engines and De Havilland DH4 and DH9 aeroplanes. By the end of the war this plant occupied 16 acres (6 hectares) and employed 5800 people.

The activities of Sizaire-Berwick split up in 1919, with F. W. Berwick making an enlarged version of the pre-war 20hp at Park Royal while the French side of the business was

Sizaire-Berwick 25/50 tourer of 1920

taken over by an American named Burke, who began by importing Park Royal-built cars and later made some of independent design at Courbevoie.

The post-war 25/50 Sizaire-Berwick was not such a good car as its predecessor, for it had a much heavier chassis – the work, it is said, of a former steamroller designer – for which the larger engine was not adequate. The Rolls-Royce radiator had been replaced by a slightly vee design; Derby had not been able to object when the Sizaire-Berwick chassis had been made in France, but now that it was an all-British product the company brought pressure to bear. Not that this worried Maurice Sizaire too much, for when he began to make cars in France under the name Sizaire Frères, what should adorn the front but a Rolls-Royce radiator!

About 250 cars were made at Park Royal, but Berwick and the Sizaires all left the company in 1922. Berwick was later involved with the Windsor light car.

Two Austin directors joined the Sizaire-Berwick board, and this resulted in some curious hybrid cars. Austin Twelve and Twenty chassis were delivered to Park Royal, fitted with Sizaire-Berwick bodies and radiators and marketed as Sizaire-Berwick 13/26 and 23/46. There was also listed a mysterious 3-litre six-cylinder 26/52 which corresponded to no Austin model. It is highly unlikely that Park Royal could have tooled up for a new six-cylinder car, and it is possible that the 26/52 never existed except on paper. All production ceased in 1925.

Now that he had no more English-built

Sizaire-Berwicks to sell, Mr Burke decided to restart production at Courbevoie. Aided by Maurice Sizaire he launched a large car with an overhead-valve version of the British 4½-litre engine. Few were made, although one ran at Le Mans in 1925.

In 1927 Burke tried again with a similar car now powered by a Lycoming straight-eight engine. A chassis and a coupé de ville were shown at the 1927 Paris Salon, but that is probably as far as it went. In December 1927 Burke organized the Compagnie Internationale Aéronautique (Automobiles Sizaire-Berwick) at the same address in Courbevoie, but nothing more was heard of Sizaire-Berwick cars. GNG

SIZAIRE FRÈRES
FRANCE 1923-1929

Maurice and Georges Sizaire made active plans to launch a car of their own name after their departure from Sizaire-Berwick in 1922, although they had registered a company called Sizaire Frères in November 1920. The first prototype of the new car was ready in 1923 and had a four-cylinder single-overhead cam 2-litre engine developing 50bhp in a chassis independently sprung by transverse leaves at front and rear. In honour of the suspension Maurice called the new car the 4RI (Quatre Roues Indépendantes).

As before, Maurice was the designer, Georges being responsible for putting the ideas into practice and making sure they were not prohibitively expensive. Financial backing, without which they could not have got going at all, came from Paul Dupuy, publisher of the popular newspapers *Le Petit Parisien* and *Le Miroir des Sports*.

Series production of the 4RI began towards the end of 1924, and by the time manufacture ended three years later about 900 had been made. Only bare chassis were sold, and the cost of having a body built to order made a complete Sizaire Frères more expensive than an equivalent Delage or Ballot.

Although the car was costly and not particularly fast, it came into its own on rough roads, and one coped without a breakdown in the punishing 3726 mile (6000km) Leningrad-Tiflis-Moscow race in 1925. They also

Sizaire-Frères 4R1 sports model of 1924

did well in the Monte Carlo Rally between 1926 and 1930.

Paul Dupuy died in 1927 and the company was reorganized as the Société Nouvelle des Automobiles Sizaire. A 3-litre six based on Maurice Sizaire's overhead-cam four was tried in one prototype, but the new owner, the Garage Saint-Didier, preferred to use proprietary engines in the search for more power. The regular services of the Sizaire brothers were also dispensed with, although Maurice was retained as a consultant for the next few years.

The new Sizaire Six for 1928 was powered by a 3-litre six-cylinder Willys-Knight sleeve-valve engine, and there were hopes that Willys might adopt the Sizaire suspension on all its cars. These came to nothing, but about 150 Willys-engined cars were made in 1928 and 1929 together with about 100 powered by the Hotchkiss AM2 engine. French production then ceased, but the design had further leases of life abroad, both in Poland and Belgium.

Two Polish cars were Sizaire-based, the Stetyz sponsored by Count Garzinsky-Ostrogog, and the Kapeka. Not more than four or five of the latter were made, and possibly only one Stetyz, which, however, won the Concours de Confort in the 1929 Monte Carlo Rally.

The Belgian venture was longer lived and was formed by the Brussels agent Richard Thielen in conjunction with Georges Sizaire. They formed the Société Belge des Automobiles Sizaire and sold under the name Belga Rise cars powered by a variety of engines, including Willys-Knight, Hotchkiss, Minerva and Talbot. They abandoned the independent rear suspension after 1932. Belga Rise cars were made in small numbers up to 1937.

Georges Sizaire died in 1934. Maurice joined the Tecalemit oil filter company and worked there until he was 83, then retired to a life of painting. He died in 1969 at the age of 92. GNG

SIZAIRE-NAUDIN
FRANCE 1905-1921

The brothers Maurice Hyppolyte Sizaire (1877-1969) and Georges Charles Sizaire (1880-1934) set up a small workshop at Puteaux, a Paris suburb, while still in their teens. While Georges was absent on National Service Maurice was joined by Louis Naudin (1876-1913). It is not certain what business the young men were engaged in at first, possibly furniture making, but there was no sign of a car before 1902.

Then a simple voiturette powered by a single cylinder De Dion-Bouton engine, with tubular frame and belt drive, was built. Its only unusual feature was independent front suspension by sliding pillars and a transverse leaf spring, which was seen on all subsequent Sizaire-Naudin cars up to 1912.

The firm of Sizaire Frères et Naudin was registered on 1 June 1903 with capital of 12,000 francs, but no cars were produced until 1905. They were of similar layout to the prototype, but had a very individual gearchange by a propeller shaft that was shifted to engage corresponding rings of teeth on the crown wheel.

First shown to the public at the Paris Salon in October 1905, the little cars attracted many orders, more than the tiny Puteaux workshop could cope with, but they also attracted the attention of a firm of bicycle importers Hammond et Monnier, that was dabbling in motorcycles as well as voiturettes. This firm took the young trio under its wing and formed the Société Anonyme des Automobiles Sizaire et Naudin, with capital of 300,000 francs and a factory in Paris 15.

Within a few months Sizaire-Naudin voiturettes were being made at the rate of one a day, but once Hammond et Monnier had established the firm they sold it. The new owner was the Duc d'Uzes, whose wife was a

pioneer lady motorist, and he remained in control for the rest of the make's life. From 1907 the cars wore the red and blue flag of the d'Uzes family above their radiators, at the front of the tubular fuel tank which typified the appearance of Sizaire-Naudin cars.

In 1906 the duke authorized a racing programme in order to gain publicity, and many successes were achieved over the next three years. The leading drivers were Georges Sizaire and Louis Naudin; victories included the Coupe des Voiturettes in 1906, 1907 and 1908, and the 1907 Sicilian Cup. They raced again, with four-cylinder cars, in 1912, but with much less success. Nevertheless the singles remained popular with sporting owners in Britain as well as France, and by 1908 production had reached over 700 a year, which was just about as many as the factory could cope with.

Sizaire-Naudin joined the four-cylinder brigade in 1910 with a car powered by a 1.8-litre F head Ballot engine, followed by a 2.6-litre model in 1911. The singles disappeared from the range in 1912, and by 1914 the Sizaire-Naudin was a much more conventional car, with beam front axle and semi-elliptic springs and an ordinary bonnet and radiator.

The failure of the four-cylinder cars in the 1912 Coupe de l'Auto triggered off a dispute within the company which led to the dismissal of the Sizaire brothers and Louis Naudin. The Sizaires were soon busy with another venture, the Sizaire-Berwick, but Naudin, who was already in poor health, died in 1913 at the age of 37.

The company survived World War I, still in the hands of the Duc d'Uzes, and in 1920 brought out two conventional four-cylinder Ballot-powered cars, of 2.3 and 3 litres capacity. In December 1920 it was re-formed as the Société des Nouveaux Etablissements Sizaire et Naudin, with François-Xavier Belas as president and the Duc d'Uzes and the Baron Lepic as directors.

In 1921 they attempted a return to the voiturette market with a small four-cylinder 1092cc car designed by a young engineer, René Le Grain-Eiffel. Sizaire-Naudin bought the licence to make this car, but after a disastrous showing in the 1921 International Voiturette race the directors closed the firm down. The Le Grain-Eiffel design was later bought by the Manufacture d'Autos, Outillage et Cycles of St Etienne, which made it for four years under the name MASE. GNG

SKODA
CZECHOSLOVAKIA 1923 to date

Skoda has been one of the leading European names in armaments and heavy engineering for more than 100 years. Emil Skoda (1839-1900) took over the small Valdstyn factory in Plzen in 1869 for general engineering, adding a steel works in 1886 and turning particularly to artillery from 1890. In 1918 Skoda had a

Sizaire-Naudin GP car (Louis Naudin driving) of 1908

workforce of 41,000.

The first venture into car building came in 1923 when the company began to make Hispano-Suizas under licence at the Plzen factory. Bodies were also made in-house, or by well-known Czech coachbuilders such as Vaclav Brozik. Only the 37.2hp Hispano was made, and about 50 were built between 1923 and 1927. Skoda's next vehicle venture was the licence manufacture of the British Sentinel steam wagon, which was carried on from 1924 to about 1930.

In 1925 Skoda acquired the old-established Laurin & Klement works at Mlada Boleslav; existing designs of cars and trucks were made, using both badges, up to 1927, after which the Laurin & Klement name disappeared. After the end of Sentinel production at Plzen, all Skoda road vehicles were made at Mlada Boleslav.

The first car of Skoda design was the 890cc four-cylinder Type A of 1928 followed by the 1270cc Rapid, which was introduced in 1929 and was made in varying sizes until 1939. Larger cars with six-cylinder engines were also made. Top of the range was the 3.9-litre straight-eight Type 860, of which about 60 were made from 1929 to 1932.

For the first five years Skoda design was very conventional, but in 1933 came the 995cc 420. This had a backbone frame, three-speed synchromesh gearbox and independent suspension all round. By 1937 the backbone frame was found on all Skodas, which now ran from the 995cc four-cylinder Popular to the 3-litre six-cylinder Superb, which car-

ried impressive coachwork and was the favoured transport of government ministers.

Although they were popular-sized family cars, Skodas were made in relatively small numbers compared with their counterparts in Germany, France or Britain. In 1933 only 1221 cars were delivered. The best pre-war year was 1937, with 4452 sales; by contrast Opel sold more than 106,000 cars in the same year.

Czechoslovakia was a small country and export markets were not easy to come by; they were mostly confined to neighbouring Poland, Hungary and Austria, although a

foothold was being established on the French market as a result of Skoda's successes in the Monte Carlo Rally in the mid-1930s. A wide range of commercial vehicles was also made, from car-based light vans to 6×6 trucks, buses and trolleybuses.

During World War II the Skoda works were kept busy making military vehicles for the German forces, including staff cars, trucks, half-tracks and the extraordinary Porsche-designed *Ostradschlepper* 4×4 tractors with 5ft (1.5m) diameter wheels and steel tyres. Plzen was used as well as Mlada Boleslav.

Skoda 1100 roadster of 1948

The post-war 1100 was in production by early 1946. Mechanically it was almost identical to the 1939 model, with 1089cc four-cylinder overhead-valve engine and all round independent suspension by transverse leaf springs and swing axles, but it had an all-new modern body style with faired-in headlights. Production soon overtook pre-war levels, and a total of 67,000 Type 1101/1102 were made from 1946 to 1951.

By this time the Skoda works had been nationalized by Czechoslovakia's new communist government. It became the Automobilove Zavody Narodny Podnik (Automobile Works National Corporation), which axed the larger six-cylinder Skoda Superb, deciding that the country's prestige cars should be made only by Tatra. Rationalization also led to the separation of Skoda's heavy vehicle department. The 8-ton Model 706 trucks were renamed LIAZ and made in a new factory at Jablonec. Apart from a few Tatra trucks made

Skoda 450 Felicia convertible of 1962

Skoda S110R coupé of 1972

by Skoda from 1951 to 1953, the only commercials to come from Mlada Boleslav have been light vans and ambulances based on passenger car components.

In 1952 the 1102 became the 1200 with engine enlarged to 1221cc and a bigger saloon body with four doors. This was made until 1962, although estate car versions were still available in 1969, by which date more than 75,000 had been made.

Up to the mid-1950s relatively few Skodas had been exported, although some found their way to Switzerland, but in 1954 came the 440, later named Octavia, which was widely exported. Both the 1089 and 1221cc engines were available, the latter in 50bhp form in the two-seater Felicia, which was the nearest that

454

Skoda got to a sports car in the post-war years. The Octavia retained the chassis and suspension of its predecessors but had a new two-door saloon body on which the curved windscreen was interchangeable with the rear window. The Octavia saloons were replaced in 1964 by the rear-engined 1000 MB, but the Kombi, or estate car, was continued until 1969, by which time total production of the Octavia in all its forms had reached 144,366.

The 1000 MB of 1964 was a break with tradition in that the engine was now at the rear, but the swing axle suspension was retained, and this combined with the rear engine led to perilous handling which earned the car much criticism in export markets. Nevertheless it sold in very large numbers in eastern Europe and quite creditably in the West, including Britain, where its roomy body and very low price – only £30 more than a basic Mini in 1969 – earned it quite a following among undiscriminating motorists. In 1972 came the S110R coupé, and some competition developments of this did well in British racing.

After some 1.5 million had been made in 13 years the 1000 MB was replaced in 1977 by the 105/120 series, sold in Britain as the Estelle. This was still a rear-engined four-door saloon, but suspension was now by coil, which led to safer handling. Production of the 105/120 was 186,400 in 1977, and up to the end of 1984 a total of about 1,417,000 had been made.

In 1981 the Skoda works at Mlada Boleslav employed 16,000 people. The current models are the 105 with 1046cc 46bhp engine, the 120 with 1174cc 52 or 58bhp engine and the 130 with 1289cc 62bhp engine. The two-door coupé version of the latter is called the Rapid. Skodas are still sold in a number of Western countries and are particularly popular in Denmark, where they were the best selling make in 1982 and the second best seller in 1983.

In the late 1960s there were two Skoda-based light utility vehicles assembled abroad, the New Zealand Trekka and the Pakistani Skopak. LIAZ heavy vehicles were made in Bulgaria under the name Skoda-Madara. GNG

SMITH
USA 1903-1911

The Smith Automobile Co of Topeka, Kansas, was founded by two brothers, Dr L. Anton Smith and Clement Smith, who operated a successful truss and artificial limb business which they founded in 1885. In 1898 they had an experimental car built by a local bicycle-maker, Terry Stafford; this 5hp single-cylinder tiller-steered light car was followed by two others in 1901, and a two-cylinder four-seater in 1902.

The favourable impression that these cars made on local people encouraged the Smiths to make cars commercially. Accordingly in 1903 the company was formed, with a capital of $100,000, subscribed mainly by the Smiths and Terry Stafford.

The first production Smith had a two-cylinder engine under the seat, and was followed by a five-seater rear-entrance tonneau. About 50 cars were made in 1903 and the same number in 1904, but by 1905 production was up to 100. The first four-cylinder Smith was made in 1906, when there were about 100 employees. Practically the whole car was made in the factory.

The two-cylinder cars were discontinued during 1906, and for 1907 the Smiths brought out a larger four-cylinder model which they named the Great Smith. It had a 5.7-litre T-head engine with separately-cast cylinders and cast aluminium crankcase. A five-seater tourer, complete with refrigerated box on the running board, cost $2500. Unfortunately the company never made any money on the Great Smiths, which were too expensive to build, and although production went up to 250 a year in 1909 this simply created greater financial problems.

The brothers parted that year, Anton Smith trading his portion of the Smith Truss Co for Clement's share in the car company. Anton was now almost sole owner as he had already bought out Terry Stafford, and he gained more capital from a Michigan furniture maker, C. Werneke, who put in $90,000.

However, the Smith Automobile Co was a sinking ship, and manufacture ceased in 1910. About 25 cars, listed as 1911 models, were sold by the receiver. One of the last cars made was an enormous 60hp six-cylinder built for the Governor of Kansas, Arthur Coppen. The plant was sold to the Perfection Metal Products Co of Kansas City.

When it was all over, Anton Smith, described as 'a rather cheerful individual', made a huge bonfire of all the company records around which he and his family gathered and sang a song, 'Broke, broke, absolutely broke. May sound funny but it ain't no joke.' He later moved to Buffalo, New York, and built up another successful business with the 'Uncle Sam Truss'. He died in 1931. Clement, who continued to make trusses in Topeka, died in 1947. GNG

SPA Tipo 235 20hp tourer of 1922

SPA Tipo 25 cabriolet of 1925

Battista Ceirano company, STAR, which had made the Rapid car, were acquired by SPA.

The collapse of the Banco di Sconto in 1922 severely weakened SPA, which had made 1000 vehicles – perhaps including its successful trucks – in both 1920 and 1921, and 600 in 1922. A further 1200 were made until 1926, when car production ceased.

Fiat acquired an interest in SPA in 1926 and from 1928 all commercial vehicle marketing was in Fiat hands. SPA was a wholly-owned Fiat subsidiary by 1931 – when the assets of Giovanni Ceirano's car firm were bought by SPA.

SPA commercials continued to be built under their own name until 1948 and thereafter heavy Fiats often carried a badge with the words Costruzione-SPA. The Turin Fiat truck factory at Stura is still known by Fiat as its SPA plant and assembles Iveco (Fiat) trucks and makes diesels of up to 350bhp. It had 9000 employees in 1980. NB

SPARTAN
GB 1973 to date

Jim McIntyre ran an accident repair company, City Bodyworks, in Nottingham, specializing in sports car work, and especially on Triumph TR6s. Dismayed by the number of rust ravaged sports cars he saw, McIntyre decided to build himself a car with a glass-fibre body – not intended as a replica but in the 'classic' style.

In 1971 City Bodyworks moved to new premises conveniently close to several car breakers' yards and he began to build his car. It took 18 months of part-time work through 1971 and 1972 to build what became the prototype Spartan. It used a Triumph Spitfire en-

Spartan two-seater of 1979

gine in a Herald chassis, with bolt on tubular frame panelled in alloy but with glassfibre wings.

A second prototype followed, and in April 1973 McIntyre formed the Spartan Car Co and announced his intention to produce cars for sale. The first Spartan was sold in kit form in July and 25 were made in the first year, at a basic £250 plus value added tax; most used Ford engines.

The kits were initially fairly crude and demanded a degree of skill and patience which many builders lacked, indirectly giving Spar-

SPA
ITALY 1906-1926

Founded in 1906 by Matteo Ceirano and Michele Ansaldi, the Societa Piemontese Automobili Ansaldi-Ceirano (SPA) had a 129,000sq ft (12,000sq m) factory in Turin with 300 workers and an output of 300 cars a year. Capital stood at 4.2 million lire. Matteo had worked for his brother Giovanni Battista's Fratelli Ceirano factory and then helped to found Itala with a former Fiat employee. Others involved at SPA were Italian car pioneer Michele Lanza and Matteo's younger brother Ernesto. The first SPAs were Italas in all but name and included 7.8-litre fours and, from 1907, 11.7-litre sixes, all of which had shaft drive.

Inadequate capital led to a merger with Fabbrica Ligure Automobili Genova (FLAG) in 1908. A Thornycroft licence was held and capital was quadrupled. Trucks were tested in 1908 and entered full production in 1909, when Aristide Faccioli from Fiat joined to

develop aero engines and then a biplane in 1910. In 1909 SPA entered a consortium with Fiat and Isotta Fraschini to build 450 trucks for the Italian army.

A monobloc 10hp twin-cylinder light car was offered in 1909 but was replaced by a 1.8-litre four in 1912. From 1910 monobloc fours were standardized in all models including a 7.6-litre 50hp luxury car. SPAs were competitive with Fiats, and in many cases cheaper. Output in 1911 was 380 cars; 500 were sold the following year, including a number in the United States. During World War I SPA made over 5000 vehicles and 3000 between 1919 and 1923.

Ansaldi had retired in 1911 and Matteo Ceirano left in 1918, when the firm came under the control of engineering giant Ansaldo, which from 1919 built Storia-designed cars in its former aero engine factory.

SPA continued producing fours and added a six in 1920 which was the basis for an exciting twin-overhead cam 4.43-litre six Super Sports model in 1922 with aluminium pistons and four valves per cylinder. In 1924 some of the remnants of another Giovanni

455

tan an early reputation for shoddiness which was not entirely deserved. Spartan reacted by steadily refining and simplifying the kits and production reached three a week in 1974. A purpose built chassis was also offered.

In May 1975 McIntyre closed his repair business to concentrate on production and offered a fully built version from December and a lengthened 2+2 from June 1976. The company expanded with new office and service space and built its 500th kit that year, before acquiring an additional factory at Pinxton, Nottingham, in 1977. The Spartan continues basically unchanged except in its use of more self made parts and more up to date engines, typically in the mid-1980s the 2-litre overhead-cam Ford Cortina unit. In 1985 the basic kit sold for £1132. BL

SPERBER
see Selve

SPHINX
see Pullman

SPYKER
HOLLAND 1900-1925

Jacobus Spijker, a blacksmith of Hilversum, Holland, had two sons, Hendrik Jan and Jacobus, born in 1856 and 1857, who started a carriage and coachwork business after having been trained in the United States. In 1895 they began to sell Benz cars in Amsterdam.

These were soon being modified and in 1900 the air-cooled, 5hp, shaft-drive Spyker appeared, the name having been simplified for export purposes.

De Industrieele Maatshcappij Trompenburg was the title of the firm formed to build the car and took its name from a famous Dutch admiral. The factory optimistically claimed a potential output of 500 vehicles a year, although only about 10 were made in the first 12 months.

Jacobus Spijker developed a range of large and well made vehicles which included a few remarkable 4×4 cars, the most unusual of which was a 1903 racer with six-cylinder engine. Many of his experiments did not reach production, but his obsession with sealing led to the famous 'Smokeless and Dustless Spykers' whose smooth undershields considerably reduced turbulence and dust. The

familiar circular radiator was adopted in 1905.

A Spyker 14/18hp successfully competed in the Peking-Paris Race and the make was widely exported, although principally to Britain where it was sold initially by the Locomobile Co of Great Britain run by Charles Jarrott and William Letts. About 250 cars were made in 1906 and 800 men were employed a year later. Virtually all parts, including bodywork, were produced in-house, although ferrous castings came from Belgium. In 1907 Hendrik Spijker and the new British importer were lost in a shipwreck.

In April 1908 the firm was declared bankrupt and although it was re-formed later that year by J. Bienfait, Jacobus Spijker was not reinstated. A Belgian, Valentin Laviolette, designed a new T-head engine in 1909 whose twin camshafts were transversely mounted, a

Spyker 50hp racer of 1903

Spyker four-cylinder tourer of 1904

system that was retained until 1917, even though Laviolette departed for Minerva in 1912. About 100 cars were made annually from 1909 to World War I. Versions of the car chassis with double reduction axles were supplied as commercial vehicles and Saurers were imported to increase the weight range.

During the war Clerget aero engines were made, along with a variety of vehicles including mobile kitchens and more than 100 aircraft. In 1916 the name of the firm was changed, in honour of its aero connections, to Nederlandsche Automobiel-en Vliegtuigenfabriek Trompenburg following its acquisition by a consortium headed by Baron F. H. Fentener van Vlissingen. Henry Wynmalen, an aviator who had held the altitude record, became a director and modernized production techniques so that the output of cars increased to 350 annually when times permitted.

An L-head 13/30 Peace model was introduced after the war. It was apparently considered unsuitable for commercial derivatives so 10hp Mathis cars and vans were imported between 1920 and 1922 and sold as Spyker-Mathis. Continental-engined 2-ton Spyker trucks were produced, of which about 85 were sold, some to the Dutch East Indies.

Fritz Koolhoven, who had worked with the makers of Bat and Armstrong-Whitworth aircraft in England, designed a new luxury car that had a 30/40hp Maybach six-cylinder engine, and bought-in axles and gearbox. This model was introduced in 1920 and received royal patronage. The Dutch royal family had a Spyker state coach and had acquired their first Spyker car in 1912.

Despite reorganization as NV Spyker Automobelfabriek with new management in 1922, and a desperate claim by the British importer that the cars were guaranteed for ever, the level of sales did not justify production and the company was wound up three years later with only about 500 post-war cars sold. NB

SS
see Jaguar

S & S
see Sayers

STABILIA
FRANCE 1908-1930

The Stabilia took its name from its maker's claim to have produced a 'non-capsizable' design, and it was made in small numbers and numerous versions from 1908 to 1930. The Stabilia was designed by a M. Vrard, who had worked for Léon Bollée from about 1906 and later for De Dion.

The first prototype was exhibited at the Paris Show in 1904. Its main feature, at a time when most cars were still very high-built and carriage-like, was an underslung chassis with rather complicated leaf springing. According to Vrard this arrangement resulted in a centre of gravity some 50 per cent lower than that of typical contemporaries – although the seats were still noticeably on rather than in the car.

The Stabilia did not go into production until late in 1907, built by the Société des Automobiles Stabilia, in Neuilly, Seine, which showed three 12-16hp four-cylinder chassis and a coupé at the 1908 Paris Show. In 1911 the company name was changed to Giraldy et Vrard, but the Stabilia name continued. To keep down the dust which such a low car might raise, the underside was fitted with a flat sheet fairing – and according to contemporary testers it did handle particularly well.

Various engine sizes were offered up to 1913, in which year a very strange rear suspension variation was tried, using coil springs in tension and connected to the bodywork by steel cables. Stabilia claimed that this counteracted the dreaded 'side-slip' by allowing the bodywork some sideways movement of its own! *The Motor* described it as 'obviously' a racing chassis.

In 1920 the maker's name changed again, to straightforward Vrard et Cie, now based at Asnières. That year's main offering was a 14hp 2815cc four-cylinder model with cantilever rear suspension.

Production virtually stopped towards the end of 1926, and after that year's Paris Show little was heard of the marque until 1930, when Stabilia showed a chassis with independent rear suspension by leaf springs and leading arms, and a rather neat 1355cc overhead-cam straight-eight engine with a claimed output of 80bhp at 2500rpm. The chassis shown had wicker seats and was obviously intended as the basis of a very light car, but it was Stabilia's final offering. BL

Standard 13.9hp Stratford all-weather tourer of 1926

Standard 6hp phaeton of 1903

STANDARD
GB 1903-1963

Reginald W. Maudslay, great-grandson of pioneer engineer Henry Maudslay, was born in 1871, educated at Marlborough and worked for London's Tower Bridge designer Sir John Wolfe Barry, who gave Maudslay £3000 of the £5000 capital employed to set up the Standard Motor Co Ltd in 1903. Alex Craig was works manager and designer at a factory in Much Park Street, Coventry, that was later to be used by bodybuilder Charlesworth and then by Lea-Francis.

The Standard name was chosen, said the company, to symbolize the use of components that had been 'tried and tested and accepted as reliable standards'. Forward control models with one-, two-, three- and four-cylinder engines were produced and engines were available for re-powering other cars and for marine and other purposes.

Twenty men were employed in 1904 and 100 by 1906, when a new factory in Bishopsgate Green, Coventry, was acquired. Front-engined six-cylinder cars soon became a speciality. Charles Friswell of London, who contracted to sell the entire output, was chairman of the company for about five years while this arrangement lasted. His shares were then bought by a Coventry solicitor and by Siegfried Bettmann, who owned Triumph and took over Friswell's position as chairman.

The Union flag or Standard became the radiator badge in 1908. Three years later 70 cars were supplied to the 1911 Delhi Durbar, including some unusual 4×4s. A four-cylinder 14hp car was launched in 1909 followed by a 9.5hp car from an additional factory in 1913, by which time the sixes had been discontinued. Output was running at 50 a week by 1914.

During World War I new works at Canley, near Coventry, made 1600 RE8 biplanes while the old works concentrated on shells and components and a few ambulances and other vehicles. The workforce rose to 2000.

By 1921 about 200 cars a month were being made. These were overhead-valve 11.6hp models which were joined by an overhead-valve 8hp in 1922, when the standard of the IX Roman Legion was temporarily adopted as a badge. Some 5000 cars, mostly of the new 13.9hp, were made in 1923 and output in 1924 doubled to 10,000. That year model names based on British towns, villages and landmarks became universal.

Canley had received a moving body assembly track by 1922 and a test circuit around the works. John Budge, chief draughtsman since 1905, was works manager during this period of rapid expansion. In 1927 an 18hp six was produced, the first for many years, and a new small four-cylinder 9hp car was designed by Ray Turner and inspired by Mathis.

John P. Black, formerly at Hillman, joined Standard in 1929 and four years later became managing director. Another recruit from Hillman after the Rootes takeover of that company was Frank Salter as planning engineer in

1930. Salter had earlier been with General Motors at Hendon and in the 1940s worked at Jowett. Edward Grinham joined as chief engineer from Humber. R. W. Maudslay, Standard's founder, died in 1934.

From 1928 special-bodied versions of Standards, styled initially by the Jensen brothers and later by C. F. Beauvais as Avon Standards, had been available and Swallow also made its own bespoke versions from 1930. For 1932 Swallow persuaded Standard to make special chassis for its new SS. Standard supplied Jaguar with engines until 1940 and its four-cylinder types until 1948. Other engine customers included Morgan and Railton.

Despite the Depression 9000 of the popular Nine model were sold from 1929 to 1930, 100 cars a day of all types were built in 1931, and in 1932, when an owners' club was started, the entire season's quota was sold by July as a result of keen pricing, modern styling and a good reputation. A total of 20,000 cars were sold in 1934, when all production took place at Canley and conveyor assembly lines were installed.

Considerable factory expansion occurred in 1935, when the Grinham, Salter and Wilde designed fastback Flying Standard range first appeared and helped to push output to 40,000 in 1937 and over 50,000 in 1939. Largest model was a 20hp six, although there were also some 200 V8 20hp models based on the chassis of the 12hp.

A new model in 1939 was the Eight, the first small British car with independent front suspension. More than 10,000 were sold before the war and 83,139 to the end of its run in 1948.

During World War II Standard made 1066 Mosquitos along with Oxford Trainers, fuselages (3000 for Beaufighters) and parts for several other aircraft, 417,000 aircraft engine cylinders, 55,000 aircraft carburettors, 20,000 Bristol Hercules engines, and numerous other items that helped to earn John Black a

knighthood. Vehicles produced included 2800 Beaverettes, 10,000 light utilities and prototypes for a 'Jungle Jeep' for the Far East that was not in fact required. When the war ended the Canley factory was undergoing a £6 million modernization programme.

A 4×4 utility Standard for farmers was not proceeded with and there was talk of a merger with Willys-Overland, which would have brought the Jeep to Coventry. Instead, Standard built Harry Ferguson's tractors from 1946. In the first year Continental engines were used, followed by a Standard engine that was to give valiant service in the Vanguard World Car from mid-1947. A diesel variant was soon produced and a total of 1930 were installed in Vanguard cars and commercials between 1954 and 1956. The Vanguard was styled by Walter Belgrove with deliberate Plymouth overtones. It was the sole Standard model made from 1948 to 1953.

Car production picked up from 2350 in 1945 to 35,000 in 1947. From 1945 Triumph, whose factory had been destroyed in the Blitz, was a wholly-owned subsidiary of Standard. Triumphs were made at Canley at a rate of 12,000 towards the end of the 1940s.

Ferguson production ran at about 50,000 a year at the Banner Lane former 'shadow' factory and in 1953 Massey-Harris acquired the tractor company. However, Standard continued to produce the tractors until it sold the Banner Lane factory to Massey-Ferguson in

Standard Eight saloon of 1953

1959. The loss of this business had serious repercussions for Standard, which had earlier hoped to be taken over by the tractor giant and had also held talks with Renault.

From 1951 Standard made the Rolls-Royce Avon jet under licence. Factory area then stood at 2.7 million sq ft (250,000sq m) and the workforce numbered 11,000.

Car exports were soon booming – 5631 in March 1951 alone – and Vanguards were soon being built in 11 foreign countries including Switzerland, South Africa, India, Australia and Belgium. Early Vanguard exports suffered chassis fractures. Versions of the Vanguard engines powered Triumph TR and Morgan sports cars. Over 270,000 Phase I and II (similar bulbous shape but not fastback) Vanguards were built during their 10-year life from 1947 to 1956.

In 1950 60,700 cars were produced and three years later, when the serious limitations of the one model policy were apparent, a new model Eight was introduced with unitary con-

Standard Flying Twelve tourer of 1938

Standard Ensign of c.1958

struction. It was the cheapest four door car in Britain and in 1954 cost £481. That year a Ten was introduced. These two 'popular' models were not a commercial success, however, even though they amassed sales of 310,000 to the end of production. In North America 57,000 Tens were sold as Triumphs.

Alick Dick, who had joined the company as an apprentice in 1934, became managing director in 1954 in place of Sir John Black. In 1958 Mulliner, the Birmingham bodymaker, was acquired as Fisher and Ludlow, Standard's previous suppliers, were by then owned by the British Motor Corporation.

In the late 1950s Standard's financial situation was weakening and was not helped by high development costs for a new small saloon that was to emerge as a Triumph, not Standard, Herald. (In India from 1961 to 1980 this car was made by Standard Motor Products of Madras and called a Gazel.) The Eights and Tens – and the Ten's variants, the Pennant and Companion – were no longer selling adequately and although there was a new Vanguard model in 1956, only about 75,000 were sold until production ended in 1963. Michelotti had been called in to revitalize the Vanguard but could do little. The Ensign, which had a similar body shell to the Vanguard, achieved sales of about 21,000.

In 1960, with car sales of about 50,000 and the tractor business ended, Standard declared a loss of £7 million. A serious attempt to enter the light commercial vehicle field had been made in 1959 with the forward control Atlas range. Merger talks took place with Rover, but it was Leyland which eventually bought Standard-Triumph in 1961.

Donald Stokes, the Leyland sales supremo, tried to boost car production, and a new assembly area with three assembly lines, each of 1300ft (400m), with a capacity of 300,000 cars a year was installed at a cost of £2.5 million. The workforce totalled 14,000.

The Standard name no longer had connotations of high quality, however. If anything it implied only average worth. Leyland therefore decided to concentrate on the Triumph marque and the last Standard cars were made in 1963. The last commercials to be badged as Standards were sold in 1965, although some designs persisted with Ley-

land badges until 1968 and Atlas engines and cabs were to be found on four wheel Scammell mechanical horses.

Much of the Standard factory has been sold for other uses and in part of it an independent research team does experimental work for several British and foreign car-makers, notably for Jaguar and BMW. NB

STANDARD (Germany)
see Gutbrod

STANDARD
USA 1912-1923

Best known as a medium-priced V8, the Standard was built by the Standard Steel Car Co of Butler, Pennsylvania, well-known maker of steel and composite railway carriages and wagons. The company's first car was a conventional six-cylinder machine powered by a 6.8-litre engine, built in open and closed models at prices up to $3600.

For 1916 Standard introduced the Eight, powered by a 50bhp 4.6-litre V8 and priced at only $1735 to $1950. By this time the Six had come down to $2100, and was dropped shortly afterwards. In 1918 the Eight's capacity went up to 5.4 litres and remained at this size for the rest of the make's life. Standard claimed that the engines were the company's own, but they carried a plate attributing manufacture to the Model Engine Works, and it is thought that they contained many components supplied by Herschell-Spillman.

Although cars were never more than a sideline for Standard, which also made armoured cars during World War I, they sold quite well, 885 being delivered in 1921. Standard discontinued the car early in 1923 and production was taken over by a new company called the Standard Auto Vehicle Co. It is possible that it did nothing more than assemble cars from parts on hand, and not more than 50 were made in 1923. Standard Steel had gone out of business by 1924 and its factory stood idle until 1930, when it was used for production of the American Austin. GNG

STANDARD (USA)
see also St Louis

STANGUELLINI
ITALY 1947-1963

Fiat-based Stanguellini of 1938

The Stanguellini engineering firm was founded in Modena in 1879 by Celso Stanguellini. Around the turn of the century Stanguellini became involved with motor cars as a Fiat dealer, when Celso's son Francesco began to compete in motor races. In 1929 Francesco's son Vittorio, born in 1910, took over the company and the main business became modifying Fiats and Fiat engines for racing – with excellent results.

In 1938 Vittorio formed a 'works' team, Squadra Stanguellini, and built special bodied Fiat racers ranging from 750cc to the new 2.8-litre six-cylinder model. He resumed racing after World War II with similar models and in 1947 introduced a four-seater sports car for the road, based on the Fiat 1100 and styled by Bertone. A 1500 Sport model, with an enlarged version of the 1100 engine, was also available.

Rebodied Fiat 750s were offered in 1948, and by 1950 Stanguellini had introduced a twin-cam engine and many other Fiat tuning parts. The 80bhp 1100-based twin-cam racing sports car could reach 120mph (193kph), and by 1956 Stanguellini was offering a 741cc twin-cam road car with a top speed of 112mph (180kph) plus an 1100 road car.

The company's main activity, however, was still building racing models. In November 1956 a new single-seater category, Formula Junior, was introduced in Italy and would gain full international status by October 1958. By 1963 some 130 marques had appeared in the formula but most of the early success went to Stanguellini's front-engined Fiat-based car, of which more than 100 were built. After 1959 Stanguellini built rear-engined Formula Junior cars, but they were now overshadowed by Cooper and others.

In 1961 the company produced another sports car, the rear-engined Delfino, and over the next two years built cars for Formula 2 and Formula 3, plus several Moto-Guzzi motorcycle-engined 250 and 350cc record breakers, known as Stanguellini-Collibris. After 1963 the company stopped building cars in order to concentrate on selling tuning equipment and designs to other manufacturers. BL

STANHOPE/AUTOGEAR, BRAMHAM
GB 1914-1925

In 1914 Harry Stanhope of Burley Road, Leeds, invented a curious three-wheeler in which the single front wheel was driven by a JAP 8hp engine as well as steered. Automatically expanding/contracting pulleys and belts with wooden idler roller took care of ratio changes, the pulley on the front axle being offset to the nearside to allow an adequate steering lock.

In 1916 Stanhope Motors (Leeds) Ltd, with £2000 capital, took over the rights to Harry Stanhope's inventions. In 1921 the company became Stanhope Motors Ltd with a capital of £7000.

The first production car appeared in 1919. Three years later a similar car, but with a Blackburne engine, went under the name Autogear. It came from a different address in Leeds, having been begun by Foster Engineering in Letchworth. The Stanhope became the Bramham and was produced from Bramham Motors at the original Stanhope address from 1922 to 1924. The Autogear variety appears to have survived until 1923. The Stanhope name reappeared in 1924 on a front-wheel-drive four-wheeler which was built until 1925 by Stanhope Brothers Ltd, a company formed by Harry and Herbert Stanhope. NB

STANLEY
USA 1897-1927

Of the few cars to succeed without relying on the internal combustion engine, the Stanley was undoubtedly the most successful, promoting the cause of steam for 30 years before finally giving in to the marketing strength and ease of use of its great rival. Its progenitors, Francis E. and Frelan Ozro Stanley, were identical twins, born in Kingsland, Maine, in 1849 to a farming family. For a while they both worked as teachers and their first business venture was making violins.

In 1893 they patented a revolutionary dry-plate photographic system and established the Stanley Dry Plate Co in Newton, Massachusetts – a business which they later sold to the Eastman Kodak Co for a substantial sum when their interests turned to cars after seeing a demonstration at a fair in Massachusetts.

In September 1897 they completed and

Stanley steam buggy of 1898

tested their first car, designed by the brothers but using bought-in engine and boiler, which imposed an unacceptable weight penalty. To overcome this the Stanleys designed their own wire-wound boiler and used it with a very light engine made by J. W. Penny & Sons of Maine. By the spring of 1898 they had built three more cars, but only for their own use, until F. O. sold his for $600.

In October 1898 F. E. won a mile race at the Charles River cycle track near Cambridge, Massachusetts, at more than 27mph (43kph), and shortly after that won a hillclimbing contest. Within two weeks the Stanleys had orders for about 200 cars and finished the first in early 1899, in a factory at Newton which they bought from a friend, the bicycle manufacturer Sterling Elliott.

Shortly after, they sold the manufacturing rights and their works, for $250,000, to John Brisben Walker and Amzi Lorenzo Barber. They also undertook not to manufacture steam cars under their own name for one year from May 1899.

In June, Walker, the publisher of *Cosmopolitan* magazine, and Barber, an asphalt manufacturer, set up the Automobile Co of America, with capital of $2.5 million and the Stanleys nominally in charge of engineering. In July the name was changed to the Locomobile Co of America when it was found that the original name was already registered. Barber and Walker parted shortly after, Barber to build the Locomobile (initially in the Newton factory) and Walker to build the near identical Mobile with the Mobile Co of America.

In 1899 the Stanleys bought the G. E. Whitney Motor Wagon Co of Boston, set up in 1897 by George E. Whitney to build steam cars based on his prototype of 1896. The Stanleys formed the Stanley Manufacturing Co and built some cars based on the Whitney and known as Stanley-Whitney. Then in 1901 they bought the old Newton factory, and many

Stanley 10hp steamer of 1911

patents, back from Locomobile for $25,000 and moved back in as the Stanley Motor Carriage Co. Shortly after, they sold various patents for $15,000 to Rollin H. White's White Sewing Machine Co of Cleveland, Ohio – probably the next most successful of the 80 or so steam manufacturers who came and went until the end of the 1920s.

The new Stanley car, announced in 1902, had a wooden frame, tiller steering and a twin-cylinder engine driving the rear axle directly. This drive system remained a Stanley characteristic throughout the company's life. The boiler, fired by pressurized kerosene, was tested to 800psi and had an automatic fuel cut-off and pressure release valve. It was considered virtually unburstable but the fire had a tendency to go out under hard acceleration and then blow back, with varying degrees of violence, on relighting. Otherwise, the car's main disadvantage over a petrol-engined model was in its starting-up time, which was typically about 20 minutes.

The Stanley certainly lacked nothing in performance, however, and was both quick and very quiet. More powerful models were added each season and by 1906 they had switched to wheel steering.

In January of that year Stanley had its finest hour when Fred Marriott drove a streamlined

Stanley 735 steamer of 1920

Stanley racer called Wogglebug to a speed of over 127mph (204kph) in the Dewar Cup at Ormond Beach, Florida. In 1907, trying for the land speed record, Marriott crashed at well over 150mph (241kph), destroying the Wogglebug but surviving his serious injuries. The Stanleys gave up racing but their road cars continued the performance tradition.

By 1911 Stanleys were being built under licence in Britain at Gateshead, and three models – two 10hps and a 20hp – were being offered, each for under £400. Already, though, the steam car market in America was almost dead; from a peak of over 40 per cent in 1900 the steamers' share had fallen to less than 2 per cent by 1909. Stanley responded with such improvements as electric lighting from 1913 and steam condensing systems (which vastly increased range) from 1915, while the cars had long been styled to resemble petrol models.

The condenser-engined cars were considerably more expensive than the simpler early cars and sales in 1915 were barely one-sixth the previous year's total of almost 750 cars. Sales revived to about 600 a year by 1918 but this was tiny by prevailing standards.

Frelan had effectively relinquished the day to day running of the company due to ill health soon after production returned to

Newton, and he moved to Colorado to open the Stanley Hotel. Both brothers continued as directors, however, until they retired officially in 1917. Francis E. Stanley was killed in a road accident in 1918 but Frelan survived until 1940, running the hotel virtually until his death.

Early in 1918 the management was taken over by Chicago businessman Prescott Warren, but prices were too high and sales too low and in 1925 the company was sold again, to the Steam Vehicle Corporation of America. The new owners continued to build Stanleys in small numbers until 1927, before stopping production completely. Plans to revive the Stanley in the mid-1930s came to nought in the face of the inevitable resistance to the steamer's few but insurmountable disadvantages over petrol's ease of operation. BL

STAR
GB 1898-1932

The Star was the longest-lived of the cars made in Wolverhampton. For most of its life it was guided by the Lisle family, who had started in business in 1883 as the bicycle-makers Sharratt & Lisle. In 1896 Edward Lisle

Sr changed the name to the Star Cycle Co Ltd and two years later a new company was formed to deal with the motor car side of the business under the name Star Motor Co Ltd. The Star Cycle Co continued to make bicycles, motorcycles and, at a later date, cars under the direction of Edward Lisle Jr.

For its first few years the Star Motor Co relied on other people's designs. From 1898 to 1902 they were based on the 3½hp belt driven Benz, and were sometimes known as Star-Benzes, although from the beginning Star was a manufacturer rather than an assembler. Every part of the Star-Benz was made in its factory, except for the Brampton roller chains and the Clipper tyres. Production was running at one car a week from October 1899.

In 1901 the Star-Benz was joined by two De Dion-engined cars, and in 1902 came an 8hp vertical twin, followed by a 10hp twin and 20hp four. All these designs were generally similar to the Panhard. The company name was changed to Star Engineering Co in 1902.

By 1904 there were 12, 18 and 24hp fours on Mercédès lines, as well as a 70hp racing car which was a close copy of the Mercédès Sixty. It competed unsuccessfully in the 1905 Gordon Bennett Eliminating Trials.

In 1905 the Star Cycle Co entered the car

Star two-seater of 1904

Star 15.9hp tourer of 1914

market with a 6hp De Dion-powered chain driven voiturette sold under the name Starling. The company was still making two-wheelers and the 1905 catalogue listed bicycles from £8 8s 0d, motorcycles from £32 and the Starling at 95 guineas. It was joined in 1907 by the 7hp shaft-driven Stuart, which was available with a four-seater tonneau body. The Stuart name was dropped in 1908, when Starlings were sold in 8 and 10hp models. In 1909 the Star Cycle Co Ltd changed its name to the Briton Motor Co Ltd and became a separate concern under the direction of Edward Lisle Jr.

Meanwhile the Star Engineering Co prospered with a range of conventional cars, the most successful of which was the four-cylinder Fifteen made from 1909 to 1914. Six-cylinder cars were made briefly in 1907 and again in 1913, but otherwise Star concentrated on fours from 10 to 20hp. By 1914, when Star was also making several commercial vehicles from a 5cwt (254kg) 10hp van to a chain-drive 4-ton lorry, it was among the six largest British vehicle producers with an annual figure of more than 1000.

During World War I Star made large numbers of army lorries as well as working on the unsuccessful ABC Dragonfly radial aero engine. In 1919 it resumed production with the pre-war 15.9 and 20.1hp cars and commercial vehicles from 1½ to 3 tons capacity. By 1920 production was running at around 1000 vehicles a year, being turned out in very cramped premises in a series of Wolverhampton back streets.

Apart from the frames which came from Thompsons of Bilston, practically the whole car was made by Star, including all body-work. One of the more unusual orders from the body department was for eight harem wagons for King Ibn Saud of Saudi Arabia; it was strictly stipulated that no men were to enter the vehicle during construction.

A new 11.9hp four-cylinder car with monobloc engine came out in 1922 and a six-cylinder Eighteen in 1923. These were gradually developed into the 12/25 and 20/50 respectively. Overhead valves were introduced in 1927, on the 14/40 four and 20/60 six, and there was also an 18/50 Light Six in 1928.

In that year the Lisle family sold out to Sydney Guy, who was eager to have a passenger car business to complement his commercial vehicles and who had given up car production a few years previously. The immediate consequences of this change of ownership were a return to the original name of Star Motor Co Ltd and a move away from the cramped factories to Star's body plant at Bushbury on the outskirts of Wolverhampton. Commercial vehicle production, never large, was gradually run down from 284 units in 1928 to 63 in 1930 and 17 in 1932.

New models of car were introduced for 1931, the 18hp Comet and 21hp Planet, both attractive looking and well-equipped sixes. They were joined by a 14hp Comet Fourteen and a Planet Twenty Four for 1932, so they covered the middle market from £345 to £695.

Unfortunately, although the Bushbury factory was more spacious, the machinery was

Star Little Comet (supercharged) of 1932

old fashioned and Star did not have the capital to modernize it. The comprehensive equipment such as one-shot chassis lubrication and thermostatically controlled radiator shutters were expensive to make, and the result was that each of the Comets and Planets was made at a loss.

Guy was not prepared to pour money into Star, particularly in a time of recession, and in March 1932 a receiver was called in. The unsold stock was sold off by David Rosenfield Ltd of Manchester, while McKenzie & Denley of Birmingham acquired manufacturing rights but never built any cars. Total production of Planets and Comets was 665. GNG

STAR (USA)
see Durant

STAVER
see Henney

Star 10-litre racer (F. R. Goodwin driving) of 1905

STEARNS/STEARNS-KNIGHT
USA 1899-1930

Frank B. Stearns (1879-1955) built his first car in the basement of his family home on fashionable Euclid Avenue, Cleveland, Ohio. The single-cylinder machine was completed in 1896, and while young Stearns was making its successor he attracted the attention of the brothers Ralph and Raymond Owen. The three of them formed F. B. Stearns & Co in 1898 and made about 50 single-cylinder two-stroke engined two-seaters before the Owens left in 1900 to pursue their own interests, which would later include the Owen Magnetic car.

The first 50 cars had been made in a workshop behind the Stearns home, but in 1900 Frank moved to a rented workshop also on Euclid Avenue. This site would remain the home of Stearns cars for the next 30 years.

Financed by profits from the cars sold, with some help from his father, Frank prospered during 1901, receiving further help from his father-in-law, Captain Thomas Wilson, founder of the Wilson Marine Transit Co and the Central National Bank of Cleveland. An enormous single-cylinder engine, of 3.8 litres capacity, was introduced in 1901 and powered a five-seater surrey.

In 1902 the company was reorganized as the F. B. Stearns Co with $200,000 capital. Frank was president, general manager and

In 1910 Frank Stearns sent his chief engineer, James G. Sterling, to England to study the Knight engine as being used by Daimler, and after exhaustive testing the Stearns company adopted sleeve valves on the 1912 models. Apart from the abortive Silent Knight car made by Charles Yale Knight himself in 1906, the Stearns was the first American car to use sleeve valves.

In 1914 a 5.1-litre four and a 6.8-litre six, both with electric lighting and starting, were offered, and for 1915 Stearns brought out a 22.5hp 4-litre Light Four selling from $1750 to $2850. This brought Stearns into a fresh market where demand was so great that a new five-storey extension to the factory had to be built. Whereas Stearns had sold fewer than 1000 cars in the first year of the Knight engine, 1916 saw 4000 cars delivered. The Light Four was joined by a V8 that year priced from $2375 to $3785.

At the end of 1917 Frank Stearns retired at the age of 37 to devote himself to experiments with diesel engines. He later obtained 16 patents in connection with diesels, and sold his engine to the US Navy in 1935. The company was reorganized with former St Louis agent George W. Booker becoming president.

Rolls-Royce aero engines were made for the war effort from late 1917, and although car production was not suspended only 1450 were delivered in 1918. Even fewer were made in 1919 – 1256 cars – of which only 53 were V8s. The latter were dropped for 1920, when production rose to 3850.

In 1921 James G. Sterling left, taking quite a number of Stearns engineering staff with him, and set up on his own at Warren, Ohio, where he made the Sterling-Knight, a six-cylinder sleeve-valve car. This design was taken over in 1925 by John N. Willys and re-worked into the 1926 Willys-Knight Model 66.

Stearns itself joined the Willys empire in December 1925 when John Willys formed a separate syndicate to acquire and manage the Cleveland company, whose name remained unchanged. H. J. Leonard was brought in as president from the Stephens Motor Car Co, a subsidiary of Moline Plow which Willys had owned until recently.

More than $500,000 was invested in Stearns for plant expansion and improvement, and in the first quarter of 1926 sales were up 89 per cent on the same period the previous year. The last year of the four-cylinder Stearns-Knight was 1926, and in 1927 the six was joined by a new 100bhp 6.3-litre straight-eight selling from $3950 up to $5800. Stearns also had exclusive US sales rights for the Daimler Double Six V12, which carried a price tag of $17,000. One wonders if any were sold.

Despite the initial euphoria, Willys soon found that Stearns was not the money-spinner he had hoped. The inventory had been written up far beyond its actual worth and the dealers were disorganized and dispirited. Good car though it was, the straight-eight faced very serious competition from Packard and Lincoln. Sales dropped from a peak of 3759 in 1925, the year before the Willys takeover, to fewer than 2000 in 1929.

The stockmarket crash of October 1929 dealt a death blow to the company, which had been shaky even when Willys bought it. The shares for which he had paid an overvalued $10 each dropped to 12½ cents, and on 30 December the stockholders voted to dissolve the company.

Car production had ceased 10 days earlier, although a number were sold off as 1930 models during the first few months of the New Year. Stearns was the second longest-lived Cleveland make, after Peerless, and built nearly 32,000 fine cars. GNG

Stearns chain-drive tonneau of 1909

treasurer, and his father F. M. Stearns was vice-president and secretary.

Two-cylinder cars as well as singles were offered in 1903, at prices up to $3000, and about 80 cars were sold. A 40hp four at $4000 came in 1905, and engine sizes were steadily enlarged, culminating in the massive 45-90hp six-cylinder of 1908 with a capacity of 13 litres and a price tag of $7500. Very few were made, but overall Stearns sales were up to 260 in 1908, 500 in 1909 and 1000 in 1910.

A 'baby Stearns' of 32hp and 4.8 litres joined the range for 1909, and was also used as the basis for a taxicab, about 30 of which were made in 1910. Heavy chain drive trucks of 3 to 5 tons capacity were made from 1911 to 1916, and from 1915 to 1916 had the Knight sleeve-valve engine.

Stearns-Knight limousine of 1926

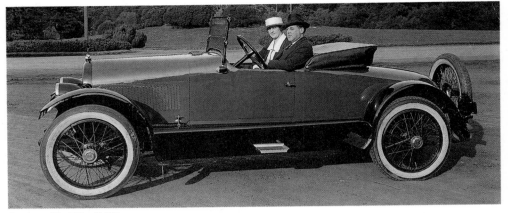

Stephens Silent Six of 1922

STEIGER
GERMANY 1914-1929

Walter Steiger was a Swiss-born engineer who set up Maschinenfabrik von Walter Steiger in Burgrieden, Germany, in 1914 to produce steel wheels for cars. During World War I the company expanded to offer repairs on aero-engines and aircraft, and at the same time Steiger began to make plans for building cars.

The first Steiger car was designed by the company's works manager, Paul Henze. Henze had previously worked for the pioneer German manufacturer Max Cudell, moved to Impéria in Belgium to design that company's first cars and then to Baron von Liebig's Austrian RAF company before joining Steiger. Prototypes of Henze's design were assembled during the war in 1917, and the renamed Walter Steiger & Co started car production in 1920.

The 10/50PS car used a 2.6-litre four-cylinder overhead-cam engine which was technically very advanced, particularly in its use of light alloys. There was also a 100mph (160kph) 3-litre sports version, which was used to good effect in competition in spite of its poor brakes.

From 1921 Steiger also built its own bodies, which had typically Germanic vee radiators. The expensive 10/50PS was Steiger's only model, partly because Paul Henze left in 1922 to design the even more advanced Simson Supra. About 2000 Steiger cars were built and the company employed up to 500 people.

In 1924 Walter Steiger and his brother took over the ailing Swiss company Société Nouvelle des Automobiles Martini, maker of Martini cars since 1897, and in 1925 Steiger's own company was reorganized as Steiger AG. Production stopped, however, in 1926 when this company went bankrupt. Steiger himself had already gone to work at Martini, where he designed the uninspired six-cylinder Martini-Steiger cars, which were built until 1929. BL

STELLA/CIEM
SWITZERLAND 1904-1913

The Compagnie de l'Industrie Electrique et Mécanique (CIEM) of Geneva made electrical machinery and as early as 1881 its chief engineer, René Thury, built a steam tricycle. Early this century CIEM added petrol engines to its products but, finding few customers, decided to build complete vehicles in 1904. A bus was available under the name Rolls in Britain in 1905 from C. S. Rolls's retail business.

Only 14 CIEM commercials were made in almost 10 years. The early ones, like the cars, had petrol-electric drive in which the engine or the batteries could independently propel

Stella 18/20hp saloon of 1910

the vehicle, a dynamotor being used, which could also be switched to start the engine. The cars had V2 8hp or V4 16hp engines until vertical types were adopted in 1905.

From 1906 the vehicles were sold under the name Stella and had conventional transmissions. About 185 cars were made until the end of production in 1913; 58 were registered as being in use in Switzerland in 1917. The works continued in the engineering business and exists today under the ownership of Ateliers de Sécheron SA. NB

STEPHENS
USA 1916-1924

The predecessors of the Moline Plow Co made farm equipment in Moline, Illinois, from 1852. George W. Stephens became a partner in 1870 and numerous acquisitions, including the Stover Engine works, Freeport Carriage Co, Henney, and the T. G. Mandt Vehicle Co, transformed it into a near rival to International Harvester Corporation. It entered the tractor business in 1913, contracting with IHC to make early examples.

In 1915 it bought the Universal Tractor Co for $150,000 and a year later started to make high-quality Continental-engined Stephens Six Cars. The cars were named after the company's president G. A. Stephens, son of the co-founder, and were built in the former Freeport Carriage and Henney Buggy factories. Paid up capital was $19 million and the chief engineer was T. T. Trumble, who had earlier worked at Chevrolet and Monroe.

In 1917 a new overhead-valve engine, designed by Alanson P. Brush and built by R&V Engineering, was introduced in the Stephens Salient Six. John N. Willys acquired an interest in the firm that year, designed a four-cylinder motor plough and was majority shareholder a year later.

Some 7000 cars were made in 1920, the year that R&V Engineering and Stephens cars were merged by Moline Plow. By that time 80 per cent of R&V Engineering's output went into Moline's tractors. Trucks were offered in 1920.

Car sales steadily declined, and with little help available from Willys, whose other interests were also struggling, production ended in 1924. Total Stephens output was between 25,000 and 30,000, peak production being 65 cars a day. Moline continued making agricultural machinery and in 1929 was one of the constituents of Minneapolis-Moline, which was acquired by the White Motor Co in 1963. NB

STEVENS-DURYEA
USA 1902-1927

In 1895 the brothers Charles E. and J. Frank Duryea founded the Duryea Motor Wagon Co in Springfield, Massachusetts. It was the first company in the United States formed specifically to produce petrol cars on a commercial basis. In 1898 the company was wound up after increasingly acrimonious arguments between the two brothers over just which had invented their car. Charles, who had conceived the idea and whose name was on the patent of June 1895 as 'inventor', continued to build cars as Duryeas through other companies; Frank, much the better engineer and the one who actually made the original Duryea a reality, went his own way.

Initially, Frank joined the proposed Automobile Co of America, which eventually built just one car. From there, in 1900, he founded the Hampden Automobile & Launch Co, also in Springfield, to build the Hampden car, although it seems that no car was actually built by the company.

In 1900, initially to earn money for the development of the Hampden, Frank started work on a new design for a well-known rifle manufacturer, the J. Stevens Arms & Tool Co of Chicopee Falls, Massachusetts, which planned to expand into the motor market. He had previously worked in Chicopee, before the Duryea was built, for the Ames Manufacturing Co.

Late in 1901, when it became apparent that the Hampden was not going to happen, Frank joined Stevens as chief engineer and by 1902 his Hampden design had emerged as the 6hp twin-cylinder two-seater Stevens-Duryea. It was built in works formerly owned by the Overman Automobile Co, maker of the Victor bicycle (to which Stevens had bought rights in 1900) and Victor steam cars, some of which were still built after Stevens acquired the works.

About 50 Stevens-Duryea cars were built during the first year and the original design continued until 1906. In 1905 it was joined by a 20hp four-cylinder model at $2500.

In 1906 a new company, the Stevens-Duryea Motor Car Co, was formed to separate car manufacture from arms manufacture and launched the huge, if conventional, 9.6-litre Big Six at $5000. From 1907 the company made only six-cylinder cars, which changed very little over the next eight years, during which production ran at about 100 cars a year.

In 1909 Frank Duryea left the company following a nervous breakdown. He returned to the management in 1914, when the J. Stevens Arms & Tool Co withdrew, but in 1915, still troubled by ill-health, he retired for good. His health improved, he travelled extensively and died in 1967 (almost 20 years after Charles) at the age of 97.

When Duryea retired the company had been doing reasonably well, following the launch of a new model, the 7.7-litre six-cylinder Model D, in 1915. As Duryea left, production stopped as World War I started and the works were sold to Westinghouse for war production.

In 1920 the Model D was relaunched as the Model E at $8000 and it sold in small numbers until 1924. From 1920 Stevens-Duryea also took over production of Raulang electric cars and taxis from the Baker, Rauch & Lang Co and made these in small numbers at Chicopee Falls.

In 1923 the company was taken over as Stevens-Duryea Motors Inc by Raymond M. Owen's Owen Magnetic Car Corporation of Wilkes Barre, Pennsylvania – itself owned by Baker, Rauch & Lang since 1915, with Owen retained as a vice-president. After Stevens-Duryea production stopped, Owen mainly used the works for building bodies, until the company folded completely in 1927. BL

STEYR
AUSTRIA 1920-1940; 1953-1977

Steyr is a town at the meeting of the rivers Steyr and Enns in Austria and has engineering connections, in iron and steelworking, extending back to 1287. Leopold Werndl was born there in 1797 and in the 1820s steered his family engineering firm towards an interest in making arms components and from the 1840s to making complete rifles, before his death in December 1855.

His son Josef, born in 1831, then took control of the workshops and in April 1864 he founded a new company, Josef und Franz Werndl & Co, Waffenfabrik und Sägemuhle in Oberletten, to mass-produce weapons. The concentric circles of today's Steyr badge represent a target.

In 1867 Josef and his father's former associate, Karl Holub, designed a breachloading rifle which was adopted by the Austrian army. The company expanded rapidly and in 1869, when the workforce totalled about 3000, it was converted to a joint-stock company, Österreichische Waffenfabriks-Gesellschaft. As such it soon became the largest arms manufacturer in Europe and Joseph Werndl was honoured by his country in 1881. By 1890 the company employed 9000 workers and was making well over 500,000 rifles a year.

In 1894 the company began to build aero-engines for airships and also Steyr-Arms bicycles, which sold in large numbers. The outbreak of World War I brought further expansion and a workforce of about 14,000 turned out 4000 rifles a day, plus machine guns, armament spares, aero-engines and bicycles. By the end of the war the company had made some 9 million rifles, 500,000 handguns and 50,000 machine guns since it started making weapons.

The post-war ban on arms manufacture forced it to look for new products and like many others it looked to motor cars. It made the decision to produce them in 1916 and started to establish new production facilities immediately after the war. The first production car, known as the Steyr Waffenauto, or Arms Car, was introduced in 1920. It was the elegant 3.3-litre six-cylinder 12/40PS Type II, designed by the talented Hans Ledwinka.

Ledwinka had started work on the design

Stevens-Duryea tourer of 1911

Steyr Type II 12/40PS of 1923

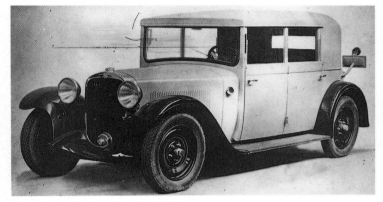

Steyr Porsche-designed Type 30 of 1929

Steyr-Puch Haflinger of c.1976

in 1916, while still working for Nesselsdorf in Czechoslovakia and before moving to Steyr full-time in 1917, taking a number of engineers with him. After the Steyr directors turned down his ideas for a small two-cylinder car, Ledwinka left the company in 1921 and returned to Nesselsdorf's successor, where his ideas emerged as the first Tatra and his own reputation burgeoned.

Several other Steyr cars were based on his original model, including the 1.8-litre four-cylinder 7/32PS Type IV and two six-cylinder models, the 4-litre 15/90PS Type VI Sport and the 4.9-litre 19/145PS Type VI Klausen, mainly for competition. Steyr built 2150 Type IIs up to 1924, 950 Type IVs up to 1925 and 85 of the Type VI Sport up to 1926. A total of just 60 of the Type VI Klausen were built, the last nine of them in 1928 after a break in production of three years.

Thereafter Steyr built a series of six-cylinder cars, several of them influenced by Ledwinka, who continued to give Steyr occasional technical advice. His influence was particularly apparent on the 1.5-litre 6/30PS Type XII, nominally designed by Steyr's new chief engineer Anton Honsig and introduced in 1926 with independent rear suspension.

In February 1926 the firm was reorganized as Steyr Werke AG and during that year production totalled 2191 cars, of which 1678 were the new Type XII. Production continued to increase, peaking at just under 5000 cars in 1929 plus just over 1000 lorries. Three of the cars built in 1929 were 5.3-litre eight-cylinder 100PS Austria models designed by the new chief engineer Ferdinand Porsche, who had joined Steyr from Daimler-Benz in January 1929. It was another excellent car but Steyr,

466

Steyr Type 55 of 1938

largely committed to big, expensive models, was suffering badly in the deepening Depression of the late 1920s.

In the autumn of 1929 Steyr production stopped completely when the company's bank, Österreichischen Bodenkreditanstalt, failed. Steyr was then obliged, by virtue of suddenly sharing the same bankers, Kreditanstalt am Hof, to enter into collaboration with Austro-Daimler-Puchwerke AG, a company formed in December 1928 by the merger of Österreichische Daimler Motoren AG and Puch Werke AG. The association prompted Porsche, who some years earlier had had an unhappy time working for Austro-Daimler, to leave Steyr in April 1930. In December he founded his own famous design bureau in Stuttgart.

Steyr's new bank was understandably reluctant to finance both that company and

Austro-Daimler-Puch to build very similar large cars, and in 1930 Steyr output amounted to four 8/40PS Type 30s and eight similarly powered Type 45 taxis. Production rose sharply in 1931, when almost 2200 of the Porsche-designed Steyr 30 were built, but the model was dropped for 1933 in favour of the low-priced 1.2-litre four-cylinder 4.5/22PS Steyr-Opel, built under licence from the German company. It was the only year for this model, which was superseded by a range of sixes developed from the 30. From 1934 there was also a popular smaller four, the 32PS Steyr 100, with all-independent suspension.

In October 1934 Steyr and Austro-Daimler-Puch agreed to a formal merger, which led to the formation of Steyr-Daimler-Puch AG in May 1935. Austro-Daimler production stopped shortly after and that company's plant was absorbed into the works in Steyr and

Graz. Car and commercial vehicle production was based in Steyr and Puch bicycles and motorcycles were built in Graz.

In March 1936 Steyr launched an even smaller car, the 1-litre 22PS flat-four Type 50. This was enlarged slightly as the 1.1-litre 55 in 1938 and was Steyr's biggest seller until the onset of World War II stopped production in 1940, when exactly 13,000 had been built.

During the war all production was turned to armaments and military equipment. New works were built at Graz early in the 1940s but by the end of the war Steyr's factories had been almost totally destroyed by repeated bombing.

In 1945 Steyr's capital stood at 80 million schillings and much of it would be needed for reconstruction, which started in 1946 and was not completed until 1955 – by which time, however, capital had risen to 320 million schillings, with almost twice that amount in reserves. The group resumed production with bicycles at Graz towards the end of 1945, then motorcycles in 1946 and later with scooters and mopeds as well. The Steyr works were among the first to be returned formally to the Austrian government after the war, in July 1946.

Steyr had decided not to resume car production, at least until both company and market were healthier, but started building petrol and diesel commercial vehicles soon after the war. In 1948 Steyr reached an agreement to assemble small Fiats in Austria, and pay for the kits with a mixture of tractors and raw materials – one of the few ways around existing import and currency restrictions.

The Steyr-Fiat was introduced in 1949, built at the main works in Steyr. Car production was transferred to Graz in 1953, after which Steyr concentrated on tractors and commercials. The year 1953 also saw the introduction of the Steyr 2000, a version of the Fiat 1900 with a 65bhp Steyr-designed 2-litre engine. Steyr built this model until 1958.

In September 1957, under the direction of Hans Ledwinka's son Erich, who now headed the design office, Steyr introduced the Steyr-Puch 500, based on the Fiat Nuova 500 but with Steyr's own engine. This was followed by larger-engined and more sporty 650T and 650TR derivatives, the latter a very successful rally car in its class. These models were offered until 1968, by which time Steyr had sold about 100,000 Fiat-based cars.

The company also built another excellent vehicle from the early 1960s, the remarkable Haflinger, or 'pony', a versatile four-wheel-drive cross-country wagon with the same air-cooled 643cc twin-cylinder engine as the 650 saloons. The last of Steyr's private cars also used this engine in a version of the Fiat 126 but it went out of production in 1978, after which the company concentrated on its commercial vehicle interests.

In 1985 the Steyr-Daimler-Puch factory also built considerable numbers of the four-wheel-drive Mercedes-Benz G-series estate cars for Daimler-Benz. BL

STIRLING
GB 1897-1903

J & C Stirling was an old-established coach-building firm of Hamilton, Lanarkshire, founded in about 1850, which began car manufacture with a stanhope (open two-seater) powered by a 4hp Daimler engine. It was the first car to be made in Scotland, and within a year the company was ordering engines from Daimler in batches of 50 and making a variety of dogcarts, waggonettes and buses.

Stirling ran the first passenger service operated by motor car in Britain (1898), and was also the first British motor firm to pay a dividend, shareholders receiving 5 per cent each year from 1897 to 1900 at least. In 1898 the company name was changed to Stirling's Motor Carriages Ltd.

In 1900 the company began to import the Clément-Panhard 5hp voiturette to which it fitted its own bodies, including an incredibly tall, sentry box-like closed coupé. Stirling moved to Granton, near Edinburgh, in 1902, by which date cars were taking very much second place to commercial vehicles.

The last Stirling-Daimler car was made in 1903, when the company was making 14-seater buses which ran in Edinburgh and London and were exported to Argentina, South Africa, Australia and New Zealand. From 1905 to 1908 buses and trucks were made under the name Scott-Stirling at Twickenham, Middlesex. GNG

STODDARD-DAYTON/
COURIER
USA 1904-1913

Son of a paint maker in Dayton, Ohio, John Stoddard was born in 1837 and by 1870 was making farm machinery, including an ad-vanced and popular hay rake. He also built bicycles. John's son Charles was sent to Europe to study the motor scene and in 1904 the Stoddard Manufacturing Co introduced a Mercédès-inspired design assembled from proprietary parts including Rutenber motors.

In 1904, when 125 cars were made, the firm became the Dayton Motor Car Co, although its growing range of large and attractive cars were still called Stoddard-Daytons. Output in 1906 was 385 cars. In 1907 engines began to be made in-house by 111 men at the rate of seven a day. Output in 1907 and 1908 was 1200 and 1400 respectively, putting Stoddard-Dayton in 10th place in the US sales league.

In 1907 an English engineer, H. J. Edwards, who had previously been at White's Cleveland Automatic Machine Co and had designed the Cleveland runabout, joined as general manager and produced an overhead-valve motor. Some 1600 cars were made in 1909, when 93 per cent of the content of all cars was said to be produced in the factory. The works were valued at $2 million and the workforce totalled 2200.

John Stoddard was president and his son Charles vice-president. Charles also controlled the Courier Car Co, a subsidiary company producing a cheaper line to the Stoddard-Dayton. John's brother Henry was involved in another Dayton make, the Speedwell.

Once H. J. Edwards obtained a Knight licence some of these sleeve-valve units were used from 1911. It was apparently interest in these engines that caused Benjamin Briscoe's United States Motor Co to acquire Dayton and Courier in 1912. The US Motor Co almost immediately went into liquidation and when Walter E. Flanders was brought in to salvage the situation he relegated the Dayton works to being simply a body, axle and casting factory for Maxwell-Briscoe. Production of the Stoddard-Dayton car ended in 1913, just when the company had ordered engines from Lyons-Atlas and planned an output of 30,000 cars. In the 1960s its factory was in use as a warehouse. NB

Stoddard-Dayton four-seat roadster of 1910

STOEWER
GERMANY 1899-1940

The Stoewer was always slightly out of the mainstream of German car production, as it was made in the Baltic port of Stettin, far from the major centres of the motor industry and probably the most easterly of all German car-making towns. It is now in Polish territory and has been renamed Szczecin.

The brothers Emil and Bernhard Stoewer owned an ironworks in Stettin, founded in 1895, and in 1897 they began to manufacture motorcycles, tricycles and quads of De Dion-Bouton type, powered by German-made De Dion engines from Cudell of Aachen. In September 1899 came their first car, a double phaeton powered by a 2.1-litre rear-mounted two-cylinder engine, with chain drive.

This seems to have been little more than a prototype, for in 1901 they came up with a front-engined two-cylinder tonneau looking very like a Panhard, followed by a four-cylinder car on the same lines in 1903. Commercial vehicles were also built, both petrol and electric buses having been completed in 1902.

When vehicle production began, the Stoewer brothers had fewer than 100 employees, but the workforce had grown to 300 in 1903, 1200 in 1913 and 2500 in 1924. Mercédès-like four-cylinder cars were introduced towards the end of 1903, chain-driven at first but with shaft drive coming on the smallest model, an 8/14PS vertical twin made from 1902 to 1905. By 1906 even the big 8.8-litre Typ P6 34/60PS six had shaft drive, although Stoewer followed its compatriots in generally avoiding the six-cylinder car, and this only lasted until 1911.

Stoewer had two involvements with other companies. The first was in 1908 when it built 200 of the 1½-litre G4 light car for NAG, which fitted its own radiators and bodies and sold them as its own Puck, and the second was from 1910 to 1912 when Emile Mathis built the Typ B6 2-litre in his Strasbourg factory, selling it under the name Stoewer-Mathis.

In 1911 Stoewer opened an aero engine department under the direction of the Rus-sian engineer Boris Loutsky, who had built a few light cars and postal vans under his own name at the turn of the century. It was Loutsky's idea to use aero engines in the largest Stoewer cars, and the first was the F4 with 8.6-litre single-overhead cam four-cylinder engine, which was made from 1911 to 1914. This gained electric lighting and starting in 1913, and a vee radiator in 1914, which was copied on all Stoewer models after the war. Most other Stoewers were quite modest motors, with engines in the 1½ to 2½-litre bracket.

During World War I Stoewer was busy making staff cars, 3- and 5-ton trucks, and Argus

Stoewer 45hp tonneau of 1902

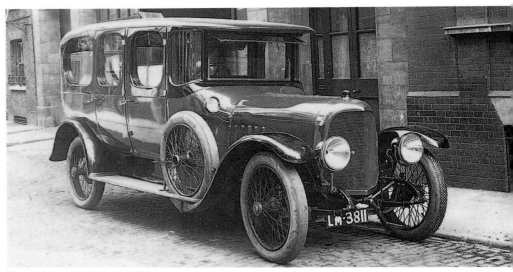

Stoewer Model F limousine of 1914

aero engines. The Argus engines went into a few post-war cars that continued Loutsky's theme and were the biggest Stoewers ever made. The D7 sporting tourer was made in 1921 only, and had an 11.2-litre single-overhead cam six-cylinder engine giving 120bhp and a top speed of 112mph (180kph). Only 20 were made. The rest of the post-war D series were more modest, running from the 1.6-litre D2 to the 4.9-litre D6, all with side-valve engines.

The best looking was the 2.6-litre D10 of 1924-25. This was a sports tourer with wire wheels and could be mistaken for a 3-litre Bentley from a distance, although its per-formance would have caused no anxiety at Cricklewood. A total of 70 D10s were made out of 1400 Stoewers delivered in 1924-25. Quite a number went to Australia, and 150 Stoewers were sold in Soviet Russia in the early 1920s.

The vee-radiatored D series was continued until 1928, but thereafter Fritz Fiedler produced a completely new series of side-valve straight-eights on American lines. They were made in various sizes from the 2-litre S8 to the 4.9-litre Repräsentant, a handsome car in the typical long-bonnetted early 1930s idiom, of which only 24 were made in two batches, 14 in 1930 and a further 10 in 1933. Total production of the Fiedler-designed straight-eight was a respectable 3274 cars.

After the designer took his talents to Horch, and later BMW, Stoewer changed direction again with the 1192cc V4-engined Model V5 with front wheel drive, all independent suspension and a DKW-like fabric saloon body. The company was backed by the city government of Stettin in the development of the V5 to safeguard local employment, and Bernhard Stoewer returned from retirement to supervise production of the new model. There was a plan for the V5 to be made in England by Morris, in return for Stoewer making Morris-Commercial trucks for the central European market, but nothing came of this.

For 1933 the V5 was replaced by the R140,

Stoewer Greif V8 cabriolet of 1935

still with front wheel drive but using a conventional in-line four of 1355cc, later 1466cc. These more popularly priced cars enabled Stoewer to climb out of the Depression, for although only 362 cars were made in 1930, 1737 were produced in 1933 and 1542 in 1934.

Emil retired in 1932 and Bernhard moved to Opel in 1934, but before he did so he produced a larger front-drive car, the 2½-litre V8 Greif, a good-looking car which was expensive to make, and at 5500 marks (about £275) the price was probably pitched too low. Only 825 Greifs were made, and they were discontinued in 1937 before they could cause more losses to the company. From October 1936 Stoewer was run by Karl Trefz, who was appointed by the city of Stettin.

In 1935 there was a bid by Ford to buy Stoewer in order to gain extra bodybuilding capacity, but the Stettin firm broke off negotiations when it received a large order from the Wehrmacht for 4×4 command cars. All Ford got out of a rumoured $500,000 investment in Stoewer was 200 Eifel roadster bodies made in 1936.

Stoewer's most successful car in the 1930s was the Greif Junior, a licence-built Tatra 1½-litre air-cooled flat four, with Stoewer-designed bodies, of which about 4000 were made between 1936 and 1939. It was joined in 1937 by the Greif's replacements, a conventional pair of pushrod overhead-valve cars, the 2½-litre four-cylinder Sedina and 3.6-litre six-cylinder Arcona, of which 924 and 201 were made respectively. Production of these continued into the first year of the war, the last Sedina being made in the spring of 1940.

Production of the Typ 40 4×4 command car lasted until 1944, after which the factory was largely destroyed by bombing. After the war Stettin became Polish territory, and the rebuilt Stoewer factory was used first for the production of Junah motorcycles and, more recently, for making components for Polski-Fiat cars. GNG

STONELEIGH
GB 1912-1924

Stoneleigh Motors Ltd of Coventry began trading in 1912 as a subsidiary of Siddeley-Deasy, making vehicles that might otherwise have demeaned the parent company's luxury image. It was named after an abbey and park that is now the Royal Agricultural Society showground.

The first car produced was an 11.9hp sleeve-valve four-cylinder engined model, very similar to the contemporary BSA. It has been suggested that all the firm's cars were made by BSA and certainly in 1912 this is borne out by overlapping chassis numbers, 500-655 being sold by Stoneleigh and 600-1038 by BSA.

Stoneleigh, though not BSA, lost interest in car production from 1913 but it made a light

truck and 14-seat bus chassis using the same engine. Several of these chassis were supplied as ambulances to Russia.

The Stoneleigh name was revived in 1922 by Siddeley-Deasy's successor, Armstrong-Siddeley, where Stoneleigh cars were known as 'Siddeley's Folly'. They were now little more than cyclecars with central steering and cloverleaf seating and had air-cooled V-twin 1-litre engines. The Stoneleigh survived into 1924, when production was halted. NB

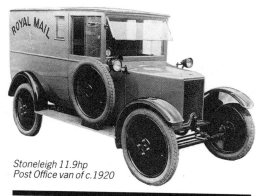

Stoneleigh 11.9hp Post Office van of c.1920

STOREY
GB 1920-1930

The Storey family were machine toolmakers of south London. William Storey experimented with steam and petrol vehicles from 1903 and, after he became managing director of the newly formed Storey Machine Tool Co Ltd in 1916, Wisconsin, Coventry-Simplex and rotary engined prototypes were built. War work, particularly the Le Rhône engines built in association with Kingsbury, precluded car production but in 1919 a 40-acre (16-hectare) factory site was acquired at Tonbridge, Kent, for this purpose.

In 1920 production began of cars with Chapuis-Dornier and Decolange engines. They were built initially in the New Cross works in south London, which also handled bodywork. Storey's own 10/12hp engine was ready towards the end of 1920.

The Tonbridge factory was almost finished when bankruptcy overtook the firm after more than 1000 cars had reportedly been

built. Works manager Jack Storey, brother of William, had planned a car called the Winchester with E. V. Varley Grossmith and is thought to have provided Varley Grossmith with components to launch the Varley-Woods motor car.

From 1921 until 1930 about 50 Storeys were built out of old Storey components by Jack Storey at Clapham Park, south London. From 1925 Storey Motors was a private limited company with £6000 capital. Its cars used various types of engine; one used a Meadows and another a Buick six. The business then sold spares for a time before becoming a garage in Norbury, south London. William Storey returned to making tools and aircraft components and owned several factories by the 1960s. He died in 1971. NB

STRAKER-SQUIRE/
CORNILLEAU ST BEUVE, SHAMROCK
GB, FRANCE 1906-1925

Born in 1861, Sidney Straker is credited with having built an experimental car in 1895 and was consulting engineer to Daimler in Coventry between 1899 and 1901. He designed steam wagons, initially with De Dion boilers, in conjunction with the London horse-drawn vehicle maker Edward Bayley. These were made from 1899 in a factory at Bristol and two years later the Straker Steam Vehicle Co was formed.

Larger works on a 5-acre (2-hectare) site opened with 460 employees in 1906 at Fishponds, Bristol. This added 30 vehicles a month to the monthly output of 13 from the old works.

By September 1907 200 steamers and 400 to 500 Büssing-based petrol-engined commercial vehicles were said to have been built since 1899. Arbenz commercials were also sold. Some or all these vehicles were imported, as were the 300 Straker buses running in London, where an office and bodyworks were maintained. From about 1909 Straker-Squire commercials were all-British. The cars that the company had begun to sell in 1906 were in fact by Cornilleau St Beuve of Paris, a

Straker-Squire 24/80hp of 1923 at Shelsley Walsh

firm which existed for five years from 1904, Pierre Cornilleau having previously been a director of Decauville.

In 1907 there appeared the firm's first home-produced car, a 12/14hp initially called the Shamrock. Designed by 21-year-old Roy Fedden, it later became the 15hp Straker-Squire. Fedden was promoted chief engineer in 1909, when George Murray from Arrol-Johnston was chief draughtsman.

In 1913 Straker-Squire (1913) Ltd, with a capital of £100,000, acquired the old business for £55,000. Mr Squire was no longer on the board and Straker himself became personally bankrupt the following year and had to step down temporarily.

The New Orleans factory at Twickenham, Middlesex, was acquired in 1914 to make 200 heavy commercials a year. At that time around 50 cars and 50 commercials were being made in Bristol each month. The wartime workforce exceeded 2000 and guns, shells and Renault aero engines were produced. Fedden controlled the aero side, which was permitted to make engines and parts to Rolls-Royce designs.

In 1918 the Cosmos Engineering Co Ltd was formed, with Fedden a director, to concentrate on aero engines. The firm was nearly bought by Siddeley-Deasy, but in 1920 Fedden and 31 key personnel left the company to start an aero engine firm that would become a cornerstone of the Bristol Aeroplane Co.

After the war Straker-Squire's Djinn boat engine business was sold and vehicle production was concentrated at a £140,000 6-acre (2.4-hectare) former National Projectile factory at Edmonton, north London, in 1919. Capital that year was increased to £500,000. The factory manager was Max Lawrence, formerly with Wolseley, and a new 4-litre six-cylinder car with aero engine influences entered production alongside the pre-war 15hp and commercials. The commercials included an unusual semi-forward control A-Type with two-bearing crankshaft, of which over 400 were sold as buses and lorries. Many suffered from mechanical problems.

Involvement in Bean's unsuccessful British Motor Trading retailing business, the effects of the post-war slump and product unreliability led to a winding up order being issued in 1921, when 1000 men were employed at Edmonton. A director acting for the creditors was S. D. Begbie of Aster who was to fulfil the same task at Arrol-Aster. An attempt to break into the popular car market in 1923 with a 1½-litre Meadows, Dorman and Aster powered car range resulted in only about 100 being sold. Straker-Clough trolleybuses were equally unsuccessful and the firm collapsed in 1925.

A final attempt to refloat the firm by W. H. Workman and J. W. Beeby came to nothing in 1925 and the spares were subsequently bought by Kryn and Lahy of Letchworth. Sidney Straker died in 1929 and the Edmonton factory was used by a clothing firm until destroyed in the Blitz of World War II. NB

STUDEBAKER
USA, CANADA 1902-1966

Studebaker had the longest history of any American car, as its ancestry reached back to the establishment of a wagon-making works at South Bend, Indiana, in 1852. That first year the Studebaker brothers, Henry and Clem, built only two wagons, but business grew as their reputation spread, and the outbreak of the Civil War in 1861 gave a tremendous boost to the wagon business. By then they had been joined by their dynamic younger brother, John Mohler Studebaker, who had already made a fortune building wheelbarrows for the gold miners in California.

By 1868 annual sales had reached $350,000 and the Studebakers could rightly claim that they were the largest vehicle builders in the world with facilities to make a wagon every seven minutes. Carriages had been added to their range in 1856, so they were complete transport suppliers to everyone from farmers to physicians. They maintained their pre-eminent position right up to the turn of the century, with annual sales in the 1890s of more than $2 million.

In 1897 they started experiments with an electric carriage and two years later they began to build bodies for electric cars. In 1902 they built an initial series of 20 two-seater electric cars designed for them by Thomas Alva Edison, and later expanded their range of electrics to include broughams and four-seater victorias, as well as commercial vehicles from 1906 in several sizes up to 5 tons.

Clem Studebaker died in 1901 and John Mohler was now president. Henry had pacifist leanings and had left the firm when it began to supply wagons to the Union Army in 1861. 'J. M.' did not favour the petrol engine, but was persuaded by younger fellow directors that the company should not rely on electrics alone.

The first petrol car was built in 1904, a 16hp two-cylinder chassis made by the General Automobile Co of Cleveland, Ohio. General supplied a few more chassis to Studebaker, but a more permanent arrangement was made with the Garford Co of Elyria, Ohio, which supplied chassis and engines, Studebaker making the bodies. This arrangement lasted until 1910 with Garford making two-cylinder cars in 1904, twins and fours in 1905 and fours thereafter. These cars were sometimes called Studebaker-Garford, but more commonly plain Studebaker.

The Garford-built cars were expensive, priced between $2600 and $4000, and Studebaker management realized that if they were to increase sales they would have to find a cheaper product. They found it in the EMF 30, a new car just put on the market by the Everitt-Metzger-Flanders Co of Detroit. This conventional four-cylinder car sold for $1250, and in 1909, a year after Studebaker had signed an exclusive contract with EMF, 7960 found customers. In 1910 sales were up to 15,020 and Studebaker ended the agreement with Garford. In 1911 a total of 26,827 Studebaker EMFs were sold, bringing the South Bend company into second place in the sales league, beaten only by Ford.

Studebaker had bought into EMF in 1908

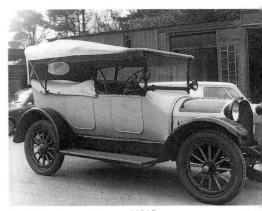

Studebaker four-seat tourer of 1915

Studebaker Land Cruiser of 1934

and gained complete control in 1910. This acquisition gave Studebaker several other factories, the car-making plants of the defunct De Luxe, Northern and Wayne, all in Detroit, the Monroe Manufacturing Co of Pontiac, Western Malleable Steel and Pressed Steel Sanitary Manufacturing, both of Detroit. It also acquired EMF's Canadian factory at Walkerville, Ontario, beginning an association with Canada which was to last beyond car production in the United States.

In 1910 Studebaker-EMF brought out a smaller car, the Flanders 20, named after one of the EMF partners, Walter E. Flanders. Built in the De Luxe factory, it had a 21hp monobloc four-cylinder engine and sold for $1050. A total of 30,707 were made from 1910 to 1913, compared with 47,619 EMF 30s between 1909 and 1912.

Studebaker discontinued its electric cars in 1912, total production since 1902 having been only 1841. The EMF and Flanders names were dropped for 1913, in which year Studebaker brought out its first six. This shared with Premier the honour of being the first monobloc six made in the USA.

In 1915 John Mohler Studebaker retired, handing over control to his son-in-law, Frederick S. Fish. Two years later J. M. died at the age of 83, the last of the pioneer brothers.

By then Fish had been replaced by Albert Russel Erskine, who was to lead Studebaker into the early 1930s. Chief engineer from 1913 to 1920 was Fred M. Zeder, aided by Carl Breer and Owen R. Skelton, all leading designers of the time.

Although Studebaker never regained its second place of 1911, it was in the top six every year to 1917, with sales rising from 28,032 in 1912 to 65,536 in 1916. The war brought a final flowering of the wagon business with large numbers being supplied to the armies of France, Britain and Russia, as well as the US Army. Studebaker also built gun carriages, staff cars and trucks.

Carriage manufacture was phased out in 1919, and two years later the last farm wagon was delivered. Horse vehicle production had lasted for just under 70 years, longer than the cars were to do. Indeed, the wagon business survived for longer as it was sold to the Kentucky Wagon Manufacturing Co of Louisville,

which continued to turn out farm wagons until the early 1940s.

Studebaker built its last four-cylinder car in 1919 and for most of the 1920s concentrated on a series of side-valve sixes of up to 5.8 litres. The company held a respected place in the middle ground of American motor car manufacture, although in fact it covered a pretty wide price range – from $975 for the Light Six roadster to $2750 for the Big Six seven-passenger sedan in 1923. Sales varied from 48,831 in 1920 to 128,258 in 1928; Studebaker's best position in the league was fourth, in 1921, and its worst was twelfth in 1929.

The company had seven factories, four in South Bend, two in Detroit and one in Walkerville, Ontario, where cars were assembled from American-made parts for the Canadian and British Empire markets. As with Buick, Chevrolet and other American makes, Canadian Studebakers could be sold in Britain with lower tariffs.

Also with an eye to the European market, a new smaller car was introduced in 1926, named after the company's president, Albert Erskine. To keep costs down many components were bought-in, including the 2.3-litre side-valve Continental engine. Even so, it cost $995 for a sedan compared with $525 for

Studebaker Golden Hawk of 1957

a Ford Model A. Dubbed by its makers 'the Little Aristocrat', the Erskine never sold as well as had been hoped – about 80,000 in four years – and in 1930 the name was dropped and the car became a small Studebaker.

At the other end of the scale was the President Eight, designed by the new chief engineer Barney Roos and launched in 1928. It had a 4.9-litre 100bhp straight-eight engine and came in five body styles; it sold at what seemed bargain prices, from $1985 to $2485. The President Eight was publicized by a number of record runs, including 30,000 miles (48,280km) in 27,000 minutes at Atlantic City. By the end of 1928 Studebaker held 114 records, 31 of which still stood 35 years later.

Also in 1928 Studebaker gained control of Pierce-Arrow, giving Erskine an automotive empire ranging from the $995 Erskine to the $5750 Pierce-Arrow eight-cylinder town car. This connection lasted until Studebaker was placed in receivership in 1933, and led to a

line of Studebaker-Pierce Arrow trucks, although the cars always retained their separate names.

Studebaker entered the 1930s with two sixes, the 68bhp Dictator and the 75bhp Commander, and the President Eight, now with 5.4 litres and 115bhp. Commanders and Presidents were continued until 1942, but the Dictator was quietly replaced by the Studebaker Six for 1938; the activities of Hitler, Mussolini and Stalin had rendered the name Dictator rather a tactless one for anyone's motor car.

In 1931 came another attempt at the smaller car, the 3.1-litre six-cylinder Rockne, named after Knute Rockne the celebrated coach of South Bend's Notre Dame University football team. It was built in the Detroit factory where the Erskine and, earlier, the EMFs had been made and sold for $585 to $675. For 1932 a 3.3-litre engine was offered as well. Despite the sound idea of a cheap car to sell in the Depression, Rockne never took off and was dropped when Studebaker went into receivership in March 1933. About 23,000 Rocknes were made.

Studebaker finances deteriorated sharply during the early 1930s; hit by the Depression, profits were inevitably lower, but Erskine insisted on paying high dividends which he paid from capital – thus reducing working capital to $3.5 million by the end of 1932. Liabilities exceeded assets by $15 million and Erskine sought a solution by merging with the White Motor Co of Cleveland, which had substantial reserves. White's bankers opposed the deal, however, and in March 1933 Studebaker went into receivership owing $6 million in bank loans. Erskine was personally bankrupt as well and three months later he committed suicide.

The Studebaker Corporation was taken over by Harold Vance and Paul Hoffman, who had been vice-presidents of sales and engineering respectively. They raised $1 million by selling off Pierce-Arrow and the banks agreed to be patient about the rest. One casualty was the big 132bhp President Eight, which was replaced for 1934 by a smaller President using the 110bhp Commander Eight engine.

After nine months of receivership Studebaker made a modest profit of $55,000 and in March 1935 the company was out of the receiver's hands. Sales picked up as the United States climbed out of the Depression, from a low of 43,024 in 1933 to 49,062 in 1935 and 85,026 in 1936.

Studebaker was meanwhile increasing production of commercial vehicles, which it had abandoned from 1919 to 1926. The company made a considerable number of parlour coaches (long distance buses) between 1929 and 1933, some powered by the President Eight engine. It also built 1- to 4-ton trucks as well as fire engines, the bigger models using Hercules engines, and in 1938 it built its first diesel truck, also Hercules powered.

Studebaker Commander Six engines pow-

Studebaker Avanti of c.1963

ered the 1937 Waterman Arrowbile, a flying car which was to be sold by selected Studebaker dealerships for $3000. No more than five demonstrators were ever built, however.

Roos left in 1936 to work for the Rootes group in Britain and was replaced by W. S. James, who set about designing another small Studebaker which appeared early in 1939 as the Champion. This did not suffer the fate of the Erskine and the Rockne, and in fact became one of the most successful Studebakers ever made.

It had a 2.7-litre 78bhp six-cylinder engine and sold for $660 to $760, according to body style and trim. This was still higher than the cheapest Ford or Chevrolet, but the Champion's excellent fuel economy – 20-22mpg, or 7.8km per litre – earned it many friends. In its first full year 72,791 were sold out of a total of 114,196 Studebakers. By the time car production was ended by the war in February 1942 a total of 215,117 Champions had been made. The engine also powered more than 15,000 amphibious Weasels for the war effort. Indeed, it was made with little change until 1960.

The Champion helped bring Studebaker back to profitability, although the company did not declare a dividend to shareholders until 1943. By this time Studebaker was contributing to the fourth war effort of its history, making 6×4 and 6×6 trucks, Weasels and Wright Cyclone aero engines. More than 210,000 vehicles and 63,789 aero engines were made between February 1942 and August 1945. Studebaker finances emerged from the war in a very healthy shape.

The first post-war cars were warmed-over 1942 models, but in March 1946 Studebaker announced the revolutionary 'coming or going models' with wraparound rear windows, styled by Raymond Loewy and Virgil Exner. Underneath their futuristic bodies their engineering was conventional, with a 2.8-litre engine in the Champion and a 3.7-litre in the Commander and Land Cruiser models. Sales boomed, reaching a record figure of 228,402 in 1949 and then being topped by 268,229 in 1950. This gave Studebaker a 4.1 per cent share of the market. The workforce reached a record 23,000.

Truck production was high, too, with a range from ½-ton pickups to tractors for 12-ton trailers, plus continuing contracts for military vehicles. Peak year for truck production was 1948, when 67,981 were sold. With the outbreak of the Korean war in 1950, Studebaker again received aero engine contracts, this time for J-47 turbo jets which were built in factories at Chicago and New Brunswick, New Jersey.

The late 1940s and early 1950s were the peak period for foreign activities. There were 11 overseas assembly plants in Brazil, Belgium, Ireland, Denmark, Sweden, Egypt, Argentina, Mexico, South Africa, India and the Philippines. Studebaker also had a full scale production plant at Hamilton, Ontario, begun in 1948. The previous Canadian plant at Walkerville had closed in 1936.

In 1951 sales declined to 222,000 and in 1952 slid further to 161,520 and a market share of only 3 per cent. As the post-war boom evaporated and the market became more competitive, Studebaker felt the pinch

in the same way as Packard, Hudson and Nash. The company also failed to modernize is ageing plants. The new Loewy-designed 1953 models were very good looking and were available with overhead-valve V8 engines, but sales were only 186,484.

The following year Studebaker merged with Packard, a move which Packard's James Nance saw as giving his company an entry to the medium priced car and the truck markets. Studebaker plant was working at well below its capacity of 250,000 vehicles a year, however, and the decline in defence contracts hit it still further. Studebaker was no help at all to Packard, which became a badge-engineered Studebaker in 1957 and disappeared altogether in 1958. In 1956 Studebaker-Packard was bought by the aircraft company Curtiss Wright, primarily as a tax-loss operation.

Studebaker-Packard sales had dropped to 56,869 in 1958, but the introduction in 1959 of the compact, low-priced Lark turned the company's fortunes again, sending sales up to 150,823 cars and earning a profit of $28.5 million. But 1960 saw the introduction of compact cars by the Big Three; sales dropped to 105,902 and profits to $750,000.

A new company president, Sherwood Egbert, set about acquiring other firms such as Gering Plastics, Gravely Tractors and Chemical Compounds Co (maker of STP oil products). He also launched the Studebaker Avanti, a sporty coupé with fibreglass body and a supercharged V8 engine which gave it a top speed of 124mph (200kph). Production problems delayed deliveries, however, and only 4643 Avantis were made before production at South Bend ended in December 1963.

Operations were now concentrated on the Canadian plant at Hamilton, where the Daytona and Cruiser models were built using Chevrolet engines made by a Canadian General Motors subsidiary at St Catharines, Ontario. The high performance Hawk and Avanti were dropped, although the latter was revived by an independent South Bend company and is still made today. Only 19,435 cars were made in 1965, and in March 1966 the Hamilton plant closed after 8947 further cars had been made.

This marked the end of a 114-year history of Studebaker vehicle-building, although the Corporation survived by merging with Wagner Electric and Worthington Corporation to form Studebaker-Worthington in 1967. In 1979 it was absorbed by the McGraw Edison Co of Illinois. GNG

STUTZ
ITALY, USA 1970 to date

During the 1960s a number of American companies started to make more or less accurate replicas of classic cars, but the sponsors of the Stutz Blackhawk simply borrowed the name of the great Indianapolis make for their strikingly styled two-door coupé of 1970. The Stutz Motor Car Co of America was formed by New York businessman William O'Donnell, but the cars were, and are, made in Italy, using General Motors mechanical components with hand-built coachwork by Carrozeria Padana of Modena. The first car was styled by Virgil Exner, who had been responsible for the Chrysler dream cars of the early 1950s, and despite Exner's death in 1973 Stutz has followed the same basic lines to the present day.

The first Blackhawk coupé was powered by a 6½-litre Pontiac V8 modified to give 425bhp. It cost $22,000, making it the most expensive car in the United States, a position Stutz has held ever since, at least with its top models. The company announced that no more than 1000 cars would be built in any one year, but in fact it has not yet reached the 1000 mark in 15 years. The best year has been 1974, when 75 cars were delivered, and in recent years annual output has varied between 45 and 60.

In 1972 a four-door sedan was introduced; it used a Cadillac chassis and sold for $31,250. Since then new models have included the Bearcat convertible and the Royale limousine. The latter is the longest car in the world at 24ft 6in (7.4m) in overall length and its 1985 price was $285,000. Optional items such as a hydraulically raised throne seat obviously add to this price; a few cars equipped with these options have been delivered to Saudi Arabia, while show business personalities are also keen buyers. One of the first Stutz cars was sold to Elvis Presley. Current Stutz prices start at $84,500 for the Blackhawk VII two-door coupé. GNG

STUTZ
USA 1911-1934

Born in Ansonia, Ohio, in 1876, Harry Clayton Stutz grew up on a farm in an austere religious atmosphere, but like that other farm boy, Henry Ford, he was more interested in machinery than in agriculture. He built his first, home-made, car in 1898 and formed the Stutz Manufacturing Co in Dayton, Ohio, the following year. In 1902 he sold this company to the Lindsay Automobile Parts Co of Indianapolis, Indiana, which he joined for a brief period.

He then worked successively for the G & J Tire Co, the Schebler Carburetor Co, the American Motor Car Co and the Marion Motor Car Co, all of Indianapolis. In 1910 he left Marion to form the Stutz Auto Parts Co, financed by his friend Henry Campbell, and while engaged on this he was also a consultant to the Empire Motor Car Co.

He built a racing car powered by a four-cylinder Wisconsin engine driving through his own design of rear-axle gearbox, and entered it in the 1911 Indianapolis 500 Mile race. Driven by Gil Anderson, the car ran steadily and finished 11th out of 22. Stutz was sufficiently encouraged to offer replicas of the car for sale, using the slogan 'The Car That Made Good in a Day'.

Stutz formed a new company to make the cars, the Ideal Motor Car Co, of which he was chief designer, while remaining president of Stutz Auto Parts Co. Much of the finance for Ideal came from former investors in Marion.

He leased a three-storey factory on North Capital Avenue, Indianapolis, and by August the first cars were being delivered. They had 6.4-litre Wisconsin T-head engines and were available as a two-passenger roadster, four-passenger toy tonneau and five-passenger touring car, with a coupé being added to the line in November. The cars remained substantially the same to the end of 1912, but during the year the roadster was given the name Bearcat, which was to become one of the best-known Stutz cars.

Harry Stutz became president of Ideal in June 1912 and a year later his two companies were merged to form the Stutz Motor Car Co of Indiana. Meanwhile a 7-litre six-cylinder engine was offered as an optional alternative to the four, providing smoother running, although the output was about the same at 60bhp.

Sales in 1913 were 759 cars and four years later they had risen to 2207, stimulated by the racing successes of the White Squadron, a team of special single-overhead cam cars led by Gil Anderson, and the independent driver Earl Cooper, who won the national championship in 1913. The Bearcat undoubtedly spearheaded Stutz sales, and the make was not particularly thought of in connection with touring cars, although these were available.

In 1915 Stutz stock was offered on the New York Stock Exchange for the first time, attracting a young financier, Alan A. Ryan. By 1916 he had a controlling interest in the company, which he re-formed as the Stutz Motor Car Co of America with himself as vice-president and Harry Stutz as president.

Although nominally at the head of the company Stutz was unable to make major decisions without Ryan's blessing, and he felt increasingly that Ryan's interest lay in stock-market manipulation rather than making motor cars. He gradually sold his holding in the company and in 1919 he left to found two independent manufacturing firms, the HCS Motor Co, which made cars from 1919 to

First Stutz 'car', 1898

Stutz Bearcat speedster of 1914

1925, and the Stutz Fire Engine Co, which was in business from 1919 to 1928 and under different ownership at Hartford City, Indiana, until 1940. Harry C. Stutz died in 1930 of complications following appendicitis.

Between 2 February and the end of March 1920 Stutz shares rose from $134 to $750 each, the latter price being fixed by Ryan who hoped to defeat the 'bears' on the stock exchange who were anticipating a fall. However, he made the mistake of antagonizing the ruling members of the stock exchange, who suspended him from trading. He owned all the Stutz stock but it was just about all he did own, and he was forced to sell his shares at auction for no more than $20 each. The result was complete ruin for Ryan, and bargain price shares for the purchaser, who turned out to be the millionaire chairman of Bethlehem Steel, Charles M. Schwab.

These financial dealings had little effect on Stutz production, although there was a certain amount of stagnation in the early 1920s as Schwab and his associates were not motor men and were slow to bring in modern designs. Stutz had been making its own engines since 1917 when its 16-valve T-head four replaced the Wisconsin unit, and this was in turn replaced in 1922 by a 4.4-litre 70bhp six, designed by former Cole engineer Charles S. Crawford. An enlarged six, the 80bhp 4.7-litre Speedway Six, followed at the end of 1923 – but what Stutz needed if it was to keep up with its competitors was an eight.

Salvation came in the person of Hungarian-born Frederick E. Moskovics, who was brought in at the end of 1925. He decided to discontinue all the existing models and concentrate on a new car of modern design, low and sleek, which completely banished the hairy-chested Bearcat image.

Known as the Stutz Vertical Eight, or the Safety Stutz, it had a 4.7-litre single-overhead cam straight-eight engine developing 92bhp designed by Charles 'Pop' Greuter, a Swiss-born engineer who had built his own cars as early as 1896 and worked for the Holyoke and Matheson companies. The low line was achieved by using worm drive instead of spiral bevel, and the cars earned their safety name by the use of wire-reinforced glass in the windscreen. The six body styles were Stutz-made but designed by Brewster.

The new Stutz caught on immediately and more than $3 million worth of orders was taken in a single day at the dealers' convention in December 1925. Sales rose from 2000 in 1925 to 5000 in 1926.

Stutz returned to racing and achieved many successes in AAA Stock Car Championships in 1927 and 1928. C. T. Weymann entered Stutz cars at Le Mans from 1928 to 1932, and in the first year Bloch and Brisson finished second to a 4½-litre Bentley. Stutz itself did no more racing after its leading driver, Frank Lockhart, was killed in a land speed record

Stutz Vertical Eight of 1926

attempt with a 16-cylinder car in April 1928.

Sales dropped in the second half of 1928 and criticism of Moskovics' leadership caused him to resign in January 1929. In an attempt to expand into a lower price market Stutz brought out the Blackhawk for 1929. This looked much like the larger cars but had a choice of a Stutz-built 3.9-litre single-overhead cam engine or a 4.4-litre pushrod overhead-valve Continental 16S. Prices ran from

Stutz Blackhawk speedster of c.1929

Stutz DV-32 saloon of 1931

$1995 to $2655 – the eights were actually cheaper by $50 than the sixes – compared with $3395 to $3895 for the 'senior Stutz'.

As with Marmon's Roosevelt, the Blackhawk was marketed as a separate make to avoid confusion with the more expensive cars, but it was not a successful venture and was discontinued after 1930. Only 1310 Blackhawks were sold in 1929 and just 280 in 1930.

The engine of the big Stutz had been increased to 5.2 litres and 113bhp in 1929, and from 1931 this model was known as the SV-16; each cylinder had single inlet and exhaust valves, giving a total of 16 valves in the engine. At the same time came the DV-32, with dual inlet and exhaust valves per cylinder. With hemispherical combustion chambers and twin overhead camshafts, the DV-32 engine gave 156bhp. The Bearcat name was revived for the two-seater models of the DV-32. This engine was theoretically available in all models, at $700 more than the equivalent SV-16. The most expensive Stutz in 1931 was the Fleetwood Town Car, priced at $7495.

Stutz was already faltering before the Depression, and the events of October 1929 simply made matters worse. Production declined sharply after 1930 and no new models

were introduced. Its last active year was 1934, when only six cars were sold.

In January 1935 Stutz announced that it would henceforth concentrate on the rear-engined Pak-Age-Car delivery van, which it had taken up in 1932 as an insurance against falling car sales. This only lasted until 1937, when Stutz went bankrupt, and Pak-Age-Car production was then taken over by Auburn Central. GNG

SUBARU
JAPAN 1958 to date

Fuji Heavy Industries Ltd, maker of the Subaru, was formed in 1953 as an amalgamation of five engineering firms which had been born as a result of the break up at the end of World War II of the giant Nakajima Aircraft Co. The company's first road vehicle was the Rabbit motor scooter, launched in 1956. Then came the 360 mini saloon powered by a rear-mounted 356cc air-cooled two-stroke engine. This was made from 1958 to 1971 and was imported to the United States by Malcolm Bricklin until it was declared by *Consumer Report* to be 'the most unsafe car on the market'.

The first full-sized Subaru was the 997cc FE of 1968, which was enlarged to 1088cc in 1970 and 1361cc in 1971. The engine was a horizontally-opposed four driving the front wheels.

In 1968 Fuji Industries became part of the Nissan group and has since assembled a number of cars for Nissan as demand requires. The mini cars were continued in improved form during the 1970s but were never re-instated on the American market. The larger Subarus, however, have become very popular in the USA, particularly since the introduction of the four-wheel-drive version of the flat four in 1973. This has since become a highly successful model in the export market as well as at home. It is currently made in saloon and estate car versions, with 1595 and 1781cc engines, including a turbocharged

version of the latter. These Subarus are also available in versions with front-wheel-drive only.

Other models are the two-cylinder 544cc Rex saloon, which is not exported to Europe or the USA, the three-cylinder 997cc Domingo four-wheel-drive minibus, and the 997cc Justy three- or five-door hatchback with front or four-wheel-drive and continuously variable transmission. This last is made under licence from the Dutch firm Van Doorne. The turbocharged 4×4 version of the Rex is the world's first 'mini turbo'. Subaru also makes a 4×4 sporting coupé, the 1.8-litre XT.

Production has risen from fewer than 20,000 cars in 1959 to 187,000 in 1971 and 545,537 in 1984, which included the assembly of 70,000 Nissan Cherries. Fuji currently has five factories, two of which are devoted to cars, Mitaka solely for engines and Gunma for assembly, while the others are concerned with aircraft, rolling stock, bus bodies and industrial power units. The workforce in the car factories is 9288 people. Fuji has three overseas assembly plants in Malaysia, New Zealand and Thailand, which between them turned out 10,380 cars in 1984. GNG

SUÈRE
FRANCE 1909-1931

J. Suère is known to have been making Velox engines in Paris in 1908 and may possibly have done so from 1905 or earlier. His company fitted these engines to its own Suère light cars from 1909. Four- and single-cylinder cars were produced and a 1½-litre sidevalve V8 prototype of 1914 entered production after World War I. In the 1920s 1.2-litre fours and 2-litre sixes were also produced and were sold in Britain by Theo of Liverpool.

Suère was listed until 1930. Production may have ended earlier, but activity returned briefly in 1930-31 with an interesting 3.2-litre eight-cylinder car that probably progressed no further than the prototype stage. NB

Subaru 1800 4WD pickup of 1984

SUNBEAM/SUNBEAM-TALBOT
GB 1901-1968

In 1859 John Marston, who had been apprenticed in the Black Country sheet metal trade, acquired a firm of japanners (metal lacquerers) and then, as an enthusiastic cyclist, started the Sunbeamland Cycle Factory in Wolverhampton in 1887. In 1895 John Marston Ltd was formed in Wolverhampton with £40,000 capital to take over the various businesses.

In 1898 another member of the family, Charles Marston, started the Villiers Engineering Co whose 20 employees made bicycle components. The line-shafting from this firm was extended into a derelict coach house and there, from 1899, John Marston allowed one of his old apprentices, Thomas Cureton, to tinker with a prototype car.

A Forman-engined 6hp twin was displayed in 1901 but the first production cars of that year were of a curious diamond wheel layout with outward facing seats. They were the work of Mabberly-Smith, had De Dion engines and were called Sunbeam Mableys.

T. C. Pullinger arrived from France to run the motor department in 1902. He obtained rights to the 12hp Berliet designed by Desgouttes and these were sold as Sunbeams from 1903. Complete chassis were at first imported but later on just engines and gearboxes were imported. A feature of the cars was the oil-bath chain cases originally perfected on Sunbeam bicycles.

In 1905 the motor department was separated as the Sunbeam Motor Car Co Ltd with a capital of £40,000. Within two years it occupied 2 acres (0.8 hectares) of factory space and was making an all-British 16/20 designed by Angus Shaw. Pullinger had gone to work for Humber in 1904 but in 1909 Louis Coatalen, with even greater continental experience plus a spell spent with Humber and Hillman, arrived as designer.

A racing programme improved the cars and their image, and profits of only £90 in 1909 rose to £95,000 net in 1913, when 2400 men were employed. A total of 429 cars were made in 1910. Louis Coatalen joined the board in 1912 and was joint managing director with W. M. Iliff in 1914. Sidney Guy was works manager before starting Guy Motors in 1914.

Staff cars and more than 1600 ambulances, many of them subcontracted by Rover, were built during World War I. Aero and naval airship engines were also produced.

After the war the four-cylinder 16 and 24 six were built at the rate of 20 a week. The factory had expanded to 30 acres (12 hectares). Most parts, including castings, were made on the premises and the workforce stood at about 4000. John Marston died in 1918.

The Sunbeam Maori-powered *R-34* airship made a trip to the United States and back in 183 hours in 1919. The following year Sunbeam became part of the £3.3 million capitalized STD Motors Ltd, which included Talbot, Darracq and commercial vehicle maker W. & G. DuCros as well as equipment makers Heenan and Froude and Jonas Woodhead. James Todd was chairman of both Sunbeam and STD and Coatalen was the group's chief engineer and competitions director.

Racing and record breaking involved much of the group's time and money, particularly at Sunbeam, which made some road-going sports models but was best known for attractive, well made and refined touring cars. Some of these used overhead-cam engines built by the under-utilized Talbot works – one of the few successful examples of integration at STD.

The company's inability to pay dividends to the preference shareholders in 1926, despite a profit of £150,000, spelled the end of the racing programme whereupon J. S. Irving, Coatalen's experimental engineer/designer at Sunbeam, and driver H. O. D. Segrave severed their connections with the STD group. Coatalen concentrated on designing land speed record cars; due to illness and long periods spent in the French factories of STD, he appeared to lose interest in Sunbeam's production side, which still employed 3000 men.

Expensive bottlenecks hindered efficient production, such as making crankshafts in-house from 410lb (185kg) billets and running-in all engines for 18 hours and then dismantling them for checks. White metal bearings were still individually poured and hand scraped in 1928. The four-cylinder cars had been discontinued in 1927, and straight-eights and double-overhead cam six-cylinder sports models ended in 1930, as did attempts to keep a foothold in the aero engine field – the last being 1000hp V12s.

Sunbeam Mabley of 1902

Sunbeam tourer of 1904

Sunbeam Tiger V12 record car of 1926

Sunbeam Talbot saloon of 1954

Hugh Rose, formerly of Guy, Crossley, Belsize and Calthorpe, designed a range of buses for Sunbeam in 1929. Sales were disappointing, but trolleybuses developed from them in 1931 did much better.

In 1934 Sunbeam Trolleybuses Ltd was formed with C. W. Reeve as managing director; Reeve was also on the boards of AEC and Napier. The firm was run jointly by Rootes and AEC until 1944, when Sunbeam Trolleybuses refused to move to the Ryton-on-Dunsmore 'shadow' factory and was bought by the engineering group Brockhouse, which sold it to Guy in 1949. When the Sunbeam name ended on trolleybuses in the early 1960s some 2000 had been sold.

Rose left for Riley in 1930 and was not replaced until H. C. M. Stephens – who had formerly worked under Coatalen and been with Thames, Adams, Oldsmobile and Citroën – returned in 1932 with a team from Singer to design a mass-market Sunbeam, the Dawn. The new model cost £3.5 million to develop and appeared in 1934 with independent front suspension and 1.6-litre overhead-valve four. It failed, however, to halt the decline of Sunbeam.

The entire board of STD had resigned in 1931 following shareholder criticism of lack of co-ordination and was replaced by Sir Thomas Clarke, Sir Daniel Neylan and J. F. Marriam, who were respectively from the boards of Express Dairies, Sir Wm Arrol and Co, and the Public Benefit Boot Co. They co-opted two members of the old Sunbeam board but were defeated when £500,000 worth of 10-year notes that had been issued to finance Coatalen's Grand Prix ambitions came due for repayment in 1934. Rootes, fresh from its success at reviving the fortunes of Humber, Hillman and Commer, salvaged Sunbeam from the chaos of STD in 1935.

Charles Marston's Villiers Engineering Co, with more than 500 employees, then moved into Sunbeam's factory. As well as motorcycle engines it made Marston Seagull outboard motors.

The Sunbeam/Marston bicycle, motorcycle and radiator firms, which had been run separ-

Sunbeam Alpine convertible of 1959

ately from the cars since 1905, were bought by ICI in 1922. ICI sold the motorcycle department to Associated Motorcycles in 1937 and the bicycles to BSA a year later. BSA acquired the motorcycle rights later on and then sold them to Raleigh. The bicycle factory at Wolverhampton was later used by Brockhouse for making machine tools. The last shaft-driven Sunbeam motorcycle was made in 1957. The Marston radiator business became Marston-Excelsior and still exists.

A straight-eight 4½-litre overhead valve engine in a Humber chassis with Dawn-type independent front suspension appeared at the 1937 London Motor Show as a Sunbeam, but did not enter production. It had been designed by Georges Roesch of Talbot. Instead the Sunbeam name was coupled with Talbot – now also owned by Rootes – for a series of upmarket or sporting versions of Hillmans and Humbers which were made at Talbot's London factory from 1938. Bodies for the more select models were made by Thrupp and Maberly. Sunbeam-Talbot Ltd was formed for this venture and had as chief en-

Sunbeam Stiletto of c.1970

gineer the Dawn designer, H. C. M. Stephens, Georges Roesch of Talbot having resigned in October 1938.

About 7000 of the Minx-based Ten were made before World War II and 4000 between 1945 and 1948. A total of 1124 2-litres, alias Hillman 14s, were produced from 1945 to 1948. The Model 80 sold 3500 in 1949-50 and the 90 about 19,000 until 1957.

To avoid confusion with Lago-Talbots, Sunbeam-Talbots were sold in France after the war as Sunbeams, and it was this name that was chosen for the Alpine sports car of 1953, made at Ryton-on-Dunsmore, near Coventry. The Sunbeam-Talbot 90 was renamed Sunbeam Mk III in 1955, and many sporting versions of Hillmans subsequently bore the Sunbeam name. These included the Rapier (Minx-based), of which 69,000 were ultimately sold including the 1967-76 fastbacks (with styling by courtesy of Chrysler's Plymouth Barracuda), the Stiletto (ex-Imp) and the Ford V8 engined and Jensen assembled Tiger of 1964, some 7000 being built before Chrysler took over the company. The Tiger used the body shell of the 1960 integral Alpine sports car, of which nearly 70,000 were made before production ended in 1968. The name has also been used by the group's subsequent owners, Peugeot-Citroën, notably on a Lotus-engined hatchback. NB

SUP
see Hinstin

SURREY/VICTORY
GB 1921-1930

Charles Alfred West of the West London Scientific Apparatus Co Ltd of Putney, south London, assembled cars from 1921 using an assortment of components including Moss drive axle, Ford T front axle and steering, Meadows gearbox (except on some friction drive versions) and Coventry-Simplex engine. He was said to have 200 orders when an investor provided £2500 in exchange for director's fees and £5 per week. Accounts and production figures were apparently withheld from this unfortunate gentleman and receivership followed in 1923.

The garage firm Surrey Service Ltd of Putney and Thames Ditton continued the Surrey until 1927 when it threw in the towel, having used only 11 Meadows engines, although possibly other makes as well. This company was also responsible for the Victory car, sometimes described as a separate brand.

The Victory had a 12/50hp four-cylinder engine of uncertain provenance and was in some way connected with the makers of Palladium cars. There was also a 19/50hp type called variously New Victory, Empire and Imperial. The Surrey marque was continued until 1930 by Surrey Light Cars of Putney. NB

SUZUKI
JAPAN 1939 to date

Michio Suzuki was born in 1887, the son of a cotton farmer in what was then the village of Hamamatsu. He was apprenticed to a carpenter who began building cotton weaving looms in 1904. In 1908 Suzuki left, to start loom manufacture himself, and in 1909 he set up the Suzuki Loom Works in Hamamatsu, in a shed provided by his father.

Suzuki expanded rapidly, as did much of Japan's industry before World War I, introducing powered looms and building up a staff of about 60 workers. In March 1920 the firm was reorganized as the Suzuki Loom Manufacturing Co, with capital of 500,000 yen.

This coincided with a crash in the Japanese textile market, but Suzuki survived on the strength of building superior machinery. By 1921 the company had doubled its capital and started a large new factory in Hamamatsu, which was already changing from a rural village to an industrial centre.

In 1936 the new Automobile Manufacturing law effectively isolated Japan from imports and encouraged domestic production. Suzuki began to consider vehicle manufacture and imported an Austin Seven which was stripped and studied in detail. In 1937 the company built a water-cooled 750cc four-cylinder engine and in 1939 put it into several vehicles for evaluation, but production was already being turned to military equipment with the approach of World War II.

Suzuki expanded greatly during the war, but in December 1944 its two main plants were partly destroyed by earthquake and then further damaged in the repeated air-raids of 1945. Loom production was resumed, however, in September 1945 and continued during post-war occupation, during which Suzuki also made such products as farm

tools, electric heaters and even a sea-water desalination plant.

Post-war revival of automobile manufacture in Japan was extremely slow and almost entirely confined to commercial vehicles. By October 1949 Suzuki's capital had reached 54 million yen but late that year and into the early 1950s the company was almost killed by a strike and another national recession in textile making.

To survive, it looked to the new market for motorized bicycles and in April 1952 introduced the Power Free, with a 36cc 'clip-on' engine. It was sold under the name SJK, for Suzuki Jidosha Kogyo, or Suzuki Automotive Industries, and the initials continued to be used until 1958, even though a new company, the Suzuki Motor Co Ltd, had been formed in June 1954.

During that year Suzuki obtained Citroën, Lloyd and Volkswagen cars, which were dismantled and studied. In August Suzuki tested its own front-wheel-drive chassis, powered by an air-cooled 360cc two-stroke twin. By October 1955 this had been developed into the production Suzulight car. With van and pickup versions added soon after its introduction, Suzulight production reached about 30 a month by the beginning of 1956 and the model continued largely unchanged until the

Suzuki Alto FX of c.1985

Suzulight TL was introduced in 1959.

In September of that year one of Suzuki's car plants was destroyed by a typhoon but by the beginning of 1960 output had reached 200 four-wheelers a month and a new plant was opened in March. In 1961 the textile machinery company, which is still a major manufacturer, and the car company were formally separated.

In 1967 Suzuki introduced a new version of the lightweight car, the 800 Fronte, a development of the Suzulight (which was still made) with a 785cc three-cylinder two-stroke engine. In 1974 water cooling was introduced on the cars, and capacity of the smallest unit was increased to 443cc in 1976 and to 539cc in 1979.

In August 1977 Suzuki showed its first four-stroke four-wheeler, the LJ80 cross-country vehicle. By 1979 four-stroke overhead-cam engines were available across the range, which included front-wheel-drive saloons, a rear-engined coupé and off-road vehicles. Two-stroke engines were still available in the Fronte saloons.

In 1981 the hatchback Alto was launched with a 797cc overhead-cam three-cylinder engine, and at the other end of the range was the SJ410 four-wheel-drive off-road vehicle. A larger engined version of the Alto was introduced in 1983 and a revised SJ410 in 1985. Suzuki's 1986 range included these and the Cultus 1.3-litre hatchback, sold in Europe as the Swift and in the US as the Chevrolet Sprint.

General Motors imported 17,000 Suzuki cars a year into America up to 1985, the maximum permissible under voluntary restraints, but with those restraints lifted from 1985 it was expecting to import many more. Suzuki's 1984 production figure of about 163,000 cars therefore looked set to be beaten quite comfortably before long.

Suzuki is also one of the world's largest motorcycle manufacturers and makes a range of other products including outboard motors, boats, industrial engines, snowmobiles, electric wheelchairs and even prefabricated houses. BL

SWALLOW DORETTI
GB 1954-1956

In January 1935 William Lyons founded SS Cars Ltd, the forerunner of Jaguar, as a nominal subsidiary of his earlier firm, the Swallow Coachbuilding Co. He then put Swallow into voluntary liquidation and set up a separate private company, the Swallow Coachbuilding Co (1935) Ltd, to continue sidecar production and sales while he concentrated his efforts on his new market for cars

In 1945 Swallow was sold to the Helliwell group and in 1946 sidecar production was taken over by Tube Investments Ltd. The Swallow Coachbuilding Co (1935) Ltd, which now did a large amount of work for the air-

Suzuki SJ410 of c.1985

Swift voiturette of c.1900

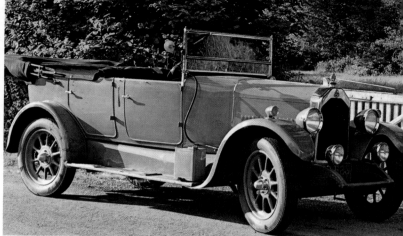

Swift 14/40 tourer of 1926

craft industry, moved to Walsall aerodrome in Staffordshire.

In January 1954 Swallow unveiled a new sports car, the Swallow Doretti, which was based on the engine and transmission of the Triumph TR2, introduced in 1952. The Doretti was largely aimed at the American market, where it was to be sold and serviced by the American branch of Standard-Triumph, and was named after Dorothy, a daughter of the American importer. It used a tubular chassis and a very strong double-skinned open two-seater body with steel inner panels and an alloy outer shell.

In Britain the car sold for £1101 compared to £844 for the TR2. In the United States it was introduced at $3295 and the price was later reduced to $2980. Strangely, British testers, who also criticized a lack of passenger and luggage space, said the car was heavier and slower than the TR2, while American reporters described it as lighter and faster.

In all, Swallow built just over 100 Dorettis, all open two-seaters except for two coupés (one of them a 1955 prototype), and, it seems, one saloon. The Doretti never really competed with the TR2, and Standard-Triumph became less enthusiastic about the car when the head of the company, Sir John Black, was badly injured while driving one. Production stopped in 1955 and in 1956 the Swallow Coachbuilding Co (1935) Ltd was sold to another sidecar manufacturer, Watsonian. BL

Swallow Doretti of c.1956

SWIFT
GB 1898-1931

The Swift Cycle Co was formed in 1896 to acquire for £375,000 the former Coventry Machinists Co that had made sewing machines from 1869 and then bicycles, some with the model name Swift. The works manager of the old firm was James Starley, known as the 'father of the cycle industry', whose relatives and friends went on to found many of the early Coventry cycle/motor firms, including Ariel, Rover, Hillman and Rudge. Original Swift directors were members of the Irish DuCros family, holders of the Dunlop patents and financiers of Ariel, and several French firms including Clément.

From 1898 Swift built De Dion-powered tricycles similar to Ariels and made motorcycles until 1915, many of which were identical to Ariels and had the same White and Poppe engines. Swift also made the 1903 Starley motorcycles and that year shared a Motor Show stand with Ariel.

From 1900 there were Swift motor quads with MMC engines and then, in 1902, the first true cars, which used a variety of engines including Fafnir. The Swift Motor Co was formed as a subsidiary in 1902 and soon moved to a separate factory in Cheylesmore, Coventry. The Swift Cycle Co then concentrated on making two-wheelers, but also produced several hundred cyclecars in 1912-13.

W. Radford, the works manager, developed two- and three-cylinder engines in 1904. General manager was Robert Burns, who had started working for Swift in 1897 and was to remain for 27 years.

Larger four-cylinder cars were added to the range. There was also a 7hp Clément-type single in 1909 of which 1030 were built, 162 having Austin radiators. Swift concentrated on the small to medium horsepower range from about 1910. These cars were well designed and lightly built and were quite popular in countries where Swift had earlier established cycle agencies.

Cars were made until 1916, by which time the works were busy producing stretcher carriers, machine gun belt fillers, fuse caps, shells and military bicycles. Then came Vickers aircraft parts and Renault, Hispano and RAF aero engines.

In 1919 the bicycle and motor firms were combined as Swift of Coventry Ltd. J. Whitcomb of Bean quietly bought 50 per cent of Swift shares for £286,700 but in the first 17 months of Bean control Swift lost £78,000. When Harper Bean collapsed in 1920 Swift nearly failed as well.

C. Sangster was now chairman of Swift and Bernard Steeley, managing director of the Lucas electrical firm, was its new general manager. J. A. Wilding was Swift's technical director from 1920 to 1926. He put an excellent 2-litre Twelve into production alongside the existing Ten with help from C. Van Eugen. Some pre-war chassis became the basis of the first Eric-Campbell cars.

The factories, totalling 150,000sq ft (13,935sq m), were reorganized to make 5000 cars a year, although only about half this quantity was produced. Swift was competing in the 'popular' class but offering more expensive cars than those of its mass-production rivals; it was a recipe for disaster.

In 1926 a creditors committee forced a major shake-up and capital was reduced from £300,000 to £140,000. The Ten was modernized and the Twelve became a Fourteen. A £150 Cadet with 8hp Coventry-Climax engine was launched in 1930 but the firm went into liquidation in April 1931.

Alfred Herbert Ltd acquired the premises and tooling, selling the spares to R. H. Collier & Co Ltd of Birmingham. The remaining 8hp engines with their SM motif were built into FSM fire pumps by Coventry-Climax. The Swift trade mark was sold to Kirk and Merrifield of Birmingham, which still uses it on bicycles. NB

SYRENA
see Warszawa

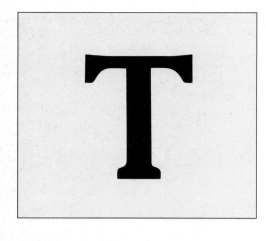

TALBOT
FRANCE 1979 to date

In July 1979 PSA Peugeot-Citroën announced that it was reviving the Talbot name for use on cars built by what until recently had been Chrysler's European factories. Chrysler was the latest acquisition in Peugeot's remarkable expansion throughout the 1960s and 1970s. It made the family controlled firm the world's fifth biggest car producer by 1978, behind General Motors, Ford, Toyota and Nissan.

In 1974 Peugeot had bought a minority holding in Citroën, which was funded at the time by Michelin and already in serious financial trouble. By 1976 Peugeot controlled the majority of Citroën shares, to create the PSA Peugeot-Citroën grouping in 1977. In August 1978 Peugeot took over the European Chrysler operations, basically comprising Chrysler

by Chrysler's takeover of Simca, which itself had acquired the original Automobiles Talbot of Suresnes in 1959.

This Talbot incarnation had appeared in June 1920 after the British-owned, but French-based, A. Darracq & Co (1905) Ltd amalgamated with the English company Clément-Talbot Ltd and the Sunbeam Motor Car Co to form the Sunbeam-Talbot-Darracq combine – with all three names remaining in use, singly or together. The French operation continued to use the Talbot name until 1960 and the takeover by Simca, which built a prototype Talbot in 1960 but then laid the name to rest.

The British version of the Talbot name continued until 1935, when the Sunbeam-Talbot-Darracq partnership collapsed. The Rootes group took over in Coventry and the Talbot name was used alone until 1938, and then in conjunction with Sunbeam until 1954.

Control of the French Talbot factory had passed to Major Anthony Lago in 1935 and he ran the company until the Simca takeover and the disappearance of that version of the Talbot name. After 1981 the Simca name, as used on the Chrysler Alpine and Horizon models, was dropped in favour of Talbot, but the first revival of the name actually came in 1980 when it was used on British-built Alpines and on the new Alpine-derived notchback Solara model.

A new Talbot model, the Tagora, was launched in 1981 with 2.2 or 2.7-litre petrol engines or a turbocharged 2.3-litre Peugeot diesel. The Talbot and Sunbeam names were found in conjunction again on the Talbot Sunbeam-Lotus high performance saloon, originally derived from the Chrysler Sunbeam in 1979. In 1982 another Talbot was added to

the range, the Peugeot 104-based Samba, which was produced in hatchback and cabriolet versions.

The company's fortunes were mixed. Poissy continued to be reasonably successful, but in 1981 one of the major British plants, at Linwood in Scotland, was closed, leaving most of the work with the plants at Ryton and Stoke, which assembled kits from France and built all-British Alpines. The former Dodge truck operation was sold to Renault, and between 1979 and 1984 the British workforce was slashed from about 25,000 to 5000 under the guidance of George Turnbull, who had returned to run Automobiles Talbot after successfully establishing the Korean Hyundai company. Turnbull left Talbot in 1984 and his problems were taken over by his former assistant, Geoff Whalen.

From 1973 to 1982 the British operation had had 10 consecutive loss making years, to an aggregate total of almost £400 million. In 1982 Peugeot gave about £55 million worth of assistance to Talbot in Britain and the group as a whole recorded losses of about £375 million during 1982 and 1983, being further hampered by protracted strikes at Poissy during 1983. The British branch made a profit of just over £3 million in 1983 but in 1984 its whole future was threatened by problems in obtaining payments, totalling about £120 million a year, from Iran for Hillman Hunter kits supplied for assembly in that country as Peykans. Shipments were stopped and large numbers of workers laid off. By 1984 Talbot's market share had fallen to less than 2 per cent.

Peugeot planned investments of about £100 million in France and £20 million in Britain leading to a new car, code-named the

Talbot 105 saloon of 1934

Talbot Samba cabriolet of 1982

France SA at Poissy, Chrysler UK Ltd in Coventry, and Chrysler España in Madrid, as the parent Chrysler Corporation in the United States attempted to generate some much needed cash to alleviate its own desperate financial problems. The Chrysler companies were renamed Automobiles Talbot.

Chrysler España was formed in 1970 when Chrysler, which had been increasing its shareholding since 1963, reorganized the company Barreiros Diesel SA, founded in 1951. Chrysler France and Chrysler UK were linked by the earlier Talbot companies; Chrysler France SA was formed in July 1970

Talbot Tagora SX of 1982

C28 hatchback and launched in late 1985 under the name Peugeot 309. This is made at Poissy and at Ryton.

In the meantime, production fell from 120,503 in 1983 to just 95,122 in 1984 – and over 70 per cent of these were Peykans, the falling numbers reflecting weeks of halted production pending payments. Production of Talbots proper in 1984 was only about 27,300, down from 35,298 in 1983. The Horizon was slightly revised in 1985 but an indication of how Talbot was clutching at straws was its mid-1985 replacement of Solara and Alpine names with Minx and Rapier – harking back to the old Hillman and Sunbeam makes. BL

TALBOT/CLÉMENT-TALBOT
GB 1902-1954

In spite of its French sounding name, Clément-Talbot Ltd was a thoroughly English company. It was formed in October 1902 as a private company with capital of £300,000 and took its name from two of its directors, the French car-maker Adolph Clément and the Earl of Shrewsbury and Talbot. Clément et Cie had been building cars at Levallois-Perret since 1899 and the Earl, in partnership with D. M. Weigel, imported them to Britain from around the turn of the century. Weigel, who later went on to build cars under his own name, became managing director of the new company, whose intention was to build cars in England with help from Clément.

While work continued on an impressive factory on a 3½-acre (1.4-hectare) site in North Kensington, London, the company imported cars from France (where they were known as Clément-Bayards from 1903) and sold them in Britain as Clément-Talbots. By late 1904 the factory was able to assemble cars from French components and by the end of that year they were being sold simply as Talbots. In January 1905 the firm exhibited a range of four twin-cylinder models and five four-cylinders, from 7/8hp to the 6.3-litre 35/50hp 4Y.

The cars had already begun to lose much of their French content and the first all-British Talbot, a 3.8-litre 20/24hp four designed by C. R. Garrard, appeared in 1906. This and the 2.7-litre 12/16hp Talbot four helped Talbot establish a very sound reputation in speed trials, hillclimbs and other competitions – prompting the slogan 'Invincible Talbot'.

The company continued to offer both its own cars and French imports, but the British cars were now much the more important. They developed along conventional lines and included six-cylinder models from 1910, by which time Talbot employed almost 600 men and was building 50 to 60 cars a month.

In 1911, G. W. A. Brown, formerly of Argyll, Humber and Austin, joined Talbot as chief engineer and began to improve the four-cylinder engines. In 1912 he prepared a stripped

and streamlined racing Talbot based on the 4.5-litre 25hp chassis and with this Percy Lambert captured numerous records, including almost 104 miles (167km) in an hour in 1913 – the first time 100 miles (160km) had ever been covered in the time. Lambert was killed shortly afterwards during another record attempt and was buried in a coffin streamlined to emulate his car!

Adolphe Clément severed his connection with the firm shortly before World War I, by which time the cars were virtually all-British anyway. During the war, Talbot built more than 1000 heavy cars and ambulances. In 1916 Brown left and was succeeded as chief engineer by a young Swiss, Georges Roesch, who had already worked for Grégoire, Delaunay-Belleville, Coventry Daimler and Renault.

His first design was the excellent 1750cc 12hp Talbot A12 prototype of 1919, but the car never reached production. In 1919 the company was taken over, for about £350,000, by Société Alexandre Darracq, based in Paris but British owned. Shortly afterwards Darracq also bought Sunbeam, which thus became part of the Sunbeam-Talbot-Darracq group – with all engineering under the direction of Louis Coatalen.

French-built Darracqs initially became Talbot Darracqs and then plain Talbots in France, but were known as Talbot-Darracqs or Darracqs in Britain.

The prewar 15/20 and 25/50 models were revised and a 1-litre 8/18 model, based on a Darracq design, was added in 1921. This was quickly upgraded by Roesch to 10/23 configuration.

The car was expensive and the other models, mainly sixes, were only made in small

Talbot coupé de ville of c.1905

numbers, so by the end of 1925 Clément-Talbot was close to bankruptcy. Roesch, whose talents had lately been spread rather too thinly over the group, was entrusted with saving the company.

The result, launched in 1926, was his famous 1666cc 14/45 Six. It had many features, including overhead valves worked by rockers on knife-edged adjusters, a flywheel fan, Delco coil ignition, Dynastart, torque tube drive and electric trafficators. It was light, roomy and cheap and dramatically revived Talbot's fortunes.

In 1930 more powerful 75 and 90 versions were developed, and with the 3-litre 105 from 1931 helped the marque to many more competition successes until financial constraints forced the company to withdraw from competition at the end of 1932.

Although both Sunbeam and Darracq now had serious problems, Talbot at last seemed reasonably successful, but in September 1934 a further £500,000 cash crisis cropped up and a receiver was appointed to the whole group. Early in 1935 the Clément-Talbot and Sunbeam companies were taken over by the Rootes group, but although the name was saved the products soon began to change for the worse. Some true Roesch models were built from parts in stock but subsequent Talbots up to 1938 were based on Hillman and Humber models and were very inferior.

Towards the end of 1938, during which year Roesch left in disgust, the marque was renamed Sunbeam-Talbot and continued to make sportier versions of the very mundane Rootes models. During World War II the company made car and aircraft components, and shortly after it transferred production to the former Rootes 'shadow' factory at Ryton-on-Dunsmore, Coventry.

The Talbot name was dropped from the cars in 1954, although it was still part of the company name until 1970. The Talbot name then reappeared in the 1980s as a marque in its own right after Peugeot-Citroën had acquired the remaining elements of the former Rootes empire from its earlier saviour, Chrysler. BL/NB

TALBOT-DARRACQ
see Darracq

Talbot 75 sports saloon of 1936

TAMPLIN
GB 1919-1927

Tamplin cyclecar of 1921

E. A. Tamplin was the proprietor of the Railway Garage in Staines, Middlesex, and in 1919 was sole agent for the Carden tandem seater cyclecar. In November of that year he bought all rights to this design, which he produced under the name Tamplin. Unlike other Carden designs it had a front-mounted V-twin JAP engine, driving by primary chain to a Sturmey-Archer three-speed gearbox and thence by a long single belt to the nearside rear wheel. The body was made of fibreboard.

In 1922 there was a more conventional car with side-by-side seating and all-chain drive. JAP engines were normally used, but there was a sports model with Blackburne engine and a handsome polished aluminium body.

At the end of 1923 Tamplin Motors moved to Cheam, Surrey, where production continued for another two years at least, although cars were listed as late as 1927. Total production of all Tamplins was about 2000, quite a respectable figure for a cyclecar. Tamplin Motors were later distributors for Chevrolet followed by Bedford commercial vehicles, and were still in business in 1950. GNG

TARRANT
AUSTRALIA 1901-1907

The Tarrant, built in Melbourne, Victoria, from 1901 to 1907, was one of the best known of early Australian cars, but like most efforts at establishing a local industry it could not really compete with American and European imports – for which its originator was a major distributor. He was Harley Tarrant, born in a small town in Victoria in 1860, the son of a printer from Oxford, England.

Harley worked first as a surveyor and civil engineer, working for the New South Wales Lands Department in the Broken Hills silver mining district. In 1888 he moved to Melbourne and established a civil engineering company with his brother Joseph. He was also becoming interested in cars, and particularly in engines. He learned mechanical engineering in his spare time and began tinkering with engines. He even built a crude two-cylinder chain-drive car in the mid-1890s but it apparently never ran on the road.

He then began work on engines for stationary use – a good market in Australia, with its many farmers and new settlers needing portable power. Early in 1898 he left his brother in charge of the civil engineering and set up the Harley Tarrant Motor Syndicate to build his engines commercially.

In 1899 he was joined by a prominent local cycle manufacturer, Howard Lewis, changed the company name to the Tarrant Engineering Co and started work on another car. In 1900 the company moved into larger premises and became the Tarrant Motor and Engineering Co.

The first Tarrant production car had a 6hp twin-cylinder De Dion engine and chain drive and was sold in September 1901. It was followed by a front-engined 10hp twin-cylinder shaft-drive model.

In 1903 Stuart Ross, who had previously worked for the Hozier Engineering Co Ltd in Glasgow, maker of the Argyll car, joined Tarrant and in 1904 the company added Argyll to its agencies for De Dion, Mercédès and Rover. Also in 1903 Tarrant opened a subsidiary, the Melbourne Motor Body Works, but most of the bodies it made must have been for the imports as Tarrant production was tiny. It took the company as long as a year to produce an individual car. Typical output was only two or three cars a year and total production was less than 20.

The final twin-cylinder models were made around 1905, with 11.9hp White & Poppe engines or a locally made 8hp unit. In 1906 Tarrant offered a 14/16hp four-cylinder model with Australian-built engine. Another larger bodyworks was opened in 1907 but this was definitely for imports, as Tarrant production stopped that year when the company became a Ford agency. As such, and with later agencies including Rolls-Royce, Fiat and Oldsmobile, Tarrant was very successful.

Harley Tarrant also followed a military career, reaching the rank of colonel and becoming Director of Automobile Transport for the Australian Army in 1914. He retired from the company due to ill health in 1917 but lived until 1949. Lewis and Ross reorganized the company as Autocar Industries Pty Ltd, and again after 1925 as the bodybuilder Ruskin Motors Pty Ltd, which was bought by the Austin Motor Co Ltd in about 1950. BL

Tarrant 14-16hp two-seater of 1907

TATRA/NESSELSDORF
CZECHOSLOVAKIA 1899 to date

In the town of Nesselsdorf in northern Moravia, Ignac Sustala, born in 1822, started a workshop in 1850. Financial backing came from Adolf Raska and the business prospered. It employed 150 men in the 1870s making 1000 carts and carriages a year. A factory was opened at Ratibor, Prussia, in 1864 and sales offices were soon set up in Wroclaw, Vienna, Berlin and Prague.

Raska died in 1877 and the firm came close to failure until a railway carriage maker asked Sustala to build flat-cars. Railway equipment then became important. A speciality was state railway carriages, bought by the crowned heads of several countries.

On Sustala's death in 1891 Hugo von Röslerstamm became manager. He was friendly with textile magnate Baron von Liebig, who in 1893 bought a Benz. This car was examined in the Sustala wagon works and a two-cylinder Benz engine was bought to power an experimental President car in 1897. Involved in the project were Dr Edmund Rumpler, Leopold Svitak and Hans Ledwinka, who had joined the firm that year. The President was driven the 204 miles (328km) to Vienna by Baron von Liebig to celebrate Kaiser Franz-Joseph's Golden Jubilee.

Tatra President of 1897

The first orders were received and 10 cars were laid down in 1899, each with a different name. From the end of 1900 the cars were known as Nesselsdorfs and had locally produced engines, some earlier ones having been made by William Hardy in Vienna.

Rumpler left for Allgemeine Motorwagen Gesellschaft in 1898 and Ledwinka worked on experimental steam cars in Vienna. In Ledwinka's absence a few De Dion-Bouton pattern steam buses were made, Lang designed petrol cars and commercial vehicles – called NW for Nesselsdorfer Wagenbau – and Kronfeld developed front-engined cars.

Ledwinka returned to the company in 1905 and in 1906 his S model 3.3-litre overhead-camshaft car put Nesselsdorf on an international footing for the first time. Six-cylinder models were made from 1913 but when Hugo von Röslerstamm retired in 1915 money for the motor department was diverted to railway wagon production and Ledwinka left for Steyr in disgust. In 1916 production amounted to 47 cars and 226 trucks.

In October 1918 Nesselsdorf was part of the new state of Czechoslovakia and the town was renamed Koprivnice. The vehicles became known as Tatras after the mountain range where they were often tested.

By 1923 Ledwinka had returned again and his revolutionary Type 11 car appeared that year with the first of the features that were to characterize the marque – air-cooled engine, swing axle and backbone chassis. The Type 11 had an opposed-twin 12bhp engine. A total of 11,070 were made of this and the four wheel braked, but otherwise similar, Type 12 until 1930. A commercial derivative was also produced and 7500 became postal vans.

which perhaps 25 were made.

In 1923 Tatra had merged with Ringhoffer of Prague, a railway rolling stock maker which had made railway equipment since 1852. Dr Hans Ringhoffer then became general manager of Tatra. The workforce numbered about 2000 and profits in 1926 were the equivalent of $65,000. Ringhoffer's Bohemia coachworks in Česká Lípa built some of the special bodies used by Tatra, as did Sodomka in Vysoké Mýto which is now the Karosa bus firm.

Rail locomotives with up to 18 air-cooled cylinders were made in the 1930s alongside cars and commercials. In 1934 the remarkable Type 77 rear engined V8 air-cooled streamlined saloon was introduced. Tatra sold 3334 cars in 1932 and was the biggest seller in Czechoslovakia. Five years later it

fringement and the company was awarded 3 million marks damages in 1967.

Diesel engines were introduced on some of the heavy commercials in 1935, air-cooled types were offered in 1939, and three years later a whole range of four-, six-, eight- and 12-cylinder air-cooled diesels with interchangeable parts was standardized for military vehicles built under German control. The Type 111 six-wheel truck appeared in 1944 and about 35,000 were built over the next 20 years; 15,000 were exported by Motokov of Prague, the export agent for Tatra from 1950.

A variation on the 57 car in 1938 took the form of basic open four-seaters, produced for the Chinese army. The 57 was revived after World War II along with a four-cylinder version of the streamlined V8.

When the communist regime in Czechoslovakia imprisoned German collaborators after the war, Hans Ledwinka spent six years in gaol. Upon release he returned to his native Austria and later ran a design consultancy in Munich. He died almost penniless and forgotten at the age of 89 in 1967.

When Tatra was nationalized Dr Julius Mackerle took over from Ledwinka and in 1948 the two current models were replaced by a 2-litre, rear engined, streamlined T600 Tatraplan which was made in small quantities for state officials. Thereafter most emphasis was placed on commercial vehicles of over 7 tons capacity.

The six-wheel T111 was succeeded by the broadly similar T138 in 1962 and in the course of the next 10 years 45,000 were built.

Tatra Type AA convertible of 1924

Tatra Type 77A saloon of 1935

There were also diminutive six-wheelers, around 500 of which were made in the 10 years from 1927. Heavier lorries included a 6×6 in 1924 and various four- and six-wheel highway models, which gradually adopted central backbones and independent suspension. Most had air-cooling, although water-cooling lasted on some into the 1930s. At opposite ends of the scale were single-cylinder three-wheelers, produced in 1929, and the Type 80 V12 car, introduced in 1931, of

was second to Skoda, selling 3241 against 4452.

A rear-engined V570 small car prototype that showed a strong similarity to the later Volkswagen was made about this time. It was based on the front engined 18bhp (later 25bhp) flat-four Type 57 launched in Prague in 1931. The 57 was made under licence by Röhr and then Stoewer and by Tatra's associates in Vienna. After World War II Ringhoffer Tatra sued Volkswagen for alleged patent in-

Tatra T600 Tatraplan of 1951

483

Exports were made to 59 countries. In 1957 the V8 T603 car was introduced receiving Vignale styling in 1969 as the 165bhp T613.

In 1969 production was around 4000 vehicles, of which perhaps 250 were cars. Truck production at Tatra's Liberec, Slovak and original factory increased to 7000 a year in the 1970s and a loan from the International Investment Bank enabled production to be doubled in the early 1980s. Tatra's most remarkable products since 1967, when they were announced, have been forward control 4×4, 6×6 (twin steer) and 8×8 military/civilian trucks and tractors for hauling up to 300 tons gross train weight or for cross-country load carrying. NB

TEILHOL
FRANCE 1975 to date

The diminutive Teilhol is fairly typical of the numerous microcars which take advantage of tax concessions for the French domestic market. It is made by Teilhol Voiture Electrique of Ambert, Puy-de-Dôme, now Teilhol SA of Courpière, one of more than 50 microcar makers to have exploited the market.

The plastic-bodied Teilhol was introduced in 1975 and has been produced in three-wheel and four-wheel and in petrol and electric versions, with various types of body. The electric cars came first, two tubular framed chain-drive three-wheelers and a four-wheeled invalid car which admitted a wheelchair through a large remotely-operated rear door. Other body styles included the inevitable golf-cart, runabout and a light delivery truck. In 1981 Teilhol introduced a petrol-engined four-wheel model with a 50cc single-cylinder Motobecane engine and automatic transmission. By 1986 this engine had been replaced by 327 or 400cc diesels. Teilhol also makes Rodeo utility vehicles for Renault. BL

TEMPELHOF
see Oryx

TEMPERINO
ITALY 1919-1924

Temperino 800cc two-seater of 1920

Maurizio Temperino was born in Italy in 1888 and brought up in the United States. When his coal miner father died he returned to Italy and with two brothers opened a bicycle repair shop in Turin in 1907. They soon assembled

484

bicycles and made an experimental light car in 1908 followed by production motorcycles with British Precision engines.

In 1919 Vetturette Temperino SA with 500,000 lire capital was founded to produce light cars at the rate of 1800 a year. Wooden bodies were made by Farina and Giovanni Farina was president of Temperino; 1-litre two-cylinder engines, air-cooled by wooden fan, came from motorcycle maker Della Ferrera, and Antonio Opessi made the chassis. Opessi had an old established firm that had helped Temperino produce its wartime motorcycles as well as 1918 car prototypes and was now entrusted with assembly of the cars. To reduce cost and complication the Temperino had drive to only one of its rear wheels. A torque tube was attached to the rear axle mounted gearbox.

A 1.1-litre improved model followed but Antonio Opessi withdrew in 1922 and the firm was reorganized as Fratelli Temperino with money provided by Banca Nazionale di Sconto, which also financed SPA. The collapse of the bank effectively wiped out Temperino in 1924 after about 1000 cars had been sold in Italy. The car's best market was Britain, where sales were handled by J. S. Wood's Kingsway Motor Co. Plans to produce cars in Britain came to nothing.

Maurizio Temperino returned to his garage business. He attempted to make a comeback as a car manufacturer in 1928 but did not get beyond building a prototype. He then devoted his talents to a variety of inventions, including economical ways of producing electricity. He died in 1975. NB

TEMPLAR
USA 1917-1924

The Templar was a quality light car made in the Cleveland, Ohio, suburb of Lakewood. Templar Motors Corporation was organized in 1916 by a group of Cleveland businessmen, deriving its name from the medieval order of Knights Templar, whose Maltese Cross emblem featured on the car. The four-cylinder 3.2-litre overhead-valve engine was of the firm's own design and manufacture, but most other parts were bought-in. Production was planned for the autumn of 1917, but the entry of America into World War I meant that most of the plant's capacity was taken up with the manufacture of 155mm shells.

Comprehensive equipment was one of the features of the Templar, among its accessories being a compass and a folding Kodak camera. Prices ran from $2085 to $3285 for the 1918 cars, of which only about 150 were made.

In 1919 the figure was 1800, quite encouraging for a new make which was aimed at a fairly small section of the market, but within two years a combination of the general depression in the auto industry and problems with discontented shareholders which dam-

aged the firm's reputation, cut sales drastically. In 1921 the workforce was down to 165 from a peak of 900 in 1919. About 850 vehicles were made in 1921, including about 100 taxicabs.

A fire in December 1921 caused more than $250,000 damage, and although production was soon resumed Templar went into receivership in October 1922. The following year it was reorganized as the Templar Motor Car Co and a 4.3-litre six-cylinder model was added to the range. Surprisingly, it was not much more expensive than the fours, at $1895 to $2045.

There were not enough buyers who wanted 'The Superfine Small Car' – 1923 production was only 125 cars – and in the autumn of 1924 a Cleveland bank acquired the company in default of a loan repayment and immediately closed down production. About 6000 Templars were built in all. GNG

TEMPO
GERMANY 1933-1940

Tempo (Hanomag) six-wheel truck of c.1966

The first Tempo was a light motorcycle-based three-wheeled delivery truck built by two Hamburg locksmiths in 1926. They turned these out at the rate of about one a week, and among their customers were coal merchants Max Vidal and his son Oscar. In 1928 they bought the manufacturing rights to the three-wheeler, founding the firm Vidal & Sohn, and went into production in 1929 aided by the engineer Otto Daus.

In 1933 they replaced the original three-wheeler with a larger machine with single driving wheel at the front instead of the rear, and made a passenger car version of this as well. Power came from a 200cc single-cylinder Ilo engine, and the body was a simple four-seater with a canvas roll top. In 1936 the Vidals brought out a 600cc four-wheeled van, and this again had its passenger car equivalent, although cars were always only a small proportion of the business. In 1937 they made about 40 per cent of all delivery vans sold in Germany.

The most unusual Tempo was the G1200 military car powered by two 596cc two-cylinder Ilo engines, one at each end of the car and each driving through its own four-speed gearbox. Made from 1936 to 1939, they were used by the Wehrmacht and also by the armies of several other countries including Sweden, Romania, Argentina and Mexico.

Thomas Flyer Model K, winner of the New York-Paris race of 1908

Tempo did not revive passenger cars after World War II, although estate car versions of the three-wheeled vans could be bought until 1956. In 1955 Oscar Vidal sold a 50 per cent share in his company to Rheinstahl-Hanomag, which 10 years later gained complete control.

From 1966 the vans, now forward control four- and six-wheelers, were sold under the Hanomag name, and when that company became part of Daimler-Benz in 1970 they became the Mercedes-Benz L206/306 series, under which name the Tempo shape survived until 1977. GNG

TERRAPLANE
see Hudson

THAMES
GB 1906-1912

Thames coach of c.1905

Started in 1857 by Mr Mare of the company Ditchborn and Mare of Blackwall, east London, the Thames Ironworks, Shipbuilding and Engineering Co built the Saltash Bridge in 1857, Queen Victoria's yacht *Fairy*, and *Warrior*, the first seagoing ironclad which was started in 1858. By 1910 it had produced 900 ships and its works covered 30 acres (12 hectares).

The original company, under chairman Peter Rolt, had gone into liquidation and been re-formed in 1899 with £600,000 capital. In 1898 the marine engine firm of John Penn and Sons, with 3 acres (1.2 hectares) of factory in Greenwich, was acquired. This company carried out experiments for steam and petrol commercial vehicles from 1901.

In 1905 lorries and buses were being produced and cars followed a year later. Charles K. Edwards, formerly of Napier, was involved with design – hence the Napier-type sixes – before departing for Iris. He was assisted by H. C. M. Stephens, who would later work for Sunbeam, Oldsmobile, Citroën and Singer. W. T. Clifford Earp handled sales through his independent agency.

In 1910 there were one-, two-, four- and six-cylinder models in production, although all but commercials had disappeared by 1912. The commercial vehicles were made for just another year, the final examples including postal vans. NB

THOMAS
USA 1902-1913

One of America's greatest cars in the pre-war era, the Thomas grew out of the bicycle industry, like so many of its contemporaries. Erwin Ross Thomas (1850-1936) began his career in railways, and then manufactured the Cleveland bicycle in Ohio and Toronto. In 1897 he and his partner H. J. Hass began to make stationary engines, and in 1900 he set up the Thomas Auto-Bi Co in Buffalo, New York, to make motorcycles.

He succeeded in attracting a lot of capital from local business interests, one of his backers being E. M. Statler, founder of the famous group of hotels. With $2 million behind him Thomas was ready to expand into four-wheelers.

His first cars were light runabouts, the 3½hp Buffalo Junior and 6hp Buffalo Senior, priced at $650 and $800 respectively. They had single-cylinder engines and single chain drive, but stood out from their contemporaries in having a three-speed sliding gearbox at a time when most American light cars had a two-speed planetary system.

In 1902 Thomas formed the E. R. Thomas Motor Co specifically for car manufacture in a new factory backing onto the old one, where motorcycles continued to be made until 1912. The Buffalo runabouts were dropped and replaced by the Thomas Model 16, a five-passenger tonneau powered by an 8hp single-cylinder engine under the driver's seat, although there was a De Dion-type bonnet at the front. The price was $1250, and 100 cars were made in the first full year of production. By the end of 1903 Thomas already had agencies in New York, Boston, Philadelphia and Chicago.

The 1904 Thomas had a 24hp vertical three-cylinder engine and cost $2500. It was the first to bear the name Thomas Flyer. For 1905 it was replaced by the Model 25, a 40hp four-cylinder car with a 60mph (96kph) top speed, priced at $3000.

In three years the Thomas had passed from being a light car no different from hundreds of others on the market to one of America's quality makes. Sales were encouraging, at 400 for the 1904-5 season. By November 1906 the company had made 1014 cars of 40hp and up, and there were orders for 1514 more. This was double the number made by the company's Buffalo rival, Pierce-Arrow.

Erwin Thomas had attracted a number of talented French engineers, including Michael Longeron (formerly of Mors and Richard Brasier) and Gustav Chedru (previously with De Dion-Bouton, Richard Brasier and Clément-Bayard). There was also a good team of Americans, led by his partner from bicycle days, H. J. Hass.

At the end of 1906 the E. R. Thomas company was riding high with orders for over $5 million worth of cars. Erwin Thomas was also marketing the Thomas-Detroit, a smaller and cheaper car which was built in Detroit by former Olds personnel, designer Howard E. Coffin and sales manager Roy D. Chapin. The E. R. Thomas-Detroit Co was capitalized at $300,000 and the plant was located in a former match factory. The 40hp four-cylinder car cost $2750, nearly $1000 less than the Buffalo-built Thomas. Production for 1906-7 was 503 cars.

The Thomas-Detroit might have had a successful career, but Chapin and Coffin wanted to be their own masters. They brought in Hugh Chalmers, vice-president of the National Cash Register Co, who bought Thomas's holding in the company and for 1908 renamed it the Chalmers Motor Co. The cars were sold under the name Chalmers-Detroit until 1910 when they became plain Chalmers. Roy Chapin and Howard Coffin were later involved with the formation of the Hudson Motor Car Co.

In 1907 Thomas began to make taxicabs powered by a 14/16hp four-cylinder engine and also fire engines. The company gained more fame from the victory in 1908 in the gruelling 169-day New York-Paris race by a stock Model K 4/60hp tourer. Driven by George Schuster and Montague Roberts, the car received no special preparation, being taken from a factory lot three days before the start. Thomas also entered cars in the 1905 and 1906 Vanderbilt Cup races and the 1908

French Grand Prix, although with no great success.

Six-cylinder cars came into the Thomas range for the first time in 1908; they were the 31hp L 6-40 and the 72hp K 6-70. The latter was the only Thomas to retain chain drive and sold for $6000 and up, depending on the body style. Sales in 1908 were 816 cars and 400 taxicabs, rising to 1036 cars in 1909, when they were boosted by the New York-Paris success.

Considerable additions to the factory area were planned, with the aim of eventually making 7500 cars a year, but production never surpassed the 1909 figure. The small six Model L had a reputation for unreliability which tarnished the whole range; this was particularly unfortunate as the L was supposed to be one of the company's bestsellers. The marque lost some of its leading agents as a result.

In 1910 Thomas retired, having reached the age of 60, selling his interests to New York banker Eugene Meyer. Sales in 1912 were only 350 cars, mostly the new long-stroke six-cylinder Model M, although the K was still listed, and a few fire engines were also made.

On 19 August 1912 the company was forced into receivership, and not more than a dozen cars were made under the receiver up to 15 February 1913, when all production ceased. At that time there was sufficient material to make 100 to 150 cars and fire engines; these and a few complete cars were sold at auction together with all jigs and factory equipment, fetching the bargain price of $256,000. The 1908 New York-Paris car went for $200. One 1914 model, with electric lighting and starting, was included in the sale. Some lists carried the Thomas up to 1919. GNG

THORNYCROFT
GB 1903-1913

Thornycroft was founded in 1864 as a boatbuilder on the Thames at Chiswick by John I. Thornycroft, born in 1843. By 1910 his firm had produced more than 300 torpedo boats,

destroyers and numerous smaller craft as well as water tube boilers totalling 1½ million horsepower. The company also built Thomas Cook's Nile tourist boats. In 1904 a shipyard had been bought in Southampton and after World War I the Chiswick yards were sold.

Steam wagons were made from 1896 and two years later special works were built at Basingstoke, Hampshire, where from 1902 petrol engined commercial vehicles were made, followed a year later by cars. Production of steamers ended in 1907; they had also been made under licence in Germany and the United States, and a licence had been sold to FLAG in Italy. They lasted a little longer in Scotland as Stewart Thornycrofts, being built by a firm that had ties with Beardmore. Sir John Thornycroft, recently knighted, was chairman of Beardmore from 1901 to 1907, the two companies being linked financially.

These good quality cars had such features as monobloc engines with overhead valves as early as 1906 and were produced until 1912, although the Model 18 was made until the end of 1913. Pre-war production totalled 1360 vehicles, of which a quarter to a third were cars. About 5000 lorries were built between 1914 and 1918.

An early manager was George A. Burls, who had been apprenticed at Maudslay. L. H. Pomeroy worked at Thornycroft before going on to hold important positions at Vauxhall and then Daimler.

Profits of about £50,000 a year shortly before the war climbed to £267,000 in 1915 and capital was increased from £350,000 to £750,000 soon after peace returned. In 1921 the workforces at Basingstoke and Southampton stood at 1550 and 3850 respectively. Losses were recorded in the early 1920s but then pre-war levels of profitability returned.

Commercial vehicles were widely exported, Thornycroft offering a broad range that included colonial and military types. The marine business was larger, however, and in 1932 the company built the water speed record breaker Miss England III at Southampton.

During World War II, in addition to marine equipment, Thornycroft made 8230 bren gun

Thornycroft two-seater of 1904

Thornycroft 18hp cabriolet of 1911

carriers, 13,000 wheeled vehicles, 2751 tons of spares and 1700 guns. Total value was £43.5 million. Chief designer at this time was Charles Burton.

In 1948 the ship and vehicle activities were separated as wholly owned subsidiaries of J. I. Thornycroft & Co Ltd. The vehicle company was called Transport Equipment (Thornycroft) Ltd and had 21½ acres (8.6 hectares) of factory on its 60-acre (24-hectare) site at Basingstoke. It built some of the largest trucks of the time, including the Mighty Antar that was powered initially by the Rover Meteorite 250bhp diesel unit. In 1961 the vehicle business was bought by AEC. Five years later the shipyard merged with Vosper Ltd and ultimately was nationalized, becoming part of British Shipbuilders as Vosper Thornycroft (UK) Ltd, a major producer of hovercraft, hydrofoils, ships – including glass reinforced plastic minesweepers used in the Falklands conflict of 1982 – and microprocessor systems.

Under AEC control the production of general purpose haulage vehicles was discontinued but military and heavy duty export vehicles and Nubian airport crash tenders were made instead. The Nubian continued after Leyland had acquired AEC and was transferred to the Scammell factory, although since 1977 the Nubian has been badged as a Scammell.

The Basingstoke factory was sold to the American-owned Eaton gearbox and axle firm in 1969. It had continued to make marine versions of automotive engines, and had earlier taken over the former HE factory on the Thames for this purpose. NB

THOROUGHBRED/MERLIN
USA, GB 1975 to date

The Thoroughbred, a glassfibre-bodied kit car with traditional open two-seater sports car styling, was first built in the United States but was designed by an Englishman, Leonard Witton. The car offered the unusual option of front or rear engined models, initially with a Ford Pinto engine in the front or the ubiquitous Volkswagen/Porsche engine in the rear. Later options included Ford or General Motors V6s or small-block V8s in the front and Mazda rotary engines front or back!

The first cars were built as the Witton Tiger but production started in 1975 as the Thoroughbred, built by Thoroughbred Cars Inc of Redmond, Washington. A Mercedes 540K cabriolet replica was also offered in the USA from 1980.

Late in 1979 another Englishman, Peter Gowing, took an interest in the original type Thoroughbred with a view to selling kits in Britain. In February 1980 he imported two shells to Britain and founded Thoroughbred Cars in Southend, Essex, to build cars on a chassis designed to take British Ford Cortina running gear. The British car was called the

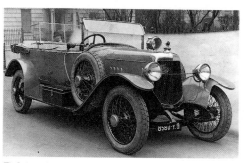
Th Schneider tourer of c.1923

Merlin TF and the first was completed in September 1980, with a VW-powered option also planned.

Early in 1982, by which time about 15 examples had been sold in Britain, a revised version was offered with running boards and bigger boot, cockpit and engine compartment. The company had plentiful orders and moved into a new 2500sq ft (225sq m) factory, with separate glassfibre shop, in 1982, where output could be increased to about two cars a week. By 1984, however, production there had stopped. But the Merlin reappeared in 1986, still backed by Peter Gowing, from new premises at Barling Magna, Essex. BL

THRIGE
DENMARK 1910-1918

The company Thomas B. Thrige AS was established in Odense, Denmark, in 1894 to make electric motors, and from about 1909 an electric lorry. In 1910 Thrige announced its first petrol-engined car, with a four-cylinder 8/22hp Ballot engine, and this was put into production in 1911. As well as the Ballot engine, most other parts, including the chassis and the axles, were bought-in from France and only assembled in Denmark.

Thrige also built a 13/35hp model, with a four-cylinder Daimler-Knight sleeve-valve engine, and a lighter 4/12hp four-cylinder Ballot-engined model, of which about 50 were built in 1914. The smaller cars were light enough to comply with a Danish regulation which limited the weight of cars used on the generally very rough minor roads to less than 992lb (450kg) and imposed a national speed limit of 30mph (48kph). They used a three-speed gearbox but they had no differential.

Thrige cars sold quite well in their own country up to the outbreak of World War I. The company continued to make cars and trucks during the war, but car production was dropped in 1918, when Thrige was faced with the imminent prospect of Ford opening a Danish plant, which in fact survived from 1919 to 1971.

During 1918 Thomas B. Thrige organized a merger of his company with two other Danish car and truck makers, Jan Hagermeister's Jan company and H. C. Frederiksen's Anglo-

Dane, both of Copenhagen. The new company, Die Fornende Danske Automobilfabriker AS, was based at Thrige's works in Odense and built Triangel trucks, buses and taxicabs until 1950. The company then imported trucks from other European makers while Thrige continued to make electric motors. BL

TH SCHNEIDER
FRANCE 1910-1928

In about 1907 Louis Ravel went to work with M. Amstoutz, owner of the original Chapuis-Dornier proprietary engine firm in the watch-making town of Besançon, and together they made engines under the name Zénith. When Amstoutz sold his interest to Théophile Schneider, Ravel helped the new owner to create Automobiles Th Schneider in 1910 and was technical director until 1920.

The company had a capital of 1 million francs and produced high-quality and expensive four- and six-cylinder cars with dashboard-mounted radiators. Capital grew to 2.5 million francs in 1912. About 200 cars were made annually by a workforce of almost 500.

The firm considered buying the ailing Mors business in 1912 but instead bought the premises of the Besançon watchmakers Antoine Antoine and the REP aircraft and engine factory at Billancourt. There on the outskirts of Paris, with a wealthy market and skilled labour force, cars were assembled from engines, gearboxes and axles produced at Besançon.

The company became a Société Anonyme in 1914 but no cars were made between 1915 and 1917, although a few ambulances were produced. During this period the factories concentrated on producing shells and other munitions. After the war the five models of 1914 were reduced to two and given frontal radiators. Fewer than 200 cars were made annually from 1918 to 1922.

A 2-litre sports tourer was added to the range in 1922 and three years later received overhead valves as the 10/45. It was described by a contemporary writer, John Prioleau, as one of the liveliest small cars he had ever driven. An even lighter VL (voiture légère) model with 1.7-litre engine joined it in 1926, a year after a 1.2-litre model.

All post-war models are thought to have been made at Boulogne sur Seine, although the office remained in Besançon. Production ended in 1928 but the London importer, Th Schneider Automobiles (England) Ltd, continued to list the 12hp SP25 model as a Schneider until 1938.

After World War I the Besançon factory had made SADIM agricultural tractors and these kept the firm going until 1939, when the SADIM business and machine tools passed to Etablissement Frey. The factory was largely demolished to make way for a technical college, but parts of it survived and are now used as classrooms. NB

THULIN
SWEDEN 1920-1928

Thulin tourer of 1920

AB Thulinverken was an aeronautical engineering company based in Landskrona, Sweden, which manufactured aero engines and also complete aircraft during World War I. At the end of the war Thulinverken was quite well aware that the market for aircraft would be seriously reduced and made moves to start car manufacture as an alternative source of income.

In 1920 it introduced a four-cylinder model which, except for some minor components, was built entirely in its own works but under licence from the German company AGA. AGA, or Aktiengesellschaft für Automobilbau, was itself a German subsidiary of an originally Swedish company – Svenska AB Gasaccumulator, manufacturer of welding equipment. The AGA design, introduced in October 1919, was in turn built under licence from the Belgian FN company.

The first Thulin was a water-cooled 20hp four-cylinder model with a distinctive German-type vee-radiator. Thulin intended to build a series of 1000 of these cars but only about 300 had been completed before bankruptcy supervened in 1924.

In 1927 the firm was reorganized and a new car, the Thulin Type B, was designed by the Swedish brothers Axel and Per Weiertz, who had previously built three prototype cyclecars under the name Self. The Type B used a 1.7-litre overhead-valve four-cylinder engine in a very low-slung chassis with four-wheel brakes. Only 13 examples – one with a sixcylinder American Hupmobile engine – were built before Thulin was again forced out of business early in 1928 by the continuing availability of American imports at low prices and the immediate success of the native Volvo from its introduction in 1927. BL

TOLEDO
see Pope

488

TONY HUBER
FRANCE 1902-1906

Born in 1874, Tony Huber trained as an engineer, co-founded the Morisse company and in 1902 started the firm bearing his name. It shared the Billancourt address of Ateliers de Billancourt and Le Blon Frères, which had made cars from 1889 to 1902, sometimes under the name Lynx.

Tony Huber cars were made from 1902 to 1906 and included 8 to 25hp models. They used Arbel steel frames. Engines were the firm's main business, however. These were supplied (possibly with chassis too) to J. J. Leonard & Co of London for its short-lived Medici model which was produced specially for doctors.

In February 1905 A. Peugeot, Tony Huber et Cie, with a capital of 410,000 francs, was formed to make motors, motor boats and electrical equipment. Directors were Armand Peugeot of Peugeot Frères, Tony Huber and Raymond Stern, formerly of Bardon. Capital was reduced to 260,000 francs in 1906 and in 1912, when the firm was dissolved, it was said to be making navigational equipment and re-engining cars.

In 1920 A. Tony Huber et Cie was listed at a different Paris address making motor boats. The Billancourt factory continued to make car engines under the control of Huguelet et Cie and in 1923 was listed as Etablissement Fivet, which made engines for a variety of companies. NB

TORINO
see Diatto

TORNADO
GB 1958-1964

The Tornado was one of the first successful kit cars in the boom period for such models in Britain in the late 1950s and early 1960s. Tornado Cars Ltd was founded in Rickmansworth, Hertfordshire, in 1957 by racing enthusiasts Colin Hextall and Bill Woodhouse. Woodhouse, born in 1933, had an excellent background for developing a glassfibre-

bodied car at a time when use of the material was still relatively new, having worked in the plastics division of ICI from 1952 to 1954 and then as a consultant engineer from 1956 to 1957.

Tornado's first car, the Typhoon, was introduced in August 1958. It used a ladder frame with coil suspension, designed to take Ford 8 or 10 engines and other parts, and several different styles of glassfibre body were available. The body was moulded in 11 sections, including front and rear bulkheads, and was available as an open two-seater, a long wheelbase four-seater or as a 2+2 GT. The chassis sold for £70 and the basic body for £130, which led Tornado to claim that a complete car could be built for £250 – although *Motor Sport* suggested a figure nearer £600 for a car in competition trim, as many were.

By 1960 Tornado offered a variety of bodies and chassis either separately or together, with chassis from as little as £39 and shells from £59. About 400 examples of the Typhoon were sold before Tornado replaced it with the less successful Tempest at £555, designed to take the Ford 105E or 109E engines, and the Triumph TR3 powered Thunderbolt at £855.

In December 1961 Tornado introduced a new model, the 109E powered two-door four-seater Talisman sports saloon. With a monocoque body and a tubular backbone frame it sold as a complete car for just under £1300, with a kit version planned for £890. About 200 Talismans were made and Bill Woodhouse raced one with great success, but Tornado never repeated the success of the Typhoon. Although the company was reorganized in 1963 as Tornado Cars (1963) Ltd, production stopped in 1964. BL

TOYOTA
JAPAN 1936 to date

The son of a carpenter, Sakichi Toyoda was born in 1867 and, at the age of 30, invented the first of many major improvements to weaving looms. In 1926 he formed the Toyoda Automatic Loom Works and three years later sold patent rights to Platt Bros in England for £100,000. This money was used by his son Kiichiro, born in 1894, to start a car department after he returned from visiting European and American plants.

Tornado Typhoon of 1958

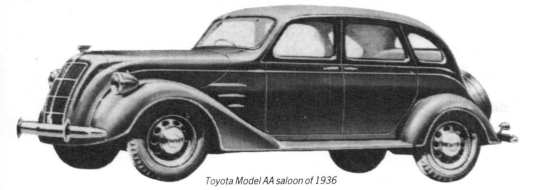

Toyota Model AA saloon of 1936

Toyota 15L Sports 800 of 1966

A 4hp two-cylinder engine was made in 1930, based on an American Smith unit. An Atsuta prototype car was made in 1932 in collaboration with Okuma-Nippon Sharyo. This appears to have been unsatisfactory, for in May 1935 a larger American-based AA model was completed. It entered production in 1936 at the rate of five a day and used Chevrolet chassis and transmission, although the Japanese company simply copied Chevrolet's six-cylinder 65bhp engine. Styling was inspired by the Chrysler Airflow.

In 1937 the Toyota Motor Co Ltd was formed. Capital stood at the equivalent of $3.5 million and the plant was located at Koromo. The factory was expanded in 1938 at a cost of $13 million to give an output of 1500 to 2000 vehicles a month. Cars, trucks and Hercules powered buses were produced. One of the original buildings is believed to have been the General Motors assembly plant for Japan.

Some 20,000 Chevrolet-type 1½-ton trucks were made from 1938 to 1942. Total truck output in 1941 was 42,813. Soon afterwards Toyota added 4×4 amphibians to the range.

The company formed the Aichi Steel Works Ltd in 1940 in order to be self-sufficient and then the Toyoda Machine Tool Works in 1941, followed by two body-pressing plants. The family version of the name was used for most non-motoring ventures.

By the end of World War II the Toyota Motor Co had grown to 3000 employees but home demand for its vehicles was minimal. A mere 5435 trucks were built in 1945 – and not a single car. Production of motor cars did not resume until 1947, and then at the rate of only about 300 a year. The Toyopet 27bhp light car was made in small numbers along with various commercials, including light 4×4s, three years later named Land Cruisers.

In 1949 Toyota formed Aisin Seiki and Nippondenso to make electrical equipment for domestic and vehicle use. Toyoda Spinning and Weaving was set up in 1950 to make thread and cloth as well as car components.

Only 304 vehicles were produced in May 1949, by which time serious losses had accrued and the workforce had been cut back from 8000 to 6000. Protracted strikes led to the resignation of Kiichiro Toyoda. Eiji Toyoda, the firm's current president, and Shoichi Saito were part of the influx of new management who visited Ford in the United States to learn the latest ideas. Car production climbed from 700 a month in 1955 to 50,000 a month 10 years later.

A separate sales firm had been organized in 1950 and spent 40 per cent of its initial capital on teaching people to drive, in order to boost demand. The plan was very successful as indicated by the fact that Toyota completed its one millionth car in 1962 and its 10 millionth in 1972, the year in which annual production reached 2 million. As well as vehicles, Toyota Motor Sales sold Esso products from 1953 under the Castle brand name.

Exports had been limited and it was not until 1956 that English language catalogues were available. In 1961 3932 cars and 7743 commercials went abroad; a decade later the figures were 604,923 cars and 181,364 commercials, and in 1981 exports had grown to 1,063,350 cars and 653,101 commercials.

The first plant devoted solely to car production in Japan came on stream at Motomachi

in 1959, two years after the 1-litre Corona made its début. Sales of the Corona family reached 5 million in 1981. Cheaper two-cylinder 697cc cars had been developed since 1954 and led on to Toyota's first mass-market car, the 1000 UP10 of 1961 which, with four cylinders, subsequently became the Starlet. At the other end of the scale were the Crowns, introduced as 1.45-litre cars in 1955 and later growing in size and refinement after a preliminary showing in the United States in 1957.

The 1.1-litre Corolla, produced from 1966, became the best-selling car in Japan. The Century 3.4-litre V8 was introduced in 1967 and the 1.6-litre Cressida in 1968, which overtook the Datsun Bluebird in domestic sales a year later. The 1.4- or 1.6-litre Carina dated from 1970, as did the 1.4- to 2-litre Celica. Many of these models later came with the option of larger engines.

After initially making rather utilitarian cars Toyota attempted to boost its image with sports models in the 1960s. Although only 3120 of the Sports 800 were made between 1964 and 1969 and only 351 of the original 2000 GT launched in 1965, the effect was achieved. Various fastback models have subsequently become best-sellers, notably the Celica.

Production of heavy commercials was left to Hino, which joined Toyota in 1966. Daihatsu came under Toyota control a year later. The original loom company had meanwhile diversified into the industrial vehicle field, making fork lift trucks – 27,000 in 1977 – and hydraulic loading shovels.

Toyota 2000 GT coupé of 1967

Toyota Starlet of 1977

Toyota Land Cruiser of 1986

The 10 millionth Toyota car was exported in 1971 and aggregate production to January 1980 reached 30 million. By then there were overseas plants in 18 countries. Kits for local assembly had first been supplied in 1960. By the end of the 1970s Toyota employed 44,000 workers in nine major plants. About half these employees lived in company owned accommodation.

In 1974 Toyota formed a joint company with General Electric to make General Avicom domestic air conditioners. Two years later it began to make complete prefabricated houses and sold 634 in the first two years. In the 1970s Toyota's shipping fleet totalled 21 car transporters. From 1976 there was a refrigerated type that brought fresh citrus fruit from the USA on each trip and returned with 3300 cars.

In 1973 electric car developments began, which in 1975 included a gas turbine/electric generator hybrid prototype. Diesel engined cars were offered in 1977. In 1978 the 1.45-litre Tercel and Corsa became Toyota's first front-wheel-drive mass-produced models.

In 1984 Toyota introduced a car that was hailed as the model that finally established Japan's coming-of-age in the car world. The MR2 was an all new mid-engined sports car powered by a 16-valve 1600cc unit and it combined relative low cost with practicality and advanced engineering. Another model, the Corolla GT, was offered in both rear-wheel-drive and front-wheel-drive forms.

The Starlet model introduced in 1973 as the 1000 appeared in hatchback form in 1978 and was gradually improved with facelifts in 1980 and 1983. However, by that time it was a slight oddity, being the only car in its class still front-engined with rear-wheel drive. In 1985 the Starlet caught up and joined the 'super-minis' with front-wheel drive and east-west engine location.

By 1985 the Land Cruiser introduced some 34 years previously had achieved the status of the world's biggest selling and most universal all-wheel-drive vehicle. It was being sold officially in 95 countries and unofficially in virtually every other. It was being assembled from component knock-down (ckd) kits in 15 countries, including Portugal, South Africa, Brazil (under the name Bandeirante), Austra-

Toyota Starlet 1-litre GL of 1986

Toyota MR2 of 1986

lia, Pakistan, Bangladesh, Kenya, Zimbabwe, Trinidad and Sarawak. Total production stood at over 1.5 million, and some 120,000 units were produced every year, of which nearly 95 per cent were for export. By any standards this was impressive.

Current output of Toyota, the world's largest motor manufacturer, averages one vehicle every 4 seconds of a 16-hour day. In 1985 total production was 2,569,284 cars, 1,096,338 commercial vehicles and 40,198 industrial vehicles. Toyota employs over 60,000 people and turnover in the year to 30 June 1985 was a staggering £18.48 billion. NB

TRABANT
see IFA

TRACTA
FRANCE 1926-1932

The Tracta was the first successful front-wheel-drive car made in any numbers. It was designed by Jean Albert Grégoire and financed by Pierre Fenaille, whose wealth came from petroleum products.

The first cars were assembled in the Gar-

age des Chantiers at Versailles, which Grégoire owned, and later in a small factory at Asnières. They were simple two-seater sports cars using 1100cc four-cylinder SCAP engines, later replaced by 1200 and 1600cc SCAPs. As well as front-wheel drive they had sliding pillar independent suspension and the option of a Cozette supercharger.

Grégoire and others raced Tractas at Le Mans and in hillclimbs up to 1930, but thereafter the direction of the firm changed from sports cars to very elegant saloons and coupés. These were powered by 2.7-litre Continental or 3-litre Hotchkiss engines which Grégoire found he could obtain for about the same price as the SCAPs.

Grégoire was meanwhile attempting to establish patents for the constant velocity universal joint which he and Fenaille had developed. He made deals with Adler and DKW in Germany and Chenard-Walcker and Citroën in France, but received little in the way of royalties from the Germans, and none from the French.

The main purpose of making Tractas was to demonstrate that front-wheel-drive was a viable principle on road and track, and once Grégoire had done this he lost interest in the cars, on which he made little if any profit. In 1932 he ended car manufacture in order to pursue his patents. Total production was 232 cars, of which 142 were the small SCAP-engined sports cars and the balance the six-cylinder models. Grégoire later designed the Hotchkiss-built Amilcar-Compound, the Aluminium-Française Grégoire which became the Dyna-Panhard, and the Hotchkiss Grégoire 2.3-litre saloon. GNG

TRIBUNE
see Pope

TRIDENT
GB 1966-1978

The Trident began life as a TVR design exercise, first seen at the 1965 Geneva Show. It originated in 1962 when Brian Hopton was chairman and managing director of TVR Cars Ltd, which was just about to go bankrupt and re-emerge as Grantura Engineering Ltd.

Hopton was looking for an Italian-styled body to fit to the new coil-sprung chassis of the Grantura Mk III. This chassis was designed by former Rolls-Royce engineer John Thurner, who had joined TVR as technical director in 1959 at the time of one of its earlier periodical reorganizations. An efficient but ugly body designed by aerodynamicist Frank Costin had been rejected, and what became the Trident was offered to TVR in 1963 by Paris based stylist Trevor Fiore – actually an Englishman called Trevor Frost.

Fiore had connections with the coachbuilder Fissore in Turin and Fissore began work on the car in 1964. It was originally intended simply as a new body for the Grantura but, prompted by American distributor Jack Griffith, the brief was modified for a slightly larger car to take the Ford 289cu in V8, as used by the American spec TVR Griffith and by the original Cobra.

Production of the glassfibre-bodied cars was planned for June 1965, and two alloy-bodied prototypes were built, one being shown in Geneva in March and shortly after in New York. Two more prototypes, one an open car, were started by Fissore but in August 1965 Grantura Engineering Ltd went bankrupt.

Martin Lilley, a TVR dealer and enthusiast, and his father, Arthur, took over the company as TVR Engineering Ltd in November 1965 and thought they had also acquired the Trident project, but this had in fact already been taken over, with help from Fiore, by another TVR dealer, Bill Last of Woodbridge, Suffolk. Last had had a stake in Grantura and had prompted another prototype from Fissore, a convertible based on Austin-Healey 3000 running gear, before Grantura went bankrupt.

Last founded Trident Cars Ltd late in 1965 and the prototype convertible, with Ford 289 V8, was shown as the first Trident at the 1966 London Racing Car Show. At the 1967 show, after a year of development, Trident exhibited its first production model, a 2+2 fastback coupé based on the big Healey chassis. The production target was three cars a week, built

initially in works at Market Harborough in Leicestershire. Most of the V8-engined cars went to the United States and a Ford V6-engined model was offered in Britain from 1967, the V6 becoming known as the Venturer and the V8 as the Clipper. Both open and closed cars were available.

Production was transferred to Woodbridge towards the end of 1968 and moved again in 1969 to Ipswich, Suffolk. In 1969 Trident began to use a lengthened Triumph TR6 floor pan and body styling was updated slightly in 1970. In 1971 a larger but milder Chrysler V8 replaced the Ford in the Clipper II and a new model, the Typhoon, was introduced with a Triumph 2.5-litre engine in place of the Ford V6, which was temporarily unavailable due to a major strike at Ford in Britain.

The cars were undoubtedly interesting, but Trident had all the traditional problems of the small volume manufacturer, particularly in meeting new regulations, and by 1973 was effectively bankrupt. Production was continued on a limited basis by Viking Performance Ltd, the subsidiary which built the glassfibre bodies, and in 1974 the company was reorganized as the Trident Motor Car Co Ltd. Even so, production all but stopped in 1975, then at the 1976 Motor Show Trident unveiled a new version of the Clipper, and the V6 was also still offered.

By 1976 the Trident board included Last, Ernest Steen (an American financier) and financial consultant Lionel Baker. They announced that negotiations were in hand for an additional factory of 30,000sq ft (2800sq m) and in November 1976 stated that export contracts were being negotiated in Australia, Holland, Belgium, the USA and Nigeria as part of a five-year expansion programme. The expansion actually turned into a further decline and Trident finally went out of business in 1978. BL

TRIUMPH
GB 1923-1984

In 1884 a 21-year-old German Jew named Siegfried Bettmann arrived in London and took on the agencies for a number of foreign firms including the White Sewing Machine Co of Cleveland, Ohio, which was later to make cars and trucks. He then began to export bicycles under the name Triumph. At first these were made for him in Birmingham, but in 1887, with a partner, Mauritz Schulte, he started his own factory in Coventry.

Business increased greatly in 1895 with an injection of £45,000 by Harvey DuCros of Dunlop, and two years later Triumph Cycle Co went public with capitalization of £170,000. Experiments with motorcycles began the following year, but production did not start until 1902 and by 1905 Triumph was making its own engines.

Business grew steadily and Bettmann became a prominent Coventry figure, being mayor in 1913. He was also chairman of the Standard Motor Co in 1911, which is interesting in view of the union of the two companies 32 years later.

World War I brought great prosperity to Triumph, which supplied more than 30,000 motorcycles to British and allied forces. Two-wheelers were so successful that Bettmann was unwilling to venture into the motor car

Trident Clipper V8 of c.1969

Triumph Gloria saloon of 1935

Triumph 10/20hp light car of 1923

Triumph Dolomite sports car of c.1935

Triumph TR2 of 1954

Triumph Dolomite roadster of 1939

field, but a new manager, Claude Holbrook, persuaded him and in 1921 they purchased the factory of the recently defunct Dawson Car Co, also of Coventry.

The first Triumph car appeared two years later. It was a conventional 10/20hp four-cylinder light car designed by Arthur Alderson of Lea-Francis who continued to work for his firm, so that Triumph had to pay Lea-Francis for the design on a contract basis. The bodies came from the Regent Carriage Co of London and prices ranged from £430 to £460, making it distinctly expensive for a light car.

It was made in small numbers until 1926, but in 1924 it was joined by a larger car, the 1873cc 13/35, which was important in being the first British car to have Lockheed hydraulic brakes on all four wheels. In 1926 the engine was enlarged to 2169cc making it a Fifteen; quite a number were exported to Australia and it was made until 1930.

In 1927 Triumph found its true *métier* with the Super Seven, a lively light car with 832cc 21bhp engine and worm drive. It was designed by Stanley Edge, who had aided Herbert Austin with the design of the Austin Seven. Sports models including a supercharged version were made as well as tourers, and a total of 17,000 were built in seven years compared with about 2000 for all previous Triumph cars. Triumph was now making its own bodies, but many other firms worked on the Super Seven chassis, notably Gordon England with its fabric saloon.

By 1931 the Depression had hit Triumph as it had other companies: motorcycle sales were down 30 per cent and no dividend was paid on ordinary shares, the first time this had happened for 30 years. The bicycle business was sold to Coventry Bicycles and Holbrook was in favour of selling off the motorcycle side as well. In 1933 Bettmann, now 70 years old, resigned and later became chairman of the motorcycle company after it was sold in 1936.

Triumph motorcycle production continued at the original Priory Street factory

until it was completely destroyed by enemy action in 1940. Post-war Triumphs were made at Meriden and from 1975 to 1983 were under the control of a workers' co-operative. In 1984 there were plans to resume Triumph motorcycle production by a new company at Newton Abbot, Devon. Siegfried Bettmann retired from the chairmanship in 1939 and died in 1951 at the age of 88.

Holbrook had never liked the small cars, which were gradually phased out and replaced by a line of very handsome cars with four- and six-cylinder engines; these were the Southern Cross, Gloria, Vitesse and Dolomite. From 1932 to 1937 Coventry-Climax engines were used; Triumph had a flourishing bodybuilding department headed by Walter Belgrove, although it also used other coachbuilders such as Tickford and Cross & Ellis. Donald Healey was technical director and had a number of competition successes. A new factory was bought from White & Poppe in 1935.

On the surface it would seem that Triumph was riding the crest of a wave, but in fact losses were piling up, reaching a catastrophic £212,000 in 1936. Even the sale of the motorcycle division to Jack Sangster of Ariel for about £50,000 did not help all that much. More capital was raised by the issuing of £200,000 more stock, and a new range of cars with Triumph's own Healey-designed engines was introduced for 1937.

In the face of financial problems one might have expected some degree of rationalization, but in fact the 1937 line up was the biggest Triumph had ever offered. There were four-cylinder Glorias with 1.2-litre inlet over exhaust Coventry-Climax engines, four-cylinder Glorias with 1½-litre Triumph engines, and four- and six-cylinder Vitesses and Dolomites with 1½- or 2-litre engines. The Dolomite with its fencer's mask grille was aimed at the SS Jaguar market; at £368 it cost £7 less than a 2½-litre Jaguar but £73 more than the 1½-litre model.

Sales improved with these new models, despite a controversial reception of the Dolo-

mite grille, and a modest profit was recorded for 1937. In 1938 there were plans to acquire Riley, which had just gone into receivership, but Lord Nuffield stepped in with a higher offer.

Despite a small trading profit in 1938 there was an overall loss due to capital investment for the new lower-priced Twelve, which was launched in March 1939, and in June 1939 Triumph went into receivership. Donald Healey sold it on behalf of the receivers to Sheffield steelmaker Thomas Ward & Co. A trickle of Twelves were assembled up to the outbreak of war, but the recently acquired Gloria factory was sold to the government, which used it for the manufacture of Claudel Hobson aero engine carburettors. In 1940 the other factory, formerly Dawson's, was let to the Armstrong-Whitworth Aircraft Co.

In 1944 Sir John Black of the Standard Motor Co bought the bomb damaged remains of this factory and the rights to the Triumph name for £75,000. He soon sold off the factory for nearly as much as he paid for it. His aim was to make a quality sports saloon to rival William Lyons' Jaguar, which had started life as an offspring of Standard.

The Triumph Motor Co (1945) Ltd was formed as a wholly-owned subsidiary of Standard and in 1946 launched its post-war cars. These used the 1776cc four-cylinder engine which Standard had built for Jaguar, a tubular chassis and either two or four seater roadster or razor-edge saloon bodywork. The latter was later christened the Renown, and in 1949 both cars received the 2.1-litre engine of the Standard Vanguard. These were made in Standard's enormous Canley factory near Coventry.

In 1953 Black launched one of the most important post-war British sports cars, the Triumph TR2. This used the Vanguard engine tuned to give 90bhp, a new chassis designed by Harry Webster and John Turnbull, and a neat two-seater body. This car and its descendants, the TR3 and TR3A, sold more than 83,000 units up to 1962.

The Renown was quietly dropped in 1954

492

and the 'baby razor edge', the 10hp Mayflower, had already preceded it into oblivion so the TRs alone bore the Triumph name until the introduction in mid-1959 of the Herald. This had been planned as a successor to the Standard Ten, but the associations of the Standard name had become those of utility and the opposite of De Luxe, so it was thought more appropriate that the new car should be called a Triumph. (Previous Standards had been badged as Triumphs for some export markets, and the name Standard was dropped altogether in 1963.)

The Herald was powered at first by the 948cc Standard Ten engine, later an 1147cc unit, and had all-round independent suspension, the first British small family car to be so equipped. It had an attractive two-door saloon body styled by Michelotti.

In 1961 Standard-Triumph was taken over

Spitfire, a Herald-engined rival for the BMC Spridgets, the TR4, 5, 6 and finally the wedge-shaped TR7.

From 1968 Triumph had been part of the British Leyland group, which meant that cars such as the Spitfire and Spridgets were under the same umbrella, as were the 2000/2500 saloons and the Rover range. Rationalization was inevitable. The Triumph saloons lost out to Rover, but the sports car had a shortlived victory over MG, whose uneconomic factory was viewed with disfavour by Sir Michael Edwardes.

The Spitfire was dropped in 1980 and the TR7 and TR8 by the autumn of 1981, thus marking the end of sports car production by the BL group. The Speke, Liverpool, factory where TRs were made was sold off.

The Triumph name was not allowed to die, being used for the Honda-Ballade-based

TROJAN
GB 1922-1937

The Trojan was a rare example of an unconventional and in many ways old-fashioned design which was a commercial success and had a loyal following among British motorists for over 14 years. It was the work of Leslie Hayward Hounsfield, born in 1877, who had worked for several well known British engineering firms including Ransomes, Sims & Jefferies and the Crompton Electrical Co. After service in the Boer war with the Electrical Reserve Volunteers he started his own small contract engineering business in Clapham, south London, in 1904. This became Trojan Ltd in 1910, the year in which he began work on his first car.

Triumph Herald of 1962

Triumph Mayflower of 1950

Triumph TR7 of 1978

by the Leyland group and the following year came a six-cylinder version of the Herald named the Vitesse. With this Triumph resumed something of its 1930s role, making well-equipped small sixes for a more discerning market. In fact 51,212 Vitesses were made compared with 443,117 of the Herald in its various forms.

With the demise of the Standard name, all cars from the Canley factory were now Triumphs. The medium-sized family car slot which had been filled for 16 years by the Standard Vanguard was filled by the Triumph 2000, which was made in various forms until 1977, while the Herald/Vitesse range was supplemented and eventually replaced by the front-wheel-drive 1300 of 1965 and rear-wheel-drive Toledo of 1970. The Toledo was a Standard type of car, but the 2-litre Dolomite using the same body shell was very much in the older Triumph image, with 91bhp 2-litre engine, and in later Dolomite Sprint form, a 16-valve single-overhead cam engine giving 127bhp.

Triumph sports cars included the popular

front-wheel-drive Acclaim saloon which was intended as a stop gap to give BL a medium sized saloon until it could launch its own. Engine and transmission were made by Honda, but the body shell was built by BL's Pressed Steel factory at Cowley, final assembly taking place at the old Morris Motors factory at Cowley.

In its short life of 32 months the Acclaim sold 133,000 units, more than Honda sold of the Ballade in the same period, but in June 1984 it was replaced by a car based on the new Honda Civic. For marketing reasons this was given the name Rover 200, so the Triumph marque finally disappeared.

Triumph engines have been used in a variety of other makes of car, from the London-built Vale Special made from 1932 to 1936 through 1950s and 1960s sports cars such as the Swallow Doretti, Peerless GT, Fairthorpe, Bond Equipe and Morgan Plus 4 to the TVR 2500 and Trident Tycoon of the 1970s. The slant-four overhead-cam engine initially used in the Dolomite was supplied to Saab for its Model 99 from 1969 to 1972. GNG

Hounsfield's chief preoccupation was with simplicity of driving and maintenance, and he drew up his specification with these aims always in view. The engine was a four-cylinder two-stroke in which each pair of cylinders had a common combustion chamber. One of the company's advertising points was that the engine had only seven moving parts – four pistons, two V-shaped con rods and a crankshaft. Transmission was by a two-speed epicyclic gearbox and final drive by duplex chain. To avoid the frequent headaches caused by punctured tyres, Hounsfield endowed his Trojan with solid tyres, which had been abandoned by most car-makers by 1900.

His first prototype ran in 1913 and was followed by two more before World War I broke out. These all had vertical engines mounted between the front seats, but in 1920 he built six more cars which had horizontal engines under the floorboards and were almost identical to those that went into production three years later.

In 1914 Hounsfield moved from Clapham

Trojan PB tourer of 1924

Trojan RE saloon of 1931

to other premises not much larger at Croydon, Surrey. The six post-war cars were built there, but Hounsfield would never have established production on a big scale had it not been for the interest shown in his cars by Leyland Motors Ltd. Already one of Britain's leading makers of commercial vehicles, Leyland had just introduced its 7.2-litre luxury Leyland Eight; wanting to try the market at the other end of the scale it put the Trojan into production at its Ham Common, Kingston-on-Thames, factory which was used for re-conditioning ex-RAF Leyland trucks.

When first exhibited at the Olympia Show in October 1922 the four-seater Trojan cost £230, but by June 1925 the price was down to £125, the same as the Model T Ford (which paid more than twice as much road tax) and £24 less than an Austin Seven. Leyland adopted the slogan 'Can You Afford to Walk?' and published some ingenious calculations to prove that over 200 miles (320km) a Trojan cost less than one would spend on shoe leather and socks.

By 1926 Trojans, both passenger cars and delivery vans, were being produced at the rate of 80 to 100 a week at Kingston, where two parallel runways could complete a car every 45 minutes. Iron castings came from Leyland's foundry at Farington, Lancashire, while the rest of the car, including the body, was made at Kingston.

In 1928, however, this came to an end as Leyland wanted the factory for a new lighter truck, which saw the light of day three years later as the Cub. Manufacturing rights for the Trojan car were sold back to Leslie Hounsfield, who enlarged his Croydon premises and continued the same models, adding the Achilles and Apollo saloons at £189 and £198.

Production at Kingston ended in May 1928 after 16,824 cars and vans had been made, but Leyland-made parts were used at Croydon for some time after that. The first entirely Croydon-built Trojan did not come off the assembly lines until January 1930.

By the time Hounsfield had established production at Croydon the sales appeal of the Trojan car was waning, although the vans continued to sell well. The RE Model, introduced at the 1929 Olympia Show, was an

attempt to take Trojan into the 1930s with an up to date looking car, but although the two-door saloon and tourer bodies were quite modern-looking, the engine, now mounted vertically in the boot, was still the same old 1488cc two-stroke, final drive was still by chain, and when first announced it had neither front wheel brakes nor an electric starter. At £198 it was competing with cars like the Standard Nine and Singer Junior, whose buyers expected such amenities as a matter of course by 1930. The result was that the RE sold disappointingly, not more than 500 in five years.

After 1934 Trojan concentrated on vans, particularly those for the Brooke Bond tea company, which took more than 5000 between the 1920s and 1950s. The old-styled mid-engined Trojan was still available for anyone who wanted one, the last going to a lady in Gloucestershire as late as 1937. A curious six-cylinder two-stroke of 1935, called the Mastra, found no buyers at all.

In 1933 Hounsfield left Trojan Ltd and set up a new company to make a patent folding camp bed which had been produced in the Trojan factory, and also the Hounsfield Tensometer metal testing instrument. He was still operating his small factory in 1953, four years before his death at the age of 80.

Trojan Ltd continued to make the old-fashioned looking mid-engined vans up to 1939, and also a light agricultural tractor, marine engines and hospital equipment such as the Tor Tilter for artificial respiration and the St Georges Open Top Oxygen Tent. The oxygen tents were made at Croydon but marketed by an independent company, Tor Equipment Ltd. During World War II Trojan made bomb racks, incendiary bomb carriers, and supply containers in which essential goods could be dropped by parachute to besieged troops. Some of this material was made at a dispersal factory at Bridgwater, Somerset.

After World War II Trojan brought out a new design of van powered by a four-cylinder two-stroke engine. While this was being readied the company made a range of stationary diesel engines and the Mini-Motor 49cc attachment for powering bicycles. A Perkins diesel engine arrived on the vans in 1952, and

these were made until 1964.

In 1959 Trojan Ltd was bought by Peter Agg, who had been the British distributor for the Lambretta motor scooter since 1950. He combined this business with running Trojan, adding the importation of Suzuki motorcycles in 1962. From 1960 to 1965 the Heinkel 200cc three-wheeler bubble car was made under licence at Croydon, while from 1966 to 1968 the company assembled the Elva Courier sports car, of which about 100 were made.

After the Elva, Trojan took on the contract to build Formula 5000 and Group Seven racing cars for the McLaren group which lasted until 1973. Its last car-building venture was an unsuccessful Formula 1 contender, driven by Tim Schenken in 1974. Trojan Ltd survives today as the company which operates Peter Agg's conference centre and car museum at Effingham Park, Sussex. GNG

TROLL
see Gutbrod

TRUMBULL
USA 1913-1915

Trumbull 13hp two-seater of 1915

The Trumbull was the most successful of the crop of American cyclecars that flourished in the years 1912 to 1915. The design originated in Detroit, where it was made by the American Cyclecar Co, but in the summer of 1913 the Connecticut Electric Manufacturing Co of Bridgeport absorbed the Detroit company and increased capital stock from $100,000 to $500,000. The name was changed to the American Cyclecar Co of Bridgeport, and the car was renamed Trumbull after company president Alexander H. Trumbull, born in 1878. His brother, Isaac B. Trumbull, was company secretary and treasurer.

The Trumbull had a 1.7-litre four-cylinder engine made by the Hermann Engineering Co of Detroit, whose designer K. L. Hermann was also on the board. Transmission was by friction disc and final drive by chain on the first 300 cars, but afterwards by a conventional three-speed gearbox and shaft drive. Bodies were mostly open two-seaters, although coupés and delivery vans were also offered. These bodies were made by Hale & Kilburn of Philadelphia, which later made many bodies for Stutz after both companies had been taken over by Charles M. Schwab.

The open two-seater cost $425, rather more than the average American cyclecar which sold at between $300 and $400. However, the Trumbull purchaser got more car for his money, without the crudities of belt drive, tandem seating or two-cylinder engine. Even so, the Trumbull sold much better in export markets, and of the 2000 built not more than 500 found buyers in the United States. The rest went to Europe or Australia, which took about 400.

Early in 1915 the company name was changed to the Trumbull Motor Car Co. In May, Isaac Trumbull was on his way to London in the *Lusitania* with 20 cars when the ship was torpedoed, and Trumbull and cars were lost, together with 117 other Americans.

It seems that Isaac had become the driving force behind the company, and without his leadership the other directors decided to close the Trumbull Motor Car Co in June 1915. It would probably not have lasted much longer anyway, as the vogue for cyclecars in America had disappeared by 1915. Alexander H. Trumbull died in 1959. GNG

TUCKER
USA 1946-1948

Shortly after World War II, Preston Thomas Tucker tried and failed to do what many had tried and failed to do before him: to break the domination of the US car market by Ford, General Motors and Chrysler. He did so with an extraordinary and advanced car, the Tucker 48, and might even have succeeded but for ruinous allegations of financial impropriety.

Tucker, of Ypsilanti, Michigan, had previously worked with the brilliant racing car designer Harry Miller and originally intended to build a radical rear-engined sports car, the Torpedo, with central driving position, three headlights and front cycle wings that steered with the wheels. Plans for the Torpedo were dropped, however, and early in 1946 Tucker set up the Tucker Corporation in Chicago and

Tucker saloon of 1948

announced his plans for 'The first new car in 50 years'.

It was now to be a rear-engined saloon with automatic transmission, disc brakes, all independent suspension and many advanced safety features, including a pop-out windscreen and armoured passenger compartment. The long, low body was styled by former Auburn-Cord-Duesenberg stylist Alex Tremulis.

Tucker raised capital, probably some $16 million, by selling dealerships in advance and by a huge common stock issue on the strength of his designs. He then leased from the government supposedly the largest single factory in the world, a giant plant in Chicago built during the war where Dodge had built aero engines for Boeing bombers. It was completely self-contained, with integral offices, conference facilities and even its own hospital.

Pressed to produce something more solid than promises, Tucker rushed to produce pilot models of his car for 1947 and did so in 100 days, by mid-June. They relied, of necessity, on commercially available engine and transmission in place of his own extreme designs, which could not be made to work in time. He settled for a flat-six originally designed for a helicopter and built by Air-Cooled Motors of Syracuse, the final offshoot of the Franklin company. Obtusely, Tucker converted the very oversquare 334cu in 166bhp motor to water cooling. It was mounted transversely and intended to drive one rear wheel from each end of the crankshaft through an infinitely variable fluid coupling, but this too was compromised in favour of a modified Cord gear train with electric selection.

Several cars were hand-built as demonstration models and early in 1948 Tucker announced completion of the first 'production-line' Tucker 48, with a projected price of $2450. Including the prototypes, 51 cars were built in all.

Early cars used the modified Cord transmission but later ones used the Y-1 system built by Tucker's Ypsilanti Machine Tool Co. Tucker bought Air-Cooled Motors and all the cars used its water-cooled flat-six! Rubber torsion suspension units were made by the

US Tire and Rubber Co and the heater system by Motorola had its own fuel pump and key start, so that it could work even when the car was not running.

With a supposed 300,000 orders, some three times the company's capacity, Tucker sought a further $30 million working capital from the government's Reconstruction Finance Committee, but in mid-1948 the watchdog Securities and Exchange Commission deemed that, in building a car materially different from his original prospectus, Tucker was acting fraudulently. The plant was closed for several weeks.

Tucker, backed by his workers, attempted to carry on and a journalist visiting the factory reported seeing 'acres of wheels, tires, body stampings . . . hundreds of cylinder blocks . . . 58 finished car bodies in the assembly line . . . 90 finished engines'. Even the respected reporter Tom McCahill later claimed to have seen more than 2000 workers on the lines and nearly 200 cars in various degrees of completion.

In August 1949 the National Tucker Shareholders Association Inc was set up to back Tucker's efforts. It claimed assets of $5 million, and available pledges, stock and orders to a total of over $25 million in 1950, offset by only $800,000 in liabilities, including the government claims for rent on the plant, which in 1949 the Federal Court had ordered Tucker to surrender to the War Assets Administration. The 44,000 stockholders and 1800 dealers claimed that they had actually paid over $1.25 million to the government, in rent and other charges, in their $175 million investment.

Furthermore, it may not have been the car that Tucker first promised, but the Tucker 48 was very special in its own right. Advertising claims of over 150mph (240kph), 0-60mph (0-96kph) in 10 seconds and the ability of two men to change a Tucker engine in less than 17 minutes may have been a little exaggerated, but a Tucker was timed at over 131mph (210kph) at Bonneville in 1950 and the few owners have reported remarkable longevity and fuel consumption.

The government, however, eventually went all the way and indicted Tucker and five of his executives for fraud. By the time he was acquitted in 1950 it was too late to save the company, which had gone into voluntary liquidation and had not even been allowed to accept offers of outside finance.

Tucker, pardonably, abandoned the 48 project but in the mid-1950s he briefly pursued a scheme to build a Tucker car, designed with Alexis de Sakhnoffsky, in Brazil, where he had been offered production facilities. It was to be a low priced sporty car with cycle wings, steering headlights (including the traditional Tucker Cyclops eye) and a rear engine. It was to be called the Carioca and sold in kit form, with an option to have it assembled by approved garages for $60. The idea was still seeking financial backing when the innovative Tucker died, in 1956. BL

TURCAT-MÉRY
FRANCE 1899-1928

Léon Turcat and his brother-in-law Simon Méry, both born in 1874, experimented with Panhard et Levassor and Peugeot designs before building an experimental car in 1896. A few more may have been built for sale from parts supplied by local engineering firms in the next two years. At Marseilles in 1899 Turcat and Méry, together with Méry's brothers, Louis and Alphonse, organized the Société des Ateliers de Construction d'Automobiles Turcat, Méry et Cie. Capital was 350,000 francs.

A four-cylinder car with five forward, two reverse ratio gearbox was offered initially but sales were very limited and by late 1901 the company's financial situation was becoming critical. Motoring journalist Paul Meyan then introduced the partners to Baron de Türkheim of De Dietrich. From 1902 Turcat-Méry designs were made by De Dietrich under the supervision of Léon and Simon. Five per cent of the price of each completed vehicle went to the inventors.

The Marseilles factory was run in their absence by Louis Méry and chairman Henri Estier, a financier who also backed the Lorraine-Dietrich factory at Lunéville. In 1905 a three-axle car was introduced and this, like many of their other models, was also made by De Dietrich. Identical racing cars were made by both firms until 1905 and in 1911 a Turcat-Méry won the first Monte Carlo Rally. Large six-cylinder models had been added in 1907.

André Citroën was technically, and possibly financially, involved with Turcat-Méry and the designer of the Cotal gearbox worked there. Emile Jellinek and Robert Bosch also both had early involvements with the firm and Paul Engelhard worked there before becoming a director of Rochet-Schneider. Turcat-Méry, like De Dietrich, was represented in Britain by Charles Jarrott and William Letts.

In 1913 capital was increased to 525,000 francs and the partners left Lorraine-Dietrich to concentrate on their Marseilles business. The factory made lorries and munitions in World War I and, with an increase in capital to 3 million francs, was expanded for an output of 1000 vehicles a year. Such quantities were wildly optimistic for the archaic designs that were revived after the war, and the partners withdrew when the firm collapsed.

Turcat-Méry was reorganized as a limited company in 1921. Capital was increased first to 6.5 million francs in 1924 and then again to 16 million francs. A more modern overhead-cam model was introduced in 1923.

In 1926 Turcat-Méry was re-formed once more by Louis Mouren, a former employee, who raised 2.5 million francs to buy it in conjunction with the Berliet representative in Nice. SCAP and CIME proprietary engines were adopted and included four-, six- and straight-eight cylinder types of up to 2.3 litres.

Turcat-Méry collapsed again in 1928 and was acquired by J. Monnerot-Dumaine. Vehicles were listed until 1933 but were probably old stock or built from spares. The original factory was subsequently used by a refrigeration firm; the wartime extension was demolished and is now the site of a housing estate. Léon Turcat became an insurance agent and his grandson was later chief test pilot of Concorde aircraft in France. NB

TURICUM
SWITZERLAND 1904-1913

Martin Fischer, the Swiss engineer who designed and built the innovative Turicum, was born in 1866 and his first trade was as a watchmaker. In about 1900 he invented an electric clock, but he gained an interest in cars after seeing a motorcycle for the first time in about 1903 and in 1904 he built his first prototype car. He built it with the help of a friend, Paul Vorbrodt, six years his junior, and with backing from a Zurich-based German financier by the name of Dr Hommel.

The car was a tiny single-seater, little more than a seat on wheels, with an air-cooled 786cc single-cylinder engine mounted right at the front and driving the rear wheels through a long chain. It was steered not by a wheel or tiller but by two foot pedals.

Fischer and Vorbrodt built this prototype in a disused skittle alley in Zurich. Later in 1904 Fischer built a slightly larger car with similar basic layout but with rudimentary bodywork and friction drive. He gave this second car the name Turicum, which is the Latinized version of Zurich.

Soon afterwards he founded Automobilfabrik Turicum AG and in 1906 moved into a larger factory in Uster, near Zurich, to begin limited production of relatively conventional Turicum cars, beginning with the wheel-steered single-cylinder 6-7hp Type A phaeton – which was first shown publicly at the Paris and Berlin Shows in 1905. Like all subsequent Turicums it used friction drive. Up to 1908 Turicum only built 7hp single-cylinder two-seater models – which had a fuel tank in the false radiator – but in 1908 the company started to build water-cooled four-cylinder models, including the 1940cc 18hp Type D.

Towards the end of 1908 Fischer and several colleagues left, and set up a new company, Fischer-Wagen AG of Zurich-Enge, early in 1909. Backed by a Zurich industrialist and in partnership with J. Weidmann, who had previously built the Brunau car, Fischer began production under his own name. His early cars were very similar to the Turicum, particularly in their use of friction drive. He continued to build cars until 1919, one of his final efforts being a twin-cylinder cyclecar, which only reached the prototype stage.

Turicum continued after Fischer's departure and had representatives in several European countries plus Russia, South Africa and South America by 1909. It built a very few examples of a twin-cylinder car in that year but mostly made four-cylinder models ranging from a 1608cc 10/12hp in various body styles to a 2613cc 16/20hp model. By 1911 Turicum employed about 150 workers and annual output was usually about 200 cars. A total of more than 1000 had been made up to that time. Shortly before World War I, however, the company ran into financial problems and was wound up in 1913. BL

Turcat-Méry Gordon Bennett car (Rougier driving) of 1904

Turicum two-seat tourer of 1914

TURKHEIMER
see OTAV

TURNER/TURNER-MIESSE
GB 1902-1913; 1922-1930

Turner two-seat tourer of c.1913

Thomas Turner and Co, a Wolverhampton engineering firm dating back to 1800, formed a subsidiary, the Miesse Steam Motor Syndicate Ltd with £50,000 capital in 1902. This company sold Belgian Miesse steam cars made in Britain under licence and the vehicles were soon being described as all-British. The Turner Motor Manufacturing Co actually built the cars and after it bought the Wulfruna Cycle Works in Villiers Street in 1904 claimed to have room for 1000 employees.

From 1906, when the company was reformed, it made a 20/25hp petrol car, the Seymour-Turner, for Seymours of London. Turner Petrol Cars Ltd was set up in 1911 with £10,000 capital to make a V-twin light car, which was followed by 10 and 15hp fours. The 10 was also sold for colonial use with high ground clearance by John Birch and Co and was known as the JB. Other variants in the range went under the name Universal.

Turner bought engines from Fondu for some of its cars but in 1914 was offering its own engines to other firms. A Turner built that year still exists and has chassis number 1250.

Steam cars were not made after 1913 and

four years later the two Turner car firms, with several members of the Dumbell family as directors, merged with the existing Turner Motor Manufacturing Co. Capital in 1922 was £50,000 and the workforce numbered 160.

After World War I Turner made chassis for Varley-Woods and the Roger for Thomas Roger and Co Ltd, which existed in Wolverhampton from 1920 to 1924. Turner resumed its own car production in 1922 and made Dorman and Meadows engined models in later years. After 1926 only a 12hp model was made and production of this had ceased by 1930.

The company was more important as a producer of motor components and in the mid-1930s it obtained a licence to make the diesels of Dr Hans List of Graz. These were offered after World War II – when Turner proudly proclaimed that they had been developed under the Marshall Aid programme – and were used to re-power Bedfords, Land-Rovers and even a Vauxhall Wyvern and Austin A70. In V4 form from 1948 they were used in Turner's own Yeoman of England farm tractor.

A complete front-wheel-drive minibus with two-cylinder supercharged diesel was offered in 1954 and there were other light commercial experiments carried out until then, including three-cylinder 4×4s. Gearboxes had gradually become the company's principal line and were supplied to many British mass-producers of medium-weight trucks.

Turner was subsequently acquired by the American Spicer transmissions firm. In 1984, when 819 were employed at Wolverhampton, the German ZF gearbox firm merged with Spicer to create ZF Spicer International with combined annual sales of $550 million. NB

TURNER
GB 1954-1966

John H. Turner was born in Wales in 1916 and from 1932 to 1936 he was apprenticed to the Abergavenny Motor Co Ltd. From 1936 to 1945 he was in charge of the toolroom at the Gloster Aircraft Co, where he worked on Sir Frank Whittle's first jet engined aeroplane. Turner was also a successful competition driver, helped by his own skill as an engine

Turner A30 sports car of 1956

tuner and builder.

In 1949 he founded Turner Sports Cars to build racing and sports cars and racing engines. He built an overhead-cam four-cylinder 500cc unit for Formula 3 and in 1955 he designed a 1960cc overhead-cam four for Raymond Flower's Phoenix sports car, which was built in Egypt to race at Le Mans but was killed by the Suez crisis. Turner's own early cars used a variety of tuned engines, including Vauxhall, Ford and Lea-Francis units, in tubular chassis.

In 1952 he expanded the company as Turner Sports Cars (Wolverhampton) Ltd with premises at Pendeford Airport in Staffordshire, and in 1954 launched a car to be built in series. It used an 803cc Austin A30 engine, or a Coventry-Climax engine for competition use, in a tubular-braced glassfibre shell. About 75 were built until 1956.

Turner then introduced a 950cc A35-engined version, which was made in similar numbers up to 1959. Many were exported to the United States, where they were introduced in 1957 at a price of about $2000.

In 1959 the open two-seater Turner Sports was introduced with the 948cc Austin-Healey Sprite engine as standard, while later versions offered various Ford and Coventry-Climax options. The Climax-engined Turner Sports was actually originated not by the works but by Turner's newly appointed northern distributor, Motorway Sales (Derby) Ltd, in 1960 and was intended mainly for racing.

On its racing début the hurriedly finished first car was described by a commentator as 'tatty'; thereafter, even when immaculately prepared, it was affectionately known as the Tatty Turner. It was one of the most successful production racing sports cars in Britain for several years and helped Turner to substantial sales, most of which were exported.

Another popular variant was the Alexander-Turner, using BMC engines tuned by Alexander Engineering and priced mid-way between Turner's own BMC-powered and Climax-powered models. Turner planned a GT version of the car, but after building fewer than 10 examples in 1962 he dropped the idea.

About 600 Turner Sports were sold until 1966, with only minor changes to the original design, but in spite of this apparent sales success production stopped that year and the firm went into liquidation in April. BL

TVR/GRIFFITH, JOMAR
GB, USA 1949 to date

The name TVR was derived from the Christian name of Trevor Wilkinson, who built the first cars and set up the first of many companies involved in the TVR story. Wilkinson was born in Blackpool, Lancashire, in 1923. He left school at 14 and was apprenticed to a local garage as a mechanic.

During World War II he worked in the family shop and in 1946 set up a car sales and repair business, Trevcar Motors. In 1947 he built an alloy-bodied open two-seater special around a pre-war Alvis chassis. Late in 1947, in partnership with Jack Pickard, he formed TVR Engineering, much of whose work was for the fairground operators in the seaside town.

He planned another special, the first to be called a TVR, and completed it in his spare time by 1949. It was intended for club racing, hillclimbs, sprints and driving tests and used the popular 1172cc side-valve Ford engine in a tubular chassis with an open two-seater alloy body. Wilkinson sold it to his cousin almost before it was finished and put the proceeds towards his next design.

This was similar to the first but had wishbone rather than trailing link front suspension – and again he sold it almost at once. He finished his third cycle-winged special in 1951 and hung onto this 1200cc Austin powered car for long enough to win several local events before he broke it up for parts.

By 1953 he was thinking of building a series of cars for sale. He started with the TVR Sports Saloon, which had a tubular frame, Austin 1200 engine, much Austin A40 running gear and a commercial glassfibre shell from RGS Atalanta. He made three cars with this shell, several more with open bodies such as the Rochdale, and some as chassis kits, to a total of about 20 cars between 1954 and 1956. Austin, Ford, MG and even Lea-Francis engines were used.

In 1955 he planned a car to use a TVR-built body, tubular backbone chassis and trailing arm torsion bar suspension all round, based on Volkswagen Beetle front units. In 1955 a rolling chassis was ordered by Ray Saidel, an American racing enthusiast who ran Saidel Sports Racing Cars in Manchester, New Hampshire. He received the chassis in 1956, fitted a Coventry-Climax engine and alloy body and renamed it a Jomar, after his children John and Margaret. It was a success and Saidel ordered six more chassis, which he sold with Climax or Ford Anglia engines.

Early in 1956 TVR moved to a larger factory at Layton, on the edge of Blackpool, with backing from industrialist Fred Thomas of Bolton, and a new director, Bernard Williams, a former dirt-track motorcycle racer who ran Grantura Plastics, TVR's body supplier. The first six TVRs with the new chassis were sold in 1957 as the Coupé – although three were open cars! In 1958, prompted by Jomar sales in the United States, TVR aimed for real series production with a development of the Coupé which became known as the Grantura, built up or in kit form.

By mid-1958 TVR was making two a month, almost all destined for the USA as Jomars, but expansion created cash problems. In December TVR Engineering was wound up and Layton Sports Cars Ltd was formed, with new backing from a group including David Scott-Moncrieff, David Hosking and Frank Lambert. Continuing uncertainty over supplies led Saidel to give up his American imports in 1959 and so end the Jomar.

In mid-1960, when about 100 cars had been built, the Grantura Mk II was introduced, most with the latest MGA engine. It was followed in 1961 by the Mk IIA, with further updated MGA units.

In September 1961 there was another reshuffle as TVR dealers Keith Aitchison and Brian Hopton took control of Layton. In April 1962 the Grantura Mk III was announced, although production did not start until September. This had a much improved coil-sprung chassis, designed by John Thurner, a former Rolls-Royce engineer who joined TVR in 1959. TVR also began a short-lived international competition programme, which it most certainly could not afford, and in April Trevor Wilkinson, disillusioned by the new directors, left – eventually to build up a very successful glassfibre accessory company.

The launch of the Mk III brought the familiar financial strain and in October 1962 Layton went out of business. Williams' Grantura Plastics, the major creditor, set up a new subsidiary, Grantura Engineering Ltd, to resume limited production, backed by Arnold Burton of the Burton tailoring chain.

Alongside the Mk III, Grantura launched the V8 Griffith, prompted by another American dealer, Jack Griffith, a former Ford dealer who ran Griffith Motors Inc of New York. Griffith modified a Grantura chassis to accept the Ford 289cu in V8, created a low-priced challenger to the Cobra and ordered chassis from Grantura to be fitted with engines and gearboxes in the USA. It was launched in April 1963 as the Griffith 200, alluding to its horsepower, and was followed in April 1964 by the improved Griffith 400. This introduced the chopped-tail style familiar on all subsequent models.

The car was available in Britain during 1965, but by then the company, which had been renamed TVR Cars Ltd during 1964, was in trouble again. A dock strike in the USA stopped the Griffith business and began the end of TVR Cars Ltd, which eventually folded in August 1965.

Some 265 Griffiths had been built and Jack Griffiths then took over what had been the Apollo, built in Turin by Intermeccanica, as the Griffith GT. In 1966 the Griffith company was taken over by Steve Wilder, who built the car as the Omega until 1968, when Intermeccanica took over again to build a similar car in Italy as the Torino, and later Indra.

In November 1965 the TVR company was taken over again, by Martin Lilley, a TVR dealer who ran the Barnet Motor Co, and his engineer father, Arthur, who already owned some TVR shares. They renamed the company TVR Engineering Ltd and resumed production soon after with the 1800S, as the clip-tailed Mk III had become in 1964.

What the Lilleys did not acquire, although they thought they had, was the TVR Trident project, a new car styled by Fiore and built by Fissore with the Ford 289 engine. This in fact passed to another dealer, Bill Last, who set up Trident Cars Ltd in 1965 and built the putative TVR as the Trident until 1978.

TVR Taimar of 1978

TVR 390SE convertible of 1986

The Lilleys looked for stability rather than rapid change and continued with similar models, the first of them the Mk IV from July 1966. They also built 10 more Griffiths up to January 1967 and appointed a new American distributor, Gerry Sagerman, to sell TVRs in America, including the smaller British engined models, *as* TVRs through TVR Cars of America.

In 1967 the Grantura range was revamped as the Vixen. This was updated through S1, S2, S3 and S4 series until 1972, after which it and the Tuscan V6 and V8 range which had replaced the Griffith in 1968 were replaced by the restyled M-series (for Martin) cars. These were made with 1.6-, 2.5- and 3-litre engines, plus a turbocharged 3-litre in 1975. The hatchback Taimar derivative was announced in 1976 and a convertible in 1978 and these, with the 3000M, were made until 1979, after which the earlier, distinctive TVR shape was replaced by the more angular Tasmin range from January 1980.

The fixed-head two-seater was soon joined by a Plus 2 and a Convertible, all with the fuel-injected Ford 2.8-litre V6 engine and redesigned chassis. A cheaper 2-litre version, the Tasmin 200 was added in October 1981.

In 1982 there was another change of ownership when Peter Wheeler, a chemical engineer who had made a large amount of money in oil rig equipment supplies, bought the company. Martin Lilley pulled out in November 1981, simply having had enough of running the firm on a shoestring. Wheeler appointed former sales director and TVR racer Stewart Halstead as managing director and the two set out to develop TVR, particularly in the USA and Middle Eastern markets, helped by Wheeler's oil connections.

The Rover V8-powered 350i was a direct result of Arab refusals to buy Ford-engined cars and its British introduction in 1983 gave TVR a neat way out of its troublesome projected turbo V6 car. TVR was now completely revitalized with sales of 397 cars in 1984, being limited only by production capacity and having finally learned the lesson of not going for a further rapid expansion. Output was instead to be increased gradually to a target of about 600 a year by adding an extra shift at the factory which the company had occupied since 1970, and which now employs about 100 people, and possibly by a move to slightly larger premises locally. Late in 1984 TVR introduced an even quicker derivative of the 350i, the 390SE, powered by a 3.9-litre 275bhp version of the Rover Vitesse V8, underlining its continuing commitment to outright performance.

The 350 series cars were updated slightly in mid-1985 so that the range comprised the four-cylinder 200 for export, the V6 280i and the 350i and 390SE V8s. A total of 472 cars was produced in that year. New models for 1987 were the S open two-seater with Ford 2.8-litre V6, and the Rover V8-powered 420 four-seater saloon. BL

UNIC
FRANCE 1904-1940

Having lost control to his partner Henri Brasier at Etablissement Georges Richard following a long absence from work caused by injuries sustained in the 1903 Paris-Madrid race, Georges Richard resigned from the company in October 1904. He then started Georges Richard et Cie with a capital of 400,000 francs split 1:4 between himself and Baron Henri de Rothschild. Richard built two-cylinder prototypes in the winter of 1904-5 and won a battle with Brasier over the use of the Georges Richard name.

The Rue Saint-Maur in the 11th *arrondissement* of Paris became too cramped for production so Rothschild organized a merger between the factory that made Bardon cars on his estate at Puteaux and Georges Richard et Cie. The new firm had a capital of 2.5 million francs, of which 2 million francs was split equally between the Bardon and Richard shareholders. It was constituted in November 1906 as Société des Automobiles Unic. The name symbolized 'unique', the components of the main two-cylinder model being used to extend the range to four- and even six-cylinder cars without having to be modified.

Georges Richard was managing director. Other directors included Baron de Rothschild and Pierre de la Ville le Roulx of Bardon, who was also on the board of French Westinghouse (a firm that had recently introduced cars).

About half the 600 to 700 chassis produced annually were sold as taxis. Hundreds went to London, where 5000 Unics were plying for hire by 1925; indeed, roughly half the 7292 Unics made in the first eight years were exported to Britain.

In 1908 Richard was awarded the Légion d'Honneur. At that time his firm had 20 overseas agents plus 49 in France and was second only to Renault in terms of output. Jules Salomon, who had joined the company from Bardon in 1908, developed his Le Zèbre model, early examples of which were produced by Unic.

In 1910 production by all Seine-based motor firms was curtailed by disastrous flooding, but thereafter Unic averaged about 1500 sales a year and made substantial profits. Roughly 100 lorries and buses were made annually, a forward control 2½-tonner having been offered from 1908, and light commercials became much more important.

During World War I shells and bombs were made as well as 17hp ambulances, and 1.2- and 2-ton lorries. Some vehicle production was undertaken by Unic's neighbour, Charron, whose factory was eventually taken over by Unic in 1930. Two companies of troops were transported to the Marne offensive by Unic taxis.

The Richard family suffered three major disasters within a few years with the loss of one son in a flying accident during the war, another through illness and the death of Georges Richard himself from complications

Unic 12/14hp taxi of 1908

Unic chassis testing, c.1924

after an accident in a vehicle with front wheel brakes in 1922. Georges Dubois, who had been with Unic from the outset and who had designed the post-war L range of family cars with Marc Clément, then took over from the founder.

A significant arrival was Gabriel Dubreuil, who had recently developed a turbine and who would be in charge of design for more than 30 years from the mid-1920s and be responsible for the introduction of turbochargers to Unic trucks in 1954. René Copin, who joined Unic in 1919, became technical director in 1936.

The relatively dull range of 9, 10 and 11hp cars was joined by a straight-eight in 1928, but most emphasis was being placed on commercial vehicles by then. The workforce had grown from 1884 in 1926 to 2820 in 1929 and several components factories as well as Charron were bought for expansion. A short-lived consortium with Donnet and Chenard et Walcker from 1927 was intended to reduce component costs.

Capital was increased to 14.5 million francs in 1931 to fund expansion. The firm was now Société Nouvelles des Automobiles Unic. Boosting exports to Britain was one of its major aims as Mann & Overton had been assembling Unic taxis in London in the late 1920s to escape import duties.

The Mercedes diesel licence for France was acquired by Unic in 1931 and 5- to 15-ton diesel trucks were soon in production as well as a range of diesel buses made in collaboration with coachbuilder Heuliez. The Unic range now covered everything from light cars to the heaviest trucks and from 1937 the trucks used Unic's own diesel engine.

Car production was discontinued at the outbreak of World War II. Instead, lorries with half-tracks were made under licence from Société d'Exploitation Kégresse. From 1938 these P107 models were produced at the rate of 15 a day and output eventually totalled 3276. These vehicles plus engines and lorries were made throughout the war despite disrupted production caused by sabotage and attempts by the Resistance to stop Unic's tooling falling into enemy hands.

In 1940 the Société Anonyme Groupe Française Automobile under Baron Petiet attempted to rationalize production by Delahaye, Hotchkiss, Latil, Licorne, French Saurer and Unic. In 1942 Hotchkiss, Latil and Saurer left the GFA while Bernard joined the group. The following year Simca also joined and that company, Delahaye and Unic became close partners. Unic did not regain its independence until 1951.

In 1952 Unic became Simca's heavy vehicle section. Ford-France was bought by Simca in 1954 and truck production was moved to Suresnes after the takeover of French Saurer in 1956. The heavy vehicle division now had 1.13 million sq ft (105,000sq m) of factory space and was second only to Berliet in sales.

Following the gradual acquisition of the Simca cars division by Chrysler, accom-

plished by 1963, Unic remained an independent company within Simca Industries. By June 1966 Fiat had gained financial control of Simca, and Someca (Fiat licence) tractors and Unic commercial vehicles were merged in the Société Anonyme Fiat France.

Diesels with Saurer injection systems went up to 270bhp in 1966 and the firm was third in importance in France in the proprietary engine market after Deutz and Perkins. V8 diesels were made between 1964 and 1975 but rationalization quickly followed the Fiat-Unic merger with Magirus in 1975 which created Iveco. Unic then became primarily an assembler.

Unic trucks were built at the former Saurer factory until 1973. Production was then moved to a new 970,000sq ft (90,000sq m) plant at Trappes, which was closed by Iveco in 1984, a year after the Unic name was finally dropped. NB

UNIPOWER
GB 1966-1970

The mid-engined Unipower was one of the better Mini-powered kit cars and was built between 1966 and 1970 by Universal Power Drives Ltd of Perivale, Middlesex. The project was started in 1963 by racing enthusiasts Val Dare-Bryan and Ernest Unger, who designed a spaceframe to take Mini running gear. The prototype was finished in 1964 in racing driver Roy Pierpoint's workshop and fitted with an aluminium body designed by a stylist who worked for Ford.

In 1965 the project was taken over by powerboat racer Tim Powell, the boss of Universal Power Drives, which made Unipower tractor units, largely for forestry work. In November he allocated space in his works for

a series of the cars to be built, now with fibreglass bodies made by Specialised Mouldings. Also involved in the project was Andrew Hedges, a long-distance racer who soon formulated competition plans for the car.

It was originally to be called the Hustler, but when two cars were shown at the January 1966 London Racing Car Show they appeared as Unipowers. A coupé and a targa model were shown but only coupés were subsequently built, the finalized production version being shown at the 1967 show. With a Cooper engine the Unipower was sold in kit form for £950, or with a Cooper S engine for £1145. About five cars were also built specifically for competition, with only limited success.

By 1968, when a total of 60 cars had been built, Powell had lost interest, having spent too much on racing and not enough on commercial development. He sold the design to Piers Weld-Forrester, who built about 15 more cars through a new company, Unipower Cars, in Willesden, north-west London, before production stopped in January 1970. About half the total output of 75 Unipowers had been exported.

Between 1968 and 1969 Weld-Forrester had also planned two new models, one with the Triumph Stag engine and one around a planned BMC 2.2-litre six-cylinder engine. The latter, a two-seater coupé, was designed by Peter Bohanna and Robin Stables and in 1972 it re-emerged in modified form with an Austin Maxi engine as the Bohanna Stables. In 1973 that car was shown as the first example of the AC ME3000. BL

UNIT
see GWK

Unipower GT of 1969

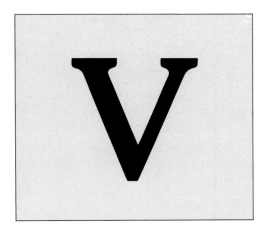

VABIS
SWEDEN 1898-1915

The Vabis car took its name from that of its maker, the Vagnfabrik i Södertalje, which was established in 1891 as a branch of the railway rolling stock company Surahammars Bruk. In 1896 the director, Major P. Peterson, set up a motor car department under the management of Gustaf Erikson, who had worked for Surahammars since 1890.

He built a four-seater car powered by a paraffin-fuelled horizontally-opposed twin engine with hot tube ignition which ran successfully in April 1898. It was followed by other experimental vehicles, and in 1902 the first machines were offered for sale, a car and truck both powered by a front-mounted 15hp V-twin engine. These were exhibited at the 1903 Stockholm Motor Exhibition, where Scania's first vehicles were also shown.

Vehicle production was sporadic until 1906, when Vabis set up a new and more modern factory specifically for car manufacture. There it made four-cylinder cars, trucks with shaft or chain drive, motorized rail trolleys and marine engines.

In 1911 the company merged with its rival, Scania of Malmö, although cars bearing the Vabis name continued to be made until 1915, after which the name Scania-Vabis was used. The Vabis factory at Södertalje was used for car and engine manufacture, while Malmö made the commercial vehicles. Total production of Vabis cars was about 100. GNG

VALVELESS
GB 1908-1914

The first Valveless car was designed and built by Ralph Lucas in Blackheath, south London. The engine was a vertical twin two-stroke with common combustion chamber, and transverse crankshafts. On the earliest models, made in 1901, reverse was provided by reversing the direction of the engine, but later an epicyclic reverse gear was provided.

Lucas worked away quietly at his two-stroke cars for six years without forming a company or selling any, until in 1907 a company called Valveless Ltd was formed, with an office in St Martin's Lane, London, and works at Blackheath. One car was exhibited at the 1907 Olympia Show on the stand of Crawshay-Williams, which had made cars under that name from 1904 to 1906.

Valveless production only got under way when Valveless Ltd sold the design to the well-established gear-making concern, David Brown of Huddersfield. The 20hp car offered on the market in 1908 had a similar design of engine to the first Lucas Valveless, but it was now mounted under a conventional bonnet with longitudinal crankshafts, driving through a sliding gearbox and propeller shaft to the rear axle. The man chiefly responsible for the David Brown version of the Valveless was F. T. Burgess, who later went to Humber as designer and driver of its 1914 twin-overhead cam Tourist Trophy cars and who worked for Bentley from 1920 to 1929.

The 20 or 25hp model was continued through the 1911 season but was then succeeded by smaller models on the same lines, of 15 and 19hp. Chassis prices ran from £315 for the 15hp to £420 for the 25hp.

Valveless tourer of 1914

Several hundred Valveless cars were made by David Brown, but the company was also making a thinly disguised Renault called the Dodson and representing the Belgian SAVA in the UK market, and Valveless production dwindled by 1914. They were not revived after World War I. David Brown had no further involvement with car manufacture until it purchased Aston Martin and Lagonda in 1947. GNG

VANDEN PLAS
see Austin

VARLEY-WOODS
GB 1919-1921

In July 1919 E. V. Varley Grossmith re-formed his High Speed Tool Co as H. S. Motors Ltd with £3000 nominal and £35,000 working capital. The objective was to make Varley-Woods cars in a former laundry in Acton, west London. J. R. Woods, his partner in the venture, had made money as a foreign trader.

Parts for the first cars were bought from Jack Storey, although most cars subsequently had Turner chassis and overhead-valve Dorman engines. Production soon moved to be near Turners in Wolverhampton and Tylor engines may then have been used. A receiver was appointed in October 1920 and the last cars were sold in 1921. In 1923 the remaining spares were acquired by Hyde Park Garage Ltd. NB

VAUXHALL
GB 1903 to date

Vauxhall 5hp two-seater of 1903

The first Vauxhall car was made by the Vauxhall Iron Works Ltd in Wandsworth Road, south-west London, but this company was originally Alex Wilson & Co, Engineers, founded in 1857 by a Scottish engineer, Alexander Wilson. He made high pressure steam engines for naval pinnaces and compound and triple expansion engines for tugboats and paddle steamers, as well as donkey engines and refrigeration plants. Within a few years the payroll consisted of 150 men.

The factory became known as the Vauxhall Iron Works, after the nearby Vauxhall Gardens, the name being a corruption of Fulk's Hall, from a 13th century knight, Fulk le Bréant, the original owner of the land. Wilson adopted Fulk's crest, the griffin, which is still carried on Vauxhall cars today.

In 1894 Wilson left the company, and three years later the name was changed officially to the Vauxhall Iron Works Co Ltd. The new chief engineer was F. W. Hodges, who designed the company's first petrol engine in about 1898 and tested it in a launch, as Frederick Lanchester also did. Five years of experimental work followed, and the first Vauxhall car was placed on the market in the middle of 1903.

The 5hp Vauxhall had a horizontal single-cylinder water-cooled engine mounted under a small bonnet, driving via a two-speed gearbox and single chain to the rear axle. Suspension was by coil springs all round. It was priced at £150 and the company sold 43 cars by the end of the year.

For 1904 the 5hp became a 6hp and it was joined by two models with vertical three-cylinder engines of 7/9 and 12/14hp. These had three speeds, double chain drive and wheel steering. Car production was still secondary to marine engines, and although at times three cars a week were being turned out the total for the year was only 76.

The London premises were very cramped, part of the car assembly taking place in the yard of a next-door brewery, and in 1905 the company moved to a new factory built on open land at Luton in Bedfordshire. The site totalled 7 acres (3 hectares) and a railway siding ran straight into the works. Marine engines were still made, and car production did not exceed three to four a week.

In 1906 the name was changed to the Vauxhall and West Hydraulic Engineering Co Ltd, and in March 1907 to its present title of Vauxhall Motors Ltd. Capital was £25,000 and the joint managing directors were Percy Kidner and Leslie Walton, both of whom were to have very long careers with the company. Hodges was still chief engineer, but in 1908 he was replaced by Laurence Pomeroy, a 26-year-old former North London Railway Co apprentice who had joined Vauxhall as chief draughtsman in 1905.

The bread-and-butter model was still the 3-litre A Type, of which about 950 were sold between 1908 and 1914, while the larger six-cylinder B Type, of 4½ and later 5.1 litres, accounted for only 75 sales from 1910 to 1915. The Prince Henry followed up its 1910 German success with good performances in Russian and Swedish trials in 1911 and 1912, while 3- and 4-litre cars with streamlined single-seater bodies set a number of records at Brooklands.

Marine engines were still made, although they were now mostly internal combustion, and played second fiddle to the cars. By 1913 the workforce was 600.

In 1914 the company was reconstructed with considerable additional capital totalling £200,000. This was increased to £300,000 in 1916, £400,000 in 1918 and £600,000 in 1920. Leslie Walton was chairman, and joint managing director with Percy Kidner, while Laurence Pomeroy was also on the board. The works manager was A. J. Hancock, who had driven Vauxhalls in both racing and record breaking.

Wartime car production was limited to the 4-litre D Type, which used the Prince Henry engine and was seen mainly as a tourer or landaulette. It survived the war, being made until 1922. The total manufactured was 4500, making it the largest production Vauxhall be-

2.2-litre four-cylinder tourer with unit construction of engine and gearbox. It was not a cheap car, at £720 to £750, but it sold well with 1800 finding buyers between 1922 and 1924. A further 3500 were sold of its successor, the LM, between 1925 and 1927. The LM was the last side-valve Vauxhall. In 1922 King gave overhead valves to the larger cars, which were now known as the OD 23/60 and the OE 30/98.

In 1923 weekly output was up to 26 cars at best and the year's production was 1444, the first time four figures had been attained. The workforce was 1200 in 1922, rising to 1600 two years later.

In 1925 came the OD's replacement, the S Type 25/70. This heavy and expensive car used a 3.9-litre six-cylinder sleeve-valve engine made under Burt McCollum patents and was quite out of line with the thinking of General Motors, which took over just after it was announced. Although production was allowed to continue until 1928, only about 50 were made.

In October 1925 General Motors made its first heavy investment in Europe when it put £300,000 capital into Vauxhall. There were no changes initially in management, and it was not until the end of 1927 that a GM-inspired Vauxhall appeared, eventually to supplant the 14/40, 23/60, 25/70 and 30/98

Vauxhall 20hp record car of 1908

Vauxhall Prince Henry of 1913

The first four-cylinder Vauxhall, an 18hp T-head design, was made in 1905, but far more significant was Pomeroy's 3-litre 20hp monobloc L-head engine of 1908. Although rated at 20hp this A Type developed 38bhp and was tuned to give 60bhp in the first of the Prince Henry sporting tourers of 1910. This car has been called the first sports car, in that it was the fastest Vauxhall of its day, but not the largest (the B Type displaced 4½ litres), while Laurence Pomeroy Jr, the designer's journalist son, called it the first of the vintage, the last of the veteran cars.

Annual production rose slowly, from 69 in 1907 to 94 in 1908, 197 in 1909 and 246 in 1910. This was the year that the tuned A Types made non stop runs in the German Prince Henry Trials, leading to a production model being catalogued as the C Type for 1911. Only 50 of these were made, but the later Prince Henry with 4-litre engine (1913-15) sold 190 units and led to the famous 30/98 sporting tourer.

fore the General Motors era.

Many were used as staff cars. Among its moments of glory was when one carried General Allenby on his entry into Jerusalem in 1917; another was the first car to cross the Rhine into Germany after the signing of the Armistice. Vauxhall also turned out several million shells for guns during World War I.

Wartime production of the D Type meant that Vauxhall was in the fortunate position of being able to go straight into the civilian market at the beginning of 1919, unlike many other car-makers. However, the D Type and the E Type 30/98 were expensive cars – £1450 and £1675 respectively – and a cheaper model was needed.

Pomeroy left at the end of 1919 to go to the Aluminium Co of America and later to Daimler. He was succeeded by Clarence E. King, who had worked with Adams at Bedford and Lorraine-Dietrich in France and was to stay with Vauxhall until 1954.

King's first design was the M Type 14/40, a

which were continued during the first two years of American ownership.

Profits in the year 1924-25 were £50,000 but the following year they were down to a derisory £36, despite a 63 per cent increase in output during the first quarter. However, this was offset by the effects of a five month coal strike in the summer of 1926.

The first product of the GM regime was the R Type 20/60, a 2.8-litre six with coupled four wheel brakes for around the same price as the four-cylinder 14/40. It sold reasonably well – 6024 in five years, including the enlarged 3.3-litre T80 – but the effects of the GM takeover were not really felt until the introduction of the Cadet in 1931.

This was a 2-litre six with three-speed gearbox on which synchromesh was introduced in 1932. Prices started at £280, the lowest since Vauxhall's earliest days. Eight factory body styles were offered, including some 'factory customs' made by outside coachbuilders at Vauxhall's request. This practice

Vauxhall J Type (left) and H Type of c.1946

Vauxhall Wyvern saloon of 1955

Vauxhall Viva HA saloon of 1964

continued on most Vauxhall models until the end of the separate chassis in 1939. Export Cadets were available with a 3.2-litre Bedford engine, and a total of 9561 were made until 1933 when it was joined, and soon replaced, by a smaller and even more popular model, the Light Six.

More important to Vauxhall's financial health than any of the cars at this time was the Bedford truck. This was developed from the Hendon-assembled 1½-ton Chevrolet, which outsold the cars by three to one in 1930.

The 2-ton Bedford, with improvements such as full-pressure lubrication, appeared in 1931. More than 10,000 Bedfords were sold in 1932 compared with 2136 Vauxhalls, and their effect was particularly felt on the export market. By 1935 Bedfords accounted for 63 per cent of British commercial vehicle exports, and assembly plants were set up at Melbourne and São Paulo.

In 1937 Bedford sales exceeded 30,000, although by that time Vauxhall had caught up, thanks to the success of the Light Six. This was available with 1½- or 1.8-litre engines and sold 82,877 units between 1933 and 1938. It was joined by a Big Six with 2.4- or 3.2-litre engine made from 1934 to 1936 in much smaller numbers, 4564.

This was succeeded by the last big six-cylinder Vauxhall and also the last model to have a separate chassis. Made from 1937 to 1940, the 3.2-litre Twenty Five was available as a saloon, drophead coupé, four-door cabriolet and limousine, as well as an ambulance version which was the only commercial vehicle ever to be badged as a Vauxhall

(all car-based vans have been, and are, sold as Bedfords). A total of 6822 Twenty Fives were made, a good proportion of which were exported to Australia, where they received various bodies by Holden.

The 1937 London Motor Show saw Vauxhall enter the 10hp family saloon market with the H-series Ten, which had 1203cc four-cylinder engine, unitary construction, and the torsion-bar independent front suspension already used on the Twenty Five. It was available as a four-door saloon and a two-door coupé, although few of the latter were sold. The chassis-less theme soon spread to the Twelve-Four (1442cc) and Fourteen-Six (1781cc). Vauxhall car sales reached a peak in 1939 of 34,367, and a surprisingly high figure of 18,543 was achieved in 1940 despite the advent of World War II.

A considerable number of J-series Fourteens were supplied to the armed forces as staff cars, but Vauxhall's main contribution lay in the manufacture of some 250,000 Bedford trucks and 5640 38-ton Churchill tanks. Vauxhall was also responsible for 95 per cent of the development work on the first 12 jet-propulsion aero engines, and also Jerricans, venturi tubes for rockets and steel helmets.

Vauxhall announced its post-war range in December 1945, although production did not start until March 1946. The Ten and Twelve shared the same four-door four-light saloon body, generally similar to the pre-war model, while the J-series Fourteen was almost unchanged from 1940. The abolition of the horsepower tax in 1947 made the Ten obsolete, and in 1948 came restyled bodies pow-

ered by 1442 and 2275cc engines, now named Wyvern and Velox respectively.

Exports loomed large during the first years of peace and in 1949 75 per cent of car production went abroad. Australasia was the best market, followed by Europe. A workforce of 12,000 made 84,167 vehicles in 1949 – 45,366 Vauxhalls and 38,801 Bedfords. This proportion was roughly maintained in 1950, although the total was up to 87,454.

A new extension programme was initiated in 1950, which would eventually cost £10 million. The first stage was the building of a new 19½-acre (8-hectare) factory at Dunstable, to which Bedford production was gradually transferred.

All-new bodies appeared on the 1952 Wyverns and Veloxes, and in the middle of the season they received new short-stroke engines of 1508 and 2262cc. The bodies bore some resemblance to Chevrolets. In 1957 American influence was more evident on the Velox/Cresta series, which had wraparound windscreens and rear windows, and on the new Victor, which replaced the Wyvern as Vauxhall's lower priced car. This proved very popular, with 390,747 being sold in five years and a further 923,193 of the later Victor FB, FC, FD, FE and high performance VX490 until 1978. By this time the Victor had grown to 2279cc and lay in the middle of the Vauxhall range rather than at the bottom of it.

The Victor took 15 months to sell its first 100,000 units but Vauxhall's new small car, the Viva, achieved this figure in 10 months and went on to become the firm's first car to sell 1 million. It was initially a two-door saloon with 1057cc engine, although four doors and larger engines later made their appearance. The Viva was significant as it showed the first signs of GM's rationalization of its European products – it shared a body style with the Opel Kadett. It was made in Vauxhall's new factory at Ellesmere Port, Cheshire.

Car production reached a peak of 247,782 in 1964, this figure nearly being equalled in 1968 when 247,034 cars were made. Exports were not so successful, despite an attempt to sell Victors in the United States through Pontiac dealers, and in Canada where they were offered under the names Envoy and Sherwood, for the saloon and estate car. In the 1970s some Vivas were sold in Canada as Pontiac Firenzas.

Bedford exports continued to flourish. By 1975 they were being built or assembled in 20 countries outside Britain, including India, where they were known as Hindusthans, and Pakistan, where they are named Rocket and are the country's best-selling truck.

In 1971 Vauxhall produced an answer to the Ford Capri in the shape of the Viva-based Firenza, available with five sizes of engine from 1256 to 2279cc. A total of 20,445 were sold in four years, including 197 of the 'droop snoot' model with lowered floorpan, fibreglass nosecap and a 131bhp 2279cc engine. A V8-powered version of this, driven by Gerry Marshall, was part of Vauxhall's return to motor sport after an absence of nearly 50 years.

Marshall had been driving Blydensteintuned Vauxhalls since 1967 and Dealer Team Vauxhall was formed in 1971, concentrating

1974, Vauxhall's version coming out a year later. It had the 1256cc Viva engine and a freshly-styled body, originally a hatchback but later joined by two- and four-door saloons and an estate car. Germany's version with Opel's own 993, 1196 or 1857cc engines was the Kadett. The T-car is also made in the USA and Japan, where it is known as the Isuzu Gemini. Vauxhall's version was made at Ellesmere Port where it gradually took over from the Viva, which was dropped in 1979.

In 1976 came another international car, the Opel Ascona-based Cavalier with 1.6- or 1.9-litre four-cylinder single-overhead cam engines. They were originally imported from Belgium, but were made at Luton from August 1977. Saloons and a coupé were offered, and from 1977 the pushrod overhead-valve 1256cc Viva engine was available in an economy version. Sales were good, at 248,440 between 1976 and 1981. The Cavalier did much to restore Vauxhall's image, languishing because of the prevalence of outdated models such as the Viva and Victor.

Replacement for the Victor came in the form of the Carlton four-door saloon and estate, British-built but on Opel lines, which was the first Vauxhall to offer the option of a diesel engine. Vauxhall's luxury model at the end of the 1970s was the 2764 or 2968cc overhead-cam six-cylinder Royale, but this was in fact an Opel Senator or Monza and was not made in Britain.

Since 1980 three important new models have been added to the Vauxhall range, all with front-wheel drive. The first was the Astra, Vauxhall's version of the Opel Kadett, with transverse four-cylinder engine in 1196, 1297

or 1598cc sizes. A diesel engine was offered in 1982.

Next came the new Cavalier, a truly international car being made by three of GM's American divisions, in Germany as the Opel Ascona and in Australia as the Holden Camira. Available in 1297, 1598 or 1796cc forms, the Cavalier is made at Luton, although some engines are sourced from Australia, as are body panels for the estate version. A 1598cc diesel is available, and from 1983 a high-performance 1796cc model with fuel injection and a sporty five-speed gearbox was offered.

The newest Vauxhall is GM's contender in the highly competitive Super Mini market, the Spanish-built Nova two-door hatchback or notchback saloon. Power options are 993, 1196 or 1297cc four-cylinder engines, the two larger with single-overhead cams and electronic ignition.

These three models have brought about a striking resurgence of Vauxhall's fortunes. UK sales of all models rose from 110,208 in 1980 to 174,183 in 1982 and 270,437 in 1984, with the market share rising from 7.28 per cent to 16.17 per cent. In February 1984 the Cavalier topped the UK sales chart, the first time a Vauxhall had been in this position for over 10 years. In the spring of 1984 Vauxhall was importing about 50 per cent of its cars, but double shift working at Luton and Ellesmere Port has since reduced this figure to around 35 per cent. In April 1984 GM Chairman Roger Smith announced a £100 million investment programme for Vauxhall and Bedford plants. Total UK production was 152,587 cars in 1985. GNG

Vauxhall Firenza coupé of 1975

Vauxhall Carlton CD of 1986

initially on racing but from 1978 on rallying only. DTV, as it was familiarly known, was organized by dealers rather than by the factory, but it brought much valuable publicity to Vauxhall, particularly when the Chevettes of Pentti Airikkala, Jimmy McRae and Tony Pond began winning international rallies from 1977. In 1982 DTV was merged with DOT (Dealer Opel Team) into GM Dealer Sport; Vauxhall's best result under this banner was Russell Brookes' win in the 1983 Circuit of Ireland.

GM's first truly international car was the Chevette, or T-car as it is known by the planners in Detroit. This was launched in Brazil in

Vauxhall Astra GTE of 1985

VAZ
SOVIET UNION 1969 to date

In 1965 and 1966 Fiat signed a series of agreements with the Soviet government whereby the Italian firm would provide the technical expertise for the setting up of a completely new Russian factory for the manufacture of popular cars. A site was chosen at Stavropol on the Volga and a new town built which was named Togliattigrad in honour of Palmiro Togliatti, the Italian communist leader. Russian engineers studied at Mirafiori and Fiat staff spent a lot of time at Togliattigrad supervising building and the choice and installation of machinery.

The factory of almost 54 million sq ft (5 million sq m) was ready by 1969 when the first cars came off the production line. They were called VAZ (Volzhsky Avtomobilny Zavod).

The VAZ-2101 saloon was to outward appearances a Fiat 124, but it had a single-

Vaz 2108 saloon of 1985

overhead cam 1197cc engine instead of the pushrod overhead-valve unit of the Italian car. The structure was reinforced, and a starting handle was provided, as was a heater capable of creating an in-car temperature of 25°C when the outside temperature was −25°C. Within a year output was 700 cars a day and the workforce totalled 34,000. In 1984 78,000 employees turned out 722,744 cars.

The original contract was worth nearly £21 million to Fiat, which signs a separate agreement with the Soviet government every time a new export market is opened up. These now include most countries of western Europe, where the cars are sold under the name Lada.

A small number of VAZ saloons have been made with single-rotor Wankel engines, some of which were sold to private buyers. A few factory-prototypes have been made with twin-rotor Wankels.

The current range includes the VAZ-2105/2107 in 1200, 1300, 1500 and 1600 forms, and the VAZ Niva 2121 4×4 two-door saloon. The latter has had a number of sporting successes in really punishing events such as the Paris-Dakar Rally. For 1985 a new VAZ was announced, the 2108, which had an all-new transverse four-cylinder engine in 1.2- or 1.5-litre sizes, and a five-speed gearbox. GNG

VELIE
USA 1909-1928

In 1860 Stephen Velie married the daughter of John Deere, the world's biggest ploughmaker, and the couple subsequently had three sons, all of whom worked for Deere. The youngest, Willard Lamb Velie, was a director until forming the Velie Carriage Co in Moline, Illinois, in 1902. It soon became the largest such firm in the American West, with an output of 25,000 a year. Most directors were also on the board of John Deere, which handled sales.

In July 1908 the Velie Motor Vehicle Co was formed with $100,000 capital. A batch of 1000 cars was laid down for 1909. They had 30hp engines made by American and British in Bridgeport, Connecticut, Brown and Lipe transmission and Timken axles. They were made on tooling acquired from the 1905-9 Monarch Motor Car Co of Chicago. Low margins and quick turnround ensured competitive pricing and good sales by John Deere, which continued to list the cars in its catalogues until 1915.

Some 3000 cars were made in 1910, Lycoming engines being used at first until chief engineer C. B. Rose produced a Velie four-cylinder unit later in the season. Production in the next four years averaged about 3500 a year.

Trucks were made from 1911 by a separate subsidiary with $200,000 capital until the two companies were merged in 1916 in the Velie Motors Corporation, which had a capital of $2 million. By then Velie trucks were in use with 360 companies. So popular were Velies in Louisiana that a new town built in 1916 was named Velie. It is nowadays a suburb of Shreveport.

Continental sixes were used from 1914 and soon replaced the fours. Falls motors appeared in the post-war Model 34. The most publicized car in the range was the polished aluminium Sport Car with wire wheels that was introduced in 1918. Car production reached a peak of 9000 in 1920 and then settled to about 5000 annually.

The Model 58 of 1922 used a Velie six-cylinder engine made in Marion, Indiana, until production was transferred to Moline three years later. Its designer, C. B. Rose, had by then left for the Moline tractor company; he was succeeded as chief engineer from 1921 by Herbert C. Snow, previously with Peerless, Willys-Overland and Winton.

The firm, by now in financial difficulties, was being run by Edwin McEwan in the absence of the ailing Willard Velie. Designer Snow left in 1927 and became chief engineer at Auburn. Willard Velie Jr handled Velie's Chicago sales until returning to Moline as vice-president when his father resumed his duties in 1927.

That year a Lycoming straight-eight model was offered and three quarters of the cars

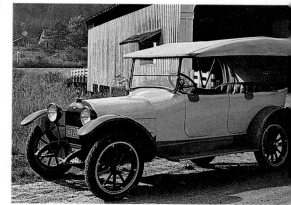

Velie 28.5hp tourer of 1917

ever built by the company were said to be still running. In 1926 Velie supplied its 6-50 engines to Apperson. The Monocoupe aircraft firm was taken over and moved into the old Velie carriage works, which also produced composite bodywork for the cars. Five- and nine-cylinder aero engines were made.

In October 1928 Willard Velie Sr died. A month later his son ended car production and decided to concentrate on making aircraft and engines. Some of the last chassis had Continental six-cylinder engines and were bodied as hearses by Rock Falls Manufacturing Co of Sterling, Illinois.

In March 1929 Willard Velie Jr died of a heart attack and the company was sold. The aircraft business moved to St Louis and car spares were subsequently handled from Indianapolis. The Velie factory was employed by John Deere and the Velie family home is now a restaurant. NB

VERITAS
GERMANY 1947-1953

The first and most successful post-war German make of sports car, the Veritas was dreamed up by three ex-BMW men while they were stationed in occupied Paris during World War II. They were Ernst Loof, Lorenz Dietrich and Georg Meier. After the war they acquired a small factory at Hausern in Bavaria and began their business by turning old BMW 328s into new Veritas.

The customer supplied the BMW engine, gearbox and transmission plus 35,000 marks and in return received a completely rebuilt engine with modified cylinder head, oversize valves and newly ground crankshafts in a modified BMW frame clothed in a slabsided aerodynamic body. Few were made before they moved in March 1948 to bigger premises at Messkirch, Baden, where some 100 people were employed.

Early Veritas cars were mostly competition machines, with which Georg Meier, Karl Kling and Tony Ulmen had a number of successes in national events such as the Hockenheim races. In 1949 Dietrich, who was the sales manager, was asked for a road going

Veritas 80PS coupé of 1948

Vermorel two-seat tourer of 1911

coupé and produced the Komet, which was simply an RS sports model with a hard top. Other orders followed and by the end of 1949 Komets were being produced at the rate of about six a month.

The company moved to new premises, part of the former Mauser arms factory at Meggensturm near Rastatt in Baden, and changed its name to Veritas Badische Automobilwerke GmbH in view of the aid it was receiving from the Baden state government. Messkirch was retained as a source of engine tuning, while assembly was to take place at Meggensturm.

By 1950 Dietrich was becoming disenchanted with racing, although the company did make a Formula 2 car called the Meteor. Work was to be concentrated on three road cars, the Saturn coupé, Skorpion convertible and Komet sports car. Early models of these had the modified BMW engine, but most used a new 1988cc single-overhead cam six designed by Erik Zipprich and built by Heinkel. It developed 100 or 140bhp according to tune, but was not sufficiently developed, and customer discontent was one of the reasons for the eventual failure of Veritas. Coachwork was by Spohn of Ravensburg.

Dietrich returned from the 1950 Geneva Show with orders for 200 cars but could not get sufficient credit to buy the necessary materials. The Baden government persuaded a consortium of Jesuits at Freiburg, together with an archbishop and Prince von Furstenburg, to advance 500,000 marks to Veritas, but they needed three times that to establish production on a viable scale, and this was not forthcoming. Only 78 cars were made at Hausern, Messkirch and Meggensturm.

Dietrich protected his interests by making a deal with Panhard whereby the French firm supplied the two-cylinder Dyna Panhard chassis to Meggensturm, where bodies made by Baur of Stuttgart were fitted, the result being known as the Dyna-Veritas. As the company had no money, Dietrich financed this out of his personal funds. About 184 Dyna-Veritas cars were made between 1950 and 1952, mostly convertibles.

Loof had meanwhile moved to the old Auto Union workshops at the Nürburgring, where he formed Automobilwerke Ernst Loof GmbH and built an improved version of the Heinkel-

powered Veritas with wider, more attractive bodywork, again made by Spohn. Unfortunately he was even more undercapitalized than before and not more than 20 Veritas-Nürburgrings were made. The last few were delivered with Ford or Opel engines as Loof could not obtain any more Heinkel units. Loof later worked for BMW as a development engineer and died in 1956, while Dietrich and Meier both ran successful businesses of their own. GNG

VERMOREL
FRANCE 1908-1930

Etablissement V. Vermorel was founded at Villefranche, Rhône, in 1850 to make woodworking machinery and agricultural implements. In 1891 it set up a research institute to study the application of machinery to farming needs, as Henry Ford did in later years.

The company's first cars were built between 1897 and 1902 but were purely experimental; they had horizontal two-cylinder engines under the seat, and chain drive. Among Vermorel's employees at this time were the brothers François and Emile Pilain, who later made cars in Lyons, and doubtless they had a hand in the Vermorel prototypes.

In 1908 Vermorel began production of a conventional car powered by a 1.8-litre T-head four-cylinder engine, and was also building a curious annular wing biplane designed by Monsieur Givaudan. This was not proceeded with, but the cars flourished and by 1911 Vermorel had 800 employees, although this was probably the total workforce, many of whom would have been working on the agricultural side.

The 1913 range consisted of three models, the 1½-litre 12CV, 2-litre 16CV and 3.3-litre 20CV, all with four-cylinder monobloc L-head engines. Light commercial vehicles were made on all chassis, including fire engines on the larger. One of these was still at the Vermorel factory when it was finally closed in 1965.

Vermorel built a 2½-ton truck for the French War Office trials of 1912 but it did not win any large orders. Wartime production

was consequently devoted to ambulances on the 16/20CV chassis.

During the 1920s a range of conventional four-cylinder cars was made; front wheel brakes were available from 1922 and in 1923 there was a 'sports model' with overhead-valve engine and wire wheels. The staple models of the mid-1920s were the 1.8-litre Type X and the 1.7-litre Type ZX, both available with a variety of open and closed bodies, all designed and built at the factory.

There were also commercial bodies, the classic 'camion Normande' beloved of the French farmer, postal vans, delivery vans and ambulances. In 1925 Vermorel built prototypes of a 5/6CV light car, which was to have been the company's answer to the 5CV Citroën, but this Type AG was never made commercially.

Vermorel's first and only six was the 1.7-litre Type AD introduced in 1928, a monobloc with overhead valves and coil ignition. This and the ZX were continued into 1930, when all car production ceased, although some lists carried the make up to 1932. Annual production in the 1920s varied between 350 and 400 cars, not enough to be viable against competition from the major manufacturers.

Victor Vermorel, son of Edouard who had started car production, died in 1927 but his son, also Edouard, carried on the agricultural implement side of the business. During World War II the company made gunsights and produced gas conversions for trucks. Edouard died in 1956, after which the firm passed out of the family, changing hands several times before it was finally closed in 1965 and the plant auctioned off in 1967. GNG

VESPA
ITALY, FRANCE 1957-1961

Rinaldo Piaggio, born in 1864, worked as a seaman with his father's shipping fleet before starting a woodworking factory in Sestri Ponente near Genoa at the age of 20. His company became a major ship refitter and from 1901 concentrated on making railway carriages and then vehicle bodywork.

During World War I it became a supplier to

the aircraft industry, building aero engines and complete planes. The bodywork side prospered and since World War II has specialized in buses and trolleybuses.

At the end of World War II when war plane production came to an end, the company began making scooters. The first Vespa (Wasp) scooters appeared in 1946 and were joined by three-wheel Ape (Bee) commercial derivatives a year later.

Scooters were assembled in Britain by Douglas and in France by Ateliers de Constructions de Motos et Accessoires of Fourchamboult. In 1957 ACMA was building 260 scooters a day and added a 100-a-day production line for a 393cc four-wheel, integrally constructed car designed by Piaggio, which felt it stood a better chance in France than in Fiat-infested Italy. Exports were planned to Belgium and Switzerland and a few right-hand-drive versions went to the Channel Islands. Claims of 55mph (88kph) and 60mpg (21km per litre) were made for the Vespa 400, a two-cylinder air-cooled two-seater, but despite talk of 200 a day if demand justified it, this model was discontinued in 1961.

Piaggio produced smaller mopeds and larger motorcycles in Genoa and acquired Gilera at Arcore in 1970. The company currently produces mopeds, motorcycles, scooters and Ape three-wheelers. NB

Vinot 12hp saloon of 1914

VIKING
see Olds

VILLARD
FRANCE 1925-1935

The Société des Automobiles Villard made three-wheel single-cylinder cars and commercials in the village of Janville, Oise, from 1925. They were unusual in having drive to the single front wheel and friction transmission. In 1927 four-wheelers with two-cylinder engines and front-wheel drive were added.

Management in 1928 was in the hands of Centralisation Automobile de Paris, although the works remained in Janville. In 1931 conventional gearboxes and V4 Chaise engines were fitted to some examples, which were reputedly exported to the United States. Few cars were made in the 1930s. Most of the Villards that were made until the collapse of the firm in 1935 were ½-ton commercials. NB

VINOT/VINOT-DEGUINGAND
FRANCE 1901-1930

This firm was founded in Puteaux in 1898 by Lucien-Marie Vinot-Préfontaine, born in 1858 in Gisors, and Albert Deguingand, born in Châtou in 1872. Their first car appeared in 1901 and had a 5½hp vertical twin engine and a vertical gate gear change that persisted for several years. It was sold in Britain as La Silencieuse. The range expanded to a 5.8-litre 30hp in 1905, by which time the workforce totalled 180 and 60 chassis and 150 engines were being made annually.

Capital had grown from 120,000 to 600,000

francs by 1907 as a result of investment in the company by the DuCros interests of Britain, a family that held investments in a number of firms, including Clément et Gladiator. This firm and Vinot had two directors in common, F. G. Fenton and L-M Vinot-Préfontaine. From 1909 Gladiator models were similar to Vinots and were made in the same factory at Puteaux. Vinots were popular as taxis in London, some still being in use in the 1930s.

Severe flooding of the Seine disrupted production in 1910 but a new monobloc 12hp was ready in 1911 and 1.7- to 4.2-litre cars were being made at the outbreak of World War I. Capital then stood at 1.2 million francs and output exceeded 500 cars a year.

L-M Vinot-Préfontaine died in 1915 soon after buying land for expansion at Nanterre. The firm moved there during the war and made trucks and 75mm shells. In 1921 the company was known as Société des Anciens Ateliers Vinot et Deguingand.

An overhead-valve 1.8-litre 10CV was added to the revived pre-war range in 1921, when the firm was being run by financiers and designs had generally stagnated. Production dwindled and very few cars, if any, were made from 1924 to 1926, when the works were acquired by Donnet, which may have had links with the company since 1919.

Albert Deguingand returned to Ateliers Deguingand at Puteaux where he completed and serviced Vinot trucks and from 1927 made a few SCAP 8hp engined Deguingand cars. Between 1927 and 1930 he offered a 735cc four-cylinder two-stroke Deguingand cyclecar designed by Violet. From 1931 it was made by Donnet. NB

VIOLET/MAJOR, VIOLET-BOGEY
FRANCE 1908-1923

Achille-Marcel Violet studied at Armentières and then at the Arts et Métiers in Lille and was a racing motorcyclist prior to 1907. With his partner Charpeaux, Violet made his first cyclecar on the sixth floor of a house in Issy-les-Moulineaux near Paris in 1908. Five were built and three sold. They had 500cc Quentin engines and were followed by La Violette production examples from 1909 which were partly financed by a restaurateur customer. The production cyclecars had engines by Cohendet, Anzani and then two-strokes made by Violet himself. Most had friction drive, but a conventional 1500cc four with sliding mesh gearbox was offered in 1914.

Violet built the similar Violet-Bogey of 1913-14 at a time when La Violette was listed in trade publications under Franc et Cie of Levallois. He was also involved with the Côte two-cylinder two-stroke engine that appeared in the Automobilette and some of the final Violet-Bogeys.

Marcel Violet served as a soldier in World War I, after which he dusted off the Violet-Bogey and produced it as a Major in 1920. The

Vinot-Deguingand 5½hp buggy of 1901

Major had the classic Violet design of two-stroke, two-cylinder 500cc engine with common combustion chambers. The model was listed until 1923.

The Mourre of 1921-23 was probably identical to the Major. It was named after M. Mourre, who raced and financially backed the marque. A very similar Weler was produced from a different address in Levallois. Violet also sold one of his vehicle designs to SICAM in 1919.

SICAM built 1058cc and 1470cc two-cylinder air-cooled engines for both Mourre and Weler. The final Mourres of 1923 had Fivet 950cc four-cylinder water-cooled engines.

Marcel Violet, a keen racing driver, produced ideas for the Bucciali brothers and was kept busy by Sima. In 1927 he developed a 735cc four-cylinder two-stroke car for Albert Deguingand and in 1929 produced the Galba. The Huascar-type cyclecar cropped up again at Donnet in 1932-33, when about 500 were made.

In 1932 Violet had revived the name Major for a single-cylinder 600cc water-cooled utility vehicle that he hoped to sell to the French army but never did. He produced a Jeep-type vehicle in 1939 and received an order for 33,000 of his 1938 oil-cooled four-cylinder motorcycles, built by Sima for the army. The project was thwarted by the fall of France, however, after only a few hundred had been delivered and seized by the Germans for use in Russia. NB

VIVINUS
BELGIUM 1899-1912

Alexis Vivinus was born in 1860 in France where he began work as a naval engineer, later moving to Belgium where in 1888 he joined a Brussels machine tool company, the Ateliers Bouton (which had no connection with Georges Bouton of Paris). In 1890 Bouton began to manufacture bicycles, but after a few years this enterprise failed and Vivinus set up on his own as a cycle-maker. In 1895 he began to import Benz cars and a year

Voisin Grand Prix car (Piccioni driving) of 1922

later installed Benz engines in two cars of his own construction. He also made a 1hp motor for attachment to a bicycle.

In 1899, with backing from the Comte de Liederkerke, he set up Société des Ateliers Vivinus with premises at Schaerbeek, Brussels. Capital was 250,000 Belgian francs. His first production cars had single cylinder air-cooled engines of 785cc, belt drive and tubular chassis. Between July 1899 and the beginning of 1901 he built 152 of these voiturettes, but more importantly he sold licences to manufacturers in three foreign countries: De Dietrich in Germany, Georges Richard in France, and Burford and Van Toll in Great Britain, where they were sold under the name New Orleans.

These licence agreements brought 400,000 francs to the company, enabling it to expand and to introduce new models with two- and then four-cylinder engines, water-cooling and then shaft drive. In 1905 the company moved to a new factory where 250 workers were producing six chassis a week.

By 1907 the voiturettes had been dropped, which was inevitable with the general trend towards larger cars, but it meant the loss of the licence agreements, with a consequent serious drop in income. The range now consisted of the four conventional four-cylinder cars of 12/14, 20/24, 22/28 and 24/30CV. The smallest chassis was widely used for taxicab work in Brussels, Stockholm, Bucharest, Vienna and Rio de Janeiro. Motorcycles and aero engines were also made and in 1909 Roger Sommer took the world's duration record in a Vivinus-powered Farman biplane.

These activities could not keep the Ateliers Vivinus going, however, and in 1911 the original company went into liquidation. It was replaced by a new one, the Société des Automobiles Vivinus, in which Alexis Vivinus played no part. This company exhibited some four-cylinder chassis at the 1912 Brussels Salon but made very few cars. Vivinus himself became the Clément-Bayard agent for Belgium, then joined Minerva for which he worked until his death in 1929, just before the launch of his greatest design, the 40CV straight-eight Minerva. GNG

VOISIN
FRANCE 1919-1939

Born in 1880, Gabriel Voisin studied architecture before making an experimental car with his brother Charles in 1899. Aircraft attracted them next. Having first made kites and then gliders in Paris they built Voisin Frères planes from 1907 with Captain Ferber, Henri Farman and Léon Delégrange at France's first aerodrome, at Issy-les-Moulineaux near Paris. In October 1908 J. T. C. Moore-Brabazon bought a Voisin biplane and became the first to exceed 250 yards (228m) of powered flight in Britain in 1909, the year in which Frederick Simms became British agent.

In 1911 a total of 59 Voisins were owned by registered aviators, making them the second most popular type. A Canard, which could fly, float and drive on the road, was tried out in 1911.

A year later Charles Voisin was killed in a motoring accident and the company, Société des Aéroplanes Voisin, was put into liquidation. It was soon re-formed, however, and went through numerous changes of name, becoming the Société Anonyme des Aéroplanes G. Voisin in 1917. A total of 10,700 biplanes with steel tube fuselages were ultimately built and played an important role in World War I, when Voisin also built Salmson and Hispano-Suiza aero engines.

In 1919 the company had a 215,000sq ft (20,000sq m) factory and 2000 employees but business was in the doldrums. The wealthy Gabriel Voisin therefore tried to diversify, producing a two-cylinder Motor Sulky, prefabricated housing, and motors for assisting bicycles. The most enduring product proved to be a four-cylinder 3969cc sleeve-valve car designed by Artaud & Dufresne which had been rejected by Citroën. Voisin also considered making steam cars.

In 1919 and 1920 1020 cars, called Avions Voisin as befitted their genesis, were completed at Issy-les-Moulineaux. From 1923 they were graced with an aluminium bird

Vivinus vis-à-vis of 1900

the 14CV six that remained in production for 10 years from October 1926 and achieved sales of 8000. Customers included the wealthy and famous such as Rudolf Valentino, who had a stable of four Voisins.

Cars were reconditioned in the factory for resale to uphold the reputation for reliability and keep staff occupied in the Depression. Gabriel Voisin disapproved of chrome and of hydraulic brakes and instead poured resources into attempting to find foolproof gear changes with Cotal or Sensaud de Lavaud systems. Two-speed axles were also used from 1928 with electric or vacuum operation.

Having made an experimental V12 car in 1920-21, several more were offered in 1931 which had capacities of 3.85 or 4.86 litres. Perhaps a dozen were built in all. Two en-

Voisin C5 of 1925, owned by Rudolf Valentino

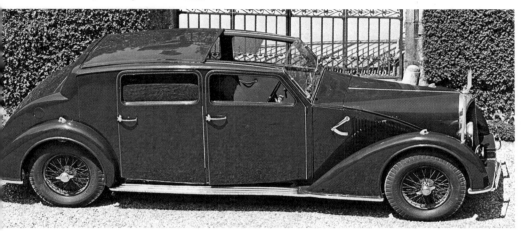
Voisin C28 Ambassador of 1936

sculpture on the distinctive radiator, reputedly first modelled from scrap sheet aluminium by Voisin himself.

Body-styling verged on the bizarre, as Gabriel Voisin had strong ideas on many subjects, including aerodynamics and functional efficiency. Bodies were usually made of fabric, wood or aluminium with angular but efficient shapes. They often had outriggers from wings to radiator, and luggage boxes on the running boards – and in the tail, when Voisin deleted running boards in the mid-1920s. He also put an extra headlamp on one rear wing that remained illuminated when one at the front dipped. Most bodywork emanated from Voisin's own factory, although some coachbuilders did their best to satisfy his demands and Weymann-type construction was favoured.

Engines were built under Knight licence and aluminium was used extensively in their construction. Front wheel brakes were standardized in 1922 and all had servo assistance from 1925. The first French six-cylinder sleeve-valve car was ready for 1927.

Marios Bernard and André Lefèbvre tackled whatever design work Voisin did not personally undertake. Bernard produced a successful 8, then 10CV sleeve-valve engine and production of these, with the 18CV models, ran at about 2000 a year by the mid-1920s. The most successful individual model was

gines were also sold to Bucciali.

Voisin acquired a licence to build Impérias in 1928 and some of these cars were assembled into the 1930s. In 1931 a Nacional Pescara was exhibited at the Paris Salon by Voisin but no commercial relationship appears to have followed.

Extraordinary prototypes were made, such as a front-wheel-drive V8 in 1930; a Cocinelle with air-cooled radial rear engine and single front and rear wheels plus one at each side in 1935; a six-wheel bus with steering axles at either end; and a 6-litre straight-twelve car in 1937 with two of its cylinders in the driving compartment to avoid an over-long bonnet. This last car was offered to the public and possibly two were sold.

In 1932-33 activity in the factory was at a very low level. All the experimental work proved very expensive and in 1937 Gabriel Voisin lost control of the firm to a financial group which he scornfully called a 'quasi GM'. Voisin loathed most American cars, although he was a friend of Fred Moskovics of Stutz.

Voisin's all enveloping pontoon bodied cars of the mid-1930s were a natural progression from the unitary construction racing models of 1923 based on an aerofoil section and which had been offered as catalogue Laboratoire models in 1924. Catalogues were personally written by Gabriel Voisin in typi-

cally arrogant style that poured ridicule on anything he did not like, including dickey seats.

The company's new management introduced the first non-sleeve valve model powered by a 3554cc supercharged side-valve Graham engine, 12 of which were probably built. Gabriel Voisin was appalled and managed to recapture control in 1939. The factory then built Gnome et Rhône aero engines, steam vans and tanks and electric cars using old Voisin dynamotors. His firm by then belonged to Gnome et Rhône, although Voisin remained president throughout the war until the company was nationalized and became part of the SNECMA aeronautics group. Total Voisin car production appears to have been about 27,200, although chassis numbering sequences run up to 65,000.

Plans to produce easy-to-assemble economy cars for under-developed countries and Panhard Dyna engined air-portable 4×4s came to nothing, and the Voisin name was discontinued by SNECMA in 1958. Gabriel Voisin, who wrote a characteristically pungent and bizarre autobiography, designed the Spanish Biscuter, which was made in considerable numbers from 1951 to 1958. He died in 1973. NB

VOLKSWAGEN
BRAZIL 1953 to date

Volkswagen do Brasil production line, c.1985

Volkswagen do Brasil was the first, and subsequently the largest, manufacturing subsidiary outside Germany for Volkswagenwerk AG. The suitability of the Volkswagen Beetle for the Brazilian market was suggested to Volkswagen at the beginning of the 1950s by the Brazilian Chrysler importer, José Thomson, who saw the strong, economical car as ideally suited to Brazil's poor roads and total dependence on imported oil.

Volkswagen's boss, Heinrich Nordoff, went to Brazil to consider the possibilities with a colleague from Wolfsburg, Friedrich Schultz-Wenk, who then went to live in Brazil and even took up Brazilian citizenship to set up the new operation. Volkswagen do Brasil was founded in March 1953, 80 per cent of its capital coming from Germany and the rest from a group of businessmen in Rio de Janeiro.

The idea was to assemble kits shipped from Germany, and the first was assembled in a rented workshop in the suburbs of São Paulo soon after the company was registered. Up to 1956 the workforce grew to about 200 and 2820 cars were assembled, which encouraged the local government to help finance a more permanent plant, started in 1956, with the intention of manufacturing rather than simply assembling cars.

The first Brazilian-built Volkswagen, a Transporter, was finished in September 1957 and had more than 50 per cent local content. In 1959 the Brazilian plant started to build Beetles, originally at a rate of about five a day, and these were joined in 1962 by Karmann-Ghia models. The cars were similar to their German counterparts except for lower compression engines and stronger suspension for local conditions.

The original premise that the car was well suited to the market was spectacularly accurate; the 500,000th Brazilian Volkswagen was built in 1963 and the one millionth in 1967. Moreover, Brazilian Volkswagens by then had almost entirely local content. By the mid-1960s Volkswagen do Brasil was the country's largest industrial organization, with a workforce of 11,000. It supplied over 65 per cent of Brazil's private cars and over 40 per cent of all vehicles.

By these standards a slip from about 80 per cent of the market, which the company once held, was cause for concern and in 1967 Rudolf Leiding was sent from Germany to improve the company's performance by developing specifically Brazilian models. The first, introduced in 1968, was a four-door version of the 1600 saloon. A fastback version of this car was added in 1971 and the SP coupé in 1972. The SP used a body styled in Brazil, under Leiding's supervision, on a modified 1600 chassis and with a 1.7-litre engine. Having achieved his objectives in Brazil, Leiding returned to Germany, where he took control of the parent company in October 1971.

In 1973 Volkswagen do Brasil built its one millionth Beetle and introduced the 1.6-litre Brasilia saloon, based on a German prototype and available in two-door, four-door and hatchback styles. A Brazilian-built Passat was launched in 1974 and the range included a cheap version called the Surf, aimed mostly at young buyers. When Volkswagen opened a Nigerian assembly plant in 1975, Brasilia and Passat kits from Brazil were the first cars to be built there.

Through the 1970s the Brasilia was second in sales only to the Beetle – with over 800,000 built until 1980. By then the company employed about 41,000 people and built more than 2000 cars a day. By the time Volkswagen worldwide passed a production total of 35 million vehicles, in June 1979, the Brazilian company had built 4,783,000 of them, and exported its products to about 50 countries – including Germany.

510

Brazilian production passed the 5 million mark in 1979 with an alcohol-fuelled Beetle. Brazil had a pressing interest in using alcohol, which it could produce in abundance from agricultural surplus to ease its dependence on oil imports. From 1979 Volkswagen do Brasil built alcohol-fuelled cars in increasing numbers, originally for use as taxis or on farms where fuel supply could be centralized, but later for general use as the government aimed for national availability of alcohol fuels as a step towards oil independence.

The Brazilian company's technical strength also led it to take over all Volkswagen's air-cooled engine development from 1980 – appropriate enough, as Brazil continued to build Beetles in large numbers. Alongside these, plus Brasilias and Passats, the company built a strange car called the Gol, which used the Beetle engine plus front-wheel drive, and the Polo, intended as the Beetle's replacement. The 1985 range still included the Beetle (known as the Fusca), the Gol (with alcohol fuel engine option from May 1984), the Voyage (a water-cooled version of the Gol), the Parati estate car, the Passat and the top-of-the-range Santana. BL

VOLKSWAGEN
GERMANY 1936 to date

The first Volkswagen was made possible by the rather unlikely juxtaposition of the dreams of two very dissimilar characters, Dr Ferdinand Porsche and Adolf Hitler. Although he never learned to drive, Hitler was a great car enthusiast, a firm believer in motor sport as a means of developing German technical excellence (and showing it off to the world), and with an avowed intent to motorize Germany's masses, including the most humble worker. Porsche was a brilliant Austrian-born engineer, conspicuously apolitical but with his own personal determination to build a 'people's car' – in German, literally, a *Volkswagen*.

Porsche, born in 1875, designed his first small car, the Austro-Daimler Sascha, in 1922. It was privately financed, by Count Sascha Kolowrat, because Austro-Daimler was not interested in Porsche's small-car ideas. With subsequent employers Porsche continued to meet resistance to a real mass-market car but in December 1930 he founded his own design office, Konstruktionsbüro für Motoren- und Fahrzeugbau Dr Ing hc Ferdinand Porsche, in Stuttgart, and continued to advocate his own ideas for a cheap car for the people.

The bureau's first project *was* a small car, for Wanderer, but its most important legacy was the first appearance of Porsche's novel torsion bar suspension. Porsche, however, saw *his* 'people's car' not like the Wanderer but as a full-sized vehicle of respectable performance and endurance but low cost – to be realised through simplified design and

manufacturing methods and economies of scale.

In September 1931 he started work on such a car, as Project 12, but could not afford to carry it through. In November, however, he was approached by the motorcycle manufacturer Zündapp, which wanted to build a popular car that it referred to as a 'Volksauto'.

Porsche based his work for Zündapp on Project 12. Where Porsche had intended to use an air-cooled flat-four engine, broadly derived from his 1912 Austro-Daimler aero-engine design, Zündapp insisted on using a complicated 1200cc five-cylinder radial engine – and this effectively rendered Porsche's goals unattainable. In any case Zündapp cancelled its contract when the motorcycle market improved, and after Porsche had built three not entirely successful prototypes.

In 1933 NSU commissioned Porsche to produce a similar car, but this time he was free to use his planned 1448cc flat-four engine – although NSU also undertook some engine development of its own. Porsche's three prototypes for NSU were very similar to what eventually appeared as the first Volkswagen, but NSU soon abandoned its car production plans in favour of its better known motorcycles.

Porsche now found an infinitely more powerful backer, in Hitler himself. Hitler and Porsche had both stated similar aims, Porsche in late 1931 and Hitler, officially, in early 1933 – shortly before work started on the ambitious autobahn building programme which was part of the same overall plan. Hitler's promise was to introduce a popular car suitable for use on the new autobahns at under 1000 marks, or less than half the price of the cheapest 'real' car available.

Porsche/VW Project 12 of 1932

VW Type 38 prototypes of 1938

Hitler knew of Porsche through his Auto Union racing designs, and in May 1934 Porsche was invited to discuss his ideas with Hitler and then submit a formal proposal. Porsche knew that the price and 1935 presentation deadline were both impossible to meet, but in June 1934 he agreed to try, backed, reluctantly, by the controlling body of the motor industry, the Reichsverband der Deutsche Automobilindustrie, or RDA.

Other manufacturers were predictably opposed to Porsche's brief and the RDA, in spite of Hitler, gave little more than token finance – paltry to the extent that Porsche had to build the first three prototypes in his own garage and the first larger test batch was subcontracted to his one-time employer Daimler-Benz, which was emphatically not concerned with small, cheap cars. In February 1936 a

VW Beetle convertible of 1949

Kubelwagen Type 82 of c.1940

meeting between other manufacturers and the RDA simply underlined their opposition, particularly that of Opel, which had the nearest thing to a vested interest as producer of Germany's then cheapest real car.

Porsche originally worked on a two-stroke design as the only way even to approach the price target and he worked on two-stroke variants until 1938, but when the first prototype was completed in October 1936 it had a low-compression 985cc version of the air-cooled flat-four four-stroke engine. Tests on the first three prototypes, over enormous mileages, were completed by December 1936 and although there were many problems, notably with breaking torsion bars and short-lived engines, Hitler told the RDA in February 1937 that Porsche's project was to be fully backed.

In May the Gesellschaft für Vorbereitung des Deutschen Volkswagens mbH (Association for the manufacture of the German people's car) was founded, with state backing of 480,000 marks, and the next batch of 30 prototypes was ordered from Daimler-Benz. While these were tested *in extremis*, mostly by military drivers, Porsche visited the United States twice in 1936 and 1937 to study modern mass-production methods – which were much admired by Hitler.

In May 1938, after another batch of prototypes had been laid down, Hitler laid the foundation stone of the factory at Fallersleben, near Hanover, where the car was to be produced by Volkswagenwerk GmbH, which was registered in October 1938. As well as the

VW Beetle saloon of 1947

factory there was to be a town for the workers, known as Kraft durch Freude Stadt after the Strength through Joy movement by which Hitler promoted the whole project. In his speech, Hitler, to Porsche's surprise and dismay, dubbed the forthcoming car the KdF-wagen. It was to be financed by advanced purchase payments and available under a stamp saving scheme run by a central agency. The scheme was popular and over 335,000 accounts were opened before World War II intervened.

Production had started in April 1939, with a workforce of 1000 and rapidly increasing. Only 210 KdF-wagens, already known as Beetles, were built before all capacity was switched to war work in 1940. An 1131cc military derivative of the car, the Kubelwagen personnel carrier, and a four-wheel-drive amphibian, the Schwimmwagen, were built in large numbers, plus many other military supplies, including aircraft components.

The workforce was supplemented by foreign internees but about half the plant was destroyed by bombing in 1944. What remained was taken over by American troops and then passed under British military control at the end of the war, when considerable further damage was caused for a short time by the liberated captive workers.

In May 1945 the British renamed KdF Stadt as Wolfsburg and in spite of material shortages began to rebuild the plant and employ the workers on vehicle repairs. The plant and the Beetle were offered to several countries as war reparations but absolutely no-one was

interested in either.

The British officer in charge, with a staff of three officers and about 30 other ranks, was Major Ivan Hirst, and he was probably the only person to see any potential at all in the Volkswagen. He organized resumption of production in August 1945, building 1785 Volkswagens by the end of that year, all for military use. More than 10,000, mostly 1131cc Beetles, were built in 1946 and although the works were closed by materials shortages in the winter, production reached 2500 a month by the end of 1947.

In January 1948 the company was returned to German administration and Hirst, by then a civilian, appointed Heinrich Nordhoff as general manager to assume complete control after Hirst left the company in August 1949. Nordhoff, born in 1899, the son of a banker, had previously worked for BMW and Opel and had studied production methods at General Motors plants in the USA. His influence at Volkswagen was enormous. In 1949 he engaged Porsche, recently released from internment, as an engineering consultant and the royalty which Porsche received on every Beetle made the Porsche car itself possible.

Nordhoff was acutely export-conscious. By 1948 about one Beetle in four was exported and towards the end of 1949 two cars, the first of several million, were sold in the USA. This quickly became Volkswagen's major market and within 10 years over half the cars Volkswagen made were sold there. Overall, about two-thirds of Volkswagen's German output has been exported to more than 150 countries – and further large numbers have been built in plants outside Germany.

A better equipped export Beetle was introduced in July 1949 and the Karmann four-seater cabriolet appeared in the same month. About 330,000 Karmann cabriolets were built until the model's demise in early 1979, three years after hardtop Beetle production had stopped in Germany. There were other convertible Beetles, but the only other type built in any quantity was the two-seater cabriolet by Hebmuller, offered between 1948 and 1953. In March 1950 Volkswagen introduced the Transporter, a ¾-ton van based on Beetle elements which is still in production, having gained larger engines and other improvements in phase with the Beetle itself.

Alongside his successes Nordhoff had the major worry of meeting the company's obligations to putative pre-war buyers who had invested in the stamp scheme. Claims appeared before the courts for many years, some as late as the late 1960s, and Volkswagen eventually allowed partial discounts on more than 120,000 cars.

In 1952 a Canadian sales company, Volkswagen Canada Ltd, was formed. It was fol-

VW 'razor edge' Karmann-Ghia coupé of 1965

VW 1500S saloon of 1963

VW Golf GTi of 1985

lowered by Volkswagen do Brasil in 1953, Volkswagen America Inc in 1955, Volkswagen Australia Pty Ltd in 1956 and Volkswagen France in 1960. Volskswagen do Brasil was the first overseas production plant and the first car was assembled in São Paulo in March 1953, while today the company still builds a wide range of models.

In Germany a larger, 1192cc engine was introduced in 1954, the first of several size and power increases which, with regular cosmetic and equipment improvements, kept the Beetle up to date without changing its basic package. In August 1955 the one millionth Volkswagen was built and the attractive Karmann-Ghia coupé was introduced, to be followed by a convertible version two years later.

Since its post-war revival there had been some ambiguity over who actually owned Volkswagen, national or local government; in 1960 the company was reorganized as Volkswagenwerk GmbH, with capital of some 600 million marks, and shares were offered to the public. National and local government took up 20 per cent each and private investors the rest.

In September 1961 Volkswagen introduced a new body shape, as a complement to rather than a replacement for the Beetle, in the 1500 saloon, whose 1493cc flat-four was also adopted by the Karmann-Ghia coupé. In 1963 the Variant estate and coupé introduced further body style options. The five millionth Volkswagen was built in December 1961 and production thereafter consistently topped 1 million units a year – and actually exceeded 2 million in the exceptional year of 1971. From 1965 Volkswagen also built various Audi models, having taken over Auto Union from

VW Passat GL 5s of 1985

Daimler-Benz which had owned it since 1956.

There were other Volkswagen models such as the 1965 TL fastback and the unitary construction 411 saloon and estate of 1969, but production was still dominated by the Beetle, with a 1285cc engine from 1965 and 1493cc from 1966.

In April 1968, shortly before his intended retirement, Nordhoff died and Kurt Lotz, his expected successor, took over early. He inherited unaccustomed problems, with growing doubts over continued reliance on the Beetle and with Volkswagen having been overtaken in 1967 as Europe's biggest carmaker by Fiat. Token new models included the jeep-like VW181 and the Volkswagen-Porsche 914 sports car, introduced in 1970

by a separate new company, Volkswagen-Porsche Vertriebgesellschaft.

In 1969 Volkswagen took over NSU and amalgamated it in August with Audi as Audi NSU Auto Union AG. In 1971 NSU's K70 prototype, a conventional derivative of the excellent but expensive Wankel-engined Ro80, re-emerged as a completely new kind of Volkswagen: a water-cooled front-engined Volkswagen!

In February 1972 Volkswagen passed the Ford Model T's production record, having built 15,007,034 Beetles. A 1584cc engine had been offered since 1970 and the last German example, a cabriolet, was built in April 1979. The Beetle was still built in Brazil, Mexico and Nigeria, at a rate of over 1000 a day. Some were even imported to Germany. The

20 millionth Beetle was built in Mexico in May 1981.

Volkswagen, however, was not as healthy as it looked. In 1971 the company lost money and in 1972 Opel overtook Volkswagen as Germany's leading manufacturer, underlining the need for a Beetle replacement. Huge investments led to the launch of several new generation Volkswagens. The first, replacing the 411 and Variant, was the water-cooled four-cylinder front-wheel-drive Passat, derived from the successful Audi 80 and introduced in 1973.

In 1974 the firm was in serious trouble, was forced to cut the workforce drastically and was in danger of going out of business completely. The revival started by the Passat (and further helped by the success of Audi) continued in 1974 with the launch of the Giugiaro-styled Scirocco and Golf – mechanically similar front-wheel-drive hatchbacks in coupé or saloon formats. A smaller hatchback, the Polo, was launched in 1975, followed by a 'three-box' derivative, the Derby, in 1977 and a 'three-box' Golf, the Jetta, in 1979. These cars helped Volkswagen back to profitability and its accustomed status of largest German manufacturer in 1976.

The Golf was also sold with great success in the USA as the Rabbit, and early in 1976 a decision was taken to manufacture that car there. Production started at New Stanton, Pennsylvania, in 1978 and soon reached 1000 vehicles a day.

The 1976 Diesel Golf and Passat models offered economy but the very rapid 110bhp fuel-injected 1588cc Golf GTi, also introduced in 1976, proved a yardstick for all other sporty hatchbacks. It quickly became something of a cult car, giving a timely boost to Volkswagen's image. A German-built Golf was the 35 millionth Volkswagen, built in June 1979. A Karmann Golf Cabriolet was added in 1979 and 1800 engines topped the range from 1982. In the same year a notchback version of the Passat, the Santana, was introduced and Volkswagen entered an agreement with Seat in Spain, whereby Seat would initially import and then build Polos and Passats under licence. By mid-1985 plans for further investment in Seat were put in jeopardy by Seat's domestic financial problems but investment continued elsewhere.

In 1982 Volkswagen signed an agreement with the Chinese government whereby the Santana would be built by the Shanghai Motor Works. Volkswagen has a 50 per cent interest in the enterprise, the balance being held by the Shanghai Tractor and Automobile Corporation, which held 35 per cent, and the Bank of China, which held 15 per cent. The Santana is also built under licence by Nissan in Japan.

Although the Golf in particular was a bestseller throughout Europe and in America, competition continued to increase and Volkswagen's financial problems returned in the early 1980s. Losses in 1982 and 1983 amounted to about £75 million a year, while most of the German industry was comfortably profitable.

The company, however, showed no lack of confidence, concluding a £155 million deal in 1984 to transfer one of its engine plants to East Germany by 1988 and continuing to introduce new models, largely with a sporting bent. Among these was the fastest Volkswagen of all, a 135mph (217kph) Scirocco with a 139bhp 16-valve engine, introduced in late 1984, and – in line with a policy of introducing four-wheel-drive options across the Volkswagen-Audi range – four-wheel-drive 'Tetra' versions of the Passat and Golf for 1985, a far cry from the original Beetle. The 16-valve engine was also available by mid-1985 in the Golf, which at the other end of the scale was also available with a turbo diesel engine.

In 1985 Volkswagen's German operations built over 1.4 million vehicles. The technical compatibility with Audi was due to result in a new range of four-, six- and eight-cylinder engines by 1988, marking the end of Audi's unusual five-cylinder units, and for its own range, Volkswagen was already working on a Scirocco replacement for 1986. BL

VOLVO
SWEDEN 1926 to date

Tradition has it, probably accurately, that the idea of the Volvo car was suggested by Assar Gabrielsson to Gustav Larson over a meal of crayfish in a Stockholm restaurant in August 1924 – leading to the first Volvo car in 1926 and production by 1927.

Gabrielsson was born in Korsberga in 1891 and moved with his family to Stockholm at the turn of the century. He studied economics and worked for four years in government administration before he joined the bearing maker Svenska Kullagerfabriken, or SKF, in Gothenburg in 1916. In 1920 he became managing director of the firm's French subsidiary and in 1923 returned to Sweden as group sales manager.

Larson was born near Orebro in 1887 and studied engineering. He had a particular interest in cars, which led him to work for White & Poppe in Coventry, England, from 1911. He went back to Sweden in 1913 and studied at the Royal Institute of Technology in Stockholm before he too joined SKF, in 1917, and got to know Gabrielsson. In 1920 he left SKF to become technical manager for AB Galco in Stockholm and it was a chance meeting with his former colleague in June 1924 which led to the famous meal.

At this time about 95 per cent of Sweden's market for about 15,000 cars a year was met by American imports. They were really no better suited to the generally appalling Swedish roads than cars from anywhere else, but at least they were readily available. Although Sweden's only car-maker of any consequence then was Thulin, Swedish industry could supply high-quality steels and made-up components at reasonable prices and Gabrielsson planned to assemble a car using as many bought-in components as possible.

By June 1925 Larson, assisted by a young engineer, Henry Westerberg, had analysed costs and produced a design, and Gabrielsson was charged with raising sufficient finance to build prototypes. By September it was apparent that no backer was forthcoming and Gabrielsson himself provided most of the 150,000 kroner needed to build nine open and one closed prototypes.

In October a Swedish painter, Helmer Mas-Olle, helped Larson evolve a suitable body design and the first open car was completed in June 1926. It used a specially commissioned four-cylinder engine built by marine-engine builder Pentaverken of Skovde and parts from many other companies. The other prototypes were completed later in the year, the last of them being the first saloon.

In August 1926 the partners showed the first car to SKF, which agreed to provide credit guarantees of 200,000 kroner to finance a trial production of 500 open and 500 closed cars. A small factory with 10 workers was established at Lundby, on Hisingen island near Gothenburg, in a rented building previously owned by another bearing company,

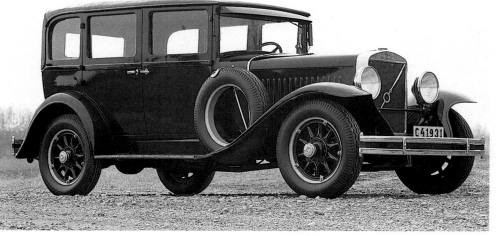

Volvo six-cylinder saloon of 1931

Nordiska Kullanger AB. Preparations for production started in October 1926. SKF also provided Larson and Gabrielsson with a company identity which the company already owned but did not use: AB Volvo – from the Latin 'I roll', an allusion to SKF's famous bearings.

The first OV4 production car, a four-cylinder 1944cc tourer nicknamed 'Jakob' by the workers, was finished in April 1927 and an assembly line was in operation within a month. Perhaps because of the local climate, the open car did not sell well and only 205 of the planned 500 were built, compared to 721 of the mechanically similar but fabric- rather than steel-bodied four-door PV4 saloon.

Both types were offered until 1929, when a six-cylinder series was started with the PV650. This used a 3010cc engine in what was essentially the PV4 chassis and the series ran sequentially through to PV659 over the years to 1937. There were capacity increases to 3266cc and eventually 3670cc for the last two models, and some offered a longer wheelbase chassis for proprietary coachwork.

From a very early stage Volvo did not rely entirely on private cars. A 1½-ton truck was introduced in February 1928 and a TR series of cars, with the PV-type engines but revised chassis and bodies, was sold as taxis from 1930 to 1937. The taxis sold well but the trucks outsold even the cars, and continued to do so right up to World War II. Volvo has continued to build commercials in large numbers ever since and built modified versions of some saloons specifically for taxi use until the late 1950s.

Commercially, Volvo initially sold fewer cars than expected but found that it was possible to make a profit on smaller numbers than originally calculated. August 1929 was the first single month in which the company did not lose money and at the end of 1929 it could show a tiny profit for the year overall.

From there it grew quite quickly. In June 1930 SKF increased its capital underwriting to 4 million kroner and Volvo was able to buy a factory where previously it had only leased, giving a new impression of permanence. Sales were helped, briefly, in 1932 by a rise in the value of the dollar, which helped Volvo compete more favourably with the still dominant American imports – and sell over 900 cars in its best year to date.

This was backed by a growing similarity to American styles, but sales were hit badly by economic depression in 1933 and 1934 and only about 600 cars were built in each of those years. In 1933 Volvo experimented with a radically streamlined prototype, designed by Gustaf Ericsson and built in secret by Nordbergs Karosserifabrik in Stockholm. It was known as the Venus Bilo but never went into production.

A less extreme streamlined model, the PV36 Carioca, was the first of the next series of cars, introduced in 1935. It used the 3670cc engine of the PV659, which it replaced, and

had Volvo's first all-steel body and independent front suspension. Only 501 Cariocas – named after a popular dance – were built, the last in 1938, compared to almost 7000 of the more conventionally styled alternatives from 1936 to 1945 as Sweden followed the almost universal resistance to 'streamlined' styling. As before, Volvo built taxi variants in the series from 1938 to 1958.

In 1935 SKF relinquished control by way of a stock flotation which valued Volvo at 13 million kroner. In the same year Volvo took over engine supplier Pentaverken, in which it had held a controlling interest since 1930.

Volvo PV444 of c.1944

Volvo 121 saloon of 1958

Volvo P1800S of 1964

The company continued as a marine engine builder and from 1949, as AB Penta, it became the marine division of AB Volvo.

Volvo was now the best-selling car in Sweden and production reached a pre-war peak of 2834 cars in 1939. Sweden's neutrality allowed the company to build cars throughout World War II but material shortages aggravated by Sweden's physical isolation kept output down, the low point being 99 cars in 1942. Commercial vehicles and military production, with which to defend neutrality, maintained Volvo's income and in September 1941 the company built its 50,000th vehicle – a truck.

The first of the next series, the PV444, was a much smaller four-cylinder 1414cc car with unitary construction and Volvo's first overhead-valve engine. Five prototypes were built

in 1942 but the car was not made public until 1944 and did not go on sale until 1947, after production had returned to full scale in 1946. It was a great success, particularly in giving Volvo a foothold in the United States, to the extent that for the first time Volvo built more cars than commercials in 1949 – 5362 cars in the course of the year. Production then increased every year up to 1973, with the one millionth car being built in 1966.

This helped finance a major investment programme in the 1950s and various types in the PV444 series, including estate cars, vans, pickups and the much improved PV544 derivative, were built until 1965, and the P210 estate to 1969 – by which time well over 500,000 of the series had been made.

Volvo had a brief aberration in 1956 when it built 67 examples of a sports car based on the

PV444, the glassfibre-bodied drophead two-seater P1900. It was styled in America by Glaspar, which built the prototype Kaiser Darrin, but wasn't really Volvo's sort of car. The Suez crisis of 1956 hurt Volvo quite badly but at least gave Gabrielsson's successor, Gunnar Engellau, a timely excuse to write the P1900 off to experience.

Gabrielsson officially retired in 1956, although he remained as chairman until shortly before his death in May 1962. Larson, who died in 1968, was already taking a less active part in the company before Gabrielsson's retirement but both he and Gabrielsson initiated independent projects to create a successor to the PV444 types. The car which did replace the 444s, however, was started as a personal project by Volvo's young designer Jan Wilsgaard and adopted in preference to either of the 'official' designs.

It was the P120 series, introduced with an attractive modern saloon, the 121, in 1956. It used the 1583 or 1778cc four-cylinder engines derived from the PV544, which was in

built in 1966 at Torslanda and in 1973, when another plant was opened at Kalmar, production was more than 250,000 cars. Also in 1973 Volvo announced plans for an assembly plant in the USA, which were later abandoned in view of world events, and opened its own test and development facility in Sweden.

A new range, the 140 series, was introduced in 1966 with the 144 saloon. Amazon running-gear was used in a stylish new shell and there was a growing emphasis on engineering for safety. The Amazon was dropped in 1970, by which time the 140 series was well established, having been expanded in 1968 by the addition of the 3-litre six-cylinder 164 variant. This basic shape has continued with regular updating, principally into the 240 family in 1974, to the present day in the form of the 244 saloons and 245 estate types, latterly with turbo and diesel engine options. They helped Volvo to a production record of 320,000 cars in 1979 and a total output of 5 million cars by 1983.

In 1969 Volvo approached DAF in Holland

until 1986 and to improve the limited popularity of the small cars, Volvo's holding fell to only 30 per cent.

The smaller Volvo cars continued with the option of 2-litre Volvo engines and models ranging from economy to sporty. Hampered more by image than by any shortcomings in ability, their sales have continued to be frustratingly limited.

Volvo forged connections with Peugeot and Renault through Société Franco-Suèdoise des Motors PRV in June 1971 to collaborate on engine development. Volvo could not afford to develop its own V8 engine, which was what the French companies were already developing jointly, but in the end the PRV engine, launched in 1974 in the new 260 series Volvo, was a 2.7-litre V6.

In 1977 Volvo's plans to merge with Saab were rejected by the latter and a proposed wide-ranging collaboration with the Norwegian government was ostensibly agreed in December 1978 and then abandoned a few weeks later. In 1979 car interests were given a

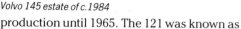

Volvo 145 estate of c.1984

Volvo 340 GL of c.1984

production until 1965. The 121 was known as the Amazon but the name was dropped for all but the home market after the German motorcycle manufacturer Kreidler claimed to have registered it already. No subsequent Volvo has used a name, all being designated by type number.

In 1959 Volvo showed the prototype of another sports car, launched in 1961 as the P1800 coupé. It was based on Amazon running-gear and its styling was started by Ghia and finished by Frua in Italy. Volvo did not have the capacity to build bodies and after agreements with Karmann in Germany fell through these were built by Pressed Steel in Scotland and the cars assembled from kits by Jensen in England. This arrangement lasted only until early 1963, when Volvo was able to move all production to Sweden, where it continued until 1973 and the last fuel-injected 1800ES sports estate derivative.

Demand had rapidly outgrown Lundby's capacity and near the end of 1959, with government backing, Volvo started work on a new facility at Torslanda, where a factory with double the earlier capacity was opened in April 1964 by King Gustav Adolf. In 1963, when production exceeded 100,000 cars for the first time, Volvo opened its first overseas assembly plant, in Canada. Works were also started in Belgium, as Volvo Europa NV.

The one millionth car, an Amazon, was

Volvo 740 GLE of c.1984

with a view to building a smaller car. In September 1972 Volvo bought a one-third share in DAF's car division which was increased to 46 per cent in 1974 and to 75 per cent a year later. The DAF division was renamed Volvo Car BV and the four-cylinder Renault-engined Variomatic-drive DAF 66 became a Volvo, to widespread indifference, until its demise in 1980. The DAF-developed Volvo 343 was introduced in 1976 as a small car supposedly more in keeping with Volvo's image and was offered with a manual transmission option from 1978.

By this time Volvo had reduced its holding in the Dutch company to 55 per cent, as the National Investment Bank of Holland took up available shares. In 1981, after substantial cash investments from the Dutch government, which was planned to continue at least

separate identity within the Volvo group as the Volvo Car Corporation, which also encompassed the Dutch interests. Initially 10 per cent (and from 1981 15 per cent) of this corporation was owned by Renault as a condition of its technical and financial support, including a planned Renault-engined front-wheel-drive replacement for the 340 types.

In merging with the giant Swedish company Beijerinvest AB in May 1981, the Volvo group became by far the largest company in Scandinavia. Its interests range from car, truck, bus, boat and aero-engine production to oil exploration and shipping.

Early in 1982 Volvo introduced a new series of large luxury cars, the 760 series, to run alongside the existing range. The in-house styling was controversial but the car, with a range of engines including a 2.8-litre

V6, a six-cylinder Volkswagen-built diesel and a turbocharged 2.3-litre four, was another success for the company.

In 1985 Volvo announced a new Electronic Traction Control system as an option on the more potent models for controlling wheel-spin, particularly important for Scandinavian conditions. At the 1985 Geneva Show the company exhibited the Bertone-styled (and built) 780 Coupé, a very pretty car based on the 760, initially aimed at the American market. The promise of a forthcoming sports car further underlined that Volvo was not about to rest on its continuing success.

An estate car version of the 760 was introduced in 1985. This was followed in 1986 by the 480ES, a front-drive sporting hatchback powered by a 1.7-litre Renault engine, and built in the Dutch factory. Production world-wide of 397,100 cars in 1985 was enough to encourage plans for a new factory at Uddevalla, even though the increased production had resulted in marginally reduced profits. BL

VOX
see Hurst

VULCAN/CHILTERN
GB 1902-1928

Southport, on the Lancashire coast, was an unlikely situation for a motor manufacturer, but it was there that the Vulcan Motor Manufacturing and Engineering Co Ltd was formed in 1903. Its mascot showed Vulcan shaping armour with hammer and anvil. Brothers Thomas and Joseph Hampson had experimented with cars since 1896, initially in Wigan. Their first car was running successfully in 1899, although sales did not begin until 1902.

In 1906 sales totalled £43,000 and the firm became Vulcan Motor and Engineering Co (1906) Ltd with capital of £40,000. It moved to nearby Crossens that year. Products in 1907 included 10 to 30hp cars, the former with two cylinders and the latter with six. Output in 1909 was about six cars a week. A comprehensive range of solid, well built models was produced. Commercials became important from 1914.

In that year 650 men were employed in 5 acres (2 hectares) of factory and a further 300 were recruited for war work. £30,000 of new machinery was installed in anticipation of a new 8hp car. Most production, however, consisted of horse-drawn limbers and aircraft such as the Be2d and Re8.

In 1916, following a 12 month profit of £44,000, the Hampson brothers left and the firm became Vulcan Motor Engineering Co (1916) Ltd. Thomas Hampson then became mayor of Southport and joined the engineers Brockhouse, where he was general manager at the time Brockhouse purchased the Vulcan factory in 1938. He died in 1949.

In 1919-20 the Vulcan Motor and Engineering Co Ltd was making the Dorman-engined Chiltern car in Dunstable. This was linked to the Crossens firm through motor dealer C. B. Wardman, who was a director of both companies.

In 1919 Harper Bean Ltd acquired 75 per cent of Vulcan's share capital which stood at £150,000, of which £88,500 had been issued. Vulcan in return took up £150,000 of Harper Bean shares. C. B. Wardman became managing director. In 1920 capital was increased to £600,000 and over 1000 ex-servicemen were employed. By the end of 1920 Harper Bean had gone into liquidation but Vulcan managed to extricate itself.

About 1000 vehicles, more than 90 per cent of them commercials, were made in eight months of 1923 and almost 6000 between August 1919 and February 1924, but it soon became obvious that this volume of production could not be sold. In 1923 the designer

for the previous 10 years, Charles E. Burton, left for Karrier and later Thornycroft.

The workforce was down to 700 in 1924 and a net profit of £19,000 was earned in the year to September 1925. The factory was largely self-sufficient, having a moving assembly track and its own foundries. It had a special press for making complete doors. Various ambitious car plans, including a V8 in 1919, came to nothing. Those that were produced had either Vulcan 20hp or Dorman 12 and 16hp engines.

From 1922 Vulcan and Lea-Francis had close ties via C. B. Wardman. Vulcan's coachworks built many Lea-Francis bodies and the two companies also sold the same cars. These were mostly Vulcans with Lea-Francis radiators and included Meadows-engined 14s in 1925 and Anzani-engined 12s in 1926.

A. O. Lord, who had built the 1923-24 Lloyd-Lord, was brought in by Wardman to run Vulcan's car business and he produced an unsuccessful 1½-litre twin-overhead cam six. Vulcan charged Lea-Francis £20,000 in 1927 for the doubtful privilege of the design work carried out on this engine. The more prosaic Vulcan cars and commercials were selling particularly well in Australia at this time but the home market was severely depressed and car production was halted in 1928.

Financial difficulties caused most of Vulcan's workforce to be laid off in 1929 and Vulcan directors left the Lea-Francis board, even though cars of Vulcan origin were sold by the Coventry firm until 1930. The commercial vehicle range from the mid-1920s included increasingly large buses and trucks as well as familiar 1½ to 3-tonners. Municipal vehicles became an important sideline.

A court order to wind up Vulcan Motor and Engineering was presented in 1931, when liabilities stood at £306,000 plus £620,000 in ordinary shares. The profits earned by Vulcan between 1907 and 1930 totalled £516,000 but losses in the same period amounted to almost double that figure. Vulcan Motor Services, formed in 1930 and which had taken over C. B. Wardman's London dealership, also got into difficulties and was liquidated in 1937.

Tilling-Stevens acquired the manufacturing rights to Vulcan commercial vehicles in 1937 and moved production to Maidstone, Kent. Vulcan Motors Ltd was registered with a capital of only £1000 in early 1938. The chief engineer was F. Sumes. The old factory was used by Brockhouse to make the air-portable motorcycle that became known as the Corgi after World War II. Many of the former staff moved to Northern Counties bus bodyworks.

Post-war Vulcan commercials used Perkins and Gardner diesels or, until 1951, Vulcan petrol engines. Rootes acquired control in 1950 and three years later Vulcan and Tilling-Stevens vehicle production ended. The Maidstone factory then made two-stroke diesels for Commer and marine applications for about 20 years. NB

Vulcan 10hp tourer of 1922

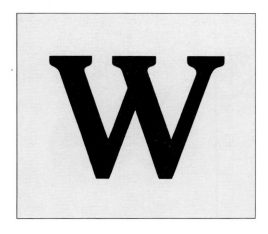

WAF
AUSTRIA 1911-1926

The Wiener Automobilfabrik was the successor to Bock & Hollender, which had sold cars since 1899 and motorcycles from 1905. The 24 and 40hp four-cylinder Bock & Hollender designs were continued under the WAF name, being the work of Ferdinand Trummer who set up WAF in order to distribute as well as to manufacture the cars. Motorcycles were not continued under the WAF name.

In 1914 came a new model, the 2.8-litre 45PS four-cylinder Alpentyp, built for the International Alpine Trial, and revived after World War I. A 70PS six was added, made mostly in closed form, but the most interesting post-war model was the 4-litre straight-eight consisting of two four-cylinder engines in-line, each with its own carburettor and ignition. This was Austria's first straight-eight engine, but it was made only in small numbers in 1924 and 1925.

During the post-war years WAF also made goods vehicles, 1½-, 2- and 3-tonners with shaft drive, and a chain-driven 5-tonner. WAF was wound up early in 1926. GNG

WALTER
CZECHOSLOVAKIA 1909-1937

Josef Walter was born the son of a locksmith and machine maker at Veprěk near Slaný in 1873. He started his own workshop, repaired bicycles and soon was assembling them. He started motor cycle experiments in 1898 and displayed machines publicly the following year.

With finance raised from relatives he built a factory in 1905 and was soon selling motorcycles and combinations to Russia and the Balkan states. A cheap Tobek-designed three-wheeler with air-cooled two-cylinder engine was produced in 1909 and about 900 of these were sold in the next four years.

Having tried Renault and Fafnir-engined four-wheelers, Jos Walter & Spol developed its own four-cylinder units and started production at a new plant at Prague-Jinonice. Design was by Zubatý. Contemporary engineers included Novak from Tatra, Plocek and Barvitius. Aero engines were developed by Smejkal. The company also built BMW aero engines under licence from 1923.

Disagreements with his financial partner Košiře led Josef Walter to start a separate firm with his sons Jan and Jaroslav in 1922. It began by making gears but soon produced motorcycles. It was taken over by CZ in 1949.

The car factory under Teny Kumpera added stationary engines and commercial vehicles in 1922. In 1928 came the first of a series of Barvitius-designed six-cylinder cars and a few, probably only five, V12 5.9-litre Royals in 1931.

From making fast and expensive high-quality cars – 2568 were in use in 1931 – the Walter company was forced to retreat to building Fiats under licence. The Bijou was based on the Fiat 514, the Junior on the Balilla and the Prince and Lord on 521 six-cylinder types. Production was 374 in 1934 but came to an end in 1937, when just 23 cars were made.

Heavy trucks and buses continued to be built for another 10 years, after which Walter made engines for Praga trucks. Aero engines and propellers, along with fuel pumps and other components, had become Walter's principal output. The company is still in business in the aeronautics field. NB

WALTER
USA 1904-1909

Walter cars were only manufactured for a short period, unlike the trucks which have had a 76 year history and are still going strong, but they were linked with the birth of the famous Mercer car. William Walter (1862-1945) went to the United States from his native Switzerland in 1883 and formed the American Chocolate Machinery Co with a factory on West 65th Street in New York City. In 1898 he imported a three-wheeled car from Switzerland, probably made by Egg & Egli, and later in the year he completed his own tiller steered four-wheeler.

Several experimental cars followed but it was not until 1904 that he put a car on the market. This was a conventional high-quality four-cylinder machine with overhead inlet valves, available in 30, 40 or 50hp models at prices up to $5700. Practically all of the car, including the body, was made in Walter's six-storey factory.

In 1905 the company name was changed to the Walter Automobile Co and the following year the business moved to larger premises at Trenton, New Jersey. The New York factory was retained, possibly continuing to make chocolate machinery for a few years, and in 1909 truck production started there. For a while car chassis were made in New York and driven to Trenton for the fitting of bodies. In 1906 the Trenton factory was bought by the John A. Roebling Co, a well-known wire manufacturer.

Among Walter's employees were fellow Swiss Louis Chevrolet and a young engineer of either Swiss or French descent, Etienne Planche. Planche had designed the Sharp Arrow car which Roebling had contracted to build for W. H. Sharp, a professional photographer who wanted to get into motor racing. Possibly as many as 10 Sharp Arrows were made in Walter's Trenton factory and were followed by two cars called Roebling-Planche, one of which was a vast 15.6-litre racing car for which $12,000 was asked.

Early in 1910 Roebling changed the name of the Walter Automobile Co to the Mercer Automobile Co, after Mercer County in which Trenton is located. Planche left afterwards to join Louis Chevrolet in Detroit, where they worked on the design of the first Chevrolet car. The famous Mercer Type 35 was designed by Finlay Robertson Porter.

Walter six-cylinder cabriolet of 1931

The Walter family had no more connection with the Trenton business but concentrated on truck manufacture in New York City until 1923, then on Long Island until 1957, when they moved to Voorheesville, New York. After bankruptcy in 1980 they were rescued by their Canadian branch, and a new company, Walter Equipment USA, was established at Guilderland, a suburb of Albany, New York. There they make snow ploughs and airport fire engines. GNG

WALTHAM
see Metz

WANDERER
GERMANY 1911-1939

Winkelhofer & Jaenicke of Schonau-Chemnitz, Saxony, was formed in 1885 and made milling machinery, typewriters and Wanderer bicycles. Motorcycles followed in 1902. A prototype two-cylinder car, reputedly dating from 1904, survives and a four-cylinder prototype was built in 1907.

Bugatti tried to interest newly-named Wanderer Fahrradwerke in a design based on the Bébé Peugeot in 1910, but the following year Wanderer introduced its own 5/12PS tandem seat, monobloc, four-cylinder light car familiarly known as the Püppchen (Doll). These cars sold well and performed adequately in trials, even winning a gold medal in the 1914 London-Edinburgh event. British sales were handled by NAG's agents.

Tandem and Sociable versions followed. Together with Wanderer motorcycles, tandem models were made in large numbers during World War I.

In 1917 the firm moved to Siegmar and became Wanderer-Werke AG. Larger cars of up to 2 litres were made in the 1920s and a six-cylinder 2.45-litre model was built under licence by Martini from 1930 to 1932. A 3-litre sports version was also made in Germany.

Alexander Novikoff's design of an advanced 498cc Wanderer motorcycle with pressed steel frame and shaft drive was sold as a complete project to Jawa in 1929. Thereafter Wanderer made motorized bicycles under NSU licence.

By 1928 the factory had a moving car assembly track with conveyor feed of components. Capacity was said to be 20 cars a day. A 3.3-litre supercharged straight-eight prototype appeared in 1931 but, like most of the older models, was not pursued after Wanderer was absorbed into the Auto Union group in 1932. Porsche had been hired to design new engines that were plainly influenced by his work for Steyr, and these appeared in Wanderers and Audis, which also shared other components and pressings.

Wanderer catered for the middle-class segment of Auto Union's range with four- and

Wanderer W25K of c.1936

six-cylinder saloons and sports models. In 1935 Wanderers accounted for 4.1 per cent of German car registrations and fifth place, just behind Mercedes-Benz. A 2-litre W25K (for *kompressor*) sports model with DKW beam rear axle was available from 1936 for about a year but could not compete with the similarly priced BMW 328.

In 1937 the new 1.8-litre W24 saloon was a little more expensive than the Mercedes 170 and there was also a 2.63-litre six-cylinder W23. The W26 version had seven-seat bodywork and swing axle rear suspension, not the DKW beam axle as used on the W23. Car production ended with the outbreak of World War II and the Wanderer name was not revived when Auto Union was re-established upon the return of peace. NB

WARSZAWA/SYRENA
POLAND 1951-1972; 1955 to 1982

Before World War II the Polish motor industry was more or less confined to the Polski-Fiat, made under licence from Fiat between 1932 and 1939. During the war the factory was destroyed and when the war ended there was virtually no private motoring in Poland; almost all vehicles were owned by the government or local organizations and sold, controlled and serviced by the Centalshandlowa Przemyslu Motorazyagjnego.

By 1949 Poland had a pressing need for more vehicles and the state-controlled Fabryka Samochodow Osobowych (FSO) had started work on a factory near Warsaw to build Fiat 1100s under licence at a rate of about 200 cars a week. Before the factory was completed, FSO ran into problems with the Fiat licencing arrangements – they had no connection with the earlier Polski-Fiat operation – and plans were changed to allow manufacture of a Russian design, the Pobieda.

The Pobieda (Victory) was designed under the direction of Andrei Lipgart and touted as the first truly Russian design, as opposed to a blatant copy. Nevertheless, its 2.1-litre four-cylinder side-valve engine owed much to the Willys Jeep and its body styling to the beetle-backed Opel. The first examples were built at the Zavod Imieni Molotova works in Gorki by the GAZ organization. They were then heavily modified for a launch in Russia in mid-1949 as the production Pobieda, also known as the GAZ M20. Production started under licence in Warsaw in November 1951, using some engine and body parts from Russia. The car was launched in Poland in 1952 as the Warszawa M20.

In 1955 FSO introduced a heavily modified version of the Warszawa which was quite different from the Pobieda. With regular modifications, including a change to three-box styling in 1965 and the addition of taxi, station wagon and light commercial variants, Warszawa production continued until 1972.

Also in 1955 FSO's works at Bielsko-Biała launched a new model to its own designs, a small front-wheel-drive saloon called the Syrena. The original versions used a water-cooled 744cc twin-cylinder two-stroke engine. The marque remained in production until 1982, with a 992cc three-cylinder engine from 1963 to 1964 and an 842cc unit replacing the original 744 as standard from 1967.

Overall control of the Soviet bloc motor industry was in the hands of the Council for Mutual Economic Co-operation (Comecon) and between the mid-1960s and the mid-1970s production expanded at about twice the average rate for the rest of the world – with considerable help from Fiat, which had involvements with Yugoslavia, Russia and Poland. By the late 1960s Comecon was not only encouraging competition between its members but also rapidly developing its interest in exporting.

In 1968 FSO began building a new Polski-Fiat, the 125P, compounded of 1300 running gear and the 124 body. From 1974 FSO also built versions of the 126 and 131, and in 1975

Fiat helped extend the Bielsko-Biała works which then became the only factory building the 126 from late in 1980.

In 1979 FSO introduced the Polonez, in saloon and hatchback variants, using many of the 125P's mechanical elements. In 1981 the Polski-Fiat name was dropped and the cars were marketed under the name FSO. BL

WASP
USA 1919-1924

The Wasp was a distinctive looking car made from standard proprietary components, designed and built by Karl Hamlen Martin. Born in 1885, Martin had worked as a coachbuilder in New York and had then designed the Roamer car for Albert Barley, the Deering Magnetic and the Kenworthy. In 1919 he moved to the small town of Bennington, Vermont, and with backing from two local residents he formed the Martin-Wasp Corporation with capital of $100,000.

The first six Wasp cars were laid down during the year, and one was ready for display at New York's Commodore Hotel in January 1920. It was of striking appearance, with cycletype wings, step plates instead of running board, and fins on top of the bonnet. The radiator had a diagonal stripe, anticipating Volvo's stripe by a good seven years. Underneath all this was a conventional specification: four-cylinder Wisconsin T-head engine, Brown-Lipe gearbox, Timken axles, Gemmer steering and Parrish & Bingham frame. The bodies were made by a wagon-builder in Bennington. The Commodore Hotel car was bought for $5500 by Douglas Fairbanks as a wedding present for Mary Pickford, which was about as exciting a first purchase as any car-maker could hope for.

By January 1923 the Martin-Wasp Corporation had 28 workers but had sold just 11 cars, all with open tourer bodies described as the 'rickshaw phaeton'. Three more four-cylinder cars were made, and in 1924 Martin decided to bring out a six. This used the familiar 5.2-litre Continental 6T engine in a larger wheelbase, but only three were made before the money ran out.

The last car could not be delivered because the purchaser had died, and it remained in chassis form at Martin's home until 1954 when it was bought by an Ohio car collector whose wife had grown up in Bennington. A replica body took seven years to build, and the last Wasp took to the road for the first time as a complete car in 1961.

The Martin-Wasp Corporation became Martin Shops, which specialized in handmade furniture, metal work and letterhead stationery. Karl Hamlen Martin died in 1954. GNG

WAVERLEY
GB 1910-1931

Vernon Trier helped build the Marlborough car for T. B. André and Co Ltd, the agent for Hartford shock absorbers, Ballot engines and Malicet et Blin components. At the 1909 London Show Andrés exhibited both the Marlborough and Trier's JAP-engined Waverley cyclecar, which had four wheels but only one of which was driven. Trier was also involved in the Trier and Martin carburettor firm which set up Light Cars Ltd with £1500 capital in September 1910 to make Waverleys in Trenmar Gardens, north-west London.

Bodies came from E. B. Hall and Co Ltd, just round the corner in Waldo Road. Four-cylinder Chapuis-Dornier engined light cars were soon being made. Sales were handled from Great Portland Street by A. H. Salmon, who left T. B. André to join Light Cars Ltd in 1910. Components were probably by Malicet et Blin, for in 1913 the Waverley was said to contain Marlborough components.

Chassis numbers ran up to 1500 by World War I but it seems unlikely that this number was built. In the absence of French engines a Coventry-Simplex was tried in 1916, and this make as well as Tylors was adopted in 1919. During the previous two years the company had been involved exclusively in war work.

The company's name became Waverley Cars Ltd in 1915 and four years later the sales office moved into the works. In the mid-1920s it was also handling Sénéchal cars. An estimated 75 cars were produced in 1923.

In 1924 a Burt-McCollum sleeve-valve four-cylinder 1½-litre engine, as found in the Argyll, was tried. The following year a six-cylinder two-litre overhead-cam Coventry-Climax was standardized in the fabric-bodied sports saloons that had become Waverley's speciality. Dorman engines were fitted in small models in 1926. Waverley's bodybuilder, to which Waverley had extended considerable credit and which worked for Waverley exclusively until 1923, went bankrupt in 1925 but was later revived as Carlton Carriage Co.

Efforts to launch a rear-engined two-cylinder £100 Waverley light car in 1926 met with failure and at the end of 1927 this whole project, including patterns, parts, drawings and three completed chassis, was offered for sale. GWK briefly toyed with the idea.

The 16/50 six appeared in some sales lists until 1935 and certainly the firm was still in business after World War II as machinists and manufacturers. Vernon Trier was then running the André components firm, having previously been managing director of the Silent-bloc motor components firm. NB

WAVERLEY (USA)
see Pope

WEIGEL/CROWDY
GB 1906-1912

D. M. Weigel came to prominence in 1900 as manager of the British Automobile Commercial Syndicate, the importer of Clément cars. When Clément-Talbot was formed with the backing of the Earl of Shrewsbury and Talbot, Weigel became managing director, remaining in this post until 1906 when he left to set up his own company, Weigel Motors Ltd, with premises in Goswell Street, London.

The first Weigel car, announced in October 1906, was a substantial machine with 40hp four-cylinder engine described by *Motoring Illustrated* as being 'on the lines of an Italian Mercédès'. This would point to Itala, and as another journal described the premises at

Waverley tourer of 1915

Weigel straight-eight racer of 1907

Goswell Street as being more of a depot than a factory, it seems that Weigel made little, if any, of the cars themselves. The chassis were finished by the Wilkinson Sword Co, and bodies were by the English branch of J. Rothschild et Fils, of which company Weigel was a director.

It is uncertain how many Weigels were made, but in January 1907 there were said to be 25 cars 'under construction' at Goswell Street, as well as six complete cars. A 25hp four and a 60hp six were announced later and at least one of the latter was made, for the Earl of Wilton, with sumptuous Rothschild limousine body. Weigel also made some unsuccessful Grand Prix cars, two 15-litre straight-eights in 1907 and three 13-litre fours in 1908.

Later in 1907 Weigel Motors was reorganized, and at the end of the year the company moved to new premises off Latimer Road in west London. In October 1909 it was in the hands of the receivers and was acquired by a new company managed by A. E. Crowdy, who had been manager of Wolseley's sales in Lancashire.

The company name became Crowdy Ltd and two lines of car were offered, 20/30 and 30/40hp fours of Weigel design, and a new 12/14hp with Hewitt piston valve engine and a dashboard radiator. For 1911 Crowdy offered a 19hp four and a 29hp six with piston valve engine as well as the old Weigel-type fours, and in August of that year the company moved to larger premises in Birmingham. However, this move overstrained resources and, within a year, in June 1912, the works and contents were sold by order of the receiver. GNG

WEISS MANFRED
HUNGARY 1924-1930; 1948

Before 1924 the Hungarian company Weiss Manfred Acel es Femmuvei R-T of Budapest was already well known for a huge variety of products, including arms, munitions, aircraft, motorcycles, bicycles and household equipment. In 1924 the company also produced a 750cc four-cylinder two-stroke engined saloon car, designed by Victor Szmick.

In 1928 it introduced a side-valve 875cc four-cylinder engine in a car which (like the original) was much larger than the engine size suggested. In 1929 Szmick himself scored an excellent second place in the Monte Carlo Rally with an 875cc model.

The company stopped building cars in 1930 but continued to build lorries, and some military cross-country vehicles to Straussler designs. It also made bodies for imported Ford Model As.

Immediately after World War II Weiss Manfred built another small rear-engined utility car, under the name of Pente 500. It was designed to government specification by Weiss Manfred's chief engineer, Janos Pen-

telenyi, and had an air-cooled 500cc twin-cylinder two-stroke engine. With Hungary now behind the Iron Curtain and starved of imported cars, there was a pressing need for basic transport which the Pente was intended to meet. Several prototypes were built from 1946, and by the end of 1948 the car was said to be in production, with a 600cc model already projected for the near future.

In the end, very few Pentes were made. Weiss Manfred, now a state-owned company, stopped car production and made Csepel lorries under licence from Steyr of Austria. BL

WELCH/WELCH-DETROIT
USA 1903-1911

The Welch brothers were bicycle-makers in Chelsea, Michigan, who began experimenting with cars in 1901. Two years later they put their Welch Tourist car on the market, exhibiting at the 1903 Chicago Show.

The two-cylinder rear-entrance tonneau was advertised as being 'replete with new and original ideas' and the same ad spoke of its genuine honeycomb radiator and noiseless spiral gear drive. What it did not mention, probably because the company thought buyers would not appreciate it, was that the cylinders had inclined overhead valves and hemispherical combustion chambers – proclaimed as a novelty by Chrysler when it adopted them in 1951!

In 1904 the brothers moved to larger premises at Pontiac, Michigan, where they formed the Welch Motor Car Co and began to make four-cylinder cars. The 36/40hp engine had a capacity of 5.2 litres and its inclined overhead valves were now operated by a single overhead camshaft, another pioneering feature shared with Maudslay which has gone largely unrecognized. A six-cylinder 75hp model followed in 1907, with prices up to $8000 which kept sales low, overhead camshafts notwithstanding.

To widen their market the Welchs set up a new factory in Detroit to make a smaller four-cylinder car under the name Welch-Detroit. General manager of the Detroit plant was A. B. C. Hardy, who had designed the Hardy or Flint roadster in 1904.

In 1911 both Welch plants were bought by William C. Durant to become part of his growing General Motors empire. The Pontiac works were closed and the big Welchs discontinued; the machinery from both plants was moved to the Rainier plant at Saginaw, Michigan. There the 40hp four-cylinder Welch-Detroit was rechristened Marquette and was made for a year alongside one surviving model of Rainier, which was also sold as a Marquette.

In July 1912 the Marquette Motor Co changed its name to Peninsular Motor Co, but no cars were made under this name. The Marquette name was revived in 1929 for a short-lived cheap model of Buick. GNG

WERNER
FRANCE 1906-1914

Michel and Eugene Werner were journalists who settled in Paris and developed phonographs, cameras, typewriters and, in 1897, bicycles with Labitte-designed motor attachments driving the front wheels. A more conventional engine position came in 1901 and by September 1902 some 6000 Werners had been produced at Levallois-Perret and licences sold to many other manufacturers.

In 1899 a Coventry factory was opened in England with backing from Harry Lawson and in 1903 a British floated Werner Frères Ltd acquired the French company and paid the founding brothers 1 million francs in cash and shares. Motor tricycles were by then also produced.

Werner went into liquidation in 1906 and was re-formed to make both motorcycles and cars. Galien et Sarda owned the motorcycle factory and rights, and built a few light cars before collapsing in 1909. Werner Frères et Cie at Billancourt did not return to motorcycle production but offered one- and two-cylinder light cars and a 1.3-litre four-cylinder De Dion-powered car in 1909. It subsequently added models of up to 4.1 litres, but the firm had ceased trading by the time war broke out in 1914. NB

WESTCAR/HERON
GB 1921-1926

Major Henry Beeston Prescott-Westcar OBE established a well-equipped workshop at the family home, Strode Park in Kent, and in 1921 began to assemble Westcars. He used such proprietary components as Dorman 11.9hp engines, Alford and Alder and Moss axles, Meadows gearboxes and Marles steering. Bodies were framed with ash from the estate and were described as being sold in 1924 as enclosed models for the trade and open models for the public. The Strode Garage Electricity Works was the name of the manufacturer. It generated its own electricity for the Strode Park estates and for customers in Herne village.

Despite being well finished and cheap, Westcars were unable to compete with the mass-producers so the major decided that something more unconventional was needed to attract buyers. A Ruby engined prototype of the Heron was built in 1924 and had Consuta plywood body. After other experiments a chassis-less type built on Marks-Moir principles with transverse Dorman mid-mounted engine and chain drive was adopted in 1925. Later there was a version with front-mounted Coventry-Climax engine.

Very few Westcars were built and under 100 were sold; 20 cars were exported to India and a petrol-electric tram was put into use on the local pier. Agencies were offered in all areas in 1925 but no-one seemed interested. In April 1926 the plant and stock-in-trade were sold by auction. The original workshops are now cottages and the major's home is a centre for the disabled. NB

WESTCOTT
USA 1910-1925

The Westcott was a conventional assembled car which made its bow in September 1910 as a four-cylinder vehicle powered by a 45/50hp Rutenber engine. It was originally made at Richmond, Indiana, but in May 1916 the factory was sold to the Davis Motor Car Co, also of Richmond. Production moved to Springfield, Ohio, and a factory formerly occupied by the Buckeye Division of the American Seeding Machine Co. At Richmond 200 men had produced 1000 cars a year, and it had been announced that the move would enable both figures to be doubled. In fact the best year was 1920, when a total of 1850 cars were delivered.

From 1914 Westcott standardized on Continental engines, fours being made until 1916 and thereafter sixes only. A complete line of open and closed bodies was offered at prices running from $1185 to $2535 in 1916. Most of the bodies came from the Central Manufacturing Co of Connersville, Indiana, which also supplied coachwork to Haynes, Moon, Stutz, Overland and other car-makers.

In 1923 Westcott announced the Closure, an all-weather sedan which could be converted to a tourer in summer. By this time two sizes of Continental engine were offered, a 3.9-litre in the Model B44, and a 4.9-litre in the Model D48.

The Westcott always had a good reputation and was sold quite widely, not only in its native Ohio, but like so many other small makes it could not compete with the mass-producers. In 1923 1000 Westcotts were sold – compared with 216,000 Buicks – but sales dwindled to a few hundred over the next two years. The 1925 models, which featured four-wheel brakes and balloon tyres, were the last. GNG

WESTINGHOUSE/ASTRA,
MARTA
USA, FRANCE, HUNGARY 1904-1912

Of Westphalian stock, George Westinghouse was born in New York in 1846. At the age of 23 he patented air brakes for railway rolling stock and established firms to exploit these patents and subsequent electrical inventions in east Pittsburgh, London and Paris.

Westinghouse masterminded the Niagara Falls hydroelectric project of 1893 and patented a gas engine in the United States in 1896. He was helped in this work by Albert

Schmid, who had been recruited from his French company. A 50-seat bus with electric hub motors was made for Chicago in 1901 and motors were sold to several car firms, including internal combustion units for Chalmers-Detroit between 1908 and 1912.

In 1901 the French brake and electrical interests were combined in Westinghouse Société Anonyme with capital of 25 million francs. Albert Schmid returned to France to run the Le Havre branch in 1902 and there introduced large, high-quality four-cylinder cars in 1904 under the name Westinghouse or Westinghouse-Schmid. Pierre la Ville le Roulx of Unic gave financial support to the company.

In August 1907 negotiations were opened with the town of Arad – then in Hungary, but part of Romania after the war – to site a factory there. The factory initially made railway engines and equipment and then produced about 150 Marta cars from 1910 to 1912. It also assembled 150 De Dion taxis from 1908 to 1910.

Westinghouse in America went into receivership in 1907 but was soon re-formed. The same fate befell the French company in 1912 which, when revived, did not return to vehicle production. The Arad factory was sold to Austro-Daimler and about 500 2½-litre Martas were made until the end of production in 1914. Under Romanian control the factory made Astra cars until 1924 and commercials to 1926.

Westinghouse, a famous manufacturer of electrical and braking products, returned to vehicle manufacture in 1953 upon the acquisition of the Le Tourneau diesel-electric construction vehicle business based in Peoria, Illinois. In 1957 dumptrucks were produced under the name Wabco – a corruption of Westinghouse Air Brake Co – and remain in production today under the auspices of the owners of Westinghouse, the American-Standard Co. The British railway brake factory belongs to Hawker-Siddeley. NB

WHITE
USA 1900-1918

Thomas H. White worked for Grout sewing machines and formed a rival company in 1866, moving it from Massachusetts to Cleveland, Ohio, in 1876 when it became the White Manufacturing Co. Sewing machine output grew from 25 to 8000 a month by 1881. The company also made bicycles, roller skates, lathes and screw cutters.

The Cleveland Automatic Machine Co was a subsidiary company where Elmer Sperry developed the car that became the Pope-Waverley and where H. J. Edwards worked on the Cleveland Runabout; A. L. Garford, who later made Garford trucks, was president. Two members of the White family were on the board of Walter C. Baker's Baker Motor Vehicle Co in the late 1890s.

White steam coupé de ville of 1903

At this time a younger member of the family, Rollin H. White, developed a steam car which entered production in 1900. Output was soon three a week. A total of 385 Whites were made in 1902, 710 in 1904 and, from 1906, 1500 a year.

In 1906 the motor business, which had included truck production from 1901, became a separate company, the White Co, with a capital of $16 million and a 17-acre (7-hectare) site in Cleveland employing 1000 men. The steamers were up to twice the cost of Stanleys but they were well made, reliable and capable of developing 150bhp in the 18hp model over short distances, which caused Whites to be banned from most hillclimb events. A 20hp four-cylinder monobloc Delahaye-based car was introduced in 1909 and the 10,000th steam car was made in 1910. Production of steamers ended in 1911. White purchased Waltham Manufacturing in order to obtain the Selden licence that was required at this time by makers of petrol cars.

Internal combustion engined trucks were made in 1910 and total output soon exceeded 2000 vehicles a year. From 1912 a monobloc 60hp six-cylinder car was offered but cars dwindled in number after the outbreak of World War I, during which time a few 16-valve large fours were made from 1916. Car production was not resumed after 1918, although occasional one-offs for family and business contacts and cars for commercial travellers on van chassis were sometimes built.

Thomas White had died in 1914 and Rollin left to start the Cleveland Motor Plow Co and later build Rollin cars. In 1915 a reorganized firm, White Motor Co, bought out the vehicle business for $16 million, although the old company was used for marketing purposes until 1938. In 1927 Rollin's brothers, Walter and Windsor, left the board.

Commercial vehicle production then occupied the company until it went bankrupt in 1980. In 1932, when production was down to 3850 vehicles, Studebaker acquired 95 per cent control. Some Studebaker-Pierce-Arrow trucks were made by White, which regained its independence in 1934. Two years before, some remarkable horizontally-opposed, 12-cylinder engines were used first in buses and then trucks. A wide assortment of military vehicles, notably 4000 half-tracks and 20,000 scout cars, were built during World War II.

A spate of takeovers added Sterling in 1951, Autocar in 1953, Superior Diesel in 1955, Reo in 1957, Diamond T in 1958 and bodymaker Montpelier Manufacturing Co in 1959. In 1960 White bought the Oliver Corporation. It also purchased Rollin White's Cletrac, whose crawlers were made in Cleveland until 1960. In 1966 the Hupp Corporation's Hercules Engine Division was bought and in the following year a factory was established in British Columbia to make Western Star trucks. In 1968 the Euclid construction vehicle business was bought, as was the Alco engine range from Studebaker-Worthington in 1969.

Financial difficulties in the 1970s led White to shed many of its interests, including Diamond-Reo in 1975, Euclid (to Daimler-Benz) in 1977 and the farm machinery business in 1980 to TIC Investment Corporation. White lost $51 million in its final 15 months.

In 1981 Volvo bought White and its Autocar subsidiary for the equivalent of £38 million to create the Volvo-White Truck Corporation. The Canadian firm was bought locally for £13 million and became Canadian Western Star Trucks Inc in 1981. Silchester Holdings bought the Australian assembly plant, which was then supplied with ckd kits from Canada. The original Cleveland plant made its last vehicle in 1978 and manufacture subsequently took place at Ogden, Utah (Autocar's base), and Dublin, Virginia. NB

WHITLOCK
GB 1903-1932

Despite its life, on paper, of 29 years, the Whitlock was a rather obscure car which made little mark on the motoring scene at any time. Henry Whitlock Ltd was an old-established coachbuilder of Holland Gate, London. The company was founded in 1778 and was able to describe itself in 1903 as 'Coachbuilders to the Royal Family, and Motor Car Manufacturers'. It is unlikely that the firm was a manufacturer as early as 1903, for the Whitlock-Century which it was selling was almost certainly a Willesden-built Century.

The Whitlock-Century was still being advertised in 1905, but by this date a separate company had been formed, with £10,000 capital, called the Whitlock Automobile Co. It advertised the Whitlock-Aster, with a French-built chassis and English coachwork, in several sizes from 10/12hp (two cylinders) to 24/30hp (four cylinders). The smaller cars had armoured wood frames, the larger ones pressed steel. A 12/14hp tourer ran in the 1905 Tourist Trophy but without success.

Wikov 1½-litre sports model of 1934

So far Whitlock could not be described as a car manufacturer in the usual sense, and nothing is known of the provenance of a very small car with 883cc monobloc four-cylinder engine which was advertised at £200 in 1906 under the name Whitlock Ideal. Although this engine has not been traced elsewhere, it is highly unlikely that it was made at Holland Gate, which was clearly a coachbuilding premises.

In 1912 the two Whitlock companies were bought by J. A. Lawton-Goodman Ltd, a Liverpool coachbuilding company established as J. A. Lawton & Co in 1871 which built quite a number of bodies on Rolls-Royce and Napier chassis. Premises were acquired in Cricklewood Broadway, north-west London, and in 1914 two cars were advertised under the name Lawton; these were a 12/16 and a 20/30 at chassis prices of £295 and £495 respectively. For 1915 and 1916 the same cars at the same prices were advertised under the name Whitlock, but whether any were made or where they came from is unknown.

The Whitlock's next appearance was more substantial, for a light car was exhibited at the 1922 London Motor Show. A two-seater powered by an 11hp Coventry-Simplex engine, it was catalogued with several body styles; there was also a slightly larger version with 11.9hp Anzani engine. Judging by the lack of reference to them in the press except at motor show time, few were probably made.

The same goes for the later, and larger, Whitlocks. These included a Light Six of 1924-26, powered by a 2-litre Coventry Climax engine that went into the almost equally obscure 16/50 Waverley, made only a few miles away at Trenmar Gardens, off the Harrow Road.

From 1927 the smaller Whitlocks were dropped in favour of a 20/70hp powered by a 2973cc six-cylinder Meadows 6EP, as used by Invicta. This was a better-looking car than its predecessors, with a Bentley-style radiator and wire wheels from 1928. Chassis price was £600, complete cars selling from £675 to £750. The 1928 and later models used the enlarged 3301cc version of the 6EP engine, and in 1930 the Bentley-style radiator was replaced by a flat-fronted design.

Although the 20/70 was listed until 1936, Whitlock's last motor show was 1929 and it is unlikely that production, such as it was, continued beyond 1931 or 1932. According to Meadows delivery figures not more than seven 20/70s were made, five of which were at the 1929 show, and the only known surviving Whitlock of any kind is one of the last, flat-radiatored models.

Lawton-Goodman, which built all the coachwork on the vintage Whitlocks, also worked on other chassis and made a saloon on a 25/30 Rolls-Royce as late as 1937. Thereafter the company concentrated on trailers and commercial bodywork such as ice-cream vans. GNG

WIKOV
CZECHOSLOVAKIA 1925-1937

The Wikov was made by a firm of agricultural engineers, Wichterle & Kovarik of Prostějov, which was founded in 1918. There was nothing agricultural about the cars, however, which were made under Ansaldo licence and featured four-cylinder single-overhead cam engines, initially of 1480cc capacity but rising later to 1750 and 1960cc. Production was never large, running at about 100 cars a year in the 1920s.

In 1929 came a sports model of the 1½-litre car, which could exceed 100mph (160kph) when equipped with a supercharger. The company's best-known driver, A. Szcyzcycki, achieved many successes in rallies and races, including the 1930 and 1931 International High Tatra Rallies and the 1931 Polish Grand Prix.

The larger engines were mostly used in

touring Wikovs, including some which were fitted with streamlined Jaray bodies, and in commercial vehicles such as 1½-ton trucks and fire engines. In 1933 a prototype 3½-litre straight-eight, again Ansaldo-based, was built but it was never put into production.

Vehicles were always a sideline to Wikov's agricultural products, which included tractors, ploughs, harrows and rollers. Only 70 cars were made in 1934, dwindling to 52 in 1935, 35 in 1936 and 17 in 1937, the last year of passenger car production. Trucks were produced for a few years more, the last being a series of 28 made in 1940 for the German army of occupation. After World War II the company name was changed to Agrostoj, and as such continues to make farm machinery. GNG

WILKINSON
see Deemster

WILLS SAINTE CLAIRE
USA 1921-1927

Childe Harold Wills, named after the hero of Byron's poem *Childe Harold's Pilgrimage*, was born in 1878. He was an early partner of Henry Ford, joining Ford & Malcolmson in 1902. He became production manager and chief engineer; among his major contributions were the design of Ford's planetary transmission and the introduction of vanadium steel. By 1919 he was disenchanted with Henry Ford's refusal to update his cars, and left the company with a settlement of nearly $1.6 million.

He was now in a position to form his own car company, the C. H. Wills Co, and set about building not only a factory but a model town containing workers' homes, schools and a park. This was supervised by an ex-Ford man, John R. Lee, who was one of the leading social planners of his day. The town was named Maryville, after Wills' wife, and the cars were christened Wills Sainte Claire after Lake Sainte Claire near Detroit.

The Wills Sainte Claire was an advanced car with a comparatively small 4.3-litre V8 engine which had a single-overhead camshaft to each bank of cylinders. Surprisingly the cylinder heads were non-detachable, which proved a mechanic's nightmare, and led to the adoption of a detachable head six-cylinder engine.

Announced in August 1920, the Wills Sainte Claire did not get into production until March 1921. Despite plans to build 10,000 a year, only 1532 were made in 1921 and many remained unsold at the end of the year. The price had risen from a planned $2000 to $2875, but 1921 was a slump year for the American car industry anyway. Matters improved in 1922, when 2840 cars were built, and with the several hundred unsold 1921

cars finding buyers total sales exceeded 3000, the best the company would ever achieve.

Profits did not equal sales, however, and Wills lost money on every car made. By the end of 1922 the company was $8 million in debt. Wills was temporarily ousted from control but came back with the support of the Boston financial firm Kidder, Peabody & Co, which reorganized the Maryville company as Wills Sainte Claire Inc and appointed its nominee, Asa Nelson, as president. C. H. Wills was vice-president.

In 1925 a 4½-litre six was introduced and this became the mainstay of the company, although the V8 was available up to the end of production two years later. Sales hovered around the 2000 mark from 1924 to 1926 but could not get Wills Sainte Claire into profit.

The company was liquidated in 1927. Wills himself was in debt to the tune of $4 million, but he eventually managed to pay it all back. He was later on the board of New Era Motors Inc, sponsors of the Ruxton, and from 1933 until his death in 1940 he was chief metallurgist at Chrysler. GNG

WILLYS
USA 1908-1963

The complex story of cars carrying the Willys name started four years before John North Willys (1873-1935) came on the scene. The Standard Wheel Co of Terre Haute, Indiana, was one of the largest wheelmakers in the country, and in June 1902 the company opened an automobile department. Initially this had a staff of one, a young polytechnic graduate called Claude E. Cox who was sent around various car-makers to study the current designs.

The machine he subsequently produced was in advance of most of its contemporaries in that, although a light single-cylinder runabout, its engine was front-mounted under a bonnet rather than under the seat. It was christened the Overland and about a dozen were made during 1903, selling for $595. By the end of the year Standard Wheel had agencies in Chicago, New York, Philadelphia, Pittsburgh, Indianapolis and Cleveland.

A two-cylinder model came in 1904, of which 25 were sold, and in January 1905 production was moved to another factory belonging to Standard Wheel in Indianapolis. This proved unsuitable for car manufacture, which Standard Wheel's President Charles Minshall decided to give up.

Cox found a new partner in buggy builder David M. Parry, and they set up the Overland Auto Co in 1906, Parry with 51 per cent of the stock and Cox with 49 per cent and the responsibility of producing the cars. He built two models, a 9/10hp two-cylinder and a 16/18hp four-cylinder, but production was erratic, and in November 1907 a dealer from Elmira, New York, called John North Willys

came to Indianapolis to find out why his cars hadn't been delivered as promised.

Willys was a successful dealer who numbered among his agencies Pierce, Rambler, American Underslung – and Overland. He sold 47 of the Overland in 1906 – the entire output – and ordered 500 in 1907. When he got to Indianapolis he found the Overland company in a very bad way, with virtually no components for making cars and a dwindling workforce.

As he had $1000 invested in the company he decided to revitalize it, talked the creditors into waiting a while, and built 465 cars in a circus tent in 1908. The next year he bought a large factory in Toledo, Ohio, where the Pope Toledo car had been made, and turned out 4907 cars to make a net profit of $1 million. On the way he had lost Claude Cox, who disapproved of Willys's barnstorming style and went on to a varied and successful career in the motor industry.

Willys Overland four-cylinder double phaeton of 1908

With the move to Toledo the company became the Willys-Overland Co, a name that was retained for the next 54 years. The new factory soon had a payroll of 5000, who turned out 15,598 cars in 1910. The cars were conventional four-cylinder machines of 25 or 40hp selling at prices from $1000 to $1500. In 1911 Willys was third in the US production league, behind Ford and Studebaker-EMF, and from 1912 to 1918 he held second place consistently. His peak year at this time was 1916, when 142,779 cars were made.

Most of these were the popular four-cylinder models selling at about $600, but in 1914 he joined the sleeve-valve brigade by buying the Edwards Motor Co, maker of the Edwards-Knight four-cylinder sleeve-valve car. He had also acquired, in 1912, the majority stock in the Garford company, and used its factory at Elyria, Ohio, to build the Willys-Knight, which was the Edwards-Knight renamed. From 1915 the Elyria factory was used for engine manufacture only, the rest of the car being made at Toledo.

Another aspect of Willys's empire building was his purchase in 1913 of the Gramm Motor Truck Co of Lima, Ohio. There he built a 1½-ton truck which was the first vehicle actually to bear the name Willys, preceding the Willys-Knight by one year. He sold Gramm in 1915 but continued to market the trucks during the years of World War I, and again from 1927 to 1931. Other acquisitions at this time included the Electric Auto Lite Corporation of Toledo, Warner Gear and Tillotson Carburetter, also of Toledo, Morrow Manufacturing Co of Elmira, New York, New Process Gear Co of Syracuse, New York, and Fisk Rubber Co of Chicopee Falls, Massachusetts.

The Willys-Knight was in the low to middle price bracket, selling for $1095 in 1914, which made it the cheapest Knight-engined car in the world. Even a short-lived V8 of 1917-18 cost less than $2000. By the 1920s Willys was making more sleeve-valve engines than all other car-makers combined, producing about 49,000 cars in 1923. Even this was small beer compared with the 130,000 Overlands built in the same year.

Willys plunged into the war effort earlier than most American manufacturers, for he was in France when war broke out and secured contracts for several thousand light trucks and ambulances. When the United States entered the war in April 1917 he embarked on a massive scheme to convert his plants for war production, although it was a year before he began to manufacture Sunbeam aero engines for the British and Curtiss OX-5 aero engines for the US government. On 1 November 1918 he announced that all passenger car production would be suspended in favour of military goods, but 11 days later the war ended.

However, he wasn't back into production for long before a disastrous strike hit the Toledo plants, largely because Willys was away in New York and negotiations were badly handled by his deputy, Clarence Earl. Attempts to hire non-union labour led to rioting, 70 men were injured and two were shot dead by an 'auxiliary police force'. Earl closed the plant and Ohio's governor placed the area under martial law. No cars were made from the spring until just before Christmas.

The delay was disastrous for the introduction of the new cheap Overland, which was supposed to rival the Ford Model T at under $500. The increased cost of materials pushed its price up to $845 when it finally did appear, which meant that it was no competitor at all for the Ford.

Added to these problems was the fact that Willys had over expanded, buying the Duesenberg plant and an additional 23 acres (9 hectares) at Elizabeth, New Jersey, just before the post-war recession dampened car sales throughout the industry. At the end of 1919 Willys-Overland owed $18 million to banks and $14 million to suppliers.

The Chase National Bank was willing to extend credit, but only if a manager of its choice was put in to sort things out. The bank's choice was Walter P. Chrysler, who had just given up the presidency of Buick. His price was a free hand in deciding Willys's future, and $1 million a year. He cut Willys's salary from $150,000 to $75,000 a year – which possibly prompted Willys to sell his

house at Pasadena, California, to Chrysler for $200,000 in April 1921.

Chrysler stayed at Willys-Overland for two years, and left it not recovered, but in a less parlous state than when he arrived. He also acquired the designs for a modern low-priced six-cylinder car which was to have been built in the New Jersey plant and which eventually saw the light of day three years later as the Chrysler 70.

John Willys divested himself of the Willys Corporation, a holding company for all his activities except Willys-Overland, and concentrated on his car-making. From 1922 onwards he began to climb back into profits, which reached $20 million in 1925. Production grew from 48,000 in 1921 to 215,000 in 1925. The one millionth Overland was delivered in June 1923.

In 1920 Willys cemented his friendship with William Letts of Crossley in England by forming Willys-Overland-Crossley Ltd, which would assemble Overland cars in a wartime extension factory at Heaton Chapel in Cheshire. The cars were given British lighting and trim, and also right hand drive. In 1924 came a hybrid in the shape of an Overland powered by a 1.8-litre Morris Oxford engine. From 1926 to 1933 Willys-Overland-Crossley made a range of trucks which became increasingly British in design.

Overland and Willys-Knight cars were little changed in the years 1920 to 1926, and were joined in 1925 by a larger and more expensive sleeve-valve car, the Stearns-Knight. In 1926 came the Overland Whippet, a 2.2-litre four which in 1927 was priced at just $545, $5 less than the Model A Ford. Willys had undercut Henry at last – and was rewarded by the company's best year ever in 1928, with 315,000 cars sold, 55,000 of which were Willys-Knights. His prices ran from the $545 Whippet Four coupé to the $5800 Stearns-Knight eight-cylinder sedan limousine.

In the summer of 1929 Willys sold his holdings in Willys-Overland for $21 million, and in March 1930 he became the first United States ambassador to Poland. This appointment lasted a little over two years, for in May

1932 he was recalled by President Hoover who thought his talents would be more valuable at home, dealing with the ravages that the Depression had wrought at Toledo.

For 1933 Willys dropped the Knight and all other models except for a new small car using a slightly smaller version of the Whippet engine (2197cc, 48bhp) in a new body which had some pretensions to streamlining with semi faired-in headlamps. The Willys 77 was no beauty, but it sold more than 45,000 in four years and helped the company through a receivership which began in February 1933, brought about by the closure of several Detroit banks. The 77 outlived its creator, who died of a heart attack in August 1935, undoubtedly brought on by his constant struggles to keep his company afloat.

Willys-Overland was still in receivership at the time of John Willys's death, and court permission had to be secured every time a new run of 5000 cars was planned. The 77 sold sufficiently well for the receivership to end in February 1936, when David R. Wilson, president of the Wilson Foundry & Machine Co of Pontiac, Michigan, and the court appointed trustee, became president of the newly constituted Willys-Overland Motors Inc. Board chairman was Ward Canaday, who had joined the company in 1916 in advertising and sales.

The 77 was completely restyled for 1937, when the new Model 37 sold 76,803 units. Styling was updated during the final years of peace, but the small side-valve engine remained basically unchanged until passenger car production was dropped in favour of the Jeep early in 1942. It was a handy and economical little car, but Americans were still wedded to the full-size six-passenger sedan with an engine of 3½ litres or more. Willys sales remained at the bottom of the league, at around 25,000 to 28,000 in 1939-41.

Barney Roos, who had worked for Pierce-Arrow, Marmon, Studebaker and the Rootes group, was chief engineer from 1938, and Joseph W. Frazer was president in 1939-43. The 1941 models were called Americars.

The Jeep was the saviour of the Willys for-

Willys Overland tourer of 1923

tunes. Although designed by Karl Probst of American Bantam, it was made in quantity only by Willys and Ford, some 361,000 coming from Toledo between 1941 and 1945. The engine was the same 2.2 litre until that had powered the Willys 77, with output increased to 54bhp.

Even while Willys was turning out Jeeps as rapidly as it could, the company was thinking about post-war production and hired the stylist Brooks Stevens to design a Jeep-based passenger car. One was built, but after it was destroyed in an accident in 1943 the plan was abandoned. Another stylist, John Tjaarda, who was responsible for the Lincoln Zephyr, proposed a series of Jeep-based cars to be built internationally, in the USA, Mexico, Britain, France and Sweden.

Nothing came of this, but the idea of Jeep-derived cars appealed to Joe Frazer's successor, Charles Sorensen, who had worked for Ford since 1905. The result was the Jeep Station Wagon and the Jeepster, an open four-passenger sports phaeton, introduced in 1946 and 1948 respectively. A 2.4-litre six was available from 1948, and two years later the four received an F-head which raised output to 72bhp.

These Jeep variants, together with civilian models of the classic military Jeep, kept Willys going until it introduced its first post-war car in 1952. This was the Aero, a compact sedan powered by a 2.6-litre version of the 1948 six-cylinder engine. Designed by Clyde Paton, the Aero was eventually made in two- and four-door sedan models, and as a hardtop coupé, the Aero Eagle.

It was well received by the press, but was too expensive to sell in large numbers. The cheapest Aero cost $1731 in 1952, when you could get a six-cylinder Ford for $1525 and a Plymouth for $1551. Nevertheless 31,363 found buyers in 1952 and a total of 41,814 in 1953.

In April 1953 Kaiser Manufacturing Co bought a controlling interest in Willys, the outcome being a change of name for the Toledo company to Kaiser-Willys Sales Division of Willys Motors Inc. Kaiser's 3.7-litre six-cylinder engine became available in the Aero, but although acceleration was improved, maximum speed only went up by 1.5mph (2.4kph), and fuel consumption was worse. Aero sales plummeted to only 8240 in 1954 and 5897 in 1955. This was the last year for the Aero, after which Kaiser-Willys concentrated on various models of Jeep.

In 1954 Willys licensed the French Hotchkiss company to manufacture the Jeep. This provided useful outlets in countries whose shortage of dollars prevented them from buying Jeeps direct from Toledo.

The Aero had a further lease of life in Brazil, where a version restyled by Brooks Stevens was made from 1960 to 1972, latterly by Ford Brasil SA, which had taken over Willys-Overland do Brasil SA in 1967. In 1963 Kaiser-Willys changed its name to the Kaiser-Jeep Corporation. GNG

Winton Bullet I racer of 1922

WILSON-PILCHER
see Armstrong-Whitworth

WINDHOFF
GERMANY 1908-1914

In 1904 Maschinenfabrik Windhoff & Co, a machinery manufacturing company run by the brothers Hans and Ernst Windhoff in Rheine, Westphalia, began building various proprietary automobile components, including engines, gearboxes, steering gear, radiators and axles. In 1907 the automobile parts branch of the company, Gebruder Windhoff Motoren und Fahrzeugfabrik, opened a new factory to build complete cars, the first of which went on sale in 1908.

Two four-cylinder and two six-cylinder models were offered at first, ranging from the 2-litre W4 to the 6.1-litre H6, and Windhoff entered two 3-litre 28PS six-cylinder W6 cars in the 1908 Prince Henry Trials, where they finished without penalty. The cars were well built, almost entirely in Windhoff's own works, and technically quite advanced. In 1909 a 2.6-litre four-cylinder 25PS model, the J4, was introduced and as production increased Windhoff began to buy in some bodies, which were originally all built in-house, from Karmann.

In 1911 Windhoff was preparing a completely new range of cars, which was introduced in 1912. It included the 1.5-litre 6/18PS and 2.6-litre 10/30PS four-cylinder Types B and A and the 3.9-litre 15/40PS six-cylinder Type C, which was probably the best of several well thought of Windhoff designs. The largest of the Windhoff range was the 17/45PS Type F, but only small numbers were built.

Windhoff stopped car production in 1914 upon the outbreak of World War I, and after the war reverted to building only components for other makes, the best known of these being radiators. From 1924 to 1933 Windhoff built some highly regarded motorcycles, including a remarkable shaft-drive model in 1927 which effectively used its oil-cooled 746cc four-cylinder engine in place of a conventional frame. BL

WINTON
USA 1898-1924

Scots-born Alexander Winton (1860-1932) founded the Winton Bicycle Co in Cleveland, Ohio, in 1891 and began to experiment with cars in 1896. The Winton Motor Carriage Co was formed on 1 March 1897 with capital of $200,000 and a factory was acquired from the Brush Electrical Co. Bicycles continued to be made at the original factory until at least 1899.

After numerous trials and long distance runs, Winton went into production with a light 1-cylinder two-passenger motor buggy, making his first sale in March 1898. Production that year was 22 buggies and eight delivery wagons, rising to more than 100 vehicles in 1899, which made the company the largest producer of petrol engined cars in the United States. (Columbia electrics and Locomobile steamers were still comfortably ahead, and the latter remained at the top of the US production league until 1903.)

The 1901 Wintons featured steering wheels, an innovation shared with their fellow Ohio make, Packard. The company also supplied steering gears to Autocar of Ardmore, Pennsylvania. Capital was increased to $1 million and a successful racing programme was begun, which led to a new 15hp two-cylinder car for 1902.

A new 11-acre (4-hectare) factory and a seven-storey downtown sales building and garage were acquired in 1902. The following year's sales, now exclusively of the two-cylinder model, were up to 850. Four-cylinder cars came in 1904, priced at up to $3200, and branches were opened in New York and London.

In 1908 a range of six-cylinder cars was launched and Winton claimed that it was the only automobile manufacturer in the world producing solely six-cylinder cars. In 1909 1200 cars were sold, all expensive sixes of 48 and 60hp with prices rising to $5750.

A new and ultimately very significant direction was taken in 1912 with the setting up of the Winton Gas Engine Manufacturing Co to make stationary and marine diesel engines. A cheaper line of six-cylinder cars came out in

Wolseley four-seat tonneau of 1903

Wolseley 21hp landaulette of 1913

1915, priced from $2285 to $3500, and by 1920 these accounted for more than 98 per cent of the year's 2500 cars. This was the last successful year for Winton cars, as the 1921 recession brought sales down to 325 cars and the plant was working at only 30 per cent capacity.

Business improved a little in 1922, when 690 cars were sold, but in November 1923 Alexander Winton offered his diesel engine plant as a separate venture and asked stockholders if they wished to continue or liquidate the car business. They chose to liquidate, and the last Winton car was built on 11 February 1924. The Winton Engine works were continued, and became General Motors' Cleveland Diesel Engine Division in 1930. It was closed down in 1961. GNG

WOLSELEY
GB 1896-1975

The Wolseley was one of Britain's most respected makes of car for much of its life, and was guided by three of the country's leading motor magnates – Herbert Austin, John Davenport Siddeley and William Morris. Yet the company never had an independent existence, being owned by Vickers for its first 26 years and Morris thereafter.

Frederick York Wolseley (1837-99) was the third of four sons, the eldest of whom became Field Marshal Sir Garnet (later Viscount) Wolseley, one of the leading British soldiers of his time. Frederick went to Australia, where he set up the Wolseley Sheep Shearing Machine Co Ltd in Sydney in 1887. Two years later he formed a British company as the quality of the Australian-made machines was not satisfactory, but at first he fared no better in England.

His premises in Broad Street, Birmingham, were the assembly point for components supplied by a variety of small engineering firms, and some of them were of very poor quality. Wolseley resigned in 1894, and the company

would probably have gone under had not the young works manager, Herbert Austin (1866-1941), persuaded the directors to set up a factory where all the components would be made under his supervision. In 1895 the business moved to Aston, Birmingham, where it added to its range of products, machine tools, bicycle parts and some complete bicycles.

In the autumn of 1895 Austin made one of several visits to France, where he was particularly struck by the Léon Bollée three-wheeled voiturette. During the winter he built a car of his own on Bollée lines but using a horizontally opposed two-cylinder engine in place of the French car's single cylinder. He did not proceed with this car, as its similarity to the Bollée would have rendered him liable to prosecution from the holders of the Bollée patents, the British Motor Syndicate Ltd.

Instead he built another three-wheeler on more individual lines, with single front-wheel and back-to-back seating for two, which was shown at the National Cycle Exhibition in December 1896. This met with the approval of the Wolseley directors, who issued a catalogue of the car, which they called the Wolseley Autocar Number 1. It was priced at £110 as a two-seater and £150 as a four-seater. In fact only the one was ever made. A four-seater would have necessitated a complete redesign, as it was much too narrow for side-by-side seating.

Herbert Austin's first four-wheeler was built during the latter part of 1899 and had several features used on subsequent production cars. These included a horizontal single cylinder engine mounted at the front, a large radiator which was wrapped around the bonnet, and chain final drive. Austin drove this car in the 1000 Mile Trial held in the spring of 1900, and his creditable performance brought orders for replicas, which were priced at £270. A steering wheel replaced the tiller on a second four-wheeler of 1900, but it seems that few, if any, cars were delivered to customers under the auspices of the Wolseley Sheep Shearing Machine Co Ltd.

For several years Herbert Austin had been friendly with the American-born machine-gun inventor Sir Hiram Maxim, to whom he had supplied some components for Maxim's steam-powered aeroplane. Maxim was a partner in the big engineering company Vickers Son & Maxim Ltd, and it was through this connection that Vickers bought the car-making interests from the Wolseley Sheep Shearing Machine Co in February 1901. The price was £12,400 in cash plus 67.5 per cent second debentures of £100 each to the company, and 33 of these debentures to Herbert Austin.

The Sheep Shearing Machine Co was free to carry on any business except that of making motor cars. It was still active in the 1920s, making its traditional products as well as horse clipping machines, cream separators and petrol engines. In 1924 Herbert Austin was chairman, despite his involvement in his own company.

Vickers registered the new company with capital of £40,000 as the Wolseley Tool & Autocar Co Ltd, and premises were acquired at Adderley Park, Birmingham, in a factory acquired from the defunct Starley Brothers & Westwood company. The works covered 3½ acres (1.4 hectares), and 323 cars were made during 1901.

There were two models, a 5hp single and 10hp twin, both of similar design with horizontal engines, wrap around radiators and chain drive. The horizontal engined theme was pursued until 1905, with a big 20hp four-cylinder model of 5.2 litres capacity being made from 1902 to 1904.

From 1902 to 1905 some remarkable racing cars were made, which competed in leading events of the day such as the Paris-Vienna, Paris-Madrid and the Gordon Bennett races, although they were never very successful. The 96hp of 1905 had a capacity of 11.9 litres.

Wolseley claimed to have 800 cars on order in 1903 and registered a profit of £12,512, paying a 10 per cent dividend on the ordinary shares. This was the peak of the company's success with the Austin-designed cars, and the following five years saw losses.

Meanwhile John Davenport Siddeley (1866-1953) was selling vertical-engined cars of Peugeot design made at Vickers' works at Crayford, Kent. These began to outsell the horizontal-engined Wolseleys in 1904, and as Austin stubbornly refused to countenance a similar design at Adderley Park, Siddeley was invited to become sales manager for Wolseley. The implied snub was too much for Austin, who resigned as general manager in 1905 and a year later set up as a manufacturer under his own name. Ironically, all his subsequent cars had vertical engines.

A few months after Austin's departure, Siddeley took his place as general manager, and stayed four years. The horizontal-engined cars remained in production through the 1906 season, but they were joined by three vertical-engined four-cylinder cars of 15, 18 and 32hp. These cars became known as Wolseley-Siddeleys, and some just carried the name Siddeley on their hub nuts.

In a speech to more than 100 dealers in November 1906 Siddeley said that the name Wolseley would not, for the present, be attached to the vertical engined cars that the company was building. This led to a feeling among the directors that their new general manager was hogging the limelight, and led eventually to a parting of the ways.

Wolseley made 453 cars in 1906, when the company employed 3000 men. Every part of the cars was made in-house except for the tyres and coils. Steel was supplied from Vickers' steel works at Sheffield.

Commercial vehicles played an important part during the Siddeley era, and during a visit to Adderley Park in 1906 it was noted that there were 24 car chassis and 40 bus chassis under construction. The London General Omnibus Co took over 100 double deckers in 1907, although a petrol-electric version with BTH motors remained a prototype.

Despite the activity on several fronts – aero and marine engines were also produced – Wolseley had made no profit since 1903. It was decided that one of the reasons for this was the widely scattered premises. In 1909, therefore, the company transferred all the machinery from Crayford to Adderley Park and also closed the London head office.

Siddeley departed at this point, joining the Deasy company in Coventry. He later had a very successful career with Armstrong-Siddeley, being knighted in 1933 and created Viscount Kenilworth in 1937. Wolseley's new managing director was Ernest Hopwood, formerly secretary of the British Electric Traction Co.

Design of the cars continued with little change. In 1910 there were five four-cylinder models and three sixes, of which the largest was a massive 60hp of 9875cc capacity. Demand was beginning to pick up, with production well over 1000 cars.

To cope with this the company expanded into the premises of the Metropolitan Railway Carriage & Wagon Co, another Vickers-owned concern, when it moved to the other side of Birmingham. Metropolitan later merged with the rolling stock divison of Cammell Laird, and then with Weymann, to become today's Metro-Cammell-Weymann, maker of MCW buses.

Wolseley used the new works for transmission and chassis assembly. Further expansion took place in 1914, when the Adderley Park factory was extended, but even so there was not sufficient space for the production of a new 9.5hp light car called the Stellite. This was made in the factory of another Vickers company, the Electric & Ordnance Accessories Co of Aston, Birmingham.

In 1913 3000 Wolseleys and 1500 Stellites were made by a total workforce of 5500. Since 1900 the company had made 13,500 vehicles, which put it among the top three or four British manufacturers.

Commercial vehicles had faded out after Siddeley's departure, but in 1912 a new line was developed under the direction of Alfred Remmington (1877-1922), who had joined the company in 1902 and became chief designer in 1905. These were a 12cwt (609kg) van and a 25cwt (1270kg) truck at first, but by 1914 there were six models up to a 5-tonner, which was made during the war.

Other pre-war activities included the manufacture of about 500 two-cylinder taxis from 1906 to 1909, engines for petrol-electric railcars operated by the Delaware & Hudson Co, V12 engines for the Duke of Westminster's racing launch *Ursula*, marine engines for lifeboats and ferry boats made by Saunders of Cowes, Isle of Wight, and aero engines up to a 120hp V8. Two unusual jobs were the manufacture of motor sleighs used in Captain R. F. Scott's Antarctic explorations, and the two-wheeled Gyrocar built to the design of Count Peter Schilowsky in 1912.

In July 1914 the company name was changed to Wolseley Motors Ltd. A month later World War I broke out and the factories were turned over to production of Wolseley Viper V8 aero engines, shells and telescopic gun mountings. From 1917 complete SE5 aeroplanes were made in a special factory, more than 700 being completed by the war's end. Among the 7000 employees during the war were 1300 women. In addition the Electric & Ordnance Co had built a 13,000 employee factory at Ward End for the manufacture of fuses and shell cases.

Like many manufacturers Wolseley emerged from the war with enlarged factory capacity, a substantial bank balance and high hopes for the future. Vickers took over the Ward End factory from its subsidiary in 1919 for £400,000. This was later to become the home of Wolseley under the Morris regime.

The 1919 models were similar to the pre-war 16/20, 24/30 and 30/40 models, but for 1920 Wolseley brought out three new designs with single-overhead cam engines, 10 and 15hp four-cylinder, and 20hp six-cylinder models. The Stellite, which had been revived in 1919, was dropped in favour of the Ten, although the old and well-established Stellite name was used in 1921 for a cheap version of the Ten.

In 1921 production reached a peak of 12,000 cars (commercials were no longer made), but thereafter demand dropped, as it did for so many other car-makers. Vickers had raised over £1.7 million in debenture stock for factory extensions and a lavish new showroom in the West End of London. There was a specific first charge on all the company's assets, and to meet the interest and to provide for redemption over 25 years the company was faced with an annual charge of £140,250. While sales were high this was not too much of a burden, but the slump, not helped by William Morris's drastic price cutting in 1922-23, took its toll. Sales declined markedly.

Wolseley Hornet sports car of 1935

A short-lived 7hp flat twin failed to capture the public's attention. The 1926 range consisted of an improved Ten called the 11/22, a 16/35hp four and 24/55hp six. Only a few hundred of these sold in the first nine months of the year, and in November the old and respected firm of Wolseley was declared bankrupt with liabilities of more than £2 million.

In February 1927 the company was put up for sale, and was bought by William Morris for £730,000. Underbidders were Herbert Austin and General Motors. The firm was renamed Wolseley Motors (1927) Ltd, and was the personal property of Morris until 1935, when he sold it to Morris Motors Ltd. This was because he was not at first sure of how successful it would be, and he did not want to burden his public company with a possible liability. Only when its future was beyond reasonable doubt did Wolseley join the Nuffield group of companies.

Morris quickly realized that one of the causes of the collapse was that factory space was too large for the company's needs. He therefore turned Adderley Park over to his newly-established Morris-Commercial truck line and concentrated Wolseley at Ward End. The mainstay of his new programme was the 16/45hp overhead-cam Silent Six, which had been launched by the old company in the autumn of 1926. This was joined by the four-

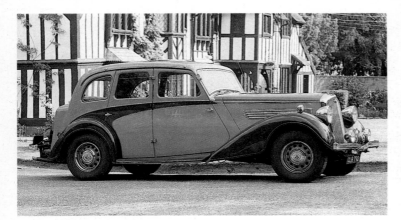

Wolseley 21hp saloon of 1936

Wolseley 4/50 saloon of 1949

cylinder 12/32hp and the straight-eight 21/60hp. Confusingly, in September 1928 there came a six, also called the 21/60, and this survived until 1935.

The eights were made in limited numbers, about 200 of the 21/60 and less than half a dozen of the 4-litre 32/80. None survived after 1931. An enlarged version of the 21/60 eight was used in the Morris-Léon Bollée.

In 1930 came the Hornet, a Morris Minor with lengthened bonnet which accommodated a 1271cc overhead-cam six-cylinder engine. At £175 it was a real bargain, and its much criticized handling did not really become acute until the engine was moved forward on the 1932 models. The Hornet special sports chassis attracted countless custom coachbuilders, of which Swallow, Maltby and Whittingham & Mitchel were the leading ones.

A total of 34,674 Hornets were made between 1930 and 1935, of which 4897 were Hornet Specials sold in chassis form only. The Hornet's engine was also used in the MG Magna.

In 1935 Wolseley became an integral part of the Nuffield empire, and the following year's models bore a distinct family resemblance to the Morris range. The chief differences were overhead-valve engines and better equipped interiors of the Wolseleys, which could be distinguished at night by their illuminated radiator badge, a feature of all models from 1933 to 1972. Many motorists heeded the slogan 'Buy Wisely, Buy Wolseley', and in 1937 sales were 30,000 compared with only 2000 a decade earlier.

The 1939 range consisted of the Ten and 12/48 four-cylinder cars, and five sixes from the 1.8-litre 14/60 to the 3½-litre 25, nearly all of which had their slightly cheaper equivalents in the Morris range. Planned for 1940, but delayed six years because of the war, was Wolseley's version of the Series E Morris Eight, with Wolseley radiator and non-faired headlights.

At the beginning of World War II the Ward End works received a contract to make Morris-Commercial's six-wheel War Office truck, of which 6000 were built until 1942. They also made 22,000 bren gun carriers, being the largest producer of tracked vehicles in the

528

country, 600 ambulance conversions on a variety of chassis, wings for the Horsa glider, and countless shell fuses and mines. Total wartime earnings of the Wolseley factory were £30 million.

A government order for some 18/85s enabled car production to be resumed in September 1945; there followed Tens, Twelves, Fourteens and the delayed Eight. All these were replaced in October 1948 by the 4/50 and 6/80, Wolseley versions of the Morris Oxford and Six.

In January 1949 production of Wolseleys was moved from Ward End to Cowley, near Oxford, where they were made on parallel assembly lines to Morrises although, it was said, 'with the same degree of individual attention, care and craftsmanship which has always been associated with the name of Wolseley since its first introduction'. Ward End was used for the manufacture of the Oxford taxicab from early 1947 to 1952, about 1800 being made.

In 1952 Morris and Austin merged to form the British Motor Corporation, and from then onwards the Wolseley's individuality was gently but firmly phased out. The overhead-cam engine disappeared in January 1953 with the demise of the 4/50, and the last Nuffield engine went with the replacement of the 4/44 by the Austin-powered 1½-litre 15/50 in the summer of 1956.

More interesting was the 1500, a mating of the 1½-litre B-series engine with a Morris Minor chassis and a compact four-door saloon body. There were 100,832 Wolseley versions of the car made between 1957 and 1965, as well as a Riley variant and, in Australia, Austin and Morris-badged versions. Otherwise the remaining Wolseleys were variants on the Mini, 1100/1300 and Austin 1800.

The last Wolseley was part of the BL 18/22 range, with transverse 2.2-litre engine, front wheel drive and Hydragas suspension. In September 1975 this range was renamed Princess, and the Wolseley name disappeared. GNG

WOLVERINE
see Reo

WOODILL
USA 1952-1958

This car was built by Woody Woodill, a Willys dealer from Downey, California. It used a fibreglass two-seater sports body supplied by Glasspar, F-head Willys 90hp engine and Willys-based chassis built by the hot rod expert Harold ('Shorty') Post.

It was first shown in Los Angeles in November 1952; Willys was very enthusiastic and wanted Woodill to build it in large numbers for them. It could have become Willys's answer to the Corvette – in fact it was released several months before the Corvette – but the Willys merger with Kaiser in 1953 put the Wildfire up against the Kaiser Darrin 161, and as the latter was already tooled up, it won out against the California car.

Woodill went ahead on his own, though, selling the Wildfire as a kit, to be powered by Ford, Buick or Cadillac engines. Most of the 300 kits plus 10 to 15 built up cars sold were Ford powered, and all but one fast-back coupé were open two-seaters.

The expected kit car boom was torpedoed by the arrival of successful complete sports cars such as the Corvette, Thunderbird and Triumph TR, and Woodill gave up in 1958. GNG

WOODS
USA 1899-1918

The Woods Motor Vehicle Co was founded in Chicago early in 1899, with a capital of $10 million, in an attempt to provide a Midwest challenge to the powerful East Coast Electric Vehicle Co, which made the Columbia. Finance came from several wealthy Chicago businessmen, and the name was provided by Clinton E. Woods, who had been designing electric cars since 1897 and who was appointed works superintendent.

Early Woods vehicles were modified horse-drawn carriages and very few were made before the company went into receivership in the autumn of 1901. By then Clinton

Woods had left the firm, which was reorganized on much more successful lines in 1902. Three years later a new factory enabled annual production to be tripled to 500. Sixteen styles were listed for 1903, including a hansom cab, full mail phaeton, delivery vans and a rear entrance tonneau with a dummy bonnet to give the appearance of a petrol car.

Genuine petrol-engined cars with 40/45hp four-cylinder engines were made from 1905 to 1907, after which Woods reverted to electrics, mostly enclosed broughams. Prices were high, in the range of $2100 to $4000. When the popularity of electric cars began to wane, Woods brought out the unusual Woods Dual Power coupé in which the electric motor powered the vehicle up to 15mph (24kph), after which a four-cylinder petrol engine took over, for speeds up to a maximum of 35mph (56kph). Regenerative braking was provided through the electric motor.

The 1916 Dual Power used an engine of Woods' own make, but for 1917 a Continental engine was employed in a longer wheelbase chassis. The price was increased from $2650 to $2950. The Dual Power was the only Woods model for the 1917 and 1918 seasons, but production ended in the autumn of the latter year. GNG

WOODS MOBILETTE
USA 1914-1917

The makers of the Woods Mobilette proclaimed it to be 'America's First Cyclecar' in its advertising, presumably on the strength of a prototype that had been built in 1910, for it did not go on sale until early 1914, when probably 20 to 30 hopefuls had already launched their little machines on an unsuspecting world. With a 12hp four-cylinder engine, two-speed gearbox and shaft drive, it was more of a light car than many of its contemporaries, but its narrow track of 36in (914mm) necessitated tandem seating.

Some cyclecars could be garaged on the front porch, but for those who did not have a porch, let alone a garage, the manufacturer offered some practical advice: 'Get some rough lumber and build a box 4½ feet high, 3½ feet wide and 8½ or 9 feet long with a door at one end. Into this box the car can be placed and locked up safe from storms, thieves, etc.' The Mobilette cost $380 free-on-board (fob) Harvey, Illinois, plus $15 for a windscreen and hood.

Staggered side-by-side seating appeared on the 1916 models, which also offered electric lighting and starting as extras. These were standardized for 1917, but the Mobilette did not last out the year. Even so, it had outlived all other American cyclecars. GNG

WYSS
see Saurer

YLN
TAIWAN 1953 to date

The Yue Loong Engineering Co Ltd of Taipei, Taiwan, was founded in 1953 to manufacture various models of Datsun under licence. This has remained the company's main business ever since, although it had a licence agreement with the Aichi Machine Industry Co Ltd to make Cony light utility vehicles in the 1960s, and also makes Jeeps under licence from American Motors Corporation. In 1960 the company name was changed to Yue Loong Motor Co Ltd.

The most popular Datsun/Nissan models to have been made by Yue Loong are the Bluebird, Cedric and Sunny. Local content is about 60 per cent, with the balance coming from Japan. There are minor styling differences between the Taiwanese and Japanese products, as well as different names to suit the different market.

The 1984 range consisted of the YLN 311SD (Nissan Sunny), 721 (Nissan Stanza 1600) and 807GX (Nissan Cedric body shell with 2.4-litre six-cylinder engine). Yue Loong also makes pickup trucks of Nissan design, scooters and stationary engines. In 1985 output was 58,221 cars. GNG

YORK
see Pullman

Z Disk torpedo of 1924

Z/ZETKA
CZECHOSLOVAKIA 1923-1939

The Zbrojovka factory was established at Brno to make arms in 1918. Falling demand after World War I led to the production of alternative products, including textile machinery. In 1923 a prototype car known as the Z or Zetka (an abbreviation of the long company title) was made in Switzerland and then five copies were built at Brno.

Bretislav Novotny, later of Aero, was the designer and production started in February 1924. Small two-stroke cars were the norm, although more complex competition types were built, including in 1931 an eight-cylinder 1500cc two-stroke that had two parallel banks of cylinders. In 1925 the Z-18 twin-cylinder 990cc car designed by Souček and Lenz was substituted for the original single-cylinder Disk model.

In 1931 a total of 2129 Zs were in use. Subsequent production peaked at 953 in 1934 and then dropped away and ended in 1939. The company then built arms again.

At the end of World War II Dr F. Musil and Dr J. Miksch developed a light tractor that was entrusted to the Zbrojovka group, by then nationalized, and a new factory was built for the production of weapons, textile machinery, ZKL bearings and Zetor tractors (which still use the Z emblem in a rifled barrel as a trade mark). More than 500,000 Zetors have now been built, additional assembly taking place in India, Iraq and Burma. NB

ZAPOROZHETS
SOVIET UNION 1960 to date

The Zaporozhets marked a move by the Soviet motor industry into the small car market with a vehicle in the Fiat 600 class. Made in the Communard tractor factory at Zaporozh'ye in the Ukraine, the original ZAZ-965 had a rear-mounted 746cc V4 engine and a monocoque two-door saloon body, with all-independent suspension. Engine capacity later went up to 887cc and then to 1197cc but the car was largely unchanged until 1967, when a new body reminiscent of the NSU was introduced. This is still made today under the designation ZAZ-968M.

In 1965 a 4×4 utility vehicle with front-mounted engine was produced by the Communard works. Known as the LUAZ-969, it is still made today. A few Zaporozhets 966s were sold in western Europe under the name Yalta and powered by a 956cc Renault R8 engine. Although no longer exported, the Zaporozhets still sells well in its homeland. About 145,000 were made in 1984. GNG

ZASTAVA
YUGOSLAVIA 1954 to date

Crevena Zastava (Red Flag) is Fiat's operation in Yugoslavia, where cars went into production at Kragujevac in a factory which had been founded in 1853 to make agricultural implements. The first models built were the Fiat 1400 and 1900, soon joined by the 600 which became the most popular Zastava; the same body is still made today, 14 years after it went out of production in Italy. By 1962 the factory had been considerably extended and could turn out 82,000 cars a year.

During the 1960s the Fiats 1100, 1300, 1500, 124, 125 and Polski-Fiat 125P were all made by Zastava. In 1971 came the Yugoslav variant of the Fiat 128, known as the Zastava 101. This had a restyled rear panel, and later came in a hatchback version which was never made at Turin. For 1983 Zastava brought out the Yugo 45, a three-door hatchback based on the Fiat 127 but with different styling.

This formed part of the 1985 range, together with the 750LE and 850 rear-engined cars using the old Fiat 600 body shell, and the 101 in 1100 or 1300 form. In Britain and most export markets the cars are sold under the name Yugo. In 1982 Zastava had 48,261 employees and production that year was 150,432 cars. GNG

ZÉDEL
see Donnet-Zédel

ZELE
ITALY 1974 to date

The Zele is an electrically-powered town car, introduced in 1974 by the famous Italian coachbuilder Zagato and built in Milan by a branch of the company, Zagato Car srl. Ugo Zagato, born in 1890, had worked in Germany between 1905 and 1909 then returned to his native Italy and worked in coachbuilding and aeronautical engineering before concentrating on coachbuilding full-time after World War I.

He built special bodies for Fiats and then for Alfa-Romeo competition cars from the late 1920s. He continued to build many bodies, particularly for Alfas, and in 1937 he founded Carrozzeria Ugo Zagato & Co, which became Carrozzeria Zagato SA in 1942 and Carrozzeria Zagato SpA in 1962.

In 1936 Ugo was joined by his elder son Elio, and in 1955 by his younger son Gianni. When Ugo died, in 1968, Elio took over the company – which still concentrated mainly on competition and GT designs.

The plastic bodied Zele was something of a departure; it was upright and boxy and less than 78in (1.9m) long. The Zele 1000 was a two-door two-seater saloon, standing on Mini wheels and with a Marelli 24-volt one-kilo-watt motor. It had two-pedal control and three-speed gears controlled by a dashboard switch. With a weight of just over 1100lb (498kg) it offered a top speed of about 25mph (40kph) and a range of about 45 miles (72km). The otherwise identical Zele 2000, which shared the 1000's coil-spring independent front suspension and drum brakes, used a two-kilowatt motor to give a better top speed at about 35mph (56kph) but slightly less range, at only about 30 miles (48km).

The car was marketed briefly in Britain in 1975 by Bristol Cars Ltd, which had long-standing connections with Zagato as coachbuilders. It was very expensive at a British price of £1995 and very few were sold. It fared no better in the United States, where it was sold by the Elcar Corporation of Elkhart, Indiana, but it is still available in Italy, now with all independent suspension. BL

ZETA
AUSTRALIA 1964-1967

Unlike earlier Australian austerity prototypes the Zeta was produced at a time of affluence and was intended as a 'second or third car' as much as for basic transport. Lightburn & Co Ltd of Camden, South Australia, first showed the Zeta in 1962. It was bodied in fibreglass but the doors and chassis were made of steel.

The car entered production in 1964 alongside the firm's other lines of concrete mixers, boats and washing machines. A transverse twin-cylinder 324cc Villiers engine drove the front wheels. A sports version based on the Meadows-made Friskysport was also offered, although only about 50 were built. Behind the Zeta project was Gordon Bedson from Kieft, and Gus Stewart, who had started Frisky and later worked at Dennis.

Of Australian new car registrations in 1965 totalling 255,000, Zeta accounted for just 108 – plus five electric powered cars apparently called Lightburn rather than Zeta. Reliability problems on long journeys and a general dislike of small cars in Australia caused the demise of the project after three years. Lightburn continued making its other products and also imported and assembled a limited number of Alfa Romeos. NB

ZETKA
see Z

ZIS/ZIL
SOVIET UNION 1936 to date

The Zavod Imieni Stalina factory was built in Moscow in 1924 and operated under the name AMO until 1933, when it was renamed in honour of Joseph Stalin. Commercial vehicles only were made until 1936, when a large

Zastava 101 of c.1975

ZIS-101 saloon of c.1936

ZIL-4104 limousine of 1983

saloon powered by a 5.6-litre overhead-valve straight-eight engine was announced under the name ZIS-101.

The 90bhp engine was based on the Buick Master Eight, the start of American influence on the top line Russian cars which has continued up to the present day. Like its successors in the ZIS/ZIL series, the 101 was available to senior government officials only, and was never on general sale.

No prices were ever quoted, but *Life* magazine estimated that, because of limited production, each ZIS cost $75,000 to build. About two a day were made up to 1940, when they were replaced by the restyled 102.

As early as 1943 consideration was being given to a new post-war ZIS, and the first five ZIS-110s took to the road in August 1945. They looked identical to the 1942 Packard 180, which indeed they were, as Packard had sold the body dies to the Soviet Union once it decided that it was no longer going to make a top-of-the-market car. There was no need for coercion from President Roosevelt for the sale, as has been alleged. The engine of the 110 was also a Packard design, and Stromberg carburettors were used.

Production of the ZIS-110 lasted until 1959. Stalin's posthumous fall from favour necessitated a change of name, and in 1956 the factory and the cars were renamed ZIL (Zavod Imieni Likhatcheva) after I. A. Likhatchev, a former minister of roads and transport. Convertibles and ambulance models of the 110 were made, and when the cars were surplus to government needs they were sold off as taxis. Production figures have never been published but probably varied from as few as 20 up to 500 a year, according to demand.

Prototypes of the 110's replacement were running in 1956, but the ZIL-111 did not appear until 1959. It was a long limousine in the Cadillac idiom, powered by a 6-litre short-stroke V8 of General Motors type. While not as close to any American design as the ZIS-110 had been, the ZIL-111 showed that designers in Moscow kept a close watch on Detroit, and who can blame them, when America led the world in large cars powered by big V8 engines. With the steady downsizing now in vogue in Detroit, and the probable demise of the big V8, it will be interesting to see what the ZIL of the 1990s is like.

In 1970 the ZIL-111 was replaced by the 114 with razor edge styling. This was made together with the shorter 117 five-seater limousine, and a restyled seven-seater limousine, the 4104, which has a 7.7-litre engine. Today the 4104 has replaced the earlier models. Production of the ZIL is claimed to be 500 a year, but in most years it is probably much less. The bulk of ZIL production is devoted to commercial vehicles, although the Moscow factory also makes bicycles and refrigerators. GNG

ZL
see Donnet-Zédel

ZÜNDAPP
GERMANY 1917-1958

The munitions company Zünder und Apparatebau GmbH was founded in Nuremberg in 1917 by Dr Fritz Neumeyer, who already ran a tube making company, and with backing from the giant armaments manufacturer, Krupps. The company was obliged to abandon munitions production with the demilitarization of Germany after World War I and Krupps' involvement also ended. Neumeyer reorganized Zünder und Apparatebau GmbH as Zündapp Gesellschaft für den Bau von Specialmaschinen and began to build tractors and electrical equipment.

In 1921 Zündapp introduced its first motorcycle, a very basic single-cylinder 2¼hp model intended for the mass market. Because it filled a post-war need for cheap basic transport it was very successful, in spite of the near total collapse of the German economy, and over 10,000 were sold by 1924.

Zündapp continued to introduce new models and produce motorcycles in increasing numbers, as well as establishing a comprehensive sales and service network. With the Depression of the late 1920s, however, motorcycle production slumped and in the early 1930s Zündapp planned to launch a car, also aimed at a mass market.

In November 1931 Zündapp approached Dr Ferdinand Porsche's recently established design bureau to produce such a car. In September 1931 Porsche had announced his own intention to build a 'people's car' and he based his work for Zündapp on his Project 12, which had earlier faltered for lack of finance.

Porsche originally planned to use an air-cooled flat-four engine, broadly derived from his twin-cylinder Austro-Daimler aero-engine design of 1912, but Zündapp insisted on using a water-cooled 1.2-litre five-cylinder radial engine in its 'Volksauto'. Porsche built three prototypes of the car, but in 1932 Zündapp paid him off and abandoned the project as the motorcycle industry began to recover. Porsche later developed the car in a similarly short-lived design exercise for NSU but its ultimate derivative was the Volkswagen.

Neumeyer died in 1935 and his son, Hans Friedrich, who had already been with the company for some years, took control and added aero engines to Zündapp's range of products. In 1938 the company was reorganized as Zündapp-Werke GmbH and throughout World War II produced military motorcycles in large numbers, the production total passing 250,000 in 1942.

The works were largely destroyed during the war and afterwards, under American control, were confined to making light machinery, including sewing machines, before resuming motorcycle production in 1947. Zündapp opened a new factory in Munich in 1950 but by the mid-1950s the motorcycle market was faltering again and in 1956 Zündapp began to build another car, the Janus, under licence from its designer, the aircraft manufacturer Dornier.

This small four-wheeled back-to-back two-seater with doors at the front and back used a 248cc single-cylinder two-stroke engine derived from the motorcycle range. It was only built until 1958, however, when Zündapp closed the Nuremberg factory. The production total for the Janus had reached about 6900 before Zündapp again concentrated on making motorcycles, now mainly small capacity models, and proprietary engines for other makers, as it still does today. BL

ZÜST
see OM

Chronology
by David Burgess-Wise

1885 Gottlieb Daimler builds motorcycle testbed.
Karl Benz constructs his three-wheeler, the first petrol car to be designed as an entity, not converted from a horse-carriage.
English inventor Butler exhibits drawings of 'Petrocycle'.

1886 Benz patents his motor car, 29 January.
First successful runs of the Benz three-wheeler.
Gottlieb Daimler and Wilhelm Maybach convert a horse-carriage to petrol power with a four-stroke engine.

1887 Butler shows improved Petrocycle.
Léon Serpollet builds his first steam tricycle.

1888 Veterinary surgeon John Boyd Dunlop re-invents the pneumatic tyre.
In Britain, Magnus Volk begins limited production of electric carriages, selling one to the Sultan of Morocco.
Karl Benz begins limited production of three-wheeled cars, but sales are few; Emile Roger of Paris becomes Benz agent.
Piano maker Steinway becomes American Daimler engine agent.

1889 Woodworking machinery makers Panhard & Levassor acquire French rights for new Daimler V-twin engine.
Peugeot builds four Serpollet steamers.

1890 Initially not interested in producing cars, Panhard & Levassor grant automotive licence for the Daimler engine to the Peugeot ironmongery business.
Daimler-Motoren-Gesellschaft established in Cannstatt, Germany, to sell engines and horseless carriages.

1891 Levassor changes his mind, designing and building a rear-engined car.
British rights to Daimler engine acquired by Frederick R. Simms, who initially applies it to motor launches.
Lambert builds America's first car, a three-wheeler.

1892 Levassor creates the archetypal motor car of the next 70 years; this layout, with front engine, sliding-gear transmission and rear-wheel drive, will be known as the Système Panhard.
British engineer Bremer begins work on tiny Benz-inspired four-wheeler.

1893 One of the first Panhard & Levassor cars is sold to the Abbé Gavois, a French parish priest; he will use it for the next 40 years.
In Springfield, Massachusetts, the brothers James and Frank Duryea build their motor buggy, America's first practicable motor car to lead to production.
Benz and Daimler cars shown at the Chicago World Exposition.
Benz begins production of the four-wheeled Viktoria.

1894 Benz introduces a lighter, more popular model, the Velo.
America's first car factory opened by Henry G. Morris and Pedro Salom of Philadelphia, building Electrobat electric carriages.
Elwood Haynes and the two Apperson brothers collaborate to build an automobile in Kokomo, Indiana; it is claimed as America's first.
Henry Hewetson imports Benz into Britain.

1895 The Benz company builds 135 motor vehicles.
After years of revision, Selden's 'master patent' is finally granted in the USA.
John Henry Knight, of Farnham, Surrey, builds a three-wheeled car.
De Dion and Bouton, previously steam-carriage builders, produce their first petrol engine.
The Lanchester brothers build the first all-British four-wheeled car.
The first car to run on Michelin pneumatic tyres is a Peugeot nicknamed 'L'Eclair' since it moves in lightning-like zig-zags.
Sir David Salomans holds Britain's first motor exhibition in October at Tunbridge Wells, Kent.
The first indoor exhibition of cars in Britain is held in London in November at the Stanley Cycle Show; one of the five exhibits is a Panhard owned by the Hon. Evelyn Ellis, in which the Prince of Wales, the future King Edward VII, has just taken his first petrol-car ride.
J. J. Henry Sturmey founds Britain's first motoring magazine, *The Autocar,* still published over 90 years later.

1896 Bollée voiturette is first car sold with pneumatic tyres as standard.
British motor industry established in January when H. J. Lawson founds the Daimler company in Coventry; Lawson tries to monopolize British motor industry through his Great Horseless Carriage Company.
Henry Ford makes first run in his experimental 'Quadricycle' in June; other American pioneers to complete their first cars this year are Charles Brady King, Ransom Eli Olds and Alexander Winton.
Britain's Locomotives on Highways Act comes into effect in November, raising speed limit to 12mph (20kph).
Lawson organizes first London–Brighton run to celebrate 'Emancipation Day'.

1897 The Stanley brothers, Francis and Freelan, are the first Americans to produce steam cars commercially.
Henry Sturmey makes first journey from John o'Groats to Land's End, in a Coventry-built Daimler.
First large-scale car-building venture in America by the Pope Manufacturing Company of Hartford, Connecticut.
Emil Jellinek orders first four-cylinder Cannstatt-Daimler.
Emile Levassor dies.
Frederick R. Simms founds Automobile Club of Great Britain and Ireland, later the Royal Automobile Club.

1898 Belgian driver Camille 'Red Devil' Jenatzy is first man to exceed 60mph (97kph), on a streamlined electric racer, 'La Jamais Contente'.
Panhard-Levassor replaces the tiller with wheel steering.
First De Dion-Bouton voiturette built.
Louis Renault constructs his first car, with a De Dion engine and live-axle drive.
First four-cylinder Coventry-Daimler appears.
Napier builds its first engine.

1899 Ransom Eli Olds puts the Oldsmobile into production.
Other companies which start manufacture this year are FIAT, Sunbeam, Wolseley, Albion, and Isotta-Fraschini.
The first Gardner-Serpollet steam cars introduced.
ACGBI organizes Motor Show in Richmond Park.

1900 The ACGBI Thousand Miles' Trial demonstrates the reliability of the motor vehicle to the British public, many of whom have never previously seen a car.
Gottlieb Daimler dies; a week later his company decides to produce the Mercédès, designed by Wilhelm Maybach and named after Jellinek's teenage daughter.
America builds 4192 automobiles, sold at an average of $1000.
Opel, famed for sewing machines and cycles, buys Lutzmann factory.

1901 Lanchester begins production.
Cannstatt-Daimler unveils the Mercédès, 'the car of the day after tomorrow'.
Winton and Shanks attempt first motor crossing of America but are halted by quicksand in Nevada.

1902 First attempt to drive round the world by Dr Lehwess's Panhard caravan 'Passe Partout' – it breaks down at Nijni Novgorod.
Frederick R. Simms founds the Society of Motor Manufacturers and Traders (SMMT).
The Mercédès-Simplex appears; it is a significant improvement over the 1901 model.

1903 British Motor Car Act passed, raising speed limit to 20mph (32kph); numbering of cars and driving licences introduced.
SMMT organizes its first motor show at the Crystal Palace (though London already has two other motor shows, the Stanley and the Cordingley).
Marius Barbarou designs the new front-engined Benz Parsifal to replace the obsolescent rear-engined belt-drive model derived from the 1885-86 prototype three-wheeler.
Henry Ford founds the Ford Motor Company in June.

Association of Licenced Automobile Manufacturers incorporated in USA to administer the Selden patent; Ford is among those sued for alleged infringement.

Spyker of Holland builds a four-wheel-drive six-cylinder racer.

Napier announces the first production six-cylinder car.

Cadillac Motor Car Company founded in Detroit; H. M. Leland is chief engineer.

Ford exports to Britain for the first time.

London marine engineering firm, the Vauxhall Iron Works, builds its first car.

First crossing of America by motor car; Jackson and Crocker drive a single-cylinder Winton from San Francisco to New York in 65 days.

1904 Motor Car Act becomes law on New Year's Day.

Danny Weigel drives a 20hp Talbot 2000 miles (3200km) non-stop.

Mr Rolls meets Mr Royce; the Rolls-Royce car is born.

France's leading boilermakers, Delaunay-Belleville, begins car manufacture.

Rover, builders of bicycles since the 1880s, begins car production.

1905 Herbert Austin, general manager of Wolseley, resigns to found his own company.

Sergeant Jarrett of Chertsey arrests so many motorists for breaking the speed limit that he is promoted to Inspector within the year.

The Automobile Association founded to combat the police 'trapping' of motorists.

1906 Rolls-Royce Limited capitalized, though the motor trade is deeply suspicious of the scheme.

Austin begins production at Longbridge, Birmingham.

Ford brings out his $500 four-cylinder Model N.

America produces 33,500 cars.

Racing driver and wealthy soup manufacturer's son Vincenzo Lancia founds his Lancia company.

Adams of Bedford makes a car with a 60hp Antoinette V8 aero-engine.

Exports of French cars to Britain total over 400 a month but exports of British cars to France are only two per month.

American millionaire Charles Glidden begins his second round-the-world trip driving a Napier.

Rolls-Royce introduces the 40/50hp six – 'the best car in the world'.

1907 The Automobile Club is awarded the Royal accolade by King Edward VII.

Over 60,000 cars are registered in Britain.

Observed by the RAC, the Rolls-Royce 40/50hp 'Silver Ghost' covers 15,000 miles (24,140km) with only one unscheduled stop.

A 45hp Hotchkiss also completes a 15,000-mile test, during which it wears out 46 tyres.

1908 William Crapo Durant founds General Motors Company.

Cadillac awarded the RAC Dewar Trophy for demonstrating standardization of production parts.

The Model T Ford is announced, costing only $850; first year's output is 8000.

1909 De Dion-Bouton introduces the first true production V8.

Daimler of Coventry fits the Knight sleeve-valve engine.

Cadillac incorporated into General Motors.

Mrs John R. Ramsey is first woman to drive across America, in a Maxwell.

1910 British parliament rejects proposal to tax petrol but taxes cars on horsepower ratings devised by the RAC.

Death of Charles S. Rolls in a flying accident at Bournemouth.

Cyclecars – 'The New Motoring' – appear, with Morgan, GN, and Bedelia in the forefront.

Ettore Bugatti begins production at Molsheim, Alsace (still German territory at that time).

Four-wheel brakes offered by Argyll, Crossley, Arrol-Johnston, Isotta-Fraschini.

Experiments with wireless installation in a car fail due to excessive bulk.

Sankey introduces pressed-steel detachable wheel.

1911 First British Ford Factory established at Trafford Park, Manchester, and quickly becomes Britain's biggest motor manufacturer, with an output of 8000 Model Ts in 1913.

After protesting that it will not abandon steam cars for petrol, White does so.

Cadillac is the first to stardardize electric lighting and starting, on its 20/30hp model.

The Selden Patent Case ends with victory for Ford – the Selden patent judged 'valid but not infringed'.

1912 S. F. Edge resigns from Napier after a dispute over company policy, accepting a £160,000 'golden handshake' to keep out of the motor industry for seven years; he successfully turns to pig farming and cattle breeding, and also backs motion-pictures.

Oxford cycle and motor agent William Morris introduces his 10hp Morris-Oxford light car.

1913 Henry Ford applies the principle of the moving conveyor belt to magneto assembly.

Mechanical direction indicators make their first tentative appearance.

In America, the Lincoln Highway Association is formed to lobby for a proper transcontinental road.

Future giant companies gather momentum; Fiat builds 3251 cars in the year, Renault 9338.

1914 Ford introduces full assembly-line production, cutting time taken to build a Model T chassis from 12.5 to 1.5 hours; sales rise to 182,809 and workers have their daily pay raised to $5, an industry record.

Over 200 makes of car are available on the British market.

Renault taxis carry French reinforcements to repel German Army's advance on Paris.

1915 Cadillac introduces its V8.

Packard announces the V12 Twin-Six, inspired by Sunbeam aero-engines.

Giacinto Ghia founds Carrozzeria Ghia in Turin.

Banker Nicola Romeo takes over Anonima Lombardo Fabbrica Automobili, forming Alfa Romeo.

Dodge Brothers adopt Budd pressed-steel bodywork.

Every customer who buys a Ford Model T this year gets a $50 rebate because sales have passed their target figure.

Fergus owner-driver car announced.

William Foster & Co of Lincoln builds the first successful tank.

1917 Herbert Austin awarded knighthood.

Henry Leland resigns from Cadillac to found Lincoln; at first, they build Liberty aero engines.

Chevrolet joins General Motors.

1918 American registrations exceed 5 million for the first time.

1919 André Citroën begins mass-production of his Model A in the former Mors factory.

Henry Ford buys out all other shareholders in the Ford Motor Company for $100 million.

Post-war models introduced by Hispano-Suiza, Guy, Enfield-Allday and Bentley all display aero-engine influence.

S. F. Edge returns to the car industry by taking over AC Cars.

Isotta-Fraschini introduces the first production straight-eight, designed by Cattaneo.

Fiat launches the popular 501.

1920 Half the motor vehicles in the world are Model T Fords.

American factories hit by sudden slump and post-war boom in new car sales collapses; Ford cuts prices to boost sales.

Britain's McKenna Duties add 33.3 per cent tax to the price of imported cars.

Sunbeam, Talbot, and Darracq combine to form the S-T-D group.

In Britain, the Motor Car Act taxes cars at £1 per RAC horsepower (slashing sales of the 22hp Model T Ford), but pre-1914 cars pay only half the horsepower tax, while cars only used to take servants to church or voters to the polls are exempt from tax.

Billy Durant loses control of General Motors to DuPont/Morgan banking interests, and Alfred P. Sloan takes over as head of the group.

Duesenberg announces America's first production straight-eight.

Work starts on Britain's first motor bypasses, the Great West Road and Purley Way.
The number of car manufacturers in France is computed at 350.

1921 Lincoln announces its V8.
The 3-litre Bentley enters production.
Morris follows the Ford lead and cuts prices by up to £100 to boost flagging market – and doubles its sales, building 3077 cars against 1932 cars in 1920.
Billy Durant borrows $7 million and founds Durant Motors.
Fiat launches the 6.8-litre V12 SuperFiat; it is a super flop.

1922 Ford takes over Lincoln.
Introduction of the Austin Seven.
Clyno abandons motorcycles and begins car production.
Marconi experiments with wireless receivers in Daimler cars.
Model T Ford production exceeds a million.
Lancia launches the Lambda, with unit body/chassis construction, independent front suspension and narrow V4 engine.
Trico (USA) introduces the electric windscreen wiper, though the Folberth vacuum wiper has been around since 1916, and manual wipers are even older.
Leyland Motors takes over manufacture of the Trojan.
In the USA, C. F. 'Boss' Kettering and T. H. Midgley introduce tetraethyl leaded petrol.
Bignan of Paris introduces a sports car with desmodromic valves.

1923 Cecil Kimber of Morris Garages builds the first MG, based on his Morris Cowley sports conversions.
Famous Coventry cycle and motorcycle manufacturers Triumph build their first car, the 10/20hp.

1924 Walter P. Chrysler, formerly with Maxwell, begins production of the car bearing his name.
In the USA, DuPont develops quick-drying enamel, enabling car production to be speeded up.
Napier ends car production to concentrate on aero engines.
Léon Bollée of Le Mans is taken over by Morris.

1925 General Motors takes over Vauxhall Motors of Luton as its European 'Trojan Horse'.
Morris produces 54,151 Bullnose Oxfords and Cowleys.
Ford's Manchester factory builds its 250,000th Model T, which makes a triumphal tour of Britain.
'Round-the-World' Buick visits 14 countries in six months and covers 16,499 miles (26,553km).
First popular British car with hydraulic four-wheel brakes is the Triumph 13/30.
Rolls-Royce replaces the Silver Ghost, in production since 1906, with the Phantom I.
Fiat launches a more modern light car, the ohc 990cc 509.

1926 In Germany, Benz and Daimler join to create Daimler-Benz.
Daimler of Coventry announces its Double-Six, with a 7136cc V12 sleeve-valve engine.
The General Strike sees London's first commuter traffic jams.
Clyno becomes Britain's third biggest motor manufacturer, turning out 300 cars a week from a cramped factory in Wolverhampton.
London sees its first traffic lights.

1927 Model T Ford ends production after some 16 million cars in 19 years; the lowest price for a new Model T during that period is $290 (£65), a record for a conventional motor car.
In Italy, Società Anonima Brevetti Automobilistici launches a 984cc 4×4 car with independent suspension all round: SABA will only last until 1928.
Wolseley fails, and is bought by Morris.
Chevrolet becomes the top-selling car in American motor industry as Ford prepares for production of the Model A.
Studebaker and Oldsmobile pioneer chromium plating.
Stanley steam cars cease production.
The first Bugatti Royale appears.
In Belgium, Imperia-Excelsior takes over Métallurgique and closes it down, selling the buildings to Minerva.

1928 Rootes buys Humber and Hillman.
Alvis produces Britain's first catalogued front-wheel-drive car.
Chrysler acquires Dodge for $175,000,000.
Cadillac pioneers synchromesh gearchange.
Clyno attempts to market a '£100' version of their new 8hp model; it finally costs £112, they still call it the 'Century', and it is a total failure.
Erstwhile aero-engine builders BMW take over Dixi and begin licence production of the Austin Seven.

1929 US car production reaches 5,337,087, a record that will not be broken until the 1950s.
US registrations total 26.5 million.
Karl Benz dies, aged 85.
Financially overstretched, Clyno goes into liquidation.
Armstrong-Siddeley offers the option of a Wilson preselector gearbox; it will be standard from 1933 (preselector gears were featured as early as 1901-1907 on the marque's forbear, the Wilson-Pilcher).
Lancia launches the 3960cc V8 DiLambda.
Renault introduces its first straight-eight, the 7100cc Reinastella.

1930 Sir Dennistoun Burney, designer of the R100 airship, builds the aerodynamic Burney Streamline, with rear engine and all-round independent suspension; he sells 12, one to Edward, Prince of Wales.
Daimler combines the fluid flywheel with the preselector gearbox to produce semi-automatic transmission.
Car sales fall as a result of the Depression.
Henry Royce is knighted.
The Veteran Car Club – the first such organization in the world – is formed to preserve early motor cars.
British Parliament abolishes the obsolete 20mph (32kph) speed limit and introduces compulsory third-party insurance.
Cadillac launches a 7.4-litre V16.
Morris fits hydraulic brakes to its larger models.

1931 With the Cadet, Vauxhall introduces synchromesh gears to the British market.

Bentley Motors goes into liquidation; Napier bids for the company, but is outflanked by Rolls-Royce, who form Bentley Motors (1931) Limited.
Daimler buys Lanchester, Britain's oldest car manufacturer.
Morris introduces a £100 utility 8hp Minor two-seater.
Only 10 per cent of all production cars are now tourers.
Ford of Britain moves into its new factory at Dagenham on the Essex bank of the Thames; all production machinery is moved south from Trafford Park at weekends so no production is lost.
The Swallow Coachbuilding Company of former sidecar maker William Lyons produces the first SS cars, adding luxury coachwork to modified Standard chassis at remarkably reasonable prices.

1932 Rootes Group formed.
The first small Ford designed for Europe, the 8hp Model Y, is unveiled in February at the Ford Motor Show in London's Albert Hall.
Ford introduces the V8 in the USA; it sells over 300,000 in its first year.

1933 Reo offers semi-automatic transmission.
Ford slips into third place in America, behind General Motors and Chrysler.

1934 Chrysler introduces its revolutionary Airflow range – with overdrive.
Morris instals its first moving production line at Cowley.
William Lyons founds SS Cars Ltd in Coventry, as a subsidiary to the Swallow Coachbuilding Company.
Sir William Morris becomes Baron Nuffield.
Nazis start building Germany's autobahn system.
Metallic paintwork first becomes available on British cars.
Citroën Traction Avant launched, but its development costs are so great that the company is ruined, and André Citroën has to sell out to Michelin.

1935 British Transport Minister Leslie Hore-Belisha introduces pedestrian crossings, a driving test, and a 30mph (48kph) limit in built-up areas.
Ford of Britain introduces the first £100 saloon car, a cheaper Model Y.
Rootes Group takes over the ailing Sunbeam-Talbot-Darracq organization.
World census reveals that 35 million motor vehicles are registered.
Triumph offers screenwash system.

1936 Morgan produces its first four-wheeler – but retaining the 1909-designed sliding-pillar independent front suspension.
Fiat introduces its 570cc '500', otherwise called 'Topolino' – 'Mickey Mouse' – which combines 55mph (88kph) performance with 55mpg (23 kmpl) economy.
Porsche manufactures the first Volkswagen, financed by the Nazi party; Hitler will propose that it can be bought for less than £50 on an instalment plan.
There are still 45 indigenous British motor manufacturers.
Sir Herbert Austin becomes Baron Austin of Longbridge.
SS Cars introduces its 'Jaguar' model.

1937 The SMMT transfers its Motor Exhibition to Earl's Court after holding the Show at Olympia since 1905.
Germany already has 800 miles (1287km) of autobahn – at a cost of some £45 million.

1938 Britain increases the horsepower tax to £1 5s (£1.25) per RAC hp – and petrol tax goes up from 8d to 9d (3.33p to 3.75p) per gallon.
The Standard Flying Eight is the first British small saloon featuring independent front suspension.
The Nuffield Group acquires Riley.
British manufacturers start building 'shadow factories' to produce war matériel.

1939 Lincoln introduces the customized Continental for Edsel Ford to the design of Eugene Turenne Gregory.
Ford builds the first Mercury.
In Britain, 4.5 million hold driving licences.

1940 Car factories in Britain go over to war production.
Germany blitzes central Coventry in November.
A total of 23 million vehicles registered in the USA.

1941 Lord Wakefield, founder of Castrol, dies aged 81.
Death of Lord Austin, aged 74.
Louis Chevrolet dies aged 62.

1942 Vauxhall builds 12-cylinder Churchill tanks.

1943 War cuts American passenger car output to 139 vehicles.

1944 Louis Renault, accused of having collaborated with the Germans, dies mysteriously in prison and his company is nationalized.

1945 Standard acquires Triumph, in liquidation since 1939.
SS Cars renamed 'Jaguar'.
Petrol still rationed in Britain; of the price of 2s (10p) per gallon, 9d (3.75p) is tax.
The 28-year-old Henry Ford II takes over the Ford Motor Company from his grandfather, Henry Ford I.
Britain's Labour government compels car makers to export half their output.
British car buyers have to sign a covenant promising not to sell their new vehicles for a year, to curb the black market in new cars.
The Bristol Aeroplane Company forms car division.

1946 British Motor Industry celebrates its Golden Jubilee.
The first post-war British designs – from Armstrong-Siddeley, Triumph, Bentley, and Jowett – appear.
Petrol ration for British motorists increased by 50 per cent.
Ford of Britain produces its millionth car in August.

1947 Fiftieth birthday of the American car industry.
Henry Ford dies, aged 84.
Bristol and Frazer-Nash acquire the BMW engine as 'war reparations'.
Ettore Bugatti dies in Paris, aged 66.
Gear maker David Brown buys Aston Martin and Lagonda.
Standard announces the Vanguard.

1948 America builds its 100,000,000th car.
First post-war London Motor Show features the Issigonis-designed Morris Minor, the Jaguar XK120, and the 'umbrella on four wheels', the Citroën 2CV.
British car taxation reformed; now all cars taxed at a flat rate, initially £10.
Rover introduces the four-wheel-drive Land-Rover.
Buick introduces Dynaflow, America's first production torque-convertor automatic transmission.
Tubeless tyres appear in America.

1949 Britain relaxes petrol restrictions; more cars become available on the British market.

1950 Petrol rationing ends in Britain, though the fuel tax is doubled.
British government halves double purchase tax on luxury cars and extends the new-car covenant to two years.
Ford regains second place in the US industry, overtaking Chrysler.
The world's first gas-turbine car is demonstrated by Rover.
Ford of Britain unveils its first post-war designs, the new Consul four and Zephyr six.

1951 Norah, Lady Docker's first 'Golden Daimler', a straight-eight, is shown at Earl's Court.
Disc braking and power steering are standard items of US Chrysler specification.
Spain attempts to re-enter luxury car market with Pegaso.
Doctor Porsche dies.

1952 Austin and Morris merge to form the British Motor Corporation; Lord Nuffield is chairman.
Mercedes announces the 300SL sports with 'gull-wing' coachwork, and Fiat launches the 8V, with all-round independent suspension.
The Triumph TR and the Healey 100 are the first popular-priced sports cars to offer 100 mph (160kph) performance.
Nissan signs seven-year agreement with Austin in December.

1953 Branded petrols again available in Britain; compression ratios rise to take advantage of the higher octane ratings.
Singer announces Britain's first plastics-bodied production car, the SMX Roadster.
New-car covenant purchase scheme abolished.
Hino of Japan signs seven-year contract with Renault for production of 4CV.
First Nissan-built Austin A40 leaves production line in April.

1954 General Motors builds its 50-millionth car.
Nash and Hudson combine to form American Motors Corporation.
The Lanchester Sprite 1.6-litre is offered with automatic transmission, still a rarity in Europe, although common on American cars.
Volkswagen, having rebuilt its factory after it was gutted in the war, is now well enough established to start a vigorous export drive.
All new American cars are now offered with tubeless tyres.
Ford of America introduces the Thunderbird.

1955 Citroën introduces the DS19, with hydropneumatic self-levelling suspension, automatic jacks, power steering, and disc braking.
The Rolls-Royce Silver Cloud and Bentley S-Type appear.
Pininfarina styles BMC cars.
America has a record year, producing 9,204,049 vehicles; some eight million are passenger cars.

1956 President Gamal Abdel Nasser nationalizes Suez Canal.
American cars begin to sprout tail fins.
Ford Motor Company stock becomes available to the public for the first time when the Ford Foundation offers over ten million shares.
The Triumph TR3 and Jensen 541 are fitted with disc brakes.
Ford is first British private company to make regular use of a computer.
Daimler discontinues production of the Lanchester.

1957 Suez Canal closed; ensuing crisis cuts oil supplies to Europe. Petrol rationing re-introduced in Britain and other European countries, resulting in production of super-economy bubble cars.
Fiat launches a new 500, with vertical-twin air-cooled engine and four-speed crash gearbox.
Lotus introduces the plastic monocoque-bodied Elite.
Ford (US) introduces a new model line, the Edsel.
American Motors discontinues Nash and Hudson marques.
Ford builds its 3-millionth Mercury.
Chrysler's 10-millionth Plymouth produced.

1958 Sir Leonard Lord takes over as chairman of BMC.
Work starts on the M1 motorway from London to Birmingham, first proposed in 1924.
Work starts on Mont Blanc tunnel.
New 40mph (64kph) speed limit on roads around London.
Britain's first motorway – the 8.2-mile (13km) Preston by-pass – opens.
Ford celebrates the 50th birthday of the Model T by assembling their 50-millionth car (and reassembling a 1909 T).
Chrysler builds its 25-millionth car.
Packard ceases production.
'Frogeye' Austin-Healey Sprite announced.
A new production record for British manufacturers – one million cars in a year.

1959 British cuts purchase tax on new cars from 60 to 50 per cent.
M1 motorway opens from St Albans to Rugby.
Lea-Francis expires vulgarly with the bulbous Lynx.
American manufacturers introduce new compact models to combat increasing imports of European small cars (though the 'compact' Chrysler Valiant has a 2.8-litre engine).
Alec Issigonis designs the diminutive front-wheel drive Mini-Minor.
NSU announces that it will manufacture cars with Wankel rotary engines.
Triumph launches the Michelotti-styled Herald, with all-round independent suspension.

Ford of Britain launches the 105E Anglia, its first-ever four-speed car, with raked-back rear window, to supplant the ultra-cheap Popular, which still uses the 1934-designed 10hp sidevalve engine and 1938 styling; the 1953 unit-construction 100E Anglia now becomes the Popular.
In Holland DAF begins producing cars with the Variomatic infinitely-variable transmission.

1960 Jaguar Cars acquires Daimler.
Japanese industry exceeds 200,000 cars for the first time.
The Hillman Minx is offered with Easidrive automatic transmission.

1961 Transport Minister Ernest Marples launches testing of all cars over ten years old in Britain.
British car tax raised to £15 from £12 10s (£12.50) a year.
Sir Leonard Lord elevated to peerage as Lord Lambury.
Morris produces its millionth Minor.
Commercial-vehicle producers Leyland Motors takes over Standard-Triumph and AEC.

1962 Morris 1100 launched with Hydrolastic suspension.
BMC production reaches 600,000 vehicles a year.
Ford of Britain launches the MkI Cortina, a full-size family five-seater at Mini prices.

1963 Formation of the Leyland Motor Corporation; its first chairman, Sir Henry Spurrier, retires through ill-health four months later and dies in 1964.
Hillman unveils 'Project Alex', the 875cc Imp, first passenger car to be built in Scotland since the Arrol-Johnston ceased production in 1931.
Death of Lord Nuffield, aged 86.
NSU launches the first Wankel-engined car, the Spyder.
Rover announces the 2000 saloon with body styling inspired by the experimental Rover T4 jet car; it is voted 'Car of the Year'.
Mercedes launches the 600, with a 6.3-litre eight-cylinder engine and an overall length of 20ft 6in (6.25m).

1964 The Triumph 2000 is introduced.

Ford of America launches the Mustang 'personal sports car', which sells a record 500,000 in under 18 months.
Chrysler acquires control of Rootes Group.
Front safety belts standard in all new US cars – but wearing them is not compulsory.

1965 BMC merges with the Pressed Steel Company.
BMC chairman and managing director George Harriman is knighted.
British motor tax increased to £17 10s (£17.50).
Britain's Labour government brings in a blanket speed limit of 70mph (113kph) as a 'four-month experiment'.
AP automatic transmission offered on the Mini.
Rolls-Royce launches its first unit-constructed car, the Silver Shadow.

1966 Jensen introduces the four-wheel-drive, 6.3-litre FF.
The Jaguar group – Jaguar, Daimler, Guy, Coventry-Climax, and Henry Meadows – merges with BMC to form British Motor Holdings.
Japan's car exports exceed 100,000 for the first time.

1967 Japanese production exceeds a million for the first time.
Citroën kills off Panhard, founded in 1889, which it finally acquired in 1965 after holding a stake in the capital for a decade.
NSU launches the Ro80, first volume-production Wankel-engined car, and signs an agreement with Citroën for joint production of the Wankel engine.
Leyland Motor Corporation takes over Rover and Alvis; Alvis car production finishes within the year.
Ford of Europe established to coordinate the programmes of British and Continental Ford companies.

1968 British Motor Holdings merges with Leyland Motors to form the British Leyland Motor Corporation.
Volkswagen produces a new model, the 411 (still with an air-cooled flat-four engine) alongside the 1936-designed Beetle.

Renault loses 100,000 cars as strikes cripple French manufacturers.
California passes clean-air act because of atmospheric pollution, opening the way for catalytic converters and lead-free petrol.

1969 Volkswagen takes over Audi.
Jaguar introduces the XJ6.

1970 Japan is now the world's second biggest motor manufacturer, with a monthly output of 200,000 cars.
Rover launches a more up-market four-wheel-drive model, the Range Rover.
Citroën introduces a new small model, the GS, and the Maserati-engined SM.
Ford takes over Ghia of Turin from Alejandro de Tomaso.
British Leyland drops the Minor and introduces the five-speed Maxi.
Simca manufactures the Chrysler 160/180 range in France for European and British markets.
Mercedes builds the experimental three-rotor Wankel-engined C III.
Volkswagen unveils the K70, its first water-cooled model.
Victoria, Australia, passes world's first compulsory safety-belt law.

1971 In seemingly perpetual financial difficulties, Aston Martin is sold by the David Brown Group to a consortium of financiers, who continue manufacture of the DBS.
Jaguar unveils its new V12 engine.
Jensen stops making the FF and is acquired by American-based, Norwegian-born, Kjell Qvale.
Ford takes 25 per cent of Mazda.
GM acquires 34.2 per cent of Isuzu.
After berating the Chevrolet Corvair in his 1965 book *Unsafe at Any Speed*, safety crusader Ralph Nader focuses on the VW Beetle.
Rolls-Royce put into liquidation following its aero-engine division's problems with the RB211 jet engine; the still-profitable car division is hived off.
Rolls-Royce announces the two-door Corniche, at prices from £12,829.

1972 Datsun of Japan becomes the second-biggest exporter of cars to Britain.
British motor industry produces 1,900,000 cars.

1973 The Arab-Israeli War restricts oil supply; Arabs increase oil prices four-fold and petrol rationing threatened in the West.
Britain imposes 50mph (80kph) speed limit to conserve fuel.
British motorists queue for petrol.
Volkswagen passes the Model T Ford's 46-year-old production record with the Beetle.
Ford opens 'greenfield' automatic transmission plant in Bordeaux.
Imported cars take 25 per cent of British market.
GM offers first car with optional airbag restraint system.

1974 Peugeot takes over Citroën.
Fiat runs into serious financial trouble.
General Motors cancels its plans to build 100,000 Wankel-engined Vegas.
American manufacturers, with a record 80 days' stock of unsold cars, abandon large-engined cars in the quest for fuel economy.
Ford researches 150-year-old Stirling 'hot-air' engine principle.
The Mercedes 600 Limousine is the first production car sold in Britain at a price of more than £20,000.
Fiat builds a million 127s.
Volkswagen introduces the modern front-wheel-drive Golf as a successor to the perennial Beetle.
Pioneers E. L. Cord and Gabriel Voisin die.

1975 UK government – whose National Enterprise Board now has a 95% stake in the company – pumps £200 million into British Leyland; the added finance does not prevent BL from being dragged down still further by industrial disputes.
Rolls-Royce unveils the £31,000 Camargue.
Imports take 33 per cent of British market.
Government bails out Chrysler-UK.
British car tax raised from £25 to £40.
Chrysler-Europe introduces French-built Alpine, which attracts vital custom.
Volvo takes control of DAF.
Volvo, Peugeot, and Renault all fit the joint-venture 'Douvrin' V6 engine in their luxury models.
Citroën replaces the 20-year-old DS with the aerodynamic CX range and wins 'Car of the Year' Award.

Jaguar replaces its E-Type sports car with the XJS sports coupé.
Triumph's last true sports car, the TR6, is replaced by the pedestrian TR7.
Lotus moves into the supercar league with the introduction of the new Esprit and Eclat.
The Toyota Corolla is the first Japanese car to become world's best-selling model.
Porsche announces the Carrera Turbo.

1976 Chrysler Alpine voted 'Car of the Year'.
Ford introduces the new front-wheel-drive Fiesta, built in a totally new factory in Valencia, Spain.
Rover launches the David Bache-styled, Ferrari Daytona-inspired, 3500 SD range.
The William Towns-designed Aston Martin Lagonda is the first production car with computerized digital instrumentation.
Audi-NSU experiments with a Wankel engine in the Audi 100.
Citroën launches the LN, with Citroën mechanics in a Peugeot body.
What is said to be America's last convertible is built by Cadillac as the demand for open-top motoring fades in the face of safety neurosis.

1977 Porsche launches 924 and 928.

1978 Fired by Ford, Lee Iacocca joins Chrysler as president.

1979 Japan builds 6.2 million cars, against 8.4 million from the USA.
Chrysler seeks US government loan guarantees.

1980 Austin introduces the Metro.
New front-wheel-drive Escort from Ford.
Audi introduces the four-wheel-drive Quattro.
US 'Big Four' lose a total of $4200 million.
Chrysler launches front-wheel-drive 'K' cars.
Imported cars sell record 2.4 million on US market.
BL signs cooperation deal with Honda.
Nissan enters agreements with Alfa Romeo and Volkswagen.

Japan builds 7 million cars, overtaking the USA (6.4 million) as the world's biggest producer, and exports 3.95 million of them.

1981 Ford Escort production world-wide reaches a million after 13 months, beating the 52-year-old 'fastest first million' record of the Model A Ford.
Japan agrees to limit American sales to 1,680,000 units.
DeLorean sports car goes on sale in US.
GM buys 5 per cent of Suzuki.
Chrysler workers forgo $622 million in pay and benefits to help company qualify for another loan.

1982 DeLorean goes out of business.
Renault and Honda cars built in the US.
Chrysler is first US maker to reintroduce convertibles.

1983 Japan out-produces the USA for the fourth successive year.
American sales pick up after three lean years.
Chrysler pays off $1.2 billion in loans seven years early.
Pontiac launches mid-engine Fiero sports car with plastic body panels.
Britain makes front safety belts compulsory.

1984 Ford starts building new 1.6-litre diesel engine at Dagenham for its small front-wheel-drive cars.
American 'Big Three' set records for sales and profits.
GM-Toyota joint venture launched in California.
Cadillac reintroduces the convertible – the $31,000 Eldorado.

1985 British car tax raised to £100.
Electronics wizard Sir Clive Sinclair miscalculates with his C5 electric tricycle.
GM announces Saturn Corporation to build sub-compact cars on 'greenfield' site in Tennessee in 1990s.
Nissan starts building cars in Tennessee.
Chrysler reveals 'Project Liberty' prototype.
John Lennon's psychedelic Rolls-Royce sells for a record $2.3 million.

1986 Oil prices plummet.
The Nissan plant in Washington, Tyne & Wear, starts building Bluebirds in Britain.
The Ford Scorpio – first mass-produced car to offer antilock braking as standard across the range – is voted 'Car of the Year'.
Hamburger king Thomas Monaghan pays a record $8.1 million for a Bugatti Royale.
Ford is invited to take over Alfa Romeo but Fiat steps in at the 11th hour and absorbs Alfa instead.
Renault chief Georges Besse is gunned down in the street by political assassins.
Ford talks on possible takeover of Austin Rover founder in tide of misplaced jingoism.
Ford builds its 20-millionth British vehicle – twice the total of any other British marque.

1987 British government writes off £680 million of accumulated Rover Group (formerly BL) debts.
Ford (GB) stops production of Capri after 18 years and 1.9 million manufactured.
BMW introduces the V12 750i model – it has an electronically governed top speed of 155mph (250kph).
For the first time since 1924, Ford's accounts show that it has earnt more money in the financial year worldwide than GM.
At the Geneva Motor Show the coachbuilders Hooper of London announce the Bentley Empress II – at £275,000 the most expensive production car ever.

Index

Pages in italics include illustrations. Abbreviations: m/cycle, motor cycle; c/car, cycle car; amph, amphibious vehicle.

Acknowledgments

The publishers wish to thank the following individuals and organisations for their kind permission to reproduce the illustrations in this book:
BPCC/Aldus Archive, Anselmi, Archivio I.G.D.A., Autocar, J. Baker Collection, Giovanni Belli, Bisconcini, G. Boschetti, Neill Bruce, D. Burgess-Wise, A. Cherrett, F.C. Crawford, Crawford Museum, Davrian, Dodge, Fairthorpe, Fiat, G. Goddard, Harrah's Motor Museum, Hillman, I.C.P., L.A.T., Marka, Moretti, National Magazine Company, The National Motor Museum at Beaulieu, Ogle, Pocklington, Quattroruote, Renault, Rheinstahl Hanowlog, V.A.G., Vauxhall Opel, Veteran Vintage Motor Museum, Von Ferson, Zagari.

The publishers would particularly like to thank NICK BALDWIN, MIRCO DECET, G.N. GEORGANO, and the NATIONAL MOTOR MUSEUM AT BEAULIEU for their assistance, advice and expertise in compiling and researching this book.